With the purcha~~se~~
New Book*

You Can Access the Real Financial Data that the Experts Use!

*Access is available to purchasers of new books only. If you purchased a used book, the site ID may have expired.

This card entitles the purchaser of a new textbook to a semester of access to the Educational Version of Standard & Poor's Market Insight®, a rich online resource featuring hundreds of the most often researched companies in the Market Insight database.

For 1,000 companies, this website provides you:

- Access to six years' worth of fundamental financial data from the renowned Standard & Poor's COMPUSTAT® database
- 12 Excel Analytics Reports, including balance sheets, income statements, ratio reports and cash flow statements; adjusted prices reports, and profitability; forecasted values and monthly valuation data reports
- Access to Financial Highlights Reports including key ratios
- S & P Stock Reports that offer fundamental, quantitative and technical analysis
- EDGAR reports updated throughout the day
- Industry Surveys, written by S & P's Equity analysts
- News feeds (updated hourly) for companies and industries.

See other side for your unique site ID access code.

Welcome to the Educational Version of Market Insight!

www.mhhe.com/edumarketinsight

Check out your textbook's website for details on how this special offer enhances the value of your purchase!

1. To get started, use your web browser to go to **www.mhhe.com/edumarketinsight**

2. Enter your site ID exactly as it appears below.

3. You may be prompted to enter the site ID for future use—please keep this card.

Your site ID is:

> ap219829

STANDARD &POOR'S

ISBN 978-0-07-128625-1
MHID 0-07-128625-X

 McGraw-Hill Irwin

*If you purchased a used book, this site ID may have expired.

Modern Financial Management

The McGraw-Hill/Irwin Series in Finance, Insurance, and Real Estate

Stephen A. Ross
Franco Modigliani Professor of Finance and Economics
Sloan School of Management
Massachusetts Institute of Technology
Consulting Editor

Financial Management

Adair
Excel Applications for Corporate Finance
First Edition

Benninga and Sarig
Corporate Finance: *A Valuation Approach*

Block and Hirt
Foundations of Financial Management
Twelfth Edition

Brealey, Myers, and Allen
Principles of Corporate Finance
Eighth Edition

Brealey, Myers, and Marcus
Fundamentals of Corporate Finance
Fifth Edition

Brooks
FinGame Online 4.0

Bruner
Case Studies in Finance: *Managing for Corporate Value Creation*
Fifth Edition

Chew
The New Corporate Finance: *Where Theory Meets Practice*
Third Edition

Chew and Gillan
Corporate Governance at the Crossroads: *A Book of Readings*
First Edition

DeMello
Cases in Finance
Second Edition

Grinblatt and Titman
Financial Markets and Corporate Strategy
Second Edition

Helfert
Techniques of Financial Analysis: *A Guide to Value Creation*
Eleventh Edition

Higgins
Analysis for Financial Management
Eighth Edition

Kester, Ruback, and Tufano
Case Problems in Finance
Twelfth Edition

Ross, Westerfield, and Jaffe
Corporate Finance
Eighth Edition

Ross, Westerfield, Jaffe, and Jordan
Corporate Finance: *Core Principles and Applications*
First Edition

Ross, Westerfield, and Jordan
Essentials of Corporate Finance
Fifth Edition

Ross, Westerfield, and Jordan
Fundamentals of Corporate Finance
Eighth Edition

Shefrin
Behavioral Corporate Finance: *Decisions That Create Value*
First Edition

White
Financial Analysis with an Electronic Calculator
Sixth Edition

Investments

Adair
Excel Applications for Investments
First Edition

Bodie, Kane, and Marcus
Essentials of Investments
Sixth Edition

Bodie, Kane, and Marcus
Investments
Seventh Edition

Hirt and Block
Fundamentals of Investment Management
Eighth Edition

Hirschey and Nofsinger
Investments: *Analysis and Behavior*
First Edition

Jordan and Miller
Fundamentals of Investments: *Valuation and Management*
Fourth Edition

Financial Institutions and Markets

Rose and Hudgins
Bank Management and Financial Services
Seventh Edition

Rose and Marquis
Money and Capital Markets: *Financial Institutions and Instruments in a Global Marketplace*
Ninth Edition

Saunders and Cornett
Financial Institutions Management: *A Risk Management Approach*
Fifth Edition

Saunders and Cornett
Financial Markets and Institutions: *An Introduction to the Risk Management Approach*
Third Edition

International Finance

Eun and Resnick
International Financial Management
Fourth Edition

Kuemmerle
Case Studies in International Entrepreneurship: *Managing and Financing Ventures in the Global Economy*
First Edition

Real Estate

Brueggeman and Fisher
Real Estate Finance and Investments
Thirteenth Edition

Corgel, Ling, and Smith
Real Estate Perspectives: *An Introduction to Real Estate*
Fourth Edition

Ling and Archer
Real Estate Principles: *A Value Approach*
Second Edition

Financial Planning and Insurance

Allen, Melone, Rosenbloom, and Mahoney
Pension Planning: *Pension, Profit-Sharing, and Other Deferred Compensation Plans*
Ninth Edition

Altfest
Personal Financial Planning
First Edition

Harrington and Niehaus
Risk Management and Insurance
Second Edition

Kapoor, Dlabay, and Hughes
Focus on Personal Finance: *An Active Approach to Help You Develop Successful Financial Skills*
First Edition

Kapoor, Dlabay, and Hughes
Personal Finance
Eighth Edition

Modern Financial Management

Eighth Edition

Stephen A. Ross
Sloan School of Management
Massachusetts Institute of Technology

Randolph W. Westerfield
Marshall School of Business
University of Southern California

Jeffrey Jaffe
Wharton School of Business
University of Pennsylvania

Bradford D. Jordan
Gatton College of Business and Economics
University of Kentucky

 **McGraw-Hill
Irwin**

Boston   Burr Ridge, IL   Dubuque, IA   New York   San Francisco   St. Louis
Bangkok   Bogotá   Caracas   Kuala Lumpur   Lisbon   London   Madrid   Mexico City
Milan   Montreal   New Delhi   Santiago   Seoul   Singapore   Sydney   Taipei   Toronto

McGraw-Hill
Irwin

MODERN FINANCIAL MANAGEMENT: INTERNATIONAL STUDENT EDITION

Published by McGraw-Hill/Irwin, a business unit of The McGraw-Hill Companies, Inc., 1221
Avenue of the Americas, New York, NY, 10020.
Some ancillaries, including electronic and print components, may not be available to customers outside the United States.

This book is printed on acid-free paper.

3 4 5 6 7 8 9 0 DOW/DOW 0 9 8

ISBN   978-0-07-110088-5
MHID 0-07-110088-1

www.mhhe.com

To our family and friends with love and gratitude.

About the Authors

STEPHEN A. ROSS *Sloan School of Management, Massachusetts Institute of Technology* Stephen A. Ross is the Franco Modigliani Professor of Financial Economics at the Sloan School of Management, Massachusetts Institute of Technology. One of the most widely published authors in finance and economics, Professor Ross is recognized for his work in developing the arbitrage pricing theory, as well as for having made substantial contributions to the discipline through his research in signaling, agency theory, option pricing, and the theory of the term structure of interest rates, among other topics. A past president of the American Finance Association, he currently serves as an associate editor of several academic and practitioner journals. He is a trustee of CalTech and Freddie Mac.

RANDOLPH W. WESTERFIELD *Marshall School of Business, University of Southern California* Randolph W. Westerfield is Dean Emeritus of the University of Southern California's Marshall School of Business and is the Charles B. Thornton Professor of Finance.

Professor Westerfield came to USC from the Wharton School, University of Pennsylvania, where he was the chairman of the finance department and member of the finance faculty for 20 years. He is a member of several public company boards of directors, including Health Management Associates, Inc., William Lyon Homes, and the Nicholas Applegate Growth Fund. His areas of expertise include corporate financial policy, investment management, and stock market price behavior.

JEFFREY F. JAFFE *Wharton School of Business, University of Pennsylvania* Jeffrey F. Jaffe has been a frequent contributor to the finance and economics literatures in such journals as the *Quarterly Economic Journal, The Journal of Finance, The Journal of Financial and Quantitative Analysis, The Journal of Financial Economics,* and *The Financial Analysts Journal.* His best-known work concerns insider trading, where he showed both that corporate insiders earn abnormal profits from their trades and that regulation has little effect on these profits. He has also made contributions concerning initial public offerings, regulation of utilities, the behavior of marketmakers, the fluctuation of gold prices, the theoretical effect of inflation on interest rates, the empirical effect of inflation on capital asset prices, the relationship between small-capitalization stocks and the January effect, and the capital structure decision.

BRADFORD D. JORDAN *Gatton College of Business and Economics, University of Kentucky* Bradford D. Jordan is Professor of Finance and holder of the Richard W. and Janis H. Furst Endowed Chair in Finance at the University of Kentucky. He has a long-standing interest in both applied and theoretical issues in corporate finance and has extensive experience teaching all levels of corporate finance and financial management policy. Professor Jordan has published numerous articles on issues such as cost of capital, capital structure, and the behavior of security prices. He is a past president of the Southern Finance Association, and he is coauthor of *Fundamentals of Investments: Valuation and Management,* 4e, a leading investments text, also published by McGraw-Hill/Irwin.

Preface

The teaching and the practice of corporate finance are more challenging and exciting than ever before. The last decade has seen fundamental changes in financial markets and financial instruments. In the early years of the 21st century, we still see announcements in the financial press about such matters as takeovers, junk bonds, financial restructuring, initial public offerings, bankruptcy, and derivatives. In addition, there is the new recognition of "real" options, private equity and venture capital, and the disappearing dividend. The world's financial markets are more integrated than ever before. Both the theory and practice of corporate finance have been moving ahead with uncommon speed, and our teaching must keep pace.

These developments place new burdens on the teaching of corporate finance. On one hand, the changing world of finance makes it more difficult to keep materials up to date. On the other hand, the teacher must distinguish the permanent from the temporary and avoid the temptation to follow fads. Our solution to this problem is to emphasize the modern fundamentals of the theory of finance and make the theory come to life with contemporary examples. Increasingly, many of these examples are outside the United States. All too often the beginning student views corporate finance as a collection of unrelated topics that are unified largely because they are bound together between the covers of one book. As in the previous editions, our aim is to present corporate finance as the working of a few integrated and powerful institutions.

The Intended Audience of This Book

This book has been written for the introductory courses in corporate finance at the MBA level and for the intermediate courses in many undergraduate programs. Some instructors will find our text appropriate for the introductory course at the undergraduate level as well.

We assume that most students either will have taken, or will be concurrently enrolled in, courses in accounting, statistics, and economics. This exposure will help students understand some of the more difficult material. However, the book is self-contained, and a prior knowledge of these areas is not essential. The only mathematics prerequisite is basic algebra.

New to the Eighth Edition

With the eight edition of *Modern Financial Management,* we have done extensive updating and reworking throughout the text. Among the more noticeable changes are opening vignettes for each chapter. Most of these present familiar companies in situations covered by the chapter, thereby motivating the discussion. The end-of-chapter material has been expanded considerably. We now have two separate sets of questions, one that focuses on concepts and critical ideas and another that is more problem oriented. The total number of questions has grown significantly. Finally, almost every chapter now ends with a mini-case that places the student in the position of needing to apply chapter concepts in a common real-world situation. These cases are suitable for a variety of pedagogical purposes, ranging from homework to group assignments to in-class discussions.

In addition to these changes and overall updating, a number of chapters have significant new material. Following are some of the more notable additions and upgrades:

Chapter 1:   Expanded discussion of goal of the firm and agency problems. New material on Sarbanes-Oxley.

Chapter 3:   Completely rewritten to cover financial statements analysis and long-term financial planning.

Chapter 5:   New discussion of bond price information, including the NASD TRACE system.

Chapter 7:   New discussion of alternative definitions of project cash flows.

Chapter 8:   Reorganized, with improved discussion of decision trees.

Chapter 9:   New discussion of geometric versus arithmetic returns.

Chapter 12:   Expanded discussion on actual cost of capital estimation.

Chapter 18:   New material on several dividend-related subjects.

Chapter 19:   New material on Dutch auction IPOs.

Chapter 20:   New material on bond price quotes and make-whole call provisions.

Chapter 22:   Expanded discussion on applications of options analysis in corporate finance.

Chapter 27:   New material on financial electronic data interchange and the Check Clearing Act for the 21st Century.

Chapter 29:   Completely rewritten with new material on a variety of merger-related topics.

Chapter 31:   Completely rewritten for clarity.

We have also worked to improve the supplements to the text, with the goal of providing far and away the most comprehensive student and instructor support at this level. For example, we now provide fully detailed step-by-step solutions to end-of-chapter problems (and spreadsheets for each one as well). The testbank has grown significantly in terms of the number of questions, and we have worked to provide a wider variety of questions and question types. The PowerPoint set also has grown.

The book's Online Learning Center (OLC) delivers several new and very rich student study aids. There is self-study software with at least 100 questions per chapter. Narrated PowerPoint slides actually talk students through the material. Our Interactive FinSims contain simulations of key finance concepts in which students are asked to provide values for key variables. These digital assets provide completely new avenues for students to explore and ways for them to comprehend the subject on a deeper level.

For a complete look at the new and updated eighth edition features, please see the next section.

Pedagogy

In this edition of *Modern Financial Management*, we have updated and improved our features to present material in a way that makes it coherent and easy to understand. In addition, *Modern Financial Management* is rich in valuable learning tools and support, to help students succeed in learning the fundamentals of financial management.

Chapter Opening Vignettes

Each chapter begins with a "roadmap" that describes the objectives of the chapter and how it connects with concepts already learned in previous chapters. Real company examples that will be discussed are highlighted in these sections.

CHAPTER

10

Return and Risk
The Capital Asset Pricing Model (CAPM)

Expected returns on common stocks can vary quite a bit. One important determinant is the industry in which a company operates. For example, according to recent estimates from Ibbotson Associates, the median expected return for department stores, which includes companies such as Sears and Kohls, is 11.63 percent, whereas computer service companies such as Microsoft and Oracle have a median expected return of 15.46 percent. Air transportation companies such as Delta and Southwest have a median expected return that is even higher: 17.93 percent.

These estimates raise some obvious questions. First, why do these industry expected returns differ so much, and how are these specific numbers calculated? Also, does the higher return offered by airline stocks mean that investors should prefer these to, say, department store stocks? As we will see in this chapter, the Nobel Prize–winning answers to these questions form the basis of our modern understanding of risk and return.

10.1 Individual Securities

In the first part of Chapter 10, we will examine the characteristics of individual securities. In particular, we will discuss:

1. *Expected return*: This is the return that an individual expects a stock to earn over the next period. Of course, because this is only an expectation, the actual return may be either higher or lower. An individual's expectation may simply be the average return per period a security has earned in the past. Alternatively, it may be based on a detailed analysis of a firm's prospects, on some computer-based model, or on special (or inside) information.

2. *Variance and standard deviation*: There are many ways to assess the volatility of a security's return. One of the most common is variance, which is a measure of the squared deviations of a security's return from its expected return. Standard deviation is the square root of the variance.

3. *Covariance and correlation*: Returns on individual securities are related to one another. Covariance is a statistic measuring the interrelationship between two securities. Alternatively, this relationship can be restated in terms of the correlation between the two securities. Covariance and correlation are building blocks to an understanding of the beta coefficient.

Table 24.2
The Case for and against Convertible Bonds (CBs)

	If Firm Subsequently Does Poorly	If Firm Subsequently Prospers
Convertible bonds (CBs)	No conversion because of low stock price.	Conversion because of high stock price.
Compared to: Straight bonds	CBs provide cheap financing because coupon rate is lower.	CBs provide expensive financing because bonds are converted, which dilutes existing equity.
Common stock	CBs provide expensive financing because firm could have issued common stock at high prices.	CBs provide cheap financing because firm issues stock at high prices when bonds are converted.

Summary   Compared with equity, the firm is better off having issued convertible debt if the underlying stock subsequently does well. The firm is worse off having issued convertible debt if the underlying stock subsequently does poorly. We cannot predict future stock price in an efficient market. Thus, we cannot argue that issuing convertibles is better or worse than issuing equity. The preceding analysis is summarized in Table 24.2.

Modigliani–Miller (MM) pointed out that, abstracting from taxes and bankruptcy costs, the firm is indifferent to whether it issues stock or issues debt. The MM relationship is a quite general one. Their pedagogy could be adjusted to show that the firm is indifferent to whether it issues convertibles or issues other instruments. To save space (and the patience of students) we have omitted a full-blown proof of MM in a world with convertibles. However, our results are perfectly consistent with MM. Now we turn to the real-world view of convertibles.

The "Free Lunch" Story

The preceding discussion suggests that issuing a convertible bond is no better and no worse than issuing other instruments. Unfortunately, many corporate executives fall into the trap of arguing that issuing convertible debt is actually better than issuing alternative instruments. This is a free lunch type of explanation, of which we are quite critical.

EXAMPLE 24.4

Are Convertibles Always Better?   The stock price of RW Company is $20. Suppose this company can issue subordinated debentures at 10 percent. It can also issue convertible bonds at 6 percent with a conversion value of $800. The conversion value means that the holders can convert a convertible bond into 40 (= $800/$20) shares of common stock.

A company treasurer who believes in free lunches might argue that convertible bonds should be issued because they represent a cheaper source of financing than either subordinated bonds or common stock. The treasurer will point out that if the company does poorly and the price does not rise above $20, the convertible bondholders will not convert the bonds into common stock. In this case the company will have obtained debt financing at below-market rates by attaching worthless equity kickers. On the other hand, if the firm does well and the price of its common stock rises to $25 or above, convertible holders will convert. The company will issue 40 shares. The company will receive a bond with face value of $1,000 in exchange for issuing 40 shares of common stock, implying a conversion price of $25. The company will have issued common stock at $25 per share, or 20 percent above the $20 common stock price prevailing when the convertible bonds were issued. This enables it to lower its cost of equity capital. Thus, the treasurer happily points out, regardless of whether the company does well or poorly, convertible bonds are the cheapest form of financing.

(continued)

Figures and Tables

This text makes extensive use of real data and presents them in various figures and tables. Explanations in the narrative, examples, and end-of-chapter problems will refer to many of these exhibits.

Examples

Separate called-out examples are integrated throughout the chapters. Each example illustrates an intuitive or mathematical application in a step-by-step format. There is enough detail in the explanations so the student doesn't have to look elsewhere for additional information.

"In Their Own Words" Boxes

Located throughout the chapters, this unique series consists of articles written by distinguished scholars or practitioners about key topics in the text. Boxes include essays by Edward I. Altman, Anthony Bourdain, Robert S. Hansen, Robert C. Higgins, Michael C. Jensen, Richard M. Levich, Merton Miller, and Jay R. Ritter.

In Their Own Words

SKILLS NEEDED FOR THE CHIEF FINANCIAL OFFICERS OF eFINANCE.COM

Chief strategist: CFOs will need to use real-time financial information to make crucial decisions fast.

Chief deal maker: CFOs must be adept at venture capital, mergers and acquisitions, and strategic partnerships.

Chief risk officer: Limiting risk will be even more important as markets become more global and hedging instruments become more complex.

Chief communicator: Gaining the confidence of Wall Street and the media will be essential.

SOURCE: *BusinessWeek*, August 28, 2000, p. 120.

The interplay of the firm's activities with the financial markets is illustrated in Figure 1.4. The arrows in Figure 1.4 trace cash flow from the firm to the financial markets and back again. Suppose we begin with the firm's financing activities. To raise money, the firm sells debt and equity shares to investors in the financial markets. This results in cash flows from the financial markets to the firm (A). This cash is invested in the investment activities (assets) of the firm (B) by the firm's management. The cash generated by the firm (C) is paid to shareholders and bondholders (F). The shareholders receive cash in the form of dividends; the bondholders who lent funds to the firm receive interest and, when the initial loan is repaid, principal. Not all of the firm's cash is paid out. Some is retained (E), and some is paid to the government as taxes (D).

Over time, if the cash paid to shareholders and bondholders (F) is greater than the cash raised in the financial markets (A), value will be created.

Identification of Cash Flows   Unfortunately, it is not easy to observe cash flows directly. Much of the information we obtain is in the form of accounting statements, and

2.2 The Income Statement

The **income statement** measures performance over a specific period—say a year. The accounting definition of income is:

$$\text{Revenue} - \text{Expenses} \equiv \text{Income}$$

If the balance sheet is like a snapshot, the income statement is like a video recording of what the people did between two snapshots. Table 2.2 gives the income statement for the U.S. Composite Corporation for 2007.

The income statement usually includes several sections. The operations section reports the firm's revenues and expenses from principal operations. One number of particular importance is earnings before interest and taxes (EBIT), which summarizes earnings before taxes and financing costs. Among other things, the nonoperating section of the income statement includes all financing costs, such as interest expense. Usually a second section reports as a separate item the amount of taxes levied on income. The last item on the income statement is the bottom line, or net income. Net income is frequently expressed per share of common stock—that is, earnings per share.

When analyzing an income statement, the financial manager should keep in mind GAAP, noncash items, time, and costs.

25.5 Interest Rate Futures Contracts

In this section we consider interest rate futures contracts. Our examples deal with futures contracts on Treasury bonds because of their high popularity. We first price Treasury bonds and Treasury bond forward contracts. Differences between futures and forward contracts are explored. Hedging examples are provided next.

Pricing of Treasury Bonds

As mentioned earlier in the text, a Treasury bond pays semiannual interest over its life. In addition, the face value of the bond is paid at maturity. Consider a 20-year, 8 percent coupon bond that was issued on March 1. The first payment is to occur in six months—that is, on September 1. The value of the bond can be determined as follows:

Pricing of Treasury Bond

$$P_{TB} = \frac{\$40}{1 + R_1} + \frac{\$40}{(1 + R_2)^2} + \frac{\$40}{(1 + R_3)^3} + \cdots + \frac{\$40}{(1 + R_{39})^{39}} + \frac{\$1,040}{(1 + R_{40})^{40}} \qquad (25.1)$$

Because an 8 percent coupon bond pays interest of $80 a year, the semiannual coupon is $40. Principal and the semiannual coupons are both paid at maturity. As we mentioned in a previous chapter, the price of the Treasury bond, P_{TB}, is determined by discounting each payment on a bond at the appropriate spot rate. Because the payments are semiannual, each spot rate is expressed in semiannual terms. That is, imagine a horizontal term structure where the effective annual yield is 12 percent for all maturities. Because each spot rate, R, is expressed in semiannual terms, each spot rate is $\sqrt{1.12} - 1 = 5.83\%$. Coupon payments

End-of-Chapter Material

The end-of-chapter material reflects and builds upon the concepts learned from the chapter and study features.

The following shows a sample textbook page:

> **Chapter 2** Financial Statements and Cash Flow   **35**
>
> go under financing activities, but unfortunately that is not how the accounting is handled. The reason is that interest is deducted as an expense when net income is computed. As a consequence, a primary difference between the accounting cash flow and the financial cash flow of the firm (see Table 2.5) is interest expense.
>
> **Summary and Conclusions**
>
> Besides introducing you to corporate accounting, the purpose of this chapter has been to teach you how to determine cash flow from the accounting statements of a typical company.
>
> 1. Cash flow is generated by the firm and paid to creditors and shareholders. It can be classified as:
>   a. Cash flow from operations.
>   b. Cash flow from changes in fixed assets.
>   c. Cash flow from changes in working capital.
> 2. Calculations of cash flow are not difficult, but they require care and particular attention to detail in properly accounting for noncash expenses such as depreciation and deferred taxes. It is especially important that you do not confuse cash flow with changes in net working capital and net income.
>
> **Concept Questions**
>
> 1. **Liquidity** True or false: All assets are liquid at some price. Explain.
> 2. **Accounting and Cash Flows** Why might the revenue and cost figures shown on a standard income statement not represent the actual cash inflows and outflows that occurred during a period?
> 3. **Accounting Statement of Cash Flows** Looking at the accounting statement of cash flows, what does the bottom line number mean? How useful is this number for analyzing a company?
> 4. **Cash Flows** How do financial cash flows and the accounting statement of cash flows differ? Which is more useful for analyzing a company?
> 5. **Book Values versus Market Values** Under standard accounting rules, it is possible for a company's liabilities to exceed assets. When this occurs, the owners' equity is negative. Can this happen with market values? Why or why not?
> 6. **Cash Flow from Assets** Why is it not necessarily bad for the cash flow from assets to be negative for a particular period?
> 7. **Operating Cash Flow** Why is it not necessarily bad for the operating cash flow to be negative for a particular period?
> 8. **Net Working Capital and Capital Spending** Could a company's change in net working capital be negative in a given year? (Hint: Yes.) Explain how this might come about. What about net capital spending?
> 9. **Cash Flow to Stockholders and Creditors** Could a company's cash flow to stockholders be negative in a given year? (Hint: Yes.) Explain how this might come about. What about cash flow to creditors?
> 10. **Firm Values** Referring back to the CBS Records example at the beginning of the chapter, note that we suggested that CBS Records' stockholders probably didn't suffer as a result of the reported loss. What do you think was the basis for our conclusion?
>
> **Questions and Problems**
>
> **BASIC**
> **(Questions 1–10)**
>
> 1. **Building a Balance Sheet** Culligan, Inc., has current assets of $5,000, net fixed assets of $23,000, current liabilities of $4,300, and long-term debt of $13,000. What is the value of the shareholders' equity account for this firm? How much is net working capital?
> 2. **Building an Income Statement** Ragsdale, Inc., has sales of $527,000, costs of $280,000, depreciation expense of $38,000, interest expense of $15,000, and a tax rate of 35 percent.

Summary and Conclusions

The summary provides a quick review of key concepts in the chapter.

Questions and Problems

Because solving problems is so critical to a student's learning, new questions and problems have been added, and existing questions and problems have been revised. All problems have also been thoroughly reviewed and accuracy-checked.

Problems have been grouped according to level of difficulty with the levels listed in the margin: Basic, Intermediate, and Challenge.

Additionally, we have tried to make the problems in the critical "concept" chapters, such as those on value, risk, and capital structure, especially challenging and interesting.

We provide answers to selected problems in Appendix B at the end of the book.

S&P Problems

Included in the end-of-chapter material are problems directly incorporating the Educational Version of Market Insight, a service based on Standard & Poor's renowned Compustat database. These problems provide you with an easy method of including current real-world data in your course.

> **S&P Problems**
>
> STANDARD & POOR'S
>
> www.mhhe.com/edumarketinsight
>
> 1. **Marginal and Average Tax Rates** Download the annual income statements for Sharper Image (SHRP). Looking back at Table 2.3, what is the marginal income tax rate for Sharper Image? Using the total income tax and the pretax income numbers, calculate the average tax rate for Sharper Image. Is this number greater than 35 percent? Why or why not?
> 2. **Net Working Capital** Find the annual balance sheets for American Electric Power (AEP) and HJ Heinz (HNZ). Calculate the net working capital for each company. Is American Electric Power's net working capital negative? If so, does this indicate potential financial difficulty for the company? What about Heinz?
> 3. **Per Share Earnings and Dividends** Find the annual income statements for Harley-Davidson (HDI), Hawaiian Electric Industries (HE), and Time Warner (TWX). What are the earnings per share (EPS Basic from operations) for each of these companies? What are the dividends per share for each company? Why do these companies pay out a different portion of income in the form of dividends?

Excel Problems

Indicated by the Excel icon in the margin, these problems can be found at the end of almost all chapters. Located on the book's Web site (see Online Resources), Excel templates have been created for each of these problems, where students can use the data in the problem to work out the solution using Excel skills.

> **CHALLENGE**
> **(Questions 15–17)**
>
> 15. **Convertible Calculations** You have been hired to value a new 25-year callable, convertible bond. The bond has a 6.80 percent coupon rate, payable annually. The conversion price is $150, and the stock currently sells for $44.75. The stock price is expected to grow at 12 percent per year. The bond is callable at $1,200; but based on prior experience, it won't be called unless the conversion value is $1,300. The required return on this bond is 10 percent. What value would you assign to this bond?
>
>
>
> 16. **Warrant Value** Superior Clamps, Inc., has a capital structure consisting of 4 million shares of common stock and 500,000 warrants. Each warrant gives its owner the right to purchase one share of newly issued common stock for an exercise price of $20. The warrants are European and will expire one year from today. The market value of the company's assets is $88 million, and the annual variance of the returns on the firm's assets is 0.04. Treasury bills that mature in one year yield a continuously compounded interest rate of 7 percent. The company does not pay a dividend. Use the Black–Scholes model to determine the value of a single warrant.

End-of-Chapter Cases

Located at the end of almost every chapter, these mini-cases focus on common company situations that embody important corporate finance topics. Each case presents a new scenario, data, and a dilemma. Several questions at the end of each case require students to analyze and focus on all of the material they learned in that chapter.

> **Mini Case**
>
> **Cash Flows at Warf Computers, Inc.**
>
> Warf Computers, Inc., was founded 15 years ago by Nick Warf, a computer programmer. The small initial investment to start the company was made by Nick and his friends. Over the years, this same group has supplied the limited additional investment needed by the company in the form of both equity and short- and long-term debt. Recently the company has developed a virtual keyboard (VK). The VK uses sophisticated artificial intelligence algorithms that allow the user to speak naturally and have the computer input the text, correct spelling and grammatical errors, and format the document according to preset user guidelines. The VK even suggests alternative phrasing and sentence structure, and it provides detailed stylistic diagnostics. Based on a proprietary, very advanced software/hardware hybrid technology, the system is a full generation beyond what is currently on the market. To introduce the VK, the company will require significant outside investment.
>
> Nick has made the decision to seek this outside financing in the form of new equity investments and bank loans. Naturally, new investors and the banks will require a detailed financial analysis. Your employer, Angus Jones & Partners, LLC, has asked you to examine the financial statements provided by Nick. Here are the balance sheet for the two most recent years and the most recent income statement:

Comprehensive Teaching

Modern Financial Management has many options in terms of the textbook, instructor supplements, student supplements, and multimedia products. Mix and match to create a package that is perfect for your course.

Instructor Supplements

Instructor's CD-ROM

This CD contains all the necessary supplements—Instructor's Manual, Test Bank, Computerized Test Bank, and PowerPoint—all in one useful product in an electronic format.

- **Instructor's Manual**

  Prepared by Steven Dolvin, Butler University and Joseph Smolira, Belmont University.

  This is a great place to find new lecture ideas. The IM has three main sections. The first section contains a chapter outline and other lecture materials. The annotated outline for each chapter includes lecture tips, real-world tips, ethics notes, suggested PowerPoint slides, and, when appropriate, a video synopsis. Detailed solutions for all end-of-chapter problems appear in section two.

- **Test Bank**

  Prepared by Patricia Ryan, Colorado State University.

  Here's a great format for a better testing process. The Test Bank has well over 100 questions per chapter that closely link with the text material and provides a variety of question formats (multiple-choice questions/problems and essay questions) and levels of difficulty (basic, intermediate, and challenge) to meet every instructor's testing needs. Problems are detailed enough to make them intuitive for students, and solutions are provided for the instructor.

- **Computerized Test Bank (Windows)**

  These additional questions are found in a computerized test bank utilizing McGraw-Hill's EZ Test testing software to quickly create customized exams. This user-friendly program allows instructors to sort questions by format; edit existing questions or add new ones; and scramble questions for multiple versions of the same test.

- **PowerPoint Presentation System**

  Prepared by Steven Dolvin, Butler University.

  Customize our content for your course. This presentation has been thoroughly revised to include more lecture-oriented slides, as well as exhibits and examples both from the book and from outside sources. Applicable slides have Web links that take you directly to specific Internet sites, or a spreadsheet link to show an example in Excel. You can also go to the Notes Page function for more tips on presenting the slides. If you already have PowerPoint installed on your PC, you can edit, print, or rearrange the complete presentation to meet your specific needs.

Solutions Manual

Prepared by Joseph Smolira, Belmont University.

This manual contains detailed, worked-out solutions for all of the problems in the end-of-chapter material. It has also been reviewed for accuracy by multiple sources. The Solutions Manual is also available for purchase by your students.

and Learning Package

Videos

Now available in DVD format: a current set of videos about hot topics! McGraw-Hill/Irwin has produced a series of finance videos that are 10-minute case studies of topics such as financial markets, careers, rightsizing, capital budgeting, EVA (economic value added), mergers and acquisitions, and foreign exchange. Discussion questions for these videos, as well as video clips, are available in the Instructor's Center at www.mhhe.com/rwj.

Digital Solutions

Online Learning Center (OLC): Online Support at www.mhhe.com/rwj

The Online Learning Center (OLC) contains FREE access to additional Web-based study and teaching aids created for this text, such as the following.

Student Support

- **New! Self-Study Software**

  With this self-study program, students can test their knowledge of one chapter or a number of chapters by using self-grading questions written specifically for this text. There are at least 100 questions per chapter. Students can set a timer function to simulate a test environment, or they can choose to have answers pop up as they finish each question. Questions were prepared by Kay Johnson, Penn State University–Erie.

- **New! Narrated PowerPoint Examples**

  Created by Kay Johnson, Penn State University–Erie, exclusively for students. Each chapter's slides follow the chapter topics and provide steps and explanations showing how to solve key problems. Because each student learns differently, a quick click on each slide will "talk through" its contents with you!

- **New! Interactive FinSims**

  Created by Eric Sandburg, Interactive Media, each module highlights a key concept of the book and simulates how to solve its problems, asking the student to input certain variables. This hands-on approach guides students through difficult and important corporate finance topics.

- **Excel Templates**

  Corresponding to most end-of-chapter problems, each template allows the student to work through the problem using Excel. Each end-of-chapter problem with a template is indicated by an Excel icon in the margin beside it.

- **More**

  Be sure to check out the other helpful features on the OLC, including links to Corporate Finance Online study problems, and Finance around the World.

Teaching Support

Along with having access to all of the same material your students can view on the book's OLC, you also have password-protected access to the Instructor's Manual, solutions to end-of-chapter problems, Instructor's PowerPoint, Excel Template Solutions, video clips, video projects and questions, and teaching notes to Corporate Finance Online.

OLCs can be delivered in multiple ways—through the textbook Web site (www.mhhe.com/rwj), through PageOut, or within a course management system like Blackboard, WebCT, TopClass, or eCollege. Ask your campus representative for more details.

Standard & Poor's Educational Version of Market Insight

McGraw-Hill/Irwin and the Institutional Market Services division of Standard & Poor's are pleased to announce an exclusive partnership that offers instructors and students FREE access to the educational version of Standard & Poor's Market Insight with each new textbook. The educational version of Market Insight is a rich online resource that provides six years of fundamental financial data for over 1,000 companies in the database. S&P–specific problems can be found at the end of almost all chapters in this text and ask students to solve a problem by using research found on this site. For more details, please see the bound-in card inside the front cover of this text or visit www.mhhe.com/edumarketinsight.

Corporate Finance Online

As part of the OLC, instructors and students will also have access to *Corporate Finance Online*, found on the opening page. Corporate Finance Online is an exclusive Web tool from McGraw-Hill/Irwin. The site provides over 54 exercises for 27 key corporate finance topics, allowing students to complete challenging exercises and discussion questions that draw on recent articles, company reports, government data, and other Web-based resources. For instructors there are also password-protected teaching notes to assist with classroom integration of the material.

PageOut at www.pageout.net

FREE to adopters, this Web page generation software is designed to help you create your own course Web site without hassle. In just a few minutes even the most novice computer user can have a functioning course Web site.

Simply type your material into the template provided and PageOut instantly converts it to HTML. Next, choose your favorite of three easy-to-navigate designs and your class Web home page is created, complete with online syllabus, lecture notes, and bookmarks. You can even include a separate instructor page and an assignment page.

PageOut offers enhanced point-and-click features, including a Syllabus Page that applies a real-world link to original text material, an automatic grade book, and a discussion board where you and your students can exchange questions and post announcements. Ask your campus representative to show you a demo.

Options Available for Purchase & Packaging

You may also package either version of the text with a variety of additional learning tools that are available for your students.

Student Problem Manual

Prepared by Robert Hanson, Eastern Michigan University.

The Student Problem Manual is a direct companion to the text. It is uniquely designed to involve the student in the learning process. Each chapter contains a mission statement, an average of 20 fill-in-the-blank concept test questions and answers, and an average of 15 problems and worked-out solutions. This product can be purchased separately or can be packaged with this text.

Solutions Manual

Prepared by Joseph Smolira, Belmont University.

This manual contains detailed, worked-out solutions for all of the problems in the end-of-chapter material. It has also been reviewed for accuracy by multiple sources. The Solutions Manual is also available for purchase by your students.

The Wall Street Journal

If you order this package, your students can subscribe to *The Wall Street Journal*—both print and online versions—for 15 weeks at a specially priced rate of $20.00 in addition to the price of the text. Students will receive a "How to Use the *WSJ*" handbook plus a card explaining how to start the subscription to both versions.

BusinessWeek

Your students can subscribe to 15 weeks of *BusinessWeek* for a specially priced rate of $8.25 in addition to the price of the text. Students will receive a pass-code card shrink-wrapped with their new text. The card directs students to a Web site where they enter the code and then gain access to *BusinessWeek's* registration page to enter address information and set up their print and online subscriptions.

Financial Times

Your students can subscribe to the *Financial Times* for 15 weeks at a specially priced rate of $10 in addition to the price of the text by ordering this special package. Students will receive a subscription card shrink-wrapped with their new text to fill in and send to the *Financial Times* to start receiving their subscription. Instructors, once you order, make sure you contact your sales representative to receive a complimentary one-year subscription.

Excel Applications for Corporate Finance

By Troy Adair, University of Michigan–Ann Arbor; can be packaged with the text at a discounted price.

This supplement teaches students how to build financial models in Excel and shows students how to use these models to solve a variety of common corporate finance problems. For more information about this supplement, visit www.mhhe.com/adair1e.

FinGame Online 4.0

By LeRoy Brooks, John Carroll University.

Just $15.00 when packaged with this text. In this comprehensive simulation game, students control a hypothetical company over numerous periods of operation. The game is now tied to the text by exercises found at the Online Learning Center. As students make major financial and operating decisions for their company, they will develop and enhance skills in financial management and financial accounting statement analysis.

Financial Analysis with an Electronic Calculator, Sixth Edition

By Mark A. White, University of Virginia, McIntire School of Commerce.

The information and procedures in this supplementary text enable students to master the use of financial calculators and develop a working knowledge of financial mathematics and problem solving. Complete instructions are included for solving all major problem types on three popular models: HP 10-B and 12-C, TI BA II Plus, and TI-84. Hands-on problems with detailed solutions allow students to practice the skills outlined in the text and obtain instant reinforcement. *Financial Analysis with an Electronic Calculator* is a self-contained supplement to the introductory financial management course.

Acknowledgments

The plan for developing this edition began with a number of our colleagues who had an interest in the book and regularly teach the MBA introductory course. We integrated their comments and recommendations throughout the Eighth Edition. Contributors to this edition include the following:

Janet Hamilton
Portland State University

Robert Hauswald
American University

Robert Krell
George Mason University

Thomas Legg
University of Minnesota

Joseph Meredith
Elon University

Vassil Mihov
Texas Christian University

Edward Morris
Lindenwood University

Betty Simkins
Oklahoma State University

Robert Wood
Tennessee Tech University

Over the years, many others have contributed their time and expertise to the development and writing of this text. We extend our thanks once again for their assistance and countless insights:

R. Aggarwal
John Carroll University

Christopher Anderson
University of Missouri–Columbia

James J. Angel
Georgetown University

Nasser Arshadi
University of Missouri–St. Louis

Kevin Bahr
University of Wisconsin–Milwaukee

Robert Balik
Western Michigan University

John W. Ballantine
Babson College

Thomas Bankston
Angelo State University

Brad Barber
University of California–Davis

Michael Barry
Boston College

Swati Bhatt
Rutgers University

Roger Bolton
Williams College

Gordon Bonner
University of Delaware

Oswald Bowlin
Texas Technical University

Ronald Braswell
Florida State University

William O. Brown
Claremont McKenna College

Kirt Butler
Michigan State University

Bill Callahan
Southern Methodist University

Steven Carvell
Cornell University

Indudeep S. Chhachhi
Western Kentucky University

Andreas Christofi
Monmouth University

Jeffrey L. Coles
Arizona State University

Mark Copper
Wayne State University

James Cotter
University of Iowa

Jay Coughenour
University of Massachusetts–Boston

Arnold Cowan
Iowa State University

Raymond Cox
Central Michigan University

John Crockett
George Mason University

Mark Cross
Louisiana Technical University

Ron Crowe
Jacksonville University

William Damon
Vanderbilt University

Sudip Datta
Bentley College

Anand Desai
University of Florida

Miranda Lam Detzler
University of Massachusetts–Boston

David Distad
University of California–Berkeley

Dennis Draper
University of Southern California

Jean-Francois Dreyfus
New York University

Gene Drzycimski
University of Wisconsin–Oshkosh

Robert Duvic
The University of Texas at Austin

Demissew Ejara
University of Massachusetts–Boston

Robert Eldridge
Fairfield University

Gary Emery
University of Oklahoma

Theodore Eytan
City University of New York–Baruch College

Don Fehrs
University of Notre Dame

Steven Ferraro
Pepperdine University

Andrew Fields
University of Delaware

Paige Fields
Texas A&M

Adlai Fisher
New York University

Michael Fishman
Northwestern University

Yee-Tien Fu
Stanford University

Bruno Gerard
University of Southern California

Frank Ghannadian
Mercer University–Atlanta

Michael Goldstein
University of Colorado

Indra Guertler
Babson College

James Haltiner
College of William and Mary

Delvin Hawley
University of Mississippi

Hal Heaton
Brigham Young University

John A. Helmuth
University of Michigan–Dearborn

John Helmuth
Rochester Institute of Technology

Michael Hemler
University of Notre Dame

Stephen Heston
Washington University

Andrea Heuson
University of Miami

Edith Hotchkiss
Boston College

Charles Hu
Claremont McKenna College

Hugh Hunter
Eastern Washington University

James Jackson
Oklahoma State University

Raymond Jackson
*University of Massachusetts–
Dartmouth*

Prem Jain
Tulane University

Narayanan Jayaraman
Georgia Institute of Technology

Brad Jordan
University of Kentucky

Jarl Kallberg
New York University

Jonathan Karpoff
University of Washington

Paul Keat
*American Graduate School of
International Management*

Dolly King
University of Wisconsin–Milwaukee

Brian Kluger
University of Cincinnati

Narayana Kocherlakota
University of Iowa

Ronald Kudla
The University of Akron

Youngsik Kwak
Delaware State University

Nelson Lacey
University of Massachusetts

Gene Lai
University of Rhode Island

Josef Lakonishok
University of Illinois

Dennis Lasser
*State University of New York–
Binghamton*

Paul Laux
Case Western Reserve University

Bong-Su Lee
University of Minnesota

Youngho Lee
Howard University

James T. Lindley
University of Southern Mississippi

Dennis Logue
Dartmouth College

Michael Long
Rutgers University

Yulong Ma
Cal State–Long Beach

Ileen Malitz
Fairleigh Dickinson University

Terry Maness
Baylor University

Surendra Mansinghka
San Francisco State University

Michael Mazzco
Michigan State University

Robert I. McDonald
Northwestern University

Hugh McLaughlin
Bentley College

Larry Merville
University of Texas–Richardson

Joe Messina
San Francisco State University

Roger Mesznik
*City College of New York–Baruch
College*

Rick Meyer
University of South Florida

Richard Miller
Wesleyan University

Naval Modani
University of Central Florida

Richard Mull
New Mexico State University

Jim Musumeci
*Southern Illinois University–
Carbondale*

Robert Nachtmann
University of Pittsburgh

Edward Nelling
Georgia Tech

Gregory Niehaus
University of South Carolina

Peder Nielsen
Oregon State University

Ingmar Nyman
Hunter College

Dennis Officer
University of Kentucky

Joseph Ogden
State University of New York

Venky Panchapagesan
Washington University–St. Louis

Bulent Parker
University of Wisconsin–Madison

Ajay Patel
University of Missouri–Columbia

Dilip Kumar Patro
Rutgers University

Gary Patterson
University of South Florida

Glenn N. Pettengill
Emporia State University

Pegaret Pichler
University of Maryland

Christo Pirinsky
Ohio State University

Jeffrey Pontiff
University of Washington

Franklin Potts
Baylor University

Annette Poulsen
University of Georgia

N. Prabhala
Yale University

Mao Qiu
University of Utah–Salt Lake City

Latha Ramchand
University of Houston

Gabriel Ramirez
Virginia Commonwealth University

Narendar Rao
Northeastern Illinois University

Steven Raymar
Indiana University

Stuart Rosenstein
East Carolina University

Bruce Rubin
Old Dominion University

Patricia Ryan
Drake University

Jaime Sabal
New York University

Anthony Sanders
Ohio State University

Andy Saporoschenko
University of Akron

William Sartoris
Indiana University

James Schallheim
University of Utah

Mary Jean Scheuer
California State University at Northridge

Faruk Selcuk
University of Bridgeport

Lemma Senbet
University of Maryland

Kuldeep Shastri
University of Pittsburgh

Sudhir Singh
Frostburg State University

Scott Smart
Indiana University

Jackie So
Southern Illinois University

John Stansfield
Columbia College

John S. Strong
College of William and Mary

A. Charlene Sullivan
Purdue University

Michael Sullivan
University of Nevada–Las Vegas

Timothy Sullivan
Bentley College

R. Bruce Swensen
Adelphi University

Ernest Swift
Georgia State University

Alex Tang
Morgan State University

Richard Taylor
Arkansas State University

Andrew C. Thompson
Virginia Polytechnic Institute

Timothy Thompson
Northwestern University

Karin Thorburn
Dartmouth College

Satish Thosar
University of Massachusetts–Dorchester

Charles Trzcinka
State University of New York–Buffalo

Haluk Unal
University of Maryland–College Park

Oscar Varela
University of New Orleans

Steven Venti
Dartmouth College

Avinash Verma
Washington University

Lankford Walker
Eastern Illinois University

Ralph Walkling
Ohio State University

F. Katherine Warne
Southern Bell College

Susan White
University of Texas–Austin

Robert Whitelaw
New York University

Berry Wilson
Georgetown University

Thomas Zorn
University of Nebraska–Lincoln

Kent Zumwalt
Colorado State University

For their help on the Eighth Edition, we would like to thank Linda De Angelo, Dennis Draper, Kim Dietrich, Harry De Angelo, Aris Protopapadakis, Suh-Pyng Ku, and Mark Westerfield all of the Marshall School of Business at the University of Southern California; Jordan Strauss Esq.; Stephen Dolvin, Butler University, for his work on the Instructor's Manual and PowerPoint; Patricia Ryan, Colorado State University, for her work on the Test Bank; Robert Hanson, Eastern Michigan University, for his work on the Student Problem Manual; Joe Smolira, Belmont University, for his work on the solutions and text; and Kay Johnson, Penn State University–Erie, for her work on the self-study software and narrated Student PowerPoint. We also owe a debt of gratitude to Bradford D. Jordan of the University of Kentucky; Edward I. Altman of New York University; Robert S. Hansen of Virginia Tech; and Jay R. Ritter of the University of Florida, who have provided several thoughtful comments and immeasurable help.

We thank Allissa Day, Hinh Khieu, Pankaj Maskara, and Theodore Phillips, Jr., for their extensive proofing and problem-checking efforts.

Over the past three years readers have provided assistance by detecting and reporting errors. Our goal is to offer the best textbook available on the subject, so this information was invaluable as we prepared the Eighth Edition. We want to ensure that all future editions are error-free—and therefore we offer $10 per arithmetic error to the first individual reporting it. Any arithmetic error resulting in subsequent errors will be counted double. All errors should be reported using the Feedback Form on the Corporate Finance Online Learning Center at www.mhhe.com/rwj.

Many talented professionals at McGraw-Hill/Irwin have contributed to the development of *Corporate Finance*, Eighth Edition. We would especially like to thank Michele Janicek, Jennifer Rizzi, Julie Phifer, Christine Vaughan, Kami Carter, Gina Hangos, Jennifer Wilson, and Beckey Szura.

Finally, we wish to thank our families and friends, Carol, Kate, Jon, Jan, Mark, and Lynne, for their forbearance and help.

Stephen A. Ross
Randolph W. Westerfield
Jeffrey F. Jaffe
Bradford D. Jordan

Brief Contents

Contents

PART II Valuation and Capital Budgeting

Chapter 7
Making Capital Investment Decisions 197

Chapter 8
Risk Analysis, Real Options, and Capital Budgeting 229

PART Ⅲ Risk

Chapter 9
Risk and Return: Lessons from Market History 256

Chapter 10
Return and Risk: The Capital Asset Pricing Model (CAPM) 279

Chapter 11
An Alternative View of Risk and Return: The Arbitrage Pricing Theory   320

Chapter 12
Risk, Cost of Capital, and Capital Budgeting   342

PART (IV) Capital Structure and Dividend Policy

Chapter 13
Corporate Financing Decisions and Efficient Capital Markets   368

PART Ⓥ Long-Term Financing

Chapter 19
Issuing Securities to the Public — 549

Chapter 20
Long-Term Debt — 580

Chapter 21
Leasing — 606

PART VI Options, Futures, and Corporate Finance

Chapter 22
Options and Corporate Finance　　630

Chapter 23
Options and Corporate Finance: Extensions and Applications　　671

Chapter 24
Warrants and Convertibles　　695

Introduction to Corporate Finance

In July 1999, Carleton "Carly" Fiorina assumed the position of CEO of Hewlett-Packard (HP). Investors were pleased with her view of HP's future: She promised 15 percent annual growth in sales and earnings, quite a goal for a company with five consecutive years of declining revenue. Ms. Fiorina also changed the way HP was run. Rather than continuing to operate as separate product groups, which essentially meant the company operated as dozens of minicompanies, Ms. Fiorina reorganized the company into just two divisions.

In 2002, HP announced that it would merge with Compaq Computers. However, in one of the more acrimonious recent corporate battles, a group led by Walter Hewlett, son of one of HP's cofounders, fought the merger. Ms. Fiorina ultimately prevailed, and the merger took place. With Compaq in the fold, the company began a two-pronged strategy. It would compete with Dell in the lower-cost, more commodity-like personal computer segment and with IBM in the more specialized, high-end computing market.

Unfortunately for HP's shareholders, Ms. Fiorina's strategy did not work out as planned; in February 2005, under pressure from HP's board of directors, Ms. Fiorina resigned her position as CEO. Evidently investors also felt a change in direction was a good idea; HP's stock price jumped almost 7 percent the day the resignation was announced.

Understanding Ms. Fiorina's rise from corporate executive to chief executive officer, and finally to ex-employee, takes us into issues involving the corporate form of organization, corporate goals, and corporate control, all of which we discuss in this chapter.

1.1 What Is Corporate Finance?

Suppose you decide to start a firm to make tennis balls. To do this you hire managers to buy raw materials, and you assemble a workforce that will produce and sell finished tennis balls. In the language of finance, you make an investment in assets such as inventory, machinery, land, and labor. The amount of cash you invest in assets must be matched by an equal amount of cash raised by financing. When you begin to sell tennis balls, your firm will generate cash. This is the basis of value creation. The purpose of the firm is to create value for you, the owner. The value is reflected in the framework of the simple balance sheet model of the firm.

The Balance Sheet Model of the Firm

Suppose we take a financial snapshot of the firm and its activities at a single point in time. Figure 1.1 shows a graphic conceptualization of the balance sheet, and it will help introduce you to corporate finance.

Figure 1.1

The Balance Sheet Model of the Firm

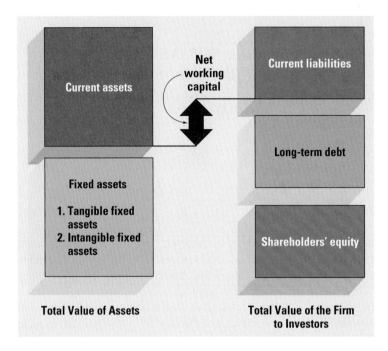

The assets of the firm are on the left side of the balance sheet. These assets can be thought of as current and fixed. *Fixed assets* are those that will last a long time, such as buildings. Some fixed assets are tangible, such as machinery and equipment. Other fixed assets are intangible, such as patents and trademarks. The other category of assets, *current assets*, comprises those that have short lives, such as inventory. The tennis balls that your firm has made, but has not yet sold, are part of its inventory. Unless you have overproduced, they will leave the firm shortly.

Before a company can invest in an asset, it must obtain financing, which means that it must raise the money to pay for the investment. The forms of financing are represented on the right side of the balance sheet. A firm will issue (sell) pieces of paper called *debt* (loan agreements) or *equity shares* (stock certificates). Just as assets are classified as long-lived or short-lived, so too are liabilities. A short-term debt is called a *current liability.* Short-term debt represents loans and other obligations that must be repaid within one year. Long-term debt is debt that does not have to be repaid within one year. Shareholders' equity represents the difference between the value of the assets and the debt of the firm. In this sense, it is a residual claim on the firm's assets.

From the balance sheet model of the firm, it is easy to see why finance can be thought of as the study of the following three questions:

1. In what long-lived assets should the firm invest? This question concerns the left side of the balance sheet. Of course the types and proportions of assets the firm needs tend to be set by the nature of the business. We use the term **capital budgeting** to describe the process of making and managing expenditures on long-lived assets.

2. How can the firm raise cash for required capital expenditures? This question concerns the right side of the balance sheet. The answer to this question involves the firm's **capital structure**, which represents the proportions of the firm's financing from current and long-term debt and equity.

3. How should short-term operating cash flows be managed? This question concerns the upper portion of the balance sheet. There is often a mismatch between the timing of

Figure 1.2

Two Pie Models of the Firm

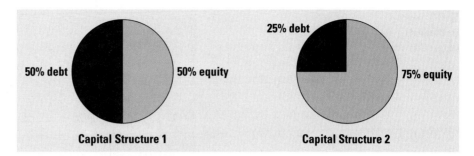

Capital Structure 1 — 50% debt, 50% equity

Capital Structure 2 — 25% debt, 75% equity

cash inflows and cash outflows during operating activities. Furthermore, the amount and timing of operating cash flows are not known with certainty. Financial managers must attempt to manage the gaps in cash flow. From a balance sheet perspective, short-term management of cash flow is associated with a firm's **net working capital**. Net working capital is defined as current assets minus current liabilities. From a financial perspective, short-term cash flow problems come from the mismatching of cash inflows and outflows. This is the subject of short-term finance.

Capital Structure

Financing arrangements determine how the value of the firm is sliced up. The people or institutions that buy debt from (i.e., lend money to) the firm are called *creditors*.[1] The holders of equity shares are called *shareholders*.

Sometimes it is useful to think of the firm as a pie. Initially the size of the pie will depend on how well the firm has made its investment decisions. After a firm has made its investment decisions, it determines the value of its assets (e.g., its buildings, land, and inventories).

The firm can then determine its capital structure. The firm might initially have raised the cash to invest in its assets by issuing more debt than equity; now it can consider changing that mix by issuing more equity and using the proceeds to buy back (pay off) some of its debt. Financing decisions like this can be made independently of the original investment decisions. The decisions to issue debt and equity affect how the pie is sliced.

The pie we are thinking of is depicted in Figure 1.2. The size of the pie is the value of the firm in the financial markets. We can write the value of the firm, V, as

$$V = B + S$$

where B is the market value of the debt and S is the market value of the equity. The pie diagrams consider two ways of slicing the pie: 50 percent debt and 50 percent equity, and 25 percent debt and 75 percent equity. The way the pie is sliced could affect its value. If so, the goal of the financial manager will be to choose the ratio of debt to equity that makes the value of the pie—that is, the value of the firm, V—as large as it can be.

The Financial Manager

In large firms, the finance activity is usually associated with a top officer of the firm, such as the vice president and chief financial officer, and some lesser officers. Figure 1.3 depicts a general organizational structure emphasizing the finance activity within the firm. Reporting to the chief financial officer are the treasurer and the controller. The treasurer is

For current issues facings CFOs, see **www.cfo.com**.

---

[1]We tend to use the words *creditors*, *debtholders*, and *bondholders* interchangeably. In later chapters we examine the differences among the kinds of creditors. In algebraic notation, we will usually refer to the firm's debt with the letter B (for bondholders).

Figure 1.3

Hypothetical Organization Chart

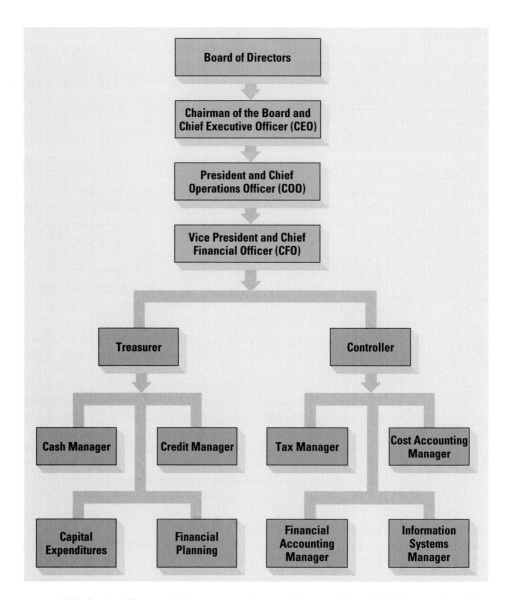

responsible for handling cash flows, managing capital expenditure decisions, and making financial plans. The controller handles the accounting function, which includes taxes, cost and financial accounting, and information systems.

The most important job of a financial manager is to create value from the firm's capital budgeting, financing, and net working capital activities. How do financial managers create value? The answer is that the firm should:

1. Try to buy assets that generate more cash than they cost.
2. Sell bonds and stocks and other financial instruments that raise more cash than they cost.

Thus, the firm must create more cash flow than it uses. The cash flows paid to bondholders and stockholders of the firm should be greater than the cash flows put into the firm by the bondholders and stockholders. To see how this is done, we can trace the cash flows from the firm to the financial markets and back again.

In Their Own Words

The interplay of the firm's activities with the financial markets is illustrated in Figure 1.4. The arrows in Figure 1.4 trace cash flow from the firm to the financial markets and back again. Suppose we begin with the firm's financing activities. To raise money, the firm sells debt and equity shares to investors in the financial markets. This results in cash flows from the financial markets to the firm (A). This cash is invested in the investment activities (assets) of the firm (B) by the firm's management. The cash generated by the firm (C) is paid to shareholders and bondholders (F). The shareholders receive cash in the form of dividends; the bondholders who lent funds to the firm receive interest and, when the initial loan is repaid, principal. Not all of the firm's cash is paid out. Some is retained (E), and some is paid to the government as taxes (D).

Over time, if the cash paid to shareholders and bondholders (F) is greater than the cash raised in the financial markets (A), value will be created.

Identification of Cash Flows Unfortunately, it is not easy to observe cash flows directly. Much of the information we obtain is in the form of accounting statements, and much of the work of financial analysis is to extract cash flow information from accounting statements. The following example illustrates how this is done.

Figure 1.4

Cash Flows between the Firm and the Financial Markets

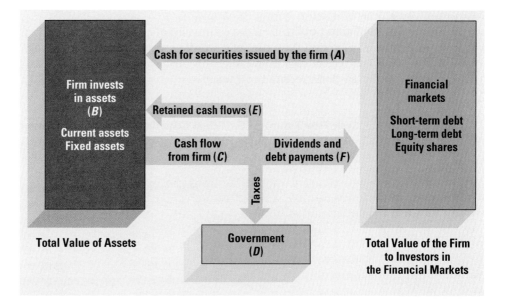

5

EXAMPLE 1.1

Accounting Profit versus Cash Flows   The Midland Company refines and trades gold. At the end of the year, it sold 2,500 ounces of gold for $1 million. The company had acquired the gold for $900,000 at the beginning of the year. The company paid cash for the gold when it was purchased. Unfortunately it has yet to collect from the customer to whom the gold was sold. The following is a standard accounting of Midland's financial circumstances at year-end:

The Midland Company	
Accounting View	
Income Statement	
Year Ended December 31	
Sales	$1,000,000
−Costs	−900,000
Profit	$ 100,000

By generally accepted accounting principles (GAAP), the sale is recorded even though the customer has yet to pay. It is assumed that the customer will pay soon. From the accounting perspective, Midland seems to be profitable. However, the perspective of corporate finance is different. It focuses on cash flows:

The Midland Company	
Financial View	
Income Statement	
Year Ended December 31	
Cash inflow	$ 0
Cash outflow	−900,000
	−$ 900,000

The perspective of corporate finance is interested in whether cash flows are being created by the gold trading operations of Midland. Value creation depends on cash flows. For Midland, value creation depends on whether and when it actually receives $1 million.

Timing of Cash Flows   The value of an investment made by a firm depends on the timing of cash flows. One of the most important principles of finance is that individuals prefer to receive cash flows earlier rather than later. One dollar received today is worth more than one dollar received next year.

EXAMPLE 1.2

Cash Flow Timing   The Midland Company is attempting to choose between two proposals for new products. Both proposals will provide additional cash flows over a four-year period and will initially cost $10,000. The cash flows from the proposals are as follows:

Year	New Product A	New Product B
1	$ 0	$ 4,000
2	0	4,000
3	0	4,000
4	20,000	4,000
Total	$20,000	$16,000

(continued)

At first it appears that new product *A* would be best. However, the cash flows from proposal *B* come earlier than those of *A*. Without more information, we cannot decide which set of cash flows would create the most value for the bondholders and shareholders. It depends on whether the value of getting cash from *B* up front outweighs the extra total cash from *A*. Bond and stock prices reflect this preference for earlier cash, and we will see how to use them to decide between *A* and *B*.

Risk of Cash Flows The firm must consider risk. The amount and timing of cash flows are not usually known with certainty. Most investors have an aversion to risk.

EXAMPLE 1.3

Risk The Midland Company is considering expanding operations overseas. It is evaluating Europe and Japan as possible sites. Europe is considered to be relatively safe, whereas operating in Japan is seen as very risky. In both cases the company would close down operations after one year.

After doing a complete financial analysis, Midland has come up with the following cash flows of the alternative plans for expansion under three scenarios—pessimistic, most likely, and optimistic:

	Pessimistic	Most Likely	Optimistic
Europe	$75,000	$100,000	$125,000
Japan	0	150,000	200,000

If we ignore the pessimistic scenario, perhaps Japan is the best alternative. When we take the pessimistic scenario into account, the choice is unclear. Japan appears to be riskier, but it also offers a higher expected level of cash flow. What is risk and how can it be defined? We must try to answer this important question. Corporate finance cannot avoid coping with risky alternatives, and much of our book is devoted to developing methods for evaluating risky opportunities.

1.2 The Corporate Firm

The firm is a way of organizing the economic activity of many individuals. A basic problem of the firm is how to raise cash. The corporate form of business—that is, organizing the firm as a corporation—is the standard method for solving problems encountered in raising large amounts of cash. However, businesses can take other forms. In this section we consider the three basic legal forms of organizing firms, and we see how firms go about the task of raising large amounts of money under each form.

The Sole Proprietorship

A **sole proprietorship** is a business owned by one person. Suppose you decide to start a business to produce mousetraps. Going into business is simple: You announce to all who will listen, "Today, I am going to build a better mousetrap."

Most large cities require that you obtain a business license. Afterward, you can begin to hire as many people as you need and borrow whatever money you need. At year-end all the profits and the losses will be yours.

Here are some factors that are important in considering a sole proprietorship:

For more about small business organization, see the "Business and Human Resources" section at **www.nolo.com**.

1. The sole proprietorship is the cheapest business to form. No formal charter is required, and few government regulations must be satisfied for most industries.

2. A sole proprietorship pays no corporate income taxes. All profits of the business are taxed as individual income.

3. The sole proprietorship has unlimited liability for business debts and obligations. No distinction is made between personal and business assets.

4. The life of the sole proprietorship is limited by the life of the sole proprietor.

5. Because the only money invested in the firm is the proprietor's, the equity money that can be raised by the sole proprietor is limited to the proprietor's personal wealth.

The Partnership

Any two or more people can get together and form a **partnership**. Partnerships fall into two categories: (1) general partnerships and (2) limited partnerships.

In a *general partnership* all partners agree to provide some fraction of the work and cash and to share the profits and losses. Each partner is liable for all of the debts of the partnership. A partnership agreement specifies the nature of the arrangement. The partnership agreement may be an oral agreement or a formal document setting forth the understanding.

Limited partnerships permit the liability of some of the partners to be limited to the amount of cash each has contributed to the partnership. Limited partnerships usually require that (1) at least one partner be a general partner and (2) the limited partners do not participate in managing the business. Here are some things that are important when considering a partnership:

1. Partnerships are usually inexpensive and easy to form. Written documents are required in complicated arrangements, including general and limited partnerships. Business licenses and filing fees may be necessary.

2. General partners have unlimited liability for all debts. The liability of limited partners is usually limited to the contribution each has made to the partnership. If one general partner is unable to meet his or her commitment, the shortfall must be made up by the other general partners.

3. The general partnership is terminated when a general partner dies or withdraws (but this is not so for a limited partner). It is difficult for a partnership to transfer ownership without dissolving. Usually all general partners must agree. However, limited partners may sell their interest in a business.

4. It is difficult for a partnership to raise large amounts of cash. Equity contributions are usually limited to a partner's ability and desire to contribute to the partnership. Many companies, such as Apple Computer, start life as a proprietorship or partnership, but at some point they choose to convert to corporate form.

5. Income from a partnership is taxed as personal income to the partners.

6. Management control resides with the general partners. Usually a majority vote is required on important matters, such as the amount of profit to be retained in the business.

It is difficult for large business organizations to exist as sole proprietorships or partnerships. The main advantage to a sole proprietorship or partnership is the cost of getting started. Afterward, the disadvantages, which may become severe, are (1) unlimited liability, (2) limited life of the enterprise, and (3) difficulty of transferring ownership. These three disadvantages lead to (4) difficulty in raising cash.

The Corporation

Of the forms of business enterprises, the **corporation** is by far the most important. It is a distinct legal entity. As such, a corporation can have a name and enjoy many of the legal powers of natural persons. For example, corporations can acquire and exchange property. Corporations can enter contracts and may sue and be sued. For jurisdictional purposes the corporation is a citizen of its state of incorporation (it cannot vote, however).

Starting a corporation is more complicated than starting a proprietorship or partnership. The incorporators must prepare articles of incorporation and a set of bylaws. The articles of incorporation must include the following:

1. Name of the corporation.
2. Intended life of the corporation (it may be forever).
3. Business purpose.
4. Number of shares of stock that the corporation is authorized to issue, with a statement of limitations and rights of different classes of shares.
5. Nature of the rights granted to shareholders.
6. Number of members of the initial board of directors.

The bylaws are the rules to be used by the corporation to regulate its own existence, and they concern its shareholders, directors, and officers. Bylaws range from the briefest possible statement of rules for the corporation's management to hundreds of pages of text.

In its simplest form, the corporation comprises three sets of distinct interests: the shareholders (the owners), the directors, and the corporation officers (the top management). Traditionally, the shareholders control the corporation's direction, policies, and activities. The shareholders elect a board of directors, who in turn select top management. Members of top management serve as corporate officers and manage the operations of the corporation in the best interest of the shareholders. In closely held corporations with few shareholders, there may be a large overlap among the shareholders, the directors, and the top management. However, in larger corporations, the shareholders, directors, and the top management are likely to be distinct groups.

The potential separation of ownership from management gives the corporation several advantages over proprietorships and partnerships:

1. Because ownership in a corporation is represented by shares of stock, ownership can be readily transferred to new owners. Because the corporation exists independently of those who own its shares, there is no limit to the transferability of shares as there is in partnerships.
2. The corporation has unlimited life. Because the corporation is separate from its owners, the death or withdrawal of an owner does not affect the corporation's legal existence. The corporation can continue on after the original owners have withdrawn.
3. The shareholders' liability is limited to the amount invested in the ownership shares. For example, if a shareholder purchased $1,000 in shares of a corporation, the potential loss would be $1,000. In a partnership, a general partner with a $1,000 contribution could lose the $1,000 plus any other indebtedness of the partnership.

Limited liability, ease of ownership transfer, and perpetual succession are the major advantages of the corporation form of business organization. These give the corporation an enhanced ability to raise cash.

Table 1.1 **A Comparison of Partnerships and Corporations**

	Corporation	Partnership
Liquidity and marketability	Shares can be exchanged without termination of the corporation. Common stock can be listed on a stock exchange.	Units are subject to substantial restrictions on transferability. There is usually no established trading market for partnership units.
Voting rights	Usually each share of common stock entitles the holder to one vote per share on matters requiring a vote and on the election of the directors. Directors determine top management.	Some voting rights by limited partners. However, general partners have exclusive control and management of operations.
Taxation	Corporations have double taxation: Corporate income is taxable, and dividends to shareholders are also taxable.	Partnerships are not taxable. Partners pay personal taxes on partnership profits.
Reinvestment and dividend payout	Corporations have broad latitude on dividend payout decisions.	Partnerships are generally prohibited from reinvesting partnership profits. All profits are distributed to partners.
Liability	Shareholders are not personally liable for obligations of the corporation.	Limited partners are not liable for obligations of partnerships. General partners may have unlimited liability.
Continuity of existence	Corporations may have a perpetual life.	Partnerships have limited life.

There is, however, one great disadvantage to incorporation. The federal government taxes corporate income (the states do as well). This tax is in addition to the personal income tax that shareholders pay on dividend income they receive. This is double taxation for shareholders when compared to taxation on proprietorships and partnerships. Table 1.1 summarizes our discussion of partnerships and corporations.

Today all 50 states have enacted laws allowing for the creation of a relatively new form of business organization, the limited liability company (LLC). The goal of this entity is to operate and be taxed like a partnership but retain limited liability for owners, so an LLC is essentially a hybrid of partnership and corporation. Although states have differing definitions for LLCs, the more important scorekeeper is the Internal Revenue Service (IRS). The IRS will consider an LLC a corporation, thereby subjecting it to double taxation, unless it meets certain specific criteria. In essence, an LLC cannot be too corporation-like, or it will be treated as one by the IRS. LLCs have become common. For example, Goldman, Sachs and Co., one of Wall Street's last remaining partnerships, decided to convert from a private partnership to an LLC (it later "went public," becoming a publicly held corporation). Large accounting firms and law firms by the score have converted to LLCs.

To find out more about LLCs, visit **www.corporate.com**.

A Corporation by Another Name . . .

The corporate form of organization has many variations around the world. The exact laws and regulations differ from country to country, of course, but the essential features of public ownership and limited liability remain. These firms are often called *joint stock companies*, *public limited companies*, or *limited liability companies*, depending on the specific nature of the firm and the country of origin.

Table 1.2 gives the names of a few well-known international corporations, their countries of origin, and a translation of the abbreviation that follows each company name.

Table 1.2

International
Corporations

Company	Country of Origin	Type of Company	
		In Original Language	Interpretation
Bayerische Moterenwerke (BMW) AG	Germany	Aktiengesellschaft	Corporation
Dornier GmBH	Germany	Gesellschaft mit Baschraenkter Haftung	Limited liability company
Rolls-Royce PLC	United Kingdom	Public limited company	Public ltd. company
Shell UK Ltd.	United Kingdom	Limited	Corporation
Unilever NV	Netherlands	Naamloze Vennootschap	Joint stock company
Fiat SpA	Italy	Societa per Azioni	Joint stock company
Volvo AB	Sweden	Aktiebolag	Joint stock company
Peugeot SA	France	Société Anonyme	Joint stock company

1.3   The Goal of Financial Management

Assuming that we restrict our discussion to for-profit businesses, the goal of financial management is to make money or add value for the owners. This goal is a little vague, of course, so we examine some different ways of formulating it to come up with a more precise definition. Such a definition is important because it leads to an objective basis for making and evaluating financial decisions.

Possible Goals

If we were to consider possible financial goals, we might come up with some ideas like the following:

- Survive.
- Avoid financial distress and bankruptcy.
- Beat the competition.
- Maximize sales or market share.
- Minimize costs.
- Maximize profits.
- Maintain steady earnings growth.

These are only a few of the goals we could list. Furthermore, each of these possibilities presents problems as a goal for the financial manager.

For example, it's easy to increase market share or unit sales: All we have to do is lower our prices or relax our credit terms. Similarly, we can always cut costs simply by doing away with things such as research and development. We can avoid bankruptcy by never borrowing any money or never taking any risks, and so on. It's not clear that any of these actions are in the stockholders' best interests.

Profit maximization would probably be the most commonly cited goal, but even this is not a precise objective. Do we mean profits this year? If so, then we should note that actions such as deferring maintenance, letting inventories run down, and taking other short-run cost-cutting measures will tend to increase profits now, but these activities aren't necessarily desirable.

The goal of maximizing profits may refer to some sort of "long-run" or "average" profits, but it's still unclear exactly what this means. First, do we mean something like accounting net income or earnings per share? As we will see in more detail in the next chapter, these accounting numbers may have little to do with what is good or bad for the firm. Second, what do we mean by the long run? As a famous economist once remarked, in the long run, we're all dead! More to the point, this goal doesn't tell us what the appropriate trade-off is between current and future profits.

The goals we've listed here are all different, but they tend to fall into two classes. The first of these relates to profitability. The goals involving sales, market share, and cost control all relate, at least potentially, to different ways of earning or increasing profits. The goals in the second group, involving bankruptcy avoidance, stability, and safety, relate in some way to controlling risk. Unfortunately, these two types of goals are somewhat contradictory. The pursuit of profit normally involves some element of risk, so it isn't really possible to maximize both safety and profit. What we need, therefore, is a goal that encompasses both factors.

The Goal of Financial Management

The financial manager in a corporation makes decisions for the stockholders of the firm. So, instead of listing possible goals for the financial manager, we really need to answer a more fundamental question: From the stockholders' point of view, what is a good financial management decision?

If we assume that stockholders buy stock because they seek to gain financially, then the answer is obvious: Good decisions increase the value of the stock, and poor decisions decrease the value of the stock.

From our observations, it follows that the financial manager acts in the shareholders' best interests by making decisions that increase the value of the stock. The appropriate goal for the financial manager can thus be stated quite easily:

The goal of financial management is to maximize the current value per share of the existing stock.

The goal of maximizing the value of the stock avoids the problems associated with the different goals we listed earlier. There is no ambiguity in the criterion, and there is no short-run versus long-run issue. We explicitly mean that our goal is to maximize the *current* stock value.

If this goal seems a little strong or one-dimensional to you, keep in mind that the stockholders in a firm are residual owners. By this we mean that they are entitled only to what is left after employees, suppliers, and creditors (and everyone else with legitimate claims) are paid their due. If any of these groups go unpaid, the stockholders get nothing. So if the stockholders are winning in the sense that the leftover, residual portion is growing, it must be true that everyone else is winning also.

Because the goal of financial management is to maximize the value of the stock, we need to learn how to identify investments and financing arrangements that favorably impact the value of the stock. This is precisely what we will be studying. In fact, we could have defined *corporate finance* as the study of the relationship between business decisions and the value of the stock in the business.

A More General Goal

If our goal is as stated in the preceding section (to maximize the value of the stock), an obvious question comes up: What is the appropriate goal when the firm has no traded stock? Corporations are certainly not the only type of business; and the stock in many corporations rarely changes hands, so it's difficult to say what the value per share is at any particular time.

Business ethics are considered at **www. business-ethics.com**.

As long as we are considering for-profit businesses, only a slight modification is needed. The total value of the stock in a corporation is simply equal to the value of the owners' equity. Therefore, a more general way of stating our goal is as follows: Maximize the market value of the existing owners' equity.

With this in mind, we don't care whether the business is a proprietorship, a partnership, or a corporation. For each of these, good financial decisions increase the market value of the owners' equity, and poor financial decisions decrease it. In fact, although we choose to focus on corporations in the chapters ahead, the principles we develop apply to all forms of business. Many of them even apply to the not-for-profit sector.

Finally, our goal does not imply that the financial manager should take illegal or unethical actions in the hope of increasing the value of the equity in thc firm. What we mean is that the financial manager best serves the owners of the business by identifying goods and services that add value to the firm because they are desired and valued in the free marketplace.

1.4 The Agency Problem and Control of the Corporation

We've seen that the financial manager acts in the best interests of the stockholders by taking actions that increase the value of the stock. However, in large corporations ownership can be spread over a huge number of stockholders. This dispersion of ownership arguably means that management effectively controls the firm. In this case, will management necessarily act in the best interests of the stockholders? Put another way, might not management pursue its own goals at the stockholders' expense? In the following pages we briefly consider some of the arguments relating to this question.

Agency Relationships

The relationship between stockholders and management is called an *agency relationship*. Such a relationship exists whenever someone (the principal) hires another (the agent) to represent his or her interests. For example, you might hire someone (an agent) to sell a car that you own while you are away at school. In all such relationships there is a possibility of a conflict of interest between the principal and the agent. Such a conflict is called an **agency problem**.

Suppose you hire someone to sell your car and you agree to pay that person a flat fee when he or she sells the car. The agent's incentive in this case is to make the sale, not necessarily to get you the best price. If you offer a commission of, say, 10 percent of the sales price instead of a flat fee, then this problem might not exist. This example illustrates that the way in which an agent is compensated is one factor that affects agency problems.

Management Goals

To see how management and stockholder interests might differ, imagine that a firm is considering a new investment. The new investment is expected to favorably impact the share value, but it is also a relatively risky venture. The owners of the firm will wish to take the investment (because the stock value will rise), but management may not because there is the possibility that things will turn out badly and management jobs will be lost. If management does not take the investment, then the stockholders may lose a valuable opportunity. This is one example of an *agency cost*.

More generally, the term *agency costs* refers to the costs of the conflict of interest between stockholders and management. These costs can be indirect or direct. An indirect agency cost is a lost opportunity, such as the one we have just described.

Direct agency costs come in two forms. The first type is a corporate expenditure that benefits management but costs the stockholders. Perhaps the purchase of a luxurious and unneeded corporate jet would fall under this heading. The second type of direct agency cost is an expense that arises from the need to monitor management actions. Paying outside auditors to assess the accuracy of financial statement information could be one example.

It is sometimes argued that, left to themselves, managers would tend to maximize the amount of resources over which they have control or, more generally, corporate power or wealth. This goal could lead to an overemphasis on corporate size or growth. For example, cases in which management is accused of overpaying to buy up another company just to increase the size of the business or to demonstrate corporate power are not uncommon. Obviously, if overpayment does take place, such a purchase does not benefit the stockholders of the purchasing company.

Our discussion indicates that management may tend to overemphasize organizational survival to protect job security. Also, management may dislike outside interference, so independence and corporate self-sufficiency may be important goals.

Do Managers Act in the Stockholders' Interests?

Whether managers will, in fact, act in the best interests of stockholders depends on two factors. First, how closely are management goals aligned with stockholder goals? This question relates, at least in part, to the way managers are compensated. Second, can managers be replaced if they do not pursue stockholder goals? This issue relates to control of the firm. As we will discuss, there are a number of reasons to think that, even in the largest firms, management has a significant incentive to act in the interests of stockholders.

Managerial Compensation   Management will frequently have a significant economic incentive to increase share value for two reasons. First, managerial compensation, particularly at the top, is usually tied to financial performance in general and often to share value in particular. For example, managers are frequently given the option to buy stock at a bargain price. The more the stock is worth, the more valuable is this option. In fact, options are often used to motivate employees of all types, not just top management.

The second incentive managers have relates to job prospects. Better performers within the firm will tend to get promoted. More generally, managers who are successful in pursuing stockholder goals will be in greater demand in the labor market and thus command higher salaries.

In fact, managers who are successful in pursuing stockholder goals can reap enormous rewards. For example, the best-paid executive in 2005 was Terry Semel, the CEO of Yahoo; according to *Forbes* magazine, he made about $231 million. By way of comparison, Semel made quite a bit more than George Lucas ($180 million), but only slightly more than Oprah Winfrey ($225 million), and way more than Judge Judy ($28 million). Over the period 2001–2005, Oracle CEO Larry Ellison was the highest-paid executive, earning about $868 million.

Control of the Firm   Control of the firm ultimately rests with stockholders. They elect the board of directors, who, in turn, hire and fire management. The fact that stockholders control the corporation was made abundantly clear by Carly Fiorina's experience at HP, which we described to open the chapter. Even though she had reorganized the corporation, there came a time when shareholders, through their elected directors, decided that HP would be better off without her, so out she went.

An important mechanism by which unhappy stockholders can replace existing management is called a *proxy fight*. A proxy is the authority to vote someone else's stock. A proxy fight develops when a group solicits proxies in order to replace the existing board and thereby replace existing management. For example, the proposed merger between HP and Compaq, which we mentioned in our chapter opener, triggered one of the most widely followed, bitterly contested, and expensive proxy fights in history, with an estimated price tag of well over $100 million.

Another way that management can be replaced is by takeover. Firms that are poorly managed are more attractive as acquisitions than well-managed firms because a greater profit potential exists. Thus, avoiding a takeover by another firm gives management another incentive to act in the stockholders' interests. For example, in 2004, Comcast, the cable television giant, announced a surprise bid to buy Disney when Disney's management was under close scrutiny for its performance. Not too surprisingly, Disney's management strongly opposed being acquired, and Comcast ultimately decided to withdraw, in part because of improvements in Disney's financial performance.

Conclusion   The available theory and evidence are consistent with the view that stockholders control the firm and that stockholder wealth maximization is the relevant goal of the corporation. Even so, there will undoubtedly be times when management goals are pursued at the expense of the stockholders, at least temporarily.

Stakeholders

Our discussion thus far implies that management and stockholders are the only parties with an interest in the firm's decisions. This is an oversimplification, of course. Employees, customers, suppliers, and even the government all have a financial interest in the firm.

Taken together, these various groups are called **stakeholders** in the firm. In general, a stakeholder is someone other than a stockholder or creditor who potentially has a claim on the cash flows of the firm. Such groups will also attempt to exert control over the firm, perhaps to the detriment of the owners.

1.5   Financial Markets

As indicated in Section 1.1, firms offer two basic types of securities to investors. *Debt securities* are contractual obligations to repay corporate borrowing. *Equity securities* are shares of common stock and preferred stock that represent noncontractual claims to the residual cash flow of the firm. Issues of debt and stock that are publicly sold by the firm are then traded in the financial markets.

The financial markets are composed of the **money markets** and the **capital markets**. Money markets are the markets for debt securities that will pay off in the short term (usually less than one year). Capital markets are the markets for long-term debt (with a maturity of over one year) and for equity shares.

The term *money market* applies to a group of loosely connected markets. They are dealer markets. Dealers are firms that make continuous quotations of prices for which they stand ready to buy and sell money market instruments for their own inventory and at their own risk. Thus, the dealer is a principal in most transactions. This is different from a stockbroker acting as an agent for a customer in buying or selling common stock on most stock exchanges; an agent does not actually acquire the securities.

At the core of the money markets are the money market banks (these are large banks mostly in New York), government securities dealers (some of which are the large banks), and many money brokers. Money brokers specialize in finding short-term money for borrowers and placing money for lenders. The financial markets can be classified further as the *primary market* and the *secondary markets*.

The Primary Market: New Issues

The primary market is used when governments and corporations initially sell securities. Corporations engage in two types of primary market sales of debt and equity: public offerings and private placements.

Most publicly offered corporate debt and equity come to the market underwritten by a syndicate of investment banking firms. The *underwriting* syndicate buys the new securities from the firm for the syndicate's own account and resells them at a higher price. Publicly issued debt and equity must be registered with the United States Securities and Exchange Commission (SEC). *Registration* requires the corporation to disclose any and all material information in a registration statement.

The legal, accounting, and other costs of preparing the registration statement are not negligible. In part to avoid these costs, privately placed debt and equity are sold on the basis of private negotiations to large financial institutions, such as insurance companies and mutual funds, and other investors. Private placements are not registered with the SEC.

Secondary Markets

A secondary market transaction involves one owner or creditor selling to another. Therefore, the secondary markets provide the means for transferring ownership of corporate securities. Although a corporation is directly involved only in a primary market transaction (when it sells securities to raise cash), the secondary markets are still critical to large corporations. The reason is that investors are much more willing to purchase securities in a primary market transaction when they know that those securities can later be resold if desired.

Dealer versus Auction Markets   There are two kinds of secondary markets: *dealer* markets and *auction* markets. Generally speaking, dealers buy and sell for themselves, at their own risk. A car dealer, for example, buys and sells automobiles. In contrast, brokers and agents match buyers and sellers, but they do not actually own the commodity that is bought or sold. A real estate agent, for example, does not normally buy and sell houses.

Dealer markets in stocks and long-term debt are called *over-the-counter* (OTC) markets. Most trading in debt securities takes place over the counter. The expression *over the counter* refers to days of old when securities were literally bought and sold at counters in offices around the country. Today a significant fraction of the market for stocks and almost all of the market for long-term debt have no central location; the many dealers are connected electronically.

Auction markets differ from dealer markets in two ways. First, an auction market or exchange has a physical location (like Wall Street). Second, in a dealer market, most of the buying and selling is done by the dealer. The primary purpose of an auction market, on the other hand, is to match those who wish to sell with those who wish to buy. Dealers play a limited role.

Trading in Corporate Securities   The equity shares of most large firms in the United States trade in organized auction markets. The largest such market is the New York Stock Exchange (NYSE), which accounts for more than 85 percent of all the shares traded in auction markets. Other auction exchanges include the American Stock Exchange (AMEX) and regional exchanges such as the Pacific Stock Exchange.

To learn more about the exchanges, visit **www.nyse.com** and **www.nasdaq.com**.

In addition to the stock exchanges, there is a large OTC market for stocks. In 1971, the National Association of Securities Dealers (NASD) made available to dealers and brokers an electronic quotation system called NASDAQ (which originally stood for NASD Automated Quotation system and is pronounced "naz-dak"). There are roughly two times as many companies on NASDAQ as there are on the NYSE, but they tend to be much smaller and trade less actively. There are exceptions, of course. Both Microsoft and Intel trade OTC, for example. Nonetheless, the total value of NASDAQ stocks is much less than the total value of NYSE stocks.

There are many large and important financial markets outside the United States, of course, and U.S. corporations are increasingly looking to these markets to raise cash. The Tokyo Stock Exchange and the London Stock Exchange (TSE and LSE, respectively) are two well-known examples. The fact that OTC markets have no physical location means that national borders do not present a great barrier, and there is now a huge international OTC debt market. Because of globalization, financial markets have reached the point where trading in many investments never stops; it just travels around the world.

Exchange Trading of Listed Stocks

Auction markets are different from dealer markets in two ways. First, trading in a given auction exchange takes place at a single site on the floor of the exchange. Second, transaction prices of shares traded on auction exchanges are communicated almost immediately to the public by computer and other devices.

The NYSE is one of the preeminent securities exchanges in the world. All transactions in stocks listed on the NYSE occur at a particular place on the floor of the exchange called a *post*. At the heart of the market is the specialist. Specialists are members of the NYSE who *make a market* in designated stocks. Specialists have an obligation to offer to buy and sell shares of their assigned NYSE stocks. It is believed that this makes the market liquid because the specialist assumes the role of a buyer for investors if they wish to sell and a seller if they wish to buy.

Listing

Stocks that trade on an organized exchange are said to be *listed* on that exchange. To be listed, firms must meet certain minimum criteria concerning, for example, asset size and number of shareholders. These criteria differ from one exchange to another.

NYSE has the most stringent requirements of the exchanges in the United States. For example, to be listed on the NYSE, a company is expected to have a market value for its publicly held shares of at least $100 million. There are additional minimums on earnings, assets, and number of shares outstanding. The listing requirements for non–U.S. companies are somewhat more stringent. Table 1.3 gives the market value of NYSE-listed stocks and bonds.

To find out more about Sarbanes-Oxley, go to **www.sarbanes-oxley.com**.

Listed companies face significant disclosure requirements. In response to corporate scandals at companies such as Enron, WorldCom, Tyco, and Adelphia, Congress enacted the Sarbanes-Oxley Act in 2002. The act, better known as "Sarbox" or "SOX," is intended to protect investors from corporate abuses. For example, one section of Sarbox prohibits personal loans from a company to its officers, such as the ones that were received by WorldCom CEO Bernie Ebbers.

One of the key sections of Sarbox took effect on November 15, 2004. Section 404 requires, among other things, that each company's annual report must have an assessment

Table 1.3

Market Value
of NYSE-Listed
Securities

End-of-Year	Number of Listed Companies	Market Value ($ in trillions)
NYSE-listed stocks*		
2005	2,779	$21.2
2004	2,768	19.8
2003	2,750	17.3
2002	2,783	13.4
2001	2,798	16.0
2000	2,862	17.1

End-of-Year	Number of Issues	Market Value ($ in trillions)
NYSE-listed bonds†		
2005	971	$1.0
2004	1,059	1.1
2003	1,273	1.4
2002	1,323	1.4
2001	1,447	1.7
2000	1,627	2.1

*Includes preferred stock and common stock.

†Includes bonds issued by U.S. companies, foreign companies, the U.S. government, international banks, foreign governments, and municipalities. The bond value shown is the face value.

SOURCE: Data from the NYSE Web site, www.nyse.com.

of the company's internal control structure and financial reporting. The auditor must then evaluate and attest to management's assessment of these issues.

Sarbox contains other key requirements. For example, the officers of the corporation must review and sign the annual reports. They must explicitly declare that the annual report does not contain any false statements or material omissions; that the financial statements fairly represent the financial results; and that they are responsible for all internal controls. Finally, the annual report must list any deficiencies in internal controls. In essence, Sarbox makes company management responsible for the accuracy of the company's financial statements.

Of course, as with any law, there are compliance costs, and Sarbox has increased the cost of corporate audits, sometimes dramatically. Estimates of the increase in company audit costs to comply with Sarbox range from $500,000 to over $5 million, which has led to some unintended consequences. For example, in 2004, 134 firms delisted their shares from exchanges, or "went dark." This was up from 30 delistings in 1999. Most of the companies that delisted stated that their reason was to avoid the cost of compliance with Sarbox. Some conservative estimates put the national Sarbox compliance tab at $35 billion in the first year alone, which is roughly 20 times the amount originally estimated by the SEC. For a large multibillion-dollar-revenue company, the cost might be .05 percent of revenues; but it could be 4 percent or so for smaller companies, an enormous cost.

A company that goes dark does not have to file quarterly or annual reports. Annual audits by independent auditors are not required, and executives do not have to certify the accuracy of the financial statements, so the savings can be huge. Of course there are costs. Stock prices typically fall when a company announces it is going dark. Further, such companies will typically have limited access to capital markets and usually will pay higher interest on bank loans.

Summary and Conclusions

This chapter introduced you to some of the basic ideas in corporate finance:

1. Corporate finance has three main areas of concern:
   a. *Capital budgeting:* What long-term investments should the firm take?
   b. *Capital structure:* Where will the firm get the long-term financing to pay for its investments? Also, what mixture of debt and equity should it use to fund operations?
   c. *Working capital management:* How should the firm manage its everyday financial activities?

2. The goal of financial management in a for-profit business is to make decisions that increase the value of the stock, or, more generally, increase the market value of the equity.

3. The corporate form of organization is superior to other forms when it comes to raising money and transferring ownership interests, but it has the significant disadvantage of double taxation.

4. There is the possibility of conflicts between stockholders and management in a large corporation. We called these conflicts *agency problems* and discussed how they might be controlled and reduced.

5. The advantages of the corporate form are enhanced by the existence of financial markets. Financial markets function as both primary and secondary markets for corporate securities and can be organized as either dealer or auction markets.

Of the topics we've discussed thus far, the most important is the goal of financial management: maximizing the value of the stock. Throughout the text we will be analyzing many different financial decisions, but we will always ask the same question: How does the decision under consideration affect the value of the stock?

Concept Questions

1. **Agency Problems**   Who owns a corporation? Describe the process whereby the owners control the firm's management. What is the main reason that an agency relationship exists in the corporate form of organization? In this context, what kinds of problems can arise?

2. **Not-for-Profit Firm Goals**   Suppose you were the financial manager of a not-for-profit business (a not-for-profit hospital, perhaps). What kinds of goals do you think would be appropriate?

3. **Goal of the Firm**   Evaluate the following statement: Managers should not focus on the current stock value because doing so will lead to an overemphasis on short-term profits at the expense of long-term profits.

4. **Ethics and Firm Goals**   Can the goal of maximizing the value of the stock conflict with other goals, such as avoiding unethical or illegal behavior? In particular, do you think subjects like customer and employee safety, the environment, and the general good of society fit in this framework, or are they essentially ignored? Think of some specific scenarios to illustrate your answer.

5. **International Firm Goal**   Would the goal of maximizing the value of the stock differ for financial management in a foreign country? Why or why not?

6. **Agency Problems**   Suppose you own stock in a company. The current price per share is $25. Another company has just announced that it wants to buy your company and will pay $35 per share to acquire all the outstanding stock. Your company's management immediately begins fighting off this hostile bid. Is management acting in the shareholders' best interests? Why or why not?

7. **Agency Problems and Corporate Ownership**   Corporate ownership varies around the world. Historically, individuals have owned the majority of shares in public corporations in the United States. In Germany and Japan, however, banks, other large financial institutions, and other companies own most of the stock in public corporations. Do you think agency problems are likely to be more or less severe in Germany and Japan than in the United States?

8. **Agency Problems and Corporate Ownership**   In recent years, large financial institutions such as mutual funds and pension funds have become the dominant owners of stock in the

United States, and these institutions are becoming more active in corporate affairs. What are the implications of this trend for agency problems and corporate control?

9. **Executive Compensation**   Critics have charged that compensation to top management in the United States is simply too high and should be cut back. For example, focusing on large corporations, Larry Ellison of Oracle has been one of the best-compensated CEOs in the United States, earning about $41 million in 2004 alone and $836 million over the 2000–2004 period. Are such amounts excessive? In answering, it might be helpful to recognize that superstar athletes such as Tiger Woods, top entertainers such as Mel Gibson and Oprah Winfrey, and many others at the top of their respective fields earn at least as much, if not a great deal more.

10. **Goal of Financial Management**   Why is the goal of financial management to maximize the current share price of the company's stock? In other words, why isn't the goal to maximize the future share price?

S&P Problems

www.mhhe.com/edumarketinsight

1. **Industry Comparison**   On the Market Insight home page, follow the "Industry" link at the top of the page. You will be on the industry page. You can use the drop-down menu to select different industries. Answer the following questions for these industries: airlines, automobile manufacturers, biotechnology, computer hardware, homebuilding, marine, restaurants, soft drinks, and wireless telecommunications.
    a. How many companies are in each industry?
    b. What are the total sales for each industry?
    c. Do the industries with the largest total sales have the most companies in the industry? What does this tell you about competition in the various industries?

Financial Statements and Cash Flow

In February 2006, CBS Records joined other companies in announcing operating results for the latest quarter. For CBS, the news was not good: Earnings amounted to a loss of $6 per share. Included in the earnings figure was a charge of about $9.4 billion to write down the value of the company's radio and television businesses. The write-off was nothing new to CBS. The company lost over $18 billion (or about $11 per share) in the same quarter of the previous year, due mostly to write-offs in its radio station and outdoor advertising businesses.

The write-offs by CBS were large, but they pale in comparison to those taken by Time Warner, which were probably the largest in history. The media giant took a charge of $45.5 billion in the fourth quarter of 2002. This enormous write-off followed an earlier, even larger charge of $54 billion earlier in the year.

So did stockholders in CBS Records lose $9.4 billion in one quarter as the result of the write-off? Fortunately for them, the answer is probably not. Understanding why leads us to the main subject of this chapter: that all-important substance known as *cash flow*.

2.1 The Balance Sheet

The **balance sheet** is an accountant's snapshot of a firm's accounting value on a particular date, as though the firm stood momentarily still. The balance sheet has two sides: On the left are the *assets* and on the right are the *liabilities* and *stockholders' equity*. The balance sheet states what the firm owns and how it is financed. The accounting definition that underlies the balance sheet and describes the balance is:

$$\text{Assets} \equiv \text{Liabilities} + \text{Stockholders' equity}$$

We have put a three-line equality in the balance equation to indicate that it must always hold, by definition. In fact, the stockholders' equity is *defined* to be the difference between the assets and the liabilities of the firm. In principle, equity is what the stockholders would have remaining after the firm discharged its obligations.

Table 2.1 gives the 2007 and 2006 balance sheet for the fictitious U.S. Composite Corporation. The assets in the balance sheet are listed in order by the length of time it normally would take an ongoing firm to convert them into cash. The asset side depends on the nature of the business and how management chooses to conduct it. Management must make decisions about cash versus marketable securities, credit versus cash sales, whether to make or buy commodities, whether to lease or purchase items, the types of business in which

Two excellent sources for company financial information are **finance.yahoo.com** and **money.cnn.com**.

Table 2.1   **The Balance Sheet of the U.S. Composite Corporation**

<table>
<tr><th colspan="7">U.S. COMPOSITE CORPORATION
Balance Sheet
2007 and 2006
($ in millions)</th></tr>
<tr><th>Assets</th><th>2007</th><th>2006</th><th>Liabilities (Debt) and
Stockholders' Equity</th><th>2007</th><th>2006</th></tr>
<tr><td>Current assets:</td><td></td><td></td><td>Current liabilities:</td><td></td><td></td></tr>
<tr><td> Cash and equivalents</td><td>$ 140</td><td>$ 107</td><td> Accounts payable</td><td>$ 213</td><td>$ 197</td></tr>
<tr><td> Accounts receivable</td><td>294</td><td>270</td><td> Notes payable</td><td>50</td><td>53</td></tr>
<tr><td> Inventories</td><td>269</td><td>280</td><td> Accrued expenses</td><td>223</td><td>205</td></tr>
<tr><td> Other</td><td>58</td><td>50</td><td>   Total current liabilities</td><td>$ 486</td><td>$ 455</td></tr>
<tr><td>   Total current assets</td><td>$ 761</td><td>$ 707</td><td></td><td></td><td></td></tr>
<tr><td></td><td></td><td></td><td>Long-term liabilities:</td><td></td><td></td></tr>
<tr><td>Fixed assets:</td><td></td><td></td><td> Deferred taxes</td><td>$ 117</td><td>$ 104</td></tr>
<tr><td> Property, plant, and equipment</td><td>$1,423</td><td>$1,274</td><td> Long-term debt*</td><td>471</td><td>458</td></tr>
<tr><td> Less accumulated depreciation</td><td>550</td><td>460</td><td>   Total long-term liabilities</td><td>$ 588</td><td>$ 562</td></tr>
<tr><td> Net property, plant, and
  equipment</td><td>873</td><td>814</td><td>Stockholders' equity:</td><td></td><td></td></tr>
<tr><td> Intangible assets and others</td><td>245</td><td>221</td><td> Preferred stock</td><td>$ 39</td><td>$ 39</td></tr>
<tr><td>   Total fixed assets</td><td>$1,118</td><td>$1,035</td><td> Common stock ($1 par value)</td><td>55</td><td>32</td></tr>
<tr><td></td><td></td><td></td><td> Capital surplus</td><td>347</td><td>327</td></tr>
<tr><td></td><td></td><td></td><td> Accumulated retained
  earnings</td><td>390</td><td>347</td></tr>
<tr><td></td><td></td><td></td><td>   Less treasury stock†</td><td>26</td><td>20</td></tr>
<tr><td></td><td></td><td></td><td>   Total equity</td><td>$ 805</td><td>$ 725</td></tr>
<tr><td>Total assets</td><td>$1,879</td><td>$1,742</td><td>Total liabilities and
  stockholders' equity‡</td><td>$1,879</td><td>$ 1,742</td></tr>
</table>

*Long-term debt rose by $471 million − $458 million = $13 million. This is the difference between $86 million new debt and $73 million in retirement of old debt.

†Treasury stock rose by $6 million. This reflects the repurchase of $6 million of U.S. Composite's company stock.

‡U.S. Composite reports $43 million in new equity. The company issued 23 million shares at a price of $1.87. The par value of common stock increased by $23 million, and capital surplus increased by $20 million.

to engage, and so on. The liabilities and the stockholders' equity are listed in the order in which they would typically be paid over time.

The liabilities and stockholders' equity side reflects the types and proportions of financing, which depend on management's choice of capital structure, as between debt and equity and between current debt and long-term debt.

When analyzing a balance sheet, the financial manager should be aware of three concerns: liquidity, debt versus equity, and value versus cost.

Annual and quarterly financial statements for most public U.S. corporations can be found in the EDGAR database at **www.sec.gov.**

Liquidity

Liquidity refers to the ease and quickness with which assets can be converted to cash (without significant loss in value). *Current assets* are the most liquid and include cash and assets that will be turned into cash within a year from the date of the balance sheet. *Accounts receivable* are amounts not yet collected from customers for goods or services sold to them (after adjustment for potential bad debts). *Inventory* is composed of raw materials to be used in production, work in process, and finished goods. *Fixed assets* are the least liquid kind of assets. Tangible fixed assets include property, plant, and equipment. These assets do not convert to cash from normal business activity, and they are not usually used to pay expenses such as payroll.

Some fixed assets are not tangible. Intangible assets have no physical existence but can be very valuable. Examples of intangible assets are the value of a trademark or the value of a patent. The more liquid a firm's assets, the less likely the firm is to experience problems meeting short-term obligations. Thus, the probability that a firm will avoid financial distress can be linked to the firm's liquidity. Unfortunately, liquid assets frequently have lower rates of return than fixed assets; for example, cash generates no investment income. To the extent a firm invests in liquid assets, it sacrifices an opportunity to invest in more profitable investment vehicles.

Debt versus Equity

Liabilities are obligations of the firm that require a payout of cash within a stipulated period. Many liabilities involve contractual obligations to repay a stated amount and interest over a period. Thus, liabilities are debts and are frequently associated with nominally fixed cash burdens, called *debt service*, that put the firm in default of a contract if they are not paid. *Stockholders' equity* is a claim against the firm's assets that is residual and not fixed. In general terms, when the firm borrows, it gives the bondholders first claim on the firm's cash flow.[1] Bondholders can sue the firm if the firm defaults on its bond contracts. This may lead the firm to declare itself bankrupt. Stockholders' equity is the residual difference between assets and liabilities:

$$\text{Assets} - \text{Liabilities} \equiv \text{Stockholders' equity}$$

This is the stockholders' share in the firm stated in accounting terms. The accounting value of stockholders' equity increases when retained earnings are added. This occurs when the firm retains part of its earnings instead of paying them out as dividends.

Value versus Cost

The home page for the Financial Accounting Standards Board (FASB) is **www.fasb.org**.

The accounting value of a firm's assets is frequently referred to as the *carrying value* or the *book value* of the assets.[2] Under **generally accepted accounting principles (GAAP)**, audited financial statements of firms in the United States carry the assets at cost.[3] Thus the terms *carrying value* and *book value* are unfortunate. They specifically say "value," when in fact the accounting numbers are based on cost. This misleads many readers of financial statements to think that the firm's assets are recorded at true market values. *Market value* is the price at which willing buyers and sellers would trade the assets. It would be only a coincidence if accounting value and market value were the same. In fact, management's job is to create value for the firm that exceeds its cost.

Many people use the balance sheet, but the information each may wish to extract is not the same. A banker may look at a balance sheet for evidence of accounting liquidity and working capital. A supplier may also note the size of accounts payable and therefore the general promptness of payments. Many users of financial statements, including managers and investors, want to know the value of the firm, not its cost. This information is not found

---

[1]Bondholders are investors in the firm's debt. They are creditors of the firm. In this discussion, the term *bondholder* means the same thing as *creditor*.

[2]Confusion often arises because many financial accounting terms have the same meaning. This presents a problem with jargon for the reader of financial statements. For example, the following terms usually refer to the same thing: *assets minus liabilities*, *net worth*, *stockholders' equity*, *owners' equity*, *book equity*, and *equity capitalization*.

[3]Generally, GAAP requires assets to be carried at the lower of cost or market value. In most instances, cost is lower than market value. However, in some cases when a fair market value can be readily determined, the assets have their value adjusted to the fair market value.

on the balance sheet. In fact, many of the true resources of the firm do not appear on the balance sheet: good management, proprietary assets, favorable economic conditions, and so on. Henceforth, whenever we speak of the value of an asset or the value of the firm, we will normally mean its market value. So, for example, when we say the goal of the financial manager is to increase the value of the stock, we mean the market value of the stock.

EXAMPLE 2.1

Market Value versus Book Value   The Cooney Corporation has fixed assets with a book value of $700 and an appraised market value of about $1,000. Net working capital is $400 on the books, but approximately $600 would be realized if all the current accounts were liquidated. Cooney has $500 in long-term debt, both book value and market value. What is the book value of the equity? What is the market value?

We can construct two simplified balance sheets, one in accounting (book value) terms and one in economic (market value) terms:

COONEY CORPORATION
Balance Sheets
Market Value versus Book Value

Assets			Liabilities and Shareholders' Equity		
	Book	**Market**		**Book**	**Market**
Net working capital	$ 400	$ 600	Long-term debt	$ 500	$ 500
Net fixed assets	700	1,000	Shareholders' equity	600	1,100
	$1,100	$1,600		$1,100	$1,600

In this example, shareholders' equity is actually worth almost twice as much as what is shown on the books. The distinction between book and market values is important precisely because book values can be so different from true economic value.

2.2 The Income Statement

The **income statement** measures performance over a specific period—say a year. The accounting definition of income is:

$$\text{Revenue} - \text{Expenses} \equiv \text{Income}$$

If the balance sheet is like a snapshot, the income statement is like a video recording of what the people did between two snapshots. Table 2.2 gives the income statement for the U.S. Composite Corporation for 2007.

The income statement usually includes several sections. The operations section reports the firm's revenues and expenses from principal operations. One number of particular importance is earnings before interest and taxes (EBIT), which summarizes earnings before taxes and financing costs. Among other things, the nonoperating section of the income statement includes all financing costs, such as interest expense. Usually a second section reports as a separate item the amount of taxes levied on income. The last item on the income statement is the bottom line, or net income. Net income is frequently expressed per share of common stock—that is, earnings per share.

When analyzing an income statement, the financial manager should keep in mind GAAP, noncash items, time, and costs.

Table 2.2

The Income Statement of the U.S. Composite Corporation

U.S. COMPOSITE CORPORATION Income Statement 2007 ($ in millions)	
Total operating revenues	$2,262
Cost of goods sold	1,655
Selling, general, and administrative expenses	327
Depreciation	90
Operating income	$ 190
Other income	29
Earnings before interest and taxes (EBIT)	$ 219
Interest expense	49
Pretax income	$ 170
Taxes	84
Current: $71	
Deferred: 13	
Net income	$ 86
Addition to retained earnings:	$ 43
Dividends:	43

Note: There are 29 million shares outstanding. Earnings per share and dividends per share can be calculated as follows:

$$\text{Earnings per share} = \frac{\text{Net income}}{\text{Total shares outstanding}}$$

$$= \frac{\$86}{29}$$

$$= \$2.97 \text{ per share}$$

$$\text{Dividends per share} = \frac{\text{Dividends}}{\text{Total shares outstanding}}$$

$$= \frac{\$43}{29}$$

$$= \$1.48 \text{ per share}$$

Generally Accepted Accounting Principles

Revenue is recognized on an income statement when the earnings process is virtually completed and an exchange of goods or services has occurred. Therefore, the unrealized appreciation from owning property will not be recognized as income. This provides a device for smoothing income by selling appreciated property at convenient times. For example, if the firm owns a tree farm that has doubled in value, then, in a year when its earnings from other businesses are down, it can raise overall earnings by selling some trees. The matching principle of GAAP dictates that revenues be matched with expenses. Thus, income is reported when it is earned, or accrued, even though no cash flow has necessarily occurred (for example, when goods are sold for credit, sales and profits are reported).

Noncash Items

The economic value of assets is intimately connected to their future incremental cash flows. However, cash flow does not appear on an income statement. There are several **noncash items** that are expenses against revenues but do not affect cash flow. The most important of these is *depreciation*. Depreciation reflects the accountant's estimate of the cost of equipment used up in the production process. For example, suppose an asset with a five-year life and no resale value is purchased for $1,000. According to accountants, the $1,000 cost must be expensed over the useful life of the asset. If straight-line depreciation is used, there will be five equal installments, and $200 of depreciation expense will be incurred each year. From a finance perspective, the cost of the asset is the actual negative cash flow incurred when the asset is acquired (that is, $1,000, *not* the accountant's smoothed $200-per-year depreciation expense).

Another noncash expense is *deferred taxes*. Deferred taxes result from differences between accounting income and true taxable income.[4] Notice that the accounting tax shown on the income statement for the U.S. Composite Corporation is $84 million. It can be broken down as current taxes and deferred taxes. The current tax portion is actually sent to the tax authorities (for example, the Internal Revenue Service). The deferred tax portion is not. However, the theory is that if taxable income is less than accounting income in the current year, it will be more than accounting income later on. Consequently, the taxes that are not paid today will have to be paid in the future, and they represent a liability of the firm. This shows up on the balance sheet as deferred tax liability. From the cash flow perspective, though, deferred tax is not a cash outflow.

In practice, the difference between cash flows and accounting income can be quite dramatic, so it is important to understand the difference. For example, through the first nine months of 2005, automobile interior supplier Lear Corporation had a total loss of almost $779 million. That sounds bad, but Lear also reported a positive cash flow of about $229 million for the same period.

Time and Costs

It is often useful to visualize all of future time as having two distinct parts, the *short run* and the *long run*. The short run is the period in which certain equipment, resources, and commitments of the firm are fixed; but the time is long enough for the firm to vary its output by using more labor and raw materials. The short run is not a precise period that will be the same for all industries. However, all firms making decisions in the short run have some fixed costs—that is, costs that will not change because of fixed commitments. In real business activity, examples of fixed costs are bond interest, overhead, and property taxes. Costs that are not fixed are variable. Variable costs change as the output of the firm changes; some examples are raw materials and wages for laborers on the production line.

In the long run, all costs are variable. Financial accountants do not distinguish between variable costs and fixed costs. Instead, accounting costs usually fit into a classification that distinguishes product costs from period costs. Product costs are the total production costs incurred during a period—raw materials, direct labor, and manufacturing overhead—and are reported on the income statement as cost of goods sold. Both variable and fixed costs are included in product costs. Period costs are costs that are allocated to a time period; they are called *selling*, *general*, and *administrative expenses*. One period cost would be the company president's salary.

2.3   Taxes

Taxes can be one of the largest cash outflows a firm experiences. For example, for the fiscal year 2005, ExxonMobil's earnings before taxes were about $59.9 billion. Its tax bill, including all taxes paid worldwide, was a whopping $23.3 billion, or about 38.9 percent

---

[4]One situation in which taxable income may be lower than accounting income is when the firm uses accelerated depreciation expense procedures for the IRS but uses straight-line procedures allowed by GAAP for reporting purposes.

Table 2.3

Corporate Tax Rates

Taxable Income	Tax Rate
$ 0– 50,000	15%
50,001– 75,000	25
75,001– 100,000	34
100,001– 335,000	39
335,001–10,000,000	34
10,000,001–15,000,000	35
15,000,001–18,333,333	38
18,333,334+	35

of its pretax earnings. The size of the tax bill is determined by the tax code, an often amended set of rules. In this section, we examine corporate tax rates and how taxes are calculated.

If the various rules of taxation seem a little bizarre or convoluted to you, keep in mind that the tax code is the result of political, not economic, forces. As a result, there is no reason why it has to make economic sense. To put the complexity of corporate taxation into perspective, General Electric's (GE's) 2006 tax return required 24,000 pages, far too much to print. The electronically filed return ran 237 megabytes.

Corporate Tax Rates

Corporate tax rates in effect for 2006 are shown in Table 2.3. A peculiar feature of taxation instituted by the Tax Reform Act of 1986 and expanded in the 1993 Omnibus Budget Reconciliation Act is that corporate tax rates are not strictly increasing. As shown, corporate tax rates rise from 15 percent to 39 percent, but they drop back to 34 percent on income over $335,000. They then rise to 38 percent and subsequently fall to 35 percent.

According to the originators of the current tax rules, there are only four corporate rates: 15 percent, 25 percent, 34 percent, and 35 percent. The 38 and 39 percent brackets arise because of "surcharges" applied on top of the 34 and 35 percent rates. A tax is a tax, however, so there are really six corporate tax brackets, as we have shown.

Average versus Marginal Tax Rates

In making financial decisions, it is frequently important to distinguish between average and marginal tax rates. Your **average tax rate** is your tax bill divided by your taxable income— in other words, the percentage of your income that goes to pay taxes. Your **marginal tax rate** is the tax you would pay (in percent) if you earned one more dollar. The percentage tax rates shown in Table 2.3 are all marginal rates. Put another way, the tax rates apply to the part of income in the indicated range only, not all income.

The difference between average and marginal tax rates can best be illustrated with a simple example. Suppose our corporation has a taxable income of $200,000. What is the tax bill? Using Table 2.3, we can figure our tax bill like this:

$$
\begin{aligned}
.15(\$\ 50,000) &= \$\ 7,500 \\
.25(\$\ 75,000 - 50,000) &=\ 6,250 \\
.34(\$100,000 - 75,000) &=\ 8,500 \\
.39(\$200,000 - 100,000) &=\ \underline{39,000} \\
&\quad\ \$61,250
\end{aligned}
$$

Our total tax is thus $61,250.

The IRS has a great Web site! **www.irs.gov**

In our example, what is the average tax rate? We had a taxable income of $200,000 and a tax bill of $61,250, so the average tax rate is $61,250/200,000 = 30.625%. What is the marginal tax rate? If we made one more dollar, the tax on that dollar would be 39 cents, so our marginal rate is 39 percent.

EXAMPLE 2.2

Deep in the Heart of Taxes　Algernon, Inc., has a taxable income of $85,000. What is its tax bill? What is its average tax rate? Its marginal tax rate?

From Table 2.3, we see that the tax rate applied to the first $50,000 is 15 percent; the rate applied to the next $25,000 is 25 percent, and the rate applied after that up to $100,000 is 34 percent. So Algernon must pay $.15 \times \$50,000 + .25 \times 25,000 + .34 \times (85,000 - 75,000) = \$17,150$. The average tax rate is thus $\$17,150/85,000 = 20.18\%$. The marginal rate is 34 percent because Algernon's taxes would rise by 34 cents if it had another dollar in taxable income.

Table 2.4 summarizes some different taxable incomes, marginal tax rates, and average tax rates for corporations. Notice how the average and marginal tax rates come together at 35 percent.

With a *flat-rate* tax, there is only one tax rate, so the rate is the same for all income levels. With such a tax, the marginal tax rate is always the same as the average tax rate. As it stands now, corporate taxation in the United States is based on a modified flat-rate tax, which becomes a true flat rate for the highest incomes.

In looking at Table 2.4, notice that the more a corporation makes, the greater is the percentage of taxable income paid in taxes. Put another way, under current tax law, the average tax rate never goes down, even though the marginal tax rate does. As illustrated, for corporations, average tax rates begin at 15 percent and rise to a maximum of 35 percent.

Normally, the marginal tax rate will be relevant for financial decision making. The reason is that any new cash flows will be taxed at that marginal rate. Because financial decisions usually involve new cash flows or changes in existing ones, this rate will tell us the marginal effect of a decision on our tax bill.

There is one last thing to notice about the tax code as it affects corporations. It's easy to verify that the corporate tax bill is just a flat 35 percent of taxable income if our taxable income is more than $18.33 million. Also, for the many midsize corporations with taxable incomes in the range of $335,000 to $10,000,000, the tax rate is a flat 34 percent. Because we will usually be talking about large corporations, you can assume that the average and marginal tax rates are 35 percent unless we explicitly say otherwise.

Before moving on, we should note that the tax rates we have discussed in this section relate to federal taxes only. Overall tax rates can be higher if state, local, and any other taxes are considered.

Table 2.4

Corporate Taxes and Tax Rates

(1) Taxable Income	(2) Marginal Tax Rate	(3) Total Tax	(3)/(1) Average Tax Rate
$ 45,000	15%	$ 6,750	15.00%
70,000	25	12,500	17.86
95,000	34	20,550	21.63
250,000	39	80,750	32.30
1,000,000	34	340,000	34.00
17,500,000	38	6,100,000	34.86
50,000,000	35	17,500,000	35.00
100,000,000	35	35,000,000	35.00

2.4 Net Working Capital

Net working capital is current assets minus current liabilities. Net working capital is positive when current assets are greater than current liabilities. This means the cash that will become available over the next 12 months will be greater than the cash that must be paid out. The net working capital of the U.S. Composite Corporation is $275 million in 2007 and $252 million in 2006:

	Current assets ($ millions)	−	Current liabilities ($ millions)	=	Net working capital ($ millions)
2007	$761	−	$486	=	$275
2006	707	−	455	=	252

In addition to investing in fixed assets (i.e., capital spending), a firm can invest in net working capital. This is called the **change in net working capital**. The change in net working capital in 2007 is the difference between the net working capital in 2007 and 2006—that is, $275 million − $252 million = $23 million. The change in net working capital is usually positive in a growing firm.

2.5 Financial Cash Flow

Perhaps the most important item that can be extracted from financial statements is the actual **cash flow** of the firm. An official accounting statement called the *statement of cash flows* helps to explain the change in accounting cash and equivalents, which for U.S. Composite is $33 million in 2007. (See Section 2.6.) Notice in Table 2.1 that cash and equivalents increase from $107 million in 2006 to $140 million in 2007. However, we will look at cash flow from a different perspective: the perspective of finance. In finance, the value of the firm is its ability to generate financial cash flow. (We will talk more about financial cash flow in a later chapter.)

The first point we should mention is that cash flow is not the same as net working capital. For example, increasing inventory requires using cash. Because both inventories and cash are current assets, this does not affect net working capital. In this case, an increase in inventory is associated with decreasing cash flow.

Just as we established that the value of a firm's assets is always equal to the combined value of the liabilities and the value of the equity, the cash flows received from the firm's assets (that is, its operating activities), CF(*A*), must equal the cash flows to the firm's creditors, CF(*B*), and equity investors, CF(*S*):

$$CF(A) \equiv CF(B) + CF(S)$$

The first step in determining cash flows of the firm is to figure out the *cash flow from operations*. As can be seen in Table 2.5, operating cash flow is the cash flow generated by business activities, including sales of goods and services. Operating cash flow reflects tax payments, but not financing, capital spending, or changes in net working capital:

	$ in millions
Earnings before interest and taxes	$219
Depreciation	90
Current taxes	−71
Operating cash flow	$238

Table 2.5

Financial Cash Flow
of the U.S. Composite
Corporation

U.S. COMPOSITE CORPORATION Financial Cash Flow 2007 ($ in millions)	
Cash flow of the firm	
Operating cash flow	$238
(Earnings before interest and taxes plus depreciation minus taxes)	
Capital spending	−173
(Acquisitions of fixed assets minus sales of fixed assets)	
Additions to net working capital	−23
Total	$ 42
Cash flow to investors in the firm	
Debt	$ 36
(Interest plus retirement of debt minus long-term debt financing)	
Equity	6
(Dividends plus repurchase of equity minus new equity financing)	
Total	$ 42

Another important component of cash flow involves *changes in fixed assets*. For example, when U.S. Composite sold its power systems subsidiary in 2007, it generated $25 million in cash flow. The net change in fixed assets equals the acquisition of fixed assets minus the sales of fixed assets. The result is the cash flow used for capital spending:

Acquisition of fixed assets	$198	
Sales of fixed assets	−25	
Capital spending	$173	($149 + 24 = Increase in property, plant, and equipment + Increase in intangible assets)

We can also calculate capital spending simply as:

$$\begin{aligned}
\text{Capital spending} &= \text{Ending net fixed assets} - \text{Beginning net fixed assets} \\
&\quad + \text{Depreciation} \\
&= \$1,118 - 1,035 + 90 \\
&= \$173
\end{aligned}$$

Cash flows are also used for making investments in net working capital. In U.S. Composite Corporation in 2007, *additions to net working capital* are:

Additions to net working capital	$23

Note that this $23 million is the change in net working capital we previously calculated.

Total cash flows generated by the firm's assets are then equal to:

Operating cash flow	$238
Capital spending	−173
Additions to net working capital	− 23
Total cash flow of the firm	**$ 42**

The total outgoing cash flow of the firm can be separated into cash flow paid to creditors and cash flow paid to stockholders. The cash flow paid to creditors represents a regrouping of the data in Table 2.5 and an explicit recording of interest expense. Creditors are paid an amount generally referred to as *debt service*. Debt service is interest payments plus repayments of principal (that is, retirement of debt).

An important source of cash flow is the sale of new debt. U.S. Composite's long-term debt increased by $13 million (the difference between $86 million in new debt and $73 million in retirement of old debt).[5] Thus, an increase in long-term debt is the net effect of new borrowing and repayment of maturing obligations plus interest expense:

Cash Flow Paid to Creditors ($ in millions)	
Interest	$ 49
Retirement of debt	73
Debt service	122
Proceeds from long-term debt sales	−86
Total	**$ 36**

Cash flow paid to creditors can also be calculated as:

$$\text{Cash flow paid to creditors} = \text{Interest paid} - \text{Net new borrowing}$$

$$= \text{Interest paid} - (\text{Ending long-term debt} - \text{Beginning long-term debt})$$

$$= \$49 - (471 - 458)$$

$$= \$36$$

Cash flow of the firm also is paid to the stockholders. It is the net effect of paying dividends plus repurchasing outstanding shares of stock and issuing new shares of stock:

Cash Flow to Stockholders ($ in millions)	
Dividends	$43
Repurchase of stock	6
Cash to stockholders	49
Proceeds from new stock issue	−43
Total	**$ 6**

---

[5]New debt and the retirement of old debt are usually found in the "notes" to the balance sheet.

In general, cash flow to stockholders can be determined as:

$$\text{Cash flow to stockholders} = \text{Dividends paid} - \text{Net new equity raised}$$
$$= \text{Dividends paid} - (\text{Stock sold}$$
$$- \text{Stock repurchased})$$

To determine stock sold, notice that the common stock and capital surplus accounts went up by a combined $23 + 20 = \$43$, which implies that the company sold $43 million worth of stock. Second, treasury stock went up by $6, indicating that the company bought back $6 million worth of stock. Net new equity is thus $43 - 6 = \$37$. Dividends paid were $43 million, so the cash flow to stockholders was:

$$\text{Cash flow to stockholders} = \$43 - (43 - 6) = \$6,$$

which is what we previously calculated.

Some important observations can be drawn from our discussion of cash flow:

1. Several types of cash flow are relevant to understanding the financial situation of the firm. **Operating cash flow**, defined as earnings before interest plus depreciation minus taxes, measures the cash generated from operations not counting capital spending or working capital requirements. It is usually positive; a firm is in trouble if operating cash flow is negative for a long time because the firm is not generating enough cash to pay operating costs. **Total cash flow of the firm** includes adjustments for capital spending and additions to net working capital. It will frequently be negative. When a firm is growing at a rapid rate, spending on inventory and fixed assets can be higher than operating cash flow.

2. Net income is not cash flow. The net income of the U.S. Composite Corporation in 2007 was $86 million, whereas cash flow was $42 million. The two numbers are not usually the same. In determining the economic and financial condition of a firm, cash flow is more revealing.

A firm's total cash flow sometimes goes by a different name, **free cash flow**. Of course, there is no such thing as "free" cash (we wish!). Instead, the name refers to cash that the firm is free to distribute to creditors and stockholders because it is not needed for working capital or fixed asset investments. We will stick with "total cash flow of the firm" as our label for this important concept because, in practice, there is some variation in exactly how free cash flow is computed. Nonetheless, whenever you hear the phrase "free cash flow," you should understand that what is being discussed is cash flow from assets or something quite similar.

2.6 The Accounting Statement of Cash Flows

As previously mentioned, there is an official accounting statement called the *statement of cash flows*. This statement helps explain the change in accounting cash, which for U.S. Composite is $33 million in 2007. It is very useful in understanding financial cash flow.

The first step in determining the change in cash is to figure out cash flow from operating activities. This is the cash flow that results from the firm's normal activities in producing and selling goods and services. The second step is to make an adjustment for cash flow from investing activities. The final step is to make an adjustment for cash flow from financing activities. Financing activities are the net payments to creditors and owners (excluding interest expense) made during the year.

The three components of the statement of cash flows are determined next.

Cash Flow from Operating Activities

To calculate cash flow from operating activities we start with net income. Net income can be found on the income statement and is equal to $86 million. We now need to add back noncash expenses and adjust for changes in current assets and liabilities (other than cash and notes payable). The result is cash flow from operating activities. Notes payable will be included in the financing activities section.

U.S. COMPOSITE CORPORATION **Cash Flow from Operating Activities** **2007** **($ in millions)**	
Net income	$ 86
Depreciation	90
Deferred taxes	13
Change in assets and liabilities	
Accounts receivable	−24
Inventories	11
Accounts payable	16
Accrued expense	18
Other	−8
Cash flow from operating activities	**$202**

Cash Flow from Investing Activities

Cash flow from investing activities involves changes in capital assets: acquisition of fixed assets and sales of fixed assets (i.e., net capital expenditures). The result for U.S. Composite is shown here:

U.S. COMPOSITE CORPORATION **Cash Flow from Investing Activities** **2007** **($ in millions)**	
Acquisition of fixed assets	−$198
Sales of fixed assets	25
Cash flow from investing activities	**−$173**

Cash Flow from Financing Activities

Cash flows to and from creditors and owners include changes in equity and debt:

U.S. COMPOSITE CORPORATION
Cash Flow from Financing Activities
2007
($ in millions)

Retirement of long-term debt	−$73
Proceeds from long-term debt sales	86
Change in notes payable	−3
Dividends	−43
Repurchase of stock	−6
Proceeds from new stock issue	43
Cash flow from financing activities	**$ 4**

The statement of cash flows is the addition of cash flows from operations, cash flows from investing activities, and cash flows from financing activities, and is produced in Table 2.6. When we add all the cash flows together, we get the change in cash on the balance sheet of $33 million.

There is a close relationship between the official accounting statement called the statement of cash flows and the total cash flow of the firm used in finance. Going back to the previous section, you should note a slight conceptual problem here. Interest paid should really

Table 2.6

Statement of
Consolidated
Cash Flows of the
U.S. Composite
Corporation

U.S. COMPOSITE CORPORATION
Statement of Cash Flows
2007
($ in millions)

Operations	
Net income	$ 86
Depreciation	90
Deferred taxes	13
Changes in assets and liabilities	
Accounts receivable	−24
Inventories	11
Accounts payable	16
Accrued expenses	18
Other	−8
Total cash flow from operations	**$202**
Investing activities	
Acquisition of fixed assets	−$198
Sales of fixed assets	25
Total cash flow from investing activities	**−$173**
Financing activities	
Retirement of long-term debt	−$ 73
Proceeds from long-term debt sales	86
Change in notes payable	−3
Dividends	−43
Repurchase of stock	−6
Proceeds from new stock issue	43
Total cash flow from financing activities	**$ 4**
Change in cash (on the balance sheet)	**$ 33**

go under financing activities, but unfortunately that is not how the accounting is handled. The reason is that interest is deducted as an expense when net income is computed. As a consequence, a primary difference between the accounting cash flow and the financial cash flow of the firm (see Table 2.5) is interest expense.

Summary and Conclusions

Besides introducing you to corporate accounting, the purpose of this chapter has been to teach you how to determine cash flow from the accounting statements of a typical company.

1. Cash flow is generated by the firm and paid to creditors and shareholders. It can be classified as:
   a. Cash flow from operations.
   b. Cash flow from changes in fixed assets.
   c. Cash flow from changes in working capital.
2. Calculations of cash flow are not difficult, but they require care and particular attention to detail in properly accounting for noncash expenses such as depreciation and deferred taxes. It is especially important that you do not confuse cash flow with changes in net working capital and net income.

Concept Questions

1. **Liquidity** True or false: All assets are liquid at some price. Explain.
2. **Accounting and Cash Flows** Why might the revenue and cost figures shown on a standard income statement not represent the actual cash inflows and outflows that occurred during a period?
3. **Accounting Statement of Cash Flows** Looking at the accounting statement of cash flows, what does the bottom line number mean? How useful is this number for analyzing a company?
4. **Cash Flows** How do financial cash flows and the accounting statement of cash flows differ? Which is more useful for analyzing a company?
5. **Book Values versus Market Values** Under standard accounting rules, it is possible for a company's liabilities to exceed its assets. When this occurs, the owners' equity is negative. Can this happen with market values? Why or why not?
6. **Cash Flow from Assets** Why is it not necessarily bad for the cash flow from assets to be negative for a particular period?
7. **Operating Cash Flow** Why is it not necessarily bad for the operating cash flow to be negative for a particular period?
8. **Net Working Capital and Capital Spending** Could a company's change in net working capital be negative in a given year? (*Hint*: Yes.) Explain how this might come about. What about net capital spending?
9. **Cash Flow to Stockholders and Creditors** Could a company's cash flow to stockholders be negative in a given year? (*Hint*: Yes.) Explain how this might come about. What about cash flow to creditors?
10. **Firm Values** Referring back to the CBS Records example at the beginning of the chapter, note that we suggested that CBS Records' stockholders probably didn't suffer as a result of the reported loss. What do you think was the basis for our conclusion?

Questions and Problems

BASIC
(Questions 1–10)

1. **Building a Balance Sheet** Culligan, Inc., has current assets of €5,000, net fixed assets of €23,000, current liabilities of €4,300, and long-term debt of €13,100. What is the value of the shareholders' equity account for this firm? How much is net working capital?
2. **Building an Income Statement** Royale, Inc., has sales of £527,000, costs of £280,000, depreciation expense of £38,000, interest expense of £15,000, and a tax rate of 35 percent.

What is the net income for the firm? Suppose the company paid out £47,000 in cash dividends. What is the addition to retained earnings?

3.   **Market Values and Book Values**   Klingon Cruisers, Inc., purchased new cloaking machinery three years ago for $7 million. The machinery can be sold to the Romulans today for $3.2 million. Klingon's current balance sheet shows net fixed assets of $4,000,000, current liabilities of $2,200,000, and net working capital of $900,000. If all the current assets were liquidated today, the company would receive $2.8 million cash. What is the book value of Klingon's assets today? What is the market value?

4.   **Calculating Taxes**   The Herrera Co. had $273,000 in taxable income. Using the rates from Table 2.3 in the chapter, calculate the company's income taxes. What is the average tax rate? What is the marginal tax rate?

5.   **Calculating OCF**   Toyada, Inc., has sales of £13,500, costs of £5,400, depreciation expense of £1,200, and interest expense of £680. If the tax rate is 30 percent, what is the operating cash flow, or OCF?

6.   **Calculating Net Capital Spending**   See Suwon's 2006 balance sheet showed net fixed assets of ₩4.2 million, and the 2007 balance sheet showed net fixed assets of ₩4.7 million. The company's 2007 income statement showed a depreciation expense of ₩925,000. What was See Suwon's net capital spending for 2007?

7.   **Building a Balance Sheet**   The following table presents the long-term liabilities and stockholders' equity of Information Control Corp. one year ago:

Long-term debt	€60,000,000
Preferred stock	18,000,000
Common stock (€1 par value)	25,000,000
Capital surplus	49,000,000
Accumulated retained earnings	89,000,000

During the past year, Information Control issued 10 million shares of new stock at a total price of €26 million, and issued €8 million in new long-term debt. The company generated €7 million in net income and paid €4 million in dividends. Construct the current balance sheet reflecting the changes that occurred at Information Control Corp. during the year.

8.   **Cash Flow to Creditors**   The 2006 balance sheet of Ganesh Enterprises showed long-term debt of Rs. 2.8 million, and the 2007 balance sheet showed long-term debt of Rs. 3.1 million. The 2007 income statement showed an interest expense of Rs. 340,000. What was the firm's cash flow to creditors during 2007?

9.   **Cash Flow to Stockholders**   The 2006 balance sheet of Ganesh Enterprises showed Rs. 820,000 in the common stock account and Rs. 6.8 million in the additional paid-in surplus account. The 2007 balance sheet showed Rs. 855,000 and Rs. 7.6 million in the same two accounts, respectively. If the company paid out Rs. 600,000 in cash dividends during 2007, what was the cash flow to stockholders for the year?

10.   **Calculating Cash Flows**   Given the information for Ganesh Enterprises in the previous two problems, suppose you also know that the firm's net capital spending for 2007 was Rs. 760,000 and that the firm reduced its net working capital investment by Rs. 165,000. What was the firm's 2007 operating cash flow, or OCF?

INTERMEDIATE
(Questions 11–24)

11.   **Cash Flows**   Thames Realty's accountants prepared the following financial statements for year-end 2007:
      a.   Explain the change in cash during 2007.
      b.   Determine the change in net working capital in 2007.
      c.   Determine the cash flow generated by the firm's assets during 2007.

THAMES REALTY
Income Statement
2007

Revenue	£500
Expenses	300
Depreciation	75
Net income	£125
Dividends	£ 65

THAMES REALTY
Balance Sheets
December 31

	2007	2006
Assets		
Cash	£ 45	£ 10
Other current assets	145	120
Net fixed assets	250	150
Total assets	£440	£280
Liabilities and Equity		
Current liabilities	£ 70	£ 60
Long-term debt	90	0
Stockholders' equity	280	220
Total liabilities and equity	£440	£280

12. **Financial Cash Flows**   The Stancil Corporation provided the following current information:

Proceeds from short-term borrowing	€ 7,000
Proceeds from long-term borrowing	18,000
Proceeds from the sale of common stock	2,000
Purchases of fixed assets	3,000
Purchases of inventories	1,000
Payment of dividends	23,000

Determine the cash flows from the firm and the cash flows to investors of the firm.

13. **Building an Income Statement**   During the year, the Senbet Discount Tire Company had gross sales of $1 million. The firm's cost of goods sold and selling expenses were $300,000 and $200,000, respectively. Senbet also had notes payable of $1 million. These notes carried an interest rate of 10 percent. Depreciation was $100,000. Senbet's tax rate was 35 percent.
    a. What was Senbet's net income?
    b. What was Senbet's operating cash flow?

14. **Calculating Total Cash Flows**   Netanya Placement Corp. shows the following information on its 2007 income statement: sales = ILS 145,000; costs = ILS 86,000; other expenses = ILS 4,900; depreciation expense = ILS 7,000; interest expense = ILS 15,000; taxes = ILS 12,840; dividends = ILS 8,700. In addition, you're told that the firm issued ILS 6,450 in new equity during 2007 and redeemed ILS 6,500 in outstanding long-term debt.
    a. What is the 2007 operating cash flow?
    b. What is the 2007 cash flow to creditors?
    c. What is the 2007 cash flow to stockholders?
    d. If net fixed assets increased by ILS 5,000 during the year, what was the addition to net working capital (NWC)?

15. **Using Income Statements**   Given the following information for Chegutu Forest Products, calculate the depreciation expense: sales = ZWD 29,000; costs = ZWD 13,000; addition to retained earnings = ZWD 4,500; dividends paid = ZWD 900; interest expense = ZWD 1,600; tax rate = 35 percent.

16. **Preparing a Balance Sheet**   Prepare a 2007 balance sheet for Smith Corp. based on the following information: cash = $175,000; patents and copyrights = $720,000; accounts payable = $430,000; accounts receivable = $140,000; tangible net fixed assets = $2,900,000; inventory = $265,000; notes payable = $180,000; accumulated retained earnings = $1,240,000; long-term debt = $1,430,000.

17. **Residual Claims**   Huang, Inc., is obligated to pay its creditors CNY 400,000 very soon.
    a. What is the market value of the shareholders' equity if assets have a market value of CNY 440,000?
    b. What if assets equal CNY 330,000?

18. **Marginal versus Average Tax Rates**   (Refer to Table 2.3.) Corporation Growth has $85,000 in taxable income, and Corporation Income has $8,500,000 in taxable income.
    a. What is the tax bill for each firm?
    b. Suppose both firms have identified a new project that will increase taxable income by $10,000. How much in additional taxes will each firm pay? Why is this amount the same?

19. **Net Income and OCF**   During 2007, Raines Umbrella Corp. had sales of £850,000. Cost of goods sold, administrative and selling expenses, and depreciation expenses were £630,000, £120,000, and £130,000, respectively. In addition, the company had an interest expense of £85,000 and a tax rate of 35 percent. (Ignore any tax loss carryback or carryforward provisions.)
    a. What is Raines's net income for 2007?
    b. What is its operating cash flow?
    c. Explain your results in (a) and (b).

20. **Accounting Values versus Cash Flows**   In Problem 19, suppose Raines Umbrella Corp. paid out £30,000 in cash dividends. Is this possible? If spending on net fixed assets and net working capital was zero, and if no new stock was issued during the year, what was the change in the firm's long-term debt account?

21. **Calculating Cash Flows**   Soignies Handcrafts had the following operating results for 2007: sales = €12,800; cost of goods sold = €10,400; depreciation expense = €1,900; interest expense = €450; dividends paid = €500. At the beginning of the year, net fixed assets were €9,100, current assets were €3,200, and current liabilities were €1,800. At the end of the year, net fixed assets were €9,700, current assets were €3,850, and current liabilities were €2,100. The tax rate for 2007 was 34 percent.
    a. What is net income for 2007?
    b. What is the operating cash flow for 2007?
    c. What is the cash flow from assets for 2007? Is this possible? Explain.
    d. If no new debt was issued during the year, what is the cash flow to creditors? What is the cash flow to stockholders? Explain and interpret the positive and negative signs of your answers in (a) through (d).

22. **Calculating Cash Flows**   Consider the following abbreviated financial statements for Berea Fireworks:

BEREA FIREWORKS 2006 and 2007 Partial Balance Sheets						
Assets			**Liabilities and Owners' Equity**			
	2006	**2007**			**2006**	**2007**
Current assets	£ 650	£ 705	Current liabilities		£ 265	£ 290
Net fixed assets	2,900	3,400	Long-term debt		1,500	1,720

BEREA FIREWORKS 2007 Income Statement	
Sales	£8,600
Costs	4,150
Depreciation	800
Interest paid	216

a. What is owners' equity for 2006 and 2007?

b. What is the change in net working capital for 2007?

c. In 2007, Berea Fireworks purchased £1,500 in new fixed assets. How much in fixed assets did Berea Fireworks sell? What is the cash flow from assets for the year? (The tax rate is 35 percent.)

d. During 2007, Berea Fireworks raised £300 in new long-term debt. How much long-term debt must Berea Fireworks have paid off during the year? What is the cash flow to creditors?

Use the following information for Ingersoll, Inc., for Problems 23 and 24 (assume the tax rate is 34 percent):

	2006	2007
Sales	$ 4,018	$ 4,312
Depreciation	577	578
Cost of goods sold	1,382	1,569
Other expenses	328	274
Interest	269	309
Cash	2,107	2,155
Accounts receivable	2,789	3,142
Short-term notes payable	407	382
Long-term debt	7,056	8,232
Net fixed assets	17,669	18,091
Accounts payable	2,213	2,146
Inventory	4,959	5,096
Dividends	488	532

23. **Financial Statements**   Draw up an income statement and balance sheet for this company for 2006 and 2007.

24. **Calculating Cash Flow**   For 2007, calculate the cash flow from assets, cash flow to creditors, and cash flow to stockholders.

CHALLENGE
(Questions 25–27)

25. **Cash Flows**   You are researching Wu Manufacturing and have found the following accounting statement of cash flows for the most recent year. You also know that the company paid CNY 110 million in current taxes and had an interest expense of CNY 57 million. Use the accounting statement of cash flows to construct the financial statement of cash flows.

WU MANUFACTURING Statement of Cash Flows (CNY in millions)	
Operations	
Net income	CNY 192
Depreciation	105
Deferred taxes	21
Changes in assets and liabilities	
Accounts receivable	−31
Inventories	24
Accounts payable	19
Accrued expenses	−10
Other	2
Total cash flow from operations	CNY 322

(continued)

Investing activities	
Acquisition of fixed assets	−CNY 198
Sale of fixed assets	25
Total cash flow from investing activities	−CNY 173
Financing activities	
Retirement of long-term debt	−CNY 84
Proceeds from long-term debt sales	129
Change in notes payable	6
Dividends	−94
Repurchase of stock	−15
Proceeds from new stock issue	49
Total cash flow from financing activities	−CNY 9
Change in cash (on balance sheet)	CNY 140

26. **Net Fixed Assets and Depreciation**   On the balance sheet, the net fixed assets (NFA) account is equal to the gross fixed assets (FA) account, which records the acquisition cost of fixed assets, minus the accumulated depreciation (AD) account, which records the total depreciation taken by the firm against its fixed assets. Using the fact that $NFA = FA - AD$, show that the expression given in the chapter for net capital spending, $NFA_{end} - NFA_{beg} + D$ (where D is the depreciation expense during the year), is equivalent to $FA_{end} - FA_{beg}$.

27. **Tax Rates**   Refer to the corporate marginal tax rate information in Table 2.3.
    a. Why do you think the marginal tax rate jumps up from 34 percent to 39 percent at a taxable income of $100,001, and then falls back to a 34 percent marginal rate at a taxable income of $335,001?
    b. Compute the average tax rate for a corporation with exactly $335,001 in taxable income. Does this confirm your explanation in part (a)? What is the average tax rate for a corporation with exactly $18,333,334? Is the same thing happening here?
    c. The 39 percent and 38 percent tax rates both represent what is called a tax "bubble." Suppose the government wanted to lower the upper threshold of the 39 percent marginal tax bracket from $335,000 to $200,000. What would the new 39 percent bubble rate have to be?

S&P Problems

www.mhhe.com/edumarketinsight

1. **Marginal and Average Tax Rates**   Download the annual income statements for Sharper Image (SHRP). Looking back at Table 2.3, what is the marginal income tax rate for Sharper Image? Using the total income tax and the pretax income numbers, calculate the average tax rate for Sharper Image. Is this number greater than 35 percent? Why or why not?

2. **Net Working Capital**   Find the annual balance sheets for American Electric Power (AEP) and HJ Heinz (HNZ). Calculate the net working capital for each company. Is American Electric Power's net working capital negative? If so, does this indicate potential financial difficulty for the company? What about Heinz?

3. **Per Share Earnings and Dividends**   Find the annual income statements for Harley-Davidson (HDI), Hawaiian Electric Industries (HE), and Time Warner (TWX). What are the earnings per share (EPS Basic from operations) for each of these companies? What are the dividends per share for each company? Why do these companies pay out a different portion of income in the form of dividends?

4. **Cash Flow Identity**   Download the annual balance sheets and income statements for Landry's Seafood Restaurants (LNY). Using the most recent year, calculate the cash flow identity for Landry Seafood. Explain your answer.

Cash Flows at Warf Computers, Inc.

Warf Computers, Inc., was founded 15 years ago by Nick Warf, a computer programmer. The small initial investment to start the company was made by Nick and his friends. Over the years, this same group has supplied the limited additional investment needed by the company in the form of both equity and short- and long-term debt. Recently the company has developed a virtual keyboard (VK). The VK uses sophisticated artificial intelligence algorithms that allow the user to speak naturally and have the computer input the text, correct spelling and grammatical errors, and format the document according to preset user guidelines. The VK even suggests alternative phrasing and sentence structure, and it provides detailed stylistic diagnostics. Based on a proprietary, very advanced software/hardware hybrid technology, the system is a full generation beyond what is currently on the market. To introduce the VK, the company will require significant outside investment.

   Nick has made the decision to seek this outside financing in the form of new equity investments and bank loans. Naturally, new investors and the banks will require a detailed financial analysis. Your employer, Angus Jones & Partners, LLC, has asked you to examine the financial statements provided by Nick. Here are the balance sheet for the two most recent years and the most recent income statement:

WARF COMPUTERS
Balance Sheet
($ in thousands)

	2007	2006		2007	2006
Current assets:			Current liabilities:		
Cash and equivalents	$ 232	$ 201	Accounts payable	$ 263	$ 197
Accounts receivable	367	342	Notes payable	68	53
Inventories	329	340	Accrued expenses	126	205
Other	47	40	Total current liabilities	$ 457	$ 455
Total current assets	$ 975	$ 923			
Fixed assets:			Long-term liabilities:		
Property, plant, and equipment	$2,105	$1,630	Deferred taxes	$ 143	$ 82
			Long-term debt	629	589
Less accumulated depreciation	687	560	Total long-term liabilities	$ 772	$ 671
Net property, plant, and equipment	$1,418	$1,070	Stockholders' equity:		
			Preferred stock	$ 10	$ 10
Intangible assets and others	406	363	Common stock	72	64
Total fixed assets	$1,824	$1,433	Capital surplus	438	399
			Accumulated retained earnings	1,147	822
			Less treasury stock	−97	−65
			Total equity	$1,570	$1,230
			Total liabilities and		
Total assets	$2,799	$2,356	shareholders' equity	$2,799	$2,356

   Nick has also provided the following information: During the year the company raised $94,000 in new long-term debt and retired $54,000 in long-term debt. The company also sold $47,000 in new stock and repurchased $32,000 in stock. The company purchased $629,000 in fixed assets and sold $111,000 in fixed assets.

WARF COMPUTERS Income Statement ($ in thousands)	
Sales	$3,875
Cost of goods sold	2,286
Selling, general, and administrative expense	434
Depreciation	127
Operating income	$1,028
Other income	38
Earnings before interest and taxes (EBIT)	$1,066
Interest expense	76
Pretax income	$ 990
Taxes	347
Current: $286	
Deferred: 61	
Net income	$ 643
Addition to retained earnings	$ 325
Dividends	$ 318

Angus has asked you to prepare the financial statement of cash flows and the accounting statement of cash flows. He has also asked you to answer the following questions:

1. How would you describe Warf Computers' cash flows?

2. Which cash flow statement more accurately describes the cash flows at the company?

3. In light of your previous answers, comment on Nick's expansion plans.

Financial Statements Analysis and Long-Term Planning

In early 2006, shares of stock in food producer Kraft were trading for about $28. At that price, Kraft had a price–earnings ratio, or PE, of 19, meaning that investors were willing to pay $19 for every dollar in income earned by Kraft. At the same time, investors were willing to pay a stunning $482 for each dollar earned by grocer Kroger, but only about $8 and $5 for each dollar earned by Gateway Computers and United States Steel, respectively. And there were stocks like Maytag, which, despite having no earnings (a loss actually), had a stock price of about $19 per share. Meanwhile, the average stock in the Standard and Poor's (S&P) 500 index, which contains 500 of the largest publicly traded companies in the United States, had a PE ratio of about 19, so Kraft was average in this regard.

What do PE ratios tell us and why are they important? To find out, this chapter explores a variety of ratios and their use in financial analysis and planning.

3.1 Financial Statements Analysis

In Chapter 2, we discussed some of the essential concepts of financial statements and cash flows. This chapter continues where our earlier discussion left off. Our goal here is to expand your understanding of the uses (and abuses) of financial statement information.

A good working knowledge of financial statements is desirable simply because such statements, and numbers derived from those statements, are the primary means of communicating financial information both within the firm and outside the firm. In short, much of the language of business finance is rooted in the ideas we discuss in this chapter.

Clearly, one important goal of the accountant is to report financial information to the user in a form useful for decision making. Ironically, the information frequently does not come to the user in such a form. In other words, financial statements don't come with a user's guide. This chapter is a first step in filling this gap.

Standardizing Statements

One obvious thing we might want to do with a company's financial statements is to compare them to those of other, similar companies. We would immediately have a problem, however. It's almost impossible to directly compare the financial statements for two companies because of differences in size.

For example, Ford and GM are obviously serious rivals in the auto market, but GM is much larger (in terms of assets), so it is difficult to compare them directly. For that matter, it's difficult even to compare financial statements from different points in time for the same company if the company's size has changed. The size problem is compounded if we try to

Table 3.1

PRUFROCK CORPORATION Balance Sheets as of December 31, 2006 and 2007 ($ in millions)		
Assets	**2006**	**2007**
Current assets		
Cash	$ 84	$ 98
Accounts receivable	165	188
Inventory	393	422
Total	$ 642	$ 708
Fixed assets		
Net plant and equipment	$2,731	$2,880
Total assets	$3,373	$3,588
Liabilities and owners' equity		
Current liabilities		
Accounts payable	$ 312	$ 344
Notes payable	231	196
Total	$ 543	$ 540
Long-term debt	$ 531	$ 457
Owners' equity		
Common stock and paid-in surplus	$ 500	$ 550
Retained earnings	1,799	2,041
Total	$2,299	$2,591
Total liabilities and owners' equity	$3,373	$3,588

compare GM and, say, Toyota. If Toyota's financial statements are denominated in yen, then we have size *and* currency differences.

To start making comparisons, one obvious thing we might try to do is to somehow standardize the financial statements. One common and useful way of doing this is to work with percentages instead of total dollars. The resulting financial statements are called **common-size statements**. We consider these next.

Common-Size Balance Sheets

For easy reference, Prufrock Corporation's 2006 and 2007 balance sheets are provided in Table 3.1. Using these, we construct common-size balance sheets by expressing each item as a percentage of total assets. Prufrock's 2006 and 2007 common-size balance sheets are shown in Table 3.2.

Notice that some of the totals don't check exactly because of rounding errors. Also notice that the total change has to be zero because the beginning and ending numbers must add up to 100 percent.

In this form, financial statements are relatively easy to read and compare. For example, just looking at the two balance sheets for Prufrock, we see that current assets were 19.7 percent of total assets in 2007, up from 19.1 percent in 2006. Current liabilities declined from 16.0 percent to 15.1 percent of total liabilities and equity over that same time. Similarly, total equity rose from 68.1 percent of total liabilities and equity to 72.2 percent.

Overall, Prufrock's liquidity, as measured by current assets compared to current liabilities, increased over the year. Simultaneously, Prufrock's indebtedness diminished as

Table 3.2

PRUFROCK CORPORATION Common-Size Balance Sheets December 31, 2006 and 2007			
Assets	**2006**	**2007**	**Change**
Current assets			
Cash	2.5%	2.7%	+ .2%
Accounts receivable	4.9	5.2	+ .3
Inventory	11.7	11.8	+ .1
Total	19.1	19.7	+ .6
Fixed assets			
Net plant and equipment	80.9	80.3	− .6
Total assets	100.0%	100.0%	.0%
Liabilities and owners' equity			
Current liabilities			
Accounts payable	9.2%	9.6%	+ .4%
Notes payable	6.8	5.5	−1.3
Total	16.0	15.1	− .9
Long-term debt	15.7	12.7	−3.0
Owners' equity			
Common stock and paid-in surplus	14.8	15.3	+ .5
Retained earnings	53.3	56.9	+3.6
Total	68.1	72.2	+4.1
Total liabilities and owners' equity	100.0%	100.0%	.0%

a percentage of total assets. We might be tempted to conclude that the balance sheet has grown "stronger."

Common-Size Income Statements

A useful way of standardizing the income statement shown in Table 3.3 is to express each item as a percentage of total sales, as illustrated for Prufrock in Table 3.4.

This income statement tells us what happens to each dollar in sales. For Prufrock, interest expense eats up $.061 out of every sales dollar, and taxes take another $.081. When all is said and done, $.157 of each dollar flows through to the bottom line (net income), and that amount is split into $.105 retained in the business and $.052 paid out in dividends.

These percentages are useful in comparisons. For example, a relevant figure is the cost percentage. For Prufrock, $.582 of each $1.00 in sales goes to pay for goods sold. It would be interesting to compute the same percentage for Prufrock's main competitors to see how Prufrock stacks up in terms of cost control.

3.2 Ratio Analysis

Another way of avoiding the problems involved in comparing companies of different sizes is to calculate and compare **financial ratios**. Such ratios are ways of comparing and investigating the relationships between different pieces of financial information. We cover some of the more common ratios next (there are many others we don't discuss here).

Table 3.3

PRUFROCK CORPORATION 2007 Income Statement ($ in millions)		
Sales		$2,311
Cost of goods sold		1,344
Depreciation		276
Earnings before interest and taxes		$ 691
Interest paid		141
Taxable income		$ 550
Taxes (34%)		187
Net income		$ 363
Dividends	$121	
Addition to retained earnings	242	

Table 3.4

PRUFROCK CORPORATION Common-Size Income Statement 2007		
Sales		100.0%
Cost of goods sold		58.2
Depreciation		11.9
Earnings before interest and taxes		29.9
Interest paid		6.1
Taxable income		23.8
Taxes (34%)		8.1
Net income		15.7%
Dividends	5.2%	
Addition to retained earnings	10.5	

One problem with ratios is that different people and different sources frequently don't compute them in exactly the same way, and this leads to much confusion. The specific definitions we use here may or may not be the same as ones you have seen or will see elsewhere. If you are using ratios as tools for analysis, you should be careful to document how you calculate each one; and, if you are comparing your numbers to those of another source, be sure you know how their numbers are computed.

We will defer much of our discussion of how ratios are used and some problems that come up with using them until later in the chapter. For now, for each ratio we discuss, several questions come to mind:

Go to **www.investor. reuters.com** and find the ratios link to examine comparative ratios for a huge number of companies

1. How is it computed?

2. What is it intended to measure, and why might we be interested?

3. What is the unit of measurement?

4. What might a high or low value be telling us? How might such values be misleading?

5. How could this measure be improved?

Financial ratios are traditionally grouped into the following categories:

1. Short-term solvency, or liquidity, ratios.
2. Long-term solvency, or financial leverage, ratios.
3. Asset management, or turnover, ratios.
4. Profitability ratios.
5. Market value ratios.

We will consider each of these in turn. In calculating these numbers for Prufrock, we will use the ending balance sheet (2007) figures unless we explicitly say otherwise.

Short-Term Solvency or Liquidity Measures

As the name suggests, short-term solvency ratios as a group are intended to provide information about a firm's liquidity, and these ratios are sometimes called *liquidity measures.* The primary concern is the firm's ability to pay its bills over the short run without undue stress. Consequently, these ratios focus on current assets and current liabilities.

For obvious reasons, liquidity ratios are particularly interesting to short-term creditors. Because financial managers are constantly working with banks and other short-term lenders, an understanding of these ratios is essential.

One advantage of looking at current assets and liabilities is that their book values and market values are likely to be similar. Often (though not always), these assets and liabilities just don't live long enough for the two to get seriously out of step. On the other hand, like any type of near-cash, current assets and liabilities can and do change fairly rapidly, so today's amounts may not be a reliable guide to the future.

Current Ratio   One of the best-known and most widely used ratios is the *current ratio.* As you might guess, the current ratio is defined as:

$$\text{Current ratio} = \frac{\text{Current assets}}{\text{Current liabilities}} \qquad \textbf{(3.1)}$$

For Prufrock, the 2007 current ratio is:

$$\text{Current ratio} = \frac{\$708}{\$540} = 1.31 \text{ times}$$

Because current assets and liabilities are, in principle, converted to cash over the following 12 months, the current ratio is a measure of short-term liquidity. The unit of measurement is either dollars or times. So, we could say Prufrock has \$1.31 in current assets for every \$1 in current liabilities, or we could say Prufrock has its current liabilities covered 1.31 times over.

To a creditor, particularly a short-term creditor such as a supplier, the higher the current ratio, the better. To the firm, a high current ratio indicates liquidity, but it also may indicate an inefficient use of cash and other short-term assets. Absent some extraordinary circumstances, we would expect to see a current ratio of at least 1; a current ratio of less than 1 would mean that net working capital (current assets less current liabilities) is negative. This would be unusual in a healthy firm, at least for most types of businesses.

The current ratio, like any ratio, is affected by various types of transactions. For example, suppose the firm borrows over the long term to raise money. The short-run effect would be an increase in cash from the issue proceeds and an increase in long-term debt. Current liabilities would not be affected, so the current ratio would rise.

EXAMPLE 3.1

Current Events   Suppose a firm were to pay off some of its suppliers and short-term creditors. What would happen to the current ratio? Suppose a firm buys some inventory. What happens in this case? What happens if a firm sells some merchandise?

The first case is a trick question. What happens is that the current ratio moves away from 1. If it is greater than 1 (the usual case), it will get bigger, but if it is less than 1, it will get smaller. To see this, suppose the firm has $4 in current assets and $2 in current liabilities for a current ratio of 2. If we use $1 in cash to reduce current liabilities, the new current ratio is ($4 − 1)/($2 − 1) = 3. If we reverse the original situation to $2 in current assets and $4 in current liabilities, the change will cause the current ratio to fall to 1/3 from 1/2.

The second case is not quite as tricky. Nothing happens to the current ratio because cash goes down while inventory goes up—total current assets are unaffected.

In the third case, the current ratio would usually rise because inventory is normally shown at cost and the sale would normally be at something greater than cost (the difference is the markup). The increase in either cash or receivables is therefore greater than the decrease in inventory. This increases current assets, and the current ratio rises.

Finally, note that an apparently low current ratio may not be a bad sign for a company with a large reserve of untapped borrowing power.

Quick (or Acid-Test) Ratio   Inventory is often the least liquid current asset. It's also the one for which the book values are least reliable as measures of market value because the quality of the inventory isn't considered. Some of the inventory may later turn out to be damaged, obsolete, or lost.

More to the point, relatively large inventories are often a sign of short-term trouble. The firm may have overestimated sales and overbought or overproduced as a result. In this case, the firm may have a substantial portion of its liquidity tied up in slow-moving inventory.

To further evaluate liquidity, the *quick*, or *acid-test*, *ratio* is computed just like the current ratio, except inventory is omitted:

$$\text{Quick ratio} = \frac{\text{Current assets} - \text{Inventory}}{\text{Current liabilities}} \tag{3.2}$$

Notice that using cash to buy inventory does not affect the current ratio, but it reduces the quick ratio. Again, the idea is that inventory is relatively illiquid compared to cash.

For Prufrock, this ratio in 2007 was:

$$\text{Quick ratio} = \frac{\$708 - 422}{\$540} = .53 \text{ times}$$

The quick ratio here tells a somewhat different story than the current ratio because inventory accounts for more than half of Prufrock's current assets. To exaggerate the point, if this inventory consisted of, say, unsold nuclear power plants, then this would be a cause for concern.

To give an example of current versus quick ratios, based on recent financial statements, Wal-Mart and Manpower, Inc., had current ratios of .89 and 1.45, respectively. However, Manpower carries no inventory to speak of, whereas Wal-Mart's current assets are virtually all inventory. As a result, Wal-Mart's quick ratio was only .13, and Manpower's was 1.37, almost the same as its current ratio.

Cash Ratio   A very short-term creditor might be interested in the *cash ratio*:

$$\text{Cash ratio} = \frac{\text{Cash}}{\text{Current liabilities}} \tag{3.3}$$

You can verify that this works out to be .18 times for Prufrock.

Long-Term Solvency Measures

Long-term solvency ratios are intended to address the firm's long-run ability to meet its obligations or, more generally, its financial leverage. These ratios are sometimes called *financial leverage ratios* or just *leverage ratios*. We consider three commonly used measures and some variations.

Total Debt Ratio   The *total debt ratio* takes into account all debts of all maturities to all creditors. It can be defined in several ways, the easiest of which is this:

$$\begin{aligned} \text{Total debt ratio} &= \frac{\text{Total assets} - \text{Total equity}}{\text{Total assets}} \\ &= \frac{\$3,588 - 2,591}{\$3,588} = .28 \text{ times} \end{aligned} \tag{3.4}$$

In this case, an analyst might say that Prufrock uses 28 percent debt.[1] Whether this is high or low or whether it even makes any difference depends on whether capital structure matters, a subject we discuss in a later chapter.

Prufrock has $.28 in debt for every $1 in assets. Therefore, there is $.72 in equity ($1 − .28) for every $.28 in debt. With this in mind, we can define two useful variations on the total debt ratio, the *debt–equity ratio* and the *equity multiplier*:

The online Women's Business Center has more information about financial statements, ratios, and small business topics at **www.onlinewbc.gov.**

$$\begin{aligned} \text{Debt–equity ratio} &= \text{Total debt/Total equity} \\ &= \$.28/\$.72 = .39 \text{ times} \end{aligned} \tag{3.5}$$

$$\begin{aligned} \text{Equity multiplier} &= \text{Total assets/Total equity} \\ &= \$1/\$.72 = 1.39 \text{ times} \end{aligned} \tag{3.6}$$

The fact that the equity multiplier is 1 plus the debt–equity ratio is not a coincidence:

$$\begin{aligned} \text{Equity multiplier} &= \text{Total assets/Total equity} = \$1/\$.72 = 1.39 \text{ times} \\ &= (\text{Total equity} + \text{Total debt})/\text{Total equity} \\ &= 1 + \text{Debt–equity ratio} = 1.39 \text{ times} \end{aligned}$$

The thing to notice here is that given any one of these three ratios, you can immediately calculate the other two, so they all say exactly the same thing.

Times Interest Earned   Another common measure of long-term solvency is the *times interest earned* (TIE) *ratio*. Once again, there are several possible (and common) definitions, but we'll stick with the most traditional:

$$\begin{aligned} \text{Times interest earned ratio} &= \frac{\text{EBIT}}{\text{Interest}} \\ &= \frac{\$691}{\$141} = 4.9 \text{ times} \end{aligned} \tag{3.7}$$

---

[1] Total equity here includes preferred stock, if there is any. An equivalent numerator in this ratio would be (Current liabilities + Long-term debt).

As the name suggests, this ratio measures how well a company has its interest obligations covered, and it is often called the *interest coverage ratio*. For Prufrock, the interest bill is covered 4.9 times over.

Cash Coverage   A problem with the TIE ratio is that it is based on EBIT, which is not really a measure of cash available to pay interest. The reason is that depreciation, a noncash expense, has been deducted out. Because interest is most definitely a cash outflow (to creditors), one way to define the *cash coverage ratio* is:

$$\text{Cash coverage ratio} = \frac{\text{EBIT} + \text{Depreciation}}{\text{Interest}}$$ (3.8)

$$= \frac{\$691 + 276}{\$141} = \frac{\$967}{\$141} = 6.9 \text{ times}$$

The numerator here, EBIT plus depreciation, is often abbreviated EBITD (earnings before interest, taxes, and depreciation). It is a basic measure of the firm's ability to generate cash from operations, and it is frequently used as a measure of cash flow available to meet financial obligations.

Asset Management or Turnover Measures

We next turn our attention to the efficiency with which Prufrock uses its assets. The measures in this section are sometimes called *asset management* or *utilization ratios*. The specific ratios we discuss can all be interpreted as measures of turnover. What they are intended to describe is how efficiently, or intensively, a firm uses its assets to generate sales. We first look at two important current assets: inventory and receivables.

Inventory Turnover and Days' Sales in Inventory   During the year, Prufrock had a cost of goods sold of $1,344. Inventory at the end of the year was $422. With these numbers, *inventory turnover* can be calculated as:

$$\text{Inventory turnover} = \frac{\text{Cost of goods sold}}{\text{Inventory}}$$ (3.9)

$$= \frac{\$1,344}{\$422} = 3.2 \text{ times}$$

In a sense, we sold off, or turned over, the entire inventory 3.2 times over the year. As long as we are not running out of stock and thereby forgoing sales, the higher this ratio is, the more efficiently we are managing inventory.

   If we know that we turned our inventory over 3.2 times during the year, we can immediately figure out how long it took us to turn it over on average. The result is the average *days' sales in inventory*:

$$\text{Days' sales in inventory} = \frac{365 \text{ days}}{\text{Inventory turnover}}$$ (3.10)

$$= \frac{365}{3.2} = 114 \text{ days}$$

This tells us that, roughly speaking, inventory sits 114 days on average before it is sold. Alternatively, assuming we used the most recent inventory and cost figures, it will take about 114 days to work off our current inventory.

For example, in February 2005, General Motors had a 123-day supply of the slow-selling Pontiac G6 and a 122-day supply of the Buick LaCrosse. This means that, at the then-current rate of sales, it would have taken General Motors 123 days to deplete the available supply, whereas a 60-day supply is considered normal in the industry. By the middle of 2005, General Motors had an overall 73-day supply of inventory. The extra 13-day supply meant that General Motors had approximately $5 billion more than normal tied up in inventory—money that could have been used elsewhere. Of course, the days in inventory is much lower for better-selling models. DaimlerChrysler had no such problem with its new (and tough-looking) Chrysler 300C. This popular model flew off dealer lots, and DaimlerChrysler had only 28 days of inventory on hand.

Receivables Turnover and Days' Sales in Receivables   Our inventory measures give some indication of how fast we can sell products. We now look at how fast we collect on those sales. The *receivables turnover* is defined in the same way as inventory turnover:

$$\text{Receivables turnover} = \frac{\text{Sales}}{\text{Accounts receivable}} \qquad (3.11)$$

$$= \frac{\$2,311}{\$188} = 12.3 \text{ times}$$

Loosely speaking, we collected our outstanding credit accounts and lent the money again 12.3 times during the year.[2]

This ratio makes more sense if we convert it to days, so the *days' sales in receivables* is:

$$\text{Days' sales in receivables} = \frac{365 \text{ days}}{\text{Receivables turnover}} \qquad (3.12)$$

$$= \frac{365}{12.3} = 30 \text{ days}$$

Therefore, on average, we collect on our credit sales in 30 days. For obvious reasons, this ratio is frequently called the *average collection period* (ACP). Also note that if we are using the most recent figures, we can also say that we have 30 days' worth of sales currently uncollected.

EXAMPLE 3.2

Payables Turnover   Here is a variation on the receivables collection period. How long, on average, does it take for Prufrock Corporation to *pay* its bills? To answer, we need to calculate the accounts payable turnover rate using cost of goods sold. We will assume that Prufrock purchases everything on credit.

The cost of goods sold is $1,344, and accounts payable are $344. The turnover is therefore $1,344/$344 = 3.9 times. So, payables turned over about every 365/3.9 = 94 days. On average, then, Prufrock takes 94 days to pay. As a potential creditor, we might take note of this fact.

---

[2]Here we have implicitly assumed that all sales are credit sales. If they were not, we would simply use total credit sales in these calculations, not total sales.

Total Asset Turnover   Moving away from specific accounts like inventory or receivables, we can consider an important "big picture" ratio, the *total asset turnover* ratio. As the name suggests, total asset turnover is:

Pricewaterhouse-
Coopers has a useful
utility for extracting
EDGAR data. Try it at
**www.edgarscan.
pwcglobal.com.**

$$\text{Total asset turnover} = \frac{\text{Sales}}{\text{Total assets}} \qquad (3.13)$$

$$= \frac{\$2,311}{\$3,588} = .64 \text{ times}$$

In other words, for every dollar in assets, we generated $.64 in sales.

EXAMPLE 3.3

More Turnover   Suppose you find that a particular company generates $.40 in annual sales for every dollar in total assets. How often does this company turn over its total assets?

   The total asset turnover here is .40 times per year. It takes $1/.40 = 2.5$ years to turn assets over completely.

Profitability Measures

The three measures we discuss in this section are probably the best-known and most widely used of all financial ratios. In one form or another, they are intended to measure how efficiently the firm uses its assets and how efficiently the firm manages its operations. The focus in this group is on the bottom line—net income.

Profit Margin   Companies pay a great deal of attention to their *profit margin*:

$$\text{Profit margin} = \frac{\text{Net income}}{\text{Sales}} \qquad (3.14)$$

$$= \frac{\$363}{\$2,311} = 15.7\%$$

This tells us that Prufrock, in an accounting sense, generates a little less than 16 cents in profit for every dollar in sales.

   All other things being equal, a relatively high profit margin is obviously desirable. This situation corresponds to low expense ratios relative to sales. However, we hasten to add that other things are often not equal.

   For example, lowering our sales price will usually increase unit volume but will normally cause profit margins to shrink. Total profit (or, more importantly, operating cash flow) may go up or down, so the fact that margins are smaller isn't necessarily bad. After all, isn't it possible that, as the saying goes, "Our prices are so low that we lose money on everything we sell, but we make it up in volume"?[3]

   Profit margins are very different for different industries. Grocery stores have a notoriously low profit margin, generally around 2 percent. In contrast, the profit margin for the pharmaceutical industry is about 18 percent. So, for example, it is not surprising that

---

[3]No, it's not.

recent profit margins for Albertson's and Pfizer were about 1.2 percent and 15.6 percent, respectively.

Return on Assets *Return on assets* (ROA) is a measure of profit per dollar of assets. It can be defined several ways, but the most common is:

$$\text{Return on assets} = \frac{\text{Net income}}{\text{Total assets}} \tag{3.15}$$

$$= \frac{\$363}{\$3,588} = 10.12\%$$

Return on Equity *Return on equity* (ROE) is a measure of how the stockholders fared during the year. Because benefiting shareholders is our goal, ROE is, in an accounting sense, the true bottom-line measure of performance. ROE is usually measured as:

$$\text{Return on equity} = \frac{\text{Net income}}{\text{Total equity}} \tag{3.16}$$

$$= \frac{\$363}{\$2,591} = 14\%$$

Therefore, for every dollar in equity, Prufrock generated 14 cents in profit; but, again, this is correct only in accounting terms.

Because ROA and ROE are such commonly cited numbers, we stress that it is important to remember they are accounting rates of return. For this reason, these measures should properly be called *return on book assets* and *return on book equity*. In addition, ROE is sometimes called *return on net worth*. Whatever it's called, it would be inappropriate to compare the result to, for example, an interest rate observed in the financial markets.

The fact that ROE exceeds ROA reflects Prufrock's use of financial leverage. We will examine the relationship between these two measures in the next section.

Market Value Measures

Our final group of measures is based, in part, on information not necessarily contained in financial statements—the market price per share of the stock. Obviously, these measures can be calculated directly only for publicly traded companies.

We assume that Prufrock has 33 million shares outstanding and the stock sold for $88 per share at the end of the year. If we recall that Prufrock's net income was $363 million, then we can calculate that its earnings per share were:

$$\text{EPS} = \frac{\text{Net income}}{\text{Shares outstanding}} = \frac{\$363}{33} = \$11 \tag{3.17}$$

Price–Earnings Ratio The first of our market value measures, the *price–earnings* or PE *ratio* (or multiple), is defined as:

$$\text{PE ratio} = \frac{\text{Price per share}}{\text{Earnings per share}} \tag{3.18}$$

$$= \frac{\$88}{\$11} = 8 \text{ times}$$

In the vernacular, we would say that Prufrock shares sell for eight times earnings, or we might say that Prufrock shares have, or "carry," a PE multiple of 8.

Because the PE ratio measures how much investors are willing to pay per dollar of current earnings, higher PEs are often taken to mean that the firm has significant prospects for future growth. Of course, if a firm had no or almost no earnings, its PE would probably be quite large; so, as always, care is needed in interpreting this ratio.

Market-to-Book Ratio   A second commonly quoted measure is the *market-to-book ratio*:

$$\text{Market-to-book-ratio} = \frac{\text{Market value per share}}{\text{Book value per share}} \qquad\qquad \textbf{(3.19)}$$

$$= \frac{\$88}{\$2,591/33} = \frac{\$88}{\$78.5} = 1.12 \text{ times}$$

Notice that book value per share is total equity (not just common stock) divided by the number of shares outstanding.

Book value per share is an accounting number that reflects historical costs. In a loose sense, the market-to-book ratio therefore compares the market value of the firm's investments to their cost. A value less than 1 could mean that the firm has not been successful overall in creating value for its stockholders.

This completes our definition of some common ratios. We could tell you about more of them, but these are enough for now. We'll leave it here and go on to discuss some ways of using these ratios instead of just how to calculate them. Table 3.5 summarizes the ratios we've discussed.

3.3   The Du Pont Identity

As we mentioned in discussing ROA and ROE, the difference between these two profitability measures reflects the use of debt financing or financial leverage. We illustrate the relationship between these measures in this section by investigating a famous way of decomposing ROE into its component parts.

A Closer Look at ROE

To begin, let's recall the definition of ROE:

$$\text{Return on equity} = \frac{\text{Net income}}{\text{Total equity}}$$

If we were so inclined, we could multiply this ratio by Assets/Assets without changing anything:

$$\text{Return on equity} = \frac{\text{Net income}}{\text{Total equity}} = \frac{\text{Net income}}{\text{Total equity}} \times \frac{\text{Assets}}{\text{Assets}}$$

$$= \frac{\text{Net income}}{\text{Assets}} \times \frac{\text{Assets}}{\text{Total equity}}$$

Notice that we have expressed the ROE as the product of two other ratios—ROA and the equity multiplier:

$$\text{ROE} = \text{ROA} \times \text{Equity multiplier} = \text{ROA} \times (1 + \text{Debt–equity ratio})$$

Table 3.5 Common Financial Ratios

I. Short-term solvency, or liquidity, ratios

$$\text{Current ratio} = \frac{\text{Current assets}}{\text{Current liabilities}}$$

$$\text{Quick ratio} = \frac{\text{Current assets} - \text{Inventory}}{\text{Current liabilities}}$$

$$\text{Cash ratio} = \frac{\text{Cash}}{\text{Current liabilities}}$$

$$\text{Days' sales in receivables} = \frac{365 \text{ days}}{\text{Receivables turnover}}$$

$$\text{Total asset turnover} = \frac{\text{Sales}}{\text{Total assets}}$$

$$\text{Capital intensity} = \frac{\text{Total assets}}{\text{Sales}}$$

II. Long-term solvency, or financial leverage, ratios

$$\text{Total debt ratio} = \frac{\text{Total assets} - \text{Total equity}}{\text{Total assets}}$$

Debt–equity ratio = Total debt/Total equity

Equity multiplier = Total assets/Total equity

$$\text{Times interest earned ratio} = \frac{\text{EBIT}}{\text{Interest}}$$

$$\text{Cash coverage ratio} = \frac{\text{EBIT} + \text{Depreciation}}{\text{Interest}}$$

IV. Profitability ratios

$$\text{Profit margin} = \frac{\text{Net income}}{\text{Sales}}$$

$$\text{Return on assets (ROA)} = \frac{\text{Net income}}{\text{Total assets}}$$

$$\text{Return on equity (ROE)} = \frac{\text{Net income}}{\text{Total equity}}$$

$$\text{ROE} = \frac{\text{Net income}}{\text{Sales}} \times \frac{\text{Sales}}{\text{Assets}} \times \frac{\text{Assets}}{\text{Equity}}$$

III. Asset utilization, or turnover, ratios

$$\text{Inventory turnover} = \frac{\text{Cost of goods sold}}{\text{Inventory}}$$

$$\text{Day's sales in inventory} = \frac{365 \text{ days}}{\text{Inventory turnover}}$$

$$\text{Receivable turnover} = \frac{\text{Sales}}{\text{Accounts receivable}}$$

V. Market value ratios

$$\text{Price–earnings ratio} = \frac{\text{Price per share}}{\text{Earnings per share}}$$

$$\text{Market-to-book ratio} = \frac{\text{Market value per share}}{\text{Book value per share}}$$

Looking back at Prufrock, for example, we see that the debt–equity ratio was .39 and ROA was 10.12 percent. Our work here implies that Prufrock's ROE, as we previously calculated, is:

$$\text{ROE} = 10.12\% \times 1.39 = 14\%$$

The difference between ROE and ROA can be substantial, particularly for certain businesses. For example based on recent financial statements, Bank of America has an ROA of only 1.44 percent, which is actually fairly typical for a bank. However, banks tend to borrow a lot of money, and, as a result, have relatively large equity multipliers. For Bank of America, ROE is about 17 percent, implying an equity multiplier of 11.8.

We can further decompose ROE by multiplying the top and bottom by total sales:

$$\text{ROE} = \frac{\text{Sales}}{\text{Sales}} \times \frac{\text{Net income}}{\text{Assets}} \times \frac{\text{Assets}}{\text{Total equity}}$$

If we rearrange things a bit, ROE is:

$$\text{ROE} = \underbrace{\frac{\text{Net income}}{\text{Sales}} \times \frac{\text{Sales}}{\text{Assets}}}_{\text{Return on assets}} \times \frac{\text{Assets}}{\text{Total equity}} \tag{3.20}$$

$$= \text{Profit margin} \times \text{Total asset turnover} \times \text{Equity multiplier}$$

What we have now done is to partition ROA into its two component parts, profit margin and total asset turnover. The last expression of the preceding equation is called the **Du Pont identity** after the Du Pont Corporation, which popularized its use.

We can check this relationship for Prufrock by noting that the profit margin was 15.7 percent and the total asset turnover was .64. ROE should thus be:

$$
\begin{aligned}
\text{ROE} &= \text{Profit margin} \times \text{Total asset turnover} \times \text{Equity multiplier} \\
&= 15.7\% \qquad\quad \times \qquad .64 \qquad \times \qquad 1.39 \\
&= 14\%
\end{aligned}
$$

This 14 percent ROE is exactly what we had before.

The Du Pont identity tells us that ROE is affected by three things:

1. Operating efficiency (as measured by profit margin).
2. Asset use efficiency (as measured by total asset turnover).
3. Financial leverage (as measured by the equity multiplier).

Weakness in either operating or asset use efficiency (or both) will show up in a diminished return on assets, which will translate into a lower ROE.

Considering the Du Pont identity, it appears that the ROE could be leveraged up by increasing the amount of debt in the firm. However, notice that increasing debt also increases interest expense, which reduces profit margins, which acts to reduce ROE. So, ROE could go up or down, depending. More important, the use of debt financing has a number of other effects, and, as we discuss at some length in later chapters, the amount of leverage a firm uses is governed by its capital structure policy.

The decomposition of ROE we've discussed in this section is a convenient way of systematically approaching financial statement analysis. If ROE is unsatisfactory by some measure, then the Du Pont identity tells you where to start looking for the reasons.

General Motors provides a good example of how Du Pont analysis can be useful and also illustrates why care must be taken in interpreting ROE values. In 1989, GM had an ROE of 12.1 percent. By 1993, its ROE had dramatically improved to 44.1 percent. On closer inspection, however, we find that over the same period GM's profit margin declined from 3.4 to 1.8 percent, and ROA declined from 2.4 to 1.3 percent. The decline in ROA was moderated only slightly by an increase in total asset turnover from .71 to .73 over the period.

Given this information, how was it possible for GM's ROE to have climbed so sharply? From our understanding of the Du Pont identity, it must be the case that GM's equity multiplier increased substantially. In fact, what happened was that GM's book equity value was almost wiped out overnight in 1992 by changes in the accounting treatment of pension liabilities. If a company's equity value declines sharply, its equity multiplier rises. In GM's case, the multiplier went from 4.95 in 1989 to 33.62 in 1993. In sum, the dramatic "improvement" in GM's ROE was almost entirely due to an accounting change that affected

Table 3.6

FINANCIAL STATEMENTS FOR DU PONT 12 months ending, April 2005 (All $ are in millions)					
Income Statement			**Balance Sheet**		
Sales	$8,912	Current assets		Current liabilities	
CoGS	5,426	Cash	$ 1,084	Accounts payable	$ 1,182
Gross profit	$3,486	Accounts receivable	1,092	Notes payable	28
SG&A expense	1,949	Inventory	1,469	Other	1,377
Depreciation	246	Total	$ 3,646	Total	$ 2,587
EBIT	$1,291				
Interest	232	Fixed assets	$ 6,932	Total long-term debt	$ 5,388
EBT	$1,059			Total equity	$ 2,603
Taxes	323				
Net income	$ 736	Total assets	$10,578	Total liabilities and equity	$10,578

the equity multiplier and doesn't really represent an improvement in financial performance at all.

An Expanded Du Pont Analysis

So far, we've seen how the Du Pont equation lets us break down ROE into its basic three components: profit margin, total asset turnover, and financial leverage. We now extend this analysis to take a closer look at how key parts of a firm's operations feed into ROE. To get going, we went to the *S&P Market Insight* Web page (www.mhhe.com/edumarketinsight) and pulled abbreviated financial statements for science and technology giant Du Pont. What we found is summarized in Table 3.6.

Using the information in Table 3.6, Figure 3.1 shows how we can construct an expanded Du Pont analysis for Du Pont and present that analysis in chart form. The advantage of the extended Du Pont chart is that it lets us examine several ratios at once, thereby getting a better overall picture of a company's performance and also allowing us to determine possible items to improve.

Looking at the left side of our Du Pont chart in Figure 3.1, we see items related to profitability. As always, profit margin is calculated as net income divided by sales. But, as our chart emphasizes, net income depends on sales and a variety of costs, such as cost of goods sold (CoGS) and selling, general, and administrative expenses (SG&A expense). Du Pont can increase its ROE by increasing sales and also by reducing one or more of these costs. In other words, if we want to improve profitability, our chart clearly shows the areas on which we should focus.

Turning to the right side of Figure 3.1, we have an analysis of the key factors underlying total asset turnover. Thus, for example, we see that reducing inventory holdings through more efficient management reduces current assets, which reduces total assets, which then improves total asset turnover.

Figure 3.1 **Expanded Du Pont Chart for Du Pont**

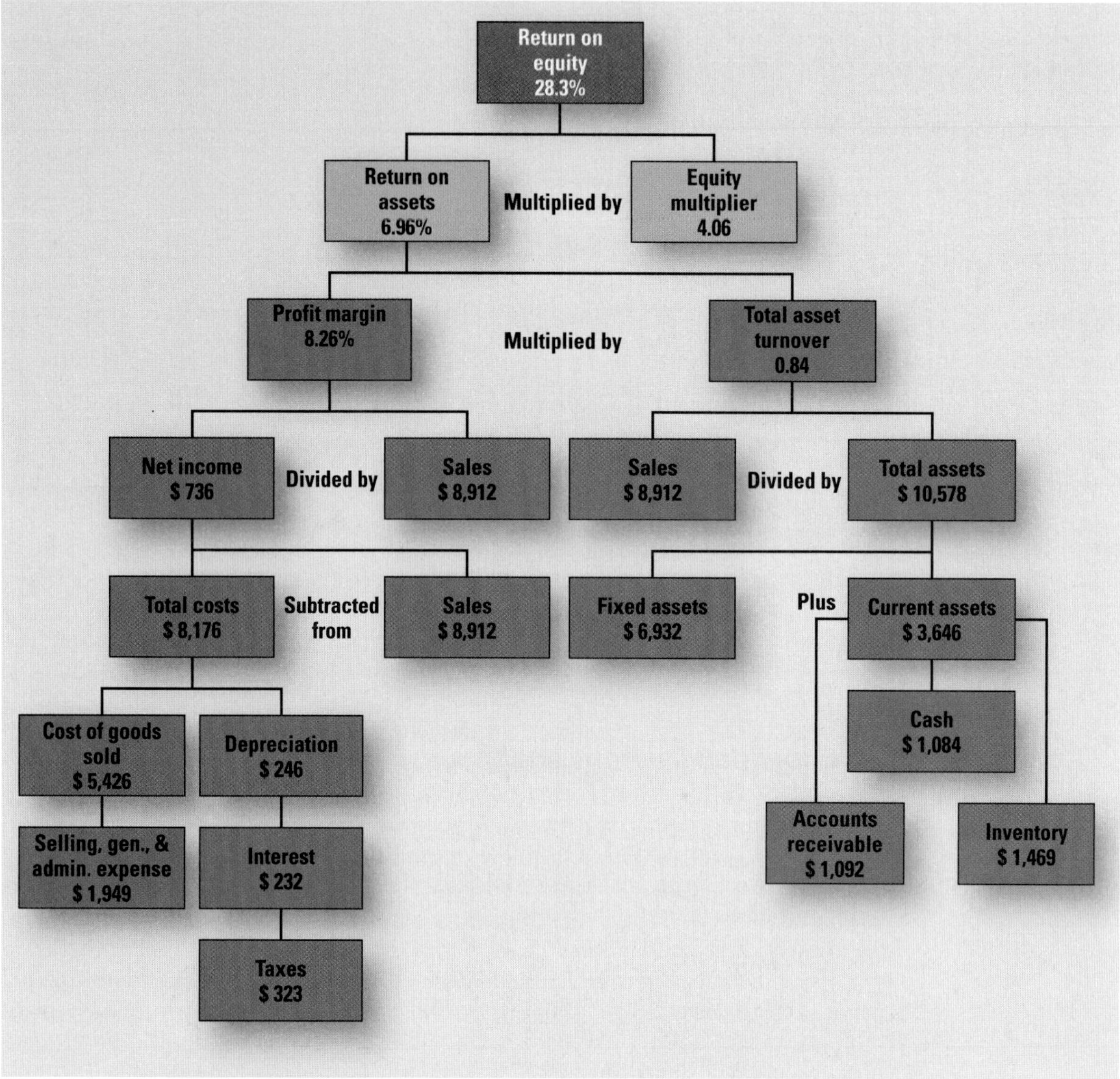

```
                          Return on
                           equity
                           28.3%

            Return on                    Equity
             assets      Multiplied by  multiplier
             6.96%                        4.06

        Profit margin               Total asset
            8.26%      Multiplied by   turnover
                                         0.84

    Net income                Sales        Sales              Total assets
     $ 736     Divided by    $ 8,912      $ 8,912  Divided by   $ 10,578

   Total costs   Subtracted    Sales     Fixed assets   Plus   Current assets
    $ 8,176         from       $ 8,912     $ 6,932               $ 3,646

 Cost of goods                                                       Cash
     sold       Depreciation                                       $ 1,084
   $ 5,426        $ 246

 Selling, gen., &                           Accounts
 admin. expense    Interest                receivable           Inventory
    $ 1,949        $ 232                     $ 1,092              $ 1,469

                    Taxes
                    $ 323
```

3.4 Using Financial Statement Information

Our next task is to discuss in more detail some practical aspects of financial statement analysis. In particular, we will look at reasons for doing financial statement analysis, how to go about getting benchmark information, and some of the problems that come up in the process.

Choosing a Benchmark

Given that we want to evaluate a division or a firm based on its financial statements, a basic problem immediately comes up. How do we choose a benchmark, or a standard of comparison? We describe some ways of getting started in this section.

Time Trend Analysis   One standard we could use is history. Suppose we found that the current ratio for a particular firm is 2.4 based on the most recent financial statement information. Looking back over the last 10 years, we might find that this ratio had declined fairly steadily over that period.

Based on this, we might wonder if the liquidity position of the firm has deteriorated. It could be, of course, that the firm has made changes that allow it to more efficiently use its current assets, that the nature of the firm's business has changed, or that business practices have changed. If we investigate, we might find any of these possible explanations behind the decline. This is an example of what we mean by management by exception—a deteriorating time trend may not be bad, but it does merit investigation.

Peer Group Analysis The second means of establishing a benchmark is to identify firms similar in the sense that they compete in the same markets, have similar assets, and operate in similar ways. In other words, we need to identify a *peer group*. There are obvious problems with doing this: No two companies are identical. Ultimately, the choice of which companies to use as a basis for comparison is subjective.

One common way of identifying potential peers is based on **Standard Industrial Classification (SIC) codes**. These are four-digit codes established by the U.S. government for statistical reporting purposes. Firms with the same SIC code are frequently assumed to be similar.

The first digit in an SIC code establishes the general type of business. For example, firms engaged in finance, insurance, and real estate have SIC codes beginning with 6. Each additional digit narrows the industry. Companies with SIC codes beginning with 60 are mostly banks and banklike businesses, those with codes beginning with 602 are mostly commercial banks, and SIC code 6025 is assigned to national banks that are members of the Federal Reserve system. Table 3.7 lists selected two-digit codes (the first two digits of the four-digit SIC codes) and the industries they represent.

SIC codes are far from perfect. For example, suppose you were examining financial statements for Wal-Mart, the largest retailer in the United States. The relevant SIC code is 5310, Department Stores. In a quick scan of the nearest financial database, you would find about 20 large, publicly owned corporations with this same SIC code, but you might not be comfortable with some of them. Target would seem to be a reasonable peer, but Neiman-Marcus also carries the same industry code. Are Wal-Mart and Neiman-Marcus really comparable?

As this example illustrates, it is probably not appropriate to blindly use SIC code–based averages. Instead, analysts often identify a set of primary competitors and then compute a set of averages based on just this group. Also, we may be more concerned with a group of the top firms in an industry, not the average firm. Such a group is called an *aspirant group* because we aspire to be like its members. In this case, a financial statement analysis reveals how far we have to go.

Beginning in 1997, a new industry classification system was initiated. Specifically, the North American Industry Classification System (NAICS, pronounced "nakes") is intended to replace the older SIC codes, and it will eventually. Currently, however, SIC codes are still widely used.

Learn more about NAICS at **www.naics.com**.

With these caveats about SIC codes in mind, we can now look at a specific industry. Suppose we are in the retail hardware business. Table 3.8 contains some condensed common-size financial statements for this industry from the Risk Management Association (RMA, formerly known as Robert Morris Associates), one of many sources of such information. Table 3.9 contains selected ratios from the same source.

There is a large amount of information here, most of which is self-explanatory. On the right in Table 3.8, we have current information reported for different groups based on sales. Within each sales group, common-size information is reported. For example, firms with

Table 3.7

Selected Two-Digit SIC Codes

Agriculture, Forestry, and Fishing	Wholesale Trade
01　Agriculture production—crops	50　Wholesale trade—durable goods
08　Forestry	51　Wholesale trade—nondurable goods
09　Fishing, hunting, and trapping	
Mining	**Retail Trade**
10　Metal mining	54　Food stores
12　Bituminous coal and lignite mining	55　Automobile dealers and gas stations
13　Oil and gas extraction	58　Eating and drinking places
Construction	**Finance, Insurance, and Real Estate**
15　Building construction	60　Banking
16　Construction other than building	63　Insurance
17　Construction—special trade contractors	65　Real estate
Manufacturing	**Services**
28　Chemicals and allied products	78　Motion pictures
29　Petroleum refining and related industries	80　Health services
35　Machinery, except electrical	82　Educational services
37　Transportation equipment	
Transportation, Communication, Electric, Gas, and Sanitary Service	
40　Railroad transportation	
45　Transportation by air	
49　Electric, gas, and sanitary services	

sales in the $10 million to $25 million range have cash and equivalents equal to 5 percent of total assets. There are 31 companies in this group, out of 309 in all.

On the left, we have three years' worth of summary historical information for the entire group. For example, operating profit rose from 1.9 percent of sales to 2.5 percent over that time.

Table 3.9 contains some selected ratios, again reported by sales groups on the right and time period on the left. To see how we might use this information, suppose our firm has a current ratio of 2. Based on these ratios, is this value unusual?

Looking at the current ratio for the overall group for the most recent year (third column from the left in Table 3.9), we see that three numbers are reported. The one in the middle, 2.2, is the median, meaning that half of the 309 firms had current ratios that were lower and half had bigger current ratios. The other two numbers are the upper and lower quartiles.

EXAMPLE 3.4

More Ratios　Take a look at the most recent numbers reported for Sales/Receivables and EBIT/ Interest in Table 3.9. What are the overall median values? What are these ratios?

If you look back at our discussion, you will see that these are the receivables turnover and the times interest earned, or TIE, ratios. The median value for receivables turnover for the entire group is 26.5 times. So, the days in receivables would be 365/26.5 = 14, which is the bold-faced number reported. The median for the TIE is 2.8 times. The number in parentheses indicates that the calculation is meaningful for, and therefore based on, only 269 of the 309 companies. In this case, the reason is that only 269 companies paid any significant amount of interest.

Table 3.8 Selected Financial Statement Information

Retail—Hardware Stores SIC# 5072, 5251 (NAICS 444130)

Comparative Historical Data				Current Data Sorted by Sales					

Type of Statement

9	11	17	Unqualified	1	1	2	1	4	8
38	42	54	Reviewed		8	10	16	14	6
88	85	110	Compiled	19	48	18	17	5	3
44	34	52	Tax returns	10	30	5	1	5	1
67	57	76	Other	14	25	13	11	3	10

4/1/00–3/31/01 All	4/1/01–3/31/02 All	4/1/02–3/31/03 All		58 (4/1–9/30/02)			251 (10/1/02–3/31/03)		
				0–1 MM	1–3 MM	3–5 MM	5–10 MM	10–25 MM	25 MM and Over
246	229	309	**Number of Statements**	44	112	48	46	31	28

Assets

5.9%	6.1%	6.0%	Cash and equivalents	5.3%	7.1%	7.4%	5.0%	5.0%	3.5%
12.2	13.3	13.8	Trade receivables (net)	7.4	11.6	15.3	19.9	20.4	13.5
52.0	48.9	50.5	Inventory	62.4	50.1	47.8	47.3	44.5	50.4
1.3	1.3	1.8	All other current	1.8	1.7	1.7	2.1	.7	2.7
71.4	69.6	72.2	Total current	76.8	70.4	72.2	74.2	70.5	70.1
17.3	17.8	17.0	Fixed assets (net)	14.7	17.4	16.4	16.0	18.3	20.2
1.9	3.1	1.7	Intangibles (net)	1.1	1.6	1.5	2.0	.5	3.5
9.4	9.5	9.2	All other noncurrent	7.3	10.5	9.9	7.8	10.7	6.2
100.0	100.0	100.0	Total	100.0	100.0	100.0	100.0	100.0	100.0

Liabilities

8.7	8.0	11.3	Notes payable—short term	11.1	10.1	8.0	13.3	11.1	18.5
3.7	3.8	3.5	Cur. mat.—L/T/D	2.9	3.6	3.5	5.2	2.6	2.0
15.7	15.6	15.5	Trade payables	13.2	14.6	15.8	19.4	15.4	15.3
.2	.2	.2	Income taxes payable	.0	.5	.1	.2	.3	.1
7.1	8.1	7.0	All other current	7.8	7.3	5.8	6.0	7.1	8.2
35.3	35.6	37.4	Total current	35.0	36.0	33.3	44.1	36.5	44.1
19.1	20.6	19.0	Long-term debt	29.0	20.6	17.9	13.6	13.7	13.9
.1	.1	.1	Deferred taxes	.1	.0	.0	.1	.3	.2
4.8	6.3	5.0	All other noncurrent	8.9	4.8	5.4	1.3	3.5	6.4
40.6	37.4	38.5	Net worth	27.0	38.6	43.3	40.9	46.0	35.5
100.0	100.0	100.0	Total liabilities and net worth	100.0	100.0	100.0	100.0	100.0	100.0

Income Data

100.0	100.0	100.0	Net sales	100.0	100.0	100.0	100.0	100.0	100.0
35.0	35.3	35.7	Gross profit	39.8	37.3	36.4	32.9	29.9	32.3
33.1	33.1	33.1	Operating expenses	38.3	34.7	33.6	30.1	27.9	29.0
1.9	2.2	2.5	Operating profit	1.5	2.7	2.8	2.8	2.0	3.4
.1	.4	.2	All other expenses (net)	.6	.2	.1	.2	−.3	.7
1.8	1.8	2.3	Profit before taxes	.9	2.5	2.7	2.6	2.3	2.7

MM = $ million.

Interpretation of statement studies figures: RMA cautions that the studies should be regarded only as a general guideline and not as an absolute industry norm. This is due to limited samples within categories, the categorization of companies by their primary Standard Industrial Classification (SIC) number only, and different methods of operations by companies within the same industry. For these reasons, RMA recommends that the figures be used only as general guidelines in addition to other methods of financial analysis.

Table 3.9   Selected Ratios

Retail—Hardware Stores SIC# 5072, 5251 (NAICS 444130)

Comparative Historical Data				Current Data Sorted by Sales					
			Type of Statement						
9	11	17	Unqualified	1	1	2	1	4	8
38	42	54	Reviewed		8	10	16	14	6
88	85	110	Compiled	19	48	18	17	5	3
44	34	52	Tax returns	10	30	5	1	5	1
67	57	76	Other	14	25	13	11	3	10
4/1/00–3/31/01 All 246	4/1/01–3/31/02 All 229	4/1/02–3/31/03 All 309	Number of Statements	58 (4/1–9/30/02) 0–1 MM 44	1–3 MM 112	251 (10/1/02–3/31/03) 3–5 MM 48	5–10 MM 46	10–25 MM 31	25 MM and Over 28
			Ratios						
3.8%	3.7%	3.7%		6.6%	4.0%	3.4%	2.6%	2.8%	2.4%
2.1	2.2	2.2	Current	2.5	2.5	2.6	1.8	1.7	1.8
1.5	1.4	1.5		1.4	1.5	1.5	1.8	1.5	1.3
1.0	1.0	1.1		.9	1.1	1.2	1.0	1.1	.7
.5	.5	(308) .5	Quick	.4	.5	(47) .6	.5	.7	.5
.3	.2	.2		.2	.2	.3	.2	.4	.2
8 43.2	7 49.8	7 49.8		4 91.2	8 48.6	6 65.0	11 33.2	11 34.6	5 68.4
14 26.7	15 24.5	14 26.5	Sales/	11 32.1	12 29.3	15 25.0	20 18.4	26 14.0	15 24.5
25 14.6	27 13.4	29 12.4	receivables	20 18.4	25 14.6	34 10.8	43 8.4	39 9.4	38 9.7
88 4.2	81 4.5	85 4.3		137 2.7	93 3.9	78 4.7	70 5.2	57 6.4	81 4.5
120 3.0	121 3.0	120 3.0	Cost of sales/	179 2.0	121 3.0	114 3.2	108 3.4	83 4.4	104 3.5
178 2.0	163 2.2	171 2.1	inventory	262 1.4	172 2.1	167 2.2	161 2.3	120 3.0	149 2.5
17 21.3	18 20.0	17 21.3		0 UND	17 22.0	17 22.0	22 16.3	15 23.8	18 19.8
29 12.8	29 12.7	30 12.3	Cost of sales/	25 14.3	30 12.3	29 12.7	34 10.6	22 16.4	30 12.1
48 7.7	46 7.9	50 7.4	payables	68 5.4	43 8.5	53 6.9	59 6.2	41 8.8	44 8.3
4.2	4.4	4.2		2.6	4.1	4.4	5.4	5.7	5.7
6.4	6.7	7.0	Sales/	4.0	6.5	6.8	9.1	7.0	10.2
11.8	12.9	12.3	working capital	10.5	11.2	10.2	14.9	12.4	16.4
5.0	4.8	8.1		7.7	7.8	8.4	15.1	9.5	8.3
(225) 2.1	(213) 2.1	(269) 2.8	EBIT/interest	(36) 2.4	(93) 2.5	(43) 4.0	(43) 3.2	(27) 4.1	(27) 3.2
.7	1.1	1.1		–.7	1.2	1.4	1.0	1.6	1.1
3.8	4.5	5.5	Net profit + depr.,		5.2	12.4	2.6	6.1	13.4
(58) 1.7	(53) 2.0	(73) 2.4	dep., amort./cur.		(21) 1.9	(10) 2.0	(15) .6	(14) 2.8	(11) 5.3
.7	1.1	.5	mat. L/T/D		.7	.1	.0	1.3	.5
.1	.2	.2		.0	.2	.1	.1	.1	.3
.4	.4	.4	Fixed/worth	.4	.4	.4	.3	.3	.6
1.1	1.1	1.0		8.1	1.1	.9	.7	.8	1.2
.7	.6	.7		.8	.6	.7	.6	.6	1.2
1.6	1.7	1.5	Debt/worth	2.8	1.6	1.4	1.7	1.0	2.2
3.8	4.8	3.7		NM	4.2	2.9	2.9	1.9	3.6
27.7	27.6	29.2	% profit before	46.5	25.3	28.4	31.0	17.6	40.4
(224) 9.9	(203) 10.4	(277) 11.9	taxes/tangible	(33) 12.3	(98) 11.5	(45) 15.0	(45) 10.9	(30) 9.6	(26) 23.7
.1	1.6	2.2	net worth	.4	.9	3.3	1.8	.3	2.5
9.4	9.1	11.5	% profit	10.6	10.5	12.4	12.7	9.2	11.3
3.6	3.2	4.7	before taxes/	4.9	4.6	4.7	5.4	5.2	4.9
–1.2	.2	.2	total assets	6.0	.2	1.5	.5	.2	.4
49.2	40.5	41.1		97.7	42.1	42.7	40.3	55.4	29.1
21.0	20.4	19.6	Sales/net	21.2	23.1	18.6	20.1	17.6	14.3
9.4	8.7	9.2	fixed assets	7.1	9.4	9.6	12.2	7.6	9.1
3.1	3.0	3.1		2.8	3.0	3.2	3.2	3.0	3.3
2.3	2.4	2.4	Sales/	2.0	2.5	2.4	2.5	2.4	2.3
1.8	1.8	1.8	total assets	1.1	1.9	1.8	1.7	2.2	1.9
.7	.7	.7		.8	.7	.7	.7	.8	.8
(222) 1.1	(200) 1.2	(266) 1.2	% depr., dep.,	(31) 1.2	(102) 1.5	(41) 1.2	(40) 1.0	(29) 1.1	(23) 1.2
2.0	2.2	2.0	amort./sales	2.4	2.5	1.6	1.3	1.8	1.7
2.9	2.0	2.3	% officers',	3.7	2.7	2.0	2.1	1.3	
(132) 4.6	(136) 4.0	(168) 4.0	directors', owners'	(21) 5.3	(75) 4.5	(32) 3.8	(22) 3.0	(14) 2.0	
7.0	6.1	7.0	comp/sales	11.6	7.1	6.7	6.2	3.3	
2,771,100M	2,517,327M	3,762,671M	Net sales ($)	27,586M	204,026M	188,955M	328,481M	469,173M	2,544,450M
990,644M	1,153,657M	1,607,310M	Total assets ($)	18,552M	93,100M	86,254M	158,179M	191,739M	1,059,486M

M = $ thousand; MM = $ million.

So, 25 percent of the firms had a current ratio larger than 3.7 and 25 percent had a current ratio smaller than 1.5. Our value of 2 falls comfortably within these bounds, so it doesn't appear too unusual. This comparison illustrates how knowledge of the range of ratios is important in addition to knowledge of the average. Notice how stable the current ratio has been for the last three years.

There are many sources of ratio information in addition to the one we examine here. For example, www.investor.reuters.com shows a variety of ratios for publicly traded companies. Below we show a screen cut of the profitability ratios (called "Management Effectiveness" on this Web site) for grocery retailer Kroger ("TTM" stands for "trailing twelve months").

Management Effectiveness				
Management Effectiveness (%)	**Company**	**Industry**	**Sector**	**S&P 500**
Return On Assets (TTM)	0.14	5.46	5.91	7.84
Return On Assets - 5 Yr. Avg.	3.54	6.07	4.90	6.22
Return On Investment (TTM)	0.21	8.20	8.48	11.81
Return On Investment - 5 Yr. Avg.	5.01	8.87	7.17	9.84
Return On Equity (TTM)	0.74	16.04	12.65	19.82
Return On Equity - 5 Yr. Avg.	20.13	20.27	11.08	17.60

In looking at numbers such as these, recall our caution about analyzing ratios that you don't calculate yourself: Different sources frequently do their calculations somewhat differently, even if the ratio names are the same.

Problems with Financial Statement Analysis

We continue our chapter on financial statements by discussing some additional problems that can arise in using financial statements. In one way or another, the basic problem with financial statement analysis is that there is no underlying theory to help us identify which quantities to look at and to guide us in establishing benchmarks.

As we discuss in other chapters, there are many cases in which financial theory and economic logic provide guidance in making judgments about value and risk. Little such help exists with financial statements. This is why we can't say which ratios matter the most and what a high or low value might be.

One particularly severe problem is that many firms are conglomerates, owning more or less unrelated lines of business. GE is a well-known example. The consolidated financial statements for such firms don't really fit any neat industry category. More generally, the kind of peer group analysis we have been describing is going to work best when the firms are strictly in the same line of business, the industry is competitive, and there is only one way of operating.

Another problem that is becoming increasingly common is that major competitors and natural peer group members in an industry may be scattered around the globe. The automobile industry is an obvious example. The problem here is that financial statements from outside the United States do not necessarily conform to GAAP. The existence of different standards and procedures makes it difficult to compare financial statements across national borders.

Even companies that are clearly in the same line of business may not be comparable. For example, electric utilities engaged primarily in power generation are all classified in the same group (SIC 4911). This group is often thought to be relatively homogeneous. However, most utilities operate as regulated monopolies, so they don't compete much with each other, at least not historically. Many have stockholders, and many are organized as cooperatives with no stockholders. There are several different ways of generating power, ranging from hydroelectric to nuclear, so the operating activities of these utilities can differ quite a bit. Finally, profitability is strongly affected by the regulatory environment, so utilities in different locations can be similar but show different profits.

Several other general problems frequently crop up. First, different firms use different accounting procedures—for inventory, for example. This makes it difficult to compare statements. Second, different firms end their fiscal years at different times. For firms in seasonal businesses (such as a retailer with a large Christmas season), this can lead to difficulties in comparing balance sheets because of fluctuations in accounts during the year. Finally, for any particular firm, unusual or transient events, such as a one-time profit from an asset sale, may affect financial performance. Such events can give misleading signals as we compare firms.

3.5 Long-Term Financial Planning

Long-term planning is another important use of financial statements. Most financial planning models output pro forma financial statements, where pro forma means "as a matter of form." In our case, this means that financial statements are the form we use to summarize the projected future financial status of a company.

A Simple Financial Planning Model

We can begin our discussion of long-term planning models with a relatively simple example. The Computerfield Corporation's financial statements from the most recent year are shown below and on the next page.

Unless otherwise stated, the financial planners at Computerfield assume that all variables are tied directly to sales and current relationships are optimal. This means that all items will grow at exactly the same rate as sales. This is obviously oversimplified; we use this assumption only to make a point.

COMPUTERFIELD CORPORATION
Financial Statements

Income Statement			Balance Sheet			
Sales	$1,000		Assets	$500	Debt	$250
Costs	800				Equity	250
Net income	$ 200		Total	$500	Total	$500

Suppose sales increase by 20 percent, rising from $1,000 to $1,200. Planners would then also forecast a 20 percent increase in costs, from $800 to $800 × 1.2 = $960. The pro forma income statement would thus look like this:

Pro Forma Income Statement	
Sales	$1,200
Costs	960
Net income	$ 240

The assumption that all variables will grow by 20 percent lets us easily construct the pro forma balance sheet as well:

Pro Forma Balance Sheet			
Assets	$600 (+100)	Debt	$300 (+50)
		Equity	300 (+50)
Total	$600 (+100)	Total	$600 (+100)

Notice we have simply increased every item by 20 percent. The numbers in parentheses are the dollar changes for the different items.

Planware provides insight into cash flow forecasting in its "White Papers" section (www.planware.org).

Now we have to reconcile these two pro forma statements. How, for example, can net income be equal to $240 and equity increase by only $50? The answer is that Computerfield must have paid out the difference of $240 – 50 = $190, possibly as a cash dividend. In this case dividends are the "plug" variable.

Suppose Computerfield does not pay out the $190. In this case, the addition to retained earnings is the full $240. Computerfield's equity will thus grow to $250 (the starting amount) plus $240 (net income), or $490, and debt must be retired to keep total assets equal to $600.

With $600 in total assets and $490 in equity, debt will have to be $600 − 490 = $110. Because we started with $250 in debt, Computerfield will have to retire $250 − 110 = $140 in debt. The resulting pro forma balance sheet would look like this:

Pro Forma Balance Sheet			
Assets	$600 (+100)	Debt	$110 (−140)
		Equity	490 (+240)
Total	$600 (+100)	Total	$600 (+100)

In this case, debt is the plug variable used to balance projected total assets and liabilities.

This example shows the interaction between sales growth and financial policy. As sales increase, so do total assets. This occurs because the firm must invest in net working capital and fixed assets to support higher sales levels. Because assets are growing, total liabilities and equity, the right side of the balance sheet, will grow as well.

The thing to notice from our simple example is that the way the liabilities and owners' equity change depends on the firm's financing policy and its dividend policy. The growth in assets requires that the firm decide on how to finance that growth. This is strictly a managerial decision. Note that in our example the firm needed no outside funds. This won't usually be the case, so we explore a more detailed situation in the next section.

The Percentage of Sales Approach

In the previous section, we described a simple planning model in which every item increased at the same rate as sales. This may be a reasonable assumption for some elements. For others, such as long-term borrowing, it probably is not: The amount of long-term borrowing is set by management, and it does not necessarily relate directly to the level of sales.

In this section, we describe an extended version of our simple model. The basic idea is to separate the income statement and balance sheet accounts into two groups, those that vary directly with sales and those that do not. Given a sales forecast, we will then be able to calculate how much financing the firm will need to support the predicted sales level.

The financial planning model we describe next is based on the **percentage of sales approach**. Our goal here is to develop a quick and practical way of generating pro forma statements. We defer discussion of some "bells and whistles" to a later section.

The Income Statement   We start out with the most recent income statement for the Rosengarten Corporation, as shown in Table 3.10. Notice that we have still simplified things by including costs, depreciation, and interest in a single cost figure.

Rosengarten has projected a 25 percent increase in sales for the coming year, so we are anticipating sales of $1,000 \times 1.25 = \$1,250$. To generate a pro forma income statement, we assume that total costs will continue to run at $800/1,000 = 80$ percent of sales. With this assumption, Rosengarten's pro forma income statement is as shown in Table 3.11. The effect here of assuming that costs are a constant percentage of sales is to assume that the profit margin is constant. To check this, notice that the profit margin was $132/1,000 =$

Table 3.10

ROSENGARTEN CORPORATION Income Statement		
Sales		$1,000
Costs		800
Taxable income		$ 200
Taxes (34%)		68
Net income		$ 132
Dividends	$44	
Addition to retained earnings	88	

Table 3.11

ROSENGARTEN CORPORATION Pro Forma Income Statement	
Sales (projected)	$1,250
Costs (80% of sales)	1,000
Taxable income	$ 250
Taxes (34%)	85
Net income	$ 165

13.2 percent. In our pro forma statement, the profit margin is $165/1,250 = 13.2 percent; so it is unchanged.

Next, we need to project the dividend payment. This amount is up to Rosengarten's management. We will assume Rosengarten has a policy of paying out a constant fraction of net income in the form of a cash dividend. For the most recent year, the **dividend payout ratio** was:

$$\text{Dividend payout ratio} = \text{Cash dividends/Net income}$$
$$= \$44/132 = 33\ 1/3\% \qquad \textbf{(3.21)}$$

We can also calculate the ratio of the addition to retained earnings to net income:

$$\text{Addition to retained earnings/Net income} = \$88/132 = 66\ 2/3\%$$

This ratio is called the **retention ratio** or **plowback ratio**, and it is equal to 1 minus the dividend payout ratio because everything not paid out is retained. Assuming that the payout ratio is constant, the projected dividends and addition to retained earnings will be:

$$\text{Projected dividends paid to shareholders} = \$165 \times 1/3 = \$\ 55$$
$$\text{Projected addition to retained earnings} = \$165 \times 2/3 = \underline{\ 110}$$
$$\underline{\underline{\$165}}$$

The Balance Sheet   To generate a pro forma balance sheet, we start with the most recent statement, as shown in Table 3.12.

On our balance sheet, we assume that some items vary directly with sales and others do not. For those items that vary with sales, we express each as a percentage of sales for the year just completed. When an item does not vary directly with sales, we write "n/a" for "not applicable."

Table 3.12

ROSENGARTEN CORPORATION Balance Sheet					
Assets			**Liabilities and Owners' Equity**		
	$	**Percentage of Sales**		**$**	**Percentage of Sales**
Current assets			Current liabilities		
Cash	$ 160	16%	Accounts payable	$ 300	30%
Accounts receivable	440	44	Notes payable	100	n/a
Inventory	600	60	Total	$ 400	n/a
Total	$1,200	120	Long-term debt	$ 800	n/a
Fixed assets			Owners' equity		
Net plant and equipment	$1,800	180	Common stock and paid-in surplus	$ 800	n/a
			Retained earnings	1,000	n/a
			Total	$1,800	n/a
Total assets	$3,000	300%	Total liabilities and owners' equity	$3,000	n/a

For example, on the asset side, inventory is equal to 60 percent of sales ($600/1,000) for the year just ended. We assume this percentage applies to the coming year, so for each $1 increase in sales, inventory will rise by $.60. More generally, the ratio of total assets to sales for the year just ended is $3,000/1,000 = 3, or 300 percent.

This ratio of total assets to sales is sometimes called the **capital intensity ratio**. It tells us the amount of assets needed to generate $1 in sales; the higher the ratio is, the more capital intensive is the firm. Notice also that this ratio is just the reciprocal of the total asset turnover ratio we defined previously.

For Rosengarten, assuming that this ratio is constant, it takes $3 in total assets to generate $1 in sales (apparently Rosengarten is in a relatively capital-intensive business). Therefore, if sales are to increase by $100, Rosengarten will have to increase total assets by three times this amount, or $300.

On the liability side of the balance sheet, we show accounts payable varying with sales. The reason is that we expect to place more orders with our suppliers as sales volume increases, so payables will change "spontaneously" with sales. Notes payable, on the other hand, represents short-term debt such as bank borrowing. This will not vary unless we take specific actions to change the amount, so we mark this item as "n/a."

Similarly, we use "n/a" for long-term debt because it won't automatically change with sales. The same is true for common stock and paid-in surplus. The last item on the right side, retained earnings, will vary with sales, but it won't be a simple percentage of sales. Instead, we will explicitly calculate the change in retained earnings based on our projected net income and dividends.

We can now construct a partial pro forma balance sheet for Rosengarten. We do this by using the percentages we have just calculated wherever possible to calculate the projected amounts. For example, net fixed assets are 180 percent of sales; so, with a new sales level of $1,250, the net fixed asset amount will be $1.80 \times \$1,250 = \$2,250$, representing an increase of $2,250 - 1,800 = \$450$ in plant and equipment. It is important to note that for items that don't vary directly with sales, we initially assume no change and simply write in the original amounts. The result is shown in Table 3.13. Notice that the change in retained earnings is equal to the $110 addition to retained earnings we calculated earlier.

Inspecting our pro forma balance sheet, we notice that assets are projected to increase by $750. However, without additional financing, liabilities and equity will increase by only $185, leaving a shortfall of $750 - 185 = \$565$. We label this amount *external financing needed* (EFN).

Rather than create pro forma statements, if we were so inclined, we could calculate EFN directly as follows:

$$EFN = \frac{\text{Assets}}{\text{Sales}} \times \Delta\text{Sales} - \frac{\text{Spontaneous liabilities}}{\text{Sales}} \times \Delta\text{Sales} - PM \qquad \textbf{(3.22)}$$
$$\times \text{Projected sales} \times (1 - d)$$

In this expression, "ΔSales" is the projected change in sales (in dollars). In our example projected sales for next year are $1,250, an increase of $250 over the previous year, so ΔSales = $250. By "Spontaneous liabilities," we mean liabilities that naturally move up and down with sales. For Rosengarten, the spontaneous liabilities are the $300 in accounts payable. Finally, *PM* and *d* are the profit margin and dividend payout ratios, which we previously calculated as 13.2 percent and 33 1/3 percent, respectively. Total assets and sales are $3,000

Table 3.13

ROSENGARTEN CORPORATION					
Partial Pro Forma Balance Sheet					
Assets			**Liabilities and Owners' Equity**		
	Next Year	**Change from Current Year**		**Next Year**	**Change from Current Year**
Current assets			Current liabilities		
Cash	$ 200	$ 40	Accounts payable	$ 375	$ 75
Accounts receivable	550	110	Notes payable	100	0
Inventory	750	150	Total	$ 475	$ 75
Total	$1,500	$300	Long-term debt	$ 800	$ 0
Fixed assets			Owners' equity		
Net plant and equipment	$2,250	$450	Common stock and paid-in surplus	$ 800	$ 0
			Retained earnings	1,110	110
			Total	$1,910	$110
			Total liabilities and owners' equity	$3,185	$185
Total assets	$3,750	$750	External financing needed	$ 565	$565

and $1,000, respectively, so we have:

$$EFN = \frac{\$3,000}{1,000} \times \$250 - \frac{\$300}{1,000} \times \$250 - .132 \times \$1,250 \times \left(1 - \frac{1}{3}\right) = \$565$$

In this calculation, notice that there are three parts. The first part is the projected increase in assets, which is calculated using the capital intensity ratio. The second is the spontaneous increase in liabilities. The third part is the product of profit margin and projected sales, which is projected net income, multiplied by the retention ratio. Thus, the third part is the projected addition to retained earnings.

A Particular Scenario   Our financial planning model now reminds us of one of those good news–bad news jokes. The good news is we're projecting a 25 percent increase in sales. The bad news is this isn't going to happen unless Rosengarten can somehow raise $565 in new financing.

This is a good example of how the planning process can point out problems and potential conflicts. If, for example, Rosengarten has a goal of not borrowing any additional funds and not selling any new equity, then a 25 percent increase in sales is probably not feasible.

If we take the need for $565 in new financing as given, we know that Rosengarten has three possible sources: short-term borrowing, long-term borrowing, and new equity. The choice of some combination among these three is up to management; we will illustrate only one of the many possibilities.

Suppose Rosengarten decides to borrow the needed funds. In this case, the firm might choose to borrow some over the short term and some over the long term. For example, current assets increased by $300 whereas current liabilities rose by only $75. Rosengarten could borrow $300 − 75 = $225 in short-term notes payable and leave total net working

Table 3.14

			ROSENGARTEN CORPORATION			
			Pro Forma Balance Sheet			
Assets			**Liabilities and Owners' Equity**			
	Next Year	**Change from Current Year**			**Next Year**	**Change from Current Year**
Current assets			Current liabilities			
Cash	$ 200	$ 40	Accounts payable		$ 375	$ 75
Accounts receivable	550	110	Notes payable		325	225
Inventory	750	150				
Total	$1,500	$300	Total		$ 700	$300
			Long-term debt		$1,140	$340
Fixed assets			Owners' equity			
Net plant and equipment	$2,250	$450	Common stock and paid-in surplus		$ 800	$ 0
			Retained earnings		1,110	110
			Total		$1,910	$110
Total assets	$3,750	$750	Total liabilities and owners' equity		$3,750	$750

capital unchanged. With $565 needed, the remaining $565 − 225 = $340 would have to come from long-term debt. Table 3.14 shows the completed pro forma balance sheet for Rosengarten.

We have used a combination of short- and long-term debt as the plug here, but we emphasize that this is just one possible strategy; it is not necessarily the best one by any means. We could (and should) investigate many other scenarios. The various ratios we discussed earlier come in handy here. For example, with the scenario we have just examined, we would surely want to examine the current ratio and the total debt ratio to see if we were comfortable with the new projected debt levels.

3.6 External Financing and Growth

External financing needed and growth are obviously related. All other things staying the same, the higher the rate of growth in sales or assets, the greater will be the need for external financing. In the previous section, we took a growth rate as given, and then we determined the amount of external financing needed to support that growth. In this section, we turn things around a bit. We will take the firm's financial policy as given and then examine the relationship between that financial policy and the firm's ability to finance new investments and thereby grow.

We emphasize that we are focusing on growth not because growth is an appropriate goal; instead, for our purposes, growth is simply a convenient means of examining the interactions between investment and financing decisions. In effect, we assume that the use of growth as a basis for planning is just a reflection of the very high level of aggregation used in the planning process.

EFN and Growth

The first thing we need to do is establish the relationship between EFN and growth. To do this, we introduce the simplified income statement and balance sheet for the Hoffman

Table 3.15

HOFFMAN COMPANY Income Statement and Balance Sheet

Income Statement

Sales	$500
Costs	400
Taxable income	$100
Taxes (34%)	34
Net income	$ 66
Dividends	$22
Addition to retained earnings	44

Balance Sheet

Assets			Liabilities and Owners' Equity		
	$	Percentage of Sales		$	Percentage of Sales
Current assets	$200	40%	Total debt	$250	n/a
Net fixed assets	300	60	Owners' equity	250	n/a
Total assets	$500	100%	Total liabilities and owners' equity	$500	n/a

Company in Table 3.15. Notice that we have simplified the balance sheet by combining short-term and long-term debt into a single total debt figure. Effectively, we are assuming that none of the current liabilities vary spontaneously with sales. This assumption isn't as restrictive as it sounds. If any current liabilities (such as accounts payable) vary with sales, we can assume that any such accounts have been netted out in current assets. Also, we continue to combine depreciation, interest, and costs on the income statement.

Suppose the Hoffman Company is forecasting next year's sales level at $600, a $100 increase. Notice that the percentage increase in sales is $100/500 = 20 percent. Using the percentage of sales approach and the figures in Table 3.15, we can prepare a pro forma income statement and balance sheet as in Table 3.16. As Table 3.16 illustrates, at a 20 percent growth rate, Hoffman needs $100 in new assets. The projected addition to retained earnings is $52.8, so the external financing needed, EFN, is $100 − 52.8 = $47.2.

Notice that the debt–equity ratio for Hoffman was originally (from Table 3.15) equal to $250/250 = 1.0. We will assume that the Hoffman Company does not wish to sell new equity. In this case, the $47.2 in EFN will have to be borrowed. What will the new debt–equity ratio be? From Table 3.16, we know that total owners' equity is projected at $302.8. The new total debt will be the original $250 plus $47.2 in new borrowing, or $297.2 total. The debt–equity ratio thus falls slightly from 1.0 to $297.2/302.8 = .98.

Table 3.17 shows EFN for several different growth rates. The projected addition to retained earnings and the projected debt–equity ratio for each scenario are also given (you should probably calculate a few of these for practice). In determining the debt–equity ratios, we assumed that any needed funds were borrowed, and we also assumed any surplus funds were used to pay off debt. Thus, for the zero growth case the debt falls by $44, from $250 to $206. In Table 3.17, notice that the increase in assets required is simply equal to the original assets of $500 multiplied by the growth rate. Similarly, the addition to retained earnings is equal to the original $44 plus $44 times the growth rate.

Table 3.16

| HOFFMAN COMPANY |
| Pro Forma Income Statement and Balance Sheet |

Income Statement

Sales (projected)	$600.0
Costs (80% of sales)	480.0
Taxable income	$120.0
Taxes (34%)	40.8
Net income	$ 79.2

Dividends	$26.4	
Addition to retained earnings	52.8	

Balance Sheet

Assets			Liabilities and Owners' Equity		
	$	**Percentage of Sales**		**$**	**Percentage of Sales**
Current assets	$240.0	40%	Total debt	$250.0	n/a
Net fixed assets	360.0	60	Owners' equity	302.8	n/a
Total assets	$600.0	100%	Total liabilities and owners' equity	$552.8	n/a
			External financing needed	$ 47.2	n/a

Table 3.17
Growth and Projected
EFN for the Hoffman
Company

Projected Sales Growth	Increase in Assets Required	Addition to Retained Earnings	External Financing Needed, EFN	Projected Debt–Equity Ratio
0%	$ 0	$44.0	−$44.0	.70
5	25	46.2	−21.2	.77
10	50	48.4	1.6	.84
15	75	50.6	24.4	.91
20	100	52.8	47.2	.98
25	125	55.0	70.0	1.05

Table 3.17 shows that for relatively low growth rates, Hoffman will run a surplus, and its debt–equity ratio will decline. Once the growth rate increases to about 10 percent, however, the surplus becomes a deficit. Furthermore, as the growth rate exceeds approximately 20 percent, the debt–equity ratio passes its original value of 1.0.

Figure 3.2 illustrates the connection between growth in sales and external financing needed in more detail by plotting asset needs and additions to retained earnings from Table 3.17 against the growth rates. As shown, the need for new assets grows at a much faster rate than the addition to retained earnings, so the internal financing provided by the addition to retained earnings rapidly disappears.

As this discussion shows, whether a firm runs a cash surplus or deficit depends on growth. Microsoft is a good example. Its revenue growth in the 1990s was amazing, averaging well over 30 percent per year for the decade. Growth slowed down noticeably over the 2000–2006 period, but, nonetheless, Microsoft's combination of growth and substantial

Figure 3.2

Growth and Related Financing Needed for the Hoffman Company

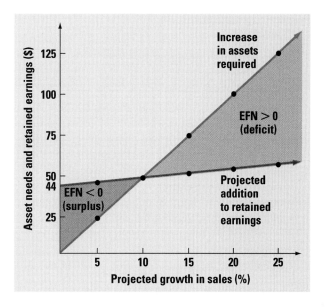

profit margins led to enormous cash surpluses. In part because Microsoft paid few or no dividends, the cash really piled up; in 2006, Microsoft's cash horde exceeded $38 billion.

Financial Policy and Growth

Based on our discussion just preceding, we see that there is a direct link between growth and external financing. In this section, we discuss two growth rates that are particularly useful in long-range planning.

The Internal Growth Rate   The first growth rate of interest is the maximum growth rate that can be achieved with no external financing of any kind. We will call this the **internal growth rate** because this is the rate the firm can maintain with internal financing only. In Figure 3.2, this internal growth rate is represented by the point where the two lines cross. At this point, the required increase in assets is exactly equal to the addition to retained earnings, and EFN is therefore zero. We have seen that this happens when the growth rate is slightly less than 10 percent. With a little algebra (see Problem 28 at the end of the chapter), we can define this growth rate more precisely as:

$$\text{Internal growth rate} = \frac{\text{ROA} \times b}{1 - \text{ROA} \times b} \tag{3.23}$$

where ROA is the return on assets we discussed earlier, and b is the plowback, or retention, ratio also defined earlier in this chapter.

For the Hoffman Company, net income was $66 and total assets were $500. ROA is thus $66/500 = 13.2$ percent. Of the $66 net income, $44 was retained, so the plowback ratio, b, is $44/66 = 2/3$. With these numbers, we can calculate the internal growth rate as:

$$
\begin{aligned}
\text{Internal growth rate} &= \frac{\text{ROA} \times b}{1 - \text{ROA} \times b} \\
&= \frac{.132 \times (2/3)}{1 - .132 \times (2/3)} \\
&= 9.65\%
\end{aligned}
$$

Thus, the Hoffman Company can expand at a maximum rate of 9.65 percent per year without external financing.

The Sustainable Growth Rate   We have seen that if the Hoffman Company wishes to grow more rapidly than at a rate of 9.65 percent per year, external financing must be arranged. The second growth rate of interest is the maximum growth rate a firm can achieve with no external *equity* financing while it maintains a constant debt–equity ratio. This rate is commonly called the **sustainable growth rate** because it is the maximum rate of growth a firm can maintain without increasing its financial leverage.

There are various reasons why a firm might wish to avoid equity sales. For example, new equity sales can be expensive because of the substantial fees that may be involved. Alternatively, the current owners may not wish to bring in new owners or contribute additional equity. Why a firm might view a particular debt–equity ratio as optimal is discussed in later chapters; for now, we will take it as given.

Based on Table 3.17, the sustainable growth rate for Hoffman is approximately 20 percent because the debt–equity ratio is near 1.0 at that growth rate. The precise value can be calculated as follows (see Problem 28 at the end of the chapter):

$$\text{Sustainable growth rate} = \frac{\text{ROE} \times b}{1 - \text{ROE} \times b} \tag{3.24}$$

This is identical to the internal growth rate except that ROE, return on equity, is used instead of ROA.

For the Hoffman Company, net income was $66 and total equity was $250; ROE is thus $66/250 = 26.4$ percent. The plowback ratio, b, is still 2/3, so we can calculate the sustainable growth rate as:

$$
\begin{aligned}
\text{Sustainable growth rate} &= \frac{\text{ROE} \times b}{1 - \text{ROE} \times b} \\
&= \frac{.264 \times (2/3)}{1 - .264 \times (2/3)} \\
&= 21.36\%
\end{aligned}
$$

Thus, the Hoffman Company can expand at a maximum rate of 21.36 percent per year without external equity financing.

EXAMPLE 3.5

Sustainable Growth   Suppose Hoffman grows at exactly the sustainable growth rate of 21.36 percent. What will the pro forma statements look like?

At a 21.36 percent growth rate, sales will rise from $500 to $606.8. The pro forma income statement will look like this:

HOFFMAN COMPANY	
Pro Forma Income Statement	
Sales (projected)	$606.8
Costs (80% of sales)	485.4
Taxable income	$121.4
Taxes (34%)	41.3
Net income	$ 80.1
Dividends	$26.7
Addition to retained earnings	53.4

(continued)

We construct the balance sheet just as we did before. Notice, in this case, that owners' equity will rise from $250 to $303.4 because the addition to retained earnings is $53.4.

HOFFMAN COMPANY Pro Forma Balance Sheet					
Assets			**Liabilities and Owners' Equity**		
	$	**Percentage of Sales**		**$**	**Percentage of Sales**
Current assets	$242.7	40%	Total debt	$250.0	n/a
Net fixed assets	364.1	60	Owners' equity	303.4	n/a
Total assets	$606.8	100%	Total liabilities and owners' equity	$553.4	n/a
			External financing needed	$ 53.4	n/a

As illustrated, EFN is $53.4. If Hoffman borrows this amount, then total debt will rise to $303.4, and the debt–equity ratio will be exactly 1.0, which verifies our earlier calculation. At any other growth rate, something would have to change.

Determinants of Growth Earlier in this chapter, we saw that the return on equity, ROE, could be decomposed into its various components using the Du Pont identity. Because ROE appears so prominently in the determination of the sustainable growth rate, it is obvious that the factors important in determining ROE are also important determinants of growth.

From our previous discussions, we know that ROE can be written as the product of three factors:

$$\text{ROE} = \text{Profit margin} \times \text{Total asset turnover} \times \text{Equity multiplier}$$

If we examine our expression for the sustainable growth rate, we see that anything that increases ROE will increase the sustainable growth rate by making the top bigger and the bottom smaller. Increasing the plowback ratio will have the same effect.

Putting it all together, what we have is that a firm's ability to sustain growth depends explicitly on the following four factors:

1. *Profit margin*: An increase in profit margin will increase the firm's ability to generate funds internally and thereby increase its sustainable growth.

2. *Dividend policy*: A decrease in the percentage of net income paid out as dividends will increase the retention ratio. This increases internally generated equity and thus increases sustainable growth.

3. *Financial policy*: An increase in the debt–equity ratio increases the firm's financial leverage. Because this makes additional debt financing available, it increases the sustainable growth rate.

4. *Total asset turnover*: An increase in the firm's total asset turnover increases the sales generated for each dollar in assets. This decreases the firm's need for new assets as sales grow and thereby increases the sustainable growth rate. Notice that increasing total asset turnover is the same thing as decreasing capital intensity.

The sustainable growth rate is a very useful planning number. What it illustrates is the explicit relationship between the firm's four major areas of concern: its operating efficiency as measured by profit margin, its asset use efficiency as measured by total asset turnover, its dividend policy as measured by the retention ratio, and its financial policy as measured by the debt–equity ratio.

Profit Margins and Sustainable Growth   The Sandar Co. has a debt–equity ratio of .5, a profit margin of 3 percent, a dividend payout ratio of 40 percent, and a capital intensity ratio of 1. What is its sustainable growth rate? If Sandar desired a 10 percent sustainable growth rate and planned to achieve this goal by improving profit margins, what would you think?

ROE is $.03 \times 1 \times 1.5 = 4.5$ percent. The retention ratio is $1 - .40 = .60$. Sustainable growth is thus $.045(.60)/[1 - .045(.60)] = 2.77$ percent.

For the company to achieve a 10 percent growth rate, the profit margin will have to rise. To see this, assume that sustainable growth is equal to 10 percent and then solve for profit margin, PM:

$$.10 = PM(1.5)(.6)/[1 - PM(1.5)(.6)]$$

$$PM = .1/.99 = 10.1\%$$

For the plan to succeed, the necessary increase in profit margin is substantial, from 3 percent to about 10 percent. This may not be feasible.

Given values for all four of these, there is only one growth rate that can be achieved. This is an important point, so it bears restating:

If a firm does not wish to sell new equity and its profit margin, dividend policy, financial policy, and total asset turnover (or capital intensity) are all fixed, then there is only one possible growth rate.

One of the primary benefits of financial planning is that it ensures internal consistency among the firm's various goals. The concept of the sustainable growth rate captures this element nicely. Also, we now see how a financial planning model can be used to test the feasibility of a planned growth rate. If sales are to grow at a rate higher than the sustainable growth rate, the firm must increase profit margins, increase total asset turnover, increase financial leverage, increase earnings retention, or sell new shares.

The two growth rates, internal and sustainable, are summarized in Table 3.18.

A Note about Sustainable Growth Rate Calculations

Very commonly, the sustainable growth rate is calculated using just the numerator in our expression, $ROE \times b$. This causes some confusion, which we can clear up here. The issue has to do with how ROE is computed. Recall that ROE is calculated as net income divided by total equity. If total equity is taken from an ending balance sheet (as we have done consistently, and is commonly done in practice), then our formula is the right one. However, if total equity is from the beginning of the period, then the simpler formula is the correct one.

In principle, you'll get exactly the same sustainable growth rate regardless of which way you calculate it (as long as you match up the ROE calculation with the right formula).

Table 3.18

Summary of Internal and Sustainable Growth Rates

I. Internal Growth Rate

$$Internal\ growth\ rate = \frac{ROA \times b}{1 - ROA \times b}$$

where

ROA = Return on assets = Net income/Total assets

    b = Plowback (retention) ratio

       = Addition to retained earnings/Net income

The internal growth rate is the maximum growth rate that can be achieved with no external financing of any kind.

II. Sustainable Growth Rate

$$Sustainable\ growth\ rate = \frac{ROE \times b}{1 - ROE \times b}$$

where

ROE = Return on equity = Net income/Total equity

    b = Plowback (retention) ratio

       = Addition to retained earnings/Net income

The sustainable growth rate is the maximum growth rate that can be achieved with no external equity financing while maintaining a constant debt–equity ratio.

In reality, you may see some differences because of accounting-related complications. By the way, if you use the average of beginning and ending equity (as some advocate), yet another formula is needed. Also, all of our comments here apply to the internal growth rate as well.

3.7 Some Caveats Regarding Financial Planning Models

Financial planning models do not always ask the right questions. A primary reason is that they tend to rely on accounting relationships and not financial relationships. In particular, the three basic elements of firm value tend to get left out—namely, cash flow size, risk, and timing.

Because of this, financial planning models sometimes do not produce output that gives the user many meaningful clues about what strategies will lead to increases in value. Instead, they divert the user's attention to questions concerning the association of, say, the debt–equity ratio and firm growth.

The financial model we used for the Hoffman Company was simple—in fact, too simple. Our model, like many in use today, is really an accounting statement generator at heart. Such models are useful for pointing out inconsistencies and reminding us of financial needs, but they offer little guidance concerning what to do about these problems.

In Their Own Words

ROBERT C. HIGGINS ON SUSTAINABLE GROWTH

Most financial officers know intuitively that it takes money to make money. Rapid sales growth requires increased assets in the form of accounts receivable, inventory, and fixed plant, which, in turn, require money to pay for assets. They also know that if their company does not have the money when needed, it can literally "grow broke." The sustainable growth equation states these intuitive truths explicitly.

Sustainable growth is often used by bankers and other external analysts to assess a company's credit-worthiness. They are aided in this exercise by several sophisticated computer software packages that provide detailed analyses of the company's past financial performance, including its annual sustainable growth rate.

Bankers use this information in several ways. Quick comparison of a company's actual growth rate to its sustainable rate tells the banker what issues will be at the top of management's financial agenda. If actual growth consistently exceeds sustainable growth, management's problem will be where to get the cash to finance growth. The banker thus can anticipate interest in loan products. Conversely, if sustainable growth consistently exceeds actual, the banker had best be prepared to talk about investment products because management's problem will be what to do with all the cash that keeps piling up in the till.

Bankers also find the sustainable growth equation useful for explaining to financially inexperienced small business owners and overly optimistic entrepreneurs that, for the long-run viability of their business, it is necessary to keep growth and profitability in proper balance.

Finally, comparison of actual to sustainable growth rates helps a banker understand why a loan applicant needs money and for how long the need might continue. In one instance, a loan applicant requested $100,000 to pay off several insistent suppliers and promised to repay in a few months when he collected some accounts receivable that were coming due. A sustainable growth analysis revealed that the firm had been growing at four to six times its sustainable growth rate and that this pattern was likely to continue in the foreseeable future. This alerted the banker that impatient suppliers were only a symptom of the much more fundamental disease of overly rapid growth, and that a $100,000 loan would likely prove to be only the down payment on a much larger, multiyear commitment.

Robert C. Higgins is Professor of Finance at the University of Washington. He pioneered the use of sustainable growth as a tool for financial analysis.

In closing our discussion, we should add that financial planning is an iterative process. Plans are created, examined, and modified over and over. The final plan will be a result negotiated between all the different parties to the process. In fact, long-term financial planning in most corporations relies on what might be called the Procrustes approach.[4] Upper-level management has a goal in mind, and it is up to the planning staff to rework and to ultimately deliver a feasible plan that meets that goal.

The final plan will therefore implicitly contain different goals in different areas and also satisfy many constraints. For this reason, such a plan need not be a dispassionate assessment of what we think the future will bring; it may instead be a means of reconciling the planned activities of different groups and a way of setting common goals for the future.

However it is done, the important thing to remember is that financial planning should not become a purely mechanical exercise. If it does, it will probably focus on the wrong things. Nevertheless, the alternative to planning is stumbling into the future. Perhaps the immortal Yogi Berra (the baseball catcher, not the cartoon character), said it best: "Ya gotta watch out if you don't know where you're goin.' You just might not get there."[5]

---

[4] In Greek mythology, Procrustes is a giant who seizes travelers and ties them to an iron bed. He stretches them or cuts off their legs as needed to make them fit the bed.

[5] We're not *exactly* sure what this means, either, but we like the sound of it.

Summary and Conclusions

This chapter focuses on working with information contained in financial statements. Specifically, we studied standardized financial statements, ratio analysis, and long-term financial planning.

1. We explained that differences in firm size make it difficult to compare financial statements, and we discussed how to form common-size statements to make comparisons easier and more meaningful.

2. Evaluating ratios of accounting numbers is another way of comparing financial statement information. We defined a number of the most commonly used ratios, and we discussed the famous Du Pont identity.

3. We showed how pro forma financial statements can be generated and used to plan for future financing needs.

After you have studied this chapter, we hope that you have some perspective on the uses and abuses of financial statement information. You should also find that your vocabulary of business and financial terms has grown substantially.

Concept Questions

1. **Financial Ratio Analysis** A financial ratio by itself tells us little about a company because financial ratios vary a great deal across industries. There are two basic methods for analyzing financial ratios for a company: time trend analysis and peer group analysis. Why might each of these analysis methods be useful? What does each tell you about the company's financial health?

2. **Industry-Specific Ratios** So-called "same-store sales" are a very important measure for companies as diverse as McDonald's and Sears. As the name suggests, examining same-store sales means comparing revenues from the same stores or restaurants at two different points in time. Why might companies focus on same-store sales rather than total sales?

3. **Sales Forecast** Why do you think most long-term financial planning begins with sales forecasts? Put differently, why are future sales the key input?

4. **Sustainable Growth** In the chapter, we used Rosengarten Corporation to demonstrate how to calculate EFN. The ROE for Rosengarten is about 7.3 percent, and the plowback ratio is about 67 percent. If you calculate the sustainable growth rate for Rosengarten, you will find it is only 5.14 percent. In our calculation for EFN, we used a growth rate of 25 percent. Is this possible? (*Hint*: Yes. How?)

5. **EFN and Growth Rate** Broslofski Co. maintains a positive retention ratio and keeps its debt–equity ratio constant every year. When sales grow by 20 percent, the firm has a negative projected EFN. What does this tell you about the firm's sustainable growth rate? Do you know, with certainty, if the internal growth rate is greater than or less than 20 percent? Why? What happens to the projected EFN if the retention ratio is increased? What if the retention ratio is decreased? What if the retention ratio is zero?

6. **Common-Size Financials** One tool of financial analysis is common-size financial statements. Why do you think common-size income statements and balance sheets are used? Note that the accounting statement of cash flows is not converted into a common-size statement. Why do you think this is?

7. **Asset Utilization and EFN** One of the implicit assumptions we made in calculating the external funds needed was that the company was operating at full capacity. If the company is operating at less than full capacity, how will this affect the external funds needed?

8. **Comparing ROE and ROA** Both ROA and ROE measure profitability. Which one is more useful for comparing two companies? Why?

9. **Ratio Analysis** Consider the ratio EBITD/Assets. What does this ratio tell us? Why might it be more useful than ROA in comparing two companies?

10. **Return on Investment**   In the chapter, we presented several ratios for Kroger from www.investor.reuters.com. One of the ratios was return on investment. Return on investment is calculated as net income divided by long-term liabilities plus equity. What do you think return on investment is intended to measure? What is the relationship between return on investment and return on assets?

Use the following information to answer the next five questions: A small business called The Grandmother Calendar Company began selling personalized photo calendar kits. The kits were a hit, and sales soon sharply exceeded forecasts. The rush of orders created a huge backlog, so the company leased more space and expanded capacity, but it still could not keep up with demand. Equipment failed from overuse and quality suffered. Working capital was drained to expand production, and, at the same time, payments from customers were often delayed until the product was shipped. Unable to deliver on orders, the company became so strapped for cash that employee paychecks began to bounce. Finally, out of cash, the company ceased operations entirely three years later.

11. **Product Sales**   Do you think the company would have suffered the same fate if its product had been less popular? Why or why not?

12. **Cash Flow**   The Grandmother Calendar Company clearly had a cash flow problem. In the context of the cash flow analysis we developed in Chapter 2, what was the impact of customers' not paying until orders were shipped?

13. **Corporate Borrowing**   If the firm was so successful at selling, why wouldn't a bank or some other lender step in and provide it with the cash it needed to continue?

14. **Cash Flow**   Which was the biggest culprit here: too many orders, too little cash, or too little production capacity?

15. **Cash Flow**   What are some actions a small company like The Grandmother Calendar Company can take (besides expansion of capacity) if it finds itself in a situation in which growth in sales outstrips production?

Questions and Problems

BASIC
(Questions 1–10)

1. **Du Pont Identity**   If Roten, Inc., has an equity multiplier of 1.75, total asset turnover of 1.30, and a profit margin of 8.2 percent, what is its ROE?

2. **Equity Multiplier and Return on Equity**   Thomsen Company has a debt–equity ratio of 1.30. Return on assets is 8.7 percent, and total equity is $520,000. What is the equity multiplier? Return on equity? Net income?

3. **Using the Du Pont Identity**   Y3K, Inc., has sales of €2,700, total assets of €1,185, and a debt–equity ratio of 1.00. If its return on equity is 16 percent, what is its net income?

4. **EFN**   The most recent financial statements for Martin, Inc., are shown here:

Income Statement		Balance Sheet			
Sales	£19,200	Assets	£93,000	Debt	£20,400
Costs	15,550			Equity	72,600
Taxable income	£ 3,650	Total	£93,000	Total	£93,000
Taxes (34%)	1,241				
Net income	£ 2,409				

Assets and costs are proportional to sales. Debt and equity are not. A dividend of £963.60 was paid, and Martin wishes to maintain a constant payout ratio. Next year's sales are projected to be £23,040. What external financing is needed?

5.   **Sales and Growth**   The most recent financial statements for Yamazaki Co. are shown here:

Income Statement		Balance Sheet			
Sales	¥54,000,000	Current assets	¥ 26,000,000	Long-term debt	¥ 58,000,000
Costs	34,800,000	Fixed assets	105,000,000	Equity	73,000,000
Taxable income	¥19,200,000	Total	¥131,000,000	Total	¥131,000,000
Taxes (34%)	6,528,000				
Net income	¥12,672,000				

Assets and costs are proportional to sales. The company maintains a constant 30 percent dividend payout ratio and a constant debt–equity ratio. What is the maximum increase in sales that can be sustained assuming no new equity is issued?

6.   **Sustainable Growth**   If the Layla Corp. has a 19 percent ROE and a 30 percent payout ratio, what is its sustainable growth rate?

 7.   **Sustainable Growth**   Assuming the following ratios are constant, what is the sustainable growth rate?

Total asset turnover = 1.40
Profit margin   = 7.6%
Equity multiplier   = 1.50
Payout ratio   = 40%

8.   **Calculating EFN**   The most recent financial statements for Yuks Times are shown here (assuming no income taxes):

Income Statement		Balance Sheet			
Sales	$4,400	Assets	$13,400	Debt	$ 9,100
Costs	2,685			Equity	4,300
Net income	$1,715	Total	$13,400	Total	$13,400

Assets and costs are proportional to sales. Debt and equity are not. No dividends are paid. Next year's sales are projected to be $5,192. What is the external financing needed?

9.   **External Funds Needed**   Surya Pradhan, CFO of Bagmati Bhoj Sewa, has created the firm's pro forma balance sheet for the next fiscal year. Sales are projected to grow by 10 percent to NPR 440 million. Current assets, fixed assets, and short-term debt are 20 percent, 140 percent, and 15 percent of sales, respectively. Bagmati Bhoj Sewa pays out 40 percent of its net income in dividends. The company currently has NPR 145 million of long-term debt and NPR 50 million in common stock par value. The profit margin is 12 percent.
   a. Construct the current balance sheet for the firm using the projected sales figure.

b. Based on Mr. Pradhan's sales growth forecast, how much does Bagmati Bhoj Sewa need in external funds for the upcoming fiscal year?

c. Construct the firm's pro forma balance sheet for the next fiscal year and confirm the external funds needed you calculated in part (b).

10. **Sustainable Growth Rate**   The Steiben Company has a ROE of 8.50 percent and a payout ratio of 35 percent.

   a. What is the company's sustainable growth rate?

   b. Can the company's actual growth rate be different from its sustainable growth rate? Why or why not?

   c. How can the company change its sustainable growth rate?

INTERMEDIATE
(Questions 11–23)

11. **Return on Equity**   Firm A and Firm B have debt–total asset ratios of 60 percent and 40 percent and returns on total assets of 20 percent and 30 percent, respectively. Which firm has a greater return on equity?

12. **Ratios and Foreign Companies**   Prince Albert Canning PLC had a net loss of £13,156 on sales of £147,318 (both in thousands of pounds). What was the company's profit margin? Does the fact that these figures are quoted in a foreign currency make any difference? Why? In dollars, sales were $267,661. What was the net loss in dollars?

13. **External Funds Needed**   The Sumata Company has forecast a 20 percent sales growth rate for next year. The current financial statements are shown here:

Income Statement	
Sales	¥38,000,000
Costs	33,400,000
Taxable income	¥ 4,600,000
Taxes	1,610,000
Net income	¥ 2,990,000
Dividends	¥1,196,000
Additions to retained earnings	1,794,000

Balance Sheet			
Assets		**Liabilities and Equity**	
Current assets	¥ 9,000,000	Short-term debt	¥ 8,000,000
		Long-term debt	6,000,000
Fixed assets	22,000,000		
		Common stock	¥ 4,000,000
		Accumulated retained earnings	13,000,000
		Total equity	¥17,000,000
Total assets	¥31,000,000	Total liabilities and equity	¥31,000,000

a. Using the equation from the chapter, calculate the external funds needed for next year.

b. Construct the firm's pro forma balance sheet for next year and confirm the external funds needed you calculated in part (a).

c. Calculate the sustainable growth rate for the company.

d. Can Sumata Company eliminate the need for external funds by changing its dividend policy? What other options are available to the company to meet its growth objectives?

14. Days' Sales in Receivables A company has net income of $173,000, a profit margin of 8.6 percent, and an accounts receivable balance of $143,200. Assuming 70 percent of sales are on credit, what is the company's days' sales in receivables?

15. Ratios and Fixed Assets The Le Bleu Company has a ratio of long-term debt to total assets of 0.70 and a current ratio of 1.20. Current liabilities are $850, sales are $4,310, profit margin is 9.5 percent, and ROE is 21.5 percent. What is the amount of the firm's net fixed assets?

16. Calculating the Cash Coverage Ratio Titan Inc.'s net income for the most recent year was $7,850. The tax rate was 40 percent. The firm paid $2,108 in total interest expense and deducted $1,687 in depreciation expense. What was Titan's cash coverage ratio for the year?

17. Cost of Goods Sold Guthrie Corp. has current liabilities of €340,000, a quick ratio of 1.8, inventory turnover of 4.2, and a current ratio of 3.3. What is the cost of goods sold for the company?

18. Common-Size and Common-Base Year Financial Statements In addition to common-size financial statements, common–base year financial statements are often used. Common–base year financial statements are constructed by dividing the current year account value by the base year account value. Thus, the result shows the growth rate in the account. Using the following financial statements, construct the common-size balance sheet and common–base year balance sheet for the company. Use 2006 as the base year.

BLAIR HORN LIMITED						
2006 and 2007 Balance Sheets						
Assets				**Liabilities and Owners' Equity**		
	2006	**2007**			**2006**	**2007**
Current assets				Current liabilities		
Cash	£ 10,168	£ 10,683		Accounts payable	£ 73,185	£ 59,309
Accounts receivable	27,145	28,613		Notes payable	39,125	48,168
Inventory	59,324	64,853		Total	£112,310	£107,477
Total	£ 96,637	£104,149		Long-term debt	£ 50,000	£ 62,000
				Owners' equity		
Fixed assets				Common stock and		
Net plant and	£304,165	£347,168		paid-in surplus	£ 80,000	£ 80,000
equipment				Retained earnings	158,492	201,840
				Total	£238,492	£281,840
				Total liabilities and		
Total assets	£400,802	£451,317		owners' equity	£400,802	£451,317

Use the following information for Problems 19, 20, and 22:

The discussion of EFN in the chapter implicitly assumed that the company was operating at full capacity. Often, this is not the case. For example, assume that Rosengarten was operating at 90 percent capacity. Full-capacity sales would be $1,000/.90 = $1,111. The balance sheet shows $1,800 in fixed assets. The capital intensity ratio for the company is

Capital intensity ratio = Fixed assets/Full-capacity sales = $1,800/$1,111 = 1.62

This means that Rosengarten needs $1.62 in fixed assets for every dollar in sales when it reaches full capacity. At the projected sales level of $1,250, it needs $1,250 × 1.62 = $2,025 in fixed assets, which is $225 lower than our projection of $2,250 in fixed assets. So, EFN is only $565 − 225 = $340.

19. **Full-Capacity Sales**   Thorpe Mfg., Inc., is currently operating at only 85 percent of fixed asset capacity. Current sales are CAD 478,000. How much can sales increase before any new fixed assets are needed?

20. **Fixed Assets and Capacity Usage**   For the company in the previous problem, suppose fixed assets are CAD 415,000 and sales are projected to grow to CAD 680,000. How much in new fixed assets are required to support this growth in sales?

21. **Calculating EFN**   The most recent financial statements for Tai Po Stationers follow. Sales for 2007 are projected to grow by 20 percent. Interest expense will remain constant; the tax rate and the dividend payout rate will also remain constant. Costs, other expenses, current assets, and accounts payable increase spontaneously with sales. If the firm is operating at full capacity and no new debt or equity is issued, what external financing is needed to support the 20 percent growth rate in sales?

TAI PO STATIONERS
2006 Income Statement

Sales	HKD 905,000
Costs	710,000
Other expenses	12,000
Earnings before interest and taxes	HKD 183,000
Interest paid	19,700
Taxable income	HKD 163,300
Taxes (35%)	57,155
Net income	HKD 106,145

Dividends	HKD 42,458	
Addition to retained earnings	63,687	

TAI PO STATIONERS
Balance Sheet as of December 31, 2006

Assets		Liabilities and Owners' Equity	
Current assets		Current liabilities	
Cash	HKD 25,000	Accounts payable	HKD 65,000
Accounts receivable	43,000	Notes payable	9,000
Inventory	76,000	Total	HKD 74,000
Total	HKD 144,000	Long-term debt	HKD 156,000
Fixed assets		Owners' equity	
		Common stock and paid-in surplus	HKD 21,000
Net plant and equipment	HKD 364,000	Retained earnings	257,000
		Total	HKD 278,000
Total assets	HKD 508,000	Total liabilities and owners' equity	HKD 508,000

22. **Capacity Usage and Growth**   In the previous problem, suppose the firm was operating at only 80 percent capacity in 2006. What is EFN now?

23. **Calculating EFN**   In Problem 21, suppose the firm wishes to keep its debt–equity ratio constant. What is EFN now?

24. **EFN and Internal Growth**   Redo Problem 21 using sales growth rates of 15 and 25 percent in addition to 20 percent. Illustrate graphically the relationship between EFN and the growth rate, and use this graph to determine the relationship between them.

25. **EFN and Sustainable Growth**   Redo Problem 23 using sales growth rates of 30 and 35 percent in addition to 20 percent. Illustrate graphically the relationship between EFN and the growth rate, and use this graph to determine the relationship between them.

26. **Constraints on Growth**   Las Pierdas Tours wishes to maintain a growth rate of 14 percent per year and a debt–equity ratio of .30. Profit margin is 6.2 percent, and the ratio of total assets to sales is constant at 1.55. Is this growth rate possible? To answer, determine what the dividend payout ratio must be. How do you interpret the result?

27. **EFN**   Define the following:

S   = Previous year's sales

A   = Total assets

D   = Total debt

E   = Total equity

g = Projected growth in sales

PM = Profit margin

b = Retention (plowback) ratio

Show that EFN can be written as:

$$\text{EFN} = -\text{PM(S)}b + [\text{A} - \text{PM(S)}b] \times g$$

Hint: Asset needs will equal A $\times$ g. The addition to retained earnings will equal PM(S)b $\times$ $(1 + g)$.

28. **Sustainable Growth Rate**   Based on the results in Problem 27, show that the internal and sustainable growth rates can be calculated as shown in Equations 3.23 and 3.24. *Hint:* For the internal growth rate, set EFN equal to zero and solve for g.

29. **Sustainable Growth Rate**   In the chapter, we discussed one calculation of the sustainable growth rate as:

$$\text{Sustainable growth rate} = \frac{\text{ROE} \times b}{1 - \text{ROE} \times b}$$

In practice, probably the most commonly used calculation of the sustainable growth rate is ROE $\times$ b. This equation is identical to the sustainable growth rate equation presented in the chapter if the ROE is calculated using the beginning of period equity. Derive this equation from the equation presented in the chapter.

30. **Sustainable Growth Rate**   Use the sustainable growth rate equations from the previous problem to answer the following questions. No Return, Inc., had total assets of £210,000 and equity of £165,000 at the beginning of the year. At the end of the year, the company had total assets of £250,000. During the year the company sold no new equity. Net income for the year was £80,000 and dividends were £49,000. What is the sustainable growth rate for the company? What is the sustainable growth rate if you calculate ROE based on the beginning of period equity?

S&P
Problems

STANDARD
&POOR'S

www.mhhe.com/edumarketinsight

1. **Calculating the Du Pont Identity**   Find the annual income statements and balance sheets for Dow Chemical (DOW) and Gateway (GTW). Calculate the Du Pont identity for each company for the most recent three years. Comment on the changes in each component of the Du Pont identity for each company over this period and compare the components between the two companies. Are the results what you expected? Why or why not?

2. **Ratio Analysis**   Find and download the "Profitability" spreadsheet for Southwest Airlines (LUV) and Continental Airlines (CAL). Find the ROA (Net ROA), ROE (Net ROE), PE ratio (P/E—high and P/E—low), and the market-to-book ratio (Price/Book—high and Price/Book—low) for each company. Because stock prices change daily, PE and market-to-book ratios are often reported as the highest and lowest values over the year, as is done in this instance. Look at these ratios for both companies over the past five years. Do you notice any trends in these ratios? Which company appears to be operating at a more efficient level based on these four ratios? If you were going to invest in an airline, which one (if either) of these companies would you choose based on this information? Why?

3. **Sustainable Growth Rate**   Use the annual income statements and balance sheets under the "Excel Analytics" link to calculate the sustainable growth rate for Coca-Cola (KO) each year for the past four years. Is the sustainable growth rate the same for every year? What are possible reasons the sustainable growth rate may vary from year to year?

4. **External Funds Needed**   Look up Black & Decker (BDK). Under the "Financial Highlights" link you can find a five-year growth rate for sales. Using this growth rate and the most recent income statement and balance sheet, compute the external funds needed for BDK next year.

Mini Case

Ratios and Financial Planning at East Coast Yachts

Dan Ervin was recently hired by East Coast Yachts to assist the company with its short-term financial planning and also to evaluate the company's financial performance. Dan graduated from college five years ago with a finance degree, and he has been employed in the treasury department of a *Fortune* 500 company since then.

East Coast Yachts was founded 10 years ago by Larisa Warren. The company's operations are located near Hilton Head Island, South Carolina, and the company is structured as an LLC. The company has manufactured custom midsize, high-performance yachts for clients over this period, and its products have received high reviews for safety and reliability. The company's yachts have also recently received the highest award for customer satisfaction. The yachts are primarily purchased by wealthy individuals for pleasure use. Occasionally, a yacht is manufactured for purchase by a company for business purposes.

The custom yacht industry is fragmented, with a number of manufacturers. As with any industry, there are market leaders, but the diverse nature of the industry ensures that no manufacturer dominates the market. The competition in the market, as well as the product cost, ensures that attention to detail is a necessity. For instance, East Coast Yachts will spend 80 to 100 hours on hand-buffing the stainless steel stem-iron, which is the metal cap on the yacht's bow that conceivably could collide with a dock or another boat.

To get Dan started with his analyses, Larisa has provided the following financial statements. Dan has gathered the industry ratios for the yacht manufacturing industry.

EAST COAST YACHTS
2006 Income Statement

Sales	$128,700,000
Cost of goods sold	90,700,000
Other expenses	15,380,000
Depreciation	4,200,000
Earnings before interest and taxes (EBIT)	$ 18,420,000
Interest	2,315,000
Taxable income	$ 16,105,000
Taxes (40%)	6,442,000
Net income	$ 9,663,000
Dividends	$5,797,800
Addition to retained earnings	3,865,200

EAST COAST YACHTS
Balance Sheet as of December 31, 2006

Assets		Liabilities & Equity	
Current assets		**Current liabilities**	
Cash	$ 2,340,000	Accounts payable	$ 4,970,000
Accounts receivable	4,210,000	Notes payable	10,060,000
Inventory	4,720,000		
Total	$11,270,000	Total	$15,030,000
Fixed assets		Long-term debt	$25,950,000
Net plant and equipment	$72,280,000		
		Shareholders' equity	
		Common stock	$ 4,000,000
		Retained earnings	38,570,000
		Total equity	$42,570,000
Total assets	$83,550,000	Total liabilities and equity	$83,550,000

Yacht Industry Ratios

	Lower Quartile	Median	Upper Quartile
Current ratio	0.50	1.43	1.89
Quick ratio	0.21	0.38	0.62
Total asset turnover	0.68	0.85	1.38
Inventory turnover	4.89	6.15	10.89
Receivables turnover	6.27	9.82	14.11
Debt ratio	0.44	0.52	0.61
Debt–equity ratio	0.79	1.08	1.56
Equity multiplier	1.79	2.08	2.56
Interest coverage	5.18	8.06	9.83
Profit margin	4.05%	6.98%	9.87%
Return on assets	6.05%	10.53%	13.21%
Return on equity	9.93%	16.54%	26.15%

1. Calculate all of the ratios listed in the industry table for East Coast Yachts.

2. Compare the performance of East Coast Yachts to the industry as a whole. For each ratio, comment on why it might be viewed as positive or negative relative to the industry. Suppose you create an inventory ratio calculated as inventory divided by current liabilities. How do you interpret this ratio? How does East Coast Yachts compare to the industry average?

3. Calculate the sustainable growth rate of East Coast Yachts. Calculate external funds needed (EFN) and prepare pro forma income statements and balance sheets assuming growth at precisely this rate. Recalculate the ratios in the previous question. What do you observe?

4. As a practical matter, East Coast Yachts is unlikely to be willing to raise external equity capital, in part because the owners don't want to dilute their existing ownership and control positions. However, East Coast Yachts is planning for a growth rate of 20 percent next year. What are your conclusions and recommendations about the feasibility of East Coast's expansion plans?

5. Most assets can be increased as a percentage of sales. For instance, cash can be increased by any amount. However, fixed assets often must be increased in specific amounts because it is impossible, as a practical matter, to buy part of a new plant or machine. In this case a company has a "staircase" or "lumpy" fixed cost structure. Assume that East Coast Yachts is currently producing at 100 percent of capacity. As a result, to expand production, the company must set up an entirely new line at a cost of $25,000,000. Calculate the new EFN with this assumption. What does this imply about capacity utilization for East Coast Yachts next year?

Discounted Cash Flow Valuation

What do baseball players Paul Konerko, A.J. Burnett, and Ramon Hernandez have in common? All three athletes signed big contracts at the end of 2005. The contract values were reported as $60 million, $55 million, and $27.5 million, respectively. But reported numbers like these are often misleading. For example, in December 2005, Ramon Hernandez signed with the Baltimore Orioles. His contract called for salaries of $4.5 million, $6.5 million, $7.5 million, and $8 million per year over the next four years (plus a guaranteed minimum $1 million in 2010, for a total of $27.5 million). Not bad, especially for someone who makes a living using the "tools of ignorance" (jock jargon for catcher's equipment).

A closer look at the numbers shows that Paul, A.J., and Ramon did pretty well, but nothing like the quoted figures. Using A.J.'s contract as an example, although the value was reported to be $55 million, it was actually payable over several years. It consisted of a $6 million signing bonus plus $49 million in future salary and bonuses. The $49 million was to be distributed as $1 million in 2006 and $12 million per year for 2007 through 2010. Because the payments were spread out over time, we must consider the time value of money, which means his contract was worth less than reported. How much did he really get? This chapter gives you the "tools of knowledge" to answer this question.

4.1 Valuation: The One-Period Case

Keith Vaughn is trying to sell a piece of raw land in Alaska. Yesterday he was offered $10,000 for the property. He was about ready to accept the offer when another individual offered him $11,424. However, the second offer was to be paid a year from now. Keith has satisfied himself that both buyers are honest and financially solvent, so he has no fear that the offer he selects will fall through. These two offers are pictured as cash flows in Figure 4.1. Which offer should Keith choose?

Mike Tuttle, Keith's financial adviser, points out that if Keith takes the first offer, he could invest the $10,000 in the bank at an insured rate of 12 percent. At the end of one year, he would have:

$$\underset{\substack{\text{Return of}\\\text{principal}}}{\$10,000} + \underset{\text{Interest}}{(0.12 \times \$10,000)} = \$10,000 \times 1.12 = \$11,200$$

Figure 4.1

Cash Flow for Keith Vaughn's Sale

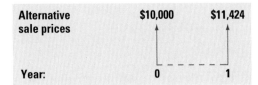

Because this is less than the $11,424 Keith could receive from the second offer, Mike recommends that he take the latter. This analysis uses the concept of **future value (FV)** or **compound value**, which is the value of a sum after investing over one or more periods. The compound or future value of $10,000 at 12 percent is $11,200.

An alternative method employs the concept of **present value (PV)**. One can determine present value by asking the following question: How much money must Keith put in the bank today so that he will have $11,424 next year? We can write this algebraically as:

$$PV \times 1.12 = \$11,424$$

We want to solve for PV, the amount of money that yields $11,424 if invested at 12 percent today. Solving for PV, we have:

$$PV = \frac{\$11,424}{1.12} = \$10,200$$

The formula for PV can be written as follows:

Present Value of Investment:

$$PV = \frac{C_1}{1 + r} \tag{4.1}$$

where C_1 is cash flow at date 1 and r is the rate of return that Keith Vaughn requires on his land sale. It is sometimes referred to as the *discount rate.*

Present value analysis tells us that a payment of $11,424 to be received next year has a present value of $10,200 today. In other words, at a 12 percent interest rate, Keith is indifferent between $10,200 today or $11,424 next year. If you gave him $10,200 today, he could put it in the bank and receive $11,424 next year.

Because the second offer has a present value of $10,200, whereas the first offer is for only $10,000, present value analysis also indicates that Keith should take the second offer. In other words, both future value analysis and present value analysis lead to the same decision. As it turns out, present value analysis and future value analysis must always lead to the same decision.

As simple as this example is, it contains the basic principles that we will be working with over the next few chapters. We now use another example to develop the concept of net present value.

EXAMPLE 4.1

Present Value   Lida Jennings, a financial analyst at Kaufman & Broad, a leading real estate firm, is thinking about recommending that Kaufman & Broad invest in a piece of land that costs $85,000. She is certain that next year the land will be worth $91,000, a sure $6,000 gain. Given that the guaranteed interest rate in the bank is 10 percent, should Kaufman & Broad undertake the investment in land? Ms. Jennings's choice is described in Figure 4.2 with the cash flow time chart.

A moment's thought should be all it takes to convince her that this is not an attractive business deal. By investing $85,000 in the land, she will have $91,000 available next year. Suppose, instead,

(continued)

Figure 4.2 **Cash Flows for Land Investment**

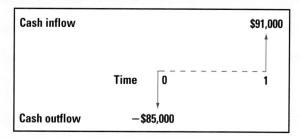

that Kaufman & Broad puts the same $85,000 into the bank. At the interest rate of 10 percent, this $85,000 would grow to:

$$(1 + .10) \times \$85,000 = \$93,500$$

next year.

It would be foolish to buy the land when investing the same $85,000 in the financial market would produce an extra $2,500 (that is, $93,500 from the bank minus $91,000 from the land investment). This is a future value calculation.

Alternatively, she could calculate the present value of the sale price next year as:

$$\text{Present value} = \frac{\$91,000}{1.10} = \$82,727.27$$

Because the present value of next year's sales price is less than this year's purchase price of $85,000, present value analysis also indicates that she should not recommend purchasing the property.

Frequently, businesspeople want to determine the exact *cost* or *benefit* of a decision. In Example 4.1, the decision to buy this year and sell next year can be evaluated as:

$$-\$2,273 \quad = \quad -\$85,000 \quad + \quad \frac{\$91,000}{1.10}$$

$$\underset{\text{Cost of land today}}{} \qquad \underset{\text{Present value of next year's sales price}}{}$$

The formula for NPV can be written as follows:

Net Present Value of Investment:

$$\text{NPV} = -\text{Cost} + \text{PV} \tag{4.2}$$

Equation 4.2 says that the value of the investment is −$2,273, after stating all the benefits and all the costs as of date 0. We say that −$2,273 is the **net present value** (NPV) of the investment. That is, NPV is the present value of future cash flows minus the present value of the cost of the investment. Because the net present value is negative, Lida Jennings should not recommend purchasing the land.

Both the Vaughn and the Jennings examples deal with perfect certainty. That is, Keith Vaughn knows with perfect certainty that he could sell his land for $11,424 next year. Similarly, Lida Jennings knows with perfect certainty that Kaufman & Broad could receive $91,000 for selling its land. Unfortunately, businesspeople frequently do not know future cash flows. This uncertainty is treated in the next example.

Uncertainty and Valuation   Professional Artworks, Inc., is a firm that speculates in modern paintings. The manager is thinking of buying an original Picasso for $400,000 with the intention of selling it at the end of one year. The manager expects that the painting will be worth $480,000 in one year. The relevant cash flows are depicted in Figure 4.3.

Of course, this is only an expectation—the painting could be worth more or less than $480,000. Suppose the guaranteed interest rate granted by banks is 10 percent. Should the firm purchase the piece of art?

Figure 4.3   **Cash Flows for Investment in Painting**

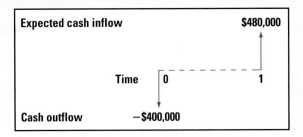

Our first thought might be to discount at the interest rate, yielding:

$$\frac{\$480,000}{1.10} = \$436,364$$

Because $436,364 is greater than $400,000, it looks at first glance as if the painting should be purchased. However, 10 percent is the return one can earn on a riskless investment. Because the painting is quite risky, a higher discount rate is called for. The manager chooses a rate of 25 percent to reflect this risk. In other words, he argues that a 25 percent expected return is fair compensation for an investment as risky as this painting.

The present value of the painting becomes:

$$\frac{\$480,000}{1.25} = \$384,000$$

Thus, the manager believes that the painting is currently overpriced at $400,000 and does not make the purchase.

The preceding analysis is typical of decision making in today's corporations, though real-world examples are, of course, much more complex. Unfortunately, any example with risk poses a problem not presented by a riskless example. In an example with riskless cash flows, the appropriate interest rate can be determined by simply checking with a few banks. The selection of the discount rate for a risky investment is quite a difficult task. We simply don't know at this point whether the discount rate on the painting in Example 4.2 should be 11 percent, 25 percent, 52 percent, or some other percentage.

Because the choice of a discount rate is so difficult, we merely wanted to broach the subject here. We must wait until the specific material on risk and return is covered in later chapters before a risk-adjusted analysis can be presented.

4.2   The Multiperiod Case

The previous section presented the calculation of future value and present value for one period only. We will now perform the calculations for the multiperiod case.

Future Value and Compounding

Suppose an individual were to make a loan of $1. At the end of the first year, the borrower would owe the lender the principal amount of $1 plus the interest on the loan at the interest rate of r. For the specific case where the interest rate is, say, 9 percent, the borrower owes the lender:

$$\$1 \times (1 + r) = \$1 \times 1.09 = \$1.09$$

At the end of the year, though, the lender has two choices. She can either take the $1.09—or, more generally, $(1 + r)$—out of the financial market, or she can leave it in and lend it again for a second year. The process of leaving the money in the financial market and lending it for another year is called **compounding**.

Suppose the lender decides to compound her loan for another year. She does this by taking the proceeds from her first one-year loan, $1.09, and lending this amount for the next year. At the end of next year, then, the borrower will owe her:

$$\$1 \times (1 + r) \times (1 + r) = \$1 \times (1 + r)^2 = 1 + 2r + r^2$$
$$\$1 \times (1.09) \times (1.09) = \$1 \times (1.09)^2 = \$1 + \$0.18 + \$0.0081 = \$1.1881$$

This is the total she will receive two years from now by compounding the loan.

In other words, the capital market enables the investor, by providing a ready opportunity for lending, to transform $1 today into $1.1881 at the end of two years. At the end of three years, the cash will be $\$1 \times (1.09)^3 = \$1.2950$.

The most important point to notice is that the total amount the lender receives is not just the $1 that she lent plus two years' worth of interest on $1:

$$2 \times r = 2 \times \$0.09 = \$0.18$$

The lender also gets back an amount r^2, which is the interest in the second year on the interest that was earned in the first year. The term $2 \times r$ represents **simple interest** over the two years, and the term r^2 is referred to as the *interest on interest.* In our example, this latter amount is exactly:

$$r^2 = (\$0.09)^2 = \$0.0081$$

When cash is invested at **compound interest**, each interest payment is reinvested. With simple interest, the interest is not reinvested. Benjamin Franklin's statement, "Money makes money and the money that money makes makes more money," is a colorful way of explaining compound interest. The difference between compound interest and simple interest is illustrated in Figure 4.4. In this example, the difference does not amount to much because the loan is for $1. If the loan were for $1 million, the lender would receive $1,188,100 in two years' time. Of this amount, $8,100 is interest on interest. The lesson is that those small numbers beyond the decimal point can add up to big dollar amounts when the transactions are for big amounts. In addition, the longer-lasting the loan, the more important interest on interest becomes.

Figure 4.4

Simple and Compound Interest

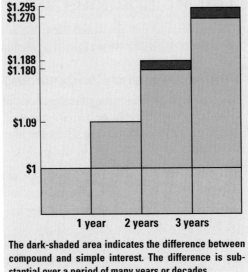

The dark-shaded area indicates the difference between compound and simple interest. The difference is substantial over a period of many years or decades.

The general formula for an investment over many periods can be written as follows:

Future Value of an Investment:

$$FV = C_0 \times (1 + r)^T \tag{4.3}$$

where C_0 is the cash to be invested at date 0 (i.e., today), r is the interest rate per period, and T is the number of periods over which the cash is invested.

EXAMPLE 4.3

Interest on Interest   Suh-Pyng Ku has put $500 in a savings account at the First National Bank of Kent. The account earns 7 percent, compounded annually. How much will Ms. Ku have at the end of three years? The answer is:

$$\$500 \times 1.07 \times 1.07 \times 1.07 = \$500 \times (1.07)^3 = \$612.52$$

Figure 4.5 illustrates the growth of Ms. Ku's account.

Figure 4.5   **Suh-Pyng Ku's Savings Account**

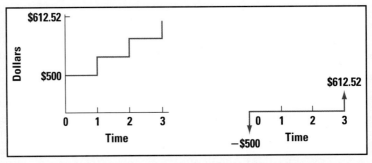

Compound Growth   Jay Ritter invested $1,000 in the stock of the SDH Company. The company pays a current dividend of $2, which is expected to grow by 20 percent per year for the next two years. What will the dividend of the SDH Company be after two years? A simple calculation gives:

$$\$2 \times (1.20)^2 = \$2.88$$

Figure 4.6 illustrates the increasing value of SDH's dividends.

Figure 4.6   **The Growth of the SDH Dividends**

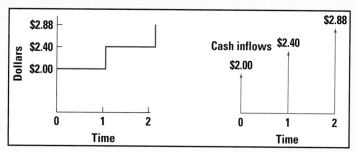

The two previous examples can be calculated in any one of several ways. The computations could be done by hand, by calculator, by spreadsheet, or with the help of a table. The appropriate table is Table A.3, which appears in the back of the text. This table presents *future value of $1 at the end of T periods*. The table is used by locating the appropriate interest rate on the horizontal and the appropriate number of periods on the vertical. For example, Suh-Pyng Ku would look at the following portion of Table A.3:

	Interest Rate		
Period	**6%**	**7%**	**8%**
1	1.0600	1.0700	1.0800
2	1.1236	1.1449	1.1664
3	1.1910	1.2250	1.2597
4	1.2625	1.3108	1.3605

She could calculate the future value of her $500 as

$$\underset{\substack{\text{Initial}\\\text{investment}}}{\$500} \quad \times \quad \underset{\substack{\text{Future value}\\\text{of }\$1}}{1.2250} \quad = \quad \$612.50$$

In the example concerning Suh-Pyng Ku, we gave you both the initial investment and the interest rate and then asked you to calculate the future value. Alternatively, the interest rate could have been unknown, as shown in the following example.

Finding the Rate   Carl Voigt, who recently won $10,000 in the lottery, wants to buy a car in five years. Carl estimates that the car will cost $16,105 at that time. His cash flows are displayed in Figure 4.7.

What interest rate must he earn to be able to afford the car?

(continued)

EXAMPLE 4.4

EXAMPLE 4.5

Figure 4.7   **Cash Flows for Purchase of Carl Voigt's Car**

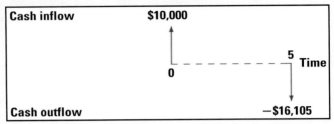

The ratio of purchase price to initial cash is:

$$\frac{\$16,105}{\$10,000} = 1.6105$$

Thus, he must earn an interest rate that allows $1 to become $1.6105 in five years. Table A.3 tells us that an interest rate of 10 percent will allow him to purchase the car.

We can express the problem algebraically as:

$$\$10,000 \times (1 + r)^5 = \$16,105$$

where r is the interest rate needed to purchase the car. Because $\$16,105/\$10,000 = 1.6105$, we have:

$$(1 + r)^5 = 1.6105$$
$$r = 10\%$$

Either the table or a hand calculator lets us solve for r.

The Power of Compounding: A Digression

Most people who have had any experience with compounding are impressed with its power over long periods. Take the stock market, for example. Ibbotson and Sinquefield have calculated what the stock market returned as a whole from 1926 through 2005.[1] They find that one dollar placed in these stocks at the beginning of 1926 would have been worth $2,657.56 at the end of 2005. This is 10.36 percent compounded annually for 80 years—that is, $(1.1036)^{80} = \$2,657.56$, ignoring a small rounding error.

The example illustrates the great difference between compound and simple interest. At 10.36 percent, simple interest on $1 is 10.36 cents a year. Simple interest over 80 years is $8.29 ($=80 \times \$.1035$). That is, an individual withdrawing 10.35 cents every year would have withdrawn $8.29 ($=80 \times \$0.1035$) over 80 years. This is quite a bit below the $2,657.56 that was obtained by reinvestment of all principal and interest.

The results are more impressive over even longer periods. A person with no experience in compounding might think that the value of $1 at the end of 160 years would be twice the value of $1 at the end of 80 years, if the yearly rate of return stayed the same. Actually the value of $1 at the end of 160 years would be the *square* of the value of $1 at the end of 80 years. That is, if the annual rate of return remained the same, a $1 investment in common stocks should be worth $7,062, 625.15 [$=\$1 \times (2,657.56 \times 2,657.56)$].

A few years ago, an archaeologist unearthed a relic stating that Julius Caesar lent the Roman equivalent of one penny to someone. Because there was no record of the penny ever being repaid, the archaeologist wondered what the interest and principal would be if a

---

[1] *Stocks, Bonds, Bills, and Inflation* [SBBI]. 2006 Yearbook. Ibbotson Associates, Chicago, 2006.

descendant of Caesar tried to collect from a descendant of the borrower in the 20th century. The archaeologist felt that a rate of 6 percent might be appropriate. To his surprise, the principal and interest due after more than 2,000 years was vastly greater than the entire wealth on earth.

The power of compounding can explain why the parents of well-to-do families frequently bequeath wealth to their grandchildren rather than to their children. That is, they skip a generation. The parents would rather make the grandchildren very rich than make the children moderately rich. We have found that in these families the grandchildren have a more positive view of the power of compounding than do the children.

EXAMPLE 4.6

How Much for That Island? Some people have said that it was the best real estate deal in history. Peter Minuit, director general of New Netherlands, the Dutch West India Company's colony in North America, in 1626 allegedly bought Manhattan Island for 60 guilders' worth of trinkets from native Americans. By 1667, the Dutch were forced by the British to exchange it for Suriname (perhaps the worst real estate deal ever). This sounds cheap; but did the Dutch really get the better end of the deal? It is reported that 60 guilders was worth about $24 at the prevailing exchange rate. If the native Americans had sold the trinkets at a fair market value and invested the $24 at 5 percent (tax free), it would now, about 380 years later, be worth more than $2.5 billion. Today, Manhattan is undoubtedly worth more than $2.5 billion, so at a 5 percent rate of return the native Americans got the worst of the deal. However, if invested at 10 percent, the amount of money they received would be worth about:

$$\$24(1 + r)^T = 24 \times 1.1^{380} \cong \$129 \text{ quadrillion}$$

This is a lot of money. In fact, $129 quadrillion is more than all the real estate in the world is worth today. Note that no one in the history of the world has ever been able to find an investment yielding 10 percent every year for 380 years.

Present Value and Discounting

We now know that an annual interest rate of 9 percent enables the investor to transform $1 today into $1.1881 two years from now. In addition, we would like to know the following:

How much would an investor need to lend today so that she could receive $1 two years from today?

Algebraically, we can write this as:

$$PV \times (1.09)^2 = \$1$$

In the preceding equation, PV stands for present value, the amount of money we must lend today to receive $1 in two years' time.

Solving for PV in this equation, we have:

$$PV = \frac{\$1}{1.1881} = \$.84$$

This process of calculating the present value of a future cash flow is called **discounting**. It is the opposite of compounding. The difference between compounding and discounting is illustrated in Figure 4.8.

To be certain that $.84 is in fact the present value of $1 to be received in two years, we must check whether or not, if we lent $.84 today and rolled over the loan for two years, we would get exactly $1 back. If this were the case, the capital markets would be saying that $1

Figure 4.8

Compounding and Discounting

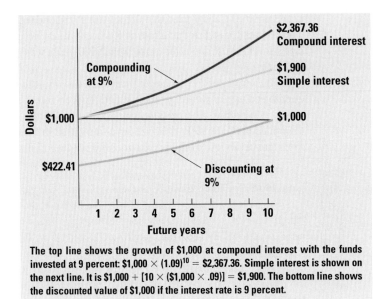

The top line shows the growth of $1,000 at compound interest with the funds invested at 9 percent: $1,000 $\times$ (1.09)^{10} = $2,367.36. Simple interest is shown on the next line. It is $1,000 + [10 $\times$ ($1,000 $\times$ .09)] = $1,900. The bottom line shows the discounted value of $1,000 if the interest rate is 9 percent.

received in two years' time is equivalent to having $.84 today. Checking the exact numbers, we get:

$$\$.84168 \times 1.09 \times 1.09 = \$1$$

In other words, when we have capital markets with a sure interest rate of 9 percent, we are indifferent between receiving $.84 today or $1 in two years. We have no reason to treat these two choices differently from each other because if we had $.84 today and lent it out for two years, it would return $1 to us at the end of that time. The value .84 $[=1/(1.09)^2]$ is called the **present value factor**. It is the factor used to calculate the present value of a future cash flow.

In the multiperiod case, the formula for PV can be written as follows:

Present Value of Investment:

$$PV = \frac{C_T}{(1+r)^T} \tag{4.4}$$

Here, C_T is the cash flow at date T and r is the appropriate discount rate.

EXAMPLE 4.7

Multiperiod Discounting   Bernard Dumas will receive $10,000 three years from now. Bernard can earn 8 percent on his investments, so the appropriate discount rate is 8 percent. What is the present value of his future cash flow? The answer is:

$$PV = \$10,000 \times \left(\frac{1}{1.08}\right)^3$$
$$= \$10,000 \times .7938$$
$$= \$7,938$$

Figure 4.9 illustrates the application of the present value factor to Bernard's investment.

When his investments grow at an 8 percent rate of interest, Bernard Dumas is equally inclined toward receiving $7,938 now and receiving $10,000 in three years' time. After all, he could convert the $7,938 he receives today into $10,000 in three years by lending it at an interest rate of 8 percent.

(continued)

Figure 4.9   **Discounting Bernard Dumas's Opportunity**

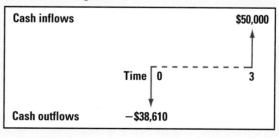

Bernard Dumas could have reached his present value calculation in one of several ways. The computation could have been done by hand, by calculator, with a spreadsheet, or with the help of Table A.1, which appears in the back of the text. This table presents the *present value of $1 to be received after T periods.* We use the table by locating the appropriate interest rate on the horizontal and the appropriate number of periods on the vertical. For example, Bernard Dumas would look at the following portion of Table A.1:

	Interest Rate		
Period	**7%**	**8%**	**9%**
1	.9346	.9259	.9174
2	.8734	.8573	.8417
3	.8163	.7938	.7722
4	.7629	.7350	.7084

The appropriate present value factor is .7938.

In the preceding example we gave both the interest rate and the future cash flow. Alternatively, the interest rate could have been unknown.

EXAMPLE 4.8

Finding the Rate   A customer of the Chaffkin Corp. wants to buy a tugboat today. Rather than paying immediately, he will pay $50,000 in three years. It will cost the Chaffkin Corp. $38,610 to build the tugboat immediately. The relevant cash flows to Chaffkin Corp. are displayed in Figure 4.10. By charging what interest rate would the Chaffkin Corp. neither gain nor lose on the sale?

Figure 4.10   **Cash Flows for Tugboat**

Cash inflows		$50,000
		↑
Time	0	3
	↓	
Cash outflows	−$38,610	

(continued)

The ratio of construction cost (present value) to sale price (future value) is:

$$\frac{\$38,610}{\$50,000} = 0.7722$$

We must determine the interest rate that allows $1 to be received in three years to have a present value of $.7722. Table A.1 tells us that 9 percent is that interest rate.

Frequently, an investor or a business will receive more than one cash flow. The present value of the set of cash flows is simply the sum of the present values of the individual cash flows. This is illustrated in the following example.

EXAMPLE 4.9

Cash Flow Valuation   Dennis Draper has won the Kentucky State Lottery and will receive the following set of cash flows over the next two years:

Year	Cash Flow
1	$2,000
2	$5,000

Mr. Draper can currently earn 6 percent in his money market account, so the appropriate discount rate is 6 percent. The present value of the cash flows is:

Year	Cash Flow × Present Value Factor = Present Value
1	$2,000 × $\dfrac{1}{1.06}$ = $2,000 × .943 = $1,887
2	$5,000 × $\left(\dfrac{1}{1.06}\right)^{2}$ = $5,000 × .890 = $4,450
	Total $6,337

In other words, Mr. Draper is equally inclined toward receiving $6,337 today and receiving $2,000 and $5,000 over the next two years.

EXAMPLE 4.10

NPV   Finance.com has an opportunity to invest in a new high-speed computer that costs $50,000. The computer will generate cash flows (from cost savings) of $25,000 one year from now, $20,000 two years from now, and $15,000 three years from now. The computer will be worthless after three years, and no additional cash flows will occur. Finance.com has determined that the appropriate discount rate is 7 percent for this investment. Should Finance.com make this investment in a new high-speed computer? What is the net present value of the investment?

(continued)

The cash flows and present value factors of the proposed computer are as follows:

	Cash Flows	Present Value Factor
Year 0	−$50,000	$1 = 1$
1	$25,000	$\dfrac{1}{1.07} = .9346$
2	$20,000	$\left(\dfrac{1}{1.07}\right)^2 = .8734$
3	$15,000	$\left(\dfrac{1}{1.07}\right)^3 = .8163$

The present value of the cash flows is:

Cash flows × Present value factor = Present value

Year 0	−$50,000 × 1	=	−$50,000
1	$25,000 × .9346	=	$23,365
2	$20,000 × .8734	=	$17,468
3	$15,000 × .8163	=	$12,244.5
		Total:	$ 3,077.5

Finance.com should invest in the new high-speed computer because the present value of its future cash flows is greater than its cost. The NPV is $3,077.5.

The Algebraic Formula

To derive an algebraic formula for the net present value of a cash flow, recall that the PV of receiving a cash flow one year from now is:

$$PV = C_1/(1 + r)$$

and the PV of receiving a cash flow two years from now is:

$$PV = C_2/(1 + r)^2$$

We can write the NPV of a T-period project as:

$$NPV = -C_0 + \frac{C_1}{1+r} + \frac{C_2}{(1+r)^2} + \cdots + \frac{C_T}{(1+r)^T} = -C_0 + \sum_{i=1}^{T} \frac{C_i}{(1+r)^i} \qquad \textbf{(4.5)}$$

The initial flow, $-C_0$, is assumed to be negative because it represents an investment. The Σ is shorthand for the sum of the series.

We will close out this section by answering the question we posed at the beginning of the chapter concerning baseball player A.J. Burnett's contract. Remember that the contract called for a signing bonus of $6 million to be paid immediately, plus salary and bonuses of $49 million to be distributed as $1 million in 2006 and $12 million per year for

2007 through 2010. If 12 percent is the appropriate interest rate, what kind of deal did the Toronto Blue Jays pitch to A.J.?

To answer, we can calculate the present value by discounting each year's salary back to the present as follows (notice we assumed the future salaries will be paid at the end of the year):

$$
\begin{array}{lll}
\text{Year 0:} & \$ 6{,}000{,}000 & = \$6{,}000{,}000 \\
\text{Year 1:} & \$ 1{,}000{,}000 \times 1/1.12^1 & = \$ \ \ 892{,}857.14 \\
\text{Year 2:} & \$12{,}000{,}000 \times 1/1.12^2 & = \$9{,}566{,}326.53 \\
\quad\vdots & \qquad\vdots & \qquad\vdots \\
\text{Year 5:} & \$12{,}000{,}000 \times 1/1.12^5 & = \$6{,}809{,}122.27
\end{array}
$$

If you fill in the missing rows and then add (do it for practice), you will see that Burnett's contract had a present value of about $39.44 million, or only about 70 percent of the $55 million reported value, but still pretty good. And of course, playing for the Toronto Blue Jays, Burnett will probably have his Octobers free as well.

4.3 Compounding Periods

So far, we have assumed that compounding and discounting occur yearly. Sometimes, compounding may occur more frequently than just once a year. For example, imagine that a bank pays a 10 percent interest rate "compounded semiannually." This means that a $1,000 deposit in the bank would be worth $1,000 \times 1.05 = $1,050 after six months, and $1,050 \times 1.05 = $1,102.50 at the end of the year.

The end-of-the-year wealth can be written as:

$$
\$1{,}000\left(1 + \frac{.10}{2}\right)^2 = \$1{,}000 \times (1.05)^2 = \$1{,}102.50
$$

Of course, a $1,000 deposit would be worth $1,100 ($1,000 \times 1.10) with yearly compounding. Note that the future value at the end of one year is greater with semiannual compounding than with yearly compounding. With yearly compounding, the original $1,000 remains the investment base for the full year. The original $1,000 is the investment base only for the first six months with semiannual compounding. The base over the second six months is $1,050. Hence one gets *interest on interest* with semiannual compounding.

Because $1,000 \times 1.1025 = $1,102.50, 10 percent compounded semiannually is the same as 10.25 percent compounded annually. In other words, a rational investor could not care less whether she is quoted a rate of 10 percent compounded semiannually or a rate of 10.25 percent compounded annually.

Quarterly compounding at 10 percent yields wealth at the end of one year of:

$$
\$1{,}000\left(1 + \frac{.10}{4}\right)^4 = \$1{,}103.81
$$

More generally, compounding an investment m times a year provides end-of-year wealth of:

$$
C_0\left(1 + \frac{r}{m}\right)^m \tag{4.6}
$$

where C_0 is the initial investment and r is the **stated annual interest rate**. The stated annual interest rate is the annual interest rate without consideration of compounding. Banks and other financial institutions may use other names for the stated annual interest rate. **Annual percentage rate (APR)** is perhaps the most common synonym.

EXAMPLE 4.11

EARs What is the end-of-year wealth if Jane Christine receives a stated annual interest rate of 24 percent compounded monthly on a $1 investment?

Using Equation 4.6, her wealth is:

$$\$1\left(1 + \frac{.24}{12}\right)^{12} = \$1 \times (1.02)^{12}$$
$$= \$1.2682$$

The annual rate of return is 26.82 percent. This annual rate of return is called either the **effective annual rate (EAR)** or the **effective annual yield (EAY)**. Due to compounding, the effective annual interest rate is greater than the stated annual interest rate of 24 percent. Algebraically, we can rewrite the effective annual interest rate as follows:

Effective Annual Rate:

$$\left(1 + \frac{r}{m}\right)^{m} - 1 \tag{4.7}$$

Students are often bothered by the subtraction of 1 in Equation 4.7. Note that end-of-year wealth is composed of both the interest earned over the year and the original principal. We remove the original principal by subtracting 1 in Equation 4.7.

EXAMPLE 4.12

Compounding Frequencies If the stated annual rate of interest, 8 percent, is compounded quarterly, what is the effective annual rate?

Using Equation 4.7, we have:

$$\left(1 + \frac{r}{m}\right)^{m} - 1 = \left(1 + \frac{.08}{4}\right)^{4} - 1 = .0824 = 8.24\%$$

Referring back to our original example where $C_0 = \$1,000$ and $r = 10\%$, we can generate the following table:

C_0	Compounding frequency (m)	C_1	Effective Annual Rate = $\left(1 + \frac{r}{m}\right)^{m} - 1$
$1,000	Yearly (m = 1)	$1,100.00	.10
1,000	Semiannually (m = 2)	1,102.50	.1025
1,000	Quarterly (m = 4)	1,103.81	.10381
1,000	Daily (m = 365)	1,105.16	.10516

Distinction between Stated Annual Interest Rate and Effective Annual Rate

The distinction between the stated annual interest rate (SAIR), or APR, and the effective annual rate (EAR) is frequently troubling to students. We can reduce the confusion by noting that the SAIR becomes meaningful only if the compounding interval is given. For example, for an SAIR of 10 percent, the future value at the end of one year with semiannual compounding is $[1 + (.10/2)]^2 = 1.1025$. The future value with quarterly compounding is $[1 + (.10/4)]^4 = 1.1038$. If the SAIR is 10 percent but no compounding interval is given, we cannot calculate future value. In other words, we do not know whether to compound semiannually, quarterly, or over some other interval.

By contrast, the EAR is meaningful *without* a compounding interval. For example, an EAR of 10.25 percent means that a $1 investment will be worth $1.1025 in one year. We can think of this as an SAIR of 10 percent with semiannual compounding or an SAIR of 10.25 percent with annual compounding, or some other possibility.

There can be a big difference between an SAIR and an EAR when interest rates are large. For example, consider "payday loans." Payday loans are short-term loans made to consumers, often for less than two weeks, and are offered by companies such as AmeriCash Advance and National Payday. The loans work like this: You write a check today that is postdated. When the check date arrives, you go to the store and pay the cash for the check, or the company cashes the check. For example, AmeriCash Advance allows you to write a postdated check for $125 for 15 days later. In this case, they would give you $100 today. So, what are the APR and EAR of this arrangement? First, we need to find the interest rate, which we can find by the FV equation as follows:

$$FV = PV\,(1 + r)^T$$
$$\$125 = \$100 \times (1 + r)^1$$
$$1.25 = (1 + r)$$
$$r = .25 \text{ or } 25\%$$

That doesn't seem too bad until you remember this is the interest rate for *15 days*! The APR of the loan is:

$$APR = .25 \times 365/15$$
$$APR = 6.0833 \text{ or } 608.33\%$$

And the EAR for this loan is:

$$EAR = (1 + r/m)^m - 1$$
$$EAR = (1 + .25)^{365/15} - 1$$
$$EAR = 227.1096 \text{ or } 22{,}710.96\%$$

Now that's an interest rate! Just to see what a difference a day (or three) makes, let's look at National Payday's terms. This company will allow you to write a postdated check for the same amount, but will allow you 18 days to repay. Check for yourself that the APR of this arrangement is 506.94 percent and the EAR is 9,128.26 percent. This is lower, but still not a loan we recommend.

Compounding over Many Years

Equation 4.6 applies for an investment over one year. For an investment over one or more (T) years, the formula becomes this:

Future Value with Compounding:

$$FV = C_0 \left(1 + \frac{r}{m}\right)^{mT} \tag{4.8}$$

Multiyear Compounding Harry DeAngelo is investing $5,000 at a stated annual interest rate of 12 percent per year, compounded quarterly, for five years. What is his wealth at the end of five years?

Using Equation 4.8, his wealth is:

$$\$5,000 \times \left(1 + \frac{.12}{4}\right)^{4 \times 5} = \$5,000 \times (1.03)^{20} = \$5,000 \times 1.8061 = \$9,030.50$$

Continuous Compounding

The previous discussion shows that we can compound much more frequently than once a year. We could compound semiannually, quarterly, monthly, daily, hourly, each minute, or even more often. The limiting case would be to compound every infinitesimal instant, which is commonly called **continuous compounding**. Surprisingly, banks and other financial institutions sometimes quote continuously compounded rates, which is why we study them.

Though the idea of compounding this rapidly may boggle the mind, a simple formula is involved. With continuous compounding, the value at the end of T years is expressed as:

$$C_0 \times e^{rT} \tag{4.9}$$

where C_0 is the initial investment, r is the stated annual interest rate, and T is the number of years over which the investment runs. The number e is a constant and is approximately equal to 2.718. It is not an unknown like C_0, r, and T.

Continuous Compounding Linda DeFond invested $1,000 at a continuously compounded rate of 10 percent for one year. What is the value of her wealth at the end of one year?

From Equation 4.9 we have:

$$\$1,000 \times e^{0.10} = \$1,000 \times 1.1052 = \$1,105.20$$

This number can easily be read from Table A.5. We merely set r, the value on the horizontal dimension, to 10 percent and T, the value on the vertical dimension, to 1. For this problem the relevant portion of the table is shown here:

Period (T)	Continuously Compounded Rate (r) 9%	10%	11%
1	1.0942	1.1052	1.1163
2	1.1972	1.2214	1.2461
3	1.3100	1.3499	1.3910

Note that a continuously compounded rate of 10 percent is equivalent to an annually compounded rate of 10.52 percent. In other words, Linda DeFond would not care whether her bank quoted a continuously compounded rate of 10 percent or a 10.52 percent rate, compounded annually.

Figure 4.11

Annual, Semiannual, and Continuous Compounding

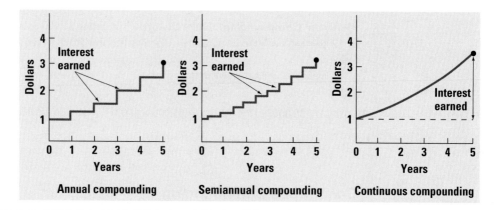

Annual compounding   Semiannual compounding   Continuous compounding

Continuous Compounding, Continued   Linda DeFond's brother, Mark, invested $1,000 at a continuously compounded rate of 10 percent for two years.

The appropriate formula here is:

$$\$1,000 \times e^{.10 \times 2} = \$1,000 \times e^{.20} = \$1,221.40$$

Using the portion of the table of continuously compounded rates shown in the previous example, we find the value to be 1.2214.

Figure 4.11 illustrates the relationship among annual, semiannual, and continuous compounding. Semiannual compounding gives rise to both a smoother curve and a higher ending value than does annual compounding. Continuous compounding has both the smoothest curve and the highest ending value of all.

Present Value with Continuous Compounding   The Michigan state lottery is going to pay you $1,000 at the end of four years. If the annual continuously compounded rate of interest is 8 percent, what is the present value of this payment?

$$\$1,000 \times \frac{1}{e^{.08 \times 4}} = \$1,000 \times \frac{1}{1.3771} = \$726.16$$

4.4   Simplifications

The first part of this chapter has examined the concepts of future value and present value. Although these concepts allow us to answer a host of problems concerning the time value of money, the human effort involved can be excessive. For example, consider a bank calculating the present value of a 20-year monthly mortgage. This mortgage has 240 ($=20 \times 12$) payments, so a lot of time is needed to perform a conceptually simple task.

Because many basic finance problems are potentially time-consuming, we search for simplifications in this section. We provide simplifying formulas for four classes of cash flow streams:

- Perpetuity.
- Growing perpetuity.

- Annuity.
- Growing annuity.

Perpetuity

A **perpetuity** is a constant stream of cash flows without end. If you are thinking that perpetuities have no relevance to reality, it will surprise you that there is a well-known case of an unending cash flow stream: the British bonds called *consols*. An investor purchasing a consol is entitled to receive yearly interest from the British government forever.

How can the price of a consol be determined? Consider a consol that pays a coupon of C dollars each year and will do so forever. Simply applying the PV formula gives us:

$$PV = \frac{C}{1+r} + \frac{C}{(1+r)^2} + \frac{C}{(1+r)^3} + \cdots$$

where the dots at the end of the formula stand for the infinite string of terms that continues the formula. Series like the preceding one are called *geometric series*. It is well known that even though they have an infinite number of terms, the whole series has a finite sum because each term is only a fraction of the preceding term. Before turning to our calculus books, though, it is worth going back to our original principles to see if a bit of financial intuition can help us find the PV.

The present value of the consol is the present value of all of its future coupons. In other words, it is an amount of money that, if an investor had it today, would enable him to achieve the same pattern of expenditures that the consol and its coupons would. Suppose an investor wanted to spend exactly C dollars each year. If he had the consol, he could do this. How much money must he have today to spend the same amount? Clearly, he would need exactly enough so that the interest on the money would be C dollars per year. If he had any more, he could spend more than C dollars each year. If he had any less, he would eventually run out of money spending C dollars per year.

The amount that will give the investor C dollars each year, and therefore the present value of the consol, is simply:

$$PV = \frac{C}{r} \qquad\qquad (4.10)$$

To confirm that this is the right answer, notice that if we lend the amount C/r, the interest it earns each year will be:

$$\text{Interest} = \frac{C}{r} \times r = C$$

which is exactly the consol payment. We have arrived at this formula for a consol:

Formula for Present Value of Perpetuity:

$$PV = \frac{C}{1+r} + \frac{C}{(1+r)^2} + \frac{C}{(1+r)^3} + \cdots$$
$$= \frac{C}{r} \qquad\qquad (4.11)$$

It is comforting to know how easily we can use a bit of financial intuition to solve this mathematical problem.

EXAMPLE 4.17

Perpetuities   Consider a perpetuity paying $100 a year. If the relevant interest rate is 8 percent, what is the value of the consol?

Using Equation 4.10 we have:

$$PV = \frac{\$100}{.08} = \$1,250$$

Now suppose that interest rates fall to 6 percent. Using Equation 4.10 the value of the perpetuity is:

$$PV = \frac{\$100}{.06} = \$1,666.67$$

Note that the value of the perpetuity rises with a drop in the interest rate. Conversely, the value of the perpetuity falls with a rise in the interest rate.

Growing Perpetuity

Imagine an apartment building where cash flows to the landlord after expenses will be $100,000 next year. These cash flows are expected to rise at 5 percent per year. If one assumes that this rise will continue indefinitely, the cash flow stream is termed a **growing perpetuity**. The relevant interest rate is 11 percent. Therefore, the appropriate discount rate is 11 percent, and the present value of the cash flows can be represented as:

$$PV = \frac{\$100,000}{1.11} + \frac{\$100,000(1.05)}{(1.11)^2} + \frac{\$100,000(1.05)^2}{(1.11)^3} + \cdots$$
$$+ \frac{\$100,000(1.05)^{N-1}}{(1.11)^N} + \cdots$$

Algebraically, we can write the formula as:

$$PV = \frac{C}{1+r} + \frac{C \times (1+g)}{(1+r)^2} + \frac{C \times (1+g)^2}{(1+r)^3} + \cdots + \frac{C \times (1+g)^{N-1}}{(1+r)^N} + \cdots$$

where C is the cash flow to be received one period hence, g is the rate of growth per period, expressed as a percentage, and r is the appropriate discount rate.

Fortunately, this formula reduces to the following simplification:

Formula for Present Value of Growing Perpetuity:

$$PV = \frac{C}{r - g} \qquad \qquad (4.12)$$

From Equation 4.12 the present value of the cash flows from the apartment building is:

$$\frac{\$100,000}{.11 - .05} = \$1,666,667$$

There are three important points concerning the growing perpetuity formula:

1. *The numerator*: The numerator in Equation 4.12 is the cash flow one period hence, not at date 0. Consider the following example.

EXAMPLE 4.18

Paying Dividends   Rothstein Corporation is *just about* to pay a dividend of $3.00 per share. Investors anticipate that the annual dividend will rise by 6 percent a year forever. The applicable discount rate is 11 percent. What is the price of the stock today?

The numerator in Equation 4.12 is the cash flow to be received next period. Since the growth rate is 6 percent, the dividend next year is $3.18 (=$3.00 × 1.06). The price of the stock today is:

$$\$66.60 \quad = \quad \$3.00 \quad + \quad \frac{\$3.18}{.11 - .06}$$

Imminent   Present value of all
dividend   dividends beginning
a year from now

The price of $66.60 includes both the dividend to be received immediately and the present value of all dividends beginning a year from now. Equation 4.12 makes it possible to calculate only the present value of all dividends beginning a year from now. Be sure you understand this example; test questions on this subject always seem to trip up a few of our students.

2. *The discount rate and the growth rate*: The discount rate r must be greater than the growth rate g for the growing perpetuity formula to work. Consider the case in which the growth rate approaches the interest rate in magnitude. Then, the denominator in the growing perpetuity formula gets infinitesimally small and the present value grows infinitely large. The present value is in fact undefined when r is less than g.

3. *The timing assumption*: Cash generally flows into and out of real-world firms both randomly and nearly continuously. However, Equation 4.12 assumes that cash flows are received and disbursed at regular and discrete points in time. In the example of the apartment, we assumed that the net cash flows of $100,000 occurred only once a year. In reality, rent checks are commonly received every month. Payments for maintenance and other expenses may occur anytime within the year.

We can apply the growing perpetuity formula of Equation 4.12 only by assuming a regular and discrete pattern of cash flow. Although this assumption is sensible because the formula saves so much time, the user should never forget that it is an *assumption*. This point will be mentioned again in the chapters ahead.

A few words should be said about terminology. Authors of financial textbooks generally use one of two conventions to refer to time. A minority of financial writers treat cash flows as being received on exact *dates*—for example date 0, date 1, and so forth. Under this convention, date 0 represents the present time. However, because a year is an interval, not a specific moment in time, the great majority of authors refer to cash flows that occur at the end of a year (or alternatively, the end of a *period*). Under this *end-of-the-year* convention, the end of year 0 is the present, the end of year 1 occurs one period hence, and so on. (The beginning of year 0 has already passed and is not generally referred to.)[2]

The interchangeability of the two conventions can be seen from the following chart:

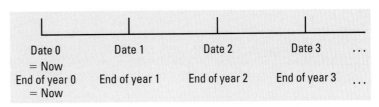

Date 0   Date 1   Date 2   Date 3   . . .
= Now
End of year 0   End of year 1   End of year 2   End of year 3   . . .
= Now

---

[2]Sometimes, financial writers merely speak of a cash flow in year x. Although this terminology is ambiguous, such writers generally mean the *end of year x*.

We strongly believe that the *dates convention* reduces ambiguity. However, we use both conventions because you are likely to see the *end-of-year convention* in later courses. In fact, both conventions may appear in the same example for the sake of practice.

Annuity

An **annuity** is a level stream of regular payments that lasts for a fixed number of periods. Not surprisingly, annuities are among the most common kinds of financial instruments. The pensions that people receive when they retire are often in the form of an annuity. Leases and mortgages are also often annuities.

To figure out the present value of an annuity we need to evaluate the following equation:

$$\frac{C}{1+r} + \frac{C}{(1+r)^2} + \frac{C}{(1+r)^3} + \cdots + \frac{C}{(1+r)^T}$$

The present value of receiving the coupons for only T periods must be less than the present value of a consol, but how much less? To answer this, we have to look at consols a bit more closely.

Consider the following time chart:

Date (or end of year)	Now 0	1	2	3	T	$(T+1)$	$(T+2)$
Consol 1		C	C	$C\ldots$	C	C	$C\ldots$
Consol 2						C	$C\ldots$
Annuity		C	C	$C\ldots$	C		

Consol 1 is a normal consol with its first payment at date 1. The first payment of consol 2 occurs at date $T + 1$.

The present value of having a cash flow of C at each of T dates is equal to the present value of consol 1 minus the present value of consol 2. The present value of consol 1 is given by:

$$PV = \frac{C}{r} \tag{4.13}$$

Consol 2 is just a consol with its first payment at date $T + 1$. From the perpetuity formula, this consol will be worth C/r at date T.[3] However, we do not want the value at date T. We want the value now, in other words, the present value at date 0. We must discount C/r back by T periods. Therefore, the present value of consol 2 is:

$$PV = \frac{C}{r}\left[\frac{1}{(1+r)^T}\right] \tag{4.14}$$

The present value of having cash flows for T years is the present value of a consol with its first payment at date 1 minus the present value of a consol with its first payment at date

---

[3]Students frequently think that C/r is the present value at date $T + 1$ because the consol's first payment is at date $T + 1$. However, the formula values the consol as of one period prior to the first payment.

$T + 1$. Thus the present value of an annuity is Equation 4.13 minus Equation 4.14. This can be written as:

$$\frac{C}{r} - \frac{C}{r}\left[\frac{1}{(1+r)^T}\right]$$

This simplifies to the following:

Formula for Present Value of Annuity:

$$PV = C\left[\frac{1}{r} - \frac{1}{r(1+r)^T}\right]$$

This can also be written as:

$$PV = C\left[\frac{1 - \dfrac{1}{(1+r)^T}}{r}\right] \tag{4.15}$$

EXAMPLE 4.19

Lottery Valuation   Mark Young has just won the state lottery, paying $50,000 a year for 20 years. He is to receive his first payment a year from now. The state advertises this as the Million Dollar Lottery because $1,000,000 = $50,000 × 20. If the interest rate is 8 percent, what is the true value of the lottery?

Equation 4.15 yields:

$$\begin{array}{l} \text{Present value of} \\ \text{Million Dollar Lottery} \end{array} = \$50,000 \times \left[\frac{1 - \dfrac{1}{(1.08)^{20}}}{.08}\right]$$

$$\begin{array}{ccc} \text{Periodic payment} & & \text{Annuity factor} \\ = \$50,000 & \times & 9.8181 \\ = \$490,905 \end{array}$$

Rather than being overjoyed at winning, Mr. Young sues the state for misrepresentation and fraud. His legal brief states that he was promised $1 million but received only $490,905.

The term we use to compute the present value of the stream of level payments, C, for T years is called an **annuity factor**. The annuity factor in the current example is 9.8181. Because the annuity factor is used so often in PV calculations, we have included it in Table A.2 in the back of this book. The table gives the values of these factors for a range of interest rates, r, and maturity dates, T.

The annuity factor as expressed in the brackets of Equation 4.15 is a complex formula. For simplification, we may from time to time refer to the annuity factor as:

$$A_r^T$$

This expression stands for the present value of $1 a year for T years at an interest rate of r.

We can also provide a formula for the future value of an annuity:

$$FV = C\left[\frac{(1+r)^T}{r} - \frac{1}{r}\right] = C\left[\frac{(1+r)^T - 1}{r}\right] \tag{4.16}$$

As with present value factors for annuities, we have compiled future value factors in Table A.3 in the back of this book.

EXAMPLE 4.20

Retirement Investing   Suppose you put $3,000 per year into a Roth IRA. The account pays 6 percent interest per year. How much will you have when you retire in 30 years?

This question asks for the future value of an annuity of $3,000 per year for 30 years at 6 percent, which we can calculate as follows:

$$FV = C \left[\frac{(1+r)^T - 1}{r} \right] = \$3,000 \times \left[\frac{1.06^{30} - 1}{.06} \right]$$
$$= \$3,000 \times 79.0582$$
$$= \$237,174.56$$

So, you'll have close to a quarter million dollars in the account.

Our experience is that annuity formulas are not hard, but tricky, for the beginning student. We present four tricks next.

Trick 1: A Delayed Annuity

One of the tricks in working with annuities or perpetuities is getting the timing exactly right. This is particularly true when an annuity or perpetuity begins at a date many periods in the future. We have found that even the brightest beginning student can make errors here. Consider the following example.

EXAMPLE 4.21

Delayed Annuities   Danielle Caravello will receive a four-year annuity of $500 per year, beginning at date 6. If the interest rate is 10 percent, what is the present value of her annuity? This situation can be graphed as follows:

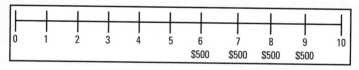

The analysis involves two steps:

1. Calculate the present value of the annuity using Equation 4.15:

Present Value of Annuity at Date 5:

$$\$500 \left[\frac{1 - \dfrac{1}{(1.10)^4}}{.10} \right] = \$500 \times A_{.10}^4$$
$$= \$500 \times 3.1699$$
$$= \$1,584.95$$

Note that $1,584.95 represents the present value at *date 5*.

Students frequently think that $1,584.95 is the present value at date 6 because the annuity begins at date 6. However, our formula values the annuity as of one period prior to the first payment. This can be seen in the most typical case where the first payment occurs at date 1. The formula values the annuity as of date 0 in that case.

2. Discount the present value of the annuity back to date 0:

Present Value at Date 0:

$$\frac{\$1,584.95}{(1.10)^5} = \$984.13$$

(continued)

Again, it is worthwhile mentioning that because the annuity formula brings Danielle's annuity back to date 5, the second calculation must discount over the remaining five periods. The two-step procedure is graphed in Figure 4.12.

Figure 4.12   **Discounting Danielle Caravello's Annuity**

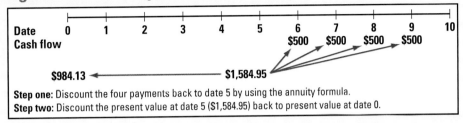

Step one: Discount the four payments back to date 5 by using the annuity formula.
Step two: Discount the present value at date 5 ($1,584.95) back to present value at date 0.

Trick 2: Annuity due   The annuity formula of Equation 4.15 assumes that the first annuity payment begins a full period hence. This type of annuity is sometimes called an *annuity in arrears* or an *ordinary annuity*. What happens if the annuity begins today—in other words, at date 0?

Annuity Due   In a previous example, Mark Young received $50,000 a year for 20 years from the state lottery. In that example, he was to receive the first payment a year from the winning date. Let us now assume that the first payment occurs immediately. The total number of payments remains 20.

Under this new assumption, we have a 19-date annuity with the first payment occurring at date 1—plus an extra payment at date 0. The present value is:

$$\$50,000 \quad + \quad \$50,000 \times A_{.08}^{19}$$

Payment at date 0 \qquad 19-year annuity

$$= \$50,000 + (\$50,000 \times 9.6036)$$
$$= \$530,180$$

$530,180, the present value in this example, is greater than $490,905, the present value in the earlier lottery example. This is to be expected because the annuity of the current example begins earlier. An annuity with an immediate initial payment is called an *annuity in advance* or, more commonly, an *annuity due*. Always remember that Equation 4.15 and Table A.2 in this book refer to an *ordinary annuity*.

Trick 3: The Infrequent Annuity   The following example treats an annuity with payments occurring less frequently than once a year.

Infrequent Annuities   Ann Chen receives an annuity of $450, payable once every two years. The annuity stretches out over 20 years. The first payment occurs at date 2—that is, two years from today. The annual interest rate is 6 percent.

The trick is to determine the interest rate over a two-year period. The interest rate over two years is:

$$(1.06 \times 1.06) - 1 = 12.36\%$$

That is, $100 invested over two years will yield $112.36.

What we want is the present value of a $450 annuity over 10 periods, with an interest rate of 12.36 percent per period:

$$\$450 \left[\frac{1 - \dfrac{1}{(1 + .1236)^{10}}}{.1236} \right] = \$450 \times A_{.1236}^{10} = \$2,505.57$$

Trick 4: Equating Present Value of Two Annuities   The following example equates the present value of inflows with the present value of outflows.

EXAMPLE 4.24

Working with Annuities   Harold and Helen Nash are saving for the college education of their newborn daughter, Susan. The Nashes estimate that college expenses will run $30,000 per year when their daughter reaches college in 18 years. The annual interest rate over the next few decades will be 14 percent. How much money must they deposit in the bank each year so that their daughter will be completely supported through four years of college?

To simplify the calculations, we assume that Susan is born today. Her parents will make the first of her four annual tuition payments on her 18th birthday. They will make equal bank deposits on each of her first 17 birthdays, but no deposit at date 0. This is illustrated as follows:

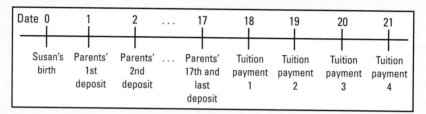

Mr. and Ms. Nash will be making deposits to the bank over the next 17 years. They will be withdrawing $30,000 per year over the following four years. We can be sure they will be able to withdraw fully $30,000 per year if the present value of the deposits is equal to the present value of the four $30,000 withdrawals.

This calculation requires three steps. The first two determine the present value of the withdrawals. The final step determines yearly deposits that will have a present value equal to that of the withdrawals.

1. We calculate the present value of the four years at college using the annuity formula:

$$\$30,000 \times \left[\frac{1 - \frac{1}{(1.14)^4}}{.14} \right] = \$30,000 \times A^4_{.14}$$

$$= \$30,000 \times 2.9137 = \$87,411$$

We assume that Susan enters college on her 18th birthday. Given our discussion in Trick 1, $87,411 represents the present value at date 17.

2. We calculate the present value of the college education at date 0 as:

$$\frac{\$87,411}{(1.14)^{17}} = \$9,422.91$$

3. Assuming that Harold and Helen Nash make deposits to the bank at the end of each of the 17 years, we calculate the annual deposit that will yield a present value of all deposits of $9,422.91. This is calculated as:

$$C \times A^{17}_{.14} = \$9,422.91$$

Because $A^{17}_{.14} = 6.3729$,

$$C = \frac{\$9,422.91}{6.3729} = \$1,478.59$$

Thus deposits of $1,478.59 made at the end of each of the first 17 years and invested at 14 percent will provide enough money to make tuition payments of $30,000 over the following four years.

An alternative method in Example 4.24 would be to (1) calculate the present value of the tuition payments at Susan's 18th birthday and (2) calculate annual deposits so that the future value of the deposits at her 18th birthday equals the present value of the tuition payments at that date. Although this technique can also provide the right answer, we have found that it is more likely to lead to errors. Therefore, we equate only present values in our presentation.

Growing Annuity

Cash flows in business are likely to grow over time, due either to real growth or to inflation. The growing perpetuity, which assumes an infinite number of cash flows, provides one formula to handle this growth. We now consider a **growing annuity**, which is a *finite* number of growing cash flows. Because perpetuities of any kind are rare, a formula for a growing annuity would be useful indeed. Here is the formula:

Formula for Present Value of Growing Annuity:

$$\text{PV} = C\left[\frac{1}{r-g} - \frac{1}{r-g} \times \left(\frac{1+g}{1+r}\right)^T \right] = C\left[\frac{1 - \left(\frac{1+g}{1+r}\right)^T}{r-g} \right] \quad \textbf{(4.17)}$$

As before, C is the payment to occur at the end of the first period, r is the interest rate, g is the rate of growth per period, expressed as a percentage, and T is the number of periods for the annuity.

Growing Annuities　Stuart Gabriel, a second-year MBA student, has just been offered a job at $80,000 a year. He anticipates his salary increasing by 9 percent a year until his retirement in 40 years. Given an interest rate of 20 percent, what is the present value of his lifetime salary?

　　We simplify by assuming he will be paid his $80,000 salary exactly one year from now, and that his salary will continue to be paid in annual installments. The appropriate discount rate is 20 percent. From Equation 4.17, the calculation is:

$$\text{Present value of Stuart's lifetime salary} = \$80,000 \times \left[\frac{1 - \left(\frac{1.09}{1.20}\right)^{40}}{.20 - .09} \right] = \$711,730.71$$

Though the growing annuity is quite useful, it is more tedious than the other simplifying formulas. Whereas most sophisticated calculators have special programs for perpetuity, growing perpetuity, and annuity, there is no special program for a growing annuity. Hence, we must calculate all the terms in Equation 4.17 directly.

More Growing Annuities　In our previous example, Helen and Harold Nash planned to make 17 identical payments to fund the college education of their daughter, Susan. Alternatively, imagine that they planned to increase their payments at 4 percent per year. What would their first payment be?

　　The first two steps of the previous Nash family example showed that the present value of the college costs was $9,422.91. These two steps would be the same here. However, the third step must be altered. Now we must ask, How much should their first payment be so that, if payments increase by 4 percent per year, the present value of all payments will be $9,422.91?

　　We set the growing annuity formula equal to $9,422.91 and solve for C:

$$C\left[\frac{1 - \left(\frac{1+g}{1+r}\right)^T}{r-g} \right] = C\left[\frac{1 - \left(\frac{1.04}{1.14}\right)^{17}}{.14 - .04} \right] = \$9,422.91$$

Here, $C = \$1,192.78$. Thus, the deposit on their daughter's first birthday is $1,192.78, the deposit on the second birthday is $1,240.49 (= 1.04 × $1,192.78), and so on.

4.5 What Is a Firm Worth?

Suppose you are a business appraiser trying to determine the value of small companies. How can you determine what a firm is worth? One way to think about the question of how much a firm is worth is to calculate the present value of its future cash flows.

Let us consider the example of a firm that is expected to generate net cash flows (cash inflows minus cash outflows) of $5,000 in the first year and $2,000 for each of the next five years. The firm can be sold for $10,000 seven years from now. The owners of the firm would like to be able to make 10 percent on their investment in the firm.

The value of the firm is found by multiplying the net cash flows by the appropriate present value factor. The value of the firm is simply the sum of the present values of the individual net cash flows.

The present value of the net cash flows is given next.

The Present Value of the Firm			
End of Year	Net Cash Flow of the Firm	Present Value Factor (10%)	Present Value of Net Cash Flows
1	$ 5,000	.90909	$ 4,545.45
2	2,000	.82645	1,652.90
3	2,000	.75131	1,502.62
4	2,000	.68301	1,366.02
5	2,000	.62092	1,241.84
6	2,000	.56447	1,128.94
7	10,000	.51316	5,131.58
		Present value of firm	$16,569.35

We can also use the simplifying formula for an annuity:

$$\frac{\$5,000}{1.1} + \frac{(2,000 \times A^5_{.10})}{1.1} + \frac{10,000}{(1.1)^7} = \$16,569.35$$

Suppose you have the opportunity to acquire the firm for $12,000. Should you acquire the firm? The answer is yes because the NPV is positive:

$$NPV = PV - Cost$$
$$\$4,569.35 = \$16,569.35 - \$12,000$$

The incremental value (NPV) of acquiring the firm is $4,569.35.

EXAMPLE 4.27

Firm Valuation   The Trojan Pizza Company is contemplating investing $1 million in four new outlets in Los Angeles. Andrew Lo, the firm's chief financial officer (CFO), has estimated that the investments will pay out cash flows of $200,000 per year for nine years and nothing thereafter. (The cash flows will occur at the end of each year and there will be no cash flow after year 9.) Mr. Lo has determined that the relevant discount rate for this investment is 15 percent. This is the rate of return that the firm can earn at comparable projects. Should the Trojan Pizza Company make the investments in the new outlets?

(continued)

The decision can be evaluated as follows:

$$\text{NPV} = -\$1,000,000 + \frac{\$200,000}{1.15} + \frac{\$200,000}{(1.15)^2} + \cdots + \frac{\$200,000}{(1.15)^9}$$

$$= -\$1,000,000 + \$200,000 \times A^9_{.15}$$

$$= -\$1,000,000 + \$954,316.78$$

$$= -\$45,683.22$$

The present value of the four new outlets is only \$954,316.78. The outlets are worth less than they cost. The Trojan Pizza Company should not make the investment because the NPV is −\$45,683.22. If the Trojan Pizza Company requires a 15 percent rate of return, the new outlets are not a good investment.

Summary and Conclusions

1. Two basic concepts, *future value* and *present value,* were introduced in the beginning of this chapter. With a 10 percent interest rate, an investor with \$1 today can generate a future value of \$1.10 in a year, \$1.21 [=\$1 × (1.10)²] in two years, and so on. Conversely, present value analysis places a current value on a future cash flow. With the same 10 percent interest rate, a dollar to be received in one year has a present value of \$0.909 (=\$1/1.10) in year 0. A dollar to be received in two years has a present value of \$0.826 [=\$1/(1.10)²].

2. We commonly express an interest rate as, say, 12 percent per year. However, we can speak of the interest rate as 3 percent per quarter. Although the stated annual interest rate remains 12 percent (=3 percent × 4), the effective annual interest rate is 12.55 percent [=(1.03)⁴ − 1]. In other words, the compounding process increases the future value of an investment. The limiting case is continuous compounding, where funds are assumed to be reinvested every infinitesimal instant.

3. A basic quantitative technique for financial decision making is net present value analysis. The net present value formula for an investment that generates cash flows (C_i) in future periods is:

$$\text{NPV} = -C_0 + \frac{C_1}{(1+r)} + \frac{C_2}{(1+r)^2} + \cdots + \frac{C_T}{(1+r)^T} = -C_0 + \sum_{i=1}^{T} \frac{C_i}{(1+r)^i}$$

The formula assumes that the cash flow at date 0 is the initial investment (a cash outflow).

4. Frequently, the actual calculation of present value is long and tedious. The computation of the present value of a long-term mortgage with monthly payments is a good example of this. We presented four simplifying formulas:

$$\text{Perpetuity: } PV = \frac{C}{r}$$

$$\text{Growing perpetuity: } PV = \frac{C}{r - g}$$

$$\text{Annuity: } PV = C \left[\frac{1 - \dfrac{1}{(1+r)^T}}{r} \right]$$

$$\text{Growing annuity: } PV = C \left[\frac{1 - \left(\dfrac{1+g}{1+r}\right)^T}{r - g} \right]$$

5. We stressed a few practical considerations in the application of these formulas:

    a. The numerator in each of the formulas, C, is the cash flow to be received *one full period hence.*

    b. Cash flows are generally irregular in practice. To avoid unwieldy problems, assumptions to create more regular cash flows are made both in this textbook and in the real world.

    c. A number of present value problems involve annuities (or perpetuities) beginning a few periods hence. Students should practice combining the annuity (or perpetuity) formula with the discounting formula to solve these problems.

    d. Annuities and perpetuities may have periods of every two or every n years, rather than once a year. The annuity and perpetuity formulas can easily handle such circumstances.

    e. We frequently encounter problems where the present value of one annuity must be equated with the present value of another annuity.

Concept Questions

1. **Compounding and Period**   As you increase the length of time involved, what happens to future values? What happens to present values?

2. **Interest Rates**   What happens to the future value of an annuity if you increase the rate r? What happens to the present value?

3. **Present Value**   Suppose two athletes sign 10-year contracts for €80 million. In one case, we're told that the €80 million will be paid in 10 equal installments. In the other case, we're told that the €80 million will be paid in 10 installments, but the installments will increase by 5 percent per year. Who got the better deal?

4. **APR and EAR**   Should lending laws be changed to require lenders to report EARs instead of APRs? Why or why not?

5. **Time Value**   On subsidized Stafford loans, a common source of financial aid for college students, interest does not begin to accrue until repayment begins. Who receives a bigger subsidy, a freshman or a senior? Explain.

Use the following information for the next five questions:

On December 2, 1982, General Motors Acceptance Corporation (GMAC), a subsidiary of General Motors, offered some securities for sale to the public. Under the terms of the deal, GMAC promised to repay the owner of one of these securities $10,000 on December 1, 2012, but the investors would receive nothing until then. Investors paid GMAC $500 for each of these securities on December 2, 1982, for the promise of a $10,000 payment 30 years later.

6. **Time Value of Money**   Why would GMAC be willing to accept such a small amount today ($500) in exchange for a promise to repay 20 times that amount ($10,000) in the future?

7. **Call Provisions**   GMAC has the right to buy back the securities anytime it wishes by paying $10,000 (this is a term of this particular deal). What impact does this feature have on the desirability of this security as an investment?

8. **Time Value of Money**   Would you be willing to pay £500 today in exchange for £10,000 in 30 years? What would be the key considerations in answering yes or no? Would your answer depend on who is making the promise to repay?

9. **Investment Comparison**   Suppose that when GMAC offered the security for $500, the U.S. Treasury had offered an essentially identical security. Do you think it would have had a higher or lower price? Why?

10. **Length of Investment**   The GMAC security is bought and sold on the New York Stock Exchange. If you looked at the price today, do you think the price would exceed the $500 original price? Why? If you looked in the year 2010, do you think the price would be higher or lower than today's price? Why?

Questions and Problems

BASIC
(Questions 1–20)

1. **Simple Interest versus Compound Interest**   First City Bank pays 7 percent simple interest on its savings account balances, whereas Second City Bank pays 7 percent interest compounded annually. If you made a $5,000 deposit in each bank, how much more money would you earn from your Second City Bank account at the end of 5 years?

2. **Calculating Future Values**   Compute the future value of €1,000 compounded annually for
   a. 10 years at 6 percent.
   b. 10 years at 7 percent.
   c. 20 years at 6 percent.
   d. Why is the interest earned in part (c) not twice the amount earned in part (a)?

3. **Calculating Present Values**   For each of the following, compute the present value:

Present Value	Years	Interest Rate	Future Value
	6	5%	£ 15,451
	9	11	51,557
	18	16	886,073
	23	19	550,164

4. **Calculating Interest Rates**   Solve for the unknown interest rate in each of the following:

Present Value	Years	Interest Rate	Future Value
$ 265	2		$ 307
360	9		896
39,000	15		162,181
46,523	30		483,500

5. **Calculating the Number of Periods**   Solve for the unknown number of years in each of the following:

Present Value	Years	Interest Rate	Future Value
¥ 625,000		9%	¥ 1,284,000
810,000		7	4,341,000
18,400,000		21	402,662,000
21,500,000		29	173,439,000

6. **Calculating the Number of Periods**   At 6 percent interest, how long does it take to double your money? To quadruple it?

7. **Calculating Present Values**   Will Do Later, Inc., has an unfunded pension liability of $800 million that must be paid in 20 years. To assess the value of the firm's stock, financial analysts want to discount this liability back to the present. If the relevant discount rate is 9.5 percent, what is the present value of this liability?

8. **Calculating Rates of Return**   Although appealing to more refined tastes, art as a collectible has not always performed so profitably. During 2003, Sotheby's sold the Edgar Degas bronze sculpture *Petite Danseuse de Quartorze Ans* at auction for a price of $10,311,500. Unfortunately for the previous owner, he had purchased it in 1999 at a price of $12,377,500. What was his annual rate of return on this sculpture?

9. **Perpetuities**   An investor purchasing a British consol is entitled to receive annual payments from the British government forever. What is the price of a consol that pays £120 annually if the next payment occurs one year from today? The market interest rate is 15 percent.

10. **Continuous Compounding**   Compute the future value of $1,000 continuously compounded for
    a. 5 years at a stated annual interest rate of 12 percent.
    b. 3 years at a stated annual interest rate of 10 percent.
    c. 10 years at a stated annual interest rate of 5 percent.
    d. 8 years at a stated annual interest rate of 7 percent.

11. **Present Value and Multiple Cash Flows**   Bawati Restoration Co. has identified an investment project with the following cash flows. If the discount rate is 10 percent, what is the present value of these cash flows? What is the present value at 18 percent? At 24 percent?

Year	Cash Flow
1	EGP 1,200
2	600
3	855
4	1,480

12. **Present Value and Multiple Cash Flows**   Investment X offers to pay you CNY 4,000 per year for nine years, whereas Investment Y offers to pay you CNY 6,000 per year for five years. Which of these cash flow streams has the higher present value if the discount rate is 5 percent? If the discount rate is 22 percent?

13. **Calculating Annuity Present Value**   An investment offers PKR 3,600 per year for 15 years, with the first payment occurring one year from now. If the required return is 10 percent, what is the value of the investment? What would the value be if the payments occurred for 40 years? For 75 years? Forever?

14. **Calculating Perpetuity Values**   The Perpetual Life Insurance Co. is trying to sell you an investment policy that will pay you and your heirs $15,000 per year forever. If the required return on this investment is 8 percent, how much will you pay for the policy? Suppose the Perpetual Life Insurance Co. told you the policy costs $195,000. At what interest rate would this be a fair deal?

15. **Calculating EAR**   Find the EAR in each of the following cases:

Stated Rate (APR)	Number of Times Compounded	Effective Rate (EAR)
11%	Quarterly	
7	Monthly	
9	Daily	
17	Infinite	

16. **Calculating APR**   Find the APR, or stated rate, in each of the following cases:

Stated Rate (APR)	Number of Times Compounded	Effective Rate (EAR)
	Semiannually	8.1%
	Monthly	7.6
	Weekly	16.8
	Infinite	26.2

17. **Calculating EAR**   First National Bank charges 12.2 percent compounded monthly on its business loans. First United Bank charges 12.5 percent compounded semiannually. As a potential borrower, to which bank would you go for a new loan?

18. **Interest Rates**   Well-known financial writer Andrew Tobias argues that he can earn 177 percent per year buying wine by the case. Specifically, he assumes that he will consume one €10 bottle of fine Bordeaux per week for the next 12 weeks. He can either pay €10 per week or buy a case of 12 bottles today. If he buys the case, he receives a 10 percent discount and, by doing so, earns the 177 percent. Assume he buys the wine and consumes the first bottle today. Do you agree with his analysis? Do you see a problem with his numbers?

19. **Calculating Number of Periods**   One of your customers is delinquent on his accounts payable balance. You've mutually agreed to a repayment schedule of KRW 500 per month. You will charge .9 percent per month interest on the overdue balance. If the current balance is KRW 16,500, how long will it take for the account to be paid off?

20. **Calculating EAR**   Friendly's Quick Loans, Inc., offers you "three for four or I knock on your door." This means you get $3 today and repay $4 when you get your paycheck in one week (or else). What's the effective annual return Friendly's earns on this lending business? If you were brave enough to ask, what APR would Friendly's say you were paying?

INTERMEDIATE
(Questions 21–50)

21. **Future Value**   What is the future value in three years of $1,000 invested in an account with a stated annual interest rate of 8 percent,
    a. Compounded annually?
    b. Compounded semiannually?
    c. Compounded monthly?
    d. Compounded continuously?
    e. Why does the future value increase as the compounding period shortens?

22. **Simple Interest versus Compound Interest**   First Simple Bank pays 8 percent simple interest on its investment accounts. If First Complex Bank pays interest on its accounts compounded annually, what rate should the bank set if it wants to match First Simple Bank over an investment horizon of 10 years?

23. **Calculating Annuities**   You are planning to save for retirement over the next 30 years. To do this, you will invest LKR 700 a month in a stock account and LKR 300 a month in a bond account. The return of the stock account is expected to be 11 percent, and the bond account will pay 7 percent. When you retire, you will combine your money into an account with a 9 percent return. How much can you withdraw each month from your account assuming a 25-year withdrawal period?

24. **Calculating Rates of Return**   Suppose an investment offers to quadruple your money in 12 months (don't believe it). What rate of return per quarter are you being offered?

25. **Calculating Rates of Return**   You're trying to choose between two different investments, both of which have up-front costs of £50,000. Investment G returns £85,000 in five years. Investment H returns £175,000 in 10 years. Which of these investments has the higher return?

26. **Growing Perpetuities**   I. M. Smart has been working on an advanced technology in laser eye surgery. His technology will be available in the near term. He anticipates his first annual cash flow from the technology to be INR 200,000, received two years from today. Subsequent annual cash flows will grow at 5 percent in perpetuity. What is the present value of the technology if the discount rate is 10 percent?

27. **Perpetuities**   Zumo Financial designed a new security that pays a quarterly dividend of ¥1,000 in perpetuity. The first dividend occurs one quarter from today. What is the price of the security if the stated annual interest rate is 12 percent, compounded quarterly?

28. **Annuity Present Values**   What is the present value of an annuity of NZD 2,000 per year, with the first cash flow received three years from today and the last one received 22 years from today? Use a discount rate of 8 percent.

29. **Annuity Present Values**   What is the value today of a 15-year annuity that pays $500 a year? The annuity's first payment occurs at the end of year 6. The annual interest rate is 12 percent for years 1 through 5, and 15 percent thereafter.

30. **Balloon Payments**   Qi Fung has just arranged to purchase a CNY 40,000,000 vacation home in the Macao with a 20 percent down payment. The mortgage has an 8 percent stated

annual interest rate, compounded monthly, and calls for equal monthly payments over the next 30 years. His first payment will be due one month from now. However, the mortgage has an eight-year balloon payment, meaning that the balance of the loan must be paid off at the end of year 8. There were no other transaction costs or finance charges. How much will Qi's balloon payment be in eight years?

31.   Calculating Interest Expense   You receive a credit card application from Shady Banks Savings and Loan offering an introductory rate of 1.90 percent per year, compounded monthly for the first six months, increasing thereafter to 16 percent compounded monthly. Assuming you transfer the £4,000 balance from your existing credit card and make no subsequent payments, how much interest will you owe at the end of the first year?

32.   Perpetuities   Upala Pharmaceuticals is considering a drug project that costs CRC 240,000 today and is expected to generate end-of-year annual cash flows of CRC 21,000, forever. At what discount rate would Upala be indifferent between accepting or rejecting the project?

33.   Growing Annuity   Southern California Publishing Company is trying to decide whether to revise its popular textbook, *Financial Psychoanalysis Made Simple.* The company has estimated that the revision will cost $50,000. Cash flows from increased sales will be $12,000 the first year. These cash flows will increase by 6 percent per year. The book will go out of print five years from now. Assume that the initial cost is paid now and revenues are received at the end of each year. If the company requires an 11 percent return for such an investment, should it undertake the revision?

34.   Growing Annuity   Your job pays you only once a year for all the work you did over the previous 12 months. Today, December 31, you just received your salary of SAR 400,000, and you plan to spend all of it. However, you want to start saving for retirement beginning next year. You have decided that one year from today you will begin depositing 2 percent of your annual salary in an account that will earn 8 percent per year. Your salary will increase at 4 percent per year throughout your career. How much money will you have on the date of your retirement 40 years from today?

35.   Present Value and Interest Rates   What is the relationship between the value of an annuity and the level of interest rates? Suppose you just bought a 10-year annuity of VND 5,000 per year at the current interest rate of 10 percent per year. What happens to the value of your investment if interest rates suddenly drop to 5 percent? What if interest rates suddenly rise to 15 percent?

36.   Calculating the Number of Payments   You're prepared to make monthly payments of €100, beginning at the end of this month, into an account that pays 10 percent interest compounded monthly. How many payments will you have made when your account balance reaches €15,000?

37.   Calculating Annuity Present Values   You want to borrow $45,000 from your local bank to buy a new sailboat. You can afford to make monthly payments of $950, but no more. Assuming monthly compounding, what is the highest APR you can afford on a 60-month loan?

38.   Calculating Loan Payments   You need a 30-year, fixed-rate mortgage to buy a new home for $200,000. Your mortgage bank will lend you the money at a 6.8 percent APR for this 360-month loan. However, you can only afford monthly payments of $1,000, so you offer to pay off any remaining loan balance at the end of the loan in the form of a single balloon payment. How large will this balloon payment have to be for you to keep your monthly payments at $1,000?

39.   Present and Future Values   The present value of the following cash flow stream is PHP 5,979 when discounted at 10 percent annually. What is the value of the missing cash flow?

Year	Cash Flow
1	PHP 1,000
2	?
3	2,000
4	2,000

40. **Calculating Present Values** You just won the TVM Lottery. You will receive ¥1 million today plus another 10 annual payments that increase by ¥400,000 per year. Thus, in one year you receive ¥1.4 million. In two years, you get ¥1.8 million, and so on. If the appropriate interest rate is 12 percent, what is the present value of your winnings?

41. **EAR versus APR** You have just purchased a new warehouse. To finance the purchase, you've arranged for a 30-year mortgage for 80 percent of the £1,600,000 purchase price. The monthly payment on this loan will be £10,000. What is the APR on this loan? The EAR?

42. **Present Value and Break-Even Interest** Consider a firm with a contract to sell an asset for $115,000 three years from now. The asset costs $72,000 to produce today. Given a relevant discount rate on this asset of 13 percent per year, will the firm make a profit on this asset? At what rate does the firm just break even?

43. **Present Value and Multiple Cash Flows** What is the present value of $2,000 per year, at a discount rate of 10 percent, if the first payment is received 9 years from now and the last payment is received 25 years from now?

44. **Variable Interest Rates** A 15-year annuity pays ILS 1,500 per month, and payments are made at the end of each month. If the interest rate is 15 percent compounded monthly for the first seven years, and 12 percent compounded monthly thereafter, what is the present value of the annuity?

45. **Comparing Cash Flow Streams** You have your choice of two investment accounts. Investment A is a 15-year annuity that features end-of-month €1,000 payments and has an interest rate of 10.5 percent compounded monthly. Investment B is a 9 percent continuously compounded lump-sum investment, also good for 15 years. How much money would you need to invest in B today for it to be worth as much as Investment A 15 years from now?

46. **Calculating Present Value of a Perpetuity** Given an interest rate of 6.5 percent per year, what is the value at date $t = 7$ of a perpetual stream of $3,000 payments that begins at date $t = 15$?

47. **Calculating EAR** A local finance company quotes a 14 percent interest rate on one-year loans. So, if you borrow £20,000, the interest for the year will be £2,800. Because you must repay a total of £22,800 in one year, the finance company requires you to pay £22,800/12, or £1,900, per month over the next 12 months. Is this a 14 percent loan? What rate would legally have to be quoted? What is the effective annual rate?

48. **Calculating Present Values** A 5-year annuity of ten semiannual payments of CAD 10,000 will begin 9 years from now, with the first payment coming 9.5 years from now. If the discount rate is 12 percent compounded monthly, what is the value of this annuity five years from now? What is the value three years from now? What is the current value of the annuity?

49. **Calculating Annuities Due** As discussed in the text, an ordinary annuity assumes equal payments at the end of each period over the life of the annuity. An *annuity due* is the same thing except the payments occur at the beginning of each period instead. Thus, a three-year annual annuity due would have periodic payment cash flows occurring at Years 0, 1, and 2, whereas a three-year annual ordinary annuity would have periodic payment cash flows occurring at Years 1, 2, and 3.
    a. At a 9.5 percent annual discount rate, find the present value of a six-year ordinary annuity contract of CNY 525 payments.
    b. Find the present value of the same contract if it is an annuity due.

50. **Calculating Annuities Due** You want to buy a new sports car from Muscle Motors for AUD 56,000. The contract is in the form of a 48-month annuity due at an 8.15 percent APR. What will your monthly payment be?

CHALLENGE
(Questions 51–76)

51. **Calculating Annuities Due** You want to lease a set of golf clubs from Hook N Shank. The lease contract is in the form of 24 equal monthly payments at a 12 percent stated annual interest rate, compounded monthly. Because the clubs cost $4,000 retail, Hook N Shank wants the PV of the lease payments to equal $4,000. Suppose that your first payment is due immediately. What will your monthly lease payments be?

52. **Annuities** You are saving for the college education of your two children. They are two years apart in age; one will begin college 15 years from today and the other will begin 17 years from today. You estimate your children's college expenses to be $23,000 per year per child, payable at the beginning of each school year. The annual interest rate is 5.5 percent. How much money must you deposit in an account each year to fund your children's education? Your deposits begin one year from today. You will make your last deposit when your oldest child enters college. Assume four years of college.

53. **Growing Annuities** Mitchai Khieu has received a job offer from a large investment bank as a clerk to an associate banker. His base salary will be VND 75,000. He will receive his first annual salary payment one year from the day he begins to work. In addition, he will get an immediate VND 10,000 bonus for joining the company. His salary will grow at 4 percent each year. Each year he will receive a bonus equal to 10 percent of his salary. Mr. Mitchai is expected to work for 25 years. What is the present value of the offer if the discount rate is 12 percent?

54. **Calculating Annuities** You have recently won the super jackpot in the Washington State Lottery. On reading the fine print, you discover that you have the following two options:
    a. You will receive 31 annual payments of $160,000, with the first payment being delivered today. The income will be taxed at a rate of 28 percent. Taxes will be withheld when the checks are issued.
    b. You will receive $446,000 now, and you will not have to pay taxes on this amount. In addition, beginning one year from today, you will receive $101,055 each year for 30 years. The cash flows from this annuity will be taxed at 28 percent.

    Using a discount rate of 10 percent, which option should you select?

55. **Calculating Growing Annuities** You have 30 years left until retirement and want to retire with INR 1 million. Your salary is paid annually, and you will receive INR 55,000 at the end of the current year. Your salary will increase at 3 percent per year, and you can earn a 10 percent return on the money you invest. If you save a constant percentage of your salary, what percentage of your salary must you save each year?

56. **Balloon Payments** On September 1, 2004, Tsing Chao bought a motorcycle for CNY 15,000. She paid CNY 1,000 down and financed the balance with a five-year loan at a stated annual interest rate of 9.6 percent, compounded monthly. She started the monthly payments exactly one month after the purchase (i.e., October 1, 2004). Two years later, at the end of October 2006, Tsing got a new job and decided to pay off the loan. If the bank charges her a 1 percent prepayment penalty based on the loan balance, how much must she pay the bank on November 1, 2006?

57. **Calculating Annuity Values** Bilbo Baggins wants to save money to meet three objectives. First, he would like to be able to retire 30 years from now with a retirement income of €25,000 per month for 20 years, with the first payment received 30 years and 1 month from now. Second, he would like to purchase a cabin in Rivendell in 10 years at an estimated cost of €350,000. Third, after he passes on at the end of the 20 years of withdrawals, he would like to leave an inheritance of €750,000 to his nephew Frodo. He can afford to save €2,100 per month for the next 10 years. If he can earn an 11 percent EAR before he retires and an 8 percent EAR after he retires, how much will he have to save each month in years 11 through 30?

58. **Calculating Annuity Values** After deciding to buy a new car, you can either lease the car or purchase it with a three-year loan. The car you wish to buy costs £35,000. The dealer has a special leasing arrangement where you pay £1 today and £450 per month for the next three years. If you purchase the car, you will pay it off in monthly payments over the next three years at an 8 percent APR. You believe that you will be able to sell the car for £23,000 in three years. Should you buy or lease the car? What break-even resale price in three years would make you indifferent between buying and leasing?

59. **Calculating Annuity Values** An All-Pro defensive lineman is in contract negotiations. The team has offered the following salary structure:

Time	Salary
0	$8,000,000
1	$4,000,000
2	$4,800,000
3	$5,700,000
4	$6,400,000
5	$7,000,000
6	$7,500,000

All salaries are to be paid in a lump sum. The player has asked you as his agent to renegotiate the terms. He wants a $9 million signing bonus payable today and a contract value increase of $750,000. He also wants an equal salary paid every three months, with the first paycheck three months from now. If the interest rate is 4.5 percent compounded daily, what is the amount of his quarterly check? Assume 365 days in a year.

60. **Discount Interest Loans** This question illustrates what is known as *discount interest*. Imagine you are discussing a loan with a somewhat unscrupulous lender. You want to borrow £20,000 for one year. The interest rate is 12 percent. You and the lender agree that the interest on the loan will be .12 × £20,000 = £2,400. So, the lender deducts this interest amount from the loan up front and gives you £17,600. In this case, we say that the discount is £2,400. What's wrong here?

61. **Calculating Annuity Values** You are serving on a jury. A plaintiff is suing the city for injuries sustained after a freak street sweeper accident. In the trial, doctors testified that it will be five years before the plaintiff is able to return to work. The jury has already decided in favor of the plaintiff. You are the foreperson of the jury and propose that the jury give the plaintiff an award to cover the following: (1) The present value of two years' back pay. The plaintiff's annual salary for the last two years would have been $40,000 and $43,000, respectively. (2) The present value of five years' future salary. You assume the salary will be $45,000 per year. (3) $100,000 for pain and suffering. (4) $20,000 for court costs. Assume that the salary payments are equal amounts paid at the end of each month. If the interest rate you choose is a 9 percent EAR, what is the size of the settlement? If you were the plaintiff, would you like to see a higher or lower interest rate?

62. **Calculating EAR with Points** You are looking at a one-year loan of PHP 10,000. The interest rate is quoted as 10 percent plus three points. A *point* on a loan is simply 1 percent (one percentage point) of the loan amount. Quotes similar to this one are very common with home mortgages. The interest rate quotation in this example requires the borrower to pay three points to the lender up front and repay the loan later with 10 percent interest. What rate would you actually be paying here? What is the EAR for a one-year loan with a quoted interest rate of 13 percent plus two points? Is your answer affected by the loan amount?

63. **EAR versus APR** Two banks in the area offer 30-year, €200,000 mortgages at 7.5 percent and charge a €1,500 loan application fee. However, the application fee charged by Insecurity Bank and Trust is refundable if the loan application is denied, whereas that charged by I. M. Greedy and Sons Mortgage Bank is not. The current disclosure law requires that any fees that will be refunded if the applicant is rejected be included in calculating the APR, but this is not required with nonrefundable fees (presumably because refundable fees are part of the loan rather than a fee). What are the EARs on these two loans? What are the APRs?

64. **Calculating EAR with Add-On Interest** This problem illustrates a deceptive way of quoting interest rates called *add-on interest*. Imagine that you see an advertisement for Crazy Qun's Stereo City that reads something like this: "CNY 1,000 Instant Credit! 15% Simple Interest! Three Years to Pay! Low, Low Monthly Payments!" You're not exactly sure what all this means and somebody has spilled ink over the APR on the loan contract, so you ask the manager for clarification.

Qun explains that if you borrow CNY 1,000 for three years at 15 percent interest, in three years you will owe:

$$\text{CNY } 1,000 \times 1.15^3 = \text{CNY } 1,000 \times 1.52088 = \text{CNY } 1,520.88$$

Qun recognizes that coming up with CNY 1,520.88 all at once might be a strain, so he lets you make "low, low monthly payments" of CNY 1,520.88/36 = CNY 42.25 per month, even though this is extra bookkeeping work for him.

Is this a 15 percent loan? Why or why not? What is the APR on this loan? What is the EAR? Why do you think this is called add-on interest?

65. **Calculating Annuity Payments**   This is a classic retirement problem. A time line will help in solving it. Your friend is celebrating her 35th birthday today and wants to start saving for her anticipated retirement at age 65. She wants to be able to withdraw £90,000 from her savings account on each birthday for 15 years following her retirement; the first withdrawal will be on her 66th birthday. Your friend intends to invest her money in the local credit union, which offers 8 percent interest per year. She wants to make equal annual payments on each birthday into the account established at the credit union for her retirement fund.

   a. If she starts making these deposits on her 36th birthday and continues to make deposits until she is 65 (the last deposit will be on her 65th birthday), what amount must she deposit annually to be able to make the desired withdrawals at retirement?

   b. Suppose your friend has just inherited a large sum of money. Rather than making equal annual payments, she has decided to make one lump-sum payment on her 35th birthday to cover her retirement needs. What amount does she have to deposit?

   c. Suppose your friend's employer will contribute £1,500 to the account every year as part of the company's profit-sharing plan. In addition, your friend expects a £25,000 distribution from a family trust fund on her 55th birthday, which she will also put into the retirement account. What amount must she deposit annually now to be able to make the desired withdrawals at retirement?

66. **Calculating the Number of Periods**   Your Christmas ski vacation was great, but it unfortunately ran a bit over budget. All is not lost: You just received an offer in the mail to transfer your €10,000 balance from your current credit card, which charges an annual rate of 19.2 percent, to a new credit card charging a rate of 9.2 percent. How much faster could you pay the loan off by making your planned monthly payments of €200 with the new card? What if there was a 2 percent fee charged on any balances transferred?

67. **Future Value and Multiple Cash Flows**   An insurance company is offering a new policy to its customers. Typically the policy is bought by a parent or grandparent for a child at the child's birth. The details of the policy are as follows: The purchaser (say, the parent) makes the following six payments to the insurance company:

First birthday:	$750
Second birthday:	$750
Third birthday:	$850
Fourth birthday:	$850
Fifth birthday:	$950
Sixth birthday:	$950

   After the child's sixth birthday, no more payments are made. When the child reaches age 65, he or she receives $250,000. If the relevant interest rate is 11 percent for the first six years and 7 percent for all subsequent years, is the policy worth buying?

68. **Annuity Present Values and Effective Rates**   You have just won the lottery. You will receive £1,000,000 today, and then receive 40 payments of £500,000. These payments will start one year from now and will be paid every six months. A representative from Get Rich Now has offered to purchase all the payments from you for £10 million. If the appropriate interest rate is a 9 percent APR compounded daily, should you take the offer? Assume there are 12 months in a year, each with 30 days.

69. **Calculating Interest Rates**   A financial planning service offers a college savings program. The plan calls for you to make six annual payments of $8,000 each, with the first payment occurring today, your child's 12th birthday. Beginning on your child's 18th birthday, the plan will provide $20,000 per year for four years. What return is this investment offering?

70. **Break-Even Investment Returns**   Your financial planner offers you two different investment plans. Plan X is a CAD 10,000 annual perpetuity. Plan Y is a 10-year, CAD 22,000 annual annuity. Both plans will make their first payment one year from today. At what discount rate would you be indifferent between these two plans?

71. **Perpetual Cash Flows**   What is the value of an investment that pays AUD 6,700 every *other* year forever, if the first payment occurs one year from today and the discount rate is 13 percent compounded daily? What is the value today if the first payment occurs four years from today?

72. **Ordinary Annuities and Annuities Due**   As discussed in the text, an annuity due is identical to an ordinary annuity except that the periodic payments occur at the beginning of each period and not at the end of the period. Show that the relationship between the value of an ordinary annuity and the value of an otherwise equivalent annuity due is:

$$\text{Annuity due value} = \text{Ordinary annuity value} \times (1 + r)$$

Show this for both present and future values.

73. **Calculating EAR**   A check-cashing store is in the business of making personal loans to walk-up customers. The store makes only one-week loans at 10 percent interest per week.
    a. What APR must the store report to its customers? What is the EAR that the customers are actually paying?
    b. Now suppose the store makes one-week loans at 10 percent discount interest per week (see Question 60). What's the APR now? The EAR?
    c. The check-cashing store also makes one-month add-on interest loans at 9 percent discount interest per week. Thus, if you borrow €100 for one month (four weeks), the interest will be $(€100 \times 1.09^4) - 100 = €41.16$. Because this is discount interest, your net loan proceeds today will be €58.84. You must then repay the store €100 at the end of the month. To help you out, though, the store lets you pay off this €100 in installments of €25 per week. What is the APR of this loan? What is the EAR?

74. **Present Value of a Growing Perpetuity**   What is the equation for the present value of a growing perpetuity with a payment of C one period from today if the payments grow by C each period?

75. **Rule of 72**   A useful rule of thumb for the time it takes an investment to double with discrete compounding is the "Rule of 72." To use the rule of 72, you simply divide 72 by the interest rate to determine the number of periods it takes for a value today to double. For example, if the interest rate is 6 percent, the rule of 72 say it will take $72/6 = 12$ years to double. This is approximately equal to the actual answer of 11.90 years. The Rule of 72 can also be applied to determine what interest rate is needed to double money in a specified period. This is a useful approximation for many interest rates and periods. At what rate is the Rule of 72 exact?

76. **Rule of 69.3**   A corollary to the Rule of 72 is the Rule of 69.3. The Rule of 69.3 is exactly correct except for rounding when interest rates are compounded continuously. Prove the Rule of 69.3 for continuously compounded interest.

S&P Problems

www.mhhe.com/edumarketinsight

1. Under the "Excel Analytics" link find the "Mthly. Adj. Price" for Elizabeth Arden (RDEN) stock. What was your annual return over the last four years assuming you purchased the stock at the close price four years ago? (Assume no dividends were paid.) Using this same return, what price will Elizabeth Arden stock sell for five years from now? Ten years from now? What if the stock price increases at 11 percent per year?

2. **Calculating the Number of Periods**   Find the monthly adjusted stock prices for Southwest Airlines (LUV). You find an analyst who projects the stock price will increase 12 percent per year for the foreseeable future. Based on the most recent monthly stock price, if the projection holds true, when will the stock price reach $150? When will it reach $200?

www.mhhe.com/rwj

Appendix 4A   Net Present Value: First Principles of Finance

To access the appendix for this chapter, please go to www.mhhe.com/rwj.

The MBA Decision

Ben Bates graduated from college six years ago with a finance undergraduate degree. Although he is satisfied with his current job, his goal is to become an investment banker. He feels that an MBA degree would allow him to achieve this goal. After examining schools, he has narrowed his choice to either Wilton University or Mount Perry College. Although internships are encouraged by both schools, to get class credit for the internship, no salary can be paid. Other than internships, neither school will allow its students to work while enrolled in its MBA program.

Ben currently works at the money management firm of Dewey and Louis. His annual salary at the firm is $50,000 per year, and his salary is expected to increase at 3 percent per year until retirement. He is currently 28 years old and expects to work for 35 more years. His current job includes a fully paid health insurance plan, and his current average tax rate is 26 percent. Ben has a savings account with enough money to cover the entire cost of his MBA program.

The Ritter College of Business at Wilton University is one of the top MBA programs in the country. The MBA degree requires two years of full-time enrollment at the university. The annual tuition is $60,000, payable at the beginning of each school year. Books and other supplies are estimated to cost $2,500 per year. Ben expects that after graduation from Wilton, he will receive a job offer for about $95,000 per year, with a $15,000 signing bonus. The salary at this job will increase at 4 percent per year. Because of the higher salary, his average income tax rate will increase to 31 percent.

The Bradley School of Business at Mount Perry College began its MBA program 16 years ago. The Bradley School is smaller and less well known than the Ritter College. Bradley offers an accelerated, one-year program, with a tuition cost of $75,000 to be paid upon matriculation. Books and other supplies for the program are expected to cost $3,500. Ben thinks that he will receive an offer of $78,000 per year upon graduation, with a $10,000 signing bonus. The salary at this job will increase at 3.5 percent per year. His average tax rate at this level of income will be 29 percent.

Both schools offer a health insurance plan that will cost $3,000 per year, payable at the beginning of the year. Ben also estimates that room and board expenses will cost $20,000 per year at either school. The appropriate discount rate is 6.5 percent.

1. How does Ben's age affect his decision to get an MBA?

2. What other, perhaps nonquantifiable factors affect Ben's decision to get an MBA?

3. Assuming all salaries are paid at the end of each year, what is the best option for Ben—from a strictly financial standpoint?

4. Ben believes that the appropriate analysis is to calculate the future value of each option. How would you evaluate this statement?

5. What initial salary would Ben need to receive to make him indifferent between attending Wilton University and staying in his current position?

6. Suppose, instead of being able to pay cash for his MBA, Ben must borrow the money. The current borrowing rate is 5.4 percent. How would this affect his decision?

How to Value Bonds and Stocks

When the stock market closed on January 20, 2006, the common stock of McGraw-Hill, publisher of high-quality college textbooks, was going for $49.34 per share. On that same day, Eastman Chemical closed at $49.96, while pharmaceutical benefits manager Caremark Rx closed at $50.02. Because the stock prices of these three companies were so similar, you might expect that they would be offering similar dividends to their stockholders, but you would be wrong. In fact, Eastman Chemical's dividend was $1.76 per share, McGraw-Hill's was $0.66 per share, and Caremark Rx paid no dividends at all!

As we will see in this chapter, the dividends currently being paid are one of the primary factors we look at when attempting to value common stocks. However, it is obvious from looking at Caremark that current dividends are not the end of the story, so this chapter explores dividends, stock values, and the connection between the two.

5.1 Definition and Example of a Bond

A *bond* is a certificate showing that a borrower owes a specified sum. To repay the money, the borrower has agreed to make interest and principal payments on designated dates. For example, imagine that Kreuger Enterprises just issued 100,000 bonds for $1,000 each, where the bonds have a coupon rate of 5 percent and a maturity of two years. Interest on the bonds is to be paid yearly. This means that:

1. $100 million (=100,000 × $1,000) has been borrowed by the firm.
2. The firm must pay interest of $5 million (=5% × $100 million) at the end of one year.
3. The firm must pay both $5 million of interest and $100 million of principal at the end of two years.

We now consider how to value a few different types of bonds.

5.2 How to Value Bonds

Pure Discount Bonds

The **pure discount bond** is perhaps the simplest kind of bond. It promises a single payment, say $1, at a fixed future date. If the payment is one year from now, it is called a *one-year discount bond*; if it is two years from now, it is called a *two-year discount bond*, and so on.

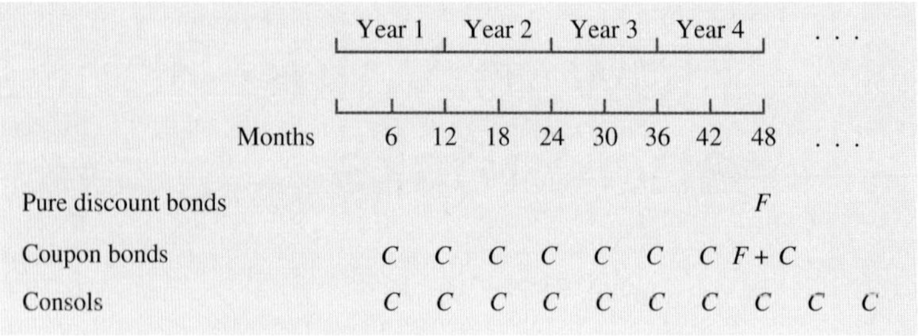

Figure 5.1

Different Types of
Bonds: *C*, Coupon
Paid Every 6 Months;
F, Face Value at
Year 4 (maturity for
pure discount and
coupon bonds)

The date when the issuer of the bond makes the last payment is called the **maturity date** of the bond, or just its *maturity* for short. The bond is said to mature or *expire* on the date of its final payment. The payment at maturity ($1 in this example) is termed the bond's **face** or **par value**.

Pure discount bonds are often called *zero coupon bonds* or *zeros* to emphasize the fact that the holder receives no cash payments until maturity. We will use the terms *zero* and *discount* interchangeably to refer to bonds that pay no coupons.

The first row of Figure 5.1 shows the pattern of cash flows from a four-year pure discount bond. Note that the face value, *F*, is paid when the bond expires in the 48th month. There are no payments of either interest or principal prior to this date.

In the previous chapter, we indicated that one discounts a future cash flow to determine its present value. The present value of a pure discount bond can easily be determined by the techniques of the previous chapter. For short, we sometimes speak of the *value* of a bond instead of its present value.

Consider a pure discount bond that pays a face value of *F* in *T* years, where the interest rate is *R* in each of the *T* years. (We also refer to this rate as the *market interest rate.*) Because the face value is the only cash flow that the bond pays, the present value of this face amount is calculated as follows:

Value of a Pure Discount Bond:

$$PV = \frac{F}{(1 + R)^T}$$

The present value formula can produce some surprising results. Suppose that the interest rate is 10 percent. Consider a bond with a face value of $1 million that matures in 20 years. Applying the formula to this bond, its PV is given by:

$$PV = \frac{\$1 \text{ million}}{(1.1)^{20}}$$
$$= \$148,644$$

or only about 15 percent of the face value.

Level Coupon Bonds

Typical bonds issued by either governments or corporations offer cash payments not just at maturity, but also at regular times in between. For example, payments on U.S. government issues and American corporate bonds are made every six months until the bonds mature.

These payments are called the **coupons** of the bond. The middle row of Figure 5.1 illustrates the case of a four-year, *level coupon bond*: The coupon, *C*, is paid every six months and is the same throughout the life of the bond.

Note that the face value of the bond, *F*, is paid at maturity (end of year 4). *F* is sometimes called the *principal* or the *denomination*. Bonds issued in the United States typically have face values of $1,000, though this can vary with the type of bond.

As we mentioned before, the value of a bond is simply the present value of its cash flows. Therefore, the value of a level coupon bond is merely the present value of its stream of coupon payments plus the present value of its repayment of principal. Because a level coupon bond is just an annuity of *C* each period, together with a payment at maturity of $1,000, the value of a level coupon bond is calculated as follows:

Value of a Level Coupon Bond:

$$PV = \frac{C}{1+R} + \frac{C}{(1+R)^2} + \cdots + \frac{C}{(1+R)^T} + \frac{\$1,000}{(1+R)^T}$$

where *C* is the coupon and the face value, *F*, is $1,000. The value of the bond can be rewritten like this:

Value of a Level Coupon Bond:

$$PV = C \times A_R^T + \frac{\$1,000}{(1+R)^T}$$

As mentioned in the previous chapter, A_R^T is the present value of an annuity of $1 per period for *T* periods at an interest rate per period of *R*.

EXAMPLE 5.1

Bond Prices   Suppose it is November 2006 and we are considering a government bond. We see in *The Wall Street Journal* some *13s* of November 2010. This is jargon that means the annual coupon rate is 13 percent.[1] The face value is $1,000, implying that the yearly coupon is $130 (=13% × $1,000). Interest is paid each May and November, implying that the coupon every six months is $65 (=$130/2). The face value will be paid out in November 2010, four years from now. By this we mean that the purchaser obtains claims to the following cash flows:

5/07	11/07	5/08	11/08	5/09	11/09	5/10	11/10
$65	$65	$65	$65	$65	$65	$65	$65 + $1,000

If the stated annual interest rate in the market is 10 percent per year, what is the present value of the bond?

Our work on compounding in the previous chapter showed that the interest rate over any six-month interval is half of the stated annual interest rate. In the current example, this semiannual rate is 5 percent (=10%/2). Because the coupon payment in each six-month period is $65, and there are

(continued)

---

[1]The coupon rate is specific to the bond. The coupon rate indicates what cash flow should appear in the numerator of the NPV equation. The coupon rate does *not* appear in the denominator of the NPV equation.

eight of these six-month periods from November 2006 to November 2010, the present value of the bond is:

$$PV = \frac{\$65}{(1.05)} + \frac{\$65}{(1.05)^2} + \cdots + \frac{\$65}{(1.05)^8} + \frac{\$1,000}{(1.05)^8}$$

$$= \$65 \times A_{0.05}^8 + \$1,000/(1.05)^8$$

$$= (\$65 \times 6.463) + (\$1,000 \times 0.677)$$

$$= \$420.095 + \$677$$

$$= \$1,097.095$$

Traders will generally quote the bond as 109.7095,[2] indicating that it is selling at 109.7095 percent of the face value of \$1,000.

At this point, it is worthwhile to relate the preceding example of bond pricing to the discussion of compounding in the previous chapter. At that time, we distinguished between the stated annual interest rate and the effective annual interest rate. In particular, we pointed out that the effective annual interest rate is:

$$(1 + R/m)^m - 1$$

where R is the stated annual interest rate and m is the number of compounding intervals. Because $R = 10\%$ and $m = 2$ (the bond makes semiannual payments), the effective annual interest rate is

$$[1 + (0.10/2)]^2 - 1 = (1.05)^2 - 1 = 10.25\%$$

In other words, because the bond is paying interest twice a year, the bondholder earns a 10.25 percent return when compounding is considered.[3]

One final note concerning level coupon bonds: Although the preceding example concerns government bonds, corporate bonds are identical in form. For example, Du Pont Corporation has a 4.75 percent bond maturing in 2012. This means that Du Pont will make semiannual payments of \$23.75 (=4.75%/2 × \$1,000) between now and 2012 for each face value of \$1,000.

Consols

Not all bonds have a final maturity date. As we mentioned in the previous chapter, consols are bonds that never stop paying a coupon, have no final maturity date, and therefore never mature. Thus, a consol is a perpetuity. In the 18th century, the Bank of England issued such bonds, called "English consols." These were bonds that the Bank of England guaranteed would pay the holder a cash flow forever! Through wars and depressions, the Bank of England continued to honor this commitment, and you can still buy such bonds in London today. The U.S. government also once sold consols to raise money to build the Panama Canal. Even though these U.S. bonds were supposed to last forever and to pay their coupons

---

[2] U.S. government bond prices are actually quoted in 32nds of a dollar, so a quote this precise would not be given for such bonds.

[3] For an excellent discussion of how to value semiannual payments, see J. T. Lindley, B. P. Helms, and M. Haddad, "A Measurement of the Errors in Intra-Period Compounding and Bond Valuation," *The Financial Review* 22 (February 1987). We benefited from several conversations with the authors of this article.

forever, don't go looking for any. There is a special clause in the bond contract that gives the government the right to buy them back from the holders, and that is what the government has done. Such clauses are known as *call provisions*, and we study them later.

An important example of a consol, though, is called *preferred stock*. Preferred stock is stock that is issued by corporations and that provides the holder a fixed dividend in perpetuity. If there were never any question that the firm would actually pay the dividend on the preferred stock, such stock would in fact be a consol.

These instruments can be valued by the perpetuity formula of the previous chapter. For example, if the marketwide interest rate is 10 percent, a consol with a yearly interest payment of $50 is valued at:

$$\frac{\$50}{0.10} = \$500$$

5.3 Bond Concepts

We complete our discussion of bonds by considering two concepts concerning them. First we examine the relationship between interest rates and bond prices. Then we define the concept of yield to maturity.

Interest Rates and Bond Prices

The discussion of level coupon bonds allows us to relate bond prices to interest rates. Consider the following example:

Bond Valuation   The interest rate is 10 percent. A two-year bond with a 10 percent coupon pays interest of $100 (=$1,000 × 10%). For simplicity we assume that the interest is paid annually. In this case, we see that the bond is priced at its face value of $1,000:

$$\$1,000 = \frac{\$100}{1.10} + \frac{\$1,000 + \$100}{(1.10)^2}$$

If the interest rate unexpectedly rises to 12 percent, the bond sells at:

$$\$966.20 = \frac{\$100}{1.12} + \frac{\$1,000 + \$100}{(1.12)^2}$$

Because $966.20 is less than $1,000, the bond is said to sell at a **discount**. This is a sensible result. Now that the interest rate is 12 percent, a newly issued bond with a 12 percent coupon rate will sell at $1,000. This newly issued bond will have coupon payments of $120 (=0.12 × $1,000). Because our bond has interest payments of only $100, investors will pay less than $1,000 for it.

If interest rates fell to 8 percent, the bond would sell at:

$$\$1,035.67 = \frac{\$100}{1.08} + \frac{\$1,000 + \$100}{(1.08)^2}$$

Because $1,035.67 is more than $1,000, the bond is said to sell at a **premium**.

Thus, we find that bond prices fall with a rise in interest rates and rise with a fall in interest rates. Furthermore, the general principle is that a level coupon bond sells in the following ways:

1. At the face value of $1,000 if the coupon rate is equal to the marketwide interest rate.
2. At a discount if the coupon rate is below the marketwide interest rate.
3. At a premium if the coupon rate is above the marketwide interest rate.

Yield to Maturity

Let's now consider the previous example *in reverse.* If our bond is selling at $1,035.67, what return is a bondholder receiving? This can be answered by considering the following equation:

$$\$1,035.67 = \frac{\$100}{1+y} + \frac{\$1,000 + \$100}{(1+y)^2}$$

The unknown, y, is the discount rate that equates the price of the bond with the discounted value of the coupons and face value. Our earlier work implies that $y = 8\%$. Thus, traders state that the bond is yielding an 8 percent return. Bond traders also state that the bond has a **yield to maturity** of 8 percent. The yield to maturity is frequently called the bond's *yield* for short. So, we would say the bond with its 10 percent coupon is priced to yield 8 percent at $1,035.67.

Bond Market Reporting

In 2002, data availability in the corporate bond market began to improve dramatically. Under new regulations, corporate bond dealers are now required to report trade information through what is known as the Transactions Report and Compliance Engine (TRACE). As this is written, transaction prices are now reported for more than 4,000 bonds. More bonds will be added over time.

The Present Value Formulas for Bonds

Pure Discount Bonds

$$PV = \frac{F}{(1+R)^T}$$

Level Coupon Bonds

$$PV = C\left[\frac{1}{R} - \frac{1}{R \times (1+R)^T}\right] + \frac{F}{(1+R)^T} = C \times A_R^T + \frac{F}{(1+R)^T}$$

where F is typically $1,000 for a level coupon bond.

Consols

$$PV = \frac{C}{R}$$

Figure 5.2

Sample *Wall Street Journal* Bond Quotation

SOURCE: Reprinted by permission of *The Wall Street Journal*, via Copyright Clearance Center. © 2006 Dow Jones and Company, Inc., January 19, 2006. All Rights Reserved Worldwide.

Corporate Bonds

Thursday, January 19, 2006

Forty most active fixed-coupon corporate bonds

COMPANY (TICKER)	COUPON	MATURITY	LAST PRICE	LAST YIELD	*EST SPREAD	UST†	EST $ VOL (000's)
Goldman Sachs Group Inc (GS)	4.500	Jun 15, 2010	97.984	5.016	71	5	116,790
JPMorgan Chase (JPM)	5.150	Oct 01, 2015	98.935	5.291	92	10	114,535
Wal-Mart Stores Inc (WMT)	5.250	Sep 01, 2035	97.286	5.435	89	30	106,785
Virginia Electric and Power Co (D)	6.000	Jan 15, 2036	101.113	5.920	138	30	102,050
Ameriprise Financial Inc (AMP)	5.650	Nov 15, 2015	101.670	5.427	105	10	78,419
Ameriprise Financial Inc (AMP)	5.350	Nov 15, 2010	101.107	5.086	78	5	77,720
AT&T Inc (SBC)	5.100	Sep 15, 2014	97.828	5.417	104	10	72,859
Telecom Italia Capital (TITIM)	6.375	Nov 15, 2033	100.195	6.359	181	30	71,279
Tyco International Group SA (TYC)	6.375	Oct 15, 2011	104.961	5.355	105	5	69,148
Marsh & McLennan Companies Inc (MMC)	5.150	Sep 15, 2010	99.773	5.204	90	5	68,850
COX Communications Inc (COXENT)	7.125	Oct 01, 2012	106.810	5.876	149	5	65,891
Mohawk Industries Inc (MHK)	6.125	Jan 15, 2016	101.159	5.969	159	10	65,400
Time Warner Inc (TWX)	7.700	May 01, 2032	113.181	6.632	209	30	63,575
iStar Financial Inc (SFI)	5.375	Apr 15, 2010	99.981	5.378	107	5	60,530
Kroger Co (KR)	5.500	Feb 01, 2013	98.542	5.755	138	10	58,626
Ohio Power Co (AEP)	5.500	Feb 15, 2013	101.661	5.215	84	10	55,150
Kroger Co (KR)	7.500	Apr 01, 2031	112.406	6.492	195	30	54,720
Toyota Motor Credit Corp (TOYOTA)	5.125	Jan 11, 2011	99.930	5.141	83	5	54,000
General Electric Capital Corp (GE)	5.875	Feb 15, 2012	104.601	4.985	61	5	53,751
Time Warner Inc (TWX)	6.875	May 01, 2012	106.527	5.623	124	5	53,436
Vale Overseas Ltd (VALE)	6.250	Jan 11, 2016	100.600	6.168	179	10	52,735
Morgan Stanley (MWD)	5.050	Jan 21, 2011	100.030	5.036	73	5	51,415
HSBC Finance Corp (HSBC)	4.625	Jan 15, 2008	99.514	4.885	53	2	51,115
Albertson's Inc (ABS)	8.000	May 01, 2031	99.093	8.083	353	30	50,549
United Technologies Corp (UTX)	7.125	Nov 15, 2010	109.487	4.885	58	5	50,420
Convergys Corp (CVG)	4.875	Dec 15, 2009	96.769	5.813	150	5	50,400
General Electric Capital Corp (GE)	6.125	Feb 22, 2011	105.465	4.895	59	5	49,912
Bear Stearns Companies Inc (BSC)	6.500	May 01, 2006	100.506	4.531	n.a.	n.a.	49,769
Wal-Mart Stores Inc (WMT)	4.550	May 01, 2013	97.800	4.912	54	10	49,352
Fortune Brands Inc (FO)	5.375	Jan 15, 2016	99.287	5.468	109	10	48,700
Lear Corp (LEA)	5.750	Aug 01, 2014	79.125	9.359	499	10	48,466
HSBC Finance Corp (HSBC)	5.500	Jan 19, 2016	100.418	5.445	107	10	48,195
Wells Fargo (WFC)	4.875	Jan 12, 2011	99.919	4.893	57	5	46,830
BellSouth Corp (BLS)	5.200	Sep 15, 2014	99.587	5.259	89	10	45,588
Johnson Controls Inc (JCI)	5.250	Jan 15, 2011	100.351	5.169	86	5	45,325
Comcast Corp (CMCSA)	4.950	Jun 15, 2016	93.867	5.741	137	10	44,279
GlaxoSmithKline Capital Inc (GSK)	4.375	Apr 15, 2014	96.153	4.949	58	10	43,249
WellPoint Inc (WLP)	5.850	Jan 15, 2036	101.016	5.778	123	30	42,600
Countrywide Home Loans Inc (CFC)	5.500	Feb 01, 2007	100.539	4.950	n.a.	n.a.	41,744
GlaxoSmithKline Capital Inc (GSK)	2.375	Apr 16, 2007	97.254	4.700	34	2	41,704
Time Warner Companies Inc (TWX)	9.150	Feb 01, 2023	122.903	6.850	230	30	41,109

Volume represents total volume for each issue; price/yield data are for trades of $1 million and greater. * Estimated spreads, in basis points (100 basis points is one percentage point), over the 2, 3, 5, 10 or 30-year hot run Treasury note/bond. 2-year: 4.375 12/07; 3-year: 4.375 11/08; 5-year: 4.250 01/11; 10-year: 4.500 11/15; 30-year: 5.375 02/31. †Comparable U.S. Treasury issue.

Source: MarketAxess Corporate BondTicker

To learn more about TRACE, visit **www.nasd.com**.

TRACE bond quotes are available at www.nasdbondinfo.com. We went to the site and entered "Deere" for the well-known manufacturer of green tractors. We found a total of eight bond issues outstanding. Here you can see the information we found for three of these:

Issue: DE.GG DEERE & CO. 7.125 03/03/2031			Time and Sales	Descriptive Data	
In Portfolio	Rating Moody's/S&P/Fitch	Date	Last Sale Price	Yield	Most Recent Date	Price	Yield
☐	A3 / A- / A	01/20/2006	122.333	5.476993	01/20/2006	122.33	5.476993

Issue: DE.GA DEERE & COMPANY 8.95 06/15/2019			Time and Sales	Descriptive Data	
In Portfolio	Rating Moody's/S&P/Fitch	Date	Last Sale Price	Yield	Most Recent Date	Price	Yield
☐	A3 / A- / A	01/20/2006	113.50	4.599	01/20/2006	113.50	4.599

Issue: DE.GB DEERE & COMPANY 8.50 01/09/2022			Time and Sales	Descriptive Data	
In Portfolio	Rating Moody's/S&P/Fitch	Date	Last Sale Price	Yield	Most Recent Date	Price	Yield
☐	A3 / A- / A	01/05/2006	132.115	5.463	01/05/2006	132.12	5.463

Most of the information is self-explanatory. The price and yield columns show the price and yield to maturity of the most recent sales. Notice the last sale dates for the issue maturing in 2022. This bond had not had a reported trade for the last two weeks. A great feature of this Web site is the "Descriptive Data" link, which gives you more information about the bond issue such as call dates and coupon dates.

As shown in Figure 5.2, *The Wall Street Journal* provides a daily snapshot of the data from TRACE by reporting the 40 most active issues. The information reported is again largely self-explanatory. The EST Spread is the estimated yield spread over a particular U.S. Treasury issue (a yield spread is just the difference in yields). The spread is reported in basis points, where 1 basis point is equal to .01 percent. The selected Treasury issue's maturity is given under UST, which is a standard abbreviation in the bond markets for U.S. Treasury. A "hot run" Treasury is the most recently issued of a particular maturity, better known as an on-the-run issue. Finally, the reported volume is the face value of bonds traded.

5.4   The Present Value of Common Stocks

Dividends versus Capital Gains

Our goal in this section is to value common stocks. We learned in the previous chapter that an asset's value is determined by the present value of its future cash flows. A stock provides two kinds of cash flows. First, stocks often pay dividends on a regular basis. Second, the stockholder receives the sale price when selling the stock. Thus, to value common stocks, we need to answer an interesting question. Which of the following is the value of a stock equal to?

1. The discounted present value of the sum of next period's dividend plus next period's stock price.
2. The discounted present value of all future dividends.

This is the kind of question that students would love to see on a multiple-choice exam: Both (1) and (2) are right.

To see that (1) and (2) are the same, let's start with an individual who will buy the stock and hold it for one year. In other words, she has a one-year *holding period*. In addition, she is willing to pay P_0 for the stock today. That is, she calculates:

$$P_0 = \frac{\text{Div}_1}{1 + R} + \frac{P_1}{1 + R} \tag{5.1}$$

Div_1 is the dividend paid at year's end, and P_1 is the price at year's end. P_0 is the PV of the common stock investment. The term in the denominator, R, is the appropriate discount rate for the stock.

That seems easy enough; but where does P_1 come from? P_1 is not pulled out of thin air. Rather, there must be a buyer at the end of year 1 who is willing to purchase the stock for P_1. This buyer determines price as follows:

$$P_1 = \frac{\text{Div}_2}{1 + R} + \frac{P_2}{1 + R} \tag{5.2}$$

Substituting the value of P_1 from Equation 5.2 into Equation 5.1 yields:

$$\begin{aligned} P_0 &= \frac{1}{1+R}\left[\text{Div}_1 + \left(\frac{\text{Div}_2 + P_2}{1+R}\right)\right] \\ &= \frac{\text{Div}_1}{1+R} + \frac{\text{Div}_2}{(1+R)^2} + \frac{P_2}{(1+R)^2} \end{aligned} \tag{5.3}$$

We can ask a similar question for Equation 5.3: Where does P_2 come from? An investor at the end of year 2 is willing to pay P_2 because of the dividend and stock price at year 3. This process can be repeated *ad nauseam*.[4] At the end, we are left with this:

$$P_0 = \frac{\text{Div}_1}{1+R} + \frac{\text{Div}_2}{(1+R)^2} + \frac{\text{Div}_3}{(1+R)^3} + \cdots = \sum_{t=1}^{\infty} \frac{\text{Div}_t}{(1+R)^t} \qquad (5.4)$$

Thus, the value of a firm's common stock to the investor is equal to the present value of all of the expected future dividends.

This is a very useful result. A common objection to applying present value analysis to stocks is that investors are too shortsighted to care about the long-run stream of dividends. These critics argue that an investor will generally not look past his or her time horizon. Thus, prices in a market dominated by short-term investors will reflect only near-term dividends. However, our discussion shows that a long-run dividend discount model holds even when investors have short-term time horizons. Although an investor may want to cash out early, she must find another investor who is willing to buy. The price this second investor pays is dependent on dividends *after* his date of purchase.

Valuation of Different Types of Stocks

The preceding discussion shows that the value of the firm is the present value of its future dividends. How do we apply this idea in practice? Equation 5.4 represents a very general model and is applicable regardless of whether the level of expected dividends is growing, fluctuating, or constant. The general model can be simplified if the firm's dividends are expected to follow some basic patterns: (1) zero growth, (2) constant growth, and (3) differential growth. These cases are illustrated in Figure 5.3.

Case 1 (Zero Growth)   The value of a stock with a constant dividend is given by

$$P_0 = \frac{\text{Div}_1}{1 + R} + \frac{\text{Div}_2}{(1 + R)^2} + \cdots = \frac{\text{Div}_1}{R}$$

Here it is assumed that $\text{Div}_1 = \text{Div}_2 = \cdots = \text{Div}$. This is just an application of the perpetuity formula from a previous chapter.

Case 2 (Constant Growth)   Dividends grow at rate g, as follows:

End of Year Dividend:				
1	2	3	4	$\cdots$
Div_1	$\text{Div}_1(1 + g)$	$\text{Div}_1(1 + g)^2$	$\text{Div}_1(1 + g)^3$	

Note that Div_1 is the dividend at the end of the *first* period.

---

[4]This procedure reminds us of the physicist lecturing about the origins of the universe. He was approached by an elderly gentleman in the audience who disagreed with the lecture. The attendee said that the universe rests on the back of a huge turtle. When the physicist asked what the turtle rested on, the gentleman said another turtle. Anticipating the physicist's objections, the attendee said, "Don't tire yourself out, young fellow. It's turtles all the way down."

Figure 5.3

Zero Growth,
Constant Growth, and
Differential Growth
Patterns

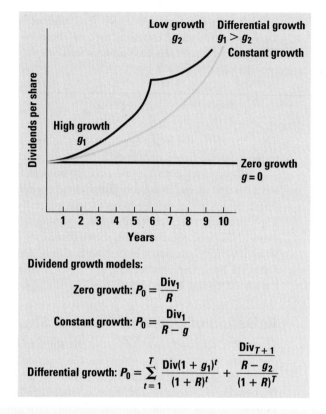

Dividend growth models:

Zero growth: $P_0 = \dfrac{Div_1}{R}$

Constant growth: $P_0 = \dfrac{Div_1}{R - g}$

Differential growth: $P_0 = \displaystyle\sum_{t=1}^{T} \dfrac{Div(1 + g_1)^t}{(1 + R)^t} + \dfrac{\dfrac{Div_{T+1}}{R - g_2}}{(1 + R)^T}$

EXAMPLE 5.3

Projected Dividends   Hampshire Products will pay a dividend of \$4 per share a year from now. Financial analysts believe that dividends will rise at 6 percent per year for the foreseeable future. What is the dividend per share at the end of each of the first five years? With 6 percent growth we have this:

End of Year Dividend:

1	2	3	4	5
\$4.00	$\$4 \times (1.06)$	$\$4 \times (1.06)^2$	$\$4 \times (1.06)^3$	$\$4 \times (1.06)^4$
	= \$4.24	= \$4.4944	= \$4.7641	= \$5.0499

The value of a common stock with dividends growing at a constant rate is

$$P_0 = \frac{Div_1}{1 + R} + \frac{Div_1\,(1 + g)}{(1 + R)^2} + \frac{Div_1\,(1 + g)^2}{(1 + R)^3} + \frac{Div_1\,(1 + g)^3}{(1 + R)^4} + \cdots = \frac{Div_1}{R - g}$$

where g is the growth rate. Div_1 is the dividend on the stock at the end of the first period. This is the formula for the present value of a growing perpetuity, which we derived in a previous chapter.

EXAMPLE 5.4

Stock Valuation   Suppose an investor is considering the purchase of a share of the Utah Mining Company. The stock will pay a \$3 dividend a year from today. This dividend is expected to grow at 10 percent per year ($g = 10\%$) for the foreseeable future. The investor thinks that the required return (R) on this stock is 15 percent, given her assessment of Utah Mining's risk. (We also refer to R as the discount rate for the stock.) What is the value of a share of Utah Mining Company's stock?

Using the constant growth formula of case 2, we assess the value to be \$60:

$$\$60 = \frac{\$3}{.15 - .10}$$

(continued)

P_0 is quite dependent on the value of g. If g had been estimated to be 12.5 percent, the value of the share would have been:

$$\$120 = \frac{\$3}{.15 - .125}$$

The stock price doubles (from \$60 to \$120) when g increases only 25 percent (from 10 percent to 12.5 percent). Because of P_0's dependence on g, one must maintain a healthy sense of skepticism when using this constant growth of dividends model.

Furthermore, note that P_0 is equal to infinity when the growth rate, g, equals the discount rate, R. Because stock prices do not grow infinitely, an estimate of g greater than R implies an error in estimation. More will be said about this point later.

Case 3 (Differential Growth) In this case, an algebraic formula would be too unwieldy. Instead we present examples.

Differential Growth Consider the stock of Elixir Drug Company, which has a new massage ointment and is enjoying rapid growth. The dividend for a share of stock a year from today will be \$1.15. During the following four years the dividend will grow at 15 percent per year ($g_1 = 15\%$). After that, growth (g_2) will equal 10 percent per year. Can you calculate the present value of the stock if the required return (R) is 15 percent?

Figure 5.4 displays the growth in the dividends. We need to apply a two-step process to discount these dividends. We first calculate the net present value of the dividends growing at 15 percent per annum. That is, we first calculate the present value of the dividends at the end of each of the first five years. Second, we calculate the present value of the dividends that begin at the end of year 6.

Figure 5.4

Growth in Dividends for Elixir Drug Company

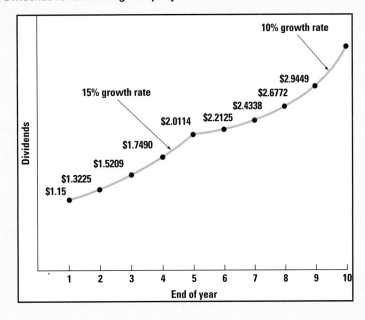

(continued)

Calculate Present Value of First Five Dividends   The present value of dividend payments in years 1 through 5 is as follows:

Future Year	Growth Rate (g_1)	Expected Dividend	Present Value
1	.15	$1.15	$1
2	.15	1.3225	1
3	.15	1.5209	1
4	.15	1.7490	1
5	.15	2.0114	1
Years 1–5	The present value of dividends = $5		

The growing annuity formula of the previous chapter could normally be used in this step. However, note that dividends grow at 15 percent, which is also the discount rate. Because $g = R$, the growing annuity formula cannot be used in this example.

Calculate Present Value of Dividends Beginning at End of Year 6   This is the procedure for deferred perpetuities and deferred annuities that we mentioned in the previous chapter. The dividends beginning at the end of year 6 are as follows:

End of Year Dividend:			
6	7	8	9
$\text{Div}_5 \times (1 + g_2)$	$\text{Div}_5 \times (1 + g_2)^2$	$\text{Div}_5 \times (1 + g_2)^3$	$\text{Div}_5 \times (1 + g_2)^4$
$\$2.0114 \times 1.10$	$\$2.0114 \times (1.10)^2$	$\$2.0114 \times (1.10)^3$	$\$2.0114 \times (1.10)^4$
$= \$2.2125$	$= \$2.4338$	$= \$2.6772$	$= \$2.9449$

As stated in the previous chapter, the growing perpetuity formula calculates present value as of one year prior to the first payment. Because the payment begins at the end of year 6, the present value formula calculates present value as of the end of year 5.

The price at the end of year 5 is given by

$$P_5 = \frac{\text{Div}_6}{R - g_2} = \frac{\$2.2125}{.15 - .10}$$
$$= \$44.25$$

The present value of P_5 today is

$$\frac{P_5}{(1 + R)^5} = \frac{\$44.25}{(1.15)^5} = \$22$$

The present value of *all* dividends today is $27 (= $22 + 5).

5.5 Estimates of Parameters in the Dividend Growth Model

The value of the firm is a function of its growth rate, g, and its discount rate, R. How do we estimate these variables?

Where Does g Come From?

The previous discussion of stocks assumed that dividends grow at the rate *g*. We now want to estimate this rate of growth. This section extends the discussion of growth contained in Chapter 3. Consider a business whose earnings next year are expected to be the same as earnings this year unless a *net investment* is made. This situation is likely to occur because net investment is equal to gross, or total, investment less depreciation. A net investment of zero occurs when *total investment* equals depreciation. If total investment is equal to depreciation, the firm's physical plant is maintained, consistent with no growth in earnings.

Net investment will be positive only if some earnings are not paid out as dividends—that is, only if some earnings are retained.[5] This leads to the following equation:

$$
\underset{\text{year}}{\underset{\text{next}}{\text{Earnings}}} = \underset{\text{year}}{\underset{\text{this}}{\text{Earnings}}} + \underbrace{\underset{\text{this year}}{\underset{\text{earnings}}{\text{Retained}}} \times \underset{\text{earnings}}{\underset{\text{retained}}{\text{Return on}}}}_{\text{Increase in earnings}} \qquad \textbf{(5.5)}
$$

The increase in earnings is a function of both the *retained earnings* and the *return on the retained earnings.*

We now divide both sides of Equation 5.5 by earnings this year, yielding

$$
\frac{\text{Earnings next year}}{\text{Earnings this year}} = \frac{\text{Earnings this year}}{\text{Earnings this year}} + \left(\frac{\text{Retained earnings this year}}{\text{Earnings this year}} \right) \qquad \textbf{(5.6)}
$$
$$
\times \text{Return on retained earnings}
$$

The left side of Equation 5.6 is simply 1 plus the growth rate in earnings, which we write as $1 + g$. The ratio of retained earnings to earnings is called the **retention ratio**. Thus we can write

$$
1 + g = 1 + \text{Retention ratio} \times \text{Return on retained earnings} \qquad \textbf{(5.7)}
$$

It is difficult for a financial analyst to determine the return to be expected on currently retained earnings: The details on forthcoming projects are not generally public information. However, it is frequently assumed that the projects selected in the current year have an anticipated return equal to returns from projects in other years. Here we can estimate the anticipated return on current retained earnings by the historical **return on equity** or ROE. After all, ROE is simply the return on the firm's entire equity, which is the return on the cumulation of all the firm's past projects.

From Equation 5.7, we have a simple way to estimate growth:

Formula for Firm's Growth Rate:
$$
g = \text{Retention ratio} \times \text{Return on retained earnings} \qquad \textbf{(5.8)}
$$

Previously, *g* referred to growth in dividends. However, the growth in earnings is equal to the growth rate in dividends in this context, because as we will presently see, the ratio of dividends to earnings is held constant. In fact, as you have probably figured out, *g* is the sustainable growth rate we introduced in Chapter 3.

---

[5]We ignore the possibility of the issuance of stocks or bonds to raise capital. These possibilities are considered in later chapters.

Earnings Growth   Pagemaster Enterprises just reported earnings of $2 million. It plans to retain 40 percent of its earnings. The historical return on equity (ROE) has been 16 percent, a figure that is expected to continue into the future. How much will earnings grow over the coming year?

We first perform the calculation without reference to Equation 5.8. Then, we use Equation 5.8 as a check.

Calculation without Reference to Equation 5.8   The firm will retain $800,000 (=40% × $2 million). Assuming that historical ROE is an appropriate estimate for future returns, the anticipated increase in earnings is:

$$\$800,000 \times .16 = \$128,000$$

The percentage growth in earnings is:

$$\frac{\text{Change in earnings}}{\text{Total earnings}} = \frac{\$128,000}{\$2 \text{ million}} = .064$$

This implies that earnings in one year will be $2,128,000 (= $2,000,000 × 1.064).

Check Using Equation 5.8   We use g = Retention ratio × ROE. We have:

$$g = .4 \times .16 = .064$$

Where Does R Come From?

Thus far, we have taken the required return, or discount rate R, as given. We will have quite a bit to say about this subject in later chapters. For now, we want to examine the implications of the dividend growth model for this required return. Earlier we calculated P_0 as follows:

$$P_0 = \text{Div}_1/(R - g)$$

If we rearrange this to solve for R, we get:

$$R - g = \text{Div}_1/P_0$$
$$R = \text{Div}_1/P_0 + g \tag{5.9}$$

This tells us that the total return, R, has two components. The first of these, Div_1/P_0, is called the **dividend yield**. Because this is calculated as the expected cash dividend divided by the current price, it is conceptually similar to the current yield on a bond, which is the annual coupon divided by the bond's price.

The second part of the total return is the growth rate, g. As we will verify shortly, the dividend growth rate is also the rate at which the stock price grows. Thus, this growth rate can be interpreted as the **capital gains yield**—that is, the rate at which the value of the investment grows.

To illustrate the components of the required return, suppose we observe a stock selling for $20 per share. The next dividend will be $1 per share. You think that the dividend will grow by 10 percent per year more or less indefinitely. What return does this stock offer you if this is correct?

The dividend growth model calculates total return as:

$$R = \text{Dividend yield} + \text{Capital gains yield}$$
$$R = \text{Div}_1/P_0 \quad + \quad g$$

In this case, total return works out to be:

$$R = \$1/20 + 10\%$$
$$= 5\% + 10\%$$
$$= 15\%$$

This stock, therefore, has an expected return of 15 percent.

We can verify this answer by calculating the price in one year, P_1, using 15 percent as the required return. Based on the dividend growth model, this price is:

$$P_1 = \text{Div}_1 \times (1 + g)/(R - g)$$
$$= \$1 \times 1.10/(.15 - .10)$$
$$= \$1.10/.05$$
$$= \$22$$

Notice that this $22 is $20 × 1.1, so the stock price has grown by 10 percent as it should. If you pay $20 for the stock today, you will get a $1 dividend at the end of the year, and you will have a $22 − 20 = $2 gain. Your dividend yield is thus $1/20 = 5 percent. Your capital gains yield is $2/20 = 10 percent, so your total return would be 5 percent + 10 percent = 15 percent.

To get a feel for actual numbers in this context, consider that, according to the 2006 Value Line *Investment Survey*, Procter & Gamble's dividends were expected to grow by 9.5 percent over the next 5 or so years, compared to a historical growth rate of 10.5 percent over the preceding 5 years and 11.5 percent over the preceding 10 years. In 2006, the projected dividend for the coming year was given as $1.12. The stock price at that time was about $58 per share. What is the return investors require on P&G? Here the dividend yield is 1.9 percent and the capital gains yield is 9.5 percent, giving a total required return of 11.4 percent on P&G stock.

EXAMPLE 5.7

Calculating the Required Return Pagemaster Enterprises, the company examined in the previous example, has 1,000,000 shares of stock outstanding. The stock is selling at $10. What is the required return on the stock?

Because the retention ratio is 40 percent, the **payout ratio** is 60 percent ($= 1 -$ retention ratio). The payout ratio is the ratio of dividends/earnings. Because earnings a year from now will be $2,128,000 ($= \$2,000,000 \times 1.064$), dividends will be $1,276,800 ($= .60 \times \$2,128,000$). Dividends per share will be $1.28 ($= \$1,276,800/1,000,000$). Given our previous result that $g = .064$, we calculate R from (5.9) as follows:

$$.192 = \frac{\$1.28}{10.00} + .064$$

A Healthy Sense of Skepticism

It is important to emphasize that our approach merely *estimates g*; our approach does not *determine g* precisely. We mentioned earlier that our estimate of g is based on a number of assumptions. For example, we assume that the return on reinvestment of future retained earnings is equal to the firm's past ROE. We assume that the future retention ratio is equal to the past retention ratio. Our estimate for g will be off if these assumptions prove to be wrong.

Unfortunately, the determination of R is highly dependent on g. For example, if g is estimated to be 0 in our example, R equals 12.8 percent ($= \$1.28/\$10.00$). If g is estimated to be 12 percent, R equals 24.8 percent ($= \$1.28/\$10.00 + 12\%$). Thus, one should view estimates of R with a healthy sense of skepticism.

Because of the preceding, some financial economists generally argue that the estimation error for R or a single security is too large to be practical. Therefore, they suggest calculating the average R for an entire industry. This R would then be used to discount the dividends of a particular stock in the same industry.

One should be particularly skeptical of two polar cases when estimating R for individual securities. First, consider a firm currently paying no dividend. The stock price will be above zero because investors believe that the firm may initiate a dividend at some point or the firm may be acquired at some point. However, when a firm goes from no dividends to a positive number of dividends, the implied growth rate is *infinite*. Thus, Equation 5.9 must be used with extreme caution here, if at all—a point we emphasize later in this chapter.

Second, we mentioned earlier that the value of the firm is infinite when g is equal to R. Because prices for stocks do not grow infinitely, an analyst whose estimate of g for a particular firm is equal to or above R must have made a mistake. Most likely the analyst's high estimate for g is correct for the next few years. However, firms simply cannot maintain an abnormally high growth rate *forever*. The analyst's error was to use a short-run estimate of g in a model requiring a perpetual growth rate.

5.6 Growth Opportunities

We previously spoke of the growth rate of dividends. We now want to address the related concept of growth opportunities. Imagine a company with a level stream of earnings per share in perpetuity. The company pays all of these earnings out to stockholders as dividends. Hence we have:

$$\text{EPS} = \text{Div}$$

where EPS is *earnings per share* and Div is dividends per share. A company of this type is frequently called a *cash cow*.

The perpetuity formula of the previous chapter gives the value of a share of stock:

Value of a Share of Stock When a Firm Acts as a Cash Cow:
$$\frac{\text{EPS}}{R} = \frac{\text{Div}}{R}$$

where R is the discount rate on the firm's stock.

This policy of paying out all earnings as dividends may not be the optimal one. Many firms have *growth* opportunities: opportunities to invest in profitable projects. Because these projects can represent a significant fraction of the firm's value, it would be foolish to forgo them in order to pay out all earnings as dividends.

Although firms frequently think in terms of a *set* of growth opportunities, let's focus on only one opportunity—that is, the opportunity to invest in a single project. Suppose the firm retains the entire dividend at date 1 to invest in a particular capital budgeting project. The net present value *per share* of the project as of date 0 is *NPVGO*, which stands for the *net present value (per share) of the growth opportunity.*

What is the price of a share of stock at date 0 if the firm decides to take on the project at date 1? Because the per share value of the project is added to the original stock price, the stock price must now be this:

Stock Price after Firm Commits to New Project:
$$\frac{\text{EPS}}{R} + \text{NPVGO} \tag{5.10}$$

Thus Equation 5.10 indicates that the price of a share of stock can be viewed as the sum of two different items. The first term (EPS/R) is the value of the firm if it rested on its laurels—that is, if it simply distributed all earnings to the stockholders. The second term is the *additional* value if the firm retains earnings to fund new projects.

EXAMPLE 5.8

Growth Opportunities   Sarro Shipping, Inc., expects to earn $1 million per year in perpetuity if it undertakes no new investment opportunities. There are 100,000 shares of stock outstanding, so earnings per share equal $10 (=$1,000,000/100,000). The firm will have an opportunity at date 1 to spend $1,000,000 on a new marketing campaign. The new campaign will increase earnings in every subsequent period by $210,000 (or $2.10 per share). This is a 21 percent return per year on the project. The firm's discount rate is 10 percent. What is the value per share before and after deciding to accept the marketing campaign?

The value of a share of Sarro Shipping before the campaign is

Value of a Share of Sarro When Firm Acts as a Cash Cow:

$$\frac{EPS}{R} = \frac{\$10}{.1} = \$100$$

The value of the marketing campaign as of date 1 is

Value of Marketing Campaign at Date 1:

$$-\$1,000,000 + \frac{\$210,000}{.1} = \$1,100,000 \qquad (5.11)$$

Because the investment is made at date 1 and the first cash inflow occurs at date 2, Equation 5.11 represents the value of the marketing campaign as of date 1. We determine the value at date 0 by discounting back one period as follows:

Value of Marketing Campaign at Date 0:

$$\frac{\$1,100,000}{1.1} = \$1,000,000$$

Thus NPVGO per share is $10 (=$1,000,000/100,000).

The price per share is

$$EPS/R + NPVGO = \$100 + 10 = \$110$$

The calculation in our example can also be made on a straight net present value basis. Because all the earnings at date 1 are spent on the marketing effort, no dividends are paid to stockholders at that date. Dividends in all subsequent periods are $1,210,000 (=$1,000,000 + $210,000). In this case $1,000,000 is the annual dividend when Sarro is a cash cow. The additional contribution to the dividend from the marketing effort is $210,000. Dividends per share are $12.10 (=$1,210,000/100,000). Because these dividends start at date 2, the price per share at date 1 is $121 (=$12.10/.1). The price per share at date 0 is $110 (=$121/1.1).

Note that value is created in this example because the project earned a 21 percent rate of return when the discount rate was only 10 percent. No value would have been created had the project earned a 10 percent rate of return. The NPVGO would have been zero, and value would have been negative had the project earned a percentage return below 10 percent. The NPVGO would be negative in that case.

Two conditions must be met in order to increase value:

1. Earnings must be retained so that projects can be funded.[6]
2. The projects must have positive net present value.

Surprisingly, a number of companies seem to invest in projects known to have *negative* net present values. For example, in the late 1970s, oil companies and tobacco companies were flush with cash. Due to declining markets in both industries, high dividends and low investment would have been the rational action. Unfortunately, a number of companies in both industries reinvested heavily in what were widely perceived to be negative NPVGO projects.

Given that NPV analysis (such as that presented in the previous chapter) is common knowledge in business, why would managers choose projects with negative NPVs? One conjecture is that some managers enjoy controlling a large company. Because paying dividends in lieu of reinvesting earnings reduces the size of the firm, some managers find it emotionally difficult to pay high dividends.

Growth in Earnings and Dividends versus Growth Opportunities

As mentioned earlier, a firm's value increases when it invests in growth opportunities with positive NPVGOs. A firm's value falls when it selects opportunities with negative NPVGOs. However, dividends grow whether projects with positive NPVs or negative NPVs are selected. This surprising result can be explained by the following example.

EXAMPLE 5.9

NPV versus Dividends   Lane Supermarkets, a new firm, will earn $100,000 a year in perpetuity if it pays out all its earnings as dividends. However, the firm plans to invest 20 percent of its earnings in projects that earn 10 percent per year. The discount rate is 18 percent. An earlier formula tells us that the growth rate of dividends is:

$$g = \text{Retention ratio} \times \text{Return on retained earnings} = .2 \times .10 = 2\%$$

For example, in this first year of the new policy, dividends are $80,000 [$= (1 - .2) \times \$100,000$]. Dividends next year are $81,600 ($= \$80,000 \times 1.02$). Dividends the following year are $83,232 [$= \$80,000 \times (1.02)^2$] and so on. Because dividends represent a fixed percentage of earnings, earnings must grow at 2 percent a year as well.

However, note that the policy reduces value because the rate of return on the projects of 10 percent is less than the discount rate of 18 percent. That is, the firm would have had a higher value at date 0 if it had a policy of paying all its earnings out as dividends. Thus, a policy of investing in projects with negative NPVs rather than paying out earnings as dividends will lead to growth in dividends and earnings, but will reduce value.

Dividends or Earnings: Which to Discount?

As mentioned earlier, this chapter applied the growing perpetuity formula to the valuation of stocks. In our application, we discounted dividends, not earnings. This is sensible because investors select a stock for what they can get out of it. They get only two things out of a stock: dividends and the ultimate sale price, which is determined by what future investors expect to receive in dividends.

---

[6]Later in the text, we speak of issuing stock or debt to fund projects.

The calculated stock price would be too high were earnings to be discounted instead of dividends. As we saw in our estimation of a firm's growth rate, only a portion of earnings goes to the stockholders as dividends. The remainder is retained to generate future dividends. In our model, retained earnings are equal to the firm's investment. To discount earnings instead of dividends would be to ignore the investment a firm must make today to generate future returns.

The No-Dividend Firm

Students frequently ask the following questions: If the dividend discount model is correct, why aren't no-dividend stocks selling at zero? This is a good question and gets at the goals of the firm. A firm with many growth opportunities faces a dilemma. The firm can pay out dividends now, or it can forgo dividends now so that it can make investments that will generate even greater dividends in the future.[7] This is often a painful choice because a strategy of dividend deferment may be optimal yet unpopular among certain stockholders.

Many firms choose to pay no dividends—and these firms sell at positive prices. For example, most Internet firms, such as Amazon.com, Google, and eBay, pay no dividends. Rational shareholders believe that either they will receive dividends at some point or they will receive something just as good. That is, the firm will be acquired in a merger, with the stockholders receiving either cash or shares of stock at that time.

Of course, the actual application of the dividend discount model is difficult for firms of this type. Clearly the model for constant growth of dividends does not apply. Though the differential growth model can work in theory, the difficulties of estimating the date of first dividend, the growth rate of dividends after that date, and the ultimate merger price make application of the model quite difficult in reality.

Empirical evidence suggests that firms with high growth rates are likely to pay lower dividends, a result consistent with the analysis here. For example, consider McDonald's Corporation. The company started in the 1950s and grew rapidly for many years. It paid its first dividend in 1975, though it was a billion-dollar company (in both sales and market value of stockholders' equity) prior to that date. Why did it wait so long to pay a dividend? It waited because it had so many positive growth opportunities (additional locations for new hamburger outlets) to take advantage of.

5.7   The Dividend Growth Model and the NPVGO Model

This chapter has revealed that the price of a share of stock is the sum of its price as a cash cow plus the per-share value of its growth opportunities. The Sarro Shipping example illustrated this formula using only one growth opportunity. We also used the growing perpetuity formula to price a stock with a steady growth in dividends. When the formula is applied to stocks, it is typically called the *dividend growth model*. A steady growth in dividends results from a continual investment in growth opportunities, not just investment in a single opportunity. Therefore, it is worthwhile to compare the dividend growth model with the *NPVGO model* when growth occurs through continual investing.

We can use an example to illustrate the main points. Suppose Cumberland Book Publishers has EPS of $10 at the end of the first year, a dividend payout ratio of 40 percent, a

---

[7]A third alternative is to issue stock so the firm has enough cash both to pay dividends and to invest. This possibility is explored in a later chapter.

discount rate of 16 percent, and a return on its retained earnings of 20 percent. Because the firm retains some of its earnings each year, it is selecting growth opportunities each year. This is different from Sarro Shipping, which had a growth opportunity in only one year. We wish to calculate the price per share using both the dividend growth model and the NPVGO model.

The Dividend Growth Model

The dividends at date 1 are $.40 \times \$10 = \$4$ per share. The retention ratio is .60 $(1 - .40)$, implying a growth rate in dividends of .12 $(= .60 \times .20)$.

From the dividend growth model, the price of a share of stock today is

$$\frac{\text{Div}_1}{R - g} = \frac{\$4}{.16 - .12} = \$100$$

The NPVGO Model

Using the NPVGO model, it is more difficult to value a firm with growth opportunities each year (like Cumberland) than a firm with growth opportunities in only one year (like Sarro). To value according to the NPVGO model, we need to calculate on a per-share basis (1) the net present value of a single growth opportunity, (2) the net present value of all growth opportunities, and (3) the stock price if the firm acts as a cash cow—that is, the value of the firm without these growth opportunities. The value of the firm is the sum of (2) + (3).

1. *Value per share of a single growth opportunity*: Out of the earnings per share of $10 at date 1, the firm retains $6 $(= .6 \times \$10)$ at that date. The firm earns $1.20 $(= \$6 \times .20)$ per year in perpetuity on that $6 investment. The NPV from the investment is calculated as follows:

   Per-Share NPV Generated from Investment of Date 1:

   $$-\$6 + \frac{\$1.20}{.16} = \$1.50 \tag{5.12}$$

   That is, the firm invests $6 to reap $1.20 per year on the investment. The earnings are discounted at 16 percent, implying a value per share from the project of $1.50. Because the investment occurs at date 1 and the first cash flow occurs at date 2, $1.50 is the value of the investment at *date 1*. In other words, the NPV from the date 1 investment has *not* yet been brought back to date 0.

2. *Value per share of all opportunities*: As pointed out earlier, the growth rate of earnings and dividends is 12 percent. Because retained earnings are a fixed percentage of total earnings, retained earnings must also grow at 12 percent a year. That is, retained earnings at date 2 are $6.72 $(= \$6 \times 1.12)$, retained earnings at date 3 are $7.5264 $[= \$6 \times (1.12)^2]$, and so on.

   Let's analyze the retained earnings at date 2 in more detail. Because projects will always earn 20 percent per year, the firm earns $1.344 $(= \$6.72 \times .20)$ in each future year on the $6.72 investment at date 2.

   Here is the NPV from the investment:

   NPV per Share Generated from Investment at Date 2:

   $$-\$6.72 + \frac{\$1.344}{.16} = \$1.68 \tag{5.13}$$

$1.68 is the NPV as of date 2 of the investment made at date 2. The NPV from the date 2 investment has *not* yet been brought back to date 0.

Now consider the retained earnings at date 3 in more detail. The firm earns $1.5053 (= $7.5264 × .20) per year on the investment of $7.5264 at date 3.

The NPV from the investment is thus:

NPV per Share Generated from Investment at Date 3:

$$-\$7.5264 + \frac{\$1.5053}{.16} = \$1.882 \tag{5.14}$$

From Equations 5.12, 5.13, and 5.14, the NPV per share of all of the growth opportunities, discounted back to date 0, is:

$$\frac{\$1.50}{1.16} + \frac{\$1.68}{(1.16)^2} + \frac{\$1.882}{(1.16)^3} + \cdots \tag{5.15}$$

Because it has an infinite number of terms, this expression looks quite difficult to compute. However, there is an easy simplification. Note that retained earnings are growing at 12 percent per year. Because all projects earn the same rate of return per year, the NPVs in Equations 5.12, 5.13, and 5.14 are also growing at 12 percent per year. Hence, we can write Equation 5.15 as:

$$\frac{\$1.50}{1.16} + \frac{\$1.50 \times 1.12}{(1.16)^2} + \frac{\$1.50 \times (1.12)^2}{(1.16)^3} + \cdots$$

This is a growth perpetuity whose value is:

$$\text{NPVGO} = \$\frac{1.50}{.16 - .12} = \$37.50$$

Because the first NPV of $1.50 occurs at date 1, the NPVGO is $37.50 as of date 0. In other words, the firm's policy of investing in new projects from retained earnings has an NPV of $37.50.

3. *Value per share if the firm is a cash cow*: We now assume that the firm pays out all of its earnings as dividends. The dividends would be $10 per year in this case. Because there would be no growth, the value per share would be evaluated by the perpetuity formula:

$$\frac{\text{Div}}{R} = \frac{\$10}{.16} = \$62.50$$

Summation

Equation 5.10 states that value per share is the value of a cash cow plus the value of the growth opportunities. This is

$$\$100 = \$62.50 + 37.50$$

Hence, value is the same whether calculated by a discounted dividend approach or a growth opportunities approach. The share prices from the two approaches must be equal because the approaches are different yet equivalent methods of applying concepts of present value.

5.8 Price–Earnings Ratio

We argued earlier that one should not discount earnings to determine price per share. Nevertheless, financial analysts frequently relate earnings and price per share, as made evident by their heavy reliance on the price–earnings (or PE) ratio.

Our previous discussion stated that:

$$\text{Price per share} = \frac{\text{EPS}}{R} + \text{NPVGO}$$

Dividing by EPS yields:

$$\frac{\text{Price per share}}{\text{EPS}} = \frac{1}{R} + \frac{\text{NPVGO}}{\text{EPS}}$$

The left side is the formula for the price–earnings ratio. The equation shows that the PE ratio is related to the net present value of growth opportunities. As an example, consider two firms, each having just reported earnings per share of $1. However, one firm has many valuable growth opportunities, whereas the other firm has no growth opportunities at all. The firm with growth opportunities should sell at a higher price because an investor is buying both current income of $1 and growth opportunities. Suppose that the firm with growth opportunities sells for $16 and the other firm sells for $8. The $1 earnings per share number appears in the denominator of the PE ratio for both firms. Thus, the PE ratio is 16 for the firm with growth opportunities but only 8 for the firm without the opportunities.

This explanation seems to hold fairly well in the real world. Electronic and other high-tech stocks generally sell at very high PE ratios (or *multiples*, as they are often called) because they are perceived to have high growth rates. In fact, some technology stocks sell at high prices even though the companies have never earned a profit. Conversely, railroads, utilities, and steel companies sell at lower multiples because of the prospects of lower growth. Table 5.1 contains PE ratios in 2006 for some well-known companies and the S&P 500 Index. Notice the variation across industries.

Of course, the market is merely pricing *perceptions* of the future, not the future itself. We will argue later in the text that the stock market generally has realistic perceptions of a firm's prospects. However, this is not always true. In the late 1960s, many electronics firms were selling at multiples of 200 times earnings. The high perceived growth rates did not materialize, causing great declines in stock prices during the early 1970s. In earlier decades, fortunes were made in stocks like IBM and Xerox because the high growth rates were not anticipated by investors. Most recently, we have experienced the dot-com collapse when many Internet stocks were trading at multiples of thousands of times annual earnings. In fact, most Internet stocks had no earnings.

There are two additional factors explaining the PE ratio. The first is the discount rate, *R*. The previous formula shows that the PE ratio is *negatively* related to the firm's discount

Table 5.1

Selected PE Ratios

Company	Industry	PE Ratio
Ford	Automobiles	7.69
Bear Stearns	Investment banking	11.60
Caterpillar	Heavy equipment	16.79
S&P 500 average	n/a	19.00
Cisco Systems	Computer networking	21.47
Amgen	Biotechnology	27.18
Starbucks	Expensive coffee	50.01

rate. We have already suggested that the discount rate is positively related to the stock's risk or variability. Thus the PE ratio is negatively related to the stock's risk. To see that this is a sensible result, consider two firms, *A* and *B*, behaving as cash cows. The stock market *expects* both firms to have annual earnings of $1 per share forever. However, the earnings of firm *A* are known with certainty, whereas the earnings of firm *B* are quite variable. A rational stockholder is likely to pay more for a share of firm *A* because of the absence of risk. If a share of firm *A* sells at a higher price and both firms have the same EPS, the PE ratio of firm *A* must be higher.

The second additional factor concerns the firm's choice of accounting methods. Under current accounting rules, companies are given a fair amount of leeway. For example, consider inventory accounting where either FIFO or LIFO may be used. In an inflationary environment, *FIFO (first in–first out)* accounting understates the true cost of inventory and hence inflates reported earnings. Inventory is valued according to more recent costs under *LIFO (last in–first out)*, implying that reported earnings are lower here than they would be under FIFO. Thus LIFO inventory accounting is a more *conservative* method than FIFO. Similar accounting leeway exists for construction costs (*completed contracts* versus *percentage-of-completion methods*) and depreciation (*accelerated depreciation* versus *straight-line depreciation*).

As an example, consider two identical firms, *C* and *D*. Firm *C* uses LIFO and reports earnings of $2 per share. Firm *D* uses the less conservative accounting assumptions of FIFO and reports earnings of $3 per share. The market knows that both firms are identical and prices both at $18 per share. This price–earnings ratio is 9 (= $18/$2) for firm *C* and 6 (= $18/$3) for firm *D*. Thus, the firm with the more conservative principles has the higher PE ratio.

This last example depends on the assumption that the market sees through differences in accounting treatments. A significant portion of the academic community believes that the market sees through virtually all accounting differences. These academics are adherents of the hypothesis of *efficient capital markets*, a theory that we explore in great detail later in the text. Though many financial people might be more moderate in their beliefs regarding this issue, the consensus view is certainly that many of the accounting differences are seen through. Thus, the proposition that firms with conservative accountants have high PE ratios is widely accepted.

5.9 Stock Market Reporting

If you look through the pages of *The Wall Street Journal* (or another financial newspaper), you will find information about a large number of stocks in several different markets. Figure 5.5 reproduces a small section of the stock page for the New York Stock Exchange from January 20, 2006. Information on most NASDAQ issues is reported in the same way. In Figure 5.5, locate the line for motorcycle maker Harley-Davidson (HarleyDav). With the column headings, the line reads:

52-WEEK			YLD		VOL		NET
HI	LO	STOCK (DIV)	%	PE	100s	CLOSE	CHG
62.49	44.40	HarleyDav .64	1.2	16	70028	54.05	2.56

You can get real-time stock quotes on the Web. See **finance.yahoo. com** for details.

The first two numbers, 62.49 and 44.40, are the highest and lowest prices for the stock over the past 52 weeks. The .64 is the annual dividend in dollars. Because Harley, like most companies, pays dividends quarterly, this $.64 is actually the latest quarterly dividend multiplied by 4. So the cash dividend paid was $.64/4 = $.16, or 16 cents per share.

Jumping ahead just a bit, "CLOSE" is the closing price of the day (i.e., the last price at which a trade took place before the NYSE closed for the day). The "Net Chg" of 2.56 tells us that the closing price of $54.05 is $2.56 higher than it was the day before; so we say that Harley was up 2.56 for the day.

The column marked "Yld %" gives the dividend yield based on the current dividend and the closing price. For Harley, this is $.64/54.05 = .0118, or about 1.2 percent, the number shown. The next column, labeled "PE," is the price–earnings ratio we discussed earlier. It is calculated as the closing price divided by annual earnings per share (based on

Figure 5.5

Sample Stock Quotation from *The Wall Street Journal*

SOURCE: Reprinted by permission of *The Wall Street Journal*, Friday, January 20, 2006. Reprinted by permission of Dow Jones & Company, Inc. via Copyright Clearance Center, Inc. © 2006 Dow Jones & Company, Inc. All Rights Reserved Worldwide.

FRIDAY, JANUARY 20, 2006 **C5**

NYSE COMPOSITE TRANSACTIONS

52-WEEK HI	LO	STOCK (DIV)	YLD %	PE	VOL 100s	CLOSE	NET CHG
		F					
33.10	25.15	♣FBL Fnl A .42	1.3	12	229	32.69	0.48
63.87	43.25	FMC	...	11	4249	53.19	-0.29
48.04	28.62	♣FMC Tech	...	25	8011	47.25	1.03
21	16.18	FNB Cp .94f	5.5	14	1006	17.19	0.20
48.11	36.89	FPL Gp s 1.42	3.3	19	19334	43.24	0.62
13.95	9.20	FTD Grp n	...	dd	755	10	-0.23
30.54	17.01	FTI Cnsltng	...	26	1264	27.73	0.39
42.30	27.06	FactstRsch s .20	.5	27	1365	39.85	0.19
48.47	32.26	FairIsaac .08	.2	25	4654	46.37	0.16
3.84	2.11	FairchldCp	...	dd	235	2.44	-0.04
▲ 18.62	12.80	FrchldSemi	...	dd	49721	19.64	1.76
179.90	126.73	FairfaxFnl 1.40e	.9	dd	431	153.70	2.45
43.75	29.90	FairmntHtlRt .12	.3	33	5864	41.90	0.20
18.55	10.01	FairpntComm n 1.59	13.2	dd	1995	12.03	...
31.15	15.42	Falconbridge .48g	...	...	696	29.74	0.41
35.25	19.40	FamilyDlr .38	1.6	19	7430	24.07	-0.11
66.50	41.34	FannieMae lf 1.04	1.9	7	27571	54.10	0.84
3.32	1.22	Fedders .09j	...	...	1040	1.33	-0.05
23.15	12.89	FedAgrMtg A .40	1.9	8	2	20.96	0.15
32.47	15.53	FedAgri C .40	1.4	11	215	29.04	0.24
▲ 65.98	46.19	FedRlty 2.22a	3.3	40	1059	66.80	1.82
17.95	13.80	FedSgnl .24	1.4	29	3843	16.63	0.50
78.05	54.20	FedDeptStr 1.00	1.4	12	17955	71.92	0.33
▲ 38.54	26.99	FedInv B .60	1.6	27	5613	38.48	0.12
105.82	76.81	FedExCp .32	.3	20	18187	102.72	2.10
18.80	11.78	Felcor .15e	.8	dd	2031	18.69	0.18
14.70	8.63	FldmnMallProp .91	7.4	...	120	12.25	0.59
22.49	20.13	Ferrellgas 2.00	9.3	14	826	21.54	...
23.22	16.27	Ferro lf .58	3.0	36	1034	19.55	0.38
10.28	5.76	Fiat ADS	...	...	304	10.11	-0.05
41.11	27.01	FidNtlFnl s 1.00	2.7	6	17489	37.50	0.10
26	19.50	FidNtlTitle n .25p	...	...	2130	25.60	0.45
45.19	32.70	FnlFed .60	1.4	20	1679	42.96	0.01
10.95	8.23	FstAcceptance	...	19	271	10.31	0.14
49.50	30	FstAmCp .72	1.6	10	3607	46.20	0.04
29.71	10.37	FstBcp slf .28	2.3	6	1830	12.39	0.16
14.70	12.63	FstCmwlthFnl .68f	5.1	15	1274	13.39	0.07
45	36.50	♣FstData .24	.6	21	28954	42.81	-0.24
44.80	34.78	FstHoriznNat 1.80	4.7	11	14298	38.62	-0.33
42.80	36.70	FstIndRlty 2.80f	7.2	23	4795	38.90	0.03
73.27	20.89	FstMarblehead .24e	.7	14	4764	32.64	-0.05
▲ 28.30	20.87	FstPotomac 1.20f	4.2	84	507	28.51	0.42
▲ 40.22	30.56	♣FstRepBnk s .50	1.2	20	2255	40.27	1.16
53.36	38.54	FstEngy 1.80f	3.5	20	7906	51.51	0.40
65.32	47.84	FstFedFnl	...	12	2309	57.40	-0.55
67.50	53.50	FisherSci	...	26	10349	65.68	0.28
22.42	12.62	Flagstar .60m	4.2	11	2071	14.41	0.09
13.69	7.33	♣FleetwdEnt	...	dd	7381	11.65	0.31
48.49	38.90	FL ECstInd .24	.5	19	1828	47.45	0.79
67.98	36	♣FL RockInd s .60	1.2	21	5062	50	-0.15
30.61	18.51	FlwrsFoods s .40	1.5	30	1459	26.92	-0.25
▲ 43.35	23.69	Flowserve lf	...	40	2966	43.77	0.61
82.50	50.11	FluorCp .64	.8	33	6302	81.75	-0.15
79.60	50.47	Fomento ADS .60e	.8	...	2188	76.51	0.61
29.95	18.74	FootLocker .36f	1.6	14	6989	22.45	-0.08
13.54	7.57	FordMotor .40	4.9	8	195015	8.22	0.01
45.15	24.77	FrdgCndn s 4.77e	...	...	8274	39.70	0.75
41	28.61	♣ForestCtyA s .24	.6	63	834	38.37	-0.18
40.90	29.05	♣ForestCtyB s .24	.6	63	10	38.16	-0.29
45.21	32.46	ForestLabs	...	22	19929	43.26	0.63
54.76	31.65	ForestOil	...	23	6110	50.24	1.14
90.57	73.02	FortBrnds 1.44	1.8	17	5826	78.59	0.16
▲ 44.30	20.65	FoundtnCoal .18e	.4	30	3641	44.37	1.46
23	15.46	♣4KidsEntn	...	25	681	17.78	0.37
82.20	46.85	FourSeasons .11g	...	...	1908	54.74	0.19
▼ 31.90	23	FraTelecm .68e	2.9	...	2255	23.15	-0.28

52-WEEK HI	LO	STOCK (DIV)	YLD %	PE	VOL 100s	CLOSE	NET CHG
62.49	44.40	HarleyDav .64	1.2	16	70028	54.05	2.56
126.69	68.54	HarmanInt .05	...	28	4741	101.80	0.68
▲ 15.41	5.96	HrmnyGld ADS	...	...	19553	15.47	0.97
79.69	57.29	HarrahEntn 1.45	2.0	22	12208	71.83	-0.11
▲ 47.60	26.94	Harris s .32	.7	31	4478	47.54	0.04
71.68	49.87	Harsco 1.20	1.7	21	2653	71.41	2.25
31.47	25.04	HarteHanks .20	.8	20	1355	26.43	-0.07
89.49	65.35	HrtfrdFnl 1.20f	1.4	11	14241	87.32	0.43
80.30	61.58	HrtfrdFnl 7.0un 3.50	4.5	...	530	78.25	0.36
79.17	60.90	HrtfrdFnl un 3.00	3.9	...	19	77.66	0.76
10.48	6.09	♣Hartmarx	...	13	2425	7.85	0.29
33.69	23.85	HrvstErgyTr nx 4.20g	12.8	...	1702	32.70	0.48
13.93	7.83	HarvstNatRes	...	7	2983	9.49	0.47
22.35	17.75	Hasbro .36	1.7	21	12330	21.76	0.30
18	11.53	HavrtyFurn .27f	2.0	19	938	13.75	0.05
17.69	11.92	HavrtyFurn A .25f	1.9	19	4	13.40	0.12
29.79	24.60	HawElInd 1.24	4.7	19	1626	26.50	0.24
4.40	2.45	Head	...	48	1	3.38	-0.01
45.75	29.08	Headwaters	...	13	9083	35.98	0.11
28.92	23.13	HlthCrProp 1.68	6.1	24	2870	27.59	0.59
39.20	31.15	HlthCr Reit 2.48	6.7	39	1493	37	0.44
27	20.75	HlthMgt A .24f	1.1	16	13862	22.27	-0.02
54.11	27.63	HealthNet	...	91	6973	51.21	-0.23
41.36	31.01	HlthcrRlty 2.64	7.7	31	2025	34.48	0.49
26.34	23.15	♣HearstArgyl .28	1.2	18	1171	23.95	0.14
27.73	20.77	HeartlndPymnt n	...	...	2032	21.75	0.03
6.22	2.95	HeclaMin	...	dd	11349	4.23	0.23
27.45	18.32	Heico .08f	.3	29	419	25.39	0.01
21.93	14.52	Heico A .08f	.4	23	106	20.26	-0.04
38.16	33.55	Heinz 1.20	3.5	17	14395	33.99	0.10
▲ 11.35	8.36	Hellenic	...	...	975	11.35	0.28
72.58	33.89	HelmPayne .33	.5	29	8435	71.66	1.61
34.10	14.52	Herbalife	...	...	1299	31.90	-0.40
15.55	10	Hercules	...	14	5657	11.10	0.05
37.89	29.16	HeritageProp 2.10	6.1	43	1995	34.63	0.40
67.37	52.49	Hershey .98	1.8	27	7545	55.16	0.06
31.43	23.94	Hewitt	...	22	9320	26.14	-0.49
▲ 31.90	18.89	HewlettPk .32	1.0	39	184228	32.24	0.57
20.15	13.81	Hexcel	...	dd	7124	19.34	...
12.24	9.78	HighlndHspty .56	5.1	78	2953	10.93	-0.01
31.86	24.27	HighwdProp lf 1.70	5.5	67	1698	30.72	0.61
40.45	31.75	♣HilbRogl .46	1.2	27	2085	39	-0.21
57	44.81	Hillenbrnd 1.13f	2.2	dd	1357	51	0.09
25.81	18.78	Hilton .16	.6	24	29325	25.03	0.65
75.40	57.36	Hitachi .96e	1.3	...	591	71.57	1.46
11.95	8.45	HolngrIntA s .20a	2.2	...	870	8.94	0.09
▲ 66.47	25.28	HollyCp .40	.6	16	2793	67.74	2.99
47	32.25	HllyEngyPtnr 2.40	5.8	...	167	41.50	-0.25
43.98	34.56	HomeDpt .60f	1.5	16	122154	41.28	-0.62
46.44	35.36	♣HmProp 2.56f	5.7	33	4920	44.70	0.45
10.14	6.70	Homebanc .95e	11.7	dd	1823	8.12	0.03
30.36	23.75	♣HondaMtr ADS .30e	1.1	...	12846	27.67	0.30
39.50	32.68	Honeywell .83	2.2	20	37918	37.19	0.17
20.80	15.86	HoraceMn .42	2.2	10	1960	19.47	0.27
13.10	10.24	HoriznLine n .11p	...	...	108	12.25	-0.12
35.44	29.16	♣HormelFood .56f	1.7	18	3270	33.59	-0.42
▲ 38.55	20.10	HrnbkOffshr	...	68	3137	38.59	1.78
42.82	26.83	♣DR Horton s .40f	1.0	8	31354	38.86	-1.14
▲ 45.50	28.35	Hospira	...	28	6291	45.40	0.15
45.04	38	HsptlyProp 2.92	6.9	26	2593	42.29	0.94
▲ 19.81	15.46	HostMar Reit .41e	2.1	60	14033	19.81	0.21
71.47	45.60	HoustonExplr	...	13	4939	55.95	2.23
73.40	42.50	♣HovnanEnt	...	7	7354	50.91	-0.32
46.75	34	HSBC Fin un 2.22a	5.2	...	10	42.85	-0.40
32.75	25.94	HuanengPwr 1.21r	4.3	...	909	28.10	0.32
▲ 27.05	16.80	HubIntl .24	.9	34	330	27	0.17
49.75	39.19	HubbellA 1.32	3.2	16	4661	41.35	-1.00
54.20	42.56	HubbellB 1.32	2.9	17	2966	45.24	-1.21
42.95	31.31	HudsnUtdBcp 1.48	3.5	17	1890	42.40	0.11

52-WEEK HI	LO	STOCK (DIV)	YLD %	PE	VOL 100s	CLOSE	NET CHG
56.22	43.54	KindrMrgEgy 3.20f	6.3	23	4768	50.62	0.52
▲ 99.97	72.47	KindrMorgan 3.50f	3.5	23	16197	101.44	5.15
49.25	37.44	KindrMrgMg 3.20f	6.9	31	1040	46.67	0.65
42.11	24.74	Kindred	...	9	19081	26.80	-0.94
74.20	33	KineticCnpts	...	27	2945	41.20	0.08
18.85	7.50	KingPharm	...	19	19771	18.03	0.04
21.07	14.70	KingswayFin .20g	...	...	110	20.74	0.03
10.68	4.61	KinrossGld lf	...	1	19305	10.46	0.46
55.54	37.19	KirbyCp	...	22	931	53.02	1.26
16.52	13.40	KiteRltyTr .75	4.9	...	691	15.28	0.03
25.07	20.71	KKR Fnl n .72e	3.1	...	1295	23.25	-0.16
11.30	7.84	KMG America	...	...	276	8.78	-0.07
22.51	13.83	KnightTrnsp s .16f	.8	29	7943	20.89	-0.38
69.09	52.42	KnghtRidder 1.48	2.3	9	7479	63.54	-0.65
19	14.75	Knoll .25e	1.5	26	356	16.81	-0.07
58.90	43.63	KohlsCp	...	19	37830	44.48	-0.10
24.10	19	Konami ADS .49e	2.1	...	8	22.99	0.59
78.65	40.65	Kookmin ADS	...	...	6436	69.57	0.74
13.29	9.50	♣KoorInd	...	...	167	10.63	0.08
▲ 21.92	13.05	KoreaElecPwr .56e	2.6	...	6622	21.90	0.85
20.40	13.92	KornFerry	...	19	1458	19.55	0.14
34.35	27.44	KftFoods .92	3.2	20	24975	29.07	0.01
9.49	3.35	KrspyKrm lf	...	dd	15355	5.19	-0.06
20.88	15.15	Kroger	...	cc	51806	19	-0.07
49.20	27.50	KronosWrldwd 1.00	3.3	20	43	30.20	0.15
45.90	24.20	Kubota ADS .37e	.9	...	503	43.39	1.25
82.97	62.58	Kyocera .92e	1.2	...	406	79.78	0.27
		L					
8.29	1.90	LLE RoyalTr j	...	...	324	3.25	-0.01
10.75	5.01	LSI Logic	...	dd	55657	8.86	0.22
23.92	16.50	LTC Prop x 1.44f	6.4	15	735	22.60	0.14
84.84	64.66	L 3Comm .50	.7	19	8717	74.58	-0.32
11.19	7.75	LaQuinta	...	dd	7502	11.19	0.01
16.40	10.13	♣LaZ Boy .44	2.9	29	4966	15.16	0.06
26.50	15.25	LaborRdy	...	20	3497	21.64	-0.01
58.14	44.63	LabCpAm	...	22	9475	57.39	0.42
11.87	5.25	LaBranche	...	23	5746	10.89	0.21
34.31	26.90	LacledeGrp 1.38	4.5	16	448	30.85	0.18
26.35	19.81	Lafarge ADS .72e	3.1	...	732	23.57	1.07
70.47	50.85	♣LafargeNoAm .96	1.6	21	5252	58.81	1.24
▲ 27.56	20.41	LaidlawInt .30e	1.1	12	6321	27.31	0.06
31.69	8.77	LamsonSes	...	29	3324	27.24	0.65
40.40	30.06	LanAirline ADS .69e	1.8	...	591	38.25	0.02
70.09	46.50	LandAmFnl .72	1.1	9	2945	66.64	-0.42
54	43.90	♣Landauer 1.80f	3.7	25	136	48.05	1.25
33	25.39	LandryRes .20	.7	13	2704	29.25	0.25
51.40	29.08	LasVegasSands	...	66	7548	47.78	-0.04
38.47	27.34	LaSalleHtl 1.20	3.1	64	1751	38.21	0.34
35.48	20.40	Lazard n .14e	.4	...	3362	34	0.70
15.35	9.20	LeapFrog A	...	dd	3217	11.77	-0.03
▼ 54.55	23.28	Lear 1.00	4.1	dd	25619	24.35	1.04
45.96	36.11	LeeEnt .72	2.0	23	1670	36.66	0.15
▲ 131.40	69.82	LeggMason .72	.5	34	12325	131.10	4.69
29.61	18.19	LegPlatt .64	2.7	17	7160	23.80	0.15
16.15	14.16	LehmnFstTrInco x 1.32m	8.9	...	345	14.87	-0.06
▲ 136.63	85.92	LehmnHldg .96f	.7	13	28223	137.49	4.12
68.86	50.30	Lennar A .64	1.0	8	13277	62.62	-0.65
64	46.90	Lennar B .64	1.1	7	1116	57.55	-0.75
31.16	18.65	♣LennoxIntl .44f	1.4	20	1861	30.70	0.42
17.94	9.85	LenoxGrp	...	11	252	12.83	0.03
49.65	32.40	LeucdaNat .25	.5	4	2203	48.94	0.46
33.85	18.86	Levitt A .08	.3	8	1773	23.90	0.43
25.26	20.26	LexgtnProp 1.46f	6.4	45	1660	22.70	0.29
86.62	39.33	LexmarkInt	...	14	8880	46.75	0.05
26.60	18.01	LG PhilipsADS	...	...	10777	21.05	0.34
▼ 25.03	10.03	Libbey .40	3.8	46	869	10.60	0.43
48.05	34.32	LbtyCp 1.00a	2.1	27	255	47.22	0.01

the most recent four quarters). In the jargon of Wall Street, we might say that Harley "sells for 16 times earnings."

Finally, the column marked "Vol 100s" tells us how many shares traded during the day (in hundreds). For example, the 70028 for Harley tells us that about 7 million shares changed hands on this day alone. If the average price during the day was $54 or so, then the dollar volume of transactions was on the order of 54×7 million = $378 million worth for Harley alone. This was a fairly heavy day of trading in Harley shares, and it serves to illustrate how active the market can be for well-known companies.

If you look over Figure 5.5, you will notice quite a few footnote indicators (small letters) and special symbols. To learn more about these, pick up any *Wall Street Journal* and consult the stock pages.

Summary and Conclusions

In this chapter, we used general present value formulas from the previous chapter to price bonds and stock.

1. Pure discount bonds and perpetuities can be viewed as the polar cases of bonds. The value of a pure discount bond (also called a zero coupon bond, or simply a zero) is:

$$PV = \frac{F}{(1 + R)^T}$$

The value of a perpetuity (also called a *consol*) is:

$$PV = \frac{C}{R}$$

2. Level payment bonds can be viewed as an intermediate case. The coupon payments form an annuity, and the principal repayment is a lump sum. The value of this type of bond is simply the sum of the values of its two parts.

3. The yield to maturity on a bond is the single rate that discounts the payments on the bond to its purchase price.

4. A stock can be valued by discounting its dividends. We mentioned three types of situations:
   a. The case of zero growth of dividends.
   b. The case of constant growth of dividends.
   c. The case of differential growth.

5. An estimate of the growth rate of a stock is needed for the formulas for situations 4(b) or 4(c). A useful estimate of the growth rate is

$$g = \text{Retention ratio} \times \text{Return on retained earnings}$$

6. It is worthwhile to view a share of stock as the sum of its worth if the company behaves like a cash cow (the company does no investing) and the value per share of its growth opportunities. We write the value of a share as:

$$\frac{EPS}{R} + NPVGO$$

We showed that, in theory, share price must be the same whether the dividend growth model or the formula here is used.

7. From accounting, we know that earnings are divided into two parts: dividends and retained earnings. Most firms continually retain earnings to create future dividends. One should not

discount earnings to obtain price per share because part of earnings must be reinvested. Only dividends reach the stockholders, and only they should be discounted to obtain share price.

8. We suggested that a firm's price–earnings ratio is a function of three factors:
    a. The per-share amount of the firm's valuable growth opportunities.
    b. The risk of the stock.
    c. The type of accounting method used by the firm.

Concept Questions

1. **Coupon Rate**   How does a bond issuer decide on the appropriate coupon rate to set on its bonds? Explain the difference between the coupon rate and the required return on a bond.

2. **Bond Market**   What are the implications for bond investors of the lack of transparency in the bond market?

3. **Stock Valuation**   Why does the value of a share of stock depend on dividends?

4. **Stock Valuation**   A substantial percentage of the companies listed on the NYSE and the NASDAQ don't pay dividends, but investors are nonetheless willing to buy shares in them. How is this possible given your answer to the previous question?

5. **Dividend Policy**   Referring to the previous two questions, under what circumstances might a company choose not to pay dividends?

6. **Dividend Growth Model**   Under what two assumptions can we use the dividend growth model presented in the chapter to determine the value of a share of stock? Comment on the reasonableness of these assumptions.

7. **Common versus Preferred Stock**   Suppose a company has a preferred stock issue and a common stock issue. Both have just paid a $2 dividend. Which do you think will have a higher price, a share of the preferred or a share of the common?

8. **Growth Rate**   In the context of the dividend growth model, is it true that the growth rate in dividends and the growth rate in the price of the stock are identical?

9. **Price–Earnings Ratio**   What are the three factors that determine a company's price–earnings ratio?

10. **Stock Valuation**   Evaluate the following statement Managers should not focus on the current stock value because doing so will lead to an overemphasis on short-term profits at the expense of long-term profits.

Questions and Problems

BASIC
(Questions 1–9)

1. **Valuing Bonds**   What is the price of a 10-year, pure discount bond paying $1,000 at maturity if the YTM is
    a. 5 percent?
    b. 10 percent?
    c. 20 percent?

2. **Valuing Bonds**   Microhard has issued a bond with the following characteristics:
    Par: £1,000
    Time to maturity: 20 years
    Coupon rate: 8 percent
    Semiannual payments

    Calculate the price of this bond if the YTM is
    a. 8 percent.
    b. 10 percent.
    c. 6 percent.

3. **Bond Yields**   Sell Hi Buy Lo issued 12-year bonds 2 years ago at a coupon rate of 8.6 percent. The bonds make semiannual payments. If these bonds currently sell for 97 percent of par value, what is the YTM?

4. **Stock Values** The Brennan Co. just paid a dividend of €1.40 per share on its stock. The dividends are expected to grow at a constant rate of 6 percent per year indefinitely. If investors require a 15 percent return on the Brennan Co. stock, what is the current price? What will the price be in three years? In 10 years?

5. **Stock Values** The next dividend payment by MUG, Inc., will be $3.10 per share. The dividends are anticipated to maintain a 5 percent growth rate forever. If MUG stock currently sells for $48.00 per share, what is the required return?

6. **Stock Values** Sugam Limited will pay a INR 3.60 per share dividend next year. The company pledges to increase its dividend by 4.5 percent per year indefinitely. If you require a 13 percent return on your investment, how much will you pay for the company's stock today?

7. **Stock Valuation** Suppose you know that a company's stock currently sells for ¥11,000 per share and the required return on the stock is 12 percent. You also know that the total return on the stock is evenly divided between a capital gains yield and a dividend yield. If it's the company's policy to always maintain a constant growth rate in its dividends, what is the current dividend per share?

8. **Stock Valuation** Gruber Corp. pays a constant $12 dividend on its stock. The company will maintain this dividend for the next eight years and will then cease paying dividends forever. If the required return on this stock is 10 percent, what is the current share price?

9. **Growth Rate** The newspaper reported last week that Maskara Enterprises earned $20 million this year. The report also stated that the firm's return on equity is 14 percent. Maskara retains 60 percent of its earnings. What is the firm's earnings growth rate? What will next year's earnings be?

INTERMEDIATE
(Questions 10–31)

10. **Bond Price Movements** Miryang Foods Corporation has a premium bond making semiannual payments. The bond pays an 8 percent coupon, has a YTM of 6 percent, and has 13 years to maturity. The Yeosu Fishing Company has a discount bond making semiannual payments. This bond pays a 6 percent coupon, has a YTM of 8 percent, and also has 13 years to maturity. If interest rates remain unchanged, what do you expect the price of these bonds to be 1 year from now? In 3 years? In 8 years? In 12 years? In 13 years? What's going on here? Illustrate your answers by graphing bond prices versus time to maturity.

11. **Bond Yields** Butuan Engineering has 8.4 percent coupon bonds on the market with nine years to maturity. The bonds make semiannual payments and currently sell for 104 percent of par. What is the current yield on the bonds? The YTM? The effective annual yield?

12. **Bond Yields** Petty Co. wants to issue new 20-year bonds for some much-needed expansion projects. The company currently has 8 percent coupon bonds on the market that sell for $1,095, make semiannual payments, and mature in 20 years. What coupon rate should the company set on its new bonds if it wants them to sell at par?

13. **Stock Valuation** Stratford Diners, Inc., just paid a dividend of £3.00 on its stock. The growth rate in dividends is expected to be a constant 5 percent per year indefinitely. Investors require a 16 percent return on the stock for the first three years, a 14 percent return for the next three years, and then an 11 percent return thereafter. What is the current share price for Stratford Diners stock?

14. **Nonconstant Growth** Yumen XI, Inc., is a young start-up company. No dividends will be paid on the stock over the next nine years because the firm needs to plow back its earnings to fuel growth. The company will pay a CNY 8 per share dividend in 10 years and will increase the dividend by 6 percent per year thereafter. If the required return on this stock is 15 percent, what is the current share price?

15. **Nonconstant Dividends** Corn, Inc., has an odd dividend policy. The company has just paid a dividend of €9 per share and has announced that it will increase the dividend by €3 per share for each of the next four years, and then never pay another dividend. If you require an 11 percent return on the company's stock, how much will you pay for a share today?

16. **Nonconstant Dividends** South Side Corporation is expected to pay the following dividends over the next four years: KRW 8, KRW 6, KRW 3, and KRW 2. Afterward the company pledges to maintain a constant 5 percent growth rate in dividends forever. If the required return on the stock is 13 percent, what is the current share price?

17. **Nonconstant Growth**   Rizzi Co. is growing quickly. Dividends are expected to grow at a 25 percent rate for the next three years, with the growth rate falling off to a constant 7 percent thereafter. If the required return is 13 percent and the company just paid an ILS 2.80 dividend, what is the current share price?

18. **Nonconstant Growth**   Yusuf & Sons is experiencing rapid growth. Dividends are expected to grow at 30 percent per year during the next three years, 18 percent over the following year, and then 8 percent per year indefinitely. The required return on this stock is 14 percent, and the stock currently sells for PKR 70.00 per share. What is the projected dividend for the coming year?

19. **Finding the Dividend**   Hollin Corporation stock currently sells for $50 per share. The market requires a 14 percent return on the firm's stock. If the company maintains a constant 8 percent growth rate in dividends, what was the most recent dividend per share paid on the stock?

20. **Valuing Preferred Stock**   Mark Bank just issued some new preferred stock. The issue will pay a €9 annual dividend in perpetuity, beginning six years from now. If the market requires a 7 percent return on this investment, how much does a share of preferred stock cost today?

21. **Negative Growth**   Xian Mining Company's iron ore reserves are being depleted, and its costs of recovering a declining quantity of ore are rising each year. As a result, the company's earnings are declining at a rate of 10 percent per year. If the dividend per share to be paid tomorrow is CNY 5 and the required rate of return is 14 percent, what is the value of the firm's stock? Assume that the dividend payments are based on a fixed percentage of the firm's earnings.

22. **Nonconstant Growth and Quarterly Dividends**   Pasqually Mineral Water, Inc., will pay a quarterly dividend per share of ¥1,000 at the end of each of the next 12 quarters. Thereafter the dividend will grow at a quarterly rate of 0.5 percent forever. The appropriate rate of return on the stock is 10 percent, compounded quarterly. What is the current stock price?

23. **Nonconstant Growth**   To buy back its own shares, Pennzoil Co. has decided to suspend its dividends for the next two years. It will resume its annual cash dividend of $2.00 in year 3 and year 4. Thereafter its dividend payments will grow at an annual growth rate of 6 percent forever. The required rate of return on Pennzoil's stock is 16 percent. According to the discounted dividend model, what should Pennzoil's current share price be?

24. **Finding the Dividend**   Allen, Inc., is expected to pay equal dividends at the end of each of the next two years. Thereafter, the dividend will grow at a constant annual rate of 4 percent forever. The current stock price is £30. What is next year's dividend payment if the required rate of return is 13 percent?

25. **Finding the Required Return**   Miyagi's Dojo earned ¥10 million for the fiscal year ending yesterday. The firm also paid out 25 percent of its earnings as dividends yesterday. The firm will continue to pay out 25 percent of its earnings as annual, end-of-year dividends. The remaining 75 percent of earnings is retained by the company for use in projects. The company has 1.25 million shares of common stock outstanding. The current stock price is ¥40. The historical return on equity (ROE) of 11 percent is expected to continue in the future. What is the required rate of return on the stock?

26. **Dividend Growth**   Four years ago, Kuruman Diamond, Inc., paid a dividend of ZAR .90 per share. Bling paid a dividend of ZAR 1.66 per share yesterday. Dividends will grow over the next five years at the same rate they grew over the last four years. Thereafter dividends will grow at 8 percent per year. The required return on the stock is 20 percent. What will Kuruman Diamond's cash dividend be in seven years?

27. **Price–Earnings Ratio**   Consider Pacific Energy Company and U.S. Bluechips, Inc., both of which reported earnings of $800,000. Without new projects, both firms will continue to generate earnings of $800,000 in perpetuity. Assume that all earnings are paid as dividends and that both firms require a 15 percent rate of return.
    a. What is the current PE ratio for each company?
    b. Pacific Energy Company has a new project that will generate additional earnings of $100,000 each year in perpetuity. Calculate the new PE ratio of the company.

c. U. S. Bluechips has a new project that will increase by $200,000 in perpetuity. Calculate the new PE ratio of the firm.

28. **Growth Opportunities**   Quebec Royal Foods currently has earnings per share of CAD 7.00. The company has no growth and pays out all earnings as dividends. It has a new project that will require an investment of CAD 1.75 per share in one year. The project will only last two years and will increase earnings in the two years following the investment by CAD 1.90 and CAD 2.10, respectively. Investors require a 12 percent return on the company's stock.

   a. What is the value per share of the company's stock assuming the firm does not undertake the investment opportunity?

   b. If the company does undertake the investment, what is the value per share now?

   c. Again assume the company undertakes the investment. What will the price per share be four years from today?

29. **Growth Opportunities**   Broome Whale Watchers' revenues last year were AUD 3 million, and total costs were AUD 1.5 million. Broome Whale Watchers has 1 million shares of common stock outstanding. Gross revenues and costs are expected to grow at 5 percent per year. Broome Whale Watchers pays no income taxes. All earnings are paid out as dividends.

   a. If the appropriate discount rate is 15 percent and all cash flows are received at year's end, what is the price per share of Broome Whale Watchers stock?

   b. Broome Whale Watchers has decided to start parasailing training. The project requires an immediate outlay of AUD 15 million. In one year, another outlay of AUD 5 million will be needed. The year after that, earnings will increase by AUD 6 million. That profit level will be maintained in perpetuity. What effect will undertaking this project have on the price per share of the stock?

30. **Growth Opportunities**   Quepos Real Estate, Inc., expects to earn CRC 110 million per year in perpetuity if it does not undertake any new projects. The firm has an opportunity to invest CRC 12 million today and CRC 7 million in one year in real estate. The new investment will generate annual earnings of CRC 10 million in perpetuity, beginning two years from today. The firm has 20 million shares of common stock outstanding, and the required rate of return on the stock is 15 percent. Land investments are not depreciable. Ignore taxes.

   a. What is the price of a share of stock if the firm does not undertake the new investment?

   b. What is the value of the investment?

   c. What is the per-share stock price if the firm undertakes the investment?

31. **Growth Opportunities**   The annual earnings of Avalanche Skis, Inc., will be £5 per share in perpetuity if the firm makes no new investments. Under such a situation the firm would pay out all of its earnings as dividends. Assume the first dividend will be received exactly one year from now.

   Alternatively, assume that three years from now, and in every subsequent year in perpetuity, the company can invest 25 percent of its earnings in new projects. Each project will earn 40 percent at year-end in perpetuity. The firm's discount rate is 14 percent.

   a. What is the price per share of Avalanche Skis, Inc., stock today without the company making the new investment?

   b. If Avalanche announces that the new investment will be made, what will the per-share stock price be today?

CHALLENGE
(Questions 32–40)

32. **Components of Bond Returns**   Bond P is a premium bond with a 10 percent coupon. Bond D is a 6 percent coupon bond currently selling at a discount. Both bonds make annual payments, have a YTM of 8 percent, and have five years to maturity. What is the current yield for Bond P? For Bond D? If interest rates remain unchanged, what is the expected capital gains yield over the next year for Bond P? For Bond D? Explain your answers and the interrelationship among the various types of yields.

33. **Holding Period Yield**   The YTM on a bond is the interest rate you earn on your investment if interest rates don't change. If you actually sell the bond before it matures, your realized return is known as the holding period yield (HPY).

a. Suppose that today you buy an 8 percent annual coupon bond for ¥1,150. The bond has 10 years to maturity. What rate of return do you expect to earn on your investment?

b. Two years from now, the YTM on your bond has declined by 1 percent, and you decide to sell. What price will your bond sell for? What is the HPY on your investment? Compare this yield to the YTM when you first bought the bond. Why are they different?

34. Valuing Bonds   The Mallory Corporation has two different bonds currently outstanding. Bond M has a face value of €20,000 and matures in 20 years. The bond makes no payments for the first six years, then pays €1,200 every six months over the subsequent eight years, and finally pays €1,500 every six months over the last six years. Bond N also has a face value of €20,000 and a maturity of 20 years; it makes no coupon payments over the life of the bond. If the required return on both these bonds is 10 percent compounded semiannually, what is the current price of Bond M? Of Bond N?

35. Capital Gains versus Income   Consider four different stocks, all of which have a required return of 15 percent and a most recent dividend of $4.50 per share. Stocks W, X, and Y are expected to maintain constant rates in dividends for the foreseeable future of 10 percent, 0 percent, and −5 percent per year, respectively. Stock Z is a growth stock that will increase its dividend by 20 percent for the next two years and then maintain a constant 12 percent growth rate thereafter. What is the dividend yield for each of these four stocks? What is the expected capital gains yield? Discuss the relationship among the various returns that you find for each of these stocks.

36. Stock Valuation   Most corporations pay quarterly rather than annual dividends on their common stock. Barring any unusual circumstances during the year, the board raises, lowers, or maintains the current dividend once a year and then pays this dividend out in equal quarterly installments to its shareholders.

a. Suppose a company currently pays a £3.00 annual dividend on its common stock in a single annual installment, and management plans on raising this dividend by 6 percent per year indefinitely. If the required return on this stock is 14 percent, what is the current share price?

b. Now suppose that the company in (a) actually pays its annual dividend in equal quarterly installments; thus this company has just paid a £.75 dividend per share, as it has for the previous three quarters. What is your value for the current share price now? (*Hint:* Find the equivalent annual end-of-year dividend for each year.) Comment on whether you think that this model of stock valuation is appropriate.

37. Growth Opportunities   Edmonton Woodworks Co., (today) expects to earn CAD 6 per share for each of the future operating periods (beginning at time 1) if the firm makes no new investments and returns the earnings as dividends to the shareholders. However, Clint Williams, president and CEO, has discovered an opportunity to retain and invest 30 percent of the earnings beginning three years from today. This opportunity to invest will continue for each period indefinitely. He expects to earn 12 percent on this new equity investment, the return beginning one year after each investment is made. The firm's equity discount rate is 14 percent throughout.

a. What is the price per share of Edmonton Woodworks Co., stock without making the new investment?

b. If the new investment is expected to be made, per the preceding information, what would the price of the stock be now?

c. Suppose the company could increase the investment in the project by whatever amount it chose. What would the retention ratio need to be to make this project attractive?

38. Nonconstant Growth   Storico Co. just paid a dividend of AUD 3.50 per share. The company will increase its dividend by 20 percent next year and will then reduce its dividend growth rate by 5 percentage points per year until it reaches the industry average of 5 percent dividend growth, after which the company will keep a constant growth rate forever. If the required return on Storico stock is 13 percent, what will a share of stock sell for today?

39. Nonconstant Growth   This one's a little harder. Suppose the current share price for the firm in the previous problem is AUD 98.65 and all the dividend information remains the same. What required return must investors be demanding on Storico stock? (*Hint:* Set up the valuation formula with all the relevant cash flows, and use trial and error to find the unknown rate of return.)

40. **Growth Opportunities**   Zhiji Qi Limited has earnings of CNY10 million and is projected to grow at a constant rate of 5 percent forever because of the benefits gained from the learning curve. Currently all earnings are paid out as dividends. The company plans to launch a new project two years from now that would be completely internally funded and require 20 percent of the earnings that year. The project would start generating revenues one year after the launch of the project, and the earnings from the new project in any year are estimated to be constant at CNY5 million. The company has 10 million shares of stock outstanding. Estimate the value of Zhiji Qi Limited stock. The discount rate is 10 percent.

S&P Problems

STANDARD &POOR'S

www.mhhe.com/edumarketinsight

1. **Dividend Discount Model**   Enter the ticker symbol "WMT" for Wal-Mart. Using the most recent balance sheet and income statement under the "Excel Analytics" link, calculate the sustainable growth rate for Wal-Mart. Now download the "Mthly. Adj. Price" and find the closing stock price for the same month as the balance sheet and income statement you used. What is the implied required return on Wal-Mart according to the dividend growth model? Does this number make sense? Why or why not?

2. **Growth Opportunities**   Assume that investors require an 11 percent return on Harley-Davidson (HDI) stock. Under the "Excel Analytics" link find the "Mthly. Adj. Price" and find the closing price for the month of the most recent fiscal year end for HDI. Using this stock price and the EPS for the most recent year, calculate the NPVGO for Harley-Davidson. What is the appropriate PE ratio for Harley-Davidson using these calculations?

Mini Case

Stock Valuation at Ragan Thermal Systems

Ragan Thermal Systems, Inc., was founded nine years ago by brother and sister Carrington and Genevieve Ragan. The company manufactures and installs commercial heating, ventilation, and cooling (HVAC) units. Ragan has experienced rapid growth because of a proprietary technology that increases the energy efficiency of its systems. The company is equally owned by Carrington and Genevieve. The original agreement between the siblings gave each 50,000 shares of stock. In the event either wished to sell the stock, the shares first had to be offered to the other at a discounted price.

Although neither sibling wants to sell any shares at this time, they have decided they should value their holdings in the company for financial planning purposes. To accomplish this, they have gathered the following information about their main competitors.

Ragan Thermal Systems, Inc., Competitors					
	EPS	DPS	Stock Price	ROE	R
Arctic Cooling, Inc.	$ .82	$ .16	$15.19	11%	10%
National Heating & Cooling	1.32	.52	12.49	14	13
Expert HVAC Corp.	−.47	.54	48.60	14	12
Industry average	$0.56	$0.41	$25.43	13%	11.67%

Expert HVAC Corp.'s negative earnings per share (EPS) were the result of an accounting write-off last year. Without the write-off, EPS for the company would have been $2.34.

Last year, Ragan had an EPS of $4.32 and paid a dividend to Carrington and Genevieve of $54,000 each. The company also had a return on equity of 25 percent. The siblings believe a required return for the company of 20 percent is appropriate.

1. Assuming the company continues its current growth rate, what is the value per share of the company's stock?

2. To verify their calculations, Carrington and Genevieve have hired Josh Schlessman as a consultant. Josh was previously an equity analyst, and he has covered the HVAC industry. Josh has examined the company's financial statements as well as those of its competitors. Although Ragan currently has a technological advantage, Josh's research indicates that Ragan's competitors are investigating other methods to improve efficiency. Given this, Josh believes that Ragan's technological advantage will last for only the next five years. After that period, the company's growth will likely slow to the industry average. Additionally, Josh believes that the required return the company uses is too high. He believes the industry average required return is more appropriate. Under Josh's assumptions, what is the estimated stock price?

3. What is the industry average price–earnings ratio? What is Ragan's price–earnings ratio? Comment on any differences and explain why they may exist.

4. Assume the company's growth rate declines to the industry average after five years. What percentage of the stock's value is attributable to growth opportunities?

5. Assume the company's growth rate slows to the industry average in five years. What future return on equity does this imply?

6. After discussions with Josh, Carrington and Genevieve agree that they would like to try to increase the value of the company stock. Like many small business owners, they want to retain control of the company and do not want to sell stock to outside investors. They also feel that the company's debt is at a manageable level and do not want to borrow more money. What steps can they take to increase the price of the stock? Are there any conditions under which this strategy would not increase the stock price?

Appendix 5A   The Term Structure of Interest Rates, Spot Rates, and Yield to Maturity

To access the appendix for this chapter, please go to www.mhhe.com/rwj.

Net Present Value and Other Investment Rules

In 2005, the automobile market in North America faced chronic overcapacity. By some estimates, General Motors may have had as many as 15 factories more than it needed. But not all automobile manufacturers faced this problem. For example, Toyota Motors announced plans for its seventh North American assembly plant, and then began a search for a site to accommodate its eighth North American plant. Each plant represents an investment of $1 billion or more. For example, Toyota's truck factory in southern Indiana was built at a cost of $2.5 billion.

Toyota's new plants are an example of a capital budgeting decision. Decisions such as these, with a price tag of over $1 billion each, are obviously major undertakings, and the risks and rewards must be carefully weighed. In this chapter, we discuss the basic tools used in making such decisions.

In Chapter 1, we saw that increasing the value of the stock in a company is the goal of financial management. Thus, what we need to know is how to tell whether a particular investment will achieve that. This chapter considers a variety of techniques that are used in practice for this purpose. More important, it shows how many of these techniques can be misleading, and it explains why the net present value approach is the right one.

6.1 Why Use Net Present Value?

This chapter, as well as the next two, focuses on *capital budgeting*, the decision-making process for accepting or rejecting projects. This chapter develops the basic capital budgeting methods, leaving much of the practical application to subsequent chapters. But we don't have to develop these methods from scratch. In Chapter 4, we pointed out that a dollar received in the future is worth less than a dollar received today. The reason, of course, is that today's dollar can be reinvested, yielding a greater amount in the future. And we showed in Chapter 4 that the exact worth of a dollar to be received in the future is its present value. Furthermore, Section 4.1 suggested calculating the *net present value* of any project. That is, the section suggested calculating the difference between the sum of the present values of the project's future cash flows and the initial cost of the project.

The net present value (NPV) method is the first one to be considered in this chapter. We begin by reviewing the approach with a simple example. Then, we ask why the method leads to good decisions.

Find out more about capital budgeting for small businesses at **www. missouribusiness.net**.

EXAMPLE 6.1

Net Present Value   The Alpha Corporation is considering investing in a riskless project costing $100. The project receives $107 in one year and has no other cash flows. The discount rate is 6 percent.

The NPV of the project can easily be calculated as

$$\$.94 = -\$100 + \frac{\$107}{1.06} \qquad (6.1)$$

From Chapter 4, we know that the project should be accepted because its NPV is positive. Had the NPV of the project been negative, as would have been the case with an interest rate greater than 7 percent, the project should be rejected.

The basic investment rule can be generalized thus:

Accept a project if the NPV is greater than zero.

Reject a project if NPV is less than zero.

We refer to this as the **NPV rule**.

Why does the NPV rule lead to good decisions? Consider the following two strategies available to the managers of Alpha Corporation:

1. Use $100 of corporate cash to invest in the project. The $107 will be paid as a dividend in one year.

2. Forgo the project and pay the $100 of corporate cash as a dividend today.

If strategy 2 is employed, the stockholder might deposit the dividend in a bank for one year. With an interest rate of 6 percent, strategy 2 would produce cash of $106 (= $100 × 1.06) at the end of the year. The stockholder would prefer strategy 1 because strategy 2 produces less than $107 at the end of the year.

Our basic point is this: Accepting positive NPV projects benefits the stockholders.

How do we interpret the exact NPV of $0.94? This is the increase in the value of the firm from the project. For example, imagine that the firm today has productive assets worth $V and has $100 of cash. If the firm forgoes the project, the value of the firm today would simply be:

$$\$V + \$100$$

If the firm accepts the project, the firm will receive $107 in one year but will have no cash today. Thus, the firm's value today would be:

$$\$V + \frac{\$107}{1.06}$$

The difference between these equations is just $0.94, the present value of Equation 6.1. Thus: The value of the firm rises by the NPV of the project.

Note that the value of the firm is merely the sum of the values of the different projects, divisions, or other entities within the firm. This property, called **value additivity**, is quite important. It implies that the contribution of any project to a firm's value is simply the NPV of the project. As we will see later, alternative methods discussed in this chapter do not generally have this nice property.

One detail remains. We assumed that the project was riskless, a rather implausible assumption. Future cash flows of real-world projects are invariably risky. In other words, cash flows can only be estimated, rather than known. Imagine that the managers of Alpha *expect* the cash flow of the project to be $107 next year. That is, the cash flow could be higher, say $117, or lower, say $97. With this slight change, the project is risky. Suppose the project is about as risky as the stock market as a whole, where the expected return this year is perhaps 10 percent. Then 10 percent becomes the discount rate, implying that the NPV of the project would be:

$$-\$2.73 = -\$100 + \frac{\$107}{1.10}$$

Because the NPV is negative, the project should be rejected. This makes sense: A stockholder of Alpha receiving a $100 dividend today could invest it in the stock market, expecting a 10 percent return. Why accept a project with the same risk as the market but with an expected return of only 7 percent?

Conceptually, the discount rate on a risky project is the return that one can expect to earn on a financial asset of comparable risk. This discount rate is often referred to as an *opportunity cost* because corporate investment in the project takes away the stockholder's opportunity to invest the dividend in a financial asset. If the actual calculation of the discount rate strikes you as extremely difficult in the real world, you are probably right. Although you can call a bank to find out the current interest rate, whom do you call to find the expected return on the market this year? And, if the risk of the project differs from that of the market, how do you make the adjustment? However, the calculation is by no means impossible. We forgo the calculation in this chapter, but we present it in later chapters of the text.

Having shown that NPV is a sensible approach, how can we tell whether alternative methods are as good as NPV? The key to NPV is its three attributes:

1. *NPV uses cash flows.* Cash flows from a project can be used for other corporate purposes (such as dividend payments, other capital budgeting projects, or payments of corporate interest). By contrast, earnings are an artificial construct. Although earnings are useful to accountants, they should not be used in capital budgeting because they do not represent cash.

2. *NPV uses all the cash flows of the project.* Other approaches ignore cash flows beyond a particular date; beware of these approaches.

3. *NPV discounts the cash flows properly.* Other approaches may ignore the time value of money when handling cash flows. Beware of these approaches as well.

6.2 The Payback Period Method

Defining the Rule

One of the most popular alternatives to NPV is **payback**. Here is how payback works: Consider a project with an initial investment of −$50,000. Cash flows are $30,000, $20,000, and $10,000 in the first three years, respectively. These flows are illustrated in Figure 6.1. A useful way of writing down investments like the preceding is with the notation

$$(-\$50,000, \$30,000, \$20,000, \$10,000)$$

Figure 6.1

Cash Flows of an
Investment Project

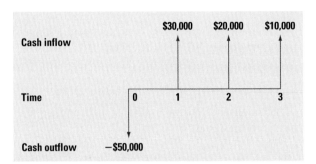

The minus sign in front of the $50,000 reminds us that this is a cash outflow for the investor, and the commas between the different numbers indicate that they are received—or if they are cash outflows, that they are paid out—at different times. In this example we are assuming that the cash flows occur one year apart, with the first one occurring the moment we decide to take on the investment.

The firm receives cash flows of $30,000 and $20,000 in the first two years, which add up to the $50,000 original investment. This means that the firm has recovered its investment within two years. In this case two years is the *payback period* of the investment.

The **payback period rule** for making investment decisions is simple. A particular cutoff date, say two years, is selected. All investment projects that have payback periods of two years or less are accepted, and all of those that pay off in more than two years—if at all—are rejected.

Problems with the Payback Method

There are at least three problems with payback. To illustrate the first two problems, we consider the three projects in Table 6.1. All three projects have the same three-year payback period, so they should all be equally attractive—right?

Actually, they are not equally attractive, as can be seen by a comparison of different *pairs* of projects.

Problem 1: Timing of Cash Flows within the Payback Period   Let us compare project *A* with project *B*. In years 1 through 3, the cash flows of project *A* rise from $20 to $50, while the cash flows of project *B* fall from $50 to $20. Because the large cash flow of $50 comes earlier with project *B*, its net present value must be higher. Nevertheless, we just saw that the payback periods of the two projects are identical. Thus, a problem with the payback method is that it does not consider the timing of the cash flows within the payback period. This example shows that the payback method is inferior to NPV because, as we pointed out earlier, the NPV method *discounts the cash flows properly.*

Problem 2: Payments after the Payback Period   Now consider projects *B* and *C*, which have identical cash flows within the payback period. However, project *C* is clearly preferred because it has a cash flow of $60,000 in the fourth year. Thus, another problem

Table 6.1

Expected Cash
Flows for Projects *A*
through *C* ($)

Year	A	B	C
0	−$100	−$100	−$100
1	20	50	50
2	30	30	30
3	50	20	20
4	60	60	60,000
Payback period (years)	3	3	3

with the payback method is that it ignores all cash flows occurring after the payback period. Because of the short-term orientation of the payback method, some valuable long-term projects are likely to be rejected. The NPV method does not have this flaw because, as we pointed out earlier, this method *uses all the cash flows of the project.*

Problem 3: Arbitrary Standard for Payback Period   We do not need to refer to Table 6.1 when considering a third problem with the payback method. Capital markets help us estimate the discount rate used in the NPV method. The riskless rate, perhaps proxied by the yield on a Treasury instrument, would be the appropriate rate for a riskless investment. Later chapters of this textbook show how to use historical returns in the capital markets to estimate the discount rate for a risky project. However, there is no comparable guide for choosing the payback cutoff date, so the choice is somewhat arbitrary.

Managerial Perspective

The payback method is often used by large, sophisticated companies when making relatively small decisions. The decision to build a small warehouse, for example, or to pay for a tune-up for a truck is the sort of decision that is often made by lower-level management. Typically, a manager might reason that a tune-up would cost, say, $200, and if it saved $120 each year in reduced fuel costs, it would pay for itself in less than two years. On such a basis the decision would be made.

Although the treasurer of the company might not have made the decision in the same way, the company endorses such decision making. Why would upper management condone or even encourage such retrograde activity in its employees? One answer would be that it is easy to make decisions using payback. Multiply the tune-up decision into 50 such decisions a month, and the appeal of this simple method becomes clearer.

The payback method also has some desirable features for managerial control. Just as important as the investment decision itself is the company's ability to evaluate the manager's decision-making ability. Under the NPV method, a long time may pass before one decides whether a decision was correct. With the payback method we know in two years whether the manager's assessment of the cash flows was correct.

It has also been suggested that firms with good investment opportunities but no available cash may justifiably use payback. For example, the payback method could be used by small, privately held firms with good growth prospects but limited access to the capital markets. Quick cash recovery enhances the reinvestment possibilities for such firms.

Finally, practitioners often argue that standard academic criticisms of payback overstate any real-world problems with the method. For example, textbooks typically make fun of payback by positing a project with low cash inflows in the early years but a huge cash inflow right after the payback cutoff date. This project is likely to be rejected under the payback method, though its acceptance would, in truth, benefit the firm. Project *C* in our Table 6.1 is an example of such a project. Practitioners point out that the pattern of cash flows in these textbook examples is much too stylized to mirror the real world. In fact, a number of executives have told us that for the overwhelming majority of real-world projects, both payback and NPV lead to the same decision. In addition, these executives indicate that if an investment like project *C* were encountered in the real world, decision makers would almost certainly make ad hoc adjustments to the payback rule so that the project would be accepted.

Notwithstanding all of the preceding rationale, it is not surprising to discover that as the decisions grow in importance, which is to say when firms look at bigger projects, NPV becomes the order of the day. When questions of controlling and evaluating the manager become less important than making the right investment decision, payback is used less frequently. For big-ticket decisions, such as whether or not to buy a machine, build a factory, or acquire a company, the payback method is seldom used.

Summary of Payback

The payback method differs from NPV and is therefore conceptually wrong. With its arbitrary cutoff date and its blindness to cash flows after that date, it can lead to some flagrantly foolish decisions if it is used too literally. Nevertheless, because of its simplicity, as well as its other mentioned advantages, companies often use it as a screen for making the myriad minor investment decisions they continually face.

Although this means that you should be wary of trying to change approaches such as the payback method when you encounter them in companies, you should probably be careful not to accept the sloppy financial thinking they represent. After this course, you would do your company a disservice if you used payback instead of NPV when you had a choice.

6.3   The Discounted Payback Period Method

Aware of the pitfalls of payback, some decision makers use a variant called the **discounted payback period method**. Under this approach, we first discount the cash flows. Then we ask how long it takes for the discounted cash flows to equal the initial investment.

For example, suppose that the discount rate is 10 percent and the cash flows on a project are given by:

$$(-\$100, \$50, \$50, \$20)$$

This investment has a payback period of two years because the investment is paid back in that time.

To compute the project's discounted payback period, we first discount each of the cash flows at the 10 percent rate. These discounted cash flows are:

$$[-\$100, \$50/1.1, \$50/(1.1)^2, \$20/(1.1)^3] = (-\$100, \$45.45, \$41.32, \$15.03)$$

The discounted payback period of the original investment is simply the payback period for these discounted cash flows. The payback period for the discounted cash flows is slightly less than three years because the discounted cash flows over the three years are \$101.80 ($=\$45.45 + 41.32 + 15.03$). As long as the cash flows and discount rate are positive, the discounted payback period will never be smaller than the payback period because discounting reduces the value of the cash flows.

At first glance discounted payback may seem like an attractive alternative, but on closer inspection we see that it has some of the same major flaws as payback. Like payback, discounted payback first requires us to make a somewhat magical choice of an arbitrary cutoff period, and then it ignores all cash flows after that date.

If we have already gone to the trouble of discounting the cash flows, any small appeal to simplicity or to managerial control that payback may have has been lost. We might just as well add up all the discounted cash flows and use NPV to make the decision. Although discounted payback looks a bit like NPV, it is just a poor compromise between the payback method and NPV.

6.4   The Average Accounting Return Method

Defining the Rule

Another attractive, but fatally flawed, approach to financial decision making is the **average accounting return**. The average accounting return is the average project earnings after taxes and depreciation, divided by the average book value of the investment during its life.

In spite of its flaws, the average accounting return method is worth examining because it is used frequently in the real world.

Average Accounting Return   Consider a company that is evaluating whether to buy a store in a new mall. The purchase price is $500,000. We will assume that the store has an estimated life of five years and will need to be completely scrapped or rebuilt at the end of that time. The projected yearly sales and expense figures are shown in Table 6.2.

Table 6.2   **Projected Yearly Revenue and Costs for Average Accounting Return**

	Year 1	Year 2	Year 3	Year 4	Year 5
Revenue	$433,333	$450,000	$266,667	$200,000	$133,333
Expenses	200,000	150,000	100,000	100,000	100,000
Before-tax cash flow	233,333	300,000	166,667	100,000	33,333
Depreciation	100,000	100,000	100,000	100,000	100,000
Earnings before taxes	133,333	200,000	66,667	0	− 66,667
Taxes ($t_c = .25$)*	33,333	50,000	16,667	0	− 16,667
Net income	$100,000	$150,000	$ 50,000	$ 0	−$ 50,000

$$\text{Average net income} = \frac{(\$100,000 + 150,000 + 50,000 + 0 - 50,000)}{5} = \$50,000$$

$$\text{Average investment} = \frac{\$500,000 + 0}{2} = \$250,000$$

$$\text{AAR} = \frac{\$50,000}{\$250,000} = 20\%$$

*Corporate tax rate $= t_c$. The tax rebate in year 5 of −$16,667 occurs if the rest of the firm is profitable. Here the loss in the project reduces the taxes of the entire firm.

It is worth examining Table 6.2 carefully. In fact, the first step in any project assessment is a careful look at projected cash flows. First-year sales for the store are estimated to be $433,333. Before-tax cash flow will be $233,333. Sales are expected to rise and expenses are expected to fall in the second year, resulting in a before-tax cash flow of $300,000. Competition from other stores and the loss in novelty will reduce before-tax cash flow to $166,667, $100,000, and $33,333, respectively, in the next three years.

To compute the average accounting return (AAR) on the project, we divide the average net income by the average amount invested. This can be done in three steps.

Step 1: Determining Average Net Income   Net income in any year is net cash flow minus depreciation and taxes. Depreciation is *not* a cash outflow.[1] Rather, it is a charge reflecting the fact that the investment in the store becomes less valuable every year.

We assume the project has a useful life of five years, at which time it will be worthless. Because the initial investment is $500,000 and because it will be worthless in five years, we assume that it loses value at the rate of $100,000 each year. This steady loss in value of $100,000 is called *straight-line depreciation*. We subtract both depreciation and taxes from before-tax cash flow to derive net income, as shown in Table 6.2. Net income is $100,000

[1]Depreciation will be treated in more detail in the next chapter.

in the first year, $150,000 in year 2, $50,000 in year 3, zero in year 4, and −$50,000 in the last year. The average net income over the life of the project is therefore:

Average Net Income:

$$[\$100,000 + 150,000 + 50,000 + 0 + (-50,000)]/5 = \$50,000$$

Step 2: Determining Average Investment   We stated earlier that, due to depreciation, the investment in the store becomes less valuable every year. Because depreciation is $100,000 per year, the value at the end of year zero is $500,000, the value at the end of year 1 is $400,000, and so on. What is the average value of the investment over the life of the investment?

The mechanical calculation is:

Average Investment:

$$(\$500,000 + 400,000 + 300,000 + 200,000 + 100,000 + 0)/6 \qquad \text{(6.2)}$$
$$= \$250,000$$

We divide by 6, not 5, because $500,000 is what the investment is worth at the beginning of the five years and $0 is what it is worth at the beginning of the sixth year. In other words, there are six terms in the parentheses of Equation 6.2.

Step 3: Determining AAR   The average return is simply:

$$\text{AAR} = \frac{\$50,000}{\$250,000} = 20\%$$

If the firm had a targeted accounting rate of return greater than 20 percent, the project would be rejected; if its targeted return were less than 20 percent, it would be accepted.

Analyzing the Average Accounting Return Method

By now you should be able to see what is wrong with the AAR method.

The most important flaw with AAR is that it does not work with the right raw materials. It uses net income and book value of the investment, both of which come from the accounting books. Accounting numbers are somewhat arbitrary. For example, certain cash outflows, such as the cost of a building, are depreciated under current accounting rules. Other flows, such as maintenance, are expensed. In real-world situations, the decision to depreciate or expense an item involves judgment. Thus, the basic inputs of the AAR method, income and average investment, are affected by the accountant's judgment. Conversely, the NPV method *uses cash flows*. Accounting judgments do not affect cash flow.

Second, AAR takes no account of timing. In the previous example, the AAR would have been the same if the $100,000 net income in the first year had occurred in the last year. However, delaying an inflow for five years would have lowered the NPV of the investment. As mentioned earlier in this chapter, the NPV approach *discounts properly*.

Third, just as payback requires an arbitrary choice of the cutoff date, the AAR method offers no guidance on what the right targeted rate of return should be. It could be the discount rate in the market. But then again, because the AAR method is not the same as the present value method, it is not obvious that this would be the right choice.

Given these problems, is the AAR method employed in practice? Like the payback method, the AAR (and variations of it) is frequently used as a "backup" to discounted cash flow methods. Perhaps this is so because it is easy to calculate and uses accounting numbers readily available from the firm's accounting system. In addition, both stockholders and the media pay a lot of attention to the overall profitability of a firm. Thus, some managers

Figure 6.2

Cash Flows for a Simple Project

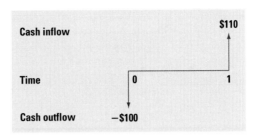

may feel pressured to select projects that are profitable in the near term, even if the projects come up short in terms of NPV. These managers may focus on the AAR of individual projects more than they should.

6.5 The Internal Rate of Return

Now we come to the most important alternative to the NPV method: the internal rate of return, universally known as the IRR. The IRR is about as close as you can get to the NPV without actually being the NPV. The basic rationale behind the IRR method is that it provides a single number summarizing the merits of a project. That number does not depend on the interest rate prevailing in the capital market. That is why it is called the internal rate of return; the number is internal or intrinsic to the project and does not depend on anything except the cash flows of the project.

For example, consider the simple project ($-\$100$, $\$110$) in Figure 6.2. For a given rate, the net present value of this project can be described as:

$$\text{NPV} = -\$100 + \frac{\$110}{1 + R}$$

where R is the discount rate. What must the discount rate be to make the NPV of the project equal to zero?

We begin by using an arbitrary discount rate of .08, which yields:

$$\$1.85 = -\$100 + \frac{\$110}{1.08}$$

Because the NPV in this equation is positive, we now try a higher discount rate, such as .12. This yields:

$$-\$1.79 = -\$100 + \frac{\$110}{1.12}$$

Because the NPV in this equation is negative, we try lowering the discount rate to .10. This yields:

$$0 = -\$100 + \frac{\$110}{1.10}$$

This trial-and-error procedure tells us that the NPV of the project is zero when R equals 10 percent.[2] Thus, we say that 10 percent is the project's **internal rate of return** (IRR). In

---

[2]Of course, we could have directly solved for R in this example after setting NPV equal to zero. However, with a long series of cash flows, one cannot generally directly solve for R. Instead, one is forced to use trial and error (or let a machine use trial and error).

Figure 6.3

Cash Flows for
a More Complex
Project

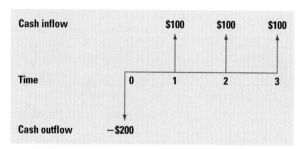

general, the IRR is the rate that causes the NPV of the project to be zero. The implication of this exercise is very simple. The firm should be equally willing to accept or reject the project if the discount rate is 10 percent. The firm should accept the project if the discount rate is below 10 percent. The firm should reject the project if the discount rate is above 10 percent.

The general investment rule is clear:

Accept the project if the IRR is greater than the discount rate. Reject the project if the IRR is less than the discount rate.

We refer to this as the **basic IRR rule**. Now we can try the more complicated example (−$200, $100, $100, $100) in Figure 6.3.

As we did previously, let's use trial and error to calculate the internal rate of return. We try 20 percent and 30 percent, yielding the following:

Discount Rate	NPV
20%	$10.65
30	−18.39

After much more trial and error, we find that the NPV of the project is zero when the discount rate is 23.37 percent. Thus, the IRR is 23.37 percent. With a 20 percent discount rate, the NPV is positive and we would accept it. However, if the discount rate were 30 percent, we would reject it.

Algebraically, IRR is the unknown in the following equation:[3]

$$0 = -\$200 + \frac{\$100}{1+IRR} + \frac{\$100}{(1+IRR)^2} + \frac{\$100}{(1+IRR)^3}$$

Figure 6.4 illustrates what the IRR of a project means. The figure plots the NPV as a function of the discount rate. The curve crosses the horizontal axis at the IRR of 23.37 percent because this is where the NPV equals zero.

It should also be clear that the NPV is positive for discount rates below the IRR and negative for discount rates above the IRR. This means that if we accept projects like this one when the discount rate is less than the IRR, we will be accepting positive NPV projects. Thus, the IRR rule coincides exactly with the NPV rule.

If this were all there were to it, the IRR rule would always coincide with the NPV rule. This would be a wonderful discovery because it would mean that just by computing the

---

[3]One can derive the IRR directly for a problem with an initial outflow and up to four subsequent inflows. In the case of two subsequent inflows, for example, the quadratic formula is needed. In general, however, only trial and error will work for an outflow and five or more subsequent inflows.

Figure 6.4

Net Present Value (NPV) and Discount Rates for a More Complex Project

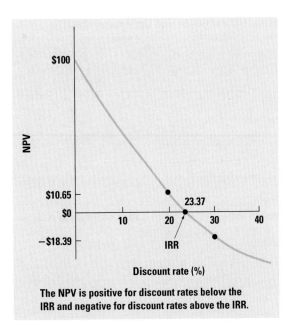

The NPV is positive for discount rates below the IRR and negative for discount rates above the IRR.

IRR for a project we would be able to tell where it ranks among all of the projects we are considering. For example, if the IRR rule really works, a project with an IRR of 20 percent will always be at least as good as one with an IRR of 15 percent.

But the world of finance is not so kind. Unfortunately, the IRR rule and the NPV rule are the same only for examples like the one just discussed. Several problems with the IRR approach occur in more complicated situations.

6.6 Problems with the IRR Approach

Definition of Independent and Mutually Exclusive Projects

An **independent project** is one whose acceptance or rejection is independent of the acceptance or rejection of other projects. For example, imagine that McDonald's is considering putting a hamburger outlet on a remote island. Acceptance or rejection of this unit is likely to be unrelated to the acceptance or rejection of any other restaurant in its system. The remoteness of the outlet in question ensures that it will not pull sales away from other outlets.

Now consider the other extreme, **mutually exclusive investments**. What does it mean for two projects, A and B, to be mutually exclusive? You can accept A or you can accept B or you can reject both of them, but you cannot accept both of them. For example, A might be a decision to build an apartment house on a corner lot that you own, and B might be a decision to build a movie theater on the same lot.

We now present two general problems with the IRR approach that affect both independent and mutually exclusive projects. Then we deal with two problems affecting mutually exclusive projects only.

Two General Problems Affecting Both Independent and Mutually Exclusive Projects

We begin our discussion with project A, which has the following cash flows:

$$(-\$100, \$130)$$

Table 6.3   **The Internal Rate of Return and Net Present Value**

Dates:	Project A			Project B			Project C		
	0	**1**	**2**	**0**	**1**	**2**	**0**	**1**	**2**
Cash flows	−$100	$130		$100	−$130		−$100	$230	−$132
IRR		30%			30%		10%	and	20%
NPV @10%		$18.2			−$18.2			0	
Accept if market rate		<30%			>30%		>10%	but	<20%
Financing or investing		Investing			Financing			Mixture	

Figure 6.5   **Net Present Value and Discount Rates for Projects *A*, *B*, and *C***

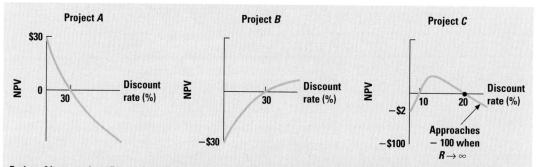

Project *A* has a cash outflow at date 0 followed by a cash inflow at date 1. Its NPV is negatively related to the discount rate.
Project *B* has a cash inflow at date 0 followed by a cash outflow at date 1. Its NPV is positively related to the discount rate.
Project *C* has two changes of sign in its cash flows. It has an outflow at date 0, an inflow at date 1, and an outflow at date 2.
Projects with more than one change of sign can have multiple rates of return.

The IRR for project *A* is 30 percent. Table 6.3 provides other relevant information about the project. The relationship between NPV and the discount rate is shown for this project in Figure 6.5. As you can see, the NPV declines as the discount rate rises.

Problem 1: Investing or Financing?   Now consider project *B*, with cash flows of:

$$(\$100, -\$130)$$

These cash flows are exactly the reverse of the flows for project *A*. In project *B*, the firm receives funds first and then pays out funds later. While unusual, projects of this type do exist. For example, consider a corporation conducting a seminar where the participants pay in advance. Because large expenses are frequently incurred at the seminar date, cash inflows precede cash outflows.

Consider our trial-and-error method to calculate IRR:

$$-\$4 = +\$100 - \frac{\$130}{1.25}$$

$$\$0 = +\$100 - \frac{\$130}{1.30}$$

$$\$3.70 = +\$100 - \frac{\$130}{1.35}$$

As with project *A*, the internal rate of return is 30 percent. However, notice that the net present value is *negative* when the discount rate is *below* 30 percent. Conversely, the net present value is positive when the discount rate is above 30 percent. The decision rule is exactly the opposite of our previous result. For this type of a project, the following rule applies:

Accept the project when the IRR is less than the discount rate. Reject the project when the IRR is greater than the discount rate.

This unusual decision rule follows from the graph of project *B* in Figure 6.5. The curve is upward sloping, implying that NPV is *positively* related to the discount rate.

The graph makes intuitive sense. Suppose the firm wants to obtain $100 immediately. It can either (1) accept project *B* or (2) borrow $100 from a bank. Thus, the project is actually a substitute for borrowing. In fact, because the IRR is 30 percent, taking on project *B* is tantamount to borrowing at 30 percent. If the firm can borrow from a bank at, say, only 25 percent, it should reject the project. However, if a firm can borrow from a bank only at, say, 35 percent, it should accept the project. Thus project *B* will be accepted if and only if the discount rate is *above* the IRR.[4]

This should be contrasted with project *A*. If the firm has $100 of cash to invest, it can either (1) accept project *A* or (2) lend $100 to the bank. The project is actually a substitute for lending. In fact, because the IRR is 30 percent, taking on project *A* is tantamount to lending at 30 percent. The firm should accept project *A* if the lending rate is below 30 percent. Conversely, the firm should reject project *A* if the lending rate is above 30 percent.

Because the firm initially pays out money with project *A* but initially receives money with project *B*, we refer to project *A* as an *investing type project* and project *B* as a *financing type project*. Investing type projects are the norm. Because the IRR rule is reversed for financing type projects, be careful when using it with this type of project.

Problem 2: Multiple Rates of Return   Suppose the cash flows from a project are:

$$(-\$100, \$230, -\$132)$$

Because this project has a negative cash flow, a positive cash flow, and another negative cash flow, we say that the project's cash flows exhibit two changes of sign, or "flip-flops." Although this pattern of cash flows might look a bit strange at first, many projects require outflows of cash after receiving some inflows. An example would be a strip-mining project. The first stage in such a project is the initial investment in excavating the mine. Profits from operating the mine are received in the second stage. The third stage involves a further investment to reclaim the land and satisfy the requirements of environmental protection legislation. Cash flows are negative at this stage.

Projects financed by lease arrangements may produce a similar pattern of cash flows. Leases often provide substantial tax subsidies, generating cash inflows after an initial investment. However, these subsidies decline over time, frequently leading to negative cash flows in later years. (The details of leasing will be discussed in a later chapter.)

It is easy to verify that this project has not one but two IRRs, 10 percent and 20 percent.[5] In a case like this, the IRR does not make any sense. What IRR are we to use—10 percent

---

[4]This paragraph implicitly assumes that the cash flows of the project are risk-free. In this way we can treat the borrowing rate as the discount rate for a firm needing $100. With risky cash flows, another discount rate would be chosen. However, the intuition behind the decision to accept when the IRR is less than the discount rate would still apply.

[5]The calculations are

$$-\$100 + \frac{\$230}{1.1} - \frac{\$132}{(1.1)^2}$$
$$-\$100 + 209.09 - 109.09 = 0$$

and

$$-\$100 + \frac{\$230}{1.2} - \frac{\$132}{(1.2)^2}$$
$$-\$100 + 191.67 - 91.67 = 0$$

Thus, we have multiple rates of return.

or 20 percent? Because there is no good reason to use one over the other, IRR simply cannot be used here.

Why does this project have multiple rates of return? Project C generates multiple internal rates of return because both an inflow and an outflow occur after the initial investment. In general, these flip-flops or changes in sign produce multiple IRRs. In theory, a cash flow stream with K changes in sign can have up to K sensible internal rates of return (IRRs above -100 percent). Therefore, because project C has two changes in sign, it can have as many as two IRRs. As we pointed out, projects whose cash flows change sign repeatedly can occur in the real world.

NPV Rule   Of course, we should not be too worried about multiple rates of return. After all, we can always fall back on the NPV rule. Figure 6.5 plots the NPV of project C ($-$100, $230, -$132) as a function of the discount rate. As the figure shows, the NPV is zero at both 10 percent and 20 percent and negative outside the range. Thus, the NPV rule tells us to accept the project if the appropriate discount rate is between 10 percent and 20 percent. The project should be rejected if the discount rate lies outside this range.

Modified IRR   As an alternative to NPV, we now introduce the **modified IRR (MIRR)** method, which handles the multiple IRR problem by combining cash flows until only one change in sign remains. To see how it works, consider project C again. With a discount rate of, say, 14 percent, the value of the last cash flow, $-$132, is:

$$-\$132/1.14 = -\$115.79$$

as of date 1. Because $230 is already received at that time, the "adjusted" cash flow at date 1 is $114.21 ($= \$230 - 115.79$). Thus, the MIRR approach produces the following two cash flows for the project:

$$(-\$100, \$114.21)$$

Note that by discounting and then combining cash flows, we are left with only one change in sign. The IRR rule can now be applied. The IRR of these two cash flows is 14.21 percent, implying that the project should be accepted given our assumed discount rate of 14 percent.

Of course, project C is relatively simple to begin with: It has only three cash flows and two changes in sign. However, the same procedure can easily be applied to more complex projects—that is, just keep discounting and combining the later cash flows until only one change of sign remains.

Although this adjustment does correct for multiple IRRs, it appears, at least to us, to violate the "spirit" of the IRR approach. As stated earlier, the basic rationale behind the IRR method is that it provides a single number summarizing the merits of a project. That number does not depend on the discount rate. In fact, that is why it is called the internal rate of return: The number is *internal*, or intrinsic, to the project and does not depend on anything except the cash flows of the project. By contrast, MIRR is clearly a function of the discount rate. However, a firm using this adjustment will avoid the multiple IRR problem, just as a firm using the NPV rule will avoid it.

The Guarantee against Multiple IRRs   If the first cash flow of a project is negative (because it is the initial investment) and if all of the remaining flows are positive, there can be only a single, unique IRR, no matter how many periods the project lasts. This is easy to understand by using the concept of the time value of money. For example, it is simple to verify that project A in Table 6.3 has an IRR of 30 percent because using a 30-percent discount rate gives

$$\text{NPV} = -\$100 + \$130/(1.3)$$
$$= \$0$$

How do we know that this is the only IRR? Suppose we were to try a discount rate greater than 30 percent. In computing the NPV, changing the discount rate does not change the value of the initial cash flow of −$100 because that cash flow is not discounted. But raising the discount rate can only lower the present value of the future cash flows. In other words, because the NPV is zero at 30 percent, any increase in the rate will push the NPV into the negative range. Similarly, if we try a discount rate of less than 30 percent, the overall NPV of the project will be positive. Though this example has only one positive flow, the above reasoning still implies a single, unique IRR if there are many inflows (but no outflows) after the initial investment.

If the initial cash flow is positive—and if all of the remaining flows are negative—there can only be a single, unique IRR. This result follows from similar reasoning. Both these cases have only one change of sign or flip-flop in the cash flows. Thus, we are safe from multiple IRRs whenever there is only one sign change in the cash flows.

General Rules The following chart summarizes our rules:

Flows	Number of IRRs	IRR Criterion	NPV Criterion
First cash flow is negative and all remaining cash flows are positive.	1	Accept if IRR > R. Reject if IRR < R.	Accept if NPV > 0. Reject if NPV < 0.
First cash flow is positive and all remaining cash flows are negative.	1	Accept if IRR < R. Reject if IRR > R.	Accept if NPV > 0. Reject if NPV < 0.
Some cash flows after first are positive and some cash flows after first are negative.	May be more than 1.	No valid IRR.	Accept if NPV > 0. Reject if NPV < 0.

Note that the NPV criterion is the same for each of the three cases. In other words, NPV analysis is always appropriate. Conversely, the IRR can be used only in certain cases. When it comes to NPV, the preacher's words, "You just can't lose with the stuff I use," clearly apply.

Problems Specific to Mutually Exclusive Projects

As mentioned earlier, two or more projects are mutually exclusive if the firm can accept only one of them. We now present two problems dealing with the application of the IRR approach to mutually exclusive projects. These two problems are quite similar, though logically distinct.

The Scale Problem A professor we know motivates class discussions of this topic with this statement: "Students, I am prepared to let one of you choose between two mutually exclusive 'business' propositions. Opportunity 1—You give me $1 now and I'll give you $1.50 back at the end of the class period. Opportunity 2—You give me $10 and I'll give you $11 back at the end of the class period. You can choose only one of the two opportunities. And you cannot choose either opportunity more than once. I'll pick the first volunteer."

Which would you choose? The correct answer is opportunity 2.[6] To see this, look at the following chart:

	Cash Flow at Beginning of Class	Cash Flow at End of Class (90 Minutes Later)	NPV[7]	IRR
Opportunity 1	−$ 1	+$ 1.50	$ .50	50%
Opportunity 2	− 10	+ 11.00	1.00	10

As we have stressed earlier in the text, one should choose the opportunity with the highest NPV. This is opportunity 2 in the example. Or, as one of the professor's students explained it, "I'm bigger than the professor, so I know I'll get my money back. And I have $10 in my pocket right now so I can choose either opportunity. At the end of the class, I'll be able to play two rounds of my favorite electronic game with opportunity 2 and still have my original investment, safe and sound.[8] The profit on opportunity 1 buys only one round."

This business proposition illustrates a defect with the internal rate of return criterion. The basic IRR rule indicates the selection of opportunity 1 because the IRR is 50 percent. The IRR is only 10 percent for opportunity 2.

Where does IRR go wrong? The problem with IRR is that it ignores issues of *scale.* Although opportunity 1 has a greater IRR, the investment is much smaller. In other words, the high percentage return on opportunity 1 is more than offset by the ability to earn at least a decent return[9] on a much bigger investment under opportunity 2.

Because IRR seems to be misguided here, can we adjust or correct it? We illustrate how in the next example.

EXAMPLE 6.3

NPV versus IRR   Stanley Jaffe and Sherry Lansing have just purchased the rights to *Corporate Finance: The Motion Picture.* They will produce this major motion picture on either a small budget or a big budget. Here are the estimated cash flows:

	Cash Flow at Date 0	Cash Flow at Date 1	NPV @25%	IRR
Small budget	−$10 million	$40 million	$22 million	300%
Large budget	− 25 million	65 million	27 million	160

Because of high risk, a 25 percent discount rate is considered appropriate. Sherry wants to adopt the large budget because the NPV is higher. Stanley wants to adopt the small budget because the IRR is higher. Who is right?

(continued)

---

[6]The professor uses real money here. Though many students have done poorly on the professor's exams over the years, no student ever chose opportunity 1. The professor claims that his students are "money players."

[7]We assume a zero rate of interest because his class lasted only 90 minutes. It just seemed like a lot longer.

[8]At press time for this text, electronic games cost $0.50 apiece.

[9]A 10 percent return is more than decent over a 90-minute interval!

For the reasons espoused in the classroom example, NPV is correct. Hence Sherry is right. However, Stanley is very stubborn where IRR is concerned. How can Sherry justify the large budget to Stanley using the IRR approach?

This is where *incremental IRR* comes in. Sherry calculates the incremental cash flows from choosing the large budget instead of the small budget as follows:

	Cash Flow at Date 0 (in $ millions)	Cash Flow at Date 1 (in $ millions)
Incremental cash flows from choosing large budget instead of small budget	$-\$25 - (-10) = -\$15$	$\$65 - 40 = \$25$

This chart shows that the incremental cash flows are $-\$15$ million at date 0 and $\$25$ million at date 1. Sherry calculates incremental IRR as follows:

Formula for Calculating the Incremental IRR:

$$0 = -\$15 \text{ million} + \frac{\$25 \text{ million}}{1 + \text{IRR}}$$

IRR equals 66.67 percent in this equation, implying that the **incremental IRR** is 66.67 percent. Incremental IRR is the IRR on the incremental investment from choosing the large project instead of the small project.

In addition, we can calculate the NPV of the incremental cash flows:

NPV of Incremental Cash Flows:

$$-\$15 \text{ million} + \frac{\$25 \text{ million}}{1.25} = \$5 \text{ million}$$

We know the small-budget picture would be acceptable as an independent project because its NPV is positive. We want to know whether it is beneficial to invest an additional $15 million to make the large-budget picture instead of the small-budget picture. In other words, is it beneficial to invest an additional $15 million to receive an additional $25 million next year? First, our calculations show the NPV on the incremental investment to be positive. Second, the incremental IRR of 66.67 percent is higher than the discount rate of 25 percent. For both reasons, the incremental investment can be justified, so the large-budget movie should be made. The second reason is what Stanley needed to hear to be convinced.

In review, we can handle this example (or any mutually exclusive example) in one of three ways:

1. *Compare the NPVs of the two choices.* The NPV of the large-budget picture is greater than the NPV of the small-budget picture. That is, $27 million is greater than $22 million.

2. *Calculate the incremental NPV from making the large-budget picture instead of the small-budget picture.* Because the incremental NPV equals $5 million, we choose the large-budget picture.

3. *Compare the incremental IRR to the discount rate.* Because the incremental IRR is 66.67 percent and the discount rate is 25 percent, we take the large-budget picture.

All three approaches always give the same decision. However, we must *not* compare the IRRs of the two pictures. If we did, we would make the wrong choice. That is, we would accept the small-budget picture.

Although students frequently think that problems of scale are relatively unimportant, the truth is just the opposite. A well-known chef on TV often says, "I don't know about your flour, but the flour I buy don't come seasoned." The same thing applies to capital budgeting. No real-world project comes in one clear-cut size. Rather, the firm has to *determine* the best size for the project. The movie budget of $25 million is not fixed in stone. Perhaps an extra $1 million to hire a bigger star or to film at a better location will increase the movie's gross. Similarly, an industrial firm must decide whether it wants a warehouse of, say, 500,000 square feet or 600,000 square feet. And, earlier in the chapter, we imagined McDonald's opening an outlet on a remote island. If it does this, it must decide how big the outlet should be. For almost any project, someone in the firm has to decide on its size, implying that problems of scale abound in the real world.

One final note here. Students often ask which project should be subtracted from the other in calculating incremental flows. Notice that we are subtracting the smaller project's cash flows from the bigger project's cash flows. This leaves an *outflow* at date 0. We then use the basic IRR rule on the incremental flows.[10]

The Timing Problem   Next we illustrate another, quite similar problem with the IRR approach to evaluating mutually exclusive projects.

EXAMPLE 6.4

Mutually Exclusive Investments   Suppose that the Kaufold Corporation has two alternative uses for a warehouse. It can store toxic waste containers (investment A) or electronic equipment (investment B). The cash flows are as follows:

	Cash Flow at Year				NPV			
Year:	0	1	2	3	@0%	@10%	@15%	IRR
Investment A	−$10,000	$10,000	$1,000	$ 1,000	$2,000	$669	$109	16.04%
Investment B	−10,000	1,000	1,000	12,000	4,000	751	−484	12.94

We find that the NPV of investment B is higher with low discount rates, and the NPV of investment A is higher with high discount rates. This is not surprising if you look closely at the cash flow patterns. The cash flows of A occur early, whereas the cash flows of B occur later. If we assume a high discount rate, we favor investment A because we are implicitly assuming that the early cash flow (for example, $10,000 in year 1) can be reinvested at that rate. Because most of investment B's cash flows occur in year 3, B's value is relatively high with low discount rates.

The patterns of cash flow for both projects appear in Figure 6.6. Project *A* has an NPV of $2,000 at a discount rate of zero. This is calculated by simply adding up the cash flows without discounting them. Project *B* has an NPV of $4,000 at the zero rate. However, the NPV of project *B* declines more rapidly as the discount rate increases than does the NPV

---

[10]Alternatively, we could have subtracted the larger project's cash flows from the smaller project's cash flows. This would have left an *inflow* at date 0, making it necessary to use the IRR rule for financing situations. This would work, but we find it more confusing.

Figure 6.6

Net Present Value and
the Internal Rate of
Return for Mutually
Exclusive Projects

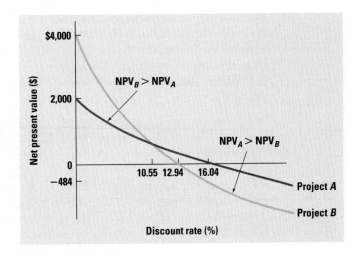

of project A. As we mentioned, this occurs because the cash flows of B occur later. Both projects have the same NPV at a discount rate of 10.55 percent. The IRR for a project is the rate at which the NPV equals zero. Because the NPV of B declines more rapidly, B actually has a lower IRR.

As with the movie example, we can select the better project with one of three different methods:

1. *Compare NPVs of the two projects.* Figure 6.6 aids our decision. If the discount rate is below 10.55 percent, we should choose project B because B has a higher NPV. If the rate is above 10.55 percent, we should choose project A because A has a higher NPV.

2. *Compare incremental IRR to discount rate.* Method 1 employed NPV. Another way of determining that B is a better project is to subtract the cash flows of A from the cash flows of B and then to calculate the IRR. This is the incremental IRR approach we spoke of earlier.

    Here are the incremental cash flows:

					NPV of Incremental Cash Flows			
Year:	0	1	2	3	Incremental IRR	@0%	@10%	@15%
B − A	0	−$9,000	0	$11,000	10.55%	$2,000	$83	−$593

This chart shows that the incremental IRR is 10.55 percent. In other words, the NPV on the incremental investment is zero when the discount rate is 10.55 percent. Thus, if the relevant discount rate is below 10.55 percent, project B is preferred to project A. If the relevant discount rate is above 10.55 percent, project A is preferred to project B.[11]

---

[11]In this example, we first showed that the NPVs of the two projects are equal when the discount rate is 10.55 percent. We next showed that the incremental IRR is also 10.55 percent. This is not a coincidence; this equality must *always* hold. The incremental IRR is the rate that causes the incremental cash flows to have zero NPV. The incremental cash flows have zero NPV when the two projects have the same NPV.

3. *Calculate NPV on incremental cash flows.* Finally, we could calculate the NPV on the incremental cash flows. The chart that appears with the previous method displays these NPVs. We find that the incremental NPV is positive when the discount rate is either 0 percent or 10 percent. The incremental NPV is negative if the discount rate is 15 percent. If the NPV is positive on the incremental flows, we should choose *B*. If the NPV is negative, we should choose *A*.

In summary, the same decision is reached whether we (1) compare the NPVs of the two projects, (2) compare the incremental IRR to the relevant discount rate, or (3) examine the NPV of the incremental cash flows. However, as mentioned earlier, we should *not* compare the IRR of project *A* with the IRR of project *B*.

We suggested earlier that we should subtract the cash flows of the smaller project from the cash flows of the bigger project. What do we do here when the two projects have the same initial investment? Our suggestion in this case is to perform the subtraction so that the *first* nonzero cash flow is negative. In the Kaufold Corp. example we achieved this by subtracting *A* from *B*. In this way, we can still use the basic IRR rule for evaluating cash flows.

The preceding examples illustrate problems with the IRR approach in evaluating mutually exclusive projects. Both the professor–student example and the motion picture example illustrate the problem that arises when mutually exclusive projects have different initial investments. The Kaufold Corp. example illustrates the problem that arises when mutually exclusive projects have different cash flow timing. When working with mutually exclusive projects, it is not necessary to determine whether it is the scale problem or the timing problem that exists. Very likely both occur in any real-world situation. Instead, the practitioner should simply use either an incremental IRR or an NPV approach.

Redeeming Qualities of IRR

IRR probably survives because it fills a need that NPV does not. People seem to want a rule that summarizes the information about a project in a single rate of return. This single rate gives people a simple way of discussing projects. For example, one manager in a firm might say to another, "Remodeling the north wing has a 20 percent IRR."

To their credit, however, companies that employ the IRR approach seem to understand its deficiencies. For example, companies frequently restrict managerial projections of cash flows to be negative at the beginning and strictly positive later. Perhaps, then, the ability of the IRR approach to capture a complex investment project in a single number and the ease of communicating that number explain the survival of the IRR.

A Test

To test your knowledge, consider the following two statements:

1. You must know the discount rate to compute the NPV of a project, but you compute the IRR without referring to the discount rate.

2. Hence, the IRR rule is easier to apply than the NPV rule because you don't use the discount rate when applying IRR.

The first statement is true. The discount rate is needed to *compute* NPV. The IRR is *computed* by solving for the rate where the NPV is zero. No mention is made of the discount rate in the mere computation. However, the second statement is false. To *apply* IRR, you must compare the internal rate of return with the discount rate. Thus the discount rate is needed for making a decision under either the NPV or IRR approach.

6.7 The Profitability Index

Another method used to evaluate projects is called the **profitability index**. It is the ratio of the present value of the future expected cash flows *after* initial investment divided by the amount of the initial investment. The profitability index can be represented like this:

$$\text{Profitability index (PI)} = \frac{\text{PV of cash flows } subsequent \text{ to initial investment}}{\text{Initial investment}}$$

EXAMPLE 6.5

Profitability Index   Hiram Finnegan Inc. (HFI) applies a 12 percent discount rate to two investment opportunities.

Project	Cash Flows ($000,000)			PV @ 12% of Cash Flows Subsequent to Initial Investment ($000,000)	Profit-ability Index	NPV @12% ($000,000)
	C_0	C_1	C_2			
1	−$20	$70	$10	$70.5	3.53	$50.5
2	− 10	15	40	45.3	4.53	35.3

Calculation of Profitability Index

The profitability index is calculated for project 1 as follows. The present value of the cash flows *after* the initial investment is:

$$\$70.5 = \frac{\$70}{1.12} + \frac{\$10}{(1.12)^2}$$

The profitability index is obtained by dividing this result by the initial investment of $20. This yields:

$$3.53 = \frac{\$70.5}{\$20}$$

Application of the Profitability Index   How do we use the profitability index? We consider three situations:

1. *Independent projects*: Assume that HFI's two projects are independent. According to the NPV rule, both projects should be accepted because NPV is positive in each case. The profitability index (PI) is greater than 1 whenever the NPV is positive. Thus, the PI *decision rule* is
   • Accept an independent project if PI > 1.
   • Reject it if PI < 1.

2. *Mutually exclusive projects*: Let us now assume that HFI can only accept one of its two projects. NPV analysis says accept project 1 because this project has the bigger NPV. Because project 2 has the higher PI, the profitability index leads to the wrong selection.

The problem with the profitability index for mutually exclusive projects is the same as the scale problem with the IRR that we mentioned earlier. Project 2 is smaller than project 1. Because the PI is a ratio, this index misses the fact that project 1 has a larger investment than project 2 has. Thus, like IRR, PI ignores differences of scale for mutually exclusive projects.

However, like IRR, the flaw with the PI approach can be corrected using incremental analysis. We write the incremental cash flows after subtracting project 2 from project 1 as follows:

	Cash Flows ($000,000)			PV @ 12% of Cash Flows Subsequent to Initial Investment ($000,000)	Profit-ability Index	NPV @12% ($000,000)
Project	C_0	C_1	C_2			
1–2	−$10	$55	−$30	$25.2	2.52	$15.2

Because the profitability index on the incremental cash flows is greater than 1.0, we should choose the bigger project—that is, project 1. This is the same decision we get with the NPV approach.

3. *Capital rationing*: The first two cases implicitly assumed that HFI could always attract enough capital to make any profitable investments. Now consider the case when the firm does not have enough capital to fund all positive NPV projects. This is the case of **capital rationing**.

Imagine that the firm has a third project, as well as the first two. Project 3 has the following cash flows:

	Cash Flows ($000,000)			PV @ 12% of Cash Flows Subsequent to Initial Investment ($000,000)	Profit-ability Index	NPV @12% ($000,000)
Project	C_0	C_1	C_2			
3	−$10	−$5	$60	$43.4	4.34	$33.4

Further, imagine that (1) the projects of Hiram Finnegan Inc. are independent, but (2) the firm has only $20 million to invest. Because project 1 has an initial investment of $20 million, the firm cannot select both this project and another one. Conversely, because projects 2 and 3 have initial investments of $10 million each, both these projects can be chosen. In other words, the cash constraint forces the firm to choose either project 1 or projects 2 and 3.

What should the firm do? Individually, projects 2 and 3 have lower NPVs than project 1 has. However, when the NPVs of projects 2 and 3 are added together, the sum is higher than the NPV of project 1. Thus, common sense dictates that projects 2 and 3 should be accepted.

What does our conclusion have to say about the NPV rule or the PI rule? In the case of limited funds, we cannot rank projects according to their NPVs. Instead we should rank them according to the ratio of present value to initial investment. This is the PI rule. Both project 2 and project 3 have higher PI ratios than does project 1. Thus they should be ranked ahead of project 1 when capital is rationed.

The usefulness of the profitability index under capital rationing can be explained in military terms. The Pentagon speaks highly of a weapon with a lot of "bang for the buck." In capital budgeting, the profitability index measures the bang (the dollar return) for the buck invested. Hence it is useful for capital rationing.

It should be noted that the profitability index does not work if funds are also limited beyond the initial time period. For example, if heavy cash outflows elsewhere in the firm were to occur at date 1, project 3, which also has a cash outflow at date 1, might need to be rejected. In other words, the profitability index cannot handle capital rationing over multiple time periods.

In addition, what economists term *indivisibilities* may reduce the effectiveness of the PI rule. Imagine that HFI has $30 million available for capital investment, not just $20 million. The firm now has enough cash for projects 1 and 2. Because the sum of the NPVs of these two projects is greater than the sum of the NPVs of projects 2 and 3, the firm would be better served by accepting projects 1 and 2. But because projects 2 and 3 still have the highest profitability indexes, the PI rule now leads to the wrong decision. Why does the PI rule lead us astray here? The key is that projects 1 and 2 use up all of the $30 million, whereas projects 2 and 3 have a combined initial investment of only $20 million (= $10 + 10). If projects 2 and 3 are accepted, the remaining $10 million must be left in the bank.

This situation points out that care should be exercised when using the profitability index in the real world. Nevertheless, while not perfect, the profitability index goes a long way toward handling capital rationing.

6.8   The Practice of Capital Budgeting

So far this chapter has asked "Which capital budgeting methods should companies be using?" An equally important question is this: Which methods *are* companies using? Table 6.4 helps answer this question. As can be seen from the table, approximately three-quarters of U.S. and Canadian companies use the IRR and NPV methods. This is not surprising, given the theoretical advantages of these approaches. Over half of these companies use the payback method, a rather surprising result given the conceptual problems with this approach. And while discounted payback represents a theoretical improvement over regular payback,

Table 6.4

Percentage of CFOs Who Always or Almost Always Use a Given Technique

	% Always or Almost Always
Internal rate of return (IRR)	75.6%
Net present value (NPV)	74.9
Payback method	56.7
Discounted payback	29.5
Accounting rate of return	30.3
Profitability index	11.9

SOURCE: Figure 2 from John R. Graham and Campbell R. Harvey, "The Theory and Practice of Corporate Finance: Evidence from the Field," *Journal of Financial Economics* 60 (2001). Based on a survey of 392 CFOs.

KITCHEN CONFIDENTIAL: ADVENTURES IN THE CULINARY UNDERBELLY BY ANTHONY BOURDAIN (BLOOMSBURY PRESS, 2000)

To want to own a restaurant can be a strange and terrible affliction. What causes such a destructive urge in so many otherwise sensible people? Why would anyone who has worked hard, saved money, and often been successful in other fields want to pump their hard-earned cash down a hole that statistically, at least, will almost surely prove dry? Why venture into an industry with enormous fixed expenses (rent, electricity, gas, water, linen, maintenance, insurance, license fees, trash removal, etc.), a notoriously transient and unstable workforce, and a highly perishable inventory of assets? The chances of ever seeing a return on your investment are about one in five. What insidious spongiform bacteria so riddles the brains of men and women that they stand there on the tracks, watching the lights of the oncoming locomotive, knowing full well it will eventually run them over? After all these years in the business, I still don't know.

Anthony Bourdain is also the author of the novels *Bone in the Throat, Gone Bamboo,* and *The Bobby Gold Stories.* He is the executive chef at Brasserie Les Halles in New York.

---

the usage here is far less. Perhaps companies are attracted to the user-friendly nature of payback. In addition, the flaws of this approach, as mentioned in the current chapter, may be relatively easy to correct. For example, while the payback method ignores all cash flows after the payback period, an alert manager can make ad hoc adjustments for a project with back-loaded cash flows.

Capital expenditures by individual corporations can add up to enormous sums for the economy as a whole. For example, in late 2005, Royal Dutch Shell announced it expected to increase its capital spending in 2006 to $19 billion, an increase of 17 percent over the previous year. About the same time, competitor Chevron Corp. announced it would increase its capital budget for 2006 to $14.8 billion, up from $11 billion in 2005. Other companies with large capital spending budgets in 2006 were ConocoPhillips, which projected capital spending of $11.4 billion, and Canadian-based Suncor Energy, which projected capital spending of $3.5 billion.

Capital spending is often an industrywide occurrence. For example, in 2006, capital spending by dynamic random access memory (DRAM) chip makers was expected to reach $16.84 billion. This amount represented only a 5 percent increase from 2005 and was a major slowdown for capital spending growth. From 2003 to 2004, the DRAM industry's capital spending had grown by an astonishing 65 percent.

According to information released by the Census Bureau in 2006, capital investment for the economy as a whole was actually $1.05 trillion in 2004, $975 billion in 2003, and $953 billion in 2002. The totals for the three years therefore were about $3 trillion! Given the sums at stake, it is not too surprising that careful analysis of capital expenditures is something at which successful corporations seek to become adept.

One might expect the capital budgeting methods of large firms to be more sophisticated than the methods of small firms. After all, large firms have the financial resources to hire more sophisticated employees. Table 6.5 provides some support for this idea. Here firms indicate frequency of use of the various capital budgeting methods on a scale of 0 (never) to 4 (always). Both the IRR and NPV methods are used more frequently, and payback less frequently, in large firms than in small firms. Conversely, large and small firms employ the last three approaches about equally.

Table 6.5

Frequency of Use
of Various Capital
Budgeting Methods

	Large Firms	Small Firms
Internal rate of return (IRR)	3.41	2.87
Net present value (NPV)	3.42	2.83
Payback method	2.25	2.72
Discounted payback	1.55	1.58
Accounting rate of return	1.25	1.41
Profitability index	0.75	0.78

Firms indicate frequency of use on a scale from 0 (never) to 4 (always). Numbers in table are averages across respondents.
SOURCE: Table 2 from Graham and Harvey (2001), op. cit.

The use of quantitative techniques in capital budgeting varies with the industry. As one would imagine, firms that are better able to estimate cash flows are more likely to use NPV. For example, estimation of cash flow in certain aspects of the oil business is quite feasible. Because of this, energy-related firms were among the first to use NPV analysis. Conversely, the cash flows in the motion picture business are very hard to project. The grosses of the great hits like *Titanic*, *Harry Potter*, and *Star Wars* were far, far greater than anyone imagined. The big failures like *Alamo* and *Waterworld* were unexpected as well. Because of this, NPV analysis is frowned upon in the movie business.

How does Hollywood perform capital budgeting? The information that a studio uses to accept or reject a movie idea comes from the *pitch*. An independent movie producer schedules an extremely brief meeting with a studio to pitch his or her idea for a movie. Consider the following four paragraphs of quotes concerning the pitch from the thoroughly delightful book *Reel Power*:[12]

"They [studio executives] don't want to know too much," says Ron Simpson. "They want to know concept. . . . They want to know what the three-liner is, because they want it to suggest the ad campaign. They want a title. . . . They don't want to hear any esoterica. And if the meeting lasts more than five minutes, they're probably not going to do the project."

"A guy comes in and says this is my idea: '*Jaws* on a spaceship,'" says writer Clay Frohman (*Under Fire*). "And they say, 'Brilliant, fantastic.' Becomes *Alien*. That is *Jaws* on a spaceship, ultimately. . . . And that's it. That's all they want to hear. Their attitude is 'Don't confuse us with the details of the story.'"

". . . Some high-concept stories are more appealing to the studios than others. The ideas liked best are sufficiently original that the audience will not feel it has already seen the movie, yet similar enough to past hits to reassure executives wary of anything too far-out. Thus, the frequently used shorthand: It's *Flashdance* in the country (*Footloose*) or *High Noon* in outer space (*Outland*)."

". . . One gambit not to use during a pitch," says executive Barbara Boyle, "is to talk about big box-office grosses your story is sure to make. Executives know as well as anyone that it's impossible to predict how much money a movie will make, and declarations to the contrary are considered pure malarkey."

---

[12]Mark Litwak, *Reel Power: The Struggle for Influence and Success in the New Hollywood* (New York: William Morrow and Company, Inc., 1986), pp. 73, 74, and 77.

Summary and Conclusions

1. In this chapter, we covered different investment decision rules. We evaluated the most popular alternatives to the NPV: the payback period, the discounted payback period, the accounting rate of return, the internal rate of return, and the profitability index. In doing so we learned more about the NPV.

2. While we found that the alternatives have some redeeming qualities, when all is said and done, they are not the NPV rule; for those of us in finance, that makes them decidedly second-rate.

3. Of the competitors to NPV, IRR must be ranked above both payback and accounting rate of return. In fact, IRR always reaches the same decision as NPV in the normal case where the initial outflows of an independent investment project are followed only by a series of inflows.

4. We classified the flaws of IRR into two types. First, we considered the general case applying to both independent and mutually exclusive projects. There appeared to be two problems here:
   a. Some projects have cash inflows followed by one or more outflows. The IRR rule is inverted here: One should accept when the IRR is *below* the discount rate.
   b. Some projects have a number of changes of sign in their cash flows. Here, there are likely to be multiple internal rates of return. The practitioner must use either NPV or modified internal rate of return here.

5. Next, we considered the specific problems with the NPV for mutually exclusive projects. We showed that, due to differences in either size or timing, the project with the highest IRR need not have the highest NPV. Hence, the IRR rule should not be applied. (Of course, NPV can still be applied.)

   However, we then calculated incremental cash flows. For ease of calculation, we suggested subtracting the cash flows of the smaller project from the cash flows of the larger project. In that way the incremental initial cash flow is negative. One can always reach a correct decision by accepting the larger project if the incremental IRR is greater than the discount rate.

6. We described capital rationing as the case where funds are limited to a fixed dollar amount. With capital rationing the profitability index is a useful method of adjusting the NPV.

Concept Questions

1. **Payback Period and Net Present Value**   If a project with conventional cash flows has a payback period less than the project's life, can you definitively state the algebraic sign of the NPV? Why or why not? If you know that the discounted payback period is less than the project's life, what can you say about the NPV? Explain.

2. **Net Present Value**   Suppose a project has conventional cash flows and a positive NPV. What do you know about its payback? Its discounted payback? Its profitability index? Its IRR? Explain.

3. **Comparing Investment Criteria**   Define each of the following investment rules and discuss any potential shortcomings of each. In your definition, state the criterion for accepting or rejecting independent projects under each rule.
   a. Payback period.
   b. Average accounting return.
   c. Internal rate of return.
   d. Profitability index.
   e. Net present value.

4. **Payback and Internal Rate of Return**   A project has perpetual cash flows of C per period, a cost of I, and a required return of R. What is the relationship between the project's payback and its IRR? What implications does your answer have for long-lived projects with relatively constant cash flows?

5. **International Investment Projects** In November 2004, automobile manufacturer Honda announced plans to build an automatic transmission plant in Georgia and expand its transmission plant in Ohio. Honda apparently felt that it would be better able to compete and create value with U.S.-based facilities. Other companies such as Fuji Film and Swiss chemical company Lonza have reached similar conclusions and taken similar actions. What are some of the reasons that foreign manufacturers of products as diverse as automobiles, film, and chemicals might arrive at this same conclusion?

6. **Capital Budgeting Problems** What are some of the difficulties that might come up in actual applications of the various criteria we discussed in this chapter? Which one would be the easiest to implement in actual applications? The most difficult?

7. **Capital Budgeting in Not-for-Profit Entities** Are the capital budgeting criteria we discussed applicable to not-for-profit corporations? How should such entities make capital budgeting decisions? What about the U.S. government? Should it evaluate spending proposals using these techniques?

8. **Net Present Value** The investment in project A is €1 million, and the investment in project B is €2 million. Both projects have a unique internal rate of return of 20 percent. Is the following statement true or false?

   For any discount rate from 0 percent to 20 percent, project B has an NPV twice as great as that of project A.

   Explain your answer.

9. **Net Present Value versus Profitability Index** Consider the following two mutually exclusive projects available to Global Investments, Inc.:

	C_0	C_1	C_2	Profitability Index	NPV
A	−£1,000	£1,000	£500	1.32	£322
B	−500	500	400	1.57	285

   The appropriate discount rate for the projects is 10 percent. Global Investments chose to undertake project A. At a luncheon for shareholders, the manager of a pension fund that owns a substantial amount of the firm's stock asks you why the firm chose project A instead of project B when project B has a higher profitability index.

   How would you, the CFO, justify your firm's action? Are there any circumstances under which Global Investments should choose project B?

10. **Internal Rate of Return** Projects A and B have the following cash flows:

Year	Project A	Project B
0	−$1,000	−$2,000
1	C1A	C1B
2	C2A	C2B
3	C3A	C3B

    a. If the cash flows from the projects are identical, which of the two projects would have a higher IRR? Why?

    b. If C1B = 2C1A, C2B = 2C2A, and C3B = 2C3A, then is $IRR_A = IRR_B$?

11. **Net Present Value** You are evaluating project A and project B. Project A has a short period of future cash flows, while project B has relatively long future cash flows. Which project will be more sensitive to changes in the required return? Why?

12. **Modified Internal Rate of Return**   One of the less flattering interpretations of the acronym MIRR is "meaningless internal rate of return." Why do you think this term is applied to MIRR?

13. **Net Present Value**   It is sometimes stated that "the net present value approach assumes reinvestment of the intermediate cash flows at the required return." Is this claim correct? To answer, suppose you calculate the NPV of a project in the usual way. Next, suppose you do the following:
    a. Calculate the future value (as of the end of the project) of all the cash flows other than the initial outlay assuming they are reinvested at the required return, producing a single future value figure for the project.
    b. Calculate the NPV of the project using the single future value calculated in the previous step and the initial outlay. It is easy to verify that you will get the same NPV as in your original calculation only if you use the required return as the reinvestment rate in the previous step.

14. **Internal Rate of Return**   It is sometimes stated that "the internal rate of return approach assumes reinvestment of the intermediate cash flows at the internal rate of return." Is this claim correct? To answer, suppose you calculate the IRR of a project in the usual way. Next, suppose you do the following:
    a. Calculate the future value (as of the end of the project) of all the cash flows other than the initial outlay assuming they are reinvested at the IRR, producing a single future value figure for the project.
    b. Calculate the IRR of the project using the single future value calculated in the previous step and the initial outlay. It is easy to verify that you will get the same IRR as in your original calculation only if you use the IRR as the reinvestment rate in the previous step.

Questions and Problems

BASIC
(Questions 1–10)

1. **Calculating Payback Period and NPV**   Incosoft, Inc., has the following mutually exclusive projects.

Year	Project A	Project B
0	−£7,500	−£5,000
1	4,000	2,500
2	3,500	1,200
3	1,500	3,000

   a. Suppose Incosoft's payback period cutoff is two years. Which of these two projects should be chosen?
   b. Suppose Incosoft uses the NPV rule to rank these two projects. Which project should be chosen if the appropriate discount rate is 15 percent?

2. **Calculating Payback**   An investment project provides cash inflows of £840 per year for eight years. What is the project payback period if the initial cost is £3,000? What if the initial cost is £5,000? What if it is £7,200?

3. **Calculating Discounted Payback**   An investment project has annual cash inflows of $7,000, $7,500, $8,000, and $8,500, and a discount rate of 14 percent. What is the discounted payback period for these cash flows if the initial cost is $8,000? What if the initial cost is $13,000? What if it is $17,500?

4. **Calculating Discounted Payback**   An investment project costs ¥1,000,000 and has annual cash flows of ¥210,000 for six years. What is the discounted payback period if the discount rate is 0 percent? What if the discount rate is 5 percent? If it is 15 percent?

5. **Average Accounting Return**   Your firm is considering purchasing a machine with the following annual, end-of-year, book investment accounts:

	Purchase Date	Year 1	Year 2	Year 3	Year 4
Gross investment	€16,000	€16,000	€16,000	€16,000	€16,000
Less: Accumulated depreciation	0	4,000	8,000	12,000	16,000
Net investment	€16,000	€12,000	€ 8,000	€ 4,000	€ 0

The machine generates, on average, €4,500 per year in additional net income.
   a. What is the average accounting return for this machine?
   b. What three flaws are inherent in this decision rule?

6. **Average Accounting Return**   Guandong Techies Co. has invested CNY 8,000 in a high-tech project lasting three years. Depreciation is CNY 4,000, CNY 2,500, and CNY 1,500 in years 1, 2, and 3, respectively. The project generates pretax income of CNY 2,000 each year. The pretax income already includes the depreciation expense. If the tax rate is 30 percent, what is the project's average accounting return (AAR)?

7. **Calculating IRR**   Bring It Again, Inc., has a project with the following cash flows:

Year	Cash Flows ($)
0	−$8,000
1	4,000
2	3,000
3	2,000

The company evaluates all projects by applying the IRR rule. If the appropriate interest rate is 8 percent, should the company accept the project?

8. **Calculating IRR**   Compute the internal rate of return for the cash flows of the following two projects:

	Cash Flows (£)	
Year	Project A	Project B
0	−£2,000	−£1,500
1	1,000	500
2	1,500	1,000
3	2,000	1,750

9. **Calculating Profitability Index**   Waqar Akhtar plans to open a self-serve grooming center in a storefront. The grooming equipment will cost PKR 160,000, to be paid immediately. Waqar expects aftertax cash inflows of PKR 40,000 annually for seven years, after which he plans to scrap the equipment and retire to the beaches of Nevis. The first cash inflow occurs at the end of the first year. Assume the required return is 15 percent. What is the project's PI? Should it be accepted?

10. **Calculating Profitability Index**   Suppose the following two independent investment opportunities are available to Greenplain, Inc. The appropriate discount rate is 10 percent.

Year	Project Alpha	Project Beta
0	−CRC 500	−CRC 2,000
1	300	300
2	700	1,800
3	600	1,700

a. Compute the profitability index for each of the two projects.

b. Which project(s) should Greenplain accept based on the profitability index rule?

INTERMEDIATE
(Questions 11–23)

11.   Cash Flow Intuition   A project has an initial cost of I, has a required return of R, and pays C annually for N years.

a. Find C in terms of I and N such that the project has a payback period just equal to its life.

b. Find C in terms of I, N, and R such that this is a profitable project according to the NPV decision rule.

c. Find C in terms of I, N, and R such that the project has a benefit–cost ratio of 2.

12.   Problems with IRR   Suppose you are offered €5,000 today but must make the following payments:

Year	Cash Flows (€)
0	€5,000
1	−2,500
2	−2,300
3	−1,000
4	−1,000

a. What is the IRR of this offer?

b. If the appropriate discount rate is 15 percent, should you accept this offer?

c. If the appropriate discount rate is 20 percent, should you accept this offer?

d. What is the NPV of the offer if the appropriate discount rate is 15 percent? 20 percent?

e. Are the decisions under the NPV rule in part (d) consistent with those of the IRR rule?

13.   NPV versus IRR   Consider the following cash flows on two mutually exclusive projects for the Jai Hindustan Patrika (JHP). Both projects require an annual return of 15 percent.

Year	Deepwater Fishing	New Submarine Ride
0	−INR 600,000	−INR 1,800,000
1	270,000	1,000,000
2	350,000	700,000
3	300,000	900,000

As a financial analyst for JHP, you are asked the following questions:

a. If your decision rule is to accept the project with the greater IRR, which project should you choose?

b. Because you are fully aware of the IRR rule's scale problem, you calculate the incremental IRR for the cash flows. Based on your computation, which project should you choose?

c. To be prudent, you compute the NPV for both projects. Which project should you choose? Is it consistent with the incremental IRR rule?

14. **Problems with Profitability Index** The Robb Computer Corporation is trying to choose between the following two mutually exclusive design projects:

Year	Cash Flow (I)	Cash Flow (II)
0	−CAD 30,000	−CAD 5,000
1	15,000	2,800
2	15,000	2,800
3	15,000	2,800

   a. If the required return is 10 percent and Robb Computer applies the profitability index decision rule, which project should the firm accept?
   b. If the company applies the NPV decision rule, which project should it take?
   c. Explain why your answers in (a) and (b) are different.

15. **Problems with IRR** Osaka Dreamworks Limited is trying to evaluate a generation project with the following cash flows:

Year	Cash Flow
0	−¥28,000,000
1	53,000,000
2	−8,000,000

   a. If the company requires a 12 percent return on its investments, should it accept this project? Why?
   b. Compute the IRR for this project. How many IRRs are there? If you apply the IRR decision rule, should you accept the project or not? What's going on here?

16. **Comparing Investment Criteria** Mario Brothers, a game manufacturer, has a new idea for an adventure game. It can market the game either as a traditional board game or as an interactive CD-ROM, but not both. Consider the following cash flows of the two mutually exclusive projects for Mario Brothers. Assume the discount rate for Mario Brothers is 10 percent.

Year	Board Game	CD-ROM
0	−€300	−€1,500
1	400	1,100
2	100	800
3	100	400

   a. Based on the payback period rule, which project should be chosen?
   b. Based on the NPV, which project should be chosen?
   c. Based on the IRR, which project should be chosen?
   d. Based on the incremental IRR, which project should be chosen?

17. **Profitability Index versus NPV** Huang Group, a consumer electronics conglomerate, is reviewing its annual budget in wireless technology. It is considering investments in three different technologies to develop wireless communication devices. Consider the following cash

flows of the three independent projects for Huang. Assume the discount rate for Huang is 10 percent. Further, Huang Group has only CNY 30 million to invest in new projects this year.

	Cash Flows (in millions)		
Year	CDMA	G4	Wi-Fi
0	−CNY 10	−CNY 20	−CNY 30
1	25	20	20
2	15	50	40
3	5	40	100

a. Based on the profitability index decision rule, rank these investments.
b. Based on the NPV, rank these investments.
c. Based on your findings in (a) and (b), what would you recommend to the CEO of Huang Group and why?

18. **Comparing Investment Criteria**   Consider the following cash flows of two mutually exclusive projects for AZ-Motorcars. Assume the discount rate for AZ-Motorcars is 10 percent.

Year	AZM Mini-SUV	AZF Full-SUV
0	−CRC 200,000	−CRC 500,000
1	200,000	200,000
2	150,000	300,000
3	150,000	300,000

a. Based on the payback period, which project should be taken?
b. Based on the NPV, which project should be taken?
c. Based on the IRR, which project should be taken?
d. Based on this analysis, is incremental IRR analysis necessary? If yes, please conduct the analysis.

19. **Comparing Investment Criteria**   The treasurer of Seoul Foods, Inc., has projected the cash flows of projects A, B, and C as follows.

Year	Project A	Project B	Project C
0	−KRW 100,000	−KRW 200,000	−KRW 100,000
1	70,000	130,000	75,000
2	70,000	130,000	60,000

Suppose the relevant discount rate is 12 percent a year.
a. Compute the profitability index for each of the three projects.
b. Compute the NPV for each of the three projects.
c. Suppose these three projects are independent. Which project(s) should Seoul Foods accept based on the profitability index rule?
d. Suppose these three projects are mutually exclusive. Which project(s) should Seoul Foods accept based on the profitability index rule?
e. Suppose Seoul Foods budget for these projects is KRW 300,000. The projects are not divisible. Which project(s) should Seoul Foods accept?

20. **Comparing Investment Criteria** Consider the following cash flows of two mutually exclusive projects for Tokyo Rubber Company. Assume the discount rate for Tokyo Rubber Company is 10 percent.

Year	Dry Prepreg	Solvent Prepreg
0	−¥1,000,000,000	−¥500,000,000
1	600,000,000	300,000,000
2	400,000,000	500,000,000
3	1,000,000,000	100,000,000

   a. Based on the payback period, which project should be taken?
   b. Based on the NPV, which project should be taken?
   c. Based on the IRR, which project should be taken?
   d. Based on this analysis, is incremental IRR analysis necessary? If yes, please conduct the analysis.

21. **Comparing Investment Criteria** Consider two mutually exclusive new product launch projects that Nagano Golf is considering. Assume the discount rate for Nagano Golf is 15 percent.

   Project *A*: Nagano NP-30.
   Professional clubs that will take an initial investment of $100,000 at time 0.
   Next five years (years 1–5) of sales will generate a consistent cash flow of $40,000 per year.
   Introduction of new product at year 6 will terminate further cash flows from this project.

   Project *B*: Nagano NX-20.
   High-end amateur clubs that will take an initial investment of $30,000 at time 0.
   Cash flow at year 1 is $20,000. In each subsequent year cash flow will grow at 15 percent per year.
   Introduction of new product at year 6 will terminate further cash flows from this project.

Year	NP-30	NX-20
0	−$100,000	−$30,000
1	40,000	20,000
2	40,000	23,000
3	40,000	26,450
4	40,000	30,418
5	40,000	34,980

Please fill in the following table:

	NP-30	NX-20	Implications
NPV			
IRR			
Incremental IRR			
PI			

22. **Comparing Investment Criteria**   Consider two mutually exclusive R&D projects that ADM is considering. Assume the discount rate for ADM is 15 percent.

   Project *A*:   Server CPU .13 micron processing project.

   By shrinking the die size to .13 micron, ADM will be able to offer server CPU chips with lower power consumption and heat generation, meaning faster CPUs.

   Project *B*:   New telecom chip project.

   Entry into this industry will require introduction of a new chip for cellphones. The know-how will require a lot of upfront capital, but success of the project will lead to large cash flows later on.

Year	A	B
0	−£100,000	−£200,000
1	50,000	60,000
2	50,000	60,000
3	40,000	60,000
4	30,000	100,000
5	20,000	200,000

Please fill in the following table:

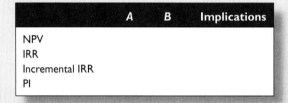

	A	B	Implications
NPV			
IRR			
Incremental IRR			
PI			

23. **Comparing Investment Criteria**   You are a senior manager at Peking Aircraft and have been authorized to spend up to CNY 200,000 for projects. The three projects you are considering have the following characteristics:

   Project *A*:   Initial investment of CNY 150,000. Cash flow of CNY 50,000 at year 1 and CNY 100,000 at year 2. This is a plant expansion project, where the required rate of return is 10 percent.

   Project *B*:   Initial investment of CNY 200,000. Cash flow of CNY 200,000 at year 1 and CNY 111,000 at year 2. This is a new product development project, where the required rate of return is 20 percent.

   Project *C*:   Initial investment of CNY 100,000. Cash flow of CNY 100,000 at year 1 and CNY 100,000 at year 2. This is a market expansion project, where the required rate of return is 20 percent.

   Assume the corporate discount rate is 12 percent.
   Please offer your recommendations, backed by your analysis:

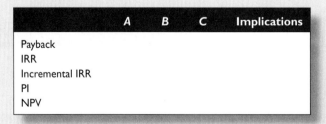

	A	B	C	Implications
Payback				
IRR				
Incremental IRR				
PI				
NPV				

24. **Payback and NPV**   An investment under consideration has a payback of seven years and a cost of PHP 5,020. If the required return is 12 percent, what is the worst-case NPV? The best-case NPV? Explain. Assume the cash flows are conventional.

25. **Multiple IRRs**   This problem is useful for testing the ability of financial calculators and computer software. Consider the following cash flows. How many different IRRs are there? (*Hint*: Search between 20 percent and 70 percent.) When should we take this project?

Year	Cash Flow
0	−£ 504
1	2,862
2	−6,070
3	5,700
4	−2,000

26. **NPV Valuation**   The Yurdone Corporation wants to set up a private cemetery business. According to the CFO, Barry M. Deep, business is "looking up." As a result, the cemetery project will provide a net cash inflow of KRW 50,000 for the firm during the first year, and the cash flows are projected to grow at a rate of 6 percent per year forever. The project requires an initial investment of KRW 780,000.
    a. If Yurdone requires a 13 percent return on such undertakings, should the cemetery business be started?
    b. The company is somewhat unsure about the assumption of a 6 percent growth rate in its cash flows. At what constant growth rate would the company just break even if it still required a 13 percent return on investment?

27. **Calculating IRR**   The Utah Mining Corporation is set to open a gold mine near Provo, Utah. According to the treasurer, Monty Goldstein, "This is a golden opportunity." The mine will cost $600,000 to open and will have an economic life of 11 years. It will generate a cash inflow of $100,000 at the end of the first year, and the cash inflows are projected to grow at 8 percent per year for the next 10 years. After 11 years, the mine will be abandoned. Abandonment costs will be $50,000 at the end of year 11.
    a. What is the IRR for the gold mine?
    b. The Utah Mining Corporation requires a 10 percent return on such undertakings. Should the mine be opened?

28. **Calculating IRR**   Consider two streams of cash flows, A and B. Stream A's first cash flow is $5,000 and is received three years from today. Future cash flows in stream A grow by 4 percent in perpetuity. Stream B's first cash flow is −$6,000, is received two years from today, and will continue in perpetuity. Assume that the appropriate discount rate is 12 percent.
    a. What is the present value of each stream?
    b. Suppose that the two streams are combined into one project, called C. What is the IRR of project C?
    c. What is the correct IRR rule for project C?

29. **Calculating Incremental Cash Flows**   Lalu Chaudhary, the CFO of MakeMoney.com, has to decide between the following two projects:

Year	Project Lakh	Project Crore
0	−INR 1,500	−INR I_o
1	I_o + 200	I_o + 500
2	1,200	1,500
3	1,500	2,000

The expected rate of return for either of the two projects is 12 percent. What is the range of initial investment (I_0) for which Project Crore is more financially attractive than Project Lakh?

30.   **Problems with IRR**   McKeekin Corp. has a project with the following cash flows:

Year	Cash Flow
0	€20,000
1	−26,000
2	13,000

What is the IRR of the project? What is happening here?

Bullock Gold Mining

Mini Case

Seth Bullock, the owner of Bullock Gold Mining, is evaluating a new gold mine in South Dakota. Dan Dority, the company's geologist, has just finished his analysis of the mine site. He has estimated that the mine would be productive for eight years, after which the gold would be completely mined. Dan has taken an estimate of the gold deposits to Alma Garrett, the company's financial officer. Alma has been asked by Seth to perform an analysis of the new mine and present her recommendation on whether the company should open the new mine.

Alma has used the estimates provided by Dan to determine the revenues that could be expected from the mine. She has also projected the expense of opening the mine and the annual operating expenses. If the company opens the mine, it will cost $500 million today, and it will have a cash outflow of $80 million nine years from today in costs associated with closing the mine and reclaiming the area surrounding it. The expected cash flows each year from the mine are shown in the following table. Bullock Mining has a 12 percent required return on all of its gold mines.

Year	Cash Flow
0	−$500,000,000
1	60,000,000
2	90,000,000
3	170,000,000
4	230,000,000
5	205,000,000
6	140,000,000
7	110,000,000
8	70,000,000
9	−80,000,000

1. Construct a spreadsheet to calculate the payback period, internal rate of return, modified internal rate of return, and net present value of the proposed mine.

2. Based on your analysis, should the company open the mine?

3. Bonus question: Most spreadsheets do not have a built-in formula to calculate the payback period. Write a VBA script that calculates the payback period for a project.

Making Capital Investment Decisions

In January 2006, Sharp Corporation, the world's leading producer of flat panel LCD TVs, announced that it would spend an additional 200 billion yen ($1.75 billion) to build a new plant to produce LCD panels. This addition brought the total investment in the new plant to 350 billion yen ($3.07 billion). The extra investment increased the production capacity of the new plant from 30,000 glass substrates per month to 90,000 glass substrates per month, and the new plant would have the capacity to produce the equivalent of 22 million 32-inch TV sets by 2008. Just several days earlier, Matsushita Electric Industrial Co., the world's leading plasma TV manufacturer, announced that it would invest 180 billion yen ($1.57 billion) to build a new plant to produce plasma panels. The new plasma plant would more than double the company's production capacity to 11.1 million units per year.

This chapter follows up on our previous one by delving more deeply into capital budgeting and the evaluation of projects such as these flat panel manufacturing facilities. We identify the relevant cash flows of a project, including initial investment outlays, requirements for net working capital, and operating cash flows. Further, we look at the effects of depreciation and taxes. We also examine the impact of inflation, and show how to evaluate consistently the NPV analysis of a project.

7.1 Incremental Cash Flows

Cash Flows—Not Accounting Income

You may not have thought about it, but there is a big difference between corporate finance courses and financial accounting courses. Techniques in corporate finance generally use cash flows, whereas financial accounting generally stresses income or earnings numbers. Certainly our text follows this tradition: Our net present value techniques discount cash flows, not earnings. When considering a single project, we discount the cash flows that the firm receives from the project. When valuing the firm as a whole, we discount dividends—not earnings—because dividends are the cash flows that an investor receives.

EXAMPLE 7.1

Relevant Cash Flows   The Weber-Decker Co. just paid $1 million in cash for a building as part of a new capital budgeting project. This entire $1 million is an immediate cash outflow. However, assuming straight-line depreciation over 20 years, only $50,000 (=$1 million/20) is considered an accounting expense in the current year. Current earnings are thereby reduced by only $50,000. The remaining $950,000 is expensed over the following 19 years. For capital budgeting purposes, the relevant cash outflow at date 0 is the full $1 million, not the reduction in earnings of only $50,000.

Always discount cash flows, not earnings, when performing a capital budgeting calculation. Earnings do not represent real money. You can't spend out of earnings, you can't eat out of earnings, and you can't pay dividends out of earnings. You can do these things only out of cash flow.

In addition, it is not enough to use cash flows. In calculating the NPV of a project, only cash flows that are *incremental* to the project should be used. These cash flows are the changes in the firm's cash flows that occur as a direct consequence of accepting the project. That is, we are interested in the difference between the cash flows of the firm with the project and the cash flows of the firm without the project.

The use of incremental cash flows sounds easy enough, but pitfalls abound in the real world. We describe how to avoid some of the pitfalls of determining incremental cash flows.

Sunk Costs

A **sunk cost** is a cost that has already occurred. Because sunk costs are in the past, they cannot be changed by the decision to accept or reject the project. Just as we "let bygones be bygones," we should ignore such costs. Sunk costs are not incremental cash outflows.

EXAMPLE 7.2

Sunk Costs   The General Milk Company is currently evaluating the NPV of establishing a line of chocolate milk. As part of the evaluation, the company had paid a consulting firm $100,000 to perform a test marketing analysis. This expenditure was made last year. Is this cost relevant for the capital budgeting decision now confronting the management of General Milk Company?

The answer is no. The $100,000 is not recoverable, so the $100,000 expenditure is a sunk cost, or spilled milk. Of course, the decision to spend $100,000 for a marketing analysis was a capital budgeting decision itself and was perfectly relevant *before* it was sunk. Our point is that once the company incurred the expense, the cost became irrelevant for any future decision.

Opportunity Costs

Your firm may have an asset that it is considering selling, leasing, or employing elsewhere in the business. If the asset is used in a new project, potential revenues from alternative uses are lost. These lost revenues can meaningfully be viewed as costs. They are called **opportunity costs** because, by taking the project, the firm forgoes other opportunities for using the assets.

EXAMPLE 7.3

Opportunity Costs   Suppose the Weinstein Trading Company has an empty warehouse in Philadelphia that can be used to store a new line of electronic pinball machines. The company hopes to sell these machines to affluent Northeastern consumers. Should the warehouse be considered a cost in the decision to sell the machines?

The answer is yes. The company could sell the warehouse if the firm decides not to market the pinball machines. Thus, the sales price of the warehouse is an opportunity cost in the pinball machine decision.

Side Effects

Another difficulty in determining incremental cash flows comes from the side effects of the proposed project on other parts of the firm. A side effect is classified as either **erosion** or **synergy**. Erosion occurs when a new product reduces the sales and, hence, the cash flows of existing products. Synergy occurs when a new project increases the cash flows of existing projects.

EXAMPLE 7.4

Synergies Suppose the Innovative Motors Corporation (IMC) is determining the NPV of a new convertible sports car. Some of the customers who would purchase the car are owners of IMC's compact sedans. Are all sales and profits from the new convertible sports car incremental?

The answer is no because some of the cash flow represents transfers from other elements of IMC's product line. This is erosion, which must be included in the NPV calculation. Without taking erosion into account, IMC might erroneously calculate the NPV of the sports car to be, say, $100 million. If half the customers are transfers from the sedan and lost sedan sales have an NPV of −$150 million, the true NPV is −$50 million (=$100 million − $150 million).

IMC is also contemplating the formation of a racing team. The team is forecast to lose money for the foreseeable future, with perhaps the best projection showing an NPV of −$35 million for the operation. However, IMC's managers are aware that the team will likely generate great publicity for all of IMC's products. A consultant estimates that the increase in cash flows elsewhere in the firm has a present value of $65 million. Assuming that the consultant's estimates of synergy are trustworthy, the net present value of the team is $30 million (=$65 million − $35 million). The managers should form the team.

Allocated Costs

Frequently a particular expenditure benefits a number of projects. Accountants allocate this cost across the different projects when determining income. However, for capital budgeting purposes, this **allocated cost** should be viewed as a cash outflow of a project only if it is an incremental cost of the project.

EXAMPLE 7.5

Allocated Costs The Voetmann Consulting Corp. devotes one wing of its suite of offices to a library requiring a cash outflow of $100,000 a year in upkeep. A proposed capital budgeting project is expected to generate revenue equal to 5 percent of the overall firm's sales. An executive at the firm, H. Sears, argues that $5,000 (=5 percent × $100,000) should be viewed as the proposed project's share of the library's costs. Is this appropriate for capital budgeting?

The answer is no. One must ask what the difference is between the cash flows of the entire firm with the project and the cash flows of the entire firm without the project. The firm will spend $100,000 on library upkeep whether or not the proposed project is accepted. Because acceptance of the proposed project does not affect this cash flow, the cash flow should be ignored when calculating the NPV of the project.

7.2 The Baldwin Company: An Example

We next consider the example of a proposed investment in machinery and related items. Our example involves the Baldwin Company and colored bowling balls.

The Baldwin Company, originally established in 1965 to make footballs, is now a leading producer of tennis balls, baseballs, footballs, and golf balls. In 1973 the company introduced "High Flite," its first line of high-performance golf balls. Baldwin management has sought opportunities in whatever businesses seem to have some potential for cash flow. Recently W. C. Meadows, vice president of the Baldwin Company, identified another segment of the sports ball market that looked promising and that he felt was not adequately served by larger manufacturers. That market was for brightly colored bowling balls, and he believed many bowlers valued appearance and style above performance. He also believed that it would be difficult for competitors to take advantage of the opportunity because of both Baldwin's cost advantages and its highly developed marketing skills.

As a result, the Baldwin Company investigated the marketing potential of brightly colored bowling balls. Baldwin sent a questionnaire to consumers in three markets: Philadelphia, Los Angeles, and New Haven. The results of the three questionnaires were much better than expected and supported the conclusion that the brightly colored bowling balls could achieve a 10 to 15 percent share of the market. Of course, some people at Baldwin complained about the cost of the test marketing, which was $250,000. (As we shall see later, this is a sunk cost and should not be included in project evaluation.)

In any case, the Baldwin Company is now considering investing in a machine to produce bowling balls. The bowling balls would be manufactured in a building owned by the firm and located near Los Angeles. This building, which is vacant, and the land can be sold for $150,000 after taxes.

Working with his staff, Meadows is preparing an analysis of the proposed new product. He summarizes his assumptions as follows: The cost of the bowling ball machine is $100,000. The machine has an estimated market value at the end of five years of $30,000. Production by year during the five-year life of the machine is expected to be as follows: 5,000 units, 8,000 units, 12,000 units, 10,000 units, and 6,000 units. The price of bowling balls in the first year will be $20. The bowling ball market is highly competitive, so Meadows believes that the price of bowling balls will increase at only 2 percent per year, as compared to the anticipated general inflation rate of 5 percent. Conversely, the plastic used to produce bowling balls is rapidly becoming more expensive. Because of this, production cash outflows are expected to grow at 10 percent per year. First-year production costs will be $10 per unit. Meadows has determined, based on Baldwin's taxable income, that the appropriate incremental corporate tax rate in the bowling ball project is 34 percent.

Net working capital is defined as the difference between current assets and current liabilities. Like any other manufacturing firm, Baldwin finds that it must maintain an investment in working capital. It will purchase raw materials before production and sale, giving rise to an investment in inventory. It will maintain cash as a buffer against unforeseen expenditures. And, its credit sales will generate accounts receivable. Management determines that an immediate (year 0) investment in the different items of working capital of $10,000 is required. Working capital is forecast to rise in the early years of the project but to fall to $0 by the project's end. In other words, the investment in working capital is to be completely recovered by the end of the project's life.

Projections based on these assumptions and Meadows's analysis appear in Tables 7.1 through 7.4. In these tables all cash flows are assumed to occur at the *end* of the year. Because of the large amount of information in these tables, it is important to see how the tables are related. Table 7.1 shows the basic data for both investment and income. Supplementary schedules on operations and depreciation, as presented in Tables 7.2 and 7.3, help explain where the numbers in Table 7.1 come from. Our goal is to obtain projections of cash flow. The data in Table 7.1 are all that are needed to calculate the relevant cash flows, as shown in Table 7.4.

An Analysis of the Project

Investments   The investment outlays for the project are summarized in the top segment of Table 7.1. They consist of three parts:

1. *The bowling ball machine*: The purchase requires an immediate (year 0) cash outflow of $100,000. The firm realizes a cash inflow when the machine is sold in year 5. These cash flows are shown in line 1 of Table 7.1. As indicated in the footnote to the table, taxes are incurred when the asset is sold.

Table 7.1   **The Worksheet for Cash Flows of the Baldwin Company (in $ thousands). (All cash flows occur at the *end* of the year.)**

	Year 0	Year 1	Year 2	Year 3	Year 4	Year 5
Investments:						
(1) Bowling ball machine	−$100.00					$21.76*
(2) Accumulated depreciation		$ 20.00	$ 52.00	$ 71.20	$ 82.72	94.24
(3) Adjusted basis of machine after depreciation (end of year)		80.00	48.00	28.80	17.28	5.76
(4) Opportunity cost (warehouse)	−150.00					150.00
(5) Net working capital (end of year)	10.00	10.00	16.32	24.97	21.22	0
(6) Change in net working capital	−10.00		−6.32	−8.65	3.75	21.22
(7) Total cash flow of investment [(1) + (4) + (6)]	−260.00		−6.32	−8.65	3.75	192.98
Income:						
(8) Sales revenues		$100.00	$163.20	$249.72	$212.20	$129.90
(9) Operating costs		−50.00	−88.00	−145.20	−133.10	−87.84
(10) Depreciation		−20.00	−32.00	−19.20	−11.52	−11.52
(11) Income before taxes [(8) + (9) + (10)]		30.00	43.20	85.32	67.58	30.54
(12) Tax at 34 percent		−10.20	−14.69	−29.01	−22.98	−10.38
(13) Net income		19.80	28.51	56.31	44.60	20.16

*We assume that the ending market value of the capital investment at year 5 is $30 (in thousands). The taxable amount is $24.24 (=$30 − $5.76). The aftertax salvage value is $30 − [.34 × ($30 − $5.76)] = $21.76.

Table 7.2

Operating Revenues and Costs of the Baldwin Company

(1) Year	(2) Quantity Produced	(3) Price	(4) Sales Revenues	(5) Cost Per Unit	(6) Operating Costs
1	5,000	$20.00	$100,000	$10.00	$ 50,000
2	8,000	20.40	163,200	11.00	88,000
3	12,000	20.81	249,720	12.10	145,200
4	10,000	21.22	212,200	13.31	133,100
5	6,000	21.65	129,900	14.64	87,840

Prices rise at 2% a year.
Unit costs rise at 10% a year.

2. *The opportunity cost of not selling the warehouse*: If Baldwin accepts the bowling ball project, it will use a warehouse and land that could otherwise be sold. The estimated sales price of the warehouse and land is therefore included as an *opportunity cost* in year 0, as presented in line 4. Opportunity costs are treated as cash outflows for purposes of capital budgeting. However, note that if the project is accepted, management assumes that the warehouse will be sold for $150,000 (after taxes) in year 5.

   The test marketing cost of $250,000 is not included. The tests occurred in the past and should be viewed as a *sunk cost*.

Table 7.3

Depreciation (in percent) under Modified Accelerated Cost Recovery System (MACRS)

Year	3 Years	5 Years	7 Years	10 Years	15 Years	20 Years
			Recovery Period Class			
1	.333	.200	.143	.100	.050	.038
2	.444	.320	.245	.180	.095	.072
3	.148	.192	.175	.144	.086	.067
4	.074	.115	.125	.115	.077	.062
5		.115	.089	.092	.069	.057
6		.058	.089	.074	.062	.053
7			.089	.066	.059	.049
8			.045	.066	.059	.045
9				.066	.059	.045
10				.066	.059	.045
11				.033	.059	.045
12–15					.059	.045
16					.030	.045
17–20						.045
21						.022

Depreciation is expressed as a percentage of the asset's cost. These schedules are based on the IRS publication *Depreciation*. Details of depreciation are presented later in the chapter. Three-year depreciation actually carries over four years because the IRS assumes the purchase is made in midyear.

Table 7.4 Incremental Cash Flows for the Baldwin Company (in $ thousands)

	Year 0	Year 1	Year 2	Year 3	Year 4	Year 5
(1) Sales revenue [line 8, Table 7.1]		$100.00	$163.20	$249.72	$212.20	$129.90
(2) Operating costs [line 9, Table 7.1]		−50.00	−88.00	−145.20	−133.10	−87.84
(3) Taxes [line 12, Table 7.1]		−10.20	−14.69	−29.01	−22.98	−10.38
(4) Cash flow from operations [(1) + (2) + (3)]		39.80	60.51	75.51	56.12	31.68
(5) Total cash flow of investment [line 7, Table 7.1]	−$260.00			−6.32	−8.65	3.75	192.98
(6) Total cash flow of project [(4) + (5)]	−260.00	39.80	54.19	66.86	59.87	224.66

NPV @		
	4%	$123.641
	10%	$51.588
	15%	$5.472
	15.67%	$0
	20%	−$31.351

3. *The investment in working capital*: Required working capital appears in line 5. Working capital rises over the early years of the project as expansion occurs. However, all working capital is assumed to be recovered at the end, a common assumption in capital budgeting. In other words, all inventory is sold by the end, the cash balance maintained as a buffer is liquidated, and all accounts receivable are collected. Increases in working capital in the early years must be funded by cash generated elsewhere in the firm. Hence, these increases are viewed as cash *outflows*. To reiterate, it is the *increase* in working capital over a year that leads to a cash outflow in that year. Even if working

capital is at a high level, there will be no cash outflow over a year if working capital stays constant over that year. Conversely, decreases in working capital in the later years are viewed as cash inflows. All of these cash flows are presented in line 6 of Table 7.1. A more complete discussion of working capital is provided later in this section.

To recap, there are three investments in this example: the bowling ball machine (line 1 in Table 7.1), the opportunity cost of the warehouse (line 4), and the changes in working capital (line 6). The total cash flow from these three investments is shown in line 7.

Income and Taxes Next the determination of income is presented in the bottom segment of Table 7.1. While we are ultimately interested in cash flow—not income—we need the income calculation to determine taxes. Lines 8 and 9 of Table 7.1 show sales revenues and operating costs, respectively. The projections in these lines are based on the sales revenues and operating costs computed in columns 4 and 6 of Table 7.2. The estimates of revenues and costs follow from assumptions made by the corporate planning staff at Baldwin. In other words, the estimates critically depend on the fact that product prices are projected to increase at 2 percent per year and costs per unit are projected to increase at 10 percent per year.

Depreciation of the $100,000 capital investment is shown in line 10 of Table 7.1. Where do these numbers come from? Depreciation for tax purposes for U.S. companies is based on the Modified Accelerated Cost Recovery System (MACRS). Each asset is assigned a useful life under MACRS, with an accompanying depreciation schedule as shown in Table 7.3. The IRS ruled that Baldwin is to depreciate its capital investment over five years, so the second column of the table applies in this case. Because depreciation in the table is expressed as a percentage of the asset's cost, multiply the percentages in this column by $100,000 to arrive at depreciation in dollars.

Income before taxes is calculated in line 11 of Table 7.1. Taxes are provided in line 12 of this table, and net income is calculated in line 13.

Salvage Value In calculating depreciation under current tax law, the expected economic life and future value of an asset are not issues. As a result, the book value of an asset can differ substantially from its actual market value. For example, consider the bowling machine the Baldwin Company is considering for its new project. The book value after the first year is $100,000 less the first year's depreciation of $20,000, or $80,000. After six years, the book value of the machine is zero.

Suppose, at the end of the project, Baldwin sold the machine. At the end of the fifth year, the book value of the machine would be $5,760; but based on Baldwin's experience, it would probably be worth about $30,000. If the company actually sold it for this amount, then it would pay taxes at the ordinary income tax rate on the difference between the sale price of $30,000 and the book value of $5,760. With a 34 percent tax rate, the tax liability would be $.34 \times (\$30,000 - 5,760) = \$8,241.60$. So, the aftertax salvage value of the equipment, a cash inflow to the company, would be $30,000 - 8,241.60 = \$21,758.40$.

Taxes must be paid in this case because the difference between the market value and the book value is "excess" depreciation, and it must be "recaptured" when the asset is sold. In this case, Baldwin would have over depreciated the asset by $30,000 - 5,760 = \$24,240$. Because the depreciation was too high, the company paid too little in taxes.

Notice this is not a tax on a long-term capital gain. Further, what is and what is not a capital gain is ultimately up to taxing authorities, and the specific rules can be very complex. We will ignore capital gains taxes for the most part.

Finally, if the book value exceeds the market value, then the difference is treated as a loss for tax purposes. For example, if Baldwin sold the machine for $4,000, then the book value exceeds the market value by $1,760. In this case, a tax savings of .34 × $1,760 = $598.40 occurs.

Cash Flow   Cash flow is finally determined in Table 7.4. We begin by reproducing lines 8, 9, and 12 in Table 7.1 as lines 1, 2, and 3 in Table 7.4. Cash flow from operations, which is sales minus both operating costs and taxes, is provided in line 4 of Table 7.4. Total investment cash flow, taken from line 7 of Table 7.1, appears as line 5 of Table 7.4. Cash flow from operations plus total cash flow of the investment equals total cash flow of the project, which is displayed as line 6 of Table 7.4.

Net Present Value   The NPV of the Baldwin bowling ball project can be calculated from the cash flows in line 6. As can be seen at the bottom of Table 7.4, the NPV is $51,588 if 10 percent is the appropriate discount rate and −$31,351 if 20 percent is the appropriate discount rate. If the discount rate is 15.67 percent, the project will have a zero NPV. In other words, the project's internal rate of return is 15.67 percent. If the discount rate of the Baldwin bowling ball project is above 15.67 percent, it should not be accepted because its NPV would be negative.

Which Set of Books?

It should be noted that the firm's management generally keeps two sets of books, one for the IRS (called the *tax books*) and another for its annual report (called the *stockholders' books*). The tax books follow the rules of the IRS. The stockholders' books follow the rules of the *Financial Accounting Standards Board* (FASB), the governing body in accounting. The two sets of rules differ widely in certain areas. For example, income on municipal bonds is ignored for tax purposes while being treated as income by the FASB. The differences almost always benefit the firm: The rules permit income on the stockholders' books to be higher than income on the tax books. That is, management can look profitable to the stockholders without needing to pay taxes on all of the reported profit. In fact, plenty of large companies consistently report positive earnings to the stockholders while reporting losses to the IRS.

A Note about Net Working Capital

The investment in net working capital is an important part of any capital budgeting analysis. While we explicitly considered net working capital in lines 5 and 6 of Table 7.1, students may be wondering where the numbers in these lines came from. An investment in net working capital arises whenever (1) inventory is purchased, (2) cash is kept in the project as a buffer against unexpected expenditures, and (3) credit sales are made, generating accounts receivable rather than cash. (The investment in net working capital is reduced by credit purchases, which generate accounts payable.) This investment in net working capital represents a cash outflow because cash generated elsewhere in the firm is tied up in the project.

To see how the investment in net working capital is built from its component parts, we focus on year 1. We see in Table 7.1 that Baldwin's managers predict sales in year 1 to be $100,000 and operating costs to be $50,000. If both the sales and costs were cash transactions, the firm would receive $50,000 (=$100,000 − $50,000). As stated earlier, this cash flow would occur at the *end* of year 1.

Now let's give you more information. The managers:

1. Forecast that $9,000 of the sales will be on credit, implying that cash receipts at the end of year 1 will be only $91,000 (=$100,000 − $9,000). The accounts receivable of $9,000 will be collected at the end of year 2.

2. Believe that they can defer payment on $3,000 of the $50,000 of costs, implying that cash disbursements at the end of year 1 will be only $47,000 (=$50,000 − $3,000). Baldwin will pay off the $3,000 of accounts payable at the end of year 2.

3. Decide that inventory of $2,500 should be left on hand at the end of year 1 to avoid *stockouts* (that is, running out of inventory).

4. Decide that cash of $1,500 should be earmarked for the project at the end of year 1 to avoid running out of cash.

Thus, net working capital at the end of year 1 is:

$$
\underset{\substack{\text{Accounts} \\ \text{receivable}}}{\$9,000} \quad - \quad \underset{\substack{\text{Accounts} \\ \text{payable}}}{\$3,000} \quad + \quad \underset{\text{Inventory}}{\$2,500} \quad + \quad \underset{\text{Cash}}{\$1,500} \quad = \quad \underset{\substack{\text{Net working} \\ \text{capital}}}{\$10,000}
$$

Because $10,000 of cash generated elsewhere in the firm must be used to offset this requirement for net working capital, Baldwin's managers correctly view the investment in net working capital as a cash outflow of the project. As the project grows over time, needs for net working capital increase. *Changes* in net working capital from year to year represent further cash flows, as indicated by the negative numbers for the first few years on line 6 of Table 7.1. However, in the declining years of the project, net working capital is reduced—ultimately to zero. That is, accounts receivable are finally collected, the project's cash buffer is returned to the rest of the corporation, and all remaining inventory is sold off. This frees up cash in the later years, as indicated by positive numbers in years 4 and 5 on line 6.

Typically corporate worksheets (such as Table 7.1) treat net working capital as a whole. The individual components of working capital (receivables, inventory, and the like) do not generally appear in the worksheets. However, the reader should remember that the working capital numbers in the worksheets are not pulled out of thin air. Rather, they result from a meticulous forecast of the components, just as we illustrated for year 1.

A Note about Depreciation

The Baldwin case made some assumptions about depreciation. Where did these assumptions come from? Assets are currently depreciated for tax purposes according to the provisions of the 1986 Tax Reform Act. There are seven classes of depreciable property:

• The three-year class includes certain specialized short-lived property. Tractor units and racehorses over two years old are among the very few items fitting into this class.

• The five-year class includes (a) cars and trucks; (b) computers and peripheral equipment, as well as calculators, copiers, and typewriters; and (c) specific items used for research.

• The seven-year class includes office furniture, equipment, books, and single-purpose agricultural structures. It is also a catchall category because any asset not designated to be in another class is included here.

• The 10-year class includes vessels, barges, tugs, and similar equipment related to water transportation.

• The 15-year class encompasses a variety of specialized items. Included are equipment of telephone distribution plants and similar equipment used for voice and data communications, and sewage treatment plants.

- The 20-year class includes farm buildings, sewer pipe, and other very long-lived equipment.
- Real property that is depreciable is separated into two classes: residential and nonresidential. The cost of residential property is recovered over 27½ years and nonresidential property over 31½ years.

Items in the three-, five-, and seven-year classes are depreciated using the 200 percent declining-balance method, with a switch to straight-line depreciation at a point specified in the Tax Reform Act. Items in the 15- and 20-year classes are depreciated using the 150 percent declining-balance method, with a switch to straight-line depreciation at a specified point. All real estate is depreciated on a straight-line basis.

All calculations of depreciation include a half-year convention, which treats all property as if it were placed in service at midyear. To be consistent, the IRS allows half a year of depreciation for the year in which property is disposed of or retired. The effect of this is to spread the deductions for property over one year more than the name of its class—for example, six tax years for five-year property.

Interest Expense

It may have bothered you that interest expense was ignored in the Baldwin example. After all, many projects are at least partially financed with debt, particularly a bowling ball machine that is likely to increase the debt capacity of the firm. As it turns out, our approach of assuming no debt financing is rather standard in the real world. Firms typically calculate a project's cash flows under the assumption that the project is financed only with equity. Any adjustments for debt financing are reflected in the discount rate, not the cash flows. The treatment of debt in capital budgeting will be covered in depth later in the text. Suffice it to say at this time that the full ramifications of debt financing are well beyond our current discussion.

7.3   Inflation and Capital Budgeting

Inflation is an important fact of economic life, and it must be considered in capital budgeting. We begin our examination of inflation by considering the relationship between interest rates and inflation.

Interest Rates and Inflation

Suppose a bank offers a one-year interest rate of 10 percent. This means that an individual who deposits $1,000 will receive $1,100 (=$1,000 × 1.10) in one year. Although 10 percent may seem like a handsome return, one can put it in perspective only after examining the rate of inflation.

Imagine that the rate of inflation is 6 percent over the year and it affects all goods equally. For example, a restaurant that charges $1.00 for a hamburger today will charge $1.06 for the same hamburger at the end of the year. You can use your $1,000 to buy 1,000 hamburgers today (date 0). Alternatively, if you put your money in the bank, you can buy 1,038 (=$1,100/$1.06) hamburgers at date 1. Thus, lending increases your hamburger consumption by only 3.8 percent.

Because the prices of all goods rise at this 6 percent rate, lending lets you increase your consumption of any single good or any combination of goods by only 3.8 percent. Thus, 3.8 percent is what you are *really* earning through your savings account, after adjusting for

Figure 7.1

Calculation of Real Rate of Interest

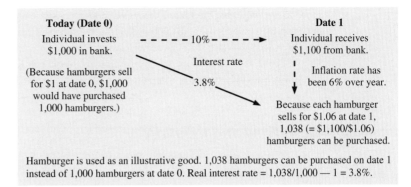

Hamburger is used as an illustrative good. 1,038 hamburgers can be purchased on date 1 instead of 1,000 hamburgers at date 0. Real interest rate = 1,038/1,000 — 1 = 3.8%.

inflation. Economists refer to the 3.8 percent number as the *real interest rate*. Economists refer to the 10 percent rate as the *nominal interest rate* or simply the *interest rate*. This discussion is illustrated in Figure 7.1.

We have used an example with a specific nominal interest rate and a specific inflation rate. In general, the formula between real and nominal interest rates can be written as follows:

$$1 + \text{Nominal interest rate} = (1 + \text{Real interest rate}) \times (1 + \text{Inflation rate})$$

Rearranging terms, we have:

$$\text{Real interest rate} = \frac{1 + \text{Nominal interest rate}}{1 + \text{Inflation rate}} - 1 \tag{7.1}$$

The formula indicates that the real interest rate in our example is 3.8 percent (=1.10/1.06 − 1).

Equation 7.1 determines the real interest rate precisely. The following formula is an approximation:

$$\text{Real interest rate} \cong \text{Nominal interest rate} - \text{Inflation rate} \tag{7.2}$$

The symbol $\cong$ indicates that the equation is approximately true. This latter formula calculates the real rate in our example like this:

$$4\% = 10\% - 6\%$$

The student should be aware that, although Equation 7.2 may seem more intuitive than Equation 7.1, 7.2 is only an approximation. This approximation is reasonably accurate for low rates of interest and inflation. In our example the difference between the approximate calculation and the exact one is only 0.2 percent (=4 percent − 3.8 percent). Unfortunately, the approximation becomes poor when rates are higher.

EXAMPLE 7.6

Real and Nominal Rates   The little-known monarchy of Gerberovia recently had a nominal interest rate of 300 percent and an inflation rate of 280 percent. According to Equation 7.2, the real interest rate is:

$$300\% - 280\% = 20\% \text{ (Approximate formula)}$$

However, according to Equation 7.1 this rate is:

$$\frac{1 + 300\%}{1 + 280\%} - 1 = 5.26\% \quad \text{(Exact formula)}$$

(continued)

How do we know that the second formula is indeed the exact one? Let's think in terms of hamburgers again. Had you deposited $1,000 in a Gerberovian bank a year ago, the account would be worth $4,000 [=$1,000 × (1 + 300%)] today. However, while a hamburger cost $1 a year ago, it costs $3.80 (=1 + 280%) today. Therefore, you would now be able to buy 1,052.6 (=$4,000/3.80) hamburgers, implying a real interest rate of 5.26 percent.

Cash Flow and Inflation

The previous analysis defines two types of interest rates, nominal rates and real rates, and relates them through Equation 7.1. Capital budgeting requires data on cash flows as well as on interest rates. Like interest rates, cash flows can be expressed in either nominal or real terms.

A **nominal cash flow** refers to the actual dollars to be received (or paid out). A **real cash flow** refers to the cash flow's purchasing power. These definitions are best explained by examples.

Nominal versus Real Cash Flow   Burrows Publishing has just purchased the rights to the next book of famed romantic novelist Barbara Musk. Still unwritten, the book should be available to the public in four years. Currently, romantic novels sell for $10.00 in softcover. The publishers believe that inflation will be 6 percent a year over the next four years. Because romantic novels are so popular, the publishers anticipate that their prices will rise about 2 percent per year more than the inflation rate over the next four years. Burrows Publishing plans to sell the novel at $13.60 [=$(1.08)^4 \times $10.00] four years from now, anticipating sales of 100,000 copies.

The expected cash flow in the fourth year of $1.36 million (=$13.60 × 100,000) is a *nominal cash flow*. That is, the firm expects to receive $1.36 million at that time. In other words, a nominal cash flow refers to the actual dollars to be received in the future.

The purchasing power of $1.36 million in four years is:

$$\$1.08 \text{ million} = \frac{\$1.36 \text{ million}}{(1.06)^4}$$

The figure of $1.08 million is a *real cash flow* because it is expressed in terms of purchasing power. Extending our hamburger example, the $1.36 million to be received in four years will only buy 1.08 million hamburgers because the price of a hamburger will rise from $1 to $1.26 [=$1 × (1.06)^4] over the period.

Depreciation   EOBII Publishers, a competitor of Burrows, recently bought a printing press for $2,000,000 to be depreciated by the straight-line method over five years. This implies yearly depreciation of $400,000 (=$2,000,000/5). Is this $400,000 figure a real or a nominal quantity?

Depreciation is a *nominal* quantity because $400,000 is the actual tax deduction over each of the next four years. Depreciation becomes a real quantity if it is adjusted for purchasing power. Hence, $316,837 [=$400,000/(1.06)^4] is depreciation in the fourth year, expressed as a real quantity.

Discounting: Nominal or Real?

Our previous discussion showed that interest rates can be expressed in either nominal or real terms. Similarly, cash flows can be expressed in either nominal or real terms. Given these choices, how should one express interest rates and cash flows when performing capital budgeting?

Financial practitioners correctly stress the need to maintain *consistency* between cash flows and discount rates. That is:

Nominal cash flows must be discounted at the *nominal* rate.

Real cash flows must be discounted at the *real* rate.

As long as one is consistent, either approach is correct. To minimize computational error, it is generally advisable in practice to choose the approach that is easiest. This idea is illustrated in the following two examples.

EXAMPLE 7.9

Real and Nominal Discounting   Shields Electric forecasts the following nominal cash flows on a particular project:

	0	1	2
Cash flow	−$1,000	$600	$650

The nominal discount rate is 14 percent, and the inflation rate is forecast to be 5 percent. What is the value of the project?

Using Nominal Quantities   The NPV can be calculated as:

$$\$26.47 = -\$1,000 + \frac{\$600}{1.14} + \frac{\$650}{(1.14)^2}$$

The project should be accepted.

Using Real Quantities   The real cash flows are these:

	0	1	2
Cash flow	−$1,000	$571.43	$589.57
		$\left(\dfrac{\$600}{1.05}\right)$	$\left(\dfrac{\$650}{(1.05)^2}\right)$

As we have discussed, the real discount rate is 8.57143 percent ($=1.14/1.05 - 1$).

The NPV can be calculated as:

$$\$26.47 = -\$1,000 + \frac{\$571.43}{1.0857143} + \frac{\$589.57}{(1.0857143)^2}$$

The NPV is the same whether cash flows are expressed in nominal or in real quantities. It must always be the case that the NPV is the same under the two different approaches.

Because both approaches always yield the same result, which one should be used? Use the approach that is simpler because the simpler approach generally leads to fewer computational errors. The Shields Electric example begins with nominal cash flows, so nominal quantities produce a simpler calculation here.

EXAMPLE 7.10

Real and Nominal NPV   Altshuler, Inc., generated the following forecast for a capital budgeting project:

	Year		
	0	1	2
Capital expenditure	$1,210		
Revenues (in real terms)		$1,900	$2,000
Cash expenses (in real terms)		950	1,000
Depreciation (straight-line)		605	605

The president, David Altshuler, estimates inflation to be 10 percent per year over the next two years. In addition, he believes that the cash flows of the project should be discounted at the nominal rate of 15.5 percent. His firm's tax rate is 40 percent.

Mr. Altshuler forecasts all cash flows in *nominal* terms, leading to the following spreadsheet:

	Year		
	0	1	2
Capital expenditure	−$1,210		
Revenues		$2,090 (= 1,900 × 1.10)	$2,420 [= 2,000 × (1.10)^2]
−Expenses		−1,045 (= 950 × 1.10)	−1,210 [= 1,000 × (1.10)^2]
−Depreciation		−605 (= 1,210/2)	−605
Taxable income		$ 440	$ 605
−Taxes (40%)		−176	−242
Income after taxes		$ 264	$ 363
+Depreciation		+605	+605
Cash flow		$ 869	$ 968

$$\text{NPV} = -\$1,210 + \frac{\$869}{1.155} + \frac{\$968}{(1.155)^2} = \$268$$

Mr. Altshuler's sidekick, Stuart Weiss, prefers working in real terms. He first calculates the real rate to be 5 percent ($= 1.155/1.10 - 1$). Next, he generates the following spreadsheet in *real* quantities:

	Year		
	0	1	2
Capital expenditure	−$1,210		
Revenues		$1,900	$ 2,000
−Expenses		−950	−1,000
−Depreciation		−550 (=605/1.1)	−500 [=605/(1.1)^2]
Taxable income		$ 400	$ 500
−Taxes (40%)		−160	−200
Income after taxes		$ 240	$ 300
+Depreciation		+550	+500
Cash flow		$ 790	$ 800

(continued)

$$\text{NPV} = -\$1{,}210 + \frac{\$790}{1.05} + \frac{\$800}{(1.05)^2} = \$268$$

In explaining his calculations to Mr. Altshuler, Mr. Weiss points out these facts:

1. The capital expenditure occurs at date 0 (today), so its nominal value and its real value are equal.
2. Because yearly depreciation of $605 is a nominal quantity, one converts it to a real quantity by discounting at the inflation rate of 10 percent.

It is no coincidence that both Mr. Altshuler and Mr. Weiss arrive at the same NPV number. Both methods must always generate the same NPV.

7.4 Alternative Definitions of Operating Cash Flow

The analysis we went through in the previous section is quite general and can be adapted to just about any capital investment problem. In the next section, we illustrate a particularly useful variation. Before we do so, we need to discuss the fact that different definitions of project operating cash flow are commonly used, both in practice and in finance texts.

As we will see, the different approaches to operating cash flow all measure the same thing. If they are used correctly, they all produce the same answer, and one is not necessarily any better or more useful than another. Unfortunately, the fact that alternative definitions are used sometimes leads to confusion. For this reason, we examine several of these variations next to see how they are related.

In the discussion that follows, keep in mind that when we speak of cash flow, we literally mean dollars in less dollars out. This is all we are concerned with. Different definitions of operating cash flow simply amount to different ways of manipulating basic information about sales, costs, depreciation, and taxes to get at cash flow.

For a particular project and year under consideration, suppose we have the following estimates:

$$\text{Sales} = \$1{,}500$$
$$\text{Costs} = \$700$$
$$\text{Depreciation} = \$600$$

With these estimates, notice that EBIT is:

$$\text{EBIT} = \text{Sales} - \text{Costs} - \text{Depreciation}$$
$$= \$1{,}500 - 700 - 600$$
$$= \$200$$

Once again, we assume that no interest is paid, so the tax bill is:

$$\text{Taxes} = \text{EBIT} \times t_c$$
$$= \$200 \times .34 = \$68$$

where t_c, the corporate tax rate, is 34 percent.

When we put all of this together, we see that project operating cash flow, OCF, is:

$$\text{OCF} = \text{EBIT} + \text{Depreciation} - \text{Taxes}$$
$$= \$200 + 600 - 68 = \$732$$

It turns out there are some other ways to determine OCF that could be (and are) used. We consider these next.

The Bottom-Up Approach

Because we are ignoring any financing expenses, such as interest, in our calculations of project OCF, we can write project net income as:

$$\text{Project net income} = \text{EBIT} - \text{Taxes}$$
$$= \$200 - 68$$
$$= \$132$$

If we simply add the depreciation to both sides, we arrive at a slightly different and very common expression for OCF:

$$\text{OCF} = \text{Net income} + \text{Depreciation}$$
$$= \$132 + 600 \qquad\qquad \textbf{(7.3)}$$
$$= \$732$$

This is the *bottom-up* approach. Here, we start with the accountant's bottom line (net income) and add back any noncash deductions such as depreciation. It is crucial to remember that this definition of operating cash flow as net income plus depreciation is correct only if there is no interest expense subtracted in the calculation of net income.

The Top-Down Approach

Perhaps the most obvious way to calculate OCF is this:

$$\text{OCF} = \text{Sales} - \text{Costs} - \text{Taxes}$$
$$= \$1,500 - 700 - 68 = \$732 \qquad\qquad \textbf{(7.4)}$$

This is the *top-down* approach, the second variation on the basic OCF definition. Here we start at the top of the income statement with sales and work our way down to net cash flow by subtracting costs, taxes, and other expenses. Along the way, we simply leave out any strictly noncash items such as depreciation.

The Tax Shield Approach

The third variation on our basic definition of OCF is the *tax shield* approach. This approach will be very useful for some problems we consider in the next chapter. The tax shield definition of OCF is:

$$\text{OCF} = (\text{Sales} - \text{Costs}) \times (1 - t_c) + \text{Depreciation} \times t_c \qquad\qquad \textbf{(7.5)}$$

where t_c is again the corporate tax rate. Assuming that $t_c = 34$ percent, the OCF works out to be:

$$\text{OCF} = (\$1,500 - 700) \times .66 + 600 \times .34$$
$$= \$528 + 204$$
$$= \$732$$

This is just as we had before.

This approach views OCF as having two components. The first part is what the project's cash flow would be if there were no depreciation expense. In this case, this would-have-been cash flow is $528.

The second part of OCF in this approach is the depreciation deduction multiplied by the tax rate. This is called the **depreciation tax shield**. We know that depreciation is a non-cash expense. The only cash flow effect of deducting depreciation is to reduce our taxes, a benefit to us. At the current 34 percent corporate tax rate, every dollar in depreciation expense saves us 34 cents in taxes. So, in our example, the $600 depreciation deduction saves us $600 \times .34 = $204 in taxes.

Conclusion

Now that we've seen that all of these approaches are the same, you're probably wondering why everybody doesn't just agree on one of them. One reason is that different approaches are useful in different circumstances. The best one to use is whichever happens to be the most convenient for the problem at hand.

7.5 Investments of Unequal Lives: The Equivalent Annual Cost Method

Suppose a firm must choose between two machines of unequal lives. Both machines can do the same job, but they have different operating costs and will last for different time periods. A simple application of the NPV rule suggests taking the machine whose costs have the lower present value. This choice might be a mistake, however, because the lower-cost machine may need to be replaced before the other one.

Let's consider an example. The Downtown Athletic Club must choose between two mechanical tennis ball throwers. Machine A costs less than machine B but will not last as long. The cash *outflows* from the two machines are shown here:

Machine	Date				
	0	**1**	**2**	**3**	**4**
A	$500	$120	$120	$120	
B	$600	$100	$100	$100	$100

Machine A costs $500 and lasts three years. There will be maintenance expenses of $120 to be paid at the end of each of the three years. Machine B costs $600 and lasts four years. There will be maintenance expenses of $100 to be paid at the end of each of the four years. We place all costs in real terms, an assumption greatly simplifying the analysis. Revenues per year are assumed to be the same, regardless of machine, so they are ignored in the analysis. Note that all numbers in the previous chart are *outflows*.

To get a handle on the decision, let's take the present value of the costs of each of the two machines. Assuming a discount rate of 10 percent, we have:

$$\text{Machine } A: \$798.42 = \$500 + \frac{\$120}{1.1} + \frac{\$120}{(1.1)^2} + \frac{\$120}{(1.1)^3}$$

$$\text{Machine } B: \$916.99 = \$600 + \frac{\$100}{1.1} + \frac{\$100}{(1.1)^2} + \frac{\$100}{(1.1)^3} + \frac{\$100}{(1.1)^4}$$

Machine B has a higher present value of outflows. A naive approach would be to select machine A because of its lower present value. However, machine B has a longer life, so perhaps its cost per year is actually lower.

How might one properly adjust for the difference in useful life when comparing the two machines? Perhaps the easiest approach involves calculating something called the *equivalent annual cost* of each machine. This approach puts costs on a per-year basis.

The previous equation showed that payments of ($500, $120, $120, $120) are equivalent to a single payment of $798.42 at date 0. We now wish to equate the single payment of $798.42 at date 0 with a three-year annuity. Using techniques of previous chapters, we have:

$$\$798.42 = C \times A_{.10}^{3}$$

$A_{.10}^{3}$ is an annuity of $1 a year for three years, discounted at 10 percent. C is the unknown— the annuity payment per year such that the present value of all payments equals $798.42. Because $A_{.10}^{3}$ equals 2.4869, C equals $321.05 (=$798.42/2.4869). Thus, a payment stream of ($500, $120, $120, $120) is equivalent to annuity payments of $321.05 made at the *end* of each year for three years. We refer to $321.05 as the *equivalent annual cost* of machine A.

This idea is summarized in the following chart:

	Date			
	0	1	2	3
Cash outflows of machine A	$500	$120	$120	$120
Equivalent annual cost of machine A		$321.05	$321.05	$321.05

The Downtown Athletic Club should be indifferent between cash outflows of ($500, $120, $120, $120) and cash outflows of ($0, $321.05, $321.05, $321.05). Alternatively, one can say that the purchase of the machine is financially equivalent to a rental agreement calling for annual lease payments of $321.05.

Now let's turn to machine B. We calculate its equivalent annual cost from:

$$\$916.99 = C \times A_{.10}^{4}$$

Because $A_{.10}^{4}$ equals 3.1699, C equals $916.99/3.1699, or $289.28.

As we did for machine A, we can create the following chart for machine B:

	Date				
	0	1	2	3	4
Cash outflows of machine B	$600	$100	$100	$100	$100
Equivalent annual cost of machine B		$289.28	$289.28	$289.28	$289.28

The decision is easy once the charts of the two machines are compared. Would you rather make annual lease payments of $321.05 or $289.28? Put this way, the problem becomes a no-brainer: A rational person would rather pay the lower amount. Thus, machine B is the preferred choice.

Two final remarks are in order. First, it is no accident that we specified the costs of the tennis ball machines in real terms. Although B would still have been the preferred machine had the costs been stated in nominal terms, the actual solution would have been much more difficult. As a general rule, always convert cash flows to real terms when working through problems of this type.

Second, such analysis applies only if one anticipates that both machines can be replaced. The analysis would differ if no replacement were possible. For example, imagine that the only company that manufactured tennis ball throwers just went out of business and no new producers are expected to enter the field. In this case, machine *B* would generate revenues in the fourth year whereas machine *A* would not. Here, simple net present value analysis for mutually exclusive projects including both revenues and costs would be appropriate.

The General Decision to Replace

The previous analysis concerned the choice between machine *A* and machine *B*, both of which were new acquisitions. More typically firms must decide when to replace an existing machine with a new one. This decision is actually quite straightforward. One should replace if the annual cost of the new machine is less than the annual cost of the old machine. As with much else in finance, an example clarifies this approach better than further explanation.

EXAMPLE 7.11

Replacement Decisions   Consider the situation of BIKE, which must decide whether to replace an existing machine. BIKE currently pays no taxes. The replacement machine costs $9,000 now and requires maintenance of $1,000 at the end of every year for eight years. At the end of eight years, the machine would be sold for $2,000 after taxes.

The existing machine requires increasing amounts of maintenance each year, and its salvage value falls each year, as shown:

Year	Maintenance	Aftertax Salvage
Present	$ 0	$4,000
1	1,000	2,500
2	2,000	1,500
3	3,000	1,000
4	4,000	0

This chart tells us that the existing machine can be sold for $4,000 now after taxes. If it is sold one year from now, the resale price will be $2,500 after taxes, and $1,000 must be spent on maintenance during the year to keep it running. For ease of calculation, we assume that this maintenance fee is paid at the end of the year. The machine will last for four more years before it falls apart. In other words, salvage value will be zero at the end of year 4. If BIKE faces an opportunity cost of capital of 15 percent, when should it replace the machine?

Our approach is to compare the annual cost of the replacement machine with the annual cost of the old machine. The annual cost of the replacement machine is simply its *equivalent annual cost* (EAC). Let's calculate that first.

Equivalent Annual Cost of New Machine   The present value of the cost of the new replacement machine is as follows:

$$PV_{costs} = \$9,000 + \$1,000 \times A_{.15}^8 - \frac{\$2,000}{(1.15)^8}$$

$$= \$9,000 + \$1,000 \times (4.4873) - \$2,000 \times (.3269)$$

$$= \$12,833$$

(continued)

Notice that the $2,000 salvage value is an inflow. It is treated as a *negative* number in this equation because it *offsets* the cost of the machine.

The EAC of a new replacement machine equals:

$$\text{PV/8-year annuity factor at 15\%} = \frac{\text{PV}}{A^8_{.15}} = \frac{\$12,833}{4.4873} = \$2,860$$

This calculation implies that buying a replacement machine is financially equivalent to renting this machine for $2,860 per year.

Cost of Old Machine   This calculation is a little trickier. If BIKE keeps the old machine for one year, the firm must pay maintenance costs of $1,000 a year from now. But this is not BIKE's only cost from keeping the machine for one year. BIKE will receive $2,500 at date 1 if the old machine is kept for one year but would receive $4,000 today if the old machine were sold immediately. This reduction in sales proceeds is clearly a cost as well.

Thus the PV of the costs of keeping the machine one more year before selling it equals:

$$\$4,000 + \frac{\$1,000}{1.15} - \frac{\$2,500}{1.15} = \$2,696$$

That is, if BIKE holds the old machine for one year, BIKE does *not* receive the $4,000 today. This $4,000 can be thought of as an opportunity cost. In addition, the firm must pay $1,000 a year from now. Finally, BIKE does receive $2,500 a year from now. This last item is treated as a negative number because it offsets the other two costs.

Although we normally express cash flows in terms of present value, the analysis to come is easier if we express the cash flow in terms of its future value one year from now. This future value is:

$$\$2,696 \times 1.15 = \$3,100$$

In other words, the cost of keeping the machine for one year is equivalent to paying $3,100 at the end of the year.

Making the Comparison   Now let's review the cash flows. If we replace the machine immediately, we can view our annual expense as $2,860, beginning at the end of the year. This annual expense occurs forever if we replace the new machine every eight years. This cash flow stream can be written as follows:

	Year 1	Year 2	Year 3	Year 4	...
Expenses from replacing machine immediately	$2,860	$2,860	$2,860	$2,860	...

If we replace the old machine in one year, our expense from using the old machine for that final year can be viewed as $3,100, payable at the end of the year. After replacement, our annual expense is $2,860, beginning at the end of two years. This annual expense occurs forever if we replace the new machine every eight years. This cash flow stream can be written like this:

	Year 1	Year 2	Year 3	Year 4	...
Expenses from using old machine for one year and then replacing it	$3,100	$2,860	$2,860	$2,860	...

(continued)

Put this way, the choice is a no-brainer. Anyone would rather pay $2,860 at the end of the year than $3,100 at the end of the year. Thus, BIKE should replace the old machine immediately to minimize the expense at year 1.[1]

Two final points should be made about the decision to replace. First, we have examined a situation where both the old machine and the replacement machine generate the same revenues. Because revenues are unaffected by the choice of machine, revenues do not enter our analysis. This situation is common in business. For example, the decision to replace either the heating system or the air conditioning system in one's home office will likely not affect firm revenues. However, sometimes revenues will be greater with a new machine. The approach here can easily be amended to handle differential revenues.

Second, we want to stress the importance of the current approach. Applications of this approach are pervasive in business because *every* machine must be replaced at some point.

---

[1]One caveat is in order. Perhaps the old machine's maintenance is high in the first year but drops after that. A decision to replace immediately might be premature in that case. Therefore, we need to check the cost of the old machine in future years.

The cost of keeping the existing machine a second year is:

$$\text{PV of costs at time 1} = \$2,500 + \frac{\$2,000}{1.15} - \frac{\$1,500}{1.15} = \$2,935$$

which has a future value of $3,375 (=$2,935 × 1.15).

The costs of keeping the existing machine for years 3 and 4 are also greater than the EAC of buying a new machine. Thus, BIKE's decision to replace the old machine immediately is still valid.

Summary and Conclusions

This chapter discussed a number of practical applications of capital budgeting.

1. Capital budgeting must be placed on an incremental basis. This means that sunk costs must be ignored, whereas both opportunity costs and side effects must be considered.

2. In the Baldwin case we computed NPV using the following two steps:
   a. Calculate the net cash flow from all sources for each period.
   b. Calculate the NPV using these cash flows.

3. Inflation must be handled consistently. One approach is to express both cash flows and the discount rate in nominal terms. The other approach is to express both cash flows and the discount rate in real terms. Because either approach yields the same NPV calculation, the simpler method should be used. The simpler method will generally depend on the type of capital budgeting problem.

4. A firm should use the equivalent annual cost approach when choosing between two machines of unequal lives.

Concept Questions

1. **Opportunity Cost**   In the context of capital budgeting, what is an opportunity cost?

2. **Incremental Cash Flows**   Which of the following should be treated as an incremental cash flow when computing the NPV of an investment?
   a. A reduction in the sales of a company's other products caused by the investment.
   b. An expenditure on plant and equipment that has not yet been made and will be made only if the project is accepted.
   c. Costs of research and development undertaken in connection with the product during the past three years.
   d. Annual depreciation expense from the investment.

  e. Dividend payments by the firm.

  f. The resale value of plant and equipment at the end of the project's life.

  g. Salary and medical costs for production personnel who will be employed only if the project is accepted.

3. **Incremental Cash Flows** Your company currently produces and sells steel shaft golf clubs. The board of directors wants you to consider the introduction of a new line of titanium bubble woods with graphite shafts. Which of the following costs are *not* relevant?

  a. Land you already own that will be used for the project, but otherwise will be sold for €700,000, its market value.

  b. A €300,000 drop in your sales of steel shaft clubs if the titanium woods with graphite shafts are introduced.

  c. €200,000 spent on research and development last year on graphite shafts.

4. **Depreciation** Given the choice, would a firm prefer to use MACRS depreciation or straight-line depreciation? Why?

5. **Net Working Capital** In our capital budgeting examples, we assumed that a firm would recover all of the working capital it invested in a project. Is this a reasonable assumption? When might it not be valid?

6. **Stand-Alone Principle** Suppose a financial manager is quoted as saying, "Our firm uses the stand-alone principle. Because we treat projects like minifirms in our evaluation process, we include financing costs because they are relevant at the firm level." Critically evaluate this statement.

7. **Equivalent Annual Cost** When is EAC analysis appropriate for comparing two or more projects? Why is this method used? Are there any implicit assumptions required by this method that you find troubling? Explain.

8. **Cash Flow and Depreciation** "When evaluating projects, we're only concerned with the relevant incremental aftertax cash flows. Therefore, because depreciation is a noncash expense, we should ignore its effects when evaluating projects." Critically evaluate this statement.

9. **Capital Budgeting Considerations** A major college textbook publisher has an existing finance textbook. The publisher is debating whether to produce an "essentialized" version, meaning a shorter (and lower-priced) book. What are some of the considerations that should come into play?

  To answer the next three questions, refer to the following example. In 2003, Porsche unveiled its new sports utility vehicle (SUV), the Cayenne. With a price tag of over $40,000, the Cayenne goes from zero to 62 mph in 8.5 seconds. Porsche's decision to enter the SUV market was in response to the runaway success of other high-priced SUVs such as the Mercedes-Benz M class. Vehicles in this class had generated years of very high profits. The Cayenne certainly spiced up the market, and, in 2006, Porsche introduced the Cayenne Turbo S, which goes from zero to 60 mph in 4.8 seconds and has a top speed of 168 mph. The base price for the Cayenne Turbo S? Almost $112,000!

  Some analysts questioned Porsche's entry into the luxury SUV market. The analysts were concerned because not only was Porsche a late entry into the market, but also the introduction of the Cayenne might damage Porsche's reputation as a maker of high-performance automobiles.

10. **Erosion** In evaluating the Cayenne, would you consider the possible damage to Porsche's reputation as erosion?

11. **Capital Budgeting** Porsche was one of the last manufacturers to enter the sports utility vehicle market. Why would one company decide to proceed with a product when other companies, at least initially, decide not to enter the market?

12. **Capital Budgeting** In evaluating the Cayenne, what do you think Porsche needs to assume regarding the substantial profit margins that exist in this market? Is it likely that they will be maintained as the market becomes more competitive, or will Porsche be able to maintain the profit margin because of its image and the performance of the Cayenne?

Questions and Problems

BASIC
(Questions 1–10)

1. **Calculating Project NPV**   Raphael Restaurant is considering the purchase of a $10,000 souffle maker. The souffle maker has an economic life of five years and will be fully depreciated by the straight-line method. The machine will produce 2,000 souffles per year, with each costing $2 to make and priced at $5. Assume that the discount rate is 15 percent and the tax rate is 34 percent. Should Raphael make the purchase?

2. **Calculating Project NPV**   The Best Manufacturing Company is considering a new investment. Financial projections for the investment are tabulated here. The corporate tax rate is 34 percent. Assume all sales revenue is received in cash, all operating costs and income taxes are paid in cash, and all cash flows occur at the end of the year. All net working capital is recovered at the end of the project.

	Year 0	Year 1	Year 2	Year 3	Year 4
Investment	$10,000	–	–	–	–
Sales revenue	–	$7,000	$7,000	$7,000	$7,000
Operating costs	–	2,000	2,000	2,000	2,000
Depreciation	–	2,500	2,500	2,500	2,500
Net working capital spending	500	250	300	200	?

   a. Compute the incremental net income of the investment for each year.
   b. Compute the incremental cash flows of the investment for each year.
   c. Suppose the appropriate discount rate is 12 percent. What is the NPV of the project?

3. **Calculating Project NPV**   Down Under Boomerang, Inc., is considering a new three-year expansion project that requires an initial fixed asset investment of ZAR 2.7 million. The fixed asset will be depreciated straight-line to zero over its three-year tax life, after which it will be worthless. The project is estimated to generate ZAR 2,400,000 in annual sales, with costs of ZAR 960,000. The tax rate is 35 percent and the required return is 15 percent. What is the project's NPV?

4. **Calculating Project Cash Flow from Assets**   In the previous problem, suppose the project requires an initial investment in net working capital of ZAR 300,000 and the fixed asset will have a market value of ZAR 210,000 at the end of the project. What is the project's year 0 net cash flow? Year 1? Year 2? Year 3? What is the new NPV?

5. **NPV and Modified ACRS**   In the previous problem, suppose the fixed asset actually falls into the three-year MACRS class. All the other facts are the same. What is the project's year 1 net cash flow now? Year 2? Year 3? What is the new NPV?

6. **Project Evaluation**   Your firm is contemplating the purchase of a new £925,000 computer-based order entry system. The system will be depreciated straight-line to zero over its five-year life. It will be worth £90,000 at the end of that time. You will save £360,000 before taxes per year in order processing costs, and you will be able to reduce working capital by £125,000 (this is a one-time reduction). If the tax rate is 35 percent, what is the IRR for this project?

7. **Project Evaluation**   Dog Up! Hong Chen is looking at a new sausage system with an installed cost of CNY 390,000. This cost will be depreciated straight-line to zero over the project's five-year life, at the end of which the sausage system can be scrapped for CNY 60,000. The sausage system will save the firm CNY 120,000 per year in pretax operating costs, and the system requires an initial investment in net working capital of CNY 28,000. If the tax rate is 34 percent and the discount rate is 10 percent, what is the NPV of this project?

8. **Calculating Salvage Value**   An asset used in a four-year project falls in the five-year MACRS class for tax purposes. The asset has an acquisition cost of $9,300,000 and will be sold for

$2,100,000 at the end of the project. If the tax rate is 35 percent, what is the aftertax salvage value of the asset?

9. **Calculating NPV**   Netanya Petroleum is considering a new project that complements its existing business. The machine required for the project costs ILS 2 million. The marketing department predicts that sales related to the project will be ILS 1.2 million per year for the next four years, after which the market will cease to exist. The machine will be depreciated down to zero over its four-year economic life using the straight-line method. Cost of goods sold and operating expenses related to the project are predicted to be 25 percent of sales. Netanya also needs to add net working capital of ILS 75,000 immediately. The additional net working capital will be recovered in full at the end of the project's life. The corporate tax rate is 35 percent. The required rate of return for Netanya is 14 percent. Should Netanya proceed with the project?

10. **Calculating EAC**   You are evaluating two different silicon wafer milling machines. The Techron I costs £210,000, has a three-year life, and has pretax operating costs of £34,000 per year. The Techron II costs £320,000, has a five-year life, and has pretax operating costs of £23,000 per year. For both milling machines, use straight-line depreciation to zero over the project's life and assume a salvage value of £20,000. If your tax rate is 35 percent and your discount rate is 14 percent, compute the EAC for both machines. Which do you prefer? Why?

INTERMEDIATE
(Questions 11–29)

11. **Cost-Cutting Proposals**   Massey Machine Shop is considering a four-year project to improve its production efficiency. Buying a new machine press for $480,000 is estimated to result in $160,000 in annual pretax cost savings. The press falls in the MACRS five-year class, and it will have a salvage value at the end of the project of $70,000. The press also requires an initial investment in spare parts inventory of $20,000, along with an additional $3,000 in inventory for each succeeding year of the project. If the shop's tax rate is 35 percent and its discount rate is 15 percent, should Massey buy and install the machine press?

12. **Comparing Mutually Exclusive Projects**   Karachi Foods Ltd. is trying to decide between two different conveyor belt systems. System A costs PKR 430,000, has a four-year life, and requires PKR 120,000 in pretax annual operating costs. System B costs PKR 540,000, has a six-year life, and requires PKR 80,000 in pretax annual operating costs. Both systems are to be depreciated straight-line to zero over their lives and will have zero salvage value. Whichever system is chosen, it will *not* be replaced when it wears out. If the tax rate is 34 percent and the discount rate is 20 percent, which system should the firm choose?

13. **Comparing Mutually Exclusive Projects**   Suppose in the previous problem that Karachi Foods always needs a conveyor belt system; when one wears out, it must be replaced. Which system should the firm choose now?

14. **Comparing Mutually Exclusive Projects**   Vandalay Industries is considering the purchase of a new machine for the production of latex. Machine A costs €2,100,000 and will last for six years. Variable costs are 35 percent of sales, and fixed costs are €150,000 per year. Machine B costs €4,500,000 and will last for nine years. Variable costs for this machine are 30 percent and fixed costs are €100,000 per year. The sales for each machine will be €9 million per year. The required return is 10 percent and the tax rate is 35 percent. Both machines will be depreciated on a straight-line basis. If the company plans to replace the machine when it wears out on a perpetual basis, which machine should you choose?

15. **Capital Budgeting with Inflation**   Consider the following cash flows on two mutually exclusive projects:

Year	Project A	Project B
0	−$40,000	−$50,000
1	20,000	10,000
2	15,000	20,000
3	15,000	40,000

The cash flows of project *A* are expressed in real terms, whereas those of project *B* are expressed in nominal terms. The appropriate nominal discount rate is 15 percent and the inflation rate is 4 percent. Which project should you choose?

16. **Inflation and Company Value**   Sparkling Water, Inc., expects to sell 2 million bottles of drinking water each year in perpetuity. This year each bottle will sell for $1.25 in real terms and will cost $0.80 in real terms. Sales income and costs occur at year-end. Revenues will rise at a real rate of 6 percent annually, while real costs will rise at a real rate of 5 percent annually. The real discount rate is 10 percent. The corporate tax rate is 34 percent. What is Sparkling worth today?

17. **Calculating Nominal Cash Flow**   Sinhalese Artworks Limited is considering an investment of LKR 250,000 in an asset with an economic life of five years. The firm estimates that the nominal annual cash revenues and expenses at the end of the first year will be LKR 200,000 and LKR 50,000, respectively. Both revenues and expenses will grow thereafter at the annual inflation rate of 3 percent. Sinhalese will use the straight-line method to depreciate its asset to zero over five years. The salvage value of the asset is estimated to be LKR 30,000 in nominal terms at that time. The one-time net working capital investment of LKR 10,000 is required immediately and will be recovered at the end of the project. All corporate cash flows are subject to a 34 percent tax rate. What is the project's total nominal cash flow from assets for each year?

18. **Cash Flow Valuation**   Calgary Auto Parts runs a small manufacturing operation. For this fiscal year, it expects real net cash flows of CAD 120,000. Calgary is an ongoing operation, but it expects competitive pressures to erode its real net cash flows at 6 percent per year in perpetuity. The appropriate real discount rate for Calgary is 12 percent. All net cash flows are received at year-end. What is the present value of the net cash flows from Calgary's operations?

19. **Equivalent Annual Cost**   Bridgton Golf Academy is evaluating different golf practice equipment. The "Dimple-Max" equipment costs $45,000, has a three-year life, and costs $5,000 per year to operate. The relevant discount rate is 12 percent. Assume that the straight-line depreciation method is used and that the equipment is fully depreciated to zero. Furthermore, assume the equipment has a salvage value of $10,000 at the end of the project's life. The relevant tax rate is 34 percent. All cash flows occur at the end of the year. What is the equivalent annual cost (EAC) of this equipment?

20. **Equivalent Annual Cost**   Ambuja University must purchase word processors for its typing lab. The university can buy 10 EVF word processors that cost INR 8,000 each and have annual, year-end maintenance costs of INR 2,000 per machine. The EVF word processors will be replaced at the end of year 4 and have no value at that time. Alternatively, Ambuja can buy 11 AEH word processors to accomplish the same work. The AEH word processors will be replaced after three years. They each cost INR 5,000 and have annual, year-end maintenance costs of INR 2,500 per machine. Each AEH word processor will have a resale value of INR 500 at the end of three years. The university's opportunity cost of funds for this type of investment is 14 percent. Because the university is a nonprofit institution, it does not pay taxes. It is anticipated that whichever manufacturer is chosen now will be the supplier of future machines. Would you recommend purchasing 10 EVF word processors or 11 AEH machines?

21. **Calculating Project NPV**   Scott Investors, Inc., is considering the purchase of an AUD 500,000 computer with an economic life of five years. The computer will be fully depreciated over five years using the straight-line method. The market value of the computer will be AUD 100,000 in five years. The computer will replace five office employees whose combined annual salaries are AUD 120,000. The machine will also immediately lower the firm's required net working capital by AUD 100,000. This amount of net working capital will need to be replaced once the machine is sold. The corporate tax rate is 34 percent. Is it worthwhile to buy the computer if the appropriate discount rate is 10 percent?

22. **Calculating NPV and IRR for a Replacement**   A firm is considering an investment in a new machine with a price of ¥32 million to replace its existing machine. The current machine has a book value of ¥1 million and a market value of ¥9 million. The new machine is expected

to have a four-year life, and the old machine has four years left in which it can be used. If the firm replaces the old machine with the new machine, it expects to save ¥8 million in operating costs each year over the next four years. Both machines will have no salvage value in four years. If the firm purchases the new machine, it will also need an investment of ¥500,000 in net working capital. The required return on the investment is 18 percent, and the tax rate is 39 percent.

a. What are the NPV and IRR of the decision to replace the old machine?

b. The new machine saves ¥32 million over the next four years and has a cost of ¥32 million. When you consider the time value of money, how is it possible that the NPV of the decision to replace the old machine has a positive NPV?

23. **Project Analysis and Inflation**   Filadelfia Spinners, Inc., has been considering the purchase of a new manufacturing facility for CRC 120,000. The facility is to be fully depreciated on a straight-line basis over seven years. It is expected to have no resale value after the seven years. Operating revenues from the facility are expected to be CRC 50,000, in nominal terms, at the end of the first year. The revenues are expected to increase at the inflation rate of 5 percent. Production costs at the end of the first year will be CRC 20,000, in nominal terms, and they are expected to increase at 7 percent per year. The real discount rate is 14 percent. The corporate tax rate is 34 percent. Filadelfia has other ongoing profitable operations. Should the company accept the project?

24. **Calculating Project NPV**   With the growing popularity of casual surf print clothing, two recent MBA graduates decided to broaden this casual surf concept to encompass a "surf lifestyle for the home." With limited capital, they decided to focus on surf print table and floor lamps to accent people's homes. They projected unit sales of these lamps to be 5,000 in the first year, with growth of 15 percent each year for the next five years. Production of these lamps will require AUD 28,000 in net working capital to start. Total fixed costs are AUD 75,000 per year, variable production costs are AUD 20 per unit, and the units are priced at AUD 45 each. The equipment needed to begin production will cost AUD 60,000. The equipment will be depreciated using the straight-line method over a five-year life and is not expected to have a salvage value. The effective tax rate is 34 percent, and the required rate of return is 25 percent. What is the NPV of this project?

25. **Calculating Project NPV**   You have been hired as a consultant for Pristine Urban-Tech Zither, Inc. (PUTZ), manufacturers of fine zithers. The market for zithers is growing quickly. The company bought some land three years ago for $1 million in anticipation of using it as a toxic waste dump site but has recently hired another company to handle all toxic materials. Based on a recent appraisal, the company believes it could sell the land for $800,000 on an aftertax basis. The company also hired a marketing firm to analyze the zither market, at a cost of $125,000. An excerpt of the marketing report is as follows:

> The zither industry will have a rapid expansion in the next four years. With the brand name recognition that PUTZ brings to bear, we feel that the company will be able to sell 2,900, 3,800, 2,700, and 1,900 units each year for the next four years, respectively. Again, capitalizing on the name recognition of PUTZ, we feel that a premium price of $700 can be charged for each zither. Because zithers appear to be a fad, we feel at the end of the four-year period, sales should be discontinued.

PUTZ feels that fixed costs for the project will be $350,000 per year, and variable costs are 15 percent of sales. The equipment necessary for production will cost $3.8 million and will be depreciated according to a three-year MACRS schedule. At the end of the project, the equipment can be scrapped for $400,000. Net working capital of $120,000 will be required by the end of the first year. PUTZ has a 38 percent tax rate, and the required return on the project is 15 percent. What is the NPV of the project? Assume the company has other profitable projects.

26. **Calculating Project NPV**   Sumami Ink is deciding when to replace its old machine. The machine's current salvage value is KRW 2 million. Its current book value is KRW 1 million. If not sold, the old machine will require maintenance costs of KRW 400,000 at the end of the year for the next five years. Depreciation on the old machine is KWR 200,000 per year. At the end of five years, it will have a salvage value of KRW 200,000 and a book value of KRW 0. A replacement machine costs KRW 3 million now and requires maintenance costs

of KRW 500,000 at the end of each year during its economic life of five years. At the end of the five years, the new machine will have a salvage value of KRW 500,000. It will be fully depreciated by the straight-line method. In five years a replacement machine will cost KRW 3,500,000. Sumami Ink will need to purchase this machine regardless of what choice it makes today. The corporate tax rate is 34 percent and the appropriate discount rate is 12 percent. The company is assumed to earn sufficient revenues to generate tax shields from depreciation. Should Sumami Ink replace the old machine now or at the end of five years?

27. **Calculating EAC**   Gold Star Industries is contemplating a purchase of computers. The firm has narrowed its choices to the SAL 5000 and the DET 1000. Gold Star would need 10 SALs, and each SAL costs $3,750 and requires $500 of maintenance each year. At the end of the computer's eight-year life, Gold Star expects to sell each one for $500. Alternatively, Gold Star could buy seven DETs. Each DET costs $5,250 and requires $700 of maintenance every year. Each DET lasts for six years and has a resale value of $600 at the end of its economic life. Gold Star will continue to purchase the model that it chooses today into perpetuity. Gold Star has a 34 percent tax rate. Assume that the maintenance costs occur at year-end. Depreciation is straight-line to zero. Which model should Gold Star buy if the appropriate discount rate is 11 percent?

28. **EAC and Inflation**   Office Automation, Inc., must choose between two copiers, the XX40 or the RH45. The XX40 costs £700 and will last for three years. The copier will require an aftertax cost of £100 per year after all relevant expenses. The RH45 costs £900 and will last five years. The real aftertax cost for the RH45 will be £110 per year. All cash flows occur at the end of the year. The inflation rate is expected to be 5 percent per year, and the nominal discount rate is 14 percent. Which copier should the company choose?

29. **Project Analysis and Inflation**   Dickinson Brothers, Inc., is considering investing in a machine to produce computer keyboards. The price of the machine will be CAD 400,000, and its economic life is five years. The machine will be fully depreciated by the straight-line method. The machine will produce 10,000 keyboards each year. The price of each keyboard will be CAD 40 in the first year and will increase by 5 percent per year. The production cost per keyboard will be CAD 20 in the first year and will increase by 10 percent per year. The project will have an annual fixed cost of CAD 50,000 and require an immediate investment of CAD 25,000 in net working capital. The corporate tax rate for the company is 34 percent. If the appropriate discount rate is 15 percent, what is the NPV of the investment?

CHALLENGE
(Questions 30–40)

30. **Project Evaluation**   Birla Acoustics (BAI), Inc., projects unit sales for a new seven-octave voice emulation implant as follows:

Year	Unit Sales
1	85,000
2	98,000
3	106,000
4	114,000
5	93,000

Production of the implants will require $1,500,000 in net working capital to start and additional net working capital investments each year equal to 15 percent of the projected sales increase for the following year. Total fixed costs are $900,000 per year, variable production costs are $240 per unit, and the units are priced at $325 each. The equipment needed to begin production has an installed cost of $21,000,000. Because the implants are intended for professional singers, this equipment is considered industrial machinery and thus qualifies as seven-year MACRS property. In five years, this equipment can be sold for about 20 percent of its acquisition cost. BAI is in the 35 percent marginal tax bracket and has a required return on all its projects of 18 percent. Based on these preliminary project estimates, what is the NPV of the project? What is the IRR?

31. **Calculating Required Savings**   A proposed cost-saving device has an installed cost of €480,000. The device will be used in a five-year project but is classified as three-year MACRS

property for tax purposes. The required initial net working capital investment is €40,000, the marginal tax rate is 35 percent, and the project discount rate is 12 percent. The device has an estimated year 5 salvage value of €45,000. What level of pretax cost savings do we require for this project to be profitable?

32.   Calculating a Bid Price   Another utilization of cash flow analysis is setting the bid price on a project. To calculate the bid price, we set the project NPV equal to zero and find the required price. Thus the bid price represents a financial break-even level for the project. Guthrie Enterprises needs someone to supply it with 150,000 cartons of machine screws per year to support its manufacturing needs over the next five years, and you've decided to bid on the contract. It will cost you $780,000 to install the equipment necessary to start production; you'll depreciate this cost straight-line to zero over the project's life. You estimate that in five years this equipment can be salvaged for $50,000. Your fixed production costs will be $240,000 per year, and your variable production costs should be $8.50 per carton. You also need an initial investment in net working capital of $75,000. If your tax rate is 35 percent and you require a 16 percent return on your investment, what bid price should you submit?

33.   Financial Break-Even Analysis   The technique for calculating a bid price can be extended to many other types of problems. Answer the following questions using the same technique as setting a bid price; that is, set the project NPV to zero and solve for the variable in question.
  a. In the previous problem, assume that the price per carton is $13 and find the project NPV. What does your answer tell you about your bid price? What do you know about the number of cartons you can sell and still break even? How about your level of costs?
  b. Solve the previous problem again with the price still at $13—but find the quantity of cartons per year that you can supply and still break even. (*Hint*: It's less than 150,000.)
  c. Repeat (b) with a price of $13 and a quantity of 150,000 cartons per year, and find the highest level of fixed costs you could afford and still break even. (*Hint*: It's more than $240,000.)

34.   Calculating a Bid Price   Your company has been approached to bid on a contract to sell 10,000 voice recognition (VR) computer keyboards a year for four years. Due to technological improvements, beyond that time they will be outdated and no sales will be possible. The equipment necessary for the production will cost INR 2.4 million and will be depreciated on a straight-line basis to a zero salvage value. Production will require an investment in net working capital of INR 75,000 to be returned at the end of the project, and the equipment can be sold for INR 200,000 at the end of production. Fixed costs are INR 500,000 per year, and variable costs are INR 165 per unit. In addition to the contract, you feel your company can sell 3,000, 6,000, 8,000, and 5,000 additional units to companies in other countries over the next four years, respectively, at a price of INR 275. This price is fixed. The tax rate is 40 percent, and the required return is 13 percent. Additionally, the president of the company will undertake the project only if it has an NPV of INR 100,000. What bid price should you set for the contract?

35.   Replacement Decisions   Suppose we are thinking about replacing an old computer with a new one. The old one cost us $650,000; the new one will cost $780,000. The new machine will be depreciated straight-line to zero over its five-year life. It will probably be worth about $140,000 after five years.
   The old computer is being depreciated at a rate of $130,000 per year. It will be completely written off in three years. If we don't replace it now, we will have to replace it in two years. We can sell it now for $230,000; in two years it will probably be worth $90,000. The new machine will save us $125,000 per year in operating costs. The tax rate is 38 percent, and the discount rate is 14 percent.
  a. Suppose we recognize that if we don't replace the computer now, we will be replacing it in two years. Should we replace now or should we wait? (*Hint*: What we effectively have here is a decision either to "invest" in the old computer—by not selling it—or to invest in the new one. Notice that the two investments have unequal lives.)
  b. Suppose we consider only whether we should replace the old computer now without worrying about what's going to happen in two years. What are the relevant cash flows? Should

we replace it or not? (*Hint*: Consider the net change in the firm's aftertax cash flows if we do the replacement.)

36.   **Project Analysis**   Altay Enterprises of Mongolia is evaluating alternative uses for a three-story manufacturing and warehousing building that it has purchased for MNT 225,000. The company can continue to rent the building to the present occupants for MNT 12,000 per year. The present occupants have indicated an interest in staying in the building for at least another 15 years. Alternatively, the company could modify the existing structure to use for its own manufacturing and warehousing needs. Altay's production engineer feels the building could be adapted to handle one of two new product lines. The cost and revenue data for the two product alternatives are as follows:

	Product A	Product B
Initial cash outlay for building modifications	MNT 36,000	MNT 54,000
Initial cash outlay for equipment	144,000	162,000
Annual pretax cash revenues (generated for 15 years)	105,000	127,500
Annual pretax expenditures (generated for 15 years)	60,000	75,000

The building will be used for only 15 years for either product *A* or product *B*. After 15 years the building will be too small for efficient production of either product line. At that time, Altay plans to rent the building to firms similar to the current occupants. To rent the building again, Altay will need to restore the building to its present layout. The estimated cash cost of restoring the building if product *A* has been undertaken is MNT 3,750. If product *B* has been manufactured, the cash cost will be MNT 28,125. These cash costs can be deducted for tax purposes in the year the expenditures occur.

Altay will depreciate the original building shell (purchased for MNT 225,000) over a 30-year life to zero, regardless of which alternative it chooses. The building modifications and equipment purchases for either product are estimated to have a 15-year life. They will be depreciated by the straight-line method. The firm's tax rate is 34 percent, and its required rate of return on such investments is 12 percent.

For simplicity, assume all cash flows occur at the end of the year. The initial outlays for modifications and equipment will occur today (year 0), and the restoration outlays will occur at the end of year 15. Altay has other profitable ongoing operations that are sufficient to cover any losses. Which use of the building would you recommend to management?

37.   **Project Analysis and Inflation**   The Biological Insect Control Corporation (BICC) has hired you as a consultant to evaluate the NPV of its proposed toad ranch. BICC plans to breed toads and sell them as ecologically desirable insect control mechanisms. They anticipate that the business will continue into perpetuity. Following the negligible start-up costs, BICC expects the following nominal cash flows at the end of the year:

Revenues	£150,000
Labor costs	80,000
Other costs	40,000

The company will lease machinery for £20,000 per year. The lease payments start at the end of year 1 and are expressed in nominal terms. Revenues will increase by 5 percent per year in real terms. Labor costs will increase by 3 percent per year in real terms. Other costs will decrease by 1 percent per year in real terms. The rate of inflation is expected to be 6 percent per year. BICC's required rate of return is 10 percent in real terms. The company has a 34 percent tax rate. All cash flows occur at year-end. What is the NPV of BICC's proposed toad ranch today?

38.   **Project Analysis and Inflation**   Yuka International has an investment opportunity to produce a new stereo color TV. The required investment on January 1 of this year is €32 million. The firm will depreciate the investment to zero using the straight-line method over four years. The investment has no resale value after completion of the project. The firm is in the 34 percent tax

bracket. The price of the product will be €400 per unit, in real terms, and will not change over the life of the project. Labor costs for year 1 will be €15.30 per hour, in real terms, and will increase at 2 percent per year in real terms. Energy costs for year 1 will be €5.15 per physical unit, in real terms, and will increase at 3 percent per year in real terms. The inflation rate is 5 percent per year. Revenues are received and costs are paid at year-end. Refer to the following table for the production schedule:

	Year 1	Year 2	Year 3	Year 4
Physical production, in units	100,000	200,000	200,000	150,000
Labor input, in hours	2,000,000	2,000,000	2,000,000	2,000,000
Energy input, physical units	200,000	200,000	200,000	200,000

The real discount rate for Yuka is 8 percent. Calculate the NPV of this project.

39. **Project Analysis and Inflation**   After extensive medical and marketing research, Pill, Inc., believes it can penetrate the pain reliever market. It is considering two alternative products. The first is a medication for headache pain. The second is a pill for headache and arthritis pain. Both products would be introduced at a price of $4 per package in real terms. The headache-only medication is projected to sell 5 million packages a year, whereas the headache and arthritis remedy would sell 10 million packages a year. Cash costs of production in the first year are expected to be $1.50 per package in real terms for the headache-only brand. Production costs are expected to be $1.70 in real terms for the headache and arthritis pill. All prices and costs are expected to rise at the general inflation rate of 5 percent.

Either product requires further investment. The headache-only pill could be produced using equipment costing $10.2 million. That equipment would last three years and have no resale value. The machinery required to produce the broader remedy would cost $12 million and last three years. The firm expects that equipment to have a $1 million resale value (in real terms) at the end of year 3.

Pill, Inc., uses straight-line depreciation. The firm faces a corporate tax rate of 34 percent and believes that the appropriate real discount rate is 12 percent. Which pain reliever should the firm produce?

40. **Calculating Project NPV**   Ganpati & Sons manufactures fine furniture. The company is deciding whether to introduce a new mahogany dining room table set. The set will sell for £5,600, including a set of eight chairs. The company feels that sales will be 1,300; 1,325; 1,375; 1,450; and 1,320 sets per year for the next five years, respectively. Variable costs will amount to 45 percent of sales, and fixed costs are £1.7 million per year. The new tables will require inventory amounting to 10 percent of sales, produced and stockpiled in the year prior to sales. It is believed that the addition of the new table will cause a loss of 200 tables per year of the oak tables the company produces. These tables sell for £4,500 and have variable costs of 40 percent of sales. The inventory for this oak table is also 10 percent. Ganpati currently has excess production capacity. If the company buys the necessary equipment today, it will cost £10.5 million. However, the excess production capacity means the company can produce the new table without buying the new equipment. The company controller has said that the current excess capacity will end in two years with current production. This means that if the company uses the current excess capacity for the new table, it will be forced to spend the £10.5 million in two years to accommodate the increased sales of its current products. In five years, the new equipment will have a market value of £2.8 million if purchased today, and £6.1 million if purchased in two years. The equipment is depreciated on a seven-year MACRS schedule. The company has a tax rate of 38 percent, and the required return for the project is 14 percent.
   a. Should Ganpati undertake the new project?
   b. Can you perform an IRR analysis on this project? How many IRRs would you expect to find?
   c. How would you interpret the profitability index?

Bethesda Mining Company

Bethesda Mining is a midsized coal mining company with 20 mines located in Ohio, Pennsylvania, West Virginia, and Kentucky. The company operates deep mines as well as strip mines. Most of the coal mined is sold under contract, with excess production sold on the spot market.

The coal mining industry, especially high-sulfur coal operations such as Bethesda, has been hard-hit by environmental regulations. Recently, however, a combination of increased demand for coal and new pollution reduction technologies has led to an improved market demand for high-sulfur coal. Bethesda has just been approached by Mid-Ohio Electric Company with a request to supply coal for its electric generators for the next four years. Bethesda Mining does not have enough excess capacity at its existing mines to guarantee the contract. The company is considering opening a strip mine in Ohio on 5,000 acres of land purchased 10 years ago for $6 million. Based on a recent appraisal, the company feels it could receive $5 million on an aftertax basis if it sold the land today.

Strip mining is a process where the layers of topsoil above a coal vein are removed and the exposed coal is removed. Some time ago, the company would simply remove the coal and leave the land in an unusable condition. Changes in mining regulations now force a company to reclaim the land; that is, when the mining is completed, the land must be restored to near its original condition. The land can then be used for other purposes. Because it is currently operating at full capacity, Bethesda will need to purchase additional necessary equipment, which will cost $30 million. The equipment will be depreciated on a seven-year MACRS schedule. The contract runs for only four years. At that time the coal from the site will be entirely mined. The company feels that the equipment can be sold for 60 percent of its initial purchase price. However, Bethesda plans to open another strip mine at that time and will use the equipment at the new mine.

The contract calls for the delivery of 600,000 tons of coal per year at a price of $34 per ton. Bethesda Mining feels that coal production will be 650,000 tons, 725,000 tons, 810,000 tons, and 740,000 tons, respectively, over the next four years. The excess production will be sold in the spot market at an average of $40 per ton. Variable costs amount to $13 per ton, and fixed costs are $2,500,000 per year. The mine will require a net working capital investment of 5 percent of sales. The NWC will be built up in the year prior to the sales.

Bethesda will be responsible for reclaiming the land at termination of the mining. This will occur in year 5. The company uses an outside company for reclamation of all the company's strip mines. It is estimated the cost of reclamation will be $4 million. After the land is reclaimed, the company plans to donate the land to the state for use as a public park and recreation area. This will occur in year 6 and result in a charitable expense deduction of $6 million. Bethesda faces a 38 percent tax rate and has a 12 percent required return on new strip mine projects. Assume that a loss in any year will result in a tax credit.

You have been approached by the president of the company with a request to analyze the project. Calculate the payback period, profitability index, average accounting return, net present value, internal rate of return, and modified internal rate of return for the new strip mine. Should Bethesda Mining take the contract and open the mine?

Goodweek Tires, Inc.

After extensive research and development, Goodweek Tires, Inc., has recently developed a new tire, the SuperTread, and must decide whether to make the investment necessary to produce and market it. The tire would be ideal for drivers doing a large amount of wet weather and off-road driving in addition to normal freeway usage. The research and development costs so far have totaled about $10 million. The SuperTread would be put on the market beginning this year, and Goodweek expects it to stay on the market for a total of four years. Test marketing costing $5 million has shown that there is a significant market for a SuperTread-type tire.

As a financial analyst at Goodweek Tires, you have been asked by your CFO, Adam Smith, to evaluate the SuperTread project and provide a recommendation on whether to go ahead with the investment. Except for the initial investment that will occur immediately, assume all cash flows will occur at year-end.

Goodweek must initially invest $120 million in production equipment to make the Super-Tread. This equipment can be sold for $51 million at the end of four years. Goodweek intends to sell the SuperTread to two distinct markets:

1. *The original equipment manufacturer (OEM) market*: The OEM market consists primarily of the large automobile companies (like General Motors) that buy tires for new cars. In the OEM market, the SuperTread is expected to sell for $36 per tire. The variable cost to produce each tire is $18.

2. *The replacement market*: The replacement market consists of all tires purchased after the automobile has left the factory. This market allows higher margins; Goodweek expects to sell the SuperTread for $59 per tire there. Variable costs are the same as in the OEM market.

Goodweek Tires intends to raise prices at 1 percent above the inflation rate; variable costs will also increase at 1 percent above the inflation rate. In addition, the SuperTread project will incur $25 million in marketing and general administration costs the first year. This cost is expected to increase at the inflation rate in the subsequent years.

Goodweek's corporate tax rate is 40 percent. Annual inflation is expected to remain constant at 3.25 percent. The company uses a 15.9 percent discount rate to evaluate new product decisions. Automotive industry analysts expect automobile manufacturers to produce 2 million new cars this year and production to grow at 2.5 percent per year thereafter. Each new car needs four tires (the spare tires are undersized and are in a different category). Goodweek Tires expects the SuperTread to capture 11 percent of the OEM market.

Industry analysts estimate that the replacement tire market size will be 14 million tires this year and that it will grow at 2 percent annually. Goodweek expects the SuperTread to capture an 8 percent market share.

The appropriate depreciation schedule for the equipment is the seven-year MACRS depreciation schedule. The immediate initial working capital requirement is $11 million. Thereafter, the net working capital requirements will be 15 percent of sales. What are the NPV, payback period, discounted payback period, AAR, IRR, and PI on this project?

CHAPTER 8

Risk Analysis, Real Options, and Capital Budgeting

In 1836, defenders of the Alamo in San Antonio, Texas, held out for 13 days against great odds, and "Remember the Alamo!" became a part of U.S. history. In contrast, Disney's 2004 movie *The Alamo*, starring Billy Bob Thornton as Davy Crockett, barely lasted a weekend at the box office, and the last thing Disney's management wants to do is remember that particular bomb. Disney spent close to $100 million making the movie, plus millions more for marketing and distribution, but the film pulled in only about $22.5 million. In fact, about 4 of 10 movies lose money at the box office, though DVD sales often help the final tally. Of course there are movies that do quite well. In 2005, the last of the Star Wars movies, *Revenge of the Sith*, pulled in about $849 million at a cost of $115 million.

Obviously, Disney didn't *plan* to lose $80 or so million on *The Alamo*, but it happened. As the short life and quick death of *The Alamo* show, projects don't always go as companies think they will. This chapter explores how this can happen, and what companies can do to analyze and possibly avoid these situations.

8.1 Sensitivity Analysis, Scenario Analysis, and Break-Even Analysis

One main point of this book is that NPV analysis is a superior capital budgeting technique. In fact, because the NPV approach uses cash flows rather than profits, uses all the cash flows, and discounts the cash flows properly, it is hard to find any theoretical fault with it. However, in our conversations with practical businesspeople, we hear the phrase "a false sense of security" frequently. These people point out that the documentation for capital budgeting proposals is often quite impressive. Cash flows are projected down to the last thousand dollars (or even the last dollar) for each year (or even each month). Opportunity costs and side effects are handled quite properly. Sunk costs are ignored—also quite properly. When a high net present value appears at the bottom, one's temptation is to say yes immediately. Nevertheless, the projected cash flow often goes unmet in practice, and the firm ends up with a money loser.

Sensitivity Analysis and Scenario Analysis

How can the firm get the net present value technique to live up to its potential? One approach is **sensitivity analysis**, which examines how sensitive a particular NPV calculation is to changes in underlying assumptions. Sensitivity analysis is also known as *what-if* analysis and *bop* (best, optimistic, and pessimistic) analysis.

Table 8.1

Cash Flow Forecasts for Solar Electronics Corporation's Jet Engine: Base Case (millions)*

	Year 1	Years 2–6
Revenues		$6,000
Variable costs		3,000
Fixed costs		1,791
Depreciation		300
Pretax profit		909
Tax ($t_c = 0.34$)		309
Net profit		$ 600
Cash flow		$ 900
Initial investment costs	$1,500	

*Assumptions: (1) Investment is depreciated in years 2 through 6 using the straight-line method; (2) tax rate is 34 percent; (3) the company receives no tax benefits for initial development costs.

Consider the following example. Solar Electronics Corporation (SEC) has recently developed a solar-powered jet engine and wants to go ahead with full-scale production. The initial (year 1)[1] investment is $1,500 million, followed by production and sales over the next five years. The preliminary cash flow projection appears in Table 8.1. Should SEC go ahead with investment in and production of the jet engine, the NPV at a discount rate of 15 percent is (in millions):

$$NPV = -\$1,500 + \sum_{t=1}^{5} \frac{\$900}{(1.15)^t}$$
$$= -\$1,500 + \$900 \times A_{0.15}^5$$
$$= \$1,517$$

Because the NPV is positive, basic financial theory implies that SEC should accept the project. However, is this all there is to say about the venture? Before actual funding, we ought to check out the project's underlying assumptions about revenues and costs.

Revenues   Let's assume that the marketing department has projected annual sales to be:

$$\begin{array}{ccccc}
\text{Number of jet engines} & & & & \text{Size of jet engine} \\
\text{sold per year} & = & \text{Market share} & \times & \text{market per year} \\
3,000 & = & 0.30 & \times & 10,000
\end{array}$$

$$\begin{array}{ccccc}
\text{Annual sales} & & \text{Number of jet} & & \text{Price per} \\
\text{revenues} & = & \text{engines sold} & \times & \text{engine} \\
\$6,000 \text{ million} & = & 3,000 & \times & \$2 \text{ million}
\end{array}$$

Thus, it turns out that the revenue estimates depend on three assumptions:

1. Market share.
2. Size of jet engine market.
3. Price per engine.

---

[1] Financial custom generally designates year 0 as "today." However, we use year 1 as today in this example because later in this chapter we will consider another decision made a year earlier. That decision will have occurred at year 0.

Table 8.2

Different Estimates for Solar Electronics' Solar Plane Engine

Variable	Pessimistic	Expected or Best	Optimistic
Market size (per year)	5,000	10,000	20,000
Market share	20%	30%	50%
Price	$1.9 million	$2 million	$2.2 million
Variable cost (per plane)	$1.2 million	$1 million	$0.8 million
Fixed cost (per year)	$1,891 million	$1,791 million	$1,741 million
Investment	$1,900 million	$1,500 million	$1,000 million

Costs Financial analysts frequently divide costs into two types: variable costs and fixed costs. **Variable costs** change as the output changes, and they are zero when production is zero. Costs of direct labor and raw materials are usually variable. It is common to assume that a variable cost is constant per unit of output, implying that total variable costs are proportional to the level of production. For example, if direct labor is variable and one unit of final output requires $10 of direct labor, then 100 units of final output should require $1,000 of direct labor.

Fixed costs are not dependent on the amount of goods or services produced during the period. Fixed costs are usually measured as costs per unit of time, such as rent per month or salaries per year. Naturally, fixed costs are not fixed forever. They are fixed only over a predetermined time period.

The engineering department has estimated variable costs to be $1 million per engine. Fixed costs are $1,791 million per year. The cost breakdowns are:

$$\begin{array}{cc} \text{Variable} \\ \text{cost per year} \end{array} = \begin{array}{cc} \text{Variable cost} \\ \text{per unit} \end{array} \times \begin{array}{cc} \text{Number of jet engines} \\ \text{sold per year} \end{array}$$

$$\$3{,}000 \text{ million} = \$1 \text{ million} \times 3{,}000$$

$$\begin{array}{cc} \text{Total cost before} \\ \text{taxes per year} \end{array} = \begin{array}{cc} \text{Variable cost} \\ \text{per year} \end{array} + \text{Fixed cost per year}$$

$$\$4{,}791 \text{ million} = \$3{,}000 \text{ million} + \$1{,}791 \text{ million}$$

These estimates for market size, market share, price, variable cost, and fixed cost, as well as the estimate of initial investment, are presented in the middle column of Table 8.2. These figures represent the firm's expectations or best estimates of the different parameters. For comparison, the firm's analysts also prepared both optimistic and pessimistic forecasts for each of the different variables. These forecasts are provided in the table as well.

Standard sensitivity analysis calls for an NPV calculation for all three possibilities of a single variable, along with the expected forecast for all other variables. This procedure is illustrated in Table 8.3. For example, consider the NPV calculation of $8,154 million provided in the upper right corner of this table. This NPV occurs when the optimistic forecast of 20,000 units per year is used for market size while all other variables are set at their expected forecasts from Table 8.2. Note that each row of the middle column of Table 8.3 shows a value of $1,517 million. This occurs because the expected forecast is used for the variable that was singled out, as well as for all other variables.

Table 8.3 can be used for a number of purposes. First, taken as a whole, the table can indicate whether NPV analysis should be trusted. In other words, it reduces the false sense of security we spoke of earlier. Suppose that NPV is positive when the expected forecast for each variable is used. However, further suppose that every number in the pessimistic

Table 8.3

NPV Calculations (in $ millions) for the Solar Plane Engine Using Sensitivity Analysis

	Pessimistic	Expected or Best	Optimistic
Market size	−$1,802*	$1,517	$8,154
Market share	−696*	1,517	5,942
Price	853	1,517	2,844
Variable cost	189	1,517	2,844
Fixed cost	1,295	1,517	1,628
Investment	1,208	1,517	1,903

Under sensitivity analysis, one input is varied while all other inputs are assumed to meet their expectation. For example, an NPV of −$1,802 occurs when the pessimistic forecast of 5,000 is used for market size, while all other variables are set at their expected forecasts from Table 8.2.

*We assume that the other divisions of the firm are profitable, implying that a loss on this project can offset income elsewhere in the firm, thereby reducing the overall taxes of the firm.

column is highly negative and every number in the optimistic column is highly positive. A change in a single forecast greatly alters the NPV estimate, making one leery of the net present value approach. A conservative manager might well scrap the entire NPV analysis in this situation. Fortunately, the solar plane engine does not exhibit this wide dispersion because all but two of the numbers in Table 8.3 are positive. Managers viewing the table will likely consider NPV analysis to be useful for the solar-powered jet engine.

Second, sensitivity analysis shows where more information is needed. For example, error in the estimate of investment appears to be relatively unimportant because, even under the pessimistic scenario, the NPV of $1,208 million is still highly positive. By contrast, the pessimistic forecast for market share leads to a negative NPV of −$696 million, and a pessimistic forecast for market size leads to a substantially negative NPV of −$1,802 million. Because the effect of incorrect estimates on revenues is so much greater than the effect of incorrect estimates on costs, more information about the factors determining revenues might be needed.

Because of these advantages, sensitivity analysis is widely used in practice. Graham and Harvey[2] report that slightly over 50 percent of the 392 firms in their sample subject their capital budgeting calculations to sensitivity analysis. This number is particularly large when one considers that only about 75 percent of the firms in their sample use NPV analysis.

Unfortunately, sensitivity analysis also suffers from some drawbacks. For example, sensitivity analysis may unwittingly *increase* the false sense of security among managers. Suppose all pessimistic forecasts yield positive NPVs. A manager might feel that there is no way the project can lose money. Of course the forecasters may simply have an optimistic view of a pessimistic forecast. To combat this, some companies do not treat optimistic and pessimistic forecasts subjectively. Rather, their pessimistic forecasts are always, say, 20 percent less than expected. Unfortunately, the cure in this case may be worse than the disease: A deviation of a fixed percentage ignores the fact that some variables are easier to forecast than others.

In addition, sensitivity analysis treats each variable in isolation when, in reality, the different variables are likely to be related. For example, if ineffective management allows costs to get out of control, it is likely that variable costs, fixed costs, and investment will all rise above expectation at the same time. If the market is not receptive to a solar plane engine, both market share and price should decline together.

---

[2] See Figure 2 of John Graham and Campbell Harvey, "The Theory and Practice of Corporate Finance: Evidence from the Field," *Journal of Financial Economics* (May/June 2001).

Table 8.4

Cash Flow Forecast (in $ millions) under the Scenario of a Plane Crash*

	Year 1	Years 2–5
Revenues		$2,800
Variable costs		1,400
Fixed costs		1,791
Depreciation		300
Pretax profit		−691
Tax ($t_c = 0.34$)[†]		235
Net profit		−$456
Cash flow		−$156
Initial investment cost	−$1,500	

*Assumptions are

   Market size   7,000 (70 percent of expectation)

   Market share 20% (2/3 of expectation)

Forecasts for all other variables are the expected forecasts as given in Table 8.2.

[†]Tax loss offsets income elsewhere in firm.

     Managers frequently perform **scenario analysis**, a variant of sensitivity analysis, to minimize this problem. Simply put, this approach examines a number of different likely scenarios, where each scenario involves a confluence of factors. As a simple example, consider the effect of a few airline crashes. These crashes are likely to reduce flying in total, thereby limiting the demand for any new engines. Furthermore, even if the crashes do not involve solar-powered aircraft, the public could become more averse to any innovative and controversial technologies. Hence, SEC's market share might fall as well. Perhaps the cash flow calculations would look like those in Table 8.4 under the scenario of a plane crash. Given the calculations in the table, the NPV (in millions) would be:

$$-\$2,023 = -\$1,500 - \$156 \times A_{0.15}^{5}$$

A series of scenarios like this might illuminate issues concerning the project better than the standard application of sensitivity analysis would.

Break-Even Analysis

Our discussion of sensitivity analysis and scenario analysis suggests that there are many ways to examine variability in forecasts. We now present another approach, **break-even analysis**. As its name implies, this approach determines the sales needed to break even. The approach is a useful complement to sensitivity analysis because it also sheds light on the severity of incorrect forecasts. We calculate the break-even point in terms of both accounting profit and present value.

Accounting Profit   Annual net profit under four different sales forecasts is as follows:

Annual Unit Sales	Net Profit (in $ millions)
0	−$1,380
1,000	−720
3,000	600
10,000	5,220

Table 8.5   Revenues and Costs of Project under Different Sales Assumptions (in $ millions, except unit sales)

Year 1			Years 2–6						
Initial Invest-ment	Annual Unit Sales	Revenues	Variable Costs	Fixed Costs	Depreci-ation	Taxes* ($t_c = 0.34$)	Net Profit	Operating Cash Flows	NPV (evaluated date 1)
$1,500	0	$ 0	$ 0	−$1,791	−$300	$ 711	−$1,380	−$1,080	−$ 5,120
1,500	1,000	2,000	−1,000	−1,791	−300	371	−720	−420	−2,908
1,500	3,000	6,000	−3,000	−1,791	−300	−309	600	900	1,517
1,500	10,000	20,000	−10,000	−1,791	−300	−2,689	5,220	5,520	17,004

*Loss is incurred in the first two rows. For tax purposes, this loss offsets income elsewhere in the firm.

Figure 8.1

Break-Even Point Using Accounting Numbers

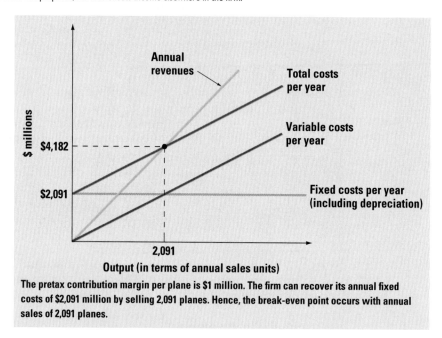

The pretax contribution margin per plane is $1 million. The firm can recover its annual fixed costs of $2,091 million by selling 2,091 planes. Hence, the break-even point occurs with annual sales of 2,091 planes.

A more complete presentation of costs and revenues appears in Table 8.5.

We plot the revenues, costs, and profits under the different assumptions about sales in Figure 8.1. The revenue and cost curves cross at 2,091 jet engines. This is the break-even point—that is, the point where the project generates no profits or losses. As long as annual sales are above 2,091 jet engines, the project will make a profit.

This break-even point can be calculated very easily. Because the sales price is $2 million per engine and the variable cost is $1 million per engine,[3] the difference between sales price and variable cost per engine is:

$$\text{Sales price} - \text{Variable cost} = \$2\text{ million} - \$1\text{ million}$$
$$= \$1\text{ million}$$

This difference is called the pretax **contribution margin** because each additional engine contributes this amount to pretax profit. (Contribution margin can also be expressed on an aftertax basis.)

---

[3]Though the previous section considered both optimistic and pessimistic forecasts for sales price and variable cost, break-even analysis uses just the expected or best estimates of these variables.

Fixed costs are $1,791 million and depreciation is $300 million, implying that the sum of these costs is:

$$\text{Fixed costs} + \text{Depreciation} = \$1,791 \text{ million} + \$300 \text{ million}$$
$$= \$2,091 \text{ million}$$

That is, the firm incurs costs of $2,091 million per year, regardless of the number of sales. Because each engine contributes $1 million, annual sales must reach the following level to offset the costs:

Accounting Profit Break-Even Point:

$$\frac{\text{Fixed costs} + \text{Depreciation}}{\text{Sales price} - \text{Variable costs}} = \frac{\$2,091 \text{ million}}{\$1 \text{ million}} = 2,091$$

Thus, 2,091 engines is the break-even point required for an accounting profit.

The astute reader might be wondering why taxes have been ignored in the calculation of break-even accounting profit. The reason is that a firm with a pretax profit of $0 will also have an aftertax profit of $0 because no taxes are paid if no pretax profit is reported. Thus, the number of units needed to break even on a pretax basis must be equal to the number of units needed to break even on an aftertax basis.

Present Value   As we have stated many times, we are more interested in present value than we are in profit. Therefore, we should calculate breakeven in terms of present value. Given a discount rate of 15 percent, the solar plane engine has the following net present values for different levels of annual sales:

Annual Unit Sales	NPV ($ millions)
0	−5,120
1,000	−2,908
3,000	1,517
10,000	17,004

These NPV calculations are reproduced from the last column of Table 8.5.

Figure 8.2 relates the net present value of both the revenues and the costs to output. There are at least two differences between Figure 8.2 and Figure 8.1, one of which is quite important and the other is much less so. First the less important point: The dollar amounts on the vertical dimension of Figure 8.2 are greater than those on the vertical dimension of Figure 8.1 because the net present values are calculated over five years. More important, accounting breakeven occurs when 2,091 units are sold annually, whereas NPV breakeven occurs when 2,315 units are sold annually.

Of course the NPV break-even point can be calculated directly. The firm originally invested $1,500 million. This initial investment can be expressed as a five-year equivalent annual cost (EAC), determined by dividing the initial investment by the appropriate five-year annuity factor:

$$\text{EAC} = \frac{\text{Initial investment}}{\text{5-year annuity factor at } 15\%} = \frac{\text{Initial investment}}{A^5_{.15}}$$

$$= \frac{\$1,500 \text{ million}}{3.3522} = \$447.5 \text{ million}$$

Figure 8.2

**Break-Even Point
Using Net Present
Value***

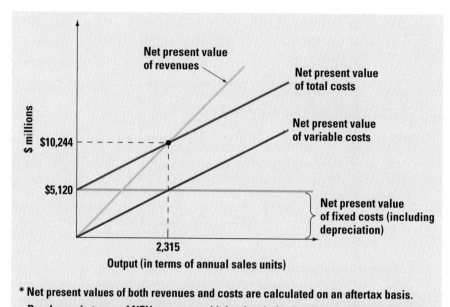

* Net present values of both revenues and costs are calculated on an aftertax basis.
Breakeven in terms of NPV occurs at a higher level of sales than does breakeven for
accounting income. Companies that just break even on an accounting basis are not
recovering the opportunity cost of the initial investment.

Note that the EAC of $447.5 million is greater than the yearly depreciation of $300 million.
This must occur because the calculation of EAC implicitly assumes that the $1,500 million
investment could have been invested at 15 percent.

Aftertax costs, regardless of output, can be viewed like this:

$$\underset{\text{million}}{\$1,528} = \underset{\text{million}}{\$447.5} + \underset{\text{million}}{\$1,791} \times .66 - \underset{\text{million}}{\$300} \times .34$$

$$= \text{EAC} + \text{Fixed costs} \times (1 - t_c) - \text{Depreciation} \times t_c$$

That is, in addition to the initial investment's equivalent annual cost of $447.5 million, the
firm pays fixed costs each year and receives a depreciation tax shield each year. The depreciation tax shield is written as a negative number because it offsets the costs in the equation.
Each plane contributes $.66 million to aftertax profit, so it will take the following sales to
offset the costs:

Present Value Break-Even Point:

$$\frac{\text{EAC} + \text{Fixed costs} \times (1 - t_c) - \text{Depreciation} \times t_c}{(\text{Sales price} - \text{Variable costs}) \times (1 - t_c)} = \frac{\$1,528 \text{ million}}{\$.66 \text{ million}} = 2,315$$

Thus, 2,315 planes is the break-even point from the perspective of present value.

Why is the accounting break-even point different from the financial break-even point?
When we use accounting profit as the basis for the break-even calculation, we subtract
depreciation. Depreciation for the solar jet engines project is $300 million per year. If 2,091
solar jet engines are sold per year, SEC will generate sufficient revenues to cover the $300
million depreciation expense plus other costs. Unfortunately, at this level of sales SEC will
not cover the economic opportunity costs of the $1,500 million laid out for the investment. If
we take into account that the $1,500 million could have been invested at 15 percent, the true
annual cost of the investment is $447.5 million, not $300 million. Depreciation understates
the true costs of recovering the initial investment. Thus companies that break even on an

accounting basis are really losing money. They are losing the opportunity cost of the initial investment.

Is break-even analysis important? Very much so: All corporate executives fear losses. Break-even analysis determines how far down sales can fall before the project is losing money, either in an accounting sense or an NPV sense.

8.2   Monte Carlo Simulation

Both sensitivity analysis and scenario analysis attempt to answer the question "What if?" However, while both analyses are frequently used in the real world, each has its own limitations. Sensitivity analysis allows only one variable to change at a time. By contrast, many variables are likely to move at the same time in the real world. Scenario analysis follows specific scenarios, such as changes in inflation, government regulation, or the number of competitors. Although this methodology is often quite helpful, it cannot cover all sources of variability. In fact, projects are likely to exhibit a lot of variability under just one economic scenario.

Monte Carlo simulation is a further attempt to model real-world uncertainty. This approach takes its name from the famous European casino because it analyzes projects the way one might analyze gambling strategies. Imagine a serious blackjack player who wonders if he should take a third card whenever his first two cards total 16. Most likely, a formal mathematical model would be too complex to be practical here. However, he could play thousands of hands in a casino, sometimes drawing a third card when his first two cards add to 16 and sometimes not drawing that third card. He could compare his winnings (or losings) under the two strategies to determine which were better. Of course he would probably lose a lot of money performing this test in a real casino, so simulating the results from the two strategies on a computer might be cheaper. Monte Carlo simulation of capital budgeting projects is in this spirit.

Imagine that Backyard Barbeques, Inc. (BBI), a manufacturer of both charcoal and gas grills, has a blueprint for a new grill that cooks with compressed hydrogen. The CFO, Edward H. Comiskey, being dissatisfied with simpler capital budgeting techniques, wants a Monte Carlo simulation for this new grill. A consultant specializing in the Monte Carlo approach, Lester Mauney, takes him through the five basic steps of the method.

Step 1: Specify the Basic Model

Les Mauney breaks up cash flow into three components: annual revenue, annual costs, and initial investment. The revenue in any year is viewed as:

$$\text{Number of grills sold} \atop \text{by entire industry} \times {\text{Market share of BBI's} \atop \text{hydrogen grill (in percent)}} \times {\text{Price per} \atop \text{hydrogen grill}} \qquad \textbf{(8.1)}$$

The cost in any year is viewed as:

$$\text{Fixed manufacturing costs} + \text{Variable manufacturing costs} + \text{Marketing costs} \\ + \text{Selling costs}$$

Initial investment is viewed as:

$$\text{Cost of patent} + \text{Test marketing costs} + \text{Cost of production facility}$$

Step 2: Specify a Distribution for Each Variable in the Model

Here comes the hard part. Let's start with revenue, which has three components in Equation 8.1. The consultant first models overall market size—that is, the number of grills sold

Figure 8.3

Probability
Distributions for
Industrywide Unit
Sales, Market Share
of BBI's Hydrogen
Grill, and Price of
Hydrogen Grill

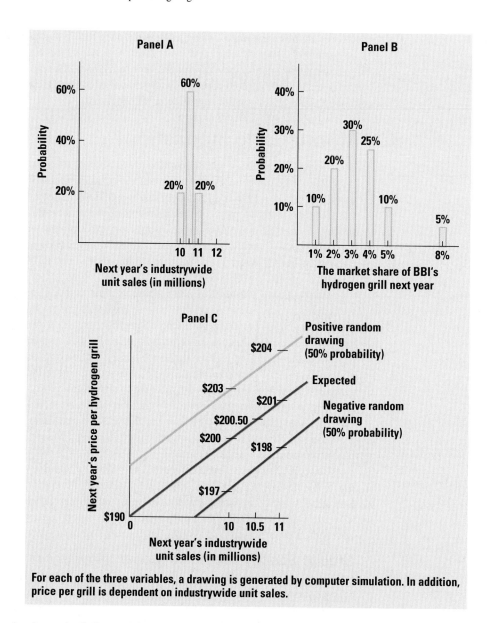

For each of the three variables, a drawing is generated by computer simulation. In addition, price per grill is dependent on industrywide unit sales.

by the entire industry. The trade publication *Outdoor Food (OF)* reported that 10 million grills of all types were sold in the continental United States last year, and it forecasts sales of 10.5 million next year. Mr. Mauney, using *OF*'s forecast and his own intuition, creates the following distribution for next year's sales of grills by the entire industry:

Probability	20%	60%	20%
Next Year's Industrywide Unit Sales	10 million	10.5 million	11 million

The tight distribution here reflects the slow but steady historical growth in the grill market. This probability distribution is graphed in Panel A of Figure 8.3.

Lester Mauney realizes that estimating the market share of BBI's hydrogen grill is more difficult. Nevertheless, after a great deal of analysis, he determines the distribution of next year's market share:

Probability	10%	20%	30%	25%	10%	5%
Market Share of BBI's Hydrogen Grill Next Year	1%	2%	3%	4%	5%	8%

Whereas the consultant assumed a symmetrical distribution for industrywide unit sales, he believes a skewed distribution makes more sense for the project's market share. In his mind there is always the small possibility that sales of the hydrogen grill will really take off. This probability distribution is graphed in Panel B of Figure 8.3.

These forecasts assume that unit sales for the overall industry are unrelated to the project's market share. In other words, the two variables are *independent* of each other. Mr. Mauney reasons that although an economic boom might increase industrywide grill sales and a recession might decrease them, the project's market share is unlikely to be related to economic conditions.

Now Mr. Mauney must determine the distribution of price per grill. Mr. Comiskey, the CFO, informs him that the price will be in the area of $200 per grill, given what other competitors are charging. However, the consultant believes that the price per hydrogen grill will almost certainly depend on the size of the overall market for grills. As in any business, you can usually charge more if demand is high.

After rejecting a number of complex models for price, Mr. Mauney settles on the following specification:

$$\text{Next year's price per hydrogen grill} = \$190 + \$1 \times \frac{\text{Industrywide unit sales}}{\text{(in millions)}} +/- \$3 \tag{8.2}$$

The grill price in Equation 8.2 depends on the unit sales of the industry. In addition, random variation is modeled via the term "$+/-\$3$," where a drawing of $+\$3$ and a drawing of $-\$3$ each occur 50 percent of the time. For example, if industrywide unit sales are 11 million, the price per share would be either of the following:

$$\$190 + \$11 + \$3 = \$204 \quad (50\% \text{ probability})$$
$$\$190 + \$11 - \$3 = \$198 \quad (50\% \text{ probability})$$

The relationship between the price of a hydrogen grill and industrywide unit sales is graphed in Panel C of Figure 8.3.

The consultant now has distributions for each of the three components of next year's revenue. However, he needs distributions for future years as well. Using forecasts from *Outdoor Food* and other publications, Mr. Mauney forecasts the distribution of growth rates for the entire industry over the second year:

Probability	20%	60%	20%
Growth Rate of Industrywide Unit Sales in Second Year	1%	3%	5%

Given both the distribution of next year's industrywide unit sales and the distribution of growth rates for this variable over the second year, we can generate the distribution of industrywide unit sales for the second year. A similar extension should give Mr. Mauney a distribution for later years as well, though we won't go into the details here. And just as the consultant extended the first component of revenue (industrywide unit sales) to later years, he would want to do the same thing for market share and unit price.

The preceding discussion shows how the three components of revenue can be modeled. Step 2 would be complete once the components of cost and investment are modeled in a similar way. Special attention must be paid to the interactions between variables here because ineffective management will likely allow the different cost components to rise together. However, you are probably getting the idea now, so we will skip the rest of this step.

Step 3: The Computer Draws One Outcome

As we said, next year's revenue in our model is the product of three components. Imagine that the computer randomly picks industrywide unit sales of 10 million, a market share for BBI's hydrogen grill of 2 percent, and a +\$3 random price variation. Given these drawings, next year's price per hydrogen grill will be:

$$\$190 + \$10 + \$3 = \$203$$

and next year's revenue for BBI's hydrogen grill will be:

$$10 \text{ million} \times 0.02 \times \$203 = \$40.6 \text{ million}$$

Of course, we are not done with the entire *outcome* yet. We would have to perform drawings for revenue in each future year. In addition, we would perform drawings for costs in each future year. Finally, a drawing for initial investment would have to be made as well. In this way, a single outcome, made up of a drawing for each variable in the model, would generate a cash flow from the project in each future year.

How likely is it that the specific outcome discussed would be drawn? We can answer this because we know the probability of each component. Because industry sales of \$10 million has a 20 percent probability, a market share of 2 percent also has a 20 percent probability, and a random price variation of +\$3 has a 50 percent probability, the probability of these three drawings together in the same outcome is:

$$0.02 = 0.20 \times 0.20 \times 0.50 \tag{8.3}$$

Of course the probability would get even smaller once drawings for future revenues, future costs, and the initial investment are included in the outcome.

This step generates the cash flow for each year from a single outcome. What we are ultimately interested in is the *distribution* of cash flow each year across many outcomes. We ask the computer to randomly draw over and over again to give us this distribution, which is just what is done in the next step.

Step 4: Repeat the Procedure

The first three steps generate one outcome, but the essence of Monte Carlo simulation is repeated outcomes. Depending on the situation, the computer may be called on to generate thousands or even millions of outcomes. The result of all these drawings is a distribution of cash flow for each future year. This distribution is the basic output of Monte Carlo simulation.

Consider Figure 8.4. Here, repeated drawings have produced the simulated distribution of the third year's cash flow. There would be, of course, a distribution like the one in this figure for each future year. This leaves us with just one more step.

Step 5: Calculate NPV

Given the distribution of cash flow for the third year in Figure 8.4, one can determine the expected cash flow for this year. In a similar manner, one can also determine the expected

Figure 8.4

Simulated Distribution of the Third Year's Cash Flow for BBI's New Hydrogen Grill

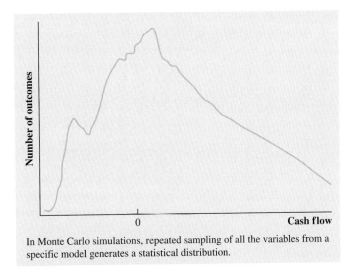

In Monte Carlo simulations, repeated sampling of all the variables from a specific model generates a statistical distribution.

cash flow for each future year and then calculate the net present value of the project by discounting these expected cash flows at an appropriate rate.

Monte Carlo simulation is often viewed as a step beyond either sensitivity analysis or scenario analysis. Interactions between the variables are explicitly specified in Monte Carlo; so (at least in theory) this methodology provides a more complete analysis. And, as a by-product, having to build a precise model deepens the forecaster's understanding of the project.

Because Monte Carlo simulations have been around for at least 35 years, you might think that most firms would be performing them by now. Surprisingly, this does not seem to be the case. In our experience, executives are frequently skeptical of the complexity. It is difficult to model either the distributions of each variable or the interactions between variables. In addition, the computer output is often devoid of economic intuition. Thus while Monte Carlo simulations are used in certain real-world situations,[4] the approach is not likely to be "the wave of the future." In fact, Graham and Harvey[5] report that only about 15 percent of the firms in their sample use capital budgeting simulations.

8.3   Real Options

In Chapter 6, we stressed the superiority of net present value (NPV) analysis over other approaches when valuing capital budgeting projects. However, both scholars and practitioners have pointed out problems with NPV. The basic idea here is that NPV analysis, as well as all the other approaches in Chapter 6, ignores the adjustments that a firm can make after a project is accepted. These adjustments are called **real options**. In this respect NPV underestimates the true value of a project. NPV's conservatism is best explained through a series of examples.

The Option to Expand

Conrad Willig, an entrepreneur, recently learned of a chemical treatment causing water to freeze at 100 degrees Fahrenheit rather than 32 degrees. Of all the many practical

---

[4]More than perhaps any other, the pharmaceutical industry has pioneered applications of this methodology. For example, see Nancy A. Nichols, "Scientific Management at Merck: An Interview with CFO Judy Lewent," *Harvard Business Review* (January/February 1994).

[5]See Figure 2 of Graham and Harvey, op. cit.

Figure 8.5

Decision Tree for Ice Hotel

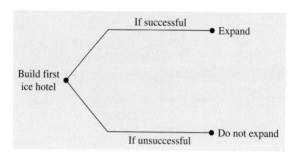

applications for this treatment, Mr. Willig liked the idea of hotels made of ice more than anything else. Conrad estimated the annual cash flows from a single ice hotel to be $2 million, based on an initial investment of $12 million. He felt that 20 percent was an appropriate discount rate, given the risk of this new venture. Believing that the cash flows would be perpetual, Mr. Willig determined the NPV of the project to be:

$$-\$12,000,000 + \$2,000,000/0.20 = -\$2 \text{ million}$$

Most entrepreneurs would have rejected this venture, given its negative NPV. But Conrad was not your typical entrepreneur. He reasoned that NPV analysis missed a hidden source of value. While he was pretty sure that the initial investment would cost $12 million, there was some uncertainty concerning annual cash flows. His cash flow estimate of $2 million per year actually reflected his belief that there was a 50 percent probability that annual cash flows will be $3 million and a 50 percent probability that annual cash flows will be $1 million.

The NPV calculations for the two forecasts are given here:

> **Optimistic forecast:** $-\$12$ million $+ \$3$ million$/0.20 = \$3$ million
> **Pessimistic forecast:** $-\$12$ million $+ \$1$ million$/0.20 = -\$7$ million

On the surface, this new calculation doesn't seem to help Mr. Willig much. An average of the two forecasts yields an NPV for the project of:

$$50\% \times \$3 \text{ million} + 50\% \times (-\$7 \text{ million}) = -\$2 \text{ million}$$

which is just the value he calculated in the first place.

However, if the optimistic forecast turns out to be correct, Mr. Willig would want to *expand*. If he believes that there are, say, 10 locations in the country that can support an ice hotel, the true NPV of the venture would be:

$$50\% \times 10 \times \$3 \text{ million} + 50\% \times (-\$7 \text{ million}) = \$11.5 \text{ million}$$

Figure 8.5, which represents Mr. Willig's decision, is often called a **decision tree.** The idea expressed in the figure is both basic and universal. The entrepreneur has the option to expand if the pilot location is successful. For example, think of all the people that start restaurants, most of them ultimately failing. These individuals are not necessarily overly optimistic. They may realize the likelihood of failure but go ahead anyway because of the small chance of starting the next McDonald's or Burger King.

The Option to Abandon

Managers also have the option to abandon existing projects. Abandonment may seem cowardly, but it can often save companies a great deal of money. Because of this, the option to abandon increases the value of any potential project.

Figure 8.6

The Abandonment Option in the Movie Industry

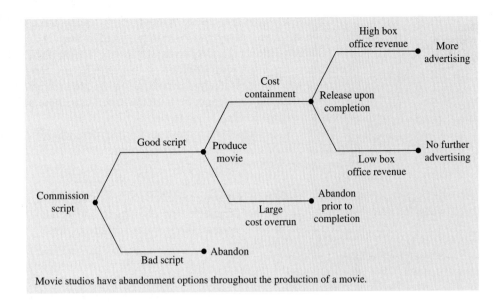

Movie studios have abandonment options throughout the production of a movie.

The example of ice hotels, which illustrated the option to expand, can also illustrate the option to abandon. To see this, imagine that Mr. Willig now believes that there is a 50 percent probability that annual cash flows will be $6 million and a 50 percent probability that annual cash flows will be −$2 million. The NPV calculations under the two forecasts become:

Optimistic forecast: −$12 million + $6 million/0.2 = $18 million
Pessimistic forecast: −$12 million − $2 million/0.2 = −$22 million

yielding an NPV for the project of:

$$50\% \times \$18 \text{ million} + 50\% \times (-\$22 \text{ million}) = -\$2 \text{ million} \qquad \textbf{(8.4)}$$

Furthermore, now imagine that Mr. Willig wants to own, at most, just one ice hotel, implying that there is no option to expand. Because the NPV in Equation 8.4 is negative, it looks as if he will not build the hotel.

But things change when we consider the abandonment option. As of date 1, the entrepreneur will know which forecast has come true. If cash flows equal those under the optimistic forecast, Conrad will keep the project alive. If, however, cash flows equal those under the pessimistic forecast, he will abandon the hotel. If Mr. Willig knows these possibilities ahead of time, the NPV of the project becomes:

$$50\% \times \$18 \text{ million} + 50\% \times (-\$12 \text{ million} - \$2 \text{ million}/1.20) = \$2.17 \text{ million}$$

Because Mr. Willig abandons after experiencing the cash flow of −$2 million at date 1, he does not have to endure this outflow in any of the later years. The NPV is now positive, so Conrad will accept the project.

The example here is clearly a stylized one. Whereas many years may pass before a project is abandoned in the real world, our ice hotel was abandoned after just one year. And, while salvage values generally accompany abandonment, we assumed no salvage value for the ice hotel. Nevertheless, abandonment options are pervasive in the real world.

For example, consider the moviemaking industry. As shown in Figure 8.6, movies begin with either the purchase or development of a script. A completed script might cost a movie studio a few million dollars and potentially lead to actual production. However, the great majority of scripts (perhaps well in excess of 80 percent) are abandoned. Why would studios abandon scripts that they commissioned in the first place? The studios know ahead of time that only a few scripts will be promising, and they don't know which ones. Thus, they cast a wide net, commissioning many scripts to get a few good ones. The studios must be ruthless with the bad scripts because the expenditure here pales in comparison to the huge losses from producing a bad movie.

The few lucky scripts then move into production, where costs might be budgeted in the tens of millions of dollars, if not much more. At this stage, the dreaded phrase is that on-location production gets "bogged down," creating cost overruns. But the studios are equally ruthless here. Should these overruns become excessive, production is likely to be abandoned midstream. Interestingly, abandonment almost always occurs due to high costs, not due to the fear that the movie won't be able to find an audience. Little information on that score will be obtained until the movie is actually released.

Release of the movie is accompanied by significant advertising expenditures, perhaps in the range of $10 to $20 million. Advertising will continue following strong ticket sales, but it will likely be abandoned after a few weeks of poor box office performance.

Moviemaking is one of the riskiest businesses around, with studios receiving hundreds of millions of dollars in a matter of weeks from a blockbuster while receiving practically nothing during this period from a flop. The abandonment options contain costs that might otherwise bankrupt the industry.

To illustrate some of these ideas, consider the case of Euro Disney. The deal to open Euro Disney occurred in 1987, and the park opened its doors outside Paris in 1992. Disney's management thought Europeans would go goofy over the new park, but trouble soon began. The number of visitors never met expectations, in part because the company priced tickets too high. Disney also decided not to serve alcohol in a country that was accustomed to wine with meals. French labor inspectors fought Disney's strict dress codes, and so on.

After several years of operations, the park began serving wine in its restaurants, lowered ticket prices, and made other adjustments. In other words, management exercised its option to reformulate the product. The park began to make a small profit. Then the company exercised the option to expand by adding a "second gate," which was another theme park next to Euro Disney named Walt Disney Studios. The second gate was intended to encourage visitors to extend their stays. But the new park flopped. The reasons ranged from high ticket prices, attractions geared toward Hollywood rather than European filmmaking, labor strikes in Paris, and a summer heat wave.

By the summer of 2003, Euro Disney was close to bankruptcy again. Executives discussed a range of options. These options ranged from letting the company go broke (the option to abandon) to pulling the Disney name from the park. In 2005, the company finally agreed to a restructuring with the help of the French government.

The whole idea of managerial options was summed up aptly by Jay Rasulo, the overseer of Disney's theme parks, when he said, "One thing we know for sure is that you never get it 100 percent right the first time. We open every one of our parks with the notion that we're going to add content."

A recent example of a company actually exercising the option to abandon occurred in 2005 when Sony Corporation announced that it was withdrawing from the handheld computer, or PDA, market in Japan. What was somewhat surprising was that the company was the market leader in sales at the time, with about one-third of the market. However, PDA sales had been shrinking over the past three years, in large part due to increased competition from smart phones that have PDA capabilities. So, Sony concluded that the future market for stand-alone devices was limited and bailed out.

Figure 8.7

**Decision Tree for
Vacant Land**

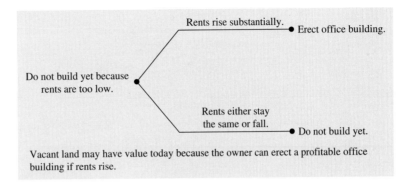

Vacant land may have value today because the owner can erect a profitable office building if rents rise.

Timing Options

One often finds urban land that has been vacant for many years. Yet this land is bought and sold from time to time. Why would anyone pay a positive price for land that has no source of revenue? Certainly, one could not arrive at a positive price through NPV analysis. However, the paradox can easily be explained in terms of real options.

Suppose that the land's highest and best use is as an office building. Total construction costs for the building are estimated to be $1 million. Currently, net rents (after all costs) are estimated to be $90,000 per year in perpetuity, and the discount rate is 10 percent. The NPV of this proposed building would be:

$$-\$1 \text{ million} + \$90{,}000/.10 = -\$100{,}000$$

Because this NPV is negative, one would not currently want to build. However, suppose that the federal government is planning various urban revitalization programs for the city. Office rents will likely increase if the programs succeed. In this case the property's owner might want to erect the office building after all. Conversely, office rents will remain the same, or even fall, if the programs fail. The owner will not build in this case.

We say that the property owner has a *timing option*. Although she does not currently want to build, she will want to build in the future should rents in the area rise substantially. This timing option explains why vacant land often has value. There are costs, such as taxes, from holding raw land, but the value of an office building after a substantial rise in rents may more than offset these holding costs. Of course the exact value of the vacant land depends on both the probability of success in the revitalization program and the extent of the rent increase. Figure 8.7 illustrates this timing option.

Mining operations almost always provide timing options as well. Suppose you own a copper mine where the cost of mining each ton of copper exceeds the sales revenue. It's a no-brainer to say that you would not want to mine the copper currently. And because there are costs of ownership such as property taxes, insurance, and security, you might actually want to pay someone to take the mine off your hands. However, we would caution you not to do so hastily. Copper prices in the future might increase enough so that production is profitable. Given that possibility, you could likely find someone to pay a positive price for the property today.

8.4 Decision Trees

As shown in the previous section, managers adjust their decisions on the basis of new information. For example, a project may be expanded if early experience is promising, whereas the same project might be abandoned in the wake of bad results. As we said earlier, the choices available to managers are called *real options* and an individual project can often be

Figure 8.8

Decision Tree for SEC ($ millions)

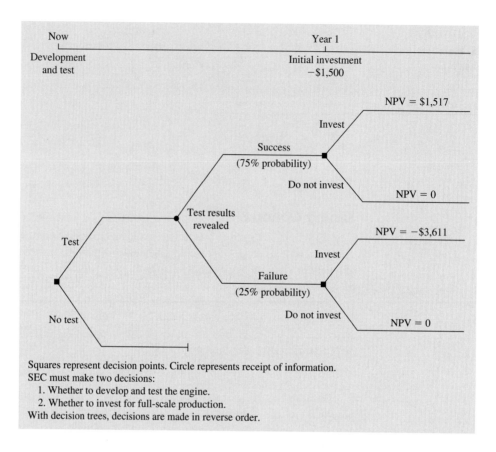

Now
Development and test

Year 1
Initial investment
−$1,500

NPV = $1,517

Invest

Success
(75% probability)

Do not invest

NPV = 0

Test results revealed

NPV = −$3,611

Invest

Test

Failure
(25% probability)

Do not invest

NPV = 0

No test

Squares represent decision points. Circle represents receipt of information.
SEC must make two decisions:
   1. Whether to develop and test the engine.
   2. Whether to invest for full-scale production.
With decision trees, decisions are made in reverse order.

viewed as a series of real options, leading to valuation approaches beyond the basic present value methodology of earlier chapters.

Earlier in this chapter, we considered Solar Electronics Corporation's (SEC's) solar-powered jet engine project, with cash flows as shown in Table 8.1. In that example, SEC planned to invest $1,500 million at year 1 and expected to receive $900 million per year in each of the next five years. Our calculations showed an NPV of $1,517 million, so the firm would presumably want to go ahead with the project.

To illustrate decision trees in more detail, let's move back one year to year 0, when SEC's decision was more complicated. At that time, the engineering group had developed the technology for a solar-powered plane engine, but test marketing had not begun. The marketing department proposed that SEC develop some prototypes and conduct test marketing of the engine. A corporate planning group, including representatives from production, marketing, and engineering, estimated that this preliminary phase would take a year and cost $100 million. Furthermore, the group believed there was a 75 percent chance that the marketing test would prove successful. After completion of the marketing tests, SEC would decide whether to engage in full-scale production, necessitating the investment of $1,500 million.

The marketing tests add a layer of complexity to the analysis. Our previous work on the example assumed that the marketing tests had already proved successful. How do we analyze whether we want to go ahead with the marketing tests in the first place? This is where decision trees come in.

To recap, SEC faces two decisions, both of which are represented in Figure 8.8. First the firm must decide whether to go ahead with the marketing tests. And if the tests are performed, the firm must decide whether the results of the tests warrant full-scale production.

The important point here, as we will see, is that decision trees answer the two questions in *reverse* order. So let's work backward, first considering what to do with the results of the tests, which can be either successful or unsuccessful.

Assume tests have been successful (75 percent probability). Table 8.1 tells us that full-scale production will cost $1,500 million and will generate an annual cash flow of $900 million for five years, yielding an NPV of:

$$= -\$1,500 + \sum_{t=1}^{5} \frac{\$900}{(1.15)^t}$$
$$= -\$1,500 + \$900 \times A_{0.15}^5$$
$$= \$1.517$$

Because the NPV is positive, successful marketing tests should lead to full-scale production. (Note that the NPV is calculated as of year 1, the time at which the investment of $1,500 million is made. Later we will discount this number back to year 0, when the decision on test marketing is to be made.)

Assume tests have not been successful (25 percent probability). Here, SEC's $1,500 million investment would produce an NPV of −$3,611 million, calculated as of year 1. (To save space, we will not provide the raw numbers leading to this calculation.) Because the NPV here is negative, SEC will not want full-scale production if the marketing tests are unsuccessful.

Decision on marketing tests. Now we know what to do with the results of the marketing tests. Let's use these results to move back one year. That is, we now want to figure out whether SEC should invest $100 million for the test marketing costs in the first place.

The expected payoff evaluated at date 1 (in millions) is:

$$
\begin{aligned}
\text{Expected} \atop \text{payoff} &= \left(\begin{array}{c} \text{Probability} \\ \text{of} \\ \text{success} \end{array} \times \begin{array}{c} \text{Payoff} \\ \text{if} \\ \text{successful} \end{array} \right) + \left(\begin{array}{c} \text{Probability} \\ \text{of} \\ \text{failure} \end{array} \times \begin{array}{c} \text{Payoff} \\ \text{if} \\ \text{failure} \end{array} \right) \\
&= \quad (0.75 \quad \times \quad \$1,517) \quad + \quad (0.25 \quad \times \quad \$0) \\
&= \$1,138
\end{aligned}
$$

The NPV of testing computed at date 0 (in millions) is:

$$
\begin{aligned}
\text{NPV} &= -\$100 + \frac{\$1,138}{1.15} \\
&= \$890
\end{aligned}
$$

Because the NPV is positive, the firm should test the market for solar-powered jet engines.

Warning We have used a discount rate of 15 percent for both the testing and the investment decisions. Perhaps a higher discount rate should have been used for the initial test marketing decision, which is likely to be riskier than the investment decision.

Recap As mentioned above, the analysis is graphed in Figure 8.8. As can be seen from the figure, SEC must make the following two decisions:

1. Whether to develop and test the solar-powered jet engine.
2. Whether to invest for full-scale production following the results of the test.

Using a decision tree, we answered the second question before we answered the first one.

Decision trees represent the best approach to solving SEC's problem, given the information presented so far in the text. However, we will examine a more sophisticated approach to valuing options in a later chapter. Though this approach was first used to value financial options traded on organized option exchanges, it can be used to value real options as well.

Summary and Conclusions

This chapter discussed a number of practical applications of capital budgeting.

1. Though NPV is the best capital budgeting approach conceptually, it has been criticized in practice for giving managers a false sense of security. Sensitivity analysis shows NPV under varying assumptions, giving managers a better feel for the project's risks. Unfortunately sensitivity analysis modifies only one variable at a time, but many variables are likely to vary together in the real world. Scenario analysis examines a project's performance under different scenarios (such as war breaking out or oil prices skyrocketing). Finally, managers want to know how bad forecasts must be before a project loses money. Break-even analysis calculates the sales figure at which the project breaks even. Though break-even analysis is frequently performed on an accounting profit basis, we suggest that a net present value basis is more appropriate.

2. Monte Carlo simulation begins with a model of the firm's cash flows, based on both the interactions between different variables and the movement of each individual variable over time. Random sampling generates a distribution of these cash flows for each period, leading to a net present value calculation.

3. We analyzed the hidden options in capital budgeting, such as the option to expand, the option to abandon, and timing options.

4. Decision trees represent an approach for valuing projects with these hidden, or real, options.

Concept Questions

1. **Forecasting Risk**   What is forecasting risk? In general, would the degree of forecasting risk be greater for a new product or a cost-cutting proposal? Why?

2. **Sensitivity Analysis and Scenario Analysis**   What is the essential difference between sensitivity analysis and scenario analysis?

3. **Marginal Cash Flows**   A coworker claims that looking at all this marginal this and incremental that is just a bunch of nonsense, and states, "Listen, if our average revenue doesn't exceed our average cost, then we will have a negative cash flow, and we will go broke!" How do you respond?

4. **Break-Even Point**   As a shareholder of a firm that is contemplating a new project, would you be more concerned with the accounting break-even point, the cash break-even point (the point at which operating cash flow is zero), or the financial break-even point? Why?

5. **Break-Even Point**   Assume a firm is considering a new project that requires an initial investment and has equal sales and costs over its life. Will the project reach the accounting, cash, or financial break-even point first? Which will it reach next? Last? Will this order always apply?

6. **Real Options**   Why does traditional NPV analysis tend to underestimate the true value of a capital budgeting project?

7. **Real Options**   The Mango Republic has just liberalized its markets and is now permitting foreign investors. Tesla Manufacturing has analyzed starting a project in the country and has determined that the project has a negative NPV. Why might the company go ahead with the project? What type of option is most likely to add value to this project?

8. **Sensitivity Analysis and Breakeven**   How does sensitivity analysis interact with break-even analysis?

9. **Option to Wait**   An option can often have more than one source of value. Consider a logging company. The company can log the timber today or wait another year (or more) to log the timber. What advantages would waiting one year potentially have?

10. **Project Analysis**   You are discussing a project analysis with a coworker. The project involves real options, such as expanding the project if successful, or abandoning the project if it fails. Your coworker makes the following statement: "This analysis is ridiculous. We looked at expanding or abandoning the project in two years, but there are many other options we should consider. For example, we could expand in one year, and expand further in two years. Or we could expand in one year, and abandon the project in two years. There are too many options for us to examine. Because of this, anything this analysis would give us is worthless." How would you evaluate this statement? Considering that with any capital budgeting project there are an infinite number of real options, when do you stop the option analysis on an individual project?

Questions and Problems

1. **Sensitivity Analysis and Break-Even Point**   We are evaluating a project that costs £896,000, has an eight-year life, and has no salvage value. Assume that depreciation is straight-line to zero over the life of the project. Sales are projected at 100,000 units per year. Price per unit is £38, variable cost per unit is £25, and fixed costs are £900,000 per year. The tax rate is 35 percent, and we require a 15 percent return on this project.
    a. Calculate the accounting break-even point.
    b. Calculate the base-case cash flow and NPV. What is the sensitivity of NPV to changes in the sales figure? Explain what your answer tells you about a 500-unit decrease in projected sales.
    c. What is the sensitivity of OCF to changes in the variable cost figure? Explain what your answer tells you about a £1 decrease in estimated variable costs.

2. **Scenario Analysis**   In the previous problem, suppose the projections given for price, quantity, variable costs, and fixed costs are all accurate to within ±10 percent. Calculate the best-case and worst-case NPV figures.

3. **Calculating Breakeven**   In each of the following cases, find the unknown variable. Ignore taxes.

Accounting Breakeven	Unit Price	Unit Variable Cost	Fixed Costs	Depreciation
130,200	$ 41	$30	$ 820,000	?
135,000	?	57	3,200,000	$1,150,000
5,478	105	?	160,000	105,000

4. **Financial Breakeven**   L.J.'s Toys Inc. just purchased a $200,000 machine to produce toy cars. The machine will be fully depreciated by the straight-line method over its five-year economic life. Each toy sells for $25. The variable cost per toy is $5, and the firm incurs fixed costs of $350,000 each year. The corporate tax rate for the company is 25 percent. The appropriate discount rate is 10 percent. What is the financial break-even point for the project?

5. **Option to Wait**   Your company is deciding whether to invest in a new machine. The new machine will increase cash flow by CAD 280,000 per year. You believe the technology used in the machine has a 10-year life; in other words, no matter when you purchase the machine, it will be obsolete 10 years from today. The machine is currently priced at CAD 1,500,000. The cost of the machine will decline by CAD 125,000 per year until it reaches CAD 1,000,000, where it will remain. If your required return is 12 percent, should you purchase the machine? If so, when should you purchase it?

6. **Decision Trees**   Akita Electronics Limited has developed a new gadget. If the gadget is successful, the present value of the payoff (when the product is brought to market) is ¥20 million. If the gadget fails, the present value of the payoff is ¥5 million. If the product goes directly to market, there is a 50 percent chance of success. Alternatively, Akita can delay the launch by one year and spend ¥2 million to test market the gadget. Test marketing would allow the firm to improve the product and increase the probability of success to 75 percent. The appropriate discount rate is 20 percent. Should the firm conduct test marketing?

7. **Decision Trees**   The manager for a growing firm is considering the launch of a new product. If the product goes directly to market, there is a 50 percent chance of success. For €120,000 the manager can conduct a focus group that will increase the product's chance of success to 70 percent. Alternatively, the manager has the option to pay a consulting firm €400,000 to research the market and refine the product. The consulting firm successfully launches new products 90 percent of the time. If the firm successfully launches the product, the payoff will be €1.2 million. If the product is a failure, the NPV is zero. Which action will result in the highest expected payoff to the firm?

8. **Decision Trees**   B&B has a new baby powder ready to market. If the firm goes directly to the market with the product, there is only a 60 percent chance of success. However, the firm can conduct customer segment research, which will take a year and cost $1 million. By going through research, B&B will be able to better target potential customers and will increase the probability of success to 70 percent. If successful, the baby powder will bring a present value profit (at time of initial selling) of $30 million. If unsuccessful, the present value payoff is only $3 million. Should the firm conduct customer segment research or go directly to market? The appropriate discount rate is 15 percent.

9. **Financial Break-Even Analysis**   You are considering investing in a company that cultivates mushrooms for sale to local restaurants. Use the following information:

Sales price per mushrooms	= CNY 2.00
Variable costs per mushrooms	= CNY .72
Fixed costs per year	= CNY 340,000
Depreciation per year	= CNY 20,000
Tax rate	= 35%

The discount rate for the company is 15 percent, the initial investment in equipment is CNY 140,000, and the project's economic life is seven years. Assume the equipment is depreciated on a straight-line basis over the project's life.
   a. What is the accounting break-even level for the project?
   b. What is the financial break-even level for the project?

10. **Financial Breakeven**   Niko has purchased a brand new machine to produce its High Flight line of shoes. The machine has an economic life of five years. The depreciation schedule for the machine is straight-line with no salvage value. The machine costs $300,000. The sales price per pair of shoes is $60, while the variable cost is $8. $100,000 of fixed costs per year are attributed to the machine. Assume that the corporate tax rate is 34 percent and the appropriate discount rate is 8 percent. What is the financial break-even point?

INTERMEDIATE
(Questions 11–25)

11. **Break-Even Intuition**   Consider a project with a required return of R percent that costs £I and will last for N years. The project uses straight-line depreciation to zero over the N-year life; there are neither salvage value nor net working capital requirements.
   a. At the accounting break-even level of output, what is the IRR of this project? The payback period? The NPV?
   b. At the cash break-even level of output, what is the IRR of this project? The payback period? The NPV?
   c. At the financial break-even level of output, what is the IRR of this project? The payback period? The NPV?

12. **Sensitivity Analysis**   Consider a four-year project with the following information: initial fixed asset investment = AUD 420,000; straight-line depreciation to zero over the four-year life; zero salvage value; price = AUD 28; variable costs = AUD 19; fixed costs = AUD 190,000; quantity sold = 110,000 units; tax rate = 34 percent. How sensitive is OCF to changes in quantity sold?

13. **Project Analysis**   You are considering a new product launch. The project will cost $720,000, have a four-year life, and have no salvage value; depreciation is straight-line to zero. Sales are projected at 190 units per year; price per unit will be $21,000; variable cost per unit will be $15,000; and fixed costs will be $225,000 per year. The required return on the project is 15 percent, and the relevant tax rate is 35 percent.

  a. Based on your experience, you think the unit sales, variable cost, and fixed cost projections given here are probably accurate to within ±10 percent. What are the upper and lower bounds for these projections? What is the base-case NPV? What are the best-case and worst-case scenarios?

  b. Evaluate the sensitivity of your base-case NPV to changes in fixed costs.

  c. What is the accounting break-even level of output for this project?

14. **Project Analysis**   Dunedin Shoewear has decided to sell a new line of tennis shoes. The shoes will sell for NZD 700 per pair and have a variable cost of NZD 320 per pair. The company has spent NZD 150,000 for a marketing study that determined the company will sell 55,000 pairs per year for seven years. The marketing study also determined that the company will lose sales of 13,000 pairs of its high-priced shoes. The high-priced shoes sell at NZD 1,100 and have variable costs of NZD 600. The company will also increase sales of its cheap shoes by 10,000 pairs. The cheap shoes sell for NZD 400 and have variable costs of NZD 180 per pair. The fixed costs each year will be NZD 7,500,000. The company has also spent NZD 1,000,000 on research and development for the new shoes. The plant and equipment required will cost NZD 18,200,000 and will be depreciated on a straight-line basis. The new shoes will also require an increase in net working capital of NZD 950,000 that will be returned at the end of the project. The tax rate is 40 percent, and the cost of capital is 14 percent. Calculate the payback period, the NPV, and the IRR.

15. **Scenario Analysis**   In the previous problem, you feel that the values are accurate to within only ±10 percent. What are the best-case and worst-case NPVs? (*Hint:* The price and variable costs for the two existing pairs of shoes are known with certainty; only the sales gained or lost are uncertain.)

16. **Sensitivity Analysis**   Dunedin Shoewear would like to know the sensitivity of NPV to changes in the price of the new shoes and the quantity of new shoes sold. What is the sensitivity of the NPV to each of these variables?

17. **Abandonment Value**   We are examining a new project. We expect to sell 7,000 units per year at CNY 60 net cash flow apiece for the next 10 years. In other words, the annual operating cash flow is projected to be CNY 60 × 7,000 = CNY 420,000. The relevant discount rate is 16 percent, and the initial investment required is CNY 1,800,000.

  a. What is the base-case NPV?

  b. After the first year, the project can be dismantled and sold for CNY 1,400,000. If expected sales are revised based on the first year's performance, when would it make sense to abandon the investment? In other words, at what level of expected sales would it make sense to abandon the project?

  c. Explain how the CNY 1,400,000 abandonment value can be viewed as the opportunity cost of keeping the project in one year.

18. **Abandonment**   In the previous problem, suppose you think it is likely that expected sales will be revised upward to 9,000 units if the first year is a success and revised downward to 4,000 units if the first year is not a success.

  a. If success and failure are equally likely, what is the NPV of the project? Consider the possibility of abandonment in answering.

  b. What is the value of the option to abandon?

19. **Abandonment and Expansion**   In the previous problem, suppose the scale of the project can be doubled in one year in the sense that twice as many units can be produced and sold.

Naturally, expansion would be desirable only if the project were a success. This implies that if the project is a success, projected sales after expansion will be 18,000. Again assuming that success and failure are equally likely, what is the NPV of the project? Note that abandonment is still an option if the project is a failure. What is the value of the option to expand?

20. **Break-Even Analysis**   Your buddy comes to you with a sure-fire way to make some quick money and help pay off your student loans. His idea is to sell T-shirts with the words "I get" on them. "You get it?" He says, "You see all those bumper stickers and T-shirts that say 'got milk' or 'got surf.' So this says, 'I get.' It's funny! All we have to do is buy a used silk screen press for $2,000 and we are in business!" Assume there are no fixed costs, and you depreciate the $2,000 in the first period. Taxes are 30 percent.
   a. What is the accounting break-even point if each shirt costs $8 to make and you can sell them for $10 apiece?

   Now assume one year has passed and you have sold 5,000 shirts! You find out that the Dairy Farmers of America have copyrighted the "got milk" slogan and are requiring you to pay $10,000 to continue operations. You expect this craze will last for another three years and that your discount rate is 12 percent.
   b. What is the financial break-even point for your enterprise now?

21. **Decision Trees**   Young screenwriter Carl Draper has just finished his first script. It has action, drama, and humor, and he thinks it will be a blockbuster. He takes the script to every motion picture studio in town and tries to sell it but to no avail. Finally, ACME studios offers to buy the script for either (a) €5,000 or (b) 1 percent of the movie's profits. There are two decisions the studio will have to make. First is to decide if the script is good or bad, and second if the movie is good or bad. First, there is a 90 percent chance that the script is bad. If it is bad, the studio does nothing more and throws the script out. If the script is good, they will shoot the movie. After the movie is shot, the studio will review it, and there is a 70 percent chance that the movie is bad. If the movie is bad, the movie will not be promoted and will not turn a profit. If the movie is good, the studio will promote heavily; the average profit for this type of movie is €10 million. Carl rejects the €5,000 and says he wants the 1 percent of profits. Was this a good decision by Carl?

22. **Accounting Breakeven**   Samuelson, Inc., has just purchased a £600,000 machine to produce calculators. The machine will be fully depreciated by the straight-line method over its economic life of five years and will produce 20,000 calculators each year. The variable production cost per calculator is £15, and total fixed costs are £900,000 per year. The corporate tax rate for the company is 40 percent. For the firm to break even in terms of accounting profit, how much should the firm charge per calculator?

23. **Abandonment Decisions**   Allied Products, Inc., is considering a new product launch. The firm expects to have an annual operating cash flow of $25 million for the next 10 years. Allied Products uses a discount rate of 20 percent for new product launches. The initial investment is $100 million. Assume that the project has no salvage value at the end of its economic life.
   a. What is the NPV of the new product?
   b. After the first year, the project can be dismantled and sold for $50 million. If the estimates of remaining cash flows are revised based on the first year's experience, at what level of expected cash flows does it make sense to abandon the project?

24. **Expansion Decisions**   Applied Nanotech is thinking about introducing a new surface cleaning machine. The marketing department has come up with the estimate that Applied Nanotech can sell 10 units per year at ¥.3 million net cash flow per unit for the next five years. The engineering department has come up with the estimate that developing the machine will take a ¥10 million initial investment. The finance department has estimated that a 25 percent discount rate should be used.
   a. What is the base-case NPV?
   b. If unsuccessful, after the first year the project can be dismantled and will have an aftertax salvage value of ¥5 million. Also, after the first year, expected cash flows will be revised up to 20 units per year or to 0 units, with equal probability. What is the revised NPV?

25. **Scenario Analysis**   You are the financial analyst for a tennis racket manufacturer. The company is considering using a graphitelike material in its tennis rackets. The company has estimated the information in the following table about the market for a racket with the new material. The company expects to sell the racket for five years. The equipment required for the project has no salvage value. The required return for projects of this type is 13 percent, and the company has a 40 percent tax rate. Should you recommend the project?

	Pessimistic	Expected	Optimistic
Market size	110,000	120,000	130,000
Market share	22%	25%	27%
Selling price	£ 115	£ 120	£ 125
Variable costs per unit	£ 72	£ 70	£ 68
Fixed costs per year	£ 850,000	£ 800,000	£ 750,000
Initial investment	£1,500,000	£1,500,000	£1,500,000

CHALLENGE
(Questions 26–30)

26. **Scenario Analysis**   Consider a project to supply Detroit with 40,000 tons of machine screws annually for automobile production. You will need an initial $1,700,000 investment in threading equipment to get the project started; the project will last for five years. The accounting department estimates that annual fixed costs will be $450,000 and that variable costs should be $210 per ton; accounting will depreciate the initial fixed asset investment straight-line to zero over the five-year project life. It also estimates a salvage value of $500,000 after dismantling costs. The marketing department estimates that the automakers will let the contract at a selling price of $230 per ton. The engineering department estimates you will need an initial net working capital investment of $450,000. You require a 13 percent return and face a marginal tax rate of 38 percent on this project.
    a. What is the estimated OCF for this project? The NPV? Should you pursue this project?
    b. Suppose you believe that the accounting department's initial cost and salvage value projections are accurate only to within ±15 percent; the marketing department's price estimate is accurate only to within ±10 percent; and the engineering department's net working capital estimate is accurate only to within ±5 percent. What is your worst-case scenario for this project? Your best-case scenario? Do you still want to pursue the project?

27. **Sensitivity Analysis**   In Problem 26, suppose you're confident about your own projections, but you're a little unsure about Detroit's actual machine screw requirement. What is the sensitivity of the project OCF to changes in the quantity supplied? What about the sensitivity of NPV to changes in quantity supplied? Given the sensitivity number you calculated, is there some minimum level of output below which you wouldn't want to operate? Why?

28. **Abandonment Decisions**   Consider the following project for Hand Clapper, Inc. The company is considering a four-year project to manufacture clap-command garage door openers. This project requires an initial investment of ZWD 8 million that will be depreciated straight-line to zero over the project's life. An initial investment in net working capital of ZWD 2 million is required to support spare parts inventory; this cost is fully recoverable whenever the project ends. The company believes it can generate ZWD 7 million in pretax revenues with ZWD 3 million in total pretax operating costs. The tax rate is 38 percent, and the discount rate is 16 percent. The market value of the equipment over the life of the project is as follows:

Year	Market Value (ZWD millions)
1	ZWD 6.50
2	6.00
3	3.00
4	0.50

a. Assuming Hand Clapper operates this project for four years, what is the NPV?

b. Now compute the project NPVs assuming the project is abandoned after only one year, after two years, and after three years. What economic life for this project maximizes its value to the firm? What does this problem tell you about not considering abandonment possibilities when evaluating projects?

29. **Abandonment Decisions**   Come Up Antakshari has hired you to perform a feasibility study of a new video game that requires an INR 4 million initial investment. Antakshari expects a total annual operating cash flow of INR 750,000 for the next 10 years. The relevant discount rate is 10 percent. Cash flows occur at year-end.

a. What is the NPV of the new video game?

b. After one year, the estimate of remaining annual cash flows will be revised either upward to INR 1.5 million or downward to INR 120,000. Each revision has an equal probability of occurring. At that time, the video game project can be sold for INR 800,000. What is the revised NPV given that the firm can abandon the project after one year?

30. **Financial Breakeven**   The Cornchopper Company is considering the purchase of a new harvester. Cornchopper has hired you to determine the break-even purchase price in terms of present value of the harvester. This break-even purchase price is the price at which the project's NPV is zero. Base your analysis on the following facts:

- The new harvester is not expected to affect revenues, but pretax operating expenses will be reduced by €10,000 per year for 10 years.
- The old harvester is now 5 years old, with 10 years of its scheduled life remaining. It was originally purchased for €45,000 and has been depreciated by the straight-line method.
- The old harvester can be sold for €20,000 today.
- The new harvester will be depreciated by the straight-line method over its 10-year life.
- The corporate tax rate is 34 percent.
- The firm's required rate of return is 15 percent.
- The initial investment, the proceeds from selling the old harvester, and any resulting tax effects occur immediately.
- All other cash flows occur at year-end.
- The market value of each harvester at the end of its economic life is zero.

Mini Case

Bunyan Lumber, LLC

Bunyan Lumber, LLC, harvests timber and delivers logs to timber mills for sale. The company was founded 70 years ago by Pete Bunyan. The current CEO is Paula Bunyan, the granddaughter of the founder. The company is currently evaluating a 5,000-acre forest it owns in Oregon. Paula has asked Steve Boles, the company's finance officer, to evaluate the project. Paula's concern is when the company should harvest the timber.

Lumber is sold by the company for its "pond value." Pond value is the amount a mill will pay for a log delivered to the mill location. The price paid for logs delivered to a mill is quoted in dollars per thousands of board feet (MBF), and the price depends on the grade of the logs. The forest Bunyan Lumber is evaluating was planted by the company 20 years ago and is made up entirely of Douglas fir trees. The table here shows the current price per MBF for the three grades of timber the company feels will come from the stand:

Timber Grade	Price Per MBF
1P	$1,050
2P	925
3P	770

Steve believes that the pond value of lumber will increase at the inflation rate. The company is planning to thin the forest today, and it expects to realize a positive cash flow of $1,000 per acre from thinning. The thinning is done to increase the growth rate of the remaining trees, and it is always done 20 years following a planting.

The major decision the company faces is when to log the forest. When the company logs the forest, it will immediately replant saplings, which will allow for a future harvest. The longer the forest is allowed to grow, the larger the harvest becomes per acre. Additionally, an older forest has a higher grade of timber. Steve has compiled the following table with the expected harvest per acre in thousands of board feet, along with the breakdown of the timber grades:

Years from Today to Begin Harvest	Harvest (MBF) Per Acre	Timber Grade		
		1P	2P	3P
20	6	10%	40%	50%
25	7.6	12	42	46
30	9	15	42	43
35	10	16	43	41

The company expects to lose 5 percent of the timber it cuts due to defects and breakage.

The forest will be clear-cut when the company harvests the timber. This method of harvesting allows for faster growth of replanted trees. All of the harvesting, processing, replanting, and transportation are to be handled by subcontractors hired by Bunyan Lumber. The cost of the logging is expected to be $140 per MBF. A road system has to be constructed and is expected to cost $50 per MBF on average. Sales preparation and administrative costs, excluding office overhead costs, are expected to be $18 per MBF.

As soon as the harvesting is complete, the company will reforest the land. Reforesting costs include the following:

	Per Acre Cost
Excavator piling	$150
Broadcast burning	300
Site preparation	145
Planting costs	225

All costs are expected to increase at the inflation rate.

Assume all cash flows occur at the year of harvest. For example, if the company begins harvesting the timber 20 years from today, the cash flow from the harvest will be received 20 years from today. When the company logs the land, it will immediately replant the land with new saplings. The harvest period chosen will be repeated for the foreseeable future. The company's nominal required return is 10 percent, and the inflation rate is expected to be 3.7 percent per year. Bunyan Lumber has a 35 percent tax rate.

Clear-cutting is a controversial method of forest management. To obtain the necessary permits, Bunyan Lumber has agreed to contribute to a conservation fund every time it harvests the lumber. If the company harvested the forest today, the required contribution would be $100,000. The company has agreed that the required contribution will grow by 3.2 percent per year. When should the company harvest the forest?

Risk and Return

Lessons from Market History

With the S&P 500 index up about 3 percent and the NASDAQ stock market index up about 1.4 percent in 2005, stock market performance overall was well below average. However, it was a great year for investors in pharmaceutical manufacturer ViroPharma, Inc., which gained a whopping 469 percent! And investors in Hansen Natural, makers of Monster energy drinks, had to be energized by the 333 percent gain of that stock. Of course, not all stocks increased in value. Stock in video game manufacturer Majesco Entertainment fell 92 percent during the year, and stock in Aphton, a biotechnology company, dropped 89 percent. These examples show that there were tremendous potential profits to be made during 2005, but there was also the risk of losing money—lots of it. So what should you, as a stock market investor, expect when you invest your own money? In this chapter, we study eight decades of market history to find out.

9.1 Returns

Dollar Returns

Suppose the Video Concept Company has several thousand shares of stock outstanding and you are a shareholder. Further suppose that you purchased some of the shares of stock in the company at the beginning of the year; it is now year-end and you want to figure out how well you have done on your investment. The return you get on an investment in stocks, like that in bonds or any other investment, comes in two forms.

First, over the year most companies pay dividends to shareholders. As the owner of stock in the Video Concept Company, you are a part owner of the company. If the company is profitable, it generally will distribute some of its profits to the shareholders. Therefore, as the owner of shares of stock, you will receive some cash, called a *dividend,* during the year. This cash is the *income component* of your return. In addition to the dividends, the other part of your return is the *capital gain*—or, if it is negative, the *capital loss* (negative capital gain)—on the investment.

For example, suppose we are considering the cash flows of the investment in Figure 9.1, showing that you purchased 100 shares of stock at the beginning of the year at a price of $37 per share. Your total investment, then, was:

$$C_0 = \$37 \times 100 = \$3,700$$

How did the market do today? Find out at **finance.yahoo.com.**

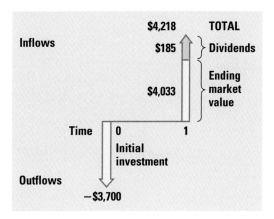

Figure 9.1
Dollar Returns

Suppose that over the year the stock paid a dividend of $1.85 per share. During the year, then, you received income of:

$$\text{Div} = \$1.85 \times 100 = \$185$$

Suppose, finally, that at the end of the year the market price of the stock is $40.33 per share. Because the stock increased in price, you had a capital gain of:

$$\text{Gain} = (\$40.33 - \$37) \times 100 = \$333$$

The capital gain, like the dividend, is part of the return that shareholders require to maintain their investment in the Video Concept Company. Of course, if the price of Video Concept stock had dropped in value to, say, $34.78, you would have recorded this capital loss:

$$\text{Loss} = (\$34.78 - \$37) \times 100 = -\$222$$

The *total dollar return* on your investment is the sum of the dividend income and the capital gain or loss on the investment:

$$\text{Total dollar return} = \text{Dividend income} + \text{Capital gain (or loss)}$$

(From now on we will refer to *capital losses* as *negative capital gains* and not distinguish them.) In our first example the total dollar return is given by:

$$\text{Total dollar return} = \$185 + \$333 = \$518$$

Notice that if you sold the stock at the end of the year, your total amount of cash would be the initial investment plus the total dollar return. In the preceding example you would have:

$$\text{Total cash if stock is sold} = \text{Initial investment} + \text{Total dollar return}$$
$$= \$3,700 + \$518$$
$$= \$4,218$$

As a check, notice that this is the same as the proceeds from the sale of stock plus the dividends:

$$\text{Proceeds from stock sale} + \text{Dividends}$$
$$= \$40.33 \times 100 + \$185$$
$$= \$4,033 + \$185$$
$$= \$4,218$$

Figure 9.2

Percentage Returns

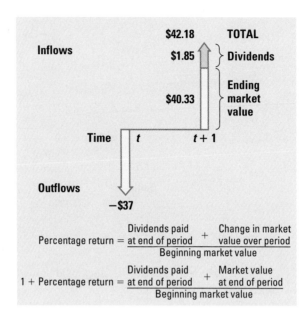

Suppose, however, that you hold your Video Concept stock and don't sell it at year-end. Should you still consider the capital gain as part of your return? Does this violate our previous present value rule that only cash matters?

The answer to the first question is a strong yes, and the answer to the second question is an equally strong no. The capital gain is every bit as much a part of your return as is the dividend, and you should certainly count it as part of your total return. That you have decided to hold onto the stock and not sell or *realize* the gain or the loss in no way changes the fact that, if you want to, you could get the cash value of the stock. After all, you could always sell the stock at year-end and immediately buy it back. The total amount of cash you would have at year-end would be the $518 gain plus your initial investment of $3,700. You would not lose this return when you bought back 100 shares of stock. In fact, you would be in exactly the same position as if you had not sold the stock (assuming, of course, that there are no tax consequences and no brokerage commissions from selling the stock).

Percentage Returns

It is more convenient to summarize the information about returns in percentage terms than in dollars because the percentages apply to any amount invested. The question we want to answer is this: How much return do we get for each dollar invested? To find this out, let t stand for the year we are looking at, let P_t be the price of the stock at the beginning of the year, and let Div_{t+1} be the dividend paid on the stock during the year. Consider the cash flows in Figure 9.2.

In our example, the price at the beginning of the year was $37 per share and the dividend paid during the year on each share was $1.85. Hence the percentage income return, sometimes called the *dividend yield*, is:

$$Dividend\ yield = Div_{t+1}/P_t$$
$$= \$1.85/\$37$$
$$= .05$$
$$= 5\%$$

The **capital gain** (or loss) is the change in the price of the stock divided by the initial price. Letting P_{t+1} be the price of the stock at year-end, we can compute the capital gain as follows:

$$\text{Capital gain} = (P_{t+1} - P_t)/P_t$$
$$= (\$40.33 - \$37)/\$37$$
$$= \$3.33/\$37$$
$$= .09$$
$$= 9\%$$

Combining these two results, we find that the *total return* on the investment in Video Concept stock over the year, which we will label R_{t+1}, was:

$$R_{t+1} = \frac{\text{Div}_{t+1}}{P_t} + \frac{(P_{t+1} - P_t)}{P_t}$$
$$= 5\% + 9\%$$
$$= 14\%$$

From now on, we will refer to returns in percentage terms.

To give a more concrete example, stock in Goldman Sachs (GS), the well-known financial services company, began 2005 at $102.90 a share. Goldman Sachs paid dividends of $1.00 during 2005, and the stock price at the end of the year was $127.47. What was the return on GS for the year? For practice, see if you agree that the answer is 24.85 percent. Of course, negative returns occur as well. For example, in 2005, General Motor's stock price at the beginning of the year was $37.64 per share, and dividends of $2.00 were paid. The stock ended the year at $19.42 per share. Verify that the loss was 43.09 percent for the year.

EXAMPLE 9.1

Calculating Returns Suppose a stock begins the year with a price of $25 per share and ends with a price of $35 per share. During the year it paid a $2 dividend per share. What are its dividend yield, its capital gain, and its total return for the year? We can imagine the cash flows in Figure 9.3.

$$R_1 = \frac{\text{Div}_1}{P_0} + \frac{P_1 - P_0}{P_0}$$
$$= \frac{\$2}{\$25} + \frac{\$35 - 25}{\$25} = \frac{\$12}{\$25}$$
$$= 8\% + 40\% = 48\%$$

Figure 9.3 Cash Flow—An Investment Example

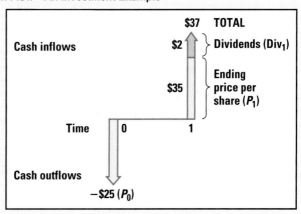

(continued)

Thus, the stock's dividend yield, its capital gain yield, and its total return are 8 percent, 40 percent, and 48 percent, respectively.

Suppose you had $5,000 invested. The total dollar return you would have received on an investment in the stock is $5,000 × .48 = $2,400. If you know the total dollar return on the stock, you do not need to know how many shares you would have had to purchase to figure out how much money you would have made on the $5,000 investment. You just use the total dollar return.

9.2 Holding Period Returns

A famous set of studies dealing with rates of return on common stocks, bonds, and Treasury bills was conducted by Roger Ibbotson and Rex Sinquefield.[1] They present year-by-year historical rates of return for the following five important types of financial instruments in the United States:

For more about market history, visit **www. globalfindata.com.**

1. *Large-company common stocks*: The common stock portfolio is based on the Standard & Poor's (S&P) composite index. At present the S&P composite includes 500 of the largest (in terms of market value) stocks in the United States.

2. *Small-company common stocks*: This is a portfolio corresponding to the bottom fifth of stocks traded on the New York Stock Exchange in which stocks are ranked by market value (that is, the price of the stock multiplied by the number of shares outstanding).

3. *Long-term corporate bonds*: This is a portfolio of high-quality corporate bonds with a 20-year maturity.

4. *Long-term U.S. government bonds*: This is based on U.S. government bonds with a maturity of 20 years.

5. *U.S. Treasury bills*: This is based on Treasury bills with a three-month maturity.

None of the returns are adjusted for taxes or transaction costs. In addition to the year-by-year returns on financial instruments, the year-to-year change in the consumer price index is computed. This is a basic measure of inflation. We can calculate year-by-year real returns by subtracting annual inflation.

Before looking closely at the different portfolio returns, we graphically present the returns and risks available from U.S. capital markets in the 80-year period from 1926 to 2005. Figure 9.4 shows the growth of $1 invested at the beginning of 1926. Notice that the vertical axis is logarithmic, so that equal distances measure the same percentage change. The figure shows that if $1 were invested in large-company common stocks and all dividends were reinvested, the dollar would have grown to $2,657.56 by the end of 2005. The biggest growth was in the small stock portfolio. If $1 were invested in small stocks in 1926, the investment would have grown to $13,706.15. However, when you look carefully at Figure 9.4, you can see great variability in the returns on small stocks, especially in the earlier part of the period. A dollar in long-term government bonds was very stable as compared with a dollar in common stocks. Figures 9.5 to 9.8 plot each year-to-year percentage return as a vertical bar drawn from the horizontal axis for large-company common stocks, for small-company stocks, for long-term bonds and Treasury bills, and for inflation, respectively.

Figure 9.4 gives the growth of a dollar investment in the stock market from 1926 through 2005. In other words, it shows what the worth of the investment would have been if

---

[1] The most recent update of this work is *Stocks, Bonds, Bills and Inflation: 2006 Yearbook*™ (Chicago: Ibbotson Associates). All rights reserved.

Figure 9.4   Wealth Indexes of Investments in the U.S. Capital Markets (Year-End 1925 = $1.00)

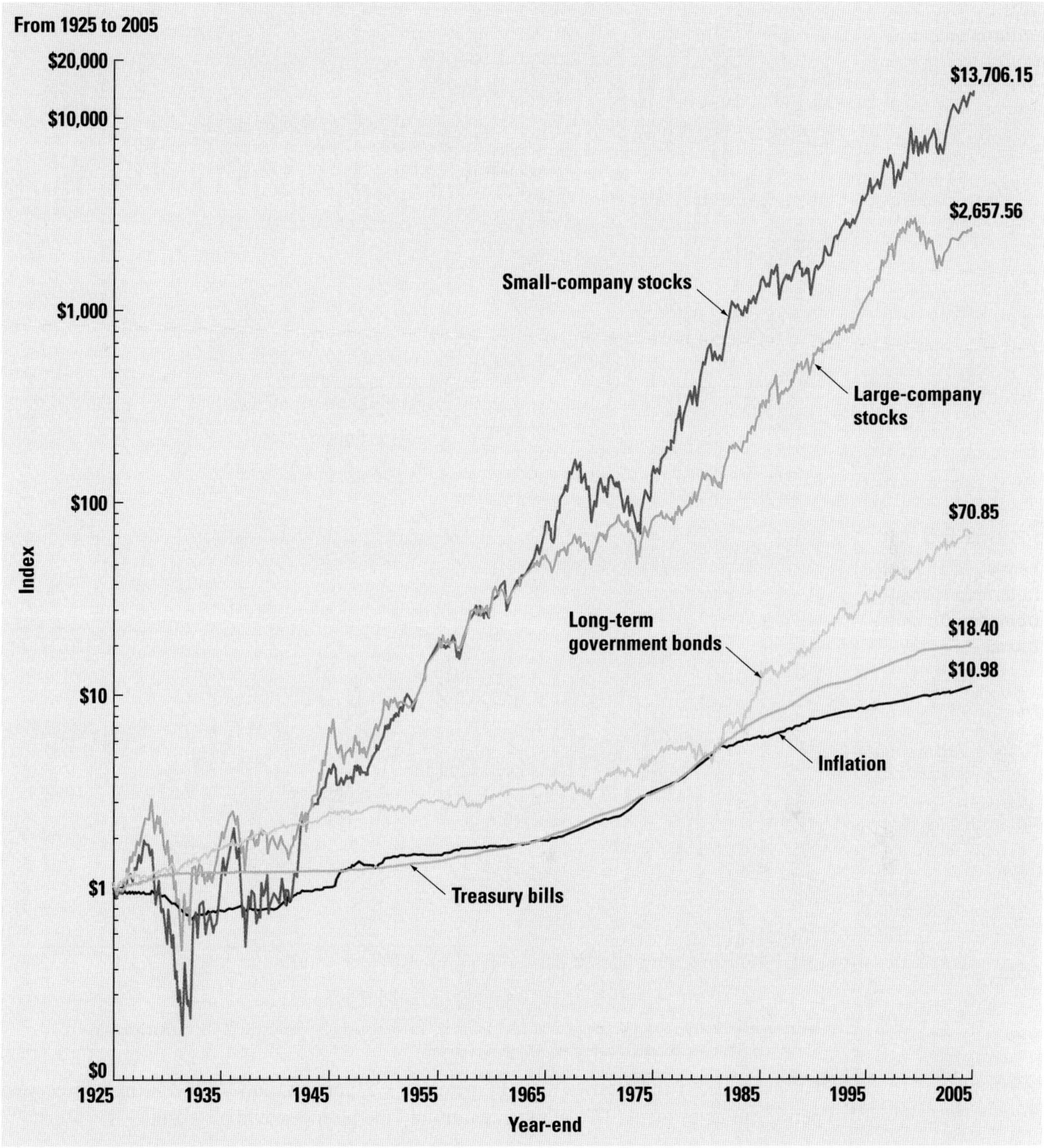

From 1925 to 2005

the dollar had been left in the stock market and if each year the dividends from the previous year had been reinvested in more stock. If R_t is the return in year t (expressed in decimals), the value you would have at the end of year T is the product of 1 plus the return in each of the years:

$$(1 + R_1) \times (1 + R_2) \times \cdots \times (1 + R_t) \times \cdots \times (1 + R_T)$$

Figure 9.5

Year-by-Year Total Returns on Large-Company Common Stocks

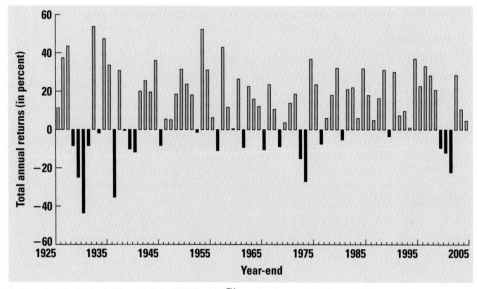

Figure 9.6

Year-by-Year Total Returns on Small-Company Common Stocks

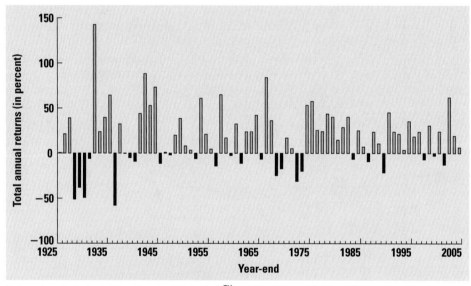

Go to **bigcharts. marketwatch.com** to see both intraday and long-term charts.

For example, if the returns were 11 percent, −5 percent, and 9 percent in a three-year period, an investment of $1 at the beginning of the period would be worth:

$$(1 + R_1) \times (1 + R_2) \times (1 + R_3) = (\$1 + .11) \times (\$1 - .05) \times (\$1 + .09)$$
$$= \$1.11 \times \$.95 \times \$1.09$$
$$= \$1.15$$

at the end of the three years. Notice that .15 or 15 percent is the total return and that it includes the return from reinvesting the first-year dividends in the stock market for two more years and reinvesting the second-year dividends for the final year. The 15 percent is called a three-year **holding period return**. Table 9.1 gives the annual returns each year for selected investments from 1926 to 2005. From this table, you can determine holding period returns for any combination of years.

Figure 9.7

Year-by-Year Total Returns on Bonds and Bills

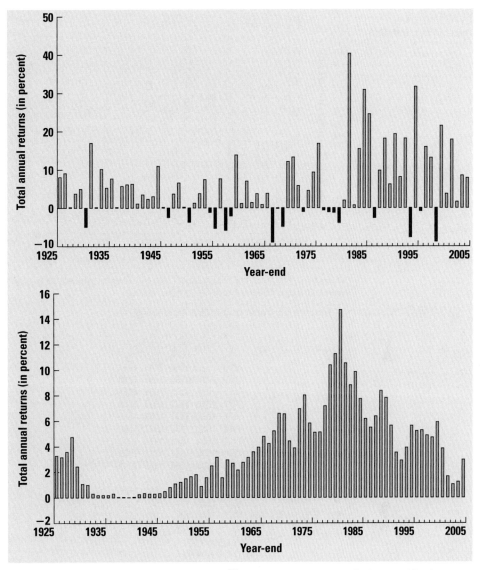

9.3   Return Statistics

The history of capital market returns is too complicated to be handled in its undigested form. To use the history, we must first find some manageable ways of describing it, dramatically condensing the detailed data into a few simple statements.

This is where two important numbers summarizing the history come in. The first and most natural number is some single measure that best describes the past annual returns on the stock market. In other words, what is our best estimate of the return that an investor could have realized in a particular year over the 1926 to 2005 period? This is the *average return*.

Figure 9.9 plots the histogram of the yearly stock market returns given in Table 9.1. This plot is the **frequency distribution** of the numbers. The height of the graph gives the number of sample observations in the range on the horizontal axis.

Figure 9.8

Year-by-Year Inflation

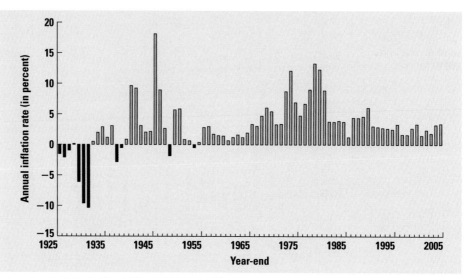

Figure 9.9   Histogram of Returns on Common Stocks, 1926–2005

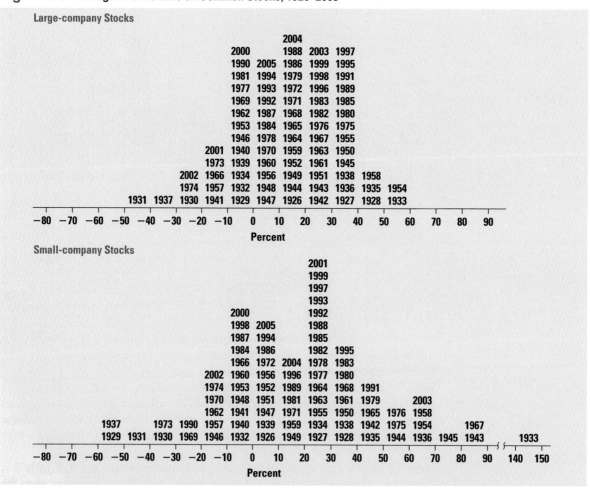

Table 9.1

Year-by-Year Total
Returns, 1926–2005

Year	Large-Company Stocks	Long-Term Government Bonds	U.S. Treasury Bills	Consumer Price Index
1926	13.75%	5.69%	3.30%	−1.12%
1927	35.70	6.58	3.15	−2.26
1928	45.08	1.15	4.05	−1.16
1929	−8.80	4.39	4.47	0.58
1930	−25.13	4.47	2.27	−6.40
1931	−43.60	−2.15	1.15	−9.32
1932	−8.75	8.51	0.88	−10.27
1933	52.95	1.92	0.52	0.76
1934	−2.31	7.59	0.27	1.52
1935	46.79	4.20	0.17	2.99
1936	32.49	5.13	0.17	1.45
1937	−35.45	1.44	0.27	2.86
1938	31.63	4.21	0.06	−2.78
1939	−1.43	3.84	0.04	0.00
1940	−10.36	5.70	0.04	0.71
1941	−12.02	0.47	0.14	9.93
1942	20.75	1.80	0.34	9.03
1943	25.38	2.01	0.38	2.96
1944	19.49	2.27	0.38	2.30
1945	36.21	5.29	0.38	2.25
1946	−8.42	0.54	0.38	18.13
1947	5.05	−1.02	0.62	8.84
1948	4.99	2.66	1.06	2.99
1949	17.81	4.58	1.12	−2.07
1950	30.05	−0.98	1.22	5.93
1951	23.79	−0.20	1.56	6.00
1952	18.39	2.43	1.75	0.75
1953	−1.07	2.28	1.87	0.75
1954	52.23	3.08	0.93	−0.74
1955	31.62	−0.73	1.80	0.37
1956	6.91	−1.72	2.66	2.99
1957	−10.50	6.82	3.28	2.90
1958	43.57	−1.72	1.71	1.76
1959	12.01	−2.02	3.48	1.73
1960	0.47	11.21	2.81	1.36
1961	26.84	2.20	2.40	0.67
1962	−8.75	5.72	2.82	1.33
1963	22.70	1.79	3.23	1.64
1964	16.43	3.71	3.62	0.97
1965	12.38	0.93	4.06	1.92
1966	−10.06	5.12	4.94	3.46
1967	23.98	−2.86	4.39	3.04
1968	11.03	2.25	5.49	4.72
1969	−8.43	−5.63	6.90	6.20
1970	3.94	18.92	6.50	5.57
1971	14.30	11.24	4.36	3.27
1972	18.99	2.39	4.23	3.41
1973	−14.69	3.30	7.29	8.71
1974	−26.47	4.00	7.99	12.34
1975	37.23	5.52	5.87	6.94

(continued)

Table 9.1

Year-by-Year Total Returns, 1926–2005

(concluded)

Year	Large-Company Stocks	Long-Term Government Bonds	U.S. Treasury Bills	Consumer Price Index
1976	23.93%	15.56%	5.07%	4.86%
1977	−7.16	0.38	5.45	6.70
1978	6.57	−1.26	7.64	9.02
1979	18.61	1.26	10.56	13.29
1980	32.50	−2.48	12.10	12.52
1981	−4.92	4.04	14.60	8.92
1982	21.55	44.28	10.94	3.83
1983	22.56	1.29	8.99	3.79
1984	6.27	15.29	9.90	3.95
1985	31.73	32.27	7.71	3.80
1986	18.67	22.39	6.09	1.10
1987	5.25	−3.03	5.88	4.43
1988	16.61	6.84	6.94	4.42
1989	31.69	18.54	8.44	4.65
1990	−3.10	7.74	7.69	6.11
1991	30.46	19.36	5.43	3.06
1992	7.62	7.34	3.48	2.90
1993	10.08	13.06	3.03	2.75
1994	1.32	−7.32	4.39	2.67
1995	37.58	25.94	5.61	2.54
1996	22.96	0.13	5.14	3.32
1997	33.36	12.02	5.19	1.70
1998	28.58	14.45	4.86	1.61
1999	21.04	−7.51	4.80	2.68
2000	−9.10	17.22	5.98	3.39
2001	−11.89	5.51	3.33	1.55
2002	−22.10	15.15	1.61	2.4
2003	28.89	2.01	0.94	1.9
2004	10.88	8.12	1.14	3.3
2005	4.91	6.89	2.79	3.4

SOURCE: Author calculations based on data obtained from *Global Financial Data*, Bloomberg, Standard and Poor's, and other sources.

Given a frequency distribution like that in Figure 9.9, we can calculate the **average** or **mean** of the distribution. To compute the average of the distribution, we add up all of the values and divide by the total (T) number (80 in our case because we have 80 years of data). The bar over the R is used to represent the mean, and the formula is the ordinary formula for the average:

$$\text{Mean} = \bar{R} = \frac{(R_1 + \cdots + R_T)}{T}$$

The mean of the 80 annual large-company stocks returns from 1926 to 2005 is 12.2 percent.

EXAMPLE 9.2

Calculating Average Returns   Suppose the returns on common stock from 1926 to 1929 are .1370, .3580, .4514, and −.0888, respectively. The average, or mean, return over these four years is:

$$\bar{R} = \frac{.1370 + .3580 + .4514 - .0888}{4} = .2144 \text{ or } 21.44\%$$

9.4 Average Stock Returns and Risk-Free Returns

Now that we have computed the average return on the stock market, it seems sensible to compare it with the returns on other securities. The most obvious comparison is with the low-variability returns in the government bond market. These are free of most of the volatility we see in the stock market.

The government borrows money by issuing bonds, which the investing public holds. As we discussed in an earlier chapter, these bonds come in many forms, and the ones we will look at here are called *Treasury bills*, or *T-bills*. Once a week the government sells some bills at an auction. A typical bill is a pure discount bond that will mature in a year or less. Because the government can raise taxes to pay for the debt it incurs—a trick that many of us would like to be able to perform—this debt is virtually free of the risk of default. Thus we will call this the *risk-free return* over a short time (one year or less).

An interesting comparison, then, is between the virtually risk-free return on T-bills and the very risky return on common stocks. This difference between risky returns and risk-free returns is often called the *excess return on the risky asset*. It is called *excess* because it is the additional return resulting from the riskiness of common stocks and is interpreted as an equity **risk premium**.

Table 9.2 shows the average stock return, bond return, T-bill return, and inflation rate for the period from 1926 through 2005. From this we can derive excess returns. The average excess return from large-company common stocks for the entire period was 8.5 percent (12.3 percent − 3.8 percent).

One of the most significant observations of stock market data is this long-term excess of the stock return over the risk-free return. An investor for this period was rewarded for investment in the stock market with an extra or excess return over what would have been achieved by simply investing in T-bills.

Why was there such a reward? Does it mean that it never pays to invest in T-bills and that someone who invested in them instead of in the stock market needs a course in finance? A complete answer to these questions lies at the heart of modern finance, and Chapter 10 is devoted entirely to this. However, part of the answer can be found in the variability of the various types of investments. We see in Table 9.1 many years when an investment in T-bills achieved higher returns than an investment in large common stocks. Also, we note that the returns from an investment in common stocks are frequently negative, whereas an investment in T-bills never produces a negative return. So, we now turn our attention to measuring the variability of returns and an introductory discussion of risk.

We first look more closely at Table 9.2. We see that the standard deviation of T-bills is substantially less than that of common stocks. This suggests that the risk of T-bills is less than that of common stocks. Because the answer turns on the riskiness of investments in common stock, we next turn our attention to measuring this risk.

9.5 Risk Statistics

The second number that we use to characterize the distribution of returns is a measure of the risk in returns. There is no universally agreed-upon definition of risk. One way to think about the risk of returns on common stock is in terms of how spread out the frequency distribution in Figure 9.9 is. The spread, or dispersion, of a distribution is a measure of how much a particular return can deviate from the mean return. If the distribution

Table 9.2   **Total Annual Returns, 1926–2005**

Series	Arithmetic Mean	Risk Premium (relative to U.S. Treasury bills)	Standard Deviation	Distribution
Large-company stocks	12.3%	8.5%	20.2%	
Small-company stocks	17.4	13.6	32.9	*
Long-term corporate bonds	6.2	2.4	8.5	
Long-term government	5.8	2.0	9.2	
Intermediate-term government	5.5	1.7	5.7	
U.S. Treasury bills	3.8		3.1	
Inflation	3.1		4.3	
				−90% 0% 90%

*The 1933 small-company stock total return was 142.9 percent.

SOURCE: Modified from *Stocks, Bonds, Bills and Inflation: 2006 Yearbook,*™ annual updates work by Roger G. Ibbotson and Rex A. Sinquefield (Chicago: Ibbotson Associates). All rights reserved.

is very spread out, the returns that will occur are very uncertain. By contrast, a distribution whose returns are all within a few percentage points of each other is tight, and the returns are less uncertain. The measures of risk we will discuss are variance and standard deviation.

Variance

The **variance** and its square root, the **standard deviation**, are the most common measures of variability or dispersion. We will use Var and σ^2 to denote the variance and SD and σ to represent the standard deviation. σ is, of course, the Greek letter sigma.

EXAMPLE 9.3

Volatility   Suppose the returns on common stocks from 1926 to 1929 are (in decimals) .1370, .3580, .4514, and −.0888, respectively. The variance of this sample is computed as follows:

$$\text{Var} = \frac{1}{T-1}[(R_1 - \bar{R})^2 + (R_2 - \bar{R})^2 + (R_3 - \bar{R})^2 + (R_4 - \bar{R})^2]$$

$$.0582 = \frac{1}{3}[(.1370 - .2144)^2 + (.3580 - .2144)^2$$
$$+ (.4514 - .2144)^2 + (-.0888 - .2144)^2]$$

$$\text{SD} = \sqrt{.0582} = .2413 \text{ or } 24.13\%$$

This formula tells us just what to do: Take the T individual returns (R_1, R_2, . . .) and subtract the average return $\bar{R}$, square the result, and add them up. Finally, this total must be divided by the number of returns less one ($T - 1$). The standard deviation is always just the square root of the variance.

Using the stock returns for the 80-year period from 1926 through 2005 in this formula, the resulting standard deviation of large stock returns is 20.2 percent. The standard deviation is the standard statistical measure of the spread of a sample, and it will be the measure we use most of the time. Its interpretation is facilitated by a discussion of the normal distribution.

Standard deviations are widely reported for mutual funds. For example, the Fidelity Magellan Fund is one of the largest mutual funds in the United States. How volatile is it? To find out, we went to www.morningstar.com, entered the ticker symbol FMAGX, and hit the "Risk/Measures" link. Here is what we found:

Fidelity Magellan FMAGX   See Fund Family Data ▸▸

Volatility Measurements	Trailing 3-Yr through 12-31-05	*Trailing 5-Yr through 12-31-05	
Standard Deviation	8.89	Sharpe Ratio	1.17
Mean	12.61	Bear Market Decile Rank*	7

Modern Portfolio Theory Statistics		Trailing 3-Yr through 12-31-05
	Standard Index S&P 500	**Best Fit Index** S&P 500
R-Squared	96	96
Beta	0.95	0.95
Alpha	-1.01	-1.01

Over the last three years, the standard deviation of the return on the Fidelity Magellan Fund was 8.89 percent. When you consider the average stock has a standard deviation of about 50 percent, this seems like a low number. But the Magellan fund is a relatively well-diversified portfolio, so this is an illustration of the power of diversification, a subject we will discuss in detail later. The mean is the average return; so over the last three years, investors in the Magellan Fund earned a 12.61 percent return per year. Also under the Volatility Measurements section, you will see the Sharpe ratio. The Sharpe ratio is calculated as the risk premium of the asset divided by the standard deviation. As such, it is a measure of return to the level of risk taken (as measured by standard deviation). The "beta" for the Fidelity Magellan Fund is .95. We will have more to say about this number—lots more—in the next chapter.

Figure 9.10

The Normal Distribution

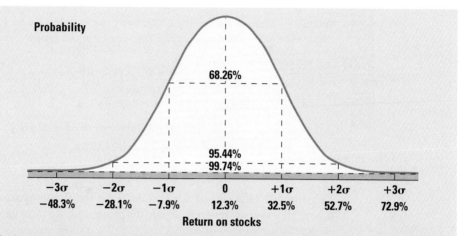

In the case of a normal distribution, there is a 68.26 percent probability that a return will be within one standard deviation of the mean. In this example, there is a 68.26 percent probability that a yearly return will be between –7.9 percent and 32.5 percent.

There is a 95.44 percent probability that a return will be within two standard deviations of the mean. In this example, there is a 95.44 percent probability that a yearly return will be between –28.1 percent and 52.7 percent.

Finally, there is a 99.74 percent probability that a return will be within three standard deviations of the mean. In this example, there is a 99.74 percent probability that a yearly return will be between –48.3 percent and 72.99 percent.

Normal Distribution and Its Implications for Standard Deviation

A large enough sample drawn from a **normal distribution** looks like the bell-shaped curve drawn in Figure 9.10. As you can see, this distribution is *symmetric* about its mean, not *skewed,* and has a much cleaner shape than the actual distribution of yearly returns drawn in Figure 9.9. Of course, if we had been able to observe stock market returns for 1,000 years, we might have filled in a lot of the jumps and jerks in Figure 9.9 and had a smoother curve.

In classical statistics, the normal distribution plays a central role, and the standard deviation is the usual way to represent the spread of a normal distribution. For the normal distribution, the probability of having a return that is above or below the mean by a certain amount depends only on the standard deviation. For example, the probability of having a return that is within one standard deviation of the mean of the distribution is approximately .68 or 2/3, and the probability of having a return that is within two standard deviations of the mean is approximately .95.

The 20.2 percent standard deviation we found for stock returns from 1926 through 2005 can now be interpreted in the following way: If stock returns are roughly normally distributed, the probability that a yearly return will fall within 20.2 percent of the mean of 12.3 percent will be approximately 2/3. That is, about 2/3 of the yearly returns will be between −7.9 percent and 32.5 percent. (Note that −7.9 = 12.3 − 20.2 and 32.5 = 12.3 + 20.2.) The probability that the return in any year will fall within two standard deviations is about .95. That is, about 95 percent of yearly returns will be between −28.1 percent and 52.7 percent.

9.6 More on Average Returns

Thus far in this chapter we have looked closely at simple average returns. But there is another way of computing an average return. The fact that average returns are calculated two different ways leads to some confusion, so our goal in this section is to explain the two approaches and also the circumstances under which each is appropriate.

Arithmetic versus Geometric Averages

Let's start with a simple example. Suppose you buy a particular stock for $100. Unfortunately, the first year you own it, it falls to $50. The second year you own it, it rises back to $100, leaving you where you started (no dividends were paid).

What was your average return on this investment? Common sense seems to say that your average return must be exactly zero because you started with $100 and ended with $100. But if we calculate the returns year-by-year, we see that you lost 50 percent the first year (you lost half of your money). The second year, you made 100 percent (you doubled your money). Your average return over the two years was thus $(-50 \text{ percent} + 100 \text{ percent})/2 = 25$ percent!

So which is correct, 0 percent or 25 percent? The answer is that both are correct; they just answer different questions. The 0 percent is called the **geometric average return**. The 25 percent is called the **arithmetic average return**. The geometric average return answers the question, *"What was your average compound return per year over a particular period?"* The arithmetic average return answers the question, *"What was your return in an average year over a particular period?"*

Notice that in previous sections, the average returns we calculated were all arithmetic averages, so we already know how to calculate them. What we need to do now is (1) learn how to calculate geometric averages and (2) learn the circumstances under which one average is more meaningful than the other.

Calculating Geometric Average Returns

First, to illustrate how we calculate a geometric average return, suppose a particular investment had annual returns of 10 percent, 12 percent, 3 percent, and −9 percent over the last four years. The geometric average return over this four-year period is calculated as $(1.10 \times 1.12 \times 1.03 \times .91)^{1/4} - 1 = 3.66$ percent. In contrast, the average arithmetic return we have been calculating is $(.10 + .12 + .03 - .09)/4 = 4.0$ percent.

In general, if we have T years of returns, the geometric average return over these T years is calculated using this formula:

$$\text{Geometric average return} = [(1 + R_1) \times (1 + R_2) \times \cdots \times (1 + R_T)]^{1/T} - 1 \qquad \textbf{(9.1)}$$

This formula tells us that four steps are required:

1. Take each of the T annual returns $R_1, R_2, \ldots, R_T$ and add 1 to each (after converting them to decimals).
2. Multiply all the numbers from step 1 together.
3. Take the result from step 2 and raise it to the power of $1/T$.
4. Finally, subtract 1 from the result of step 3. The result is the geometric average return.

EXAMPLE 9.4

Calculating the Geometric Average Return Calculate the geometric average return for S&P 500 large-cap stocks for 1926–1930 using the numbers given here.

First convert percentages to decimal returns, add 1, and then calculate their product:

S&P 500 Returns	Product
13.75%	1.1375
35.70	× 1.3570
45.08	× 1.4508
−8.80	× .9120
−25.13	× .7487
	1.5291

(continued)

Notice that the number 1.5291 is what our investment is worth after five years if we started with a $1 investment. The geometric average return is then calculated as:

$$\text{Geometric average return} = 1.5291^{1/5} - 1 = .0887, \text{ or } 8.87\%$$

Thus the geometric average return is about 8.87 percent in this example. Here is a tip: If you are using a financial calculator, you can put $1 in as the present value, $1.5291 as the future value, and 5 as the number of periods. Then solve for the unknown rate. You should get the same answer we did.

You may have noticed in our examples thus far that the geometric average returns seem to be smaller. It turns out that this will always be true (as long as the returns are not all identical, in which case the two "averages" would be the same). To illustrate, Table 9.3 shows the arithmetic averages and standard deviations from Table 9.2, along with the geometric average returns.

As shown in Table 9.3, the geometric averages are all smaller, but the magnitude of the difference varies quite a bit. The reason is that the difference is greater for more volatile investments. In fact, there is a useful approximation. Assuming all the numbers are expressed in decimals (as opposed to percentages), the geometric average return is approximately equal to the arithmetic average return minus half the variance. For example, looking at the large-company stocks, the arithmetic average is 12.3 and the standard deviation is 20.2, implying that the variance is .0408. The approximate geometric average is thus 12.3% − .0408/2 = 10.26%, which is quite close to the actual value.

More Geometric Averages   Take a look back at Figure 9.4. There we showed the value of a $1 investment after 80 years. Use the value for the large-company stock investment to check the geometric average in Table 9.3.

In Figure 9.4, the large-company investment grew to $2,657.56 over 80 years. The geometric average return is thus:

$$\text{Geometric average return} = \$2,657.56^{1/80} - 1 = .1036, \text{ or } 10.4\%$$

This 10.4 percent is the value shown in Table 9.3. For practice, check some of the other numbers in Table 9.3 the same way.

Arithmetic Average Return or Geometric Average Return?

When we look at historical returns, the difference between the geometric and arithmetic average returns isn't too hard to understand. To put it slightly differently, the geometric average tells you what you actually earned per year on average, compounded annually. The arithmetic average tells you what you earned in a typical year. You should use whichever one answers the question you want answered.

A somewhat trickier question concerns forecasting the future, and there's a lot of confusion about this point among analysts and financial planners. The problem is this: If we

Table 9.3

Geometric versus Arithmetic Average Returns: 1926–2005

Series	Geometric Mean	Arithmetic Mean	Standard Deviation
Large-company stocks	10.4%	12.3%	20.2%
Small-company stocks	12.6	17.4	32.9
Long-term corporate bonds	5.9	6.2	8.5
Long-term government bonds	5.5	5.8	9.2
Intermediate-term government bonds	5.3	5.5	5.7
U.S. Treasury bills	3.7	3.8	3.1
Inflation	3.0	3.1	4.3

have *estimates* of both the arithmetic and geometric average returns, then the arithmetic average is probably too high for longer periods and the geometric average is probably too low for shorter periods.

The good news is that there is a simple way of combining the two averages, which we will call *Blume's formula*.[2] Suppose we calculated geometric and arithmetic return averages from N years of data and we wish to use these averages to form a T-year average return forecast, $R(T)$, where T is less than N. Here's how we do it:

$$R(T) = \frac{T-1}{N-1} \times \text{Geometric average} + \frac{N-T}{N-1} \times \text{Arithmetic average} \qquad \textbf{(9.2)}$$

For example, suppose that from 25 years of annual returns data, we calculate an arithmetic average return of 12 percent and a geometric average return of 9 percent. From these averages, we wish to make 1-year, 5-year, and 10-year average return forecasts. These three average return forecasts are calculated as follows:

$$R(1) = \frac{1-1}{24} \times 9\% + \frac{25-1}{24} \times 12\% = 12\%$$

$$R(5) = \frac{5-1}{24} \times 9\% + \frac{25-5}{24} \times 12\% = 11.5\%$$

$$R(10) = \frac{10-1}{24} \times 9\% + \frac{25-10}{24} \times 12\% = 10.875\%$$

Thus, we see that 1-year, 5-year, and 10-year forecasts are 12 percent, 11.5 percent, and 10.875 percent, respectively.

This concludes our discussion of geometric versus arithmetic averages. One last note: In the future, when we say "average return," we mean arithmetic average unless we explicitly say otherwise.

---

[2] This elegant result is due to Marshal Blume ("Unbiased Estimates of Long-Run Expected Rates of Return," *Journal of the American Statistical Association*, September 1974, pp. 634–638).

Summary and Conclusions

1. This chapter presented returns for a number of different asset classes. The general conclusion is that stocks have outperformed bonds over most of the 20th century, though stocks have also exhibited more risk.

2. The statistical measures in this chapter are necessary building blocks for the material of the next three chapters. In particular, standard deviation and variance measure the variability of the return on an individual security and on portfolios of securities. In the next chapter, we will argue that standard deviation and variance are appropriate measures of the risk of an individual security if an investor's portfolio is composed of that security only.

Concept Questions

1. **Investment Selection** Given that ViroPharma was up by almost 469 percent for 2005, why didn't all investors hold ViroPharma?

2. **Investment Selection** Given that Majesco Entertainment was down by 92 percent for 2005, why did some investors hold the stock? Why didn't they sell out before the price declined so sharply?

3. **Risk and Return** We have seen that over long periods stock investments have tended to substantially outperform bond investments. However, it is not at all uncommon to observe investors with long horizons holding their investments entirely in bonds. Are such investors irrational?

4. **Stocks versus Gambling** Critically evaluate the following statement: Playing the stock market is like gambling. Such speculative investing has no social value, other than the pleasure people get from this form of gambling.

5. **Effects of Inflation**   Look at Table 9.1 and Figure 9.7 in the text. When were T-bill rates at their highest over the period from 1926 through 2005? Why do you think they were so high during this period? What relationship underlies your answer?

6. **Risk Premiums**   Is it possible for the risk premium to be negative before an investment is undertaken? Can the risk premium be negative after the fact? Explain.

7. **Returns**   Two years ago, General Materials' and Standard Fixtures' stock prices were the same. During the first year, General Materials' stock price increased by 10 percent while Standard Fixtures' stock price decreased by 10 percent. During the second year, General Materials' stock price decreased by 10 percent and Standard Fixtures' stock price increased by 10 percent. Do these two stocks have the same price today? Explain.

8. **Returns**   Two years ago, the Lake Minerals and Small Town Furniture stock prices were the same. The annual return for both stocks over the past two years was 10 percent. Lake Minerals' stock price increased 10 percent each year. Small Town Furniture's stock price increased 25 percent in the first year and lost 5 percent last year. Do these two stocks have the same price today?

9. **Arithmetic versus Geometric Returns**   What is the difference between arithmetic and geometric returns? Suppose you have invested in a stock for the last 10 years. Which number is more important to you, the arithmetic or geometric return?

10. **Historical Returns**   The historical asset class returns presented in the chapter are not adjusted for inflation. What would happen to the estimated risk premium if we did account for inflation? The returns are also not adjusted for taxes. What would happen to the returns if we accounted for taxes? What would happen to the volatility?

Questions and Problems

BASIC
(Questions 1–20)

1. **Calculating Returns**   Suppose a stock had an initial price of $83 per share, paid a dividend of $1.40 per share during the year, and had an ending share price of $94. Compute the percentage total return.

2. **Calculating Yields**   In Problem 1, what was the dividend yield? The capital gains yield?

3. **Calculating Returns**   Rework Problems 1 and 2 assuming the ending share price is $76.

4. **Calculating Returns**   Suppose you bought a 9 percent coupon bond one year ago for £1,120. The bond sells for £1,074 today.
   a. Assuming a £1,000 face value, what was your total return on this investment over the past year?
   b. What was your total nominal rate of return on this investment over the past year?
   c. If the inflation rate last year was 3 percent, what was your total real rate of return on this investment?

5. **Nominal versus Real Returns**   What was the arithmetic average annual return on large-company stocks from 1926 through 2005.
   a. In nominal terms?
   b. In real terms?

6. **Bond Returns**   What is the historical real return on long-term government bonds? On long-term corporate bonds?

7. **Calculating Returns and Variability**   Using the following returns, calculate the average returns, the variances, and the standard deviations for X and Y:

Year	Returns	
	X	**Y**
1	11%	36%
2	6	−7
3	−8	21
4	28	−12
5	13	43

8.   **Risk Premiums**   Refer to Table 9.1 in the text and look at the period from 1973 through 1978.
   a. Calculate the arithmetic average returns for large-company stocks and T-bills over this period.
   b. Calculate the standard deviation of the returns for large-company stocks and T-bills over this period.
   c. Calculate the observed risk premium in each year for the large-company stocks versus the T-bills. What was the arithmetic average risk premium over this period? What was the standard deviation of the risk premium over this period?

9.   **Calculating Returns and Variability**   You've observed the following returns on Potatochipper.com's stock over the past five years: 216 percent, 21 percent, 4 percent, 16 percent, and 19 percent.
   a. What was the arithmetic average return on Potatochipper.com's stock over this five-year period?
   b. What was the variance of Potatochipper.com's returns over this period? The standard deviation?

10.   **Calculating Real Returns and Risk Premiums**   In Problem 9, suppose the average inflation rate over this period was 4.2 percent and the average T-bill rate over the period was 5.1 percent.
   a. What was the average real return on Potatochipper.com's stock?
   b. What was the average nominal risk premium on Potatochipper.com's stock?

11.   **Calculating Real Rates**   Given the information in Problem 10, what was the average real risk-free rate over this time period? What was the average real risk premium?

12.   **Holding Period Return**   A stock has had returns of −4.91 percent, 21.67 percent, 32.57 percent, 6.19 percent, and 31.85 percent over the past five years, respectively. What was the holding period return for the stock?

13.   **Calculating Returns**   You purchased a zero coupon bond one year ago for £152.37. The market interest rate is now 10 percent. If the bond had 20 years to maturity when you originally purchased it, what was your total return for the past year?

14.   **Calculating Returns**   You bought a share of 5 percent preferred stock for €84.12 last year. The market price for your stock is now €80.27. What is your total return for last year?

15.   **Calculating Returns**   You bought a stock three months ago for AUD 38.65 per share. The stock paid no dividends. The current share price is AUD 42.02. What is the APR of your investment? The EAR?

16.   **Calculating Real Returns**   Refer to Table 9.1. What was the average real return for Treasury bills from 1926 through 1932?

17.   **Return Distributions**   Refer back to Figure 9.10. What range of returns would you expect to see 68 percent of the time for long-term corporate bonds? What about 95 percent of the time?

18.   **Return Distributions**   Refer back to Figure 9.10. What range of returns would you expect to see 68 percent of the time for large-company stocks? What about 95 percent of the time?

19.   **Blume's Formula**   Over a 30-year period an asset had an arithmetic return of 12.8 percent and a geometric return of 10.7 percent. Using Blume's formula, what is your best estimate of the future annual returns over 5 years? 10 years? 20 years?

20.   **Blume's Formula**   Assume that the historical return on large-company stocks is a predictor of the future returns. What return would you estimate for large-company stocks over the next year? The next 5 years? 20 years? 30 years?

INTERMEDIATE
(Questions 21–28)

21.   **Calculating Returns and Variability**   You find a certain stock that had returns of 8 percent, −13 percent, −7 percent, and 22 percent for four of the last five years. If the average return of the stock over this period was 11 percent, what was the stock's return for the missing year? What is the standard deviation of the stock's returns?

22.   **Arithmetic and Geometric Returns**   A stock has had returns of 21 percent, 14 percent, 23 percent, −8 percent, 9 percent, and −14 percent over the last six years. What are the arithmetic and geometric returns for the stock?

www.mhhe.com/rwj

23. **Arithmetic and Geometric Returns**   A stock has had the following year-end prices and
    dividends:

Year	Price	Dividend
1	€43.12	—
2	49.07	€0.55
3	51.19	0.60
4	47.24	0.63
5	56.09	0.72
6	67.21	0.81

    What are the arithmetic and geometric returns for the stock?

24. **Calculating Returns**   Refer to Table 9.1 in the text and look at the period from 1973 through
    1980.
    a. Calculate the average return for Treasury bills and the average annual inflation rate (con-
       sumer price index) for this period.
    b. Calculate the standard deviation of Treasury bill returns and inflation over this period.
    c. Calculate the real return for each year. What is the average real return for Treasury bills?
    d. Many people consider Treasury bills to be risk-free. What do these calculations tell you
       about the potential risks of Treasury bills?

25. **Calculating Investment Returns**   You bought one of Butter Sweet's 8 percent coupon bonds
    one year ago for $1,028.50. These bonds make annual payments and mature six years from
    now. Suppose you decide to sell your bonds today, when the required return on the bonds is
    7 percent. If the inflation rate was 4.8 percent over the past year, what would be your total real
    return on the investment?

26. **Using Return Distributions**   Suppose the returns on long-term government bonds are nor-
    mally distributed. Based on the historical record, what is the approximate probability that your
    return on these bonds will be less than −3.5 percent in a given year? What range of returns
    would you expect to see 95 percent of the time? What range would you expect to see 99 percent
    of the time?

27. **Using Return Distributions**   Assuming that the returns from holding small-company stocks
    are normally distributed, what is the approximate probability that your money will double in
    value in a single year? Triple in value?

28. **Distributions**   In the previous problem, what is the probability that the return is less than
    −100 percent? (Think.) What are the implications for the distribution of returns?

CHALLENGE
(Questions 29–30)

29. **Using Probability Distributions**   Suppose the returns on large-company stocks are nor-
    mally distributed. Based on the historical record, use the cumulative normal probability table
    (rounded to the nearest table value) in Chapter 22 to determine the probability that in any given
    year you will lose money by investing in common stock.

30. **Using Probability Distributions**   Suppose the returns on long-term corporate bonds and T-
    bills are normally distributed. Based on the historical record, use the cumulative normal proba-
    bility table (rounded to the nearest table value) in Chapter 22 to answer the following questions:
    a. What is the probability that in any given year, the return on long-term corporate bonds will
       be greater than 10 percent? Less than 0 percent?
    b. What is the probability that in any given year, the return on T-bills will be greater than
       10 percent? Less than 0 percent?
    c. In 1979, the return on long-term corporate bonds was −4.18 percent. How likely is it that
       this low of a return will recur at some point in the future? T-bills had a return of 10.32 per-
       cent in this same year. How likely is it that this high of a return on T-bills will recur at some
       point in the future?

S&P Problems

STANDARD &POOR'S

www.mhhe.com/edumarketinsight

1. **Calculating Yields** Download the historical stock prices for Duke Energy (DUK) under the "Mthly. Adj. Prices" link. Find the closing stock price for the beginning and end of the prior two years. Now use the annual financial statements to find the dividend for each of these years. What was the capital gains yield and dividend yield for Duke Energy stock for each of these years? Now calculate the capital gains yield and dividend yield for Abercrombie & Fitch (ANF). How do the returns for these two companies compare?

2. **Calculating Average Returns** Download the Monthly Adjusted Prices for Microsoft (MSFT). What is the return on the stock over the past 12 months? Now use the 1 Month Total Return and calculate the average monthly return. Is this one-twelfth of the annual return you calculated? Why or why not? What is the monthly standard deviation of Microsoft's stock over the past year?

Mini Case

A Job at East Coast Yachts

You recently graduated from college, and your job search led you to East Coast Yachts. Because you felt the company's business was seaworthy, you accepted a job offer. The first day on the job, while you are finishing your employment paperwork, Dan Ervin, who works in Finance, stops by to inform you about the company's 401(k) plan.

A 401(k) plan is a retirement plan offered by many companies. Such plans are tax-deferred savings vehicles, meaning that any deposits you make into the plan are deducted from your current pretax income, so no current taxes are paid on the money. For example, assume your salary will be $50,000 per year. If you contribute $3,000 to the 401(k) plan, you will pay taxes on only $47,000 in income. There are also no taxes paid on any capital gains or income while you are invested in the plan, but you do pay taxes when you withdraw money at retirement. As is fairly common, the company also has a 5 percent match. This means that the company will match your contribution up to 5 percent of your salary, but you must contribute to get the match.

The 401(k) plan has several options for investments, most of which are mutual funds. A mutual fund is a portfolio of assets. When you purchase shares in a mutual fund, you are actually purchasing partial ownership of the fund's assets. The return of the fund is the weighted average of the return of the assets owned by the fund, minus any expenses. The largest expense is typically the management fee, paid to the fund manager. The management fee is compensation for the manager, who makes all of the investment decisions for the fund.

East Coast Yachts uses Bledsoe Financial Services as its 401(k) plan administrator. Here are the investment options offered for employees:

Company Stock One option in the 401(k) plan is stock in East Coast Yachts. The company is currently privately held. However, when you interviewed with the owner, Larissa Warren, she informed you the company stock was expected to go public in the next three to four years. Until then, a company stock price is simply set each year by the board of directors.

Bledsoe S&P 500 Index Fund This mutual fund tracks the S&P 500. Stocks in the fund are weighted exactly the same as the S&P 500. This means the fund return is approximately the return on the S&P 500, minus expenses. Because an index fund purchases assets based on the compensation of the index it is following, the fund manager is not required to research stocks and make investment decisions. The result is that the fund expenses are usually low. The Bledsoe S&P 500 Index Fund charges expenses of .15 percent of assets per year.

Bledsoe Small-Cap Fund This fund primarily invests in small-capitalization stocks. As such, the returns of the fund are more volatile. The fund can also invest 10 percent of its assets in companies based outside the United States. This fund charges 1.70 percent in expenses.

Bledsoe Large-Company Stock Fund   This fund invests primarily in large-capitalization stocks of companies based in the United States. The fund is managed by Evan Bledsoe and has outperformed the market in six of the last eight years. The fund charges 1.50 percent in expenses.

Bledsoe Bond Fund   This fund invests in long-term corporate bonds issued by U.S.–domiciled companies. The fund is restricted to investments in bonds with an investment-grade credit rating. This fund charges 1.40 percent in expenses.

Bledsoe Money Market Fund   This fund invests in short-term, high–credit quality debt instruments, which include Treasury bills. As such, the return on the money market fund is only slightly higher than the return on Treasury bills. Because of the credit quality and short-term nature of the investments, there is only a very slight risk of negative return. The fund charges .60 percent in expenses.

1. What advantages do the mutual funds offer compared to the company stock?

2. Assume that you invest 5 percent of your salary and receive the full 5 percent match from East Coast Yachts. What EAR do you earn from the match? What conclusions do you draw about matching plans?

3. Assume you decide you should invest at least part of your money in large-capitalization stocks of companies based in the United States. What are the advantages and disadvantages of choosing the Bledsoe Large-Company Stock Fund compared to the Bledsoe S&P 500 Index Fund?

4. The returns on the Bledsoe Small-Cap Fund are the most volatile of all the mutual funds offered in the 401(k) plan. Why would you ever want to invest in this fund? When you examine the expenses of the mutual funds, you will notice that this fund also has the highest expenses. Does this affect your decision to invest in this fund?

5. A measure of risk-adjusted performance that is often used is the Sharpe ratio. The Sharpe ratio is calculated as the risk premium of an asset divided by its standard deviation. The standard deviation and return of the funds over the past 10 years are listed here. Calculate the Sharpe ratio for each of these funds. Assume that the expected return and standard deviation of the company stock will be 18 percent and 70 percent, respectively. Calculate the Sharpe ratio for the company stock. How appropriate is the Sharpe ratio for these assets? When would you use the Sharpe ratio?

	10-Year Annual Return	Standard Deviation
Bledsoe S&P 500 Index Fund	11.48%	15.82%
Bledsoe Small-Cap Fund	16.68	19.64
Bledsoe Large-Company Stock Fund	11.85	15.41
Bledsoe Bond Fund	9.67	10.83

6. What portfolio allocation would you choose? Why? Explain your thinking carefully.

Appendix 9A   The Historical Market Risk Premium: The Very Long Run

To access Appendix 9A, please go to www.mhhe.com/rwj.

Return and Risk

The Capital Asset Pricing Model (CAPM)

Expected returns on common stocks can vary quite a bit. One important determinant is the industry in which a company operates. For example, according to recent estimates from Ibbotson Associates, the median expected return for department stores, which includes companies such as Sears and Kohls, is 11.63 percent, whereas computer service companies such as Microsoft and Oracle have a median expected return of 15.46 percent. Air transportation companies such as Delta and Southwest have a median expected return that is even higher: 17.93 percent.

These estimates raise some obvious questions. First, why do these industry expected returns differ so much, and how are these specific numbers calculated? Also, does the higher return offered by airline stocks mean that investors should prefer these to, say, department store stocks? As we will see in this chapter, the Nobel Prize–winning answers to these questions form the basis of our modern understanding of risk and return.

10.1 Individual Securities

In the first part of Chapter 10, we will examine the characteristics of individual securities. In particular, we will discuss:

1. *Expected return*: This is the return that an individual expects a stock to earn over the next period. Of course, because this is only an expectation, the actual return may be either higher or lower. An individual's expectation may simply be the average return per period a security has earned in the past. Alternatively, it may be based on a detailed analysis of a firm's prospects, on some computer-based model, or on special (or inside) information.

2. *Variance and standard deviation*: There are many ways to assess the volatility of a security's return. One of the most common is variance, which is a measure of the squared deviations of a security's return from its expected return. Standard deviation is the square root of the variance.

3. *Covariance and correlation*: Returns on individual securities are related to one another. Covariance is a statistic measuring the interrelationship between two securities. Alternatively, this relationship can be restated in terms of the correlation between the two securities. Covariance and correlation are building blocks to an understanding of the beta coefficient.

10.2 Expected Return, Variance, and Covariance

Expected Return and Variance

Suppose financial analysts believe that there are four equally likely states of the economy: depression, recession, normal, and boom. The returns on the Supertech Company are expected to follow the economy closely, while the returns on the Slowpoke Company are not. The return predictions are as follows:

	Supertech Returns R_{At}	Slowpoke Returns R_{Bt}
Depression	−20%	5%
Recession	10	20
Normal	30	−12
Boom	50	9

Variance can be calculated in four steps. An additional step is needed to calculate standard deviation. (The calculations are presented in Table 10.1.) The steps are these:

1. Calculate the expected return:

   Supertech

   $$\frac{-0.20 + 0.10 + 0.30 + 0.50}{4} = 0.175 = 17.5\% = \overline{R}_A$$

   Slowpoke

   $$\frac{0.05 + 0.20 - 0.12 + 0.09}{4} = 0.055 = 5.5\% = \overline{R}_B$$

2. For each company, calculate the deviation of each possible return from the company's expected return given previously. This is presented in the third column of Table 10.1.

3. The deviations we have calculated are indications of the dispersion of returns. However, because some are positive and some are negative, it is difficult to work with them in this form. For example, if we were to simply add up all the deviations for a single company, we would get zero as the sum.

   To make the deviations more meaningful, we multiply each one by itself. Now all the numbers are positive, implying that their sum must be positive as well. The squared deviations are presented in the last column of Table 10.1.

4. For each company, calculate the average squared deviation, which is the variance:[1]

   Supertech

   $$\frac{0.140625 + 0.005625 + 0.015625 + 0.105625}{4} = 0.066875$$

---

[1] In this example, the four states give rise to four *possible* outcomes for each stock. Had we used past data, the outcomes would have actually occurred. In that case, statisticians argue that the correct divisor is $N - 1$, where N is the number of observations. Thus the denominator would be 3 [= (4 − 1)] in the case of past data, not 4. Note that the example in Section 9.5 involved past data and we used a divisor of $N - 1$. While this difference causes grief to both students and textbook writers, it is a minor point in practice. In the real world, samples are generally so large that using N or $N - 1$ in the denominator has virtually no effect on the calculation of variance.

Table 10.1

Calculating Variance and Standard Deviation

(1) State of Economy	(2) Rate of Return	(3) Deviation from Expected Return	(4) Squared Value of Deviation
	Supertech*	**(Expected return = 0.175)**	
	R_{At}	$(R_{At} - \bar{R}_A)$	$(R_{At} - \bar{R}_A)^2$
Depression	−0.20	−0.375	0.140625
		$(= -0.20 - 0.175)$	$[= (-0.375)^2]$
Recession	0.10	−0.075	0.005625
Normal	0.30	0.125	0.015625
Boom	0.50	0.325	0.105625
			0.267500
	Slowpoke†	**(Expected return = 0.055)**	
	R_{Bt}	$(R_{Bt} - \bar{R}_B)$	$(R_{Bt} - \bar{R}_B)^2$
Depression	0.05	−0.005	0.000025
		$(= 0.05 - 0.055)$	$[= (-0.005)^2]$
Recession	0.20	0.145	0.021025
Normal	−0.12	−0.175	0.030625
Boom	0.09	0.035	0.001225
			0.052900

$$*\bar{R}_A = \frac{-0.20 + 0.10 + 0.30 + 0.50}{4} = 0.175 = 17.5\%$$

$$\text{Var}(R_A) = \sigma_A^2 = \frac{0.2675}{4} = 0.066875$$

$$\text{SD}(R_A) = \sigma_A = \sqrt{0.066875} = 0.2586 = 25.86\%$$

$$†\bar{R}_B = \frac{0.05 + 0.20 - 0.12 - 0.09}{4} = 0.055 = 5.5\%$$

$$\text{Var}(R_B) = \sigma_B^2 = \frac{0.0529}{4} = 0.013225$$

$$\text{SD}(R_B) = \sigma_B = \sqrt{0.013225} = 0.1150 = 11.50\%$$

Slowpoke

$$\frac{0.000025 + 0.021025 + 0.030625 + 0.001225}{4} = 0.013225$$

Thus, the variance of Supertech is 0.066875, and the variance of Slowpoke is: 0.013225.

5. Calculate standard deviation by taking the square root of the variance:

Supertech

$$\sqrt{0.066875} = 0.2586 = 25.86\%$$

Slowpoke

$$\sqrt{0.013225} = 0.1150 = 11.50\%$$

Algebraically, the formula for variance can be expressed as:

$$\text{Var}(R) = \text{Expected value of } (R - \bar{R})^2$$

where $\bar{R}$ is the security's expected return and R is the actual return.

A look at the four-step calculation for variance makes it clear why it is a measure of the spread of the sample of returns. For each observation we square the difference between the actual return and the expected return. We then take an average of these squared differences. Squaring the differences makes them all positive. If we used the differences between each return and the expected return and then averaged these differences, we would get zero because the returns that were above the mean would cancel the ones below.

However, because the variance is still expressed in squared terms, it is difficult to interpret. Standard deviation has a much simpler interpretation, which was provided in Section 9.5. Standard deviation is simply the square root of the variance. The general formula for the standard deviation is:

$$SD(R) = \sqrt{\text{Var}(R)}$$

Covariance and Correlation

Variance and standard deviation measure the variability of individual stocks. We now wish to measure the relationship between the return on one stock and the return on another. Enter **covariance** and **correlation**.

Covariance and correlation measure how two random variables are related. We explain these terms by extending the Supertech and Slowpoke example.

Calculating Covariance and Correlation   We have already determined the expected returns and standard deviations for both Supertech and Slowpoke. (The expected returns are 0.175 and 0.055 for Supertech and Slowpoke, respectively. The standard deviations are 0.2586 and 0.1150, respectively.) In addition, we calculated the deviation of each possible return from the expected return for each firm. Using these data, we can calculate covariance in two steps. An extra step is needed to calculate correlation.

1. For each state of the economy, multiply Supertech's deviation from its expected return and Slowpoke's deviation from its expected return together. For example, Supertech's rate of return in a depression is -0.20, which is -0.375 ($=-0.20 - 0.175$) from its expected return. Slowpoke's rate of return in a depression is 0.05, which is -0.005 ($=0.05 - 0.055$) from its expected return. Multiplying the two deviations together yields 0.001875 [$=(-0.375) \times (-0.005)$]. The actual calculations are given in the last column of Table 10.2. This procedure can be written algebraically as:

$$(R_{At} - \bar{R}_A) \times (R_{Bt} - \bar{R}_B) \tag{10.1}$$

where R_{At} and R_{Bt} are the returns on Supertech and Slowpoke in state t. $\bar{R}_A$ and $\bar{R}_B$ are the expected returns on the two securities.

2. Calculate the average value of the four states in the last column. This average is the covariance. That is:[2]

$$\sigma_{AB} = \text{Cov}(R_A, R_B) = \frac{-0.0195}{4} = -0.004875$$

Note that we represent the covariance between Supertech and Slowpoke as either $\text{Cov}(R_A, R_B)$ or σ_{AB}. Equation 10.1 illustrates the intuition of covariance. Suppose Supertech's return is generally above its average when Slowpoke's return is above its average, and Supertech's return is generally

(continued)

---

[2] As with variance, we divided by N (4 in this example) because the four states give rise to four *possible* outcomes. However, had we used past data, the correct divisor would be $N - 1$ (3 in this example).

Table 10.2 **Calculating Covariance and Correlation**

State of Economy	Rate of Return of Supertech R_{At}	Deviation from Expected Return $(R_{At} - \bar{R}_A)$	Rate of Return of Slowpoke R_{Bt}	Deviation from Expected Return $(R_{Bt} - \bar{R}_B)$	Product of Deviations $(R_{At} - \bar{R}_A) \times (R_{Bt} - \bar{R}_B)$
		(Expected return $= 0.175$)		(Expected return $= 0.055$)	
Depression	-0.20	-0.375 $(= -0.20 - 0.175)$	0.05	-0.005 $(= 0.05 - 0.055)$	0.001875 $(= -0.375 \times -0.005)$
Recession	0.10	-0.075	0.20	0.145	-0.010875 $(= -0.075 \times 0.145)$
Normal	0.30	0.125	-0.12	-0.175	-0.021875 $(= 0.125 \times -0.175)$
Boom	0.50	0.325	0.09	0.035	0.011375 $(= 0.325 \times 0.035)$
	$\overline{0.70}$		$\overline{0.22}$		$\overline{-0.0195}$

$$\sigma_{AB} = \text{Cov}(R_A, R_B) = \frac{-0.0195}{4} = -0.004875$$

$$\rho_{AB} = \text{Corr}(R_A, R_B) = \frac{\text{Cov}(R_A, R_B)}{\text{SD}(R_A) \times \text{SD}(R_B)} = \frac{-0.004875}{0.2586 \times 0.1150} = -0.1639$$

below its average when Slowpoke's return is below its average. This shows a positive dependency or a positive relationship between the two returns. Note that the term in Equation 10.1 will be *positive* in any state where both returns are *above* their averages. In addition, 10.1 will still be *positive* in any state where both terms are *below* their averages. Thus a positive relationship between the two returns will give rise to a positive value for covariance.

Conversely, suppose Supertech's return is generally above its average when Slowpoke's return is below its average, and Supertech's return is generally below its average when Slowpoke's return is above its average. This demonstrates a negative dependency or a negative relationship between the two returns. Note that the term in Equation 10.1 will be *negative* in any state where one return is above its average and the other return is below its average. Thus a negative relationship between the two returns will give rise to a negative value for covariance.

Finally, suppose there is no relationship between the two returns. In this case, knowing whether the return on Supertech is above or below its expected return tells us nothing about the return on Slowpoke. In the covariance formula, then, there will be no tendency for the deviations to be positive or negative together. On average, they will tend to offset each other and cancel out, making the covariance zero.

Of course, even if the two returns are unrelated to each other, the covariance formula will not equal zero exactly in any actual history. This is due to sampling error; randomness alone will make the calculation positive or negative. But for a historical sample that is long enough, if the two returns are not related to each other, we should expect the covariance to come close to zero.

The covariance formula seems to capture what we are looking for. If the two returns are positively related to each other, they will have a positive covariance, and if they are negatively related to each other, the covariance will be negative. Last, and very important, if they are unrelated, the covariance should be zero.

The formula for covariance can be written algebraically as:

$$\sigma_{AB} = \text{Cov}(R_A, R_B) = \text{Expected value of } [(R_A - \bar{R}_A) \times (R_B - \bar{R}_B)]$$

(continued)

where $\bar{R}_A$ and $\bar{R}_B$ are the expected returns for the two securities, and R_A and R_B are the actual returns. The ordering of the two variables is unimportant. That is, the covariance of A with B is equal to the covariance of B with A. This can be stated more formally as $Cov(R_A, R_B) = Cov(R_B, R_A)$ or $\sigma_{AB} = \sigma_{BA}$.

The covariance we calculated is -0.004875. A negative number like this implies that the return on one stock is likely to be above its average when the return on the other stock is below its average, and vice versa. However, the size of the number is difficult to interpret. Like the variance figure, the covariance is in squared deviation units. Until we can put it in perspective, we don't know what to make of it.

We solve the problem by computing the correlation.

3. To calculate the correlation, divide the covariance by the standard deviations of both of the two securities. For our example, we have:

$$\rho_{AB} = Corr(R_A, R_B) = \frac{Cov(R_A, R_B)}{\sigma_A \times \sigma_B} = \frac{-0.004875}{0.2586 \times 0.1150} = -0.1639 \qquad \textbf{(10.2)}$$

where σ_A and σ_B are the standard deviations of Supertech and Slowpoke, respectively. Note that we represent the correlation between Supertech and Slowpoke either as $Corr(R_A, R_B)$ or ρ_{AB}. As with covariance, the ordering of the two variables is unimportant. That is, the correlation of A with B is equal to the correlation of B with A. More formally, $Corr(R_A, R_B) = Corr(R_B, R_A)$ or $\rho_{AB} = \rho_{BA}$.

Figure 10.1

Examples of Different Correlation Coefficients—Graphs Plotting the Separate Returns on Two Securities through Time

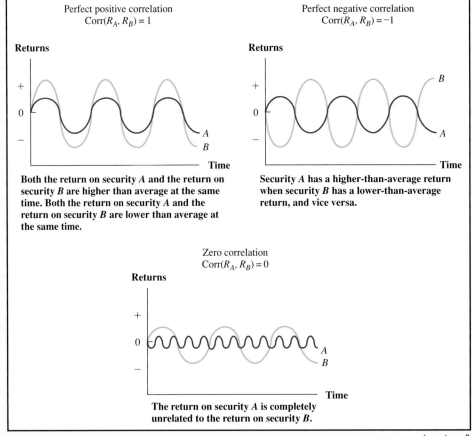

(continued)

Because the standard deviation is always positive, the sign of the correlation between two variables must be the same as that of the covariance between the two variables. If the correlation is positive, we say that the variables are *positively correlated*; if it is negative, we say that they are *negatively correlated*; and if it is zero, we say that they are *uncorrelated*. Furthermore, it can be proved that the correlation is always between $+1$ and -1. This is due to the standardizing procedure of dividing by the two standard deviations.

We can compare the correlation between different *pairs* of securities. For example, it turns out that the correlation between General Motors and Ford is much higher than the correlation between General Motors and IBM. Hence, we can state that the first pair of securities is more interrelated than the second pair.

Figure 10.1 shows the three benchmark cases for two assets, *A* and *B*. The figure shows two assets with return correlations of $+1$, -1, and 0. This implies perfect positive correlation, perfect negative correlation, and no correlation, respectively. The graphs in the figure plot the separate returns on the two securities through time.

10.3   The Return and Risk for Portfolios

Suppose an investor has estimates of the expected returns and standard deviations on individual securities and the correlations between securities. How does the investor choose the best combination or **portfolio** of securities to hold? Obviously, the investor would like a portfolio with a high expected return and a low standard deviation of return. It is therefore worthwhile to consider:

1. The relationship between the expected return on individual securities and the expected return on a portfolio made up of these securities.
2. The relationship between the standard deviations of individual securities, the correlations between these securities, and the standard deviation of a portfolio made up of these securities.

To analyze these two relationships, we will use the same example of Supertech and Slowpoke. The relevant calculations follow.

The Expected Return on a Portfolio

The formula for expected return on a portfolio is very simple:

The expected return on a portfolio is simply a weighted average of the expected returns on the individual securities.

Relevant Data from Example of Supertech and Slowpoke		
Item	**Symbol**	**Value**
Expected return on Supertech	$\bar{R}_{Super}$	$0.175 = 17.5\%$
Expected return on Slowpoke	$\bar{R}_{Slow}$	$0.055 = 5.5\%$
Variance of Supertech	σ^2_{Super}	0.066875
Variance of Slowpoke	σ^2_{Slow}	0.013225
Standard deviation of Supertech	σ_{Super}	$0.2586 = 25.86\%$
Standard deviation of Slowpoke	σ_{Slow}	$0.1150 = 11.50\%$
Covariance between Supertech and Slowpoke	$\sigma_{Super, Slow}$	-0.004875
Correlation between Supertech and Slowpoke	$\rho_{Super, Slow}$	-0.1639

Portfolio Expected Returns   Consider Supertech and Slowpoke. From our earlier calculations, we find that the expected returns on these two securities are 17.5 percent and 5.5 percent, respectively.

The expected return on a portfolio of these two securities alone can be written as:

$$\text{Expected return on portfolio} = X_{\text{Super}}(17.5\%) + X_{\text{Slow}}(5.5\%) = \bar{R}_P$$

where X_{Super} is the percentage of the portfolio in Supertech and X_{Slow} is the percentage of the portfolio in Slowpoke. If the investor with $100 invests $60 in Supertech and $40 in Slowpoke, the expected return on the portfolio can be written as:

$$\text{Expected return on portfolio} = 0.6 \times 17.5\% + 0.4 \times 5.5\% = 12.7\%$$

Algebraically, we can write:

$$\text{Expected return on portfolio} = X_A\bar{R}_A + X_B\bar{R}_B = \bar{R}_P \tag{10.3}$$

where X_A and X_B are the proportions of the total portfolio in the assets A and B, respectively. (Because our investor can invest in only two securities, $X_A + X_B$ must equal 1 or 100 percent.) $\bar{R}_A$ and $\bar{R}_B$ are the expected returns on the two securities.

Now consider two stocks, each with an expected return of 10 percent. The expected return on a portfolio composed of these two stocks must be 10 percent, regardless of the proportions of the two stocks held. This result may seem obvious at this point, but it will become important later. The result implies that you do not reduce or *dissipate* your expected return by investing in a number of securities. Rather, the expected return on your portfolio is simply a weighted average of the expected returns on the individual assets in the portfolio.

Variance and Standard Deviation of a Portfolio

The Variance   The formula for the variance of a portfolio composed of two securities, A and B, is:

The Variance of the Portfolio

$$\text{Var(portfolio)} = X_A^2\sigma_A^2 + 2X_AX_B\sigma_{A,B} + X_B^2\sigma_B^2$$

Note that there are three terms on the right side of the equation. The first term involves the variance of $A(\sigma_A^2)$, the second term involves the covariance between the two securities $(\sigma_{A,B})$, and the third term involves the variance of $B(\sigma_B^2)$. (As stated earlier in this chapter, $\sigma_{A,B} = \sigma_{B,A}$. That is, the ordering of the variables is not relevant when we are expressing the covariance between two securities.)

The formula indicates an important point. The variance of a portfolio depends on both the variances of the individual securities and the covariance between the two securities. The variance of a security measures the variability of an individual security's return. Covariance measures the relationship between the two securities. For given variances of the individual securities, a positive relationship or covariance between the two securities increases the variance of the entire portfolio. A negative relationship or covariance between the two securities decreases the variance of the entire portfolio. This important result seems to square with common sense. If one of your securities tends to go up when the other goes down, or vice versa, your two securities are offsetting each other. You are achieving what we call a *hedge* in finance, and the risk of your entire portfolio will be low. However, if both your securities rise and fall together, you are not hedging at all. Hence, the risk of your entire portfolio will be higher.

The variance formula for our two securities, Super and Slow, is:

$$\text{Var(portfolio)} = X_{\text{Super}}^2 \sigma_{\text{Super}}^2 + 2X_{\text{Super}}X_{\text{Slow}}\sigma_{\text{Super, Slow}} + X_{\text{Slow}}^2 \sigma_{\text{Slow}}^2 \quad \textbf{(10.4)}$$

Given our earlier assumption that an individual with \$100 invests \$60 in Supertech and \$40 in Slowpoke, $X_{\text{Super}} = 0.6$ and $X_{\text{Slow}} = 0.4$. Using this assumption and the relevant data from our previous calculations, the variance of the portfolio is:

$$0.023851 = 0.36 \times 0.066875 + 2 \times [0.6 \times 0.4 \times (-0.004875)] + 0.16 \times 0.013225$$
$$\textbf{(10.4}')$$

The Matrix Approach   Alternatively, Equation 10.4 can be expressed in the following matrix format:

	Supertech	**Slowpoke**
Supertech	$X_{\text{Super}}^2 \sigma_{\text{Super}}^2$ $0.024075 = 0.36 \times 0.066875$	$X_{\text{Super}}X_{\text{Slow}}\sigma_{\text{Super, Slow}}$ $-0.00117 = 0.6 \times 0.4 \times (-0.004875)$
Slowpoke	$X_{\text{Super}}X_{\text{Slow}}\sigma_{\text{Super, Slow}}$ $-0.00117 = 0.6 \times 0.4 \times (-0.004875)$	$X_{\text{Slow}}^2 \sigma_{\text{Slow}}^2$ $0.002116 = 0.16 \times 0.013225$

There are four boxes in the matrix. We can add the terms in the boxes to obtain Equation 10.4, the variance of a portfolio composed of the two securities. The term in the upper left corner involves the variance of Supertech. The term in the lower right corner involves the variance of Slowpoke. The other two boxes contain the term involving the covariance. These two boxes are identical, indicating why the covariance term is multiplied by 2 in Equation 10.4.

At this point, students often find the box approach to be more confusing than Equation 10.4. However, the box approach is easily generalized to more than two securities, a task we perform later in this chapter.

Standard Deviation of a Portfolio   Given Equation 10.4$'$, we can now determine the standard deviation of the portfolio's return. This is:

$$\sigma_P = \text{SD(portfolio)} = \sqrt{\text{Var(portfolio)}} = \sqrt{0.023851} \quad \textbf{(10.5)}$$
$$= 0.1544 = 15.44\%$$

The interpretation of the standard deviation of the portfolio is the same as the interpretation of the standard deviation of an individual security. The expected return on our portfolio is 12.7 percent. A return of -2.74 percent ($=12.7\% - 15.44\%$) is one standard deviation below the mean, and a return of 28.14 percent ($=12.7\% + 15.44\%$) is one standard deviation above the mean. If the return on the portfolio is normally distributed, a return between -2.74 percent and $+28.14$ percent occurs about 68 percent of the time.[3]

The Diversification Effect   It is instructive to compare the standard deviation of the portfolio with the standard deviation of the individual securities. The weighted average of the standard deviations of the individual securities is:

$$\text{Weighted average of standard deviations} = X_{\text{Super}}\sigma_{\text{Super}} + X_{\text{Slow}}\sigma_{\text{Slow}} \quad \textbf{(10.6)}$$
$$0.2012 = 0.6 \times 0.2586 + 0.4 \times 0.115$$

---

[3] There are only four equally probable returns for Supertech and Slowpoke, so neither security possesses a normal distribution. Thus, probabilities would be slightly different in our example.

One of the most important results in this chapter concerns the difference between Equations 10.5 and 10.6. In our example, the standard deviation of the portfolio is *less* than a weighted average of the standard deviations of the individual securities.

We pointed out earlier that the expected return on the portfolio is a weighted average of the expected returns on the individual securities. Thus, we get a different type of result for the standard deviation of a portfolio than we do for the expected return on a portfolio.

It is generally argued that our result for the standard deviation of a portfolio is due to diversification. For example, Supertech and Slowpoke are slightly negatively correlated ($\rho = -0.1639$). Supertech's return is likely to be a little below average if Slowpoke's return is above average. Similarly, Supertech's return is likely to be a little above average if Slowpoke's return is below average. Thus, the standard deviation of a portfolio composed of the two securities is less than a weighted average of the standard deviations of the two securities.

Our example has negative correlation. Clearly, there will be less benefit from diversification if the two securities exhibit positive correlation. How high must the positive correlation be before all diversification benefits vanish?

To answer this question, let us rewrite Equation 10.4 in terms of correlation rather than covariance. The covariance can be rewritten as:[4]

$$\sigma_{\text{Super, Slow}} = \rho_{\text{Super, Slow}} \sigma_{\text{Super}} \sigma_{\text{Slow}} \qquad \textbf{(10.7)}$$

This formula states that the covariance between any two securities is simply the correlation between the two securities multiplied by the standard deviations of each. In other words, covariance incorporates both (1) the correlation between the two assets and (2) the variability of each of the two securities as measured by standard deviation.

From our calculations earlier in this chapter we know that the correlation between the two securities is -0.1639. Given the variances used in Equation 10.4', the standard deviations are 0.2586 and 0.115 for Supertech and Slowpoke, respectively. Thus, the variance of a portfolio can be expressed as follows:

Variance of the Portfolio's Return

$$= X_{\text{Super}}^2 \sigma_{\text{Super}}^2 + 2X_{\text{Super}} X_{\text{Slow}} \rho_{\text{Super, Slow}} \sigma_{\text{Super}} \sigma_{\text{Slow}} + X_{\text{Slow}}^2 \sigma_{\text{Slow}}^2 \qquad \textbf{(10.8)}$$

$$0.023851 = 0.36 \times 0.066875 + 2 \times 0.6 \times 0.4 \times (-0.1639)$$
$$\times 0.2586 \times 0.115 + 0.16 \times 0.013225$$

The middle term on the right side is now written in terms of correlation, ρ, not covariance.

Suppose $\rho_{\text{Super, Slow}} = 1$, the highest possible value for correlation. Assume all the other parameters in the example are the same. The variance of the portfolio is:

Variance of the $\quad = 0.040466 = 0.36 \times 0.066875 + 2 \times (0.6 \times 0.4 \times 1 \times 0.2586$
portfolio's return $\qquad\qquad\qquad \times 0.115) + 0.16 \times 0.013225$

The standard deviation is:

$$\text{Standard deviation of portfolio's return} = \sqrt{0.040466} = 0.2012 = 20.12\% \quad \textbf{(10.9)}$$

Note that Equations 10.9 and 10.6 are equal. That is, the standard deviation of a portfolio's return is equal to the weighted average of the standard deviations of the individual returns when $\rho = 1$. Inspection of Equation 10.8 indicates that the variance and hence the

---

[4] As with covariance, the ordering of the two securities is not relevant when we express the correlation between the two securities. That is, $\rho_{\text{Super,Slow}} = \rho_{\text{Slow,Super}}$.

Table 10.3

Standard Deviations for Standard & Poor's 500 Index and for Selected Stocks in the Index

Asset	Standard Deviation
S&P 500 Index	16.35%
Verizon	33.96
Ford Motor Co.	43.61
Walt Disney Co.	32.55
General Electric	25.18
IBM	35.96
McDonald's	28.61
Sears	44.06
Toys "R" Us Inc.	50.77
Amazon.com	69.19

As long as the correlations between pairs of securities are less than 1, the standard deviation of an index is less than the weighted average of the standard deviations of the individual securities within the index.

standard deviation of the portfolio must fall as the correlation drops below 1. This leads to the following result:

As long as $\rho < 1$, the standard deviation of a portfolio of two securities is *less* than the weighted average of the standard deviations of the individual securities.

In other words, the diversification effect applies as long as there is less than perfect correlation (as long as $\rho < 1$). Thus, our Supertech–Slowpoke example is a case of overkill. We illustrated diversification by an example with negative correlation. We could have illustrated diversification by an example with positive correlation—as long as it was not *perfect* positive correlation.

An Extension to Many Assets   The preceding insight can be extended to the case of many assets. That is, as long as correlations between pairs of securities are less than 1, the standard deviation of a portfolio of many assets is less than the weighted average of the standard deviations of the individual securities.

Now consider Table 10.3, which shows the standard deviation of the Standard & Poor's 500 Index and the standard deviations of some of the individual securities listed in the index over a recent 10-year period. Note that all of the individual securities in the table have higher standard deviations than that of the index. In general, the standard deviations of most of the individual securities in an index will be above the standard deviation of the index itself, though a few of the securities could have lower standard deviations than that of the index.

10.4   The Efficient Set for Two Assets

Our results for expected returns and standard deviations are graphed in Figure 10.2. The figure shows a dot labeled Slowpoke and a dot labeled Supertech. Each dot represents both the expected return and the standard deviation for an individual security. As can be seen, Supertech has both a higher expected return and a higher standard deviation.

The box or "☐" in the graph represents a portfolio with 60 percent invested in Supertech and 40 percent invested in Slowpoke. You will recall that we previously calculated both the expected return and the standard deviation for this portfolio.

The choice of 60 percent in Supertech and 40 percent in Slowpoke is just one of an infinite number of portfolios that can be created. The set of portfolios is sketched by the curved line in Figure 10.3.

Figure 10.2

Expected Returns and Standard Deviations for Supertech, Slowpoke, and a Portfolio Composed of 60 Percent in Supertech and 40 Percent in Slowpoke

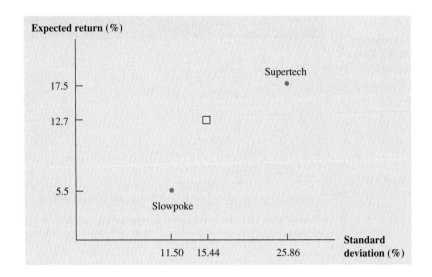

Figure 10.3

Set of Portfolios Composed of Holdings in Supertech and Slowpoke (correlation between the two securities is −0.1639)

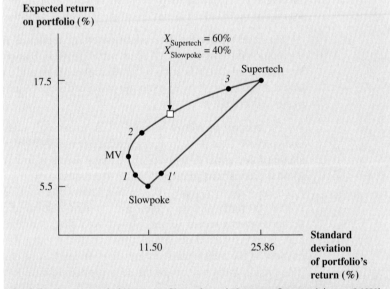

Portfolio *1* is composed of 90 percent Slowpoke and 10 percent Supertech ($\rho = -0.1639$).
Portfolio *2* is composed of 50 percent Slowpoke and 50 percent Supertech ($\rho = -0.1639$).
Portfolio *3* is composed of 10 percent Slowpoke and 90 percent Supertech ($\rho = -0.1639$).
Portfolio *1'* is composed of 90 percent Slowpoke and 10 percent Supertech ($\rho = 1$).
Point **MV** denotes the minimum variance portfolio. This is the portfolio with the lowest possible variance. By definition, the same portfolio must also have the lowest possible standard deviation.

Consider portfolio *1*. This is a portfolio composed of 90 percent Slowpoke and 10 percent Supertech. Because it is weighted so heavily toward Slowpoke, it appears close to the Slowpoke point on the graph. Portfolio *2* is higher on the curve because it is composed of 50 percent Slowpoke and 50 percent Supertech. Portfolio *3* is close to the Supertech point on the graph because it is composed of 90 percent Supertech and 10 percent Slowpoke.

There are a few important points concerning this graph:

1. We argued that the diversification effect occurs whenever the correlation between the two securities is below 1. The correlation between Supertech and Slowpoke is −0.1639. The diversification effect can be illustrated by comparison with the straight line between the Supertech point and the Slowpoke point. The straight line represents points that would have been generated had the correlation coefficient between the two securities been 1. The diversification effect is illustrated in the figure because the curved line is always to the left of the straight line. Consider point *1'*. This represents a portfolio composed of 90 percent in Slowpoke and 10 percent in Supertech *if* the correlation between the two were exactly 1. We argue that there is no diversification effect if $\rho = 1$. However, the diversification effect applies to the curved line because point *1* has the same expected return as point *1'* but has a lower standard deviation. (Points *2'* and *3'* are omitted to reduce the clutter of Figure 10.3.)

   Though the straight line and the curved line are both represented in Figure 10.3, they do not simultaneously exist in the same world. *Either* $\rho = -0.1639$ and the curve exists *or* $\rho = 1$ and the straight line exists. In other words, though an investor can choose between different points on the curve if $\rho = -0.1639$, she cannot choose between points on the curve and points on the straight line.

2. The point MV represents the minimum variance portfolio. This is the portfolio with the lowest possible variance. By definition, this portfolio must also have the lowest possible standard deviation. (The term *minimum variance portfolio* is standard in the literature, and we will use that term. Perhaps minimum standard deviation would actually be better because standard deviation, not variance, is measured on the horizontal axis of Figure 10.3.)

3. An individual contemplating an investment in a portfolio of Slowpoke and Supertech faces an **opportunity set** or **feasible set** represented by the curved line in Figure 10.3. That is, he can achieve any point on the curve by selecting the appropriate mix between the two securities. He cannot achieve any point above the curve because he cannot increase the return on the individual securities, decrease the standard deviations of the securities, or decrease the correlation between the two securities. Neither can he achieve points below the curve because he cannot lower the returns on the individual securities, increase the standard deviations of the securities, or increase the correlation. (Of course, he would not want to achieve points below the curve, even if he were able to do so.)

   Were he relatively tolerant of risk, he might choose portfolio *3*. (In fact, he could even choose the end point by investing all his money in Supertech.) An investor with less tolerance for risk might choose portfolio *2*. An investor wanting as little risk as possible would choose MV, the portfolio with minimum variance or minimum standard deviation.

4. Note that the curve is backward bending between the Slowpoke point and MV. This indicates that, for a portion of the feasible set, standard deviation actually decreases as we increase expected return. Students frequently ask, "How can an increase in the proportion of the risky security, Supertech, lead to a reduction in the risk of the portfolio?"

   This surprising finding is due to the diversification effect. The returns on the two securities are negatively correlated with each other. One security tends to go up when the other goes down and vice versa. Thus, an addition of a small amount of Supertech acts as a hedge to a portfolio composed only of Slowpoke. The risk of the portfolio is reduced, implying backward bending. Actually, backward bending always occurs if $\rho \le 0$. It may or may not occur when $\rho > 0$. Of course, the curve bends backward

Figure 10.4

Opportunity Sets Composed of Holdings in Supertech and Slowpoke

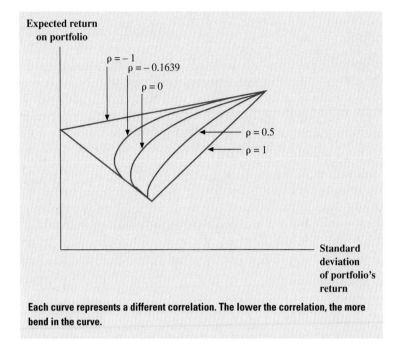

Each curve represents a different correlation. The lower the correlation, the more bend in the curve.

only for a portion of its length. As we continue to increase the percentage of Super-tech in the portfolio, the high standard deviation of this security eventually causes the standard deviation of the entire portfolio to rise.

5. No investor would want to hold a portfolio with an expected return below that of the minimum variance portfolio. For example, no investor would choose portfolio *1*. This portfolio has less expected return but more standard deviation than the minimum variance portfolio has. We say that portfolios such as portfolio *1* are *dominated* by the minimum variance portfolio. Though the entire curve from Slowpoke to Supertech is called the *feasible set*, investors consider only the curve from MV to Supertech. Hence the curve from MV to Supertech is called the **efficient set** or the **efficient frontier**.

Figure 10.3 represents the opportunity set where $\rho = -0.1639$. It is worthwhile to examine Figure 10.4, which shows different curves for different correlations. As can be seen, the lower the correlation, the more bend there is in the curve. This indicates that the diversification effect rises as ρ declines. The greatest bend occurs in the limiting case where $\rho = -1$. This is perfect negative correlation. While this extreme case where $\rho = -1$ seems to fascinate students, it has little practical importance. Most pairs of securities ex-hibit positive correlation. Strong negative correlations, let alone perfect negative correla-tion, are unlikely occurrences indeed.[5]

Note that there is only one correlation between a pair of securities. We stated ear-lier that the correlation between Slowpoke and Supertech is -0.1639. Thus, the curve in Figure 10.4 representing this correlation is the correct one, and the other curves should be viewed as merely hypothetical.

The graphs we examined are not mere intellectual curiosities. Rather, efficient sets can easily be calculated in the real world. As mentioned earlier, data on returns, standard devia-tions, and correlations are generally taken from past observations, though subjective no-tions can be used to determine the values of these parameters as well. Once the parameters

---

[5] A major exception occurs with derivative securities. For example, the correlation between a stock and a put on the stock is generally strongly negative. Puts will be treated later in the text.

Figure 10.5

Return/Risk Trade-off for World Stocks: Portfolio of U.S. and Foreign Stocks

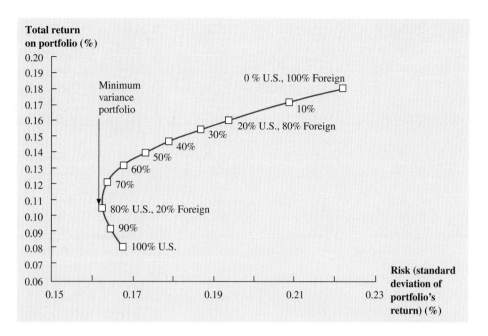

have been determined, any one of a whole host of software packages can be purchased to generate an efficient set. However, the choice of the preferred portfolio within the efficient set is up to you. As with other important decisions like what job to choose, what house or car to buy, and how much time to allocate to this course, there is no computer program to choose the preferred portfolio.

An efficient set can be generated where the two individual assets are portfolios them-selves. For example, the two assets in Figure 10.5 are a diversified portfolio of American stocks and a diversified portfolio of foreign stocks. Expected returns, standard deviations, and the correlation coefficient were calculated over the recent past. No subjectivity entered the analysis. The U.S. stock portfolio with a standard deviation of about 0.173 is less risky than the foreign stock portfolio, which has a standard deviation of about 0.222. However, combining a small percentage of the foreign stock portfolio with the U.S. portfolio actually reduces risk, as can be seen by the backward-bending nature of the curve. In other words, the diversification benefits from combining two different portfolios more than offset the intro-duction of a riskier set of stocks into our holdings. The minimum variance portfolio occurs with about 80 percent of our funds in American stocks and about 20 percent in foreign stocks. Addition of foreign securities beyond this point increases the risk of the entire portfolio.

The backward-bending curve in Figure 10.5 is important information that has not by-passed American money managers. In recent years, pension fund and mutual fund manag-ers in the United States have sought investment opportunities overseas. Another point worth pondering concerns the potential pitfalls of using only past data to estimate future returns. The stock markets of many foreign countries have had phenomenal growth in the past 25 years. Thus, a graph like Figure 10.5 makes a large investment in these foreign markets seem attractive. However, because abnormally high returns cannot be sustained forever, some subjectivity must be used in forecasting future expected returns.

10.5 The Efficient Set for Many Securities

The previous discussion concerned two securities. We found that a simple curve sketched out all the possible portfolios. Because investors generally hold more than two securities, we should look at the same graph when more than two securities are held. The shaded area in

Figure 10.6

The Feasible
Set of Portfolios
Constructed from
Many Securities

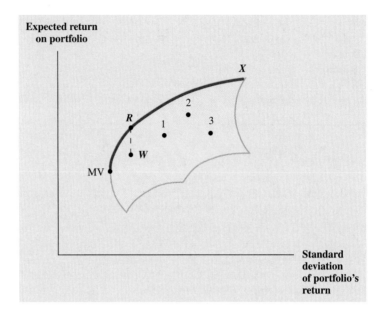

Figure 10.6 represents the opportunity set or feasible set when many securities are considered. The shaded area represents all the possible combinations of expected return and standard deviation for a portfolio. For example, in a universe of 100 securities, point 1 might represent a portfolio of, say, 40 securities. Point 2 might represent a portfolio of 80 securities. Point 3 might represent a different set of 80 securities, or the same 80 securities held in different proportions, or something else. Obviously, the combinations are virtually endless. However, note that all possible combinations fit into a confined region. No security or combination of securities can fall outside the shaded region. That is, no one can choose a portfolio with an expected return above that given by the shaded region. Furthermore, no one can choose a portfolio with a standard deviation below that given in the shaded area. Perhaps more surprisingly, no one can choose an expected return below that given in the curve. In other words, the capital markets actually prevent a self-destructive person from taking on a guaranteed loss.[6]

So far, Figure 10.6 is different from the earlier graphs. When only two securities are involved, all the combinations lie on a single curve. Conversely, with many securities the combinations cover an entire area. However, notice that an individual will want to be somewhere on the upper edge between MV and X. The upper edge, which we indicate in Figure 10.6 by a thick curve, is called the *efficient set*. Any point below the efficient set would receive less expected return and the same standard deviation as a point on the efficient set. For example, consider R on the efficient set and W directly below it. If W contains the risk level you desire, you should choose R instead to receive a higher expected return.

In the final analysis, Figure 10.6 is quite similar to Figure 10.3. The efficient set in Figure 10.3 runs from MV to Supertech. It contains various combinations of the securities Supertech and Slowpoke. The efficient set in Figure 10.6 runs from MV to X. It contains various combinations of many securities. The fact that a whole shaded area appears in Figure 10.6 but not in Figure 10.3 is just not an important difference; no investor would choose any point below the efficient set in Figure 10.6 anyway.

We mentioned before that an efficient set for two securities can be traced out easily in the real world. The task becomes more difficult when additional securities are included

---

[6]Of course, someone dead set on parting with his money can do so. For example, he can trade frequently without purpose, so that commissions more than offset the positive expected returns on the portfolio.

Table 10.4

Matrix Used to Calculate the Variance of a Portfolio

Stock	1	2	3	...	N
1	$X_1^2\sigma_1^2$	$X_1X_2\text{Cov}(R_1,R_2)$	$X_1X_3\text{Cov}(R_1,R_3)$		$X_1X_N\text{Cov}(R_1,R_N)$
2	$X_2X_1\text{Cov}(R_2,R_1)$	$X_2^2\sigma_2^2$	$X_2X_3\text{Cov}(R_2,R_3)$		$X_2X_N\text{Cov}(R_2,R_N)$
3	$X_3X_1\text{Cov}(R_3,R_1)$	$X_3X_2\text{Cov}(R_3,R_2)$	$X_3^2\sigma_3^2$		$X_3X_N\text{Cov}(R_3,R_N)$
.					
.					
.					
N	$X_NX_1\text{Cov}(R_N,R_1)$	$X_NX_2\text{Cov}(R_N,R_2)$	$X_NX_3\text{Cov}(R_N,R_3)$		$X_N^2\sigma_N^2$

The variance of the portfolio is the sum of the terms in all the boxes.

σ_i is the standard deviation of stock i.

$\text{Cov}(R_i, R_j)$ is the covariance between stock i and stock j.

Terms involving the standard deviation of a single security appear on the diagonal. Terms involving covariance between two securities appear off the diagonal.

because the number of observations grows. For example, using subjective analysis to estimate expected returns and standard deviations for, say, 100 or 500 securities may very well become overwhelming, and the difficulties with correlations may be greater still. There are almost 5,000 correlations between pairs of securities from a universe of 100 securities.

Though much of the mathematics of efficient set computation had been derived in the 1950s,[7] the high cost of computer time restricted application of the principles. In recent years this cost has been drastically reduced. A number of software packages allow the calculation of an efficient set for portfolios of moderate size. By all accounts these packages sell quite briskly, so our discussion would appear to be important in practice.

Variance and Standard Deviation in a Portfolio of Many Assets

We earlier calculated the formulas for variance and standard deviation in the two-asset case. Because we considered a portfolio of many assets in Figure 10.6, it is worthwhile to calculate the formulas for variance and standard deviation in the many-asset case. The formula for the variance of a portfolio of many assets can be viewed as an extension of the formula for the variance of two assets.

To develop the formula, we employ the same type of matrix that we used in the two-asset case. This matrix is displayed in Table 10.4. Assuming that there are N assets, we write the numbers 1 through N on the horizontal axis and 1 through N on the vertical axis. This creates a matrix of $N \times N = N^2$ boxes. The variance of the portfolio is the sum of the terms in all the boxes.

Consider, for example, the box in the second row and the third column. The term in the box is $X_2X_3\,\text{Cov}(R_2,R_3)$. X_2 and X_3 are the percentages of the entire portfolio that are invested in the second asset and the third asset, respectively. For example, if an individual with a portfolio of \$1,000 invests \$100 in the second asset, $X_2 = 10\%$ (=\$100/\$1,000). $\text{Cov}(R_3,R_2)$ is the covariance between the returns on the third asset and the returns on the second asset. Next, note the box in the third row and the second column. The term in this box is $X_3X_2\,\text{Cov}(R_3,R_2)$. Because $\text{Cov}(R_3,R_2) = \text{Cov}(R_2,R_3)$, both boxes have the same value. The second security and the third security make up one pair of stocks. In fact, every pair of stocks appears twice in the table: once in the lower left side and once in the upper right side.

Now consider boxes on the diagonal. For example, the term in the first box on the diagonal is $X_1^2\sigma_1^2$. Here, σ_1^2 is the variance of the return on the first security.

---

[7]The classic treatise is Harry Markowitz, *Portfolio Selection* (New York: John Wiley & Sons, 1959). Markowitz won the Nobel Prize in economics in 1990 for his work on modern portfolio theory.

Table 10.5

Number of Variance and Covariance Terms as a Function of the Number of Stocks in the Portfolio

Number of Stocks in Portfolio	Total Number of Terms	Number of Variance Terms (number of terms on diagonal)	Number of Covariance Terms (number of terms off diagonal)
1	1	1	0
2	4	2	2
3	9	3	6
10	100	10	90
100	10,000	100	9,900
.	.	.	.
.	.	.	.
.	.	.	.
N	N^2	N	$N^2 - N$

In a large portfolio, the number of terms involving covariance between two securities is much greater than the number of terms involving variance of a single security.

Thus, the diagonal terms in the matrix contain the variances of the different stocks. The off-diagonal terms contain the covariances. Table 10.5 relates the numbers of diagonal and off-diagonal elements to the size of the matrix. The number of diagonal terms (number of variance terms) is always the same as the number of stocks in the portfolio. The number of off-diagonal terms (number of covariance terms) rises much faster than the number of diagonal terms. For example, a portfolio of 100 stocks has 9,900 covariance terms. Because the variance of a portfolio's return is the sum of all the boxes, we have the following:

The variance of the return on a portfolio with many securities is more dependent on the covariances between the individual securities than on the variances of the individual securities.

To give a recent example of the impact of diversification, the Dow Jones Industrial Average (DJIA), which contains 30 large, well-known U.S. stocks, was about flat in 2005, meaning no gain or loss. As we saw in our previous chapter, this performance represents a fairly bad year for a portfolio of large-cap stocks. The biggest individual gainers for the year were Hewlett Packard (up 37 percent). Boeing (up 36 percent), and Altria Group (up 22 percent). However, offsetting these nice gains were General Motors (down 52 percent), Verizon Communications (down 26 percent), and IBM (down 17 percent). So, there were big winners and big losers, and they more or less offset in this particular year.

10.6　Diversification: An Example

The preceding point can be illustrated by altering the matrix in Table 10.4 slightly. Suppose we make the following three assumptions:

1. All securities possess the same variance, which we write as $\overline{var}$. In other words, $\sigma_i^2 = \overline{var}$ for every security.

2. All covariances in Table 10.4 are the same. We represent this uniform covariance as $\overline{cov}$. In other words. $Cov(R_i, R_j) = \overline{cov}$ for every pair of securities. It can easily be shown that $\overline{var} > \overline{cov}$.

3. All securities are equally weighted in the portfolio. Because there are N assets, the weight of each asset in the portfolio is $1/N$. In other words, $X_i = 1/N$ for each security i.

Table 10.6   **Matrix Used to Calculate the Variance of a Portfolio When (a) All Securities Possess the Same Variance, Which We Represent as $\overline{\text{var}}$; (b) All Pairs of Securities Possess the Same Covariance, Which We Represent as $\overline{\text{cov}}$; (c) All Securities Are Held in the Same Proportion, Which Is $1/N$**

Stock	*1*	*2*	*3*	...	*N*
1	$(1/N^2)\,\overline{\text{var}}$	$(1/N^2)\,\overline{\text{cov}}$	$(1/N^2)\,\overline{\text{cov}}$		$(1/N^2)\,\overline{\text{cov}}$
2	$(1/N^2)\,\overline{\text{cov}}$	$(1/N^2)\,\overline{\text{var}}$	$(1/N^2)\,\overline{\text{cov}}$		$(1/N^2)\,\overline{\text{cov}}$
3	$(1/N^2)\,\overline{\text{cov}}$	$(1/N^2)\,\overline{\text{cov}}$	$(1/N^2)\,\overline{\text{var}}$		$(1/N^2)\,\overline{\text{cov}}$
.					
.					
.					
N	$(1/N^2)\,\overline{\text{cov}}$	$(1/N^2)\,\overline{\text{cov}}$	$(1/N^2)\,\overline{\text{cov}}$		$(1/N^2)\,\overline{\text{var}}$

Table 10.6 is the matrix of variances and covariances under these three simplifying assumptions. Note that all of the diagonal terms are identical. Similarly, all of the off-diagonal terms are identical. As with Table 10.4, the variance of the portfolio is the sum of the terms in the boxes in Table 10.6. We know that there are N diagonal terms involving variance. Similarly, there are $N \times (N - 1)$ off-diagonal terms involving covariance. Summing across all the boxes in Table 10.6, we can express the variance of the portfolio as:

$$\text{Variance of portfolio} = \underset{\substack{\text{Number of}\\ \text{diagonal}\\ \text{terms}}}{N} \times \underset{\substack{\text{Each}\\ \text{diagonal}\\ \text{term}}}{\left(\frac{1}{N^2}\right)\overline{\text{var}}} + \underset{\substack{\text{Number of}\\ \text{off-diagonal}\\ \text{terms}}}{N(N-1)} \times \underset{\substack{\text{Each}\\ \text{off-diagonal}\\ \text{term}}}{\left(\frac{1}{N^2}\right)\overline{\text{cov}}} \quad \textbf{(10.10)}$$

$$= \left(\frac{1}{N}\right)\overline{\text{var}} + \left(\frac{N^2 - N}{N^2}\right)\overline{\text{cov}}$$

$$= \left(\frac{1}{N}\right)\overline{\text{var}} + \left(1 - \frac{1}{N}\right)\overline{\text{cov}}$$

Equation 10.10 expresses the variance of our special portfolio as a weighted sum of the average security variance and the average covariance.[8]

Now, let's increase the number of securities in the portfolio without limit. The variance of the portfolio becomes:

$$\text{Variance of portfolio (when } N \to \infty) = \overline{\text{cov}} \quad \textbf{(10.11)}$$

This occurs because (1) the weight on the variance term, $1/N$, goes to 0 as N goes to infinity, and (2) the weight on the covariance term, $1 - 1/N$, goes to 1 as N goes to infinity.

Equation 10.11 provides an interesting and important result. In our special portfolio, the variances of the individual securities completely vanish as the number of securities becomes large. However, the covariance terms remain. In fact, the variance of the portfolio becomes the average covariance, $\overline{\text{cov}}$. We often hear that we should diversify. In other words, we should not put all our eggs in one basket. The effect of diversification on the risk of a portfolio can be illustrated in this example. The variances of the individual securities are diversified away, but the covariance terms cannot be diversified away.

---

[8] Equation 10.10 is actually a weighted *average* of the variance and covariance terms because the weights, $1/N$ and $1 - 1/N$, sum to 1.

Figure 10.7

Relationship between
the Variance of a
Portfolio's Return
and the Number of
Securities in the
Portfolio*

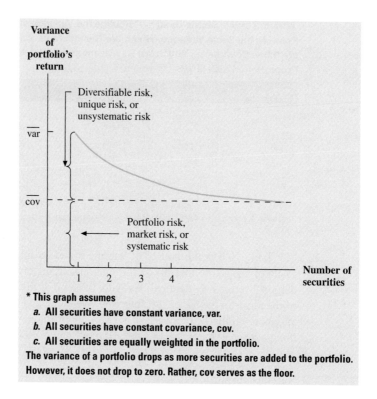

* **This graph assumes**
    a. **All securities have constant variance, var.**
    b. **All securities have constant covariance, cov.**
    c. **All securities are equally weighted in the portfolio.**
The variance of a portfolio drops as more securities are added to the portfolio.
However, it does not drop to zero. Rather, cov serves as the floor.

The fact that part, but not all, of our risk can be diversified away should be explored. Consider Mr. Smith, who brings $1,000 to the roulette table at a casino. It would be very risky if he put all his money on one spin of the wheel. For example, imagine that he put the full $1,000 on red at the table. If the wheel showed red, he would get $2,000; but if the wheel showed black, he would lose everything. Suppose instead he divided his money over 1,000 different spins by betting $1 at a time on red. Probability theory tells us that he could count on winning about 50 percent of the time. This means he could count on pretty nearly getting all his original $1,000 back.[9] In other words, risk is essentially eliminated with 1,000 different spins.

Now, let's contrast this with our stock market example, which we illustrate in Figure 10.7. The variance of the portfolio with only one security is, of course, $\overline{var}$ because the variance of a portfolio with one security is the variance of the security. The variance of the portfolio drops as more securities are added, which is evidence of the diversification effect. However, unlike Mr. Smith's roulette example, the portfolio's variance can never drop to zero. Rather it reaches a floor of $\overline{cov}$, which is the covariance of each pair of securities.[10]

Because the variance of the portfolio asymptotically approaches $\overline{cov}$, each additional security continues to reduce risk. Thus, if there were neither commissions nor other transactions costs, it could be argued that we can never achieve too much diversification. However, there is a cost to diversification in the real world. Commissions per dollar invested fall as we make larger purchases in a single stock. Unfortunately, we must buy fewer shares of each security when buying more and more different securities. Comparing the costs

---

[9]This example ignores the casino's cut.

[10]Though it is harder to show, this risk reduction effect also applies to the general case where variances and covariances are *not* equal.

and benefits of diversification, Meir Statman argues that a portfolio of about 30 stocks is needed to achieve optimal diversification.[11]

We mentioned earlier that $\overline{\text{var}}$ must be greater than $\overline{\text{cov}}$. Thus, the variance of a security's return can be broken down in the following way:

$$
\begin{array}{ccc}
\text{Total risk of} & & \text{Unsystematic or} \\
\text{individual security} & = \quad \text{Portfolio risk} \quad + & \text{diversifiable risk} \\
(\overline{\text{var}}) & (\overline{\text{cov}}) & (\overline{\text{var}} - \overline{\text{cov}})
\end{array}
$$

Total risk, which is $\overline{\text{var}}$ in our example, is the risk we bear by holding onto one security only. *Portfolio risk* is the risk we still bear after achieving full diversification, which is $\overline{\text{cov}}$ in our example. Portfolio risk is often called **systematic** or **market risk** as well. **Diversifiable**, **unique**, or **unsystematic risk** is the risk that can be diversified away in a large portfolio, which must be ($\overline{\text{var}} - \overline{\text{cov}}$) by definition.

To an individual who selects a diversified portfolio, the total risk of an individual security is not important. When considering adding a security to a diversified portfolio, the individual cares about only that portion of the risk of a security that cannot be diversified away. This risk can alternatively be viewed as the *contribution* of a security to the risk of an entire portfolio. We will talk later about the case where securities make different contributions to the risk of the entire portfolio.

Risk and the Sensible Investor

Having gone to all this trouble to show that unsystematic risk disappears in a well-diversified portfolio, how do we know that investors even want such portfolios? What if they like risk and don't want it to disappear?

We must admit that, theoretically at least, this is possible, but we will argue that it does not describe what we think of as the typical investor. Our typical investor is **risk-averse**. Risk-averse behavior can be defined in many ways, but we prefer the following example: A fair gamble is one with zero expected return; a risk-averse investor would prefer to avoid fair gambles.

Why do investors choose well-diversified portfolios? Our answer is that they are risk-averse, and risk-averse people avoid unnecessary risk, such as the unsystematic risk on a stock. If you do not think this is much of an answer, consider whether you would take on such a risk. For example, suppose you had worked all summer and had saved $5,000, which you intended to use for your college expenses. Now, suppose someone came up to you and offered to flip a coin for the money: heads, you would double your money, and tails, you would lose it all.

Would you take such a bet? Perhaps you would, but most people would not. Leaving aside any moral question that might surround gambling and recognizing that some people would take such a bet, it's our view that the average investor would not.

To induce the typical risk-averse investor to take a fair gamble, you must sweeten the pot. For example, you might need to raise the odds of winning from 50–50 to 70–30 or higher. The risk-averse investor can be induced to take fair gambles only if they are sweetened so that they become unfair to the investor's advantage.

10.7   Riskless Borrowing and Lending

Figure 10.6 assumes that all the securities in the efficient set are risky. Alternatively, an investor could combine a risky investment with an investment in a riskless or *risk-free* security, such as an investment in U.S. Treasury bills. This is illustrated in the following example.

---

[11]Meir Statman, "How Many Stocks Make a Diversified Portfolio?" *Journal of Financial and Quantitative Analysis* (September 1987).

EXAMPLE 10.3

Riskless Lending and Portfolio Risk   Ms. Bagwell is considering investing in the common stock of Merville Enterprises. In addition, Ms. Bagwell will either borrow or lend at the risk-free rate. The relevant parameters are these:

	Common Stock of Merville	Risk-Free Asset
Expected return	14%	10%
Standard deviation	0.20	0

Suppose Ms. Bagwell chooses to invest a total of $1,000, $350 of which is to be invested in Merville Enterprises and $650 placed in the risk-free asset. The expected return on her total investment is simply a weighted average of the two returns:

$$\text{Expected return on portfolio composed of one riskless and one risky asset} = 0.114 = (0.35 \times 0.14) + (0.65 \times 0.10) \quad \textbf{(10.12)}$$

Because the expected return on the portfolio is a weighted average of the expected return on the risky asset (Merville Enterprises) and the risk-free return, the calculation is analogous to the way we treated two risky assets. In other words, Equation 10.3 applies here.

Using Equation 10.4, the formula for the variance of the portfolio can be written as:

$$X^2_{\text{Merville}} \sigma^2_{\text{Merville}} + 2X_{\text{Merville}} X_{\text{Risk-free}} \sigma_{\text{Merville, Risk-free}} + X^2_{\text{Risk-free}} \sigma^2_{\text{Risk-free}}$$

However, by definition, the risk-free asset has no variability. Thus both $\sigma_{\text{Merville, Risk-free}}$ and $\sigma^2_{\text{Risk-free}}$ are equal to zero, reducing the above expression to:

$$\text{Variance of portfolio composed of one riskless and one risky asset} = X^2_{\text{Merville}} \sigma^2_{\text{Merville}} \quad \textbf{(10.13)}$$

$$= (0.35)^2 \times (0.20)^2$$
$$= 0.0049$$

The standard deviation of the portfolio is:

$$\text{Standard deviation of portfolio composed of one riskless and one risky asset} = X_{\text{Merville}} \sigma_{\text{Merville}} \quad \textbf{(10.14)}$$

$$= 0.35 \times 0.20$$
$$= 0.07$$

The relationship between risk and expected return for one risky and one riskless asset can be seen in Figure 10.8. Ms. Bagwell's split of 35–65 percent between the two assets is represented on a *straight* line between the risk-free rate and a pure investment in Merville Enterprises. Note that, unlike the case of two risky assets, the opportunity set is straight, not curved.

Suppose that, alternatively, Ms. Bagwell borrows $200 at the risk-free rate. Combining this with her original sum of $1,000, she invests a total of $1,200 in Merville. Her expected return would be:

$$\text{Expected return on portfolio formed by borrowing to invest in risky asset} = 14.8\% = 1.20 \times 0.14 + (-0.2 \times 0.10)$$

Here, she invests 120 percent of her original investment of $1,000 by borrowing 20 percent of her original investment. Note that the return of 14.8 percent is greater than the 14 percent expected return on Merville Enterprises. This occurs because she is borrowing at 10 percent to invest in a security with an expected return greater than 10 percent.

(continued)

Figure 10.8 Relationship between Expected Return and Risk for a Portfolio of One Risky Asset and One Riskless Asset

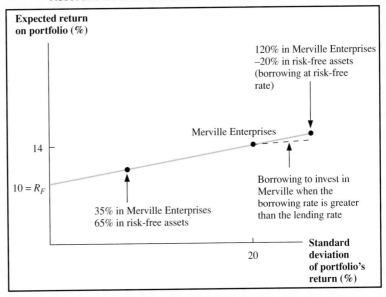

The standard deviation is:

$$\text{Standard deviation of portfolio formed by borrowing to invest in risky asset} = 0.24 = 1.20 \times 0.2$$

The standard deviation of 0.24 is greater than 0.20, the standard deviation of the Merville investment, because borrowing increases the variability of the investment. This investment also appears in Figure 10.8.

So far, we have assumed that Ms. Bagwell is able to borrow at the same rate at which she can lend.[12] Now let us consider the case where the borrowing rate is above the lending rate. The dotted line in Figure 10.8 illustrates the opportunity set for borrowing opportunities in this case. The dotted line is below the solid line because a higher borrowing rate lowers the expected return on the investment.

The Optimal Portfolio

The previous section concerned a portfolio formed between one riskless asset and one risky asset. In reality, an investor is likely to combine an investment in the riskless asset with a *portfolio* of risky assets. This is illustrated in Figure 10.9.

Consider point Q, representing a portfolio of securities. Point Q is in the interior of the feasible set of risky securities. Let us assume the point represents a portfolio of 30 percent in AT&T, 45 percent in General Motors (GM), and 25 percent in IBM. Individuals combining investments in Q with investments in the riskless asset would achieve points along the straight line from R_F to Q. We refer to this as line I. For example, point I on the line represents a portfolio of 70 percent in the riskless asset and 30 percent in stocks represented by Q. An investor with $100 choosing point I as his portfolio would put $70 in

---

[12] Surprisingly, this appears to be a decent approximation because many investors can borrow from a stockbroker (called *going on margin*) when purchasing stocks. The borrowing rate here is very near the riskless rate of interest, particularly for large investors. More will be said about this in a later chapter.

Figure 10.9

Relationship between Expected Return and Standard Deviation for an Investment in a Combination of Risky Securities and the Riskless Asset

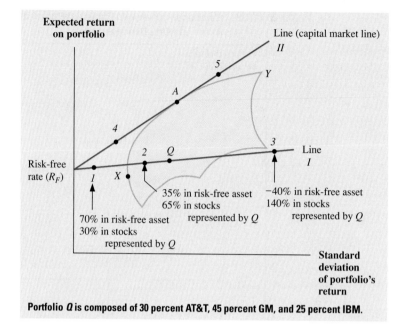

Portfolio *Q* is composed of 30 percent AT&T, 45 percent GM, and 25 percent IBM.

the risk-free asset and $30 in Q. This can be restated as $70 in the riskless asset, $9 ($=0.3 \times$ 30) in AT&T, $13.50 ($=0.45 \times 30) in GM, and $7.50 ($=0.25 \times 30) in IBM. Point *2* also represents a portfolio of the risk-free asset and Q, with more (65%) being invested in Q.

Point *3* is obtained by borrowing to invest in Q. For example, an investor with $100 of her own would borrow $40 from the bank or broker to invest $140 in Q. This can be stated as borrowing $40 and contributing $100 of her money to invest $42 ($=0.3 \times 140) in AT&T, $63 ($=0.45 \times 140) in GM, and $35 ($=0.25 \times 140) in IBM.

These investments can be summarized as follows:

	Point Q	Point *I* (Lending $70)	Point 3 (Borrowing $40)
AT&T	$ 30	$ 9	$ 42
GM	45	13.50	63
IBM	25	7.50	35
Risk-free	0	70.00	−40
Total investment	$100	$100	$100

Though any investor can obtain any point on line *I*, no point on the line is optimal. To see this, consider line *II*, a line running from R_F through *A*. Point *A* represents a portfolio of risky securities. Line *II* represents portfolios formed by combinations of the risk-free asset and the securities in *A*. Points between R_F and *A* are portfolios in which some money is invested in the riskless asset and the rest is placed in *A*. Points past *A* are achieved by borrowing at the riskless rate to buy more of *A* than we could with our original funds alone.

As drawn, line *II* is tangent to the efficient set of risky securities. Whatever point an individual can obtain on line *I*, he can obtain a point with the same standard deviation and a higher expected return on line *II*. In fact, because line *II* is tangent to the efficient set of risky assets, it provides the investor with the best possible opportunities. In other words, line *II* can be viewed as the efficient set of *all* assets, both risky and riskless. An investor with a fair degree of risk aversion might choose a point between R_F and A, perhaps point *4*. An individual with less risk aversion might choose a point closer to A or even beyond A. For example, point *5* corresponds to an individual borrowing money to increase investment in A.

The graph illustrates an important point. With riskless borrowing and lending, the portfolio of *risky* assets held by any investor would always be point A. Regardless of the investor's tolerance for risk, she would never choose any other point on the efficient set of risky assets (represented by curve XAY) nor any point in the interior of the feasible region. Rather, she would combine the securities of A with the riskless assets if she had high aversion to risk. She would borrow the riskless asset to invest more funds in A had she low aversion to risk.

This result establishes what financial economists call the **separation principle**. That is, the investor's investment decision consists of two separate steps:

1. After estimating (*a*) the expected returns and variances of individual securities, and (*b*) the covariances between pairs of securities, the investor calculates the efficient set of risky assets, represented by curve XAY in Figure 10.9. He then determines point A, the tangency between the risk-free rate and the efficient set of risky assets (curve XAY). Point A represents the portfolio of risky assets that the investor will hold. This point is determined solely from his estimates of returns, variances, and covariances. No personal characteristics, such as degree of risk aversion, are needed in this step.

2. The investor must now determine how he will combine point A, his portfolio of risky assets, with the riskless asset. He might invest some of his funds in the riskless asset and some in portfolio A. He would end up at a point on the line between R_F and A in this case. Alternatively, he might borrow at the risk-free rate and contribute some of his own funds as well, investing the sum in portfolio A. He would end up at a point on line *II* beyond A. His position in the riskless asset—that is, his choice of where on the line he wants to be—is determined by his internal characteristics, such as his ability to tolerate risk.

10.8   Market Equilibrium

Definition of the Market Equilibrium Portfolio

The preceding analysis concerns one investor. His estimates of the expected returns and variances for individual securities and the covariances between pairs of securities are his and his alone. Other investors would obviously have different estimates of these variables. However, the estimates might not vary much because all investors would be forming expectations from the same data about past price movements and other publicly available information.

Financial economists often imagine a world where all investors possess the *same* estimates of expected returns, variances, and covariances. Though this can never be literally true, it can be thought of as a useful simplifying assumption in a world where investors have access to similar sources of information. This assumption is called **homogeneous expectations**.[13]

If all investors had homogeneous expectations, Figure 10.9 would be the same for all individuals. That is, all investors would sketch out the same efficient set of risky assets because they would be working with the same inputs. This efficient set of risky assets is

---

[13]The assumption of homogeneous expectations states that all investors have the same beliefs concerning returns, variances, and covariances. It does not say that all investors have the same aversion to risk.

represented by the curve *XAY*. Because the same risk-free rate would apply to everyone, all investors would view point *A* as the portfolio of risky assets to be held.

This point *A* takes on great importance because all investors would purchase the risky securities that it represents. Investors with a high degree of risk aversion might combine *A* with an investment in the riskless asset, achieving point *4*, for example. Others with low aversion to risk might borrow to achieve, say, point *5*. Because this is a very important conclusion, we restate it:

In a world with homogeneous expectations, all investors would hold the portfolio of risky assets represented by point *A*.

If all investors choose the same portfolio of risky assets, it is possible to determine what that portfolio is. Common sense tells us that it is a market value weighted portfolio of all existing securities. It is the **market portfolio**.

In practice, economists use a broad-based index such as the Standard & Poor's (S&P) 500 as a proxy for the market portfolio. Of course all investors do not hold the same portfolio in practice. However, we know that many investors hold diversified portfolios, particularly when mutual funds or pension funds are included. A broad-based index is a good proxy for the highly diversified portfolios of many investors.

Definition of Risk When Investors Hold the Market Portfolio

The previous section states that many investors hold diversified portfolios similar to broad-based indexes. This result allows us to be more precise about the risk of a security in the context of a diversified portfolio.

Researchers have shown that the best measure of the risk of a security in a large portfolio is the *beta* of the security. We illustrate beta by an example.

EXAMPLE 10.4

Beta   Consider the following possible returns both on the stock of Jelco, Inc., and on the market:

State	Type of Economy	Return on Market (percent)	Return on Jelco, Inc. (percent)
I	Bull	15	25
II	Bull	15	15
III	Bear	−5	−5
IV	Bear	−5	−15

Though the return on the market has only two possible outcomes (15% and −5%), the return on Jelco has four possible outcomes. It is helpful to consider the expected return on a security for a given return on the market. Assuming each state is equally likely, we have:

Type of Economy	Return on Market (percent)	Expected Return on Jelco, Inc. (percent)
Bull	15%	$20\% = 25\% \times \frac{1}{2} + 15\% \times \frac{1}{2}$
Bear	−5%	$-10\% = -5\% \times \frac{1}{2} + (-15\%) \times \frac{1}{2}$

(continued)

Figure 10.10   Performance of Jelco, Inc., and the Market Portfolio

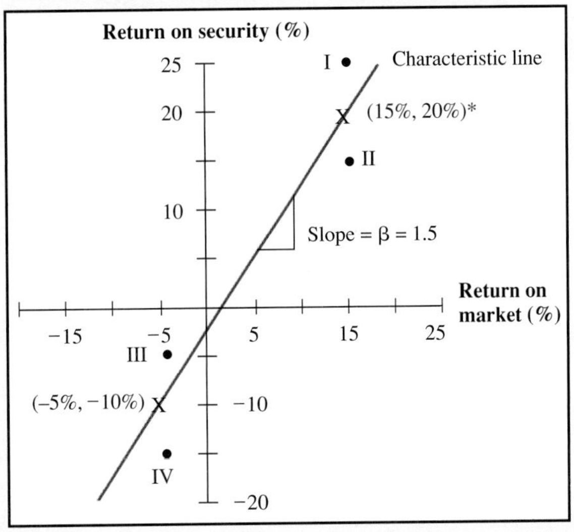

The two points marked X represent the expected return on Jelco for each possible outcome of the market portfolio. The expected return on Jelco is positively related to the return on the market. Because the slop is 1.5, we say that Jelco's beta is 1.5. Beta measures the responsiveness of the security's return to movement in the market.

* (15%, 20%) refers to the point where the return on the market is 15 percent and the return on the security is 20 percent.

Jelco, Inc., responds to market movements because its expected return is greater in bullish states than in bearish states. We now calculate exactly how responsive the security is to market movements. The market's return in a bullish economy is 20 percent [= 15% − (−5%)] greater than the market's return in a bearish economy. However, the expected return on Jelco in a bullish economy is 30 percent [= 20% − (−10%)] greater than its expected return in a bearish state. Thus Jelco, Inc., has a responsiveness coefficient of 1.5 (= 30%/20%).

This relationship appears in Figure 10.10. The returns for both Jelco and the market in each state are plotted as four points. In addition, we plot the expected return on the security for each of the two possible returns on the market. These two points, each of which we designate by an X, are joined by a line called the **characteristic line** of the security. The slope of the line is 1.5, the number calculated in the previous paragraph. This responsiveness coefficient of 1.5 is the **beta** of Jelco.

The interpretation of beta from Figure 10.10 is intuitive. The graph tells us that the returns of Jelco are magnified 1.5 times over those of the market. When the market does well, Jelco's stock is expected to do even better. When the market does poorly, Jelco's stock is expected to do even worse. Now imagine an individual with a portfolio near that of the market who is considering the addition of Jelco to her portfolio. Because of Jelco's *magnification factor* of 1.5, she will view this stock as contributing much to the risk of the portfolio. (We will show shortly that the beta of the average security in the market is 1.) Jelco contributes more to the risk of a large, diversified portfolio than does an average security because Jelco is more responsive to movements in the market.

Further insight can be gleaned by examining securities with negative betas. One should view these securities as either hedges or insurance policies. The security is expected to do well when the market does poorly and vice versa. Because of this, adding a negative-beta security to a large, diversified portfolio actually reduces the risk of the portfolio.[14]

---

[14]Unfortunately, empirical evidence shows that virtually no stocks have negative betas.

Table 10.7

Estimates of Beta for Selected Individual Stocks

Stock	Beta
McGraw-Hill Co.	.52
3M	.66
General Electric	.83
Bed, Bath & Beyond	.98
Dell	1.22
Home Depot	1.44
eBay	2.06
Computer Associates	2.58

The beta is defined as $\text{Cov}(R_i, R_M)/\text{Var}(R_M)$, where $\text{Cov}(R_i, R_M)$ is the covariance of the return on an individual stock, R_i, and the return on the market, R_M. $\text{Var}(R_M)$ is the variance of the return on the market, R_M.

Table 10.7 presents empirical estimates of betas for individual securities. As can be seen, some securities are more responsive to the market than others. For example, eBay has a beta of 2.06. This means that for every 1 percent movement in the market,[15] eBay is expected to move 2.06 percent in the same direction. Conversely, General Electric has a beta of only 0.83. This means that for every 1 percent movement in the market, General Electric is expected to move 0.83 percent in the same direction.

We can summarize our discussion of beta by saying this:

Beta measures the responsiveness of a security to movements in the market portfolio.

The Formula for Beta

Our discussion so far has stressed the intuition behind beta. The actual definition of beta is:

$$\beta_i = \frac{\text{Cov}(R_i, R_M)}{\sigma^2(R_M)} \qquad (10.15)$$

where $\text{Cov}(R_i, R_M)$ is the covariance between the return on asset i and the return on the market portfolio and $\sigma^2(R_M)$ is the variance of the market.

One useful property is that the average beta across all securities, when weighted by the proportion of each security's market value to that of the market portfolio, is 1. That is:

$$\sum_{i=1}^{N} X_i \beta_i = 1 \qquad (10.16)$$

where X_i is the proportion of security i's market value to that of the entire market and N is the number of securities in the market.

Equation 10.16 is intuitive, once you think about it. If you weight all securities by their market values, the resulting portfolio is the market. By definition, the beta of the market portfolio is 1. That is, for every 1 percent movement in the market, the market must move 1 percent—*by definition*.

A Test

We have put these questions on past corporate finance examinations:

1. What sort of investor rationally views the variance (or standard deviation) of an individual security's return as the security's proper measure of risk?

2. What sort of investor rationally views the beta of a security as the security's proper measure of risk?

---

[15] In Table 10.7, we use the Standard & Poor's 500 Index as a proxy for the market portfolio.

A good answer might be something like the following:

> A rational, risk-averse investor views the variance (or standard deviation) of her portfolio's return as the proper measure of the risk of her portfolio. If for some reason the investor can hold only one security, the variance of that security's return becomes the variance of the portfolio's return. Hence, the variance of the security's return is the security's proper measure of risk.
>
> If an individual holds a diversified portfolio, she still views the variance (or standard deviation) of her portfolio's return as the proper measure of the risk of her portfolio. However, she is no longer interested in the variance of each individual security's return. Rather, she is interested in the contribution of an individual security to the variance of the portfolio.

Under the assumption of homogeneous expectations, all individuals hold the market portfolio. Thus, we measure risk as the contribution of an individual security to the variance of the market portfolio. This contribution, when standardized properly, is the beta of the security. Although few investors hold the market portfolio exactly, many hold reasonably diversified portfolios. These portfolios are close enough to the market portfolio so that the beta of a security is likely to be a reasonable measure of its risk.

10.9   Relationship between Risk and Expected Return (CAPM)

It is commonplace to argue that the expected return on an asset should be positively related to its risk. That is, individuals will hold a risky asset only if its expected return compensates for its risk. In this section, we first estimate the expected return on the stock market as a whole. Next, we estimate expected returns on individual securities.

Expected Return on Market

Economists frequently argue that the expected return on the market can be represented as:

$$\overline{R}_M = R_F + \text{Risk premium}$$

In words, the expected return on the market is the sum of the risk-free rate plus some compensation for the risk inherent in the market portfolio. Note that the equation refers to the *expected* return on the market, not the actual return in a particular month or year. Because stocks have risk, the actual return on the market over a particular period can, of course, be below R_F or can even be negative.

Because investors want compensation for risk, the risk premium is presumably positive. But exactly how positive is it? It is generally argued that the place to start looking for the risk premium in the future is the average risk premium in the past. As reported in Chapter 9, Ibbotson and Sinquefield found that the average return on large-company common stocks was 12.3 percent over 1926–2005. The average risk-free rate over the same interval was 3.8 percent. Thus, the average difference between the two was 8.5 percent ($=12.3\% - 3.8\%$). Financial economists find this to be a useful estimate of the difference to occur in the future.

For example, if the risk-free rate, estimated by the current yield on a one-year Treasury bill, is 1 percent, the expected return on the market is:

$$9.5\% = 1\% + 8.5\%$$

Figure 10.11

Relationship between Expected Return on an individual Security and Beta of the Security

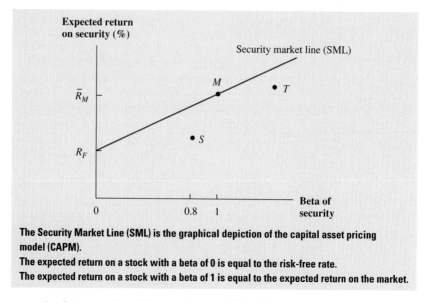

The Security Market Line (SML) is the graphical depiction of the capital asset pricing model (CAPM).
The expected return on a stock with a beta of 0 is equal to the risk-free rate.
The expected return on a stock with a beta of 1 is equal to the expected return on the market.

Of course, the future equity risk premium could be higher or lower than the historical equity risk premium. This could be true if future risk is higher or lower than past risk or if individual risk aversions are higher or lower than those of the past.

Expected Return on Individual Security

Now that we have estimated the expected return on the market as a whole, what is the expected return on an individual security? We have argued that the beta of a security is the appropriate measure of risk in a large, diversified portfolio. Because most investors are diversified, the expected return on a security should be positively related to its beta. This is illustrated in Figure 10.11.

Actually, economists can be more precise about the relationship between expected return and beta. They posit that under plausible conditions the relationship between expected return and beta can be represented by the following equation:[16]

Capital Asset Pricing Model

$$\overline{R} \quad = \quad R_F \quad + \quad \beta \quad \times \quad (\overline{R}_M - R_F) \qquad \textbf{(10.17)}$$

Expected return on a security	=	Risk-free rate	+	Beta of the security	×	Difference between expected return on market and risk-free rate

This formula, which is called the **capital asset pricing model** (or CAPM for short), implies that the expected return on a security is linearly related to its beta. Because the average return on the market has been higher than the average risk-free rate over long periods of time, $\overline{R}_M - R_F$ is presumably positive. Thus, the formula implies that the expected return on a security is *positively* related to its beta. The formula can be illustrated by assuming a few special cases:

- *Assume that* $\beta = 0$. Here $\overline{R} = R_F$—that is, the expected return on the security is equal to the risk-free rate. Because a security with zero beta has no relevant risk, its expected return should equal the risk-free rate.

---

[16]This relationship was first proposed independently by John Lintner and William F. Sharpe.

- *Assume that* $\beta = 1$. Equation 10.17 reduces to $\bar{R} = \bar{R}_M$. That is, the expected return on the security is equal to the expected return on the market. This makes sense because the beta of the market portfolio is also 1.

Equation 10.17 can be represented graphically by the upward-sloping line in Figure 10.11. Note that the line begins at R_F and rises to $\bar{R}_M$ when beta is 1. This line is frequently called the **security market line** (SML).

As with any line, the SML has both a slope and an intercept. R_F, the risk-free rate, is the intercept. Because the beta of a security is the horizontal axis, $R_M - R_F$ is the slope. The line will be upward-sloping as long as the expected return on the market is greater than the risk-free rate. Because the market portfolio is a risky asset, theory suggests that its expected return is above the risk-free rate. As mentioned, the empirical evidence of the previous chapter showed that the average return per year on the market portfolio (for large-company stocks as an example) over the past 80 years was 8.5 percent above the risk-free rate.

The stock of Aardvark Enterprises has a beta of 1.5 and that of Zebra Enterprises has a beta of 0.7. The risk-free rate is assumed to be 3 percent, and the difference between the expected return on the market and the risk-free rate is assumed to be 8.0 percent. The expected returns on the two securities are

Expected Return for Aardvark

$$15.0\% = 3\% + 1.5 \times 8.0\% \tag{10.18}$$

Expected Return for Zebra

$$8.6\% = 3\% + 0.7 \times 8.0\%$$

Three additional points concerning the CAPM should be mentioned:

1. *Linearity*: The intuition behind an upwardly sloping curve is clear. Because beta is the appropriate measure of risk, high-beta securities should have an expected return above that of low-beta securities. However, both Figure 10.11 and Equation 10.17 show something more than an upwardly sloping curve: The relationship between expected return and beta corresponds to a *straight* line.

   It is easy to show that the line of Figure 10.11 is straight. To see this, consider security S with, say, a beta of 0.8. This security is represented by a point below the security market line in the figure. Any investor could duplicate the beta of security S by buying a portfolio with 20 percent in the risk-free asset and 80 percent in a security with a beta of 1. However, the homemade portfolio would itself lie on the SML. In other words, the portfolio dominates security S because the portfolio has a higher expected return and the same beta.

   Now consider security T with, say, a beta greater than 1. This security is also below the SML in Figure 10.11. Any investor could duplicate the beta of security T by borrowing to invest in a security with a beta of 1. This portfolio must also lie on the SML, thereby dominating security T.

   Because no one would hold either S or T, their stock prices would drop. This price adjustment would raise the expected returns on the two securities. The price adjustment would continue until the two securities lay on the security market line. The preceding example considered two overpriced stocks and a straight SML. Securities lying above the SML are *underpriced*. Their prices must rise until their expected returns lie on the line. If the SML is itself curved, many stocks would be mispriced. In equilibrium, all securities would be held only when prices changed so that the SML became straight. In other words, linearity would be achieved.

2. *Portfolios as well as securities*: Our discussion of the CAPM considered individual securities. Does the relationship in Figure 10.11 and Equation 10.17 hold for portfolios as well?

Yes. To see this, consider a portfolio formed by investing equally in our two securities from Example 10.5, Aardvark and Zebra. The expected return on the portfolio is:

Expected Return on Portfolio

$$11.8\% = 0.5 \times 15.0\% + 0.5 \times 8.6\% \qquad (10.19)$$

The beta of the portfolio is simply a weighted average of the betas of the two securities. Thus, we have:

Beta of Portfolio

$$1.1 = 0.5 \times 1.5 + 0.5 \times 0.7$$

Under the CAPM, the expected return on the portfolio is

$$11.8\% = 3\% + 1.1 \times 8.0\% \qquad (10.20)$$

Because the expected return in Equation 10.19 is the same as the expected return in Equation 10.20, the example shows that the CAPM holds for portfolios as well as for individual securities.

3. *A potential confusion*: Students often confuse the SML in Figure 10.11 with line *II* in Figure 10.9. Actually, the lines are quite different. Line *II* traces the efficient set of portfolios formed from both risky assets and the riskless asset. Each point on the line represents an entire portfolio. Point *A* is a portfolio composed entirely of risky assets. Every other point on the line represents a portfolio of the securities in *A* combined with the riskless asset. The axes on Figure 10.9 are the expected return on a *portfolio* and the standard deviation of a *portfolio*. Individual securities do not lie along line *II*.

The SML in Figure 10.11 relates expected return to beta. Figure 10.11 differs from Figure 10.9 in at least two ways. First, beta appears in the horizontal axis of Figure 10.11, but standard deviation appears in the horizontal axis of Figure 10.9. Second, the SML in Figure 10.11 holds both for all individual securities and for all possible portfolios, whereas line *II* in Figure 10.9 holds only for efficient portfolios.

We stated earlier that, under homogeneous expectations, point *A* in Figure 10.9 becomes the market portfolio. In this situation, line *II* is referred to as the **capital market line** (CML).

Summary and Conclusions

This chapter set forth the fundamentals of modern portfolio theory. Our basic points are these:

1. This chapter showed us how to calculate the expected return and variance for individual securities, and the covariance and correlation for pairs of securities. Given these statistics, the expected return and variance for a portfolio of two securities *A* and *B* can be written as:

$$\text{Expected return on portfolio} = X_A \bar{R}_A + X_B \bar{R}_B$$
$$\text{Var(portfolio)} = X_A^2 \sigma_A^2 + 2 X_A X_B \sigma_{AB} + X_B^2 \sigma_B^2$$

2. In our notation, X stands for the proportion of a security in a portfolio. By varying X we can trace out the efficient set of portfolios. We graphed the efficient set for the two-asset case as a curve, pointing out that the degree of curvature or bend in the graph reflects the diversification effect: The lower the correlation between the two securities, the greater the bend. The same general shape of the efficient set holds in a world of many assets.

3. Just as the formula for variance in the two-asset case is computed from a 2×2 matrix, the variance formula is computed from an $N\times N$ matrix in the N-asset case. We showed that with a large number of assets, there are many more covariance terms than variance terms in the matrix. In fact the variance terms are effectively diversified away in a large portfolio, but the covariance terms are not. Thus, a diversified portfolio can eliminate some, but not all, of the risk of the individual securities.

4. The efficient set of risky assets can be combined with riskless borrowing and lending. In this case a rational investor will always choose to hold the portfolio of risky securities represented by point A in Figure 10.9. Then he can either borrow or lend at the riskless rate to achieve any desired point on line II in the figure.

5. The contribution of a security to the risk of a large, well-diversified portfolio is proportional to the covariance of the security's return with the market's return. This contribution, when standardized, is called the beta. The beta of a security can also be interpreted as the responsiveness of a security's return to that of the market.

6. The CAPM states that:

$$\bar{R} = R_F + \beta(\bar{R}_M - R_F)$$

In other words, the expected return on a security is positively (and linearly) related to the security's beta.

Concept Questions

1. **Diversifiable and Nondiversifiable Risks**   In broad terms, why is some risk diversifiable? Why are some risks nondiversifiable? Does it follow that an investor can control the level of unsystematic risk in a portfolio, but not the level of systematic risk?

2. **Systematic versus Unsystematic Risk**   Classify the following events as mostly systematic or mostly unsystematic. Is the distinction clear in every case?
   a. Short-term interest rates increase unexpectedly.
   b. The interest rate a company pays on its short-term debt borrowing is increased by its bank.
   c. Oil prices unexpectedly decline.
   d. An oil tanker ruptures, creating a large oil spill.
   e. A manufacturer loses a multimillion-dollar product liability suit.
   f. A Supreme Court decision substantially broadens producer liability for injuries suffered by product users.

3. **Expected Portfolio Returns**   If a portfolio has a positive investment in every asset, can the expected return on the portfolio be greater than that on every asset in the portfolio? Can it be less than that on every asset in the portfolio? If you answer yes to one or both of these questions, give an example to support your answer.

4. **Diversification**   True or false: The most important characteristic in determining the expected return of a well-diversified portfolio is the variances of the individual assets in the portfolio. Explain.

5. **Portfolio Risk**   If a portfolio has a positive investment in every asset, can the standard deviation on the portfolio be less than that on every asset in the portfolio? What about the portfolio beta?

6. **Beta and CAPM**   Is it possible that a risky asset could have a beta of zero? Explain. Based on the CAPM, what is the expected return on such an asset? Is it possible that a risky asset could have a negative beta? What does the CAPM predict about the expected return on such an asset? Can you give an explanation for your answer?

7.   **Covariance**   Briefly explain why the covariance of a security with the rest of a well-diversified portfolio is a more appropriate measure of the risk of the security than the security's variance.

8.   **Beta**   Consider the following quotation from a leading investment manager: "The shares of Southern Co. have traded close to £12 for most of the past three years. Since Southern's stock has demonstrated very little price movement, the stock has a low beta. Texas Instruments, on the other hand, has traded as high as £150 and as low as its current £75. Since TI's stock has demonstrated a large amount of price movement, the stock has a very high beta." Do you agree with this analysis? Explain.

9.   **Risk**   A broker has advised you not to invest in oil industry stocks because they have high standard deviations. Is the broker's advice sound for a risk-averse investor like yourself? Why or why not?

10.   **Security Selection**   Is the following statement true or false? A risky security cannot have an expected return that is less than the risk-free rate because no risk-averse investor would be willing to hold this asset in equilibrium. Explain.

Questions and Problems

BASIC
(Questions 1–20)

1.   **Determining Portfolio Weights**   What are the portfolio weights for a portfolio that has 70 shares of Stock *A* that sell for $40 per share and 110 shares of Stock *B* that sell for $21 per share?

2.   **Portfolio Expected Return**   You own a portfolio that has $1,200 invested in Stock *A* and $1,900 invested in Stock *B*. If the expected returns on these stocks are 10 percent and 16 percent, respectively, what is the expected return on the portfolio?

3.   **Portfolio Expected Return**   You own a portfolio that is 50 percent invested in Stock *X*, 30 percent in Stock *Y*, and 20 percent in Stock *Z*. The expected returns on these three stocks are 11 percent, 17 percent, and 14 percent, respectively. What is the expected return on the portfolio?

4.   **Portfolio Expected Return**   You have ¥1,000,000 to invest in a stock portfolio. Your choices are Stock *X* with an expected return of 14 percent and Stock *Y* with an expected return of 9 percent. If your goal is to create a portfolio with an expected return of 12.2 percent, how much money will you invest in Stock *X*? In Stock *Y*?

5.   **Calculating Expected Return**   Based on the following information, calculate the expected return:

State of Economy	Probability of State of Economy	Rate of Return If State Occurs
Recession	.20	−.05
Normal	.50	.12
Boom	.30	.25

6.   **Calculating Returns and Standard Deviations**   Based on the following information, calculate the expected return and standard deviation for the two stocks:

State of Economy	Probability of State of Economy	Rate of Return If State Occurs	
		Stock *A*	Stock *B*
Recession	.10	.06	−.20
Normal	.60	.07	.13
Boom	.30	.11	.33

7. **Calculating Returns and Standard Deviations**   Based on the following information, calculate the expected return and standard deviation:

State of Economy	Probability of State of Economy	Rate of Return If State Occurs
Depression	.10	−.045
Recession	.30	.044
Normal	.50	.120
Boom	.10	.207

8. **Calculating Expected Returns**   A portfolio is invested 20 percent in Stock *G*, 70 percent in Stock *J*, and 10 percent in Stock *K*. The expected returns on these stocks are 8 percent, 15 percent, and 24 percent, respectively. What is the portfolio's expected return? How do you interpret your answer?

9. **Returns and Standard Deviations**   Consider the following information:

State of Economy	Probability of State of Economy	Rate of Return If State Occurs		
		Stock A	Stock B	Stock C
Boom	.70	.07	.15	.33
Bust	.30	.13	.03	−.06

   a. What is the expected return on an equally weighted portfolio of these three stocks?

   b. What is the variance of a portfolio invested 20 percent each in *A* and *B*, and 60 percent in *C*?

10. **Returns and Standard Deviations**   Consider the following information:

State of Economy	Probability of State of Economy	Rate of Return If State Occurs		
		Stock A	Stock B	Stock C
Boom	.30	.30	.45	.33
Good	.40	.12	.10	.15
Poor	.25	.01	−.15	−.05
Bust	.05	−.06	−.30	−.09

   a. Your portfolio is invested 30 percent each in *A* and *C*, and 40 percent in *B*. What is the expected return of the portfolio?

   b. What is the variance of this portfolio? The standard deviation?

11. **Calculating Portfolio Betas**   You own a stock portfolio invested 25 percent in Stock *Q*, 20 percent in Stock *R*, 15 percent in Stock *S*, and 40 percent in Stock *T*. The betas for these four stocks are .6, 1.70, 1.15, and 1.90, respectively. What is the portfolio beta?

12. **Calculating Portfolio Betas**   You own a portfolio equally invested in a risk-free asset and two stocks. If one of the stocks has a beta of 1.5 and the total portfolio is equally as risky as the market, what must the beta be for the other stock in your portfolio?

13. **Using CAPM**   A stock has a beta of 1.3, the expected return on the market is 14 percent, and the risk-free rate is 4 percent. What must the expected return on this stock be?

14. **Using CAPM**   A stock has an expected return of 14 percent, the risk-free rate is 4 percent, and the market risk premium is 6 percent. What must the beta of this stock be?

15. **Using CAPM**   A stock has an expected return of 11 percent, its beta is .85, and the risk-free rate is 4.5 percent. What must the expected return on the market be?

16. **Using CAPM**   A stock has an expected return of 17 percent, a beta of 1.9, and the expected return on the market is 11 percent. What must the risk-free rate be?

17. **Using CAPM**   A stock has a beta of 1.2 and an expected return of 16 percent. A risk-free asset currently earns 5 percent.
    a. What is the expected return on a portfolio that is equally invested in the two assets?
    b. If a portfolio of the two assets has a beta of .75, what are the portfolio weights?
    c. If a portfolio of the two assets has an expected return of 8 percent, what is its beta?
    d. If a portfolio of the two assets has a beta of 2.3, what are the portfolio weights? How do you interpret the weights for the two assets in this case? Explain.

 18. **Using the SML**   Asset *W* has an expected return of 16 percent and a beta of 1.3. If the risk-free rate is 5 percent, complete the following table for portfolios of Asset *W* and a risk-free asset. Illustrate the relationship between portfolio expected return and portfolio beta by plotting the expected returns against the betas. What is the slope of the line that results?

Percentage of Portfolio in Asset W	Portfolio Expected Return	Portfolio Beta
0%		
25		
50		
75		
100		
125		
150		

 19. **Reward-to-Risk Ratios**   Stock *Y* has a beta of 1.50 and an expected return of 17 percent. Stock *Z* has a beta of .80 and an expected return of 10.5 percent. If the risk-free rate is 5.5 percent and the market risk premium is 7.5 percent, are these stocks correctly priced?

20. **Reward-to-Risk Ratios**   In the previous problem, what would the risk-free rate have to be for the two stocks to be correctly priced?

INTERMEDIATE
(Questions 21–33)

21. **Portfolio Returns**   Using information from the previous chapter about capital market history, determine the return on a portfolio that is equally invested in large-company stocks and long-term government bonds. What is the return on a portfolio that is equally invested in small-company stocks and Treasury bills?

22. **CAPM**   Using the CAPM, show that the ratio of the risk premiums on two assets is equal to the ratio of their betas.

23. **Portfolio Returns and Deviations**   Consider the following information about three stocks:

State of Economy	Probability of State of Economy	Rate of Return If State Occurs		
		Stock A	Stock B	Stock C
Boom	.4	.20	.35	.60
Normal	.4	.15	.12	.05
Bust	.2	.01	−.25	−.50

    a. If your portfolio is invested 40 percent each in *A* and *B* and 20 percent in *C*, what is the portfolio expected return? The variance? The standard deviation?

    b. If the expected T-bill rate is 3.80 percent, what is the expected risk premium on the portfolio?

    c. If the expected inflation rate is 3.40 percent, what are the approximate and exact expected real returns on the portfolio? What are the approximate and exact expected real risk premiums on the portfolio?

24. **Analyzing a Portfolio**   You want to create a portfolio equally as risky as the market, and you have ¥1,000,000 to invest. Given this information, fill in the rest of the following table:

Asset	Investment	Beta
Stock *A*	¥200,000	.80
Stock *B*	¥250,000	1.30
Stock *C*		1.50
Risk-free asset		

25. **Analyzing a Portfolio**   You have EGP 100,000 to invest in a portfolio containing Stock *X*, Stock *Y*, and a risk-free asset. You must invest all of your money. Your goal is to create a portfolio that has an expected return of 13.5 percent and that has only 70 percent of the risk of the overall market. If *X* has an expected return of 31 percent and a beta of 1.8, *Y* has an expected return of 20 percent and a beta of 1.3, and the risk-free rate is 7 percent, how much money will you invest in Stock *X*? How do you interpret your answer?

26. **Covariance and Correlation**   Based on the following information, calculate the expected return and standard deviation of each of the following stocks. Assume each state of the economy is equally likely to happen. What are the covariance and correlation between the returns of the two stocks?

State of Economy	Return on Stock *A*	Return on Stock *B*
Bear	.063	−.037
Normal	.105	.064
Bull	.167	.253

27. **Covariance and Correlation**   Based on the following information, calculate the expected return and standard deviation for each of the following stocks. What are the covariance and correlation between the returns of the two stocks?

State of Economy	Probability of State of Economy	Return on Stock *J*	Return on Stock *K*
Bear	.25	−.020	.050
Normal	.60	.092	.062
Bull	.15	.154	.074

28. **Portfolio Standard Deviation**   Security *U* has an expected return of 12 percent and a standard deviation of 34 percent per year. Security *I* has an expected return of 18 percent and a standard deviation of 50 percent per year.

    a. What is the expected return on a portfolio composed of 30 percent of security *U* and 70 percent of security *I*?

b. If the correlation between the returns of security U and security I is .2, what is the standard deviation of the portfolio described in part (a)?

29. **Portfolio Standard Deviation**   Suppose the expected returns and standard deviations of stocks A and B are $E(R_A)$ = .15, $E(R_B)$ = .25, σ_A = .40, and σ_B = .65, respectively.

   a. Calculate the expected return and standard deviation of a portfolio that is composed of 40 percent A and 60 percent B when the correlation between the returns on A and B is .5.

   b. Calculate the standard deviation of a portfolio that is composed of 40 percent A and 60 percent B when the correlation coefficient between the returns on A and B is $-.5$.

   c. How does the correlation between the returns on A and B affect the standard deviation of the portfolio?

30. **Correlation and Beta**   You have been provided the following data about the securities of three firms, the market portfolio, and the risk-free asset:

Security	Expected Return	Standard Deviation	Correlation*	Beta
Firm A	.13	.38	(i)	.9
Firm B	.16	(ii)	.4	1.1
Firm C	.25	.65	.35	(iii)
The market portfolio	.15	.20	(iv)	(v)
The risk-free asset	.05	(vi)	(vii)	(viii)

*With the market portfolio.

   a. Fill in the missing values in the table.

   b. Is the stock of Firm A correctly priced according to the capital asset pricing model (CAPM)? What about the stock of Firm B? Firm C? If these securities are not correctly priced, what is your investment recommendation for someone with a well-diversified portfolio?

31. **CML**   The market portfolio has an expected return of 12 percent and a standard deviation of 10 percent. The risk-free rate is 4 percent.

   a. What is the expected return on a well-diversified portfolio with a standard deviation of 7 percent?

   b. What is the standard deviation of a well-diversified portfolio with an expected return of 20 percent?

32. **Beta and CAPM**   A portfolio that combines the risk-free asset and the market portfolio has an expected return of 12 percent and a standard deviation of 18 percent. The risk-free rate is 5 percent, and the expected return on the market portfolio is 14 percent. Assume the capital asset pricing model holds. What expected rate of return would a security earn if it had a .40 correlation with the market portfolio and a standard deviation of 40 percent?

33. **Beta and CAPM**   Suppose the risk-free rate is 6.2 percent and the market portfolio has an expected return of 14.8 percent. The market portfolio has a variance of .0498. Portfolio Z has a correlation coefficient with the market of .45 and a variance of .1783. According to the capital asset pricing model, what is the expected return on portfolio Z?

CHALLENGE
(Questions 34–39)

34. **Systematic versus Unsystematic Risk**   Consider the following information about Stocks Y and Z:

State of Economy	Probability of State of Economy	Rate of Return If State Occurs	
		Stock Y	Stock Z
Recession	.15	.09	$-.30$
Normal	.70	.42	.12
Irrational exuberance	.15	.26	.44

The market risk premium is 9 percent, and the risk-free rate is 4 percent. Which stock has the most systematic risk? Which one has the most unsystematic risk? Which stock is "riskier"? Explain.

35.   **SML**   Suppose you observe the following situation:

Security	Beta	Expected Return
Reliance Co.	1.3	.23
Alliance Co.	.6	.13

Assume these securities are correctly priced. Based on the CAPM, what is the expected return on the market? What is the risk-free rate?

36.   **Covariance and Portfolio Standard Deviation**   There are three securities in the market. The following chart shows their possible payoffs:

State	Probability of Outcome	Return on Security 1	Return on Security 2	Return on Security 3
1	.10	.25	.25	.10
2	.40	.20	.15	.15
3	.40	.15	.20	.20
4	.10	.10	.10	.25

a.   What are the expected return and standard deviation of each security?
b.   What are the covariances and correlations between the pairs of securities?
c.   What are the expected return and standard deviation of a portfolio with half of its funds invested in security 1 and half in security 2?
d.   What are the expected return and standard deviation of a portfolio with half of its funds invested in security 1 and half in security 3?
e.   What are the expected return and standard deviation of a portfolio with half of its funds invested in security 2 and half in security 3?
f.   What do your answers in parts (a), (c), (d), and (e) imply about diversification?

37.   **SML**   Suppose you observe the following situation:

State of Economy	Probability of State	Return If State Occurs	
		Stock A	Stock B
Bust	.25	−.10	−.30
Normal	.50	.10	.05
Boom	.25	.20	.40

a.   Calculate the expected return on each stock.
b.   Assuming the capital asset pricing model holds and stock *A*'s beta is greater than stock *B*'s beta by .20, what is the expected market risk premium?

38.   Standard Deviation and Beta   There are two stocks in the market, stock A and stock B. The price of stock A today is €50. The price of stock A next year will be €40 if the economy is in a recession, €55 if the economy is normal, and €60 if the economy is expanding. The probabilities of recession, normal times, and expansion are .1, .8, and .1, respectively. Stock A pays no dividends and has a correlation of .8 with the market portfolio. Stock B has an expected return of 9 percent, a standard deviation of 12 percent, a correlation with the market portfolio of .2, and a correlation with stock A of .6. The market portfolio has a standard deviation of 10 percent. Assume the CAPM holds.

   a. If you are a typical, risk-averse investor with a well-diversified portfolio, which stock would you prefer? Why?

   b. What are the expected return and standard deviation of a portfolio consisting of 70 percent of stock A and 30 percent of stock B?

   c. What is the beta of the portfolio in part (b)?

39.   Minimum Variance Portfolio   Assume stocks A and B have the following characteristics:

Stock	Expected Return (%)	Standard Deviation (%)
A	5	10
B	10	20

The covariance between the returns on the two stocks is .001.

   a. Suppose an investor holds a portfolio consisting of only stock A and stock B. Find the portfolio weights, X_A and X_B, such that the variance of her portfolio is minimized. (*Hint*: Remember that the sum of the two weights must equal 1.)

   b. What is the expected return on the minimum variance portfolio?

   c. If the covariance between the returns on the two stocks is $-.02$, what are the minimum variance weights?

   d. What is the variance of the portfolio in part (c)?

S&P
Problem

www.mhhe.com/edumarketinsight

1.   Using CAPM   You can find estimates of beta for companies under the "Mthly. Val. Data" link. Locate the beta for Amazon.com (AMZN) and Dow Chemical (DOW). How has the beta for each of these companies changed over the period reported? Using the historical risk-free rate and market risk premium found in the chapter, calculate the expected return for each company based on the most recent beta. Is the expected return for each company what you would expect? Why or why not?

Appendix 10A   Is Beta Dead?

To access Appendix 10A, please go to www.mhhe.com/rwj.

A Job at East Coast Yachts, Part 2

You are discussing your 401(k) with Dan Ervin when he mentions that Sarah Brown, a representative from Bledsoe Financial Services, is visiting East Coast Yachts today. You decide that you should meet with Sarah, so Dan sets up an appointment for you later in the day.

When you sit down with Sarah, she discusses the various investment options available in the company's 401(k) account. You mention to Sarah that you researched East Coast Yachts before you accepted your new job. You are confident in management's ability to lead the company. Analysis of the company has led to your belief that the company is growing and will achieve a greater market share in the future. You also feel you should support your employer. Given these considerations, along with the fact that you are a conservative investor, you are leaning toward investing 100 percent of your 401(k) account in East Coast Yachts.

Assume the risk-free rate is the historical average risk-free rate (in Chapter 9). The correlation between the Bledsoe bond fund and large-cap stock fund is .27. Note that the spreadsheet graphing and "solver" functions may assist you in answering the following questions.

1. Considering the effects of diversification, how should Sarah respond to the suggestion that you invest 100 percent of your 401(k) account in East Coast Yachts stock?

2. Sarah's response to investing your 401(k) account entirely in East Coast Yachts stock has convinced you that this may not be the best alternative. Because you are a conservative investor, you tell Sarah that a 100 percent investment in the bond fund may be the best alternative. Is it?

3. Using the returns for the Bledsoe Large-Cap Stock Fund and the Bledsoe Bond Fund, graph the opportunity set of feasible portfolios.

4. After examining the opportunity set, you notice that you can invest in a portfolio consisting of the bond fund and the large-cap stock fund that will have exactly the same standard deviation as the bond fund. This portfolio will also have a greater expected return. What are the portfolio weights and expected return of this portfolio?

5. Examining the opportunity set, notice there is a portfolio that has the lowest standard deviation. This is the minimum variance portfolio. What are the portfolio weights, expected return, and standard deviation of this portfolio? Why is the minimum variance portfolio important?

6. A measure of risk-adjusted performance that is often used is the Sharpe ratio. The Sharpe ratio is calculated as the risk premium of an asset divided by its standard deviation. The portfolio with the highest possible Sharpe ratio on the opportunity set is called the Sharpe optimal portfolio. What are the portfolio weights, expected return, and standard deviation of the Sharpe optimal portfolio? How does the Sharpe ratio of this portfolio compare to the Sharpe ratios of the bond fund and the large-cap stock fund? Do you see a connection between the Sharpe optimal portfolio and the CAPM? What is the connection?

CHAPTER

11

An Alternative View of Risk and Return

The Arbitrage Pricing Theory

In January 2006, Yahoo!, Apple Computer, and Dutch semiconductor company ASML joined a host of other companies in announcing operating results. As you might expect, news such as this tends to move stock prices.

Yahoo!, for example, reported a profit increase of 83 percent and a revenue increase of 39 percent. But investors didn't say "Yahoo!" Instead, the stock price dropped by 12 percent when the market opened. Apple announced revenues for the most recent quarter of $5.75 billion, an increase of 65 percent over the same quarter in the previous year, and the company's net income nearly doubled to $565 million. So, did investors cheer?

Not exactly: The stock price fell by 2 percent. Finally, ASML announced its earnings were less than half of the earnings from the same quarter in the previous year, on a sales decline of 30 percent. Even with this apparently troubling news, the company's stock jumped over 6 percent.

Two of these announcements seem positive, yet the stock price fell. The third announcement seems negative, yet the stock price jumped. So when is good news really good news? The answer is fundamental to understanding risk and return, and the good news is this chapter explores it in some detail.

11.1 Factor Models: Announcements, Surprises, and Expected Returns

We learned in the previous chapter how to construct portfolios and how to evaluate their returns. We now step back and examine the returns on individual securities more closely. By doing this we will find that the portfolios inherit and alter the properties of the securities they comprise.

To be concrete, let us consider the return on the stock of a company called Flyers. What will determine this stock's return in, say, the coming month?

The return on any stock traded in a financial market consists of two parts. First, the *normal* or *expected return* from the stock is the part of the return that shareholders in the market predict or expect. It depends on all of the information shareholders have that bears on the stock, and it uses all of our understanding of what will influence the stock in the next month.

The second part is the *uncertain* or *risky return* on the stock. This is the portion that comes from information that will be revealed within the month. The list of such information is endless, but here are some examples:

- News about Flyers' research.
- Government figures released for the gross national product (GNP).

- Results of the latest arms control talks.

- Discovery that a rival's product has been tampered with.

- News that Flyers' sales figures are higher than expected.

- A sudden drop in interest rates.

- The unexpected retirement of Flyers' founder and president.

A way to write the return on Flyers' stock in the coming month, then, is:

$$R = \bar{R} + U$$

where R is the actual total return in the month, $\bar{R}$ is the expected part of the return, and U stands for the unexpected part of the return.

We must exercise some care in studying the effect of these or other news items on the return. For example, the government might give us GNP or unemployment figures for this month, but how much of that is new information for shareholders? Surely, at the beginning of the month, shareholders will have some idea or forecast of what the monthly GNP will be. To the extent to which the shareholders had forecast the government's announcement, that forecast should be factored into the expected part of the return as of the beginning of the month, $\bar{R}$. On the other hand, insofar as the announcement by the government is a surprise and to the extent to which it influences the return on the stock, it will be part of U, the unanticipated part of the return.

As an example, suppose shareholders in the market had forecast that the GNP increase this month would be 0.5 percent. If GNP influences our company's stock, this forecast will be part of the information shareholders use to form the expectation, $\bar{R}$, of the monthly return. If the actual announcement this month is exactly 0.5 percent, the same as the forecast, then the shareholders learned nothing new, and the announcement is not news. It is like hearing a rumor about a friend when you knew it all along. Another way of saying this is that shareholders had already discounted the announcement. This use of the word *discount* is different from that in computing present value, but the spirit is similar. When we discount a dollar in the future, we say that it is worth less to us because of the time value of money. When we discount an announcement or a news item in the future, we mean that it has less impact on the market because the market already knew much of it.

On the other hand, suppose the government announced that the actual GNP increase during the year was 1.5 percent. Now shareholders have learned something—that the increase is one percentage point higher than they had forecast. This difference between the actual result and the forecast, one percentage point in this example, is sometimes called the *innovation* or *surprise*.

Any announcement can be broken into two parts, the anticipated or expected part and the surprise or innovation:

Announcement = Expected part + Surprise

The expected part of any announcement is part of the information the market uses to form the expectation, $\bar{R}$, of the return on the stock. The surprise is the news that influences the unanticipated return on the stock, U.

For example, to open the chapter, we compared Yahoo!, Apple Computer, and ASML. In Yahoo!'s case, even though the company's revenue and profits jumped substantially, neither number met investor expectations. In Apple's case, in addition to the good earnings, the company announced that sales in the next quarter would be lower than previously expected. And for ASML, even though sales and profits were below the previous year, both numbers exceeded expectations.

To give another example, if shareholders of a company knew in January that the president of a firm was going to resign, the official announcement in February will be fully expected and will be discounted by the market. Because the announcement was expected before February, its influence on the stock will have taken place before February. The announcement itself in February will contain no surprise, and the stock's price should not change at all at the announcement in February.

When we speak of news, then, we refer to the surprise part of any announcement and not the portion that the market has expected and therefore has already discounted.

11.2   Risk: Systematic and Unsystematic

The unanticipated part of the return—that portion resulting from surprises—is the true risk of any investment. After all, if we got what we had expected, there would be no risk and no uncertainty.

There are important differences, though, among various sources of risk. Look at our previous list of news stories. Some of these stories are directed specifically at Flyers, and some are more general. Which of the news items are of specific importance to Flyers?

Announcements about interest rates or GNP are clearly important for nearly all companies, whereas the news about Flyers' president, its research, its sales, or the affairs of a rival company are of specific interest to Flyers. We will divide these two types of announcements and the resulting risk, then, into two components: a systematic portion, called *systematic risk*, and the remainder, which we call *specific* or *unsystematic risk*. The following definitions describe the difference:

- A *systematic risk* is any risk that affects a large number of assets, each to a greater or lesser degree.
- An *unsystematic risk* is a risk that specifically affects a single asset or a small group of assets.[1]

Uncertainty about general economic conditions, such as GNP, interest rates, or inflation, is an example of systematic risk. These conditions affect nearly all stocks to some degree. An unanticipated or surprise increase in inflation affects wages and the costs of the supplies that companies buy, the value of the assets that companies own, and the prices at which companies sell their products. These forces to which all companies are susceptible are the essence of systematic risk.

In contrast, the announcement of a small oil strike by a company may affect that company alone or a few other companies. Certainly, it is unlikely to have an effect on the world oil market. To stress that such information is unsystematic and affects only some specific companies, we sometimes call it an *idiosyncratic risk*.

The distinction between a systematic risk and an unsystematic risk is never as exact as we make it out to be. Even the most narrow and peculiar bit of news about a company ripples through the economy. It reminds us of the tale of the war that was lost because one horse lost a shoe; even a minor event may have an impact on the world. But this degree of hairsplitting should not trouble us much. To paraphrase a Supreme Court justice's comment when speaking of pornography, we may not be able to define a systematic risk and an unsystematic risk exactly, but we know them when we see them.

---

[1] In the previous chapter, we briefly mentioned that unsystematic risk is risk that can be diversified away in a large portfolio. This result will also follow from the present analysis.

This permits us to break down the risk of Flyers' stock into its two components: the systematic and the unsystematic. As is traditional, we will use the Greek epsilon, ϵ, to represent the unsystematic risk and write:

$$R = \bar{R} + U$$
$$= \bar{R} + m + \epsilon$$

where we have used the letter m to stand for the systematic risk. Sometimes systematic risk is referred to as *market risk*. This emphasizes the fact that m influences all assets in the market to some extent.

The important point about the way we have broken the total risk, U, into its two components, m and ϵ, is that ϵ, because it is specific to the company, is unrelated to the specific risk of most other companies. For example, the unsystematic risk on Flyers' stock, ϵ_F, is unrelated to the unsystematic risk of Xerox's stock, ϵ_X. The risk that Flyers' stock will go up or down because of a discovery by its research team—or its failure to discover something—probably is unrelated to any of the specific uncertainties that affect Xerox stock.

Using the terms of the previous chapter, this means that the unsystematic risks of Flyers' stock and Xerox's stock are unrelated to each other, or uncorrelated. In the symbols of statistics:

$$\text{Corr}(\epsilon_F, \epsilon_X) = 0$$

11.3 Systematic Risk and Betas

The fact that the unsystematic parts of the returns on two companies are unrelated to each other does not mean that the systematic portions are unrelated. On the contrary, because both companies are influenced by the same systematic risks, individual companies' systematic risks and therefore their total returns will be related.

For example, a surprise about inflation will influence almost all companies to some extent. How sensitive is Flyers' stock return to unanticipated changes in inflation? If Flyers' stock tends to go up on news that inflation is exceeding expectations, we would say that it is positively related to inflation. If the stock goes down when inflation exceeds expectations and up when inflation falls short of expectations, it is negatively related. In the unusual case where a stock's return is uncorrelated with inflation surprises, inflation has no effect on it.

We capture the influence of a systematic risk like inflation on a stock by using the **beta coefficient**. The beta coefficient, β, tells us the response of the stock's return to a systematic risk. In the previous chapter, beta measured the responsiveness of a security's return to a specific risk factor, the return on the market portfolio. We used this type of responsiveness to develop the capital asset pricing model. Because we now consider many types of systematic risks, our current work can be viewed as a generalization of our work in the previous chapter.

If a company's stock is positively related to the risk of inflation, that stock has a positive inflation beta. If it is negatively related to inflation, its inflation beta is negative; and if it is uncorrelated with inflation, its inflation beta is zero.

It's not hard to imagine some stocks with positive inflation betas and other stocks with negative inflation betas. The stock of a company owning gold mines will probably have a positive inflation beta because an unanticipated rise in inflation is usually associated with an increase in gold prices. On the other hand, an automobile company facing stiff foreign competition might find that an increase in inflation means that the wages it pays are higher, but that it cannot raise its prices to cover the increase. This profit squeeze, as the company's expenses rise faster than its revenues, would give its stock a negative inflation beta.

Some companies that have few assets and that act as brokers—buying items in competitive markets and reselling them in other markets—might be relatively unaffected by inflation because their costs and their revenues would rise and fall together. Their stock would have an inflation beta of zero.

Some structure is useful at this point. Suppose we have identified three systematic risks on which we want to focus. We may believe that these three are sufficient to describe the systematic risks that influence stock returns. Three likely candidates are inflation, GNP, and interest rates. Thus, every stock will have a beta associated with each of these systematic risks: an inflation beta, a GNP beta, and an interest rate beta. We can write the return on the stock, then, in the following form:

$$R = \bar{R} + U$$
$$= \bar{R} + m + \epsilon$$
$$= \bar{R} + \beta_I F_I + \beta_{GNP} F_{GNP} + \beta_r F_r + \epsilon$$

where we have used the symbol β_I to denote the stock's inflation beta, β_{GNP} for its GNP beta, and β_r to stand for its interest rate beta. In the equation, F stands for a surprise, whether it be in inflation, GNP, or interest rates.

Let us go through an example to see how the surprises and the expected return add up to produce the total return, R, on a given stock. To make it more familiar, suppose that the return is over a horizon of a year and not just a month. Suppose that at the beginning of the year, inflation is forecast to be 5 percent for the year, GNP is forecast to increase by 2 percent and interest rates are expected not to change. Suppose the stock we are looking at has the following betas:

$$\beta_I = 2$$
$$\beta_{GNP} = 1$$
$$\beta_r = -1.8$$

The magnitude of the beta describes how great an impact a systematic risk has on a stock's returns. A beta of $+1$ indicates that the stock's return rises and falls one for one with the systematic factor. This means, in our example, that because the stock has a GNP beta of 1, it experiences a 1 percent increase in return for every 1 percent surprise increase in GNP. If its GNP beta were -2, it would fall by 2 percent when there was an unanticipated increase of 1 percent in GNP, and it would rise by 2 percent if GNP experienced a surprise 1 percent decline.

Let us suppose that during the year the following events occur: Inflation rises by 7 percent, GNP rises by only 1 percent, and interest rates fall by 2 percent. Suppose we learn some good news about the company, perhaps that it is succeeding quickly with some new business strategy, and that this unanticipated development contributes 5 percent to its return. In other words:

$$\epsilon = 5\%$$

Let us assemble all of this information to find what return the stock had during the year.

First we must determine what news or surprises took place in the systematic factors. From our information we know that:

$$\text{Expected inflation} = 5\%$$
$$\text{Expected GNP change} = 2\%$$

and:

$$\text{Expected change in interest rates} = 0\%$$

This means that the market had discounted these changes, and the surprises will be the difference between what actually takes place and these expectations:

$$F_I = \text{Surprise in inflation}$$
$$= \text{Actual inflation} - \text{Expected inflation}$$
$$= 7\% - 5\%$$
$$= 2\%$$

Similarly:

$$F_{\text{GNP}} = \text{Surprise in GNP}$$
$$= \text{Actual GNP} - \text{Expected GNP}$$
$$= 1\% - 2\%$$
$$= -1\%$$

and:

$$F_r = \text{Surprise in change in interest rates}$$
$$= \text{Actual change} - \text{Expected change}$$
$$= -2\% - 0\%$$
$$= -2\%$$

The total effect of the systematic risks on the stock return, then, is:

$$m = \text{Systematic risk portion of return}$$
$$= \beta_I F_I + \beta_{\text{GNP}} F_{\text{GNP}} + \beta_r F_r$$
$$= [2 \times 2\%] + [1 \times (-1\%)] + [(-1.8) \times (-2\%)]$$
$$= 6.6\%$$

Combining this with the unsystematic risk portion, the total risky portion of the return on the stock is:

$$m + \epsilon = 6.6\% + 5\% = 11.6\%$$

Last, if the expected return on the stock for the year was, say, 4 percent, the total return from all three components will be:

$$R = \bar{R} + m + \epsilon$$
$$= 4\% + 6.6\% + 5\%$$
$$= 15.6\%$$

The model we have been looking at is called a **factor model**, and the systematic sources of risk, designated F, are called the *factors*. To be perfectly formal, a *k-factor model* is a model where each stock's return is generated by:

$$R = \bar{R} + \beta_1 F_1 + \beta_2 F_2 + \cdots + \beta_k F_k + \epsilon$$

where ϵ is specific to a particular stock and uncorrelated with the ϵ term for other stocks. In our preceding example we had a three-factor model. We used inflation, GNP, and the change in interest rates as examples of systematic sources of risk, or factors. Researchers have not settled on what is the correct set of factors. Like so many other questions, this might be one of those matters that is never laid to rest.

In practice, researchers frequently use a one-factor model for returns. They do not use all of the sorts of economic factors we used previously as examples; instead they use an index of stock market returns—like the S&P 500, or even a more broadly based index with more stocks in it—as the single factor. Using the single-factor model we can write returns like this:

$$R = \bar{R} + \beta(R_{S\&P500} - \bar{R}_{S\&P500}) + \epsilon$$

Where there is only one factor (the returns on the S&P 500 portfolio index), we do not need to put a subscript on the beta. In this form (with minor modifications) the factor model is called a **market model**. This term is employed because the index that is used for the factor is an index of returns on the whole (stock) market. The market model is written as:

$$R = \bar{R} + \beta(R_M - \bar{R}_M) + \epsilon$$

where R_M is the return on the market portfolio.[2] The single β is called the *beta coefficient*.

11.4 Portfolios and Factor Models

Now let us see what happens to portfolios of stocks when each of the stocks follows a one-factor model. For purposes of discussion, we will take the coming one-month period and examine returns. We could have used a day or a year or any other period. If the period represents the time between decisions, however, we would rather it be short than long, and a month is a reasonable time frame to use.

We will create portfolios from a list of N stocks, and we will use a one-factor model to capture the systematic risk. The ith stock in the list will therefore have returns:

$$R_i = \bar{R}_i + \beta_i F + \epsilon_i \qquad (11.1)$$

where we have subscripted the variables to indicate that they relate to the ith stock. Notice that the factor F is not subscripted. The factor that represents systematic risk could be a surprise in GNP, or we could use the market model and let the difference between the S&P 500 return and what we expect that return to be, $R_{S\&P500} - \bar{R}_{S\&P500}$, be the factor. In either case, the factor applies to all of the stocks.

The β_i is subscripted because it represents the unique way the factor influences the ith stock. To recapitulate our discussion of factor models, if β_i is zero, the returns on the ith stock are:

$$R_i = \bar{R}_i + \epsilon_i$$

In words, the ith stock's returns are unaffected by the factor, F, if β_i is zero. If β_i is positive, positive changes in the factor raise the ith stock's returns, and negative changes lower them. Conversely, if β_i is negative, its returns and the factor move in opposite directions.

Figure 11.1 illustrates the relationship between a stock's excess returns, $R_i - \bar{R}_i$, and the factor F for different betas, where $\beta_i > 0$. The lines in Figure 11.1 plot Equation 11.1 on the assumption that there has been no unsystematic risk. That is, $\epsilon_i = 0$. Because we are assuming positive betas, the lines slope upward, indicating that the return on the stock rises with F. Notice that if the factor is zero ($F = 0$), the line passes through zero on the y-axis.

Now let us see what happens when we create stock portfolios where each stock follows a one-factor model. Let X_i be the proportion of security i in the portfolio. That is, if an individual with a portfolio of $100 wants $20 in General Motors, we say $X_{GM} = 20\%$.

---

[2] Alternatively, the market model could be written as:

$$R = \alpha + \beta R_M + \epsilon$$

Here alpha (α) is an intercept term equal to $\bar{R} - \beta\bar{R}_M$.

Figure 11.1

The One-Factor Model

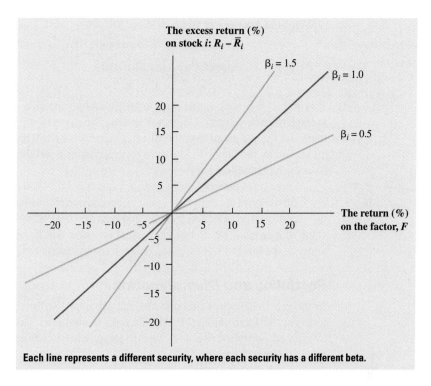

The excess return (%) on stock i: $R_i - \bar{R}_i$

$\beta_i = 1.5$
$\beta_i = 1.0$
$\beta_i = 0.5$

The return (%) on the factor, F

Each line represents a different security, where each security has a different beta.

Because the Xs represent the proportions of wealth we are investing in each of the stocks, we know that they must add up to 100 percent or 1:

$$X_1 + X_2 + X_3 + \cdots + X_N = 1$$

We know that the portfolio return is the weighted average of the returns on the individual assets in the portfolio. Algebraically, this can be written as follows:

$$R_P = X_1 R_1 + X_2 R_2 + X_3 R_3 + \cdots + X_N R_N \tag{11.2}$$

We saw from Equation 11.1 that each asset, in turn, is determined by both the factor F and the unsystematic risk of ϵ_i. Thus by substituting Equation 11.1 for each R_i in Equation 11.2, we have:

$$R_P = X_1(\bar{R}_1 + \beta_1 F + \epsilon_1) \qquad + X_2(\bar{R}_2 + \beta_2 F + \epsilon_2) \tag{11.3}$$
$$\text{(Return on stock 1)} \qquad\qquad \text{(Return on stock 2)}$$
$$+ X_3(\bar{R}_3 + \beta_3 F + \epsilon_3) + \cdots + X_N(\bar{R}_N + \beta_N F + \epsilon_N)$$
$$\text{(Return on stock 3)} \qquad\qquad \text{(Return on stock } N)$$

Equation 11.3 shows us that the return on a portfolio is determined by three sets of parameters:

1. The expected return on each individual security, $\bar{R}_i$.
2. The beta of each security multiplied by the factor F.
3. The unsystematic risk of each individual security, ϵ_i.

We express Equation 11.3 in terms of these three sets of parameters like this:

Weighted Average of Expected Returns

$$R_P = X_1 \bar{R}_1 + X_2 \bar{R}_2 + X_3 \bar{R}_3 + \cdots + X_N \bar{R}_N \tag{11.4}$$

Weighted Average of Betas $\times$ F

$$+ (X_1\beta_1 + X_2\beta_2 + X_3\beta_3 + \cdots + X_N\beta_N)F$$

Weighted Average of Unsystematic Risks

$$+ X_1\epsilon_1 + X_2\epsilon_2 + X_3\epsilon_3 + \cdots + X_N\epsilon_N$$

This rather imposing equation is actually straightforward. The first row is the weighted average of each security's expected return. The items in the parentheses of the second row represent the weighted average of each security's beta. This weighted average is, in turn, multiplied by the factor F. The third row represents a weighted average of the unsystematic risks of the individual securities.

Where does uncertainty appear in Equation 11.4? There is no uncertainty in the first row because only the expected value of each security's return appears there. Uncertainty in the second row is reflected by only one item, F. That is, while we know that the expected value of F is zero, we do not know what its value will be over a particular period. Uncertainty in the third row is reflected by each unsystematic risk, ϵ_i.

Portfolios and Diversification

In the previous sections of this chapter, we expressed the return on a single security in terms of our factor model. Portfolios were treated next. Because investors generally hold diversified portfolios, we now want to know what Equation 11.4 looks like in a *large* or diversified portfolio.[3]

As it turns out, something unusual occurs to Equation 11.4: The third row actually *disappears* in a large portfolio. To see this, consider a gambler who divides $1,000 by betting on red over many spins of the roulette wheel. For example, he may participate in 1,000 spins, betting $1 at a time. Though we do not know ahead of time whether a particular spin will yield red or black, we can be confident that red will win about 50 percent of the time. Ignoring the house take, the investor can be expected to end up with just about his original $1,000.

Though we are concerned with stocks, not roulette wheels, the same principle applies. Each security has its own unsystematic risk, where the surprise for one stock is unrelated to the surprise of another stock. By investing a small amount in each security, we bring the weighted average of the unsystematic risks close to zero in a large portfolio.[4]

Although the third row completely vanishes in a large portfolio, nothing unusual occurs in either row 1 or row 2. Row 1 remains a weighted average of the expected returns on the individual securities as securities are added to the portfolio. Because there is no uncertainty at all in the first row, there is no way for diversification to cause this row to vanish. The terms inside the parentheses of the second row remain a weighted average of the betas. They do not vanish, either, when securities are added. Because the factor F is unaffected when securities are added to the portfolios, the second row does not vanish.

Why does the third row vanish while the second row does not, though both rows reflect uncertainty? The key is that there are many unsystematic risks in row 3. Because these risks are independent of each other, the effect of diversification becomes stronger as we add more assets to the portfolio. The resulting portfolio becomes less and less risky, and the

---

[3]Technically, we can think of a large portfolio as one where an investor keeps increasing the number of securities without limit. In practice, *effective* diversification would occur if at least a few dozen securities were held.

[4]More precisely, we say that the weighted average of the unsystematic risk approaches zero as the number of equally weighted securities in a portfolio approaches infinity.

return becomes more certain. However, the systematic risk, F, affects all securities because it is outside the parentheses in row 2. Because we cannot avoid this factor by investing in many securities, diversification does not occur in this row.

EXAMPLE 11.1

Diversification and Unsystematic Risk   The preceding material can be further explained by the following example. We keep our one-factor model here but make three specific assumptions:

1. All securities have the same expected return of 10 percent. This assumption implies that the first row of Equation 11.4 must also equal 10 percent because this row is a weighted average of the expected returns of the individual securities.

2. All securities have a beta of 1. The sum of the terms inside the parentheses in the second row of Equation 11.4 must equal 1 because these terms are a weighted average of the individual betas. Because the terms inside the parentheses are multiplied by F, the value of the second row is $1 \times F = F$.

3. In this example, we focus on the behavior of one individual, Walter V. Bagehot. Mr. Bagehot decides to hold an equally weighted portfolio. That is, the proportion of each security in his portfolio is $1/N$.

We can express the return on Mr. Bagehot's portfolio as follows:

Return on Walter V. Bagehot's Portfolio

$$R_P = 10\% + F + \left(\frac{1}{N}\epsilon_1 + \frac{1}{N}\epsilon_2 + \frac{1}{N}\epsilon_3 + \cdots + \frac{1}{N}\epsilon_N \right) \quad \textbf{(11.4$'$)}$$

From row 1 of Equation 11.4   From row 2 of Equation 11.4   From row 3 of Equation 11.4

We mentioned before that as N increases without limit, row 3 of Equation 11.4 becomes equal to zero.[5] Thus, the return to Walter Bagehot's portfolio when the number of securities is very large is

$$R_P = 10\% + F \quad \textbf{(11.4$''$)}$$

The key to diversification is exhibited in Equation 11.4$''$. The unsystematic risk of row 3 vanishes while the systematic risk of row 2 remains.

This is illustrated in Figure 11.2. Systematic risk, captured by variation in the factor F, is not reduced through diversification. Conversely, unsystematic risk diminishes as securities are added, vanishing as the number of securities becomes infinite. Our result is analogous to the diversification example of the previous chapter. In that chapter, we said that undiversifiable or systematic risk arises from positive covariances between securities. In this chapter, we say that systematic risk arises from a common factor F. Because a common factor causes positive covariances, the arguments of the two chapters are parallel.

(continued)

---

[5]Our presentation on this point has been nonrigorous. The student interested in more rigor should note that the variance of row 3 is:

$$\frac{1}{N^2}\sigma_\epsilon^2 + \frac{1}{N^2}\sigma_\epsilon^2 + \frac{1}{N^2}\sigma_\epsilon^2 + \cdots + \frac{1}{N^2}\sigma_\epsilon^2 = \frac{1}{N^2}N\sigma_\epsilon^2$$

where σ_ϵ^2 is the variance of each ϵ. This can be rewritten as σ_ϵ^2/N, which tends to 0 as N goes to infinity.

Figure 11.2 **Diversification and the Portfolio Risk for an Equally Weighted Portfolio**

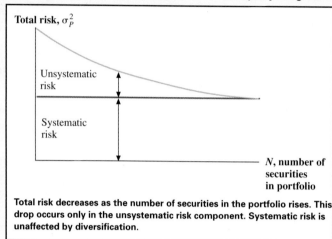

Total risk decreases as the number of securities in the portfolio rises. This drop occurs only in the unsystematic risk component. Systematic risk is unaffected by diversification.

11.5 Betas and Expected Returns

The Linear Relationship

We have argued many times that the expected return on a security compensates for its risk. In the previous chapter we showed that market beta (the standardized covariance of the security's returns with those of the market) was the appropriate measure of risk under the assumptions of homogeneous expectations and riskless borrowing and lending. The capital asset pricing model, which posited these assumptions, implied that the expected return on a security was positively (and linearly) related to its beta. We will find a similar relationship between risk and return in the one-factor model of this chapter.

We begin by noting that the relevant risk in large and well-diversified portfolios is all systematic because unsystematic risk is diversified away. An implication is that when a well-diversified shareholder considers changing her holdings of a particular stock, she can ignore the security's unsystematic risk.

Notice that we are not claiming that stocks, like portfolios, have no unsystematic risk. Nor are we saying that the unsystematic risk of a stock will not affect its returns. Stocks do have unsystematic risk, and their actual returns do depend on the unsystematic risk. Because this risk washes out in a well-diversified portfolio, however, shareholders can ignore this unsystematic risk when they consider whether to add a stock to their portfolio. Therefore, if shareholders are ignoring the unsystematic risk, only the systematic risk of a stock can be related to its *expected* return.

This relationship is illustrated in the security market line of Figure 11.3. Points P, C, A, and L all lie on the line emanating from the risk-free rate of 10 percent. The points representing each of these four assets can be created by combinations of the risk-free rate and any of the other three assets. For example, because A has a beta of 2.0 and P has a beta of 1.0, a portfolio of 50 percent in asset A and 50 percent in the riskless rate has the same beta as asset P. The risk-free rate is 10 percent and the expected return on security A is 35 percent, implying that the combination's return of 22.5 percent [(10% + 35%)/2] is identical to security P's expected return. Because security P has both the same beta and the same expected return as a combination of the riskless asset and security A, an individual is

Figure 11.3

A Graph of Beta and Expected Return for Individual Stocks under the One-Factor Model

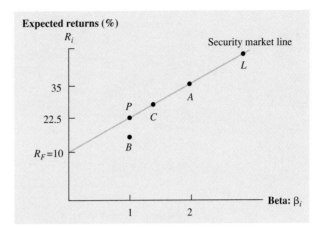

equally inclined to add a small amount of security P and to add a small amount of this combination to her portfolio. However, the unsystematic risk of security P need not be equal to the unsystematic risk of the combination of security A and the risk-free rate because unsystematic risk is diversified away in a large portfolio.

Of course, the potential combinations of points on the security market line are endless. We can duplicate P by combinations of the risk-free rate and either C or L (or both of them). We can duplicate C (or A or L) by borrowing at the risk-free rate to invest in P. The infinite number of points on the security market line that are not labeled can be used as well.

Now consider security B. Because its expected return is below the line, no investor would hold it. Instead, the investor would prefer security P, a combination of security A and the riskless asset, or some other combination. Thus, security B's price is too high. Its price will fall in a competitive market, forcing its expected return back up to the line in equilibrium.

The preceding discussion allows us to provide an equation for the security market line of Figure 11.3. We know that a line can be described algebraically from two points. It is perhaps easiest to focus on the risk-free rate and asset P because the risk-free rate has a beta of 0 and P has a beta of 1.

Because we know that the return on any zero-beta asset is R_F and the expected return on asset P is $\bar{R}_P$, it can easily be shown that:

$$\bar{R} = R_F + \beta(\bar{R}_P - R_F) \qquad (11.5)$$

In Equation 11.5, $\bar{R}$ can be thought of as the expected return on any security or portfolio lying on the security market line. β is the beta of that security or portfolio.

The Market Portfolio and the Single Factor

In the CAPM the beta of a security measures the security's responsiveness to movements in the market portfolio. In the one-factor model of the arbitrage pricing theory (APT) the beta of a security measures its responsiveness to the factor. We now relate the market portfolio to the single factor.

A large, diversified portfolio has no unsystematic risk because the unsystematic risks of the individual securities are diversified away. Assuming enough securities so that the market portfolio is fully diversified and assuming that no security has a disproportionate market share, this portfolio is fully diversified and contains no unsystematic risk.[6] In other

---

[6]This assumption is plausible in the real world. For example, even the market value of General Electric is only 3 percent to 4 percent of the market value of the S&P 500 Index.

Figure 11.4

A Graph of Beta and
Expected Return for
Individual Stocks
under the One-Factor
Model

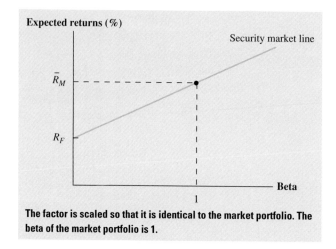

The factor is scaled so that it is identical to the market portfolio. The
beta of the market portfolio is 1.

words, the market portfolio is perfectly correlated with the single factor, implying that the
market portfolio is really a scaled-up or scaled-down version of the factor. After scaling
properly, we can treat the market portfolio as the factor itself.

The market portfolio, like every security or portfolio, lies on the security market line.
When the market portfolio is the factor, the beta of the market portfolio is 1 by definition.
This is shown in Figure 11.4. (We deleted the securities and the specific expected returns
from Figure 11.3 for clarity: The two graphs are otherwise identical.) With the market portfolio as the factor, Equation 11.5 becomes:

$$\bar{R} = R_F + \beta(\bar{R}_M - R_F)$$

where $\bar{R}_M$ is the expected return on the market. This equation shows that the expected return on any asset, $\bar{R}$, is linearly related to the security's beta. The equation is identical to that
of the CAPM, which we developed in the previous chapter.

11.6   The Capital Asset Pricing Model and the Arbitrage Pricing Theory

The CAPM and the APT are alternative models of risk and return. It is worthwhile to consider the differences between the two models, both in terms of pedagogy and in terms of
application.

Differences in Pedagogy

We feel that the CAPM has at least one strong advantage from the student's point of view.
The derivation of the CAPM necessarily brings the reader through a discussion of efficient
sets. This treatment—beginning with the case of two risky assets, moving to the case of
many risky assets, and finishing when a riskless asset is added to the many risky ones—is of
great intuitive value. This sort of presentation is not as easily accomplished with the APT.

However, the APT has an offsetting advantage. The model adds factors until the
unsystematic risk of any security is uncorrelated with the unsystematic risk of every other
security. Under this formulation, it is easily shown that (1) unsystematic risk steadily falls
(and ultimately vanishes) as the number of securities in the portfolio increases but (2) the
systematic risks do not decrease. This result was also shown in the CAPM, though the intuition was cloudier because the unsystematic risks could be correlated across securities.

Differences in Application

One advantage of the APT is that it can handle multiple factors while the CAPM ignores them. Although the bulk of our presentation in this chapter focused on the one-factor model, a multifactor model is probably more reflective of reality. That is, we must abstract from many marketwide and industrywide factors before the unsystematic risk of one security becomes uncorrelated with the unsystematic risks of other securities. Under this multifactor version of the APT, the relationship between risk and return can be expressed as:

$$\overline{R} = R_F + (\overline{R}_1 - R_F)\beta_1 + (\overline{R}_2 - R_F)\beta_2 + (\overline{R}_3 - R_F)\beta_3 + \cdots + (\overline{R}_K - R_F)\beta_K \quad \textbf{(11.6)}$$

In this equation, β_1 stands for the security's beta with respect to the first factor, β_2 stands for the security's beta with respect to the second factor, and so on. For example, if the first factor is GNP, β_1 is the security's GNP beta. The term $\overline{R}_1$ is the expected return on a security (or portfolio) whose beta with respect to the first factor is 1 and whose beta with respect to all other factors is zero. Because the market compensates for risk, $(\overline{R}_1 - R_F)$ will be positive in the normal case.[7] (An analogous interpretation can be given to $\overline{R}_2$, $\overline{R}_3$, and so on.)

The equation states that the security's expected return is related to the security's factor betas. The intuition in Equation 11.6 is straightforward. Each factor represents risk that cannot be diversified away. The higher a security's beta with regard to a particular factor is, the higher is the risk that the security bears. In a rational world, the expected return on the security should compensate for this risk. Equation 11.6 states that the expected return is a summation of the risk-free rate plus the compensation for each type of risk that the security bears.

As an example, consider a study where the factors were monthly growth in industrial production (IP), change in expected inflation (ΔEI), unanticipated inflation (UI), unanticipated change in the risk premium between risky bonds and default-free bonds (URP), and unanticipated change in the difference between the return on long-term government bonds and the return on short-term government bonds (UBR).[8] Using the period 1958–1984, the empirical results of the study indicated that the expected monthly return on any stock, $\overline{R}_S$, can be described as:

$$\overline{R}_S = 0.0041 + 0.0136\beta_{IP} - 0.0001\beta_{\Delta EI} - 0.0006\beta_{UI} + 0.0072\beta_{URP} - 0.0052\beta_{UBR}$$

Suppose a particular stock had the following betas: $\beta_{IP} = 1.1$, $\beta_{\Delta EI} = 2$, $\beta_{UI} = 3$, $\beta_{URP} = 0.1$, $\beta_{UBR} = 1.6$. The expected monthly return on that security would be:

$$\begin{aligned}
\overline{R}_S &= 0.0041 + 0.0136 \times 1.1 - 0.0001 \times 2 - 0.0006 \times 3 + 0.0072 \times 0.1 - \\
&\quad 0.0052 \times 1.6 \\
&= 0.0095
\end{aligned}$$

Assuming that a firm is unlevered and that one of the firm's projects has risk equivalent to that of the firm, this value of 0.0095 (i.e., .95%) can be used as the monthly discount rate for the project. (Because annual data are often supplied for capital budgeting purposes, the annual rate of 0.120 $[= (1.0095)^{12} - 1]$ might be used instead.)

Because many factors appear on the right side of Equation 11.6, the APT formulation has the potential to measure expected returns more accurately than does the CAPM. However, as we mentioned earlier, we cannot easily determine which are the appropriate factors. The factors in the preceding study were included for reasons of both common sense and convenience. They were not derived from theory.

---

[7] Actually, $(\overline{R}_i - R_F)$ could be negative in the case where factor i is perceived as a hedge of some sort.

[8] N. Chen, R. Roll, and S. Ross, "Economic Forces and the Stock Market," *Journal of Business* (July 1986).

By contrast, the use of the market index in the CAPM formulation is implied by the theory of the previous chapter. We suggested in earlier chapters that the S&P 500 index mirrors stock market movements quite well. Using the Ibbotson-Sinquefield results showing that the yearly return on the S&P 500 index was, on average, 8.5 percent greater than the risk-free rate, the last chapter easily calculated expected returns on different securities from the CAPM.[9]

11.7   Empirical Approaches to Asset Pricing

Empirical Models

The CAPM and the APT by no means exhaust the models and techniques used in practice to measure the expected return on risky assets. Both the CAPM and the APT are *risk-based models*. They each measure the risk of a security by its beta(s) on some systematic factor(s), and they each argue that the expected excess return must be proportional to the beta(s). Although we have seen that this is intuitively appealing and has a strong basis in theory, there are alternative approaches.

Most of these alternatives can be lumped under the broad heading of parametric or **empirical models**. The word *empirical* refers to the fact that these approaches are based less on some theory of how financial markets work and more on simply looking for regularities and relations in the history of market data. In these approaches the researcher specifies some parameters or attributes associated with the securities in question and then examines the data directly for a relation between these attributes and expected returns. For example, an extensive amount of research has been done on whether the expected return on a firm is related to its size. Is it true that small firms have higher average returns than large firms? Researchers have also examined a variety of accounting measures such as the ratio of the price of a stock to its accounting earnings, its P/E ratio, and the closely related ratio of the market value of the stock to the book value of the company, the M/B ratio. Here it might be argued that companies with low P/E's or low M/B's are "undervalued" and can be expected to have higher returns in the future.

To use the empirical approach to determine the expected return, we would estimate the following equation:

$$\overline{R}_i = R_F + k_{P/E} \, (P/E)_i + k_{M/B} \, (M/B)_i + k_{size} \, (size)_P$$

where $\overline{R}_i$ is the expected return of firm i, and where the k's are coefficients that we estimate from stock market data. Notice that this is the same form as Equation 11.6 with the firm's attributes in place of betas and with the k's in place of the excess factor portfolio returns.

When tested with data, these parametric approaches seem to do quite well. In fact, when comparisons are made between using parameters and using betas to predict stock returns, the parameters, such as P/E and M/B, seem to work better. There are a variety of possible explanations for these results, and the issues have certainly not been settled. Critics of the empirical approach are skeptical of what they call *data mining*. The particular parameters that researchers work with are often chosen because they have been shown to be related to returns. For instance, suppose that you were asked to explain the change in SAT test scores over the past 40 years in some particular state. Suppose that to do this you searched through all of the data series you could find. After much searching, you might discover, for example, that the change in the scores was directly related to the jackrabbit

---

[9]Though many researchers assume that surrogates for the market portfolio are easily found, Richard Roll, "A Critique of the Asset Pricing Theory's Tests," *Journal of Financial Economics* (March 1977), argues that the absence of a universally acceptable proxy for the market portfolio seriously impairs application of the theory. After all, the market must include real estate, racehorses, and other assets that are not in the stock market.

population in Arizona. We know that any such relation is purely accidental; but if you search long enough and have enough choices, you will find something even if it is not really there. It's a bit like staring at clouds. After a while you will see clouds that look like anything you want—clowns, bears, or whatever—but all you are really doing is data mining.

Needless to say, the researchers on these matters defend their work by arguing that they have not mined the data and have been very careful to avoid such traps by not snooping at the data to see what will work.

Of course, as a matter of pure theory, because anyone in the market can easily look up the P/E ratio of a firm, we would certainly not expect to find that firms with low P/E's did better than firms with high P/E's simply because they were undervalued. In an efficient market, such public measures of undervaluation would be quickly exploited and would not last.

Perhaps a better explanation for the success of empirical approaches lies in a synthesis of the risk-based approaches and the empirical methods. In an efficient market risk and return are related; so perhaps the parameters or attributes that appear to be related to returns are also better measures of risk. For example, if we were to find that low P/E firms outperformed high P/E firms and that this was true even for firms that had the same beta(s), then we would have at least two possible explanations. First, we could simply discard the risk-based theories as incorrect. Furthermore, we could argue that markets are inefficient and that buying low P/E stocks provides us with an opportunity to make higher than predicted returns. Second, we could argue that *both* views of the world are correct and that the P/E is really just a better way to measure systematic risk—that is, beta(s)—than directly estimating beta from the data.

Style Portfolios

In addition to their use as a platform for estimating expected returns, stock attributes are also widely used as a way of characterizing money management styles. For example, a portfolio that has a P/E ratio much in excess of the market average might be characterized as a high P/E or a **growth stock portfolio**. Similarly, a portfolio made up of stocks with an average P/E less than that for a market index might be characterized as a low P/E or a **value portfolio**.

To evaluate how well portfolio managers are doing, often their performance is compared with the performance of some basic indexes. For example, the portfolio returns of managers who purchase large U.S. stocks might be compared to the performance of the S&P 500 index. In such a case the S&P 500 is said to be the **benchmark** against which their performance is measured. Similarly, an international manager might be compared against some common index of international stocks. In choosing an appropriate benchmark, care should be taken to identify a benchmark that contains only those types of stocks that the manager targets as representative of his or her style and that are also available to be purchased. A manager who was told not to purchase any stocks in the S&P 500 index would not consider it legitimate to be compared against the S&P 500.

Increasingly, too, managers are compared not only against an index but also against a peer group of similar managers. The performance of a fund that advertises itself as a growth fund might be measured against the performance of a large sample of similar funds. For instance, the performance over some period commonly is assigned to quartiles. The top 25 percent of the funds are said to be in the first quartile, the next 25 percent in the second quartile, the next 25 percent in the third quartile, and the worst-performing 25 percent of the funds in the last quartile. If the fund we are examining happens to have a performance that falls in the second quartile, then we speak of its manager as a second quartile manager.

Similarly, we call a fund that purchases low M/B stocks a value fund and would measure its performance against a sample of similar value funds. These approaches to measuring performance are relatively new, and they are part of an active and exciting effort to refine our ability to identify and use investment skills.

Summary and Conclusions

The previous chapter developed the capital asset pricing model (CAPM). As an alternative, this chapter developed the arbitrage pricing theory (APT).

1. The APT assumes that stock returns are generated according to factor models. For example, we might describe a stock's return as:

$$R = \bar{R} + \beta_I F_I + \beta_{GNP} F_{GNP} + \beta_r F_r + \epsilon$$

where I, GNP, and r stand for inflation, gross national product, and the interest rate, respectively. The three factors F_I, F_{GNP}, and F_r represent systematic risk because these factors affect many securities. The term ϵ is considered unsystematic risk because it is unique to each individual security.

2. For convenience, we frequently describe a security's return according to a one-factor model:

$$R = \bar{R} + \beta F + \epsilon$$

3. As securities are added to a portfolio, the unsystematic risks of the individual securities offset each other. A fully diversified portfolio has no unsystematic risk but still has systematic risk. This result indicates that diversification can eliminate some, but not all, of the risk of individual securities.

4. Because of this, the expected return on a stock is positively related to its systematic risk. In a one-factor model, the systematic risk of a security is simply the beta of the CAPM. Thus, the implications of the CAPM and the one-factor APT are identical. However, each security has many risks in a multifactor model. The expected return on a security is positively related to the beta of the security with each factor.

5. Empirical or parametric models that capture the relations between returns and stock attributes such as P/E or M/B ratios can be estimated directly from the data without any appeal to theory. These ratios are also used to measure the styles of portfolio managers and to construct benchmarks and samples against which they are measured.

Concept Questions

1. **Systematic versus Unsystematic Risk**   Describe the difference between systematic risk and unsystematic risk.

2. **APT**   Consider the following statement: For the APT to be useful, the number of systematic risk factors must be small. Do you agree or disagree with this statement? Why?

3. **APT**   David McClemore, the CFO of Ultra Bread, has decided to use an APT model to estimate the required return on the company's stock. The risk factors he plans to use are the risk premium on the stock market, the inflation rate, and the price of wheat. Because wheat is one of the biggest costs Ultra Bread faces, he feels this is a significant risk factor for Ultra Bread. How would you evaluate his choice of risk factors? Are there other risk factors you might suggest?

4. **Systematic and Usystematic Risk**   You own stock in the Lewis-Striden Drug Company. Suppose you had expected the following events to occur last month:
   a. The government would announce that real GNP had grown 1.2 percent during the previous quarter. The returns of Lewis-Striden are positively related to real GNP.
   b. The government would announce that inflation over the previous quarter was 3.7 percent. The returns of Lewis-Striden are negatively related to inflation.
   c. Interest rates would rise 2.5 percentage points. The returns of Lewis-Striden are negatively related to interest rates.
   d. The president of the firm would announce his retirement. The retirement would be effective six months from the announcement day. The president is well liked: In general, he is considered an asset to the firm.

e. Research data would conclusively prove the efficacy of an experimental drug. Completion of the efficacy testing means the drug will be on the market soon.

Suppose the following events actually occurred:

a. The government announced that real GNP grew 2.3 percent during the previous quarter.
b. The government announced that inflation over the previous quarter was 3.7 percent.
c. Interest rates rose 2.1 percentage points.
d. The president of the firm died suddenly of a heart attack.
e. Research results in the efficacy testing were not as strong as expected. The drug must be tested for another six months, and the efficacy results must be resubmitted to the FDA.
f. Lab researchers had a breakthrough with another drug.
g. A competitor announced that it will begin distribution and sale of a medicine that will compete directly with one of Lewis-Striden's top-selling products.

Discuss how each of the actual occurrences affects the returns on your Lewis-Striden stock. Which events represent systematic risk? Which events represent unsystematic risk?

5. **Market Model versus APT**   What are the differences between a k-factor model and the market model?

6. **APT**   In contrast to the CAPM, the APT does not indicate which factors are expected to determine the risk premium of an asset. How can we determine which factors should be included? For example, one risk factor suggested is the company size. Why might this be an important risk factor in an APT model?

7. **CAPM versus APT**   What is the relationship between the one-factor model and the CAPM?

8. **Factor Models**   How can the return on a portfolio be expressed in terms of a factor model?

9. **Data Mining**   What is data mining? Why might it overstate the relation between some stock attribute and returns?

10. **Factor Selection**   What is wrong with measuring the performance of a U.S. growth stock manager against a benchmark composed of British stocks?

Questions and Problems

BASIC
(Questions 1–4)

1. **Factor Models**   A researcher has determined that a two-factor model is appropriate to determine the return of a stock. The factors are the percentage change in GNP and an interest rate. GNP is expected to grow by 3 percent, and the interest rate is expected to be 4.5 percent. A stock has a beta of 1.2 on the percentage change in GNP and a beta of −0.8 on the interest rate. If the expected rate of return for the stock is 11 percent, what is the revised expected return of the stock if GNP actually grows by 4.2 percent and interest rates are 4.4 percent?

2. **Factor Models**   Suppose a three-factor model is appropriate to describe the returns of a stock. Information about those three factors is presented in the following chart:

Factor	β	Expected Value	Actual Value
GNP	0.000586	$5,396	$5,436
Inflation	−1.40	3.1%	3.8%
Interest rates	−0.70	9.5%	10.3%

a. What is the systematic risk of the stock return?
b. Suppose unexpected bad news about the firm was announced that causes the stock price to drop by 2.6 percent. If the expected return of the stock is 9.5 percent, what is the total return on this stock?

3. Factors Models Suppose a factor model is appropriate to describe the returns on a stock. The current expected return on the stock is 10.5 percent. Information about those factors is presented in the following chart:

Factor	β	Expected Value	Actual Value
Growth in GNP	2.04	3.5%	4.8%
Inflation	−1.90	7.1%	7.8%

a. What is the systematic risk of the stock return?
b. The firm announced that its market share had unexpectedly increased from 23 percent to 28 percent. Investors know from past experience that the stock return will increase by 0.36 percent for every 1 percent increase in its market share. What is the unsystematic risk of the stock?
c. What is the total return on this stock?

4. Multifactor Models Suppose stock returns can be explained by the following three-factor model:

$$R_i = R_F + \beta_1 F_1 + \beta_2 F_2 + \beta_3 F_3$$

Assume there is no firm-specific risk. The information for each stock is presented here:

	β_1	β_2	β_3
Stock A	1.20	0.90	0.20
Stock B	0.80	1.40	−0.30
Stock C	0.95	−0.05	1.50

The risk premiums for the factors are 5.5 percent, 4.2 percent, and 4.9 percent, respectively. If you create a portfolio with 20 percent invested in stock A, 20 percent invested in stock B, and the remainder in stock C, what is the expression for the return of your portfolio? If the risk-free rate is 6 percent, what is the expected return of your portfolio?

INTERMEDIATE
(Questions 5–7)

5. Multifactor Models Suppose stock returns can be explained by a two-factor model. The firm-specific risks for all stocks are independent. The following table shows the information for two diversified portfolios:

	β_1	β_2	E(R)
Portfolio A	0.75	1.20	18%
Portfolio B	1.60	−0.20	14

If the risk-free rate is 6 percent, what are the risk premiums for each factor in this model?

6. Market Model The following three stocks are available in the market:

	E(R)	β
Chocolate	10.5%	1.20
Vanilla	13.0	0.98
Strawberry	15.7	1.37
Market	14.2	1.00

Assume the market model is valid.
a. Write the market model equation for each stock.
b. What is the return on a portfolio with weights of 30 percent chocolate, 45 percent vanilla, and 25 percent strawberry?
c. Suppose the return on the market is 15 percent and there are no unsystematic surprises in the returns. What is the return on each stock? What is the return on the portfolio?

7. **Portfolio Risk** You are forming an equally weighted portfolio of stocks. Many stocks have the same beta of 0.72 for factor 1 and the same beta of 1.69 for factor 2. All stocks also have the same expected return of 11 percent. Assume a two-factor model describes the return on each of these stocks.
a. Write the equation of the returns on your portfolio if you place only five stocks in it.
b. Write the equation of the returns on your portfolio if you place in it a very large number of stocks that all have the same expected returns and the same betas.

CHALLENGE
(Questions 8–10)

8. **APT** There are two stock markets, each driven by the same common force F with an expected value of zero and standard deviation of 10 percent. There are many securities in each market; thus you can invest in as many stocks as you wish. Due to restrictions, however, you can invest in only one of the two markets. The expected return on every security in both markets is 10 percent.

The returns for each security i in the first market are generated by the relationship

$$R_{1i} = 0.10 + 1.5F + \epsilon_{1i}$$

where ϵ_{1i} is the term that measures the surprises in the returns of stock i in market 1. These surprises are normally distributed; their mean is zero. The returns for security j in the second market are generated by relationship

$$R_{2j} = 0.10 + 0.5F + \epsilon_{2j}$$

where ϵ_{2j} is the term that measures the surprises in the returns of stock j in market 2. These surprises are normally distributed; their mean is zero. The standard deviation of ϵ_{1i} and ϵ_{2j} for any two stocks, i and j, is 20 percent.
a. If the correlation between the surprises in the returns of any two stocks in the first market is zero, and if the correlation between the surprises in the returns of any two stocks in the second market is zero, in which market would a risk-averse person prefer to invest? (Note: The correlation between ϵ_{1i} and ϵ_{1j} for any i and j is zero, and the correlation between ϵ_{2i} and ϵ_{2j} for any i and j is zero.)
b. If the correlation between ϵ_{1i} and ϵ_{1j} in the first market is 0.9 and the correlation between ϵ_{2i} and ϵ_{2j} in the second market is zero, in which market would a risk-averse person prefer to invest?
c. If the correlation between ϵ_{1i} and ϵ_{1j} in the first market is zero and the correlation between ϵ_{2i} and ϵ_{2j} in the second market is 0.5, in which market would a risk-averse person prefer to invest?
d. In general, what is the relationship between the correlations of the disturbances in the two markets that would make a risk-averse person equally willing to invest in either of the two markets?

9. **APT** Assume that the following market model adequately describes the return-generating behavior of risky assets:

$$R_{it} = \alpha_i + \beta_i R_{Mt} + \epsilon_{it}$$

Here:
R_{it} = The return for the ith asset at time t.
R_{Mt} = The return on a portfolio containing all risky assets in some proportion at time t.
R_{Mt} and ϵ_{it} are statistically independent.

www.mhhe.com/rwj

Short selling (i.e., negative positions) is allowed in the market. You are given the following information:

Asset	β_i	$E(R_i)$	$Var(\epsilon_i)$
A	0.7	8.41%	0.0100
B	1.2	12.06	0.0144
C	1.5	13.95	0.0225

The variance of the market is 0.0121, and there are no transaction costs.

a. Calculate the standard deviation of returns for each asset.

b. Calculate the variance of return of three portfolios containing an infinite number of asset types A, B, or C, respectively.

c. Assume the risk-free rate is 3.5 percent and the expected return on the market is 10.6 percent. Which asset will not be held by rational investors?

d. What equilibrium state will emerge such that no arbitrage opportunities exist? Why?

10. **APT** Assume that the returns of individual securities are generated by the following two-factor model:

$$R_{it} = E(R_{it}) + \beta_{ij}F_{1t} + \beta_{i2}F_{2t}$$

Here:

R_{it} is the return for security i at time t.

F_{1t} and F_{2t} are market factors with zero expectation and zero covariance.

In addition, assume that there is a capital market for four securities, and the capital market for these four assets is perfect in the sense that there are no transaction costs and short sales (i.e., negative positions) are permitted. The characteristics of the four securities follow:

Security	β_1	β_2	$E(R)$
1	1.0	1.5	20%
2	0.5	2.0	20
3	1.0	0.5	10
4	1.5	0.75	10

a. Construct a portfolio containing (long or short) securities 1 and 2, with a return that does not depend on the market factor, F_{1t}, in any way. (*Hint:* Such a portfolio will have $\beta_1 = 0$.) Compute the expected return and β_2 coefficient for this portfolio.

b. Following the procedure in (a), construct a portfolio containing securities 3 and 4 with a return that does not depend on the market factor F_{1t}. Compute the expected return and β_2 coefficient for this portfolio.

c. There is a risk-free asset with expected return equal to 4.9 percent, $\beta_1 = 0$, and $\beta_2 = 0$. Describe a possible arbitrage opportunity in such detail that an investor could implement it.

d. What effect would the existence of these kinds of arbitrage opportunities have on the capital markets for these securities in the short and long run? Graph your analysis.

The Fama–French Multifactor Model and Mutual Fund Returns

Dawn Browne, an investment broker, has been approached by client Jack Thomas about the risk of his investments. Dawn has recently read several articles concerning the risk factors that can potentially affect asset returns, and she has decided to examine Jack's mutual fund holdings. Jack is currently invested in the Fidelity Magellan Fund (FMAGX), the Fidelity Low-Priced Stock Fund (FLPSX), and the Baron Small Cap Fund (BSCFX).

Dawn would like to estimate the well-known multifactor model proposed by Eugene Fama and Ken French to determine the risk of each mutual fund. Here is the regression equation for the multifactor model she proposes to use:

$$R_{it} - R_{Ft} = \alpha_i + \beta_1(R_{Mt} - R_{Ft}) + \beta_2(SMB_t) + \beta_3(HML_t) + \epsilon_t$$

In the regression equation, R_{it} is the return of asset i at time t, R_{Ft} is the risk-free rate at time t, and R_{Mt} is the return on the market at time t. Thus, the first risk factor in the Fama–French regression is the market factor often used with the CAPM.

The second risk factor, SMB or "small minus big," is calculated by taking the difference in the returns on a portfolio of small-cap stocks and a portfolio of big-cap stocks. This factor is intended to pick up the so-called small firm effect. Similarly, the third factor, HML or "high minus low," is calculated by taking the difference in the returns between a portfolio of "value" stocks and a portfolio of "growth" stocks. Stocks with low market-to-book ratios are classified as value stocks and vice versa for growth stocks. This factor is included because of the historical tendency for value stocks to earn a higher return.

In models such as the one Dawn is considering, the alpha (α) term is of particular interest. It is the regression intercept; but more important, it is also the excess return the asset earned. In other words, if the alpha is positive, the asset earned a return greater than it should have given its level of risk; if the alpha is negative, the asset earned a return lower than it should have given its level of risk. This measure is called "Jensen's alpha," and it is a very widely used tool for mutual fund evaluation.

1. For a large-company stock mutual fund, would you expect the betas to be positive or negative for each of the factors in a Fama–French multifactor model?

2. The Fama–French factors and risk-free rates are available at Ken French's Web site: mba.tuck.dartmouth.edu/pages/faculty/ken.french/. Download the monthly factors and save the most recent 60 months for each factor. The historical prices for each of the mutual funds can be found on various Web sites, including finance.yahoo.com. Find the prices of each mutual fund for the same time as the Fama–French factors and calculate the returns for each month. Be sure to include dividends. For each mutual fund, estimate the multifactor regression equation using the Fama–French factors. How well do the regression estimates explain the variation in the return of each mutual fund?

3. What do you observe about the beta coefficients for the different mutual funds? Comment on any similarities or differences.

4. If the market is efficient, what value would you expect for alpha? Do your estimates support market efficiency?

5. Which fund has performed best considering its risk? Why?

CHAPTER 1

Risk, Cost of Capital, and Capital Budgeting

In late 2005, Swiss Re, one of the world's leading reinsurers, published a report discussing how insurance companies create value for shareholders. One of the key components addressed in the report was the cost of capital. According to Swiss Re, the cost of capital for the U.S. non-life insurance industry during the 1980s was about 15 percent. By 2005, the cost of capital for the industry had dropped to 7 to 8 percent. But the cost of capital is important in more than just the insurance industry. One of the major reasons given for the possible sale of General Motors Acceptance Corporation (GMAC) by General Motors was that the lowering of GM's debt rating had increased the cost of capital for GMAC.

In this chapter, we learn how to compute a firm's cost of capital and find out what it means to the firm and its investors. We will also learn when to use the firm's cost of capital—and perhaps more important, when not to use it.

12.1 The Cost of Equity Capital

Whenever a firm has extra cash, it can take one of two actions. It can pay out the cash immediately as a dividend. Alternatively, the firm can invest extra cash in a project, paying out the future cash flows of the project as dividends. Which procedure would the stockholders prefer? If a stockholder can reinvest the dividend in a financial asset (a stock or bond) with the same risk as that of the project, the stockholders would desire the alternative with the highest expected return. In other words, the project should be undertaken only if its expected return is greater than that of a financial asset of comparable risk. This is illustrated in Figure 12.1. This discussion implies a very simple capital budgeting rule:

The discount rate of a project should be the expected return on a financial asset of comparable risk.

From the firm's perspective, the expected return is the cost of equity capital. Under the CAPM, the expected return on the stock can be written as:

$$R_S = R_F + \beta \times (R_M - R_F) \tag{12.1}$$

where R_F is the risk-free rate and $R_M - R_F$ is the difference between the expected return on the market portfolio and the riskless rate. This difference is often called the expected *excess* market return or market risk premium. Note we have dropped the bar denoting expectations from our expression to simplify the notation, but remember that we are always thinking about expected returns with the CAPM.

Figure 12.1

Choices of a Firm with Extra Cash

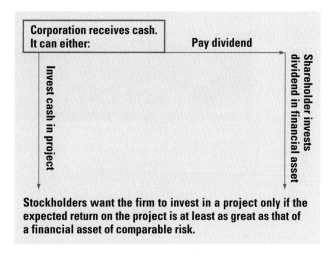

Corporation receives cash. It can either:

Pay dividend

Invest cash in project

Shareholder invests dividend in financial asset

Stockholders want the firm to invest in a project only if the expected return on the project is at least as great as that of a financial asset of comparable risk.

We now have the tools to estimate a firm's cost of equity capital. To do this, we need to know three things:

- The risk-free rate, R_F.
- The market risk premium, $R_M - R_F$.
- The company beta, β.

Cost of Equity   Suppose the stock of the Quatram Company, a publisher of college textbooks, has a beta (β) of 1.3. The firm is 100 percent equity financed; that is, it has no debt. Quatram is considering a number of capital budgeting projects that will double its size. Because these new projects are similar to the firm's existing ones, the average beta on the new projects is assumed to be equal to Quatram's existing beta. The risk-free rate is 5 percent. What is the appropriate discount rate for these new projects, assuming a market risk premium of 8.4 percent?

We estimate the cost of equity, R_S, for Quatram as:

$$R_S = 5\% + (8.4\% \times 1.3)$$
$$= 5\% + 10.92\%$$
$$= 15.92\%$$

Two key assumptions were made in this example: (1) The beta risk of the new projects is the same as the risk of the firm, and (2) the firm is all equity financed. Given these assumptions, it follows that the cash flows of the new projects should be discounted at the 15.92 percent rate.

Project Evaluation and Beta   Suppose Alpha Air Freight is an all-equity firm with a beta of 1.21. Further suppose the market risk premium is 9.5 percent, and the risk-free rate is 5 percent. We can determine the expected return on the common stock of Alpha Air Freight by using the SML of Equation 12.1. We find that the expected return is:

$$5\% + (1.21 \times 9.5\%) = 16.495\%$$

Because this is the return that shareholders can expect in the financial markets on a stock with a β of 1.21, it is the return they expect on Alpha Air Freight's stock.

(continued)

Further suppose Alpha is evaluating the following non–mutually exclusive projects:

Project	Project's Beta (β)	Project's Expected Cash Flows Next Year	Project's Internal Rate of Return	Project's NPV When Cash Flows Are Discounted At 16.495%	Accept or Reject
A	1.21	$140	40%	$20.2	Accept
B	1.21	120	20	3.0	Accept
C	1.21	110	10	−5.6	Reject

Each project initially costs $100. All projects are assumed to have the same risk as the firm as a whole. Because the cost of equity capital is 16.495 percent, projects in an all-equity firm are discounted at this rate. Projects A and B have positive NPVs, and C has a negative NPV. Thus, only A and B will be accepted. This is illustrated in Figure 12.2.

Figure 12.2   Using the Security Market Line to Estimate the Risk-Adjusted Discount Rate for Risky Projects

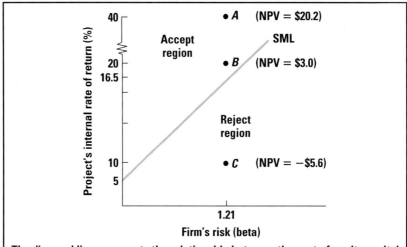

The diagonal line represents the relationship between the cost of equity capital and the firm's beta. An all-equity firm should accept a project whose internal rate of return is greater than the cost of equity capital, and should reject a project whose internal rate of return is less than the cost of equity capital. (This graph assumes that all projects are as risky as the firm.)

12.2 Estimation of Beta

In the previous section, we assumed that the beta of the company was known. Of course, beta must be estimated in the real world. We pointed out earlier that the beta of a security is the standardized covariance of a security's return with the return on the market portfolio. As we have seen, the formula for security i is

$$\text{Beta of security } i = \frac{\text{Cov}(R_i, R_M)}{\text{Var}(R_M)} = \frac{\sigma_{i,M}}{\sigma_M^2}$$

In words, the beta is the covariance of a security with the market, divided by the variance of the market. Because we calculated both covariance and variance in earlier chapters, calculating beta involves no new material.

Measuring Company Betas

The basic method of measuring company betas is to estimate:

$$\frac{\text{Cov}(R_i, R_M)}{\text{Var}(R_M)}$$

using $t = 1, 2, \ldots, T$ observations

Problems

1. Betas may vary over time.
2. The sample size may be inadequate.
3. Betas are influenced by changing financial leverage and business risk.

Solutions

1. Problems 1 and 2 can be moderated by more sophisticated statistical techniques.
2. Problem 3 can be lessened by adjusting for changes in business and financial risk.
3. Look at average beta estimates of several comparable firms in the industry.

Real-World Betas

It is instructive to see how betas are determined for actual real-world companies. Figure 12.3 plots monthly returns for four large firms against monthly returns on the Standard & Poor's (S&P) 500 index. Using a standard regression technique, we fit a straight line through data points. The result is called the "characteristic" line for the security. The slope of the characteristic line is beta. Though we have not shown it in the table, we can also determine the intercept (commonly called alpha) of the characteristic line by regression.

We use five years of monthly data for each plot. Although this choice is arbitrary, it is in line with calculations performed in the real world. Practitioners know that the accuracy of the beta coefficient is suspect when too few observations are used. Conversely, because firms may change their industry over time, observations from the distant past are out of date.

We stated in a previous chapter that the average beta across all stocks in an index is 1. Of course, this need not be true for a subset of the index. For example, of the four securities in our figure, two have betas above 1 and two have betas below 1. Because beta is a measure of the risk of a single security for someone holding a large, diversified portfolio, our results indicate that Philip Morris has relatively low risk and Amazon.com has relatively high risk. A more detailed discussion of the determinants of beta is presented in Section 12.3.

Stability of Beta

We have stated that the beta of a firm is likely to change if the firm changes its industry. It is also interesting to ask the reverse question: Does the beta of a firm stay the same if its industry stays the same?

Take the case of General Electric, a large, diversified firm that for the most part has stayed in the same industries for many decades. Figure 12.4 plots the returns on General Electric and the returns on the S&P 500 for four successive five-year periods. As can be seen from the figure, GE's beta drops slightly from the first to the third subperiod, decreasing

Figure 12.3   Plots of Five Years of Monthly Returns (2000–2004) on Four Individual Securities against Five Years of Monthly Returns on the Standard & Poor's (S&P) 500 Index

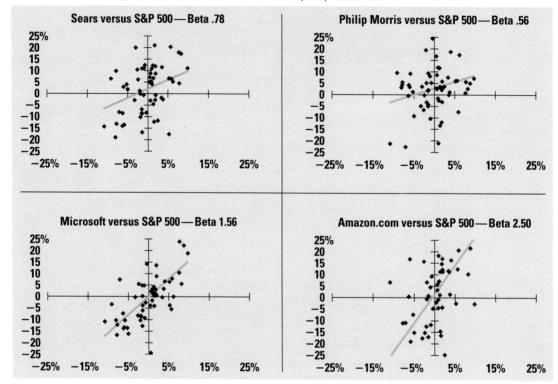

a bit more in the last subperiod. However, this movement in beta is probably nothing more than random variation.[1] Thus, for practical purposes, GE's beta has been approximately constant over the two decades covered in the figure. Although GE is just one company, most analysts argue that betas are generally stable for firms remaining in the same industry.

However, this is not to say that, as long as a firm stays in the same industry, its beta will *never* change. Changes in product line, changes in technology, or changes in the market may affect a firm's beta. For example, the deregulation of the airline industry has increased the betas of airline firms. Furthermore, as we will show in a later section, an increase in the leverage of a firm (i.e., the amount of debt in its capital structure) will increase the firm's beta.

Using an Industry Beta

Our approach to estimating the beta of a company from its own past data may seem commonsensical to you. However, it is frequently argued that people can better estimate a firm's beta by involving the whole industry. Consider Table 12.1, which shows the betas of some prominent firms in the software industry. The average beta across all of the firms in the table is 1.45. Imagine a financial executive at Symantec trying to estimate the firm's beta. Because beta estimation is subject to large random variation in this volatile industry, the executive may be uncomfortable with the estimate of 1.57. However, the error in beta

---

[1]More precisely, we can say that the beta coefficients over the four periods are not statistically different from each other.

Figure 12.4   **Plots of Monthly Returns on General Electric against the Standard & Poor's 500 Index for Four Consecutive Five-Year Periods**

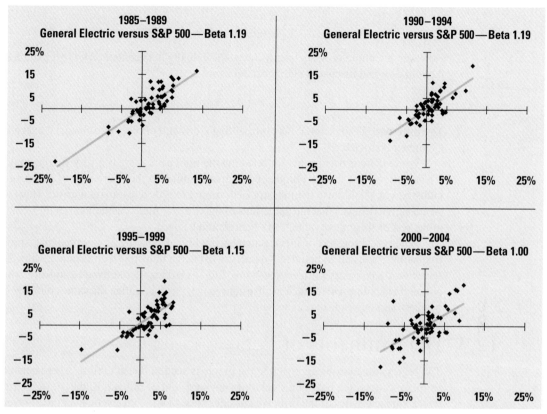

Table 12.1

Betas for Firms in the Computer Software Industry

Company	Beta
Microsoft	1.23
First Data Corp.	.97
Automatic Data Processing	1.07
Electronic Data Systems	1.60
Oracle Corp.	1.40
Computer Sciences	1.76
Computer Associates	2.60
Fiserv Inc.	1.14
Accenture Ltd.	1.71
Symantec Corp.	1.57
Paychex, Inc.	.94
Equally weighted portfolio	1.45

estimation on a single stock is much higher than the error for a portfolio of securities. Thus the executive of Symantec may use the industry beta of 1.45 as the estimate of its own firm's beta. (As it turns out, the choice is unimportant here because the industry beta is so close to that of the firm.)

In contrast, consider Computer Associates. Assuming a risk-free rate of 3.7 percent and a risk premium of 8.7 percent, Computer Associates might estimate its cost of equity capital as:

$$3.7\% + 2.60 \times 8.7\% = 26.32\%$$

However, if Computer Associates believed the industry beta contained less estimation error, it could estimate its cost of equity capital as:

$$3.7\% + 1.45 \times 8.7\% = 16.32\%$$

The difference is substantial here, presenting a difficult choice for a financial executive at Computer Associates.

While there is no formula for selecting the right beta, there is a very simple guideline. If you believe that the operations of a firm are similar to the operations of the rest of the industry, you should use the industry beta simply to reduce estimation error.[2] However, if an executive believes that the operations of the firm are fundamentally different from those in the rest of the industry, the firm's beta should be used.

When we discussed financial statement analysis in Chapter 3, we noted that a problem frequently comes up in practice—namely, what is the industry? For example, Value Line's *Investment Survey* categorizes Accenture, Ltd., as a computer software company, whereas online financial providers such as investor.reuters.com categorize the same company in the business services industry.

12.3   Determinants of Beta

The regression analysis approach in the previous section doesn't tell us where beta comes from. Of course, the beta of a stock does not come out of thin air. Rather, it is determined by the characteristics of the firm. We consider three factors: the cyclical nature of revenues, operating leverage, and financial leverage.

Cyclicality of Revenues

The revenues of some firms are quite cyclical. That is, these firms do well in the expansion phase of the business cycle and do poorly in the contraction phase. Empirical evidence suggests high-tech firms, retailers, and automotive firms fluctuate with the business cycle. Firms in industries such as utilities, railroads, food, and airlines are less dependent on the cycle. Because beta is the standardized covariability of a stock's return with the market's return, it is not surprising that highly cyclical stocks have high betas.

It is worthwhile to point out that cyclicality is not the same as variability. For example, a moviemaking firm has highly variable revenues because hits and flops are not easily pre-dicted. However, because the revenues of a studio are more dependent on the quality of its releases than the phase of the business cycle, motion picture companies are not particularly cyclical. In other words, stocks with high standard deviations need not have high betas, a point we have stressed before.

Operating Leverage

We distinguished fixed costs from variable costs earlier in the text. At that time, we men-tioned that fixed costs do not change as quantity changes. Conversely, variable costs increase

---

[2]As we will see later, an adjustment must be made when the debt level in the industry is different from that of the firm. However, we ignore this adjustment here because firms in the software industry generally have little debt.

as the quantity of output rises. This difference between variable and fixed costs allows us to define operating leverage.

EXAMPLE 12.3

Operating Leverage Illustrated Consider a firm that can choose either technology A or technology B when making a particular product. The relevant differences between the two technologies are displayed here:

Technology A	Technology B
Fixed cost: $1,000/year	Fixed cost: $2,000/year
Variable cost: $8/unit	Variable cost: $6/unit
Price: $10/unit	Price: $10/unit
Contribution margin: $2 (= $10 − $8)	Contribution margin: $4 (= $10 − $6)

Technology A has lower fixed costs and higher variable costs than does technology B. Perhaps technology A involves less mechanization than does B. Or the equipment in A may be leased, whereas the equipment in B must be purchased. Alternatively, perhaps technology A involves few employees but many subcontractors, whereas B involves only highly skilled employees who must be retained in bad times. Because technology B has both lower variable costs and higher fixed costs, we say that it has higher **operating leverage**.[3]

Figure 12.5 graphs the costs under both technologies. The slope of each total cost line represents variable costs under a single technology. The slope of A's line is steeper, indicating greater variable costs.

Figure 12.5   **Illustration of Two Different Technologies**

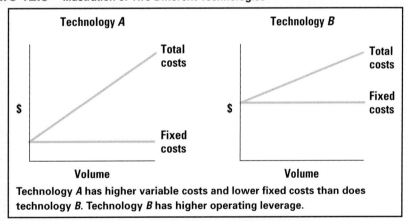

Technology A has higher variable costs and lower fixed costs than does technology B. Technology B has higher operating leverage.

Because the two technologies are used to produce the same products, a unit price of $10 applies for both cases. We mentioned in an earlier chapter that contribution margin is the difference

(continued)

---

[3]The standard definition of operating leverage is

$$\frac{\text{Change in EBIT}}{\text{EBIT}} \times \frac{\text{Sales}}{\text{Change in sales}}$$

where EBIT is the earnings before interest and taxes. That is, operating leverage measures the percentage change in EBIT for a given percentage change in sales or revenues. It can be shown that operating leverage increases as fixed costs rise and as variable costs fall.

Figure 12.6   Illustration of the Effect of a Change in Volume on the Change in Earnings before Interest and Taxes (EBIT)

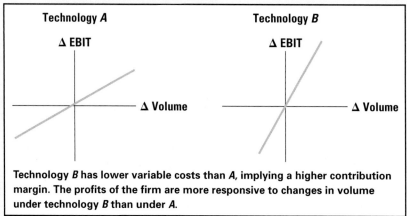

Technology *B* has lower variable costs than *A*, implying a higher contribution margin. The profits of the firm are more responsive to changes in volume under technology *B* than under *A*.

between price and variable cost. It measures the incremental profit from one additional unit. Because the contribution margin in *B* is greater, its technology is riskier. An unexpected sale increases profit by $2 under *A* but increases profit by $4 under *B*. Similarly, an unexpected sale cancellation reduces profit by $2 under *A* but reduces profit by $4 under *B*. This is illustrated in Figure 12.6. This figure shows the change in earnings before interest and taxes for a given change in volume. The slope of the right graph is greater, indicating that technology *B* is riskier.

The cyclicality of a firm's revenues is a determinant of the firm's beta. Operating leverage magnifies the effect of cyclicality on beta. As mentioned earlier, business risk is generally defined as the risk of the firm without financial leverage. Business risk depends both on the responsiveness of the firm's revenues to the business cycle and on the firm's operating leverage.

Although the preceding discussion concerns firms, it applies to projects as well. If we cannot estimate a project's beta in another way, we can examine the project's revenues and operating leverage. Projects whose revenues appear strongly cyclical and whose operating leverage appears high are likely to have high betas. Conversely, weak cyclicality and low operating leverage imply low betas. As mentioned earlier, this approach is unfortunately qualitative in nature. Because start-up projects have little data, quantitative estimates of beta generally are not feasible.

Financial Leverage and Beta

As suggested by their names, operating leverage and financial leverage are analogous concepts. Operating leverage refers to the firm's fixed costs of *production*. Financial leverage is the extent to which a firm relies on debt, and a levered firm is a firm with some debt in its capital structure. Because a *levered* firm must make interest payments regardless of the firm's sales, financial leverage refers to the firm's fixed costs of *finance*.

Consider our discussion in Chapter 10 concerning the beta of Jelco, Inc. In that example, we estimated beta from the returns on Jelco *stock*. Furthermore, the betas in Figures 12.3 and 12.4 from real-world firms were estimated from returns on stock. Thus, in each case, we estimated the firm's stock or **equity beta**. The beta of the assets of a levered firm is different from the beta of its equity. As the name suggests, the **asset beta** is the beta of the assets of the firm. The asset beta could also be thought of as the beta of the common stock had the firm been financed only with equity.

Imagine an individual who owns all the firm's debt and all its equity. In other words, this individual owns the entire firm. What is the beta of her portfolio of the firm's debt and equity?

As with any portfolio, the beta of this portfolio is a weighted average of the betas of the individual items in the portfolio. Let B stand for the market value of the firm's debt and S stand for the market value of the firm's equity. We have:

$$\beta_{Asset} = \frac{S}{B+S} \times \beta_{Equity} + \frac{B}{B+S} \times \beta_{Debt} \tag{12.2}$$

where β_{Equity} is the beta of the stock of the *levered* firm. Notice that the beta of debt, β_{Debt}, is multiplied by $B/(B + S)$, the percentage of debt in the capital structure. Similarly, the beta of equity is multiplied by the percentage of equity in the capital structure. Because the portfolio contains both the debt of the firm and the equity of the firm, the beta of the portfolio is the *asset beta*. As we just said, the asset beta can also be viewed as the beta of the common stock had the firm been all equity.

The beta of debt is very low in practice. If we make the common assumption that the beta of debt is zero, we have:

$$\beta_{Asset} = \frac{S}{B+S} \times \beta_{Equity} \tag{12.3}$$

Because $S/(B + S)$ must be below 1 for a levered firm, it follows that $\beta_{Asset} < \beta_{Equity}$. Rearranging this equation, we have:

$$\beta_{Equity} = \beta_{Asset}\left(1 + \frac{B}{S}\right)$$

The equity beta will always be greater than the asset beta with financial leverage (assuming the asset beta is positive).[4]

EXAMPLE 12.4

Asset versus Equity Betas Consider a tree growing company, Rapid Cedars, Inc., which is currently all equity and has a beta of .8. The firm has decided to move to a capital structure of one part debt to two parts equity. Because the firm is staying in the same industry, its asset beta should remain at .8. However, assuming a zero beta for its debt, its equity beta would become:

$$\beta_{Equity} = \beta_{Asset}\left(1 + \frac{B}{S}\right)$$

$$1.2 = .8\left(1 + \frac{1}{2}\right)$$

If the firm had one part debt to one part equity in its capital structure, its equity beta would be:

$$1.6 = .8(1 + 1)$$

However, as long as it stayed in the same industry, its asset beta would remain at .8. The effect of leverage, then, is to increase the equity beta.

---

[4]It can be shown that the relationship between a firm's asset beta and its equity beta with corporate taxes is

$$\beta_{Equity} = \beta_{Asset}\left[1 + (1 - t_C)\frac{B}{S}\right]$$

In this expression, t_C is the corporate tax rate. Tax effects are considered in more detail in a later chapter.

12.4 Extensions of the Basic Model

The Firm versus the Project: Vive la Différence

We now assume that the risk of a project differs from that of the firm, while going back to the all-equity assumption. We began the chapter by pointing out that each project should be paired with a financial asset of comparable risk. If a project's beta differs from that of the firm, the project should be discounted at the rate commensurate with its own beta. This is a very important point because firms frequently speak of a *corporate discount rate*. (*Hurdle rate*, *cutoff rate*, *benchmark*, and *cost of capital* are frequently used synonymously.) Unless all projects in the corporation are of the same risk, choosing the same discount rate for all projects is incorrect.

EXAMPLE 12.5

Project Risk   D. D. Ronnelley Co., a publishing firm, may accept a project in computer software. Noting that computer software companies have high betas, the publishing firm views the software venture as more risky than the rest of its business. It should discount the project at a rate commensurate with the risk of software companies. For example, it might use the average beta of a portfolio of publicly traded software firms. Instead, if all projects in D. D. Ronnelley Co. were discounted at the same rate, a bias would result. The firm would accept too many high-risk projects (software ventures) and reject too many low-risk projects (books and magazines). This point is illustrated in Figure 12.7.

Figure 12.7   **Relationship between the Firm's Cost of Capital and the Security Market Line**

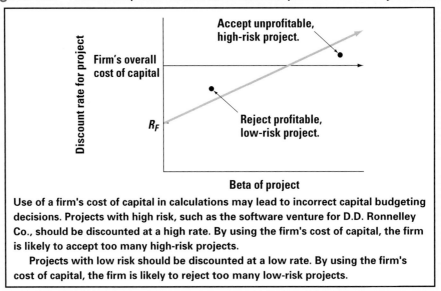

Use of a firm's cost of capital in calculations may lead to incorrect capital budgeting decisions. Projects with high risk, such as the software venture for D.D. Ronnelley Co., should be discounted at a high rate. By using the firm's cost of capital, the firm is likely to accept too many high-risk projects.

Projects with low risk should be discounted at a low rate. By using the firm's cost of capital, the firm is likely to reject too many low-risk projects.

The D. D. Ronnelley example assumes that the proposed project has identical risk to that of the software industry, allowing the industry beta to be used. However, the beta of a new project may be greater than the beta of existing firms in the same industry because the very newness of the project likely increases its responsiveness to economywide movements. For example, a start-up computer venture may fail in a recession, whereas IBM or Hewlett-Packard will still be around. Conversely, in an economywide expansion, the venture may grow much faster than the old-line computer firms.

Fortunately, a slight adjustment is all that is needed here. The new venture should be assigned a somewhat higher beta than that of the industry to reflect added risk. The adjustment is necessarily ad hoc, so no formula can be given. Our experience indicates that this approach is widespread in practice today.

However, a problem does arise for the rare project constituting its own industry. For example, consider the firms providing consumer shopping by television. Today, we can obtain a reasonable estimate for the beta of this industry because a few of the firms have publicly traded stock. However, when the ventures began in the 1980s, any beta estimate was suspect. At that time, no one knew whether shopping by TV belonged in the television industry, the retail industry, or in an entirely new industry.

What beta should be used in the rare case when an industrywide beta is not appropriate? One approach, which considers the determinants of the project's beta, was treated earlier in this chapter. Unfortunately, that approach is only qualitative in nature.

The Cost of Capital with Debt

Section 12.1 showed how to choose the discount rate when a project is all equity financed. In this section we discuss an adjustment when the project is financed with both debt and equity.

Suppose a firm uses both debt and equity to finance its investments. If the firm pays R_B for its debt financing and R_S for its equity, what is the overall or average cost of its capital? The cost of equity is R_S, as discussed in earlier sections. The cost of debt is the firm's borrowing rate, R_B, which we can often observe by looking at the yield to maturity on the firm's debt. If a firm uses both debt and equity, the cost of capital is a weighted average of each. This works out to be:

$$\frac{S}{S+B} \times R_S + \frac{B}{S+B} \times R_B$$

The weights in the formula are, respectively, the proportion of total value represented by the equity:

$$\left(\frac{S}{S+B}\right)$$

and the proportion of total value represented by debt:

$$\left(\frac{B}{S+B}\right)$$

This is only natural. If the firm had issued no debt and was therefore an all-equity firm, its average cost of capital would equal its cost of equity, R_S. At the other extreme, if the firm had issued so much debt that its equity was valueless, it would be an all-debt firm, and its average cost of capital would be its cost of debt, R_B.

Of course, interest is tax deductible at the corporate level, a point to be treated in more detail in a later chapter. The aftertax cost of debt is:

$$\text{Cost of debt (after corporate tax)} = R_B \times (1 - t_C)$$

where t_C is the corporation's tax rate.

Assembling these results, we get the average cost of capital (after tax) for the firm:

$$\text{Average cost of capital} = \left(\frac{S}{S+B}\right) \times R_S + \left(\frac{B}{S+B}\right) \times R_B \times (1 - t_C) \quad \textbf{(12.4)}$$

Because the average cost of capital is a weighting of its cost of equity and its cost of debt, it is usually referred to as the **weighted average cost of capital**, R_{WACC}, and from now on we will use this term.

EXAMPLE 12.6

WACC   Consider a firm whose debt has a market value of $40 million and whose stock has a market value of $60 million (3 million outstanding shares of stock, each selling for $20 per share). The firm pays a 15 percent rate of interest on its new debt and has a beta of 1.41. The corporate tax rate is 34 percent. (Assume that the SML holds, that the risk premium on the market is 9.5 percent [slightly higher than the historical equity risk premium], and that the current Treasury bill rate is 11 percent [much higher than the current Treasury bill rate].) What is this firm's R_{WACC}?

To compute the R_{WACC} using Equation 12.4, we must know (1) the aftertax cost of debt, $R_B \times (1 - t_C)$, (2) the cost of equity, R_S, and (3) the proportions of debt and equity used by the firm. These three values are computed next:

1. The pretax cost of debt is 15 percent, implying an aftertax cost of 9.9 percent [15% × (1 − .34)].

2. We compute the cost of equity capital by using the SML:

$$R_S = R_F + \beta \times [R_M - R_F]$$
$$= 11\% + 1.41 \times 9.5\%$$
$$= 24.40\%$$

3. We compute the proportions of debt and equity from the market values of debt and equity. Because the market value of the firm is $100 million (=$40 million + $60 million), the proportions of debt and equity are 40 and 60 percent, respectively.

The cost of equity, R_S, is 24.40 percent, and the aftertax cost of debt, $R_B \times (1 - t_C)$, is 9.9 percent. B is $40 million and S is $60 million. Therefore:

$$R_{WACC} = \frac{S}{B + S} \times R_S + \frac{B}{B + S} \times R_B \times (1 - t_C)$$
$$= \left(\frac{40}{100} \times 9.9\% \right) + \left(\frac{60}{100} \times 24.40\% \right) = 18.60\%$$

This procedure is presented in table form next:

(1) Financing Components	(2) Market Values	(3) Weight	(4) Cost of Capital (after Corporate Tax)	(5) Weighted Cost of Capital
Debt	$ 40,000,000	.40	15% × (1 − .34) = 9.9%	3.96%
Equity	60,000,000	.60	11% + 1.41 × 9.5% = 24.40	14.64
	$100,000,000	1.00		18.60%

The weights we used in the previous example were market value weights. Market value weights are more appropriate than book value weights because the market values of the securities are closer to the actual dollars that would be received from their sale. Actually, it is usually useful to think in terms of "target" market weights. These are the market weights expected to prevail over the life of the firm or project.

EXAMPLE 12.7

Project Evaluation and the WACC   Suppose a firm has both a current and a target debt–equity ratio of .6, a cost of debt of 15.15 percent, and a cost of equity of 20 percent. The corporate tax rate is 34 percent.

Our first step calls for transforming the debt–equity (B/S) ratio to a debt–value ratio. A B/S ratio of .6 implies 6 parts debt for 10 parts equity. Because value is equal to the sum of the debt plus the equity, the debt–value ratio is 6/(6 + 10) = .375. Similarly, the equity–value ratio is 10/(6 + 10) = .625. The R_{WACC} will then be:

(continued)

$$R_{WACC} = \left(\frac{S}{S+B}\right) \times R_S + \left(\frac{B}{S+B}\right) \times R_B \times (1 - t_C)$$

$$= .625 \times 20\% + .375 \times 15.15\% \times .66 = 16.25\%$$

Suppose the firm is considering taking on a warehouse renovation costing $50 million that is expected to yield cost savings of $12 million a year for six years. Using the NPV equation and discounting the six years of expected cash flows from the renovation at the R_{WACC}, we have:

$$NPV = -\$50 + \frac{\$12}{(1 + R_{WACC})} + \cdots + \frac{\$12}{(1 + R_{WACC})^6}$$

$$= -\$50 + \$12 \times A_{.1625}^6$$

$$= -\$50 + (12 \times 3.66)$$

$$= -\$6.07$$

Should the firm take on the warehouse renovation? The project has a negative NPV using the firm's R_{WACC}. This means that the financial markets offer superior projects in the same risk class (namely, the firm's risk class). The answer is clear: The firm should reject the project.

12.5   Estimating Eastman Chemical's Cost of Capital

In our previous sections, we calculated the cost of capital in examples. We will now calculate the cost of capital for a real company, Eastman Chemical Co., a leading international chemical company and maker of plastics such as that used in soft drink containers. It was created in 1993 when its former parent company, Eastman Kodak, split off the division as a separate company.

Eastman's Cost of Equity

Our first stop for Eastman is investor.reuters.com (ticker: "EMN"). As of February 2006, the relevant pieces of what we found are shown in the next box:

Key Ratios & Statistics

Price & Volume		Valuation Ratios	
Recent Price $	48.45	Price/Earnings (TTM)	7.11
52 Week High $	61.80	Price/Sales (TTM)	0.56
52 Week Low $	44.10	Price/Book (MRQ)	2.45
Avg Daily Vol (Mil)	0.77	Price/Cash Flow (TTM)	4.60
Beta	0.80	**Per Share Data**	
Share Related Items		Earnings (TTM) $	6.82
Mkt. Cap. (Mil) $	3,947.71	Sales (TTM) $	86.32
Shares Out (Mil)	81.48	Book Value (MRQ) $	19.82
Float (Mil)	80.80	Cash Flow (TTM) $	10.53
Dividend Information		Cash (MRQ) $	NM
Yield %	3.63	**Mgmt Effectiveness**	
Annual Dividend	1.76	Return on Equity (TTM)	38.42
Payout Ratio (TTM) %	19.09	Return on Assets (TTM)	9.67
Financial Strength		Return on Investment (TTM)	11.87
Quick Ratio (MRQ)	0.00	**Profitability**	
Current Ratio (MRQ)	1.80	Gross Margin (TTM) %	19.89
LT Debt/Equity (MRQ)	1.00	Operating Margin (TTM) %	10.07
Total Debt/Equity (MRQ)	1.01	Profit Margin (TTM) %	7.89

Mil = Millions   MRQ = Most Recent Quarter   TTM = Trailing Twelve Months
Asterisks (*) Indicates numbers are derived from Earnings Announcements

Table 12.2

Betas for Companies in the Diversified Chemical Industry

Company	Beta
3M Company	.65
Air Products & Chemical	.70
Monsanto Co.	1.05
PPG Industries	.86
Eastman Chemical	.80
Albemarle Corp.	1.00
Cabot Corp.	.84
Pall Corp.	1.23
Cytec Industries	.77
Millipore Corp.	1.10
Cambrex Corp.	.61
Equally weighted portfolio	.87

According to this screen, Eastman has 81.48 million shares of stock outstanding. The book value per share is $19.82, but the stock sells for $48.45. Total equity is therefore about $1.615 billion on a book value basis, but it is closer to $3.948 billion on a market value basis.

To estimate Eastman's cost of equity, we will assume a market risk premium of 8.7 percent, similar to what we calculated in Chapter 9. Eastman's beta on Reuters is .80. Table 12.2 shows the betas for other U.S.-based diversified chemical companies. As you can see, the industry average beta is .87, which is slightly higher than Eastman's beta. According to the bond section of finance.yahoo.com, T-bills were paying about 4.26 percent. Using Eastman's own beta in the CAPM to estimate the cost of equity, we find:

$$R_S = .0426 + .80(.087) = .1122 \text{ or } 11.22\%$$

If we use the industry beta, we would find that the estimate for the cost of equity capital is:

$$R_S = .0426 + .87(.087) = .1183 \text{ or } 11.83\%$$

Notice that the estimates for the cost of equity are close because Eastman's beta is relatively close to the industry beta. The decision of which cost of equity estimate to use is up to the financial executive, based on knowledge and experience of both the company and the industry. In this case, we will choose to use the cost of equity using Eastman's estimated beta.

Eastman's Cost of Debt

Eastman has six long-term bond issues that account for essentially all of its long-term debt. To calculate the cost of debt, we will have to combine these six issues and compute a weighted average. We will go to www.nasdbondinfo.com to find quotes on the bonds. We should note here that finding the yield to maturity for all of a company's outstanding bond issues on a single day is unusual. In our previous discussion of bonds, we found that the bond market is not as liquid as the stock market, and on many days individual bond issues may not trade. To find the book value of the bonds we go to www.sec.gov and find the 10Q report (i.e., the most recent financial report) dated September 30, 2005, and filed with the SEC on November 1, 2005. The basic information is as follows:

Coupon Rate	Maturity	Book Value (Face Value, in Millions)	Price (% of Par)	Yield to Maturity
3.25%	2008	$ 72	96.092%	5.02%
7.00	2012	187	108.515	5.36
6.30	2018	143	100.835	6.20
7.25	2024	497	108.448	6.45
7.625	2024	200	113.006	6.41
7.60	2027	297	113.610	6.41

To calculate the weighted average cost of debt, we take the percentage of the total debt represented by each issue and multiply by the yield on the issue. We then add to get the overall weighted average debt cost. We use both book values and market values here for comparison. The results of the calculations are as follows:

Coupon Rate	Book Value (Face Value, in Millions)	Percentage of Total	Market Value (in Millions)	Percentage of Total	Yield to Maturity	Book Value Weights	Market Value Weights
3.25%	$ 72	0.05	$ 69.19	0.05	5.02%	0.26%	0.23%
7.00	187	0.13	202.92	0.13	5.36	0.72	0.72
6.30	143	0.10	144.19	0.09	6.20	0.64	0.59
7.60	497	0.36	538.99	0.35	6.45	2.30	2.29
7.625	200	0.14	226.01	0.15	6.41	0.92	0.95
7.60	297	0.21	337.42	0.22	6.41	1.36	1.42
Total	$1,396	1.00	$1,518.72	1.00		6.19%	6.20%

As these calculations show, Eastman's cost of debt is 6.19 percent on a book value basis and 6.20 percent on a market value basis. Thus, for Eastman, whether market values or book values are used makes no difference. The reason is simply that the market values and book values are similar. This will often be the case and explains why companies frequently use book values for debt in WACC calculations.

Eastman's WACC

We now have the various pieces necessary to calculate Eastman's WACC. First, we need to calculate the capital structure weights. On a book value basis, Eastman's equity and debt are worth $1.615 billion and $1.396 billion, respectively. The total value is $3.011 billion, so the equity and debt percentages are $1.615 billion/$3.011 billion = .54 and $1.396 billion/$3.011 billion = .46, respectively. Assuming a tax rate of 35 percent, Eastman's WACC is:

$$R_{WACC} = .54 \times 11.22\% + .46 \times 6.20\% \times (1 - .35)$$
$$= 7.91\%$$

Thus, using book value capital structure weights, we get about 7.91 percent for Eastman's R_{WACC}.

If we use market value weights, however, the R_{WACC} will be higher. To see why, notice that on a market value basis, Eastman's equity and debt are worth $3.948 billion and $1.519 billion, respectively. The capital structure weights are therefore $3.948 billion/$5.467 billion = .72

and $1.519 billion/$5.467 billion $= .28$, so the equity percentage is much higher. With these weights, Eastman's R_{WACC} is:

$$R_{WACC} = .72 \times 11.22\% + .28 \times 6.20\% \times (1 - .35)$$
$$= 9.21\%$$

Thus, using market value weights, we get 9.21 percent for Eastman's R_{WACC}, which is more than a full percent higher than the 7.91 percent R_{WACC} we got using book value weights.

So how does our estimate of the R_{WACC} for Eastman compare to others? One place to find estimates for a company's R_{WACC} is www.valuepro.net. We went there and found the following information for Eastman:

Online Valuation for EMN - 2 / 3 / 2006

Intrinsic Stock Value	245.16	Recalculate	Value Another Stock

Excess Return Period (yrs)	10	Depreciation Rate (% of Rev)	4.89
Revenues ($mil)	6988.0	Investment Rate (% of Rev)	3.77
Growth Rate (%)	29	Working Capital (% of Rev)	11.9
Net Oper. Profit Margin (%)	3.88	Short-Term Assets ($mil)	1844.0
Tax Rate (%)	23.529	Short-Term Liab. ($mil)	889
Stock Price ($)	50.1400	Equity Risk Premium (%)	3
Shares Outstanding (mil)	81.4	Company Beta	1.1025
10-Yr Treasury Yield (%)	5	Value Debt Out. ($mil)	1436
Bond Spread Treasury (%)	1.5	Value Pref. Stock Out. ($mil)	0
Preferred Stock Yield (%)	7.5	Company WACC (%)	7.44

As you can see, ValuePro estimates the R_{WACC} for Eastman as 7.44 percent, which is lower than our estimate of 9.21 percent. The methods used by this site are not identical to ours, but they are similar in many important regards. You can visit the site to learn more if you are so inclined.

12.6   Reducing the Cost of Capital

Chapters 9–12 develop the idea that both the expected return on a stock and the cost of capital of the firm are positively related to risk. Recently, a number of academics have argued that expected return and cost of capital are negatively related to liquidity as well.[5] In addition, these scholars make the interesting point that although it is quite difficult to lower the risk of a firm, it is much easier to increase the liquidity of the firm's stock. Therefore they suggest that a firm can actually lower its cost of capital through liquidity enhancement. We develop this idea next.

What Is Liquidity?

Anyone who owns a home probably thinks of liquidity in terms of the time it takes to buy or sell the home. For example, condominiums in large metropolitan areas are generally quite liquid. Particularly in good times, a condominium may sell within days of being placed on the market. By contrast, single-family homes in suburban areas may take weeks or months to sell. Special properties such as multimillion-dollar mansions may take longer still.

The concept of liquidity is similar, but not identical, in stocks. Here, we speak of the *cost* of buying and selling instead. That is, stocks that are expensive to trade are considered less liquid than those that trade cheaply. What do we mean by the cost to trade? We generally think of three costs here: brokerage fees, the bid–ask spread, and market impact costs.

Brokerage fees are the easiest to understand because you must pay a broker to execute a trade. More difficult is the bid–ask spread. Consider the New York Stock Exchange (NYSE), where all trades on a particular stock must go through the stock's specialist, who is physically on the floor of the exchange. If you want to trade 100 shares of XYZ Co., your broker must get the *quote* from XYZ's specialist. Suppose the specialist provides a quote of 100.00–100.07. This means that you can buy from the specialist at $100.07 per share and sell to the specialist at $100 per share. Note that the specialist makes money here, because she buys from you at $100 and sells to you (or to someone else) at $100.07. The gain to the specialist is a cost to you because you are losing $0.07 per share over a round-trip transaction (over a purchase and a subsequent sale).

Finally, we have *market impact costs*. Suppose a trader wants to sell 10,000 shares instead of just 100 shares. Here, the specialist has to take on extra risk when buying. First, she has to pay out $1,000,000 (= 10,000 × $100), cash that may not be easily available to her. Second, the trader may be selling this large amount because she has special information that the stock will fall imminently. The specialist bears the risk of losing a lot of money on that trade. Consequently, to compensate for these risks, the specialist may buy not at $100/share but at a lower price. Similarly, the specialist may be willing to sell a large block of stock only at a price above $100.07. The price drop associated with a large sale and the price rise associated with a large purchase are the market impact costs.

Liquidity, Expected Returns, and the Cost of Capital

The cost of trading a nonliquid stock reduces the total return that an investor receives. That is, if you buy a stock for $100 and sell it later for $105, the gain before trading costs is $5. If you must pay a dollar of commission when buying and another dollar when selling, the gain after trading costs is only $3. Both the bid–ask spread and market impact costs would reduce this gain still further.

As we will see later, trading costs vary across securities. In the last four chapters we have stressed that investors demand a high expected return as compensation when investing in high-risk (e.g., high-beta) stocks. Because the expected return to the investor is the

----

[5]For example, see Y. Amihud and H. Mendelson, "The Liquidity Route to a Lower Cost of Capital," *Journal of Applied Corporate Finance* (Winter 2000), and M. J. Brennan and C. Tamarowski, "Investor Relations, Liquidity, and Stock Prices," *Journal of Applied Corporate Finance* (Winter 2000).

Figure 12.8
Liquidity and the Cost of Capital

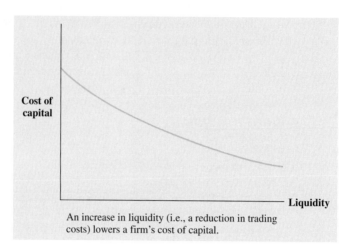

An increase in liquidity (i.e., a reduction in trading costs) lowers a firm's cost of capital.

cost of capital to the firm, the cost of capital is positively related to beta. Now we are saying the same thing for trading costs. Investors demand a high expected return when investing in stocks with high trading costs—that is, with low liquidity. This high expected return implies a high cost of capital to the firm. This idea is illustrated in Figure 12.8.

Liquidity and Adverse Selection

Liquidity varies across stocks because the factors determining liquidity vary across stocks. Although there are a number of factors, we focus on just one: *adverse selection*. As mentioned before, the specialist will lose money on a trade if the trader has information that the specialist does not have. If you have special information that the stock is worth $110 in the preceding example, you will want to buy shares at $100.07. The specialist is obligated to sell to you at this price, which is considerably below the true price of $110. Conversely, if you know that the stock is worth only $90 and you currently own 100 shares, you will be happy to sell these shares to the specialist at $100. Again, the specialist loses because he pays $100/share for a stock worth only $90. In either of these cases, we say that the specialist has been *picked off,* or has been subject to adverse selection.

The specialist must protect himself in some way here. Of course, he cannot forbid informed individuals from trading because he does not know ahead of time who these investors are. His next best alternative is to widen the bid–ask spread, thereby increasing the costs of trading to *all* traders—both informed and uninformed. That is, if the spread is widened to, say, $99.98–$100.11, each trader pays a round-trip cost of $0.13 per share.

The key here is that the spread should be positively related to the ratio of informed to uninformed traders. That is, informed traders will pick off the specialist and uninformed traders will not. Thus, informed traders in a stock raise the required return on equity, thereby increasing the cost of capital.

What the Corporation Can Do

The corporation has an incentive to lower trading costs because (given the preceding discussion) a lower cost of capital should result. Amihud and Mendelson identify two general strategies for corporations. First, they argue that firms should try to bring in more uninformed investors. Stock splits may be a useful tool here. Imagine that a company has 1 million shares outstanding with a price per share of $100. Because investors generally buy in round lots of 100 shares, these investors would need $10,000 (=$100 × 100 shares) for a purchase. A number of small investors might be "priced out" of the stock, although large investors would not be. Thus, the ratio of large investors to small investors would be high. Because large investors are generally more likely than small investors to be informed, the ratio of informed investors to uninformed investors will likely be high.

A 2:1 stock split would give two shares of stock for every one that the investor previously held. Because every investor would still hold the same proportional interest in the firm, each investor would be no better off than before. Thus, it is likely that the price per share will fall to $50 from $100. Here, an individual with 100 shares worth $10,000 (=$100 × 100 shares) finds herself still worth $10,000 (= $50 × 200 shares) after the split.

However, a round lot becomes more affordable, thereby bringing more small and uninformed investors into the firm. Consequently, the adverse selection costs are reduced, allowing the specialist to lower the bid–ask spread. In turn, it is hoped that the expected return on the stock, and the cost of equity capital, will fall as well. If this happens, the stock might actually trade at a price slightly above $50.

This idea is a new one, and empirical evidence is not yet in. Amihud and Mendelson themselves point out the possibility that this strategy might backfire because brokerage commissions are often higher on lower-priced securities. We must await confirmation of this intriguing suggestion.

Companies can also attract small investors by facilitating stock purchases through the Internet. Direct stock purchase plans and dividend reinvestment programs handled online allow small investors to buy securities cheaply. In addition, Amihud and Mendelson state, "And when these plans are administered over the Internet using Web sites like Stockpower .com, moneypaper.com, and Netstockdirect.com, the process is fast and efficient for both the company and the investor."[6]

Second, companies can disclose more information. This narrows the gap between uninformed and informed investors, thereby lowering the cost of capital. Suggestions include providing more financial data about corporate segments and more management forecasts. An interesting study by Coller and Yohn[7] concludes that the bid–ask spread is reduced after the release of these forecasts.

This section would not be complete without a discussion of security analysts. These analysts are employed by brokerage houses to follow the companies in individual industries. For example, an analyst for a particular brokerage house might follow all the firms in, say, the auto industry. This analyst distributes reports and other information to the clients of the brokerage house. Virtually all brokerage houses have analysts following the major industries. Again, through dissemination of the information, these analysts narrow the gap between the informed and the uninformed investors, thereby tending to reduce the bid–ask spread.

Although all major industries are covered, the smaller firms in these industries are often ignored, implying a higher bid–ask spread and a higher cost of capital for these firms. Analysts frequently state that they avoid following companies that release little information, pointing out that these companies are more trouble than they are worth. Thus, it behooves companies that are not followed to release as much information as possible to security analysts to attract their interest. Friendliness toward security analysts would be helpful as well. The argument here is not to get the analysts to make buy recommendations. Rather, it is simply to interest the analysts in following the company, thereby reducing the information asymmetry between informed and uninformed investors.

---

[6]Ibid., p. 19.

[7]M. Coller and T. Yohn, "Management Forecasts and Information Asymmetry: An Examination of Bid–Ask Spreads," *Journal of Accounting Research* (Fall 1997).

Summary and Conclusions

Earlier chapters about capital budgeting assumed that projects generate riskless cash flows. The appropriate discount rate in that case is the riskless interest rate. Of course, most cash flows from real-world capital budgeting projects are risky. This chapter discussed the discount rate when cash flows are risky.

1. A firm with excess cash can either pay a dividend or make a capital expenditure. Because stockholders can reinvest the dividend in risky financial assets, the expected return on a capital budgeting project should be at least as great as the expected return on a financial asset of comparable risk.

2. The expected return on any asset is dependent on its beta. Thus, we showed how to estimate the beta of a stock. The appropriate procedure employs regression analysis on historical returns.

3. We considered the case of a project whose beta risk was equal to that of the firm. If the firm is unlevered, the discount rate on the project is equal to:

$$R_F + \beta \times (R_M - R_F)$$

where R_M is the expected return on the market portfolio and R_F is the risk-free rate. In words, the discount rate on the project is equal to the CAPM's estimate of the expected return on the security.

4. If the project's beta differs from that of the firm, the discount rate should be based on the project's beta. We can generally estimate the project's beta by determining the average beta of the project's industry.

5. The beta of a company is a function of a number of factors. Perhaps the three most important are:
   - Cyclicality of revenues.
   - Operating leverage.
   - Financial leverage.

6. Sometimes we cannot use the average beta of the project's industry as an estimate of the beta of the project. For example, a new project may not fall neatly into any existing industry. In this case, we can estimate the project's beta by considering the project's cyclicality of revenues and its operating leverage. This approach is qualitative.

7. If a firm uses debt, the discount rate to use is the R_{WACC}. To calculate R_{WACC}, we must estimate the cost of equity and the cost of debt applicable to a project. If the project is similar to the firm, the cost of equity can be estimated using the SML for the firm's equity. Conceptually, a dividend growth model could be used as well, though it is likely to be far less accurate in practice.

8. Liquidity probably plays a role in determining a firm's cost of capital. A firm may be able to reduce its cost of capital by taking steps to improve liquidity.

Concept Questions

1. **Project Risk**   If you can borrow all the money you need for a project at 6 percent, doesn't it follow that 6 percent is your cost of capital for the project?

2. **WACC and Taxes**   Why do we use an aftertax figure for cost of debt but not for cost of equity?

3. **SML Cost of Equity Estimation**   If you use the stock beta and the security market line to compute the discount rate for a project, what assumptions are you implicitly making?

4. **SML Cost of Equity Estimation**   What are the advantages of using the SML approach to finding the cost of equity capital? What are the disadvantages? What are the specific pieces of information needed to use this method? Are all of these variables observable, or do they need to be estimated? What are some of the ways in which you could get these estimates?

5. **Cost of Debt Estimation**   How do you determine the appropriate cost of debt for a company? Does it make a difference if the company's debt is privately placed as opposed to being publicly traded? How would you estimate the cost of debt for a firm whose only debt issues are privately held by institutional investors?

6. **Cost of Capital**   Suppose Tom O'Bedlam, president of Bedlam Products, Inc., has hired you to determine the firm's cost of debt and cost of equity capital.

a. The stock currently sells for ARS 50 per share, and the dividend per share will probably be about ARS 5. Tom argues, "It will cost us ARS 5 per share to use the stockholders' money this year, so the cost of equity is equal to 10 percent (ARS 5/50)." What's wrong with this conclusion?

b. Based on the most recent financial statements, Bedlam Products' total liabilities are ARS 8 million. Total interest expense for the coming year will be about ARS 1 million. Tom therefore reasons, "We owe ARS 8 million, and we will pay ARS 1 million interest. Therefore, our cost of debt is obviously ARS 1 million/8 million = 12.5 percent." What's wrong with this conclusion?

c. Based on his own analysis, Tom is recommending that the company increase its use of equity financing because "debt costs 12.5 percent, but equity only costs 10 percent; thus equity is cheaper." Ignoring all the other issues, what do you think about the conclusion that the cost of equity is less than the cost of debt?

7. Company Risk versus Project Risk   Both Dow Chemical Company, a large natural gas user, and Superior Oil, a major natural gas producer, are thinking of investing in natural gas wells near Houston. Both are all equity financed companies. Dow and Superior are looking at identical projects. They've analyzed their respective investments, which would involve a negative cash flow now and positive expected cash flows in the future. These cash flows would be the same for both firms. No debt would be used to finance the projects. Both companies estimate that their projects would have a net present value of BBD 1 million at an 18 percent discount rate and a −BBD 1.1 million NPV at a 22 percent discount rate. Dow has a beta of 1.25, whereas Superior has a beta of .75. The expected risk premium on the market is 8 percent, and risk-free bonds are yielding 12 percent. Should either company proceed? Should both? Explain.

8. Divisional Cost of Capital   Under what circumstances would it be appropriate for a firm to use different costs of capital for its different operating divisions? If the overall firm WACC were used as the hurdle rate for all divisions, would the riskier divisions or the more conservative divisions tend to get most of the investment projects? Why? If you were to try to estimate the appropriate cost of capital for different divisions, what problems might you encounter? What are two techniques you could use to develop a rough estimate for each division's cost of capital?

9. Leverage   Consider a levered firm's projects that have similar risks to the firm as a whole. Is the discount rate for the projects higher or lower than the rate computed using the security market line? Why?

10. Beta   What factors determine the beta of a stock? Define and describe each.

Questions and Problems

BASIC
(Questions 1–13)

1. Calculating Cost of Equity   The Dybvig Corporation's common stock has a beta of 1.3. If the risk-free rate is 4.5 percent and the expected return on the market is 13 percent, what is Dybvig's cost of equity capital?

2. Calculating Cost of Debt   Joanne's Food Stalls is trying to determine its cost of debt. The firm has a debt issue outstanding with 12 years to maturity that is quoted at 105 percent of face value. The issue makes semiannual payments and has a coupon rate of 8 percent annually. What is Joanne's Food Stall's pretax cost of debt? If the tax rate is 30 percent, what is the aftertax cost of debt?

3. Calculating Cost of Debt   Shanken Corp. issued a 30-year, 10 percent semiannual bond 7 years ago. The bond currently sells for 108 percent of its face value. The company's tax rate is 40 percent.

a. What is the pretax cost of debt?

b. What is the aftertax cost of debt?

c. Which is more relevant, the pretax or the aftertax cost of debt? Why?

4. Calculating Cost of Debt   For the firm in the previous problem, suppose the book value of the debt issue is €20 million. In addition, the company has a second debt issue on the market, a zero coupon bond with seven years left to maturity; the book value of this issue is €80 million and the bonds sell for 58 percent of par. What is the company's total book value of debt? The total market value? What is your best estimate of the aftertax cost of debt now?

5. **Calculating WACC** Mullineaux Corporation has a target capital structure of 60 percent common stock and 40 percent debt. Its cost of equity is 16 percent, and the cost of debt is 9 percent. The relevant tax rate is 35 percent. What is Mullineaux's WACC?

6. **Taxes and WACC** Miller Manufacturing has a target debt–equity ratio of .60. Its cost of equity is 18 percent, and its cost of debt is 9 percent. If the tax rate is 40 percent, what is Miller's WACC?

7. **Finding the Capital Structure** Fama's Llamas has a weighted average cost of capital of 11.5 percent. The company's cost of equity is 16 percent, and its cost of debt is 8.5 percent. The tax rate is 35 percent. What is Fama's debt–equity ratio?

8. **Book Value versus Market Value** Filer Manufacturing has 9.5 million shares of common stock outstanding. The current share price is £53, and the book value per share is £5. Filer Manufacturing also has two bond issues outstanding. The first bond issue has a face value of £75 million and an 8 percent coupon and sells for 93 percent of par. The second issue has a face value of £60 million and a 7.5 percent coupon and sells for 96.5 percent of par. The first issue matures in 10 years, the second in 6 years.
   a. What are Filer's capital structure weights on a book value basis?
   b. What are Filer's capital structure weights on a market value basis?
   c. Which are more relevant, the book or market value weights? Why?

9. **Calculating the WACC** In the previous problem, suppose the company's stock has a beta of 1.5. The risk-free rate is 5.2 percent, and the market risk premium is 9 percent. Assume that the overall cost of debt is the weighted average implied by the two outstanding debt issues. Both bonds make semiannual payments. The tax rate is 35 percent. What is the company's WACC?

10. **WACC** Aussalam Caterers has a target debt–equity ratio of .80. Its WACC is 10.5 percent, and the tax rate is 35 percent.
   a. If Aussalam's cost of equity is 15 percent, what is its pretax cost of debt?
   b. If instead you know that the aftertax cost of debt is 6.4 percent, what is the cost of equity?

11. **Finding the WACC** Given the following information for Javed Naqvi and Sons, find the WACC. Assume the company's tax rate is 35 percent.

Debt:	4,000 7 percent coupon bonds outstanding, PKR 1,000 par value, 20 years to maturity, selling for 103 percent of par; the bonds make semiannual payments.
Common stock:	90,000 shares outstanding, selling for PKR 57 per share; the beta is 1.10.
Market:	8 percent market risk premium and 6 percent risk-free rate.

12. **Finding the WACC** Aasim Mining Corporation has 9 million shares of common stock outstanding and 120,000 8.5 percent semiannual bonds outstanding, par value BND 1,000 each. The common stock currently sells for BND 34 per share and has a beta of 1.20, and the bonds have 15 years to maturity and sell for 93 percent of par. The market risk premium is 10 percent, T-bills are yielding 5 percent, and Aasim Mining's tax rate is 35 percent.
   a. What is the firm's market value capital structure?
   b. If Aasim Mining is evaluating a new investment project that has the same risk as the firm's typical project, what rate should the firm use to discount the project's cash flows?

13. **SML and WACC** An all-equity firm is considering the following projects:

Project	Beta	Expected Return
W	.60	11%
X	.90	13
Y	1.20	14
Z	1.70	16

The T-bill rate is 5 percent, and the expected return on the market is 12 percent.

a. Which projects have a higher expected return than the firm's 12 percent cost of capital?

b. Which projects should be accepted?

c. Which projects would be incorrectly accepted or rejected if the firm's overall cost of capital were used as a hurdle rate?

INTERMEDIATE
(Questions 14–15)

14. **WACC and NPV**   Och, Inc., is considering a project that will result in initial aftertax cash savings of BOB 3.5 million at the end of the first year, and these savings will grow at a rate of 5 percent per year indefinitely. The firm has a target debt–equity ratio of .65, a cost of equity of 15 percent, and an aftertax cost of debt of 5.5 percent. The cost-saving proposal is somewhat riskier than the usual project the firm undertakes; management uses the subjective approach and applies an adjustment factor of +2 percent to the cost of capital for such risky projects. Under what circumstances should Och take on the project?

15. **Preferred Stock and WACC**   The Saunders Investment Bank has the following financing outstanding. What is the WACC for the company?

Debt:	50,000 bonds with an 8 percent coupon rate and a quoted price of £119.80; the bonds have 25 years to maturity. 150,000 zero coupon bonds with a quoted price of 13.85 and 30 years until maturity.
Preferred stock:	120,000 shares of 6.5 percent preferred with a current price of £112, and a par value = £100.
Common stock:	2,000,000 shares of common stock; the current price is £65, and the beta of the stock is 1.1.
Market:	The corporate tax rate is 40 percent, the market risk premium is 9 percent, and the risk-free rate is 4 percent.

CHALLENGE
(Questions 16–17)

16. **WACC and NPV**   Photochronograph Corporation (PC) manufactures time series photographic equipment. It is currently at its target debt–equity ratio of 1.3. It's considering building a new ¥45 million manufacturing facility. This new plant is expected to generate aftertax cash flows of ¥5.7 million in perpetuity. There are three financing options:

- A new issue of common stock. The required return on the company's equity is 17 percent.
- A new issue of 20-year bonds. If the company issues these new bonds at an annual coupon rate of 9 percent, they will sell at par.
- Increased use of accounts payable financing. Because this financing is part of the company's ongoing daily business, the company assigns it a cost that is the same as the overall firm WACC. Management has a target ratio of accounts payable to long-term debt of .20. (Assume there is no difference between the pretax and aftertax accounts payable cost.)

What is the NPV of the new plant? Assume that PC has a 35 percent tax rate.

17. **Project Evaluation**   This is a comprehensive project evaluation problem bringing together much of what you have learned in this and previous chapters. Suppose you have been hired as a financial consultant to Patsy Engineers Ltd. (PEL), a large, publicly traded firm that is the market share leader in radar detection systems (RDSs). The company is looking at setting up a manufacturing plant overseas to produce a new line of RDSs. This will be a five-year project. The company bought some land three years ago for €7 million in anticipation of using it as a toxic dump site for waste chemicals, but it built a piping system to safely discard the chemicals instead. If the company sold the land today, it would receive €6.5 million after taxes. In five years the land can be sold for €4.5 million after taxes and reclamation costs. The company wants to build its new manufacturing plant on this land; the plant will cost €15 million to build. The following market data on PEL's securities are current:

Debt:	15,000 7 percent coupon bonds outstanding, 15 years to maturity, selling for 92 percent of par; the bonds have a €1,000 par value each and make semiannual payments.
Common stock:	300,000 shares outstanding, selling for €75 per share; the beta is 1.3.

www.mhhe.com/rwj

> *Preferred stock*:   20,000 shares of 5 percent preferred stock outstanding, selling for
> €72 per share.
>
> *Market*:   8 percent expected market risk premium; 5 percent risk-free rate.

PEL's tax rate is 35 percent. The project requires €900,000 in initial net working capital investment to become operational.

a. Calculate the project's initial time 0 cash flow, taking into account all side effects.

b. The new RDS project is somewhat riskier than a typical project for PEL, primarily because the plant is being located overseas. Management has told you to use an adjustment factor of +2 percent to account for this increased riskiness. Calculate the appropriate discount rate to use when evaluating PEL's project.

c. The manufacturing plant has an eight-year tax life, and PEL uses straight-line depreciation. At the end of the project (i.e., the end of year 5), the plant can be scrapped for €5 million. What is the aftertax salvage value of this manufacturing plant?

d. The company will incur €400,000 in annual fixed costs. The plan is to manufacture 12,000 RDSs per year and sell them at €10,000 per machine; the variable production costs are €9,000 per RDS. What is the annual operating cash flow (OCF) from this project?

e. PEL's comptroller is primarily interested in the impact of PEL's investments on the bottom line of reported accounting statements. What will you tell her is the accounting break-even quantity of RDSs sold for this project?

f. Finally, PEL's president wants you to throw all your calculations, assumptions, and everything else into the report for the chief financial officer; all he wants to know is the RDS project's internal rate of return, IRR, and net present value, NPV. What will you report?

Mini Case

The Cost of Capital for Goff Computer, Inc.

You have recently been hired by Goff Computer, Inc. (GCI), in the finance area. GCI was founded eight years ago by Chris Goff and currently operates 74 stores in the Southeast. GCI is privately owned by Chris and his family and had sales of $97 million last year.

GCI sells primarily to in-store customers. Customers come to the store and talk with a sales representative. The sales representative assists the customer in determining the type of computer and peripherals that are necessary for the individual customer's computing needs. After the order is taken, the customer pays for the order immediately, and the computer is assembled to fill the order. Delivery of the computer averages 15 days but is guaranteed in 30 days.

GCI's growth to date has been financed from its profits. Whenever the company had sufficient capital, it would open a new store. Relatively little formal analysis has been used in the capital budgeting process. Chris has just read about capital budgeting techniques and has come to you for help. The company has never attempted to determine its cost of capital, and Chris would like you to perform the analysis. Because the company is privately owned, it is difficult to determine the cost of equity for the company. You have determined that to estimate the cost of capital for GCI, you will use Dell as a representative company. The following steps will allow you to calculate this estimate:

1. Most publicly traded corporations are required to submit 10Q (quarterly) and 10K (annual) reports to the SEC detailing their financial operations over the previous quarter or year, respectively. These corporate filings are available on the SEC Web site at www.sec.gov. Go to the SEC Web site, follow the "Search for Company Filings" link and the "Companies & Other Filers" link, enter "Dell Computer," and search for SEC filings made by Dell. Find the most recent 10Q and 10K and download the forms. Look on the balance sheet to find the book value of debt and the book value of equity. If you look further down the report, you should find a section titled either "Long-Term Debt" or "Long-Term Debt and Interest Rate Risk Management" that will list a breakdown of Dell's long-term debt.

2. To estimate the cost of equity for Dell, go to finance.yahoo.com and enter the ticker symbol "DELL." Follow the various links to find answers to the following questions: What is the most recent stock price listed for Dell? What is the market value of equity, or market capitalization? How many shares of stock does Dell have outstanding? What is the beta for Dell? Now go back to finance.yahoo.com and follow the "Bonds" link. What is the yield on 3-month Treasury bills? Using the historical market risk premium, what is the cost of equity for Dell using the CAPM?

3. Go to investor.reuters.com and find the list of competitors in the industry. Find the beta for each of these competitors, and then calculate the industry average beta. Using the industry average beta, what is the cost of equity? Does it matter if you use the beta for Dell or the beta for the industry in this case?

4. You now need to calculate the cost of debt for Dell. Go to www.nasdbondinfo.com, enter Dell as the company, and find the yield to maturity for each of Dell's bonds. What is the weighted average cost of debt for Dell using the book value weights and the market value weights? Does it make a difference in this case if you use book value weights or market value weights?

5. You now have all the necessary information to calculate the weighted average cost of capital for Dell. Calculate the weighted average cost of capital for Dell using book value weights and market value weights assuming Dell has a 35 percent marginal tax rate. Which cost of capital number is more relevant?

6. You used Dell as a representative company to estimate the cost of capital for GCI. What are some of the potential problems with this approach in this situation? What improvements might you suggest?

Appendix 12A   Economic Value Added and the Measurement of Financial Performance

To access the appendix for this chapter, please visit www.mhhe.com/rwj.

Corporate Financing Decisions and Efficient Capital Markets

The NASDAQ stock market was raging in the late 1990s, gaining about 23 percent, 14 percent, 35 percent, and 62 percent in 1996 to 1999, respectively. Of course, that spectacular run came to a jarring halt, and the NASDAQ lost about 40 percent in 2000, followed by another 30 percent in 2001. The ISDEX, an index of Internet-related stocks, rose from 100 in January 1996 to 1,100 in February 2000, a gain of about 1,000 percent! It then fell like a rock to 600 by May 2000.

The performance of the NASDAQ over this period, and particularly the rise and fall of Internet stocks, has been described by many as one of the greatest market "bubbles" in history. The argument is that prices were inflated to economically ridiculous levels before investors came to their senses, which then caused the bubble to pop and prices to plunge. Debate over whether the stock market of the late 1990s really was a bubble has generated much controversy. In this chapter, we discuss the competing ideas, present some evidence on both sides, and then examine the implications for financial managers.

13.1 Can Financing Decisions Create Value?

Earlier parts of the book showed how to evaluate projects according to the net present value criterion. The real world is a competitive one where projects with positive net present value are not always easy to come by. However, through hard work or through good fortune, a firm can identify winning projects. For example, to create value from capital budgeting decisions, the firm is likely to:

1. Locate an unsatisfied demand for a particular product or service.
2. Create a barrier to make it more difficult for other firms to compete.
3. Produce products or services at lower cost than the competition.
4. Be the first to develop a new product.

The next five chapters concern *financing* decisions. Typical financing decisions include how much debt and equity to sell, what types of debt and equity to sell, and when to sell them. Just as the net present value criterion was used to evaluate capital budgeting projects, we now want to use the same criterion to evaluate financing decisions.

Though the procedure for evaluating financing decisions is identical to the procedure for evaluating projects, the results are different. It turns out that the typical firm has many more capital expenditure opportunities with positive net present values than financing opportunities with positive net present values. In fact, we later show that some plausible financial models imply that no valuable financial opportunities exist at all.

Though this dearth of profitable financing opportunities will be examined in detail later, a few remarks are in order now. We maintain that there are basically three ways to create valuable financing opportunities:

1. *Fool investors.* Assume that a firm can raise capital either by issuing stock or by issuing a more complex security—say, a combination of stock and warrants. Suppose that, in truth, 100 shares of stock are worth the same as 50 units of our complex security. If investors have a misguided, overly optimistic view of the complex security, perhaps the 50 units can be sold for more than the 100 shares of stock can be. Clearly this complex security provides a valuable financing opportunity because the firm is getting more than fair value for it.

    Financial managers try to package securities to receive the greatest value. A cynic might view this as attempting to fool investors.

    However, the theory of efficient capital markets implies that investors cannot easily be fooled. It says that securities are appropriately priced at all times, implying that the market as a whole is shrewd indeed. In our example, 50 units of the complex security would sell for the same price as 100 shares of stock. Thus, corporate managers cannot attempt to create value by fooling investors. Instead, managers must create value in other ways.

2. *Reduce costs or increase subsidies.* We show later in the book that certain forms of financing have greater tax advantages than other forms. Clearly, a firm packaging securities to minimize taxes can increase firm value. In addition, any financing technique involves other costs. For example, investment bankers, lawyers, and accountants must be paid. A firm packaging securities to minimize these costs can also increase its value.

EXAMPLE 13.1

Valuing Financial Subsidies   Suppose Vermont Electronics Company is thinking about relocating its plant to Mexico where labor costs are lower. In the hope that it can stay in Vermont, the company has submitted an application to the state of Vermont to issue $2 million in five-year, tax-exempt industrial bonds. The coupon rate on industrial revenue bonds in Vermont is currently 5 percent. This is an attractive rate because the normal cost of debt capital for Vermont Electronics Company is 10 percent. What is the NPV of this potential financing transaction?

If the application is accepted and the industrial revenue bonds are issued by the Vermont Electronics Company, the NPV (ignoring corporate taxes) is:

$$\text{NPV} = \$2,000,000 - \left[\frac{\$100,000}{1.1} + \frac{\$100,000}{(1.1)^2} + \frac{\$100,000}{(1.1)^3} + \frac{\$100,000}{(1.1)^4} + \frac{\$2,100,000}{(1.1)^5} \right]$$

$$= \$2,000,000 - \$1,620,921$$

$$= \$379,079$$

This transaction has a positive NPV. The Vermont Electronics Company obtains subsidized financing where the value of the subsidy is $379,079.

3. *Create a new security.* There has been a surge in financial innovation in recent decades. For example, in a speech on financial innovation, Nobel laureate Merton Miller asked the rhetorical question, "Can any 20-year period in recorded history have witnessed even a tenth as much new development? Where corporations once issued only straight debt and straight common stock, they now issue zero coupon

bonds, adjustable rate notes, floating-rate notes, putable bonds, credit-enhanced debt securities, receivable-backed securities, adjusted-rate preferred stock, convertible adjustable preferred stock, auction rate preferred stock, single-point adjustable rate stock, convertible exchangeable preferred stock, adjustable-rate convertible debt, zero coupon convertible debt, debt with mandatory common stock purchase contracts—to name just a few!"[1] And financial innovation has occurred even more rapidly in the years following Miller's speech.

Though the advantage of each instrument is different, one general theme is that these new securities cannot easily be duplicated by combinations of existing securities. Thus, a previously unsatisfied clientele may pay extra for a specialized security catering to its needs. For example, putable bonds let the purchaser sell the bond at a fixed price back to the firm. This innovation creates a price floor, allowing the investor to reduce his or her downside risk. Perhaps risk-averse investors or investors with little knowledge of the bond market would find this feature particularly attractive.

Corporations gain by issuing these unique securities at high prices. However, the value captured by the innovator may well be small in the long run because the innovator usually cannot patent or copyright an idea. Soon many firms are issuing securities of the same kind, forcing prices down as a result.

This brief introduction sets the stage for the next several chapters of the book. The rest of this chapter examines the efficient capital markets hypothesis. We show that if capital markets are efficient, corporate managers cannot create value by fooling investors. This is quite important because managers must create value in other, perhaps more difficult, ways. The following chapters concern the costs and subsidies of various forms of financing.

13.2 A Description of Efficient Capital Markets

An efficient capital market is one in which stock prices fully reflect available information. To illustrate how an efficient market works, suppose the F-stop Camera Corporation (FCC) is attempting to develop a camera that will double the speed of the auto-focusing system now available. FCC believes this research has positive NPV.

Now consider a share of stock in FCC. What determines the willingness of investors to hold shares of FCC at a particular price? One important factor is the probability that FCC will be the first company to develop the new auto-focusing system. In an efficient market, we would expect the price of the shares of FCC to increase if this probability increases.

Suppose FCC hires a well-known engineer to develop the new auto-focusing system. In an efficient market, what will happen to FCC's share price when this is announced? If the well-known scientist is paid a salary that fully reflects his or her contribution to the firm, the price of the stock will not necessarily change. Suppose instead that hiring the scientist is a positive NPV transaction. In this case, the price of shares in FCC will increase because the firm can pay the scientist a salary below his or her true value to the company.

[1] M. Miller, "Financial Innovation: The Last Twenty Years and the Next," *Journal of Financial and Quantitative Analysis* (December 1986). However, Peter Tufano, "Securities Innovations: A Historical and Functional Perspective," *Journal of Applied Corporate Finance* (Winter 1995), shows that many securities commonly believed to have been invented in the 1970s and 1980s can be traced as far back as the 1830s.

Figure 13.1

Reaction of
Stock Price to
New Information
in Efficient and
Inefficient Markets

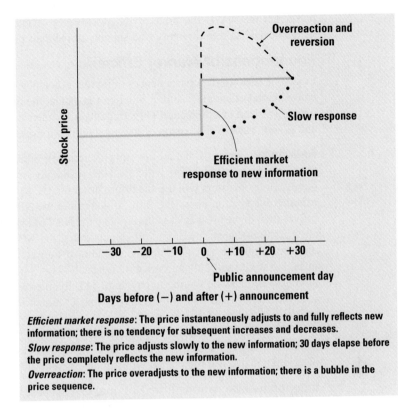

Efficient market response: The price instantaneously adjusts to and fully reflects new information; there is no tendency for subsequent increases and decreases.

Slow response: The price adjusts slowly to the new information; 30 days elapse before the price completely reflects the new information.

Overreaction: The price overadjusts to the new information; there is a bubble in the price sequence.

When will the increase in the price of FCC's shares occur? Assume that the hiring announcement is made in a press release on Wednesday morning. In an efficient market, the price of shares in FCC will *immediately* adjust to this new information. Investors should not be able to buy the stock on Wednesday afternoon and make a profit on Thursday. This would imply that it took the stock market a day to realize the implication of the FCC press release. The efficient market hypothesis predicts that the price of shares of FCC stock on Wednesday afternoon will already reflect the information contained in the Wednesday morning press release.

The **efficient market hypothesis** (EMH) has implications for investors and for firms:

- Because information is reflected in prices immediately, investors should only expect to obtain a normal rate of return. Awareness of information when it is released does an investor no good. The price adjusts before the investor has time to trade on it.

- Firms should expect to receive fair value for securities that they sell. *Fair* means that the price they receive from issuing securities is the present value. Thus, valuable financing opportunities that arise from fooling investors are unavailable in efficient capital markets.

Figure 13.1 presents several possible adjustments in stock prices. The solid line represents the path taken by the stock in an efficient market. In this case the price adjusts immediately to the new information with no further price changes. The dotted line depicts a slow reaction. Here it takes the market 30 days to fully absorb the information. Finally, the broken line illustrates an overreaction and subsequent correction back to the true price. The broken line and the dotted line show the paths that the stock price might take in an inefficient market. If the price of the stock takes several days to adjust, trading profits would be available to investors who suitably timed their purchases and sales.[2]

Foundations of Market Efficiency

Figure 13.1 shows the consequences of market efficiency. But what are the conditions that *cause* market efficiency? Andrei Shleifer argues that there are three conditions, any one of which will lead to efficiency:[3] (1) rationality, (2) independent deviations from rationality, and (3) arbitrage. A discussion of these conditions follows.

Rationality   Imagine that all investors are rational. When new information is released in the marketplace, all investors will adjust their estimates of stock prices in a rational way. In our example, investors will use the information in FCC's press release, in conjunction with existing information about the firm, to determine the NPV of FCC's new venture. If the information in the press release implies that the NPV of the venture is $10 million and there are 2 million shares, investors will calculate that the NPV is $5 per share. While FCC's old price might be, say, $40, no one would now transact at that price. Anyone interested in selling would sell only at a price of at least $45 (= $40 + 5). And anyone interested in buying would now be willing to pay up to $45. In other words, the price would rise by $5. And the price would rise immediately because rational investors would see no reason to wait before trading at the new price.

Of course, we all know times when family members, friends, and yes, even we seem to behave less than perfectly rationally. Thus, perhaps it is too much to ask that *all* investors behave rationally. But the market will still be efficient if the following scenario holds.

Independent Deviations from Rationality   Suppose that FCC's press release is not all that clear. How many new cameras are likely to be sold? At what price? What is the likely cost per camera? Will other camera companies be able to develop competing products? How long will this likely take? If these and other questions cannot be answered easily, it will be difficult to estimate NPV.

Now imagine that with so many questions going unanswered, many investors do not think clearly. Some investors might get caught up in the romance of a new product, hoping for and ultimately believing in sales projections well above what is rational. They would overpay for new shares. And if they needed to sell shares (perhaps to finance current consumption), they would do so only at a high price. If these individuals dominate the market, the stock price would likely rise beyond what market efficiency would predict.

However, due to emotional resistance, investors could just as easily react to new information in a pessimistic manner. After all, business historians tell us that investors were initially quite skeptical about the benefits of the telephone, the copier, the automobile, and the motion picture. Certainly, they could be overly skeptical about this new camera. If investors were primarily of this type, the stock price would likely rise less than market efficiency would predict.

---

[2]Now you should appreciate the following short story. A student was walking down the hall with her finance professor when they both saw a $20 bill on the ground. As the student bent down to pick it up, the professor shook his head slowly and, with a look of disappointment on his face, said patiently to the student, "Don't bother. If it was really there, someone else would have already picked it up."

The moral of the story reflects the logic of the efficient market hypothesis: If you think you have found a pattern in stock prices or a simple device for picking winners, you probably have not. If there were such a simple way to make money, someone else would have found it before. Furthermore, if people tried to exploit the information, their efforts would become self-defeating and the pattern would disappear.

[3]Andrei Shleifer, *Inefficient Markets: An Introduction to Behavioral Finance* (Oxford: Oxford University Press, 2000).

But suppose that about as many individuals were irrationally optimistic as were irrationally pessimistic. Prices would likely rise in a manner consistent with market efficiency, even though most investors would be classified as less than fully rational. Thus market efficiency does not require rational individuals—only countervailing irrationalities.

However, this assumption of offsetting irrationalities at *all* times may be unrealistic. Perhaps at certain times most investors are swept away by excessive optimism and at other times are caught in the throes of extreme pessimism. But even here there is an assumption that will produce efficiency.

Arbitrage   Imagine a world with two types of individuals: the irrational amateurs and the rational professionals. The amateurs get caught up in their emotions, at times believing irrationally that a stock is undervalued and at other times believing the opposite. If the passions of the different amateurs do not cancel each other out, these amateurs, by themselves, would tend to carry stocks either above or below their efficient prices.

Now let's bring in the professionals. Suppose professionals go about their business methodically and rationally. They study companies thoroughly, they evaluate the evidence objectively, they estimate stock prices coldly and clearly, and they act accordingly. If a stock is underpriced, they would buy it. If it is overpriced, they would sell it. And their confidence would likely be greater than that of the amateurs. Whereas an amateur might risk only a small sum, these professionals might risk large ones, *knowing* as they do that the stock is mispriced. Furthermore, they would be willing to rearrange their entire portfolio in search of a profit. If they find that General Motors is underpriced, they might sell the Ford stock they own to buy GM. *Arbitrage* is the word that comes to mind here because arbitrage generates profit from the simultaneous purchase and sale of different, but substitute, securities. If the arbitrage of professionals dominates the speculation of amateurs, markets would still be efficient.

13.3 The Different Types of Efficiency

In our previous discussion, we assumed that the market responds immediately to all available information. In actuality, certain information may affect stock prices more quickly than other information. To handle differential response rates, researchers separate information into different types. The most common classification system identifies three types: information about past prices, publicly available information, and all information. The effect of these three information sets on prices is examined next.

The Weak Form

Imagine a trading strategy that recommends buying a stock after it has gone up three days in a row and recommends selling a stock after it has gone down three days in a row. This strategy uses information based only on past prices. It does not use any other information, such as earnings, forecasts, merger announcements, or money supply figures. A capital market is said to be *weakly efficient* or to satisfy **weak form efficiency** if it fully incorporates the information in past stock prices. Thus, the preceding strategy would not be able to generate profits if weak form efficiency holds.

Often weak form efficiency is represented mathematically as:

$$P_t = P_{t-1} + \text{Expected return} + \text{Random error}_t \qquad \textbf{(13.1)}$$

Equation 13.1 states that the price today is equal to the sum of the last observed price plus the expected return on the stock (in dollars) plus a random component occuring over the interval. The last observed price could have occurred yesterday, last week, or last month, depending on

Figure 13.2

Investor Behavior
Tends to Eliminate
Cyclical Patterns

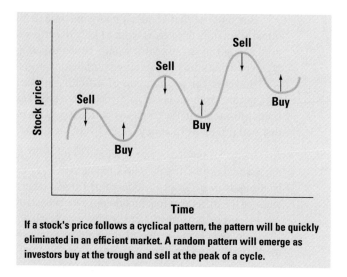

If a stock's price follows a cyclical pattern, the pattern will be quickly
eliminated in an efficient market. A random pattern will emerge as
investors buy at the trough and sell at the peak of a cycle.

the sampling interval. The expected return is a function of a security's risk and would be
based on the models of risk and return in previous chapters. The random component is due
to new information about the stock. It could be either positive or negative and has an expectation of zero. The random component in any period is unrelated to the random component
in any past period. Hence this component is not predictable from past prices. If stock prices
follow Equation 13.1 they are said to follow a **random walk**.[4]

Weak form efficiency is about the weakest type of efficiency that we would expect a
financial market to display because historical price information is the easiest kind of information about a stock to acquire. If it were possible to make extraordinary profits simply
by finding patterns in stock price movements, everyone would do it, and any profits would
disappear in the scramble.

This effect of competition can be seen in Figure 13.2. Suppose the price of a stock
displays a cyclical pattern, as indicated by the wavy curve. Shrewd investors would buy at
the low points, forcing those prices up. Conversely, they would sell at the high points, forcing prices down. Via competition, cyclical regularities would be eliminated, leaving only
random fluctuations.

The Semistrong and Strong Forms

If weak form efficiency is controversial, even more contentious are the two stronger types
of efficiency, **semistrong form efficiency** and **strong form efficiency**. A market is semistrong form efficient if prices reflect (incorporate) all publicly available information,
including information such as published accounting statements for the firm as well as historical price information. A market is strong form efficient if prices reflect all information,
public or private.

The information set of past prices is a subset of the information set of publicly available
information, which in turn is a subset of all information. This is shown in Figure 13.3. Thus,
strong form efficiency implies semistrong form efficiency, and semistrong form efficiency
implies weak form efficiency. The distinction between semistrong form efficiency and
weak form efficiency is that semistrong form efficiency requires not only that the market be

---

[4]For purposes of this text, the random walk can be considered synonymous with weak form efficiency. Technically, the random walk is a slightly more restrictive hypothesis because it assumes that stock returns are
identically distributed through time.

Figure 13.3

Relationship among Three Different Information Sets

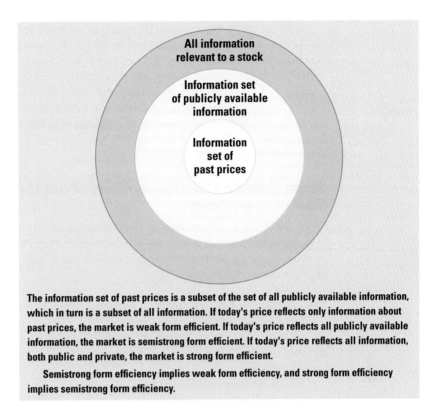

The information set of past prices is a subset of the set of all publicly available information, which in turn is a subset of all information. If today's price reflects only information about past prices, the market is weak form efficient. If today's price reflects all publicly available information, the market is semistrong form efficient. If today's price reflects all information, both public and private, the market is strong form efficient.

Semistrong form efficiency implies weak form efficiency, and strong form efficiency implies semistrong form efficiency.

efficient with respect to historical price information, but that *all* of the information available to the public be reflected in prices.

To illustrate the different forms of efficiency, imagine an investor who always sold a particular stock after its price had risen. A market that was only weak form efficient and not semistrong form efficient would still prevent such a strategy from generating positive profits. According to weak form efficiency, a recent price rise does not imply that the stock is overvalued.

Now consider a firm reporting increased earnings. An individual might consider investing in the stock after reading the news release providing this information. However, if the market is semistrong form efficient, the price should rise immediately upon the news release. Thus, the investor would end up paying the higher price, eliminating all chance for profit.

At the furthest end of the spectrum is strong form efficiency. This form says that anything that is pertinent to the value of the stock and that is known to at least one investor is, in fact, fully incorporated into the stock price. A strict believer in strong form efficiency would deny that an insider who knew whether a company mining operation had struck gold could profit from that information. Such a devotee of the strong form efficient market hypothesis might argue that as soon as the insider tried to trade on his or her information, the market would recognize what was happening, and the price would shoot up before he or she could buy any of the stock. Alternatively, believers in strong form efficiency argue that there are no secrets, and as soon as the gold is discovered, the secret gets out.

One reason to expect that markets are weak form efficient is that it is so cheap and easy to find patterns in stock prices. Anyone who can program a computer and knows a little bit of statistics can search for such patterns. It stands to reason that if there were such patterns, people would find and exploit them, in the process causing them to disappear.

Semistrong form efficiency, though, implies more sophisticated investors than does weak form efficiency. An investor must be skilled at economics and statistics and steeped in the idiosyncrasies of individual industries and companies. Furthermore, to acquire and use such skills requires talent, ability, and time. In the jargon of the economist, such an effort is costly, and the ability to be successful at it is probably in scarce supply.

As for strong form efficiency, this is just further down the road than semistrong form efficiency. It is difficult to believe that the market is so efficient that someone with valuable inside information cannot prosper from it. And empirical evidence tends to be unfavorable to this form of market efficiency.

Some Common Misconceptions about the Efficient Market Hypothesis

No idea in finance has attracted as much attention as that of efficient markets, and not all of the attention has been flattering. To a certain extent this is because much of the criticism has been based on a misunderstanding of what the hypothesis does and does not say. We illustrate three misconceptions next.

The Efficacy of Dart Throwing   When the notion of market efficiency was first publicized and debated in the popular financial press, it was often characterized by the following quote: ". . . throwing darts at the financial page will produce a portfolio that can be expected to do as well as any managed by professional security analysts."[5,6] This is almost, but not quite, true.

All the efficient market hypothesis really says is that, on average, the manager will not be able to achieve an abnormal or excess return. The excess return is defined with respect to some benchmark expected return, such as that from the security market line of Chapter 11 (SML). The investor must still decide how risky a portfolio he or she wants. In addition, a random dart thrower might wind up with all of the darts sticking into one or two high-risk stocks that deal in genetic engineering. Would you really want all of your stock investments in two such stocks?

The failure to understand this has often led to confusion about market efficiency. For example, sometimes it is wrongly argued that market efficiency means that it does not matter what you do because the efficiency of the market will protect the unwary. However, someone once remarked, "The efficient market protects the sheep from the wolves, but nothing can protect the sheep from themselves."

What efficiency does say is that the price that a firm obtains when it sells a share of its stock is a fair price in the sense that it reflects the value of that stock given the information that is available about it. Shareholders need not worry that they are paying too much for a stock with a low dividend or some other characteristic because the market has already incorporated it into the price. However, investors still have to worry about such things as their level of risk exposure and their degree of diversification.

Price Fluctuations   Much of the public is skeptical of efficiency because stock prices fluctuate from day to day. However, daily price movement is in no way inconsistent with efficiency; a stock in an efficient market adjusts to new information by changing price. A great deal of new information comes into the stock market each day. In fact, the *absence* of daily price movements in a changing world might suggest an inefficiency.

---

[5]B. G. Malkiel, *A Random Walk Down Wall Street*, 8th ed. (New York: Norton, 2003).

[6]Older articles often referred to the benchmark of "dart-throwing monkeys." As government involvement in the securities industry grew, the benchmark was often restated as "dart-throwing congressional representatives."

Stockholder Disinterest   Many laypeople are skeptical that the market price can be efficient if only a fraction of the outstanding shares changes hands on any given day. However, the number of traders in a stock on a given day is generally far less than the number of people following the stock. This is true because an individual will trade only when his appraisal of the value of the stock differs enough from the market price to justify incurring brokerage commissions and other transaction costs. Furthermore, even if the number of traders following a stock is small relative to the number of outstanding shareholders, the stock can be expected to be efficiently priced as long as a number of interested traders use the publicly available information. That is, the stock price can reflect the available information even if many stockholders never follow the stock and are not considering trading in the near future.

13.4   The Evidence

The evidence on the efficient market hypothesis is extensive, with studies covering the broad categories of weak form, semistrong form, and strong form efficiency. In the first category we investigate whether stock price changes are random. We review both *event studies* and studies of the performance of mutual funds in the second category. In the third category, we look at the performance of corporate insiders.

The Weak Form

Weak form efficiency implies that a stock's price movement in the past is unrelated to its price movement in the future. The work of Chapter 10 allows us to test this implication. In that chapter we discussed the concept of correlation between the returns on two different stocks. For example, the correlation between the return on General Motors and the return on Ford is likely to be relatively high because both stocks are in the same industry. Conversely, the correlation between the return on General Motors and the return on the stock of, say, a European fast-food chain is likely to be low.

Financial economists frequently speak of **serial correlation**, which involves only one security. This is the correlation between the current return on a security and the return on the same security over a later period. A positive coefficient of serial correlation for a particular stock indicates a tendency toward *continuation*. That is, a higher-than-average return today is likely to be followed by higher-than-average returns in the future. Similarly, a lower-than-average return today is likely to be followed by lower-than-average returns in the future.

A negative coefficient of serial correlation for a particular stock indicates a tendency toward *reversal*. A higher-than-average return today is likely to be followed by lower-than-average returns in the future. Similarly, a lower-than-average return today is likely to be followed by higher-than-average returns in the future. Both significantly positive and significantly negative serial correlation coefficients are indications of market inefficiencies; in either case, returns today can be used to predict future returns.

Serial correlation coefficients for stock returns near zero would be consistent with weak form efficiency. Thus, a current stock return that is higher than average is as likely to be followed by lower-than-average returns as by higher-than-average returns. Similarly, a current stock return that is lower than average is as likely to be followed by higher-than-average returns as by lower-than-average returns.

Table 13.1 shows the serial correlation for daily stock price changes for eight large U.S. companies. These coefficients indicate whether there are relationships between yesterday's return and today's return. As can be seen, the correlation coefficients are predominantly positive, implying that a higher-than-average return today makes a higher-than-average return tomorrow slightly more likely. Conversely, Citigroup's coefficient is slightly negative,

Table 13.1

Serial Correlation
Coefficients for
Selected Companies,
2001–2005

Company	Serial Correlation Coefficient
Boeing	.0025
Citigroup	−.0078
Coca-Cola	.0189
IBM	.0126
McDonald's	.0054
Merck	.0409
Pfizer	.0225
The Gap	.0193

McDonald's coefficient of .0054 is slightly positive, implying that a positive return today makes a positive return tomorrow slightly more likely. Citigroup's coefficient is negative, implying that a positive return today makes a negative return tomorrow slightly more likely. However, the coefficients are so small relative to estimation error and transaction costs that the results are generally considered to be consistent with efficient capital markets.

implying that a higher-than-average return today makes a lower-than-average return tomorrow slightly more likely.

However, because correlation coefficients can, in principle, vary between −1 and 1, the reported coefficients are quite small. In fact, the coefficients are so small relative to both estimation errors and to transaction costs that the results are generally considered to be consistent with weak form efficiency.

The weak form of the efficient market hypothesis has been tested in many other ways as well. Our view of the literature is that the evidence, taken as a whole, is consistent with weak form efficiency.

This finding raises an interesting thought: If price changes are truly random, why do so many believe that prices follow patterns? The work of both psychologists and statisticians suggests that most people simply do not know what randomness looks like. For example, consider Figure 13.4. The top graph was generated by a computer using random numbers and Equation 13.1. Yet we have found that people examining the chart generally see patterns. Different people see different patterns and forecast different future price movements. However, in our experience, viewers are all quite confident of the patterns they see.

Next consider the bottom graph, which tracks actual movements in The Gap's stock price. This graph may look quite nonrandom to some, suggesting weak form inefficiency. However, it also bears a close visual resemblance to the simulated series, and statistical tests indicate that it indeed behaves like a purely random series. Thus, in our opinion, people claiming to see patterns in stock price data are probably seeing optical illusions.

The Semistrong Form

The semistrong form of the efficient market hypothesis implies that prices should reflect all publicly available information. We present two types of tests of this form.

Event Studies   The *abnormal return* (AR) on a given stock for a particular day can be calculated by subtracting the market's return on the same day (R_m)—as measured by a broad-based index such as the S&P composite index—from the actual return (R) on the stock for that day.[7] We write this algebraically as:

$$AR = R - R_m$$

---

[7]We can also measure the abnormal return by using the market model. In this case the abnormal return is:

$$AR = R - (\alpha + \beta R_m)$$

Figure 13.4

Simulated and
Actual Stock Price
Movements

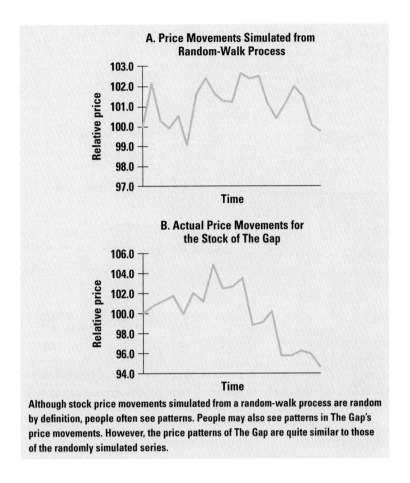

Although stock price movements simulated from a random-walk process are random by definition, people often see patterns. People may also see patterns in The Gap's price movements. However, the price patterns of The Gap are quite similar to those of the randomly simulated series.

The following system will help us understand tests of the semistrong form:

$$\text{Information released at time } t-1 \rightarrow \text{AR}_{t-1}$$
$$\text{Information released at time } t \quad\;\; \rightarrow \text{AR}_{t}$$
$$\text{Information released at time } t+1 \rightarrow \text{AR}_{t+1}$$

The arrows indicate that the abnormal return in any time period is related only to the information released during that period.

According to the efficient market hypothesis, a stock's abnormal return at time t, AR_t, should reflect the release of information at the same time, t. Any information released before then should have no effect on abnormal returns in this period because all of its influence should have been felt before. In other words, an efficient market would already have incorporated previous information into prices. Because a stock's return today cannot depend on what the market does not yet know, information that will be known only in the future cannot influence the stock's return either. Hence the arrows point in the direction that is shown, with information in any period affecting only that period's abnormal return. *Event studies* are statistical studies that examine whether the arrows are as shown or whether the release of information influences returns on other days.

These studies also speak of *cumulative abnormal returns* (CARs), as well as abnormal returns (ARs). As an example, consider a firm with ARs of 1 percent, −3 percent, and 6 percent for dates −1, 0, and 1, respectively, relative to a corporate announcement. The

Figure 13.5   Cumulative Abnormal Returns for Companies Announcing Dividend Omissions

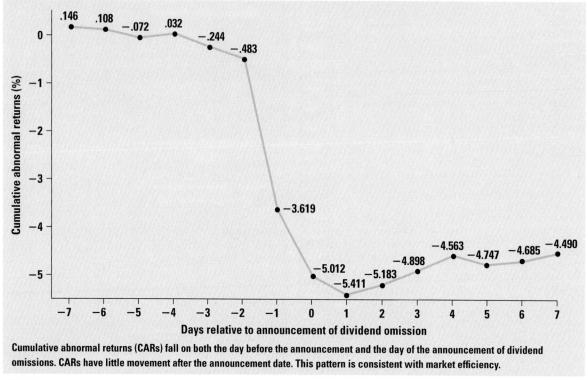

Cumulative abnormal returns (CARs) fall on both the day before the announcement and the day of the announcement of dividend omissions. CARs have little movement after the announcement date. This pattern is consistent with market efficiency.

SOURCE: From Exhibit 2 in S. H. Szewczyk, George P. Tsetsekos, and Zaher Z. Zantout, "Do Dividend Omissions Signal Future Earnings or Past Earnings?" *Journal of Investing* (Spring 1997).

CARs for dates −1, 0, and 1 would be 1 percent, −2 percent [=1 percent + (−3 percent)], and 4 percent [=1 percent + (−3 percent) + 6 percent], respectively.

As an example, consider the study by Szewczyk, Tsetsekos, and Zantout[8] on dividend omissions. Figure 13.5 shows the plot of CARs for a sample of companies announcing dividend omissions. Because dividend omissions are generally considered to be bad events, we would expect abnormal returns to be negative around the time of the announcements. They are, as evidenced by a drop in the CAR on both the day before the announcement (day −1) and the day of the announcement (day 0).[9] However, note that there is virtually no movement in the CARs in the days following the announcement. This implies that the bad

---

[8] Samuel H. Szewczyk, George P. Tsetsekos, and Zaher Z. Zantout, "Do Dividend Omissions Signal Future Earnings or Past Earnings?" *Journal of Investing* (Spring 1997).

[9] An astute reader may wonder why the abnormal return is negative on day −1 as well as on day 0. To see why, first note that the announcement date is generally taken in academic studies to be the publication date of the story in *The Wall Street Journal (WSJ)*. Then consider a company announcing a dividend omission via a press release at noon on Tuesday. The stock should fall on Tuesday. The announcement will be reported in the *WSJ* on Wednesday because the Tuesday edition of the *WSJ* has already been printed. For this firm the stock price falls on the day *before* the announcement in the *WSJ*.

Alternatively, imagine another firm announcing a dividend omission via a press release on Tuesday at 8 p.m. Because the stock market is closed at that late hour, the stock price will fall on Wednesday. Because the *WSJ* will report the announcement on Wednesday, the stock price falls on the day of the announcement in the *WSJ*.

Firms may either make announcements during trading hours or after trading hours, so stocks should fall on both day −1 and day 0 relative to publication in the *WSJ*.

Figure 13.6   Annual Return Performance* of Different Types of U.S. Mutual Funds Relative to a Broad-Based Market Index (1963–1998)

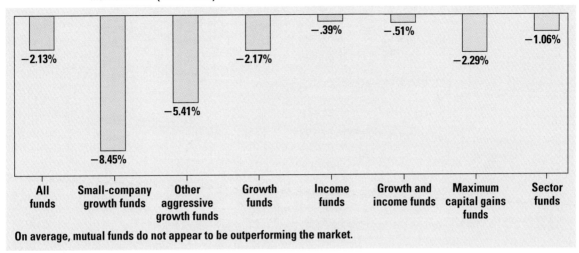

*Performance is relative to the market model.

SOURCE: Taken from Table 2 of Lubos Pastor and Robert F. Stambaugh, "Mutual Fund Performance and Seemingly Unrelated Assets," *Journal of Financial Economics* 63 (2002).

news is fully incorporated into the stock price by the announcement day, a result consistent with market efficiency.

Over the years this type of methodology has been applied to many events. Announcements of dividends, earnings, mergers, capital expenditures, and new issues of stock are a few examples of the vast literature in the area. The early event study tests generally supported the view that the market is semistrong form (and therefore also weak form) efficient. However, a number of more recent studies present evidence that the market does not impound all relevant information immediately. Some conclude from this that the market is not efficient. Others argue that this conclusion is unwarranted, given statistical and methodological problems in the studies. This issue will be addressed in more detail later in the chapter.

The Record of Mutual Funds   If the market is efficient in the semistrong form, then no matter what publicly available information mutual fund managers rely on to pick stocks, their average returns should be the same as those of the average investor in the market as a whole. We can test efficiency, then, by comparing the performance of these professionals with that of a market index.

Consider Figure 13.6, which presents the performance of various types of mutual funds relative to the stock market as a whole. The far left of the figure shows that the universe of all funds covered in the study underperforms the market by 2.13 percent per year after an appropriate adjustment for risk. Thus, rather than outperforming the market, the evidence shows underperformance. This underperformance holds for a number of types of funds as well. Returns in this study are net of fees, expenses, and commissions, so fund returns would be higher if these costs were added back. However, the study shows no evidence that funds, as a whole, are *beating* the market.

Perhaps nothing rankles successful stock market investors more than to have some professor tell them that they are not necessarily smart, just lucky. However, while Figure 13.6 represents only one study, there have been many papers on mutual funds. The overwhelming evidence here is that mutual funds, on average, do not beat broad-based indexes.

By and large, mutual fund managers rely on publicly available information. Thus the finding that they do not outperform market indexes is consistent with semistrong form and weak form efficiency.

However, this evidence does not imply that mutual funds are bad investments for individuals. Though these funds fail to achieve better returns than some indexes of the market, they permit the investor to buy a portfolio of many stocks (the phrase "a well-diversified portfolio" is often used). They might also provide a variety of services such as keeping custody and records of all the stocks.

The Strong Form

Even the strongest adherents to the efficient market hypothesis would not be surprised to find that markets are inefficient in the strong form. After all, if an individual has information that no one else has, it is likely that she can profit from it.

One group of studies of strong form efficiency investigates insider trading. Insiders in firms have access to information that is not generally available. But if the strong form of the efficient market hypothesis holds, they should not be able to profit by trading on their information. A government agency, the Securities and Exchange Commission, requires insiders in companies to reveal any trading they might do in their own company's stock. By examining the record of such trades, we can see whether they made abnormal returns. A number of studies support the view that these trades were abnormally profitable. Thus, strong form efficiency does not seem to be substantiated by the evidence.

13.5   The Behavioral Challenge to Market Efficiency

In Section 13.2 we presented Prof. Shleifer's three conditions, any one of which will lead to market efficiency. In that section we made a case that at least one of the conditions is likely to hold in the real world. However, there is definitely disagreement here. Many members of the academic community (including Prof. Shleifer) argue that none of the three conditions is likely to hold in reality. This point of view is based on what is called *behavioral finance*. Let us examine the behavioral view of each of these three conditions.

Rationality   Are people really rational? Not always. Just travel to Atlantic City or Las Vegas to see people gambling, sometimes with large sums of money. The casino's take implies a negative expected return for the gambler. Because gambling is risky and has a negative expected return, it can never be on the efficient frontier of our Chapter 10. In addition, gamblers will often bet on black at a roulette table after black has occurred a number of consecutive times, thinking that the run will continue. This strategy is faulty because roulette tables have no memory.

But, of course, gambling is only a sideshow as far as finance is concerned. Do we see irrationality in financial markets as well? The answer may well be yes. Many investors do not achieve the degree of diversification that they should. Others trade frequently, generating both commissions and taxes. In fact, taxes can be handled optimally by selling losers and holding onto winners. Although some individuals invest with tax minimization in mind, plenty of them do just the opposite. Many are more likely to sell their winners than their losers, a strategy leading to high tax payments.[10] The behavioral view is not that *all* investors are irrational. Rather, it is that some, perhaps many, investors are.

---

[10]For example, see Brad Barber and Terrance Odean, "The Courage of Misguided Convictions," *Financial Analysts Journal* (November/December 1999).

Independent Deviations from Rationality   Are deviations from rationality generally random, thereby likely to cancel out in a whole population of investors? To the contrary, psychologists have long argued that people deviate from rationality in accordance with a number of basic principles. Not all of these principles have an application to finance and market efficiency, but at least two seem to do so.

The first principle, called *representativeness*, can be explained with the gambling example just used. The gambler believing a run of black will continue is in error because the probability of a black spin is still only about 50 percent. Gamblers behaving in this way exhibit the psychological trait of representativeness. That is, they draw conclusions from insufficient data. In other words, the gambler believes the small sample he observed is more representative of the population than it really is.

How is this related to finance? Perhaps a market dominated by representativeness leads to bubbles. People see a sector of the market—for example, Internet stocks—having a short history of high revenue growth and extrapolate that it will continue forever. When the growth inevitably stalls, prices have nowhere to go but down.

The second principle is *conservatism*, which means that people are too slow in adjusting their beliefs to new information. Suppose that your goal since childhood was to become a dentist. Perhaps you came from a family of dentists, perhaps you liked the security and relatively high income that comes with that profession, or perhaps teeth always fascinated you. As things stand now, you could probably look forward to a long and productive career in that occupation. However, suppose a new drug was developed that would prevent tooth decay. That drug would clearly reduce the demand for dentists. How quickly would you realize the implications as stated here? If you were emotionally attached to dentistry, you might adjust your beliefs slowly. Family and friends could tell you to switch out of predental courses in college, but you just might not be psychologically ready to do that. Instead, you might cling to your rosy view of dentistry's future.

Perhaps there is a relationship to finance here. For example, many studies report that prices seem to adjust slowly to the information contained in earnings announcements.[11] Could it be that because of conservatism, investors are slow in adjusting their beliefs to new information? More will be said about this in the next section.

Arbitrage   In Section 13.2 we suggested that professional investors, knowing that securities are mispriced, could buy the underpriced ones while selling correctly priced (or even overpriced) substitutes. This might undo any mispricing caused by emotional amateurs.

Trading of this sort is likely to be more risky than it appears at first glance. Suppose professionals generally believed that McDonald's stock was underpriced. They would buy it while selling their holdings in, say, Burger King and Wendy's. However, if amateurs were taking opposite positions, prices would adjust to correct levels only if the positions of amateurs were small relative to those of the professionals. In a world of many amateurs, a few professionals would have to take big positions to bring prices into line, perhaps even engaging heavily in short selling. Buying large amounts of one stock and short selling large amounts of other stocks is quite risky, even if the two stocks are in the same industry. Here, unanticipated bad news about McDonald's and unanticipated good news about the other two stocks would cause the professionals to register large losses.

In addition, if amateurs mispriced McDonald's today, what is to prevent McDonald's from being even *more* mispriced tomorrow? This risk of further mispricing, even in the

---

[11] For example, see Vijay Singal, *Beyond the Random Walk* (New York: Oxford University Press, 2004), chapter 4.

presence of no new information, may also cause professionals to cut back their arbitrage positions. As an example, imagine a shrewd professional who believed Internet stocks were overpriced in 1998. Had he bet on a decline at that time, he would have lost in the near term: Prices rose through March of 2000. Yet, he would have eventually made money because prices later fell. However, near-term risk may reduce the size of arbitrage strategies.

In conclusion, the arguments presented here suggest that the theoretical underpinnings of the efficient capital markets hypothesis, presented in Section 13.2, might not hold in reality. That is, investors may be irrational, irrationality may be related across investors rather than canceling out across investors, and arbitrage strategies may involve too much risk to eliminate market efficiencies.

13.6 Empirical Challenges to Market Efficiency

Section 13.4 presented empirical evidence supportive of market efficiency. We now present evidence challenging this hypothesis. (Adherents of market efficiency generally refer to results of this type as *anomalies*.)

1. *Limits to arbitrage*: Royal Dutch Petroleum and Shell Transport merged their interests in 1907, with all subsequent cash flows being split on a 60 percent−40 percent basis between the two companies. However, both companies continued to be publicly traded. You might imagine that the market value of Royal Dutch would always be 1.5 (=60/40) times that of Shell. That is, if Royal Dutch ever became overpriced, rational investors would buy Shell instead of Royal Dutch. If Royal Dutch were underpriced, investors would buy Royal Dutch. In addition, arbitrageurs would go further by buying the underpriced security and selling the overpriced security short.

   However, Figure 13.7 shows that Royal Dutch and Shell have rarely traded at parity (i.e., 60/40) over the 1962 to 2004 period. Why would these deviations occur? As stated in the previous section, behavioral finance suggests that there are limits to arbitrage. That is, an investor buying the overpriced asset and selling the underpriced

Figure 13.7

Deviations of the Ratio of the Market Value of Royal Dutch to the Market Value of Shell from Parity

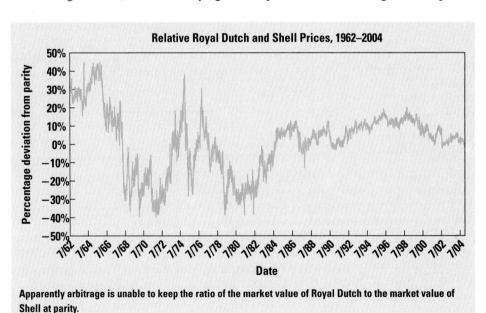

Relative Royal Dutch and Shell Prices, 1962–2004

Apparently arbitrage is unable to keep the ratio of the market value of Royal Dutch to the market value of Shell at parity.

SOURCE: Author calculations.

asset does not have a sure thing. Deviations from parity could actually *increase* in the short run, implying losses for the arbitrageur. The well-known statement, "Markets can stay irrational longer than you can stay solvent," attributed to John Maynard Keynes, applies here. Thus, risk considerations may force arbitrageurs to take positions that are too small to move prices back to parity.

Academics have documented a number of these deviations from parity. Froot and Dabora show similar results for both the twin companies of Unilever N.V. and Unilever PLC and for two classes of SmithKline Beecham stock.[12] Lamont and Thaler present similar findings for 3Com and its subsidiary Palm Inc. (see Example 13.2 for more about 3Com and Palm).[13] Other researchers find price behavior in closed-end mutual funds suggestive of parity deviations.

EXAMPLE 13.2

Can Stock Market Investors Add and Subtract?   On March 2, 2000, 3Com, a profitable provider of computer networking products and services, sold 5 percent of one of its subsidiaries to the public via an initial public offering (IPO). At the time the subsidiary was known as Palm (now it is known as palmOne).

3Com planned to distribute the remaining Palm shares to 3Com shareholders at a later date. Under the plan, if you owned one share of 3Com, you would receive 1.5 shares of Palm. So after 3Com sold part of Palm via the IPO, investors could buy Palm shares directly, or indirectly by purchasing shares of 3Com and waiting.

What makes this case interesting is what happened in the days that followed the Palm IPO. If you owned one 3Com share, you would be entitled, eventually, to 1.5 shares of Palm. Therefore each 3Com share should be worth *at least* 1.5 times the value of each Palm share. We say *at least* because the other parts of 3Com were profitable. As a result, each 3Com share should have been worth much more than 1.5 times the value of one Palm share. But as you might guess, things did not work out this way.

The day before the Palm IPO, shares in 3Com sold for $104.13. After the first day of trading, Palm closed at $95.06 per share. Multiplying $95.06 by 1.5 results in $142.59, which is the minimum value we would expect to pay for 3Com. But the day Palm closed at $95.06, 3Com shares closed at $81.81, more than $60 lower than the price implied by Palm. It gets stranger.

A 3Com price of $81.81 when Palm was selling for $95.06 implies that the market valued the rest of 3Com's businesses (per share) at $81.81 − 142.59 = −$60.78. Given the number of 3Com shares outstanding at the time, this means the market placed a *negative* value of about $22 billion on the rest of 3Com's businesses. Of course, a stock price cannot be negative. This means that the price of Palm relative to 3Com was much too high.

To profit from this mispricing, investors would purchase shares of 3Com and sell shares of Palm. This trade was a no-brainer. In a well-functioning market arbitrage traders would force the prices into alignment quickly. What happened?

As you can see in the accompanying figure, the market valued 3Com and Palm shares in such a way that the non-Palm part of 3Com had a negative value for about two months from March 2, 2000, until May 8, 2000. Thus the pricing error was corrected by market forces, but not instantly, which is consistent with the existence of limits to arbitrage.

(continued)

---

[12] Kenneth A. Froot and Emil M. Dabora, "How Are Stock Prices Affected by the Location of Trade?" *Journal of Financial Economics* 53 (August 1999).

[13] Owen Lamont and Richard Thaler, "Can the Market Add and Subtract? Mispricing in Tech Stock Carve-Outs," *Journal of Political Economy* (April 2003).

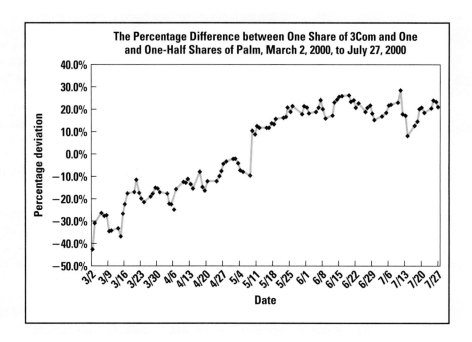

2. *Earnings surprises*: Common sense suggests that prices should rise when earnings are reported to be higher than expected and prices should fall when the reverse occurs. However, market efficiency implies that prices will adjust immediately to the announcement, while behavioral finance would predict another pattern. Kolasinski and Li rank companies by the extent of their *earnings surprise*—that is, the difference between current quarterly earnings and quarterly earnings four quarters ago, divided by the current stock price.[14] They form a portfolio of companies with the most extreme positive surprises and another portfolio of companies with the most extreme negative surprises. Figure 13.8 shows returns from buying the two portfolios, net of the return on the overall market. As can be seen, prices adjust slowly to the earnings announcements, with the portfolio with the positive surprises outperforming the portfolio with the negative surprises over both the next month and the next six months. Many other researchers obtain similar results.

   Why do prices adjust slowly? Behavioral finance suggests that investors exhibit conservatism because they are slow to adjust to the information contained in the announcements.

3. *Size*: In 1981, two important papers presented evidence that in the United States, the returns on stocks with small market capitalizations were greater than the returns on stocks with large market capitalizations over most of the 20th century.[15] The studies have since been replicated over different periods and in different countries. For example, Figure 13.9 shows average returns over the period from 1963 to 1995 for five portfolios of U.S. stocks ranked by size. As can be seen, the average return on small stocks is quite a bit higher than the average return on large stocks. Although

---

[14] Adam Kolasinski and Xu Li, "Do Managers Detect Mispricing? Evidence from Insider Trading and Post-Earnings-Announcement Drift" (Massachusetts Institute of Technology: unpublished paper, 2005).

[15] See R. W. Banz, "The Relationship between Return and Market Value of Common Stocks," *Journal of Financial Economics* (March 1981), and M. R. Reinganum, "Misspecification of Capital Asset Pricing: Empirical Anomalies Based on Earnings Yields and Market Values," *Journal of Financial Economics* (March 1981).

Figure 13.8

Returns to Two Investment Strategies Based on Earnings Surprise

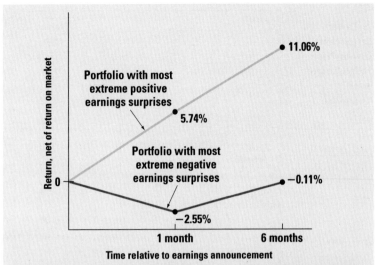

This figure shows returns net of the market return to a strategy of buying stocks with extremely high positive earnings surprise (the difference between current quarterly earnings and quarterly earnings four quarters ago, divided by the current stock price) and to a strategy of buying stocks with extremely high negative earnings surprise. The graph shows a slow adjustment to the information in the earnings announcement.

SOURCE: Adapted from Table 1 of Adam Kolasinski and Xu Li, "Do Managers Detect Mispricing? Evidence from Insider Trading and Post-Earnings-Announcement Drift" (Massachusetts Institute of Technology: unpublished paper, 2005).

Figure 13.9

Annual Stock Returns on Portfolios Sorted by Size (Market Capitalization)

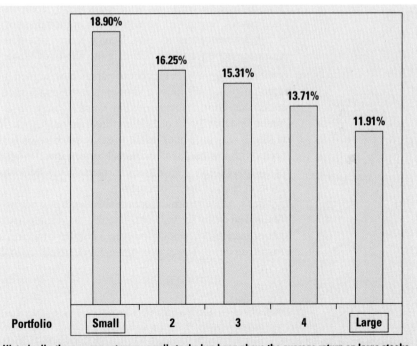

Historically, the average return on small stocks has been above the average return on large stocks.

SOURCE: Tim Loughran, "Book-to-Market across Firm Size, Exchange and Seasonality," *Journal of Financial and Quantitative Analysis* 32 (1997).

Figure 13.10

Annual U.S. Dollar Returns* (in percent) on Low Book-to-Price Firms and High Book-to-Price Firms in Selected Countries

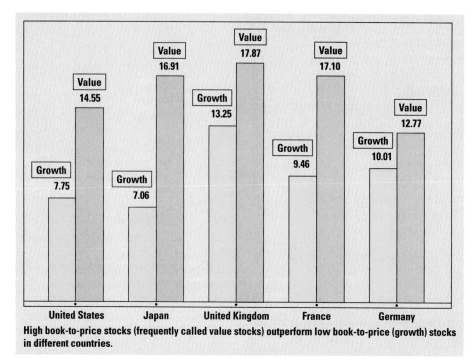

High book-to-price stocks (frequently called value stocks) outperform low book-to-price (growth) stocks in different countries.

*Returns are expressed as the excess over the return on U.S. Treasury bills.

SOURCE: Eugene F. Fama and Kenneth R. French, "Value versus Growth: The International Evidence," *Journal of Finance* (December 1998).

much of the differential performance is merely compensation for the extra risk of small stocks, researchers have generally argued that not all of it can be explained by risk differences. In addition, Donald Keim presented evidence that most of the difference in performance occurs in the month of January.[16]

4. *Value versus growth*: A number of papers have argued that stocks with high book-value-to-stock-price ratios and/or high earnings-to-price ratios (generally called *value stocks*) outperform stocks with low ratios (*growth stocks*). For example, Fama and French find that for 12 of 13 major international stock markets, the average return on stocks with high book-value-to-stock-price ratios is above the average return on stocks with low book-value-to-stock-price ratios.[17] Figure 13.10 shows these returns for the world's five largest stock markets. Value stocks have outperformed growth stocks in each of these five markets.

Because the return difference is so large and because these ratios can be obtained so easily for individual stocks, the results may constitute strong evidence against market efficiency. However, a number of papers suggest that the unusual returns are due to biases in commercial databases or to differences in risk, not to

[16]D. B. Keim, "Size-Related Anomalies and Stock Return Seasonality: Further Empirical Evidence," *Journal of Financial Economics* (June 1983). Also see Kathryn Easterday, "The Declining January Effect? An Examination of Monthly Return for Firms Trading on NYSE, AMEX, and NASDAQ" (University of Cincinnati: unpublished paper, 2005), for similar conclusions with more recent data.

[17]Taken from Table III of Eugene F. Fama and Kenneth R. French, "Value versus Growth: The International Evidence," *Journal of Finance* 53 (December 1998).

Figure 13.11

Value of Index of
Internet Stocks

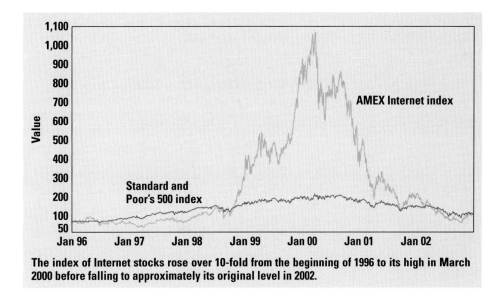

The index of Internet stocks rose over 10-fold from the beginning of 1996 to its high in March 2000 before falling to approximately its original level in 2002.

a true inefficiency.[18] Because the debate revolves around arcane statistical issues, we will not pursue the issue further. However, it is safe to say that no conclusion is warranted at this time. As with so many other topics in finance and economics, further research is needed.

5. *Crashes and bubbles*: The stock market crash of October 19, 1987, is extremely puzzling. The market dropped between 20 percent and 25 percent on a Monday following a weekend during which little surprising news was released. A drop of this magnitude for no apparent reason is not consistent with market efficiency. Because the crash of 1929 is still an enigma, it is doubtful that the more recent 1987 debacle will be explained anytime soon. The recent comments of an eminent historian are apt here: When asked what, in his opinion, the effect of the French Revolution of 1789 was, he replied that it was too early to tell.

Perhaps the two stock market crashes are evidence consistent with the **bubble theory** of speculative markets. That is, security prices sometimes move wildly above their true values. Eventually, prices fall back to their original level, causing great losses for investors. Consider, for example, the behavior of Internet stocks of the late 1990s. Figure 13.11 shows values of an index of Internet stocks from 1996 through 2002. The index rose over 10-fold from January 1996 to its high in March 2000 before retreating to approximately its original level in 2002. For comparison, the figure also shows price movement for the Standard & Poor 500 index. While this index rose and fell over the same period, the price movement was quite muted relative to that of Internet stocks.

Many commentators describe the rise and fall of Internet stocks as a *bubble*. Is it correct to do so? Unfortunately, there is no precise definition of the term. Some academics argue that the price movement in the figure is consistent with rationality. Prices rose initially, they say, because it appeared that the Internet would soon capture a large chunk of international commerce. Prices fell when later evidence suggested this would not occur quite so quickly. However, others argue that the initial

---

[18]For example, see S. P. Kothari, J. Shanken, and R. G. Sloan, "Another Look at the Cross Section of Expected Stock Returns," *Journal of Finance* 50 (March 1995), and E. F. Fama and K. R. French, "Multifactor Explanations of Asset Pricing Anomalies," *Journal of Finance* 51 (March 1996).

rosy scenario was never supported by the facts. Rather, prices rose due to nothing more than "irrational exuberance."

13.7 Reviewing the Differences

It is fair to say that the controversy over efficient capital markets has not yet been resolved. Rather, academic financial economists have sorted themselves into three camps, with some adhering to market efficiency, some believing in behavioral finance, and others (perhaps the majority) not yet convinced that either side has won the argument. This state of affairs is certainly different from, say, 20 years ago, when market efficiency went unchallenged. In addition, the controversy here is perhaps the most contentious of any area of financial economics. Only in this area do grown-up finance professors come close to fisticuffs over an idea.

Because of the controversy, it does not appear that our textbook, or any textbook, can easily resolve the differing points of view. However, we can illustrate the differences between the camps by relating the two psychological principles mentioned earlier, representativeness and conservatism, to stock returns.

Representativeness

This principle implies overweighting the results of small samples, as with the gambler who thinks a few consecutive spins of black on the roulette wheel make black a more likely outcome than red on the next spin. Financial economists have argued that representativeness leads to *overreaction* in stock returns. We mentioned earlier that financial bubbles are likely overreactions to news. Internet companies showed great revenue growth for a short time in the late 1990s, causing many to believe that this growth would continue indefinitely. Stock prices rose (too much) at this point. When at last investors realized that this growth could not be sustained, prices plummeted.

Conservatism

This principle states that individuals adjust their beliefs too slowly to new information. A market composed of this type of investor would likely lead to stock prices that *underreact* in the presence of new information. The example concerning earnings surprises may illustrate this underreaction. Prices rose slowly following announcements of positive earnings surprises. Announcements of negative surprises had a similar, but opposite, reaction.

The Academic Viewpoints

The academic camps have different views of these results. The efficient market believers stress that representativeness and conservatism have opposite implications for stock prices. Which principle, they ask, should dominate in any particular situation? In other words, why should investors overreact to news about Internet stocks but underreact to earnings news? Proponents of market efficiency say that unless behaviorists can answer these two questions satisfactorily, we should not reject market efficiency in favor of behavioral finance. In addition, Eugene Fama[19] reviewed the academic studies on anomalies, finding that about half of them show overreaction and half show underreaction. He concluded that this evidence is consistent with the market efficiency hypothesis that anomalies are chance events.

Adherents of behavioral finance see things a little differently. First, they point out that, as discussed in Section 13.5, the three theoretical foundations of market efficiency appear

---

[19]Eugene F. Fama, "Market Efficiency, Long-Term Returns, and Behavioral Finance," *Journal of Financial Economics* 49 (September 1998).

to be violated in the real world. Second, there are simply too many anomalies, with a number of them being replicated in out-of-sample tests. This argues against anomalies being mere chance events. Finally, though the field has not yet determined why either overreaction or underreaction should dominate in a particular situation, much progress has already been made in a short time.[20]

13.8 Implications for Corporate Finance

So far this chapter has examined both theoretical arguments and empirical evidence concerning efficient markets. We now ask whether market efficiency has any relevance for corporate financial managers. The answer is that it does. Next we consider four implications of efficiency for managers.

1. Accounting Choices, Financial Choices, and Market Efficiency

The accounting profession provides firms with a significant amount of leeway in their reporting practices. For example, companies may choose between the last-in, first-out (LIFO) or the first-in, first-out (FIFO) method in valuing inventories. They may choose either the percentage-of-completion or the completed-contract method for construction projects. They may depreciate physical assets by either accelerated or straight-line depreciation.

Managers clearly prefer high stock prices to low stock prices. Should managers use the leeway in accounting choices to report the highest possible income? Not necessarily. That is, accounting choice should not affect stock price if two conditions hold. First, enough information must be provided in the annual report so that financial analysts can construct earnings under the alternative accounting methods. This appears to be the case for many, though not necessarily all, accounting choices. Second, the market must be efficient in the semistrong form. In other words, the market must appropriately use all of this accounting information in determining the market price.

Of course, the issue of whether accounting choice affects stock price is ultimately an empirical matter. A number of academic papers have addressed this issue. Kaplan and Roll found that the switch from accelerated to straight-line depreciation did not affect stock prices.[21] Kaplan and Roll also looked at changes from the deferral method of accounting for the investment tax credit to the flow-through method.[22] They found that a switch would increase accounting earnings but had no effect on stock prices.

Several other accounting procedures have been studied. Hong, Kaplan, and Mandelker found no evidence that the stock market was affected by the artificially higher earnings reported using the pooling method, compared to the purchase method, for reporting mergers and acquisitions.[23] Biddle and Lindahl found that firms switching to the LIFO method

---

[20]Excellent reviews of this progress can be found in Andrei Shleifer, *Inefficient Markets: An Introduction to Behavioral Finance*, op. cit. and in Nicholas Barberis and Richard Thaler, "A Survey of Behavioral Finance," in the *Handbook of the Economics of Finance*, eds. George Constantinides, Milton Harris, and Rene Stultz (Amsterdam: North Holland, 2003).

[21]R. S. Kaplan and R. Roll, "Investor Evaluation of Accounting Information: Some Empirical Evidence," *Journal of Business* 45 (April 1972).

[22]Before 1987 U.S. tax law allowed a 10 percent tax credit on the purchase of most kinds of capital equipment.

[23]H. Hong, R. S. Kaplan, and G. Mandelker, "Pooling vs. Purchase: The Effects of Accounting for Mergers on Stock Prices," *Accounting Review* 53 (1978). The pooling method for mergers is no longer allowed under generally accepted accounting principles.

of inventory valuation experienced an increase in stock price.[24] This is to be expected in inflationary environments because LIFO valuation can reduce taxes compared to FIFO. They found that the larger the tax decrease resulting from the use of LIFO, the greater was the increase in stock price. In summary, empirical evidence suggests that accounting changes do not fool the market. Therefore, the evidence does not suggest that managers can boost stock price through accounting practices. In other words, the market appears efficient enough to see through different accounting choices.

One caveat is called for here. Our discussion specifically assumed that "financial analysts can construct earnings under the alternative accounting methods." However, companies like Enron, WorldCom, Global Crossing, and Xerox simply reported fraudulent numbers in recent years. There was no way for financial analysts to construct alternative earnings numbers because these analysts were unaware how the reported numbers were determined. So it was not surprising that the prices of these stocks initially rose well above fair value. Yes, managers can boost prices in this way—as long as they are willing to serve time once they are caught!

Is there anything else that investors can be expected to see through in an efficient market? Consider stock splits and stock dividends. Today Amarillo Corporation has 1 million shares outstanding and reports $10 million of earnings. In the hopes of boosting stock price, the firm's chief financial officer (CFO), Ms. Green, recommends to the board of directors that Amarillo have a 2-for-1 stock split. That is, a shareholder with 100 shares prior to the split would have 200 shares after the split. The CFO contends that each investor would feel richer after the split because he would own more shares.

However, this thinking runs counter to market efficiency. A rational investor knows that he would own the same proportion of the firm after the split as before the split. For example, our investor with 100 shares owns 1/10,000 (=100/1 million) of Amarillo's shares prior to the split. His share of the earnings would be $1,000 (=$10 million/10,000). Although he would own 200 shares after the split, there would now be 2 million shares outstanding. Thus, he still would own 1/10,000 of the firm. His share of the earnings would still be $1,000 because the stock split would not affect the earnings of the entire firm.

2. *The Timing Decision*

Imagine a firm whose managers are contemplating the date to issue equity. This decision is frequently called the *timing* decision. If managers believe that their stock is overpriced, they are likely to issue equity immediately. Here, they are creating value for their current stockholders because they are selling stock for more than it is worth. Conversely, if the managers believe that their stock is underpriced, they are more likely to wait, hoping that the stock price will eventually rise to its true value.

However, if markets are efficient, securities are always correctly priced. Efficiency implies that stock is sold for its true worth, so the timing decision becomes unimportant. Figure 13.12 shows three possible stock price adjustments to the issuance of new stock.

Of course market efficiency is ultimately an empirical issue. Surprisingly, recent research has called market efficiency into question. Ritter presents evidence that annual stock returns over the five years following an initial public offering (IPO) are about 2 percent less for the issuing company than the returns on a nonissuing company of similar book-to-market ratio.[25] Annual stock returns over this period following a seasoned equity offering

---

[24]G. C. Biddle and F. W. Lindahl, "Stock Price Reactions to LIFO Adoptions: The Association between Excess Returns and LIFO Tax Savings," *Journal of Accounting Research* (1982).

[25]Jay Ritter, "Investment Banking and Security Issuance," Chapter 9 of *Handbook of the Economics of Finance*, ed. George Constantinides, Milton Harris, and Rene Stulz (Amsterdam: North Holland, 2003).

Figure 13.12

Three Stock Price Adjustments after Issuing Equity

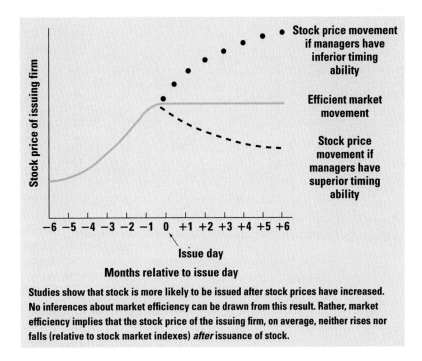

Stock price movement if managers have inferior timing ability

Efficient market movement

Stock price movement if managers have superior timing ability

Issue day

Months relative to issue day

Studies show that stock is more likely to be issued after stock prices have increased. No inferences about market efficiency can be drawn from this result. Rather, market efficiency implies that the stock price of the issuing firm, on average, neither rises nor falls (relative to stock market indexes) *after* issuance of stock.

(SEO) are between 3 percent and 4 percent less for the issuing company than for a comparable nonissuing company. A company's first public offering is called an IPO and all subsequent offerings are termed SEOs. The upper half of Figure 13.13 shows average annual returns of both IPOs and their control group, and the lower half of the figure shows average annual returns of both SEOs and their control group.

The evidence in Ritter's paper suggests that corporate managers issue SEOs when the company's stock is overpriced. In other words, managers appear to time the market successfully. The evidence that managers time their IPOs is less compelling: Returns following IPOs are closer to those of their control group.

Does the ability of a corporate official to issue an SEO when the security is overpriced indicate that the market is inefficient in the semistrong form or the strong form? The answer is actually somewhat more complex than it may first appear. On one hand, officials are likely to have special information that the rest of us do not have, suggesting that the market need only be inefficient in the strong form. On the other hand, if the market were truly semistrong efficient, the price would drop immediately and completely upon the announcement of an upcoming SEO. That is, rational investors would realize that stock is being issued because corporate officials have special information that the stock is overpriced. Indeed, many empirical studies report a price drop on the announcement date. However, Figure 13.13 shows a further price drop in the subsequent years, suggesting that the market is inefficient in the semistrong form.

If firms can time the issuance of common stock, perhaps they can also time the repurchase of stock. Here a firm would like to repurchase when its stock is undervalued. Ikenberry, Lakonishok, and Vermaelen find that stock returns of repurchasing firms are abnormally high in the two years following repurchase, suggesting that timing is effective here.[26]

---

[26]D. Ikenberry, J. Lakonishok, and T. Vermaelen, "Market Underreaction to Open Market Share Repurchases," *Journal of Financial Economics* (October–November 1995).

Figure 13.13

Returns on Initial
Public Offerings
(IPOs) and Seasoned
Equity Offerings
(SEOs) in Years
Following Issue

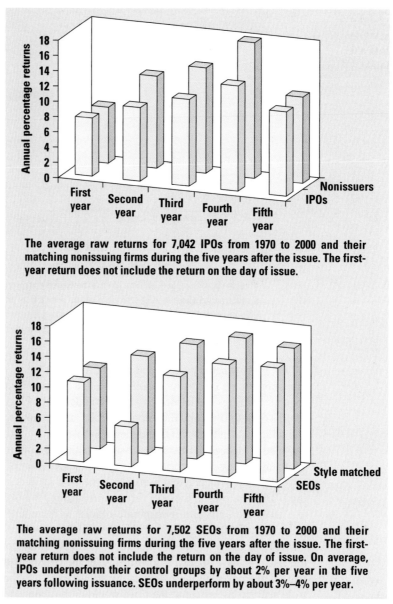

The average raw returns for 7,042 IPOs from 1970 to 2000 and their matching nonissuing firms during the five years after the issue. The first-year return does not include the return on the day of issue.

The average raw returns for 7,502 SEOs from 1970 to 2000 and their matching nonissuing firms during the five years after the issue. The first-year return does not include the return on the day of issue. On average, IPOs underperform their control groups by about 2% per year in the five years following issuance. SEOs underperform by about 3%–4% per year.

SOURCE: Jay Ritter, "Investment Banking and Security Issuance," Chapter 9 of *Handbook of the Economics of Finance,* ed. George Constantinides, Milton Harris, and Rene Stulz (Amsterdam: North Holland, 2003).

3.   *Speculation and Efficient Markets*

We normally think of individuals and financial institutions as the primary speculators in financial markets. However, industrial corporations speculate as well. For example, many companies make interest rate bets. If the managers of a firm believe that interest rates are likely to rise, they have an incentive to borrow because the present value of the liability will fall with the rate increase. In addition, these managers will have an incentive to borrow long term rather than short term in order to lock in the low rates for a longer period. The thinking can get more sophisticated. Suppose that the long-term rate is already higher than the short-term rate. The manager might argue that this differential reflects the market's view that rates will rise. However, perhaps he anticipates a rate increase even greater than what the market anticipates, as implied by the upward-sloping term structure. Again, the manager will want to borrow long term rather than short term.

Firms also speculate in foreign currencies. Suppose that the CFO of a multinational corporation based in the United States believes that the euro will decline relative to the dollar. She would probably issue euro-denominated debt rather than dollar-denominated debt because she expects the value of the foreign liability to fall. Conversely, she would issue debt domestically if she believes foreign currencies will appreciate relative to the dollar.

We are perhaps getting a little ahead of our story: The subtleties of the term structure and exchange rates are treated in other chapters, not this one. However, the big picture question is this: What does market efficiency have to say about such activity? The answer is clear. If financial markets are efficient, managers should not waste their time trying to forecast the movements of interest rates and foreign currencies. Their forecasts will likely be no better than chance. And they will be using up valuable executive time. This is not to say, however, that firms should flippantly pick the maturity or the denomination of their debt in a random fashion. A firm must *choose* these parameters carefully. However, the choice should be based on other rationales, not on an attempt to beat the market. For example, a firm with a project lasting five years might decide to issue five-year debt. A firm might issue yen-denominated debt because it anticipates expanding into Japan in a big way.

The same thinking applies to acquisitions. Many corporations buy up other firms because they think these targets are underpriced. Unfortunately, the empirical evidence suggests that the market is too efficient for this type of speculation to be profitable. And the acquirer never pays just the current market price. The bidding firm must pay a premium above market to induce a majority of shareholders of the target firm to sell their shares. However, this is not to say that firms should never be acquired. Rather, managers should consider an acquisition if there are benefits (synergies) from the union. Improved marketing, economies in production, replacement of bad management, and even tax reduction are typical synergies. These synergies are distinct from the perception that the acquired firm is underpriced.

One final point should be mentioned. We talked earlier about empirical evidence suggesting that SEOs are timed to take advantage of overpriced stock. This makes sense—managers are likely to know more about their own firms than the market does. However, while managers may have special information about their own firms, it is unlikely that they have special information about interest rates, foreign currencies, and other firms. There are simply too many participants in these markets, many of whom are devoting all of their time to forecasting. Managers typically spend most of their effort running their own firms, with only a small amount of time devoted to studying financial markets.

4.   *Information in Market Prices*

The previous section argued that it is quite difficult to forecast future market prices. However, the current and past prices of any asset are known—and of great use. Consider, for example, Becher's study of bank mergers.[27] The author finds that stock prices of acquired banks rise about 23 percent on average upon the first announcement of a merger. This is not surprising because companies are generally bought out at a premium above current stock price. However, the same study shows that prices of acquiring banks fall almost 5 percent on average upon the same announcement. This is pretty strong evidence that bank mergers do not benefit, and may even hurt, acquiring companies. The reason for this result is unclear,

---

[27]David A. Becher, "The Valuation Effects of Bank Mergers," *Journal of Corporate Finance* 6 (2000).

Figure 13.14

Stock Performance Prior to Forced Departures of Management

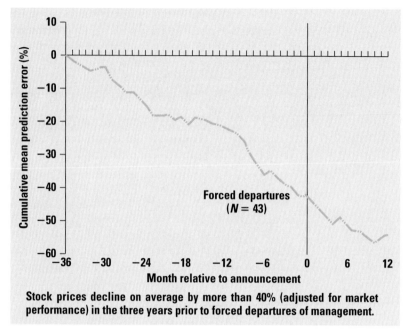

Stock prices decline on average by more than 40% (adjusted for market performance) in the three years prior to forced departures of management.

SOURCE: Adapted from Figure 1 of Warner, Watts, and Wruck, "Stock Prices and Management Changes," *Journal of Financial Economics* 20 (1988).

though perhaps acquirers simply overpay for acquisitions. Regardless of the reason, the *implication* is clear. A bank should think deeply before acquiring another bank.

Furthermore, suppose you are the CFO of a company whose stock price drops much more than 5 percent upon announcement of an acquisition. The market is telling you that the merger is bad for your firm. Serious consideration should be given to canceling the merger, even if, prior to the announcement, you thought the merger was a good idea.

Of course, mergers are only one type of corporate event. Managers should pay attention to the stock price reaction to any of their announcements, whether it concerns a new venture, a divestiture, a restructuring, or something else.

This is not the only way in which corporations can use the information in market prices. Suppose you are on the board of directors of a company whose stock price has declined precipitously since the current chief executive officer (CEO) was hired. In addition, the prices of competitors have risen over the same time. Though there may be extenuating circumstances, this can be viewed as evidence that the CEO is doing a poor job. Perhaps he should be fired. If this seems harsh, consider that Warner, Watts, and Wruck find a strong negative correlation between managerial turnover and prior stock performance.[28] Figure 13.14 shows that stocks fall on average about 40 percent in price (relative to market movements) in the three years prior to the forced departure of a top manager.

If managers are fired for bad stock price performance, perhaps they are rewarded for stock price appreciation. Hall and Liebman state,

> Our main empirical finding is that CEO wealth often changes by millions of dollars for typical changes in firm value. For example, the median total compensation for CEOs is about $1 million if their firm's stock has a 30th percentile annual return (−7.0 percent) and is

---

[28]Jerold B. Warner, Ross L. Watts, and Karen H. Wruck, "Stock Prices and Top Management Changes," *Journal of Financial Economics* 20 (1988).

$5 million if the firm's stock has a 70th percentile annual return (20.5 percent). Thus, there is a difference of about $4 million in compensation for achieving a moderately above average performance relative to a moderately below average performance.[29]

Market efficiency implies that stock prices reflect all available information. We recommend using this information as much as possible in corporate decisions. And at least with respect to executive firings and executive compensation, it looks as if real-world corporations do pay attention to market prices. The following box summarizes some key issues in the efficient markets debate:

Efficient Market Hypothesis: A Summary

Does Not Say

- Prices are uncaused.
- Investors are foolish and too stupid to be in the market.
- All shares of stock have the same expected returns.
- Investors should throw darts to select stocks.
- There is no upward trend in stock prices.

Does Say

- Prices reflect underlying value.
- Financial managers cannot time stock and bond sales.
- Managers cannot profitably speculate in foreign currencies.
- Managers cannot boost stock prices through creative accounting.

Why Doesn't Everybody Believe It?

- There are optical illusions, mirages, and apparent patterns in charts of stock market returns.
- The truth is less interesting.
- There is evidence against efficiency:
  - Two different, but financially identical, classes of stock of the same firm selling at different prices.
  - Earnings surprises.
  - Small versus large stocks.
  - Value versus growth stocks.
  - Crashes and bubbles.

Three Forms

Weak form: Current prices reflect past prices; chartism (technical analysis) is useless.

Semistrong form: Prices reflect all public information; most financial analysis is useless.

Strong form: Prices reflect all that is knowable; nobody consistently makes superior profits.

---

[29]Brian J. Hall and Jeffrey B. Liebman, "Are CEOs Really Paid Like Bureaucrats?" *Quarterly Journal of Economics* (August 1998), p. 654.

Summary and Conclusions

1. An efficient financial market processes the information available to investors and incorporates it into the prices of securities. Market efficiency has two general implications. First, in any given time period, a stock's abnormal return depends on information or news received by the market in that period. Second, an investor who uses the same information as the market cannot expect to earn abnormal returns. In other words, systems for playing the market are doomed to fail.

2. What information does the market use to determine prices? The weak form of the efficient market hypothesis says that the market uses the history of prices and is therefore efficient with respect to these past prices. This implies that stock selection based on patterns of past stock price movements is no better than random stock selection.

3. The semistrong form states that the market uses all publicly available information in setting prices.

4. Strong form efficiency states that the market uses all of the information that anybody knows about stocks, even inside information.

5. Much evidence from different financial markets supports weak form and semistrong form efficiency but not strong form efficiency.

6. Behavioral finance states that the market is not efficient. Adherents argue that:
   a. Investors are not rational.
   b. Deviations from rationality are similar across investors.
   c. Arbitrage, being costly, will not eliminate inefficiencies.

7. Behaviorists point to many studies, including those showing that small stocks outperform large stocks, value stocks outperform growth stocks, and stock prices adjust slowly to earnings surprises, as empirical confirmation of their beliefs.

8. Four implications of market efficiency for corporate finance are:
   a. Managers cannot fool the market through creative accounting.
   b. Firms cannot successfully time issues of debt and equity.
   c. Managers cannot profitably speculate in foreign currencies and other instruments.
   d. Managers can reap many benefits by paying attention to market prices.

Concept Questions

1. **Firm Value**   What rule should a firm follow when making financing decisions? How can firms create valuable financing opportunities?

2. **Efficient Market Hypothesis**   Define the three forms of market efficiency.

3. **Efficient Market Hypothesis**   Which of the following statements are true about the efficient market hypothesis?
   a. It implies perfect forecasting ability.
   b. It implies that prices reflect all available information.
   c. It implies an irrational market.
   d. It implies that prices do not fluctuate.
   e. It results from keen competition among investors.

4. **Market Efficiency Implications**   Explain why a characteristic of an efficient market is that investments in that market have zero NPVs.

5. **Efficient Market Hypothesis**   A stock market analyst is able to identify mispriced stocks by comparing the average price for the last 10 days to the average price for the last 60 days. If this is true, what do you know about the market?

6. **Semistrong Efficiency**   If a market is semistrong form efficient, is it also weak form efficient? Explain.

7.   **Efficient Market Hypothesis**   What are the implications of the efficient markets hypothesis for investors who buy and sell stocks in an attempt to "beat the market"?

8.   **Stocks versus Gambling**   Critically evaluate the following statement: Playing the stock market is like gambling. Such speculative investing has no social value other than the pleasure people get from this form of gambling.

9.   **Efficient Market Hypothesis**   Several celebrated investors and stock pickers frequently mentioned in the financial press have recorded huge returns on their investments over the past two decades. Does the success of these particular investors invalidate the EMH? Explain.

10. **Efficient Market Hypothesis**   For each of the following scenarios, discuss whether profit opportunities exist from trading in the stock of the firm under the conditions that (1) the market is not weak form efficient, (2) the market is weak form but not semistrong form efficient, (3) the market is semistrong form but not strong form efficient, and (4) the market is strong form efficient.
   a. The stock price has risen steadily each day for the past 30 days.
   b. The financial statements for a company were released three days ago, and you believe you've uncovered some anomalies in the company's inventory and cost control reporting techniques that are causing the firm's true liquidity strength to be understated.
   c. You observe that the senior management of a company has been buying a lot of the company's stock on the open market over the past week.

   Use the following information for the next two questions:
   Technical analysis is a controversial investment practice. Technical analysis covers a wide array of techniques, which are all used in an attempt to predict the direction of a particular stock or the market. Technical analysts look at two major types of information: historical stock prices and investor sentiment. A technical analyst would argue these two information sets provide information about the future direction of a particular stock or the market as a whole.

11. **Technical Analysis**   What would a technical analyst say about market efficiency?

12. **Investor Sentiment**   A technical analysis tool that is sometimes used to predict market movements is an investor sentiment index. AAII, the American Association of Individual Investors, publishes an investor sentiment index based on a survey of its members. In the following table you will find the percentage of investors who were bullish, bearish, or neutral during a four-week period:

Week	Bullish	Bearish	Neutral
1	37%	25%	38%
2	52	14	34
3	29	35	36
4	43	26	31

   What is the investor sentiment index intended to capture? How might it be useful in technical analysis?

13. **Performance of the Pros**   In the middle to late 1990s the performance of the pros was unusually poor—on the order of 90 percent of all equity mutual funds underperformed a passively managed index fund. How does this bear on the issue of market efficiency?

14. **Efficient Markets**   A hundred years ago or so, companies did not compile annual reports. Even if you owned stock in a particular company, you were unlikely to be allowed to see the balance sheet and income statement for the company. Assuming the market is semistrong form efficient, what does this say about market efficiency then compared to now?

15. **Efficient Markets Hypothesis**   Aerotech, an aerospace technology research firm, announced this morning that it has hired the world's most knowledgeable and prolific space researchers. Before today Aerotech's stock had been selling for £100. Assume that no other information is received over the next week and the stock market as a whole does not move.
    a. What do you expect will happen to Aerotech's stock?
    b. Consider the following scenarios:
        i.   The stock price jumps to £118 on the day of the announcement. In subsequent days it floats up to £123, then falls back to £116.
        ii. The stock price jumps to £116 and remains at that level.
        iii. The stock price gradually climbs to £116 over the next week.
    Which scenario(s) indicate market efficiency? Which do not? Why?

16. **Efficient Markets Hypothesis**   When the 56-year-old founder of Gulf & Western, Inc., died of a heart attack, the stock price immediately jumped from $18.00 a share to $20.25, a 12.5 percent increase. This is evidence of market inefficiency because an efficient stock market would have anticipated his death and adjusted the price beforehand. Assume that no other information is received and the stock market as a whole does not move. Is this statement about market efficiency true or false? Explain.

17. **Efficient Markets Hypothesis**   Today, the following announcement was made: "Early today the Justice Department reached a decision in the Universal Product Care (UPC) case. UPC has been found guilty of discriminatory practices in hiring. For the next five years, UPC must pay $2 million each year to a fund representing victims of UPC's policies." Assuming the market is efficient, should investors not buy UPC stock after the announcement because the litigation will cause an abnormally low rate of return? Explain.

18. **Efficient Markets Hypothesis**   Newtech Corp. is going to adopt a new chip-testing device that can greatly improve its production efficiency. Do you think the lead engineer can profit from purchasing the firm's stock before the news release on the device? After reading the announcement in *The Wall Street Journal,* should you be able to earn an abnormal return from purchasing the stock if the market is efficient?

19. **Efficient Markets Hypothesis**   TransTrust Corp. has changed how it accounts for inventory. Taxes are unaffected, although the resulting earnings report released this quarter is 20 percent higher than what it would have been under the old accounting system. There is no other surprise in the earnings report, and the change in the accounting treatment was publicly announced. If the market is efficient, will the stock price be higher when the market learns that the reported earnings are higher?

20. **Efficient Markets Hypothesis**   The Durkin Investing Agency has been the best stock picker in the country for the past two years. Before this rise to fame occurred, the Durkin newsletter had 200 subscribers. Those subscribers beat the market consistently, earning substantially higher returns after adjustment for risk and transaction costs. Subscriptions have skyrocketed to 10,000. Now, when the Durkin Investing Agency recommends a stock, the price instantly rises several points. The subscribers currently earn only a normal return when they buy recommended stock because the price rises before anybody can act on the information. Briefly explain this phenomenon. Is Durkin's ability to pick stocks consistent with market efficiency?

21. **Efficient Markets Hypothesis**   Your broker commented that well-managed firms are better investments than poorly managed firms. As evidence your broker cited a recent study examining 100 small manufacturing firms that eight years earlier had been listed in an industry magazine as the best-managed small manufacturers in the country. In the ensuing eight years, the 100 firms listed have not earned more than the normal market return. Your broker continued to say that if the firms were well managed, they should have produced better-than-average returns. If the market is efficient, do you agree with your broker?

22. **Efficient Markets Hypothesis**   A famous economist just announced in *The Wall Street Journal* his findings that the recession is over and the economy is again entering an expansion.

Assume market efficiency. Can you profit from investing in the stock market after you read this announcement?

23. **Efficient Markets Hypothesis**   Suppose the market is semistrong form efficient. Can you expect to earn excess returns if you make trades based on
   a. Your broker's information about record earnings for a stock?
   b. Rumors about a merger of a firm?
   c. Yesterday's announcement of a successful new product test?

24. **Efficient Markets Hypothesis**   Imagine that a particular macroeconomic variable that influences your firm's net earnings is positively serially correlated. Assume market efficiency. Would you expect price changes in your stock to be serially correlated? Why or why not?

25. **Efficient Markets Hypothesis**   The efficient market hypothesis implies that all mutual funds should obtain the same expected risk-adjusted returns. Therefore, we can simply pick mutual funds at random. Is this statement true or false? Explain.

26. **Efficient Markets Hypothesis**   Assume that markets are efficient. During a trading day American Golf Inc. announces that it has lost a contract for a large golfing project that, prior to the news, it was widely believed to have secured. If the market is efficient, how should the stock price react to this information if no additional information is released?

27. **Efficient Markets Hypothesis**   Prospectors, Inc., is a publicly traded gold prospecting company in Alaska. Although the firm's searches for gold usually fail, the prospectors occasionally find a rich vein of ore. What pattern would you expect to observe for Prospectors' cumulative abnormal returns if the market is efficient?

28. **Evidence on Market Efficiency**   Some people argue that the efficient market hypothesis cannot explain the 1987 market crash or the high price-to-earnings ratio of Internet stocks during the late 1990s. What alternative hypothesis is currently used for these two phenomena?

Questions and Problems

BASIC
(Questions 1–4)

1. **Cumulative Abnormal Returns**   Delta, United, and American Airlines announced purchases of planes on July 18 (7/18), February 12 (2/12), and October 7 (10/7), respectively. Given the following information, calculate the cumulative abnormal return (CAR) for these stocks as a group. Graph the result and provide an explanation. All of the stocks have a beta of 1, and no other announcements are made.

Delta			United			American		
Date	Market Return	Company Return	Date	Market Return	Company Return	Date	Market Return	Company Return
7/12	−.3	−.5	2/8	−.9	−1.1	10/1	.5	.3
7/13	.0	.2	2/9	−1.0	−1.1	10/2	.4	.6
7/16	.5	.7	2/10	.4	.2	10/3	1.1	1.1
7/17	−.5	−.3	2/11	.6	.8	10/6	.1	−.3
7/18	−2.2	1.1	2/12	−.3	−.1	10/7	−2.2	−.3
7/19	−.9	−.7	2/15	1.1	1.2	10/8	.5	.5
7/20	−1.0	−1.1	2/16	.5	.5	10/9	−.3	−.2
7/23	.7	.5	2/17	−.3	−.2	10/10	.3	.1
7/24	.2	.1	2/18	.3	.2	10/13	.0	−.1

2. **Cumulative Abnormal Returns**   The following diagram shows the cumulative abnormal returns (CAR) for 386 oil exploration companies announcing oil discoveries between 1950

and 1980. Month 0 in the diagram is the announcement month. Assume that no other information is received and the stock market as a whole does not move. Is the diagram consistent with market efficiency? Why or why not?

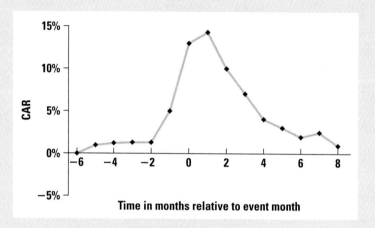

Time in months relative to event month

3. **Cumulative Abnormal Returns**   The following figures present the results of four cumulative abnormal returns (CAR) studies. Indicate whether the results of each study support, reject, or are inconclusive about the semistrong form of the efficient market hypothesis. In each figure time 0 is the date of an event.

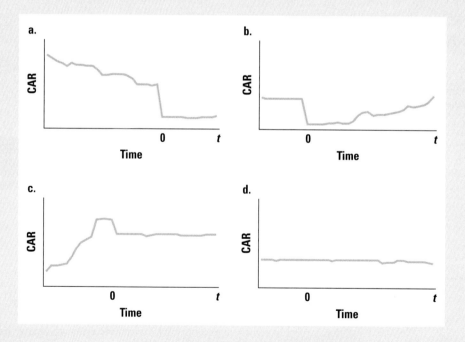

4. **Cumulative Abnormal Returns**   A study analyzed the behavior of the stock prices of firms that had lost antitrust cases. Included in the diagram are all firms that lost the initial court decision, even if the decision was later overturned on appeal. The event at time 0 is the initial,

preappeal court decision. Assume no other information was released, aside from that disclosed in the initial trial. The stock prices all have a beta of 1. Is the diagram consistent with market efficiency? Why or why not?

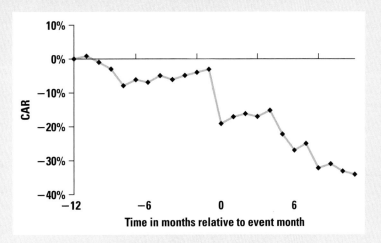

www.mhhe.com/rwj

Mini Case

Your 401(K) Account at East Coast Yachts

You have been at your job for East Coast Yachts for a week now and have decided you need to sign up for the company's 401(k) plan. Even after your discussion with Sarah Brown, the Bledsoe Financial Services representative, you are still unsure which investment option you should choose. Recall that the options available to you are stock in East Coast Yachts, the Bledsoe S&P 500 Index Fund, the Bledsoe Small-Cap Fund, the Bledsoe Large-Company Stock Fund, the Bledsoe Bond Fund, and the Bledsoe Money Market Fund. You have decided that you should invest in a diversified portfolio, with 70 percent of your investment in equity, 25 percent in bonds, and 5 percent in the money market fund. You have also decided to focus your equity investment on large-cap stocks, but you are debating whether to select the S&P 500 Index Fund or the Large-Company Stock Fund.

In thinking it over, you understand the basic difference in the two funds. One is a purely passive fund that replicates a widely followed large-cap index, the S&P 500, and has low fees. The other is actively managed with the intention that the skill of the portfolio manager will result in improved performance relative to an index. Fees are higher in the latter fund. You're just not certain which way to go, so you ask Dan Ervin, who works in the company's finance area, for advice.

After discussing your concerns, Dan gives you some information comparing the performance of equity mutual funds and the Vanguard 500 Index Fund. The Vanguard 500 is the world's largest equity index mutual fund. It replicates the S&P 500, and its return is only negligibly different from the S&P 500. Fees are very low. As a result, the Vanguard 500 is essentially identical to the Bledsoe S&P 500 Index Fund offered in the 401(k) plan, but it has been in existence for much longer, so you can study its track record for over two decades. The graph on the following page summarizes Dan's comments by showing the percentage of equity mutual funds that outperformed the Vanguard 500 Fund over the previous 10 years.[30] So for example,

---

[30]Note that this graph is not hypothetical; it reflects the actual performance of the Vanguard 500 Index Fund relative to a very large population of diversified equity mutual funds. Specialty funds, such as international funds, are excluded. All returns are net of management fees but do not include sales charges (which are known as "loads"), if any. As a result, the performance of actively managed funds is overstated.

from January 1977 to December 1986, about 70 percent of equity mutual funds outperformed the Vanguard 500. Dan suggests that you study the graph and answer the following questions:

1. What implications do you draw from the graph for mutual fund investors?

2. Is the graph consistent or inconsistent with market efficiency? Explain carefully.

3. What investment decision would you make for the equity portion of your 401(k) account? Why?

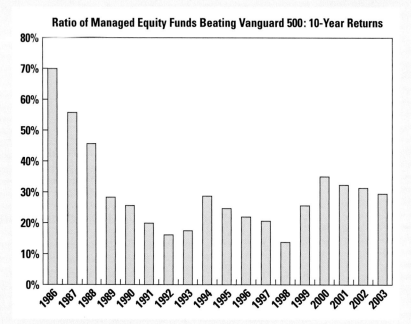

SOURCE: Author calculations using data from the Center for Research in Security Prices (CRSP) Survivor Bias-Free U.S. Mutual Fund Database.

Long-Term Financing

An Introduction

In February 2006, Japanese conglomerate Sanyo Electric Co. announced a massive recapitalization plan. An investor group that included Goldman Sachs, Daiwa Securities, and Sumitomo Mitsui Financial Group purchased 429 million shares of new preferred stock worth about 300 billion yen ($2.6 billion). Each of the shares of preferred stock could later be converted into 10 shares of common stock, which would triple the number of shares of Sanyo Electric stock.

What forms of long-term financing are available to companies, and why would companies like Sanyo choose to engage in transactions such as this one? This chapter introduces the basic sources of long-term financing: common stock, preferred stock, and long-term debt. Subsequent chapters address the optimal mix of these sources. We will also discuss how companies have financed themselves in recent years.

14.1 Common Stock

The term **common stock** has no precise meaning. It is usually applied to stock that has no special preference in either dividends or in bankruptcy. A description of the common stock of Anheuser-Busch in 2005 is presented here:

ANHEUSER-BUSCH Common Stock and Other Shareholders' Equity December 31, 2005 (in millions)	
Common stock, $1 par value, authorized 1.6 billion shares, issued 1,468.6 million shares	$1,468.6
Capital in excess of par value	1,601.8
Retained earnings	16,445.6
Treasury stock at cost	(15,258.9)
Accumulated nonowner changes in shareholder equity	(913.8)
Total equity	$3,343.3

Par and No-Par Stock

Owners of common stock in a corporation are referred to as *shareholders* or *stockholders*. They receive stock certificates for the *shares* they own. There is usually a stated value on each stock certificate called the *par value*. However, some stocks have no par value. The par value of each share of the common stock of Anheuser-Busch is $1.

The total par value is the number of shares issued multiplied by the par value of each share and is sometimes referred to as the *dedicated capital* of a corporation. The dedicated capital of Anheuser-Busch is $1 \times 1,468.6$ million shares = $1,468.6 million.

Authorized versus Issued Common Stock

Shares of common stock are the fundamental ownership units of the corporation. The articles of incorporation of a new corporation must state the number of shares of common stock the corporation is authorized to issue.

The board of directors of the corporation, after a vote of the shareholders, can amend the articles of incorporation to increase the number of shares authorized; there is no limit to the number of shares that can be authorized. In 2005, Anheuser-Busch had authorized 1.6 billion shares and had issued 1,468.6 million shares. There is no requirement that all of the authorized shares actually be issued. Although there are no legal limits to authorizing shares of stock, some practical considerations may exist:

1. Some states impose taxes based on the number of authorized shares.

2. Authorizing a large number of shares may create concern on the part of investors because authorized shares can be issued later *with* the approval of the board of directors but *without* a vote of the shareholders.

Capital Surplus

Capital surplus usually refers to amounts of directly contributed equity capital in excess of the par value.

Par Value and Surplus   Suppose 100 shares of common stock have a par value of $2 each and are sold to shareholders for $10 per share. The capital surplus would be ($10 − $2) × 100 = $8 × 100 = $800, and the total par value would be $2 × 100 = $200. What difference does it make if the total capital contribution is reported as par value or capital surplus?

About the only difference is that in most states the par value is locked in and cannot be distributed to stockholders except upon the liquidation of the corporation.

The capital surplus of Anheuser-Busch is $1,601.8 million. This figure indicates that the price of new shares issued by Anheuser-Busch has exceeded the par value and the difference has been entered as *capital in excess of par value*. In most states shares of stock cannot be issued below par value, implying that capital in excess of par value cannot be negative.

Retained Earnings

Anheuser-Busch usually pays out less than half of its net income as dividends; the rest is retained in the business and is called **retained earnings**. The cumulative amount of retained earnings (since original incorporation) was $16,445.6 million in 2005.

The sum of the par value, capital surplus, and accumulated retained earnings is the *common equity* of the firm, which is usually referred to as the firm's **book value**. The book value represents the amount contributed directly and indirectly to the corporation by equity investors.

EXAMPLE 14.2

Equity Accounting Suppose Western Redwood Corporation was formed in 1906 with 10,000 shares of stock issued and sold at its $1 par value. Because the stock was sold for $1, the first balance sheet showed a zero amount for capital surplus. By 2005, the company had become very profitable and had retained profits of $100,000. The stockholders' equity of Western Redwood Corporation in 2005 is as follows:

WESTERN REDWOOD CORPORATION
Equity Accounts
January 1, 2005

Common stock, $1 par, 10,000 shares outstanding	$ 10,000
Capital surplus	0
Retained earnings	100,000
Total stockholders' equity	$110,000

$$\text{Book value per share} = \frac{\$110,000}{10,000} = \$11$$

Suppose the company has profitable investment opportunities and decides to sell 10,000 shares of new stock. The current market price is $20 per share. The effect of the sale of stock on the balance sheet at the end of the year will be:

WESTERN REDWOOD CORPORATION
Equity Accounts
December 31, 2005

Common stock, $1 par, 20,000 shares outstanding	$ 20,000
Capital surplus ($20 − $1) × 10,000 shares	190,000
Retained earnings	100,000
Total stockholders' equity	$310,000

$$\text{Book value per share} = \frac{\$310,000}{20,000} = \$15.5$$

What happened?

1. Because 10,000 shares of new stock were issued with par value of $1, the par value rose $10,000.
2. The total amount raised by the new issue was $20 × 10,000 = $200,000, and $190,000 was entered into capital surplus.
3. The book value per share increased because the market price of the new stock was higher than the book value of the old stock.

Market Value, Book Value, and Replacement Value

The book value of Anheuser-Busch in 2005 was $3,443.3 million. This figure is based on the number of shares outstanding. The company had issued 1,468.6 million shares and bought back approximately 690.9 million shares, so that the total number of outstanding shares was 1,468.6 million − 690.9 million = 777.7 million. The shares bought back are called *treasury stock*.

The book value per share was equal to:

$$\frac{\text{Total common shareholders' equity}}{\text{Shares outstanding}} = \frac{\$3,443.3 \text{ million}}{777.7 \text{ million}} = \$4.43$$

Anheuser-Busch is a publicly owned company. Its common stock trades on the New York Stock Exchange (NYSE), and thousands of shares change hands every day. In March 2006, the market price of Anheuser-Busch stock was about $43. Thus, the market price was above the book value.

Shareholders' Rights

The conceptual structure of the corporation assumes that shareholders elect directors who in turn elect corporate officers—more generally, the management—to carry out their directives. The right to elect the directors of the corporation by vote constitutes the most important control device of shareholders.

Directors are elected each year at an annual meeting by a vote of the holders of a majority of shares who are present and entitled to vote. The exact election mechanism differs among different companies. The most important difference is whether shares must be voted cumulatively or must be voted straight.

EXAMPLE 14.3

Voting   Imagine that a corporation has two shareholders: Smith with 25 shares and Marshall with 75 shares. Both want to be on the board of directors. Marshall does not want Smith to be a director. Let us assume that there are four directors to be elected and each shareholder nominates four candidates. As we discuss next, whether Marshall will get her wish depends on whether shares are voted cumulatively or straight.

Cumulative Voting   The effect of **cumulative voting** is to permit minority participation. If cumulative voting is permitted, the total number of votes that each shareholder may cast is determined first. That number is usually calculated as the number of shares (owned or controlled) multiplied by the number of directors to be elected. Each shareholder can distribute these votes as he or she wishes over one or more candidates. Smith will get $25 \times 4 = 100$ votes, and Marshall is entitled to $75 \times 4 = 300$ votes. If Smith gives all his votes to himself, he is assured of a directorship. It is not possible for Marshall to divide 300 votes among the four candidates in such a way as to preclude Smith's election to the board.

Straight Voting   If **straight voting** is permitted, Smith may cast 25 votes for each candidate and Marshall may cast 75 votes for each. As a consequence, Marshall will elect all of the candidates.

Straight voting can freeze out minority shareholders; that is the reason many states have mandatory cumulative voting. In states where cumulative voting is mandatory, devices have been worked out to minimize its impact. One such device is to *stagger* the voting for the board of directors. Staggering permits a fraction of the directorships to come to a vote at a particular time. It has two basic effects:

1. Staggering makes it more difficult for a minority to elect a director when there is cumulative voting.

2. Staggering makes successful takeover attempts less likely by making the election of new directors more difficult.

Proxy Voting   A **proxy** is the legal grant of authority by a shareholder to someone else to vote his or her shares. For convenience, the actual voting in large public corporations usually is done by proxy.

Many companies such as Anheuser-Busch have hundreds of thousands of shareholders. Shareholders can come to the annual meeting and vote in person, or they can transfer their right to vote to another party by proxy.

Obviously, management always tries to get as many proxies transferred to it as possible. However, if shareholders are not satisfied with management, an outside group of shareholders can try to obtain as many votes as possible via proxy. They can vote to replace management by adding enough directors. This is called a *proxy fight*.

Other Rights   The value of a share of common stock in a corporation is directly related to the general rights of shareholders. In addition to the right to vote for directors, shareholders usually have the following rights:

1. The right to share proportionally in dividends paid.
2. The right to share proportionally in assets remaining after liabilities have been paid in a liquidation.
3. The right to vote on matters of great importance to stockholders, such as a merger, usually decided at the annual meeting or a special meeting.
4. The right to share proportionally in any new stock sold. This is called the *preemptive right* and will be discussed in detail in later chapters.

Dividends

A distinctive feature of corporations is that they issue shares of stock and are authorized by law to pay dividends to the holders of those shares. **Dividends** paid to shareholders represent a return on the capital directly or indirectly contributed to the corporation by the shareholders. The payment of dividends occurs at the discretion of the board of directors.

Here are some important characteristics of dividends:

1. Unless a dividend is declared by the board of directors of a corporation, it is not a liability of the corporation. A corporation cannot *default* on an undeclared dividend. As a consequence, corporations cannot become *bankrupt* because of nonpayment of dividends. The amount of the dividend—and even whether or not it is paid—are decisions based on the business judgment of the board of directors.
2. The payment of dividends by the corporation is not a business expense. Dividends are not deductible for corporate tax purposes. In short, dividends are paid out of aftertax profits of the corporation.
3. Dividends received by individual shareholders are for the most part considered ordinary income by the IRS and are fully taxable. However, corporations that own stock in other corporations are permitted to exclude 70 percent of the amounts they receive as dividends. In other words, they are taxed only on the remaining 30 percent.

Classes of Stock

Some firms issue more than one class of common stock. The classes are usually created with unequal voting rights. The Ford Motor Company has class B common stock, which is not publicly traded (it is held by Ford family interests and trusts). This class has about

40 percent of the voting power, but these shares comprise only about 15 percent of the total outstanding stock. Another example is Google, the Web search company. Google has two classes of common stock, A and B. Class A shares are held by the public, and each share has one vote. Class B shares are held by company insiders, and each class B share has 10 votes. As a result, Google's founders and management control the company.

Many companies issue dual classes of common stock. The reason has to do with control of the firm. Management of a firm can raise equity capital by issuing nonvoting common stock while maintaining voting control. Harry and Linda DeAngelo found that managements' holdings of common stock are usually tilted toward the stock with the superior voting rights.[1] Thus, managerial vote ownership is an important element of corporate control structure.

Lease, McConnell, and Mikkelson found the market prices of stocks with superior voting rights to be about 5 percent higher than the prices of otherwise identical stocks with inferior voting rights.[2] However, DeAngelo and DeAngelo found some evidence that the market value of differences in voting rights may be much higher when control of the firm is involved.

14.2 Corporate Long-Term Debt: The Basics

Securities issued by corporations may be classified roughly as *equity* securities and *debt* securities. The distinction between equity and debt is basic to much of the modern theory and practice of corporate finance.

At its crudest level, debt represents something that must be repaid; it is the result of borrowing money. When corporations borrow, they promise to make regularly scheduled interest payments and to repay the original amount borrowed (that is, the *principal*). The person or firm making the loan is called a *creditor* or *lender*.

Interest versus Dividends

The corporation borrowing the money is called a *debtor* or *borrower*. The amount owed the creditor is a liability of the corporation; however, it is a liability of limited value. The corporation can legally default at any time on its liability.[3] This can be a valuable option. The creditors benefit if the assets have a value greater than the value of the liability, but this would happen only if management were foolish. On the other hand, the corporation and the equity investors benefit if the value of the assets is less than the value of the liabilities because equity investors can walk away from the liabilities and default on their payment.

From a financial point of view, the main differences between debt and equity are the following:

1. Debt is not an ownership interest in the firm. Creditors do not usually have voting power. The device used by creditors to protect themselves is the loan contract (that is, the *indenture*).

2. The corporation's payment of interest on debt is considered a cost of doing business and is fully tax deductible. Thus interest expense is paid out to creditors before the

---

[1] H. DeAngelo and L. DeAngelo, "Managerial Ownership of Voting Rights: A Study of Public Corporations with Dual Classes of Common Stock," *Journal of Financial Economics* 14 (1985).

[2] R. C. Lease, J. J. McConnell, and W. H. Mikkelson, "The Market Value of Control in Publicly Traded Corporations," *Journal of Financial Economics* (April 1983).

[3] In practice, creditors can make a claim against the assets of the firm and a court will administer the legal remedy.

corporate tax liability is computed. Dividends on common and preferred stock are paid to shareholders after the tax liability has been determined. Dividends are considered a return to shareholders on their contributed capital. Because interest expense can be used to reduce taxes, the government (that is, the IRS) provides a direct tax subsidy on the use of debt when compared to equity. This point is discussed in detail in the next two chapters.

3. Unpaid debt is a liability of the firm. If it is not paid, the creditors can legally claim the assets of the firm. This action may result in *liquidation* and *bankruptcy*. Thus one of the costs of issuing debt is the possibility of *financial failure*, which does not arise when equity is issued.

Is It Debt or Equity?

Sometimes it is not clear whether a particular security is debt or equity. For example, suppose a 50-year bond is issued with interest payable solely from corporate income if and only if earned, and repayment is subordinate to all other debts of the business. Corporations are very adept at creating hybrid securities that look like equity but are called *debt*. Obviously the distinction between debt and equity is important for tax purposes. When corporations try to create a debt security that is really equity, they are trying to obtain the tax benefits of debt while eliminating its bankruptcy costs.

Basic Features of Long-Term Debt

Long-term corporate debt usually is denominated in units of $1,000 called the *principal* or *face value*.[4] Long-term debt is a promise by the borrowing firm to repay the principal amount by a certain date, called the *maturity date*. Long-term debt almost always has a par value equal to the face value, and debt price is often expressed as a percentage of the par value. For example, it might be said that General Motors' debt is selling at 90, which means that a bond with a par value of $1,000 can be purchased for $900. In this case, the debt is selling at a discount because the market price is less than the par value. Debt can also sell at a premium with respect to par value. The borrower using long-term debt generally pays interest at a rate expressed as a fraction of par value. Thus, at $1,000 par value, General Motors' 7 percent debt means that $70 of interest is paid to holders of the debt, usually in semiannual installments (for example, $35 on June 30 and December 31). These payments are referred to as "coupons," and the 7 percent is called the *coupon rate*.

Different Types of Debt

Typical debt securities are called *notes*, *debentures*, or *bonds*. A debenture is an unsecured corporate debt, whereas a bond is secured by a mortgage on the corporate property. However, in common parlance the word *bond* is used indiscriminately and often refers to both secured and unsecured debt. A note usually refers to an unsecured debt with a maturity shorter than that of a debenture, perhaps under 10 years.

Debentures and bonds are long-term debt. *Long-term debt* is any obligation that is payable more than one year from the date it was originally issued. Sometimes long-term debt—debentures and bonds—is called *funded debt*. Debt that is due in less than one year

---

[4]Many government bonds have larger principal denominations, up to $10,000 or $25,000, and most municipal bonds come in denominations of $5,000.

is unfunded and is accounted for as a current liability. Some debt is perpetual and has no specific maturity. This type of debt is referred to as a *consol*.

Repayment

Long-term debt is typically repaid in regular amounts over the life of the debt. The payment of long-term debt by installments is called *amortization*. At the end of the amortization the entire indebtedness is said to be *extinguished*. Amortization is typically arranged by a *sinking fund*. Each year the corporation places money into a sinking fund, and the money is used to buy back the bonds.

Debt may be extinguished before maturity by a call. Historically, almost all publicly issued corporate long-term debt has been *callable*. These are debentures or bonds for which the firm has the right to pay a specific amount, the *call price*, to retire (extinguish) the debt before the stated maturity date. The call price is always higher than the par value of the debt. Debt that is callable at 105 is debt that the firm can buy back from the holder at a price of $1,050 per debenture or bond, regardless of what the market value of the debt might be. Call prices are always specified when the debt is originally issued. As discussed in an earlier chapter, "make-whole" call provisions have become the norm.

Seniority

In general terms **seniority** indicates preference in position over other lenders. Some debt is **subordinated**. In the event of default, holders of subordinated debt must give preference to other specified creditors. Usually, this means that the subordinated lenders will be paid off only after the specified creditors have been compensated. However, debt cannot be subordinated to equity.

Security

Security is a form of attachment to property; it provides that the property can be sold in the event of default to satisfy the debt for which security is given. A mortgage is used for security in tangible property; for example, debt can be secured by mortgages on plant and equipment. Holders of such debt have prior claim on the mortgaged assets in case of default. Debentures are not secured by a mortgage. Thus, if mortgaged property is sold in the event of default, debenture holders will obtain something only if the mortgage bondholders have been fully satisfied.

Indenture

The written agreement between the corporate debt issuer and the lender, setting forth maturity date, interest rate, and all other terms, is called an *indenture*. We treat this in detail in later chapters. For now, we note that:

1. The indenture completely describes the nature of the indebtedness.
2. It lists all restrictions placed on the firm by the lenders. These restrictions are placed in *restrictive covenants*.

Some typical restrictive covenants are the following:

1. Restrictions on further indebtedness.
2. A maximum on the amount of dividends that can be paid.
3. A minimum level of working capital.

EXAMPLE 14.4

Long-Term Debt   The following table shows some of the many debt securities of Anheuser-Busch at the end of 2005 (in millions):

U.S. dollar notes due 2006 to 2023, interest rates from 4.375% to 7.5%	$3,576.2
U.S. dollar debentures due 2009 to 2043, interest rates from 5.95% to 9.0%	2,600.0
Commercial paper, interest rates of 4.39% and 2.18%, respectively, at year-end	1,102.6
Industrial revenue bonds due 2006 to 2038, interest rates from 4.6% to 7.4%	271.7
Medium-term notes due 2010, interest rate 5.625%	200.0
Chinese renminbi-denominated bank loans due 2006 to 2009, interest rates from 4.7% to 6.7%	75.8
U.S. dollar EuroNotes due 2006, interest rate 4.51%	100.0
Miscellaneous items	66.1
Unamortized debt discounts	(20.3)
Total debt	$7,972.1

Anheuser-Busch has many different notes and debentures. As can be seen, there is $1,102.6 million of commercial paper. Commercial paper refers to short-term unsecured notes. It is listed as long-term debt because it will be maintained on a long-term basis by "rolling it over."

14.3   Preferred Stock

Preferred stock represents equity of a corporation, but it is different from common stock because it has preference over common stock in the payment of dividends and in the assets of the corporation in the event of bankruptcy. *Preference* means only that the holder of the preferred share must receive a dividend (in the case of an ongoing firm) before holders of common shares are entitled to anything.

Stated Value

Preferred shares have a stated liquidating value, usually $100 per share. The dividend preference is described in terms of dollars per share. For example, General Motors' "$5 preferred" translates into a dividend yield of 5 percent of stated value.

Cumulative and Noncumulative Dividends

A preferred dividend is not like interest on a bond. The board of directors may decide not to pay the dividends on preferred shares, and their decision may not have anything to do with current net income of the corporation. Dividends payable on preferred stock are either *cumulative* or *noncumulative*. If preferred dividends are cumulative and are not paid in a particular year, they will be carried forward. Usually both the cumulated (past) preferred dividends plus the current preferred dividends must be paid before the common shareholders can receive anything. Unpaid preferred dividends are *not* debts of the firm. Directors elected by the common shareholders can defer preferred dividends indefinitely. However, if so,

1. Common shareholders must forgo dividends.
2. Though holders of preferred shares do not always have voting rights, they will typically be granted these rights if preferred dividends have not been paid for some time.

Because preferred stockholders receive no interest on the cumulated dividends, some have argued that firms have an incentive to delay paying preferred dividends.

Is Preferred Stock Really Debt?

A good case can be made that preferred stock is really debt in disguise. Preferred shareholders receive a stated dividend only, and if the corporation is liquidated, preferred shareholders get a stated value. In recent years, many new issues of preferred stock have had obligatory sinking funds.

For all these reasons, preferred stock seems like debt; but unlike debt, preferred stock dividends cannot be deducted as interest expense in determining taxable corporate income. From the individual investor's point of view, preferred dividends are ordinary income for tax purposes. For corporate investors, however, 70 percent of the amounts they receive as dividends from preferred stock is exempt from income taxes.

The yields on preferred stock are typically very low. For example, Citigroup has a Series F preferred stock with a stated $3.18 dividend. This dividend is perpetual—that is, it will be paid each year by Citigroup forever unless called. However, holders of Series F preferred stock have no voting rights. In March 2006, the market price of the Citigroup preferred stock was about $51. The current dividend yield on the Citigroup preferred of 6.2 percent $(=\$3.18/51)$ was slightly more than U.S. government bond yields on the same date, and it was less than the yield on Citigroup's long-term debt.

Corporate investors have an incentive to hold the preferred stock issued by other corporations over holding their debt because of the 70 percent income tax exemption they receive on preferred stock dividends. Because of this tax exclusion, corporate investors pay a premium for preferred stock; as a consequence, the yields are low. Individual investors do not receive this tax break. So most preferred stock in the United States is owned by corporate investors.

Thus, there are two offsetting tax effects to consider in evaluating preferred stock:

1. Dividends are not deducted from corporate income in computing the tax liability of the issuing corporation. This is the bad news.

2. When a corporation purchases preferred stock, 70 percent of the dividends received is exempt from corporate taxation. This is the good news.

The Preferred Stock Puzzle

Effect (1) just listed represents a clear tax disadvantage to the issuance of preferred stock. Although (2) represents a tax advantage, both academics and practitioners generally agree that (2) does *not* fully offset (1). In addition, preferred stock requires a regular dividend payment and thus lacks the flexibility of common stock. For these reasons, some have argued that preferred stock should not exist.

Why then do firms issue preferred stock? While the nondeductibility of dividends from taxable corporate income is the most serious obstacle to issuing preferred stock, there are several reasons why preferred stock is issued:

1. Because of the way utility rates are determined in regulatory environments, regulated public utilities can pass the tax disadvantage of issuing preferred stock on to their customers. Consequently, a substantial amount of straight preferred stock is issued by utilities.

2. Companies reporting losses to the IRS may issue preferred stock. Because they have no taxable income from which interest on debt can be deducted, preferred stock imposes no tax penalty relative to debt. In other words, (1) does not apply.

3. Firms issuing preferred stock can avoid the threat of bankruptcy that exists with debt financing. Unpaid preferred dividends are not debts of a corporation, and preferred shareholders cannot force a corporation into bankruptcy because of unpaid dividends.

Equity versus Debt

Feature	Equity	Debt
Income	Dividends	Interest
Tax status	Dividends are taxed as personal income. Dividends are not a business expense.	Interest is taxed as personal income. Interest is a business expense, and corporations can deduct interest when computing corporate tax liability.
Control	Common stock usually has voting rights.	Control is exercised with loan agreement.
Default	Firms cannot be forced into bankruptcy for nonpayment of dividends.	Unpaid debt is a liability of the firm. Nonpayment results in bankruptcy.

Bottom line: Tax status favors debt, but default favors equity. Control features of debt and equity are different, but one is not better than the other.

14.4 Patterns of Financing

Firms use cash flow for capital spending and net working capital. Historically, U.S. firms have spent about 80 percent of cash flow on capital spending and 20 percent on net working capital. Table 14.1 summarizes the patterns of long-term financing for U.S. industrial firms from 1993 to 2004. Here we observe internal financing, debt financing, and external equity financing as a percentage of total financing. For example, in 2004, gross capital spending by U.S. industrial firms was $900 billion and increases in net working capital were $187 billion. In other words, total business investment spending was $1,087 (=$900 + 187) billion. Capital spending was $900/1,087 = 82.8% of the total, whereas net working capital was $187/1,087 = 17.2% of the total.

Table 14.1 **Historical U.S. Financing Patterns (percent), 1993 to 2004**

	1993	1994	1995	1996	1997	1998	1999	2000	2001	2002	2003	2004
Uses of funds (investments)												
Capital spending	74%	72%	66%	80%	71%	83%	81%	89%	87%	98%	95%	83%
Net working capital and other	26%	28%	34%	20%	29%	17%	19%	11%	13%	2%	5%	17%
Total uses %	100	100	100	100	100	100	100	100	100	100	100	100
Sources of funds												
Internal financing	88%	85%	77%	87%	79%	79%	74%	74%	79%	97%	74%	97%
External financing	12	15	23	13	21	21	26	26	21	3	26	3
New debt	8	22	31	23	35	45	37	38	26	8	33	22
New equity	4	−7	−7	−10	−13	−24	−11	−12	−5	−5	−7	−19

SOURCE: Board of Governors of the Federal Reserve System, *Flow of Funds Accounts.* www.federalreserve.gov/release/21/current/data.htm.

Figure 14.1   Financing Decisions by U.S. Nonfinancial Corporations

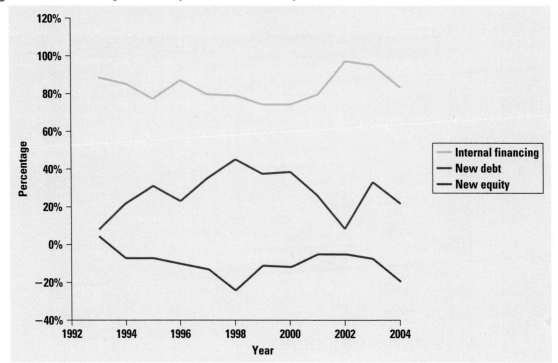

In 2004, U.S. industrial firms generated $1,057 billion of internal cash flow. Because total business spending exceeded internally generated cash flow (i.e., 1,087 > 1,057), there was a *financial gap*. This is very typical of U.S. business finance. The financial gap is made up by external financing.

One of the challenges of the financial manager is to finance the gap. In 2004, this meant issuing $240 billion of new debt because net new equity actually shrank (by $210 billion) due to stock buybacks. Figure 14.1 charts these patterns of finance.

Internal financing comes from internally generated cash flow and is defined as net income plus depreciation minus dividends. External financing is net new debt and new shares of equity net of buybacks.

Several features of long-term financing seem clear from Table 14.1:

1. Internally generated cash flow has dominated as a source of financing. Typically, between 70 and 90 percent of long-term financing comes from cash flows that corporations generate internally.

2. Typically, total firm spending is greater than internally generated cash flow. A financial deficit is created by the difference between total firm spending and internally generated cash flow. For example, 79 percent of financing came from internal cash flow in 2001, implying a financial deficit in that year of 21 percent (=100% − 79%). Debt was 26 percent of total financing, and −5 percent was financed from new stock issues. This financial deficit has averaged about 20 percent in recent years (Figure 14.2).

3. In general, the financial deficit is covered by borrowing and issuing new equity, the two sources of external financing. However, one of the most prominent aspects of

Figure 14.2

The Long-Term Financial Deficit

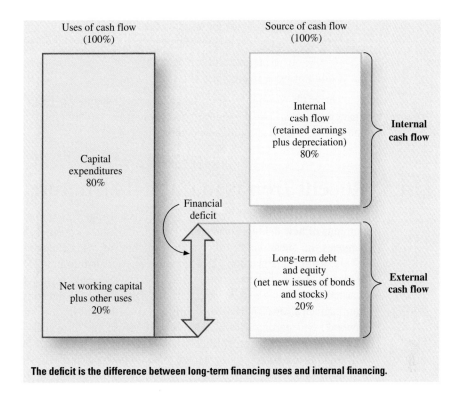

The deficit is the difference between long-term financing uses and internal financing.

Table 14.2

Recent International Financing Patterns: Sources of Funds as a Percentage of Total Sources

	United States	Japan	Canada
Internally generated funds	76.9	56.1	56.9
Externally generated funds	23.1	43.9	43.1
Increase in long-term debt	7.1	16.7	13.9
Increase in short-term debt	20.8	21.7	15.8
Increase in stock	−4.9	5.6	13.4

SOURCE: OECD, *Financial Statements of Non-financial Enterprises*, 1993–1995

external financing is that new issues of equity (both common stock and preferred stock) in the aggregate seem to be unimportant. Net new issues of equity typically account for a small part of total financing; in the late 1980s and very recently this figure has been negative.

4. Table 14.2 shows that firms in the United States generate more financing from internally generated cash than firms in other countries. Firms in other countries rely to a greater extent than U.S. firms on external equity.

These data are consistent with the results of a survey conducted by Gordon Donaldson on the way firms establish long-term financing strategies.[5] He found that:

―――――――――

[5]G. G. Donaldson, *Corporate Debt Capacity: A Study of Corporate Debt Policy and Determination of Corporate Debt Capacity* (Boston: Harvard Graduate School of Business Administration, 1961). See also S. C. Myers, "The Capital Structure Puzzle," *Journal of Finance* (July 1984).

1. The first form of financing used by firms for positive NPV projects is internally generated cash flow: net income plus depreciation minus dividends.

2. As a last resort a firm will use externally generated cash flow. First, debt is used. Common stock is used last.

These observations, when taken together, suggest a **pecking order** to long-term financing strategy. At the top of the pecking order is using internally generated cash flow, and at the bottom is issuing new equity.

14.5   Recent Trends in Capital Structure

The previous section of this chapter established that U.S. firms after 1993 issued large amounts of new debt to finance the retirement of shares of stock. This pattern of financing suggests the question: Did the capital structure of firms change significantly in the mid-1990s? Unfortunately there is no precise answer to this important question. If we used book values (i.e., balance sheet values) the answer would be less dramatic than if we used market values. Figure 14.3 charts the book value of debt to the book value of equity for U.S. nonfinancial firms. There is a slightly downward trend throughout the 1990s and then an upward trend starting in 2000. However, if we use market values instead of book values, a more dramatic picture emerges. As can be seen in Figure 14.4, when we use market values this trend is much more pronounced, reflecting the sharp rise in stock market values in the 1990s and the crash starting in 2000. Therefore, when observing the capital structures of firms, it is important to distinguish between market values and book values. For example,

Figure 14.3

Book Debt Ratio: Total Debt as a Percentage of Equity for U.S. Nonfarm, Nonfinancial Firms from 1995 to 2004

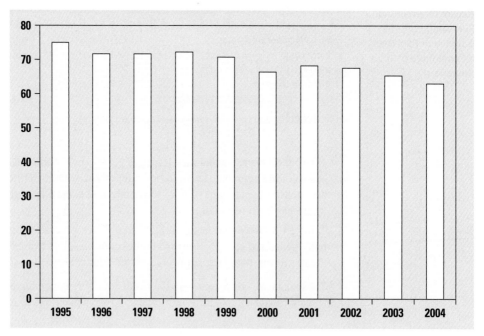

SOURCE: Board of Governors of the Federal Reserve System, *Flow of Accounts.*

Figure 14.4

**Market Debt
Ratio: Total Debt
as a Percentage
of the Market
Value of Equity
for U.S. Nonfarm,
Nonfinancial Firms
from 1995 to 2004**

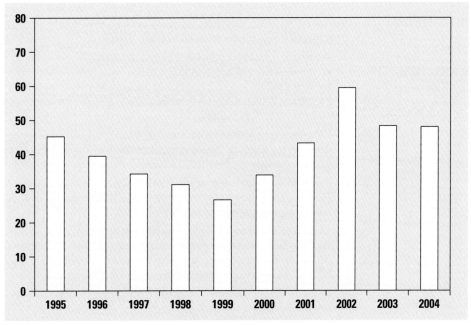

SOURCE: Board of Governors of the Federal Reserve System, *Flow of Funds.*

suppose a firm buys back shares of its own stock and finances the purchase with new debt. This would seem to suggest that the firm's reliance on debt should go up and its reliance on equity should go down. After all, the firm has fewer shares of stock outstanding and more debt. The analysis is more complicated than it seems because the market value of the firm's remaining shares of stock may go up and offset the effect of the increased debt. This is exactly what happened in the 1990s.

Which Are Best: Book or Market Values?

In general, financial economists prefer the use of market values when measuring debt ratios. This is true because market values reflect current rather than historical values. Most financial economists believe that current market values better reflect true intrinsic values than do historically based values. However, the use of market values contrasts with the perspective of many corporate practitioners.

Our conversations with corporate treasurers suggest to us that the use of book values is popular because of the volatility of the stock market. It is frequently claimed that the inherent volatility of the stock market makes market-based debt ratios move around too much. It is also true that restrictions of debt in bond covenants are usually expressed in book values rather than market values. Moreover, firms such as Standard & Poor's and Moody's use debt ratios expressed in book values to measure creditworthiness.

A key fact is that whether we use book or market values, debt ratios for U.S. nonfinancial firms generally have been well below 100 percent of total equity in recent years; that is, firms generally use less debt than equity.

Summary and Conclusions

The basic sources of long-term financing are long-term debt, preferred stock, and common stock. This chapter described the essential features of each.

1. We emphasized that common shareholders have
   a. Residual risk and return in a corporation.
   b. Voting rights.
   c. Limited liability if the corporation elects to default on its debt and must transfer some or all of its assets to the creditors.

2. Long-term debt involves contractual obligations set out in indentures. There are many kinds of debt, but the essential feature is that debt involves a stated amount that must be repaid. Interest payments on debt are considered a business expense and are tax deductible.

3. Preferred stock has some of the features of debt and some of the features of common equity. Holders of preferred stock have preference in liquidation and in dividend payments compared to holders of common equity.

4. Firms need financing for capital expenditures, working capital, and other long-term uses. Most of the financing is provided from internally generated cash flow. In the United States only about 25 percent of financing comes from new debt and new equity. Only firms in Japan have historically relied more on external financing than on internal financing.

5. In the 1980s and recently, U.S. firms retired massive amounts of equity. These share buybacks have been financed with new debt.

Concept Questions

1. **Preferred Stock and Debt**   What are the differences between preferred stock and debt?

2. **Preferred Stock**   Preferred stock doesn't offer a corporate tax shield on the dividends paid. Why do we still observe some firms issuing preferred stock?

3. **Preferred Stock and Bond Yields**   The yields on nonconvertible preferred stock are lower than the yields on corporate bonds. Why is there a difference? Which investors are the primary holders of preferred stock? Why?

4. **Corporate Financing**   What are the main differences between corporate debt and equity? Why do some firms try to issue equity in the guise of debt?

5. **Corporate Financing**   The Cable Company has £1 million of positive NPV projects it would like to accept. If Cable's managers follow the historical pattern of long-term financing for U.S. industrial firms, what will their financing strategy be?

6. **Proxy**   What is a proxy?

7. **Preferred Stock**   Do you think preferred stock is more like debt or equity? Why?

8. **Long-Term Financing**   As was mentioned in the chapter, new equity issues are generally only a small portion of all new issues. At the same time, companies continue to issue new debt. Why do companies tend to issue little new equity but continue to issue new debt?

9. **Internal versus External Financing**   What is the difference between internal financing and external financing?

10. **Internal versus External Financing**   What factors influence a firm's choices of external versus internal equity financing?

Questions and Problems

BASIC
(Questions 1–7)

1. **Equity Accounts**   Following are the equity accounts for Brigham Tire and Lube:

Common stock, €0.50 par value	€ 165,320
Capital surplus	2,876,145
Retained earnings	2,370,025
Total	€5,411,490

    a. How many shares are outstanding?

    b. At what average price were the shares sold?

    c. What is the book value per share?

2.   **Equity Accounts**   The Eastern Spruce equity accounts for last year are as follows:

Common stock, £2 par value	
500 shares outstanding	?
Capital surplus	£250,000
Retained earnings	750,000
Total	?

    a. What are the common stock and total equity values for the equity account?

    b. The company has decided to issue 5,000 shares of stock at a price of £30 per share. Show the effects of the new issue on the equity accounts.

3.   **Equity Accounts**   Niha Telephony Co.'s articles of incorporation authorize the firm to issue 500,000 shares of CNY 5 par value common stock, of which 410,000 shares have been issued. Those shares were sold at an average of 30 percent over par. In the quarter that ended last week, net income was CNY 650,000; 30 percent of that income was paid as a dividend. The previous balance sheet showed a retained earnings balance of CNY 3,545,000.

    a. Create the equity statement for the company.

    b. Suppose the company sells 25,000 of the authorized but unissued shares at the price of CNY 4 per share. What will the new equity statement look like?

4.   **Corporate Voting**   The shareholders of the Unicorn Company need to elect seven new directors. There are 500,000 shares outstanding currently trading at ¥10,572 per share. You would like to serve on the board of directors; unfortunately no one else will be voting for you. How much will it cost you to be certain that you can be elected if the company uses straight voting? How much will it cost you if the company uses cumulative voting?

5.   **Cumulative Voting**   An election is being held to fill three seats on the board of directors of a firm in which you hold stock. The company has 2,500 shares outstanding. If the election is conducted under cumulative voting and you own 300 shares, how many more shares must you buy to be assured of earning a seat on the board?

6.   **Cumulative Voting**   The shareholders of Ridhi Sidhi Garments need to elect three new directors to the board. There are 2,000,000 shares of common stock outstanding, and the current share price is INR 420. If the company uses cumulative voting procedures, how much will it cost to guarantee yourself one seat on the board of directors?

7.   **Corporate Voting**   Power Inc. is going to elect eight board members next month. Betty Brown owns 17.3 percent of the total shares outstanding. How confident can she be of having one of her candidate friends elected under the cumulative voting rule? Will her friend be elected for certain if the voting procedure is changed to the staggering rule, under which shareholders vote on four board members at a time?

Capital Structure

Basic Concepts

In early 2006, conglomerate Tyco International, Ltd., was evaluating a plan to break up the company. The breakup would result in three separate companies: electronics, health care, and fire and security services. Under the plan Tyco's shareholders would end up with shares in the three new companies. But one looming question was how the company would split its existing debt load among the three new companies. With the current debt on its balance sheet and an additional $1 billion in costs associated with the breakup, Tyco would have about $12.5 billion in total debt to allocate. The company offered little guidance on the capital structures it planned for new companies, other than to say the debt for each company would have "solid investment grade" ratings. So how should a company choose a capital structure for itself or, in Tyco's case, for its offspring? We will explore this and other issues in this chapter.

15.1 The Capital Structure Question and the Pie Theory

How should a firm choose its debt–equity ratio? We call our approach to the capital structure question the **pie model**. If you are wondering why we chose this name, just take a look at Figure 15.1. The pie in question is the sum of the financial claims of the firm, debt and equity in this case. We *define* the value of the firm to be this sum. Hence the value of the firm, V, is:

$$V \equiv B + S \tag{15.1}$$

where B is the market value of the debt and S is the market value of the equity. Figure 15.1 presents two possible ways of slicing this pie between stock and debt: 40 percent–60 percent and 60 percent–40 percent. If the goal of the management of the firm is to make the firm as valuable as possible, then the firm should pick the debt–equity ratio that makes the pie—the total value—as big as possible.

This discussion begs two important questions:

1. Why should the stockholders in the firm care about maximizing the value of the entire firm? After all, the value of the firm is, by definition, the sum of both the debt and the equity. Instead, why should the stockholders not prefer the strategy that maximizes their interests only?

2. What ratio of debt to equity maximizes the shareholders' interests?

Let us examine each of the two questions in turn.

Figure 15.1

Two Pie Models of Capital Structure

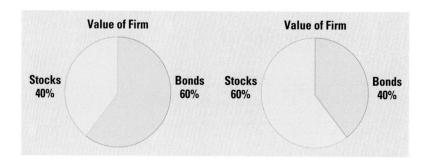

15.2 Maximizing Firm Value versus Maximizing Stockholder Interests

The following example illustrates that the capital structure that maximizes the value of the firm is the one that financial managers should choose for the shareholders.

EXAMPLE 15.1

Debt and Firm Value   Suppose the market value of the J. J. Sprint Company is $1,000. The company currently has no debt, and each of J. J. Sprint's 100 shares of stock sells for $10. A company such as J. J. Sprint with no debt is called an *unlevered* company. Further suppose that J. J. Sprint plans to borrow $500 and pay the $500 proceeds to shareholders as an extra cash dividend of $5 per share. After the issuance of debt, the firm becomes *levered*. The investments of the firm will not change as a result of this transaction. What will the value of the firm be after the proposed restructuring?

Management recognizes that, by definition, only one of three outcomes can occur from restructuring. Firm value after restructuring can be (1) greater than the original firm value of $1,000, (2) equal to $1,000, or (3) less than $1,000. After consulting with investment bankers, management believes that restructuring will not change firm value more than $250 in either direction. Thus it views firm values of $1,250, $1,000, and $750 as the relevant range. The original capital structure and these three possibilities under the new capital structure are presented next:

	No Debt (Original Capital Structure)	Value of Debt plus Equity after Payment of Dividend (Three Possibilities)		
		I	**II**	**III**
Debt	$ 0	$ 500	$ 500	$500
Equity	1,000	750	500	250
Firm value	$1,000	$1,250	$1,000	$750

Note that the value of equity is below $1,000 under any of the three possibilities. This can be explained in one of two ways. First, the table shows the value of the equity *after* the extra cash dividend is paid. Because cash is paid out, a dividend represents a partial liquidation of the firm. Consequently there is less value in the firm for the equityholders after the dividend payment. Second, in the event of a future liquidation, stockholders will be paid only after bondholders have been paid in full. Thus the debt is an encumbrance of the firm, reducing the value of the equity.

(continued)

Of course management recognizes that there are infinite possible outcomes. These three are to be viewed as *representative* outcomes only. We can now determine the payoff to stockholders under the three possibilities:

| | Payoff to Shareholders after Restructuring | | |
	I	II	III
Capital gains	−$250	−$500	−$750
Dividends	500	500	500
Net gain or loss to stockholders	$250	$ 0	−$250

No one can be sure ahead of time which of the three outcomes will occur. However, imagine that managers believe that outcome I is most likely. They should definitely restructure the firm because the stockholders would gain $250. That is, although the price of the stock declines by $250 to $750, they receive $500 in dividends. Their net gain is $250 = −$250 + $500. Also, notice that the value of the firm would rise by $250 = $1,250 − $1,000.

Alternatively, imagine that managers believe that outcome III is most likely. In this case they should not restructure the firm because the stockholders would expect a $250 loss. That is, the stock falls by $750 to $250 and they receive $500 in dividends. Their net loss is −$250 = −$750 + $500. Also, notice that the value of the firm would change by −$250 = $750 − $1,000.

Finally, imagine that the managers believe that outcome II is most likely. Restructuring would not affect the stockholders' interest because the net gain to stockholders in this case is zero. Also notice that the value of the firm is unchanged if outcome II occurs.

This example explains why managers should attempt to maximize the value of the firm. In other words, it answers question (1) in Section 15.1. We find in this example the following wisdom:

Changes in capital structure benefit the stockholders *if and only if* the value of the firm increases.

Conversely, these changes hurt the stockholders if and only if the value of the firm decreases. This result holds true for capital structure changes of many different types.[1] As a corollary, we can say the following:

Managers should choose the capital structure that they believe will have the highest firm value because this capital structure will be most beneficial to the firm's stockholders.

Note however that this example does not tell us which of the three outcomes is most likely to occur. Thus it does not tell us whether debt should be added to J. J. Sprint's capital structure. In other words, it does not answer question (2) in Section 15.1. This second question is treated in the next section.

---

[1] This result may not hold exactly in a more complex case where debt has a significant possibility of default. Issues of default are treated in the next chapter.

Table 15.1

Financial Structure of Trans Am Corporation

	Current	Proposed
Assets	$8,000	$8,000
Debt	$ 0	$4,000
Equity (market and book)	$8,000	$4,000
Interest rate	10%	10%
Market value/share	$ 20	$ 20
Shares outstanding	400	200

The proposed capital structure has leverage, whereas the current structure is all equity.

Table 15.2

Trans Am's Current Capital Structure: No Debt

	Recession	Expected	Expansion
Return on assets (ROA)	5%	15%	25%
Earnings	$ 400	$1,200	$2,000
Return on equity (ROE) = Earnings/Equity	5%	15%	25%
Earnings per share (EPS)	$1.00	$ 3.00	$ 5.00

15.3   Financial Leverage and Firm Value: An Example

Leverage and Returns to Shareholders

The previous section shows that the capital structure producing the highest firm value is the one that maximizes shareholder wealth. In this section, we wish to determine that optimal capital structure. We begin by illustrating the effect of capital structure on returns to stockholders. We will use a detailed example that we encourage students to study carefully. Once we have this example under our belts, we will be ready to determine the optimal capital structure.

Trans Am Corporation currently has no debt in its capital structure. The firm is considering issuing debt to buy back some of its equity. Both its current and proposed capital structures are presented in Table 15.1. The firm's assets are $8,000. There are 400 shares of the all-equity firm, implying a market value per share of $20. The proposed debt issue is for $4,000, leaving $4,000 in equity. The interest rate is 10 percent.

The effect of economic conditions on earnings per share is shown in Table 15.2 for the current capital structure (all-equity). Consider first the middle column where earnings are expected to be $1,200. Because assets are $8,000, the return on assets (ROA) is 15 percent (= $1,200/$8,000). Assets equal equity for this all-equity firm, so return on equity (ROE) is also 15 percent. Earnings per share (EPS) is $3.00 (= $1,200/400). Similar calculations yield EPS of $1.00 and $5.00 in the cases of recession and expansion, respectively.

The case of leverage is presented in Table 15.3. ROA in the three economic states is identical in Tables 15.2 and 15.3 because this ratio is calculated before interest is considered. Debt is $4,000 here, so interest is $400 (= .10 × $4,000). Thus earnings after interest are $800 (= $1,200 − $400) in the middle (expected) case. Because equity is $4,000, ROE is 20 percent (= $800/$4,000). Earnings per share are $4.00 (= $800/200). Similar calculations yield earnings of $0 and $8.00 for recession and expansion, respectively.

Table 15.3

Trans Am's Proposed Capital Structure: Debt = $4,000

	Recession	Expected	Expansion
Return on assets (ROA)	5%	15%	25%
Earnings before interest (EBI)	$400	$1,200	$2,000
Interest	−400	−400	−400
Earnings after interest	$ 0	$ 800	$1,600
Return on equity (ROE)			
= Earnings after interest/Equity	0	20%	40%
Earnings per share (EPS)	0	$4.00	$ 8.00

Figure 15.2

Financial Leverage: EPS and EBI for the Trans Am Corporation

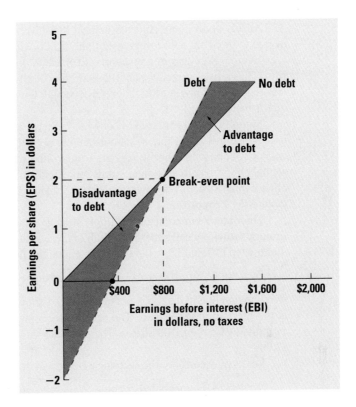

Tables 15.2 and 15.3 show that the effect of financial leverage depends on the company's earnings before interest. If earnings before interest are equal to $1,200, the return on equity (ROE) is higher under the proposed structure. If earnings before interest are equal to $400, the ROE is higher under the current structure.

This idea is represented in Figure 15.2. The solid line represents the case of no leverage. The line begins at the origin, indicating that earnings per share (EPS) would be zero if earnings before interest (EBI) were zero. The EPS rise in tandem with a rise in EBI.

The dotted line represents the case of $4,000 of debt. Here EPS are negative if EBI are zero. This follows because $400 of interest must be paid regardless of the firm's profits.

Now consider the slopes of the two lines. The slope of the dotted line (the line with debt) is higher than the slope of the solid line. This occurs because the levered firm has *fewer* shares of stock outstanding than the unlevered firm. Therefore, any increase in EBI leads to a greater rise in EPS for the levered firm because the earnings increase is distributed over fewer shares of stock.

Because the dotted line has a lower intercept but a higher slope, the two lines must intersect. The *break-even* point occurs at $800 of EBI. Were earnings before interest to be $800, both firms would produce $2 of earnings per share (EPS). Because $800 is breakeven, earnings above $800 lead to greater EPS for the levered firm. Earnings below $800 lead to greater EPS for the unlevered firm.

The Choice between Debt and Equity

Tables 15.2 and 15.3 and Figure 15.2 are important because they show the effect of leverage on earnings per share. Students should study the tables and figure until they feel comfortable with the calculation of each number in them. However, we have not yet presented the punch line. That is, we have not yet stated which capital structure is better for Trans Am.

At this point many students believe that leverage is beneficial because EPS are expected to be $4.00 with leverage and only $3.00 without leverage. However, leverage also creates *risk*. Note that in a recession, EPS are higher ($1.00 versus $0) for the unlevered firm. Thus a risk-averse investor might prefer the all-equity firm, whereas a risk-neutral (or less risk-averse) investor might prefer leverage. Given this ambiguity, which capital structure *is* better?

Modigliani and Miller (MM or M & M) have a convincing argument that a firm cannot change the total value of its outstanding securities by changing the proportions of its capital structure. In other words, the value of the firm is always the same under different capital structures. In still other words, no capital structure is any better or worse than any other capital structure for the firm's stockholders. This rather pessimistic result is the famous **MM Proposition I**.[2]

Their argument compares a simple strategy, which we call strategy *A*, with a two-part strategy, which we call strategy *B*. Both of these strategies for shareholders of Trans Am are illuminated in Table 15.4. Let us now examine the first strategy.

Strategy A: Buy 100 shares of the levered equity:

The first line in the top panel of Table 15.4 shows EPS for the proposed levered equity in the three economic states. The second line shows the earnings in the three states for an individual buying 100 shares. The next line shows that the cost of these 100 shares is $2,000.

Let us now consider the second strategy, which has two parts to it.

Strategy B: Homemade Leverage

1. Borrow $2,000 from either a bank or, more likely, a brokerage house. (If the brokerage house is the lender, we say that this activity is *going on margin*.)

2. Use the borrowed proceeds plus your own investment of $2,000 (a total of $4,000) to buy 200 shares of the current unlevered equity at $20 per share.

The bottom panel of Table 15.4 shows payoffs under strategy *B*, which we call the *homemade leverage* strategy. First observe the middle column, which indicates that 200 shares of the unlevered equity are expected to generate $600 of earnings. Assuming that the $2,000 is borrowed at a 10 percent interest rate, the interest expense is $200 ($= .10 \times \$2,000$). Thus the net earnings are expected to be $400. A similar calculation generates net earnings of either $0 or $800 in recession or expansion, respectively.

---

[2]The original paper is F. Modigliani and M. Miller, "The Cost of Capital, Corporation Finance and the Theory of Investment," *American Economic Review* (June 1958).

Table 15.4 Payoff and Cost to Shareholders of Trans Am Corporation under the Proposed Structure and under the Current Structure with Homemade Leverage

	Recession	Expected	Expansion
Strategy A: Buy 100 Shares of Levered Equity			
EPS of *levered* equity (taken from last line of Table 15.3)	$0	$ 4	$ 8
Earnings per 100 shares	0	400	800
Initial cost = 100 shares @ $20/share = $2,000			
Strategy B: Homemade Leverage			
Earnings per 200 shares in current	$1 × 200 =	$3 × 200 =	$5 × 200 =
unlevered Trans Am	200	600	1,000
Interest at 10% on $2,000	−200	−200	−200
Net earnings	$ 0	$ 400	$ 800

Initial cost = 200 shares @ $20/share − $2,000 = $2,000
           Cost of stock   Amount
                               borrowed

Investor receives the same payoff whether she (1) buys shares in a levered corporation or (2) buys shares in an unlevered firm and borrows on personal account. Her initial investment is the same in either case. Thus the firm neither helps nor hurts her by adding debt to capital structure.

Now let us compare these two strategies, both in terms of earnings per year and in terms of initial cost. The top panel of the table shows that strategy *A* generates earnings of $0, $400, and $800 in the three states. The bottom panel of the table shows that strategy *B* generates the *same* net earnings in the three states.

The top panel of the table shows that strategy *A* involves an initial cost of $2,000. Similarly, the bottom panel shows an *identical* net cost of $2,000 for strategy *B*.

This shows a very important result. Both the cost and the payoff from the two strategies are the same. Thus we must conclude that Trans Am is neither helping nor hurting its stockholders by restructuring. In other words, an investor is not receiving anything from corporate leverage that she could not receive on her own.

Note that, as shown in Table 15.1, the equity of the unlevered firm is valued at $8,000. Because the equity of the levered firm is $4,000 and its debt is $4,000, the value of the levered firm is also $8,000. Now suppose that, for whatever reason, the value of the levered firm were actually greater than the value of the unlevered firm. Here strategy *A* would cost more than strategy *B*. In this case an investor would prefer to borrow on his own account and invest in the stock of the unlevered firm. He would get the same net earnings each year as if he had invested in the stock of the levered firm. However, his cost would be less. The strategy would not be unique to our investor. Given the higher value of the levered firm, no rational investor would invest in the stock of the levered firm. Anyone desiring shares in the levered firm would get the same dollar return more cheaply by borrowing to finance a purchase of the unlevered firm's shares. The equilibrium result would be, of course, that the value of the levered firm would fall and the value of the unlevered firm would rise until they became equal. At this point individuals would be indifferent between strategy *A* and strategy *B*.

This example illustrates the basic result of Modigliani—Miller (MM) and is, as we have noted, commonly called their Proposition I. We restate this proposition as follows:

MM Proposition I (no taxes): The value of the levered firm is the same as the value of the unlevered firm.

This is perhaps the most important result in all of corporate finance. In fact, it is generally considered the beginning point of modern managerial finance. Before MM, the effect of leverage on the value of the firm was considered complex and convoluted. Modigliani and Miller showed a blindingly simple result: If levered firms are priced too high, rational investors will simply borrow on their personal accounts to buy shares in unlevered firms. This substitution is oftentimes called *homemade leverage*. As long as individuals borrow (and lend) on the same terms as the firms, they can duplicate the effects of corporate leverage on their own.

The example of Trans Am Corporation shows that leverage does not affect the value of the firm. Because we showed earlier that stockholders' welfare is directly related to the firm's value, the example indicates that changes in capital structure cannot affect the stockholders' welfare.

A Key Assumption

The MM result hinges on the assumption that individuals can borrow as cheaply as corporations. If, alternatively, individuals can borrow only at a higher rate, we can easily show that corporations can increase firm value by borrowing.

Is this assumption of equal borrowing costs a good one? Individuals who want to buy stock and borrow can do so by establishing a margin account with a broker. Under this arrangement the broker lends the individual a portion of the purchase price. For example, the individual might buy $10,000 of stock by investing $6,000 of her own funds and borrowing $4,000 from the broker. Should the stock be worth $9,000 on the next day, the individual's net worth or equity in the account would be $5,000 = $9,000 − $4,000.[3]

The broker fears that a sudden price drop will cause the equity in the individual's account to be negative, implying that the broker may not get her loan repaid in full. To guard against this possibility, stock exchange rules require that the individual make additional cash contributions (replenish her margin account) as the stock price falls. Because (1) the procedures for replenishing the account have developed over many years and (2) the broker holds the stock as collateral, there is little default risk to the broker.[4] In particular, if margin contributions are not made on time, the broker can sell the stock to satisfy her loan. Therefore, brokers generally charge low interest, with many rates being only slightly above the risk-free rate.

By contrast, corporations frequently borrow using illiquid assets (e.g., plant and equipment) as collateral. The costs to the lender of initial negotiation and ongoing supervision, as well as of working out arrangements in the event of financial distress, can be quite substantial. Thus it is difficult to argue that individuals must borrow at higher rates than corporations.

15.4 Modigliani and Miller: Proposition II (No Taxes)

Risk to Equityholders Rises with Leverage

At a Trans Am corporate meeting, a corporate officer said, "Well, maybe it does not matter whether the corporation or the individual levers—as long as some leverage takes place. Leverage benefits investors. After all, an investor's expected return rises with the amount of the leverage present." He then pointed out that, as shown in Tables 15.2 and 15.3, the expected return on unlevered equity is 15 percent whereas the expected return on levered equity is 20 percent.

---

[3] We are ignoring the one-day interest charge on the loan.

[4] Had this text been published before October 19, 1987, when stock prices declined by more than 20 percent in a single day, we might have used the phrase "virtually no" risk instead of "little" risk.

However, another officer replied, "Not necessarily. Though the expected return rises with leverage, the *risk* rises as well." This point can be seen from an examination of Tables 15.2 and 15.3. With earnings before interest (EBI) varying between $400 and $2,000, earnings per share (EPS) for the stockholders of the unlevered firm vary between $1.00 and $5.00. EPS for the stockholders of the levered firm vary between $0 and $8.00. This greater range for the EPS of the levered firm implies greater risk for the levered firm's stockholders. In other words, levered stockholders have better returns in good times than do unlevered stockholders but have worse returns in bad times. The two tables also show greater range for the ROE of the levered firm's stockholders. The earlier interpretation concerning risk applies here as well.

The same insight can be taken from Figure 15.2. The slope of the line for the levered firm is greater than the slope of the line for the unlevered firm. This means that the levered stockholders have better returns in good times than do unlevered stockholders but have worse returns in bad times, implying greater risk with leverage. In other words, the slope of the line measures the risk to stockholders because the slope indicates the responsiveness of ROE to changes in firm performance (earnings before interest).

Proposition II: Required Return to Equityholders Rises with Leverage

Because levered equity has greater risk, it should have a greater expected return as compensation. In our example, the market *requires* only a 15 percent expected return for the unlevered equity, but it requires a 20 percent expected return for the levered equity.

This type of reasoning allows us to develop **MM Proposition II**. Here MM argue that the expected return on equity is positively related to leverage because the risk to equityholders increases with leverage.

To develop this position recall that the firm's weighted average cost of capital, R_{WACC}, can be written as[5]

$$R_{\text{WACC}} = \frac{S}{B+S} \times R_S + \frac{B}{B+S} \times R_B \qquad (15.2)$$

where

R_B	is the cost of debt.
R_S	is the expected return on equity or stock, also called the *cost of equity* or the *required return on equity*.
R_{WACC}	is the firm's weighted average cost of capital.
B	is the value of the firm's debt or bonds.
S	is the value of the firm's stock or equity.

Equation 15.2 is quite intuitive. It simply says that a firm's weighted average cost of capital is a weighted average of its cost of debt and its cost of equity. The weight applied to debt is the proportion of debt in the capital structure, and the weight applied to equity is the proportion of equity in the capital structure. Calculations of R_{WACC} from Equation 15.2 for both the unlevered and the levered firm are presented in Table 15.5.

An implication of MM Proposition I is that R_{WACC} is a constant for a given firm, regardless of the capital structure.[6] For example, Table 15.5 shows that R_{WACC} for Trans Am is 15 percent, with or without leverage.

---

[5]Because we do not have taxes here, the cost of debt is R_B, not $R_B(1 - t_C)$ as it was in Chapter 12.

[6]This statement holds in a world of no taxes. It does not hold in a world with taxes, a point to be brought out later in this chapter (see Figure 15.6).

Table 15.5

Cost of Capital Calculations for Trans Am

$$R_{WACC} = \frac{B}{B+S} \times R_B + \frac{S}{B+S} \times R_S$$

Unlevered firm: $15\% = \dfrac{0}{\$8,000} \times 10\%^* + \dfrac{\$8,000}{\$8,000} \times 15\%^\dagger$

Levered firm: $15\% = \dfrac{\$4,000}{\$8,000} \times 10\%^* + \dfrac{\$4,000}{\$8,000} \times 20\%^\ddagger$

*10% is the cost of debt.

†From the "Expected" column in Table 15.2, we learn that expected earnings after interest for the unlevered firm are $1,200. From Table 15.1 we learn that equity for the unlevered firm is $8,000. Thus R_S for the unlevered firm is

$$\frac{\text{Expected earnings after interest}}{\text{Equity}} = \frac{\$1,200}{\$8,000} = 15\%$$

‡From the "Expected" column in Table 15.3, we learn that expected earnings after interest for the levered firm are $800. From Table 15.1 we learn that equity for the levered firm is $4,000. Thus R_S for the levered firm is

$$\frac{\text{Expected earnings after interest}}{\text{Equity}} = \frac{\$800}{\$4,000} = 20\%$$

Let us now define R_0 to be the *cost of capital for an all-equity firm*. For the Trans Am Corp., R_0 is calculated as

$$R_0 = \frac{\text{Expected earnings to unlevered firm}}{\text{Unlevered equity}} = \frac{\$1,200}{\$8,000} = 15\%$$

As can be seen from Table 15.5, R_{WACC} is equal to R_0 for Trans Am. In fact, R_{WACC} must *always* equal R_0 in a world without corporate taxes.[7]

Proposition II states the expected return of equity, R_S, in terms of leverage. The exact relationship, derived by setting $R_{WACC} = R_0$ and then rearranging Equation 15.2, is[8]

MM Proposition II (No Taxes)

$$R_S = R_0 + \frac{B}{S}(R_0 - R_B) \tag{15.3}$$

Equation 15.3 implies that the required return on equity is a linear function of the firm's debt–equity ratio. Examining Equation 15.3, we see that if R_0 exceeds the cost of debt, R_B,

---

[7]This statement holds in a world of no taxes. It does not hold in a world with taxes, a point to be brought out later in this chapter (see Figure 15.6).

[8]This can be derived from Equation 15.2 by setting $R_{WACC} = R_0$, yielding

$$\frac{B}{B+S} R_B + \frac{S}{B+S} R_S = R_0$$

Multiplying both sides by $(B+S)/S$ yields

$$\frac{B}{S} R_B + R_S = \frac{B+S}{S} R_0$$

We can rewrite the right side as

$$\frac{B}{S} R_B + R_S = \frac{B}{S} R_0 + R_0$$

Moving $(B/S)R_B$ to the right side and rearranging yields

$$R_S = R_0 + \frac{B}{S}(R_0 - R_B)$$

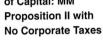

Figure 15.3

The Cost of Equity, the Cost of Debt, and the Weighted Average Cost of Capital: MM Proposition II with No Corporate Taxes

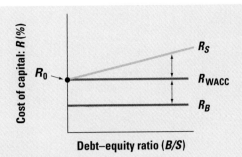

$R_S = R_0 + (R_0 - R_B)B/S$

    R_S is the cost of equity.

    R_B is the cost of debt.

    R_0 is the cost of capital for an all-equity firm.

    R_{WACC} is a firm's weighted average cost of capital. In a world with no taxes, R_{WACC} for a levered firm is equal to R_0.

    R_0 is a single point whereas R_S, R_B, and R_{WACC} are all entire lines.

The cost of equity capital, R_S, is positively related to the firm's debt–equity ratio. The firm's weighted average cost of capital, R_{WACC}, is invariant to the firm's debt–equity ratio.

then the cost of equity rises with increases in the debt–equity ratio, B/S. Normally R_0 should exceed R_B. That is, because even unlevered equity is risky, it should have an expected return greater than that of riskless debt. Note that Equation 15.3 holds for Trans Am in its levered state:

$$.20 = .15 + \frac{\$4{,}000}{\$4{,}000}(.15 - .10)$$

Figure 15.3 graphs Equation 15.3. As you can see, we have plotted the relation between the cost of equity, R_S, and the debt–equity ratio, B/S, as a straight line. What we witness in Equation 15.3 and illustrate in Figure 15.3 is the effect of leverage on the cost of equity. As the firm raises the debt–equity ratio, each dollar of equity is levered with additional debt. This raises the risk of equity and therefore the required return, R_S, on the equity.

Figure 15.3 also shows that R_{WACC} is unaffected by leverage, a point we have already made. (It is important for students to realize that R_0, the cost of capital for an all-equity firm, is represented by a single dot on the graph. By contrast, R_{WACC} is an entire line.)

EXAMPLE 15.2

MM Propositions I and II   Luteran Motors, an all-equity firm, has expected earnings of $10 million per year in perpetuity. The firm pays all of its earnings out as dividends, so the $10 million may also be viewed as the stockholders' expected cash flow. There are 10 million shares outstanding, implying expected annual cash flow of $1 per share. The cost of capital for this unlevered firm is 10 percent. In addition, the firm will soon build a new plant for $4 million. The plant is expected to generate additional cash flow of $1 million per year. These figures can be described as follows:

Current Company	New Plant
Cash flow: $10 million	Initial outlay: $4 million
Number of outstanding shares: 10 million	Additional annual cash flow: $1 million

(continued)

The project's net present value is

$$-\$4 \text{ million} + \frac{\$1 \text{ million}}{.1} = \$6 \text{ million}$$

assuming that the project is discounted at the same rate as the firm as a whole. Before the market knows of the project, the *market value* balance sheet of the firm is this:

LUTERAN MOTORS **Balance Sheet (All Equity)**		
Old assets: $\dfrac{\$10 \text{ million}}{.1} = \$100 \text{ million}$	Equity:	$100 million (10 million shares of stock)

The value of the firm is $100 million because the cash flow of $10 million per year is capitalized (discounted) at 10 percent. A share of stock sells for $10 ($= \$100$ million/10 million) because there are 10 million shares outstanding.

The market value balance sheet is a useful tool for financial analysis. Because students are often thrown off guard by it initially, we recommend extra study here. The key is that the market value balance sheet has the same form as the balance sheet that accountants use. That is, assets are placed on the left side whereas liabilities and owners' equity are placed on the right side. In addition, the left and right sides must be equal. The difference between a market value balance sheet and the accountant's balance sheet is in the numbers. Accountants value items in terms of historical cost (original purchase price less depreciation), whereas financial analysts value items in terms of market value.

The firm will issue $4 million of either equity or debt. Let us consider the effect of equity and debt financing in turn.

Stock Financing   Imagine that the firm announces that in the near future it will raise $4 million in equity to build a new plant. The stock price, and therefore the value of the firm, will rise to reflect the positive net present value of the plant. According to efficient markets, the increase occurs immediately. That is, the rise occurs on the day of the announcement, not on the date of either the onset of construction of the plant or the forthcoming stock offering. The market value balance sheet becomes this:

LUTERAN MOTORS **Balance Sheet** **(Upon Announcement of Equity Issue to Construct Plant)**		
Old assets	$100 million	Equity	$106 million (10 million shares of stock)
NPV of plant: $-4 \text{ million} + \dfrac{\$1 \text{ million}}{.1} = 6 \text{ million}$		
Total assets	$106 million	

Note that the NPV of the plant is included in the market value balance sheet. Because the new shares have not yet been issued, the number of outstanding shares remains 10 million. The price per share has now risen to $10.60 ($= \$106$ million/10 million) to reflect news concerning the plant.

(continued)

Shortly thereafter, $4 million of stock is issued or *floated*. Because the stock is selling at $10.60 per share, 377,358 (= $4 million/$10.60) shares of stock are issued. Imagine that funds are put in the bank *temporarily* before being used to build the plant. The market value balance sheet becomes this:

LUTERAN MOTORS Balance Sheet (Upon Issuance of Stock but Before Construction Begins on Plant)			
Old assets	$100 million	Equity	$110 million
			(10,377,358 shares of stock)
NPV of plant	6 million		
Proceeds from new issue of stock (currently placed in bank)	4 million		
Total assets	$110 million		

The number of shares outstanding is now 10,377,358 because 377,358 new shares were issued. The price per share is $10.60 (= $110,000,000/10,377,358). Note that the price has not changed. This is consistent with efficient capital markets because the stock price should move due only to new information.

Of course the funds are placed in the bank only temporarily. Shortly after the new issue, the $4 million is given to a contractor who builds the plant. To avoid problems in discounting, we assume that the plant is built immediately. The balance sheet then looks like this:

LUTERAN MOTORS Balance Sheet (Upon Completion of the Plant)			
Old assets	$100 million	Equity	$110 million
			(10,377,358 shares of stock)
PV of plant: $\dfrac{\$1 \text{ million}}{.1} =$	10 million		
Total assets	$110 million		

Though total assets do not change, the composition of the assets does change. The bank account has been emptied to pay the contractor. The present value of cash flows of $1 million a year from the plant is reflected as an asset worth $10 million. Because the building expenditures of $4 million have already been paid, they no longer represent a future cost. Hence they no longer reduce the value of the plant. According to efficient capital markets, the price per share of stock remains $10.60.

Expected yearly cash flow from the firm is $11 million, $10 million of which comes from the old assets and $1 million from the new. The expected return to equityholders is

$$R_S = \frac{\$11 \text{ million}}{\$110 \text{ million}} = .10$$

Because the firm is all equity, $R_S = R_0 = .10$.

Debt Financing Alternatively, imagine the firm announces that in the near future it will borrow $4 million at 6 percent to build a new plant. This implies yearly interest payments of $240,000

(continued)

(= \$4,000,000 × 6%). Again the stock price rises immediately to reflect the positive net present value of the plant. Thus we have the following:

LUTERAN MOTORS Balance Sheet (Upon Announcement of Debt Issue to Construct Plant)			
Old assets	\$100 million	Equity	\$106 million
			(10 million shares of stock)
NPV of plant:			
$-\$4 \text{ million} + \dfrac{\$1 \text{ million}}{.1} = \quad 6 \text{ million}$			
Total assets	\$106 million		

The value of the firm is the same as in the equity financing case because (1) the same plant is to be built and (2) MM proved that debt financing is neither better nor worse than equity financing.

At some point \$4 million of debt is issued. As before, the funds are placed in the bank temporarily. The market value balance sheet becomes this:

LUTERAN MOTORS Balance Sheet (Upon Debt Issuance but Before Construction Begins on Plant)			
Old assets	\$100 million	Debt	\$ 4 million
NPV of plant	6 million	Equity	106 million
			(10 million shares of stock)
Proceeds from debt issue (currently invested in bank)	4 million		
Total assets	\$110 million	Debt plus equity	\$110 million

Note that debt appears on the right side of the balance sheet. The stock price is still \$10.60 in accordance with our discussion of efficient capital markets.

Finally the contractor receives \$4 million and builds the plant. The market value balance sheet turns into this:

LUTERAN MOTORS Balance Sheet (Upon Completion of the Plant)			
Old assets	\$100 million	Debt	\$ 4 million
PV of plant	10 million	Equity	106 million
			(10 million shares of stock)
Total assets	\$110 million	Debt plus equity	\$110 million

The only change here is that the bank account has been depleted to pay the contractor. The equityholders expect yearly cash flow after interest of

$$\underset{\substack{\text{Cash flow on} \\ \text{old assets}}}{\$10,000,000} + \underset{\substack{\text{Cash flow on} \\ \text{new assets}}}{\$1,000,000} - \underset{\substack{\text{Interest:} \\ \$4 \text{ million} \times 6\%}}{\$240,000} = \$10,760,000$$

(continued)

The equityholders expect to earn a return of

$$\frac{\$10,760,000}{\$106,000,000} = 10.15\%$$

This return of 10.15 percent for levered equityholders is higher than the 10 percent return for the unlevered equityholders. This result is sensible because, as we argued earlier, levered equity is riskier. In fact, the return of 10.15 percent should be exactly what MM Proposition II predicts. This prediction can be verified by plugging values into

$$R_S = R_0 + \frac{B}{S} \times (R_0 - R_B) \qquad\qquad (15.3)$$

We obtain

$$10.15\% = 10\% + \frac{\$4,000,000}{\$106,000,000} \times (10\% - 6\%)$$

This example was useful for two reasons. First, we wanted to introduce the concept of market value balance sheets, a tool that will prove useful elsewhere in the text. Among other things, this technique allows us to calculate the price per share of a new issue of stock. Second, the example illustrates three aspects of Modigliani and Miller:

1. The example is consistent with MM Proposition I because the value of the firm is $110 million after either equity or debt financing.

2. Students are often more interested in stock price than in firm value. We show that the stock price is always $10.60, regardless of whether debt or equity financing is used.

3. The example is consistent with MM Proposition II. The expected return to equityholders rises from 10 to 10.15 percent, just as Equation 15.3 states. This rise occurs because the equityholders of a levered firm face more risk than do the equityholders of an unlevered firm.

MM: An Interpretation

The Modigliani–Miller results indicate that managers cannot change the value of a firm by repackaging the firm's securities. Though this idea was considered revolutionary when it was originally proposed in the late 1950s, the MM approach and proof have since met with wide acclaim.[9]

MM argue that the firm's overall cost of capital cannot be reduced as debt is substituted for equity, even though debt appears to be cheaper than equity. The reason for this is that as the firm adds debt, the remaining equity becomes more risky. As this risk rises, the cost of equity capital rises as a result. The increase in the cost of the remaining equity capital offsets the higher proportion of the firm financed by low-cost debt. In fact, MM prove that the two effects exactly offset each other, so that both the value of the firm and the firm's overall cost of capital are invariant to leverage.

MM use an interesting analogy to food. They consider a dairy farmer with two choices. On the one hand, he can sell whole milk. On the other hand, by skimming he can sell a combination of cream and lowfat milk. Though the farmer can get a high price for the cream, he gets a low price for the lowfat milk, implying no net gain. In fact, imagine that the proceeds from the whole-milk strategy were less than those from the cream–lowfat milk strategy. Arbitrageurs would buy the whole milk, perform the skimming operation themselves, and resell the cream and lowfat milk separately. Competition between arbitrageurs would tend to boost the price of whole milk until proceeds from the two strategies became equal. Thus the value of the farmer's milk is invariant to the way in which the milk is packaged.

---

[9]Both Merton Miller and Franco Modigliani were awarded separate Nobel Prizes, in part for their work on capital structure.

In Their Own Words

IN PROFESSOR MILLER'S WORDS . . .

The Modigliani–Miller results are not easy to understand fully. This point is related in a story told by Merton Miller.*

"How difficult it is to summarize briefly the contribution of the [Modigliani–Miller] papers was brought home to me very clearly last October after Franco Modigliani was awarded the Nobel Prize in Economics in part—but, of course, only in part—for the work in finance. The television camera crews from our local stations in Chicago immediately descended upon me. 'We understand,' they said, 'that you worked with Modigliani some years back in developing these M and M theorems and we wonder if you could explain them briefly to our television viewers.'

"'How briefly?' I asked.

"'Oh, take ten seconds,' was the reply.

"Ten seconds to explain the work of a lifetime! Ten seconds to describe two carefully reasoned articles, each running to more than thirty printed pages and each with sixty or so long footnotes! When they saw the look of dismay on my face, they said, 'You don't have to go into details. Just give us the main points in simple, commonsense terms.'

"The main point of the first or cost-of-capital article was, in principle at least, simple enough to make. It said that in an economist's ideal world of complete and perfect capital markets and with full and symmetric information among all market participants, the total market value of all the securities issued by a firm was governed by the earning power and risk of its underlying real assets and was independent of how the mix of securities issued to finance it was divided between debt instruments and equity capital. . . .

"Such a summary, however, uses too many short-handed terms and concepts, like perfect capital markets, that are rich in connotations to economists but hardly so to the general public. So I thought, instead, of an analogy that we ourselves had invoked in the original paper. . . .

"'Think of the firm,' I said, 'as a gigantic tub of whole milk. The farmer can sell the whole milk as is. Or he can separate out the cream and sell it at a considerably higher price than the whole milk would bring. (That's the analogy of a firm selling low-yield and hence high-priced debt securities.) But, of course, what the farmer would have left would be skim milk with low butterfat content and that would sell for much less than whole milk. That corresponds to the levered equity. The M and M proposition says that if there were no costs of separation (and, of course, no government dairy support programs), the cream plus the skim milk would bring the same price as the whole milk.'

"The television people conferred among themselves and came back to inform me that it was too long, too complicated, and too academic.

"'Don't you have anything simpler?' they asked. I though of another way that the M and M proposition is presented these days, which emphasizes the notion of market completeness and stresses the role of securities as devices for 'partitioning' a firm's payoffs in each possible state of the world among the group of its capital suppliers.

"'Think of the firm,' I said, 'as a gigantic pizza, divided into quarters. If now you cut each quarter in half into eighths, the M and M proposition says that you will have more pieces but not more pizza.'

"Again there was a whispered conference among the camera crew, and the director came back and said:

"'Professor, we understand from the press releases that there were two M and M propositions. Can we try the other one?'"

[Professor Miller tried valiantly to explain the second proposition, though this was apparently even more difficult to get across. After his attempt:]

"Once again there was a whispered conversation. They shut the lights off. They folded up their equipment. They thanked me for giving them the time. They said that they'd get back to me. But I knew that I had somehow lost my chance to start a new career as a packager of economic wisdom for TV viewers in convenient ten-second bites. Some have the talent for it . . . and some just don't."

*Taken from *GSB Chicago*, University of Chicago (Autumn 1986).

Food found its way into this chapter earlier when we viewed the firm as a pie. MM argue that the size of the pie does not change no matter how stockholders and bondholders divide it. MM say that a firm's capital structure is irrelevant; it is what it is by some historical accident. The theory implies that firms' debt–equity ratios could be anything. They are what they are because of whimsical and random managerial decisions about how much to borrow and how much stock to issue.

Summary of Modigliani–Miller Propositions without Taxes

Assumptions

- No taxes.
- No transaction costs.
- Individuals and corporations borrow at same rate.

Results

Proposition I: $V_L = V_U$ (Value of levered firm equals value of unlevered firm)

Proposition II: $R_S = R_0 + \dfrac{B}{S}(R_0 - R_B)$

Intuition

Proposition I: Through homemade leverage individuals can either duplicate or undo the effects of corporate leverage.

Proposition II: The cost of equity rises with leverage because the risk to equity rises with leverage.

Although scholars are always fascinated with far-reaching theories, students are perhaps more concerned with real-world applications. Do real-world managers follow MM by treating capital structure decisions with indifference? Unfortunately for the theory, virtually all companies in certain industries, such as banking, choose high debt–equity ratios. Conversely, companies in other industries, such as pharmaceuticals, choose low debt–equity ratios. In fact, almost any industry has a debt–equity ratio to which companies in that industry tend to adhere. Thus companies do not appear to be selecting their degree of leverage in a frivolous or random manner. Because of this, financial economists (including MM themselves) have argued that real-world factors may have been left out of the theory.

Though many of our students have argued that individuals can borrow only at rates above the corporate borrowing rate, we disagreed with this argument earlier in the chapter. But when we look elsewhere for unrealistic assumptions in the theory, we find two:[10]

1. Taxes were ignored.
2. Bankruptcy costs and other agency costs were not considered.

We turn to taxes in the next section. Bankruptcy costs and other agency costs will be treated in the next chapter. A summary of the main Modigliani–Miller results without taxes is presented in the nearby boxed section.

15.5 Taxes

The Basic Insight

The previous part of this chapter showed that firm value is unrelated to debt in a world without taxes. We now show that in the presence of corporate taxes, the firm's value is positively related to its debt. The basic intuition can be seen from a pie chart, such as the

---

[10]MM were aware of both of these issues, as can be seen in their original paper.

Figure 15.4

Two Pie Models of Capital Structure under Corporate Taxes

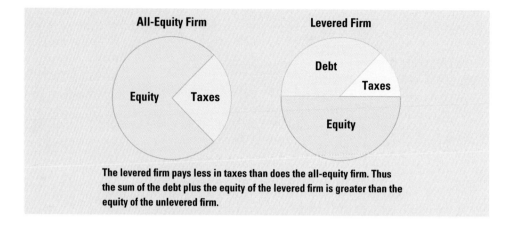

All-Equity Firm

Equity   Taxes

Levered Firm

Debt

Taxes

Equity

The levered firm pays less in taxes than does the all-equity firm. Thus the sum of the debt plus the equity of the levered firm is greater than the equity of the unlevered firm.

one in Figure 15.4. Consider the all-equity firm on the left. Here both equityholders and the IRS have claims on the firm. The value of the all-equity firm is, of course, that part of the pie owned by the equityholders. The proportion going to taxes is simply a cost.

The pie on the right for the levered firm shows three claims: equityholders, debtholders, and taxes. The value of the levered firm is the sum of the value of the debt and the value of the equity. In selecting between the two capital structures in the picture, a financial manager should select the one with the higher value. Assuming that the total area is the same for both pies[11] value is maximized for the capital structure paying the least in taxes. In other words, the manager should choose the capital structure that the IRS hates the most.

We will show that due to a quirk in U.S. tax law, the proportion of the pie allocated to taxes is less for the levered firm than it is for the unlevered firm. Thus, managers should select high leverage.

EXAMPLE 15.3

Taxes and Cash Flow   The Water Products Company has a corporate tax rate, t_C, of 35 percent and expected earnings before interest and taxes (EBIT) of $1 million each year. Its entire earnings after taxes are paid out as dividends.

The firm is considering two alternative capital structures. Under Plan I, Water Products would have no debt in its capital structure. Under Plan II, the company would have $4,000,000 of debt, B. The cost of debt, R_B, is 10 percent.

The chief financial officer for Water Products makes the following calculations:

	Plan I	Plan II
Earnings before interest and corporate taxes (EBIT)	$1,000,000	$1,000,000
Interest ($R_B B$)	0	400,000
Earnings before taxes (EBT) = (EBIT − $R_B B$)	1,000,000	600,000
Taxes (t_C = .35)	350,000	210,000
Earnings after corporate taxes (EAT) = [(EBIT − $R_B B$) × (1 − t_C)]	650,000	390,000
Total cash flow to both stockholders and bondholders [EBIT × (1 − t_C) + $t_C R_B B$]	$ 650,000	$ 790,000

(continued)

[11] Under the MM propositions developed earlier, the two pies should be of the same size.

The most relevant numbers for our purposes are the two on the bottom line. Dividends, which are equal to earnings after taxes in this example, are the cash flow to stockholders, and interest is the cash flow to bondholders. Here we see that more cash flow reaches the owners of the firm (both stockholders and bondholders) under Plan II. The difference is $140,000 = $790,000 − $650,000. It does not take us long to realize the source of this difference. The IRS receives less tax under Plan II ($210,000) than it does under Plan I ($350,000). The difference here is $140,000 = $350,000 − $210,000.

This difference occurs because the way the IRS treats interest is different from the way it treats earnings going to stockholders.[12] Interest totally escapes corporate taxation, whereas earnings after interest but before corporate taxes (EBT) are taxed at the 35 percent rate.

Present Value of the Tax Shield

The previous discussion shows a tax advantage to debt or, equivalently, a tax disadvantage to equity. We now want to value this advantage. The dollar interest is

$$\text{Interest} = \underbrace{R_B}_{\text{Interest rate}} \times \underbrace{B}_{\text{Amount borrowed}}$$

This interest is $400,000 (= 10 percent × $4,000,000) for Water Products. All this interest is tax deductible. That is, whatever the taxable income of Water Products would have been without the debt, the taxable income is now $400,000 *less* with the debt.

Because the corporate tax rate is .35 in our example, the reduction in corporate taxes is $140,000 (= .35 × $400,000). This number is identical to the reduction in corporate taxes calculated previously.

Algebraically, the reduction in corporate taxes is

$$\underbrace{t_C}_{\text{Corporate tax rate}} \times \underbrace{R_B \times B}_{\text{Dollar amount of interest}} \tag{15.4}$$

That is, whatever the taxes that a firm would pay each year without debt, the firm will pay $t_C R_B B$ less with the debt of B. Expression 15.4 is often called the *tax shield from debt*. Note that it is an *annual* amount.

As long as the firm expects to be in a positive tax bracket, we can assume that the cash flow in Expression 15.4 has the same risk as the interest on the debt. Thus its value can be determined by discounting at the cost of debt, R_B. Assuming that the cash flows are perpetual, the present value of the tax shield is

$$\frac{t_C R_B B}{R_B} = t_C B$$

Value of the Levered Firm ·

We have just calculated the present value of the tax shield from debt. Our next step is to calculate the value of the levered firm. The annual aftertax cash flow of an unlevered firm is

$$\text{EBIT} \times (1 - t_C)$$

---

[12]Note that stockholders actually receive more under Plan I ($650,000) than under Plan II ($390,000). Students are often bothered by this because it seems to imply that stockholders are better off without leverage. However, remember that there are more shares outstanding in Plan I than in Plan II. A full-blown model would show that earnings *per share* are higher with leverage.

where EBIT is earnings before interest and taxes. The value of an unlevered firm (that is, a firm with no debt) is the present value of EBIT $\times (1 - t_C)$:

$$V_U = \frac{\text{EBIT} \times (1 - t_C)}{R_0}$$

Here

$$V_U = \text{Present value of an unlevered firm.}$$

$$\text{EBIT} \times (1 - t_C) = \text{Firm cash flows after corporate taxes.}$$

$$t_C = \text{Corporate tax rate.}$$

$$R_0 = \text{The cost of capital to an all-equity firm. As can be seen from the formula, } R_0 \text{ now discounts } \textit{aftertax} \text{ cash flows.}$$

As shown previously, leverage increases the value of the firm by the tax shield, which is $t_C B$ for perpetual debt. Thus we merely add this tax shield to the value of the unlevered firm to get the value of the levered firm.

We can write this algebraically as follows:[13]

MM Proposition I (Corporate Taxes)

$$V_L = \frac{\text{EBIT} \times (1 - t_C)}{R_0} + \frac{t_C R_B B}{R_B} = V_U + t_C B \qquad \textbf{(15.5)}$$

Equation 15.5 is MM Proposition I under corporate taxes. The first term in Equation 15.5 is the value of the cash flows of the firm with no debt tax shield. In other words, this term is equal to V_U, the value of the all-equity firm. The value of the levered firm is the value of an all-equity firm plus $t_C B$, the tax rate times the value of the debt. $t_C B$ is the present value of the tax shield in the case of perpetual cash flows.[14] Because the tax shield

---

[13]This relationship holds when the debt level is assumed to be constant through time. A different formula would apply if the debt–equity ratio was assumed to be a nonconstant over time. For a deeper treatment of this point, see J. A. Miles and J. R. Ezzel, "The Weighted Average Cost of Capital, Perfect Capital Markets and Project Life," *Journal of Financial and Quantitative Analysis* (September 1980).

[14]The following example calculates the present value if we assume the debt has a finite life. Suppose the Maxwell Company has $1 million in debt with an 8 percent coupon rate. If the debt matures in two years and the cost of debt capital, R_B, is 10 percent, what is the present value of the tax shields if the corporate tax rate is 35 percent? The debt is amortized in equal installments over two years.

Year	Loan Balance	Interest	Tax Shield	Present Value of Tax Shield
0	$1,000,000			
1	500,000	$80,000	0.35 × $80,000	$25,454.54
2	0	40,000	0.35 × $40,000	11,570.25
				$37,024.79

The present value of the tax saving is

$$\text{PV} = \frac{0.35 \times \$80,000}{1.10} + \frac{0.35 \times \$40,000}{(1.10)^2} = \$37,024.79$$

The Maxwell Company's value is higher than that of a comparable unlevered firm by $37,024.79.

increases with the amount of debt, the firm can raise its total cash flow and its value by substituting debt for equity.

MM with Corporate Taxes   Divided Airlines is currently an unlevered firm. The company expects to generate $153.85 in earnings before interest and taxes (EBIT) in perpetuity. The corporate tax rate is 35 percent, implying aftertax earnings of $100. All earnings after tax are paid out as dividends.

The firm is considering a capital restructuring to allow $200 of debt. Its cost of debt capital is 10 percent. Unlevered firms in the same industry have a cost of equity capital of 20 percent. What will the new value of Divided Airlines be?

Figure 15.5   **The Effect of Financial Leverage on Firm Value: MM with Corporate Taxes in the Case of Divided Airlines**

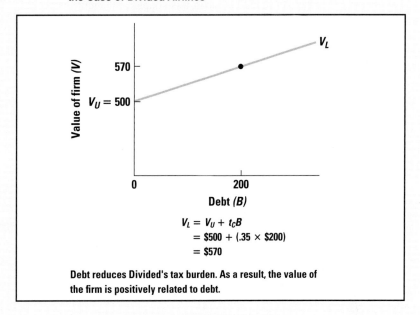

$$V_L = V_U + t_C B$$
$$= \$500 + (.35 \times \$200)$$
$$= \$570$$

Debt reduces Divided's tax burden. As a result, the value of the firm is positively related to debt.

The value of Divided Airlines will be equal to

$$V_L = \frac{EBIT \times (1 - t_C)}{R_0} + t_C B$$

$$= \frac{\$100}{.20} + (.35 \times \$200)$$

$$= \$500 + \$70 = \$570$$

The value of the levered firm is $570, which is greater than the unlevered value of $500. Because $V_L = B + S$, the value of levered equity, S, is equal to $570 - \$200 = \$370$. The value of Divided Airlines as a function of leverage is illustrated in Figure 15.5.

Expected Return and Leverage under Corporate Taxes

MM Proposition II under no taxes posits a positive relationship between the expected return on equity and leverage. This result occurs because the risk of equity increases with leverage. The same intuition also holds in a world of corporate taxes. The exact formula in a world of corporate taxes is this:[15]

MM Proposition II (Corporate Taxes)

$$R_S = R_0 + \frac{B}{S} \times (1 - t_C) \times (R_0 - R_B) \tag{15.6}$$

Applying the formula to Divided Airlines, we get

$$R_S = .2351 = .20 + \frac{200}{370} \times (1 - .35) \times (.20 - .10)$$

This calculation is illustrated in Figure 15.6.

Whenever $R_0 > R_B$, R_S increases with leverage, a result that we also found in the no-tax case. As stated earlier in this chapter, R_0 should exceed R_B. That is, because equity (even unlevered equity) is risky, it should have an expected return greater than that on the less risky debt.

Let's check our calculations by determining the value of the levered equity in another way. The algebraic formula for the value of levered equity is

$$S = \frac{(\text{EBIT} - R_B B) \times (1 - t_C)}{R_S}$$

---

[15]This relationship can be shown as follows: Given MM Proposition I under taxes, a levered firm's market value balance sheet can be written as:

V_U = Value of unlevered firm	B = Debt
$t_C B$ = Tax shield	S = Equity

The value of the unlevered firm is simply the value of the assets without benefit of leverage. The balance sheet indicates that the firm's value increases by $t_C B$ when debt of B is added. The expected cash flow *from* the left side of the balance sheet can be written as

$$V_U R_0 + t_C B R_B \tag{a}$$

Because assets are risky, their expected rate of return is R_0. The tax shield has the same risk as the debt, so its expected rate of return is R_B.

The expected cash *to* bondholders and stockholders together is

$$S R_S + B R_B \tag{b}$$

Expression (b) reflects the fact that stock earns an expected return of R_S and debt earns the interest rate R_B.

Because all cash flows are paid out as dividends in our no-growth perpetuity model, the cash flows going into the firm equal those going to stockholders. Hence (a) and (b) are equal:

$$S R_S + B R_B = V_U R_0 + t_C B R_B \tag{c}$$

Dividing both sides of (c) by S, subtracting $B R_B$ from both sides, and rearranging yields

$$R_S = \frac{V_U}{S} \times R_0 - (1 - t_C) \times \frac{B}{S} R_B \tag{d}$$

Because the value of the levered firm, V_L, equals $V_U + t_C B = B + S$, it follows that $V_U = S + (1 - t_C) \times B$. Thus (d) can be rewritten as

$$R_S = \frac{S + (1 - t_C) \times B}{S} \times R_0 - (1 - t_C) \times \frac{B}{S} R_B \tag{e}$$

Bringing the terms involving $(1 - t_C) \times (B/S)$ together produces Equation 15.6.

Figure 15.6

The Effect of Financial Leverage on the Cost of Debt and Equity Capital

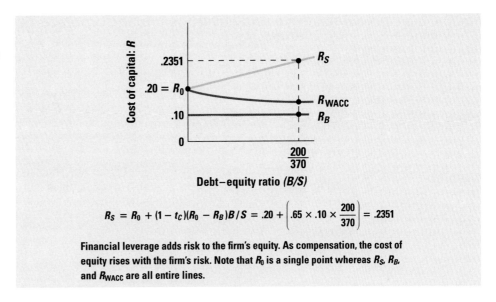

$$R_S = R_0 + (1 - t_C)(R_0 - R_B)B/S = .20 + \left(.65 \times .10 \times \frac{200}{370} \right) = .2351$$

Financial leverage adds risk to the firm's equity. As compensation, the cost of equity rises with the firm's risk. Note that R_0 is a single point whereas R_S, R_B, and R_{WACC} are all entire lines.

The numerator is the expected cash flow to levered equity after interest and taxes. The denominator is the rate at which the cash flow to equity is discounted.

For Divided Airlines we get

$$\frac{(\$153.85 - .10 \times \$200)(1 - .35)}{.2351} = \$370$$

the same result we obtained earlier (ignoring a small rounding error).

The Weighted Average Cost of Capital, R_{WACC}, and Corporate Taxes

In Chapter 12, we defined the weighted average cost of capital (with corporate taxes) as follows (note that $V_L = S + B$):

$$R_{WACC} = \frac{S}{V_L} R_S + \frac{B}{V_L} R_B(1 - t_C)$$

Note that the cost of debt capital, R_B, is multiplied by $(1 - t_C)$ because interest is tax deductible at the corporate level. However, the cost of equity, R_S, is not multiplied by this factor because dividends are not deductible. In the no-tax case, R_{WACC} is not affected by leverage. This result is reflected in Figure 15.3, which we discussed earlier. However, because debt is tax advantaged relative to equity, it can be shown that R_{WACC} declines with leverage in a world with corporate taxes. This result can be seen in Figure 15.6.

For Divided Airlines, R_{WACC} is equal to

$$R_{WACC} = \left(\frac{370}{570} \times .2351 \right) + \left(\frac{200}{570} \times .10 \times .65 \right) = .1754$$

Divided Airlines has reduced its R_{WACC} from .20 (with no debt) to .1754 with reliance on debt. This result is intuitively pleasing because it suggests that when a firm lowers its R_{WACC}, the firm's value will increase. Using the R_{WACC} approach, we can confirm that the value of Divided Airlines is $570:

$$V_L = \frac{EBIT \times (1 - t_C)}{R_{WACC}} = \frac{\$100}{.1754} = \$570$$

Stock Price and Leverage under Corporate Taxes

At this point students often believe the numbers—or at least are too intimidated to dispute them. However, they sometimes think we have asked the wrong question. "Why are we choosing to maximize the value of the firm?" they will say. "If managers are looking out for the stockholders' interest, why aren't they trying to maximize stock price?" If this question occurred to you, you have come to the right section.

Our response is twofold: First, we showed in the first section of this chapter that the capital structure that maximizes firm value is also the one that most benefits the interests of the stockholders.

However, that general explanation is not always convincing to students. As a second procedure, we calculate the stock price of Divided Airlines both before and after the exchange of debt for stock. We do this by presenting a set of market value balance sheets. The market value balance sheet for the company in its all-equity form can be represented as follows:

DIVIDED AIRLINES Balance Sheet (All-Equity Firm)		
Physical assets	Equity	$500
$\dfrac{\$153.85}{.20} \times (1 - .35) = \$500$		(100 shares)

Assuming that there are 100 shares outstanding, each share is worth $5 = $500/100.

Next imagine the company announces that in the near future it will issue $200 of debt to buy back $200 of stock. We know from our previous discussion that the value of the firm will rise to reflect the tax shield of debt. If we assume that capital markets efficiently price securities, the increase occurs immediately. That is, the rise occurs on the day of the announcement, not on the date of the debt-for-equity exchange. The market value balance sheet now becomes this:

DIVIDED AIRLINES Balance Sheet (Upon Announcement of Debt Issue)			
Physical assets	$500	Equity	$570
			(100 shares)
Present value of tax shield:			
$t_C B = 35\% \times \$200 =$	70		
Total assets	$570		

Note that the debt has not yet been issued. Therefore, only equity appears on the right side of the balance sheet. Each share is now worth $570/100 = $5.70, implying that the stockholders have benefited by $70. The equityholders gain because they are the owners of a firm that has improved its financial policy.

The introduction of the tax shield to the balance sheet is perplexing to many students. Although physical assets are tangible, the ethereal nature of the tax shield bothers these students. However, remember that an asset is any item with value. The tax shield has value because it reduces the stream of future taxes. The fact that one cannot touch the shield in the way that one can touch a physical asset is a philosophical, not financial, consideration.

At some point the exchange of debt for equity occurs. Debt of $200 is issued, and the proceeds are used to buy back shares. How many shares of stock are repurchased? Because shares are now selling at $5.70 each, the number of shares that the firm acquires is $200/$5.70 = 35.09. This leaves 64.91 (= 100 − 35.09) shares of stock outstanding. The market value balance sheet is now this:

DIVIDED AIRLINES Balance Sheet (After Exchange Has Taken Place)			
Physical assets	$500	Equity	$370
		(100 − 35.09 = 64.91 shares)	
Present value of tax shield	70	Debt	200
Total assets	$570	Debt plus equity	$570

Each share of stock is worth $370/64.91 = $5.70 after the exchange. Notice that the stock price does not change on the exchange date. As we mentioned, the stock price moves on the date of the announcement only. Because the shareholders participating in the exchange receive a price equal to the market price per share after the exchange, they do not care whether they exchange their stock.

This example was provided for two reasons. First, it shows that an increase in the value of the firm from debt financing leads to an increase in the price of the stock. In fact, the stockholders capture the entire $70 tax shield. Second, we wanted to provide more work with market value balance sheets.

A summary of the main results of Modigliani–Miller with corporate taxes is presented in the following boxed section:

Summary of Modigliani–Miller Propositions with Corporate Taxes

Assumptions

- Corporations are taxed at the rate t_C, on earnings after interest.
- No transaction costs.
- Individuals and corporations borrow at same rate.

Results

Proposition I: $V_L = V_U + t_C B$ (for a firm with perpetual debt)

Proposition II: $R_S = R_0 + \dfrac{B}{S}(1 - t_C)(R_0 - R_B)$

Intuition

Proposition I: Because corporations can deduct interest payments but not dividend payments, corporate leverage lowers tax payments.

Proposition II: The cost of equity rises with leverage because the risk to equity rises with leverage.

Summary and Conclusions

1. We began our discussion of the capital structure decision by arguing that the particular capital structure that maximizes the value of the firm is also the one that provides the most benefit to the stockholders.

2. In a world of no taxes, the famous Proposition I of Modigliani and Miller proves that the value of the firm is unaffected by the debt–equity ratio. In other words, a firm's capital structure is a matter of indifference in that world. The authors obtain their results by showing that either a high or a low corporate ratio of debt to equity can be offset by homemade leverage. The result hinges on the assumption that individuals can borrow at the same rate as corporations, an assumption we believe to be quite plausible.

3. MM's Proposition II in a world without taxes states that

$$R_S = R_0 + \frac{B}{S}(R_0 - R_B)$$

This implies that the expected rate of return on equity (also called the *cost of equity* or the *required return on equity*) is positively related to the firm's leverage. This makes intuitive sense because the risk of equity rises with leverage, a point illustrated by Figure 15.2.

4. Although the above work of MM is quite elegant, it does not explain the empirical findings on capital structure very well. MM imply that the capital structure decision is a matter of indifference, whereas the decision appears to be a weighty one in the real world. To achieve real-world applicability, we next considered corporate taxes.

5. In a world with corporate taxes but no bankruptcy costs, firm value is an increasing function of leverage. The formula for the value of the firm is

$$V_L = V_U + t_C B$$

Expected return on levered equity can be expressed as

$$R_S = R_0 + (1 - t_C) \times (R_0 - R_B) \times \frac{B}{S}$$

Here, value is positively related to leverage. This result implies that firms should have a capital structure almost entirely composed of debt. Because real-world firms select more moderate levels of debt, the next chapter considers modifications to the results of this chapter.

Concept Questions

1. **MM Assumptions**   List the three assumptions that lie behind the Modigliani–Miller theory in a world without taxes. Are these assumptions reasonable in the real world? Explain.

2. **MM Propositions**   In a world with no taxes, no transaction costs, and no costs of financial distress, is the following statement true, false, or uncertain? If a firm issues equity to repurchase some of its debt, the price per share of the firm's stock will rise because the shares are less risky. Explain.

3. **MM Propositions**   In a world with no taxes, no transaction costs, and no costs of financial distress, is the following statement true, false, or uncertain? Moderate borrowing will not increase the required return on a firm's equity. Explain.

4. **MM Propositions**   What is the quirk in the tax code that makes a levered firm more valuable than an otherwise identical unlevered firm?

5. **Business Risk versus Financial Risk**   Explain what is meant by business and financial risk. Suppose firm A has greater business risk than firm B. Is it true that firm A also has a higher cost of equity capital? Explain.

6. **MM Propositions**   How would you answer in the following debate?

    Q: Isn't it true that the riskiness of a firm's equity will rise if the firm increases its use of debt financing?

    A: Yes, that's the essence of MM Proposition II.

    Q: And isn't it true that, as a firm increases its use of borrowing, the likelihood of default increases, thereby increasing the risk of the firm's debt?

    A: Yes.

    Q: In other words, increased borrowing increases the risk of the equity *and* the debt?

    A: That's right.

    Q: Well, given that the firm uses only debt and equity financing, and given that the risks of both are increased by increased borrowing, does it not follow that increasing debt increases the overall risk of the firm and therefore decreases the value of the firm?

    A: ??

7. **Optimal Capital Structure**   Is there an easily identifiable debt–equity ratio that will maximize the value of a firm? Why or why not?

8. **Financial Leverage**   Why is the use of debt financing referred to as financial "leverage"?

9. **Homemade Leverage**   What is homemade leverage?

10. **Capital Structure Goal**   What is the basic goal of financial management with regard to capital structure?

Questions and Problems

BASIC
(Questions 1–16)

1. **EBIT and Leverage**   Money, Inc., has no debt outstanding and a total market value of $150,000. Earnings before interest and taxes, EBIT, are projected to be $14,000 if economic conditions are normal. If there is strong expansion in the economy, then EBIT will be 40 percent higher. If there is a recession, then EBIT will be 70 percent lower. Money is considering a $60,000 debt issue with a 5 percent interest rate. The proceeds will be used to repurchase shares of stock. There are currently 2,500 shares outstanding. Ignore taxes for this problem.
    a. Calculate earnings per share, EPS, under each of the three economic scenarios before any debt is issued. Also calculate the percentage changes in EPS when the economy expands or enters a recession.
    b. Repeat part (a) assuming that Money goes through with recapitalization. What do you observe?

2. **EBIT, Taxes, and Leverage**   Repeat parts (a) and (b) in Problem 1 assuming Money has a tax rate of 40 percent.

3. **ROE and Leverage**   Suppose the company in Problem 1 has a market-to-book ratio of 1.0.
    a. Calculate return on equity, ROE, under each of the three economic scenarios before any debt is issued. Also calculate the percentage changes in ROE for economic expansion and recession, assuming no taxes.
    b. Repeat part (a) assuming the firm goes through with the proposed recapitalization.
    c. Repeat parts (a) and (b) of this problem assuming the firm has a tax rate of 40 percent.

4. **Break-Even EBIT**   Visit Campina Grande is comparing two different capital structures, an all-equity plan (Plan I) and a levered plan (Plan II). Under Plan I, the company would have 150,000 shares of stock outstanding. Under Plan II, there would be 60,000 shares of stock outstanding and BRL 1.5 million in debt outstanding. The interest rate on the debt is 10 percent and there are no taxes.
    a. If EBIT is BRL 200,000, which plan will result in the higher EPS?
    b. If EBIT is BRL 700,000, which plan will result in the higher EPS?
    c. What are the break-even EBIT?

5. **MM and Stock Value**   In Problem 4, use MM Proposition I to find the price per share of equity under each of the two proposed plans. What is the value of the firm?

6. **Break-Even EBIT and Leverage**   Kolby Corp. is comparing two different capital structures. Plan I would result in 1,100 shares of stock and BSD 16,500 in debt. Plan II would result in 900 shares of stock and BSD 27,500 in debt. The interest rate on the debt is 10 percent.
    a. Ignoring taxes, compare both of these plans to an all-equity plan assuming that EBIT will be BSD 10,000. The all-equity plan would result in 1,400 shares of stock outstanding. Which of the three plans has the highest EPS? The lowest?
    b. In part (a) what are the break-even levels of EBIT for each plan as compared to that for an all-equity plan? Is one higher than the other? Why?
    c. Ignoring taxes, when will EPS be identical for Plans I and II?
    d. Repeat parts (a), (b), and (c) assuming that the corporate tax rate is 40 percent. Are the break-even levels of EBIT different from before? Why or why not?

7. **Leverage and Stock Value**   Ignoring taxes in Problem 6, what is the price per share of equity under Plan I? Plan II? What principle is illustrated by your answers?

8. **Homemade Leverage**   Amarasuriya Lever, Inc., a prominent consumer products firm, is debating whether or not to convert its all-equity capital structure to one that is 40 percent debt. Currently there are 2,000 shares outstanding and the price per share is LKR 70. EBIT is expected to remain at LKR 16,000 per year forever. The interest rate on new debt is 8 percent, and there are no taxes.
    a. Ms. Tirichati, a shareholder of the firm, owns 100 shares of stock. What is her cash flow under the current capital structure, assuming the firm has a dividend payout rate of 100 percent?
    b. What will Ms. Tirichati's cash flow be under the proposed capital structure of the firm? Assume that she keeps all 100 of her shares.
    c. Suppose Amarasuriya Lever does convert, but Ms. Tirichati prefers the current all-equity capital structure. Show how she could unlever her shares of stock to recreate the original capital structure.
    d. Using your answer to part (c), explain why Amarasuriya Lever's choice of capital structure is irrelevant.

9. **Homemade Leverage and WACC**   ABC Co. and XYZ Co. are identical firms in all respects except for their capital structure. ABC is all equity financed with $600,000 in stock. XYZ uses both stock and perpetual debt; its stock is worth $300,000 and the interest rate on its debt is 10 percent. Both firms expect EBIT to be $73,000. Ignore taxes.
    a. Richard owns $30,000 worth of XYZ's stock. What rate of return is he expecting?
    b. Show how Richard could generate exactly the same cash flows and rate of return by investing in ABC and using homemade leverage.
    c. What is the cost of equity for ABC? What is it for XYZ?
    d. What is the WACC for ABC? For XYZ? What principle have you illustrated?

10. **MM**   Nina Corp. uses no debt. The weighted average cost of capital is 15 percent. If the current market value of the equity is $35 million and there are no taxes, what is EBIT?

11. **MM and Taxes**   In the previous question, suppose the corporate tax rate is 40 percent. What is EBIT in this case? What is the WACC? Explain.

12. **Calculating WACC**   Staunton Industries has a debt–equity ratio of 1.5. Its WACC is 12 percent, and its cost of debt is 12 percent. The corporate tax rate is 35 percent.
    a. What is Staunton's cost of equity capital?
    b. What is Staunton's unlevered cost of equity capital?
    c. What would the cost of equity be if the debt–equity ratio were 2? What if it were 1.0? What if it were zero?

13. **Calculating WACC**   Fontaine has no debt but can borrow at 8 percent. The firm's WACC is currently 12 percent, and the tax rate is 35 percent.
    a. What is Fontaine's cost of equity?
    b. If the firm converts to 25 percent debt, what will its cost of equity be?
    c. If the firm converts to 50 percent debt, what will its cost of equity be?
    d. What is Fontaine's WACC in part (b)? In part (c)?

14. **MM and Taxes**   Bruce & Co. expects its EBIT to be BZD 95,000 every year forever. The firm can borrow at 11 percent. Bruce currently has no debt, and its cost of equity is 22 percent.

If the tax rate is 35 percent, what is the value of the firm? What will the value be if Bruce borrows BZD 60,000 and uses the proceeds to repurchase shares?

15. **MM and Taxes**   In Problem 14, what is the cost of equity after recapitalization? What is the WACC? What are the implications for the firm's capital structure decision?

16. **MM Proposition I**   Levered, Inc., and Unlevered, Inc., are identical in every way except their capital structures. Each company expects to earn €96 million before interest per year in perpetuity, with each company distributing all its earnings as dividends. Levered's perpetual debt has a market value of €275 million and costs 8 percent per year. Levered has 4.5 million shares outstanding, currently worth €100 per share. Unlevered has no debt and 10 million shares outstanding, currently worth €80 per share. Neither firm pays taxes. Is Levered's stock a better buy than Unlevered's stock?

INTERMEDIATE
(Questions 17–25)

17. **MM**   Tool Manufacturing has an expected EBIT of $35,000 in perpetuity and a tax rate of 35 percent. The firm has $70,000 in outstanding debt at an interest rate of 9 percent, and its unlevered cost of capital is 14 percent. What is the value of the firm according to MM Proposition I with taxes? Should Tool change its debt–equity ratio if the goal is to maximize the value of the firm? Explain.

18. **Firm Value**   Tamang Sukuti Udhyog expects an EBIT of NPR 40,000,000 every year forever. Tamang currently has no debt, and its cost of equity is 17 percent. The firm can borrow at 10 percent. If the corporate tax rate is 35 percent, what is the value of the firm? What will the value be if Tamang converts to 50 percent debt? To 100 percent debt?

19. **MM Proposition I with Taxes**   Makurdi Refiners is financed entirely with equity. The company is considering a loan of NGN 1 billion. The loan will be repaid in equal installments over the next two years, and it has an 8 percent interest rate. The company's tax rate is 35 percent. According to MM Proposition I with taxes, what would be the increase in the value of the company after the loan?

20. **MM Proposition I without Taxes**   Alpha Corporation and Beta Corporation are identical in every way except their capital structures. Alpha Corporation, an all-equity firm, has 5,000 shares of stock outstanding, currently worth $20 per share. Beta Corporation uses leverage in its capital structure. The market value of Beta's debt is $25,000, and its cost of debt is 12 percent. Each firm is expected to have earnings before interest of $35,000 in perpetuity. Neither firm pays taxes. Assume that every investor can borrow at 12 percent per year.
    a. What is the value of Alpha Corporation?
    b. What is the value of Beta Corporation?
    c. What is the market value of Beta Corporation's equity?
    d. How much will it cost to purchase 20 percent of each firm's equity?
    e. Assuming each firm meets its earnings estimates, what will be the dollar return to each position in part (d) over the next year?
    f. Construct an investment strategy in which an investor purchases 20 percent of Alpha's equity and replicates both the cost and dollar return of purchasing 20 percent of Beta's equity.
    g. Is Alpha's equity more or less risky than Beta's equity? Explain.

21. **Cost of Capital**   Acetate, Inc., has equity with a market value of £20 million and debt with a market value of £10 million. Treasury bills that mature in one year yield 8 percent per year, and the expected return on the market portfolio over the next year is 18 percent. The beta of Acetate's equity is .90. The firm pays no taxes.
    a. What is Acetate's debt–equity ratio?
    b. What is the firm's weighted average cost of capital?
    c. What is the cost of capital for an otherwise identical all-equity firm?

22. **Homemade Leverage**   The WHAT Company and the WHY Company are identical in every respect except that WHAT is not levered. The market value of WHY Company's 6 percent bonds is AUD 1 million. Financial information for the two firms appears here. All earnings streams are perpetuities. Neither firm pays taxes. Both firms distribute all earnings available to common stockholders immediately.

	WHAT	WHY
Projected operating income	AUD 300,000	AUD 300,000
Year-end interest on debt	—	AUD 60,000
Market value of stock	AUD 2,400,000	AUD 1,714,000
Market value of debt	—	AUD 1,000,000

a. An investor who can borrow at 6 percent per year wishes to purchase 5 percent of WHY's equity. Can he increase his dollar return by purchasing 5 percent of WHAT's equity if he borrows so that the initial net costs of the two strategies are the same?

b. Given the two investment strategies in (a), which will investors choose? When will this process cease?

23. **MM Propositions**   Locomotive Corporation is planning to repurchase part of its common stock by issuing corporate debt. As a result, the firm's debt–equity ratio is expected to rise from 40 percent to 50 percent. The firm currently has CAD 7.5 million worth of debt outstanding. The cost of this debt is 10 percent per year. Locomotive expects to have an EBIT of CAD 3.75 million per year in perpetuity. Locomotive pays no taxes.

a. What is the market value of Locomotive Corporation before and after the repurchase announcement?

b. What is the expected return on the firm's equity before the announcement of the stock repurchase plan?

c. What is the expected return on the equity of an otherwise identical all-equity firm?

d. What is the expected return on the firm's equity after the announcement of the stock repurchase plan?

24. **Stock Value and Leverage**   Lauria Manufacturing, Inc., plans to announce that it will issue MXN 2 million of perpetual debt and use the proceeds to repurchase common stock. The bonds will sell at par with a 6 percent annual coupon rate. Lauria is currently an all-equity firm worth MXN 10 million with 500,000 shares of common stock outstanding. After the sale of the bonds, Lauria will maintain the new capital structure indefinitely. Lauria currently generates annual pretax earnings of MXN 1.5 million. This level of earnings is expected to remain constant in perpetuity. Lauria is subject to a corporate tax rate of 40 percent.

a. What is the expected return on Lauria's equity before the announcement of the debt issue?

b. Construct Lauria's market value balance sheet before the announcement of the debt issue. What is the price per share of the firm's equity?

c. Construct Lauria's market value balance sheet immediately after the announcement of the debt issue.

d. What is Lauria's stock price per share immediately after the repurchase announcement?

e. How many shares will Lauria repurchase as a result of the debt issue? How many shares of common stock will remain after the repurchase?

f. Construct the market value balance sheet after the restructuring.

g. What is the required return on Lauria's equity after the restructuring?

25. **MM with Taxes**   Rajan, Inc., has a debt–equity ratio of 2.5. The firm's weighted average cost of capital is 15 percent, and its pretax cost of debt is 10 percent. Rajan is subject to a corporate tax rate of 35 percent.

a. What is Rajan's cost of equity capital?

b. What is Rajan's unlevered cost of equity capital?

c. What would Rajan's weighted average cost of capital be if the firm's debt–equity ratio were .75? What if it were 1.5?

CHALLENGE
(Questions 26–30)

26. **Weighted Average Cost of Capital**   In a world of corporate taxes only, show that the R_{WACC} can be written as $R_{WACC} = R_0 \times [1 - t_C(B/V)]$.

27. **Cost of Equity and Leverage**   Assuming a world of corporate taxes only, show that the cost of equity, R_S, is as given in the chapter by MM Proposition II with corporate taxes.

28. **Business and Financial Risk**   Assume a firm's debt is risk-free, so that the cost of debt equals the risk-free rate, R_f. Define β_A as the firm's *asset* beta—that is, the systematic risk of the firm's assets. Define β_S to be the beta of the firm's equity. Use the capital asset pricing model, CAPM, along with MM Proposition II to show that $\beta_S = \beta_A \times (1 + B/S)$, where B/S is the debt–equity ratio. Assume the tax rate is zero.

29. **Stockholder Risk**   Suppose a firm's business operations mirror movements in the economy as a whole very closely—that is, the firm's asset beta is 1.0. Use the result of previous problem to find the equity beta for this firm for debt–equity ratios of 0, 1, 5, and 20. What does this tell you about the relationship between capital structure and shareholder risk? How is the shareholders' required return on equity affected? Explain.

30. **Unlevered Cost of Equity**   Beginning with the cost of capital equation—that is:

$$R_{WACC} = \frac{S}{B + S}R_S + \frac{B}{B + S}R_B$$

show that the cost of equity capital for a levered firm can be written as follows:

$$R_S = R_0 + \frac{B}{S}(R_0 - R_B)$$

S&P Problems

www.mhhe.com/edumarketinsight

1. Locate the annual balance sheets for General Motors (GM), Merck (MRK), and Kellogg (K). For each company calculate the long-term debt–equity ratio for the prior two years. Why would these companies use such different capital structures?

2. Look up Georgia Pacific (GP) and download the annual income statements. For the most recent year, calculate the average tax rate and EBIT, and find the total interest expense. From the annual balance sheets calculate the total long-term debt (including the portion due within one year). Using the interest expense and total long-term debt, calculate the average cost of debt. Next, find the estimated beta for Georgia Pacific on the S&P Stock Report. Use this reported beta, a current T-bill rate, and the historical average market risk premium found in a previous chapter to calculate the levered cost of equity. Now calculate the unlevered cost of equity, then the unlevered EBIT. What is the unlevered value of Georgia Pacific? What is the value of the interest tax shield and the value of the levered Georgia Pacific?

Mini Case

Stephenson Real Estate Recapitalization

Stephenson Real Estate Company was founded 25 years ago by the current CEO, Robert Stephenson. The company purchases real estate, including land and buildings, and rents the property to tenants. The company has shown a profit every year for the past 18 years, and the shareholders are satisfied with the company's management. Prior to founding Stephenson Real Estate, Robert was the founder and CEO of a failed alpaca farming operation. The resulting bankruptcy made him extremely averse to debt financing. As a result, the company is entirely equity financed, with 15 million shares of common stock outstanding. The stock currently trades at $32.50 per share.

Stephenson is evaluating a plan to purchase a huge tract of land in the southeastern United States for $100 million. The land will subsequently be leased to tenant farmers. This purchase is expected to increase Stephenson's annual pretax earnings by $25 million in perpetuity. Kim Weyand, the company's new CFO, has been put in charge of the project. Kim has determined that the company's current cost of capital is 12.5 percent. She feels that the company would be more valuable if it included debt in its capital structure, so she is evaluating whether the company should issue debt to entirely finance the project. Based on some conversations with investment banks, she thinks that the company can issue bonds at par value with an 8 percent coupon rate. Based on her analysis, she also believes that a capital structure in the range of 70 percent equity/30 percent debt would be optimal. If the company goes beyond 30 percent debt, its bonds would carry a lower rating and a much higher coupon because the possibility of financial distress and the associated costs would rise sharply. Stephenson has a 40 percent corporate tax rate (state and federal).

1. If Stephenson wishes to maximize its total market value, would you recommend that it issue debt or equity to finance the land purchase? Explain.

2. Construct Stephenson's market value balance sheet before it announces the purchase.

3. Suppose Stephenson decides to issue equity to finance the purchase.
   a. What is the net present value of the project?
   b. Construct Stephenson's market value balance sheet after it announces that the firm will finance the purchase using equity. What would be the new price per share of the firm's stock? How many shares will Stephenson need to issue to finance the purchase?
   c. Construct Stephenson's market value balance sheet after the equity issue but before the purchase has been made. How many shares of common stock does Stephenson have outstanding? What is the price per share of the firm's stock?
   d. Construct Stephenson's market value balance sheet after the purchase has been made.

4. Suppose Stephenson decides to issue debt to finance the purchase.
   a. What will the market value of the Stephenson company be if the purchase is financed with debt?
   b. Construct Stephenson's market value balance sheet after both the debt issue and the land purchase. What is the price per share of the firm's stock?

5. Which method of financing maximizes the per-share stock price of Stephenson's equity?

CHAPTER

16

Capital Structure

Limits to the Use of Debt

Airlines have traditionally relied heavily on the use of financial leverage. Unfortunately, this practice can have adverse consequences when things don't work out as planned, as the airline industry has plainly (and painfully) showed. For example, on February 1, 2006, United Airlines emerged from Chapter 11 bankruptcy after spending 38 months in the bankruptcy process. Even though the company reorganized its balance sheet, it still faced problems. During 2005, United posted a loss of $741 million, and its loss in the fourth quarter of the year was its 22nd consecutive quarter with red ink.

Of course, other big airlines were still in bankruptcy. Delta Air Lines lost $3.8 billion in 2005, including $1.2 billion in the fourth quarter, and entered bankruptcy in September 2005. Northwest Airlines, also facing huge losses, filed at the same time as Delta. In both cases, it is likely to be some time before the companies emerge from the bankruptcy process. In early 2006, another five smaller airlines were also in bankruptcy.

As these situations point out, there is a limit to the financial leverage a company can undertake, and the risk of too much leverage is bankruptcy. In this chapter, we discuss the costs associated with bankruptcies and how companies attempt to avoid this process.

16.1 Costs of Financial Distress

Bankruptcy Risk or Bankruptcy Cost?

As mentioned throughout the previous chapter, debt provides tax benefits to the firm. However, debt puts pressure on the firm because interest and principal payments are obligations. If these obligations are not met, the firm may risk some sort of financial distress. The ultimate distress is *bankruptcy*, where ownership of the firm's assets is legally transferred from the stockholders to the bondholders. These debt obligations are fundamentally different from stock obligations. Although stockholders like and expect dividends, they are not legally entitled to dividends in the way bondholders are legally entitled to interest and principal payments.

We show next that bankruptcy costs, or more generally financial distress costs, tend to offset the advantages to debt. We begin by positing a simple example of bankruptcy. All taxes are ignored to focus only on the costs of debt.

455

EXAMPLE 16.1

Bankruptcy Costs The Knight Corporation plans to be in business for one more year. It forecasts a cash flow of either $100 or $50 in the coming year, each occurring with 50 percent probability. The firm has no other assets. Previously issued debt requires payments of $49 of interest and principal. The Day Corporation has identical cash flow prospects but has $60 of interest and principal obligations. The cash flows of these two firms can be represented as follows:

	Knight Corporation		Day Corporation	
	Boom Times (prob. 50%)	**Recession (prob. 50%)**	**Boom Times (prob. 50%)**	**Recession (prob. 50%)**
Cash flow	$100	$50	$100	$50
Payment of interest and principal on debt	49	49	60	50
Distribution to stockholders	$ 51	$ 1	$ 40	$ 0

For Knight Corporation in both boom times and recession and for Day Corporation in boom times, cash flow exceeds interest and principal payments. In these situations the bondholders are paid in full, and the stockholders receive any residual. However, the most interesting of the four columns involves Day Corporation in a recession. Here the bondholders are owed $60, but the firm has only $50 in cash. Because we assumed that the firm has no other assets, the bondholders cannot be satisfied in full. If bankruptcy occurs, the bondholders will receive all of the firm's cash, and the stockholders will receive nothing. Importantly, the stockholders do not have to come up with the additional $10 ($= \$60 - \$50$). Corporations have limited liability in America and most other countries, implying that bondholders cannot sue the stockholders for the extra $10.[1]

We assume that (1) both bondholders and stockholders are risk-neutral and (2) the interest rate is 10 percent. Due to this risk neutrality, cash flows to both stockholders and bondholders are to be discounted at the 10 percent rate.[2] We can evaluate the debt, the equity, and the entire firm for both Knight and Day as follows:

$$S_{KNIGHT} = \$23.64 = \frac{\$51 \times \frac{1}{2} + \$1 \times \frac{1}{2}}{1.10} \qquad S_{DAY} = \$18.18 = \frac{\$40 \times \frac{1}{2} + 0 \times \frac{1}{2}}{1.10}$$

$$B_{KNIGHT} = \$44.54 = \frac{\$49 \times \frac{1}{2} + \$49 \times \frac{1}{2}}{1.10} \qquad B_{DAY} = \$50 \quad = \frac{\$60 \times \frac{1}{2} + \$50 \times \frac{1}{2}}{1.10}$$

$$V_{KNIGHT} = \overline{\$68.18} \qquad\qquad\qquad V_{DAY} = \overline{\$68.18}$$

Note that the two firms have the same value, even though Day runs the risk of bankruptcy. Furthermore, notice that Day's bondholders are valuing the bonds with "their eyes open." Though the

---

[1] There are situations where the limited liability of corporations can be "pierced." Typically, fraud or misrepresentation must be present.

[2] Normally, we assume that investors are *averse* to risk. In that case, the cost of debt capital, R_B, is less than the cost of equity capital, R_S, which rises with leverage as shown in the previous chapter. In addition, R_B may rise when the increase in leverage allows the possibility of default.

For simplicity, we assume *risk neutrality* in this example. This means that investors are indifferent to the level of risk. Here, $R_S = R_B$ because risk-neutral investors do not demand compensation for bearing risk. In addition, neither R_S nor R_B rises with leverage. Because the interest rate is 10 percent, our assumption of risk neutrality implies that $R_S = 10\%$ as well.

Though financial economists believe that investors are risk-averse, they frequently develop examples based on risk neutrality to isolate a point unrelated to risk. This is our approach because we want to focus on bankruptcy costs—not bankruptcy risk. The same qualitative conclusions from this example can be drawn in a world of risk aversion, albeit with *much* more difficulty for the reader.

(continued)

promised payment of principal and interest is $60, the bondholders are willing to pay only $50. Hence their *promised* return or yield is:

$$\frac{\$60}{\$50} - 1 = 20\%$$

Day's debt can be viewed as a *junk bond* because the probability of default is so high. As with all junk bonds, Day's bondholders demand a high promised yield.

Day's example is not realistic because it ignores an important cash flow to be discussed next. A more realistic set of numbers might be these:

Day Corporation			
	Boom Times (prob. 50%)	**Recession (prob. 50%)**	
Earnings	$100	$50	$S_{DAY} = \$18.18 = \dfrac{\$40 \times \frac{1}{2} + 0 \times \frac{1}{2}}{1.10}$
Debt repayment	60	35	$B_{DAY} = \$43.18 = \dfrac{\$60 \times \frac{1}{2} + \$35 \times \frac{1}{2}}{1.10}$
Distribution to stockholders	$\underline{\$\ 40}$	$\underline{\$\ 0}$	$V_{DAY} = \underline{\underline{\$61.36}}$

Why do the bondholders receive only $35 in a recession? If cash flow is only $50, bondholders will be informed that they will not be paid in full. These bondholders are likely to hire lawyers to negotiate or even to sue the company. Similarly, the firm is likely to hire lawyers to defend itself. Further costs will be incurred if the case gets to a bankruptcy court. These fees are always paid before the bondholders get paid. In this example, we are assuming that bankruptcy costs total $15 (= $50 − 35).

The value of the firm is now $61.36, an amount below the $68.18 figure calculated earlier. By comparing Day's value in a world with no bankruptcy costs to Day's value in a world with these costs, we conclude the following:

The possibility of bankruptcy has a negative effect on the value of the firm. However, it is not the *risk* of bankruptcy itself that lowers value. Rather it is the costs associated with bankruptcy that lower value.

The explanation follows from our pie example. In a world without bankruptcy costs, the bondholders and the stockholders share the entire pie. However, bankruptcy costs eat up some of the pie in the real world, leaving less for the stockholders and bondholders.

Because the bondholders are aware that they would receive little in a recession, they pay the low price of $43.18. In this case, their promised return is:

$$\frac{\$60}{\$43.18} - 1 = 39.0\%$$

The bondholders are paying a fair price if they are realistic about both the probability and the cost of bankruptcy. It is the *stockholders* who bear these future bankruptcy costs. To see this, imagine that Day Corporation was originally all equity. The stockholders want the firm to issue debt with a promised payment of $60 and use the proceeds to pay a dividend. If there had been no bankruptcy costs, our results show that bondholders would pay $50 to purchase debt with a promised payment of $60. Hence, a dividend of $50 could be paid to the stockholders. However, if bankruptcy costs exist, bondholders would only pay $43.18 for the debt. In that case, only a dividend of $43.18 could be paid to the stockholders. Because the dividend is smaller with bankruptcy costs, the stockholders are hurt by these costs.

16.2 Description of Financial Distress Costs

The preceding example showed that bankruptcy costs can lower the value of the firm. In fact, the same general result holds even if a legal bankruptcy is prevented. Thus *financial distress costs* may be a better phrase than *bankruptcy costs*. It is worthwhile to describe these costs in more detail.

Direct Costs of Financial Distress: Legal and Administrative Costs of Liquidation or Reorganization

As mentioned earlier, lawyers are involved throughout all the stages before and during bankruptcy. With fees often in the hundreds of dollars an hour, these costs can add up quickly. A wag once remarked that bankruptcies are to lawyers what blood is to sharks. In addition, administrative and accounting fees can substantially add to the total bill. And if a trial takes place, we must not forget expert witnesses. Each side may hire a number of these witnesses to testify about the fairness of a proposed settlement. Their fees can easily rival those of lawyers or accountants. (However, we personally look upon these witnesses more kindly because they are frequently drawn from the ranks of finance professors.)

One of the most well-publicized bankruptcies in recent years concerned a municipality, Orange County, California, not a corporation. This bankruptcy followed large bond trading losses in the county's financial portfolio. The *Los Angeles Times* stated:

> Orange County taxpayers lost $1.69 billion, and their government, one year ago today, sank into bankruptcy. Now they are spending millions more to get out of it.
>
> Accountants pore over fiscal ledgers at $325 an hour. Lawyers toil into the night—at $385 an hour. Financial advisers from one of the nation's most prominent investment houses labor for the taxpayers at $150,000 a month. Clerks stand by the photocopy machines, running up bills that sometimes exceed $3,000.
>
> Total so far: $29 million. And it's nowhere near over.
>
> The multipronged effort to lift Orange County out of the nation's worst municipal bankruptcy has become a money-eating machine, gobbling up taxpayer funds at a rate of $2.4 million a month. That's $115,000 a day.
>
> County administrators are not alarmed.
>
> They say Orange County's bankruptcy was an epic disaster that will require equally dramatic expenditures of taxpayer cash to help it survive. While they have refused to pay several thousand dollars worth of claimed expenses—lavish dinners, big hotel bills—they have rarely questioned the sky-high hourly fees. They predict the costs could climb much higher.
>
> Indeed, participants in the county's investment pool have agreed to create a separate $50 million fund to pay the costs of doing legal battle with Wall Street.[3]

Bankruptcy costs in the private sector are often far larger than those in Orange County. For example, as of 2005, the direct costs of Enron's and WorldCom's bankruptcies were commonly estimated to exceed $1 billion and $600 million, respectively.

A number of academic studies have measured the direct costs of financial distress. Although large in absolute amount, these costs are actually small as a percentage of firm value. White, Altman, and Weiss estimate the direct costs of financial distress to be about 3 percent of the market value of the firm.[4] In a study of direct financial distress costs of

---

[3] "The High Cost of Going Bankrupt," *Los Angeles Times Orange County Edition*, December 6, 1995. Taken from Lexis/Nexis.

[4] M. J. White, "Bankruptcy Costs and the New Bankruptcy Code," *Journal of Finance* (May 1983); E. I. Altman, "A Further Empirical Investigation of the Bankruptcy Cost Question," *Journal of Finance* (September 1984); and Lawrence A. Weiss, "Bankruptcy Resolution: Direct Costs and Violation of Priority of Claims," *Journal of Financial Economics* 27 (1990).

20 railroad bankruptcies, Warner finds that net financial distress costs were, on average, 1 percent of the market value of the firm seven years before bankruptcy and were somewhat larger percentages as bankruptcy approached (for example, 2.5 percent of the market value of the firm three years before bankruptcy).[5] Lubben estimates the average cost of legal fees alone to be about 1.5 percent of total assets for bankrupt firms.[6]

Of course, few firms end up in bankruptcy. Thus, the preceding cost estimates must be multiplied by the probability of bankruptcy to yield the *expected* cost of bankruptcy. Warner states:

> Suppose, for example, that a given railroad picks a level of debt such that bankruptcy would occur on average once every 20 years (i.e., the probability of going bankrupt is 5 percent in any given year). Assume that when bankruptcy occurs, the firm would pay a lump sum penalty equal to 3 percent of its now current market value. . . .
>
> [Then] the firm's expected cost of bankruptcy is equal to fifteen one-hundredths of one percent of its now current market value.

Indirect Costs of Financial Distress

Impaired Ability to Conduct Business   Bankruptcy hampers conduct with customers and suppliers. Sales are frequently lost because of both fear of impaired service and loss of trust. For example, many loyal Chrysler customers switched to other manufacturers when Chrysler skirted insolvency in the 1970s. These buyers questioned whether parts and servicing would be available were Chrysler to fail. Sometimes the taint of impending bankruptcy is enough to drive customers away. For example, gamblers avoided Atlantis casino in Atlantic City after it became technically insolvent. Gamblers are a superstitious bunch. Many wondered, "If the casino itself cannot make money, how can I expect to make money there?" A particularly outrageous story concerned two unrelated stores both named Mitchells in New York City. When one Mitchells declared bankruptcy, customers stayed away from both stores. In time, the second store was forced to declare bankruptcy as well.

Though these costs clearly exist, it is quite difficult to measure them. Altman estimates that both direct and indirect costs of financial distress are frequently greater than 20 percent of firm value.[7] Andrade and Kaplan estimate total distress costs to be between 10 percent and 20 percent of firm value.[8] Bar-Or estimates expected future distress costs for firms that are currently healthy to be 8 to 10 percent of operating value, a number below the estimates of either Altman or Andrade and Kaplan.[9] However, unlike Bar-Or, these authors consider distress costs for firms already in distress, not expected distress costs for currently healthy firms.

Cutler and Summers examine the costs of the well-publicized Texaco bankruptcy.[10] In January 1984, Pennzoil reached what it believed to be a binding agreement to acquire

[5] J. B. Warner, "Bankruptcy Costs: Some Evidence," *Journal of Finance* (May 1977).

[6] Stephen J. Lubben, "The Direct Costs of Corporate Reorganization: An Empirical Examination of Professional Fees in Large Chapter 11 Cases," *American Bankruptcy Law Journal* (2000).

[7] E. I. Altman, *op. cit.*

[8] Gregor Andrade and Steven N. Kaplan, "How Costly Is Financial (Not Economic) Distress? Evidence from Highly Leveraged Transactions That Became Distressed," *Journal of Finance* (October 1998).

[9] Yuval Bar-Or, "An Investigation of Expected Financial Distress Costs," unpublished paper, Wharton School, University of Pennsylvania (March 2000).

[10] David M. Cutler and Lawrence H. Summers, "The Costs of Conflict Resolution and Financial Distress: Evidence from the Texaco–Pennzoil Litigation," *Rand Journal of Economics* (Summer 1988).

three-sevenths of Getty Oil. However, less than a week later, Texaco acquired all of Getty at a higher per-share price. Pennzoil then sued Getty for breach of contract. Because Texaco had previously indemnified Getty against litigation, Texaco became liable for damages.

In November 1985, the Texas State Court awarded damages of $12 billion to Pennzoil, although this amount was later reduced. As a result, Texaco filed for bankruptcy. Cutler and Summers identify nine important events over the course of the litigation. They find that Texaco's market value (stock price times number of shares outstanding) fell a cumulative $4.1 billion over these events, whereas Pennzoil rose only $682 million. Thus, Pennzoil gained about one-sixth of what Texaco lost, resulting in a net loss to the two firms of almost $3.5 billion.

What could explain this net loss? Cutler and Summers suggest that it is likely due to costs that Texaco and Pennzoil incurred from the litigation and subsequent bankruptcy. The authors argue that direct bankruptcy fees represent only a small part of these costs, estimating Texaco's aftertax legal expenses to be about $165 million. Legal costs to Pennzoil were more difficult to assess because Pennzoil's lead lawyer, Joe Jamail, stated publicly that he had no set fee. However, using a clever statistical analysis, the authors estimate his fee to be about $200 million. Thus we must search elsewhere for the bulk of the costs.

Indirect costs of financial distress may be the culprit. An affidavit by Texaco stated that, following the lawsuit, some of its suppliers were demanding cash payment. Other suppliers halted or canceled shipments of crude oil. Certain banks restricted Texaco's use of futures contracts on foreign exchange. The affidavit stressed that these constraints were reducing Texaco's ability to run its business, leading to deterioration of its financial condition. Could these sorts of indirect costs explain the $3.5 billion disparity between Texaco's drop and Pennzoil's rise in market value? Unfortunately, although it is quite likely that indirect costs play a role here, there is simply no way to obtain a decent quantitative estimate for them.

Agency Costs

When a firm has debt, conflicts of interest arise between stockholders and bondholders. Because of this, stockholders are tempted to pursue selfish strategies. These conflicts of interest, which are magnified when financial distress is incurred, impose **agency costs** on the firm. We describe three kinds of selfish strategies that stockholders use to hurt the bondholders and help themselves. These strategies are costly because they will lower the market value of the whole firm.

Selfish Investment Strategy 1:   *Incentive to Take Large Risks*   Firms near bankruptcy often take great chances because they believe that they are playing with someone else's money. To see this, imagine a levered firm considering two *mutually exclusive* projects, a low-risk one and a high-risk one. There are two equally likely outcomes, recession and boom. The firm is in such dire straits that should a recession hit, it will come near to bankruptcy with one project and actually fall into bankruptcy with the other. The cash flows for the entire firm if the low-risk project is taken can be described as follows:

Value of Entire Firm if Low-Risk Project Is Chosen						
	Probability	Value of Firm	=	Stock	+	Bonds
Recession	0.5	$100	=	$ 0	+	$100
Boom	0.5	200	=	100	+	100

If recession occurs, the value of the firm will be $100; if boom occurs, the value of the firm will be $200. The expected value of the firm is $150 (= 0.5 × $100 + 0.5 × $200).

The firm has promised to pay bondholders $100. Shareholders will obtain the difference between the total payoff and the amount paid to the bondholders. In other words, the bond-holders have the prior claim on the payoffs, and the shareholders have the residual claim.

Now suppose that the riskier project can be substituted for the low-risk project. The payoffs and probabilities are as follows:

Value of Entire Firm if High-Risk Project Is Chosen						
	Probability	Value of Firm	=	Stock	+	Bonds
Recession	0.5	$ 50	=	$ 0	+	$ 50
Boom	0.5	240	=	140	+	100

The expected value of the *firm* is $145 (= 0.5 × $50 + 0.5 × $240), which is lower than the expected value of the firm with the low-risk project. Thus the low-risk project would be accepted if the firm were all equity. However, note that the expected value of the *stock* is $70 (= 0.5 × 0 + 0.5 × $140) with the high-risk project, but only $50 (= 0.5 × 0 + 0.5 × $100) with the low-risk project. Given the firm's present levered state, stockholders will select the high-risk project, even though the high-risk project has a *lower* NPV.

The key is that relative to the low-risk project, the high-risk project increases firm value in a boom and decreases firm value in a recession. The increase in value in a boom is captured by the stockholders because the bondholders are paid in full (they receive $100) regardless of which project is accepted. Conversely, the drop in value in a recession is lost by the bondholders because they are paid in full with the low-risk project but receive only $50 with the high-risk one. The stockholders will receive nothing in a recession anyway, whether the high-risk or low-risk project is selected. Thus, financial economists argue that stockholders expropriate value from the bondholders by selecting high-risk projects.

A story, perhaps apocryphal, illustrates this idea. It seems that Federal Express was near financial collapse within a few years of its inception. The founder, Frederick Smith, took $20,000 of corporate funds to Las Vegas in despair. He won at the gaming tables, providing enough capital to allow the firm to survive. Had he lost, the banks would simply have received $20,000 less when the firm reached bankruptcy.

Selfish Investment Strategy 2:   *Incentive toward Underinvestment*   Stockholders of a firm with a significant probability of bankruptcy often find that new investment helps the bondholders at the stockholders' expense. The simplest case might be a real estate owner facing imminent bankruptcy. If he took $100,000 out of his own pocket to refurbish the building, he could increase the building's value by, say, $150,000. Though this investment has a positive net present value, he will turn it down if the increase in value cannot prevent bankruptcy. "Why," he asks, "should I use my own funds to improve the value of a building that the bank will soon repossess?"

This idea is formalized by the following simple example. Consider the firm in Table 16.1, which must decide whether to accept or reject a new project. The first two columns in the table show cash flows without the project. The firm receives cash inflows of $5,000 and $2,400 under a boom and a recession, respectively. Because the firm must pay principal and interest of $4,000, the firm will default in a recession.

Table 16.1

Example Illustrating Incentive to Underinvest

	Firm without Project		Firm with Project Costing $1,000	
	Boom	**Recession**	**Boom**	**Recession**
Firm cash flows	$5,000	$2,400	$6,700	$4,100
Bondholders' claim	4,000	2,400	4,000	4,000
Stockholders' claim	$1,000	$ 0	$2,700	$ 100

The project has positive NPV. However, much of its value is captured by bondholders. Rational managers, acting in the stockholders' interest, will reject the project.

Alternatively, as indicated in the next two columns of the table, the firm could raise equity to invest in a new project. The project brings in $1,700 in either state, which is enough to prevent bankruptcy even in a recession. Because $1,700 is much greater than the project's cost of $1,000, the project has a positive NPV at any plausible interest rate. Clearly, an all-equity firm would accept the project.

However, the project hurts the stockholders of the levered firm. To see this, imagine the old stockholders contribute the $1,000 *themselves*.[11] Assuming that a boom and a recession are equally likely, the expected value of the stockholders' interest without the project is $500 (= 0.5 × $1,000 + 0.5 × 0). The expected value with the project is $1,400 (= 0.5 × $2,700 + 0.5 × $100). The stockholders' interest rises by only $900 (= $1,400 − $500) while costing $1,000.

Why does a project with a positive NPV hurt the stockholders? The key is that the stockholders contribute the full $1,000 investment, but the stockholders and bondholders *share* the benefits. The stockholders take the entire gain if boom times occur. Conversely, the bondholders reap most of the cash flow from the project in a recession.

The discussion of selfish strategy 1 is quite similar to the discussion of selfish strategy 2. In both cases, an investment strategy for the levered firm is different from the one for the unlevered firm. Thus, leverage results in distorted investment policy. Whereas the unlevered corporation always chooses projects with positive net present value, the levered firm may deviate from this policy.

Selfish Investment Strategy 3: *Milking the Property*   Another strategy is to pay out extra dividends or other distributions in times of financial distress, leaving less in the firm for the bondholders. This is known as *milking the property*, a phrase taken from real estate. Strategies 2 and 3 are very similar. In Strategy 2, the firm chooses not to raise new equity. Strategy 3 goes one step further because equity is actually withdrawn through the dividend.

Summary of Selfish Strategies   The distortions just discussed occur only when there is a probability of bankruptcy or financial distress. Thus, these distortions *should not* affect, say, General Electric because bankruptcy is not a realistic possibility for a diversified blue-chip firm such as this. In other words, General Electric's debt will be virtually risk-free, regardless of the projects it accepts. The same argument could be made for regulated companies that are protected by state utility commissions. By contrast, small firms in risky industries, such as computers, are more likely to experience financial distress and, in turn, to be affected by such distortions.

---

[11] The same qualitative results will obtain if the $1,000 is raised from new stockholders. However, the arithmetic becomes much more difficult because we must determine how many new shares are issued.

Who pays for the cost of selfish investment strategies? We argue that it is ultimately the stockholders. Rational bondholders know that when financial distress is imminent, they cannot expect help from stockholders. Rather, stockholders are likely to choose investment strategies that reduce the value of the bonds. Bondholders protect themselves accordingly by raising the interest rate that they require on the bonds. Because the stockholders must pay these high rates, they ultimately bear the costs of selfish strategies. For firms that face these distortions, debt will be difficult and costly to obtain. These firms will have low leverage ratios.

The relationship between stockholders and bondholders is very similar to the relationship between Erroll Flynn and David Niven, good friends and movie stars in the 1930s. Niven reportedly said that the good thing about Flynn was that you knew exactly where you stood with him. When you needed his help, you could always count on him to let you down.

16.3 Can Costs of Debt Be Reduced?

As U.S. senators are prone to say, "A billion here, a billion there. Pretty soon it all adds up." Each of the costs of financial distress we have mentioned is substantial in its own right. The sum of them may well affect debt financing severely. Thus, managers have an incentive to reduce these costs. We now turn to some of their methods. However, it should be mentioned at the outset that the methods here can, at most, reduce the costs of debt. They cannot *eliminate* them entirely.

Protective Covenants

Because the stockholders must pay higher interest rates as insurance against their own selfish strategies, they frequently make agreements with bondholders in hopes of lower rates. These agreements, called **protective covenants**, are incorporated as part of the loan document (or *indenture*) between stockholders and bondholders. The covenants must be taken seriously because a broken covenant can lead to default. Protective covenants can be classified into two types: negative covenants and positive covenants.

A **negative covenant** limits or prohibits actions that the company may take. Here are some typical negative covenants:

1. Limitations are placed on the amount of dividends a company may pay.
2. The firm may not pledge any of its assets to other lenders.
3. The firm may not merge with another firm.
4. The firm may not sell or lease its major assets without approval by the lender.
5. The firm may not issue additional long-term debt.

A **positive covenant** specifies an action that the company agrees to take or a condition the company must abide by. Here are some examples:

1. The company agrees to maintain its working capital at a minimum level.
2. The company must furnish periodic financial statements to the lender.

These lists of covenants are not exhaustive. The authors have seen loan agreements with more than 30 covenants.

Smith and Warner examined public issues of debt and found that 91 percent of the bond indentures included covenants that restricted the issuance of additional debt, 23 percent

Table 16.2   **Loan Covenants**

Shareholder Action or Firm Circumstances	Covenant Type	Reason for Covenant
As firm approaches financial distress, shareholders may want firm to make high-risk investments.	Financial statement restrictions 1. Minimum working capital 2. Minimum interest coverage 3. Minimum net worth	High-risk investments transfer value from bondholders to stockholders when financial distress is a realistic possibility. Covenants reduce probability of financial distress.
Shareholders may attempt to transfer corporate assets to themselves.	Restrictions on asset disposition 1. Limit on dividends 2. Limit on sale of assets 3. Collateral and mortgages	Covenants limit the ability of shareholders to transfer assets to themselves and to *underinvest.*
Shareholders may attempt to increase risk of firm.	Restrictions on switching assets	Increased firm risk helps shareholders and hurts bondholders.
Shareholders may attempt to issue new debt of equal or greater priority.	Dilution restrictions 1. Limit on leasing 2. Limit on further borrowing	Covenants restrict *dilution of the claim of existing bondholders.*

restricted dividends, 39 percent restricted mergers, and 36 percent limited the sale of assets.[12]

Protective covenants should reduce the costs of bankruptcy, ultimately increasing the value of the firm. Thus, stockholders are likely to favor all reasonable covenants. To see this, consider three choices by stockholders to reduce bankruptcy costs:

1. *Issue no debt.* Because of the tax advantages to debt, this is a very costly way of avoiding conflicts.

2. *Issue debt with no restrictive and protective covenants.* In this case, bondholders will demand high interest rates to compensate for the unprotected status of their debt.

3. *Write protective and restrictive covenants into the loan contracts.* If the covenants are clearly written, the creditors may receive protection without large costs being imposed on the shareholders. The creditors will gladly accept a lower interest rate.

Thus, bond covenants, even if they reduce flexibility, can increase the value of the firm. They can be the lowest-cost solution to the stockholder–bondholder conflict. A list of typical bond covenants and their uses appears in Table 16.2.

Consolidation of Debt

One reason bankruptcy costs are so high is that different creditors (and their lawyers) contend with each other. This problem can be alleviated by proper arrangement of bondholders and stockholders. For example, perhaps one, or at most a few, lenders can shoulder the entire debt. Should financial distress occur, negotiating costs are minimized under this arrangement. In addition, bondholders can purchase stock as well. In this way, stockholders and debtholders are not pitted against each other because they are not separate entities. This appears to be the approach in Japan, where large banks generally take significant stock

---

[12]C. W. Smith and J. B. Warner, "On Financial Contracting: An Analysis of Bond Covenants," *Journal of Financial Economics* 7 (1979).

Figure 16.1

The Optimal Amount of Debt and the Value of the Firm

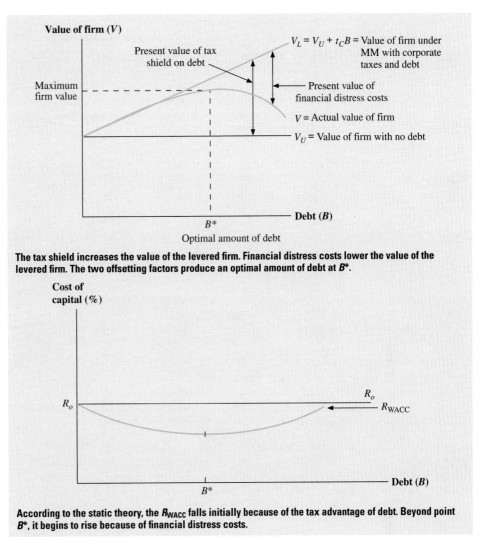

The tax shield increases the value of the levered firm. Financial distress costs lower the value of the levered firm. The two offsetting factors produce an optimal amount of debt at **B***.

According to the static theory, the R_{WACC} falls initially because of the tax advantage of debt. Beyond point **B***, it begins to rise because of financial distress costs.

positions in the firms to which they lend money.[13] Debt–equity ratios in Japan are far higher than those in the United States.

16.4 Integration of Tax Effects and Financial Distress Costs

Modigliani and Miller argue that the firm's value rises with leverage in the presence of corporate taxes. Because this relationship implies that all firms should choose maximum debt, the theory does not predict the behavior of firms in the real world. Other authors have suggested that bankruptcy and related costs reduce the value of the levered firm.

The integration of tax effects and distress costs appears in Figure 16.1. In the top graph of the figure, the diagonal straight line represents the value of the firm in a world

---

[13] Legal limitations may prevent this practice in the United States.

without bankruptcy costs. The ∩-shaped curve represents the value of the firm with these costs. This curve rises as the firm moves from all equity to a small amount of debt. Here, the present value of the distress costs is minimal because the probability of distress is so small. However, as more and more debt is added, the present value of these costs rises at an *increasing* rate. At some point, the increase in the present value of these costs from an additional dollar of debt equals the increase in the present value of the tax shield. This is the debt level maximizing the value of the firm and is represented by B^* in Figure 16.1. In other words, B^* is the optimal amount of debt. Bankruptcy costs increase faster than the tax shield beyond this point, implying a reduction in firm value from further leverage.

In the bottom graph of Figure 16.1, the weighted average cost of capital (R_{WACC}) falls as debt is added to the capital structure. After reaching B^* the weighted average cost of capital rises. The optimal amount of debt produces the lowest weighted average cost of capital.

Our discussion implies that a firm's capital structure decision involves a trade-off between the tax benefits of debt and the costs of financial distress. In fact, this approach is frequently called the *trade-off* or the *static trade-off* theory of capital structure. The implication is that there is an optimal amount of debt for any individual firm. This amount of debt becomes the firm's target debt level. Because financial distress costs cannot be expressed in a precise way, no formula has yet been developed to determine a firm's optimal debt level exactly. However, the last section of this chapter offers some rules of thumb for selecting a debt–equity ratio in the real world. Our situation reminds us of a quote of John Maynard Keynes. He reputedly said that although most historians would agree that Queen Elizabeth I was both a better monarch and an unhappier woman than Queen Victoria, no one has yet been able to express the statement in a precise and rigorous formula.

Pie Again

Now that we have considered bankruptcy costs, let's return to the pie approach of the previous chapter. The cash flows of the firm go to four different claimants: stockholders, bondholders, the government (in the form of taxes), and, during the bankruptcy process, lawyers (and others). Algebraically, we must have:

$$CF = \text{Payments to stockholders}$$
$$+$$
$$\text{Payments to bondholders}$$
$$+$$
$$\text{Payments to the government}$$
$$+$$
$$\text{Payments to lawyers (and others)}$$

It follows that the total value of the firm, V_T, equals the sum of the following four components:

$$V_T = S + B + G + L$$

where S is the value of the equity, B is the value of the bonds, G is the value of the government claims from taxes, and L stands for the value that lawyers and others receive when the firm is under financial distress. This relationship is illustrated in Figure 16.2.

Nor have we even begun to exhaust the list of financial claims to the firm's cash flows. To give an unusual example, everyone reading this book has an economic claim to the cash flows of General Motors. After all, if you are injured in an accident, you might sue

Figure 16.2

The Pie Model with Real-World Factors

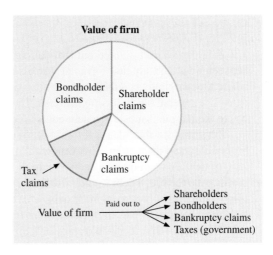

GM. Win or lose, GM will expend resources dealing with the matter. If you think this is far-fetched and unimportant, ask yourself what GM might be willing to pay every man, woman, and child in the country to have them promise that they would never sue GM, no matter what happened. The law does not permit such payments, but that does not mean that a value to all of those potential claims does not exist. We guess that it would run into the billions of dollars, and, for GM or any other company, there should be a slice of the pie labeled *LS* for "potential lawsuits."

Figure 16.2 illustrates the essence of MM's intuition. While V_T is determined by the firm's cash flows, the firm's capital structure merely cuts V_T into slices. Capital structure does *not* affect the total value, V_T.

There is, however, a difference between claims such as those of stockholders and bondholders on the one hand and those of government and potential litigants in lawsuits on the other. The first set of claims are **marketable claims**, and the second set are **nonmarketable claims**. Marketable claims can be bought and sold in financial markets, and the nonmarketable claims cannot. This distinction between marketable and nonmarketable claims is important. When stock is issued, stockholders pay cash to the firm for the privilege of later receiving dividends. Similarly, bondholders pay cash to the firm for the privilege of receiving interest in the future. However, the IRS pays nothing to the firm for the privilege of receiving taxes in the future. Similarly, lawyers pay nothing to the firm for the privilege of receiving fees from the firm in the future.

When we speak of the *value of the firm*, we are referring just to the value of the marketable claims, V_M, and not the value of nonmarketable claims, V_N. What we have shown is that capital structure does not affect the total value:

$$V_T = S + B + G + L$$
$$= V_M + V_N$$

But as we saw, the value of the marketable claims, V_M, can change with changes in the capital structure.

By the pie theory, any increase in V_M must imply an identical decrease in V_N. Rational financial managers will choose a capital structure to maximize the value of the marketable claims, V_M. Equivalently, rational managers will work to minimize the value of the nonmarketable claims, V_N. These are taxes and bankruptcy costs in the previous example, but they also include all the other nonmarketable claims such as the *LS* claim.

16.5   Signaling

The previous section pointed out that the corporate leverage decision involves a trade-off between a tax subsidy and financial distress costs. This idea was graphed in Figure 16.1, where the marginal tax subsidy of debt exceeds the distress costs of debt for low levels of debt. The reverse holds for high levels of debt. The firm's capital structure is optimized where the marginal subsidy to debt equals the marginal cost.

Let's explore this idea a little more. What is the relationship between a company's profitability and its debt level? A firm with low anticipated profits will likely take on a low level of debt. A small interest deduction is all that is needed to offset all of this firm's pretax profits. And too much debt would raise the firm's expected distress costs. A more successful firm would probably take on more debt. This firm could use the extra interest to reduce the taxes from its greater earnings. Being more financially secure, this firm would find its extra debt increasing the risk of bankruptcy only slightly. In other words, rational firms raise debt levels (and the concomitant interest payments) when profits are expected to increase.

How do investors react to an increase in debt? Rational investors are likely to infer a higher firm value from a higher debt level. Thus, these investors are likely to bid up a firm's stock price after the firm has, say, issued debt in order to buy back equity. We say that investors view debt as a *signal* of firm value.

Now we get to the incentives of managers to fool the public. Consider a firm whose level of debt is optimal. That is, the marginal tax benefit of debt exactly equals the marginal distress costs of debt. However, imagine that the firm's manager desires to increase the firm's current stock price, perhaps because he knows that many of his stockholders want to sell their stock soon. This manager might want to increase the level of debt just to make investors *think* that the firm is more valuable than it really is. If the strategy works, investors will push up the price of the stock.

This implies that firms can fool investors by taking on *some* additional leverage. Now let's ask the big question. Are there benefits to extra debt but no costs, implying that all firms will take on as much debt as possible? The answer, fortunately, is that there are costs as well. Imagine that a firm has issued extra debt just to fool the public. At some point, the market will learn that the company is not that valuable after all. At this time the stock price should actually fall *below* what it would have been had the debt never been increased. Why? Because the firm's debt level is now above the optimal level. That is, the marginal tax benefit of debt is below the marginal cost of debt. Thus if the current stockholders plan to sell, say, half of their shares now and retain the other half, an increase in debt will help them on immediate sales but likely hurt them on later ones.

Now here is the important point: We said that in a world where managers do not attempt to fool investors, valuable firms issue more debt than less valuable ones. It turns out that even when managers attempt to fool investors, the more valuable firms will still want to issue more debt than the less valuable firms. That is, while all firms will increase debt levels somewhat to fool investors, the costs of extra debt prevent the less valuable firms from issuing more debt than the more valuable firms issue. Thus, investors can still treat debt level as a signal of firm value. In other words, investors can still view an announcement of debt as a positive sign for the firm.

The foregoing is a simplified example of debt signaling, and you might argue that it is too simplified. For example, perhaps the stockholders of some firms want to sell most of their stock immediately, whereas the stockholders of other firms want to sell only a little of theirs now. It is impossible to tell here whether the firms with the most debt are the most valuable or merely the ones with the most impatient stockholders. Because other objections can be brought up as well, signaling theory is best validated by empirical evidence. And fortunately, the empirical evidence tends to support the theory.

Figure 16.3

Stock Returns at the Time of Announcements of Exchange Offers

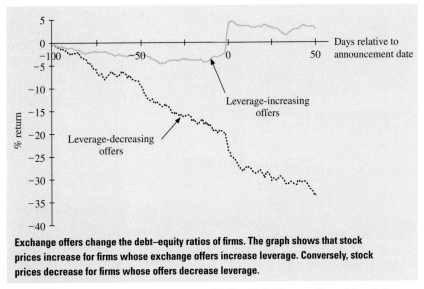

Exchange offers change the debt–equity ratios of firms. The graph shows that stock prices increase for firms whose exchange offers increase leverage. Conversely, stock prices decrease for firms whose offers decrease leverage.

SOURCE: K. Shah, "The Nature of Information Conveyed by Pure Capital Structure Changes," *Journal of Financial Economics* 36 (August 1994).

For example, consider the evidence concerning **exchange offers**. Firms often change their debt levels through exchange offers, of which there are two types. The first type of offer allows stockholders to exchange some of their stock for debt, thereby increasing leverage. The second type allows bondholders to exchange some of their debt for stock, decreasing leverage. Figure 16.3 shows the stock price behavior of firms that change their proportions of debt and equity via exchange offers. The solid line in the figure indicates that stock prices rise substantially on the date when an exchange offering increasing leverage is announced. (This date is referred to as date 0 in the figure.) Conversely, the dotted line in the figure indicates that stock price falls substantially when an offer decreasing leverage is announced.

The market infers from an increase in debt that the firm is better off, leading to a stock price rise. Conversely, the market infers the reverse from a decrease in debt, implying a stock price fall. Thus, we say that managers signal information when they change leverage.

16.6 Shirking, Perquisites, and Bad Investments: A Note on Agency Cost of Equity

A previous section introduced the static trade-off model, where a rise in debt increases both the tax shield and the costs of distress. We now extend the trade-off model by considering an important agency cost of equity. A discussion of this cost of equity is contained in a well-known quote from Adam Smith:[14]

> The directors of such [joint-stock] companies, however, being the managers of other people's money than of their own, it cannot well be expected that they should watch over it with the same anxious vigilance with which the partners in a private copartnery frequently watch over their own. Like the stewards of a rich man, they are apt to consider attention to small matters as not for their master's honor, and very easily give themselves a dispensation from having it. Negligence and profusion, therefore, must always prevail, more or less, in the management of the affairs of such a company.

[14] Adam Smith, *The Wealth of Nations* [1776], Cannon edition (New York: Modern Library, 1937), p. 700, as quoted in M. C. Jensen and W. Meckling, "Theory of the Firm: Managerial Behavior, Agency Costs, and Ownership Structure," *Journal of Financial Economics* 3 (1978).

This elegant prose can be restated in modern vocabulary. An individual will work harder for a firm if she is one of its owners than if she is just an employee. In addition, the individual will work harder if she owns a large percentage of the company than if she owns a small percentage. This idea has an important implication for capital structure, which we illustrate with the following example.

EXAMPLE 16.2

Agency Costs   Ms. Pagell is an owner–entrepreneur running a computer services firm worth $1 million. She currently owns 100 percent of the firm. Because of the need to expand, she must raise another $2 million. She can either issue $2 million of debt at 12 percent interest or issue $2 million in stock. The cash flows under the two alternatives are presented here:

		Debt Issue				Stock Issue		
Work Intensity	**Cash Flow**	**Interest**	**Cash Flow to Equity**	**Cash Flow to Ms. Pagell (100% of equity)**	**Cash Flow**	**Interest**	**Cash Flow to Equity**	**Cash Flow to Ms. Pagell ($33\frac{1}{3}$% of equity)**
6-hour days	$300,000	$240,000	$ 60,000	$ 60,000	$300,000	0	$300,000	$100,000
10-hour days	400,000	240,000	160,000	160,000	400,000	0	400,000	133,333

Like any entrepreneur, Ms. Pagell can choose the degree of intensity with which she works. In our example, she can work either a 6- or a 10-hour day. With the debt issue, the extra work brings her $100,000 (= $160,000 − $60,000) more income. However, let's assume that with a stock issue she retains only a one-third interest in the equity. Here, the extra work brings her merely $33,333 (= $133,333 − $100,000). Being human, she is likely to work harder if she issues debt. In other words, she has more incentive to *shirk* if she issues equity.

In addition, she is likely to obtain more *perquisites* (a big office, a company car, more expense account meals) if she issues stock. If she is a one-third stockholder, two-thirds of these costs are paid for by the other stockholders. If she is the sole owner, any additional perquisites reduce her equity stake alone.

Finally, she is more likely to take on capital budgeting projects with negative net present values. It might seem surprising that a manager with any equity interest at all would take on negative NPV projects: Stock price would clearly fall here. However, managerial salaries generally rise with firm size, providing managers with an incentive to accept some unprofitable projects after all the profitable ones have been taken on. That is, when an unprofitable project is accepted, the loss in stock value to a manager with only a small equity interest may be less than the increase in salary. In fact, it is our opinion that losses from accepting bad projects are far greater than losses from either shirking or excessive perquisites. Hugely unprofitable projects have bankrupted whole firms, something that even the largest expense account is unlikely to do.

Thus, as the firm issues more equity, our entrepreneur will likely increase leisure time, work-related perquisites, and unprofitable investments. These three items are called *agency costs* because managers of the firm are agents of the stockholders.[15]

This example is quite applicable to a small company considering a large stock offering. Because a manager–owner will greatly dilute his or her share of the total equity in this case,

---

[15] As previously discussed, *agency costs* are generally defined as the costs from the conflicts of interest among stockholders, bondholders, and managers.

a significant drop in work intensity or a significant increase in fringe benefits is possible. However, the example may be less applicable for a large corporation with many stockholders. For example, consider a large company such as General Motors issuing stock for the umpteenth time. The typical manager there already has such a small percentage stake in the firm that any temptation for negligence has probably been experienced before. An additional offering cannot be expected to increase this temptation.

Who bears the burden of these agency costs? Stockholders do not bear these costs as long as they invest with their eyes open. Knowing that Ms. Pagell may work shorter hours, they will pay only a low price for the stock. Thus, it is the owner who is hurt by agency costs. However, Ms. Pagell can protect herself to some extent. Just as stockholders reduce bankruptcy costs through protective covenants, an owner may allow monitoring by new stockholders. However, though proper reporting and surveillance may reduce the agency costs of equity, these techniques are unlikely to eliminate them.

It is commonly suggested that leveraged buyouts (LBOs) significantly reduce these costs of equity. In an LBO, a purchaser (usually a team of existing management) buys out the stockholders at a price above the current market. In other words, the company goes private: The stock is placed in the hands of only a few people. Because the managers now own a substantial chunk of the business, they are likely to work harder than when they were simply hired hands.[16]

Effect of Agency Costs of Equity on Debt–Equity Financing

The preceding discussion of the agency costs of equity should be viewed as an extension of the static trade-off model. That is, we stated in Section 16.4 that the change in the value of the firm when debt is substituted for equity is the difference between (1) the tax shield on debt and (2) the increase in the costs of financial distress (including the agency costs of debt). Now the change in the value of the firm is (1) the tax shield on debt plus (2) the reduction in the agency costs of equity minus (3) the increase in the costs of financial distress (including the agency costs of debt). The optimal debt–equity ratio would be higher in a world with agency costs of equity than in a world without these costs. However, because costs of financial distress are so significant, the costs of equity do not imply 100 percent debt financing.

Free Cash Flow

Any reader of murder mysteries knows that a criminal must have both motive and opportunity. The discussion thus far has been about motive. Managers with only a small ownership interest have an incentive for wasteful behavior. For example, they bear only a small portion of the costs of, say, excessive expense accounts, and they reap all of the benefits.

Now let's talk about opportunity. A manager can pad his expense account only if the firm has the cash flow to cover it. Thus, we might expect to see more wasteful activity in a firm with a capacity to generate large cash flows than in one with a capacity to generate

---

[16]One professor we know introduces his classes to LBOs by asking the students three questions:

1. How many of you have ever owned a car?
2. How many of you have ever rented a car?
3. How many of you took better care of the car you owned than the car you rented?

Just as it is human nature to take better care of your own car, it is human nature to work harder when you own more of the company.

only small cash flows. This simple idea, which is formally called the *free cash flow hypothesis*,[17] is backed by a fair amount of empirical research. For example, a frequently cited paper found that firms with high free cash flow are more likely to make bad acquisitions than firms with low free cash flow.[18]

The hypothesis has important implications for capital structure. Since dividends leave the firm, they reduce free cash flow. Thus, according to the free cash flow hypothesis, an increase in dividends should benefit the stockholders by reducing the ability of managers to pursue wasteful activities. Furthermore, since interest and principal also leave the firm, debt reduces free cash flow as well. In fact, interest and principal should have a greater effect than dividends have on the free-spending ways of managers, because bankruptcy will occur if the firm is unable to make future debt payments. By contrast, a future dividend reduction will cause fewer problems to the managers, since the firm has no legal obligation to pay dividends. Because of this, the free cash flow hypothesis argues that a shift from equity to debt will boost firm value.

In summary, the free cash flow hypothesis provides still another reason for firms to issue debt. We previously discussed the cost of equity; new equity dilutes the holdings of managers with equity interests, increasing their *motive* to waste corporate resources. We now state that debt reduces free cash flow, because the firm must make interest and principal payments. The free cash flow hypothesis implies that debt reduces the *opportunity* for managers to waste resources.

16.7   The Pecking-Order Theory

Although the trade-off theory has dominated corporate finance circles for a long time, attention is also being paid to the *pecking-order theory*.[19] To understand this view of the world, let's put ourselves in the position of a corporate financial manager whose firm needs new capital. The manager faces a choice between issuing debt and issuing equity. Previously, we evaluated the choice in terms of tax benefits, distress costs, and agency costs. However, there is one consideration that we have so far neglected: timing.

Imagine the manager saying:

> I want to issue stock in one situation only—when it is overvalued. If the stock of my firm is selling at $50 per share, but I think that it is actually worth $60, I will not issue stock. I would actually be giving new stockholders a gift because they would receive stock worth $60 but would only have to pay $50 for it. More important, my current stockholders would be upset because the firm would be receiving $50 in cash but giving away something worth $60. So if I believe that my stock is undervalued, I would issue bonds. Bonds, particularly those with little or no risk of default, are likely to be priced correctly. Their value is determined primarily by the marketwide interest rate, a variable that is publicly known.
>
> But suppose our stock is selling at $70. Now I'd like to issue stock. If I can get some fool to buy our stock for $70 while the stock is really worth only $60, I will be making $10 for our current shareholders.

Although this may strike you as a cynical view, it seems to square well with reality. Before the United States adopted insider trading and disclosure laws, many managers were

---

[17]The seminal theoretical article is Michael C. Jensen, "The Agency Costs of Free Cash Flow: Corporate Finance and Takeovers," *American Economic Review* (May 1986), pp. 323–39.

[18]L. Lang, R. Stulz, and R. Walkling, "Managerial Performance, Tobin's Q and the Gains in Tender Offers," *Journal of Financial Economics* (1989).

[19]The pecking-order theory is generally attributed to S. C. Myers, "The Capital Structure Puzzle," *Journal of Finance* 39 (July 1984).

alleged to have unfairly trumpeted their firm's prospects prior to equity issuance. And even today, managers seem more willing to issue equity after the price of their stock has risen than after their stock has fallen in price. Thus, timing might be an important motive in equity issuance, perhaps even more important than the motives in the trade-off model. After all, the firm in the preceding example *immediately* makes $10 by properly timing the issuance of equity. Ten dollars' worth of agency costs and bankruptcy cost reduction might take many years to realize.

The key that makes the example work is asymmetric information: The manager must know more about his firm's prospects than does the typical investor. If the manager's estimate of the true worth of the company is no better than the estimate of a typical investor, any attempts by the manager to time will fail. This assumption of asymmetry is quite plausible. Managers should know more about their company than do outsiders because managers work at the company every day. (One caveat is that some managers are perpetually optimistic about their firm, blurring good judgment.)

But we are not done with this example yet; we must consider the investor. Imagine an investor saying:

> I make investments carefully because they involve my hard-earned money. However, even with all the time I put into studying stocks, I can't possibly know what the managers themselves know. After all, I've got a day job to be concerned with. So I watch what the managers do. If a firm issues stock, the firm was likely overvalued beforehand. If a firm issues debt, it was likely undervalued.

When we look at both issuers and investors, we see a kind of poker game, with each side trying to outwit the other. What should the issuing firm do in this poker game? Clearly, the firm should issue debt if the equity is undervalued. But what if the equity is overvalued? Here it gets tricky because a first thought is that the firm should issue equity. However, if a firm issues equity, investors will infer that the stock is overvalued. They will not buy it until the stock has fallen enough to eliminate any advantage from equity issuance. In fact, it can be shown that only the most overvalued firms have any incentive to issue equity. Should even a moderately overpriced firm issue equity, investors will infer that this firm is among the *most* overpriced, causing the stock to fall more than is deserved. Thus, the end result is that virtually no one will issue equity.[20]

This result that essentially all firms should issue debt is clearly an extreme one. It is as extreme as (1) the Modigliani—Miller (MM) result that in a world without taxes, firms are indifferent to capital structure and (2) the MM result that in a world of corporate taxes but no financial distress costs, all firms should be 100 percent debt-financed. Perhaps we in finance have a penchant for extreme models!

But just as we can temper MM's conclusions by combining financial distress costs with corporate taxes, we can temper those of the pure pecking-order theory. This pure version assumes that timing is the financial manager's only consideration. In reality, a manager must consider taxes, financial distress costs, and agency costs as well. Thus, a firm may issue debt only up to a point. If financial distress becomes a real possibility beyond that point, the firm may issue equity instead.

Rules of the Pecking Order

The previous discussion presented the basic ideas behind the pecking-order theory. What are the practical implications of the theory for financial managers? The theory provides the following two rules for the real world.

---

[20]In the interest of simplicity, we have not presented our results in the form of a rigorous model. To the extent that a reader wants a deeper explanation, we refer him or her to S. C. Myers, "The Capital Structure Puzzle," *Journal of Finance* (July 1984).

Rule #1 Use Internal Financing   For expository purposes, we have oversimplified by comparing equity to *riskless* debt. Managers cannot use special knowledge of their firm to determine if this type of debt is mispriced because the price of riskless debt is determined solely by the marketwide interest rate. However, in reality, corporate debt has the possibility of default. Thus, just as managers tend to issue equity when they think it is overvalued, managers also tend to issue debt when they think it is overvalued.

When would managers view their debt as overvalued? Probably in the same situations when they think their equity is overvalued. For example, if the public thinks that the firm's prospects are rosy but the managers see trouble ahead, these managers would view their debt—as well as their equity—as being overvalued. That is, the public might see the debt as nearly risk-free, whereas the managers see a strong possibility of default.

Thus, investors are likely to price a debt issue with the same skepticism that they have when pricing an equity issue. The way managers get out of this box is to finance projects out of retained earnings. You don't have to worry about investor skepticism if you can avoid going to investors in the first place. So the first rule of the pecking order is this:

Use internal financing.

Rule #2 Issue Safe Securities First   Although investors fear mispricing of both debt and equity, the fear is much greater for equity. Corporate debt still has relatively little risk compared to equity because if financial distress is avoided, investors receive a fixed return. Thus, the pecking-order theory implies that if outside financing is required, debt should be issued before equity. Only when the firm's debt capacity is reached should the firm consider equity.

Of course, there are many types of debt. For example, because convertible debt is more risky than straight debt, the pecking-order theory implies that managers should issue straight debt before issuing convertibles. So, the second rule of pecking-order theory is this:

Issue the safest securities first.

Implications

A number of implications associated with the pecking-order theory are at odds with those of the trade-off theory.

1. *There is no target amount of leverage.* According to the trade-off model, each firm balances the benefits of debt, such as the tax shield, with the costs of debt, such as distress costs. The optimal amount of leverage occurs where the marginal benefit of debt equals the marginal cost of debt.

   By contrast, the pecking-order theory does not imply a target amount of leverage. Rather, each firm chooses its leverage ratio based on financing needs. Firms first fund projects out of retained earnings. This should lower the percentage of debt in the capital structure because profitable, internally funded projects raise both the book value and the market value of equity. Additional projects are funded with debt, clearly raising the debt level. However, at some point the debt capacity of the firm may be exhausted, giving way to equity issuance. Thus, the amount of leverage is determined by the happenstance of available projects. Firms do not pursue a target ratio of debt to equity.

2. *Profitable firms use less debt.* Profitable firms generate cash internally, implying less need for outside financing. Because firms desiring outside capital turn to debt first, profitable firms end up relying on less debt. The trade-off model does not have this implication. Here the greater cash flow of more profitable firms creates greater debt

capacity. These firms will use that debt capacity to capture the tax shield and the other benefits of leverage.

3. *Companies like financial slack.* The pecking-order theory is based on the difficulties of obtaining financing at a reasonable cost. A skeptical investing public thinks a stock is overvalued if the managers try to issue more of it, thereby leading to a stock price decline. Because this happens with bonds only to a lesser extent, managers rely first on bond financing. However, firms can only issue so much debt before encountering the potential costs of financial distress.

Wouldn't it be easier to have the cash ahead of time? This is the idea behind *financial slack.* Because firms know that they will have to fund profitable projects at various times in the future, they accumulate cash today. They are then not forced to go to the capital markets when a project comes up. However, there is a limit to the amount of cash a firm will want to accumulate. As mentioned earlier in this chapter, too much free cash may tempt managers to pursue wasteful activities.

16.8 Growth and the Debt–Equity Ratio

Although the trade-off between the tax shield and bankruptcy costs (as illustrated in Figure 16.1) is often viewed as the "standard model" of capital structure, it has its critics. For example, some point out that bankruptcy costs in the real world appear to be much smaller than the tax subsidy. Thus, the model implies that the optimal debt/value ratio should be near 100 percent, an implication at odds with reality.[21]

Perhaps the pecking-order theory is more consistent with the real world here. That is, firms are likely to have more equity in their capital structure than implied by the static trade-off theory because internal financing is preferred to external financing.

There is another approach that implies significant equity financing, even in a world with low bankruptcy costs. This idea, developed by Berens and Cuny,[22] argues that equity financing follows from growth. To explain the idea, we first consider an example of a no-growth firm. Next, we examine the effect of growth on firm leverage.

No Growth

Imagine a world of perfect certainty[23] where a firm has annual earnings before interest and taxes (EBIT) of $100. In addition, the firm has issued $1,000 of debt at an interest rate of 10 percent, implying interest payments of $100 per year. Here are the cash flows to the firm:

	Date			
	1	**2**	**3**	**4 ...**
Earnings before interest and taxes (EBIT)	$100	$100	$100	$100 ...
Interest	−100	−100	−100	−100 ...
Taxable income	$ 0	$ 0	$ 0	$ 0

---

[21] See Merton Miller's Presidential Address to the American Finance Association, reprinted as "Debt and Taxes," *Journal of Finance* (May 1977).

[22] J. L. Berens and C. L. Cuny, "Inflation, Growth and Capital Structure," *Review of Financial Studies* 8 (Winter 1995).

[23] The same qualitative results occur under uncertainty, though the mathematics is more troublesome.

The firm has issued just enough debt so that all EBIT are paid out as interest. Because interest is tax deductible, the firm pays no taxes. In this example, the equity is worthless because stockholders receive no cash flows. Since debt is worth $1,000, the firm is also valued at $1,000. Therefore the debt-to-value ratio is 100 percent (= $1,000/$1,000).

Had the firm issued less than $1,000 of debt, the corporation would have positive taxable income and, consequently, would have ended up paying some taxes. Had the firm issued more than $1,000 of debt, interest would have exceeded EBIT, causing default. Consequently, the optimal debt-to-value ratio is 100 percent.

Growth

Now imagine another firm where EBIT is also $100 at date 1 but are growing at 5 percent per year.[24] To eliminate taxes, this firm also wants to issue enough debt so that interest equals EBIT. Because EBIT are growing at 5 percent per year, interest must also grow at this rate. This is achieved by increasing debt by 5 percent per year.[25] The debt, EBIT, interest, and taxable income levels are these:

			Date		
	0	**1**	**2**	**3**	**4 . . .**
Debt	$1,000	$1,050	$1,102.50	$1,157.63 . . .	
New debt issued		50	52.50	55.13 . . .	
EBIT		$ 100	$ 105	$ 110.25	$115.76 . . .
Interest		−100	−105	−110.25	−115.76 . . .
Taxable income		$ 0	$ 0	$ 0	$ 0

Note that interest on a particular date is always 10 percent of the debt on the previous date. Debt is set so that interest is exactly equal to EBIT. As in the no-growth case, the levered firm has the maximum amount of debt at each date. Default would occur if interest payments were increased.

Because growth is 5 percent per year, the value of the firm is:[26]

$$V_{\text{Firm}} = \frac{\$100}{0.10 - 0.05} = \$2,000$$

The equity at date 0 is the difference between the value of the firm at that time, $2,000, and the debt of $1,000. Hence, equity must be equal to $1,000,[27] implying a debt-to-value ratio

---

[24] For simplicity, assume that growth is achieved without earnings retention. The same conclusions would be reached with retained earnings, though the arithmetic would become more involved. Of course, growth without earnings retention is less realistic than growth with retention.

[25] Because the firm makes no real investment, the new debt is used to buy back shares of stock.

[26] The firm can also be valued by a variant of Equation 15.5:

$$V_L = V_U + PVTS$$

$$= \frac{\$100(1 - t_C)}{0.10 - 0.05} + \frac{t_C \times \$100}{0.10 - 0.05} = \$2,000$$

Because of firm growth, both V_U and $PVTS$ are growing perpetuities.

[27] Students are often surprised that equity has value when taxable income is zero. Actually, the equityholders are receiving cash flow each period. The proceeds from the new debt can be used either to pay dividends or to buy back stock.

of 50 percent ($= \$1,000/\$2,000$). Note the important difference between the no-growth and the growth example. The no-growth example has no equity; the value of the firm is simply the value of the debt. With growth, there is equity as well as debt.

We can also value the equity in another way. It may appear at first glance that the stockholders receive nothing because the EBIT are paid out as interest each year. However, the new debt issued each year can be paid as a dividend to the stockholders. Because the new debt is $50 at date 1 and grows at 5 percent per year, the value of the stockholders' interest is:

$$\frac{\$50}{0.10 - 0.05} = \$1,000$$

the same number that we obtained in the previous paragraph.

As we mentioned earlier, any further increase in debt above $1,000 at date 0 would lower the value of the firm in a world with bankruptcy costs. Thus, with growth, the optimal amount of debt is less than 100 percent. Note, however, that bankruptcy costs need not be as large as the tax subsidy. In fact, even with infinitesimally small bankruptcy costs, firm value would decline if promised interest rose above $100 in the first year. The key to this example is that *today's* interest is set equal to *today's* income. Although the introduction of future growth opportunities increases firm value, it does not increase the current level of debt needed to shield today's income from today's taxes. Because equity is the difference between firm value and debt, growth increases the value of equity.

The preceding example captures an essential feature of the real world: growth. The same conclusion is reached in a world of inflation but with no growth opportunities. Thus, the result of this section, that 100 percent debt financing is suboptimal, holds whether inflation or growth opportunities are present. Furthermore, high-growth firms should have lower debt ratios than low-growth firms. Most firms have growth opportunities and inflation has been with us for most of this and the previous centuries, so this section's example is based on realistic assumptions.[28]

16.9 Personal Taxes

So far in this chapter, we have considered corporate taxes only. Because interest on debt is tax deductible whereas dividends on stock are not deductible, we argued that the tax code gives firms an incentive to issue debt. But corporations are not the only ones paying taxes; individuals must pay taxes on both the dividends and the interest that they receive. We cannot fully understand the effect of taxes on capital structure until all taxes, both corporate and personal, are considered.

The Basics of Personal Taxes

Let's begin by examining an all-equity firm that receives $1 of pretax earnings. If the corporate tax rate is t_C, the firm pays taxes t_C, leaving itself with earnings after taxes of $1 - t_C$. Let's assume that this entire amount is distributed to the stockholders as dividends. If the

---

[28] Our example assumes a single perpetual bond with level coupon payments. Berens and Cuny (BC) point out (p. 1201) that, with a number of different bonds, a firm might be able to construct an equally optimal capital structure with a greater debt-to-value (D/V) ratio. Because both capital structures are equally optimal, a firm might choose either one.

Although the analysis with many financing instruments is more complex, a firm can still choose a low D/V with no ill effect. Thus, BC's conclusion that firms *can* employ a significant amount of equity in a world with a low level of bankruptcy costs still holds.

personal tax rate on stock dividends is t_S, the stockholders pay taxes of $(1 - t_C) \times t_S$, leaving them with $(1 - t_C) \times (1 - t_S)$ after taxes.

Alternatively, imagine that the firm is financed with debt. Here, the entire $1 of earnings will be paid out as interest because interest is deductible at the corporate level. If the personal tax rate on interest is t_B, the bondholders pay taxes of t_B, leaving them with $1 - t_B$ after taxes.

The Effect of Personal Taxes on Capital Structure

To explore the effect of personal taxes on capital structure, let's consider three questions:

1. Ignoring costs of financial distress, what is the firm's optimal capital structure if dividends and interest are taxed at the same personal rate—that is, $t_S = t_B$?

    The firm should select the capital structure that gets the most cash into hands of its investors. This is tantamount to selecting a capital structure that minimizes the total amount of taxes at both the corporate and personal levels.

    As we have said, beginning with $1 of pretax corporate earnings, stockholders receive $(1 - t_C) \times (1 - t_S)$, and bondholders receive $1 - t_B$. We can see that if $t_S = t_B$, bondholders receive more than stockholders. Thus, the firm should issue debt, not equity, in this situation. Intuitively, income is taxed twice—once at the corporate level and once at the personal level—if it is paid to stockholders. Conversely, income is taxed only at the personal level if it is paid to bondholders.

    Note that the assumption of no personal taxes, which we used in the previous chapter, is a special case of the assumption that both interest and dividends are taxed at the same rate. Without personal taxes, the stockholders receive $1 - t_C$ while the bondholders receive $1. Thus, as we stated in a previous chapter, firms should issue debt in a world without personal taxes.

2. Under what conditions will the firm be indifferent between issuing equity or debt?

    The firm will be indifferent if the cash flow to stockholders equals the cash flow to bondholders. That is, the firm is indifferent when:

$$(1 - t_C) \times (1 - t_S) = 1 - t_B \tag{16.1}$$

3. What should companies do in the real world?

    Although this is clearly an important question, it is, unfortunately, a hard one—perhaps too hard to answer definitely. Nevertheless, let's begin by working with the highest tax rates. As of 2005, the corporate tax rate was 35 percent. For investors in the highest marginal tax bracket, interest income was also taxed at 35 percent. Investors in this highest bracket faced a 15 percent tax rate on dividends.

    At these rates, the left side of Equation 16.1 becomes $(1 - 0.35) \times (1 - 0.15)$, which equals 0.55. The right side of the equation becomes $1 - 0.35$, which equals 0.65. Because any rational firm would rather get $0.65 instead of $0.55 into its investors' hands, it appears at first glance that firms should prefer debt over equity, just as we argued in the previous chapter.

    Does anything else in the real world alter this conclusion? Perhaps: Our discussion on equity income is not yet complete. Firms can repurchase shares with excess cash instead of paying a dividend. Although capital gains are also taxed at a maximum of 15 percent, the shareholder pays a capital gains tax only on the gain from sale, not on the entire proceeds from the repurchase. Thus, the *effective* tax rate on capital gains is actually lower than 15 percent. Because firms both pay dividends and repurchase shares, the effective personal tax rate on *stock distributions* must be below 15 percent.

This lower effective tax rate makes equity issuance less burdensome, but the lower rate will not induce any firm to choose stocks over bonds. For example, suppose that the effective tax rate on stock distributions is 10 percent. From every dollar of pretax corporate income, stockholders receive $(1 - 0.35) \times (1 - 0.10)$, which equals $0.59. This amount is less than the $0.65 that bondholders receive. In fact, as long as the effective tax rate on stock income is positive, bondholders will still receive more than stockholders from a dollar of pretax corporate income. And we have assumed that all bondholders face a tax rate of 0.35 on interest income. In reality, plenty of bondholders are in lower tax brackets, further tipping the scales toward bond financing.

Was there ever a time when stocks had a tax advantage over bonds? Very likely, yes. Consider the 1970s, when the marginal tax rate on interest income was as high as 70 percent. While dividends were taxed at the same rate as interest, capital gains were taxed at a much lower rate. Corporate income was taxed at 46 percent. Thus, both the effective tax rate on equity income and the corporate tax rate were well below the maximum rate on interest. Under reasonable assumptions we can make a case that stocks had the tax advantage at that time.[29]

However, given that bonds appear to have the tax advantage today, is there anything that might cause firms to issue stock rather than bonds? Yes—the same costs of financial distress we discussed earlier in the chapter. We previously said that these costs are an offset to debt's tax advantage, causing firms to employ less than 100 percent leverage. The same point applies in the presence of personal taxes. And as long as the personal tax rate on equity income is below the personal tax rate on interest, the tax advantage to debt is smaller in a world with personal taxes than in a world without personal taxes. Thus, the optimal amount of debt will be lower in a world with personal taxes than in a world without them.

16.10 How Firms Establish Capital Structure

The theories of capital structure are among the most elegant and sophisticated in the field of finance. Financial economists should (and do!) pat themselves on the back for contributions in this area. However, the practical applications of the theories are less than fully satisfying. Consider that our work on net present value produced an *exact* formula for evaluating projects. Prescriptions for capital structure under either the trade-off model or the pecking-order theory are vague by comparison. No exact formula is available for evaluating the optimal debt–equity ratio. Because of this, we turn to evidence from the real world.

The following empirical regularities are worthwhile to consider when formulating capital structure policy.

1. *Most corporations have low debt–asset ratios.* How much debt is used in the real world? The average debt ratio is never greater than 100 percent. Figure 16.4 shows the debt-to-total-value ratios of firms in different countries in recent years.

---

[29]Actually, a well-known model of capital structure argues that an equilibrium would have occurred with firms issuing both debt and equity. Investors in low-tax brackets would buy the debt and investors in high-tax brackets would buy the equity. See Merton Miller, "Debt and Taxes," *Journal of Finance* (May 1977).

Figure 16.4   **Estimated Ratios of Debt to Total Value (Accounting Value) of Nonfinancial Firms, Various Countries**

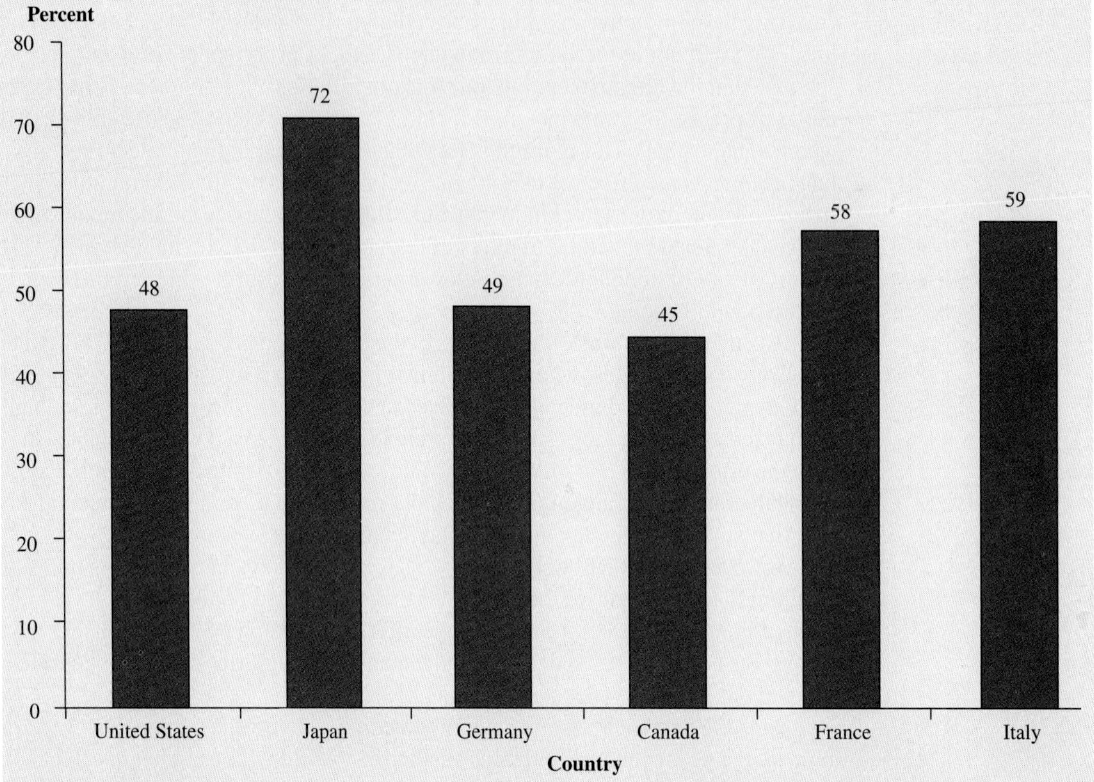

Percent

Country	Percent
United States	48
Japan	72
Germany	49
Canada	45
France	58
Italy	59

Country

Definition: Debt is short-term debt plus long-term debt. Total value is debt plus equity (in book value terms).

SOURCE: OECD financial statistics.

Differences in accounting procedures make the figures somewhat difficult to interpret. However, the debt ratios of U.S. and Canadian firms are the lowest.

Should we view these ratios as being high or low? Because academics generally see corporate tax reduction as the chief motivation for debt, we might wonder if real-world companies issue enough debt to greatly reduce, if not downright eliminate, corporate taxes. The empirical evidence suggests that this is not the case. For example, corporate taxes in the United States for 2004 were over $250 billion. Thus, it is clear that corporations do not issue debt up to the point where tax shelters are completely used up.[30] There are clearly limits to the amount of debt corporations can issue, perhaps because of the financial distress costs discussed earlier in this chapter.

2. *A number of firms use no debt.* In a fascinating study, Agrawal and Nagarajan examined approximately 100 firms on the New York Stock Exchange without long-term debt.[31] They found that these firms are averse to leverage of any kind, with

---

[30] For further insight, see John Graham, "How Big Are the Tax Benefits of Debt?" *Journal of Finance* (2000).

[31] Anup Agrawal and Nandu Nagarajan, "Corporate Capital Structure, Agency Costs, and Ownership Control: The Case of All-Equity Firms," *Journal of Finance* 45 (September 1990).

Table 16.3

Capital Structure
Ratios for Selected
U.S. Nonfinancial
Firms (Medians),
Five-Year Average

	Debt as a Percentage of the Market Value of Equity and Debt
High leverage	
Air transport	59.67
Building construction	40.39
Hotel and lodging	57.78
Paper mills	53.61
Real estate operators and lessors	49.35
Low leverage	
Biological products	4.44
Computers	3.77
Drugs	5.81
Electronics	7.09
Prepackaged software	2.27

Definition: Debt is the total of short-term debt and long-term debt.
SOURCE: Ibbotson Associates, *2005 Cost of Capital Yearbook.*

little short-term debt as well. In addition, they have levels of cash and marketable securities well above their levered counterparts. Typically, the managers of these firms have high equity ownership. Furthermore, there is significantly greater family involvement in all-equity firms than in levered firms.

Thus, a story emerges. Managers of all-equity firms are less diversified than the managers of similar, but levered, firms. Because of this, significant leverage represents an added risk that the managers of all-equity firms are loath to accept.

3. *There are differences in the capital structures of different industries.* There are significant interindustry differences in debt ratios that persist over time. As can be seen in Table 16.3, debt ratios tend to be quite low in high-growth industries with ample future investment opportunities, such as the drug and electronics industries. This is true even when the need for external financing is great. Industries with large investments in tangible assets, such as real estate, tend to have high leverage.

4. *Most corporations employ target debt–equity ratios.* Graham and Harvey asked 392 chief financial officers (CFOs) whether their firms use target debt–equity ratios, with the results being presented in Figure 16.5.[32] As can be seen, the great majority of the firms use targets, though the strictness of the targets varies across companies. Only 19 percent of the firms avoid target ratios. Results elsewhere in the paper indicate that large firms are more likely than small firms to employ these targets. The CFOs did not specify what they meant by either *flexible* or *strict* targets. However, elsewhere in the study, the respondents indicated that, by and large, they did not rebalance in response to changes in their firm's stock price, suggesting some flexibility in target ratios.

How should companies establish target debt–equity ratios? While there is no mathematical formula for establishing a target ratio, we present three important factors affecting the ratio:

---

[32] John Graham and Campbell Harvey, "The Theory and Practice of Corporate Finance," *Journal of Financial Economics* (May/June 2001).

Figure 16.5

Survey Results on the Use of Target Debt–Equity Ratios

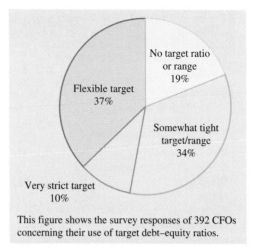

This figure shows the survey responses of 392 CFOs concerning their use of target debt–equity ratios.

SOURCE: Figure 6 of John Graham and Campbell Harvey, "The Theory and Practice of Corporate Finance," *Journal of Financial Economics* (May/June 2001).

- *Taxes:* As we pointed out earlier, firms can deduct interest for tax purposes only to the extent of their profits before interest. Thus, highly profitable firms are more likely to have larger target ratios than less profitable firms.[33]

- *Types of assets:* Financial distress is costly with or without formal bankruptcy proceedings. The costs of financial distress depend on the types of assets that the firm has. For example, if a firm has a large investment in land, buildings, and other tangible assets, it will have smaller costs of financial distress than a firm with a large investment in research and development. Research and development typically has less resale value than land; thus, most of its value disappears in financial distress. Therefore, firms with large investments in tangible assets are likely to have higher target debt–equity ratios than firms with large investments in research and development.

- *Uncertainty of operating income:* Firms with uncertain operating income have a high probability of experiencing financial distress, even without debt. Thus, these firms must finance mostly with equity. For example, pharmaceutical firms have uncertain operating income because no one can predict whether today's research will generate new, profitable drugs. Consequently, these firms issue little debt. By contrast, the operating income of firms in regulated industries, such as utilities, generally has low volatility. Relative to other industries, utilities use a great deal of debt.

One final note is in order. Because no formula supports them, the preceding points may seem too nebulous to assist financial decision making. Instead, many real-world firms simply base their capital structure decisions on industry averages. This may strike some as a cowardly approach, but it at least keeps firms from deviating far from accepted practice. After all, the existing firms in any industry are the survivors. Therefore we should pay at least some attention to their decisions.

---

[33] By contrast, the pecking-order theory argues that profitable firms will employ less debt because they can invest out of retained earnings. However, the pecking-order theory argues against the use of target ratios in the first place.

Summary and Conclusions

1. We mentioned in the last chapter that according to theory, firms should create all-debt capital structures under corporate taxation. Because firms generally employ moderate amounts of debt in the real world, the theory must have been missing something at that point. We stated in this chapter that costs of financial distress cause firms to restrain their issuance of debt. These costs are of two types: direct and indirect. Lawyers' and accountants' fees during the bankruptcy process are examples of direct costs. We mentioned four examples of indirect costs:

   Impaired ability to conduct business.
   Incentive to take on risky projects.
   Incentive toward underinvestment.
   Distribution of funds to stockholders prior to bankruptcy.

2. Because financial distress costs are substantial and the stockholders ultimately bear them, firms have an incentive to reduce costs. Protective covenants and debt consolidation are two common cost reduction techniques.

3. Because costs of financial distress can be reduced but not eliminated, firms will not finance entirely with debt. Figure 16.1 illustrates the relationship between firm value and debt. In the figure, firms select the debt–equity ratio at which firm value is maximized.

4. Signaling theory argues that profitable firms are likely to increase their leverage because the extra interest payments will offset some of the pretax profits. Rational stockholders will infer higher firm value from a higher debt level. Thus investors view debt as a signal of firm value.

5. Managers owning a small proportion of a firm's equity can be expected to work less, maintain more lavish expense accounts, and accept more pet projects with negative NPVs than managers owning a large proportion of equity. Because new issues of equity dilute a manager's percentage interest in the firm, such agency costs are likely to increase when a firm's growth is financed through new equity rather than through new debt.

6. The pecking-order theory implies that managers prefer internal to external financing. If external financing is required, managers tend to choose the safest securities, such as debt. Firms may accumulate slack to avoid external equity.

7. Berens and Cuny argue that significant equity financing can be explained by real growth and inflation, even in a world of low bankruptcy costs.

8. The results so far have ignored personal taxes. If distributions to equityholders are taxed at a lower effective personal tax rate than are interest payments, the tax advantage to debt at the corporate level is partially offset.

9. Debt–equity ratios vary across industries. We present three factors determining the target debt–equity ratio:
   a. *Taxes*: Firms with high taxable income should rely more on debt than firms with low taxable income.
   b. *Types of assets*: Firms with a high percentage of intangible assets such as research and development should have low debt. Firms with primarily tangible assets should have higher debt.
   c. *Uncertainty of operating income*: Firms with high uncertainty of operating income should rely mostly on equity.

Concept Questions

1. **Bankruptcy Costs** What are the direct and indirect costs of bankruptcy? Briefly explain each.

2. **Stockholder Incentives** Do you agree or disagree with the following statement? A firm's stockholders will never want the firm to invest in projects with negative net present values. Why?

3. **Capital Structure Decisions** Due to large losses incurred in the past several years, a firm has $1 billion in tax loss carryforwards. This means that the next $1 billion of the firm's income will be free from corporate income taxes. Security analysts estimate that it will take many years for the firm to generate $1 billion in earnings. The firm has a moderate amount of debt in its

capital structure. The firm's CEO is deciding whether to issue debt or equity to raise the funds needed to finance an upcoming project. Which method of financing would you recommend? Why?

4. **Cost of Debt**   What steps can stockholders take to reduce the costs of debt?

5. **M&M and Bankruptcy Costs**   How does the existence of financial distress costs and agency costs affect Modigliani and Miller's theory in a world where corporations pay taxes?

6. **Agency Costs of Equity**   What are the sources of agency costs of equity?

7. **Observed Capital Structures**   Refer to the observed capital structures given in Table 16.3 of the text. What do you notice about the types of industries with respect to their average debt–equity ratios? Are certain types of industries more likely to be highly leveraged than others? What are some possible reasons for this observed segmentation? Do the operating results and tax history of the firms play a role? How about their future earnings prospects? Explain.

8. **Bankruptcy and Corporate Ethics**   As mentioned in the text, some firms have filed for bankruptcy because of actual or likely litigation-related losses. Is this a proper use of the bankruptcy process?

9. **Bankruptcy and Corporate Ethics**   Firms sometimes use the threat of a bankruptcy filing to force creditors to renegotiate terms. Critics argue that in such cases the firm is using bankruptcy laws "as a sword rather than a shield." Is this an ethical tactic?

10. **Bankruptcy and Corporate Ethics**   Continental Airlines once filed for bankruptcy, at least in part, as a means of reducing labor costs. Whether this move was ethical or proper was hotly debated. Give both sides of the argument.

Questions and Problems

BASIC
(Questions 1–5)

1. **Firm Value**   Janetta Corp. has an EBIT rate of DOP 750,000 per year that is expected to continue in perpetuity. The unlevered cost of equity for the company is 15 percent, and the corporate tax rate is 35 percent. The company also has a perpetual bond issue outstanding with a market value of DOP 1.5 million.
   a. What is the value of the company?
   b. The CFO of the company informs the company president that the value of the company is DOP 3.2 million. Is the CFO correct?

2. **Agency Costs**   Tharu Annamalai is the owner, president, and primary salesperson for Annamalai Manufacturing. Because of this, the company's profits are driven by the amount of work Tharu does. If he works 40 hours each week, the company's EBIT will be FJD 500,000 per year; if he works a 50-hour week, the company's EBIT will be FJD 600,000 per year. The company is currently worth FJD 3 million. The company needs a cash infusion of FJD 2 million, and it can issue equity or issue debt with an interest rate of 9 percent. Assume there are no corporate taxes.
   a. What are the cash flows to Tharu under each scenario?
   b. Under which form of financing is Tharu likely to work harder?
   c. What specific new costs will occur with each form of financing?

3. **Capital Structure and Growth**   Edwards Construction currently has debt outstanding with a market value of GIP 80,000 and a cost of 12 percent. The company has an EBIT rate of GIP 9,600 that is expected to continue in perpetuity. Assume there are no taxes.
   a. What is the value of the company's equity? What is the debt-to-value ratio?
   b. What are the equity value and debt-to-value ratio if the company's growth rate is 5 percent?
   c. What are the equity value and debt-to-value ratio if the company's growth rate is 8 percent?

4. **Nonmarketed Claims**   Dream, Inc., has debt outstanding with a face value of XCD 4 million. The value of the firm if it were entirely financed by equity would be XCD 12 million. The company also has 250,000 shares of stock outstanding that sell at a price of XCD 35 per share. The corporate tax rate is 35 percent. What is the decrease in the value of the company due to expected bankruptcy costs?

5. Capital Structure and Nonmarketed Claims Suppose the president of the company in the previous problem stated that the company should increase the amount of debt in its capital structure because of the tax-advantaged status of its interest payments. His argument is that this action would increase the value of the company. How would you respond?

INTERMEDIATE
(Questions 6–8)

6. Costs of Financial Distress Steinberg Corporation and Dietrich Corporation are identical firms except that Dietrich is more levered. Both companies will remain in business for one more year. The companies' economists agree that the probability of the continuation of the current expansion is 80 percent for the next year, and the probability of a recession is 20 percent. If the expansion continues, each firm will generate earnings before interest and taxes (EBIT) of $2 million. If a recession occurs, each firm will generate earnings before interest and taxes (EBIT) of $800,000. Steinberg's debt obligation requires the firm to pay $750,000 at the end of the year. Dietrich's debt obligation requires the firm to pay $1 million at the end of the year. Neither firm pays taxes. Assume a discount rate of 13 percent.

    a. What are the potential payoffs in one year to Steinberg's stockholders and bondholders? What about those for Dietrich's?

    b. Steinberg's CEO recently stated that Steinberg's value should be higher than Dietrich's because the firm has less debt and therefore less bankruptcy risk. Do you agree or disagree with this statement?

7. Agency Costs Economists at European Outlook estimate that a good business environment and a bad business environment are equally likely for the coming year. The managers of Royal Dining must choose between two mutually exclusive projects. Assume that the project Royal Dining chooses will be the firm's only activity and that the firm will close one year from today. Royal Dining is obligated to make a £500 payment to bondholders at the end of the year. The projects have the same systematic risk but different volatilities. Consider the following information pertaining to the two projects:

Economy	Probability	Low-Volatility Project Payoff	High-Volatility Project Payoff
Bad	.50	£500	£100
Good	.50	700	800

    a. What is the expected value of the firm if the low-volatility project is undertaken? What if the high-volatility project is undertaken? Which of the two strategies maximizes the expected value of the firm?

    b. What is the expected value of the firm's equity if the low-volatility project is undertaken? What is it if the high-volatility project is undertaken?

    c. Which project would Royal Dining's stockholders prefer? Explain.

    d. Suppose bondholders are fully aware that stockholders might choose to maximize equity value rather than total firm value and opt for the high-volatility project. To minimize this agency cost, the firm's bondholders decide to use a bond covenant to stipulate that the bondholders can demand a higher payment if Royal Dining chooses to take on the high-volatility project. What payment to bondholders would make stockholders indifferent between the two projects?

8. Financial Distress Good Time Company is a regional chain department store. It will remain in business for one more year. The probability of a boom year is 60 percent and the probability of a recession is 40 percent. It is projected that the company will generate a total cash flow of ¥250 million in a boom year and ¥100 million in a recession. The company's required debt payment at the end of the year is ¥150 million. The market value of the company's outstanding debt is ¥108.93 million. The company pays no taxes. Assume a discount rate of 10 percent.

a. What payoff do bondholders expect to receive in the event of a recession?

b. What is the promised return on the company's debt?

c. What is the expected return on the company's debt?

CHALLENGE
(Questions 9–10)

9. **Personal Taxes, Bankruptcy Costs, and Firm Value**   When personal taxes on interest income and bankruptcy costs are considered, the general expression for the value of a levered firm in a world in which the tax rate on equity distributions equals zero is:

$$V_L = V_U + \{1 - [(1 - t_C)/(1 - t_B)]\} \times B - C(B)$$

where

V_L = The value of a levered firm.
V_U = The value of an unlevered firm.
B = The value of the firm's debt.
t_C = The tax rate on corporate income.
t_B = The personal tax rate on interest income.
$C(B)$ = The present value of the costs of financial distress.

a. In their no-tax model, what do Modigliani and Miller assume about t_C, t_B, and $C(B)$? What do these assumptions imply about a firm's optimal debt–equity ratio?

b. In their model with corporate taxes, what do Modigliani and Miller assume about t_C, t_B, and $C(B)$? What do these assumptions imply about a firm's optimal debt–equity ratio?

c. Consider an all-equity firm that is certain to be able to use interest deductions to reduce its corporate tax bill. If the corporate tax rate is 34 percent, the personal tax rate on interest income is 20 percent, and there are no costs of financial distress, by how much will the value of the firm change if it issues TWD 1 million in debt and uses the proceeds to repurchase equity?

d. Consider another all-equity firm that does not pay taxes due to large tax loss carryforwards from previous years. The personal tax rate on interest income is 20 percent, and there are no costs of financial distress. What would be the change in the value of this firm from adding TWD 1 of perpetual debt rather than TWD 1 of equity?

10. **Personal Taxes, Bankruptcy Costs, and Firm Value**   Overnight Publishing Company (OPC) has UYU 2 million in excess cash. The firm plans to use this cash either to retire all of its outstanding debt or to repurchase equity. The firm's debt is held by one institution that is willing to sell it back to OPC for UYU 2 million. The institution will not charge OPC any transaction costs. Once OPC becomes an all-equity firm, it will remain unlevered forever. If OPC does not retire the debt, the company will use the UYU 2 million in cash to buy back some of its stock on the open market. Repurchasing stock also has no transaction costs. The company will generate UYU 1,100,000 of annual earnings before interest and taxes in perpetuity regardless of its capital structure. The firm immediately pays out all earnings as dividends at the end of each year. OPC is subject to a corporate tax rate of 35 percent, and the required rate of return on the firm's unlevered equity is 20 percent. The personal tax rate on interest income is 25 percent, and there are no taxes on equity distribution. Assume there are no bankruptcy costs.

a. What is the value of OPC if it chooses to retire all of its debt and become an unlevered firm?

b. What is the value of OPC it is decides to repurchase stock instead of retiring its debt?
(*Hint*: Use the equation for the value of a levered firm with personal tax on interest income from the previous problem.)

c. Assume that expected bankruptcy costs have a present value of UYU 300,000. How does this influence OPC's decision?

Appendix 16A   Some Useful Formulas of Financial Structure

Appendix 16B   The Miller Model and the Graduated Income Tax

To access the appendixes for this chapter, please visit **www.mhhe.com/rwj**.

McKenzie Corporation's Capital Budgeting

Sam McKenzie is the founder and CEO of McKenzie Restaurants, Inc., a regional company. Sam is considering opening several new restaurants. Sally Thornton, the company's CFO, has been put in charge of the capital budgeting analysis. She has examined the potential for the company's expansion and determined that the success of the new restaurants will depend critically on the state of the economy over the next few years.

McKenzie currently has a bond issue outstanding with a face value of $25 million that is due in one year. Covenants associated with this bond issue prohibit the issuance of any additional debt. This restriction means that the expansion will be entirely financed with equity at a cost of $9 million. Sally has summarized her analysis in the following table, which shows the value of the company in each state of the economy next year, both with and without expansion:

Economic Growth	Probability	Without Expansion	With Expansion
Low	.30	$20,000,000	$24,000,000
Normal	.50	$34,000,000	$45,000,000
High	.20	$41,000,000	$53,000,000

1. What is the expected value of the company in one year, with and without expansion? Would the company's stockholders be better off with or without expansion? Why?

2. What is the expected value of the company's debt in one year, with and without the expansion?

3. One year from now, how much value creation is expected from the expansion? How much value is expected for stockholders? Bondholders?

4. If the company announces that it is not expanding, what do you think will happen to the price of its bonds? What will happen to the price of the bonds if the company does expand?

5. If the company opts not to expand, what are the implications for the company's future borrowing needs? What are the implications if the company does expand?

6. Because of the bond covenant, the expansion would have to be financed with equity. How would it affect your answer if the expansion were financed with cash on hand instead of new equity?

Valuation and Capital Budgeting for the Levered Firm

17

In late 2005, the state of Tennessee convinced Nissan to move its U.S. headquarters from California to Nashville. So why did Nissan make the move? One of the reasons was a package consisting of $197 million in state and local tax credits. When a corporation opens a major plant or considers relocation, municipalities often create a package loaded with subsidies, including tax credits, subsidized debt, educational training, road and infrastructure creation, and other incentives.

With subsidized debt, a municipality guarantees the debt, which allows the company to borrow at a much lower interest rate. If the interest rate on the debt is lower than the company's normal cost of debt, how does a company evaluate the financial benefits of this and other such subsidies? In this chapter, we illustrate how to evaluate projects using the adjusted present value and flow to equity approaches to capital budgeting to answer this question.

17.1 Adjusted Present Value Approach

The **adjusted present value (APV)** method is best described by the following formula:

$$APV = NPV + NPVF$$

In words, the value of a project to a levered firm (APV) is equal to the value of the project to an unlevered firm (NPV) plus the net present value of the financing side effects (NPVF). We can generally think of four side effects:

1. *The tax subsidy to debt*: This was discussed in Chapter 15, where we pointed out that for perpetual debt the value of the tax subsidy is $t_C B$. (t_C is the corporate tax rate, and B is the value of the debt.) The material about valuation under corporate taxes in Chapter 15 is actually an application of the APV approach.

2. *The costs of issuing new securities*: As we will discuss in detail in Chapter 20, investment bankers participate in the public issuance of corporate debt. These bankers must be compensated for their time and effort, a cost that lowers the value of the project.

3. *The costs of financial distress*: The possibility of financial distress, and bankruptcy in particular, arises with debt financing. As stated in the previous chapter, financial distress imposes costs, thereby lowering value.

4. *Subsidies to debt financing*: The interest on debt issued by state and local governments is not taxable to the investor. Because of this, the yield on tax-exempt debt is generally substantially below the yield on taxable debt. Frequently corporations can obtain financing from a municipality at the tax-exempt rate because the municipality can borrow at that rate as well. As with any subsidy, this subsidy adds value.

Although each of the preceding four side effects is important, the tax deduction to debt almost certainly has the highest dollar value in most actual situations. For this reason, the following example considers the tax subsidy but not the other three side effects.[1]

Consider a project of the P. B. Singer Co. with the following characteristics:

Cash inflows: $500,000 per year for the indefinite future.

Cash costs: 72% of sales.

Initial investment: $475,000.

$t_C = 34\%$

$R_0 = 20\%$, where R_0 is the cost of capital for a project of an all-equity firm.

If both the project and the firm are financed with only equity, the project's cash flow is as follows:

Cash inflows	$500,000
Cash costs	−360,000
Operating income	140,000
Corporate tax (34% tax rate)	−47,600
Unlevered cash flow (UCF)	$ 92,400

The distinction between present value and net present value is important for this example. The *present value* of a project is determined before the initial investment at date 0 is subtracted. The initial investment is subtracted for the calculation of *net* present value.

Given a discount rate of 20 percent, the present value of the project is:

$$\frac{\$92,400}{0.20} = \$462,000$$

The net present value (NPV) of the project—that is, the value of the project to an all-equity firm—is:

$$\$462,000 - \$475,000 = -\$13,000$$

Because the NPV is negative, the project would be rejected by an all-equity firm.

Now imagine that the firm finances the project with exactly $126,229.50 in debt, so that the remaining investment of $348,770.50 (= $475,000 − $126,229.50) is financed with equity. The net present value of the project under leverage, which we call the adjusted present value, or the APV, is:

$$\text{APV} = \text{NPV} + t_C \times B$$
$$\$29,918 = -\$13,000 + 0.34 \times \$126,229.50$$

That is, the value of the project when financed with some leverage is equal to the value of the project when financed with all equity plus the tax shield from the debt. Because this number is positive, the project should be accepted.[2]

---

[1] The Bicksler Enterprises example of Section 17.6 handles both flotation costs and interest subsidies.

[2] This example is meant to dramatize the potential importance of the tax benefits of debt. In practice, the firm will likely find the value of a project to an all-equity firm to have at least an NPV of zero.

You may be wondering why we chose such a precise amount of debt. Actually, we chose it so that the ratio of debt to the present value of the project under leverage is 0.25.[3]

In this example, debt is a fixed proportion of the present value of the project, not a fixed proportion of the initial investment of $475,000. This is consistent with the goal of a target debt-to-*market*-value ratio, which we find in the real world. For example, commercial banks typically lend to real estate developers a fixed percentage of the appraised market value of a project, not a fixed percentage of the initial investment.

17.2 Flow to Equity Approach

The **flow to equity (FTE)** approach is an alternative capital budgeting approach. The formula simply calls for discounting the cash flow from the project to the equityholders of the levered firm at the cost of equity capital, R_S. For a perpetuity this becomes:

$$\frac{\text{Cash flow from project to equityholders of the levered firm}}{R_S}$$

There are three steps to the FTE approach.

Step 1: Calculating Levered Cash Flow (LCF)[4]

Assuming an interest rate of 10 percent, the perpetual cash flow to equityholders in our P. B. Singer Co. example is:

Cash inflows	$500,000.00
Cash costs	−360,000.00
Interest (10% × $126,229.50)	−12,622.95
Income after interest	127,377.05
Corporate tax (34% tax rate)	−43,308.20
Levered cash flow (LCF)	$ 84,068.85

Alternatively, we can calculate levered cash flow (LCF) directly from unlevered cash flow (UCF). The key here is that the difference between the cash flow that equityholders receive in an unlevered firm and the cash flow that equityholders receive in a levered firm is the aftertax interest payment. (Repayment of principal does not appear in this example because the debt is perpetual.) We write this algebraically as:

$$\text{UCF} - \text{LCF} = (1 - t_C)\, R_B B$$

---

[3] That is, the present value of the project after the initial investment has been made is $504,918 (= $29,918 + $475,000). Thus, the debt-to-value ratio of the project is 0.25 (= $126,229.50/$504,918).

This level of debt can be calculated directly. Note that:

$$\text{Present value of levered project} = \text{Present value of unlevered project} + t_C \times B$$
$$V_{\text{With debt}} = \$462,000 + 0.34 \times .25 \times V_{\text{With debt}}$$

Rearranging the last line, we have:

$$V_{\text{With debt}} \times (1 - 0.34 \times 0.25) = \$462,000$$
$$V_{\text{With debt}} = \$504,918$$

Debt is 0.25 of value: $126,229.50 (= 0.25 × $504,918).

[4] We use the term *levered cash flow* (LCF) for simplicity. A more complete term would be *cash flow from the project to the equityholders of a levered firm*. Similarly, a more complete term for *unlevered cash flow* (UCF) would be *cash flow from the project to the equityholders of an unlevered firm*.

The term on the right side of this expression is the aftertax interest payment. Thus, because cash flow to the unlevered equityholders (UCF) is $92,400 and the aftertax interest payment is $8,331.15 [= .66 × .10 × $126,229.50], cash flow to the levered equityholders (LCF) is:

$$\$92,400 - \$8,331.15 = \$84,068.85$$

which is exactly the number we calculated earlier.

Step 2: Calculating R_S

The next step is to calculate the discount rate, R_S. Note that we assumed that the discount rate on unlevered equity, R_0, is .20. As we saw in an earlier chapter, the formula for R_S is:

$$R_S = R_0 + \frac{B}{S}(1 - t_C)(R_0 - R_B)$$

Note that our target debt-to-value ratio of 1/4 implies a target debt-to-equity ratio of 1/3. Applying the preceding formula to this example, we have:

$$R_S = .222 = .20 + \frac{1}{3}(.66)(.20 - .10)$$

Step 3: Valuation

The present value of the project's LCF is:

$$\frac{\text{LCF}}{R_S} = \frac{\$84,068.85}{.222} = \$378,688.50$$

Because the initial investment is $475,000 and $126,299.50 is borrowed, the firm must advance the project $348,770.50 (= $475,000 − $126,229.50) out of its own cash reserves. The *net* present value of the project is simply the difference between the present value of the project's LCF and the investment not borrowed. Thus, the NPV is:

$$\$378,688.50 - \$348,770.50 = \$29,918$$

which is identical to the result found with the APV approach.

17.3 Weighted Average Cost of Capital Method

Finally, we can value a project using the **weighted average cost of capital** (WACC) method. Although this method was discussed in earlier chapters, it is worthwhile to review it here. The WACC approach begins with the insight that projects of levered firms are simultaneously financed with both debt and equity. The cost of capital is a weighted average of the cost of debt and the cost of equity. The cost of equity is R_S. Ignoring taxes, the cost of debt is simply the borrowing rate, R_B. However, with corporate taxes, the appropriate cost of debt is $(1 - t_C)R_B$, the aftertax cost of debt.

The formula for determining the weighted average cost of capital, R_{WACC}, is:

$$R_{\text{WACC}} = \frac{S}{S + B}R_S + \frac{B}{S + B}R_B(1 - t_C)$$

The weight for equity, $S/(S + B)$, and the weight for debt, $B/(S + B)$, are target ratios. Target ratios are generally expressed in terms of market values, not accounting values. (Recall that another phrase for accounting value is *book value*.)

The formula calls for discounting the *unlevered* cash flow of the project (UCF) at the weighted average cost of capital, R_{WACC}. The net present value of the project can be written algebraically as:

$$\sum_{t=1}^{\infty} \frac{UCF_t}{(1 + R_{WACC})^t} - \text{Initial investment}$$

If the project is a perpetuity, the net present value is:

$$\frac{UCF}{R_{WACC}} - \text{Initial investment}$$

We previously stated that the target debt-to-value ratio of our project is 1/4 and the corporate tax rate is .34, implying that the weighted average cost of capital is:

$$R_{WACC} = \frac{3}{4} \times 0.222 + \frac{1}{4} \times 0.10 \times 0.66 = 0.183$$

Note that R_{WACC}, 0.183, is lower than the cost of equity capital for an all-equity firm, 0.20. This must always be the case because debt financing provides a tax subsidy that lowers the average cost of capital.

We previously determined the UCF of the project to be $92,400, implying that the present value of the project is:

$$\frac{\$92,400}{0.183} = \$504,918$$

This initial investment is $475,000, so the NPV of the project is:

$$\$504,918 - \$475,000 = \$29,918$$

Note that all three approaches yield the same value.

17.4   A Comparison of the APV, FTE, and WACC Approaches

Capital budgeting techniques in the early chapters of this text applied to all-equity firms. Capital budgeting for the levered firm could not be handled early in the book because the effects of debt on firm value were deferred until the previous two chapters. We learned there that debt increases firm value through tax benefits but decreases value through bankruptcy and related costs.

In this chapter, we provide three approaches to capital budgeting for the levered firm. The adjusted present value (APV) approach first values the project on an all-equity basis. That is, the project's aftertax cash flows under all-equity financing (called unlevered cash flows, or UCF) are placed in the numerator of the capital budgeting equation. The discount rate, assuming all-equity financing, appears in the denominator. At this point, the calculation is identical to that performed in the early chapters of this book. We then add the net present value of the debt. We point out that the net present value of the debt is likely to be the sum of four parameters: tax effects, flotation costs, bankruptcy costs, and interest subsidies.

The flow to equity (FTE) approach discounts the aftertax cash flow from a project going to the equityholders of a levered firm (LCF). LCF, which stands for levered cash flow, is the residual to equityholders after interest has been deducted. The discount rate is R_S, the cost of capital to the equityholders of a levered firm. For a firm with leverage, R_S must be greater than R_0, the cost of capital for an unlevered firm. This follows from our material in Chapter 15 showing that leverage raises the risk to the equityholders.

The last approach is the weighted average cost of capital (WACC) method. This technique calculates the project's aftertax cash flows assuming all-equity financing (UCF). The UCF is placed in the numerator of the capital budgeting equation. The denominator, R_{WACC}, is a weighted average of the cost of equity capital and the cost of debt capital. The tax advantage of debt is reflected in the denominator because the cost of debt capital is determined net of corporate tax. The numerator does not reflect debt at all.

All three approaches perform the same task: valuation in the presence of debt financing. And as illustrated by the previous example, all three provide the same valuation estimate. However, as we saw before, the approaches are markedly different in technique. Because of this, students often ask questions of the following sort: "How can this be? How can the three approaches look so different and yet give the same answer?" We believe that the best way to handle questions like these is through the following two points:

1. *APV versus WACC*: Of the three approaches, APV and WACC display the greatest similarity. After all, both approaches put the unlevered cash flow (UCF) in the numerator. However, the APV approach discounts these flows at R_0, yielding the value of the unlevered project. Adding the present value of the tax shield gives the value of the project under leverage. The WACC approach discounts UCF at R_{WACC}, which is lower than R_0.

   Thus, both approaches adjust the basic NPV formula for unlevered firms to reflect the tax benefit of leverage. The APV approach makes this adjustment directly. It simply adds in the present value of the tax shield as a separate term. The WACC approach makes the adjustment in a more subtle way. Here, the discount rate is lowered below R_0. Although we do not provide a proof in this book, it can be shown that these two adjustments always have the same quantitative effect.

2. *Entity being valued*: The FTE approach appears at first glance to be far different from the other two. For both the APV and the WACC approaches, the initial investment is subtracted out in the final step ($475,000 in our example). However, for the FTE approach, only the firm's contribution to the initial investment ($348,770.50 = $475,000 − $126,229.50) is subtracted out. This occurs because under the FTE approach only the future cash flows to the levered equityholders (LCF) are valued. By contrast, future cash flows to the unlevered equityholders (UCF) are valued in both the APV and WACC approaches. Thus, because LCFs are net of interest payments, whereas UCFs are not, the initial investment under the FTE approach is correspondingly reduced by debt financing. In this way, the FTE approach produces the same answer that the other two approaches do.

A Suggested Guideline

The net present value of our project is exactly the same under each of the three methods. In theory, this should always be the case.[5] However, one method usually provides an easier computation than another, and, in many cases, one or more of the methods are virtually impossible computationally. We first consider when it is best to use the WACC and FTE approaches.

---

[5]See I. Inselbag and H. Kaufold, "Two DCF Approaches for Valuing Companies under Alternative Financial Strategies (and How to Choose between Them)," *Journal of Applied Corporate Finance* (Spring 1997).

If the risk of a project stays constant throughout its life, it is plausible to assume that R_0 remains constant throughout the project's life. This assumption of constant risk appears to be reasonable for most real-world projects. In addition, if the debt-to-value ratio remains constant over the life of the project, both R_S and R_{WACC} will remain constant as well. Under this latter assumption, either the FTE or the WACC approach is easy to apply. However, if the debt-to-value ratio varies from year to year, both R_S and R_{WACC} vary from year to year as well. Using the FTE or the WACC approach when the denominator changes every year is computationally quite complex, and when computations become complex, the error rate rises. Thus, both the FTE and WACC approaches present difficulties when the debt-to-value *ratio* changes over time.

The APV approach is based on the *level* of debt in each future period. Consequently, when the debt level can be specified precisely for future periods, the APV approach is quite easy to use. However, when the debt level is uncertain, the APV approach becomes more problematic. For example, when the debt-to-value ratio is constant, the debt level varies with the value of the project. Because the value of the project in a future year cannot be easily forecast, the level of debt cannot be easily forecast either.

Thus, we suggest the following guideline:

Use WACC or FTE if the firm's target debt-to-value *ratio* applies to the project over its life. Use APV if the project's *level* of debt is known over the life of the project.

There are a number of situations where the APV approach is preferred. For example, in a leveraged buyout (LBO) the firm begins with a large amount of debt but rapidly pays down the debt over a number of years. Because the schedule of debt reduction in the future is known when the LBO is arranged, tax shields in every future year can be easily forecast. Thus, the APV approach is easy to use here. (An illustration of the APV approach applied to LBOs is provided in the appendix to this chapter.) By contrast, the WACC and FTE approaches are virtually impossible to apply here because the debt-to-equity value cannot be expected to be constant over time. In addition, situations involving interest subsidies and flotation costs are much easier to handle with the APV approach. (The Bicksler Enterprises example in Section 17.6 applies the APV approach to subsidies and flotation costs.) Finally, the APV approach handles the lease-versus-buy decision much more easily than does either the FTE or the WACC approach. (A full treatment of the lease-versus-buy decision appears in a later chapter.)

The preceding examples are special cases. Typical capital budgeting situations are more amenable to either the WACC or the FTE approach than to the APV approach. Financial managers generally think in terms of target debt-to-value *ratios*. If a project does better than expected, both its value and its debt capacity will likely rise. The manager will increase debt correspondingly here. Conversely, the manager would be likely to reduce debt if the value of the project were to decline unexpectedly. Of course, because financing is a time-consuming task, the ratio cannot be adjusted daily or monthly. Rather, the adjustment can be expected to occur over the long run. As mentioned before, the WACC and FTE approaches are more appropriate than is the APV approach when a firm focuses on a target debt-to-value ratio.

Because of this, we recommend that the WACC and the FTE approaches, rather than the APV approach, be used in most real-world situations. In addition, frequent discussions with business executives have convinced us that the WACC is by far the most widely used method in the real world. Thus, practitioners seem to agree with us that, outside of the special situations mentioned, the APV approach is a less important method of capital budgeting.

The Three Methods of Capital Budgeting with Leverage

1. Adjusted present value (APV) method:

$$\sum_{t=1}^{\infty} \frac{\text{UCF}_t}{(1 + R_0)^t} + \text{Additional effects of debt} - \text{Initial investment}$$

   UCF_t = The project's cash flow at date t to the equityholders of an unlevered firm.

     R_0 = Cost of capital for project in an unlevered firm.

2. Flow to equity (FTE) method:

$$\sum_{t=1}^{\infty} \frac{\text{LCF}_t}{(1 + R_S)^t} - (\text{Initial investment} - \text{Amount borrowed})$$

   LCF_t = The project's cash flow at date t to the equityholders of a levered firm.

     R_S = Cost of equity capital with leverage.

3. Weighted average cost of capital (WACC) method:

$$\sum_{t=1}^{\infty} \frac{\text{UCF}_t}{(1 + R_{\text{WACC}})^t} - \text{Initial investment}$$

   R_{WACC} = Weighted average cost of capital.

Notes

1. The middle term in the APV formula implies that the value of a project with leverage is greater than the value of the project without leverage. Because $R_{\text{WACC}} < R_0$, the WACC formula implies that the value of a project with leverage is greater than the value of the project without leverage.
2. In the FTE method, cash flow *after interest* (LCF) is used. Initial investment is reduced by *amount borrowed* as well.

Guidelines

1. Use WACC or FTE if the firm's target debt-to-value *ratio* applies to the project over its life.
2. Use APV if the project's *level* of debt is known over the life of the project.

17.5 Capital Budgeting When the Discount Rate Must Be Estimated

The previous sections of this chapter introduced APV, FTE, and WACC—the three basic approaches to valuing a levered firm. However, one important detail remains. The example in Sections 17.1 through 17.3 *assumed* a discount rate. We now want to show how this rate is determined for real-world firms with leverage, with an application to the three preceding approaches. The example in this section brings together the work in Chapters 9–12 on the discount rate for unlevered firms with that in Chapter 15 on the effect of leverage on the cost of capital.

EXAMPLE 17.1

Cost of Capital World-Wide Enterprises (WWE) is a large conglomerate thinking of entering the widget business, where it plans to finance projects with a debt-to-value ratio of 25 percent (or, alternatively, a debt-to-equity ratio of 1/3). There is currently one firm in the widget industry, American Widgets (AW). This firm is financed with 40 percent debt and 60 percent equity. The beta of AW's equity is 1.5. AW has a borrowing rate of 12 percent, and WWE expects to borrow for its widget venture at 10 percent. The corporate tax rate for both firms is 0.40, the market risk premium is 8.5 percent, and the riskless interest rate is 8 percent. What is the appropriate discount rate for WWE to use for its widget venture?

As shown in Sections 17.1–17.3, a corporation may use one of three capital budgeting approaches: APV, FTE, or WACC. The appropriate discount rates for these three approaches are R_0, R_S, and R_{WACC}, respectively. Because AW is WWE's only competitor in widgets, we look at AW's cost of capital to calculate R_0, R_S, and R_{WACC} for WWE's widget venture. The following four-step procedure will allow us to calculate all three discount rates:

1. *Determining AW's cost of equity capital*: First, we determine AW's cost of equity capital using the security market line (SML):

   AW's Cost of Equity Capital

   $$R_S = R_F + \beta \times (\bar{R}_M - R_F)$$
   $$20.75\% = 8\% + 1.5 \times 8.5\%$$

   where $\bar{R}_M$ is the expected return on the market portfolio and R_F is the risk-free rate.

2. *Determining AW's hypothetical all-equity cost of capital*: We must standardize the preceding number in some way because AW and WWE's widget ventures have different target debt-to-value ratios. The easiest approach is to calculate the hypothetical cost of equity capital for AW, assuming all-equity financing. This can be determined from MM's Proposition II under taxes:

   AW's Cost of Capital if All Equity

   $$R_S = R_0 + \frac{B}{S}(1 - t_C)(R_0 - R_B)$$

   $$20.75\% = R_0 + \frac{0.4}{0.6}(0.60)(R_0 - 12\%)$$

   By solving the equation, we find that $R_0 = 0.1825$. Of course, R_0 is less than R_S because the cost of equity capital would be less when the firm employs no leverage.

   At this point, firms in the real world generally make the assumption that the business risk of their venture is about equal to the business risk of the firms already in the business. Applying this assumption to our problem, we assert that the hypothetical discount rate of WWE's widget venture if all equity financed is also 0.1825.[6] This discount rate would be employed if WWE uses the APV approach because the APV approach calls for R_0, the project's cost of capital in a firm with no leverage.

3. *Determining R_S for WWE's widget venture*: Alternatively, WWE might use the FTE approach, where the discount rate for levered equity is determined like this:

   Cost of Equity Capital for WWE's Widget Venture

   $$R_S = R_0 + \frac{B}{S}(1 - t_C)(R_0 - R_B)$$

   (continued)

---

[6]Alternatively, a firm might assume that its venture would be somewhat riskier because it is a new entrant. Thus, the firm might select a discount rate slightly higher than 0.1825. Of course, no exact formula exists for adjusting the discount rate upward.

$$19.9\% = 18.25\% + \frac{1}{3}(0.60)(18.25\% - 10\%)$$

Note that the cost of equity capital for WWE's widget venture, 0.199, is less than the cost of equity capital for AW, 0.2075. This occurs because AW has a higher debt-to-equity ratio. (As mentioned, both firms are assumed to have the same business risk.)

4. *Determining R_{WACC} for WWE's widget venture:* Finally, WWE might use the WACC approach. Here is the appropriate calculation:

R_{WACC} for WWE's Widget Venture

$$R_{WACC} = \frac{B}{S+B}R_B(1-t_C) + \frac{S}{S+B}R_S$$

$$16.425\% = \frac{1}{4}10\%(0.60) + \frac{3}{4}19.9\%$$

The preceding example shows how the three discount rates, R_0, R_S, and R_{WACC}, are determined in the real world. These are the appropriate rates for the APV, FTE, and WACC approaches, respectively. Note that R_S for American Widgets is determined first because the cost of equity capital can be determined from the beta of the firm's stock. As discussed in an earlier chapter, beta can easily be estimated for any publicly traded firm such as AW.

17.6   APV Example

As mentioned earlier in this chapter, firms generally set a target debt-to-equity ratio, allowing the use of WACC and FTE for capital budgeting. APV does not work as well here. However, as we also mentioned earlier, APV is the preferred approach when there are side benefits and side costs to debt. Because the analysis here can be tricky, we now devote an entire section to an example where, in addition to the tax subsidy to debt, both flotation costs and interest subsidies come into play.

EXAMPLE 17.2

APV   Bicksler Enterprises is considering a $10 million project that will last five years, implying straight-line depreciation per year of $2 million. The cash revenues less cash expenses per year are $3,500,000. The corporate tax bracket is 34 percent. The risk-free rate is 10 percent, and the cost of unlevered equity is 20 percent.

The cash flow projections each year are these:

	C_0	C_1	C_2	C_3	C_4	C_5
Initial outlay	−$10,000,000					
Depreciation tax shield		0.34 × $2,000,000 = $680,000	$ 680,000	$ 680,000	$ 680,000	$ 680,000
Revenue less expenses		(1 − 0.34) × $3,500,000 = $2,310,000	$2,310,000	$2,310,000	$2,310,000	$2,310,000

(continued)

We stated before that the APV of a project is the sum of its all-equity value plus the additional effects of debt. We examine each in turn.

All-Equity Value   Assuming the project is financed with all equity, the value of the project is:

$$-\$10,000,000 + \frac{\$680,000}{0.10} \times \left[1 - \left(\frac{1}{1.10}\right)^5\right] + \frac{\$2,310,000}{0.20} \times \left[1 - \left(\frac{1}{1.20}\right)^5\right] = -\$513,951$$

     Initial cost   Depreciation tax shield   Present value of (Cash revenues − Cash expenses)

This calculation uses the techniques presented in the early chapters of this book. Notice that the depreciation tax shield is discounted at the riskless rate of 10 percent. The revenues and expenses are discounted at the higher rate of 20 percent.

An all-equity firm would clearly *reject* this project because the NPV is −$513,951. And equity flotation costs (not mentioned yet) would only make the NPV more negative. However, debt financing may add enough value to the project to justify acceptance. We consider the effects of debt next.

Additional Effects of Debt   Bicksler Enterprises can obtain a five-year, nonamortizing loan for $7,500,000 after flotation costs at the risk-free rate of 10 percent. Flotation costs are fees paid when stock or debt is issued. These fees may go to printers, lawyers, and investment bankers, among others. Bicksler Enterprises is informed that flotation costs will be 1 percent of the gross proceeds of its loan. The previous chapter indicates that debt financing alters the NPV of a typical project. We look at the effects of debt next.

Flotation Costs   Given that flotation costs are 1 percent of the gross proceeds, we have:

$$\$7,500,000 = (1 - 0.01) \times \text{Gross proceeds} = 0.99 \times \text{Gross proceeds}$$

Thus, the gross proceeds are:

$$\frac{\$7,500,000}{1 - 0.01} = \frac{\$7,500,000}{0.99} = \$7,575,758$$

This implies flotation costs of $75,758 ($= 1\% \times \$7,575,758$). To check the calculation, note that net proceeds are $7,500,000 ($= \$7,575,758 - \$75,758$). In other words, Bicksler Enterprises receives only $7,500,000. The flotation costs of $75,758 are received by intermediaries such as investment bankers.

Flotation costs are paid immediately but are deducted from taxes by amortizing on a straight-line basis over the life of the loan. The cash flows from flotation costs are as follows:

	Date 0	Date 1	Date 2	Date 3	Date 4	Date 5
Flotation costs	−$75,758					
Deduction		$\dfrac{\$75,758}{5} = \$15,152$	$15,152	$15,152	$15,152	$15,152
Tax shield from flotation costs		$0.34 \times \$15,152$ $= \$5,152$	$5,152	$5,152	$5,152	$5,152

The relevant cash flows from flotation costs are in boldface. When we discount at 10 percent, the tax shield has a net present value of:

$$\$5,152 \times A^5_{0.10} = \$19,530$$

(continued)

This implies a net cost of flotation of:

$$-\$75,758 + \$19,530 = -\$56,228$$

The net present value of the project after the flotation costs of debt but before the benefits of debt is:

$$-\$513,951 - \$56,228 = -\$570,179$$

Tax Subsidy Interest must be paid on the gross proceeds of the loan, even though intermediaries receive the flotation costs. Because the gross proceeds of the loan are \$7,575,578, annual interest is \$757,576 (= \$7,575,758 × 0.10). The interest cost after taxes is \$500,000 [= \$757,576 × (1 − 0.34)]. Because the loan is nonamortizing, the entire debt of \$7,575,758 is repaid at date 5. These terms are indicated here:

	Date 0	Date 1	Date 2	Date 3	Date 4	Date 5
Loan (gross proceeds)	**\$7,575,758**					
Interest paid		10% × \$7,575,758 = \$757,576	\$ 757,576	\$ 757,576	\$ 757,576	\$ 757,576
Interest cost after taxes		(1 − 0.34) × \$757,576 = **\$500,000**	**\$500,000**	**\$500,000**	**\$500,000**	**\$ 500,000**
Repayment of debt						**\$7,575,758**

The relevant cash flows are listed in boldface in the preceding table. They are (1) loan received, (2) annual interest cost after taxes, and (3) repayment of debt. Note that we include the *gross* proceeds of the loan as an inflow because the flotation costs have previously been subtracted.

In Chapter 15 we mentioned that the financing decision can be evaluated in terms of net present value. The net present value of the loan is simply the sum of the net present values of each of the three cash flows. This can be represented as follows:

$$\text{NPV (loan)} = + \begin{matrix}\text{Amount}\\\text{borrowed}\end{matrix} - \begin{matrix}\text{Present value}\\\text{of aftertax}\\\text{interest payments}\end{matrix} - \begin{matrix}\text{Present value}\\\text{of loan}\\\text{repayments}\end{matrix} \qquad (17.1)$$

The calculations for this example are:

$$\$976,415 = +\$7,575,758 - \frac{\$500,000}{0.10} \times \left[1 - \left(\frac{1}{1.10}\right)^5\right] - \frac{\$7,575,758}{(1.10)^5} \qquad (17.1')$$

The NPV (loan) is positive, reflecting the interest tax shield.[7]

The adjusted present value of the project with this financing is:

$$\text{APV} = \text{All-equity value} - \text{Flotation costs of debt} + \text{NPV (loan)} \qquad (17.2)$$

$$\$406,236 = -\$513,951 - \$56,228 + \$976,415 \qquad (17.2')$$

(continued)

---

[7]The NPV (loan) must be zero in a no-tax world because interest provides no tax shield there. To check this intuition, we calculate:

$$\text{No-tax case: } 0 = +\$7,575,758 - \frac{\$757,576}{0.10} \times \left[1 - \left(\frac{1}{1.10}\right)^5\right] - \frac{\$7,575,758}{(1.10)^5}$$

Though we previously saw that an all-equity firm would reject the project, a firm would *accept* the project if a $7,500,000 (net) loan could be obtained.

Because the loan just discussed was at the market rate of 10 percent, we have considered only two of the three additional effects of debt (flotation costs and tax subsidy) so far. We now examine another loan where the third effect arises.

Non–Market-Rate Financing   A number of companies are fortunate enough to obtain subsidized financing from a governmental authority. Suppose that the project of Bicksler Enterprises is deemed socially beneficial and the state of New Jersey grants the firm a $7,500,000 loan at 8 percent interest. In addition, all flotation costs are absorbed by the state. Clearly, the company will choose this loan over the one we previously calculated. Here are the cash flows from the loan:

	Date 0	Date 1	Date 2	Date 3	Date 4	Date 5
Loan received	**$7,500,000**					
Interest paid		8% × $7,500,000 = $600,000	$ 600,000	$ 600,000	$ 600,000	$ 600,000
Aftertax interest		(1 − 0.34) × $600,000 = **$396,000**	**$396,000**	**$396,000**	**$396,000**	**$ 396,000**
Repayment of debt						**$ 7,500,000**

The relevant cash flows are listed in boldface in the preceding table. Using Equation 17.1, the NPV (loan) is:

$$\$1,341,939 = +\$7,500,000 - \frac{\$396,000}{0.10} \times \left[1 - \left(\frac{1}{1.10}\right)^5\right] - \frac{\$7,500,000}{(1.10)^5} \qquad \textbf{(17.1'')}$$

Why do we discount the cash flows in Equation 17.1″ at 10 percent when the firm is borrowing at 8 percent? We discount at 10 percent because that is the fair or marketwide rate. That is, 10 percent is the rate at which the firm could borrow *without* benefit of subsidization. The net present value of the subsidized loan is larger than the net present value of the earlier loan because the firm is now borrowing at the below-market rate of 8 percent. Note that the NPV (loan) calculation in Equation 17.1″ captures both the tax effect *and* the non–market-rate effect.

The net present value of the project with subsidized debt financing is:

$$\text{APV} = \text{All-equity value} - \text{Flotation costs of debt} + \text{NPV (loan)} \qquad \textbf{(17.2)}$$

$$+\$827,988 = -\$513,951 \quad - \qquad 0 \qquad + \ \$1,341,939 \qquad \textbf{(17.2'')}$$

The preceding example illustrates the adjusted present value (APV) approach. The approach begins with the present value of a project for the all-equity firm. Next, the effects of debt are added in. The approach has much to recommend it. It is intuitively appealing because individual components are calculated separately and added together in a simple way. And, if the debt from the project can be specified precisely, the present value of the debt can be calculated precisely.

17.7 Beta and Leverage

A previous chapter provides the formula for the relationship between the beta of the common stock and leverage of the firm in a world without taxes. We reproduce this formula here:

The No-Tax Case

$$\beta_{\text{Equity}} = \beta_{\text{Asset}}\left(1 + \frac{\text{Debt}}{\text{Equity}}\right) \tag{17.3}$$

As pointed out earlier, this relationship holds under the assumption that the beta of debt is zero.

Because firms must pay corporate taxes in practice, it is worthwhile to provide the relationship in a world with corporate taxes. It can be shown that the relationship between the beta of the unlevered firm and the beta of the levered equity is this:[8]

The Corporate Tax Case

$$\beta_{\text{Equity}} = \left(1 + \frac{(1 - t_C)\text{Debt}}{\text{Equity}}\right)\beta_{\text{Unlevered firm}} \tag{17.4}$$

when (1) the corporation is taxed at the rate of t_C and (2) the debt has a zero beta.

---

[8]This result holds only if the beta of debt equals zero. To see this, note that:

$$V_U + t_C B = V_L = B + S \tag{a}$$

where:

V_U = Value of unlevered firm.

V_L = Value of levered firm.

B = Value of debt in a levered firm.

S = Value of equity in a levered firm.

As we stated in the text, the beta of the levered firm is a weighted average of the debt beta and the equity beta:

$$\frac{B}{B + S} \times \beta_B + \frac{S}{B + S} \times \beta_S$$

where β_B and β_S are the betas of the debt and the equity of the levered firm, respectively. Because $V_L = B + S$, we have:

$$\frac{B}{V_L} \times \beta_B + \frac{S}{V_L} \times \beta_S \tag{b}$$

The beta of the levered firm can *also* be expressed as a weighted average of the beta of the unlevered firm and the beta of the tax shield:

$$\frac{V_U}{V_U + t_C B} \times \beta_U + \frac{t_C B}{V_U + t_C B} \times \beta_B$$

where β_U is the beta of the unlevered firm. This follows from Equation (a). Because $V_L = V_U + t_C B$, we have:

$$\frac{V_U}{V_L} \times \beta_U + \frac{t_C B}{V_L} \times \beta_B \tag{c}$$

We can equate (b) and (c) because both represent the beta of a levered firm. Equation (a) tells us that $V_U = S + (1 - t_C) \times B$. Under the assumption that $\beta_B = 0$, equating (b) and (c) and using Equation (a) yields Equation 17.4.

The generalized formula for the levered beta (where β_B is not zero) is:

$$\beta_S = \beta_U + (1 - t_C)(\beta_U - \beta_B)\frac{B}{S}$$

and:

$$\beta_U = \frac{S}{B(1 - t_C) + S}\beta_S + \frac{B(1 - t_C)}{B(1 - t_C) + S}\beta_B$$

Because $[1 + (1 - t_C)\text{Debt/Equity}]$ must be more than 1 for a levered firm, it follows that $\beta_{\text{Unlevered firm}} < \beta_{\text{Equity}}$. The corporate tax case of Equation 17.4 is quite similar to the no-tax case of Equation 17.3 because the beta of levered equity must be greater than the beta of the unlevered firm in either case. The intuition that leverage increases the risk of equity applies in both cases.

However, notice that the two equations are not equal. It can be shown that leverage increases the equity beta less rapidly under corporate taxes. This occurs because, under taxes, leverage creates a *riskless* tax shield, thereby lowering the risk of the entire firm.

EXAMPLE 17.3

Unlevered Betas   C. F. Lee Incorporated is considering a scale-enhancing project. The market value of the firm's debt is $100 million, and the market value of the firm's equity is $200 million. The debt is considered riskless. The corporate tax rate is 34 percent. Regression analysis indicates that the beta of the firm's equity is 2. The risk-free rate is 10 percent, and the expected market premium is 8.5 percent. What would the project's discount rate be in the hypothetical case that C. F. Lee, Inc., is all-equity?

We can answer this question in two steps.

1. *Determining beta of hypothetical all-equity firm:* Rearranging Equation 17.4, we have this:

Unlevered Beta

$$\frac{\text{Equity}}{\text{Equity} + (1 - t_C) \times \text{Debt}} \times \beta_{\text{Equity}} = \beta_{\text{Unlevered firm}} \qquad (17.5)$$

$$\frac{\$200 \text{ million}}{\$200 \text{ million} + (1 - 0.34) \times \$100 \text{ million}} \times 2 = 1.50$$

2. *Determining discount rate:* We calculate the discount rate from the security market line (SML) as follows:

Discount Rate

$$R_S = R_F + \beta \times [R_M - R_F]$$
$$22.75\% = 10\% + 1.50 \times 8.5\%$$

The Project Is Not Scale Enhancing

Because the previous example assumed that the project is scale enhancing, we began with the beta of the firm's equity. If the project is not scale enhancing, we could begin with the equity betas of firms in the industry of the project. For each firm, we could calculate the hypothetical beta of the unlevered equity by Equation 17.5. The SML could then be used to determine the project's discount rate from the average of these betas.

EXAMPLE 17.4

More Unlevered Betas   The J. Lowes Corporation, which currently manufactures staples, is considering a $1 million investment in a project in the aircraft adhesives industry. The corporation estimates unlevered aftertax cash flows (UCF) of $300,000 per year into perpetuity from the project. The firm will finance the project with a debt-to-value ratio of 0.5 (or, equivalently, a debt-to-equity ratio of 1:1).

The three competitors in this new industry are currently unlevered, with betas of 1.2, 1.3, and 1.4. Assuming a risk-free rate of 5 percent, a market risk premium of 9 percent, and a corporate tax rate of 34 percent, what is the net present value of the project?

(continued)

We can answer this question in five steps.

1. *Calculating the average unlevered beta in the industry:* The average unlevered beta across all three existing competitors in the aircraft adhesives industry is:

$$\frac{1.2 + 1.3 + 1.4}{3} = 1.3$$

2. *Calculating the levered beta for J. Lowes's new project:* Assuming the same unlevered beta for this new project as for the existing competitors, we have, from Equation 17.4,

Levered Beta

$$\beta_{Equity} = \left(1 + \frac{(1 - t_C)\,\text{Debt}}{\text{Equity}}\right)\beta_{Unlevered\ firm}$$

$$2.16 = \left(1 + \frac{0.66 \times 1}{1}\right) \times 1.3$$

3. *Calculating the cost of levered equity for the new project:* We calculate the discount rate from the security market line (SML) as follows:

Discount Rate

$$R_S = R_F + \beta \times [R_M - R_F]$$
$$0.244 = 0.05 + 2.16 \times 0.09$$

4. *Calculating the WACC for the new project:* The formula for determining the weighted average cost of capital, R_{WACC}, is:

$$R_{WACC} = \frac{B}{V} R_B (1 - t_C) + \frac{S}{V} R_S$$

$$0.139 = \frac{1}{2} \times 0.05 \times 0.66 + \frac{1}{2} \times 0.244$$

5. *Determining the project's value:* Because the cash flows are perpetual, the NPV of the project is:

$$\frac{\text{Unlevered cash flows (UCF)}}{R_{WACC}} - \text{Initial investment}$$

$$\frac{\$300,000}{0.139} - \$1\ \text{million} = \$1.16\ \text{million}$$

Summary and Conclusions

Earlier chapters of this text showed how to calculate net present value for projects of all-equity firms. We pointed out in the last two chapters that the introduction of taxes and bankruptcy costs changes a firm's financing decisions. Rational corporations should employ some debt in a world of this type. Because of the benefits and costs associated with debt, the capital budgeting decision is different for levered firms than for unlevered firms. The present chapter has discussed three methods for capital budgeting by levered firms: the adjusted present value (APV), flows to equity (FTE), and weighted average cost of capital (WACC) approaches.

1. The APV formula can be written as:

$$\sum_{t=1}^{\infty} \frac{UCF_t}{(1 + R_0)^t} + \text{Additional effects of debt} - \text{Initial investment}$$

There are four additional effects of debt:

- Tax shield from debt financing.
- Flotation costs.
- Bankruptcy costs.
- Benefit of non–market-rate financing.

2. The FTE formula can be written as:

$$\sum_{t=1}^{\infty} \frac{LCF_t}{(1 + R_S)^t} - (\text{Initial investment} - \text{Amount borrowed})$$

3. The WACC formula can be written as:

$$\sum_{t=1}^{\infty} \frac{UCF_t}{(1 + R_{WACC})^t} - \text{Initial investment}$$

4. Corporations frequently follow this guideline:

- Use WACC or FTE if the firm's target debt-to-value *ratio* applies to the project over its life.
- Use APV if the project's *level* of debt is known over the life of the project.

5. The APV method is used frequently for special situations like interest subsidies, LBOs, and leases. The WACC and FTE methods are commonly used for more typical capital budgeting situations. The APV approach is a rather unimportant method for typical capital budgeting situations.

6. The beta of the equity of the firm is positively related to the leverage of the firm.

Concept Questions

1. **APV**   How is the APV of a project calculated?

2. **WACC and APV**   What is the main difference between the WACC and APV methods?

3. **FTE**   What is the main difference between the FTE approach and the other two approaches?

4. **Capital Budgeting**   You are determining whether your company should undertake a new project and have calculated the NPV of the project using the WACC method when the CFO, a former accountant, notices that you did not use the interest payments in calculating the cash flows of the project. What should you tell him? If he insists that you include the interest payments in calculating the cash flows, what method can you use?

5. **Beta and Leverage**   What are the two types of risk that are measured by a levered beta?

Questions and Problems

BASIC
(Questions 1–9)

1. **NPV and APV**   Zoso is a rental car company that is trying to determine whether to add 25 cars to its fleet. The company fully depreciates all its rental cars over five years using the straight-line method. The new cars are expected to generate TVD 120,000 per year in earnings before taxes and depreciation for five years. The company is entirely financed by equity and has a 35 percent tax rate. The required return on the company's unlevered equity is 12 percent, and the new fleet will not change the risk of the company.

   a. What is the maximum price that the company should be willing to pay for the new fleet of cars if it remains an all-equity company?

b. Suppose the company can purchase the fleet of cars for TVD 375,000. Additionally assume the company can issue TVD 250,000 of five-year, 8 percent debt to finance the project. All principal will be repaid in one balloon payment at the end of the fifth year. What is the adjusted present value (APV) of the project?

2. APV   Gemini, Inc., an all-equity firm, is considering a GYD 2.4 million investment that will be depreciated according to the straight-line method over its four-year life. The project is expected to generate earnings before taxes and depreciation of GYD 850,000 per year for four years. The investment will not change the risk level of the firm. The company can obtain a four-year, 9.5 percent loan to finance the project from a local bank. All principal will be repaid in one balloon payment at the end of the fourth year. The bank will charge the firm GYD 24,000 in flotation fees, which will be amortized over the four-year life of the loan. If the company financed the project entirely with equity, the firm's cost of capital would be 13 percent. The corporate tax rate is 30 percent. Using the adjusted present value method, determine whether the company should undertake the project.

3. Flow to Equity   Milano Pizza Club owns three identical restaurants popular for their specialty pizzas. Each restaurant has a debt–equity ratio of 40 percent and makes interest payments of €29,500 at the end of each year. The cost of the firm's levered equity is 19 percent. Each store estimates that annual sales will be €1 million; annual cost of goods sold will be €450,000; and annual general and administrative costs will be €325,000. These cash flows are expected to remain the same forever. The corporate tax rate is 30 percent.
a. Use the flow to equity approach to determine the value of the company's equity.
b. What is the total value of the company?

4. WACC   If Wild Widgets, Inc., were an all-equity company, it would have a beta of 1.1. The company has a target debt–equity ratio of 0.40. The expected return on the market portfolio is 13 percent, and Treasury bills currently yield 7 percent. The company has one bond issue outstanding that matures in 20 years and has a 9 percent coupon rate. The bond currently sells for $970. The corporate tax rate is 40 percent.
a. What is the company's cost of debt?
b. What is the company's cost of equity?
c. What is the company's weighted average cost of capital?

5. Beta and Leverage   North Pole Fishing Equipment Corporation and South Pole Fishing Equipment Corporation would have identical equity betas of 1.25 if both were all equity financed. The market value information for each company is shown here:

	North Pole	South Pole
Debt	HKD 1,400,000	HKD 2,600,000
Equity	HKD 2,600,000	HKD 1,400,000

The expected return on the market portfolio is 12.25 percent, and the risk-free rate is 5.30 percent. Both companies are subject to a corporate tax rate of 35 percent. Assume the beta of debt is zero.
a. What is the equity beta of each of the two companies?
b. What is the required rate of return on each of the two companies' equity?

6. NPV of Loans   Daniel Kaffe, CFO of Kendrick Enterprises, is evaluating a 10-year, 9 percent loan with gross proceeds of $4,250,000. The interest payments on the loan will be made annually. Flotation costs are estimated to be 1.25 percent of gross proceeds and will be amortized using a straight-line schedule over the 10-year life of the loan. The company has a tax rate of 40 percent, and the loan will not increase the risk of financial distress for the company.

a. Calculate the net present value of the loan excluding flotation costs.

b. Calculate the net present value of the loan including flotation costs.

7. **NPV for an All-Equity Company**   Shattered Glass, Inc., is an all-equity firm. The cost of the company's equity is currently 16 percent, and the risk-free rate is 6 percent. The company is currently considering a project that will cost JMD 12.6 million and last six years. The project will generate revenues minus expenses each year in the amount of JMD 4.4 million. If the company has a tax rate of 40 percent, should it accept the project?

8. **WACC**   Moneague Electric Company (MEC) is considering a TTD 50 million project in its power systems division. Tom Edison, the company's chief financial officer, has evaluated the project and determined that the project's unlevered cash flows will be TTD 3.5 million per year in perpetuity. Mr. Edison has devised two possibilities for raising the initial investment: issuing 10-year bonds or issuing common stock. MEC's pretax cost of debt is 7.2 percent, and its cost of equity is 10.9 percent. The company's target debt-to-value ratio is 80 percent. The project has the same risk as MEC's existing businesses, and it will support the same amount of debt. MEC is in the 35 percent tax bracket. Should MEC accept the project?

9. **WACC**   Bojnurd Energy has compiled the following information on its financing costs:

Type of Financing	Book Value	Market Value	Cost
Long-term debt	IRR 2,000,000	IRR 2,000,000	3.5%
Short-term debt	9,000,000	8,000,000	6.8
Common stock	6,000,000	22,000,000	14.5
Total	IRR 17,000,000	IRR 32,000,000	

The company is in the 35 percent tax bracket and has a target debt–equity ratio of 60 percent. The target short-term debt/long-term debt ratio is 20 percent.

a. What is the company's weighted average cost of capital using book value weights?

b. What is the company's weighted average cost of capital using market value weights?

c. What is the company's weighted average cost of capital using target capital structure weights?

d. What is the difference between WACCs? Which is the correct WACC to use for project evaluation?

INTERMEDIATE
(Questions 10–13)

10. **APV**   Triad Corporation has established a joint venture with Ottoman Road Construction, Inc., to build a toll road in Adana. The initial investment in paving equipment is TRL 25 million. The equipment will be fully depreciated using the straight-line method over its economic life of five years. Earnings before interest, taxes, and depreciation collected from the toll road are projected to be TRL 3.4 million per annum for 20 years starting from the end of the first year. The corporate tax rate is 35 percent. The required rate of return for the project under all-equity financing is 13 percent. The pretax cost of debt for the joint partnership is 8.5 percent. To encourage investment in the country's infrastructure, the Turkish government will subsidize the project with a TRL 15 million, 15-year loan at an interest rate of 5 percent per year. All principal will be repaid in one balloon payment at the end of year 15. What is the adjusted present value of this project?

11. **APV**   For the company in the previous problem, what is the value of being able to issue subsidized debt instead of having to issue debt at the terms it would normally receive? Assume the face amount and maturity of the debt issue are the same.

12. **APV**   Arabian Nightlife has produced energy-efficient bulbs for over 20 years. The company currently has a debt–equity ratio of 50 percent and is in the 40 percent tax bracket. The required return on the firm's levered equity is 16 percent. Arabian Nightlife is planning to

expand its production capacity. The equipment to be purchased is expected to generate the following unlevered cash flows:

Year	Cash flow
0	–SAR 24,000,000
1	8,000,000
2	13,000,000
3	10,000,000

The company has arranged an SAR 12 million debt issue to partially finance the expansion. Under the loan, the company would pay interest of 9 percent at the end of each year on the outstanding balance at the beginning of the year. The company would also make year-end principal payments of SAR 4 million per year, completely retiring the issue by the end of the third year. Using the adjusted present value method, should the company proceed with the expansion?

13. **WACC**   Neon Corporation's stock returns have a covariance with the market portfolio of 0.048. The standard deviation of the returns on the market portfolio is 20 percent, and the expected market risk premium is 7.5 percent. The company has bonds outstanding with a total market value of ¥30 million and a yield to maturity of 8 percent. The company also has 5 million shares of common stock outstanding, each selling for ¥20. The company's CEO considers the firm's current debt–equity ratio optimal. The corporate tax rate is 38 percent, and Treasury bills currently yield 6 percent. The company is considering the purchase of additional equipment that would cost ¥40 million. The expected unlevered cash flows from the equipment are ¥13 million per year for five years. Purchasing the equipment will not change the risk level of the firm.
    a. Use the weighted average cost of capital approach to determine whether Neon should purchase the equipment.
    b. Suppose the company decides to fund the purchase of the equipment entirely with debt. What is the cost of capital for the project now? Explain.

CHALLENGE
(Questions 14–17)

14. **APV, FTE, and WACC**   Seger, Inc., is an unlevered firm with expected annual earnings before taxes of $35 million in perpetuity. The current required return on the firm's equity is 20 percent, and the firm distributes all of its earnings as dividends at the end of each year. The company has 1.5 million shares of common stock outstanding and is subject to a corporate tax rate of 35 percent. The firm is planning a recapitalization under which it will issue $40 million of perpetual 9 percent debt and use the proceeds to buy back shares.
    a. Calculate the value of the company before the recapitalization plan is announced. What is the value of equity before the announcement? What is the price per share?
    b. Use the APV method to calculate the company value after the recapitalization plan is announced. What is the value of equity after the announcement? What is the price per share?
    c. How many shares will be repurchased? What is the value of equity after the repurchase has been completed? What is the price per share?
    d. Use the flow to equity method to calculate the value of the company's equity after the recapitalization.

15. **APV, FTE, and WACC**   Thani Mint Company has a debt–equity ratio of 0.45. The required return on the company's unlevered equity is 17 percent, and the pretax cost of the firm's debt is 9 percent. Sales revenue for the company is expected to remain stable indefinitely at last year's level of THB 23,500,000. Variable costs amount to 60 percent of sales. The tax rate is 40 percent, and the company distributes all its earnings as dividends at the end of each year.
    a. If the company were financed entirely by equity, how much would it be worth?
    b. What is the required return on the firm's levered equity?
    c. Use the weighted average cost of capital method to calculate the value of the company. What is the value of the company's equity? What is the value of the company's debt?
    d. Use the flow to equity method to calculate the value of the company's equity.

16. **APV, FTE, and WACC**   Damour Industries just issued LBP 160,000 of perpetual 10 percent debt and used the proceeds to repurchase stock. The company expects to generate LBP 75,000 of earnings before interest and taxes in perpetuity. The company distributes all its earnings as dividends at the end of each year. The firm's unlevered cost of capital is 18 percent, and the corporate tax rate is 40 percent.
    a. What is the value of the company as an unlevered firm?
    b. Use the adjusted present value method to calculate the value of the company with leverage.
    c. What is the required return on the firm's levered equity?
    d. Use the flow to equity method to calculate the value of the company's equity.

17. **Projects That Are Not Scale Enhancing**   Blue Angel, Inc., a private firm in the holiday gift industry, is considering a new project. The company currently has a target debt–equity ratio of .40, but the industry target debt–equity ratio is .35. The industry average beta is 1.2. The market risk premium is 8 percent, and the risk-free rate is 7 percent. Assume all companies in this industry can issue debt at the risk-free rate. The corporate tax rate is 40 percent. The project requires an initial outlay of £450,000 and is expected to result in a £75,000 cash inflow at the end of the first year. The project will be financed at Blue Angel's target debt–equity ratio. Annual cash flows from the project will grow at a constant rate of 5 percent until the end of the fifth year and remain constant forever thereafter. Should Blue Angel invest in the project?

S&P Problem

STANDARD &POOR'S

www.mhhe.com/edumarketinsight

1. Locate the annual income statements for Walt Disney (DIS) and calculate the marginal tax rate for the company for the last year. Next, find the beta for Disney in the S&P stock report. Using the current debt and equity from the most recent annual balance sheet, calculate the unlevered beta for Disney.

Appendix 17A # The Adjusted Present Value Approach to Valuing Leveraged Buyouts

To access the appendix for this chapter, please visit **www.mhhe.com/rwj.**

Mini Case

The Leveraged Buyout of Cheek Products, Inc.

Cheek Products, Inc. (CPI), was founded 53 years ago by Joe Cheek and originally sold snack foods such as potato chips and pretzels. Through acquisitions, the company has grown into a conglomerate with major divisions in the snack food industry, home security systems, cosmetics, and plastics. Additionally, the company has several smaller divisions. In recent years the company has been underperforming, but the company's management doesn't seem to be aggressively pursuing opportunities to improve operations (and the stock price).

Meg Whalen is a financial analyst specializing in identifying potential buyout targets. She believes that two major changes are needed at Cheek. First, she thinks that the company would be better off if it sold several divisions and concentrated on its core competencies in snack foods and home security systems. Second, the company is financed entirely with equity. Because the cash flows of the company are relatively steady, Meg thinks the company's debt–equity ratio should be at least .25. She believes these changes would significantly enhance shareholder wealth, but she also believes that the existing board and company management are unlikely to take the necessary actions. As a result, Meg thinks the company is a good candidate for a leveraged buyout.

A leveraged buyout (LBO) is the acquisition by a small group of equity investors of a public or private company. Generally, an LBO is financed primarily with debt. The new shareholders service the heavy interest and principal payments with cash from operations and/or asset sales. Shareholders generally hope to reverse the LBO within three to seven years by way of a public offering or sale of the company to another firm. A buyout is therefore likely to be successful only if the firm generates enough cash to serve the debt in the early years and if the company is attractive to other buyers a few years down the road.

Meg has suggested the potential LBO to her partners, Ben Feller and Brenton Flynn. Ben and Brenton have asked Meg to provide projections of the cash flows for the company. Meg has provided the following estimates (in millions):

	2007	2008	2009	2010	2011
Sales	$1,627	$1,824	$1,965	$2,012	$2,106
Costs	432	568	597	645	680
Depreciation	287	305	318	334	340
EBT	$ 908	$ 951	$1,050	$1,033	$1,086
Capital expenditures	$ 165	$ 143	$ 180	$ 182	$ 195
Change in NWC	$ (72)	$ (110)	$ 60	$ 56	$ 64
Asset sales	$ 840	$ 610			

At the end of five years, Meg estimates that the growth rate in cash flows will be 3.5 percent per year. The capital expenditures are for new projects and the replacement of equipment that wears out. Additionally, the company would realize cash flow from the sale of several divisions. Even though the company will sell these divisions, overall sales should increase because of a more concentrated effort on the remaining divisions.

After plowing through the company's financials and various pro forma scenarios, Ben and Brenton feel that in five years they will be able to sell the company to another party or take it public again. They are also aware that they will have to borrow a considerable amount of the purchase price. The interest payments on the debt for each of the next five years if the LBO is undertaken will be these (in millions):

	2007	2008	2009	2010	2011
Interest payments	$1,140	$1,100	$1,180	$1,150	$1,190

The company currently has a required return on assets of 14 percent. Because of the high debt level, the debt will carry a yield to maturity of 12.5 percent for the next five years. When the debt is refinanced in five years, they believe the new yield to maturity will be 8 percent.

CPI currently has 104 million shares of stock outstanding that sell for $53 per share. The corporate tax rate is 40 percent. If Meg, Ben, and Brenton decide to undertake the LBO, what is the most they should offer per share?

18

Dividends and Other Payouts

In July 2004, Microsoft was sitting on a cash hoard of nearly $60 billion. Under growing pressure from shareholders, the company announced it was going to use some of that cash to (1) increase the annual dividend to $.32 per share, (2) repurchase about $30 billion of the company's stock over the next four years, and (3) make a special dividend payment of $3 per share to shareholders. Microsoft had over 10 billion shares outstanding, so the special dividend payment totaled a remarkable $32.6 billion, making it the largest corporate cash disbursement in history.

To put the size of Microsoft's special dividend in perspective, the total dividends paid by all the companies in the S&P 500 for the year totaled $213.6 billion. This means Microsoft's special dividend amounted to about 15 percent of all dividends paid by 500 of the largest companies for the year. Still not impressed? Well, consider that when the dividend was sent to investors in December, personal income in the United States rose 3.7 percent. Without the dividend, personal income rose only .3 percent. This means the dividend payment accounted for over 3 percent of all personal income in the United States for the month!

18.1 Different Types of Dividends

The term *dividend* usually refers to a cash distribution of earnings. If a distribution is made from sources other than current or accumulated retained earnings, the term *distribution* rather than dividend is used. However, it is acceptable to refer to a distribution from earnings as a *dividend* and a distribution from capital as a *liquidating dividend*. More generally, any direct payment by the corporation to the shareholders may be considered part of dividend policy.

The most common type of dividend is in the form of cash. Public companies usually pay **regular cash dividends** four times a year. Sometimes firms will pay a regular cash dividend and an *extra cash dividend*. Paying a cash dividend reduces corporate cash and retained earnings—except in the case of a liquidating dividend (where paid-in capital may be reduced).

Another type of dividend is paid out in shares of stock. This dividend is referred to as a **stock dividend**. It is not a true dividend because no cash leaves the firm. Rather, a stock dividend increases the number of shares outstanding, thereby reducing the value of each share. A stock dividend is commonly expressed as a ratio; for example, with a 2 percent stock dividend a shareholder receives 1 new share for every 50 currently owned.

When a firm declares a **stock split**, it increases the number of shares outstanding. Because each share is now entitled to a smaller percentage of the firm's cash flow, the stock price should fall. For example, if the managers of a firm whose stock is selling at $90 declare a 3:1 stock split, the price of a share of stock should fall to about $30. A stock split strongly resembles a stock dividend except that it is usually much larger.

18.2 Standard Method of Cash Dividend Payment

The decision to pay a dividend rests in the hands of the board of directors of the corporation. A dividend is distributable to shareholders of record on a specific date. When a dividend has been declared, it becomes a liability of the firm and cannot be easily rescinded by the corporation. The amount of the dividend is expressed as dollars per share (*dividend per share*), as a percentage of the market price (*dividend yield*), or as a percentage of earnings per share (*dividend payout*).

The mechanics of a dividend payment can be illustrated by the example in Figure 18.1 and the following chronology:

For a list of today's dividends, go to **www.company boardroom.com**.

1. *Declaration date*: On January 15 (the declaration date), the board of directors passes a resolution to pay a dividend of $1 per share on February 16 to all holders of record on January 30.

2. *Date of record*: The corporation prepares a list on January 30 of all individuals believed to be stockholders as of this date. The word *believed* is important here: The dividend will not be paid to individuals whose notification of purchase is received by the company after January 30.

3. *Ex-dividend date*: The procedure for the date of record would be unfair if efficient brokerage houses could notify the corporation by January 30 of a trade occurring on January 29, whereas the same trade might not reach the corporation until February 2 if executed by a less efficient house. To eliminate this problem, all brokerage firms entitle stockholders to receive the dividend if they purchased the stock three business days before the date of record. The second day before the date of record, which is Wednesday, January 28, in our example, is called the *ex-dividend date*. Before this date the stock is said to trade *cum dividend*.

4. *Date of payment*: The dividend checks are mailed to the stockholders on February 16.

Obviously, the ex-dividend date is important because an individual purchasing the security before the ex-dividend date will receive the current dividend, whereas another individual purchasing the security on or after this date will not receive the dividend. The stock price will therefore fall on the ex-dividend date (assuming no other events occur). It is worthwhile to note that this drop is an indication of efficiency, not inefficiency, because the market rationally attaches value to a cash dividend. In a world with neither taxes nor transaction costs, the stock price would be expected to fall by the amount of the dividend:

$$\text{Before ex-dividend date} \qquad \text{Price} = \$(P + 1)$$
$$\text{On or after ex-dividend date} \qquad \text{Price} = \$P$$

Figure 18.1

Example of Procedure for Dividend Payment

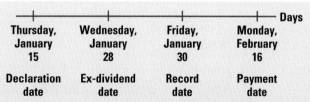

1. *Declaration date*: The board of directors declares a payment of dividends.
2. *Record date*: The declared dividends are distributable to shareholders of record on a specific date.
3. *Ex-dividend date*: A share of stock becomes ex dividend on the date the seller is entitled to keep the dividend; under NYSE rules, shares are traded ex dividend on and after the second business day before the record date.
4. *Payment date*: The dividend checks are mailed to shareholders of record.

Figure 18.2

Price Behavior around the Ex-Dividend Date for a $1 Cash Dividend

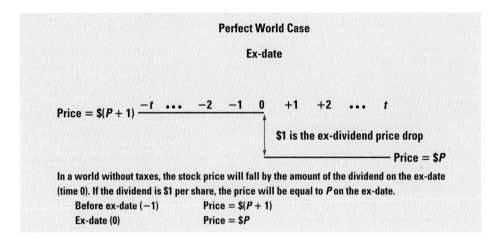

Perfect World Case

Ex-date

$$\text{Price} = \$(P + 1) \quad \frac{-t \quad \cdots \quad -2 \quad -1 \quad 0 \quad +1 \quad +2 \quad \cdots \quad t}{}$$

$1 is the ex-dividend price drop

Price = $P

In a world without taxes, the stock price will fall by the amount of the dividend on the ex-date (time 0). If the dividend is $1 per share, the price will be equal to P on the ex-date.

Before ex-date (−1)	Price = $(P + 1)$
Ex-date (0)	Price = P

This is illustrated in Figure 18.2.

The amount of the price drop may depend on tax rates. For example, consider the case with no capital gains taxes. On the day before a stock goes ex dividend, a purchaser must decide either (1) to buy the stock immediately and pay tax on the forthcoming dividend or (2) to buy the stock tomorrow, thereby missing the dividend. If all investors are in the 15 percent bracket and the quarterly dividend is $1, the stock price should fall by $.85 on the ex-dividend date. That is, if the stock price falls by this amount on the ex-dividend date, purchasers will receive the same return from either strategy.

As an example of the price drop on the ex-dividend date, consider the Microsoft dividend we discussed at the beginning of the chapter. The stock went ex dividend on November 15, 2004, with a total dividend of $3.08 per share, consisting of a $3 special dividend and a $.08 regular dividend. The following stock price chart shows the price of Microsoft stock on each of the four days prior to the ex-dividend date and on the ex-dividend date:

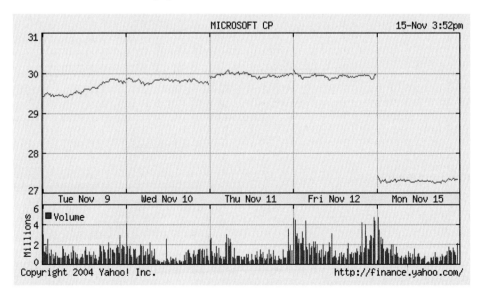

The stock closed at $29.97 on November 12 (a Friday) and opened at $27.34 on November 15, a drop of $2.63. With a 15 percent tax rate on dividends, we would have expected a drop of $2.62, and the actual price drop was almost exactly that amount.

18.3 The Benchmark Case: An Illustration of the Irrelevance of Dividend Policy

A powerful argument can be made that dividend policy does not matter. This will be illustrated with the Bristol Corporation. Bristol is an all-equity firm started 10 years ago. The current financial managers know at the present time (date 0) that the firm will dissolve in one year (date 1). At date 0 the managers are able to forecast cash flows with perfect certainty. The managers know that the firm will receive a cash flow of $10,000 immediately and another $10,000 next year. Bristol has no additional positive NPV projects.

Current Policy: Dividends Set Equal to Cash Flow

At the present time, dividends (Div) at each date are set equal to the cash flow of $10,000. The value of the firm can be calculated by discounting these dividends. This value is expressed as:

$$V_0 = \text{Div}_0 + \frac{\text{Div}_1}{1 + R_S}$$

where Div_0 and Div_1 are the cash flows paid out in dividends, and R_S is the discount rate. The first dividend is not discounted because it will be paid immediately.

Assuming $R_S = 10$ percent, the value of the firm is:

$$\$19,090.91 = \$10,000 + \frac{\$10,000}{1.1}$$

If 1,000 shares are outstanding, the value of each share is:

$$\$19.09 = \$10 + \frac{\$10}{1.1} \tag{18.1}$$

To simplify the example, we assume that the ex-dividend date is the same as the date of payment. After the imminent dividend is paid, the stock price will immediately fall to $9.09 ($= \$19.09 - \$10$). Several members of Bristol's board have expressed dissatisfaction with the current dividend policy and have asked you to analyze an alternative policy.

Alternative Policy: Initial Dividend Is Greater Than Cash Flow

Another policy is for the firm to pay a dividend of $11 per share immediately, which is, of course, a total dividend payout of $11,000. Because the cash runoff is only $10,000, the extra $1,000 must be raised in one of a few ways. Perhaps the simplest would be to issue $1,000 of bonds or stock now (at date 0). Assume that stock is issued and the new stockholders will desire enough cash flow at date 1 to let them earn the required 10 percent return on their date 0 investment. The new stockholders will demand $1,100 of the date 1 cash flow, leaving only $8,900 to the old stockholders. The dividends to the old stockholders will be these:

	Date 0	Date 1
Aggregate dividends to old stockholders	$11,000	$8,900
Dividends per share	$ 11.00	$ 8.90

Figure 18.3

Current and
Alternative Dividend
Policies

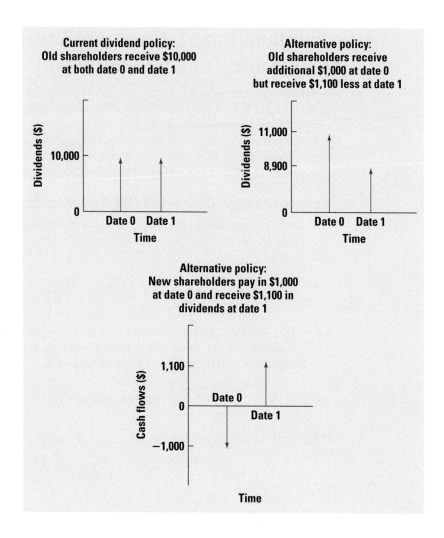

The present value of the dividends per share is therefore:

$$\$19.09 = \$11 + \frac{\$8.90}{1.1} \tag{18.2}$$

Students often find it instructive to determine the price at which the new stock is issued. Because the new stockholders are not entitled to the immediate dividend, they would pay $8.09 (= $8.90/1.1) per share. Thus, 123.61 (= $1,000/$8.09) new shares are issued.

The Indifference Proposition

Note that the values in Equations 18.1 and 18.2 are equal. This leads to the initially surprising conclusion that the change in dividend policy did not affect the value of a share of stock. However, on reflection, the result seems sensible. The new stockholders are parting with their money at date 0 and receiving it back with the appropriate return at date 1. In other words, they are taking on a zero NPV investment. As illustrated in Figure 18.3, old stockholders are receiving additional funds at date 0 but must pay the new stockholders their money with the appropriate return at date 1. Because the old stockholders must pay back principal plus the appropriate return, the act of issuing new stock at date 0 will not increase or decrease the value of the old stockholders' holdings. That is, they are giving up a zero NPV investment to the new stockholders. An increase in dividends at date 0 leads to the necessary reduction of dividends at date 1, so the value of the old stockholders' holdings remains unchanged.

This illustration is based on the pioneering work of Miller and Modigliani (MM). Although our presentation is in the form of a numerical example, the MM paper proves that investors are indifferent to dividend policy in a more general setting.

Homemade Dividends

To illustrate the indifference investors have toward dividend policy in our example, we used present value equations. An alternative and perhaps more intuitively appealing explanation avoids the mathematics of discounted cash flows.

Suppose individual investor X prefers dividends per share of $10 at both dates 0 and 1. Would she be disappointed when informed that the firm's management is adopting the alternative dividend policy (dividends of $11 and $8.90 on the two dates, respectively)? Not necessarily: She could easily reinvest the $1 of unneeded funds received on date 0, yielding an incremental return of $1.10 at date 1. Thus, she would receive her desired net cash flow of $11 − $1 = $10 at date 0 and $8.90 + $1.10 = $10 at date 1.

Conversely, imagine investor Z preferring $11 of cash flow at date 0 and $8.90 of cash flow at date 1, who finds that management will pay dividends of $10 at both dates 0 and 1. He can sell off shares of stock at date 0 to receive the desired amount of cash flow. That is, if he sells off shares (or fractions of shares) at date 0 totaling $1, his cash flow at date 0 becomes $10 + $1 = $11. Because a $1 sale of stock at date 0 will reduce his dividends by $1.10 at date 1, his net cash flow at date 1 would be $10 − $1.10 = $8.90.

The example illustrates how investors can make **homemade dividends**. In this instance, corporate dividend policy is being undone by a potentially dissatisfied stockholder. This homemade dividend is illustrated by Figure 18.4. Here the firm's cash flows of $10 per share at both dates 0 and 1 are represented by point *A*. This point also represents the initial dividend payout. However, as we just saw, the firm could alternatively pay out $11 per share at date 0 and $8.90 per share at date 1, a strategy represented by point *B*. Similarly, by either issuing new stock or buying back old stock, the firm could achieve a dividend payout represented by any point on the diagonal line.

The previous paragraph describes the choices available to the managers of the firm. The same diagonal line also represents the choices available to the shareholder. For example, if the shareholder receives a per-share dividend distribution of ($11, $8.90), he or she can either reinvest some of the dividends to move down and to the right on the graph or sell off shares of stock and move up and to the left.

The implications of the graph can be summarized in two sentences:

1. By varying dividend policy, managers can achieve any payout along the diagonal line in Figure 18.4.

2. Either by reinvesting excess dividends at date 0 or by selling off shares of stock at this date, an individual investor can achieve any net cash payout along the diagonal line.

Thus, because both the corporation and the individual investor can move only along the diagonal line, dividend policy in this model is irrelevant. The changes the managers make in dividend policy can be undone by an individual who, by either reinvesting dividends or selling off stock, can move to a desired point on the diagonal line.

Figure 18.4

Homemade
Dividends: A
Trade-Off between
Dividends per
Share at Date 0 and
Dividends per Share
at Date 1

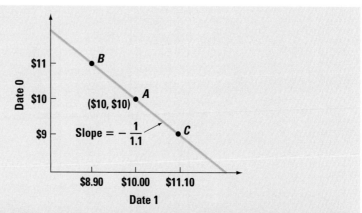

The graph illustrates both (1) how managers can vary dividend policy and (2) how individuals can undo the firm's dividend policy.

Managers varying dividend policy: A firm paying out all cash flows immediately is at point *A* on the graph. The firm could achieve point *B* by issuing stock to pay extra dividends or achieve point *C* by buying back old stock with some of its cash.

Individuals undoing the firm's dividend policy: Suppose the firm adopts the dividend policy represented by point *B*: dividends per share of $11 at date 0 and $8.90 at date 1. An investor can reinvest $1 of the dividends at 10 percent, which will place her at point *A*. Suppose, alternatively, the firm adopts the dividend policy represented by point *A*. An investor can sell off $1 of stock at date 0, placing him at point *B*. No matter what dividend policy the firm establishes, a shareholder can undo it.

A Test

You can test your knowledge of this material by examining these true statements:

1. Dividends are relevant.
2. Dividend policy is irrelevant.

The first statement follows from common sense. Clearly, investors prefer higher dividends to lower dividends at any single date if the dividend level is held constant at every other date. In other words, if the dividend per share at a given date is raised while the dividend per share for each other date is held constant, the stock price will rise. This act can be accomplished by management decisions that improve productivity, increase tax savings, or strengthen product marketing. In fact, you may recall that in Chapter 5 we argued that the value of a firm's equity is equal to the discounted present value of all its future dividends.

The second statement is understandable once we realize that dividend policy cannot raise the dividend per share at one date while holding the dividend level per share constant at all other dates. Rather, dividend policy merely establishes the trade-off between dividends at one date and dividends at another date. As we saw in Figure 18.4, an increase in date 0 dividends can be accomplished only by a decrease in date 1 dividends. The extent of the decrease is such that the present value of all dividends is not affected.

Thus, in this simple world, dividend policy does not matter. That is, managers choosing either to raise or to lower the current dividend do not affect the current value of their firm. This theory is powerful, and the work of MM is generally considered a classic in modern finance. With relatively few assumptions, a rather surprising result is shown to be perfectly true. Nevertheless, because we want to examine many real-world factors ignored by MM, their work is only a starting point in this chapter's discussion of dividends. Later parts of this chapter investigate these real-world considerations.

Dividends and Investment Policy

The preceding argument shows that an increase in dividends through issuance of new shares neither helps nor hurts the stockholders. Similarly, a reduction in dividends through share repurchase neither helps nor hurts stockholders.

What about reducing capital expenditures to increase dividends? Earlier chapters show that a firm should accept all positive net present value projects. To do otherwise would reduce the value of the firm. Thus, we have an important point:

Firms should never give up a positive NPV project to increase a dividend (or to pay a dividend for the first time).

This idea was implicitly considered by Miller and Modigliani. One of the assumptions underlying their dividend irrelevance proposition was this: "The investment policy of the firm is set ahead of time and is not altered by changes in dividend policy."

18.4 Repurchase of Stock

Instead of paying dividends, a firm may use cash to repurchase shares of its own stock. Share repurchases have taken on increased importance in recent years. Consider Figure 18.5, which shows the average ratios of dividends to earnings, repurchases to earnings, and total payout (both dividends and repurchases) to earnings for U.S. industrial firms over

Figure 18.5 **Ratios of Various Payouts to Earnings**

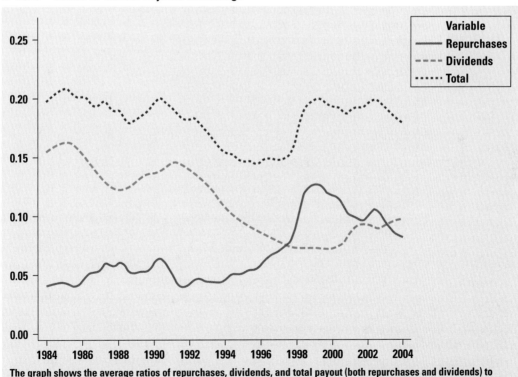

The graph shows the average ratios of repurchases, dividends, and total payout (both repurchases and dividends) to earnings for U.S. industrial companies over the years from 1984 to 2004. The graph indicates growth in repurchases over much of the sample period.

SOURCE: Figure 3 of Brandon Julio and David Ikenberry, "Reappearing Dividends," unpublished paper, University of Illinois (2004).

the years from 1984 to 2004. As can be seen, the ratio of repurchases to earnings was far less than the ratio of dividends to earnings in the early years. However, the ratio of repurchases to earnings exceeded the ratio of dividends to earnings by 1998. This trend reversed after 1999, with the ratio of repurchases to earnings falling slightly below the ratio of dividends to earnings by 2004.

Share repurchases are typically accomplished in one of three ways. First, companies may simply purchase their own stock, just as anyone would buy shares of a particular stock. In these *open market purchases*, the firm does not reveal itself as the buyer. Thus, the seller does not know whether the shares were sold back to the firm or to just another investor.

Second, the firm could institute a *tender offer*. Here, the firm announces to all of its stockholders that it is willing to buy a fixed number of shares at a specific price. For example, suppose Arts and Crafts (A&C), Inc., has 1 million shares of stock outstanding, with a stock price of $50 per share. The firm makes a tender offer to buy back 300,000 shares at $60 per share. A&C chooses a price above $50 to induce shareholders to sell—that is, tender—their shares. In fact, if the tender price is set high enough, shareholders may want to sell more than the 300,000 shares. In the extreme case where all outstanding shares are tendered, A&C will buy back 3 out of every 10 shares that a shareholder has.

Finally, firms may repurchase shares from specific individual stockholders, a procedure called a *targeted repurchase*. For example, suppose the International Biotechnology Corporation purchased approximately 10 percent of the outstanding stock of the Prime Robotics Company (P-R Co.) in April at around $38 per share. At that time, International Biotechnology announced to the Securities and Exchange Commission that it might eventually try to take control of P-R Co. In May, P-R Co. repurchased the International Biotechnology holdings at $48 per share, well above the market price at that time. This offer was not extended to other shareholders.

Companies engage in targeted repurchases for a variety of reasons. In some rare cases, a single large stockholder can be bought out at a price lower than that in a tender offer. The legal fees in a targeted repurchase may also be lower than those in a more typical buyback. In addition, the shares of large stockholders are often repurchased to avoid a takeover unfavorable to management.

We now consider an example of a repurchase presented in the theoretical world of a perfect capital market. We next discuss real-world factors involved in the repurchase decision.

Dividend versus Repurchase: Conceptual Example

Imagine that Telephonic Industries has excess cash of $300,000 (or $3 per share) and is considering an immediate payment of this amount as an extra dividend. The firm forecasts that, after the dividend, earnings will be $450,000 per year, or $4.50 for each of the 100,000 shares outstanding. Because the price–earnings ratio is 6 for comparable companies, the shares of the firm should sell for $27 (= $4.50 × 6) after the dividend is paid. These figures are presented in the top half of Table 18.1. Because the dividend is $3 per share, the stock would have sold for $30 a share *before* payment of the dividend.

Alternatively, the firm could use the excess cash to repurchase some of its own stock. Imagine that a tender offer of $30 a share is made. Here, 10,000 shares are repurchased so that the total number of shares remaining is 90,000. With fewer shares outstanding, the earnings per share will rise to $5 (= $450,000/90,000). The price–earnings ratio remains at 6 because both the business and financial risks of the firm are the same in the repurchase case as they were in the dividend case. Thus, the price of a share after the repurchase is $30 (= $5 × 6). These results are presented in the bottom half of Table 18.1.

If commissions, taxes, and other imperfections are ignored in our example, the stockholders are indifferent between a dividend and a repurchase. With dividends each

Table 18.1   Dividend versus Repurchase Example for Telephonic Industries

	For Entire Firm	Per Share
Extra Dividend		**(100,000 shares outstanding)**
Proposed dividend	$ 300,000	$ 3.00
Forecast annual earnings after dividend	450,000	4.50
Market value of stock after dividend	2,700,000	27.00
Repurchase		**(90,000 shares outstanding)**
Forecast annual earnings after repurchase	$ 450,000	$ 5.00
Market value of stock after repurchase	2,700,000	30.00

stockholder owns a share worth $27 and receives $3 in dividends, so that the total value is $30. This figure is the same as both the amount received by the selling stockholders and the value of the stock for the remaining stockholders in the repurchase case.

This example illustrates the important point that, in a perfect market, the firm is indifferent between a dividend payment and a share repurchase. This result is quite similar to the indifference propositions established by MM for debt versus equity financing and for dividends versus capital gains.

You may often read in the popular financial press that a repurchase agreement is beneficial because earnings per share increase. Earnings per share do rise for Telephonic Industries if a repurchase is substituted for a cash dividend: The EPS is $4.50 after a dividend and $5 after the repurchase. This result holds because the drop in shares after a repurchase implies a reduction in the denominator of the EPS ratio.

However, the financial press frequently places undue emphasis on EPS figures in a repurchase agreement. Given the irrelevance propositions we have discussed, the increase in EPS here is not beneficial. Table 18.1 shows that, in a perfect capital market, the total value to the stockholder is the same under the dividend payment strategy as under the repurchase strategy.

Dividends versus Repurchases: Real-World Considerations

We previously referred to Figure 18.5, which showed growth in share repurchases relative to dividends. Why do some firms choose repurchases over dividends? Here are perhaps five of the most common reasons.

1. Flexibility   Firms often view dividends as a commitment to their stockholders and are quite hesitant to reduce an existing dividend. Repurchases do not represent a similar commitment. Thus, a firm with a permanent increase in cash flow is likely to increase its dividend. Conversely, a firm whose cash flow increase is only temporary is likely to repurchase shares of stock.

2. Executive Compensation   Executives are frequently given stock options as part of their overall compensation. Let's revisit the Telephonic Industries example of Table 18.1, where the firm's stock was selling at $30 when the firm was considering either a dividend or a repurchase. Further imagine that Telephonic had granted 1,000 stock options to its CEO, Ralph Taylor, two years earlier. At that time, the stock price was, say, only $20. This means that Mr. Taylor can buy 1,000 shares for $20 a share at any time between the grant of the options and their expiration, a procedure called *exercising* the options. His gain from exercising is directly proportional to the rise in the stock price above $20. As we saw in the example, the price of the stock would fall to $27 following a dividend but would remain at $30 following a repurchase. The CEO would clearly prefer a repurchase to a dividend because the difference between the stock price and the exercise price of $20 would be $10 (= $30 − $20) following the repurchase but only $7 (= $27 − $20) following the dividend. Existing stock options will always have greater value when the firm repurchases shares instead of paying a dividend because the stock price will be greater after a repurchase than after a dividend.

3. Offset to Dilution   In addition, the exercise of stock options increases the number of shares outstanding. In other words, exercise causes dilution of the stock. Firms frequently buy back shares of stock to offset this dilution. However, it is hard to argue that this is a valid reason for repurchase. As we showed in Table 18.1, repurchase is neither better nor worse for the stockholders than a dividend. Our argument holds whether or not stock options have been exercised previously.

4. Undervaluation   Many companies buy back stock because they believe that a repurchase is their best investment. This occurs more frequently when managers believe that the stock price is temporarily depressed.

The fact that some companies repurchase their stock when they believe it is undervalued does not imply that the management of the company must be correct; only empirical studies can make this determination. The immediate stock market reaction to the announcement of a stock repurchase is usually quite favorable. In addition, some empirical work has shown that the long-term stock price performance of securities after a buyback is better than the stock price performance of comparable companies that do not repurchase.

5. Taxes   Because taxes for both dividends and share repurchases are treated in depth in the next section, suffice it to say at this point that repurchases provide a tax advantage over dividends.

18.5   Personal Taxes and Dividends

Section 18.3 asserted that in a world without taxes and other frictions, dividend policy is irrelevant. Similarly, Section 18.4 concluded that the choice between a share repurchase and a dividend is irrelevant in a world of this type. This section examines the effect of taxes on both dividends and repurchases. Our discussion is facilitated by classifying firms into two types: those without sufficient cash to pay a dividend and those with sufficient cash to do so.

Firms without Sufficient Cash to Pay a Dividend

It is simplest to begin with a firm without cash and owned by a single entrepreneur. If this firm should decide to pay a dividend of $100, it must raise capital. The firm might choose among a number of different stock and bond issues to pay the dividend. However, for simplicity, we assume that the entrepreneur contributes cash to the firm by issuing stock to himself. This transaction, diagrammed in the left side of Figure 18.6, would clearly be a *wash* in a world of no taxes. $100 cash goes into the firm when stock is issued and is immediately paid out as a dividend. Thus, the entrepreneur neither benefits nor loses when the dividend is paid, a result consistent with Miller–Modigliani.

Now assume that dividends are taxed at the owner's personal tax rate of 15 percent. The firm still receives $100 upon issuance of stock. However, the entrepreneur does not get to keep the full $100 dividend. Instead the dividend payment is taxed, implying that the owner receives only $85 net after tax. Thus, the entrepreneur loses $15.

Though the example is clearly contrived and unrealistic, similar results can be reached for more plausible situations. Thus, financial economists generally agree that in a world of personal taxes, firms should not issue stock to pay dividends.

Figure 18.6

Firm Issues Stock to
Pay a Dividend

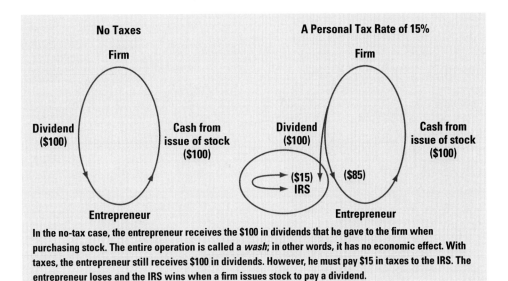

In the no-tax case, the entrepreneur receives the $100 in dividends that he gave to the firm when purchasing stock. The entire operation is called a *wash*; in other words, it has no economic effect. With taxes, the entrepreneur still receives $100 in dividends. However, he must pay $15 in taxes to the IRS. The entrepreneur loses and the IRS wins when a firm issues stock to pay a dividend.

The direct costs of issuance will add to this effect. Investment bankers must be paid when new capital is raised. Thus, the net receipts due to the firm from a new issue are less than 100 percent of total capital raised. Because the size of new issues can be lowered by a reduction in dividends, we have another argument in favor of a low-dividend policy.

Of course, our advice not to finance dividends through new stock issues might need to be modified somewhat in the real world. A company with a large and steady cash flow for many years in the past might be paying a regular dividend. If the cash flow unexpectedly dried up for a single year, should new stock be issued so that dividends could be continued? Although our previous discussion would imply that new stock should not be issued, many managers might issue the stock anyway for practical reasons. In particular, stockholders appear to prefer dividend stability. Thus, managers might be forced to issue stock to achieve this stability, knowing full well the adverse tax consequences.

Firms with Sufficient Cash to Pay a Dividend

The previous discussion argued that in a world with personal taxes, a firm should not issue stock to pay a dividend. Does the tax disadvantage of dividends imply the stronger policy, "Never, under any circumstances, pay dividends in a world with personal taxes"?

We argue next that this prescription does not necessarily apply to firms with excess cash. To see this, imagine a firm with $1 million in extra cash after selecting all positive NPV projects and determining the level of prudent cash balances. The firm might consider the following alternatives to a dividend:

1. *Select additional capital budgeting projects.* Because the firm has taken all the available positive NPV projects already, it must invest its excess cash in negative NPV projects. This is clearly a policy at variance with the principles of corporate finance.

   In spite of our distaste for this policy, researchers have suggested that many managers purposely take on negative NPV projects in lieu of paying dividends.[1]
   The idea here is that managers would rather keep the funds in the firm because their

---

[1] See, for example, M.C. Jensen, "Agency Costs of Free Cash Flows, Corporate Finance, and Takeovers," *American Economic Review* (May 1986).

prestige, pay, and perquisites are often tied to the firm's size. Although managers may help themselves here, they are hurting stockholders. We broached this subject in the section titled "Free Cash Flow" in Chapter 16, and we will have more to say about it later in this chapter.

2. *Acquire other companies*. To avoid the payment of dividends, a firm might use excess cash to acquire another company. This strategy has the advantage of acquiring profitable assets. However, a firm often incurs heavy costs when it embarks on an acquisition program. In addition, acquisitions are invariably made above the market price. Premiums of 20 to 80 percent are not uncommon. Because of this, a number of researchers have argued that mergers are not generally profitable to the acquiring company, even when firms are merged for a valid business purpose. Therefore, a company making an acquisition merely to avoid a dividend is unlikely to succeed.

3. *Purchase financial assets*. The strategy of purchasing financial assets in lieu of a dividend payment can be illustrated with the following example.

EXAMPLE 18.1

Dividends and Taxes   The Regional Electric Company has $1,000 of extra cash. It can retain the cash and invest it in Treasury bills yielding 10 percent, or it can pay the cash to shareholders as a dividend. Shareholders can also invest in Treasury bills with the same yield. Suppose the corporate tax rate is 34 percent, and the personal tax rate is 28 percent for all individuals. However, the maximum tax rate on dividends is 15 percent. How much cash will investors have after five years under each policy?

If dividends are paid now, shareholders will receive:

$$\$1,000 \times (1 - 0.15) = \$850$$

today after taxes. Because their return after personal tax on Treasury bills is 7.2 [$= 10 \times (1 - .28)$] percent, shareholders will have:

$$\$850 \times (1.072)^5 = \$1,203.35 \tag{18.3}$$

in five years. Note that interest income is taxed at the personal tax rate (28 percent in this example), but dividends are taxed at the lower rate of 15 percent.

If Regional Electric Company retains the cash to invest in Treasury bills, its aftertax interest rate will be .066 [$= .10 \times (1 - .34)$]. At the end of five years, the firm will have:

$$\$1,000 \times (1.066)^5 = \$1,376.53$$

If these proceeds are then paid as a dividend, the stockholders will receive:

$$\$1,376.53 \times (1 - 0.15) = \$1,170.05 \tag{18.4}$$

after personal taxes at date 5. The value in Equation 18.3 is greater than that in Equation 18.4, implying that cash to stockholders will be greater if the firm pays the dividend now.

This example shows that for a firm with extra cash, the dividend payout decision will depend on personal and corporate tax rates. If personal tax rates are higher than corporate tax rates, a firm will have an incentive to reduce dividend payouts. However, if personal tax rates are lower than corporate tax rates, a firm will have an incentive to pay out any excess cash as dividends.

In the United States both the highest marginal tax rate for individuals and the corporate tax rate were 35 percent in 2006. Because many investors face marginal tax rates well below the maximum, it appears that firms have an incentive not to hoard cash.

However, a quirk in the tax code provides an offsetting incentive. In particular, 70 percent of the dividends that one corporation receives from another corporation are excluded from corporate tax.[2] Individuals are not granted this exclusion. The quirk increases the likelihood that proceeds will be higher if the firm invests cash in other dividend-paying stocks rather than paying out cash as a dividend.

The firm's decision to invest in financial assets or to pay a dividend is a complex one, depending on the tax rate of the firm, the marginal tax rates of its investors, and the application of the dividend exclusion. While there are likely many real-world situations where the numbers favor investment in financial assets, few companies actually seem to hoard cash in this manner without limit. The reason is that Section 532 of the Internal Revenue Code penalizes firms exhibiting "improper accumulation of surplus." Thus, in the final analysis, the purchase of financial assets, like selecting negative NPV projects and acquiring other companies, does not obviate the need for companies with excess cash to pay dividends.

4. *Repurchase shares.* The example we described in the previous section showed that investors are indifferent between share repurchase and dividends in a world without taxes and transaction costs. However, under current tax law, stockholders generally prefer a repurchase to a dividend.

As an example, consider an individual receiving a dividend of $1 on each of 100 shares of a stock. With a 15 percent tax rate, that individual would pay taxes of $15 on the dividend. Selling shareholders would pay lower taxes if the firm repurchased $100 of existing shares. This occurs because taxes are paid only on the *profit* from a sale. The individual's gain on a sale would be only $40 if the shares sold for $100 were originally purchased for, say, $60. The capital gains tax would be $6 ($= 0.15 \times \$40$), a number below the tax on dividends of $15. Note that the tax from a repurchase is less than the tax on a dividend even though the same 15 percent tax rate applies to both the repurchase and the dividend.

Of all the alternatives to dividends mentioned in this section, the strongest case can be made for repurchases. In fact, academics have long wondered why firms *ever* pay a dividend instead of repurchasing stock. There have been at least two possible reasons for avoiding repurchases. First, Grullon and Michaely point out that in the past the Securities and Exchange Commission (SEC) had accused some firms undergoing share repurchase programs of illegal price manipulation.[3] However, these authors indicate that SEC Rule 10b-18, adopted in 1982, provides guidelines for firms to avoid the charge of price manipulation. These guidelines are relatively easy to follow, so firms should not have to worry about this charge today. In fact, Grullon and Michaely believe that the large increase in buyback programs in recent years is at least partially the result of 10b-18. Second, the IRS can penalize firms repurchasing their own stocks if the only reason is to avoid the taxes that would be levied on dividends. However, this threat has not materialized with the growth in corporate repurchases. Thus, these two reasons do not seem to justify the avoidance of repurchases.

---

[2]This exclusion applies if the firm owns less than 20 percent of the stock in the other company. The exclusion rises to 80 percent if the firm owns more than 20 percent of the stock of the other company and is 100 percent if the firm owns more than 80 percent of the stock of the other company. Corporations are not granted an exclusion for interest earned on bonds.

[3]See Gustavo Grullon and Roni Michaely, "Dividends, Share Repurchases, and the Substitution Hypothesis," *Journal of Finance* (August 2002), p. 1677.

Summary of Personal Taxes

This section suggests that because of personal taxes, firms have an incentive to reduce dividends. For example, they might increase capital expenditures, acquire other companies, or purchase financial assets. However, due to financial considerations and legal constraints, rational firms with large cash flows will likely exhaust these activities with plenty of cash left over for dividends.

It is harder to explain why firms pay dividends instead of repurchasing shares. The tax savings from buybacks are significant, and fear of either the SEC or the IRS seems overblown. Academics are of two minds here. Some argue that corporations were simply slow to grasp the benefits from repurchases. However, since the idea has firmly caught on, the trend toward replacement of dividends with buybacks will continue. We might even conjecture that dividends will be as unimportant in the future as repurchases were in the past. Conversely, others argue that companies have paid dividends all along for good reason. Perhaps the legal hassles, particularly from the IRS, are significant after all. Or there may be other, more subtle benefits from dividends. We consider potential benefits of dividends in the next section.

18.6 Real-World Factors Favoring a High-Dividend Policy

The previous section pointed out that because individuals pay taxes on dividends, financial managers might seek ways to reduce dividends. While we discussed the problems with taking on more capital budgeting projects, acquiring other firms, and hoarding cash, we stated that share repurchase has many of the benefits of a dividend with less of a tax disadvantage. This section considers reasons why a firm might pay its shareholders high dividends even in the presence of personal taxes on these dividends.

Desire for Current Income

It has been argued that many individuals desire current income. The classic example is the group of retired people and others living on a fixed income. The argument further states that these individuals would bid up the stock price should dividends rise and bid down the stock price should dividends fall.

This argument does not hold in Miller and Modigliani's theoretical model. An individual preferring high current cash flow but holding low-dividend securities could easily sell off shares to provide the necessary funds. Thus in a world of no transactions costs, a high–current-dividend policy would be of no value to the stockholder.

However, the current income argument is relevant in the real world. Stock sales involve brokerage fees and other transaction costs—direct cash expenses that could be avoided by an investment in high-dividend securities. In addition, stock sales are time-consuming, further leading investors to buy high-dividend securities.

To put this argument in perspective, remember that financial intermediaries such as mutual funds can perform repackaging transactions at low cost. Such intermediaries could buy low-dividend stocks and, by a controlled policy of realizing gains, pay their investors at a higher rate.

Behavioral Finance

Suppose it turned out that the transaction costs in selling no-dividend securities could not account for the preference of investors for dividends. Would there still be a reason for high dividends? We introduced the topic of behavioral finance in Chapter 13, pointing out that the ideas of behaviorists represent a strong challenge to the theory of efficient capital markets. It turns out that behavioral finance also has an argument for high dividends.

The basic idea here concerns *self-control*, a concept that, though quite important in psychology, has received virtually no emphasis in finance. Although we cannot review all that psychology has to say about self-control, let's focus on one example—losing weight. Suppose Alfred Martin, a college student, just got back from the Christmas break more than a few pounds heavier than he would like. Everyone would probably agree that diet and exercise are the two ways to lose weight. But how should Alfred put this approach into practice? (We'll focus on exercise, though the same principle would apply to diet as well.) One way—let's call it the economists' way—would involve trying to make rational decisions. Each day Al would balance the costs and the benefits of exercising. Perhaps he would choose to exercise on most days because losing the weight is important to him. However, when he is too busy with exams, he might rationally choose not to exercise because he cannot afford the time. And he wants to be socially active as well. So he may rationally choose to avoid exercise on days when parties and other social commitments become too time-consuming.

This seems sensible—at first glance. The problem is that he must make a choice every day, and there may simply be too many days when his lack of self-control gets the better of him. He may tell himself that he doesn't have the time to exercise on a particular day, simply because he is starting to find exercise boring, not because he really doesn't have the time. Before long, he is avoiding exercise on most days—and overeating in reaction to the guilt from not exercising!

Is there an alternative? One way would be to set rigid rules. Perhaps Alfred decides to exercise five days a week *no matter what*. This is not necessarily the best approach for everyone, but there is no question that many of us (perhaps most of us) live by a set of rules. For example, Shefrin and Statman[4] suggest some typical rules:

- Jog at least two miles a day.
- Do not consume more than 1,200 calories per day.
- Bank the wife's salary and spend from only the husband's paycheck.
- Save at least 2 percent of every paycheck for children's college education and never withdraw from this fund.
- Never touch a drop of alcohol.

What does this have to do with dividends? Investors must also deal with self-control. Suppose a retiree wants to consume $20,000 a year from savings, in addition to Social Security and her pension. On one hand, she could buy stocks with a dividend yield high enough to generate $20,000 in dividends. On the other hand, she could place her savings in no-dividend stocks, selling off $20,000 each year for consumption. Though these two approaches seem equivalent financially, the second one may allow for too much leeway. If lack of self-control gets the better of her, she might sell off too much, leaving little for her later years. Better, perhaps, to short-circuit this possibility by investing in dividend-paying stocks with a firm personal rule of *never* "dipping into principal." Although behaviorists do not claim that this approach is for everyone, they argue that enough people think this way to explain why firms pay dividends—even though, as we said earlier, dividends are tax disadvantaged.

Does behavioral finance argue for increased stock repurchases as well as increased dividends? The answer is no because investors will sell the stock that firms repurchase. As

---

[4]Hersh M. Shefrin and Meir Statman, "Explaining Investor Preference for Cash Dividends," *Journal of Financial Economics* 13 (1984).

we have said, selling stock involves too much leeway. Investors might sell too many shares of stock, leaving little for later years. Thus, the behaviorist argument may explain why companies pay dividends in a world with personal taxes.

Agency Costs

Although stockholders, bondholders, and management form firms for mutually beneficial reasons, one party may later gain at the other's expense. For example, take the potential conflict between bondholders and stockholders. Bondholders would like stockholders to leave as much cash as possible in the firm so that this cash would be available to pay the bondholders during times of financial distress. Conversely, stockholders would like to keep this extra cash for themselves. That's where dividends come in. Managers, acting on behalf of the stockholders, may pay dividends simply to keep the cash away from the bondholders. In other words, a dividend can be viewed as a wealth transfer from bondholders to stockholders. There is empirical evidence for this view of things. For example, DeAngelo and DeAngelo find that firms in financial distress are reluctant to cut dividends.[5] Of course, bondholders know about the propensity of stockholders to transfer money out of the firm. To protect themselves, bondholders frequently create loan agreements stating that dividends can be paid only if the firm has earnings, cash flow, and working capital above specified levels.

Although managers may be looking out for stockholders in any conflict with bondholders, managers may pursue selfish goals at the expense of stockholders in other situations. For example, as discussed in a previous chapter, managers might pad expense accounts, take on pet projects with negative NPVs, or simply not work hard. Managers find it easier to pursue these selfish goals when the firm has plenty of free cash flow. After all, one cannot squander funds if the funds are not available in the first place. And that is where dividends come in. Several scholars have suggested that the board of directors can use dividends to reduce agency costs.[6] By paying dividends equal to the amount of "surplus" cash flow, a firm can reduce management's ability to squander the firm's resources.

This discussion suggests a reason for increased dividends, but the same argument applies to share repurchases as well. Managers, acting on behalf of stockholders, can just as easily keep cash from bondholders through repurchases as through dividends. And the board of directors, also acting on behalf of stockholders, can reduce the cash available to spendthrift managers just as easily through repurchases as through dividends. Thus, the presence of agency costs is not an argument for dividends over repurchases. Rather, agency costs imply firms may increase either dividends or share repurchases rather than hoard large amounts of cash.

Information Content of Dividends and Dividend Signaling

Information Content   While there are many things researchers do not know about dividends, we know one thing for sure: The stock price of a firm generally rises when the firm announces a dividend increase and generally falls when a dividend reduction is announced. For example, Asquith and Mullins estimate that stock prices rise about 3 percent following

---

[5]H. DeAngelo and L. DeAngelo, "Dividend Policy and Financial Distress: An Empirical Investigation of Troubled NYSE Firms," *Journal of Finance* 45 (1990).

[6]Michael Rozeff, "How Companies Set Their Dividend Payout Ratios," in *The Revolution in Corporate Finance,* edited by Joel M. Stern and Donald H. Chew (New York: Basil Blackwell, 1986). See also Robert S. Hansen, Raman Kumar, and Dilip K. Shome, "Dividend Policy and Corporate Monitoring: Evidence from the Regulated Electric Utility Industry," *Financial Management* (Spring 1994).

announcements of dividend initiations.[7] Michaely, Thaler, and Womack find that stock prices fall about 7 percent following announcements of dividend omissions.[8]

The question is how we should *interpret* this empirical evidence. Consider the following three positions on dividends:

1. From the homemade dividend argument of MM, dividend policy is irrelevant, given that future earnings (and cash flows) are held constant.

2. Because of tax effects, a firm's stock price is negatively related to the current dividend when future earnings (or cash flows) are held constant.

3. Because of stockholders' desire for current income, a firm's stock price is positively related to its current dividend, even when future earnings (or cash flows) are held constant.

At first glance, the empirical evidence that stock prices rise when dividend increases are announced may seem consistent with position 3 and inconsistent with positions 1 and 2. In fact, many writers have said this. However, other authors have countered that the observation itself is consistent with all three positions. They point out that companies do not like to cut a dividend. Thus, firms will raise the dividend only when future earnings, cash flow, and so on are expected to rise enough so that the dividend is not likely to be reduced later to its original level. A dividend increase is management's *signal* to the market that the firm is expected to do well.

It is the expectation of good times, and not only the stockholders' affinity for current income, that raises stock price. The rise in the stock price following the dividend signal is called the **information content effect** of the dividend. To recapitulate, imagine that the stock price is unaffected or even negatively affected by the level of dividends, given that future earnings (or cash flows) are held constant. Nevertheless, the information content effect implies that stock price may rise when dividends are raised—if dividends simultaneously cause stockholders to *increase* their expectations of future earnings and cash flows.

Dividend Signaling   We just argued that the market infers a rise in earnings and cash flows from a dividend increase, leading to a higher stock price. Conversely, the market infers a decrease in cash flows from a dividend reduction, leading to a fall in stock price. This raises an interesting corporate strategy: Could management increase dividends just to make the market *think* that cash flows will be higher, even when management knows that cash flows will not rise?

While this strategy may seem dishonest, academics take the position that managers frequently attempt the strategy. Academics begin with the following accounting identity for an all-equity firm:

$$\text{Cash flow}^9 = \text{Capital expenditures} + \text{Dividends} \qquad \textbf{(18.5)}$$

Equation 18.5 must hold if a firm is neither issuing nor repurchasing stock. That is, the cash flow from the firm must go somewhere. If it is not paid out in dividends, it must be used in some expenditure. Whether the expenditure involves a capital budgeting project or a purchase of Treasury bills, it is still an expenditure.

Imagine that we are in the middle of the year and investors are trying to make some forecast of cash flow over the entire year. These investors may use Equation 18.5 to estimate

---

[7]P. Asquith and D. Mullins, Jr., "The Impact of Initiating Dividend Payments on Shareholder Wealth," *Journal of Business* (January 1983).

[8]R. Michaely, R. H. Thaler, and K. Womack, "Price Reactions to Dividend Initiations and Omissions: Overreactions or Drift," *Journal of Finance* 50 (1995).

[9]The correct representation of Equation 18.5 involves cash flow, not earnings. However, with little loss of understanding, we could discuss dividend signaling in terms of earnings, not cash flow.

cash flow. For example, suppose the firm announces that current dividends will be $50 million and the market believes that capital expenditures are $80 million. The market would then determine cash flow to be $130 million (= $50 + 80).

Now, suppose that the firm had, alternatively, announced a dividend of $70 million. The market might assume that cash flow remains at $130 million, implying capital expenditures of $60 million (= $130 − 70). Here, the increase in dividends would hurt stock price because the market anticipates valuable capital expenditures will be crowded out. Alternatively, the market might assume that capital expenditures remain at $80 million, implying the estimate of cash flow to be $150 million (= $70 + 80). Stock price would likely rise here because stock prices usually increase with cash flow. In general, academics believe that models where investors assume capital expenditures remain the same are more realistic. Thus, an increase in dividends raises stock price.

Now we come to the incentives of managers to fool the public. Suppose you are a manager who wants to boost stock price, perhaps because you are planning to sell some of your personal holdings of the company's stock immediately. You might increase dividends so that the market would raise its estimate of the firm's cash flow, thereby also boosting the current stock price.

If this strategy is appealing, would anything prevent you from raising dividends without limit? The answer is yes because there is also a *cost* to raising dividends. That is, the firm will have to forgo some of its profitable projects. Remember that cash flow in Equation 18.5 is a constant, so an increase in dividends is obtained only by a reduction in capital expenditures. At some point the market will learn that cash flow has not increased, but instead profitable capital expenditures have been cut. Once the market absorbs this information, stock price should fall below what it would have been had dividends never been raised. Thus, if you plan to sell, say, half of your shares and retain the other half, an increase in dividends should help you on the immediate sale but hurt you when you sell your remaining shares years later. So your decision on the level of dividends will be based, among other things, on the timing of your personal stock sales.

This is a simplified example of dividend signaling, where the manager sets dividend policy based on maximum benefit for himself.[10] Alternatively, a given manager may have no desire to sell his shares immediately but knows that, at any one time, plenty of ordinary shareholders will want to do so. Thus, for the benefit of shareholders in general, a manager will always be aware of the trade-off between current and future stock price. And this, then, is the essence of signaling with dividends. It is not enough for a manager to set dividend policy to maximize the true (or intrinsic) value of the firm. He must also consider the effect of dividend policy on the current stock price, even if the current stock price does not reflect true value.

Does a motive to signal imply that managers will increase dividends rather than share repurchases? The answer is likely no: Most academic models imply that dividends and share repurchases are perfect substitutes.[11] Rather, these models indicate that managers will consider reducing capital spending (even on projects with positive NPVs) to increase either dividends or share repurchases.

---

[10]Papers examining fully developed models of signaling include S. Bhattacharya, "Imperfect Information, Dividend Policy, and 'the Bird in the Hand' Fallacy," *Bell Journal of Economics* 10 (1979); S. Bhattacharya, "Non-dissipative Signaling Structure and Dividend Policy," *Quarterly Journal of Economics* 95 (1980), p. 1; S. Ross, "The Determination of Financial Structure: The Incentive Signaling Approach," *Bell Journal of Economics* 8 (1977), p. 1; M. Miller and K. Rock, "Dividend Policy under Asymmetric Information," *Journal of Finance* (1985).

[11]Signaling models where dividends and repurchases are not perfect substitutes are contained in Franklin Allen, Antonio Bernardo, and Ivo Welch, "A Theory of Dividends Based on Tax Clienteles," *Journal of Finance* (2002) and John Kose and Joseph Williams, "Dividends, Dilution and Taxes: A Signaling Equilibrium," *Journal of Finance* (1985).

18.7   The Clientele Effect: A Resolution of Real-World Factors?

In the previous two sections, we pointed out that the existence of personal taxes favors a low-dividend policy, whereas other factors favor high dividends. The financial profession had hoped that it would be easy to determine which of these sets of factors dominates. Unfortunately, after years of research, no one has been able to conclude which of the two is more important. This is surprising: We might be skeptical that the two sets of factors would cancel each other out so perfectly.

However, one particular idea, known as the *clientele effect*, implies that the two sets of factors are likely to cancel each other out after all. To understand this idea, let's separate investors in high tax brackets from those in low tax brackets. Individuals in high tax brackets likely prefer either no or low dividends. Low tax bracket investors generally fall into three categories. First, there are individual investors in low brackets. They are likely to prefer some dividends if they desire current income. Second, pension funds pay no taxes on either dividends or capital gains. Because they face no tax consequences, pension funds will also prefer dividends if they have a preference for current income. Finally, corporations can exclude at least 70 percent of their dividend income but cannot exclude any of their capital gains. Thus, corporations are likely to prefer high-dividend stocks, even without a preference for current income.

Suppose that 40 percent of all investors prefer high dividends and 60 percent prefer low dividends, yet only 20 percent of firms pay high dividends while 80 percent pay low dividends. Here, the high-dividend firms will be in short supply, implying that their stock should be bid up while the stock of low-dividend firms should be bid down.

However, the dividend policies of all firms need not be fixed in the long run. In this example, we would expect enough low-dividend firms to increase their payout so that 40 percent of the firms pay high dividends and 60 percent of the firms pay low dividends. After this adjustment, no firm will gain from changing its dividend policy. Once payouts of corporations conform to the desires of stockholders, no single firm can affect its market value by switching from one dividend strategy to another.

Clienteles are likely to form in the following way:

Group	Stocks
Individuals in high tax brackets	Zero- to low-payout stocks
Individuals in low tax brackets	Low- to medium-payout stocks
Tax-free institutions	Medium-payout stocks
Corporations	High-payout stocks

To see if you understand the clientele effect, consider the following statement: "In a world where many investors like high dividends, a firm can boost its share price by increasing its dividend payout ratio." True or false?

The statement is likely to be false. As long as there are already enough high-dividend firms to satisfy dividend-loving investors, a firm will not be able to boost its share price by paying high dividends. A firm can boost its stock price only if an *unsatisfied* clientele exists.

Figure 18.7

Preferences of
Investors for
Dividend Yield

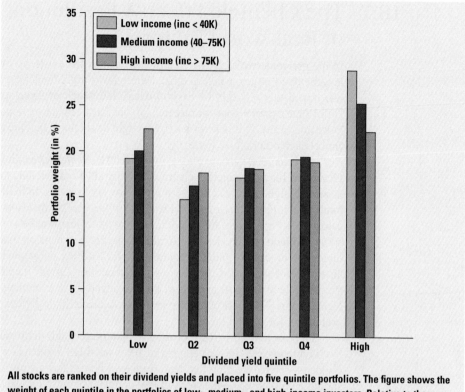

All stocks are ranked on their dividend yields and placed into five quintile portfolios. The figure shows the weight of each quintile in the portfolios of low-, medium-, and high-income investors. Relative to those with lower income, high-income investors place a greater percentage of their assets in low-dividend stocks and a smaller percentage in high-dividend stocks.

SOURCE: Adapted from Figure 2 of John Graham and Alok Kumar, "Do Dividend Clienteles Exist? Evidence on Dividend Preferences of Retail Investors," forthcoming *Journal of Finance*.

Our discussion of clienteles followed from the fact that tax brackets vary across investors. If shareholders care about taxes, stocks should attract clienteles based on dividend yield. Is there any evidence that this is the case?

Consider Figure 18.7. Here, John Graham and Alok Kumar[12] rank common stocks by their dividend yields (the ratio of dividend to stock price) and place them into five portfolios, called quintiles. The bottom quintile contains the 20 percent of stocks with the lowest dividend yields; the next quintile contains the 20 percent of stocks with the next lowest dividend yields; and so on. The figure shows the weight of each quintile in the portfolios of low-, medium-, and high-income investors. As can be seen, relative to low-income investors, high-income investors put a greater percentage of their assets into low-dividend securities. Conversely, again relative to low-income investors, high-income investors put a smaller percentage of their assets into high-dividend securities.

---

[12] John Graham and Alok Kumar, "Do Dividend Clienteles Exist? Evidence on Dividend Preferences of Retail Investors," forthcoming *Journal of Finance*.

18.8 What We Know and Do Not Know about Dividend Policy

Corporate Dividends Are Substantial

We pointed out earlier in the chapter that dividends are tax disadvantaged relative to capital gains because dividends are taxed upon payment whereas taxes on capital gains are deferred until sale. Nevertheless, dividends in the U.S. economy are substantial. For example, consider Figure 18.8, which shows the ratio of aggregate dividends to aggregate earnings for firms on the New York Stock Exchange (NYSE), the American Stock Exchange (AMEX), and NASDAQ over various periods. The ratio is approximately 43 percent for the

Figure 18.8 **Ratio of Aggregate Dividends to Aggregate Earnings in the United States**

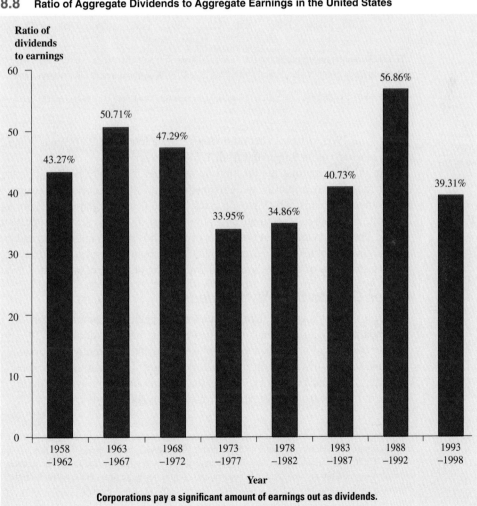

Corporations pay a significant amount of earnings out as dividends.

SOURCE: Table 11 of E. F. Fama and K. R. French, "Disappearing Dividends: Changing Firm Characteristics or Lower Propensity to Pay?" *Journal of Financial Economics* (April 2001).

Figure 18.9

Proportion of
Dividend Payers
Among All U.S.
Industrial Firms

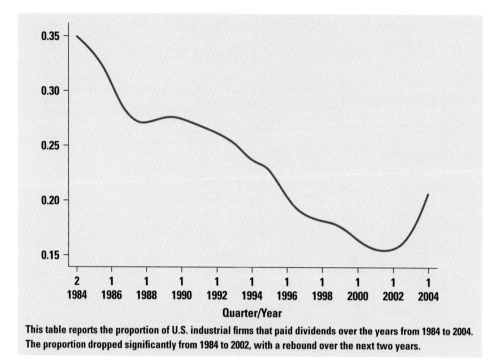

This table reports the proportion of U.S. industrial firms that paid dividends over the years from 1984 to 2004. The proportion dropped significantly from 1984 to 2002, with a rebound over the next two years.

SOURCE: Figure 1 of Brandon Julio and David Ikenberry, "Reappearing Dividends," unpublished paper, University of Illinois (July 2004).

period from 1963 to 1998. This ratio varies from a low of 33.95 percent in the 1973–1977 period to a high of 56.86 percent from 1988 to 1992.[13]

We might argue that the taxation on dividends is actually minimal, perhaps because dividends are paid primarily to individuals in low tax brackets or because institutions such as pension funds, which pay no taxes, are the primary recipients. However, Peterson, Peterson, and Ang conducted an in-depth study of dividends for one representative year, 1979.[14] They found that about two-thirds of dividends went to individuals and that the average marginal tax bracket for these individuals was about 40 percent. Thus, we must conclude that large amounts of dividends are paid, even in the presence of substantial taxation.

Fewer Companies Pay Dividends

Although dividends are substantial, Fama and French (FF) point out that the percentage of companies paying dividends has fallen over the last few decades.[15] FF argue that the decline was caused primarily by an explosion of small, currently unprofitable companies that have recently listed on various stock exchanges. For the most part, firms of this type do not pay dividends. Figure 18.9 shows that the proportion of dividend payers among U.S. industrial firms dropped substantially from 1984 to 2002.

---

[13] An astute reader may note that the year-by-year ratios of dividends to earnings in Figure 18.5 are lower than those in Figure 18.8. However, Figure 18.5 calculates an equal-weighted average for the ratio across all firms, whereas Figure 18.8 calculates the ratio of aggregate dividends to aggregate earnings. The ratios in Figure 18.8 are higher because the ratio of dividends to earnings is higher for large firms than for small firms.

[14] P. Peterson, D. Peterson, and J. Ang, "Direct Evidence on the Marginal Rate of Taxation on Dividend Income," *Journal of Financial Economics* 14 (1985).

[15] E. F. Fama and K. R. French, "Disappearing Dividends: Changing Firm Characteristics or Lower Propensity to Pay?" *Journal of Financial Economics* (April 2001).

This figure, presented in a paper by Julio and Ikenberry,[16] also shows an *increase* in the proportion of dividend payers from 2002 to 2004. One obvious explanation is the cut in the maximum tax rate on dividends to 15 percent, signed into law in May 2003. However, JI downplay the effect of the tax cut, suggesting a number of other reasons. Furthermore, the resurgence in dividend payers has been observed only over the two-year period from 2002 to 2004. Perhaps this trend is just a statistical aberration.

Figure 18.9 does not imply that dividends across *all* firms declined from 1984 to 2002. DeAngelo, DeAngelo, and Skinner[17] point out that while small firms have shied away from dividends, the largest firms have substantially increased their dividends over recent decades. This increase has created such concentration in dividends that the 25 top dividend-paying firms accounted for more than 50 percent of aggregate dividends in the United States in 2000. DeAngelo and colleagues conclude (p. 425), "Industrial firms exhibit a two-tier structure in which a small number of firms with very high earnings collectively generates the majority of earnings and dominates the dividend supply, while the vast majority of firms has at best a modest collective impact on aggregate earnings and dividends."

Corporations Smooth Dividends

In 1956, John Lintner made two important observations concerning dividend policy.[18] First, real-world companies typically set long-term target ratios of dividends to earnings. A firm is likely to set a low target ratio if it has many positive NPV projects relative to available cash flow and a high ratio if it has few positive NPV projects. Second, managers know that only part of any change in earnings is likely to be permanent. Because managers need time to assess the permanence of any earnings rise, dividend changes appear to lag earnings changes by a number of periods.

Taken together, Lintner's observations suggest that two parameters describe dividend policy: the target payout ratio (t) and the speed of adjustment of current dividends to the target (s). Dividend changes will tend to conform to the following model:

$$\text{Dividend change} \equiv \text{Div}_1 - \text{Div}_0 = s \cdot (t\text{EPS}_1 - \text{Div}_0) \qquad \textbf{(18.6)}$$

where Div_1 and Div_0 are dividends in the next year and dividends in the current year, respectively. EPS_1 is earnings per share in the next year.

EXAMPLE 18.2

Dividend Smoothing   Calculator Graphics, Inc., (CGI) has a target payout ratio of 0.30. Last year's earnings per share were $10, and in accordance with the target, CGI paid dividends of $3 per share last year. However, earnings have jumped to $20 this year. Because the managers do not believe that this increase is permanent, they do *not* plan to raise dividends all the way to $6 (= 0.30 × $20). Rather, their speed of adjustment coefficient, s, is 0.5, implying that the *increase* in dividends from last year to this year will be

$$0.5 \times (\$6 - \$3) = \$1.50$$

(continued)

---

[16]Brandon Julio and David Ikenberry, "Reappearing Dividends," unpublished paper, University of Illinois (July 2004).

[17]Harry DeAngelo, Linda DeAngelo, and Douglas Skinner, "Are Dividends Disappearing? Dividend Concentration and the Consolidation of Earnings," *Journal of Financial Economics* (2004).

[18]J. Lintner, "Distribution and Incomes of Corporations among Dividends, Retained Earnings, and Taxes," *American Economic Review* (May 1956).

That is, the increase in dividends is the product of the speed of adjustment coefficient, 0.50, times the difference between what dividends would be with full adjustment [$6 (= 0.30 × $20)] and last year's dividends. Dividends will increase by $1.50, so dividends this year will be $4.50 (= $3 + $1.50).

Now, suppose that earnings stay at $20 next year. The increase in dividends next year will be

$$0.5 \times (\$6 - \$4.50) = \$0.75$$

In words, the increase in dividends from this year to next year will be the speed of adjustment coefficient (0.50) times the difference between what dividends would have been next year with full adjustment ($6) and this year's dividends ($4.50). Because dividends will increase by $0.75, dividends next year will be $5.25 (= $4.50 + $0.75). In this way, dividends will slowly rise every year if earnings in all future years remain at $20. However, dividends will reach $6 only at infinity.

The limiting cases in Equation 18.6 occur when $s = 1$ and $s = 0$. If $s = 1$, the actual change in dividends will be equal to the target change in dividends. Here, full adjustment occurs immediately. If $s = 0$, $\text{Div}_1 = \text{Div}_0$. In other words, there is no change in dividends at all. Real-world companies can be expected to set s between 0 and 1.

An implication of Lintner's model is that the dividends-to-earnings ratio rises when a company begins a period of bad times, and the ratio falls when a company starts a period of good times. Thus, dividends display less variability than do earnings. In other words, firms *smooth* dividends.

Payouts Provide Information to the Market

We previously observed that the price of a firm's stock frequently rises when either its current dividend is increased or a stock repurchase is announced. Conversely, the price of a firm's stock can fall significantly when its dividend is cut. In other words, there is information content in payouts. For example, consider what happened to Pacific Enterprises a number of years ago. Faced with poor operating results, Pacific Enterprises omitted its regular quarterly dividend. The next day the common stock dropped from $24\frac{7}{8}$ to $18\frac{7}{8}$. One reason may be that investors are looking at current dividends for clues concerning the level of future earnings and dividends.

A Sensible Payout Policy

The knowledge of the finance profession varies across topic areas. For example, capital budgeting techniques are both powerful and precise. A single net present value equation can accurately determine whether a multimillion-dollar project should be accepted or rejected. The capital asset pricing model and the arbitrage pricing model provide empirically validated relationships between expected return and risk.

However, the field has less knowledge of capital structure policy. Though a number of elegant theories relate firm value to the level of debt, no formula can be used to calculate the firm's optimal debt–equity ratio. Our profession is forced too frequently to employ rules of thumb, such as treating the industry's average ratio as the optimal one for the firm. The field's knowledge of dividend policy is, perhaps, similar to its knowledge of capital structure policy. We do know the following:

1. The intrinsic value of a firm is reduced when positive NPV projects are rejected to pay a dividend.

2. Firms should avoid issuing stock to pay a dividend in a world with personal taxes.

3. Stock repurchases represent a sensible alternative to dividends.

In Their Own Words

The preceding recommendations suggest that firms with many positive NPV projects relative to available cash flow should have low payout ratios. Firms with fewer positive NPV projects relative to available cash flow might want to consider higher payouts. In addition, there is some benefit to dividend stability, and most firms avoid unnecessary changes in dividend payout.

However, there is no formula for calculating the optimal dividend-to-earnings ratio. In addition, there is no formula for determining the optimal mix between stock repurchases and dividends. It can be argued that for tax reasons, firms should always substitute stock repurchases for dividends. But while the volume of repurchases has greatly increased over time, Figure 18.5 does not suggest that dividends are on the way out.

The Pros and Cons of Paying Dividends

Pros	Cons
1. Dividends may appeal to investors who desire stable cash flow but do not want to incur the transaction costs from periodically selling shares of stock.	1. Dividends are taxed as ordinary income.
2. Behavioral finance argues that investors with limited self-control can meet current consumption needs with high-dividend stocks while adhering to the policy of never dipping into principal.	2. Dividends can reduce internal sources of financing. Dividends may force the firm to forgo positive NPV projects or to rely on costly external equity financing.
3. Managers, acting on behalf of stockholders, can pay dividends in order to keep cash from bondholders.	3. Once established, dividend cuts are hard to make without adversely affecting a firm's stock price.
4. The board of directors, acting on behalf of stockholders, can use dividends to reduce the cash available to spendthrift managers.	
5. Managers may increase dividends to signal their optimism concerning future cash flow.	

Some Survey Evidence about Dividends

A recent study surveyed a large number of financial executives regarding dividend policy. One of the questions asked was this: "Do these statements describe factors that affect your company's dividend decisions?" Table 18.2 shows some of the results.

As shown in Table 18.2, financial managers are very disinclined to cut dividends. Moreover, they are very conscious of their previous dividends and desire to maintain a relatively steady dividend. In contrast, the cost of external capital and the desire to attract "prudent man" investors (those with fiduciary duties) are less important.

Table 18.3 is drawn from the same survey, but here the responses are to the question, "How important are the following factors to your company's dividend decisions?" Not surprisingly given the responses in Table 18.2 and our earlier discussion, the highest priority is maintaining a consistent dividend policy. The next several items are also consistent with our previous analysis. Financial managers are very concerned about earnings stability

Table 18.2

Survey Responses on
Dividend Decisions*

Policy Statements	Percentage Who Agree or Strongly Agree
1. We try to avoid reducing dividends per share.	93.8%
2. We try to maintain a smooth dividend from year to year.	89.6
3. We consider the level of dividends per share that we have paid in recent quarters.	88.2
4. We are reluctant to make dividend changes that might have to be reversed in the future.	77.9
5. We consider the change or growth in dividends per share.	66.7
6. We consider the cost of raising external capital to be smaller than the cost of cutting dividends.	42.8
7. We pay dividends to attract investors subject to "prudent man" investment restrictions.	41.7

*Survey respondents were asked the question, "Do these statements describe factors that affect your company's dividend decisions?"

SOURCE: Adapted from Table 4 of A. Brav, J.R. Graham, C.R. Harvey, and R. Michaely, "Payout Policy in the 21st Century," *Journal of Financial Economics*, 2005.

Table 18.3

Survey Responses on
Dividend Decisions*

Policy Statements	Percentage Who Think This Is Important or Very Important
1. Maintaining consistency with our historic dividend policy.	84.1%
2. Stability of future earnings.	71.9
3. A sustainable change in earnings.	67.1
4. Attracting institutional investors to purchase our stock.	52.5
5. The availability of good investment opportunities for our firm to pursue.	47.6
6. Attracting retail investors to purchase our stock.	44.5
7. Personal taxes our stockholders pay when receiving dividends.	21.1
8. Flotation costs to issuing new equity.	9.3

*Survey respondents were asked the question, "How important are the following factors to your company's dividend decisions?"

SOURCE: Adapted from Table 5 of A. Brav, J.R. Graham, C.R. Harvey, and R. Michaely, "Payout Policy in the 21st Century," *Journal of Financial Economics*, 2005.

and future earnings levels in making dividend decisions, and they consider the availability of good investment opportunities. Survey respondents also believed that attracting both institutional and individual (retail) investors was relatively important.

In contrast to our discussion in the earlier part of this chapter of taxes and flotation costs, the financial managers in this survey did not think that personal taxes paid on dividends by shareholders are very important. And even fewer think that equity flotation costs are relevant.

18.9 Stock Dividends and Stock Splits

Another type of dividend is paid out in shares of stock. This type of dividend is called a **stock dividend**. A stock dividend is not a true dividend because it is not paid in cash. The effect of a stock dividend is to increase the number of shares that each owner holds. Because there are more shares outstanding, each is simply worth less.

A stock dividend is commonly expressed as a percentage; for example, a 20 percent stock dividend means that a shareholder receives one new share for every five currently owned (a 20 percent increase). Because every shareholder receives 20 percent more stock, the total number of shares outstanding rises by 20 percent. As we will see in a moment, the result is that each share of stock is worth about 20 percent less.

A **stock split** is essentially the same thing as a stock dividend, except that a split is expressed as a ratio instead of a percentage. When a split is declared, each share is split up to create additional shares. For example, in a three-for-one stock split, each old share is split into three new shares.

Some Details about Stock Splits and Stock Dividends

Stock splits and stock dividends have essentially the same impacts on the corporation and the shareholder: They increase the number of shares outstanding and reduce the value per share. The accounting treatment is not the same, however, and it depends on two things: (1) whether the distribution is a stock split or a stock dividend and (2) the size of the stock dividend if it is called a dividend.

By convention, stock dividends of less than 20 to 25 percent are called *small stock dividends*. The accounting procedure for such a dividend is discussed next. A stock dividend greater than this value of 20 to 25 percent is called a *large stock dividend*. Large stock dividends are not uncommon. For example, in April 2005, WellPoint (health insurer) and Gentex (manufacturer of automatic dimming rearview mirrors) both announced a 100 percent stock dividend, to name a few. Except for some relatively minor accounting differences, this has the same effect as a two-for-one stock split.

Example of a Small Stock Dividend   The Peterson Co., a consulting firm specializing in difficult accounting problems, has 10,000 shares of stock outstanding, each selling at $66. The total market value of the equity is $66 \times 10,000 = $660,000$. With a 10 percent stock dividend, each stockholder receives one additional share for each 10 owned, and the total number of shares outstanding after the dividend is 11,000.

Before the stock dividend, the equity portion of Peterson's balance sheet might look like this:

Common stock ($1 par, 10,000 shares outstanding)	$ 10,000
Capital in excess of par value	200,000
Retained earnings	290,000
Total owners' equity	$500,000

A seemingly arbitrary accounting procedure is used to adjust the balance sheet after a small stock dividend. Because 1,000 new shares are issued, the common stock account is increased by $1,000 (1,000 shares at $1 par value each), for a total of $11,000. The market price of $66 is $65 greater than the par value, so the "excess" of $65 × 1,000 shares = $65,000 is added to the capital surplus account (capital in excess of par value), producing a total of $265,000.

Total owners' equity is unaffected by the stock dividend because no cash has come in or out, so retained earnings are reduced by the entire $66,000, leaving $224,000. The net effect of these machinations is that Peterson's equity accounts now look like this:

Common stock ($1 par, 11,000 shares outstanding)	$ 11,000
Capital in excess of par value	265,000
Retained earnings	224,000
Total owners' equity	$500,000

Example of a Stock Split   A stock split is conceptually similar to a stock dividend, but it is commonly expressed as a ratio. For example, in a three-for-two split, each shareholder receives one additional share of stock for each two held originally, so a three-for-two split amounts to a 50 percent stock dividend. Again, no cash is paid out, and the percentage of the entire firm that each shareholder owns is unaffected.

The accounting treatment of a stock split is a little different from (and simpler than) that of a stock dividend. Suppose Peterson decides to declare a two-for-one stock split. The number of shares outstanding will double to 20,000, and the par value will be halved to $.50 per share. The owners' equity after the split is represented as follows:

For a list of recent stock splits, try **www.stocksplits.net**.

Common stock ($.50 par, 20,000 shares outstanding)	$ 10,000
Capital in excess of par value	200,000
Retained earnings	290,000
Total owners' equity	$500,000

Note that for all three of the categories, the figures on the right are completely unaffected by the split. The only changes are in the par value per share and the number of shares outstanding. Because the number of shares has doubled, the par value of each is cut in half.

Example of a Large Stock Dividend   In our example, if a 100 percent stock dividend were declared, 10,000 new shares would be distributed, so 20,000 shares would be outstanding. At a $1 par value per share, the common stock account would rise by $10,000, for a total of $20,000. The retained earnings account would be reduced by $10,000, leaving $280,000. The result would be the following:

Common stock ($1 par, 20,000 shares outstanding)	$ 20,000
Capital in excess of par value	200,000
Retained earnings	280,000
Total owners' equity	$500,000

Value of Stock Splits and Stock Dividends

The laws of logic tell us that stock splits and stock dividends can (1) leave the value of the firm unaffected, (2) increase its value, or (3) decrease its value. Unfortunately, the issues are complex enough that we cannot easily determine which of the three relationships holds.

The Benchmark Case   A strong case can be made that stock dividends and splits do not change either the wealth of any shareholder or the wealth of the firm as a whole. In our preceding example, the equity had a total market value of $660,000. With the small stock dividend, the number of shares increased to 11,000, so it seems that each would be worth $660,000/11,000 = $60.

For example, a shareholder who had 100 shares worth $66 each before the dividend would have 110 shares worth $60 each afterward. The total value of the stock is $6,600 either way; so the stock dividend doesn't really have any economic effect.

After the stock split, there are 20,000 shares outstanding, so each should be worth $660,000/20,000 = $33. In other words, the number of shares doubles and the price halves. From these calculations, it appears that stock dividends and splits are just paper transactions.

Although these results are relatively obvious, there are reasons that are often given to suggest that there may be some benefits to these actions. The typical financial manager is aware of many real-world complexities, and for that reason the stock split or stock dividend decision is not treated lightly in practice.

Popular Trading Range   Proponents of stock dividends and stock splits frequently argue that a security has a proper **trading range**. When the security is priced above this level, many investors do not have the funds to buy the common trading unit of 100 shares, called a *round lot*. Although securities can be purchased in *odd-lot* form (fewer than 100 shares), the commissions are greater. Thus, firms will split the stock to keep the price in this trading range.

For example, in early 2003, Microsoft announced a two-for-one stock split. This was the ninth split for Microsoft since the company went public in 1986. The stock had split three-for-two on two occasions and two-for-one a total of seven times. So for every share of Microsoft you owned in 1986 when the company first went public, you would own 288 shares as of the most recent stock split in 2003. Similarly, since Wal-Mart went public in 1970, it has split its stock two-for-one 11 times, and Dell Computer has split three-for-two once and two-for-one six times since going public in 1988.

Although this argument of a trading range is a popular one, its validity is questionable for a number of reasons. Mutual funds, pension funds, and other institutions have steadily increased their trading activity since World War II and now handle a sizable percentage of total trading volume (on the order of 80 percent of NYSE trading volume, for example). Because these institutions buy and sell in huge amounts, the individual share price is of little concern.

Furthermore, we sometimes observe share prices that are quite large that do not appear to cause problems. To take an extreme case, consider the Swiss chocolatier Lindt. In February 2006, Lindt shares were selling for around 24,595 Swiss francs each, or about $18,818. A round lot would have cost a cool $1.88 million. This is fairly expensive, but also consider Berkshire-Hathaway, the company run by legendary investor Warren Buffet. In February 2006, each share in the company sold for about $88,000, down from a high of $95,700 in February 2004.

Finally, there is evidence that stock splits may actually decrease the liquidity of the company's shares. Following a two-for-one split, the number of shares traded should more than double if liquidity is increased by the split. This doesn't appear to happen, and the reverse is sometimes observed.

Reverse Splits

A less frequently encountered financial maneuver is the **reverse split**. For example, in February 2006, Avitar, Inc., a medical products manufacturer, underwent a one-for-fifty reverse stock split, and AVANIR Pharmaceuticals undertook a one-for-four reverse stock split in January 2006. In a one-for-five reverse split, each investor exchanges five old shares for one new share. The par value is quintupled in the process. As with stock splits and stock dividends, a case can be made that a reverse split has no real effect.

Given real-world imperfections, three related reasons are cited for reverse splits. First, transaction costs to shareholders may be less after the reverse split. Second, the liquidity and marketability of a company's stock might be improved when its price is raised to the popular trading range. Third, stocks selling at prices below a certain level are not considered respectable, meaning that investors underestimate these firms' earnings, cash flow, growth, and stability. Some financial analysts argue that a reverse split can achieve instant respectability. As was the case with stock splits, none of these reasons is particularly compelling, especially not the third one.

There are two other reasons for reverse splits. First, stock exchanges have minimum price per share requirements. A reverse split may bring the stock price up to such a minimum. In 2001–2002, in the wake of a bear market, this motive became an increasingly important one. In 2001, 106 companies asked their shareholders to approve reverse splits. There were 111 reverse splits in 2002 and 75 in 2003, but only 14 by mid-year 2004. The most common reason for these reverse splits is that NASDAQ delists companies whose stock price drops below $1 per share for 30 days. Many companies, particularly Internet-related technology companies, found themselves in danger of being delisted and used reverse splits to boost their stock prices. Second, companies sometimes perform reverse splits and, at the same time, buy out any stockholders who end up with less than a certain number of shares.

For example, in October 2005, Sagient Research Systems, a publisher of independent financial research, announced a 1-for-101 reverse stock split. At the same time, the company would repurchase all shares held by shareholders with fewer than 100 shares. The purpose of the reverse split was to allow the company to go dark. The reverse split and share repurchase meant the company would have fewer than 300 shareholders, so it would no longer be required to file periodic reports with the SEC. What made the proposal especially imaginative was that immediately after the reverse stock split, the company underwent a 101-for-1 split to restore the stock to its original cost!

Summary and Conclusions

1. The dividend policy of a firm is irrelevant in a perfect capital market because the shareholder can effectively undo the firm's dividend strategy. If a shareholder receives a greater dividend than desired, he or she can reinvest the excess. Conversely, if the shareholder receives a smaller dividend than desired, he or she can sell off extra shares of stock. This argument is due to MM and is similar to their homemade leverage concept, discussed in a previous chapter.

2. Stockholders will be indifferent between dividends and share repurchases in a perfect capital market.

3. Because dividends in the United States are taxed, companies should not issue stock to pay out a dividend.

4. Also because of taxes, firms have an incentive to reduce dividends. For example, they might consider increasing capital expenditures, acquiring other companies, or purchasing financial assets. However, due to financial considerations and legal constraints, rational firms with large cash flows will likely exhaust these activities with plenty of cash left over for dividends.

5. In a world with personal taxes, a strong case can be made for repurchasing shares instead of paying dividends.

6. Nevertheless, there are a number of justifications for dividends even in a world with personal taxes:

   a. Investors in no-dividend stocks incur transaction costs when selling off shares for current consumption.

   b. Behavioral finance argues that investors with limited self-control can meet current consumption needs via high-dividend stocks while adhering to a policy of "never dipping into principal."

   c. Managers, acting on behalf of stockholders, can pay dividends to keep cash from bondholders. The board of directors, also acting on behalf of stockholders, can use dividends to reduce the cash available to spendthrift managers.

7. The stock market reacts positively to increases in dividends (or an initial payment) and negatively to decreases in dividends. This suggests that there is information content in dividend payments.

8. High (low) dividend firms should arise to meet the demands of dividend-preferring (capital gains–preferring) investors. Because of these clienteles, it is not clear that a firm can create value by changing its dividend policy.

Concept Questions

1. **Dividend Policy Irrelevance**   How is it possible that dividends are so important, but at the same time dividend policy is irrelevant?

2. **Stock Repurchases**   What is the impact of a stock repurchase on a company's debt ratio? Does this suggest another use for excess cash?

3. **Dividend Policy**   It is sometimes suggested that firms should follow a "residual" dividend policy. With such a policy, the main idea is that a firm should focus on meeting its investment needs and maintaining its desired debt–equity ratio. Having done so, a firm pays out any leftover, or residual, income as dividends. What do you think would be the chief drawback to a residual dividend policy?

4. **Dividend Chronology**   On Tuesday, December 8, Hometown Power Co.'s board of directors declares a dividend of 75 cents per share payable on Wednesday, January 17, to shareholders of record as of Wednesday, January 3. When is the ex-dividend date? If a shareholder buys stock before that date, who gets the dividends on those shares—the buyer or the seller?

5. **Alternative Dividends**   Some corporations, like one British company that offers its large shareholders free crematorium use, pay dividends in kind (that is, offer their services to shareholders at below-market cost). Should mutual funds invest in stocks that pay these dividends in kind? (The fundholders do not receive these services.)

6. **Dividends and Stock Price**   If increases in dividends tend to be followed by (immediate) increases in share prices, how can it be said that dividend policy is irrelevant?

7. **Dividends and Stock Price**   Last month, Central Virginia Power Company, which had been having trouble with cost overruns on a nuclear power plant that it had been building, announced that it was "temporarily suspending payments due to the cash flow crunch associated with its investment program." The company's stock price dropped from $28.50 to $25 when this announcement was made. How would you interpret this change in the stock price? (That is, what would you say caused it?)

8. **Dividend Reinvestment Plans**   The DRK Corporation has recently developed a dividend reinvestment plan, or DRIP. The plan allows investors to reinvest cash dividends automatically in DRK in exchange for new shares of stock. Over time, investors in DRK will be able to build their holdings by reinvesting dividends to purchase additional shares of the company.

   Over 1,000 companies offer dividend reinvestment plans. Most companies with DRIPs charge no brokerage or service fees. In fact, the shares of DRK will be purchased at a 10 percent discount from the market price.

   A consultant for DRK estimates that about 75 percent of DRK's shareholders will take part in this plan. This is somewhat higher than the average.

Evaluate DRK's dividend reinvestment plan. Will it increase shareholder wealth? Discuss the advantages and disadvantages involved here.

9. **Dividend Policy**   For initial public offerings of common stock, 2005 was a relatively slow year, with only about $28.4 billion raised by the process. Relatively few of the 162 firms involved paid cash dividends. Why do you think that most chose not to pay cash dividends?

10. **Investment and Dividends**   The Phew Charitable Trust pays no taxes on its capital gains or on its dividend income or interest income. Would it be irrational for it to have low-dividend, high-growth stocks in its portfolio? Would it be irrational for it to have municipal bonds in its portfolio? Explain.

Use the following information to answer the next two questions:

Historically, the U.S. tax code treated dividend payments made to shareholders as ordinary income. Thus, dividends were taxed at the investor's marginal tax rate, which was as high as 38.6 percent in 2002. Capital gains were taxed at a capital gains tax rate, which was the same for most investors and fluctuated through the years. In 2002, the capital gains tax rate stood at 20 percent. In an effort to stimulate the economy, President George W. Bush presided over a tax plan overhaul that included changes in dividend and capital gains tax rates. The new tax plan, which was implemented in 2003, called for a 15 percent tax rate on both dividends and capital gains for investors in higher tax brackets. For lower tax bracket investors, the tax rate on dividends and capital gains was set at 5 percent through 2007, dropping to zero in 2008.

11. **Ex-Dividend Stock Prices**   How do you think this tax law change affects ex-dividend stock prices?

12. **Stock Repurchases**   How do you think this tax law change affected the relative attractiveness of stock repurchases compared to dividend payments?

13.. **Dividends and Stock Value**   The growing perpetuity model expresses the value of a share of stock as the present value of the expected dividends from that stock. How can you conclude that dividend policy is irrelevant when this model is valid?

14. **Bird-in-the-Hand Argument**   The bird-in-the-hand argument, which states that a dividend today is safer than the uncertain prospect of a capital gain tomorrow, is often used to justify high dividend payout ratios. Explain the fallacy behind this argument.

15. **Dividends and Income Preference**   The desire for current income is not a valid explanation of preference for high current dividend policy because investors can always create homemade dividends by selling a portion of their stocks. Is this statement true or false? Why?

16. **Dividends and Clientele**   Cap Henderson owns Neotech stock because its price has been steadily rising over the past few years and he expects this performance to continue. Cap is trying to convince Sarah Jones to purchase some Neotech stock, but she is reluctant because Neotech has never paid a dividend. She depends on steady dividends to provide her with income.
    a. What preferences are these two investors demonstrating?
    b. What argument should Cap use to convince Sarah that Neotech stock is the stock for her?
    c. Why might Cap's argument not convince Sarah?

17. **Dividends and Taxes**   Your aunt is in a high tax bracket and would like to minimize the tax burden of her investment portfolio. She is willing to buy and sell to maximize her aftertax returns, and she has asked for your advice. What would you suggest she do?

18. **Dividends versus Capital Gains**   If the market places the same value on $1 of dividends as on $1 of capital gains, then firms with different payout ratios will appeal to different clienteles of investors. One clientele is as good as another; therefore, a firm cannot increase its value by changing its dividend policy. Yet empirical investigations reveal a strong correlation between dividend payout ratios and other firm characteristics. For example, small, rapidly growing firms that have recently gone public almost always have payout ratios that are zero; all earnings are reinvested in the business. Explain this phenomenon if dividend policy is irrelevant.

19. **Dividend Irrelevancy**   In spite of the theoretical argument that dividend policy should be irrelevant, the fact remains that many investors like high dividends. If this preference exists, a firm can boost its share price by increasing its dividend payout ratio. Explain the fallacy in this argument.

20. **Dividends and Stock Price**   Empirical research has found that there have been significant increases in stock price on the day an initial dividend (i.e., the first time a firm pays a cash dividend) is announced. What does this finding imply about the information content of initial dividends?

Questions and Problems

BASIC
(Questions 1–14)

1. **Dividends and Taxes**   Lee Ann, Inc., has declared a $6 per-share dividend. Suppose capital gains are not taxed, but dividends are taxed at 15 percent. New IRS regulations require that taxes be withheld when the dividend is paid. Lee Ann sells for $90 per share, and the stock is about to go ex dividend. What do you think the ex-dividend price will be?

2. **Stock Dividends**   The owners' equity accounts for Surin International are shown here:

Common stock (THB 1 par value)	THB 10,000
Capital surplus	180,000
Retained earnings	586,500
Total owners' equity	THB 776,500

   a. If Surin stock currently sells for THB 25 per share and a 10 percent stock dividend is declared, how many new shares will be distributed? Show how the equity accounts would change.
   b. If Surin declared a 25 percent stock dividend, how would the accounts change?

3. **Stock Splits**   For the company in Problem 2, show how the equity accounts will change if
   a. Surin declares a four-for-one stock split. How many shares are outstanding now? What is the new par value per share?
   b. Surin declares a one-for-four reverse stock split. How many shares are outstanding now? What is the new par value per share?

4. **Stock Splits and Stock Dividends**   Snuol Corporation (SC) currently has 150,000 shares of stock outstanding that sell for KHR 65 per share. Assuming no market imperfections or tax effects exist, what will the share price be after
   a. SC has a five-for-three stock split?
   b. SC has a 20 percent stock dividend?
   c. SC has a 42.5 percent stock dividend?
   d. SC has a three-for-seven reverse stock split?

   Determine the new number of shares outstanding in parts (a) through (d).

5. **Regular Dividends**   The balance sheet for Suriname Mouthpiece is shown here in market value terms. There are 10,000 shares of stock outstanding.

Market Value Balance Sheet			
Cash	SRD 20,000	Equity	SRD 175,000
Fixed assets	155,000		
Total	SRD 175,000	Total	SRD 175,000

   The company has declared a dividend of SRD 1.50 per share. The stock goes ex dividend tomorrow. Ignoring any tax effects, what is the stock selling for today? What will it sell for tomorrow? What will the balance sheet look like after the dividends are paid?

6.   Share Repurchase   In the previous problem, suppose Suriname Mouthpiece has announced it is going to repurchase SRD 4,025 worth of stock. What effect will this transaction have on the equity of the firm? How many shares will be outstanding? What will the price per share be after the repurchase? Ignoring tax effects, show how the share repurchase is effectively the same as a cash dividend.

7.   Stock Dividends   The market value balance sheet for Outbox Manufacturing is shown here. Outbox has declared a 25 percent stock dividend. The stock goes ex dividend tomorrow (the chronology for a stock dividend is similar to that for a cash dividend). There are 20,000 shares of stock outstanding. What will the ex-dividend price be?

Market Value Balance Sheet			
Cash	TRY 190,000	Debt	TRY 160,000
Fixed assets	330,000	Equity	360,000
Total	TRY 520,000	Total	TRY 520,000

8.   Stock Dividends   The company with the common equity accounts shown here has declared a 12 percent stock dividend when the market value of its stock is SYP 20 per share. What effects on the equity accounts will the distribution of the stock dividend have?

Common stock (SYP 1 par value)	SYP 350,000
Capital surplus	1,650,000
Retained earnings	3,000,000
Total owners' equity	SYP 5,000,000

9.   Stock Splits   In the previous problem, suppose the company instead decides on a five-for-one stock split. The firm's 70 cent per share cash dividend on the new (postsplit) shares represents an increase of 10 percent over last year's dividend on the presplit stock. What effect does this have on the equity accounts? What was last year's dividend per share?

10.   Residual Dividend Policy   Soprano, Inc., a litter recycling company, uses a residual dividend policy. (See Concept Question 3.) A debt–equity ratio of .80 is considered optimal. Earnings for the period just ended were €1,200, and a dividend of €450 was declared. How much in new debt was borrowed? What were total capital outlays?

11.   Residual Dividend Policy   Al Khawr Mining has declared an annual dividend of QAR 0.80 per share. For the year just ended, earnings were QAR 7 per share.
  a. What is Al Khawr's payout ratio?
  b. Suppose Al Khawr has 7 million shares outstanding. Borrowing for the coming year is planned at QAR 18 million. What are planned investment outlays assuming a residual dividend policy? (See Concept Question 3.) What target capital structure is implicit in these calculations?

12.   Residual Dividend Policy   Red Zeppelin Corporation follows a strict residual dividend policy. (See Concept Question 3.) Its debt–equity ratio is 3.
  a. If earnings for the year are SBD 180,000, what is the maximum amount of capital spending possible with no new equity?
  b. If planned investment outlays for the coming year are SBD 730,000, will Red Zeppelin pay a dividend? If so, how much?
  c. Does Red Zeppelin maintain a constant dividend payout? Why or why not?

13.   Residual Dividend Policy   Uppsala Farming predicts that earnings in the coming year will be SEK 56 million. There are 12 million shares, and Uppsala maintains a debt–equity ratio of 2.
  a. Calculate the maximum investment funds available without issuing new equity and the increase in borrowing that goes along with it.

b. Suppose the firm uses a residual dividend policy. (See Concept Question 3.) Planned capital expenditures total SEK 72 million. Based on this information, what will the dividend per share be?

c. In part (b), how much borrowing will take place? What is the addition to retained earnings?

d. Suppose Uppsala plans no capital outlays for the coming year. What will the dividend be under a residual policy? What will new borrowing be?

14.   Dividends and Stock Price   The Mann Company belongs to a risk class for which the appropriate discount rate is 10 percent. Mann currently has 100,000 outstanding shares selling at $100 each. The firm is contemplating the declaration of a $5 dividend at the end of the fiscal year that just began. Assume there are no taxes on dividends. Answer the following questions based on the Miller and Modigliani model, which is discussed in the text.

a. What will be the price of the stock on the ex-dividend date if the dividend is declared?

b. What will be the price of the stock at the end of the year if the dividend is not declared?

c. If Mann makes $2 million of new investments at the beginning of the period, earns net income of $1 million, and pays the dividend at the end of the year, how many shares of new stock must the firm issue to meet its funding needs?

d. Is it realistic to use the MM model in the real world to value stock? Why or why not?

INTERMEDIATE
(Questions 15–20)

15.   Homemade Dividends   You own 1,000 shares of stock in Avondale Corporation. You will receive a 70 cent per share dividend in one year. In two years, Avondale will pay a liquidating dividend of SHP 40 per share. The required return on Avondale stock is 15 percent. What is the current share price of your stock (ignoring taxes)? If you would rather have equal dividends in each of the next two years, show how you can accomplish this by creating homemade dividends. (*Hint*: Dividends will be in the form of an annuity.)

16.   Homemade Dividends   In the previous problem, suppose you want only SHP 200 total in dividends the first year. What will your homemade dividend be in two years?

17.   Stock Repurchase   Flychucker Corporation is evaluating an extra dividend versus a share repurchase. In either case €5,000 would be spent. Current earnings are €0.95 per share, and the stock currently sells for €40 per share. There are 1,000 shares outstanding. Ignore taxes and other imperfections in answering parts (a) and (b).

a. Evaluate the two alternatives in terms of the effect on the price per share of the stock and shareholder wealth.

b. What will be the effect on Flychucker's EPS and PE ratio under the two different scenarios?

c. In the real world, which of these actions would you recommend? Why?

18.   Dividends and Firm Value   The net income of Takamaka Cruises is SCR 32,000. The company has 10,000 outstanding shares and a 100 percent payout policy. The expected value of the firm one year from now is SCR 1,545,600. The appropriate discount rate for Takamaka is 12 percent, and the dividend tax rate is zero.

a. What is the current value of the firm assuming the current dividend has not yet been paid?

b. What is the ex-dividend price of Takamaka's stock if the board follows its current policy?

c. At the dividend declaration meeting, several board members claimed that the dividend is too meager and is probably depressing Takamaka's price. They proposed that Takamaka sell enough new shares to finance an SCR 4.25 dividend.

   i. Comment on the claim that the low dividend is depressing the stock price. Support your argument with calculations.

   ii. If the proposal is adopted, at what price will the new shares sell? How many will be sold?

19.   Dividend Policy   Saint Helena Realtors has a current period cash flow of SHP 1.2 million and pays no dividends. The present value of the company's future cash flows is SHP 15 million. The company is entirely financed with equity and has 1 million shares outstanding. Assume the dividend tax rate is zero.

a. What is the share price of the Saint Helena Realtors stock?

    b. Suppose the board of directors of Saint Helena Realtors announces its plan to pay out 50 percent of its current cash flow as cash dividends to its shareholders. How can Jeff Miller, who owns 1,000 shares of Saint Helena Realtors stock, achieve a zero payout policy on his own?

20. **Dividend Smoothing**   The Sharpe Co. just paid a dividend of $1.25 per share of stock. Its target payout ratio is 40 percent. The company expects to have an earnings per share of $4.50 one year from now.

    a. If the adjustment rate is .3 as defined in the Lintner model, what is the dividend one year from now?

    b. If the adjustment rate is .5 instead, what is the dividend one year from now?

    c. Which adjustment rate is more conservative? Why?

CHALLENGE
(Questions 21–24)

21. **Expected Return, Dividends, and Taxes**   The Gecko Company and the Gordon Company are two firms whose business risk is the same but that have different dividend policies. Gecko pays no dividend, whereas Gordon has an expected dividend yield of 6 percent. Suppose the capital gains tax rate is zero, whereas the dividend tax rate is 35 percent. Gecko has an expected earnings growth rate of 15 percent annually, and its stock price is expected to grow at this same rate. If the aftertax expected returns on the two stocks are equal (because they are in the same risk class), what is the pretax required return on Gordon's stock?

22. **Dividends and Taxes**   As discussed in the text, in the absence of market imperfections and tax effects, we would expect the share price to decline by the amount of the dividend payment when the stock goes ex dividend. Once we consider the role of taxes, however, this is not necessarily true. One model has been proposed that incorporates tax effects into determining the ex-dividend price:[19]

$$(P_0 - P_X)/D = (1 - t_P)/(1 - t_G)$$

Here P_0 is the price just before the stock goes ex, P_X is the ex-dividend share price, D is the amount of the dividend per share, t_P is the relevant marginal personal tax rate on dividends, and t_G is the effective marginal tax rate on capital gains.

    a. If $t_P = t_G = 0$, how much will the share price fall when the stock goes ex?

    b. If $t_P = 15$ percent and $t_G = 0$, how much will the share price fall?

    c. If $t_P = 15$ percent and $t_G = 20$ percent, how much will the share price fall?

    d. Suppose the only owners of stock are corporations. Recall that corporations get at least a 70 percent exemption from taxation on the dividend income they receive, but they do not get such an exemption on capital gains. If the corporation's income and capital gains tax rates are both 35 percent, what does this model predict the ex-dividend share price will be?

    e. What does this problem tell you about real-world tax considerations and the dividend policy of the firm?

23. **Dividends versus Reinvestment**   Santa Ana Preservatives (SAP) has SVC 2 million of extra cash after taxes have been paid. SAP has two choices to make use of this cash. One alternative is to invest the cash in financial assets. The resulting investment income will be paid out as a special dividend at the end of three years. In this case, the firm can invest in either Treasury bills yielding 7 percent or an 11 percent preferred stock. IRS regulations allow the company to exclude from taxable income 70 percent of the dividends received from investing in another company's stock. Another alternative is to pay out the cash now as dividends. This would allow the shareholders to invest on their own in Treasury bills with the same yield or in preferred stock. The corporate tax rate is 35 percent. Assume the investor has a 31 percent personal income tax rate, which is applied to interest income and preferred stock dividends. The personal dividend tax rate is 15 percent on common stock dividends. Should the cash be paid today or in three years? Which of the two options generates the highest aftertax income for the shareholders?

[19]N. Elton and M. Gruber, "Marginal Stockholder Tax Rates and the Clientele Effect," *Review of Economics and Statistics* 52 (February 1970).

24. **Dividends versus Reinvestment**   After completing its capital spending for the year, Salon Jean Elitor has €1,000 extra cash. The Company's managers must choose between investing the cash in Treasury bonds that yield 8 percent or paying the cash out to investors who would invest in the bonds themselves.

    a. If the corporate tax rate is 35 percent, what personal tax rate would make the investors equally willing to receive the dividend or to let the company invest the money?

    b. Is the answer to (a) reasonable? Why or why not?

    c. Suppose the only investment choice is a preferred stock that yields 12 percent. The corporate dividend exclusion of 70 percent applies. What personal tax rate will make the stockholders indifferent to the outcome of the company's dividend decision?

    d. Is this a compelling argument for a low dividend payout ratio? Why or why not?

S&P Problem

www.mhhe.com/edumarketinsight

1. **Dividend Payouts**   Use the annual financial statements for General Mills (GIS), Boston Beer (SAM), and US Steel (X) to find the dividend payout ratio for each company for the last three years. Why would these companies pay out a different percentage of income as dividends? Is there anything unusual about the dividends paid by US Steel? How is this possible?

Appendix 18A   Stock Dividends and Stock Splits

To access the appendix for this chapter, please visit **www.mhhe.com/rwj**.

Mini Case

Electronic Timing, Inc.

Electronic Timing, Inc. (ETI), is a small company founded 15 years ago by electronics engineers Tom Miller and Jessica Kerr. ETI manufactures integrated circuits to capitalize on the complex mixed-signal design technology and has recently entered the market for frequency timing generators, or silicon timing devices, which provide the timing signals or "clocks" necessary to synchronize electronic systems. Its clock products originally were used in PC video graphics applications, but the market subsequently expanded to include motherboards, PC peripheral devices, and other digital consumer electronics, such as digital television boxes and game consoles. ETI also designs and markets custom application-specific integrated circuits (ASICs) for industrial customers. The ASIC's design combines analog and digital, or mixed-signal, technology. In addition to Tom and Jessica, Nolan Pittman, who provided capital for the company, is the third primary owner. Each owns 25 percent of the 1 million shares outstanding. Several other individuals, including current employees, own the remaining company shares.

Recently, the company designed a new computer motherboard. The company's design is both more efficient and less expensive to manufacture, and the ETI design is expected to become standard in many personal computers. After investigating the possibility of manufacturing the new motherboard, ETI determined that the costs involved in building a new plant would be prohibitive. The owners also decided that they were unwilling to bring in another large outside owner. Instead, ETI sold the design to an outside firm. The sale of the motherboard design was completed for an aftertax payment of $30 million.

1. Tom believes the company should use the extra cash to pay a special one-time dividend. How will this proposal affect the stock price? How will it affect the value of the company?

2. Jessica believes that the company should use the extra cash to pay off debt and upgrade and expand its existing manufacturing capability. How would Jessica's proposals affect the company?

3. Nolan is in favor of a share repurchase. He argues that a repurchase will increase the company's P/E ratio, return on assets, and return on equity. Are his arguments correct? How will a share repurchase affect the value of the company?

4. Another option discussed by Tom, Jessica, and Nolan would be to begin a regular dividend payment to shareholders. How would you evaluate this proposal?

5. One way to value a share of stock is the dividend growth, or growing perpetuity, model. Consider the following: The dividend payout ratio is 1 minus b, where b is the "retention" or "plowback" ratio. So, the dividend next year will be the earnings next year, E_1, times 1 minus the retention ratio. The most commonly used equation to calculate the sustainable growth rate is the return on equity times the retention ratio. Substituting these relationships into the dividend growth model, we get the following equation to calculate the price of a share of stock today:

$$P_0 = \frac{E_1(1 - b)}{R_S - \text{ROE} \times b}$$

What are the implications of this result in terms of whether the company should pay a dividend or upgrade and expand its manufacturing capability? Explain.

6. Does the question of whether the company should pay a dividend depend on whether the company is organized as a corporation or an LLC?

Issuing Securities to the Public

On August 19, 2004, in an eagerly awaited initial public offering (IPO), the Internet search engine company Google went public. Initially the company expected to sell about 26 million shares of stock at a price of $108 to $135 per share through an unusual (for an IPO) "Dutch auction" process. Just before the company went public, it reduced the price to $85 per share and cut the number of shares offered to 19.6 million. Even with these lower numbers, the company's value when it first sold shares to investors was $23 billion. By some standards the IPO was successful, but several missteps plagued the offering, including confusion over the Dutch auction process, unregistered stock given to employees, and comments made in interviews given by the company's founders. The IPO appears to have been very successful

for investors, however. On July 11, 2006, the stock was selling for $417.43 per share. In this chapter, we examine the process by which companies such as Google sell stock to the public, the costs of doing so, and the role of investment banks in the process.

Businesses large and small have one thing in common: They need long-term capital. This chapter describes how they get it. We pay particular attention to what is probably the most important stage in a company's financial life cycle—the initial public offering. Such offerings are the process by which companies convert from being privately owned to being publicly owned. For many people, starting a company, growing it, and taking it public are the ultimate entrepreneurial dream.

19.1 The Public Issue

The basic steps in a public offering are depicted in Table 19.1. The Securities Act of 1933 sets forth the federal regulation for all new interstate securities issues. The Securities Exchange Act of 1934 is the basis for regulating securities already outstanding. The SEC administers both acts.

The Basic Procedure for a New Issue

1. Management's first step in any issue of securities to the public is to obtain approval from the board of directors.

2. Next the firm must prepare and file a **registration statement** with the SEC. This statement contains a great deal of financial information, including a financial history, details of the existing business, proposed financing, and plans for the future. It can easily run to 50 or more pages. The document is required for all public issues of securities with two principal exceptions:

   a. Loans that mature within nine months.
   b. Issues that involve less than $5.0 million.

Table 19.1   **The Process of Raising Capital**

Steps in Public Offering	Time	Activities
1. Preunderwriting conferences	Several months	The amount of money to be raised and the type of security to be issued are discussed. The underwriting syndicate and selling group are put together. The underwriting contract is negotiated. Board approval is obtained.
2. Registration statements filed and approved	A 20-day waiting period	The registration statement contains all relevant financial and business information.
3. Pricing the issue	Usually not before the last day of the registration period	For seasoned offerings the price is set close to the prevailing market price. For initial public offerings intensive research and analysis are required.
4. Public offering and sale	Shortly after the last day of the registration period	In a typical firm commitment contract, the underwriter buys a stipulated amount of stock from the firm and sells it at a higher price. The selling group assists in the sale.
5. Market stabilization	Usually 30 days after the offering	The underwriter stands ready to place orders to buy at a specified price on the market.

The second exception is known as the *small-issues exemption.* Issues of less than $5.0 million are governed by **Regulation A**, for which only a brief offering statement—rather than the full registration statement—is needed. For Regulation A to be operative, no more than $1.5 million may be sold by insiders.

3. The SEC studies the registration statement during a *waiting period.* During this time, the firm may distribute copies of a preliminary **prospectus.** The preliminary prospectus is called a **red herring** because bold red letters are printed on the cover. A prospectus contains much of the information put into the registration statement, and it is given to potential investors by the firm. The company cannot sell the securities during the waiting period. However, oral offers can be made.

   A registration statement will become effective on the 20th day after its filing unless the SEC sends a *letter of comment* suggesting changes. After the changes are made, the 20-day waiting period starts anew.

4. The registration statement does not initially contain the price of the new issue. On the effective date of the registration statement, a price is determined and a full-fledged selling effort gets under way. A final prospectus must accompany the delivery of securities or confirmation of sale, whichever comes first.

5. **Tombstone** advertisements are used during and after the waiting period. An example is reproduced in Figure 19.1.

19.2   Alternative Issue Methods

When a company decides to issue a new security, it can sell it as a public issue or a private issue. If it is a public issue, the firm is required to register the issue with the SEC. If the issue is sold to fewer than 35 investors, it can be treated as a private issue. A registration statement is not required in this case.[1]

---

[1] However, regulation significantly restricts the resale of unregistered securities. The purchaser must hold the securities at least two years.

Figure 19.1

An Example of a Tombstone Advertisement

This announcement is neither an offer to sell nor a solicitation of an offer to buy any of these securities. The offering is made only by the Prospectus.

New Issue

11,500,000 Shares

World Wrestling Federation Entertainment, Inc.

Class A Common Stock

Price $17.00 Per Share

Copies of the Prospectus may be obtained in any State in which this announcement is circulated from only such of the Underwriters, including the undersigned, as may lawfully offer these securities in such State.

U.S. Offering

9,200,000 Shares

This portion of the underwriting is being offered in the United States and Canada.

Bear, Stearns & Co. Inc.

Credit Suisse First Boston

Merrill Lynch & Co.

Wit Capital Corporation

Allen & Company Incorporated	Banc of America Securities LLC	Deutsche Banc Alex. Brown
Donaldson, Lufkin & Jenrette	A.G. Edwards & Sons, Inc.	Hambrecht & Quist ING Barings
Prudential Securities	SG Cowen	Wasserstein Perella Securities, Inc. Advest, Inc.
Axiom Capital Management, Inc.	Blackford Securities Corp.	J.C. Bradford & Co.
Joseph Charles & Assoc., Inc.	Chatsworth Securities LLC	Gabelli & Company, Inc.
Gaines, Berland Inc. Jefferies & Company, Inc.	Josephthal & Co. Inc.	Neuberger Berman, LLC
Raymond James & Associates, Inc.		Sanders Morris Mundy
Tucker Anthony Cleary Gull		Wachovia Securities, Inc.

International Offering

2,300,000 Shares

This portion of the underwriting is being offered outside of the United States and Canada.

Bear, Stearns International Limited

Credit Suisse First Boston

Merrill Lynch International

Table 19.2   **The Methods of Issuing New Securities**

Method	Type	Definition
Public		
Traditional negotiated cash offer	Firm commitment cash offer	Company negotiates an agreement with an investment banker to underwrite and distribute the new shares. A specified number of shares are bought by underwriters and sold at a higher price.
	Best efforts cash offer	Company has investment bankers sell as many of the new shares as possible at the agreed-upon price. There is no guarantee concerning how much cash will be raised. Some best efforts offerings do not use an underwriter.
	Dutch auction cash offer	Company has investment bankers auction shares to determine the highest offer price obtainable for a given number of shares to be sold.
Privileged subscription	Direct rights offer	Company offers the new stock directly to its existing shareholders.
	Standby rights offer	Like the direct rights offer, this contains a privileged subscription arrangement with existing shareholders. The net proceeds are guaranteed by the underwriters.
Nontraditional cash offer	Shelf cash offer	Qualifying companies can authorize all the shares they expect to sell over a two-year period and sell them when needed.
	Competitive firm cash offer	Company can elect to award the underwriting contract through a public auction instead of negotiation.
Private	Direct placement	Securities are sold directly to the purchaser, who, at least until recently, generally could not resell the securities for at least two years.

There are two kinds of public issues: the *general cash offer* and the *rights offer*. Cash offers are sold to all interested investors, and rights offers are sold to existing shareholders. Equity is sold by both the cash offer and the rights offer, though almost all debt is sold by cash offer.

The first public equity issue that is made by a company is referred to as an **initial public offering (IPO)** or an **unseasoned new issue**. All initial public offerings are cash offers because, if the firm's existing shareholders wanted to buy the shares, the firm would not need to sell them publicly. More than $28 billion was raised in 162 IPOs in 2005. A **seasoned new issue** refers to a new issue where the company's securities have been previously issued. A seasoned new issue of common stock may be made by using a cash offer or a rights offer.

These methods of issuing new securities are shown in Table 19.2 and discussed in the next few sections.[2]

19.3   The Cash Offer

As just mentioned, stock is sold to all interested investors in a **cash offer**. If the cash offer is a public one, **investment banks** are usually involved. Investment banks are financial intermediaries that perform a wide variety of services. In addition to aiding in the sale of

---

[2] Table 19.2 describes the main methods for issuing new securities in the United States. Most initial public offerings in the United States use the negotiated cash offer method known as *bookbuilding*. Bookbuilding refers to the way an underwriter builds a book of potential orders and uses the book to set a price. Bookbuilding is the method of equity underwriting choice in most (but not all) countries.

securities, they may facilitate mergers and other corporate reorganizations, act as brokers to both individual and institutional clients, and trade for their own accounts. You may well have heard of large Wall Street investment banking houses such as Goldman Sachs, Merrill Lynch, and Smith Barney.

For corporate issuers, investment bankers perform services such as the following:

Formulating the method used to issue the securities.

Pricing the new securities.

Selling the new securities.

There are three basic methods of issuing securities for cash:

1. *Firm commitment*: Under this method, the investment bank (or a group of investment banks) buys the securities for less than the offering price and accepts the risk of not being able to sell them. Because this function involves risk, we say that the investment banker *underwrites* the securities in a firm commitment. In other words, when participating in a firm commitment offering, the investment banker acts as an *underwriter*. (Because firm commitments are so prevalent, we will use *investment banker* and *underwriter* interchangeably in this chapter.)

   To minimize the risks here, investment bankers combine to form an underwriting group (**syndicate**) to share the risk and to help sell the issue. In such a group, one or more managers arrange or comanage the deal. The manager is designated as the lead manager or principal manager. The lead manager typically has responsibility for all aspects of the issue. The other investment bankers in the syndicate serve primarily to sell the issue to their clients.

   The difference between the underwriter's buying price and the offering price is called the *spread* or *discount*. It is the basic compensation received by the underwriter. Sometimes the underwriter will get noncash compensation in the form of warrants or stock in addition to the spread.

   Firm commitment underwriting is really just a purchase–sale arrangement, and the syndicate's fee is the spread. The issuer receives the full amount of the proceeds less the spread, and all the risk is transferred to the underwriter. If the underwriter cannot sell all of the issue at the agreed-upon offering price, it may need to lower the price on the unsold shares. However, because the offering price usually is not set until the underwriters have investigated how receptive the market is to the issue, this risk is usually minimal. This is particularly true with seasoned new issues because the price of the new issue can be based on prior trades in the security.

2. *Best efforts*: The underwriter bears risk with a firm commitment because it buys the entire issue. Conversely, the syndicate avoids this risk under a best-efforts offering because it does not purchase the shares. Instead it merely acts as an agent, receiving a commission for each share sold. The syndicate is legally bound to use its best efforts to sell the securities at the agreed-upon offering price. If the issue cannot be sold at the offering price, it is usually withdrawn. This form of underwriting has become relatively rare.

3. *Dutch auction underwriting*: With **Dutch auction underwriting** the underwriter does not set a fixed price for the shares to be sold. Instead the underwriter conducts an auction in which investors bid for shares. The offer price is determined based on the submitted bids. A Dutch auction is also known by the more descriptive name *uniform price auction*. This approach to selling securities to the public is relatively new in the IPO market and has not been widely used there, but it is very common in the

bond markets. For example, it is the sole procedure used by the U.S. Treasury to sell enormous quantities of notes, bonds, and bills to the public.

Dutch auction underwriting was much in the news in 2004 because, as we mentioned to open the chapter, Web search company Google elected to use this approach. The best way to understand a Dutch or uniform price auction is to consider a simple example. Suppose the Rial Company wants to sell 400 shares to the public. The company receives five bids as follows:

Bidder	Quantity	Price
A	100 shares	$16
B	100 shares	14
C	100 shares	12
D	200 shares	12
E	200 shares	10

Thus, bidder A is willing to buy 100 shares at $16 each, bidder B is willing to buy 100 shares at $14, and so on. The Rial Company examines the bids to determine the highest price that will result in all 400 shares being sold. For example, at $14, A and B would buy only 200 shares, so that price is too high. Working our way down, all 400 shares won't be sold until we hit a price of $12, so $12 will be the offer price in the IPO. Bidders A through D will receive shares; bidder E will not.

There are two additional important points to observe in our example. First, all the winning bidders will pay $12—even bidders A and B, who actually bid a higher price. The fact that all successful bidders pay the same price is the reason for the name "uniform price auction." The idea in such an auction is to encourage bidders to bid aggressively by providing some protection against bidding a price that is too high.

Second, notice that at the $12 offer price, there are actually bids for 500 shares, which exceeds the 400 shares Rial wants to sell. Thus, there has to be some sort of allocation. How this is done varies a bit; but in the IPO market the approach has been to simply compute the ratio of shares offered to shares bid at the offer price or better, which, in our example, is 400/500 = .8, and allocate bidders that percentage of their bids. In other words, bidders A through D would each receive 80 percent of the shares they bid at a price of $12 per share.

In most offerings, the principal underwriter is permitted to buy shares if the market price falls below the offering price. The purpose is to *support* the market and *stabilize* the price from temporary downward pressure. If the issue remains unsold after a time (for example, 30 days), members may leave the group and sell their shares at whatever price the market will allow.

Many underwriting contracts contain a **Green Shoe provision**, which gives the members of the underwriting group the option to purchase additional shares at the offering price.[3] The stated reason for the Green Shoe option is to cover excess demand and oversubscription. Green Shoe options usually last for about 30 days and involve no more than 15 percent of the newly issued shares. The Green Shoe option is a benefit to the underwriting syndicate and a cost to the issuer. If the market price of the new issue goes above the offering price within 30 days, the underwriters can buy shares from the issuer and immediately resell the shares to the public.

---

[3] The Green Shoe Corp. was the first firm to allow this provision.

The period after a new issue is initially sold to the public is called the *aftermarket*. During this period, the members of the underwriting syndicate generally do not sell shares of the new issue for less than the offer price.

Almost all underwriting agreements contain *lockups*. Such arrangements specify how long insiders must wait after an IPO before they can sell some of their stock. Typically, lockup periods are set at 180 days. Lockups are important because it is not unusual for the number of locked-up insider shares to be larger than the number of shares held by the public. Thus, there is the possibility that, when the lockup period ends, a large number of shares will be sold by insiders, thereby depressing share prices.

Beginning well before an offering and extending for 40 calendar days following an IPO, the SEC requires that a firm and its managing underwriters observe a "quiet period." This means that all communications with the public must be limited to ordinary announcements and other purely factual matters. The SEC's logic is that all relevant information should be contained in the prospectus. An important result of this requirement is that the underwriter's analysts are prohibited from making recommendations to investors. As soon as the quiet period ends, however, the managing underwriters typically publish research reports, usually accompanied by a favorable "buy" recommendation.

Firms that don't stay quiet can have their IPOs delayed. For example, just before Google's IPO, an interview with cofounders Sergy Brin and Larry Page appeared in *Playboy*. The interview almost caused a postponement of the IPO, but Google was able to amend its prospectus in time (by including the article!). However, in May 2004, Salesforce.com's IPO was delayed because an interview with CEO Mark Benioff appeared in *The New York Times*. Salesforce.com finally went public two months later.

Investment Banks

Investment banks are at the heart of new security issues. They provide advice, market the securities (after investigating the market's receptiveness to the issue), and underwrite the proceeds. They accept the risk that the market price may fall between the date the offering price is set and the time the issue is sold.

In addition, investment banks have the responsibility of pricing fairly. When a firm goes public, particularly for the first time, the buyers know relatively little about the firm's operations. After all, it is not rational for a buyer of, say, only 1,000 shares of stock to study the company at length. Instead, the buyer must rely on the judgment of the investment bank, which has presumably examined the firm in detail. Given this asymmetry of information, what prevents the investment banker from pricing the issued securities too high? Although the underwriter has a short-term incentive to price high, it has a long-term incentive to make sure its customers do not pay too much; they might desert the underwriter in future deals if they lose money on this one. Thus, as long as investment banks plan to stay in business over time, it is in their self-interest to price fairly.

In other words, financial economists argue that each investment bank has a reservoir of "reputation capital."[4] Mispricing of new issues or unethical dealings are likely to reduce this reputation capital.

One measure of this reputation capital is the pecking order among the investment banks. MBA students are aware of this order because they know that accepting a job with a top-tier firm is universally regarded as more prestigious than accepting a job with a lower-tier firm. This pecking order can be seen in Figure 19.1. The investment banks listed

---

[4]For example, see R. Carter and S. Manaster, "Initial Public Offerings and Underwriter Reputation," *Journal of Finance* (1990): and R. Beatty and J. Ritter, "Investment Banking, Reputation, and the Underpricing of Initial Public Offerings," *Journal of Financial Economics* (1986).

In Their Own Words

ROBERT S. HANSEN ON THE ECONOMIC RATIONALE FOR THE FIRM COMMITMENT OFFER

Underwriters provide four main functions: certification, monitoring, marketing, and risk bearing.

Certification assures investors that the offer price is fair. Investors have concerns about whether the offer price is unfairly above the stock's intrinsic value. Certification increases issuer value by reducing investor doubt about fairness, making a better offer price possible.

Monitoring of issuing firm management and performance builds value because it adds to shareholders' ordinary monitoring. Underwriters provide collective monitoring on behalf of both capital suppliers and current shareholders. Individual shareholder monitoring is limited because the shareholder bears the entire cost, whereas all owners collectively share the benefit, pro rata. By contrast, in underwriter monitoring all stockholders share both the costs and benefits, pro rata.

Due diligence and legal liability for the proceeds give investors assurance. However, what makes certification and monitoring credible is lead bank reputation in competitive capital markets, where they are disciplined over time. Evidence that irreputable behavior is damaging to a bank's future abounds. Capital market participants punish poorly performing banks by refusing to hire them. The participants pay banks for certification and meaningful monitoring in "quasi-rents" in the spread, which represent the fair cost of "renting" the reputations.

Marketing is finding long-term investors who can be persuaded to buy the securities at the offer price. This would not be needed if demand for new shares were "horizontal." There is much evidence that issuers and syndicates repeatedly invest in costly marketing practices, such as expensive road shows to identify and expand investor interest. Another is organizing members to avoid redundant pursuit of the same customers. Lead banks provide trading support in the issuer's stock for several weeks after the offer.

Underwriting risk is like the risk of selling a put option. The syndicate agrees to buy all new shares at the offer price and resell them at that price or at the market price, whichever is lower. Thus, once the offer begins, the syndicate is exposed to potential losses on unsold inventory should the market price fall below the offer price. The risk is likely to be small, because offerings are typically well prepared for quick sale.

Robert S. Hansen is the Freeman Senior Research Professor of Finance at Tulane University.

---

diagonally in the figure are considered the most prestigious. These appear alphabetically so that one cannot distinguish the relative status of these firms from the figure. The next set of firms is also in alphabetical order. By noting when the alphabetical order begins anew, we can determine the number of firms in each tier.

Investment banks put great importance in their relative rankings and view downward movement in their placement with much distaste. While this jockeying for position may seem as unimportant as the currying of royal favor in the court of Louis XVI, it is explained by the preceding discussion. In any industry where reputation is so important, the firms in the industry must guard theirs with great vigilance.

There are two basic methods for selecting the syndicate. In a **competitive offer** the issuing firm can offer its securities to the underwriter bidding highest. In a **negotiated offer** the issuing firm works with one underwriter. Because the firm generally does not negotiate with many underwriters concurrently, negotiated deals may suffer from lack of competition.

Whereas competitive bidding occurs frequently in other areas of commerce, it may surprise you that negotiated deals in investment banking occur with all but the largest issuing firms. Investment bankers argue that they must expend much time and effort learning about the issuer before setting an issue price and a fee schedule. Except in the case of large issues, these underwriters could not expend the time and effort without the near certainty of receiving the contract.

Table 19.3

Number of Offerings, Average First-Day Return, and Gross Proceeds of Initial Public Offerings: 1975–2005

Year	Number of Offerings*	Average First-Day Return, %[†]	Gross Proceeds ($ in millions)[‡]
1975–1979	112	5.7	1,124
1980–1989	2,380	6.8	61,880
1990–1999	4,146	21.1	291,531
2000–2005	959	29.0	193,310
1975–2005	**7,597**	**17.3**	**547,845**

*The number of offerings excludes IPOs with an offer price of less than $5.00, ADRs, best-efforts offers, unit offers, Regulation A offerings (small issues raising less than $1.5 million during the 1980s), real estate investment trusts (REITs), partnerships, and closed-end funds.
[†]First-day returns are computed as the percentage return from the offering price to the first closing market price.
[‡]Gross proceeds data are from Securities Data Co. and exclude overallotment options but include the international tranche, if any. No adjustments for inflation have been made.
SOURCE: Professor Jay R. Ritter, University of Florida.

Studies generally show that issuing costs are higher in negotiated deals than in competitive ones. However, many financial economists argue that issuing firms are not necessarily hurt by negotiated deals. They point out that the underwriter gains much information about the issuing firm through negotiation—information likely to increase the probability of a successful offering.[5]

The Offering Price

Determining the correct offering price is the most difficult thing the lead investment bank must do for an initial public offering. The issuing firm faces a potential cost if the offering price is set too high or too low. If the issue is priced too high, it may be unsuccessful and be withdrawn. If the issue is priced below the true market price, the issuer's existing shareholders will experience an opportunity loss.

Ibbotson has found that unseasoned new equity issues typically have been offered at 11 percent below their true market price.[6] Underpricing helps new shareholders earn a higher return on the shares they buy. However, the existing shareholders of the issuing firm are not necessarily helped by underpricing. To them it is an indirect cost of issuing new securities.

Several studies have confirmed the early research of Ibbotson. For example, Ritter examined approximately 7,600 firms that went public from 1975 through 2005 in the United States. He found that the average IPO rose in price 17.3 percent in the first day of trading following issuance (see Table 19.3). These figures are not annualized!

In a recent example, on January 21, 2006, McDonald's sold shares in its Chipotle Mexican Grill chain through an IPO. The initial offering was for 7.9 million shares at a price of $22 per share. The stock opened at $39.51 and rose to a first-day high of $48.28 before closing at $44.00, a 100 percent gain in the first day.

---

[5]This choice has been studied recently by Robert S. Hansen and Naveen Khanna, "Why Negotiation with a Single Syndicate May Be Preferred to Making Syndicates Compete: The Problem of Trapped Bidders," *Journal of Business* 67 (1994); S. Bhagat, "The Effect of Management's Choice between Negotiated and Competitive Equity Offerings on Shareholder Wealth," *Journal of Financial and Quantitative Analysis* (1986); and D. Logue and R. Jarrow, "Negotiation vs. Competitive Bidding in the Sales of Securities by Public Utilities," *Financial Management* 7 (1978).

[6]R. Ibbotson, "Price Performance of Common Stock New Issues," *Journal of Financial Economics* 2 (1975).

Table 19.4   Average First-Day Returns, Categorized by Sales, for IPOs: 1980–2005*

Annual Sales of Issuing Firms	Number of Firms	1980–1989 First-Day Average Return	Number of Firms	1990–1998 First-Day Average Return	Number of Firms	1999–2000 First-Day Average Return	Number of Firms	2001–2005 First-Day Average Return
0 ≤ Sales < $10 m	393	10.1%	671	17.2%	328	69.8%	77	6.1%
$10 m ≤ Sales < $20 m	253	8.7	377	18.7	139	79.9	27	10.5
$20 m ≤ Sales < $50 m	492	7.6	777	18.7	152	74.5	70	9.7
$50 m ≤ Sales < $100 m	345	6.5	574	13.0	89	60.4	72	16.1
$100 m ≤ Sales < $200 m	241	4.6	444	11.9	54	35.5	79	14.7
$200 m ≤ Sales	278	3.5	628	8.7	87	26.0	209	10.9
All	2,002	7.1%	3,471	14.8%	849	64.6%	534	11.3%

*Data are from Securities Data Co., with corrections by the authors. Sales, measured in millions, are for the last twelve months prior to going public. All sales have been converted into dollars of 2003 purchasing power, using the Consumer Price Index. There are 6,854 IPOs, after excluding IPOs with an offer price of less than $5.00 per share, units, REITs, ADRs, closed-end funds, banks and S&Ls, firms not listed on CRSP within six months of the offer date, and 140 firms with missing sales. The average first-day return is 18.5 percent.

SOURCE: Professor Jay R. Ritter, University of Florida.

Underpricing: A Possible Explanation

There are several possible explanations for underpricing. But so far there is no agreement among scholars as to which explanation is correct. In our opinion, there are two important facts associated with the underpricing puzzle that are key elements to a unifying theory. First, much of the apparent underpricing is concentrated in smaller issues. This point is documented in Table 19.4, which shows that underpricing tends to be attributable to firms with few or no sales in the prior year. These firms tend to be young firms with uncertain future prospects. The increased uncertainty in some way probably attracts risk-averse investors only if underpricing exists. Second, when the price of a new issue is too low, the issue is often *oversubscribed*. This means investors will not be able to buy all of the shares they want, and the underwriters will allocate the shares among investors. The average investor will find it difficult to get shares in an oversubscribed offering because there will not be enough shares to go around. Although initial public offerings have positive initial returns on average, a significant fraction of them have price drops. An investor submitting an order for all new issues may find that he or she will be allocated more shares in issues that go down in price.

Consider this tale of two investors. Ms. Smarts knows precisely what companies are worth when their shares are offered. Mr. Average knows only that prices usually rise one month after the IPO. Armed with this information, Mr. Average decides to buy 1,000 shares of every IPO. Does Mr. Average actually earn an abnormally high average return across all initial offerings?

The answer is no, and at least one reason is Ms. Smarts. For example, because Ms. Smarts knows that company *XYZ* is underpriced, she invests all her money in its IPO. When the issue is oversubscribed, the underwriters must allocate the shares between Ms. Smarts and Mr. Average. If they do this on a pro rata basis and if Ms. Smarts has bid for twice as many shares as Mr. Average, she will get two shares for each one Mr. Average receives. The net result is that when an issue is underpriced, Mr. Average cannot buy as much of it as he wants.

Ms. Smarts also knows that company *ABC* is overpriced. In this case, she avoids its IPO altogether, and Mr. Average ends up with a full 1,000 shares. To summarize, Mr. Average receives fewer shares when more knowledgeable investors swarm to buy an underpriced issue, but he gets all he wants when the smart money avoids the issue.

In Their Own Words

JAY RITTER ON IPO UNDERPRICING AROUND THE WORLD

The United States is not the only country in which initial public offerings of common stock (IPOs) are underpriced. The phenomenon exists in every country with a stock market, although the extent of underpricing varies from country to country.

In general, countries with developed capital markets have more moderate underpricing than those with emerging markets. During the Internet bubble of 1999–2000, however, underpricing in the developed capital markets increased dramatically. In the United States, for example, the average first-day return during 1999–2000 was 65 percent. At the same time that underpricing in the developed capital markets increased, the underpricing of IPOs sold to residents of China moderated. The Chinese average has come down to a mere 267 percent, which is lower than it had been in the early 1990s. After the bursting of the Internet bubble in mid-2000, the level of underpricing in the United States, Germany, and other developed capital markets returned to more traditional levels.

The table here gives a summary of the average first-day returns on IPOs for 39 countries around the world, with the figures collected from a number of studies by various authors. In countries where the first-day price change is limited by regulations, the return is measured until price limits are no longer binding.

Country	Sample Size	Time Period	Average First-Day Return	Country	Sample Size	Time Period	Average First-Day Return
Australia	381	1976–1995	12.1%	Malaysia	401	1980–1998	104.1%
Austria	76	1984–1999	6.5	Mexico	37	1987–1990	33.0
Belgium	86	1984–1999	14.6	Netherlands	143	1982–1999	10.2
Brazil	62	1979–1990	78.5	New Zealand	201	1979–1999	23.0
Canada	500	1971–1999	6.3	Nigeria	63	1989–1993	19.1
Chile	55	1982–1997	8.8	Norway	68	1984–1996	12.5
China	1,124	1992–2000	267.0	Philippines	104	1987–1997	22.7
Denmark	117	1984–1998	5.4	Poland	149	1991–1998	35.6
Finland	99	1984–1997	10.1	Portugal	21	1992–1998	10.6
France	571	1983–2000	11.6	Singapore	128	1973–1992	31.4
Germany	407	1978–1999	27.7	South Africa	118	1980–1991	32.7
Greece	129	1987–1994	51.7	Spain	99	1986–1998	10.7
Hong Kong	334	1980–1996	15.9	Sweden	251	1980–1994	34.1
India	98	1992–1993	35.3	Switzerland	120	1983–2000	34.9
Indonesia	106	1989–1994	15.1	Taiwan	293	1986–1998	31.1
Iran	279	1991–2004	22.4	Thailand	292	1987–1997	46.7
Israel	285	1990–1994	12.1	Turkey	138	1990–1996	13.6
Italy	164	1985–2000	23.9	United Kingdom	3,122	1959–2001	17.4
Japan	1,689	1970–2001	28.4	United States	14,840	1960–2001	18.4
Korea	477	1980–1996	74.3				

SOURCE: Jay R. Ritter is Cordell Professor of Finance at the University of Florida. An outstanding scholar, he is well-respected for his insightful analyses of new issues and companies going public.

This is called the *winner's curse*, and it explains much of the reason why IPOs have such a large average return. When the average investor wins and gets his allocation, it is because those who knew better avoided the issue. To counteract the winner's curse and attract the average investor, underwriters underprice issues.[7]

---

[7]This explanation was first suggested in K. Rock, "Why New Issues Are Underpriced," *Journal of Financial Economics* 15 (1986).

19.4   The Announcement of New Equity and the Value of the Firm

It seems reasonable to believe that new long-term financing is arranged by firms after positive net present value projects are put together. As a consequence, when the announcement of external financing is made, the firm's market value should go up. As we mentioned in an earlier chapter, this is precisely the opposite of what actually happens in the case of new equity financing. Asquith and Mullins, Masulis and Korwar, and Mikkelson and Partch have all found that the market value of existing equity drops on the announcement of a new issue of common stock.[8] Plausible reasons for this strange result include these:

1. *Managerial information*: If managers have superior information about the market value of the firm, they may know when the firm is overvalued. If they do, they might attempt to issue new shares of stock when the market value exceeds the correct value. This will benefit existing shareholders. However, the potential new shareholders are not stupid. They will infer overvaluation from the new issue, thereby bidding down the stock price on the announcement date of the issue.

2. *Debt capacity*: The stereotypical firm chooses a debt–equity ratio that balances the tax shield from the debt with the cost of financial distress. When the managers of a firm have special information that the probability of financial distress has risen, the firm is more likely to raise capital through stock than through debt. If the market infers this chain of events, the stock price should fall on the announcement date of an equity issue.

3. *Falling earnings:*[9] When managers raise capital in amounts that are unexpectedly large (as most unanticipated financings will be) and if investors have a reasonable fix on the firm's upcoming investments and dividend payouts (as they do because capital expenditure announcements are often well known, as are future dividends), the unanticipated financings are roughly equal to unanticipated shortfalls in earnings (this follows directly from the firm's sources and uses of funds identity). Therefore, an announcement of a new stock issue will also reveal a future earnings shortfall.

19.5   The Cost of New Issues

Issuing securities to the public is not free, and the costs of different issuing methods are important determinants of which will be used. The costs fall into six categories:

1. Spread or underwriting discount:	The spread is the difference between the price the issuer receives and the price offered to the public.
2. Other direct expenses:	These are costs incurred by the issuer that are not part of the compensation to underwriters. They include filing fees, legal fees, and taxes—all reported in the prospectus.

---

[8]P. Asquith and D. Mullins, "Equity Issues and Offering Dilution," *Journal of Financial Economics* 15 (1986); R. Masulis and A. N. Korwar, "Seasoned Equity Offerings: An Empirical Investigation," *Journal of Financial Economics* 15 (1986); and W. H. Mikkelson and M. M. Partch, "The Valuation Effects of Security Offerings and the Issuance Process," *Journal of Financial Economics* 15 (1986).

[9]Robert S. Haugen and Claire Crutchley, "Corporate Earnings and Financings: An Empirical Analysis," *Journal of Business* 20 (1990).

3. Indirect expenses: These costs are not reported in the prospectus and include management time spent on the new issue.

4. Abnormal returns: In a seasoned issue of stock, the price drops by 3 to 4 percent upon the announcement of the issue. The drop protects new shareholders against the firm's selling overpriced stock to new shareholders.

5. Underpricing: For initial public offerings, the stock typically rises substantially after the issue date. This is a cost to the firm because the stock is sold for less than its efficient price in the aftermarket.[10]

6. Green Shoe option: The Green Shoe option gives the underwriters the right to buy additional shares at the offer price to cover overallotments. This is a cost to the firm because the underwriter will buy additional shares only when the offer price is below the price in the aftermarket.

An interesting study by Lee, Lockhead, Ritter, and Zhao reports two of these six costs—underwriting discount and other direct expenses.[11] An updated version of their findings for both equity offerings and debt offerings are presented in Tables 19.5–19.7. Three conclusions emerge from the tables:

1. The costs in each category, for both equity offerings and debt offerings, decline as the gross proceeds of the offering increase. Thus, it appears that issuance costs are subject to substantial economies of scale.[12]

2. The bottom line of Table 19.5 indicates that across all offerings, direct expenses are higher for equity offers than for debt offers.

3. Last, and perhaps most important, the costs of issuing securities to the public are quite large. For example, total direct expenses are approximately 17 percent for an initial public offering of less than $10,000,000. In addition, Table 19.6 establishes that underpricing costs are another 16.36 percent. This implies that going public for the first time is a weighty decision. Although there are many benefits, such as raising needed capital and spreading ownership, the costs cannot be ignored.

19.6 Rights

When new shares of common stock are offered to the general public, the proportionate ownership of existing shareholders is likely to be reduced. However, if a preemptive right

---

[10]Some people have argued that the price in the aftermarket is not efficient after all. However, R. Ibbotson, "Price Performance of Common Stock New Issues," *Journal of Financial Economics* 2 (1975), shows that, on average, new issues exhibit no abnormal price performance over the first five years following issuance. This result is generally viewed as being consistent with market efficiency. That is, the stock obtains an efficient price immediately following issuance and remains at an efficient price.

[11]The notion of economies of scale has been contested by Oya Altinkilic and Robert S. Hansen, "Are There Scale Economies in Underwriting Spreads? Evidence of Rising External Financing Costs," *Review of Financial Studies* 13 (2000). They provide data and analysis showing that underwriter cost will be U-shaped.

[12]Among the most interesting developments in the initial public offering market is that almost all underwriter spreads in recent offerings have been exactly 7 percent. This is documented in H. C. Chen and Jay R. Ritter, "The Seven-Percent Solution," *Journal of Finance* (June 2000); and Robert S. Hansen, "Do Investment Banks Compete in IPO's? The Advent of the 7% Plus Contract," *Journal of Financial Economics* (August 2001).

Table 19.5   Direct Costs as a Percentage of Gross Proceeds for Equity (IPOs and SEOs) and Straight and Convertible Bonds Offered by Domestic Operating Companies: 1990–2003

	Equity							
	IPOs				SEOs			
Proceeds ($ millions)	Number of Issues	Gross Spread	Other Direct Expense	Total Direct Cost	Number of Issues	Gross Spread	Other Direct Expense	Total Direct Cost
2– 9.99	624	9.15%	6.21%	15.36%	267	7.56%	5.32%	12.88%
10– 19.99	704	7.33	4.30	11.63	519	6.32	2.49	8.81
20– 39.99	1,336	6.99	2.82	9.81	904	5.73	1.51	7.24
40– 59.99	771	6.96	2.25	9.21	677	5.28	0.92	6.20
60– 79.99	403	6.88	1.77	8.65	489	5.07	0.74	5.81
80– 99.99	245	6.79	1.55	8.34	292	4.95	0.61	5.56
100–199.99	438	6.48	1.19	7.67	657	4.57	0.43	5.00
200–499.99	197	5.91	0.81	6.72	275	3.99	0.27	4.26
500 and up	72	4.66	0.49	5.15	83	3.48	0.16	3.64
Total	4,790	7.17%	3.22%	10.39%	4,163	5.37%	1.35%	6.72%

	Bonds							
	Convertible Bonds				Straight Bonds			
Proceeds ($ millions)	Number of Issues	Gross Spread	Other Direct Expense	Total Direct Cost	Number of Issues	Gross Spread	Other Direct Expense	Total Direct Cost
2– 9.99	8	5.73%	2.78%	8.51%	70	1.39%	2.35%	3.74%
10– 19.99	20	5.26	2.90	8.16	104	1.33	1.59	2.92
20– 39.99	27	4.74	1.72	6.46	159	1.22	0.90	2.12
40– 59.99	33	3.29	1.01	4.30	152	0.72	0.63	1.35
60– 79.99	61	2.70	0.61	3.31	113	1.52	0.76	2.28
80– 99.99	17	2.16	0.56	2.72	159	1.39	0.56	1.95
100–199.99	100	2.56	0.39	2.95	677	1.60	0.52	2.12
200–499.99	53	2.34	0.22	2.56	333	1.43	0.37	1.80
500 and up	17	2.05	0.11	2.16	118	0.62	0.20	0.82
Total	336	2.99%	0.81%	3.80%	1,885	1.36%	0.61%	1.97%

SOURCE: Inmoo Lee, Scott Lockhead, Jay Ritter, and Quanshui Zhao,"The Costs of Raising Capital," *Journal of Financial Research* 1 (Spring 1996), calculations and updates by the authors.

is contained in the firm's articles of incorporation, the firm must first offer any new issue of common stock to existing shareholders. This assures each owner his or her proportionate owner's share.

An issue of common stock to existing stockholders is called a *rights offering.* Here each shareholder is issued an *option* to buy a specified number of new shares from the firm at a specified price within a specified time, after which the rights expire. For example, a firm whose stock is selling at $30 may let current stockholders buy a fixed number of shares at $10 per share within two months. The terms of the option are evidenced by certificates known as *share warrants* or *rights.* Such rights are often traded on securities exchanges or over the counter.

Table 19.6

Direct and
Indirect Costs, in
Percentages, of
Equity IPOs:
1990–2003

Proceeds ($ in millions)	Number of Issues	Gross Spread	Other Direct Expense	Total Direct Cost	Underpricing
2– 9.99	624	9.15%	6.21%	15.36%	18.18%
10– 19.99	704	7.33	4.30	11.63	10.02
20– 39.99	1,336	6.99	2.82	9.81	17.91
40– 59.99	771	6.96	2.25	9.21	29.57
60– 79.99	403	6.88	1.77	8.65	39.20
80– 99.99	245	6.79	1.55	8.34	45.36
100–199.99	438	6.48	1.19	7.67	37.10
200–499.99	197	5.91	0.81	6.72	17.12
500 and up	72	4.66	0.49	5.15	12.19
Total	4,790	7.17%	3.22%	10.39%	23.55%

SOURCE: Inmoo Lee, Scott Lockhead, Jay Ritter, and Quanshui Zhao, "The Costs of Raising Capital," *Journal of Financial Research* 1 (Spring 1996), calculations and updates by the authors.

Table 19.7

Average Gross
Spreads and Total
Direct Costs for
Domestic Debt
Issues: 1990–2003

Convertible Bonds

Proceeds ($ in millions)	Investment Grade			Noninvestment Grade		
	Number of Issues	Gross Spread	Total Direct Cost	Number of Issues	Gross Spread	Total Direct Cost
2– 9.99	0	—	—	0	—	—
10– 19.99	0	—	—	1	4.00%	5.67%
20– 39.99	0	—	—	11	3.47	5.02
40– 59.99	3	1.92%	2.43%	21	3.33	4.48
60– 79.99	4	1.65	2.09	47	2.78	3.40
80– 99.99	3	0.89	1.16	9	2.54	3.19
100–199.99	28	2.22	2.55	50	2.57	3.00
200–499.99	26	1.99	2.18	17	2.62	2.85
500 and up	12	1.96	2.09	1	2.50	2.57
Total	76	1.99%	2.26%	157	2.81%	3.47%

Straight Bonds

Proceeds ($ in millions)	Investment Grade			Noninvestment Grade		
	Number of Issues	Gross Spread	Total Direct Cost	Number of Issues	Gross Spread	Total Direct Cost
2– 9.99	40	0.62%	1.90%	0	—	—
10– 19.99	68	0.50	1.35	2	2.74%	4.80%
20– 39.99	119	0.58	1.21	13	3.06	4.36
40– 59.99	132	0.39	0.86	12	3.01	3.93
60– 79.99	68	0.57	0.97	43	2.99	4.07
80– 99.99	100	0.66	0.94	56	2.74	3.66
100–199.99	341	0.55	0.80	321	2.71	3.39
200–499.99	173	0.50	0.81	156	2.49	2.90
500 and up	97	0.28	0.38	20	2.45	2.71
Total	1,138	0.51%	0.85%	623	2.68%	3.35%

SOURCE: Inmoo Lee, Scott Lockhead, Jay Ritter, and Quanshui Zhao, "The Costs of Raising Capital," *Journal of Financial Research* 1 (Spring 1996), calculations and updates by the authors.

Table 19.8

Financial Statement
before Rights
Offering

NATIONAL POWER COMPANY Balance Sheet and Income Statement		
Balance Sheet		
Assets	Shareholder Equity	
	Common stock	$10,000,000
	Retained earnings	10,000,000
Total $20,000,000	Total	$20,000,000
Income Statement		
Earnings before taxes	$ 3,030,303	
Taxes (34%)	1,030,303	
Net income	$ 2,000,000	
Earnings per share	2	
Shares outstanding	1,000,000	
Market price per share	20	
Total market value	$20,000,000	

The Mechanics of a Rights Offering

The various considerations confronting a financial manager in a rights offering are illustrated by the situation of the National Power Company, whose initial financial statements are given in Table 19.8.

National Power earns $2 million after taxes and has 1 million shares outstanding. Earnings per share are $2, and the stock sells at 10 times earnings (that is, its price–earnings ratio is 10). The market price of each share is therefore $20. The company plans to raise $5 million of new equity funds by a rights offering.

The process of issuing rights differs from the process of issuing shares of stock for cash. Existing stockholders are notified that they have been given one right for each share of stock they own. Exercise occurs when a shareholder sends payment to the firm's subscription agent (usually a bank) and turns in the required number of rights. Shareholders of National Power will have several choices: (1) subscribe for the full number of entitled shares, (2) order all the rights sold, or (3) do nothing and let the rights expire.

The financial management of National Power must answer the following questions:

1. What price should the existing shareholders be allowed to pay for a share of new stock?
2. How many rights will be required to purchase one share of stock?
3. What effect will the rights offering have on the existing price of the stock?

Subscription Price

In a rights offering the **subscription price** is the price that existing shareholders are allowed to pay for a share of stock. A rational shareholder will subscribe to the rights offering only if the subscription price is below the market price of the stock on the offer's expiration date. For example, if the stock price at expiration is $13 and the subscription price is $15, no rational shareholder will subscribe. Why pay $15 for something worth $13? National Power chooses a price of $10, which is well below the current market price of $20. As long as the market price does not fall by half before expiration, the rights offering will succeed.

Number of Rights Needed to Purchase a Share

National Power wants to raise $5 million in new equity. With a subscription price of $10, it must issue 500,000 new shares. This can be determined by dividing the total amount to be raised by the subscription price:

$$\text{Number of new shares} = \frac{\text{Funds to be raised}}{\text{Subscription price}} = \frac{\$5,000,000}{\$10} = 500,000 \text{ shares}$$

Because stockholders typically get one right for each share of stock they own, 1 million rights will be issued by National Power. To determine how many rights must be exercised to get one share of stock, we can divide the number of existing outstanding shares of stock by the number of new shares:

$$\begin{array}{c}\text{Number of rights needed} \\ \text{to buy a share of stock}\end{array} = \frac{\text{"Old" shares}}{\text{"New" shares}} = \frac{1,000,000}{500,000} = 2 \text{ rights}$$

Thus a shareholder must give up two rights plus $10 to receive a share of new stock. If all the stockholders do this, National Power will raise the required $5 million.

It should be clear that the subscription price, the number of new shares, and the number of rights needed to buy a new share of stock are interrelated. If National Power lowers the subscription price, it must issue more new shares to raise $5 million in new equity. Several alternatives appear here:

Subscription Price	Number of New Shares	Number of Rights Needed to Buy a Share of Stock
$20	250,000	4
10	500,000	2
5	1,000,000	1

Effect of Rights Offering on Price of Stock

Rights clearly have value. In the case of National Power, the right to be able to buy a share of stock worth $20 for $10 is valuable.

Suppose a shareholder of National Power owns two shares of stock just before the rights offering. This situation is depicted in Table 19.9. Initially the price of National Power is $20 per share, so the shareholder's total holding is worth $2 \times \$20 = \$40$. The stockholder who has two shares will receive two rights. The National Power rights offer gives shareholders with two rights the opportunity to purchase one additional share for $10. The holding of the shareholder who exercises these rights and buys the new share would increase to three shares. The value of the new holding would be $40 + $10 = $50 (the $40 initial value plus the $10 paid to the company). Because the stockholder now holds three shares, the price per share would drop to $50/3 = $16.67 (rounded to two decimal places).

The difference between the old share price of $20 and the new share price of $16.67 reflects the fact that the old shares carried rights to subscribe to the new issue. The difference must be equal to the value of one right—that is, $20 − $16.67 = $3.33.

Just as we learned of an ex-dividend date in the previous chapter, there is an **ex-rights date** here. An individual buying the stock prior to the ex-rights date will receive the rights when they are distributed. An individual buying the stock on or after the ex-rights date will

Table 19.9

The Value to
the Individual
Shareholder of
National Power's
Rights

	The Shareholder
Initial position	
Number of shares	2
Share price	$20
Value of holding	$40
Terms of offer	
Subscription price	$10
Number of rights issued	2
Number of rights for a share	2
After offer	
Number of shares	3
Value of holding	$50
Share price	$16.67
Value of a right	
Old price − New price	$20 − $16.67 = $3.33
$\dfrac{\text{New price} - \text{Subscription price}}{\text{Number of rights for a share}}$	($16.67 − $10)/2 = $3.33

Table 19.10

National Power
Company Rights
Offering

Initial position	
Number of shares	1 million
Share price	$20
Value of firm	$20 million
Terms of offer	
Subscription price	$10
Number of rights issued	1 million
Number of rights for a share	2
After offer	
Number of shares	1.5 million
Share price	$16.67
Value of firm	$25 million
Value of one right	$20 − $16.67 = $3.33
	or ($16.67 − $10)/2 = $3.33

not receive the rights. In our example the price of the stock prior to the ex-rights date is $20. An individual buying on or after the ex-rights date is not entitled to the rights. The price on or after the ex-rights date is $16.67.

Table 19.10 shows what happens to National Power. If all shareholders exercise their rights, the number of shares will increase to 1.5 million and the value of the firm will increase to $25 million. After the rights offering the value of each share will drop to $16.67 (= $25 million/1.5 million).

An investor holding no shares of National Power stock who wants to subscribe to the new issue can do so by buying rights. An outside investor buying two rights will pay $3.33 × 2 = $6.67 (to account for previous rounding). If the investor exercises the rights at a subscription cost of $10, the total cost would be $10 + $6.67 = $16.67. In return for this expenditure, the investor will receive a share of the new stock, which is worth $16.67.

Of course, outside investors can also buy National Power stock directly at $16.67 per share. In an efficient stock market it will make no difference whether new stock is obtained via rights or via direct purchase.

Effects on Shareholders

Shareholders can exercise their rights or sell them. In either case, the stockholder will nei-ther win nor lose by the rights offering. The hypothetical holder of two shares of National Power has a portfolio worth $40. On the one hand, if the shareholder exercises the rights, he or she ends up with three shares worth a total of $50. In other words, by spending $10, the investor increases the value of the holding by $10, which means that he or she is neither better nor worse off.

On the other hand, a shareholder who sells the two rights for $3.33 each obtains $3.33 × 2 = $6.67 in cash. Because the two shares are each worth $16.67, the holdings are valued at

$$
\begin{array}{llll}
\text{Shares} & = 2 \times \$16.67 & = \$33.33 \\
\text{Sold rights} & = 2 \times \$\ 3.33 & = \underline{\$\ 6.67} \\
\text{Total} & & = \$40.00
\end{array}
$$

The new $33.33 market value plus $6.67 in cash is exactly the same as the original holding of $40. Thus, stockholders can neither lose nor gain from exercising or selling rights.

It is obvious that the new market price of the firm's stock will be lower after the rights offering than it was before the rights offering. The lower the subscription price, the greater the price decline of a rights offering. However, our analysis shows that the stockholders have suffered no loss because of the rights offering.

The Underwriting Arrangements

Undersubscription can occur if investors throw away rights or if bad news causes the market price of the stock to fall below the subscription price. To ensure against these possibili-ties, rights offerings are typically arranged by **standby underwriting**. Here the underwriter makes a firm commitment to purchase the unsubscribed portion of the issue at the subscrip-tion price less a take-up fee. The underwriter usually receives a **standby fee** as compensa-tion for this risk-bearing function.

In practice the subscription price is usually set well below the current market price, making the probability of a rights failure quite small. Though a small percentage (less than 10 percent) of shareholders fail to exercise valuable rights, shareholders are usually allowed to purchase unsubscribed shares at the subscription price. This **oversubscription privilege** makes it unlikely that the corporate issuer would need to turn to its underwriter for help.

19.7   The Rights Puzzle

Smith calculated the issuance costs from three alternative methods: an equity issue with underwriting, a rights issue with standby underwriting, and a pure rights issue.[13] The re-sults of his study, which appear in Table 19.11, suggest that a pure rights issue is the cheap-est of the three alternatives. The bottom line of the table shows that total costs as a percent-age of proceeds are 6.17 percent, 6.05 percent, and 2.45 percent for the three alternatives, respectively. As the body of the table indicates, this disparity holds when issues of different sizes are separated.

If corporate executives are rational, they will raise equity in the cheapest manner. Thus the preceding evidence suggests that issues of pure rights should dominate. Surprisingly,

---

[13]C.W. Smith, Jr., "Alternative Methods for Raising Capital: Rights versus Underwritten Offerings," *Journal of Financial Economics* 5 (December 1977).

Table 19.11 Costs of Flotation as a Percentage of Proceeds*

Size of Issue (in $ millions)	Underwriting				Rights with Standby Underwriting				Pure Rights	
	Number	Compensation as a Percentage of Proceeds	Other Expenses as a Percentage of Proceeds	Total Cost as a Percentage of Proceeds	Number	Compensation as a Percentage of Proceeds	Other Expenses as a Percentage of Proceeds	Total Cost as a Percentage of Proceeds	Number	Total Cost as a Percentage of Proceeds
Under 0.50	0	—	—	—	—	—	—	—	3	8.99
0.50 to 0.99	6	6.96	6.78	13.74	2	3.43	4.80	8.24	2	4.59
1.00 to 1.99	18	10.40	4.89	15.29	5	6.36	4.15	10.51	5	4.90
2.00 to 4.99	61	6.59	2.87	9.47	9	5.20	2.85	8.06	7	2.85
5.00 to 9.99	66	5.50	1.53	7.03	4	3.92	2.18	6.10	6	1.39
10.00 to 19.99	91	4.84	0.71	5.55	10	4.14	1.21	5.35	3	0.72
20.00 to 49.99	156	4.30	0.37	4.67	12	3.84	0.90	4.74	1	0.52
50.00 to 99.99	70	3.97	0.21	4.18	9	3.96	0.74	4.70	2	0.21
100.00 to 500.00	16	3.81	0.14	3.95	5	3.50	0.50	4.00	9	0.13
Total/average	484	5.02	1.15	6.17	56	4.32	1.73	6.05	38	2.45

*Based on 578 common stock issues registered under the Securities Act of 1933 during 1971–1975. The issues are subdivided by size of issue and method of financing: underwriting, rights with standby underwriting, and pure rights offering.

Issues are included only if the company's stock was listed on the NYSE, AMEX, or regional exchanges before the offering; any associated secondary distribution represents less than 10 percent of the total proceeds of the issue, and the offering contains no other types of securities. The costs reported are (1) compensation received by investment bankers for underwriting services rendered, (2) legal fees, (3) accounting fees, (4) engineering fees, (5) trustees' fees, (6) printing and engraving expenses, (7) SEC registration fees, (8) federal revenue stamps, and (9) state taxes.

SOURCE: Modified from C. W. Smith, Jr., "Costs of Underwritten versus Rights Issues," *Journal of Financial Economics* 5 (December 1977), p. 277 (Table 1).

Smith points out that over 90 percent of new issues are underwritten. This is generally viewed as an anomaly in the finance profession, though a few explanations have been advanced:[14]

1. Underwriters increase the stock price. This is supposedly accomplished because of increased public confidence or by the selling effort of the underwriting group. However, Smith could find no evidence of this in an examination of 52 rights offerings and 344 underwritten offerings.

2. Because the underwriter buys the shares at the agreed-upon price, it is providing insurance to the firm. That is, the underwriter loses if it is unable to sell all the shares to the public. This potential loss might mean that the underwriter's effective compensation is less than that measured in Table 19.11. However, the potential economic loss is probably not large. In most cases the offer price is set within 24 hours of the offering, by which time the underwriter has usually made a careful assessment of the market for the shares.

3. Other arguments include these: (*a*) The proceeds of underwritten issues are available sooner than are the proceeds from a rights offer; (*b*) underwriters provide a wider distribution of ownership than would be true with a rights offering; (*c*) consulting advice from investment bankers may be beneficial; and (*d*) stockholders find exercising rights a nuisance.

All of the preceding arguments are pieces of the puzzle, but none seems very convincing. Booth and Smith have identified a function of the underwriter that had not been taken into account in previous cost studies.[15] They argue that the underwriter *certifies* that the offering price is consistent with the true value of the issue. This certification is implied in the underwriting relationship and is provided when the underwriting firm gets access to inside information and puts its reputation for correct pricing on the line.

19.8 Shelf Registration

To simplify the procedures for issuing securities, the SEC currently allows **shelf registration**. Shelf registration permits a corporation to register an offering that it reasonably expects to sell within the next two years. A master registration statement is filed at the time of registration. The company is permitted to sell the issue whenever it wants over those two years as long as it distributes a short-form statement.

Not all companies are allowed shelf registration. The major qualifications are as follows:

1. The company must be rated *investment grade.*

2. The firm cannot have defaulted on its debt in the past 12 months.

3. The aggregate market value of the firm's outstanding stock must be more than $75 million.

4. The firm must not have violated the Securities Act of 1934 in the past 12 months.

Hershman reports on the use of the *dribble* method of new equity issuance.[16] With dribbling, a company registers the issue and hires an underwriter to be its selling agent.

---

[14] It is even more anomalous because rights offerings are used around the world. In fact, they are required by law in many other countries.

[15] J. Booth and R. Smith, "The Certification Role of the Investment Banker in New Issue Pricing," *Midland Corporate Finance Journal* (Spring 1986).

[16] A. Hershman, "New Strategies in Equity Financing," *Dunn's Business Monthly* (June 1983).

The company sells shares in small amounts from time to time via a stock exchange. For example, in June 2006, Internet search provider Ask Jeeves filed a $400 million shelf registration to sell a combination of common stock, debt securities, and other instruments.[17]

The rule has been very controversial. Several arguments have been made against shelf registration:

1. The timeliness of disclosure is reduced with shelf registration because the master registration statement may have been prepared up to two years before the actual issue occurs.

2. Some investment bankers have argued that shelf registration will cause a market overhang because registration informs the market of future issues. It has been suggested that this overhang will depress market prices. However, an empirical analysis by Bhagat, Marr, and Thompson found that shelf registration is less costly than conventional underwriting and found no evidence to suggest a market overhang effect.[18]

19.9 The Private Equity Market

The previous sections of this chapter assumed that a company is big enough, successful enough, and old enough to raise capital in the public equity market. Of course many firms have not reached this stage and cannot use the public equity market. For start-up firms or firms in financial trouble, the public equity market is often not available. The market for **venture capital** is part of the private equity market.[19]

Private Placement

Private placements avoid the costly procedures associated with the registration requirements that are part of public issues. The Securities and Exchange Commission (SEC) restricts private placement issues to no more than a couple of dozen knowledgeable investors, including institutions such as insurance companies and pension funds. The biggest drawback of privately placed securities is that the securities cannot be easily resold. Most private placements involve debt securities, but equity securities can also be privately placed.

In 1990, Rule 144A was adopted by the SEC to establish a framework for the issuance of private securities to certain qualified institutional investors. As illustrated in Figure 19.2, the rule has generated a substantial market for privately underwritten issues. Largely because of Rule 144A, companies raise about one-sixth of the proceeds from all new issues without registration with the SEC. To qualify to buy Rule 144A offerings, investors must have at least $100 million in assets under management. Most private placements are in straight bonds or convertible bonds. However, preferred stock is frequently issued as a private placement.

The Private Equity Firm

A large amount of private equity investment is undertaken by professional private equity managers representing large institutional investors such as mutual funds and pension funds. The limited partnership is the dominant form of intermediation in this market. Typically,

---

[17]D. J. Dennis, "Shelf Registration and the Market in Seasonal Equity Offerings," *Journal of Business* 64 (1991).

[18]S. Bhagat, M.W. Marr, and G. R. Thompson, "The Rule 415 Experiment: Equity Markets," *Journal of Finance* 19 (December 1985).

[19]S. E. Pratt, "Overview and Introduction to the Venture Capital Industry," *Guide to Venture Capital Sources*, 10th ed., 1987 (Venture Economics. Laurel Avenue, Box 348, Wellesley Hills, MA 02181).

Figure 19.2

Corporate Equity Security Offerings

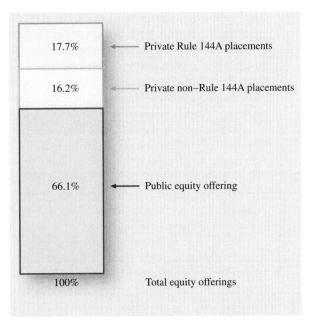

SOURCE: Jennifer E. Bethal and Erik R. Sirri, "Express Lane or Toll Booth in the Desert: The SEC Framework for Securities Issuance," *Journal of Applied Corporate Finance* (Spring 1998).

the institutional investors act as the limited partners, and the professional managers act as general partners. The general partners are firms that specialize in funding and managing equity investments in closely held private firms. The private equity market has been important for both traditional start-up companies and established public firms. Thus, the private equity market can be divided into venture equity and nonventure equity markets. A large part of the nonventure market is made up of firms in financial distress. Firms in financial distress are not likely to be able to issue public equity and typically cannot use traditional forms of debt such as bank loans or public debt. For these firms, the best alternative is to find a private equity market firm.

Suppliers of Venture Capital

As we have pointed out, venture capital is an important part of the private equity market. There are at least four types of suppliers of venture capital. First, a few old-line, wealthy families have traditionally provided start-up capital to promising businesses. For example, over the years, the Rockefeller family has made the initial capital contribution to a number of successful businesses. These families have been involved in venture capital for at least a century.

Second, a number of private partnerships and corporations have been formed to provide investment funds. The organizer behind the partnership might raise capital from institutional investors, such as insurance companies and pension funds. Alternatively, a group of individuals might provide the funds to be ultimately invested with budding entrepreneurs.

Of the early partnerships, the most well-known is clearly American Research and Development (ARD), which was formed in 1946. Though ARD invested in many companies, its success was largely due to its investment in Digital Equipment Company (DEC). When Textron acquired ARD in 1972, over 85 percent of the shareholders' distribution was due to the investment in DEC.[20] Among the more recent venture capitalists, Arthur Rock & Co. of

---

[20]H. Stevenson, D. Muzka, and J. Timmons, "Venture Capital in Transition: A Monte Carlo Simulation of Changes in Investment Patterns," *Journal of Business Venturing* (Spring 1987).

San Francisco may be the best known. Because of its huge success with Apple Computer and other high-tech firms, it has achieved near mythic stature in the venture capital industry.

Recent estimates put the number of venture capital firms at about 2,000. Pratt's *Guide to Venture Capital* (Venture Economics) provides a list of the names of many of these firms.[21] The average amount invested per venture has been estimated to be between $1 million and $2 million. However, one should not make too much of this figure because the amount of financing varies considerably with the venture to be funded.

Stories used to abound about how easily an individual could obtain venture capital. Though that may have been the case in an earlier era, it is certainly not the case today. Venture capital firms employ various screening procedures to prevent inappropriate funding. For example, because of the large demand for funds, many venture capitalists have at least one employee whose full-time job consists of reading business plans. Only the very best plans can expect to attract funds. Maier and Walker indicate that only about 2 percent of requests actually receive financing.[22]

Third, large industrial or financial corporations have established venture capital subsidiaries. Manufacturers Hanover Venture Capital Corp., Citicorp Venture Capital, and Chemical Venture Capital Corporation of Chemical Bank are examples of this type. However, subsidiaries of this type appear to make up only a small portion of the venture capital market.

Fourth, participants in an informal venture capital market have recently been identified.[23] Rather than belonging to any venture capital firm, these investors (often referred to as *angels*) act as individuals when providing financing. However, they should not, by any means, be viewed as isolated. Wetzel and others indicate that there is a rich network of angels, continually relying on each other for advice. A number of researchers have stressed that in any informal network there is likely one knowledgeable and trustworthy individual who, when backing a venture, brings a few less experienced investors in with him.

The venture capital community has unfortunately chosen to refer to these individuals as "dumb dentists." Although a number indeed may be dentists, their intelligence should not be called into question. Wetzel asserts that the prototypical angel has income over $100,000, net worth over $1,000,000, and substantial business experience and knowledge. As we might expect, the informal venture capitalist is able to tolerate high risks.

Though this informal market may seem small and unimportant, it is perhaps the largest of all sources of venture capital. Wetzel says that aggregate investments from this source total around $50 billion, about twice the amount invested by more professional venture capitalists. The size of each contribution is smaller here. Perhaps, on average, only $250,000 per venture is raised when the informal market is tapped.

Stages of Financing

Bruno and Tyebjee identify six stages in venture capital financing:[24]

1. *Seed money stage*: A small amount of financing needed to prove a concept or develop a product. Marketing is not included in this stage.

---

[21] Pratt, "Overview and Introduction to the Venture Capital Industry."

[22] J. B. Maier and D. Walker, "The Role of Venture Capital in Financing Small Business," *Journal of Business Venturing* (Summer 1987).

[23] See W. E. Wetzel, "The Informal Venture Capital Market: Aspects of Scale and Market Efficiency," *Journal of Business Venturing* (Fall 1987).

[24] A. V. Bruno and T. T. Tyebjee, "The Entrepreneur's Search for Capital," *Journal of Business Venturing* (Winter 1985).

Figure 19.3

Initial Public Offerings by Venture Capital–Backed Biotechnology Firms, January 1978 to January 1992

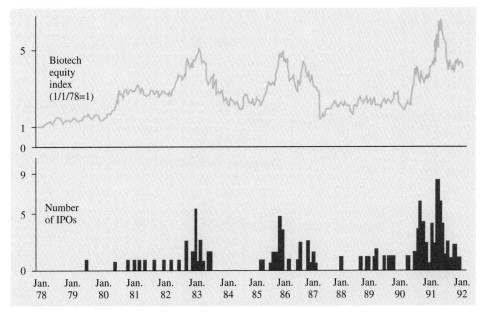

SOURCE: Joshua Lerner, "Venture Capitalists and the Decision to Go Public," *Journal of Financial Economics* 35 (June 1994).

2. *Start-up*: Financing for firms that started within the past year. Funds are likely to pay for marketing and product development expenditures.

3. *First-round financing*: Additional money to begin sales and manufacturing after a firm has spent its start-up funds.

4. *Second-round financing*: Funds earmarked for working capital for a firm that is currently selling its product but still losing money.

5. *Third-round financing*: Financing for a company that is at least breaking even and is contemplating an expansion. This is also known as *mezzanine financing*.

6. *Fourth-round financing*: Money provided for firms that are likely to go public within half a year. This round is also known as *bridge financing*.

Although these categories may seem vague to the reader, we have found that the terms are well-accepted within the industry. For example, the venture capital firms listed in Pratt's *Guide to Venture Capital* indicate which of these stages they are interested in financing.

The penultimate stage in venture capital finance is the initial public offering.[25] Venture capitalists are very important participants in initial public offerings. Venture capitalists rarely sell all of the shares they own at the time of the initial public offering. Instead they usually sell out in subsequent public offerings. However, there is considerable evidence that venture capitalists can successfully time IPOs by taking firms public when the market values are at the highest. Figure 19.3 shows the number of IPOs of privately held venture capital–backed biotechnology companies in each month from 1978 to 1992. The venture capital–backed IPOs clearly coincide with the ups and downs in the biotech market index in the top panel.

---

[25] A very influential paper by Christopher Barry, Chris J. Muscarella, John W. Peavey III, and Michael R. Vetsuypens, "The Role of Venture Capital in the Creation of Public Companies: Evidence from the Going Public Process," *Journal of Financial Economics* 27 (1990), shows that venture capitalists do not usually sell shares at the time of the initial public offering, but they usually have board seats and act as advisers to managers.

Summary and Conclusions

This chapter looked closely at how equity is issued. The main points follow:

1. Large issues have proportionately much lower costs of issuing equity than small ones.

2. Firm commitment underwriting is far more prevalent for large issues than is best-efforts underwriting. Smaller issues probably primarily use best efforts because of the greater uncertainty of these issues. For an offering of a given size, the direct expenses of best-efforts underwriting and firm commitment underwriting are of the same magnitude.

3. Rights offerings are cheaper than general cash offers and eliminate the problem of underpricing. Yet most new equity issues are underwritten general cash offers.

4. Shelf registration is a new method of issuing new debt and equity. The direct costs of shelf issues seem to be substantially lower than those of traditional issues.

5. Venture capitalists are an increasingly important influence in start-up firms and subsequent financing.

Concept Questions

1. **Debt versus Equity Offering Size**   In the aggregate, debt offerings are much more common than equity offerings and typically much larger as well. Why?

2. **Debt versus Equity Flotation Costs**   Why are the costs of selling equity so much larger than the costs of selling debt?

3. **Bond Ratings and Flotation Costs**   Why do noninvestment-grade bonds have much higher direct costs than investment-grade issues?

4. **Underpricing in Debt Offerings**   Why is underpricing not a great concern with bond offerings?

Use the following information to answer the next three questions. Eyetech Pharmaceuticals, Inc., a company that develops treatments for eye problems, went public in January 2004. Assisted by the investment bank Merrill Lynch, Eyetech sold 6.5 million shares at £21 each, thereby raising a total of £136.5 million. At the end of the first day of trading, the stock sold for £32.40 per share, down slightly from a high of £33.00. Based on the end-of-day numbers, Eyetech shares were apparently underpriced by about £11 each, meaning that the company missed out on an additional £67 million.

5. **IPO Pricing**   The Eyetech IPO was underpriced by about 54 percent. Should Eyetech be upset at Merrill Lynch over the underpricing?

6. **IPO Pricing**   In the previous question, would it affect your thinking to know that the company was incorporated less than four years earlier, had only £30 million in revenues for the first nine months of 2003, and had never earned a profit? Additionally, the company had only one product, Macugen, which had won fast-track status from the FDA but still did not have approval to be sold.

7. **IPO Pricing**   In the previous two questions, how would it affect your thinking to know that in addition to the 6.5 million shares offered in the IPO, Eyetech had an additional 32 million shares outstanding? Of the 32 million shares, 10 million shares were owned by pharmaceutical giant Pfizer, and 12 million shares were owned by the 13 directors and executive officers.

8. **Cash Offer versus Rights Offer**   Ren-Stimpy International is planning to raise fresh equity capital by selling a large new issue of common stock. Ren-Stimpy is currently a publicly traded corporation, and it is trying to choose between an underwritten cash offer and a rights offering (not underwritten) to current shareholders. Ren-Stimpy management is interested in minimizing the selling costs and has asked you for advice on the choice of issue methods. What is your recommendation and why?

9. **IPO Underpricing**   In 1980, a certain assistant professor of finance bought 12 initial public offerings of common stock. He held each of these for approximately one month and then sold. The investment rule he followed was to submit a purchase order for every firm commitment

initial public offering of oil and gas exploration companies. There were 22 of these offerings, and he submitted a purchase order for approximately €1,000 in stock for each of the companies. With 10 of these, no shares were allocated to this assistant professor. With 5 of the 12 offerings that were purchased, fewer than the requested number of shares were allocated.

The year 1980 was very good for oil and gas exploration company owners: On average, for the 22 companies that went public, the stocks were selling for 80 percent above the offering price a month after the initial offering date. The assistant professor looked at his performance record and found that the €8,400 invested in the 12 companies had grown to €10,000, representing a return of only about 20 percent (commissions were negligible). Did he have bad luck, or should he have expected to do worse than the average initial public offering investor? Explain.

10. **IPO Pricing** The following material represents the cover page and summary of the prospectus for the initial public offering of the Pest Investigation Control Corporation (PICC), which is going public tomorrow with a firm commitment initial public offering managed by the investment banking firm of Erlanger and Ritter.

Answer the following questions:

a. Assume that you know nothing about PICC other than the information contained in the prospectus. Based on your knowledge of finance, what is your prediction for the price of PICC tomorrow? Provide a short explanation of why you think this will occur.

b. Assume that you have several thousand dollars to invest. When you get home from class tonight, you find that your stockbroker, whom you have not talked to for weeks, has called. She has left a message that PICC is going public tomorrow and that she can get you several hundred shares at the offering price if you call her back first thing in the morning. Discuss the merits of this opportunity.

PROSPECTUS   **PICC**

200,000 shares
PEST INVESTIGATION CONTROL CORPORATION

Of the shares being offered hereby, all 200,000 are being sold by the Pest Investigation Control Corporation, Inc. ("the Company"). Before the offering there has been no public market for the shares of PICC, and no guarantee can be given that any such market will develop.

These securities have not been approved or disapproved by the SEC, nor has the commission passed judgment upon the accuracy or adequacy of this prospectus. Any representation to the contrary is a criminal offense.

	Price to Public	Underwriting Discount	Proceeds to Company*
Per share	$11.00	$1.10	$9.90
Total	$2,200,000	$220,000	$1,980,000

*Before deducting expenses estimated at $27,000 and payable by the company.

This is an initial public offering. The common shares are being offered, subject to prior sale, when, as, and if delivered to and accepted by the Underwriters and subject to approval of certain legal matters by their Counsel and by Counsel for the Company. The Underwriters reserve the right to withdraw, cancel, or modify such offer and to reject offers in whole or in part.

Erlanger and Ritter, Investment Bankers
July 12, 2006

Prospectus Summary

The Company	The Pest Investigation Control Corporation (PICC) breeds and markets toads and tree frogs as ecologically safe insect-control mechanisms.
The Offering	200,000 shares of common stock, no par value.
Listing	The Company will seek listing on NASDAQ and will trade over the counter.
Shares Outstanding	As of June 30, 2006, 400,000 shares of common stock were outstanding. After the offering, 600,000 shares of common stock will be outstanding.

(continued)

Use of Proceeds	To finance expansion of inventory and receivables and general working capital, and to pay for country club memberships for certain finance professors.

Selected Financial Information
(amounts in thousands except per-share data)

	Fiscal Year Ended June 30				As of June 30, 2006	
	2004	**2005**	**2006**		**Actual**	**As Adjusted for This Offering**
Revenues	$60.00	$120.00	$240.00	Working capital	$ 8	$1,961
Net earnings	3.80	15.90	36.10	Total assets	511	2,464
Earnings per share	0.01	0.04	0.09	Stockholders' equity	423	2,376

11. **Competitive and Negotiated Offers**   What are the comparative advantages of a competitive offer and a negotiated offer, respectively?

12. **Seasoned Equity Offers**   What are the possible reasons why the stock price typically drops on the announcement of a seasoned new equity issue?

13. **Raising Capital**   Megabucks Industries is planning to raise fresh equity capital by selling a large new issue of common stock. Megabucks, a publicly traded corporation, is trying to choose between an underwritten cash offer and a rights offering (not underwritten) to current shareholders. Megabucks' management is interested in maximizing the wealth of current shareholders and has asked you for advice on the choice of issue methods. What is your recommendation? Why?

14. **Shelf Registration**   Explain why shelf registration has been used by many firms instead of syndication.

15. **IPOs**   Every IPO is unique, but what are the basic empirical regularities in IPOs?

Questions and Problems

BASIC
(Questions 1–9)

1. **Rights Offerings**   Again, Inc., is proposing a rights offering. Presently there are 400,000 shares outstanding at KYD 85 each. There will be 70,000 new shares offered at KYD 70 each.
   a. What is the new market value of the company?
   b. How many rights are associated with one of the new shares?
   c. What is the ex-rights price?
   d. What is the value of a right?
   e. Why might a company have a rights offering rather than a general cash offer?

2. **Rights Offering**   Tapeta Publishing has announced a rights offer to raise LRD 50 million for a new journal, the *Liberian Journal of Financial*. This journal will review potential articles after the author pays a nonrefundable reviewing fee of LRD 5,000 per page. The stock currently sells for LRD 40 per share, and there are 5.2 million shares outstanding.
   a. What is the maximum possible subscription price? What is the minimum?
   b. If the subscription price is set at LRD 35 per share, how many shares must be sold? How many rights will it take to buy one share?
   c. What is the ex-rights price? What is the value of a right?
   d. Show how a shareholder with 100 shares before the offering and no desire (or money) to buy additional shares is not harmed by the rights offer.

3. **Rights**   Stone Shoe Co. has concluded that additional equity financing will be needed to expand operations and that the needed funds will be best obtained through a rights offering. It has correctly determined that as a result of the rights offering, the share price will fall from €80 to €74.50 (€80 is the "rights-on" price; €74.50 is the ex-rights price, also known as the *when-issued* price). The company is seeking €15 million in additional funds with a per-share subscription price equal to €40. How many shares are there currently, before the offering? (Assume that the increment to the market value of the equity equals the gross proceeds from the offering.)

4. **IPO Underpricing** The Piura Co. and the Callao Co. have both announced IPOs at PEN 40 per share. One of these is undervalued by PEN 11, and the other is overvalued by PEN 6, but you have no way of knowing which is which. You plan on buying 1,000 shares of each issue. If an issue is underpriced, it will be rationed, and only half your order will be filled. If you *could* get 1,000 shares in Piura and 1,000 shares in Callao, what would your profit be? What profit do you actually expect? What principle have you illustrated?

5. **Calculating Flotation Costs** The St. Anger Corporation needs to raise MTL 85 million to finance its expansion into new markets. The company will sell new shares of equity via a general cash offering to raise the needed funds. If the offer price is MTL 450 per share and the company's underwriters charge an 8 percent spread, how many shares need to be sold?

6. **Calculating Flotation Costs** In the previous problem, if the exchange filing fee and associated administrative expenses of the offering are MTL 900,000, how many shares need to be sold?

7. **Calculating Flotation Costs** The Pattani Driving School has just gone public. Under a firm commitment agreement, Pattani Driving School received THB 19.75 for each of the 5 million shares sold. The initial offering price was THB 21 per share, and the stock rose to THB 26 per share in the first few minutes of trading. Pattani Driving School paid THB 800,000 in direct legal and other costs and THB 250,000 in indirect costs. What was the flotation cost as a percentage of funds raised?

8. **Price Dilution** Raggio, Inc., has 100,000 shares of stock outstanding. Each share is worth $90, so the company's market value of equity is $9,000,000. Suppose the firm issues 20,000 new shares at the following prices: $90, $85, and $70. What will the effect be of each of these alternative offering prices on the existing price per share?

9. **Stock Offerings** Harbin Ski Resort has 10,000 shares of stock that each sell for CNY 40. Suppose the company issues 5,000 shares of the new stock at the following prices: CNY 40, CNY 20, and CNY 10. What is the effect of each of the alternative offering prices on the existing price per share?

INTERMEDIATE
(Questions 10–18)

10. **Dilution** Teardrop Inc., wishes to expand its facilities. The company currently has 10 million shares outstanding and no debt. The stock sells for $50 per share, but the book value per share is $40. Net income for Teardrop is currently $15 million. The new facility will cost $35 million, and it will increase net income by $500,000.
    a. Assuming a constant price–earnings ratio, what will the effect be of issuing new equity to finance the investment? To answer, calculate the new book value per share, the new total earnings, the new EPS, the new stock price, and the new market-to-book ratio. What is going on here?
    b. What would the new net income for Teardrop have to be for the stock price to remain unchanged?

11. **Dilution** The Metallica Heavy Metal Mining (MHMM) Corporation wants to diversify its operations. Some recent financial information for the company is shown here:

Stock price	£ 98
Number of shares	14,000
Total assets	£6,000,000
Total liabilities	£2,400,000
Net income	£ 630,000

MHMM is considering an investment that has the same PE ratio as the firm. The cost of the investment is £1,100,000, and it will be financed with a new equity issue. The return on the investment will equal MHMM's current ROE. What will happen to the book value per share, the market value per share, and the EPS? What is the NPV of this investment? Does dilution take place?

12. **Dilution** In the previous problem, what would the ROE on the investment have to be if we wanted the price after the offering to be £98 per share? (Assume the PE ratio remains constant.) What is the NPV of this investment? Does any dilution take place?

13. **Rights**   A company's stock currently sells for ¥4,500 per share. Last week the firm issued rights to raise new equity. To purchase a new share, a stockholder must remit ¥1,000 and three rights.

 a. What is the ex-rights stock price?

 b. What is the price of one right?

 c. When will the price drop occur? Why will it occur then?

14. **Rights**   Summit Corp.'s stock is currently selling at $13 per share. There are 1 million shares outstanding. The firm is planning to raise $2 million to finance a new project. What are the ex-rights stock price, the value of a right, and the appropriate subscription prices under the following scenarios?

 a. Two shares of outstanding stock are entitled to purchase one additional share of the new issue.

 b. Four shares of outstanding stock are entitled to purchase one additional share of the new issue.

 c. How does the stockholders' wealth change from part (a) to part (b)?

15. **Rights**   Bon Acceuil Cruising Co. is considering a rights offer. The company has determined that the ex-rights price would be MUR 52. The current price is MUR 55 per share, and there are 5 million shares outstanding. The rights offer would raise a total of MUR 60 million. What is the subscription price?

16. **Value of Right**   Show that the value of a right can be written as

$$\text{Value of a right} = P_{RO} - P_X = (P_{RO} - P_S)/(N + 1)$$

where P_{RO}, P_S, and P_X stand for the "rights-on" price, the subscription price, and the ex-rights price, respectively, and N is the number of rights needed to buy one new share at the subscription price.

17. **Selling Rights**   Windhoek Investment Bank wants to raise NAD 3.65 million via a rights offering. The company currently has 490,000 shares of common stock outstanding that sell for NAD 30 per share. Its underwriter has set a subscription price of NAD 22 per share and will charge Windhoek Investment Bank a 6 percent spread. If you currently own 6,000 shares of stock in the company and decide not to participate in the rights offering, how much money can you get by selling your rights?

18. **Valuing a Right**   Dhafar Trucking has announced a rights offer. The company has announced that it will take four rights to buy a new share in the offering at a subscription price of OMR 40. At the close of business the day before the ex-rights day, the company's stock sells for OMR 80 per share. The next morning you notice that the stock sells for OMR 72 per share and the rights sell for OMR 6 each. Are the stock and/or the rights correctly priced on the ex-rights day? Describe a transaction in which you could use these prices to create an immediate profit.

Mini Case

East Coast Yachts Goes Public

Larissa Warren and Dan Ervin have been discussing the future of East Coast Yachts. The company has been experiencing fast growth, and the future looks like clear sailing. However, the fast growth means that the company's growth can no longer be funded by internal sources, so Larissa and Dan have decided the time is right to take the company public. To this end, they have entered into discussions with the investment bank of Crowe & Mallard. The company has a working relationship with Robin Perry, the underwriter who assisted with the company's previous bond offering. Crowe & Mallard have helped numerous small companies in the IPO process, so Larissa and Dan feel confident with this choice.

Robin begins by telling Larissa and Dan about the process. Although Crowe & Mallard charged an underwriter fee of 4 percent on the bond offering, the underwriter fee is 7 percent on all initial stock offerings of the size of East Coast Yachts' initial offering. Robin tells Larissa and Dan that the company can expect to pay about $1,200,000 in legal fees and expenses, $12,000 in SEC registration fees, and $15,000 in other filing fees. Additionally, to be listed on the NASDAQ, the company must pay $100,000. There are also transfer agent fees of

$6,500 and engraving expenses of $450,000. The company should also expect to pay $75,000 for other expenses associated with the IPO.

Finally, Robin tells Larissa and Dan that to file with the SEC, the company must provide three years' worth of audited financial statements. She is unsure of the costs of the audit. Dan tells Robin that the company provides audited financial statements as part of its bond indenture, and the company pays $300,000 per year for the outside auditor.

1. At the end of the discussion Dan asks Robin about the Dutch auction IPO process. What are the differences in the expenses to East Coast Yachts if it uses a Dutch auction IPO versus a traditional IPO? Should the company go public with a Dutch auction or use a traditional underwritten offering?

2. During the discussion of the potential IPO and East Coast Yachts' future, Dan states that he feels the company should raise $50 million. However, Larissa points out that if the company needs more cash soon, a secondary offerings close to the IPO would be potentially problematic. Instead she suggests that the company should raise $80 million in the IPO. How can we calculate the optimal size of the IPO? What are the advantages and disadvantage of increasing the size of the IPO to $80 million?

3. After deliberation, Larissa and Dan have decided that the company should use a firm commitment offering with Crowe & Mallard as the lead underwriter. The IPO will be for $60 million. Ignoring underpricing, how much will the IPO cost the company as a percentage of the funds received?

4. Many of the employees of East Coast Yachts have shares of stock in the company because of an existing employee stock purchase plan. To sell the stock, the employees can tender their shares to be sold in the IPO at the offering price, or the employees can retain their stock and sell it in the secondary market after East Coast Yachts goes public (once the 180-day lockup expires). Larissa asks you to advise the employees about which option is best. What would you suggest to the employees?

CHAPTER 20

Long-Term Debt

In its basic form, a bond is a simple financial instrument. You lend a company some amount, say $10,000. The company pays you interest on a regular basis, and it repays the original loan amount of $10,000 at some point in the future. But bonds can also have unusual characteristics. For example, in 2002, Berkshire Hathaway, the company run by legendary investor Warren Buffett, issued some bonds with a surprising feature. Bond buyers were required to *make* interest payments to Berkshire Hathaway for the privilege of owning the bonds, and the interest payments had to be made up front! Furthermore, if you paid $10,663.63 for one of these bonds, Berkshire Hathaway promised to pay you $10,000 in five years. Does this sound like a good deal? Investors must have thought it did; they bought $400 million worth!

20.1 Long-Term Debt: A Review

Long-term debt securities are promises by the issuing firm to pay interest and principal on the unpaid balance. The *maturity* of a long-term debt instrument refers to the length of time the debt remains outstanding with some unpaid balance. Debt securities can be *short-term* (maturities of one year or less) or *long-term* (maturities of more than one year).[1] Short-term debt is sometimes referred to as *unfunded debt* and long-term debt as *funded debt.*[2]

The two major forms of long-term debt are public issue and privately placed debt. We discuss public-issue bonds first, and most of what we say about them holds true for privately placed long-term debt as well. The main difference between publicly issued and privately placed debt is that private debt is directly placed with a lending institution.

There are many other attributes to long-term debt, including security, call features, sinking funds, ratings, and protective covenants. The following table illustrates the features for a bond recently issued by Cisco Systems, Inc.

---

[1] In addition, people often refer to intermediate-term debt, which has a maturity of more than one year and less than three to five years.

[2] The word *funding* generally implies long-term. Thus, a firm planning to *fund* its debt requirements may be replacing short-term debt with long-term debt.

Features of a Cisco Systems, Inc., Company Bond

	Term	Explanation
Amount of issue	$3 billion	The company issued $3 billion worth of bonds.
Date of issue	02/22/2006	The bonds were sold on 02/22/2006.
Maturity	02/22/2016	The bonds mature on 02/22/2016.
Face value	$1,000	The denomination of the bonds is $1,000.
Annual coupon	5.50	Each bondholder will receive $55 per bond per year (5.50% of face value).
Offer price	99.543	The offer price will be 99.543% of the $1,000 face value, or $995.43, per bond.
Coupon payment dates	2/22, 8/22	Coupons of $55/2 = $27.50 will be paid on these dates.
Security	Senior	The bonds are the first claim for all bondholders on all property owned by the company.
Sinking fund	None	The bonds have no sinking fund.
Call provision	At any time	The bonds do not have a deferred call.
Call price	Treasury rate plus 0.20%	The bonds have a "make whole" call price.
Rating	Moody's A1 S&P A+	The bond's are in the middle of the investment grade rating.

20.2 The Public Issue of Bonds

The general procedures followed for a **public issue** of bonds are the same as those for stocks, as described in the previous chapter. First, the offering must be approved by the board of directors. Sometimes a vote of stockholders is also required. Second, a registration statement is prepared for review by the Securities and Exchange Commission. Third, if accepted, the registration statement becomes *effective* 20 days later, and the securities are sold.

However, the registration statement for a public issue of bonds must include an indenture, a document not relevant for the issue of common stock. An **indenture** is a written agreement between the corporation (the borrower) and a trust company. It is sometimes referred to as the *deed of trust*.[3] The trust company is appointed by the corporation to represent the bondholders. The trust company must (1) make sure the terms of the indenture are obeyed, (2) manage the sinking fund, and (3) represent bondholders if the company defaults on its payments.

The typical bond indenture can be a document of several hundred pages, and it generally includes the following provisions:

1. The basic terms of the bonds.
2. A description of property used as security.
3. Details of the protective covenants.
4. The sinking fund arrangements.
5. The call provision.

Each of these is discussed next.

---

[3] The term *loan agreement* or *loan contract* is usually used for privately placed debt and term loans.

The Basic Terms

Bonds usually have a *face value* of $1,000. This is also called the *principal value* or the *denomination*, and it is stated on the bond certificate. In addition, the *par value* (i.e., initial accounting value) of a bond is almost always the same as the face value.

Transactions between bond buyers and bond sellers determine the market value of the bond. Actual bond market values depend on the general level of interest rates, among other factors, and need not equal the face value. Bond prices are quoted as a percentage of the denomination. This is illustrated in the following example.

EXAMPLE 20.1

Bond Prices   Suppose the Black Corporation has issued 100 bonds. The amount stated on each bond certificate is $1,000. The total face value or principal value of the bonds is $100,000. Further suppose the bonds are currently *priced* at 100, which means 100 percent of $1,000. This means that buyers and sellers are holding bonds at a price per bond of $1,000. If interest rates rise, the price of the bond might fall to, say, 97, which means 97 percent of $1,000, or $970.

Suppose the bonds have a stated interest rate of 12 percent due on January 1, 2050. The bond indenture might read as follows:

> The bond will mature on January 1, 2050, and will be limited in aggregate principal amount to $100,000. Each bond will bear interest at the rate of 12.0% per annum from January 1, 1990, or from the most recent Interest Payment Date to which interest has been paid or provided for. Interest is payable semiannually on July 1 and January 1 of each year.

As is typical of industrial bonds, the Black bonds are registered. The indenture might read as follows:

> Interest is payable semiannually on July 1 and January 1 of each year to the person in whose name the bond is registered at the close of business on June 15 or December 15, respectively.

This means that the company has a registrar who will record the ownership of each bond. The company will pay the interest and principal by check mailed directly to the address of the owner of record.

When a bond is registered with attached coupons, the bondholder must separate a coupon from the bond certificate and send it to the company registrar (paying agent). Some bonds are in **bearer** form. This means that ownership is not recorded in the company books. As with a registered bond with attached coupons, the holder of the bond certificate separates the coupons and sends them to the company to receive payment.

There are two drawbacks to bearer bonds. First, they can be easily lost or stolen. Second, because the company does not know who owns its bonds, it cannot notify bondholders of important events. Consider, for example, Mr. and Mrs. Smith, who go to their safe deposit box and clip the coupon on their 12 percent, $1,000 bond issued by the Black Corporation. They send the coupon to the paying agent and feel richer. A few days later a notice comes from the paying agent that the bond was retired and its principal paid off one year earlier. In other words, the bond no longer exists. Mr. and Mrs. Smith must forfeit one year of interest. (Of course, they can turn their bond in for $1,000.)

However, bearer bonds have the advantage of secrecy because even the issuing company does not know who the bond's owners are. This secrecy is particularly vexing to taxing authorities because tax collection on interest is difficult if the holder is unknown.

A Note on Bond Price Quotes

If you buy a bond between coupon payment dates, the price you pay is usually more than the price you are quoted. The reason is that standard convention in the bond market is to quote prices net of "accrued interest," meaning that accrued interest is deducted to arrive at the quoted price. This quoted price is called the **clean price**. The price you actually pay, however, includes the accrued interest. This price is the **dirty price**, also known as the "full" or "invoice" price.

An example is the easiest way to understand these issues. Suppose you buy a bond with a 12 percent annual coupon, payable semiannually. You actually pay $1,080 for this bond, so $1,080 is the dirty, or invoice, price. Further, on the day you buy it, the next coupon is due in four months, so you are between coupon dates. Notice that the next coupon will be $60.

The accrued interest on a bond is calculated by taking the fraction of the coupon period that has passed, in this case two months out of six, and multiplying this fraction by the next coupon, $60. So, the accrued interest in this example is $2/6 \times \$60 = \$20$. The bond's quoted price (i.e., its clean price) would be $1,080 - \$20 = \$1,060$.

Security

Debt securities are also classified according to the *collateral* protecting the bondholder. Collateral is a general term for the assets that are pledged as security for payment of debt. For example, *collateral trust bonds* involve a pledge of common stock held by the corporation.

EXAMPLE 20.2

Collateral Trust Bonds   Suppose Railroad Holding Company owns all of the common stock of Track, Inc.; that is, Track, Inc., is a wholly owned subsidiary of the Railroad Holding Company. Railroad issues debt securities that pledge the common stock of Track, Inc., as collateral. The debts are collateral trust bonds; U.S. Sur Bank will hold them. If Railroad Holding Company defaults on the debt, U.S. Sur Bank will be able to sell the stock of Track, Inc., to satisfy Railroad's obligation.

Mortgage securities are secured by a mortgage on real estate or other long-term assets of the borrower.[4] The legal document that describes the mortgage is called a *mortgage trust indenture* or *trust deed*. The mortgage can be *closed-end*, so that there is a limit on the amount of bonds that can be issued. More frequently it is *open-end*, without limit to the amount of bonds that may be issued.

EXAMPLE 20.3

Mortgage Securities   Suppose the Miami Bond Company has buildings and land worth $10 million and a $4 million mortgage on these properties. If the mortgage is closed-end, the Miami Bond Company cannot issue more bonds on this property.

If the bond indenture contains no clause limiting the amount of additional bonds that can be issued, it is an open-end mortgage. In this case, the Miami Bond Company can issue additional bonds on its property, making the existing bonds riskier. For example, if additional mortgage bonds of $2 million

(continued)

---

[4]A set of railroad cars is an example of "other long-term assets" used as security.

are issued, the property has been pledged for a total of $6 million of bonds. If Miami Bond Company must liquidate its property for $4 million, the original bondholders will receive $\frac{4}{6}$, or 67 percent, of their investment. If the mortgage had been closed-end, they would have received 100 percent of the stated value.

The value of a mortgage depends on the market value of the underlying property. Because of this, mortgage bonds sometimes require that the property be properly maintained and insured. Of course, a building and equipment bought in 1914 for manufacturing slide rules might not have much value no matter how well the company maintains it. The value of any property ultimately depends on its next best economic use. Bond indentures cannot easily insure against losses in economic value.

Sometimes mortgages are on specific property—for example, a single building. More often, blanket mortgages are used. A blanket mortgage pledges many assets owned by the company.

Some bonds represent unsecured obligations of the company. A **debenture** is an unsecured bond, where no specific pledge of property is made. Debenture holders have a claim on property not otherwise pledged: the property that remains after mortgages and collateral trusts are taken into account. At the current time, almost all public bonds issued by industrial and finance companies are debentures. However, most utility and railroad bonds are secured by a pledge of assets.

Protective Covenants

A **protective covenant** is that part of the indenture or loan agreement that limits certain actions of the borrowing company. Protective covenants can be classified into two types: negative covenants and positive covenants. A **negative covenant** limits or prohibits actions that the company may take. Here are some typical examples:

1. Limitations are placed on the amount of dividends a company may pay.
2. The firm cannot pledge any of its assets to other lenders.
3. The firm cannot merge with another firm.
4. The firm may not sell or lease its major assets without approval by the lender.
5. The firm cannot issue additional long-term debt.

A **positive covenant** specifies an action that the company agrees to take or a condition the company must abide by. Here are some examples:

1. The company agrees to maintain its working capital at a minimum level.
2. The company must furnish periodic financial statements to the lender.

The financial implications of protective covenants were treated in detail in the chapters about capital structure. In that discussion, we argued that protective covenants can benefit stockholders because if bondholders are assured that they will be protected in times of financial stress, they will accept a lower interest rate.

The Sinking Fund

Bonds can be entirely repaid at maturity, at which time the bondholder will receive the stated value of the bond; or they can be repaid before maturity. Early repayment is more typical.

In a direct placement of debt, the repayment schedule is specified in the loan contract. For public issues, the repayment takes place through the use of a sinking fund and a call provision.

A *sinking fund* is an account managed by the bond trustee for the purpose of repaying the bonds. Typically, the company makes yearly payments to the trustee. The trustee can purchase bonds in the market or can select bonds randomly using a lottery and purchase them, generally at face value. There are many different kinds of sinking fund arrangements:

- Most sinking funds start between 5 and 10 years after the initial issuance.
- Some sinking funds establish equal payments over the life of the bond.
- Most high-quality bond issues establish payments to the sinking fund that are not sufficient to redeem the entire issue. As a consequence, there is the possibility of a large *balloon* payment at maturity.

Sinking funds have two opposing effects on bondholders:

1. *Sinking funds provide extra protection to bondholders.* A firm experiencing financial difficulties would have trouble making sinking fund payments. Thus, sinking fund payments provide an early warning system to bondholders.
2. *Sinking funds give the firm an attractive option.* If bond prices fall below the face value, the firm will satisfy the sinking fund by buying bonds at the lower market prices. If bond prices rise above the face value, the firm will buy the bonds back at the lower face value (or other fixed price, depending on the specific terms).

The Call Provision

A *call provision* lets the company repurchase or *call* the entire bond issue at a predetermined price over a specified period.

Generally the call price is above the bond's face value of $1,000. The difference between the call price and the face value is the **call premium**. For example, if the call price is 105—that is, 105 percent of $1,000—the call premium is 50. The amount of the call premium usually becomes smaller over time. One typical arrangement is to set the call premium initially equal to the annual coupon payment and then make it decline to zero over the life of the bond.

Call provisions are not usually operative during the first few years of a bond's life. For example, a company may be prohibited from calling its bonds for the first 10 years. This is referred to as a **deferred call**. During this period the bond is said to be **call-protected**.

In just the last few years, a new type of call provision, a "make-whole" call, has become widespread in the corporate bond market. With such a feature, bondholders receive approximately what the bonds are worth if they are called. Because bondholders don't suffer a loss in the event of a call, they are "made whole."

To determine the make-whole call price, we calculate the present value of the remaining interest and principal payments at a rate specified in the indenture. For example, looking at the Cisco Systems issue, we see that the discount rate is "Treasury rate plus .20%." What this means is that we determine the discount rate by first finding a U.S. Treasury issue with the same maturity. We calculate the yield to maturity on the Treasury issue and then add on an additional .20 percent to get the discount rate we use.

Notice that with a make-whole call provision, the call price is higher when interest rates are lower and vice versa. (Why?) Also notice that, as is common with a make-whole call, the Cisco Systems issue does not have a deferred call feature. Why might investors not be too concerned about the absence of this feature?

20.3 Bond Refunding

Replacing all or part of an issue of outstanding bonds is called bond **refunding**. Usually, the first step in a typical bond refunding is to call the entire issue of bonds at the call price. Bond refunding raises two questions:

1. Should firms issue callable bonds?

2. Given that callable bonds have been issued, when should the bonds be called?

We attempt to answer these questions in this section, focusing on traditional fixed-price call features.

Should Firms Issue Callable Bonds?

Common sense tells us that call provisions have value. First, many publicly issued bonds have call provisions. Second, it is obvious that a call works to the advantage of the issuer. If interest rates fall and bond prices go up, the option to buy back the bonds at the call price is valuable. In bond refunding, firms will typically replace the called bonds with a new bond issue. The new bonds will have a lower coupon rate than the called bonds.

However, bondholders will take the call provision into account when they buy the bond. For this reason we can expect that bondholders will demand higher interest rates on callable bonds than on noncallable bonds. In fact, financial economists view call provisions as being zero-sum in efficient capital markets.[5] Any expected gains to the issuer from being allowed to refund the bond at lower rates will be offset by higher initial interest rates. We illustrate the zero-sum aspect to callable bonds in the following example.

Suppose Kraus Intercable Company intends to issue perpetual bonds of $1,000 face value at a 10 percent interest rate.[6] Annual coupons have been set at $100. There is an equal chance that by the end of the year interest rates will do one of the following:

1. Fall to $6\frac{2}{3}$ percent. If so, the bond price will increase to $1,500.

2. Increase to 20 percent. If so, the bond price will fall to $500.

Noncallable Bond   Suppose the market price of the noncallable bond is the expected price it will have next year plus the coupon, all discounted at the current 10 percent interest rate.[7] The value of the noncallable bond is this:

Value of Noncallable Bond

$$\frac{\text{First-year coupon} + \text{Expected price at end of year}}{1 + r}$$

$$= \frac{\$100 + (0.5 \times \$1,500) + (0.5 \times \$500)}{1.10}$$

$$= \$1,000$$

(continued)

---

[5] See A. Kraus, "An Analysis of Call Provisions and the Corporate Refunding Decision, " *Midland Corporate Finance Journal* 1 (Spring 1983), p. 1.

[6] Recall that perpetual bonds have no maturity date.

[7] We are assuming that the current price of the noncallable bonds is the expected value discounted at the risk-free rate of 10 percent. This is equivalent to assuming that the risk is unsystematic and carries no risk premium.

Callable Bond Now suppose the Kraus Intercable Company decides to issue callable bonds. The call premium is set at $100 over par value, and the bonds can be called *only* at the end of the first year.[8] In this case, the call provision will allow the company to buy back its bonds at $1,100 ($1,000 par value plus the $100 call premium). Should interest rates fall, the company will buy a bond for $1,100 that would be worth $1,500 in the absence of a call provision. Of course, if interest rates rise, Kraus would not want to call the bonds for $1,100 because they are worth only $500 on the market.

Suppose rates fall and Kraus calls the bonds by paying $1,100. If the firm simultaneously issues new bonds with a coupon of $100, it will bring in $1,500 ($100/0.0667) at the $6\frac{2}{3}$ percent interest rate. This will allow Kraus to pay an extra dividend to shareholders of $400 ($1,500 − $1,100). In other words, if rates fall from 10 percent to $6\frac{2}{3}$ percent, exercise of the call will transfer $400 of potential bondholder gains to the shareholders.

When investors purchase callable bonds, they realize that they will forfeit their anticipated gains to shareholders if the bonds are called. As a consequence, they will not pay $1,000 for a callable bond with a coupon of $100.

How high must the coupon on the callable bond be so that it can be issued at the par value of $1,000? We can answer this in three steps.

Step 1: Determining End-of-Year Value If Interest Rates Drop
If the interest rate drops to $6\frac{2}{3}$ percent by the end of the year, the bond will be called for $1,100. The bondholder will receive both this and the annual coupon payment. If we let C represent the coupon on the callable bond, the bondholder gets the following at the end of the year:

$$\$1,100 + C$$

Step 2: Determining End-of-Year Value If Interest Rates Rise
If interest rates rise to 20 percent, the value of the bondholder's position at the end of the year is:

$$\frac{C}{0.20} + C$$

That is, the perpetuity formula tells us that the bond will sell at $C/0.20$. In addition, the bondholder receives the coupon payment at the end of the year.

Step 3: Solving for C
Because interest rates are equally likely to rise or to fall, the expected value of the bondholder's end-of-year position is:

$$(\$1,000 + C) \times 0.5 + \left(\frac{C}{0.20} + C\right) \times 0.5$$

Using the current interest rate of 10 percent, we set the present value of these payments equal to par:

$$\$1,000 = \frac{(\$1,100 + C) \times 0.5 + \left(\frac{C}{0.20} + C\right) \times 0.5}{1.10}$$

C is the unknown in the equation. The equation holds if $C = \$157.14$. In other words, callable bonds can sell at par only if their coupon rate is 15.714 percent.

(continued)

---

[8]Normally, bonds can be called over a period of many years. Our assumption that the bond can be called only at the end of the first year was introduced for simplicity.

The Paradox Restated   If Kraus issues a noncallable bond, it will need to only pay a 10 percent interest rate. By contrast, Kraus must pay an interest rate of 15.7 percent on a callable bond. The interest rate differential makes an investor indifferent to whether she buys one of the two bonds in our example or the other. Because the return to the investor is the same with either bond, the cost of debt capital is the same to Kraus with either bond. Thus, our example suggests that there is neither an advantage nor a disadvantage to issuing callable bonds.

Why, therefore, are callable bonds issued in the real world? This question has vexed financial economists for a long time. We now consider four specific reasons why a company might use a call provision:

1. Superior interest rate predictions.

2. Taxes.

3. Financial flexibility for future investment opportunities.

4. Less interest rate risk.

Superior Interest Rate Forecasting   Company insiders may know more about interest rate changes on the company's bonds than does the investing public. For example, managers may be better informed about potential changes in the firm's credit rating. Thus, a company may prefer the call provision at a particular time because it believes that the expected fall in interest rates (the probability of a fall multiplied by the amount of the fall) is greater than the bondholders believe.

Although this is possible, there is reason to doubt that inside information is the rationale for call provisions. Suppose firms really had superior ability to predict changes that would affect them. Bondholders would infer that a company expected an improvement in its credit rating whenever it issued callable bonds. Bondholders would require an increase in the coupon rate to protect them against a call if this occurred. As a result, we would expect that there would be no financial advantage to the firm from callable bonds over noncallable bonds.

Of course, there are many non–company-specific reasons why interest rates can fall. For example, the interest rate level is connected to the anticipated inflation rate. But it is difficult to see how companies could have more information about the general level of interest rates than other participants in the bond markets.

Taxes   Call provisions may have tax advantages if the bondholder is taxed at a lower rate than the company. We have seen that callable bonds have higher coupon rates than noncallable bonds. Because the coupons provide a deductible interest expense to the corporation and are taxable income to the bondholder, the corporation will gain more than a bondholder in a low tax bracket will lose. Presumably, some of the tax savings can be passed on to the bondholders in the form of a high coupon.

Future Investment Opportunities   As we have explained, bond indentures contain protective covenants that restrict a company's investment opportunities. For example, protective covenants may limit the company's ability to acquire another firm or to sell certain assets (for example, a division of the company). If the covenants are sufficiently restrictive, the cost to the shareholders in lost net present value can be large. However, if bonds are callable, the company can buy back the bonds at the call price and take advantage of a superior investment opportunity.[9]

---

[9]This argument is from Z. Bodie and R. A. Taggart, "Future Investment Opportunities and the Value of the Call Provision on a Bond," *Journal of Finance* 33 (1978), p. 4.

Less Interest Rate Risk   The call provision will reduce the sensitivity of a bond's value to changes in the level of interest rates. As interest rates increase, the value of a noncallable bond will fall. Because the callable bond has a higher coupon rate, the value of a callable bond will fall less than the value of a noncallable bond. Kraus has argued that by reducing the sensitivity of a bond's value to changes in interest rates, the call provision may reduce the risk of shareholders as well as bondholders.[10] He argues that because the bond is a liability of the corporation, the equityholders bear risk as the bond changes value over time. Thus, it can be shown that, under certain conditions, reducing the risk of bonds through a call provision will also reduce the risk of equity.

Calling Bonds: When Does It Make Sense?

The value of the company is the value of the stock plus the value of the bonds. From the Modigliani–Miller theory and the pie model in earlier chapters, we know that firm value is unchanged by how it is divided between these two instruments. Therefore, maximizing shareholder wealth means minimizing the value of the callable bond. In a world with no transaction costs, it can be shown that the company should call its bonds whenever the callable bond value exceeds the call price. This policy minimizes the value of the callable bonds.

The preceding analysis is modified slightly by including the costs from issuing new bonds. These extra costs change the refunding rule to allow bonds to trade at prices above the call price. The objective of the company is to minimize the sum of the value of the callable bonds plus new issue costs. It has been observed that many real-world firms do not call their bonds when the market value of the bonds reaches the call price. Instead, they wait until the market value of the bonds exceeds the call price. Perhaps these issue costs are an explanation. Also, when a bond is called, the holder has about 30 days to surrender the bond and receive the call price in cash. In 30 days the market value of the bonds could fall below the call price. If so, the firm is giving away money. To forestall this possibility, it can be argued that firms should wait until the market value of the bond exceeds the call price before calling bonds.

20.4 Bond Ratings

Firms frequently pay to have their debt rated. The two leading bond-rating firms are Moody's Investors Service and Standard & Poor's. The debt ratings depend on (1) the likelihood that the firm will default and (2) the protection afforded by the loan contract in the event of default. The ratings are constructed from information supplied by the corporation, primarily the financial statements of the firm. The rating classes are shown in the accompanying box.

The highest rating debt can have is AAA or Aaa. Debt rated AAA or Aaa is judged to be the best quality and to have the lowest degree of risk. The lowest rating is D, which indicates that the firm is in default. Since the 1980s, a growing part of corporate borrowing has taken the form of *low-grade bonds*. These bonds are also known as either *high-yield bonds* or *junk bonds*. Low-grade bonds are corporate bonds that are rated below *investment grade* by the major rating agencies (that is, below BBB for Standard & Poor's or Baa for Moody's).

---

[10]A. Kraus, "An Analysis of Call Provisions and the Corporate Refunding Decision," *Midland Corporate Finance Journal* 1 (Spring 1983). Kraus points out that the call provision will not always reduce the equity's interest rate risk. If the firm as a whole bears interest rate risk, more of this risk may be shifted from equityholders to bondholders with noncallable debt. In this case, equityholders may actually bear more risk with callable debt.

Bond ratings are important because bonds with lower ratings tend to have higher inter-est costs. However, the most recent evidence is that bond ratings merely reflect bond risk. There is no conclusive evidence that bond ratings affect risk.[11] It is not surprising that

Bond Ratings

	Very High Quality	High Quality	Speculative	Very Poor
Standard & Poor's	AAA AA	A BBB	BB B	CCC CC C D
Moody's	Aaa Aa	A Baa	Ba B	Caa Ca C D

At times both Moody's and Standard & Poor's adjust these ratings. S&P uses plus and minus signs: A+ is the strongest A rating and A– the weakest. Moody's uses a 1, 2, or 3 designation, with 1 indicating the strongest. These increments are called notches.

Moody's	S&P	
Aaa	AAA	Debt rated Aaa and AAA has the highest rating. Capacity to pay interest and principal is extremely strong.
Aa	AA	Debt rated Aa and AA has a very strong capacity to pay interest and repay principal. Together with the highest rating, this group comprises the high-grade bond class.
A	A	Debt rated A has a strong capacity to pay interest and repay principal. However, it is somewhat more susceptible to adverse changes in circumstances and economic conditions.
Baa	BBB	Debt rated Baa and BBB is regarded as having an adequate capacity to pay interest and repay principal. Whereas it normally exhibits adequate protection parameters, adverse economic conditions or changing circumstances are more likely to lead to a weakened capacity to pay interest and repay principal for debt in this category than in higher-rated categories. These bonds are medium-grade obligations.
Ba	BB	Debt rated in these categories is regarded, on balance, as predominantly speculative. Ba and BB indicate the lowest degree of speculation, and Ca and CC the highest.
B	B	
Caa	CCC	
Ca	CC	Although such debt is likely to have some quality and protec-tive characteristics, these are outweighed by large uncertain-ties or major risk exposure to adverse conditions.
C	C	This rating is reserved for income bonds on which no interest is being paid.
D	D	Debt rated D is in default, and payment of interest and/or repayment of principal is in arrears.

SOURCE: Data from various editions of *Standard & Poor's Bond Guide* and *Moody's Bond Guide*.

---

[11] M. Weinstein, "The Systematic Risk of Corporate Bonds," *Journal of Financial and Quantitative Analy-sis* (September 1981); J. P. Ogden, "Determinants of Relative Interest Rate Sensitivity of Corporate Bonds," *Financial Management* (Spring 1987); and F. Reilly and M. Joehnk, "The Association between Market-Based Risk Measures for Bonds and Bond Ratings," *Journal of Finance* (December 1976).

the stock prices and bond prices of firms do not show any unusual behavior on the days around a rating change. Because the ratings are based on publicly available information, they probably do not, in themselves, supply new information to the market.[12]

Rating agencies don't always agree. For example, some bonds are known as "cross-over" or "5B" bonds. The reason is that they are rated triple-B (or Baa) by one rating agency and double-B (or Ba) by another: a "split rating." For example, in January 2005, Coventry Health sold $250 million of 10-year notes rated BBB– by S&P and Ba1 by Moody's.

Junk Bonds

The investment community has labeled bonds with a Standard & Poor's rating of BB and below or a Moody's rating of Ba and below as **junk bonds**. These bonds are also called *high-yield* or *low-grade*; we shall use all three terms interchangeably. Issuance of junk bonds has grown greatly in recent years, leading to increased public interest in this form of financing.

Table 20.1 presents data on junk bond financing in the recent past. Column (1) shows the great growth in junk bond issuance over a 34-year period. Column (3) shows that the default rate on junk bonds increased from 1.24 percent in 1971 to 12.8 percent in 2002. In 2005, the default rate was 2.5 percent. Table 20.2 presents data on default rates by Standard & Poor's on cumulative bases for 10 years. It shows that junk bonds can have a 10-year cumulative (if rated CCC) rate as high as 58.3 percent.

In our opinion, the growth in junk bond financing in the 1970s and 1980s can better be explained by the activities of one man than by a number of economic factors. While a graduate student at the Wharton School in the 1970s, Michael Milken observed a large difference between the return on high-yield bonds and the return on safer bonds. Believing that this difference was greater than what the extra default risk would justify, he concluded that institutional investors would benefit from purchases of junk bonds.

His later employment at Drexel Burnham Lambert allowed him to develop the junk bond market. Milken's salesmanship simultaneously increased the demand for junk bonds among institutional investors and the supply of junk bonds among corporations. Corporations were particularly impressed with Drexel's vast network of institutional clients, allowing capital to be raised quickly. However, with the demise of the junk bond market and with Michael Milken's conviction of securities fraud, Drexel found it necessary to declare bankruptcy.

The junk bond market took on increased importance when these bonds were used to finance mergers and other corporate restructurings. Whereas a firm can issue only a small amount of high-grade debt, the same firm can issue much more debt if low-grade financing is allowed as well. Therefore, the use of junk bonds lets acquirers effect takeovers that they could not do with only traditional bond financing techniques. Drexel was particularly successful with this technique, primarily because its huge base of institutional clients allowed it to raise large sums of money quickly.

At this time, it is not clear how the great growth in junk bond financing has altered the returns on these instruments. On the one hand, financial theory indicates that the expected returns on an asset should be negatively related to its marketability.[13] Because trading

---

[12]M. Weinstein, "The Effect of a Ratings Change Announcement on Bond Price," *Journal of Financial Economics* 5 (1977). However, Robert W. Holthausen and Richard W. Leftwich, "The Effect of Bond Rating Changes on Common Stock Prices," *Journal of Financial Economics* 17 (September 1986), find that bond rating downgrades are associated with abnormal negative returns on the stock of the issuing firm.

[13]For example, see Y. Amihud and H. Mendelson, "Asset Pricing and the Bid–Ask Spread," *Journal of Financial Economics* (December 1986).

Table 20.1

Historical Default
Rates—Straight
Bonds Only: 1971–
September 30, 2005
($ millions)

Year	Par Value Outstanding*	Par Value Defaults	Default Rates		Standard Deviation
September 30, 2005	$1,073,000	$26,320	2.453%		
2004	933,100	11,657	1.249		
2003	825,000	38,451	4.661		
2002	757,000	96,858	12.795		
2001	649,000	63,609	9.801		
2000	597,200	30,295	5.073		
1999	567,400	23,532	4.147		
1998	465,500	7,464	1.603		
1997	335,400	4,200	1.252		
1996	271,000	3,336	1.231		
1995	240,000	4,551	1.896		
1994	235,000	3,418	1.454		
1993	206,907	2,287	1.105		
1992	163,000	5,545	3.402		
1991	183,600	18,862	10.273		
1990	181,000	18,354	10.140		
1989	189,258	8,110	4.285		
1988	148,187	3,944	2.662		
1987	129,557	7,486	5.778		
1986	90,243	3,156	3.497		
1985	58,088	992	1.708		
1984	40,939	344	0.840		
1983	27,492	301	1.095		
1982	18,109	577	3.186		
1981	17,115	27	0.158		
1980	14,935	224	1.500		
1979	10,356	20	0.193		
1978	8,946	119	1.330		
1977	8,157	381	4.671		
1976	7,735	30	0.388		
1975	7,471	204	2.731		
1974	10,894	123	1.129		
1973	7,824	49	0.626		
1972	6,928	193	2.786		
1971	6,602	82	1.242		
Arithmetic average default rate		1971 to 2004	3.232%		3.134%
		1978 to 2004	3.567%		3.361%
		1985 to 2004	4.401%		3.501%
Weighted average default rate†		1971 to 2004	4.836%		
		1978 to 2004	4.858%		
		1985 to 2004	4.929%		
Median annual default rate		1971 to 2004	1.802%		

*As of midyear.

†Weighted by par value of amount outstanding for each year.

SOURCE: Author's compilations and Citigroup estimates.

Table 20.2   Mortality Rates by Original Rating—All Rated Corporate Bonds*

| | | \multicolumn{10}{c}{(1971–2004)} |
| | | \multicolumn{10}{c}{Years after Issuance} |
		1	2	3	4	5	6	7	8	9	10
AAA	Marginal	0.00%	0.00%	0.00%	0.00%	0.03%	0.00%	0.00%	0.00%	0.00%	0.00%
	Cumulative	0.00	0.00	0.00	0.00	0.03	0.03	0.03	0.03	0.03	0.03
AA	Marginal	0.00	0.00	0.32	0.16	0.03	0.03	0.00	0.00	0.03	0.02
	Cumulative	0.00	0.00	0.32	0.48	0.51	0.54	0.54	0.59	0.57	0.59
A	Marginal	0.01	0.10	0.02	0.09	0.06	0.11	0.06	0.21	0.11	0.06
	Cumulative	0.01	0.11	0.13	0.22	0.28	0.39	0.45	0.65	0.76	0.82
BBB	Marginal	0.36	3.22	1.43	1.28	0.77	0.45	0.20	0.20	0.14	0.40
	Cumulative	0.36	3.56	4.49	6.16	6.89	7.31	7.50	7.68	7.87	8.18
BB	Marginal	1.19	2.48	4.40	2.01	2.51	1.16	1.60	0.88	1.70	3.60
	Cumulative	1.19	3.64	7.88	9.74	12.00	12.93	14.36	15.07	16.52	19.60
B	Marginal	2.85	6.85	7.40	8.55	6.00	4.16	3.72	2.28	1.96	0.86
	Cumulative	2.85	9.51	16.20	23.37	27.94	30.96	33.46	34.97	36.25	36.80
CCC	Marginal	7.98	15.57	19.55	12.10	4.26	9.45	5.60	3.15	0.00	4.28
	Cumulative	7.98	22.31	37.50	45.06	47.37	52.35	55.01	56.43	56.43	58.30

*Rated by S&P at issuance.
Based on 1,719 issues.
SOURCE: Edward I. Altman, NYU Salomon Center.

volume in junk bonds has greatly increased in recent years, the marketability has risen as well. This should lower the expected return on junk bonds, thereby benefiting corporate issuers. On the other hand, the increased interest in junk bond financing by corporations (the increase in the supply schedule of junk bonds) is likely to raise the expected returns on these assets. The net effect of these two forces is unclear.[14]

Junk bond financing has recently created much controversy. First, because the use of junk bonds increases the firm's interest deduction, Congress and the IRS have registered strong disapproval. Several legislators have suggested denying interest deductibility on junk bonds, particularly when the bonds are used to finance mergers. Second, the media have focused on the effect of junk bond financing on corporate solvency. Clearly, this form of financing permits the possibility of higher debt–equity ratios. Whether or not this increased leverage will lead to wholesale defaults in an economic downturn, as some commentators have suggested, remains to be seen. Third, the recent wave of mergers has often resulted in dislocations and loss of jobs. Because junk bond financing has played a role in mergers, it has come under much criticism. The social policy implications of mergers are quite complex, and any final judgment on them is likely to be reserved for the distant future. At any

[14]The actual risk of junk bonds is not known with certainty because it is not easy to measure default rate. Paul Asquith, David W. Mullins, Jr., and Eric D. Wolff, "Original-Issue High-Yield Bonds: Aging Analysis of Defaults, Exchanges, and Calls," *Journal of Finance* (September 1989), show that the default rate on junk bonds can be greater than 30 percent over the life of the bond. They look at cumulative default rates and find that of all junk bonds issued in 1977 and 1978, 34 percent had defaulted by December 31, 1988. Table 20.1 shows yearly default rates. Edward I. Altman, "Setting the Record Straight on Junk Bonds: A Review of the Research on Default Rates and Returns," *Journal of Applied Corporate Finance* (Summer 1990), shows that yearly default rates of 5 percent are consistent with cumulative default rates of over 30 percent.

In Their Own Words

EDWARD I. ALTMAN ON HIGH-YIELD "JUNK" BONDS

One of the most important developments in corporate finance over the last 25 years has been the reemergence of publicly owned and traded low-rated corporate debt. Originally offered to the public in the early 1900s to help finance some of our emerging growth industries, these high-yield/high-risk bonds virtually disappeared after the rash of bond defaults during the Depression. Recently, however, the junk bond market has been catapulted from an insignificant element in the corporate fixed income market to one of the fastest-growing and most controversial types of financing mechanisms.

The term *junk* emanates from the dominant type of low-rated bond issues outstanding prior to 1977 when the "market" consisted almost exclusively of original-issue investment-grade bonds that fell from their lofty status to a higher default risk, speculative-grade level. These so-called fallen angels amounted to about $8.5 billion in 1977. The proportion of these once investment-grade bonds subsequently dropped to as low as 10 percent in the late 1990s, but due to the huge number of rating downgrades in 2001/2002 the proportion jumped to over 20 percent in 2003. The balance of the high-yield market comprises original-issue "junk" bonds.

Beginning in 1977, issuers began to go directly to the public to raise capital for growth purposes. Early users of junk bonds were energy-related firms, cable TV companies, airlines, and assorted other industrial companies. The emerging growth company rationale coupled with relatively high returns to early investors helped legitimize this sector. Most investment banks ignored junk bonds until 1983–1984, when their merits and profit potential became more evident.

Synonymous with the market's growth was the emergence of the investment banking firm Drexel Burnham Lambert and its junk bond wizard, Michael Milken. Drexel established a potent network of issuers and investors and rode the wave of new financing and the consequent surge in secondary trading to become one of the powerful investment banks in the late 1980s. The incredible rise in power of this firm was followed by an equally incredible fall resulting first in government civil and criminal convictions and huge fines for various misdealings and finally the firm's total collapse and bankruptcy in February 1990.

By far the most controversial aspect of junk bond financing was its role in the corporate restructuring movement from 1985 through 1989. High-leverage transactions, such as leveraged buyouts (LBOs), which occur when a firm is taken private, transformed the face of corporate America, leading to a heated debate as to the economic and social consequences of corporate control changes with debt–equity ratios of at least 6:1. These transactions involved increasingly large companies, and the multibillion-dollar takeover became fairly common, capped by the huge $25 billion RJR Nabisco LBO in 1989. LBOs were

rate, junk bond financing should not be implicated too strongly in either the social benefits or the social costs of the recent wave of mergers. Perry and Taggart point out that, contrary to popular belief, this form of financing accounts for only a few percent of all mergers.[15]

We discussed the costs of issuing securities in a previous chapter and established that the costs of issuing debt are substantially less than the costs of issuing equity. Table 20.3 clarifies several questions regarding the costs of issuing debt securities. It contains a breakdown of direct costs for bond issues after the investment and noninvestment grades have been separated.

First, there are substantial economies of scale here as well. Second, investment-grade issues have much lower direct costs, particularly for straight bonds. Finally, there are relatively few noninvestment-grade issues in the smaller size categories, reflecting the fact that such issues are more commonly handled as private placements, which we discuss in a later section.

---

[15] K. Perry and R. Taggart, "The Growing Role of Junk Bonds in Corporate Finance," *Journal of Applied Corporate Finance* (Spring 1988).

typically financed with 60 percent senior bank and insurance company debt, about 25 to 30 percent subordinated public debt (junk bonds), and 10 to 15 percent equity. The junk bond segment is sometimes referred to as *mezzanine financing* because it lies between the "balcony" senior debt and the "basement" equity.

These restructurings resulted in large fees to advisers and underwriters and huge premiums to the old shareholders, and they continued as long as the market was willing to buy these new debt offerings at what appeared to be a favorable risk/return trade-off. The bottom fell out of the market in the last six months of 1989 due to a number of factors including a marked increase in defaults, government regulation against S&Ls holding junk bonds, higher interest rates, a recession, and finally, the growing realization of the leverage excesses of certain ill-conceived restructurings.

The default rate rose dramatically to over 4 percent in 1989 and then skyrocketed in 1990 and 1991 to over 10 percent each year, with about $19 billion of defaults in 1991. Throughout 1990, the pendulum of growth in new junk bond issues and returns to investors swung dramatically downward as prices plummeted and the new-issue market all but dried up. The following year (1991) was a pivotal period in that despite record defaults, bond prices and new issues rebounded strongly as the prospects for the future brightened.

In the early 1990s, the financial market was questioning the very survival of the junk bond market. The answer was a resounding yes, as the amount of new issuance soared to record annual levels of $38 billion in 1992 and steadily grew to $120 billion in 1997! Coupled with plummeting annual default rates (under 2.0 percent from 1993 to 1997 compared to about 3.5 percent for 1971 through 1997) and returns in these years between 10 and 20 percent, the risk–return characteristics were extremely favorable.

Defaults again erupted, however, in 2001–2002, with the dollar-denominated default rate reaching a record 12.8 percent of the market in 2002. This time, however, nobody questioned the survival or legitimacy of the market, and most analysts expected default rates to return to their historical mean—estimated to be over 5 percent per year. What did change, however, was a greater emphasis on bringing more creditworthy companies to the market and reliance on prudent credit analysis and hedging techniques. Time will tell if these lessons will persist. Newer dimensions of the junk bond market include the pooling of large numbers of bonds into collateralized bond obligations (CBOs), the establishment of emerging market international issuance, and the now common use of the nonregistered 144a new-issuance mechanism.

Dr. Edward I. Altman is Max L. Heine Professor of Finance and Vice Director of the Salomon Center at the Stern School of Business of New York University. He is widely recognized as one of the world's experts on bankruptcy and credit analysis as well as the high-yield bond market.

20.5 Some Different Types of Bonds

Until now we have considered "plain vanilla" bonds. In this section we look at some more unusual types: floating-rate bonds, deep-discount bonds, and income bonds.

Floating-Rate Bonds

The conventional bonds we have discussed in this chapter have *fixed dollar obligations*. That is, the coupon rate is set as a fixed percentage of the par value.

With **floating-rate bonds**, the coupon payments are adjustable. The adjustments are tied to an *interest rate index* such as the Treasury bill interest rate or the London Interbank Offered Rate (LIBOR). For example, on the same day Cisco Systems sold the bonds we discussed earlier, it also sold $500 million worth of three-year maturity bonds with a coupon rate equal to the three-month LIBOR plus eight basis points.

In most cases the coupon adjusts with a lag to some base rate. For example, suppose a coupon rate adjustment is made on June 1. The adjustment may be from a simple average

Table 20.3   Average Gross Spreads and Total Direct Costs for Domestic Debt Issues: 1990–2003

	Convertible Bonds						Straight Bonds					
	Investment Grade			Noninvestment Grade			Investment Grade			Noninvestment Grade		
Proceeds ($ in millions)	Number of Issues	Gross Spread	Total Direct Cost	Number of Issues	Gross Spread	Total Direct Cost	Number of Issues	Gross Spread	Total Direct Cost	Number of Issues	Gross Spread	Total Direct Cost
2–9.99	0	—	—	0	—	—	40	0.62%	1.90%	0	—	—
10–19.99	0	—	—	1	4.00%	5.67%	68	0.50	1.35	2	2.74%	4.80%
20–39.99	0	—	—	11	3.47	5.02	119	0.58	1.21	13	3.06	4.36
40–59.99	3	1.92%	2.43%	21	3.33	4.48	132	0.39	0.86	12	3.01	3.93
60–79.99	4	1.65	2.09	47	2.78	3.40	68	0.57	0.97	43	2.99	4.07
80–99.99	3	0.89	1.16	9	2.54	3.19	100	0.66	0.94	56	2.74	3.66
100–199.99	28	2.22	2.55	50	2.57	3.00	341	0.55	0.80	321	2.71	3.39
200–499.99	26	1.99	2.18	17	2.62	2.85	173	0.50	0.81	156	2.49	2.90
500 and up	12	1.96	2.09	1	2.50	2.57	97	0.28	0.38	20	2.45	2.71
Total	76	1.99	2.26	157	2.81	3.47	1,138	0.51	0.85	623	2.68	3.35

SOURCE: Inmoo Lee, Scott Lockhead, Jay Ritter, and Quanshui Zhao, "The Costs of Raising Capital," *Journal of Financial Research* 19 (Spring 1996); updated by the authors.

of yields on six-month Treasury bills issued during March, April, and May. In addition, the majority of these *floaters* have put provisions and floor and ceiling provisions:

1. With a *put provision* the holder has the right to redeem his or her note at par on the coupon payment date. Frequently, the investor is prohibited from redeeming at par during the first few years of the bond's life.

2. With floor and ceiling provisions the coupon rate is subject to a minimum and maximum. For example, the minimum coupon rate might be 8 percent and the maximum rate might be 14 percent.

The popularity of floating-rate bonds is connected to *inflation risk*. When inflation is higher than expected, issuers of fixed-rate bonds tend to make gains at the expense of lenders; and when inflation is less than expected, lenders make gains at the expense of borrowers. Because the inflation risk of long-term bonds is borne by both issuers and bondholders, it is in their interests to devise loan agreements that minimize inflation risk.[16]

Floaters reduce inflation risk because the coupon rate is tied to the current interest rate, which, in turn, is influenced by the rate of inflation. We can see this most clearly by considering the formula for the present value of a bond. As inflation increases the interest rate (the denominator of the formula), inflation increases a floater's coupon rate (the numerator of the formula). Hence, bond value is hardly affected by inflation. Conversely, the coupon rate of fixed-rate bonds cannot change, implying that the prices of these bonds are at the mercy of inflation.

As an alternative, an individual who is concerned with inflation risk can invest in short-term notes, such as Treasury bills, and *roll them over*.[17] The investor can accomplish essentially the same objective by buying a floater that is adjusted to the Treasury bill rate. However, the purchaser of a floater can reduce transactions costs relative to rolling over short-term Treasury bills because floaters are long-term bonds. The same type of reduction in transaction costs makes floaters attractive to some corporations.[18] They benefit from issuing a floater instead of issuing a series of short-term notes.

In an earlier section, we discussed callable bonds. Because the coupon on floaters varies with marketwide interest rates, floaters always sell at or near par. Therefore, it is not surprising that floaters do not generally have call features.

A particularly interesting type of floating-rate bond is an *inflation-linked* bond. Such bonds have coupons that are adjusted according to the rate of inflation (the principal amount may be adjusted as well). The U.S. Treasury began issuing such bonds in January 1997. The issues are sometimes called "TIPS," or Treasury Inflation Protection Securities. Other countries, including Canada, Israel, and Britain, have issued similar securities.

Deep-Discount Bonds

A bond that pays no coupon must be offered at a price that is much lower than its face value. Such bonds are known as **original-issue discount bonds**, **deep-discount bonds**, **pure discount bonds**, or **zero coupon bonds**. They are frequently called *zeroes* for short.

---

[16] See B. Cornell, "The Future of Floating-Rate Bonds," in *The Revolution in Corporate Finance*, ed. by J. M. Stern and D. H. Chew, Jr. (New York: Basil Blackwell, 1986).

[17] That is, the investor could buy a bill, receive the face value at maturity, use these proceeds to buy a second bill, receive the face value from the second bill at maturity, and so on.

[18] Cox, Ingersoll, and Ross developed a framework for pricing floating-rate notes; see J. Cox, J. Ingersoll, and S. A. Ross, "An Analysis of Variable Rate Loan Contracts," *Journal of Finance* 35 (May 1980).

Suppose the DDB Company issues $1,000 of five-year deep-discount bonds when the marketwide interest rate is 10 percent. These bonds do not pay any coupons. The initial price is set at $621 because $621 = \$1,000/(1.10)^5$.

Because these bonds have no intermediate coupon payments, they are attractive to certain investors and unattractive to others. For example, consider an insurance company forecasting death benefit payments of $1,000,000 five years from today. The company would like to be sure that it will have the funds to pay off the liability in five years' time. The company could buy five-year zero coupon bonds with a face value of $1,000,000. The company is matching assets with liabilities here, a procedure that eliminates interest rate risk. That is, regardless of the movement of interest rates, the firm's set of zeros will always be able to pay off the $1,000,000 liability.

Conversely, the firm would be at risk if it bought coupon bonds instead. For example, if it bought five-year coupon bonds, it would need to reinvest the coupon payments through to the fifth year. Because interest rates in the future are not known with certainty today, we cannot be sure if these bonds will be worth more or less than $1,000,000 by the fifth year.

Now, consider a couple saving for their child's college education in 15 years. They *expect* that, with inflation, four years of college should cost $150,000 in 15 years. Thus they buy 15-year zero coupon bonds with a face value of $150,000.[19] If they have forecast inflation perfectly (and if college costs keep pace with inflation), their child's tuition will be fully funded. However, if inflation rises more than expected, the tuition will be more than $150,000. Because the zero coupon bonds produce a shortfall, the child might end up working his way through school. As an alternative, the parents might have considered rolling over Treasury bills. Because the yields on Treasury bills rise and fall with the inflation rate, this simple strategy is likely to cause less risk than the strategy with zeros.

The key to these examples concerns the distinction between nominal and real quantities. The insurance company's liability is $1,000,000 in *nominal* dollars. Because the face value of a zero coupon bond is a nominal quantity, the purchase of zeros eliminates risk. However, it is easier to forecast college costs in real terms than in nominal terms. Thus, a zero coupon bond is a poor choice to reduce the financial risk of a child's college education.

Income Bonds

Income bonds are similar to conventional bonds, except that coupon payments depend on company income. Specifically, coupons are paid to bondholders only if the firm's income is sufficient.

Income bonds are a financial puzzle because, from the firm's standpoint, they appear to be a cheaper form of debt than conventional bonds. Income bonds provide the same tax advantage to corporations from interest deductions that conventional bonds do. However, a company that issues income bonds is less likely to experience financial distress. When a coupon payment is omitted because of insufficient corporate income, an income bond is not in default.

Why don't firms issue more income bonds? Two explanations have been offered:

1. *The "smell of death" explanation*: Firms that issue income bonds signal the capital markets of their increased prospect of financial distress.

2. *The "deadweight costs" explanation*: The calculation of corporate income is crucial to determining the status of bondholders' income, and stockholders and bondholders will not necessarily agree on how to calculate the income. This creates agency costs associated with the firm's accounting methods.

---

[19] A more precise strategy would be to buy zeros maturing in years 15, 16, 17, and 18, respectively. In this way the bonds might mature just in time to meet tuition payments.

Although these are possibilities, the work of McConnell and Schlarbaum suggests that no truly satisfactory reason exists for the lack of more investor interest in income bonds.[20]

Other Types of Bonds

Many bonds have unusual or exotic features. One such feature explains why the Berkshire Hathaway bond we described at the beginning of the chapter actually had what amounts to a negative coupon rate. The buyers of these bonds also received the right to purchase shares of stock in Berkshire at a fixed price per share over the subsequent five years. Such a right, which is called a *warrant*, would be very valuable if the stock price climbed substantially (a later chapter discusses this subject in greater depth).

Bond features are really limited only by the imaginations of the parties involved. Unfortunately, there are far too many variations for us to cover in detail here. We therefore close this section by mentioning only a few of the more common types.

A *convertible bond* can be swapped for a fixed number of shares of stock anytime before maturity at the holder's option. Convertibles are relatively common, but the number has been decreasing in recent years.

A *put bond* allows the *holder* to force the issuer to buy the bond back at a stated price. For example, International Paper Co. has bonds outstanding that allow the holder to force International Paper to buy the bonds back at 100 percent of face value given that certain "risk" events happen. One such event is a change in credit rating from investment grade to lower than investment grade by Moody's or S&P. The put feature is therefore just the reverse of the call provision.

A given bond may have many unusual features. Two of the most recent exotic bonds are CoCo bonds, which have a coupon payment, and NoNo bonds, which are zero coupon bonds. CoCo and NoNo bonds are contingent convertible, putable, callable, subordinated bonds. The contingent convertible clause is similar to the normal conversion feature, except the contingent feature must be met. For example, a contingent feature may require that the company stock trade at 110 percent of the conversion price for 20 out of the most recent 30 days. Valuing a bond of this sort can be quite complex, and the yield to maturity calculation is often meaningless. For example, in 2006, a NoNo issued by Merrill Lynch was selling at a price of $939.99, with a yield to maturity of negative 1.63 percent. At the same time, a NoNo issued by Countrywide Financial was selling for $1,640, which implied a yield to maturity of negative 59 percent!

20.6 Direct Placement Compared to Public Issues

Earlier in this chapter we described the mechanics of issuing debt to the public. However, more than 50 percent of all debt is privately placed. There are two basic forms of direct private long-term financing: term loans and private placement.

Term loans are direct business loans with maturities of 1–15 years. The typical term loan is amortized over the life of the loan. That is, the loan is repaid by equal annual payments of interest and principal. The lenders are commercial banks and insurance companies. A **private placement**, which also involves the sale of a bond or loan directly to a limited number of investors, is similar to a term loan except that the maturity is longer.

Here are some important differences between direct long-term financing and public issues:

1. A direct long-term loan avoids the cost of registration with the Securities and Exchange Commission.

---

[20] J. McConnell and G. Schlarbaum, "The Income Bond Puzzle," in *The Revolution in Corporate Finance*, ed. by J. M. Stern and D. H. Chew, Jr. (New York: Basil Blackwell, 1986).

2. Direct placement is likely to have more restrictive covenants.

3. It is easier to renegotiate a term loan and a private placement in the event of a default. It is harder to renegotiate a public issue because hundreds of holders are usually involved.

4. Life insurance companies and pension funds dominate the private placement segment of the bond market. Commercial banks are significant participants in the term loan market.

5. The costs of distributing bonds are lower in the private market.

The interest rates on term loans and private placements are usually higher than those on an equivalent public issue. Hayes, Joehnk, and Melicher found that the yield to maturity on private placements was 0.46 percent higher than on similar public issues.[21] This finding reflects the trade-off between a higher interest rate and more flexible arrangements in the event of financial distress, as well as the lower transaction costs associated with private placements.

20.7 Long-Term Syndicated Bank Loans

Most bank loans are for less than a year. They serve as a short-term "bridge" for the acquisition of inventory and are typically self-liquidating—that is, when the firm sells the inventory, the cash is used to repay the bank loan. We talk about the need for short-term bank loans in the next section of the text. Now we focus on long-term bank loans.

First, we introduce the concept of commitment. Most bank loans are made with a commitment to a firm. That commitment establishes a line of credit and allows the firm to borrow up to a predetermined limit. Most commitments are in the form of a revolving credit commitment (i.e., a revolver) with a fixed term of up to three years or more. Revolving credit commitments are drawn or undrawn depending on whether the firm has a current need for the funds.

Now we turn to the concept of syndication. Very large banks such as Citigroup typically have a larger demand for loans than they can supply, and small regional banks frequently have more funds on hand than they can profitably lend to existing customers. Basically, they cannot generate enough good loans with the funds they have available. As a result, a very large bank may arrange a loan with a firm or country and then sell portions of it to a syndicate of other banks. With a syndicated loan, each bank has a separate loan agreement with the borrowers.

A syndicated loan is a corporate loan made by a group (or syndicate) of banks and other institutional investors. A syndicated loan may be publicly traded. It may be a line of credit and be "undrawn," or it may be drawn and be used by a firm. Syndicated loans are always rated investment grade. However, a *leveraged* syndicated loan is rated speculative grade (i.e., it is "junk"). In addition, syndicated loan prices are reported for a group of publicly traded loans. Altman and Suggitt report slightly higher default rates for syndicated loans than for comparable corporate bonds.[22]

---

[21] P. A. Hayes, M. D. Joehnk, and R. W. Melicher, "Determinants of Risk Premiums in the Public and Private Bond Market," *Journal of Financial Research* (Fall 1979).

[22] Edward I. Altman and Heather J. Suggitt, "Default Rates in the Syndicated Bank Loan Market: A Longitudinal Analysis," *Journal of Banking and Finance* 24 (2000).

Summary and Conclusions

This chapter described some important aspects of long-term debt financing:

1. The written agreement describing the details of the long-term debt contract is called an *indenture*. Some of the main provisions are security, repayment, protective covenants, and call provisions.

2. There are many ways that shareholders can take advantage of bondholders. Protective covenants are designed to protect bondholders from management decisions that favor stockholders at bondholders' expense.

3. Unsecured bonds are called *debentures* or *notes*. They are general claims on the company's value. Most public industrial bonds are unsecured. In contrast, utility bonds are usually secured. Mortgage bonds are secured by tangible property, and collateral trust bonds are secured by financial securities such as stocks and bonds. If the company defaults on secured bonds, the trustee can repossess the assets. This makes secured bonds more valuable.

4. Long-term bonds usually provide for repayment of principal before maturity. This is accomplished by a sinking fund. With a sinking fund, the company retires a certain number of bonds each year. A sinking fund protects bondholders because it reduces the average maturity of the bond, and its payment signals the financial condition of the company.

5. Most publicly issued bonds are callable. A callable bond is less attractive to bondholders than a noncallable bond. A callable bond can be bought back by the company at a call price that is less than the true value of the bond. As a consequence, callable bonds are priced to obtain higher stated interest rates for bondholders than noncallable bonds.

   Generally, companies should exercise the call provision whenever the bond's value is greater than the call price.

   There is no single reason for call provisions. Some sensible reasons include taxes, greater flexibility, management's ability to predict interest rates, and the fact that callable bonds are less sensitive to interest rate changes.

6. There are many different types of bonds, including floating-rate bonds, deep-discount bonds, and income bonds. This chapter also compared private placement with public issuance.

Concept Questions

1. **Call Provisions** A company is contemplating a long-term bond issue. It is debating whether to include a call provision. What are the benefits to the company from including a call provision? What are the costs? How do these answers change for a put provision?

2. **Coupon Rate** How does a bond issuer decide on the appropriate coupon rate to set on its bonds? Explain the difference between the coupon rate and the required return on a bond.

3. **Bond Ratings** Companies pay rating agencies such as Moody's and S&P to rate their bonds, and the costs can be substantial. However, companies are not required to have their bonds rated in the first place; doing so is strictly voluntary. Why do you think they do it?

4. **Bond Ratings** U.S. Treasury bonds are not rated. Why? Often, junk bonds are not rated. Why?

5. **Crossover Bonds** Looking back at the crossover bonds we discussed in the chapter, why do you think split ratings such as these occur?

6. **Bond Market** What are the implications for bond investors of the lack of transparency in the bond market?

7. **Rating Agencies** A controversy erupted regarding bond rating agencies when some agencies began to provide unsolicited bond ratings. Why do you think this is controversial?

8. **Bonds as Equity** Recently several companies have issued bonds with 100-year maturities. Critics charge that the issuers are really selling equity in disguise. What are the issues here? Why would a company want to sell "equity in disguise"?

9. **Callable Bonds**   Do you agree or disagree with the following statement? In an efficient market callable and noncallable bonds will be priced in such a way that there will be no advantage or disadvantage to the call provision. Why?

10. **Bond Prices**   If interest rates fall, will the price of noncallable bonds move up higher than that of callable bonds? Why or why not?

11. **Junk Bonds**   What is a "junk bond"? What are some of the controversies created by junk bond financing?

12. **Sinking Funds**   Sinking funds have both positive and negative characteristics for bondholders. Why?

13. **Mortgage Bonds**   Which is riskier to a prospective creditor—an open-end mortgage or closed-end mortgage? Why?

14. **Public Issues versus Direct Financing**   Which of the following are characteristics of public issues, and which are characteristics of direct financing?

   a. SEC registration required.
   b. Higher interest cost.
   c. Higher fixed cost.
   d. Quicker access to funds.
   e. Active secondary market.
   f. Easily renegotiated.
   g. Lower flotation costs.
   h. Regular amortization required.
   i. Ease of repurchase at favorable prices.
   j. High total cost to small borrowers.
   k. Flexible terms.
   l. Less intensive investigation required.

15. **Bond Ratings**   In general, why don't bond prices change when bond ratings change?

Questions and Problems

BASIC
(Questions 1–4)

1. **Accrued Interest**   You purchase a bond with an invoice price of $1,140. The bond has a coupon rate of 7.2 percent, and there are four months to the next semiannual coupon date. What is the clean price of the bond?

2. **Accrued Interest**   You purchase a bond with a coupon rate of 6.5 percent and a clean price of £865. If the next semiannual coupon payment is due in three months, what is the invoice price?

3. **Bond Refunding**   Feel Good Clothing, Inc., plans to issue $5 million of bonds with a coupon rate of 12 percent and 30 years to maturity. The current market interest rates on these bonds is 11 percent. In one year, the interest rate on the bonds will be either 14 percent or 7 percent with equal probability. Assume investors are risk-neutral.
   a. If the bonds are noncallable, what is the price of the bonds today?
   b. If the bonds are callable one year from today at $1,450, will their price be greater than or less than the price you computed in (a)? Why?

4. **Bond Refunding**   New Business Ventures, Inc., has an outstanding perpetual bond with a 10 percent coupon rate that can be called in one year. The bonds make annual coupon payments. The call premium is set at $150 over par value. There is a 40 percent chance that the interest rate in one year will be 12 percent, and a 60 percent chance that the interest rate will be 7 percent. If the current interest rate is 9 percent, what is the current market price of the bond?

INTERMEDIATE
(Questions 5–8)

5. **Bond Refunding**   Linz Stylers intends to issue callable, perpetual bonds with annual coupon payments. The bonds are callable at €1,250. One-year interest rates are 11 percent. There is a 60 percent probability that long-term interest rates one year from today will be 13 percent, and a 40 percent probability that long-term interest rates will be 9 percent. Assume that if interest

rates fall the bonds will be called. What coupon rate should the bonds have in order to sell at par value?

6. **Bond Refunding** Bujumbura Mining Ltd., has decided to borrow money by issuing perpetual bonds with a coupon rate of 8 percent, payable annually. The one-year interest rate is 8 percent. Next year, there is a 35 percent probability that interest rates will increase to 9 percent, and there is a 65 percent probability that they will fall to 6 percent.
   a. What will the market value of these bonds be if they are noncallable?
   b. If the company instead decides to make the bonds callable in one year, what coupon will be demanded by the bondholders for the bonds to sell at par? Assume that the bonds will be called if interest rates rise and that the call premium is equal to the annual coupon.
   c. What will be the value of the call provision to the company?

7. **Bond Refunding** An outstanding issue of Public Express Airlines debentures has a call provision attached. The total principal value of the bonds is NGN 450 million, and the bonds have an annual coupon rate of 8 percent. The total cost of refunding would be 12 percent of the principal amount raised. The appropriate tax rate for the company is 35 percent. How low does the borrowing cost need to drop to justify refunding with a new bond issue?

8. **Bond Refunding** Charles River Associates is considering whether to refinance either of the two perpetual bond issues the company currently has outstanding. Here is information about the two bond issues:

	Bond A	Bond B
Coupon rate	8%	9%
Value outstanding	£75,000,000	£87,500,000
Call premium	8.5%	9.5%
Transaction cost of refunding	£10,000,000	£12,000,000
Current interest rate	7%	7.25%

The corporate tax rate is 40 percent. What is the NPV of the refunding for each bond? Which bond should the company refinance?

CHALLENGE
(Questions 9–10)

9. **Valuing the Call Feature** Consider the prices in the following three Treasury issues as of February 24, 2006:

6.500	May 12n	106:10	106:12	−13	5.28
8.250	May 12	103:14	103:16	−3	5.24
12.000	May 12	134:25	134:31	−15	5.32

The bond in the middle is callable in February 2007. What is the implied value of the call feature? (*Hint*: Is there a way to combine the two noncallable issues to create an issue that has the same coupon as the callable bond?)

10. **Treasury Bonds** The following Treasury bond quote appeared in *The Wall Street Journal* on May 11, 2004:

| 9.125 | May 09 | 100:03 | 100:04 | ... | −2.15 |

Why would anyone buy this Treasury bond with a negative yield to maturity? How is this possible?

S&P Problems

STANDARD &POOR'S

1. **Bond Ratings** Look up Coca-Cola (KO), Gateway (GTW), AT&T (T), and Navistar International (NAV). For each company, follow the "Financial Highlights" link and find the bond rating. Which companies have an investment-grade rating? Which companies are rated below investment grade? Are any unrated? When you find the credit rating for one of the companies, click on the "S&P Issuer Credit Rating" link. What are the considerations listed that Standard & Poor's uses to issue a credit rating?

2. **Bond Indentures** Look under the Edgar link for American Electric Power (AEP) and find the most recent bond issue for the company. What was the amount of bonds issued? What are the coupon rate, maturity date, payment dates, ranking, and restrictive covenants on the bonds? What are the risk factors of the bonds outlined in the prospectus?

Mini Case

Financing East Coast Yachts' Expansion Plans with a Bond Issue

Larissa Warren, the owner of East Coast Yachts, has decided to expand her operations. She asked her newly hired financial analyst, Dan Ervin, to enlist an underwriter to help sell $30 million in new 20-year bonds to finance new construction. Dan has entered into discussions with Robin Perry, an underwriter from the firm of Crowe & Mallard, about which bond features East Coast Yachts should consider and also what coupon rate the issue will likely have. Although Dan is aware of bond features, he is uncertain of the costs and benefits of some features, so he isn't sure how each feature would affect the coupon rate of the bond issue.

1. You are Robin's assistant, and she has asked you to prepare a memo to Dan describing the effect of each of the following bond features on the coupon rate of the bond. She would also like you to list any advantages or disadvantages of each feature.

   a. The security of the bond—that is, whether the bond has collateral.
   b. The seniority of the bond.
   c. The presence of a sinking fund.
   d. A call provision with specified call dates and call prices.
   e. A deferred call accompanying the call provision in (d).
   f. A make-whole call provision.
   g. Any positive covenants. Also, discuss several possible positive covenants East Coast Yachts might consider.
   h. Any negative covenants. Also, discuss several possible negative covenants East Coast Yachts might consider.
   i. A conversion feature (note that East Coast Yachts is not a publicly traded company).
   j. A floating-rate coupon.

   Dan is also considering whether to issue coupon bearing bonds or zero coupon bonds. The YTM on either bond issue will be 8 percent. The coupon bond would have an 8 percent coupon rate. The company's tax rate is 35 percent.

2. How many of the coupon bonds must East Coast Yachts issue to raise the $30 million? How many of the zeroes must it issue?

3. In 20 years, what will be the principal repayment due if East Coast Yachts issues the coupon bonds? What if it issues the zeroes?

4. What are the company's considerations in issuing a coupon bond compared to a zero coupon bond?

5. Suppose East Coast Yachts issues the coupon bonds with a make-whole call provision. The make-whole call rate is the Treasury rate plus 0.40 percent. If East Coast calls the bonds in 7 years when the Treasury rate is 5.6 percent, what is the call price of the bond? What if it is 9.1 percent?

6. Are investors really made whole with a make-whole call provision?

7. After considering all the relevant factors, would you recommend a zero coupon issue or a regular coupon issue? Why? Would you recommend an ordinary call feature or a make-whole call feature? Why?

CHAPTER 21

Leasing

Have you ever flown on an airplane owned by ILFC? You may have and not even known it. The International Lease Finance Corporation, which is the world's largest airplane leasing company by fleet value, leases airplanes to airlines such as American, Continental, and Southwest. The company currently owns more than 750 jets and has contracts to purchase 308 more aircraft at a cost of $20.1 billion through 2010. So why is ILFC in the business of buying airplanes, only to lease them out? And why don't companies that lease from ILFC simply purchase the airplanes themselves? This chapter provides answers to these and other questions associated with leasing.

21.1 Types of Leases

The Basics

A *lease* is a contractual agreement between a lessee and lessor. The agreement establishes that the lessee has the right to use an asset and in return must make periodic payments to the lessor, the owner of the asset. The lessor is either the asset's manufacturer or an independent leasing company. If the lessor is an independent leasing company, it must buy the asset from a manufacturer. Then the lessor delivers the asset to the lessee, and the lease goes into effect.

As far as the lessee is concerned, it is the use of the asset that is most important, not who owns the asset. The use of an asset can be obtained by a lease contract. Because the user can also buy the asset, leasing and buying involve alternative financing arrangements for the use of an asset. This is illustrated in Figure 21.1.

The specific example in Figure 21.1 happens often in the computer industry. Firm *U*, the lessee, might be a hospital, a law firm, or any other firm that uses computers. The lessor is an independent leasing company that purchased the equipment from a manufacturer such as IBM or Apple. Leases of this type are called **direct leases**. In the figure, the lessor issued both debt and equity to finance the purchase.

Of course, a manufacturer like IBM could lease its *own* computers, though we do not show this situation in the example. Leases of this type are called **sales-type leasing**. In this case, IBM would compete with the independent computer leasing company.

Operating Leases

Years ago, a lease where the lessee received an operator along with the equipment was called an **operating lease**. Though the operating lease defies an exact definition today, this form for leasing has several important characteristics:

Figure 21.1 **Buying versus Leasing**

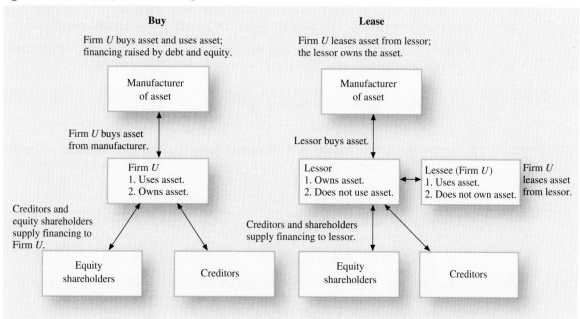

1. Operating leases are usually not fully amortized. This means that the payments required under the terms of the lease are not enough to recover the full cost of the asset for the lessor. This occurs because the term or life of the operating lease is usually less than the economic life of the asset. Thus, the lessor must expect to recover the costs of the asset by renewing the lease or by selling the asset for its residual value.

2. Operating leases usually require the lessor to maintain and insure the leased assets.

3. Perhaps the most interesting feature of an operating lease is the cancellation option. This option gives the lessee the right to cancel the lease contract before the expiration date. If the option to cancel is exercised, the lessee must return the equipment to the lessor. The value of a cancellation clause depends on whether future technological or economic conditions are likely to make the value of the asset to the lessee less than the value of the future lease payments under the lease.

To leasing practitioners, the preceding characteristics constitute an operating lease. However, accountants use the term in a slightly different way, as we will see shortly.

Financial Leases

Financial leases are the exact opposite of operating leases, as is seen from their important characteristics:

1. Financial leases do not provide for maintenance or service by the lessor.

2. Financial leases are fully amortized.

3. The lessee usually has a right to renew the lease on expiration.

4. Generally, financial leases cannot be canceled. In other words, the lessee must make all payments or face the risk of bankruptcy.

Because of these characteristics, particularly (2), this lease provides an alternative method of financing to purchase. Hence, its name is a sensible one. Two special types of financial leases are the sale and lease-back arrangement and the leveraged lease.

Sale and Leaseback   A **sale and leaseback** occurs when a company sells an asset it owns to another firm and immediately leases it back. In a sale and leaseback two things happen:

1. The lessee receives cash from the sale of the asset.
2. The lessee makes periodic lease payments, thereby retaining use of the asset.

For example, in January 2006, Franklin Electronic Publishers, distributor of Rolodex electronic organizers, closed the sale and leaseback of its corporate headquarters building. The company sold the building for $10.3 million, and at the same time agreed to a 10-year lease with the purchaser with an initial annual payment of $736,000.

Leveraged Leases   A **leveraged lease** is a three-sided arrangement among the lessee, the lessor, and the lenders:

1. As in other leases, the lessee uses the assets and makes periodic lease payments.
2. As in other leases, the lessor purchases the assets, delivers them to the lessee, and collects the lease payments. However, the lessor puts up no more than 40 to 50 percent of the purchase price.
3. The lenders supply the remaining financing and receive interest payments from the lessor. Thus, the arrangement on the right side of Figure 21.1 would be a leveraged lease if the bulk of the financing was supplied by creditors.

The lenders in a leveraged lease typically use a nonrecourse loan. This means that the lessor is not obligated to the lender in case of a default. However, the lender is protected in two ways:

1. The lender has a first lien on the asset.
2. In the event of loan default, the lease payments are made directly to the lender.

The lessor puts up only part of the funds but gets the lease payments and all the tax benefits of ownership. These lease payments are used to pay the debt service of the nonrecourse loan. The lessee benefits because, in a competitive market, the lease payment is lowered when the lessor saves taxes.

21.2 Accounting and Leasing

Before November 1976, a firm could arrange to use an asset through a lease and not disclose the asset or the lease contract on the balance sheet. Lessees needed to report information on leasing activity only in the footnotes of their financial statements. Thus leasing led to **off–balance sheet financing**.

In November 1976, the Financial Accounting Standards Board (FASB) issued its *Statement of Financial Accounting Standards No. 13* (FAS 13), "Accounting for Leases." Under FAS 13, certain leases are classified as capital leases. For a capital lease, the present value of the lease payments appears on the right side of the balance sheet. The identical value appears on the left side of the balance sheet as an asset.

FASB classifies all other leases as operating leases, though FASB's definition differs from that of nonaccountants. No mention of the lease appears on the balance sheet for operating leases.

Table 21.1

Example of Balance Sheet under FAS 13

Balance Sheet			
Truck is purchased with debt (the company owns a $100,000 truck):			
Truck	$100,000	Debt	$100,000
Land	100,000	Equity	100,000
Total assets	$200,000	Total debt plus equity	$200,000
Operating lease (the company has an operating lease for the truck):			
Truck	$ 0	Debt	$ 0
Land	100,000	Equity	100,000
Total assets	$100,000	Total debt plus equity	$100,000
Capital lease (the company has a capital lease for the truck):			
Assets under capital lease	$100,000	Obligations under capital lease	$100,000
Land	100,000	Equity	100,000
Total assets	$200,000	Total debt plus equity	$200,000

The accounting implications of this distinction are illustrated in Table 21.1. Imagine a firm that, years ago, issued $100,000 of equity to purchase land. It now wants to use a $100,000 truck, which it can either purchase or lease. The balance sheet reflecting purchase of the truck is shown at the top of the table. (We assume that the truck is financed entirely with debt.) Alternatively, imagine that the firm leases the truck. If the lease is judged to be an operating one, the middle balance sheet is created. Here, neither the lease liability nor the truck appears on the balance sheet. The bottom balance sheet reflects a capital lease. The truck is shown as an asset and the lease is shown as a liability.

Accountants generally argue that a firm's financial strength is inversely related to the amount of its liabilities. Because the lease liability is hidden with an operating lease, the balance sheet of a firm with an operating lease *looks* stronger than the balance sheet of a firm with an otherwise identical capital lease. Given the choice, firms would probably classify all their leases as operating ones. Because of this tendency, *FAS 13* states that a lease must be classified as a capital one if at least one of the following four criteria is met:

1. The present value of the lease payments is at least 90 percent of the fair market value of the asset at the start of the lease.

2. The lease transfers ownership of the property to the lessee by the end of the term of the lease.

3. The lease term is 75 percent or more of the estimated economic life of the asset.

4. The lessee can purchase the asset at a price below fair market value when the lease expires. This is frequently called a *bargain purchase price option.*

These rules capitalize leases that are similar to purchases. For example, the first two rules capitalize leases where the asset is likely to be purchased at the end of the lease period. The last two rules capitalize long-term leases.

Some firms have tried to cook the books by exploiting this classification scheme. Suppose a trucking firm wants to lease a $200,000 truck that it expects to use for 15 years. A clever financial manager could try to negotiate a lease contract for 10 years with lease payments having a present value of $178,000. These terms would get around criteria (1) and (3). If criteria (2) and (4) could be circumvented, the arrangement would be an operating lease and would not show up on the balance sheet.

Does this sort of gimmickry pay? The semistrong form of the efficient capital markets hypothesis implies that stock prices reflect all publicly available information. As we discussed earlier in this text, the empirical evidence generally supports this form of the hypothesis. Though operating leases do not appear in the firm's balance sheet, information about these leases must be disclosed elsewhere in the annual report. Because of this, attempts to keep leases off the balance sheet will not affect stock price in an efficient capital market.

21.3   Taxes, the IRS, and Leases

The lessee can deduct lease payments for income tax purposes if the lease is qualified by the Internal Revenue Service. Because tax shields are critical to the economic viability of any lease, all interested parties generally obtain an opinion from the IRS before agreeing to a major lease transaction. The opinion of the IRS will reflect the following guidelines:

1. The term of the lease must be less than 30 years. If the term is greater than 30 years, the transaction will be regarded as a conditional sale.

2. The lease should not have an option to acquire the asset at a price below its fair market value. This type of bargain option would give the lessee the asset's residual scrap value, implying an equity interest.

3. The lease should not have a schedule of payments that is very high at the start of the lease term and thereafter very low. Early *balloon* payments would be evidence that the lease was being used to avoid taxes and not for a legitimate business purpose.

4. The lease payments must provide the lessor with a fair market rate of return. The profit potential of the lease to the lessor should be apart from the deal's tax benefits.

5. The lease should not limit the lessee's right to issue debt or pay dividends while the lease is operative.

6. Renewal options must be reasonable and reflect the fair market value of the asset. This requirement can be met by granting the lessee the first option to meet a competing outside offer.

The reason the IRS is concerned about lease contracts is that many times they appear to be set up solely to avoid taxes. To see how this could happen, suppose a firm plans to purchase a $1 million bus that has a five-year class life. Depreciation expense would be $200,000 per year, assuming straight-line depreciation. Now suppose that firm can lease the bus for $500,000 per year for two years and buy the bus for $1 at the end of the two-year term. The present value of the tax benefits from acquiring the bus would clearly be less than if the bus were leased. The speedup of lease payments would greatly benefit the firm and give it a form of accelerated depreciation. If the tax rates of the lessor and lessee are different, leasing can be a form of tax avoidance.

21.4   The Cash Flows of Leasing

In this section we identify the basic cash flows used in evaluating a lease. Consider the decision confronting the Xomox corporation, which manufactures pipe. Business has been expanding, and Xomox currently has a five-year backlog of pipe orders for the Trans-Honduran Pipeline.

The International Boring Machine Corporation (IBMC) makes a pipe-boring machine that can be purchased for $10,000. Xomox has determined that it needs a new machine, and the IBMC model will save Xomox $6,000 per year in reduced electricity bills for the next five years. These savings are known with certainty because Xomox has a long-term electricity purchase agreement with State Electric Utilities, Inc.

Table 21.2

Cash Flows to Xomox from Using the IBMC Pipe-Boring Machine: Buy versus Lease

	Year 0	Year 1	Year 2	Year 3	Year 4	Year 5
Buy						
Cost of machine	−$10,000					
Aftertax operating savings [$3,960 = $6,000 × (1 − 0.34)]		$3,960	$3,960	$3,960	$3,960	$3,960
Depreciation tax benefit		680	680	680	680	680
	−$10,000	$4,640	$4,640	$4,640	$4,640	$4,640
Lease						
Lease payments		−$2,500	−$2,500	−$2,500	−$2,500	−$2,500
Tax benefits of lease payments ($850 = $2,500 × 0.34)		850	850	850	850	850
Aftertax operating savings		3,960	3,960	3,960	3,960	3,960
Total		$2,310	$2,310	$2,310	$2,310	$2,310

Depreciation is straight-line. Because the depreciable base is $10,000, depreciation expense per year is $10,000/5 = $2,000. The depreciation tax benefit per year is equal to:

Tax rate × Depreciation expense per year = Depreciation tax benefit
0.34 × $2,000 = $680

Xomox has a corporate tax rate of 34 percent. We assume that five-year straight-line depreciation is used for the pipe-boring machine, and the machine will be worthless after five years.[1]

However, Friendly Leasing Corporation has offered to lease the same pipe-boring machine to Xomox for $2,500 per year for five years. With the lease, Xomox would remain responsible for maintenance, insurance, and operating expenses.[2]

Simon Smart, a recently hired MBA, has been asked to calculate the incremental cash flows from leasing the IBMC machine in lieu of buying it. He has prepared Table 21.2, which shows the direct cash flow consequences of buying the pipe-boring machine and also signing the lease agreement with Friendly Leasing.

To simplify matters, Simon Smart has prepared Table 21.3, which subtracts the direct cash flows of buying the pipe-boring machine from those of leasing it. Noting that only the net advantage of leasing is relevant to Xomox, he concludes the following from his analysis:

1. Operating costs are not directly affected by leasing. Xomox will save $3,960 (after taxes) from use of the IBMC boring machine regardless of whether the machine is owned or leased. Thus, this cash flow stream does not appear in Table 21.3.

2. If the machine is leased, Xomox will save the $10,000 it would have used to purchase the machine. This saving shows up as an initial cash *inflow* of $10,000 in year 0.

3. If Xomox leases the pipe-boring machine, it will no longer own this machine and must give up the depreciation tax benefits. These lost tax benefits show up as an *outflow*.

---

[1] This is a simplifying assumption because current tax law allows the accelerated method as well. The accelerated method will almost always be the best choice.

[2] For simplicity, we have assumed that lease payments are made at the end of each year. Actually, most leases require lease payments to be made at the beginning of the year.

Table 21.3

Incremental Cash Flow Consequences for Xomox from Leasing Instead of Purchasing

Lease Minus Buy	Year 0	Year 1	Year 2	Year 3	Year 4	Year 5
Lease						
Lease payment		−$2,500	−$2,500	−$2,500	−$2,500	−$2,500
Tax benefit of lease payment		850	850	850	850	850
Buy (minus)						
Cost of machine	−(−$10,000)					
Lost depreciation tax benefit		−680	−680	−680	−680	−680
Total	$10,000	−$2,330	−$2,330	−$2,330	−$2,330	−$2,330

The bottom line presents the cash flows from leasing relative to the cash flows from purchase. The cash flows would be exactly the *opposite* if we considered the purchase relative to the lease.

4. If Xomox chooses to lease the machine, it must pay $2,500 per year for five years. The first payment is due at the end of the first year. (This is a break: Sometimes the first payment is due immediately.) The lease payments are tax deductible and, as a consequence, generate tax benefits of $850 ($= 0.34 \times \$2,500$).

The net cash flows have been placed in the bottom line of Table 21.3. These numbers represent the cash flows from *leasing* relative to the cash flows from the purchase. It is arbitrary that we express the flows in this way. We could have expressed the cash flows from the *purchase* relative to the cash flows from leasing. These cash flows would look like this:

	Year 0	Year 1	Year 2	Year 3	Year 4	Year 5
Net cash flows from purchase alternative relative to lease alternative	−$10,000	$2,330	$2,330	$2,330	$2,330	$2,330

Of course, the cash flows here are the opposite of those in the bottom line of Table 21.3. Depending on our purpose, we may look at either the purchase relative to the lease or vice versa. Thus, the student should become comfortable with either viewpoint.

Now that we have the cash flows, we can make our decision by discounting the flows properly. However, because the discount rate is tricky, we take a detour in the next section before moving back to the Xomox case. In this next section, we show that cash flows in the lease-versus-buy decision should be discounted at the *aftertax* interest rate (i.e., the aftertax cost of debt capital).

21.5 A Detour for Discounting and Debt Capacity with Corporate Taxes

The analysis of leases is difficult, and both financial practitioners and academics have made conceptual errors. These errors revolve around taxes. We hope to avoid their mistakes by beginning with the simplest type of example: a loan for one year. Though this example is unrelated to our lease-versus-buy situation, principles developed here will apply directly to lease–buy analysis.

Table 21.4

Lending and
Borrowing in a World
with Corporate
Taxes (Interest Rate
Is 10 Percent and
Corporate Tax Rate
Is 34 Percent)

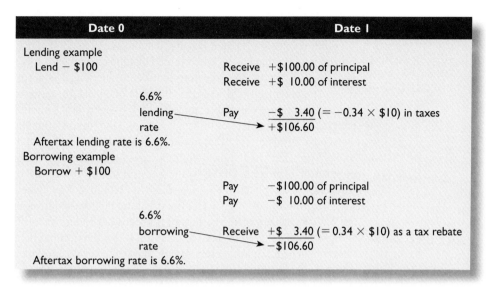

General principle: In a world with corporate taxes, riskless cash flows should be discounted at the aftertax interest rate.

Present Value of Riskless Cash Flows

Consider a corporation that lends $100 for a year. If the interest rate is 10 percent, the firm will receive $110 at the end of the year. Of this amount, $10 is interest and the remaining $100 is the original principal. A corporate tax rate of 34 percent implies taxes on the interest of $3.40 (0.34 × $10). Thus, the firm ends up with $106.60 (= $110 − $3.40) after taxes on a $100 investment.

Now, consider a company that borrows $100 for a year. With a 10 percent interest rate, the firm must pay $110 to the bank at the end of the year. However, the borrowing firm can take the $10 of interest as a tax deduction. The corporation pays $3.40 (= 0.34 × $10) less in taxes than it would have paid had it not borrowed the money at all. Thus, considering this reduction in taxes, the firm must pay $106.60 (= $110 − $3.40) on a $100 loan. The cash flows from both lending and borrowing are displayed in Table 21.4.

The previous two paragraphs show a very important result: The firm could not care less whether it received $100 today or $106.60 next year.[3] If it received $100 today, it could lend it out, thereby receiving $106.60 after corporate taxes at the end of the year. Conversely, if it knows today that it will receive $106.60 at the end of the year, it could borrow $100 today. The aftertax interest and principal payments on the loan would be paid with the $106.60 that the firm will receive at the end of the year. Because of this interchangeability, we say that a payment of $106.60 next year has a present value of $100. Because $100 = $106.60/1.066, a riskless cash flow should be discounted at the aftertax interest rate of 0.066 [= 0.10 × (1 − 0.34)].

Of course, the preceding discussion considered a specific example. The general principle is this:

In a world with corporate taxes, the firm should discount riskless cash flows at the aftertax riskless rate of interest.

---

[3]For simplicity, assume that the firm received $100 or $106.60 *after* corporate taxes. Because 0.66 = 1 − 0.34, the pretax inflows would be $151.52 ($100/0.66) and $161.52 ($106.60/0.66), respectively.

Optimal Debt Level and Riskless Cash Flows

In addition, our simple example can illustrate a related point concerning optimal debt level. Consider a firm that has just determined that the current level of debt in its capital structure is optimal. Immediately following that determination, it is surprised to learn that it will receive a guaranteed payment of $106.60 in one year from, say, a tax-exempt government lottery. This future windfall is an asset that, like any asset, should raise the firm's optimal debt level. How much does this payment raise the firm's optimal level?

Our analysis implies that the firm's optimal debt level must be $100 more than it previously was. That is, the firm could borrow $100 today, perhaps paying the entire amount out as a dividend. It would owe the bank $110 at the end of the year. However, because it receives a tax rebate of $3.40 $(= 0.34 \times \$10)$, its net repayment will be $106.60. Thus, its borrowing of $100 today is fully offset by next year's government lottery proceeds of $106.60. In other words, the lottery proceeds act as an irrevocable trust that can service the increased debt. Note that we need not know the optimal debt level before the lottery was announced. We are merely saying that whatever this prelottery optimal level was, the optimal debt level is $100 more after the lottery announcement.

Of course, this is just one example. The general principle is this:[4]

In a world with corporate taxes, we determine the increase in the firm's optimal debt level by discounting a future guaranteed aftertax inflow at the aftertax riskless interest rate.

Conversely, suppose that a second, unrelated firm is surprised to learn that it must pay $106.60 next year to the government for back taxes. Clearly, this additional liability impinges on the second firm's debt capacity. By the previous reasoning, it follows that the second firm's optimal debt level must be lowered by exactly $100.

21.6 NPV Analysis of the Lease-versus-Buy Decision

Our detour leads to a simple method for evaluating leases: Discount all cash flows at the aftertax interest rate. From the bottom line of Table 21.3, Xomox's incremental cash flows from leasing versus purchasing are these:

	Year 0	Year 1	Year 2	Year 3	Year 4	Year 5
Net cash flows from lease alternative relative to purchase alternative	$10,000	−$2,330	−$2,330	−$2,330	−$2,330	−$2,330

Let us assume that Xomox can either borrow or lend at the interest rate of 7.57575 percent. If the corporate tax rate is 34 percent, the correct discount rate is the aftertax rate of 5 percent $[= 7.57575\% \times (1 - 0.34)]$. When 5 percent is used to compute the NPV of the lease, we have:

$$\text{NPV} = \$10,000 - \$2,330 \times A_{0.05}^{5} = -\$87.68 \tag{21.1}$$

Because the net present value of the incremental cash flows from leasing relative to purchasing is negative, Xomox prefers to purchase.

---

[4]This principle holds for riskless or guaranteed cash flows only. Unfortunately, there is no easy formula for determining the increase in optimal debt level from a *risky* cash flow.

Equation 21.1 is the correct approach to lease-versus-buy analysis. However, students are often bothered by two things. First, they question whether the cash flows in Table 21.3 are truly riskless. We examine this issue next. Second, they feel that this approach lacks intuition. We address this concern a little later.

The Discount Rate

Because we discounted at the aftertax riskless rate of interest, we have implicitly assumed that the cash flows in the Xomox example are riskless. Is this appropriate?

A lease payment is like the debt service on a secured bond issued by the lessee, and the discount rate should be approximately the same as the interest rate on such debt. In general, this rate will be slightly higher than the riskless rate considered in the previous section. The various tax shields could be somewhat riskier than the lease payments for two reasons. First, the value of the depreciation tax benefits depends on the ability of Xomox to generate enough taxable income to use them. Second, the corporate tax rate may change in the future, just as it fell in 1986 and increased in 1993. For these two reasons, a firm might be justified in discounting the depreciation tax benefits at a rate higher than that used for the lease payments. However, our experience is that real-world companies discount both the depreciation shield and lease payments at the same rate. This implies that financial practitioners view these two risks as minor. We adopt the real-world convention of discounting the two flows at the same rate. This rate is the aftertax interest rate on secured debt issued by the lessee.

At this point some students still ask, Why not use R_{WACC} as the discount rate in lease-versus-buy analysis? Of course, R_{WACC} should not be used for lease analysis because the cash flows are more like debt service cash flows than operating cash flows and, as such, the risk is much less. The discount rate should reflect the risk of the incremental cash flows.

21.7 Debt Displacement and Lease Valuation

The Basic Concept of Debt Displacement

The previous analysis allows us to calculate the right answer in a simple manner. This clearly must be viewed as an important benefit. However, the analysis has little intuitive appeal. To remedy this, we hope to make lease–buy analysis more intuitive by considering the issue of debt displacement.

A firm that purchases equipment will generally issue debt to finance the purchase. The debt becomes a liability of the firm. A lessee incurs a liability equal to the present value of all future lease payments. Because of this, we argue that leases displace debt. The balance sheets in Table 21.5 illustrate how leasing might affect debt.

Suppose a firm initially has $100,000 of assets and a 150 percent optimal debt–equity ratio. The firm's debt is $60,000, and its equity is $40,000. As in the Xomox case, suppose the firm must use a new $10,000 machine. The firm has two alternatives:

1. *The firm can purchase the machine.* If it does, it will finance the purchase with a secured loan and with equity. The debt capacity of the machine is assumed to be the same as for the firm as a whole.

2. *The firm can lease the asset and get 100 percent financing.* That is, the present value of the future lease payments will be $10,000.

If the firm finances the machine with both secured debt and new equity, its debt will increase by $6,000 and its equity by $4,000. Its optimal debt–equity ratio of 150 percent will be maintained.

Table 21.5

Debt Displacement Elsewhere in the Firm When a Lease Is Instituted

Assets		Liabilities	
Initial situation			
Current	$ 50,000	Debt	$ 60,000
Fixed	50,000	Equity	40,000
Total	$100,000	Total	$100,000
Buy with secured loan			
Current	$ 50,000	Debt	$ 66,000
Fixed	50,000	Equity	44,000
Machine	10,000	Total	$110,000
Total	$110,000		
Lease			
Current	$ 50,000	Lease	$ 10,000
Fixed	50,000	Debt	56,000
Machine	10,000	Equity	44,000
Total	$110,000	Total	$110,000

This example shows that leases reduce the level of debt elsewhere in the firm. Though the example illustrates a point, it is not meant to show a precise method for calculating debt displacement.

Conversely, consider the lease alternative. Because the lessee views the lease payment as a liability, the lessee thinks in terms of a *liability-to-equity* ratio, not just a debt-to-equity ratio. As just mentioned, the present value of the lease liability is $10,000. If the leasing firm is to maintain a liability-to-equity ratio of 150 percent, debt elsewhere in the firm must fall by $4,000 when the lease is instituted. Because debt must be repurchased, net liabilities rise by only $6,000 (= $10,000 − $4,000) when $10,000 of assets are placed under lease.[5]

Debt displacement is a hidden cost of leasing. If a firm leases, it will not use as much regular debt as it would otherwise. The benefits of debt capacity will be lost—particularly the lower taxes associated with interest expense.

Optimal Debt Level in the Xomox Example

The previous section showed that leasing displaces debt. Though the section illustrated a point, it was not meant to show the *precise* method for calculating debt displacement. Here we describe the precise method for calculating the difference in optimal debt levels between purchase and lease in the Xomox example.

From the last line of Table 21.3, we know these cash flows from the *purchase* alternative relative to the cash flows from the lease alternative:[6]

	Year 0	Year 1	Year 2	Year 3	Year 4	Year 5
Net cash flows from purchase alternative relative to lease alternative	−$10,000	$2,330	$2,330	$2,330	$2,330	$2,330

---

[5] Growing firms in the real world will not generally repurchase debt when instituting a lease. Rather, they will issue less debt in the future than they would have without the lease.

[6] The last line of Table 21.3 presents the cash flows from the lease alternative relative to the purchase alternative. As pointed out earlier, our cash flows are now reversed because we are now presenting the cash flows from the purchase alternative relative to the lease alternative.

An increase in the optimal debt level at year 0 occurs because the firm learns at that time of guaranteed cash flows beginning at year 1. Our detour into discounting and debt capacity told us to calculate this increased debt level by discounting the future riskless cash inflows at the aftertax interest rate.[7] Thus, the additional debt level of the purchase alternative relative to the lease alternative is:

Increase in optimal
debt level from
purchase alternative
relative to lease
alternative:

$$\$10{,}087.68 = \frac{\$2{,}330}{1.05} + \frac{\$2{,}330}{(1.05)^2} + \frac{\$2{,}330}{(1.05)^3} + \frac{\$2{,}330}{(1.05)^4} + \frac{\$2{,}330}{(1.05)^5}$$

That is, whatever the optimal amount of debt would be under the lease alternative, the optimal amount of debt would be $10,087.68 more under the purchase alternative.

This result can be stated in another way. Imagine there are two identical firms except that one firm purchases the boring machine and the other leases it. From Table 21.3, we know that the purchasing firm generates $2,330 more cash flow after taxes in each of the five years than does the leasing firm. Further imagine that the same bank lends money to both firms. The bank should lend the purchasing firm more money because it has a greater cash flow each period. How much extra money should the bank lend the purchasing firm so that the incremental loan can be paid off by the extra cash flows of $2,330 per year? The answer is exactly $10,087.68—the increase in the optimal debt level we calculated earlier.

To see this, let us work through the example year by year. Because the purchasing firm borrows $10,087.68 more at year 0 than does the leasing firm, the purchasing firm will pay interest of $764.22 ($= \$10{,}087.68 \times 0.0757575$) at year 1 on the additional debt. The interest allows the firm to reduce its taxes by $259.83 ($= \$764.22 \times 0.34$), leaving an aftertax outflow of $504.39 ($= \$764.22 - \$259.83$) at year 1.

We know from Table 21.3 that the purchasing firm generates $2,330 more cash at year 1 than does the leasing firm. Because the purchasing firm has the extra $2,330 coming in at year 1 but must pay interest on its loan, how much of the loan can the firm repay at year 1 and still have the same cash flow as the leasing firm has? The purchasing firm can repay $1,825.61 ($= \$2{,}330 - \$504.39$) of the loan at year 1 and still have the same net cash flow that the leasing firm has. After the repayment, the purchasing firm will have a remaining balance of $8,262.07 ($= \$10{,}087.68 - \$1{,}825.61$) at year 1. For each of the five years, this sequence of cash flows is displayed in Table 21.6. The outstanding balance goes to zero over the five years. Thus, the annual cash flow of $2,330, which represents the extra cash from purchasing instead of leasing, fully amortizes the loan of $10,087.68.

Our analysis of debt capacity has two purposes. First, we want to show the additional debt capacity from purchasing. We just completed this task. Second, we want to determine whether the lease is preferred to the purchase. This decision rule follows easily from our discussion. By leasing the equipment and having $10,087.68 less debt than under the purchase alternative, the firm has exactly the same cash flow in years 1 to 5 that it would have through a levered purchase. Thus, we can ignore cash flows beginning in year 1 when comparing the lease alternative with the purchase with debt alternative. However, the cash flows differ between the alternatives at year 0:

1. *The purchase cost at year 0 of $10,000 is avoided by leasing.* This should be viewed as a cash inflow under the leasing alternative.

---

[7] Though our detour considered only riskless cash flows, the cash flows in a leasing example are not necessarily riskless. As we explained earlier, we therefore adopt the real-world convention of discounting at the aftertax interest rate on secured debt issued by the lessee.

Table 21.6   Calculation of Increase in Optimal Debt Level If Xomox Purchases Instead of Leases

	Year 0	Year 1	Year 2	Year 3	Year 4	Year 5
Outstanding balance of loan	$10,087.68	$8,262.07*	$6,345.17	$4,332.42	$2,219.05	$ 0
Interest		764.22	625.91	480.69	328.22	168.11
Tax deduction on interest		259.83	212.81	163.44	111.59	57.16
Aftertax interest expense		$ 504.39	$ 413.10	$ 317.25	$ 216.63	$ 110.95
Extra cash that purchasing firm generates over leasing firm (from Table 21.3)		$2,330.00	$2,330.00	$2,330.00	$2,330.00	$2,330.00
Repayment of loan		$1,825.61†	$1,916.90	$2,012.75	$2,113.37	$2,219.05

Assume that there are two otherwise identical firms: One leases and the other purchases. The purchasing firm can borrow $10,087.68 more than the leasing firm. The extra cash flow each year of $2,330 from purchasing instead of leasing can be used to pay off the loan in five years.
*$8,262.07 = $10,087.68 − $1,825.61.
†$1,825.61 = $2,330 − $504.39.

2. *The firm borrows $10,087.68 less at year 0 under the lease alternative than it can under the purchase alternative.* This should be viewed as a cash outflow under the leasing alternative.

Because the firm borrows $10,087.68 less by leasing but saves only $10,000 on the equipment, the lease alternative requires an extra cash outflow at year 0 relative to the purchase alternative of −$87.68 (= $10,000 − $10,087.68). Because cash flows in later years from leasing are identical to those from purchasing with debt, the firm should purchase.

This is exactly the same answer we got when, earlier in this chapter, we discounted all cash flows at the aftertax interest rate. Of course, this is no coincidence: The increase in the optimal debt level is also determined by discounting all flows at the aftertax interest rate. The accompanying box presents both methods. The numbers in the box are in terms of the NPV of the lease relative to the purchase. Thus, a negative NPV indicates that the purchase alternative should be taken. The NPV of a lease is often called the net advantage of leasing or NAL.

Two Methods for Calculating Net Present Value of Lease Relative to Purchase*

Method 1: Discount all cash flows at the aftertax interest rate:

$$-\$87.68 = \$10,000 - \$2,330 \times A_{0.05}^{5}$$

Method 2: Compare purchase price with reduction in optimal debt level under leasing alternative:

$$-\$87.68 = \$10,000 - \$10,087.68$$

$$\begin{array}{cc} \text{Purchase} & \text{Reduction in} \\ \text{price} & \text{optimal debt} \\ & \text{level if leasing} \end{array}$$

*Because we are calculating the NPV of the lease relative to the purchase, a negative value indicates that the purchase alternative is preferred.

21.8 Does Leasing Ever Pay? The Base Case

We previously looked at the lease–buy decision from the point of view of the potential lessee, Xomox. Let's now look at the decision from the point of view of the lessor, Friendly Leasing. This firm faces three cash flows, all of which are displayed in Table 21.7. First, Friendly purchases the machine for $10,000 at year 0. Second, because the asset is depreciated straight-line over five years, the depreciation expense at the end of each of the five years is $2,000 (= $10,000/5). The yearly depreciation tax shield is $680 (= $2,000 × 0.34). Third, because the yearly lease payment is $2,500, the aftertax lease payment is $1,650 [= $2,500 × (1 − 0.34)].

Now examine the total cash flows to Friendly Leasing, displayed in the bottom line of Table 21.7. Those of you with a healthy memory will notice something interesting. These cash flows are exactly the *opposite* of those of Xomox, displayed in the bottom line of Table 21.3. Those of you with a healthy sense of skepticism may be thinking something interesting: "If the cash flows of the lessor are exactly the opposite of those of the lessee, the combined cash flow of the two parties must be zero each year. Thus, there does not seem to be any joint benefit to this lease. Because the net present value to the lessee was −$87.68, the NPV to the lessor must be $87.68. The joint NPV is $0 (= −$87.68 + $87.68). There does not appear to be any way for the NPV of both the lessor and the lessee to be positive at the same time. Because one party would inevitably lose money, the leasing deal could never fly."

This is one of the most important results of leasing. Though Table 21.7 concerns one particular leasing deal, the principle can be generalized. As long as (1) both parties are subject to the same interest and tax rates and (2) transaction costs are ignored, there can be no leasing deal that benefits both parties. However, there is a lease payment for which both parties would calculate an NPV of zero. Given that fee, Xomox would be indifferent to whether it leased or bought, and Friendly Leasing would be indifferent to whether it leased or not.[8]

A student with an even healthier sense of skepticism might be thinking, "This textbook appears to be arguing that leasing is not beneficial. Yet we know that leasing occurs frequently in the real world. Maybe, just maybe, the textbook is wrong." Although we will not admit to being wrong (what authors would?!), we freely admit that our explanation is incomplete at this point. The next section considers factors that give benefits to leasing.

Table 21.7 **Cash Flows to Friendly Leasing as Lessor of IBMC Pipe-Boring Machine**

	Year 0	Year I	Year 2	Year 3	Year 4	Year 5
Cash for machine	−$10,000					
Depreciation tax benefit ($680 = $2,000 × 0.34)		$ 680	$ 680	$ 680	$ 680	$ 680
Aftertax lease payment [$1,650 = $2,500 × (1 − 0.34)]		1,650	1,650	1,650	1,650	1,650
Total	−$10,000	$2,330	$2,330	$2,330	$2,330	$2,330

These cash flows are the opposite of the cash flows to Xomox, the lessee (see the bottom line of Table 21.3).

---

[8]The break-even lease payment is $2,469.32 in our example. Both the lessor and lessee can solve for this as follows:

$$\$10,000 = \$680 \times A^5_{0.05} + L \times (1 - 0.34) \times A^5_{0.05}$$

In this case, $L = \$2,469.32$.

21.9 Reasons for Leasing

Proponents of leasing make many claims about why firms should lease assets rather than buy them. Some of the reasons given to support leasing are good, and some are not. We discuss here the reasons for leasing we think are good and some of the ones we think are not.

Good Reasons for Leasing

Leasing is a good choice if at least one of the following is true:

1. Taxes may be reduced by leasing.
2. The lease contract may reduce certain types of uncertainty.
3. Transaction costs can be higher for buying an asset and financing it with debt or equity than for leasing the asset.

Tax Advantages   The most important reason for long-term leasing is tax reduction. If the corporate income tax were repealed, long-term leasing would probably disappear. The tax advantages of leasing exist because firms are in different tax brackets.

Should a user in a low tax bracket purchase, he will receive little tax benefit from depreciation and interest deductions. Should the user lease, the lessor will receive the depreciation shield and the interest deductions. In a competitive market, the lessor must charge a low lease payment to reflect these tax shields. Thus, the user is likely to lease rather than purchase.

In our example with Xomox and Friendly Leasing, the value of the lease to Friendly was $87.68:

$$\$87.68 = -\$10,000 + \$2,330 \times A_{0.05}^{5}$$

However, the value of the lease to Xomox was exactly the opposite ($-\$87.68$). Because the lessor's gains came at the expense of the lessee, no deal could be arranged.

However, if Xomox pays no taxes and the lease payments are reduced to $2,475 from $2,500, both Friendly and Xomox will find positive NPV in leasing. Xomox can rework Table 21.3 with $t_C = 0$, finding that its cash flows from leasing are now these:

	Year 0	Year 1	Year 2	Year 3	Year 4	Year 5
Cost of machine	$10,000					
Lease payment		−$2,475	−$2,475	−$2,475	−$2,475	−$2,475

The value of the lease to Xomox is:

$$\text{Value of lease} = \$10,000 - \$2,475 \times A_{0.0757575}^{5}$$
$$= \$6.55$$

Notice that the discount rate is the interest rate of 7.57575 percent because tax rates are zero. In addition, the full lease payment of $2,475—and not some lower aftertax number—is used because there are no taxes. Finally, note that depreciation is ignored, also because no taxes apply.

Given a lease payment of $2,475, the cash flows to Friendly Leasing look like this:

	Year 0	Year 1	Year 2	Year 3	Year 4	Year 5
Cost of machine	−$10,000					
Depreciation tax shield ($680 = $2,000 × 0.34)		$ 680	$ 680	$ 680	$ 680	$ 680
Aftertax lease payment [$1,633.50 = $2,475 × (1 − 0.34)]		$1,633.50	$1,633.50	$1,633.50	$1,633.50	$1,633.50
Total		$2,313.50	$2,313.50	$2,313.50	$2,313.50	$2,313.50

The value of the lease to Friendly is:

$$\text{Value of lease} = -\$10,000 + \$2,313.50 \times A_{0.05}^5$$
$$= -\$10,000 + \$10,016.24$$
$$= \$16.24$$

As a consequence of different tax rates, the lessee (Xomox) gains $6.55 and the lessor (Friendly) gains $16.24. Both the lessor and the lessee can gain if their tax rates are different because the lessor uses the depreciation and interest tax shields that cannot be used by the lessee. The IRS loses tax revenue, and some of the tax gains to the lessor are passed on to the lessee in the form of lower lease payments.

Because both parties can gain when tax rates differ, the lease payment is agreed upon through negotiation. Before negotiation begins, each party needs to know the *reservation* payment of both parties. This is the payment that will make one party indifferent to whether it enters the lease deal. In other words, this is the payment that makes the value of the lease zero. These payments are calculated next.

Reservation Payment of Lessee   We now solve for L_{MAX}, the payment that makes the value of the lease to the lessee zero. When the lessee is in a zero tax bracket, his cash flows, in terms of L_{MAX}, are as follows:

	Year 0	Year 1	Year 2	Year 3	Year 4	Year 5
Cost of machine	$10,000					
Lease payment		$-L_{MAX}$	$-L_{MAX}$	$-L_{MAX}$	$-L_{MAX}$	$-L_{MAX}$

This chart implies that:

$$\text{Value of lease} = \$10,000 - L_{MAX} \times A_{0.0757575}^5$$

The value of the lease equals zero when:

$$L_{MAX} = \frac{\$10,000}{A_{0.0757575}^5} = \$2,476.62$$

After performing this calculation, the lessor knows that he will never be able to charge a payment above $2,476.62.

Reservation Payment of Lessor   We now solve for L_{MIN}, the payment that makes the value of the lease to the lessor zero. The cash flows to the lessor, in terms of L_{MIN}, are these:

	Year 0	Year 1	Year 2	Year 3	Year 4	Year 5
Cost of machine	−$10,000					
Depreciation tax shield						
($680 = $2,000 × 0.34)		$680	$680	$680	$680	$680
Aftertax lease payment						
($t_C = 0.34$)		$L_{MIN} \times (0.66)$	$L_{MIN} \times (0.66)$	$L_{MIN} \times (0.66)$	$L_{MIN} \times (0.66)$	$L_{MIN} \times (0.66)$

This chart implies that:

$$\text{Value of lease} = -\$10,000 + \$680 \times A_{0.05}^5 + L_{MIN} \times (0.66) \times A_{0.05}^5$$

The value of the lease equals zero when:

$$L_{MIN} = \frac{\$10,000}{0.66 \times A_{0.05}^5} - \frac{\$680}{0.66}$$

$$= \$3,499.62 - \$1,030.30$$

$$= \$2,469.32$$

After performing this calculation, the lessee knows that the lessor will never agree to a lease payment below $2,469.32.

A Reduction of Uncertainty

We have noted that the lessee does not own the property when the lease expires. The value of the property at this time is called the *residual value*, and the lessor has a firm claim to it. When the lease contract is signed, there may be substantial uncertainty about what the residual value of the asset will be. Thus, under a lease contract, this residual risk is borne by the lessor. Conversely, the user bears this risk when purchasing.

It is common sense that the party best able to bear a particular risk should do so. If the user has little risk aversion, she will not suffer by purchasing. However, if the user is highly averse to risk, she should find a third-party lessor more capable of assuming this burden.

This latter situation frequently arises when the user is a small or newly formed firm. Because the risk of the entire firm is likely to be quite high and because the principal stockholders are likely to be undiversified, the firm desires to minimize risk wherever possible. A potential lessor, such as a large, publicly held financial institution, is far more capable of bearing the risk. Conversely, this situation is not expected to happen when the user is a blue chip corporation. That potential lessee is more able to bear risk.

Transaction Costs

The costs of changing an asset's ownership are generally greater than the costs of writing a lease agreement. Consider the choice that confronts a person who lives in Los Angeles but must do business in New York for two days. It will clearly be cheaper to rent a hotel room for two nights than it would be to buy an apartment condominium for two days and then to sell it.

Unfortunately, leases generate agency costs as well. For example, the lessee might misuse or overuse the asset because she has no interest in the asset's residual value. This cost will be implicitly paid by the lessee through a high lease payment. Although the lessor can reduce these agency costs through monitoring, monitoring itself is costly.

Thus, leasing is most beneficial when the transaction costs of purchase and resale outweigh the agency costs and monitoring costs of a lease. Flath argues that this occurs in short-term leases but not in long-term leases.[9]

Bad Reasons for Leasing

Leasing and Accounting Income   In our discussion of accounting and leasing we pointed out that a firm's balance sheet shows fewer liabilities with an operating lease than with either a capitalized lease or a purchase financed with debt. We indicated that a firm desiring to project a strong balance sheet might select an operating lease. In addition, the firm's return on assets (ROA) is generally higher with an operating lease than with either a capitalized lease or a purchase. To see this, we look at the numerator and denominator of the ROA formula in turn.

With an operating lease, lease payments are treated as an expense. If the asset is purchased, both depreciation and interest charges are expenses. At least in the early part of the asset's life, the yearly lease payment is generally less than the sum of yearly depreciation and yearly interest. Thus, accounting income, the numerator of the ROA formula, is higher with an operating lease than with a purchase. Because accounting expenses with a capitalized lease are analogous to depreciation and interest with a purchase, the increase in accounting income does not occur when a lease is capitalized.

In addition, leased assets do not appear on the balance sheet with an operating lease. Thus, the total asset value of a firm, the denominator of the ROA formula, is less with an operating lease than it is with either a purchase or a capitalized lease. The two preceding effects imply that the firm's ROA should be higher with an operating lease than with either a purchase or a capitalized lease.

Of course, in an efficient capital market, accounting information cannot be used to fool investors. It is unlikely, then, that leasing's impact on accounting numbers should create value for the firm. Savvy investors should be able to see through attempts by management to improve the firm's financial statements.

One Hundred Percent Financing   It is often claimed that leasing provides 100 percent financing, whereas secured equipment loans require an initial down payment. However, we argued earlier that leases tend to displace debt elsewhere in the firm. Our earlier analysis suggests that leases do not permit a greater level of total liabilities than do purchases with borrowing.

Other Reasons   There are, of course, many special reasons that some companies find advantages in leasing. In one celebrated case, the U.S. Navy leased a fleet of tankers instead of asking Congress for appropriations. Thus, leasing may be used to circumvent capital expenditure control systems set up by bureaucratic firms.

21.10 Some Unanswered Questions

Our analysis suggests that the primary advantage of long-term leasing results from the differential tax rates of the lessor and the lessee. Other valid reasons for leasing are lower contracting costs and risk reduction. There are several questions our analysis has not specifically answered.

---

[9]D. Flath, "The Economics of Short-Term Leasing," *Economic Inquiry* 18 (April 1980).

Are the Uses of Leases and Debt Complementary?

Ang and Peterson find that firms with high debt tend to lease frequently as well.[10] This result should not be puzzling. The corporate attributes that provide high debt capacity may also make leasing advantageous. Thus, even though leasing displaces debt (that is, leasing and borrowing are substitutes) for an individual firm, high debt and high leasing can be positively associated when we look at a number of firms.

Why Are Leases Offered by Both Manufacturers and Third-Party Lessors?

The offsetting effects of taxes can explain why both manufacturers (for example, computer firms) and third-party lessors offer leases.

1. For manufacturer lessors, the basis for determining depreciation is the manufacturer's cost. For third-party lessors, the basis is the sales price that the lessor paid to the manufacturer. Because the sales price is generally greater than the manufacturer's cost, this is an advantage to third-party lessors.

2. However, the manufacturer must recognize a profit for tax purposes when selling the asset to the third-party lessor. The manufacturer's profit for some equipment can be deferred if the manufacturer becomes the lessor. This provides an incentive for manufacturers to lease.

Why Are Some Assets Leased More Than Others?

Certain assets appear to be leased more frequently than others. Smith and Wakeman have looked at nontax incentives affecting leasing.[11] Their analysis suggests many asset and firm characteristics that are important in the lease-or-buy decision. The following are among the things they mention:

1. The more sensitive the value of an asset is to use and maintenance decisions, the more likely it is that the asset will be purchased instead of leased. They argue that ownership provides a better incentive to minimize maintenance costs than does leasing.

2. Price discrimination opportunities may be important. Leasing may be a way of circumventing laws against charging too *low* a price.

Summary and Conclusions

A large fraction of America's equipment is leased rather than purchased. This chapter both described the institutional arrangements surrounding leases and showed how to evaluate leases financially.

1. Leases can be separated into two polar types. Though operating leases allow the lessee to use the equipment, ownership remains with the lessor. Although the lessor in a financial lease legally owns the equipment, the lessee maintains effective ownership because financial leases are fully amortized.

2. When a firm purchases an asset with debt, both the asset and the liability appear on the firm's balance sheet. If a lease meets at least one of a number of criteria, it must be capitalized. This means

---

[10] J. Ang and P. P. Peterson, "The Leasing Puzzle," *Journal of Finance* 39 (September 1984).

[11] C. W. Smith, Jr., and L. M. Wakeman, "Determinants of Corporate Leasing Policy," *Journal of Finance* (July 1985).

that the present value of the lease appears as both an asset and a liability. A lease escapes capital-ization if it does not meet any of these criteria. Leases not meeting the criteria are called *operat-ing leases*, though the accountant's definition differs somewhat from the practitioner's definition. Operating leases do not appear on the balance sheet. For cosmetic reasons, many firms prefer that a lease be called *operating*.

3. Firms generally lease for tax purposes. To protect its interests, the IRS allows financial arrange-ments to be classified as leases only if a number of criteria are met.

4. We showed that risk-free cash flows should be discounted at the aftertax risk-free rate. Because both lease payments and depreciation tax shields are nearly riskless, all relevant cash flows in the lease–buy decision should be discounted at a rate near this aftertax rate. We use the real-world convention of discounting at the aftertax interest rate on the lessee's secured debt.

5. Though this method is simple, it lacks certain intuitive appeal. We presented an alternative method in the hopes of increasing the reader's intuition. Relative to a lease, a purchase generates debt capacity. This increase in debt capacity can be calculated by discounting the difference be-tween the cash flows of the purchase and the cash flows of the lease by the aftertax interest rate. The increase in debt capacity from a purchase is compared to the extra outflow at year 0 from a purchase.

6. If the lessor is in the same tax bracket as the lessee, the cash flows to the lessor are exactly the opposite of the cash flows to the lessee. Thus, the sum of the value of the lease to the lessee plus the value of the lease to the lessor must be zero. Although this suggests that leases can never fly, there are actually at least three good reasons for leasing:
   a. Differences in tax brackets between lessor and lessee.
   b. Shift of risk bearing to the lessor.
   c. Minimization of transaction costs.

   We also documented a number of bad reasons for leasing.

Concept Questions

1. **Leasing versus Borrowing**   What are the key differences between leasing and borrowing? Are they perfect substitutes?

2. **Leasing and Taxes**   Taxes are an important consideration in the leasing decision. Which is more likely to lease: a profitable corporation in a high tax bracket or a less profitable one in a low tax bracket? Why?

3. **Leasing and IRR**   What are some of the potential problems with looking at IRRs in evaluat-ing a leasing decision?

4. **Leasing**   Comment on the following remarks:
   a. Leasing reduces risk and can reduce a firm's cost of capital.
   b. Leasing provides 100 percent financing.
   c. If the tax advantages of leasing were eliminating, leasing would disappear.

5. **Accounting for Leases**   Discuss the accounting criteria for determining whether a lease must be reported on the balance sheet. In each case, give a rationale for the criterion.

6. **IRS Criteria**   Discuss the IRS criteria for determining whether a lease is tax deductible. In each case give a rationale for the criterion.

7. **Off–Balance Sheet Financing**   What is meant by the term *off–balance sheet financing*? When do leases provide such financing, and what are the accounting and economic conse-quences of such activity?

8. **Sale and Leaseback**   Why might a firm choose to engage in a sale and leaseback transac-tion? Give two reasons.

9. **Leasing Cost**   Explain why the aftertax borrowing rate is the appropriate discount rate to use in lease evaluation.

Refer to the following example for Questions 10–12. In June 2004, Skymark Airlines Co. of Japan announced that it would lease a Boeing B767 from Royal Brunei Airlines beginning in July. The lease of the B767 was necessary because Skymark had an existing lease for a B767 with All Nippon Airways that was set to expire in September.

10.   **Leasing versus Purchase**   Why wouldn't Skymark purchase the plane since it was obviously needed for the company's operations?

11.   **Reasons to Lease**   Why would Royal Brunei Airlines be willing to buy a plane from Boeing and then lease it to Skymark? How is this different from just lending money to Skymark to buy the plane?

12.   **Leasing**   What do you suppose happens to the plane at the end of the lease period?

Questions and Problems

BASIC
(Questions 1–8)

Use the following information to work Problems 1–6. You work for a nuclear research laboratory that is contemplating leasing a diagnostic scanner (leasing is a common practice with expensive, high-tech equipment). The scanner costs €3,000,000, and it would be depreciated straight-line to zero over four years. Because of radiation contamination, it will actually be completely valueless in four years. You can lease it for €895,000 per year for four years.

1.   **Lease or Buy**   Assume that the tax rate is 35 percent. You can borrow at 9 percent before taxes. Should you lease or buy?

2.   **Leasing Cash Flows**   What are the cash flows from the lease from the lessor's viewpoint? Assume a 35 percent tax bracket.

3.   **Finding the Break-Even Payment**   What would the lease payment have to be for both lessor and lessee to be indifferent about the lease?

4.   **Taxes and Leasing Cash Flows**   Assume that your company does not contemplate paying taxes for the next several years. What are the cash flows from leasing in this case?

5.   **Setting the Lease Payment**   In the previous question, over what range of lease payments will the lease be profitable for both parties?

6.   **MACRS Depreciation and Leasing**   Rework Problem 1 assuming that the scanner will be depreciated as three-year property under MACRS (see Chapter 7 for the depreciation allowances).

7.   **Lease or Buy**   Liverpool Autoshop Ltd., is considering buying a machine that costs £350,000. The machine will be depreciated over five years by the straight-line method and will be worthless at that time. The company can lease the machine with year-end payments of £94,200. The company can issue bonds at a 9 percent interest rate. If the corporate tax rate is 35 percent, should the company buy or lease?

8.   **Setting the Lease Payment**   Quartz Corporation is a relatively new firm. Quartz has experienced enough losses during its early years to provide it with at least eight years of tax loss carryforwards. Thus, Quartz's effective tax rate is zero. Quartz plans to lease equipment from New Leasing Company. The term of the lease is five years. The purchase cost of the equipment is $650,000. New Leasing Company is in the 35 percent tax bracket. There are no transaction costs to the lease. Each firm can borrow at 8 percent.
  a.   What is Quartz's reservation price?
  b.   What is New Leasing Company's reservation price?
  c.   Explain why these reservation prices determine the negotiating range of the lease.

INTERMEDIATE
(Questions 9–15)

Use the following information to work Problems 9–11. The Wildcat Oil Company is trying to decide whether to lease or buy a new computer-assisted drilling system for its oil exploration business. Management has decided that it must use the system to stay competitive; it will provide AUD 700,000 in annual pretax cost savings. The system costs AUD 6 million and will be depreciated straight-line to zero over five years. Wildcat's tax rate is 40 percent, and the firm can borrow at 9 percent. Lambert Leasing Company has offered to lease the drilling equipment to Wildcat for payments of AUD 1,400,000 per year. Lambert's policy is to require its lessees to make payments at the start of the year.

9. **Lease or Buy**   What is the NAL for Wildcat? What is the maximum lease payment that would be acceptable to the company?

10. **Leasing and Salvage Value**   Suppose it is estimated that the equipment will have an aftertax residual value of AUD 500,000 at the end of the lease. What is the maximum lease payment acceptable to Wildcat now?

11. **Deposits in Leasing**   Many lessors require a security deposit in the form of a cash payment or other pledged collateral. Suppose Lambert requires Wildcat to pay an AUD 250,000 security deposit at the inception of the lease. If the lease payment is still AUD 1,400,000, is it advantageous for Wildcat to lease the equipment now?

12. **Setting the Lease Price**   Andheri Water Corporation wants to expand its manufacturing facilities. Liberty Leasing Corporation has offered Andheri the opportunity to lease a machine for INR 1,500,000 for six years. The machine will be fully depreciated by the straight-line method. The corporate tax rate for Andheri is 25 percent, whereas Liberty Leasing has a corporate tax rate of 40 percent. Both companies can borrow at 8 percent. Assume lease payments occur at year-end. What is Andheri's reservation price? What is Liberty's reservation price?

13. **Setting the Lease Price**   An asset costs CRC 360,000 and will be depreciated in a straight-line manner over its three-year life. It will have no salvage value. The corporate tax rate is 34 percent, and the appropriate interest rate is 10 percent.
    a. What set of lease payments will make the lessee and the lessor equally well off?
    b. Show the general condition that will make the value of a lease to the lessor the negative of the value to the lessee.
    c. Assume that the lessee pays no taxes and the lessor is in the 34 percent tax bracket. For what range of lease payments does the lease have a positive NPV for both parties?

14. **Lease or Buy**   Wolfson Corporation has decided to purchase a new machine that costs SEK 4.2 million. The machine will be depreciated on a straight-line basis and will be worthless after four years. The corporate tax rate is 35 percent. The Sur Bank has offered Wolfson a four-year loan for SEK 4.2 million. The repayment schedule is four yearly principal repayments of SEK 1.05 million and an interest charge of 9 percent on the outstanding balance of the loan at the beginning of each year. Both principal repayments and interest are due at the end of each year. Cal Leasing Corporation offers to lease the same machine to Wolfson. Lease payments of SEK 1.2 million per year are due at the beginning of each of the four years of the lease.
    a. Should Wolfson lease the machine or buy it with bank financing?
    b. What is the annual lease payment that will make Wolfson indifferent to whether it leases the machine or purchases it?

15. **Automobile Lease Payments**   Automobiles are often leased, and there are several terms unique to auto leases. Suppose you are considering leasing a car. The price you and the dealer agree on for the car is $40,000. This is the base capitalized cost. Other costs added to the capitalized cost price include the acquisition (bank) fee, insurance, or extended warranty. Assume these costs are $450. Capitalization cost reductions include any down payment, credit for trade-in, or dealer rebate. Assume you make a down payment of $2,000, and there is no trade-in or rebate. If you drive 12,000 miles per year, the lease-end residual value for this car will be $20,400 after three years. The lease factor, which is the interest rate on the loan, is the APR of the loan divided by 2,400. (We're not really sure where the 2,400 comes from, either.) The lease factor the dealer quotes you is 0.00385. The monthly lease payment consists of three parts: a depreciation fee, a finance fee, and sales tax. The depreciation fee is the net capitalization cost minus the residual value, divided by the term of the lease. The net capitalization cost is the cost of the car minus any cost reductions plus any additional costs. The finance fee is the net capitalization cost plus the residual, times the money factor, and the monthly sales tax is simply the monthly lease payment times the tax rate. What APR is the dealer quoting you? What is your monthly lease payment for a 36-month lease if the sales tax is 8 percent?

CHALLENGE
(Questions 16–17)

16. **Lease versus Borrow**   Return to the case of the diagnostic scanner discussed in Problems 1 through 6. Suppose the entire €3,000,000 purchase price of the scanner is borrowed. The rate on the loan in 9 percent, and the loan will be repaid in equal installments. Create a lease-versus-buy analysis that explicitly incorporates the loan payments. Show that the NPV of leasing instead of buying is not changed from what it was in Problem 1. Why is this so?

17. **Lease or Buy**   High electricity costs have made Tikka Masala's chicken-plucking machine economically worthless. Only two machines are available to replace it. The International Pluck-ing Machine (IPM) model is available only on a lease basis. The lease payments will be €2,100 for five years, due at the beginning of the year. This machine will save Tikka Masala €6,000 per year through reductions in electricity costs in every year. As an alternative, Tikka Masala can purchase a more energy-efficient machine from Basic Machine Corporation (BMC) for €15,000. This machine will save €9,000 per year in electricity costs. A local bank has offered to finance the machine with a €15,000 loan. The interest rate on the loan will be 10 percent on the remaining balance and five annual principal payments of €3,000. Tikka Masala has a target debt-to-asset ratio of 67 percent. Tikka Masala is in the 34 percent tax bracket. After five years, both machines will be worthless. The machines will be depreciated on a straight-line basis.
   a. Should Tikka Masala lease the IPM machine or purchase the more efficient BMC machine?
   b. Does your answer depend on the form of financing for direct purchase?
   c. How much debt is displaced by this lease?

Appendix 21A   APV Approach to Leasing

To access the appendix for this chapter, please visit **www.mhhe.com/rwj**.

The Decision to Lease or Buy at Warf Computers

Warf Computers has decided to proceed with the manufacture and distribution of the virtual keyboard (VK) the company has developed. To undertake this venture, the company needs to obtain equipment for the production of the microphone for the keyboard. Because of the re-quired sensitivity of the microphone and its small size, the company needs specialized equip-ment for production.

Nick Warf, the company president, has found a vendor for the equipment. Clapton Acous-tical Equipment has offered to sell Warf Computers the necessary equipment at a price of $5 million. Because of the rapid development of new technology, the equipment falls in the three-year MACRS depreciation class. At the end of four years, the market value of the equipment is expected to be $600,000.

Alternatively, the company can lease the equipment from Hendrix Leasing. The lease con-tract calls for four annual payments of $1.3 million due at the beginning of the year. Addition-ally, Warf Computers must make a security deposit of $300,000 that will be returned when the lease expires. Warf Computers can issue bonds with a yield of 11 percent, and the company has a marginal tax rate of 35 percent.

1. Should Warf buy or lease the equipment?
2. Nick mentions to James Hendrix, the president of Hendrix Leasing, that although the company will need the equipment for four years, he would like a lease contract for two years instead. At the end of the two years, the lease could be renewed. Nick would also like to eliminate the security deposit, but he would be willing to increase the lease payments to $2.3 million for each of the two years. When the lease is renewed in two years, Hendrix would consider the increased lease payments in the first two years when

calculating the terms of the renewal. The equipment is expected to have a market value of $2 million in two years. What is the NAL of the lease contract under these terms? Why might Nick prefer this lease? What are the potential ethical issues concerning the new lease terms?

3. In the leasing discussion, James informs Nick that the contract could include a purchase option for the equipment at the end of the lease. Hendrix Leasing offers three purchase options:

   a. An option to purchase the equipment at the fair market value.
   b. An option to purchase the equipment at a fixed price. The price will negotiated before the lease is signed.
   c. An option to purchase the equipment at a price of $250,000.

   How would the inclusion of a purchase option affect the value of the lease?

4. James also informs Nick that the lease contract can include a cancellation option. The cancellation option would allow Warf Computers to cancel the lease on any anniversary date of the contract. In order to cancel the lease, Warf Computers would be required to give 30 days' notice prior to the anniversary date. How would the inclusion of a cancellation option affect the value of the lease?

22 Options and Corporate Finance

On February 21, 2006, the closing stock prices for the Boeing, Dun and Bradstreet, and Caterpillar Companies were $72.96, $72, and $72.05, respectively. Each company had a call option trading on the Chicago Board Options Exchange with a $75 strike price and an expiration date of May 19, 87 days away. You might expect that the prices on these call options would be similar, but they weren't. The Boeing options sold for $0.80; Dun and Bradstreet options traded at $1.60; and Caterpillar options traded at $2.70. Why were these options priced so differently when the underlying stock prices, strike prices, and expiration dates were all essentially the same? A big reason is that the volatility of the underlying stock is an important determinant of an option's underlying value; and, in fact, these three stocks had very different volatilities. In this chapter, we explore this issue—and many others—in much greater depth using the Noble Prize–winning Black–Scholes option pricing model.

22.1 Options

An **option** is a contract giving its owner the right to buy or sell an asset at a fixed price on or before a given date. For example, an option on a building might give the buyer the right to buy the building for $1 million on or anytime before the Saturday prior to the third Wednesday in January 2010. Options are a unique type of financial contract because they give the buyer the right, but not the *obligation*, to do something. The buyer uses the option only if it is advantageous to do so; otherwise the option can be thrown away.

There is a special vocabulary associated with options. Here are some important definitions:

The Options Industry Council has a Web page with lots of educational material at **www.888options.com.**

1. *Exercising the option*: The act of buying or selling the underlying asset via the option contract.
2. *Strike or exercise price*: The fixed price in the option contract at which the holder can buy or sell the underlying asset.
3. *Expiration date*: The maturity date of the option; after this date, the option is dead.
4. *American and European options*: An American option may be exercised anytime up to the expiration date. A European option differs from an American option in that it can be exercised only on the expiration date.

22.2 Call Options

The most common type of option is a **call option**. A call option gives the owner the right to buy an asset at a fixed price during a particular period. There is no restriction on the kind of asset, but the most common ones traded on exchanges are options on stocks and bonds.

For example, call options on IBM stock can be purchased on the Chicago Board Options Exchange. IBM does not issue (that is, sell) call options on its common stock. Instead, individual investors are the original buyers and sellers of call options on IBM common stock. A representative call option on IBM stock enables an investor to buy 100 shares of IBM on or before July 15 at an exercise price of $100. This is a valuable option if there is some probability that the price of IBM common stock will exceed $100 on or before July 15.

The Value of a Call Option at Expiration

What is the value of a call option contract on common stock at expiration? The answer depends on the value of the underlying stock at expiration.

Let's continue with the IBM example. Suppose the stock price is $130 at expiration. The buyer[1] of the call option has the right to buy the underlying stock at the exercise price of $100. In other words, he has the right to exercise the call. Having the right to buy something for $100 when it is worth $130 is obviously a good thing. The value of this right is $30 (= $130 − $100) on the expiration day.[2]

The call would be worth even more if the stock price were higher on expiration day. For example, if IBM were selling for $150 on the date of expiration, the call would be worth $50 (= $150 − $100) at that time. In fact, the call's value increases $1 for every $1 rise in the stock price.

If the stock price is greater than the exercise price, we say that the call is *in the money*. Of course, it is also possible that the value of the common stock will turn out to be less than the exercise price, in which case we say that the call is *out of the money*. The holder will not exercise in this case. For example, if the stock price at the expiration date is $90, no rational investor would exercise. Why pay $100 for stock worth only $90? Because the option holder has no obligation to exercise the call, she can *walk away* from the option. As a consequence, if IBM's stock price is less than $100 on the expiration date, the value of the call option will be $0. In this case, the value of the call option is not the difference between IBM's stock price and $100, as it would be if the holder of the call option had the *obligation* to exercise the call.

Here is the payoff of this call option at expiration:

	Payoff on the Expiration Date	
	If Stock Price Is Less Than $100	**If Stock Price Is Greater Than $100**
Call option value	$0	Stock price − $100

---

[1]We use *buyer*, *owner*, and *holder* interchangeably.

[2]This example assumes that the call lets the holder purchase one share of stock at $100. In reality, one call option contract would let the holder purchase 100 shares. The profit would then equal $3,000 [= ($130 − $100) × 100].

Figure 22.1

The Value of a Call
Option on the
Expiration Date

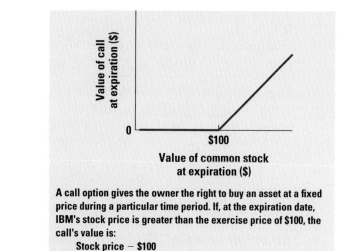

A call option gives the owner the right to buy an asset at a fixed price during a particular time period. If, at the expiration date, IBM's stock price is greater than the exercise price of $100, the call's value is:

Stock price − $100

If IBM's stock price is less than $100 at this time, the value of the call is zero.

Figure 22.1 plots the value of the call at expiration against the value of IBM's stock. This is referred to as the *hockey stick diagram* of call option values. If the stock price is less than $100, the call is out of the money and worthless. If the stock price is greater than $100, the call is in the money and its value rises one-for-one with increases in the stock price. Notice that the call can never have a negative value. It is a *limited liability instrument*, which means that all the holder can lose is the initial amount she paid for it.

EXAMPLE 22.1

Call Option Payoffs   Suppose Mr. Optimist holds a one-year call option on TIX common stock. It is a European call option and can be exercised at $150. Assume that the expiration date has arrived. What is the value of the TIX call option on the expiration date? If TIX is selling for $200 per share, Mr. Optimist can exercise the option—purchase TIX at $150—and then immediately sell the share at $200. Mr. Optimist will have made $50 (= $200 − $150). Thus, the price of this call option must be $50 at expiration.

Instead, assume that TIX is selling for $100 per share on the expiration date. If Mr. Optimist still holds the call option, he will throw it out. The value of the TIX call on the expiration date will be zero in this case.

22.3 Put Options

A **put option** can be viewed as the opposite of a call option. Just as a call gives the holder the right to buy the stock at a fixed price, a put gives the holder the right to *sell* the stock for a fixed exercise price.

The Value of a Put Option at Expiration

The circumstances that determine the value of the put are the opposite of those for a call option because a put option gives the holder the right to sell shares. Let us assume that the exercise price of the put is $50 and the stock price at expiration is $40. The owner of this put option has the right to sell the stock for *more* than it is worth, something that is clearly profitable. That is, he can buy the stock at the market price of $40 and immediately sell it at

Figure 22.2

The Value of a Put Option on the Expiration Date

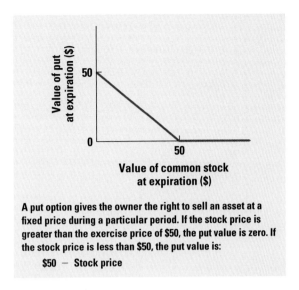

A put option gives the owner the right to sell an asset at a fixed price during a particular period. If the stock price is greater than the exercise price of $50, the put value is zero. If the stock price is less than $50, the put value is:

$50 − Stock price

the exercise price of $50, generating a profit of $10 (= $50 − $40). Thus, the value of the option at expiration must be $10.

The profit would be greater still if the stock price were lower. For example, if the stock price were only $30, the value of the option would be $20 (= $50 − $30). In fact, for every $1 that the stock price declines at expiration, the value of the put rises by $1.

However, suppose that the stock at expiration is trading at $60—or any price above the exercise price of $50. The owner of the put would not want to exercise here. It is a losing proposition to sell stock for $50 when it trades in the open market at $60. Instead, the owner of the put will walk away from the option. That is, he will let the put option expire.

Here is the payoff of this put option:

	Payoff on the Expiration Date	
	If Stock Price Is Less Than $50	If Stock Price Is Greater Than $50
Put option value	$50 − Stock price	$0

Figure 22.2 plots the values of a put option for all possible values of the underlying stock. It is instructive to compare Figure 22.2 with Figure 22.1 for the call option. The call option is valuable when the stock price is above the exercise price, and the put is valuable when the stock price is below the exercise price.

EXAMPLE 22.2

Put Option Payoffs   Ms. Pessimist believes that BMI will fall from its current $160 per-share price. She buys a put. Her put option contract gives her the right to sell a share of BMI stock at $150 one year from now. If the price of BMI is $200 on the expiration date, she will tear up the put option contract because it is worthless. That is, she will not want to sell stock worth $200 for the exercise price of $150.

On the other hand, if BMI is selling for $100 on the expiration date, she will exercise the option. In this case she can buy a share of BMI in the market for $100 per share and turn around and sell the share at the exercise price of $150. Her profit will be $50 (= $150 − $100). The value of the put option on the expiration date therefore will be $50.

22.4 Selling Options

An investor who sells (or *writes*) a call on common stock must deliver shares of the common stock if required to do so by the call option holder. Notice that the seller is *obligated* to do so.

Check out these option
exchanges:
www.cboe.com
www.pacificex.com
www.phlx.com
www.kcbt.com
www.euronext.com

If, at expiration date, the price of the common stock is greater than the exercise price, the holder will exercise the call and the seller must give the holder shares of stock in exchange for the exercise price. The seller loses the difference between the stock price and the exercise price. For example, assume that the stock price is $60 and the exercise price is $50. Knowing that exercise is imminent, the option seller buys stock in the open market at $60. Because she is obligated to sell at $50, she loses $10 (= $50 − $60). Conversely, if at the expiration date the price of the common stock is below the exercise price, the call option will not be exercised and the seller's liability is zero.

Why would the seller of a call place himself in such a precarious position? After all, the seller loses money if the stock price ends up above the exercise price, and he merely avoids losing money if the stock price ends up below the exercise price. The answer is that the seller is paid to take this risk. On the day that the option transaction takes place, the seller receives the price that the buyer pays.

Now let's look at the seller of puts. An investor who sells a put on common stock agrees to purchase shares of common stock if the put holder should so request. The seller loses on this deal if the stock price falls below the exercise price. For example, assume that the stock price is $40 and the exercise price is $50. The holder of the put will exercise in this case. In other words, she will sell the underlying stock at the exercise price of $50. This means that the seller of the put must buy the underlying stock at the exercise price of $50. Because the stock is worth only $40, the loss here is $10 (= $40 − $50).

The values of the "sell-a-call" and "sell-a-put" positions are depicted in Figure 22.3. The graph on the left side of the figure shows that the seller of a call loses nothing when the stock price at expiration date is below $50. However, the seller loses a dollar for every dollar that the stock rises above $50. The graph in the center of the figure shows that the seller of a put loses nothing when the stock price at expiration date is above $50. However, the seller loses a dollar for every dollar that the stock falls below $50.

It is worthwhile to spend a few minutes comparing the graphs in Figure 22.3 to those in Figures 22.1 and 22.2. The graph of selling a call (the graph in the left side of Figure 22.3)

Figure 22.3   **The Payoffs to Sellers of Calls and Puts and to Buyers of Common Stock**

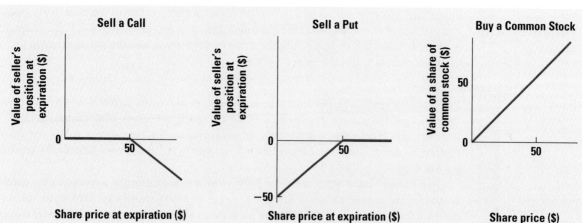

is the mirror image of the graph of buying a call (Figure 22.1).[3] This occurs because options are a zero-sum game. The seller of a call loses what the buyer makes. Similarly, the graph of selling a put (the middle graph in Figure 22.3) is the mirror image of the graph of buying a put (Figure 22.2). Again, the seller of a put loses what the buyer makes.

Figure 22.3 also shows the value at expiration of simply buying common stock. Notice that buying the stock is the same as buying a call option on the stock with an exercise price of zero. This is not surprising. If the exercise price is zero, the call holder can buy the stock for nothing, which is really the same as owning it.

22.5   Option Quotes

For more about option ticker symbols, go to the "Symbol Directory" link under "Trading Tools" at **www.cboe.com.**

Now that we understand the definitions for calls and puts, let's see how these options are quoted. Table 22.1 presents information about Intel Corporation options expiring in July 2006, obtained from finance.yahoo.com. At the time of these quotes, Intel was selling for $20.55.

Table 22.1

Information about the Options of Intel Corporation

View By Expiration: Mar 06 | Apr 06 | **Jul 06** | Jan 07 | Jan 08

CALL OPTIONS					Expire at close Fri, Jul 21, 2006		
Strike	Symbol	Last	Chg	Bid	Ask	Vol	Open Int
15.00	NQGC.X	5.90	0.00	5.80	5.90	63	992
17.50	NQGW.X	3.60	↓0.10	3.50	3.70	410	7,551
20.00	NQGD.X	1.80	↓0.05	1.75	1.85	1,057	30,155
22.50	NQGX.X	0.70	↓0.05	0.70	0.75	401	29,256
25.00	INQGE.X	0.25	↓0.05	0.25	0.30	12	33,431
27.50	INQGY.X	0.15	0.00	0.10	0.15	9	25,027
30.00	INQGF.X	0.05	0.00	0.05	0.10	90	14,076
32.50	INQGZ.X	0.05	0.00	N/A	0.05	34	2,826
35.00	INQGG.X	0.05	0.00	N/A	0.05	3	299

PUT OPTIONS					Expire at close Fri, Jul 21, 2006		
Strike	Symbol	Last	Chg	Bid	Ask	Vol	Open Int
15.00	NQSC.X	0.10	0.00	0.05	0.10	16	514
17.50	NQSW.X	0.30	↑0.05	0.25	0.30	132	5,182
20.00	NQSD.X	0.95	↑0.05	0.95	1.00	1,688	28,906
22.50	NQSX.X	2.40	↑0.05	2.35	2.45	904	22,474
25.00	INQSE.X	4.50	↑0.10	4.40	4.60	75	16,658
27.50	INQSY.X	6.10	0.00	6.90	7.00	10	7,003
30.00	INQSF.X	9.20	0.00	9.40	9.50	32	234
32.50	INQSZ.X	11.20	0.00	11.90	12.00	102	59

---

[3]Actually, because of differing exercise prices, the two graphs are not quite mirror images of each other. The exercise price in Figure 22.1 is $100, and the exercise price in Figure 22.3 is $50.

On the left in the table are the available strike prices. On the top are call option quotes; put option quotes are on the bottom. The second column contains ticker symbols, which uniquely indicate the underlying stock; the type of option; the expiration month; and the strike price. Next, we have the most recent prices on the options ("Last") and the change from the previous day ("Change"). Bid and ask prices follow. Note that option prices are quoted on a per-option basis, but trading actually occurs in standardized contracts, where each contract calls for the purchase (for calls) or sale (for puts) of 100 shares. Thus, the call option with a strike price of $25 last traded at $.25 per option, or $25 per contract. The final two columns contain volume, quoted in contracts, and the open interest ("Open Int"), which is the number of contracts currently outstanding.

22.6   Combinations of Options

For information about options and the underlying companies, see **www. optionsnewsletter.com.**

Puts and calls can serve as building blocks for more complex option contracts. For example, Figure 22.4 illustrates the payoff from buying a put option on a stock and simultaneously buying the stock.

If the share price is greater than the exercise price, the put option is worthless, and the value of the combined position is equal to the value of the common stock. If instead the exercise price is greater than the share price, the decline in the value of the shares will be exactly offset by the rise in the value of the put.

The strategy of buying a put and buying the underlying stock is called a *protective* put. It is as if we are buying insurance for the stock. The stock can always be sold at the exercise price, regardless of how far the market price of the stock falls.

Note that the combination of buying a put and buying the underlying stock has the same *shape* in Figure 22.4 as the call purchase in Figure 22.1. To pursue this point, let's consider the graph for buying a call, which is shown at the far left of Figure 22.5. This graph is the same as Figure 22.1, except that the exercise price is $50 here. Now, let's try the strategy of:

(Leg *A*) Buying a call.

(Leg *B*) Buying a risk-free, zero coupon bond (i.e., a T-bill) with a face value of $50 that matures on the same day that the option expires.

We have drawn the graph of leg *A* of this strategy at the far left of Figure 22.5, but what does the graph of leg *B* look like? It looks like the middle graph of the figure. That is, anyone buying this zero coupon bond will be guaranteed to receive $50, regardless of the price of the stock at expiration.

Figure 22.4   **Payoff to the Combination of Buying a Put and Buying the Underlying Stock**

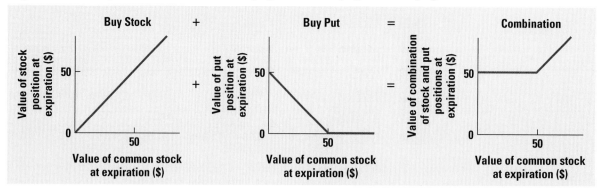

Figure 22.5 Payoff to the Combination of Buying a Call and Buying a Zero Coupon Bond

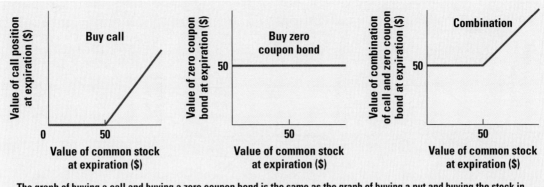

The graph of buying a call and buying a zero coupon bond is the same as the graph of buying a put and buying the stock in Figure 22.4.

What does the graph of *simultaneously* buying both leg *A* and leg *B* of this strategy look like? It looks like the far right graph of Figure 22.5. That is, the investor receives a guaranteed $50 from the bond, regardless of what happens to the stock. In addition, the investor receives a payoff from the call of $1 for every $1 that the price of the stock rises above the exercise price of $50.

The far right graph of Figure 22.5 looks *exactly* like the far right graph of Figure 22.4. Thus, an investor gets the same payoff from the strategy of Figure 22.4 and the strategy of Figure 22.5, regardless of what happens to the price of the underlying stock. In other words, the investor gets the same payoff from:

1. Buying a put and buying the underlying stock.

2. Buying a call and buying a risk-free, zero coupon bond.

If investors have the same payoffs from the two strategies, the two strategies must have the same cost. Otherwise, all investors will choose the strategy with the lower cost and avoid the strategy with the higher cost. This leads to the following interesting result:

$$\begin{matrix} \text{Price of underlying} \\ \text{stock} \end{matrix} + \begin{matrix} \text{Price of} \\ \text{put} \end{matrix} = \begin{matrix} \text{Price of} \\ \text{call} \end{matrix} + \begin{matrix} \text{Present value of} \\ \text{exercise price} \end{matrix} \qquad \textbf{(22.1)}$$

$$\text{Cost of first strategy} = \text{Cost of second strategy}$$

This relationship is known as **put–call parity** and is one of the most fundamental relationships concerning options. It says that there are two ways of buying a protective put. You can buy a put and buy the underlying stock simultaneously. Here, your total cost is the price of the underlying stock plus the price of the put. Or you can buy the call and buy a zero coupon bond. Here, your total cost is the price of the call plus the price of the zero coupon bond. The price of the zero coupon bond is equal to the present value of the exercise price—that is, the present value of $50 in our example.

Equation (22.1) is a very precise relationship. It holds only if the put and the call have both the same exercise price and the same expiration date. In addition, the maturity date of the zero coupon bond must be the same as the expiration date of the options.

To see how fundamental put–call parity is, let's rearrange the formula, yielding:

$$\begin{matrix} \text{Price of underlying} \\ \text{stock} \end{matrix} = \begin{matrix} \text{Price of} \\ \text{call} \end{matrix} - \begin{matrix} \text{Price of} \\ \text{put} \end{matrix} + \begin{matrix} \text{Present value of} \\ \text{exercise price} \end{matrix}$$

Figure 22.6   **Payoff to the Combination of Buying a Stock and Selling a Call**

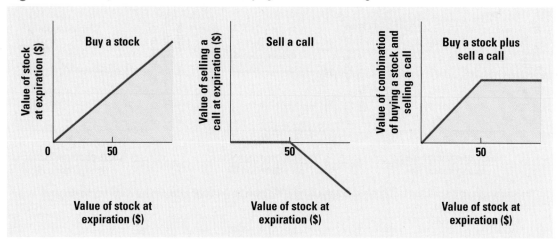

This relationship now states that you can replicate the purchase of a share of stock by buying a call, selling a put, and buying a zero coupon bond. (Note that because a minus sign comes before "Price of put," the put is sold, not bought.) Investors in this three-legged strategy are said to have purchased a *synthetic* stock.

Let's do one more transformation:

Covered Call Strategy

$$\text{Price of underlying stock} - \text{Price of call} = \frac{-\text{Price}}{\text{of put}} + \text{Present value of exercise price}$$

Many investors like to buy a stock and write the call on the stock simultaneously. This is a conservative strategy known as *selling a covered call*. The preceding put–call parity relationship tells us that this strategy is equivalent to selling a put and buying a zero coupon bond. Figure 22.6 develops the graph for the covered call. You can verify that the covered call can be replicated by selling a put and simultaneously buying a zero coupon bond.

Of course, there are other ways of rearranging the basic put–call relationship. For each rearrangement, the strategy on the left side is equivalent to the strategy on the right side. The beauty of put–call parity is that it shows how any strategy in options can be achieved in two different ways.

To test your understanding of put–call parity, suppose shares of stock in Joseph–Belmont, Inc., are selling for $80. A three-month call option with an $85 strike price goes for $6. The risk-free rate is .5 percent per month. What's the value of a three-month put option with an $85 strike price?

We can rearrange the put–call parity relationship to solve for the price of the put as follows:

$$\text{Price of put} = \frac{-\text{Price of underlying stock}}{} + \text{Price of call} + \text{Present value of strike price}$$

$$= -\$80 + \$6 + \$85/1.005^3$$

$$= \$9.74$$

As shown, the value of the put is $9.74.

EXAMPLE 22.3

A Synthetic T-Bill Suppose shares of stock in Smolira Corp. are selling for $110. A call option on Smolira with one year to maturity and a $110 strike price sells for $15. A put with the same terms sells for $5. What's the risk-free rate?

To answer, we need to use put–call parity to determine the price of a risk-free, zero coupon bond:

Price of underlying stock + Price of put − Price of call = Present value of exercise price

Plugging in the numbers, we get:

$$\$110 + \$5 - \$15 = \$100$$

Because the present value of the $110 strike price is $100, the implied risk-free rate is 10 percent.

22.7 Valuing Options

In the last section we determined what options are worth on the expiration date. Now we wish to determine the value of options when you buy them well before expiration.[4] We begin by considering the lower and upper bounds on the value of a call.

Bounding the Value of a Call

Lower Bound Consider an American call that is in the money prior to expiration. For example, assume that the stock price is $60 and the exercise price is $50. In this case, the option cannot sell below $10. To see this, note the following simple strategy if the option sells at, say, $9:

Date		Transaction	
Today	(1)	Buy call.	−$ 9
Today	(2)	Exercise call—that is, buy underlying stock at exercise price.	−$50
Today	(3)	Sell stock at current market price.	+$60
Arbitrage profit			+$ 1

The type of profit that is described in this transaction is an *arbitrage* profit. Arbitrage profits come from transactions that have no risk or cost and cannot occur regularly in normal, well-functioning financial markets. The excess demand for these options would quickly force the option price up to at least $10 (= $60 − $50).

Of course, the price of the option is likely to be above $10. Investors will rationally pay more than $10 because of the possibility that the stock will rise above $60 before expiration. For example, suppose the call actually sells for $12. In this case, we say that the *intrinsic value* of the option is $10, meaning it must always be worth at least this much. The remaining $12 − $10 = $2 is sometimes called the *time premium*, and it represents the extra amount that investors are willing to pay because of the possibility that the stock price will rise before the option expires.

---

[4]Our discussion in this section is of American options because they are more commonly traded in the real world. As necessary, we will indicate differences for European options.

Figure 22.7

The Upper and
Lower Boundaries
of Call Option
Values

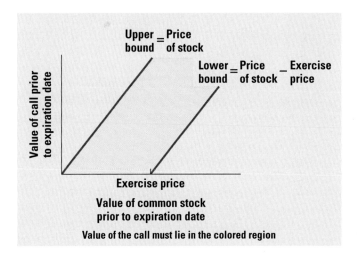

The Factors Determining Call Option Values

Upper Bound   Is there an upper boundary for the option price as well? It turns out that the upper boundary is the price of the underlying stock. That is, an option to buy common stock cannot have a greater value than the common stock itself. A call option can be used to buy common stock with a payment of the exercise price. It would be foolish to buy stock this way if the stock could be purchased directly at a lower price. The upper and lower bounds are represented in Figure 22.7.

The Factors Determining Call Option Values

The previous discussion indicated that the price of a call option must fall somewhere in the shaded region of Figure 22.7. We now will determine more precisely where in the shaded region it should be. The factors that determine a call's value can be broken into two sets. The first set contains the features of the option contract. The two basic contractual features are the exercise price and the expiration date. The second set of factors affecting the call price concerns characteristics of the stock and the market.

Exercise Price   An increase in the exercise price reduces the value of the call. For example, imagine that there are two calls on a stock selling at $60. The first call has an exercise price of $50 and the second one has an exercise price of $40. Which call would you rather have? Clearly, you would rather have the call with an exercise price of $40 because that one is $20 (= $60 − $40) in the money. In other words, the call with an exercise price of $40 should sell for more than an otherwise identical call with an exercise price of $50.

Expiration Date   The value of an American call option must be at least as great as the value of an otherwise identical option with a shorter term to expiration. Consider two American calls: One has a maturity of nine months and the other expires in six months. Obviously, the nine-month call has the same rights as the six-month call, and it also has an additional three months within which these rights can be exercised. It cannot be worth less and will generally be more valuable.[5]

---

[5]This relationship need not hold for a European call option. Consider a firm with two otherwise identical European call options, one expiring at the end of May and the other expiring a few months later. Further assume that a *huge* dividend is paid in early June. If the first call is exercised at the end of May, its holder will receive the underlying stock. If he does not sell the stock, he will receive the large dividend shortly thereafter. However, the holder of the second call will receive the stock through exercise after the dividend is paid. Because the market knows that the holder of this option will miss the dividend, the value of the second call option could be less than the value of the first.

Figure 22.8

Value of an American Call as a Function of Stock Price

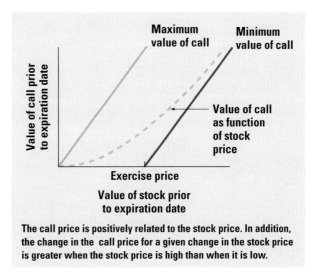

The call price is positively related to the stock price. In addition, the change in the call price for a given change in the stock price is greater when the stock price is high than when it is low.

The Philadelphia Stock Exchange has a good discussion of options at **www.phlx.com/ products.**

Stock Price   Other things being equal, the higher the stock price, the more valuable the call option will be. For example, if a stock is worth $80, a call with an exercise price of $100 isn't worth very much. If the stock soars to $120, the call becomes much more valuable.

Now consider Figure 22.8, which shows the relationship between the call price and the stock price prior to expiration. The curve indicates that the call price increases as the stock price increases. Furthermore, it can be shown that the relationship is represented not by a straight line, but by a *convex* curve. That is, the increase in the call price for a given change in the stock price is greater when the stock price is high than when the stock price is low.

There are two special points on the curve in Figure 22.8:

1. *The stock is worthless.* The call must be worthless if the underlying stock is worthless. That is, if the stock has no chance of attaining any value, it is not worthwhile to pay the exercise price to obtain the stock.

2. *The stock price is very high relative to the exercise price.* In this situation, the owner of the call knows that she will end up exercising the call. She can view herself as the owner of the stock now, with one difference: She must pay the exercise price at expiration.

Thus, the value of her position—that is, the value of the call—is:

$$\text{Stock price} - \text{Present value of exercise price}$$

These two points on the curve are summarized in the bottom half of Table 22.2.

The Key Factor: The Variability of the Underlying Asset   The greater the variability of the underlying asset, the more valuable the call option will be. Consider the following example. Suppose that just before the call expires, the stock price will be either $100 with probability .5 or $80 with probability .5. What will be the value of a call with an exercise price of $110? Clearly, it will be worthless because no matter what happens to the stock, its price will always be below the exercise price.

What happens if the stock is more variable? Suppose we add $20 to the best case and take $20 away from the worst case. Now the stock has a one-half chance of being worth $60 and a one-half chance of being worth $120. We have spread the stock returns, but of course the expected value of the stock has stayed the same:

For an option-oriented site focusing on volatilities, visit **www.ivolatility.com.**

$$(1/2 \times \$80) + (1/2 \times \$100) = \$90 = (1/2 \times \$60) + (1/2 \times \$120)$$

Table 22.2

Factors Affecting American Option Values

Increase in	Call Option*	Put Option*
Value of underlying asset (stock price)	+	−
Exercise price	−	+
Stock volatility	+	+
Interest rate	+	−
Time to expiration	+	+

In addition to the preceding, we have presented the following four relationships for American calls:

1. The call price can never be greater than the stock price (*upper bound*).
2. The call price can never be less than either zero or the difference between the stock price and the exercise price (*lower bound*).
3. The call is worth zero if the stock is worth zero.
4. When the stock price is much greater than the exercise price, the call price tends toward the difference between the stock price and the present value of the exercise price.

*The signs (+, −) indicate the effect of the variables on the value of the option. For example, the two +s for stock volatility indicate that an increase in volatility will increase both the value of a call and the value of a put.

Notice that the call option has value now because there is a one-half chance that the stock price will be $120, or $10 above the exercise price of $110. This illustrates an important point. There is a fundamental distinction between holding an option on an underlying asset and holding the underlying asset. If investors in the marketplace are risk-averse, a rise in the variability of the stock will decrease its market value. However, the holder of a call receives payoffs from the positive tail of the probability distribution. As a consequence, a rise in the variability in the underlying stock increases the market value of the call.

This result can also be seen from Figure 22.9. Consider two stocks, *A* and *B*, each of which is normally distributed. For each security, the figure illustrates the probability of different stock prices on the expiration date. As can be seen from the figures, stock *B* has more volatility than does stock *A*. This means that stock *B* has a higher probability of both

Figure 22.9

Distribution of Common Stock Price at Expiration for Both Security *A* and Security *B*. Options on the Two Securities Have the Same Exercise Price.

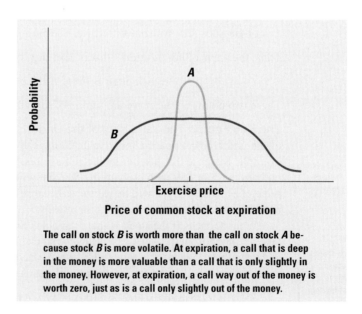

The call on stock *B* is worth more than the call on stock *A* because stock *B* is more volatile. At expiration, a call that is deep in the money is more valuable than a call that is only slightly in the money. However, at expiration, a call way out of the money is worth zero, just as is a call only slightly out of the money.

abnormally high returns and abnormally low returns. Let us assume that options on each of the two securities have the same exercise price. To option holders, a return much below average on stock *B* is no worse than a return only moderately below average on stock *A*. In either situation, the option expires out of the money. However, to option holders, a return much above average on stock *B* is better than a return only moderately above average on stock *A*. Because a call's price at the expiration date is the difference between the stock price and the exercise price, the value of the call on *B* at expiration will be higher in this case.

The Interest Rate   Call prices are also a function of the level of interest rates. Buyers of calls do not pay the exercise price until they exercise the option, if they do so at all. The ability to delay payment is more valuable when interest rates are high and less valuable when interest rates are low. Thus, the value of a call is positively related to interest rates.

A Quick Discussion of Factors Determining Put Option Values

Given our extended discussion of the factors influencing a call's value, we can examine the effect of these factors on puts very easily. Table 22.2 summarizes the five factors influencing the prices of both American calls and American puts. The effect of three factors on puts are the opposite of the effect of these three factors on calls:

1. The put's market value *decreases* as the stock price increases because puts are in the money when the stock sells below the exercise price.

2. The value of a put with a high exercise price is *greater* than the value of an otherwise identical put with a low exercise price for the reason given in (1).

3. A high interest rate *adversely* affects the value of a put. The ability to sell a stock at a fixed exercise price sometime in the future is worth less if the present value of the exercise price is reduced by a high interest rate.

The effect of the other two factors on puts is the same as the effect of these factors on calls:

4. The value of an American put with a distant expiration date is greater than an otherwise identical put with an earlier expiration.[6] The longer time to maturity gives the put holder more flexibility, just as it did in the case of a call.

5. Volatility of the underlying stock increases the value of the put. The reasoning is analogous to that for a call. At expiration, a put that is way in the money is more valuable than a put only slightly in the money. However, at expiration, a put way out of the money is worth zero, just as is a put only slightly out of the money.

22.8   An Option Pricing Formula

We have explained *qualitatively* that the value of a call option is a function of five variables:

1. The current price of the underlying asset, which for stock options is the price of a share of common stock.

2. The exercise price.

3. The time to expiration date.

4. The variance of the underlying asset.

5. The risk-free interest rate.

---

[6]Though this result must hold in the case of an American put, it need not hold for a European put.

It is time to replace the qualitative model with a precise option valuation model. The model we choose is the famous Black–Scholes option pricing model. You can put numbers into the Black–Scholes model and get values back.

The Black–Scholes model is represented by a rather imposing formula. A derivation of the formula is simply not possible in this textbook, as many students will be happy to learn. However, some appreciation for the achievement as well as some intuitive understanding is in order.

In the early chapters of this book, we showed how to discount capital budgeting projects using the net present value formula. We also used this approach to value stocks and bonds. Why, students sometimes ask, can't the same NPV formula be used to value puts and calls? This is a good question: The earliest attempts at valuing options used NPV. Unfortunately the attempts were not successful because no one could determine the appropriate discount rate. An option is generally riskier than the underlying stock, but no one knew exactly how much riskier.

Black and Scholes attacked the problem by pointing out that a strategy of borrowing to finance a stock purchase duplicates the risk of a call. Then, knowing the price of a stock already, we can determine the price of a call such that its return is identical to that of the stock-with-borrowing alternative.

We illustrate the intuition behind the Black–Scholes approach by considering a simple example where a combination of a call and a stock eliminates all risk. This example works because we let the future stock price be one of only *two* values. Hence, the example is called a *two-state* or *binomial option model*. By eliminating the possibility that the stock price can take on other values, we are able to duplicate the call exactly.

A Two-State Option Model

Consider the following example. Suppose the current market price of a stock is $50 and the stock will either be $60 or $40 at the end of the year. Further, imagine a call option on this stock with a one-year expiration date and a $50 exercise price. Investors can borrow at 10 percent. Our goal is to determine the value of the call.

To value the call correctly, we need to examine two strategies. The first is to simply buy the call. The second is to:

1. Buy one-half a share of stock.
2. Borrow $18.18, implying a payment of principal and interest at the end of the year of $20 ($= \$18.18 \times 1.10$).

As you will see shortly, the cash flows from the second strategy match the cash flows from buying a call. (A little later, we will show how we came up with the exact fraction of a share of stock to buy and the exact borrowing amount.) Because the cash flows match, we say that we are *duplicating* the call with the second strategy.

At the end of the year, the future payoffs are set out as follows:

	Future Payoffs	
Initial Transactions	**If Stock Price Is $60**	**If Stock Price Is $40**
1. Buy a call	$60 − $50 = $10	$ 0
2. Buy $\frac{1}{2}$ share of stock	$\frac{1}{2} \times \$60 =$ $30	$\frac{1}{2} \times \$40 = \$20$
Borrow $18.18 at 10%	−($18.18 × 1.10) = −$20	−$20
Total from stock and borrowing strategy	$20	$ 0

Note that the future payoff structure of the "buy-a-call" strategy is duplicated by the strategy of "buy stock and borrow." That is, under either strategy an investor would end up with $10 if the stock price rose and $0 if the stock price fell. Thus these two strategies are equivalent as far as traders are concerned.

If two strategies always have the same cash flows at the end of the year, how must their initial costs be related? The two strategies must have the *same* initial cost. Otherwise, there will be an arbitrage possibility. We can easily calculate this cost for our strategy of buying stock and borrowing:

$$
\begin{array}{lll}
\text{Buy } \tfrac{1}{2} \text{ share of stock} & \tfrac{1}{2} \times \$50 = & \$25.00 \\
\text{Borrow } \$18.18 & & -\$18.18 \\
\hline
& & \$ \ 6.82
\end{array}
$$

Because the call option provides the same payoffs at expiration as does the strategy of buying stock and borrowing, the call must be priced at $6.82. This is the value of the call option in a market without arbitrage profits.

We left two issues unexplained in the preceding example.

Determining the Delta   How did we know to buy one-half share of stock in the duplicating strategy? Actually, the answer is easier than it might at first appear. The call price at the end of the year will be either $10 or $0, whereas the stock price will be either $60 or $40. Thus, the call price has a potential swing of $10 (= $10 − $0) next period, whereas the stock price has a potential swing of $20 (= $60 − $40). We can write this in terms of the following ratio:

$$
\text{Delta} = \frac{\text{Swing of call}}{\text{Swing of stock}} = \frac{\$10 - \$0}{\$60 - \$40} = \frac{1}{2}
$$

As indicated, this ratio is called the *delta* of the call. In words, a $1 swing in the price of the stock gives rise to a $1/2 swing in the price of the call. Because we are trying to duplicate the call with the stock, it seems sensible to buy one-half share of stock instead of buying one call. In other words, the risk of buying one-half share of stock should be the same as the risk of buying one call.

Determining the Amount of Borrowing   How did we know how much to borrow? Buying one-half share of stock brings us either $30 or $20 at expiration, which is exactly $20 more than the payoffs of $10 and $0, respectively, from the call. To duplicate the call through a purchase of stock, we should also borrow enough money so that we have to pay back exactly $20 of interest and principal. This amount of borrowing is merely the present value of $20, which is $18.18 (= $20/1.10).

Now that we know how to determine both the delta and the borrowing, we can write the value of the call as follows:

$$
\text{Value of call} = \text{Stock price} \times \text{Delta} - \text{Amount borrowed} \qquad \textbf{(22.2)}
$$
$$
\$6.82 \quad = \quad \$50 \quad \times \quad \tfrac{1}{2} \quad - \quad \$18.18
$$

We will find this intuition useful in explaining the Black–Scholes model.

Risk-Neutral Valuation   Before leaving this simple example, we should comment on a remarkable feature. We found the exact value of the option without even knowing the probability that the stock would go up or down! If an optimist thought the probability of an up move was high and a pessimist thought it was low, they would still agree on the option value. How can that be? The answer is that the current $50 stock price already balances the views of the optimists and the pessimists. The option reflects that balance because its value depends on the stock price.

This insight provides us with another approach to valuing the call. If we don't need the probabilities of the two states to value the call, perhaps we can select *any* probabilities we want and still come up with the right answer. Suppose we selected probabilities such that the return on the stock is equal to the risk-free rate of 10 percent. We know that the stock return given a rise is 20 percent (= $60/$50 − 1) and the stock return given a fall is −20 percent (= $40/$50 − 1). Thus, we can solve for the probability of a rise necessary to achieve an expected return of 10 percent as follows:

$$10\% = \text{Probability of a rise} \times 20\% + (1 - \text{Probability of rise}) \times -20\%$$

Solving this formula, we find that the probability of a rise is 3/4 and the probability of a fall is 1/4. If we apply these probabilities to the call, we can value it as:

$$\text{Value of call} = \frac{\frac{3}{4} \times \$10 + \frac{1}{4} \times \$0}{1.10} = \$6.82$$

the same value we got from the duplicating approach.

Why did we select probabilities such that the expected return on the stock is 10 percent? We wanted to work with the special case where investors are *risk-neutral*. This case occurs when the expected return on *any* asset (including both the stock and the call) is equal to the risk-free rate. In other words, this case occurs when investors demand no additional compensation beyond the risk-free rate, regardless of the risk of the asset in question.

What would have happened if we had assumed that the expected return on a stock was greater than the risk-free rate? The value of the call would still be $6.82. However, the calculations would be difficult. For example, if we assumed that the expected return on the stock was, say 11 percent, we would have had to derive the expected return on the call. Although the expected return on the call would be higher than 11 percent, it would take a lot of work to determine the expected return precisely. Why do any more work than you have to? Because we can't think of any good reason, we (and most other financial economists) choose to assume risk neutrality.

Thus, the preceding material allows us to value a call in the following two ways:

1. Determine the cost of a strategy duplicating the call. This strategy involves an investment in a fractional share of stock financed by partial borrowing.

2. Calculate the probabilities of a rise and a fall under the assumption of risk neutrality. Use these probabilities, in conjunction with the risk-free rate, to discount the payoffs of the call at expiration.

The Black–Scholes Model

There's a Black–Scholes calculator (and a lot more) at **www.numa.com.**

The preceding example illustrates the duplicating strategy. Unfortunately, a strategy such as this will not work in the real world over, say, a one-year time frame because there are many more than two possibilities for next year's stock price. However, the number of possibilities is reduced as the period is shortened. Is there a time period over which the stock price can only have two outcomes? Academics argue that the assumption that there are only two possibilities for the stock price over the next infinitesimal instant is quite plausible.[7]

In our opinion, the fundamental insight of Black and Scholes is to shorten the time period. They show that a specific combination of stock and borrowing can indeed duplicate a call over an infinitesimal time horizon. Because the price of the stock will change over

---

[7]A full treatment of this assumption can be found in John C. Hull, *Options, Futures and Other Derivatives*, 6th ed. (Upper Saddle River, N J: Prentice Hall, 2005).

the first instant, another combination of stock and borrowing is needed to duplicate the call over the second instant and so on. By adjusting the combination from moment to moment, they can continually duplicate the call. It may boggle the mind that a formula can (1) determine the duplicating combination at any moment and (2) value the option based on this duplicating strategy. Suffice it to say that their dynamic strategy allows them to value a call in the real world, just as we showed how to value the call in the two-state model.

This is the basic intuition behind the Black–Scholes (BS) model. Because the actual derivation of their formula is, alas, far beyond the scope of this text, we simply present the formula itself:

Black–Scholes Model

$$C = SN(d_1) - Ee^{-Rt} N(d_2)$$

where

$$d_1 = [\ln(S/E) + (R + \sigma^2/2)t]/\sqrt{\sigma^2 t}$$
$$d_2 = d_1 - \sqrt{\sigma^2 t}$$

This formula for the value of a call, C, is one of the most complex in finance. However, it involves only five parameters:

1. S = Current stock price.
2. E = Exercise price of call.
3. R = Annual risk-free rate of return, continuously compounded.
4. σ^2 = Variance (per year) of the continuous return on the stock.
5. t = Time (in years) to expiration date.

In addition, there is this statistical concept:

$$N(d) = \text{Probability that a standardized, normally distributed,}$$
$$\text{random variable will be less than or equal to } d.$$

Rather than discuss the formula in its algebraic state, we illustrate the formula with an example.

EXAMPLE 22.4

Black–Scholes   Consider Private Equipment Company (PEC). On October 4 of year 0, the PEC April 49 call option had a closing value of $4. The stock itself was selling at $50. On October 4, the option had 199 days to expiration (maturity date = April 21, year 1). The annual risk-free interest rate, continuously compounded, was 7 percent.

This information determines three variables directly:

1. The stock price, S, is $50.
2. The exercise price, E, is $49.
3. The risk-free rate, R, is .07.

In addition, the time to maturity, t, can be calculated quickly: The formula calls for t to be expressed in *years*.

4. We express the 199-day interval in years as $t = 199/365$.

In the real world, an option trader would know S and E exactly. Traders generally view U.S. Treasury bills as riskless, so a current quote from *The Wall Street Journal* or a similar source would be obtained for the interest rate. The trader would also know (or could count) the number of days to expiration exactly. Thus, the fraction of a year to expiration, t, could be calculated quickly.

(continued)

The problem comes in determining the variance of the stock's return. The formula calls for the variance between the purchase date of October 4 and the expiration date. Unfortunately, this represents the future, so the correct value for variance is not available. Instead, traders frequently estimate variance from past data, just as we calculated variance in an earlier chapter. In addition, some traders may use intuition to adjust their estimate. For example, if anticipation of an upcoming event is likely to increase the volatility of the stock, the trader might adjust her estimate of variance upward to reflect this. (This problem was most severe right after the October 19, 1987, crash. The stock market was quite risky in the aftermath, so estimates using precrash data were too low.)

The preceding discussion was intended merely to mention the difficulties in variance estimation, not to present a solution. For our purposes, we assume that a trader has come up with an estimate of variance:

5. The variance of Private Equipment Co. has been estimated to be .09 per year.

Using these five parameters, we calculate the Black–Scholes value of the PEC option in three steps:

Step 1: *Calculate d_1 and d_2*. These values can be determined by a straightforward, albeit tedious, insertion of our parameters into the basic formula. We have

$$d_1 = \left[\ln\left(\frac{S}{E}\right) + (R + \sigma^2/2)t \right] \Big/ \sqrt{\sigma^2 t}$$

$$= \left[\ln\left(\frac{50}{49}\right) + (.07 + .09/2) \times \frac{199}{365} \right] \Big/ \sqrt{.09 \times \frac{199}{365}}$$

$$= [.0202 + .0627]/.2215 = .3742$$

$$d_2 = d_1 - \sqrt{\sigma^2 t}$$

$$= .1527$$

Step 2: *Calculate $N(d_1)$ and $N(d_2)$*. We can best understand the values $N(d_1)$ and $N(d_2)$ by examining Figure 22.10. The figure shows the normal distribution with an expected value of 0 and a standard deviation of 1. This is frequently called the **standardized normal distribution**. We mentioned in an earlier chapter that the probability that a drawing from this distribution will be between −1 and +1 (within one standard deviation of its mean, in other words) is 68.26 percent.

Now let us ask a different question: What is the probability that a drawing from the standardized normal distribution will be *below* a particular value? For example, the probability that a drawing will be below 0 is clearly 50 percent because the normal distribution is symmetric. Using statistical

Figure 22.10   **Graph of Cumulative Probability**

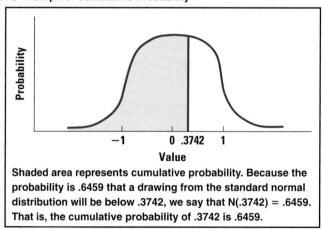

Shaded area represents cumulative probability. Because the probability is .6459 that a drawing from the standard normal distribution will be below .3742, we say that N(.3742) = .6459. That is, the cumulative probability of .3742 is .6459.

(continued)

terminology, we say that the **cumulative probability** of 0 is 50 percent. Statisticians also say that $N(0) = 50\%$. It turns out that:

$$N(d_1) = N(.3742) = .6459$$
$$N(d_2) = N(.1527) = .5607$$

The first value means that there is a 64.59 percent probability that a drawing from the standardized normal distribution will be below .3742. The second value means that there is a 56.07 percent probability that a drawing from the standardized normal distribution will be below .1527. More generally, $N(d)$ is the probability that a drawing from the standardized normal distribution will be below d. In other words, $N(d)$ is the cumulative probability of d. Note that d_1 and d_2 in our example are slightly above zero, so $N(d_1)$ and $N(d_2)$ are slightly greater than .50.

Perhaps the easiest way to determine $N(d_1)$ and $N(d_2)$ is from the EXCEL function NORMSDIST. In our example, NORMSDIST(.3742) and NORMSDIST(.1527) are .6459 and .5607, respectively.

We can also determine the cumulative probability from Table 22.3. For example, consider $d = .37$. This can be found in the table as .3 on the vertical and .07 on the horizontal. The value in the table for

Table 22.3 **Cumulative Probabilities of the Standard Normal Distribution Function**

d	.00	.01	.02	.03	.04	.05	.06	.07	.08	.09
.0	.0000	.0040	.0080	.0120	.0160	.0199	.0239	.0279	.0319	.0359
.1	.0398	.0438	.0478	.0517	.0557	.0596	.0636	.0675	.0714	.0753
.2	.0793	.0832	.0871	.0910	.0948	.0987	.1026	.1064	.1103	.1141
.3	.1179	.1217	.1255	.1293	.1331	.1368	.1406	.1443	.1480	.1517
.4	.1554	.1591	.1628	.1664	.1700	.1736	.1772	.1808	.1844	.1879
.5	.1915	.1950	.1985	.2019	.2054	.2088	.2123	.2157	.2190	.2224
.6	.2257	.2291	.2324	.2357	.2389	.2422	.2454	.2486	.2517	.2549
.7	.2580	.2611	.2642	.2673	.2704	.2734	.2764	.2794	.2823	.2852
.8	.2881	.2910	.2939	.2967	.2995	.3023	.3051	.3078	.3106	.3133
.9	.3159	.3186	.3212	.3238	.3264	.3289	.3315	.3340	.3365	.3389
1.0	.3413	.3438	.3461	.3485	.3508	.3531	.3554	.3577	.3599	.3621
1.1	.3643	.3665	.3686	.3708	.3729	.3749	.3770	.3790	.3810	.3830
1.2	.3849	.3869	.3888	.3907	.3925	.3944	.3962	.3980	.3997	.4015
1.3	.4032	.4049	.4066	.4082	.4099	.4115	.4131	.4147	.4162	.4177
1.4	.4192	.4207	.4222	.4236	.4251	.4265	.4279	.4292	.4306	.4319
1.5	.4332	.4345	.4357	.4370	.4382	.4394	.4406	.4418	.4429	.4441
1.6	.4452	.4463	.4474	.4484	.4495	.4505	.4515	.4525	.4535	.4545
1.7	.4554	.4564	.4573	.4582	.4591	.4599	.4608	.4616	.4625	.4633
1.8	.4641	.4649	.4656	.4664	.4671	.4678	.4686	.4693	.4699	.4706
1.9	.4713	.4719	.4726	.4732	.4738	.4744	.4750	.4756	.4761	.4767
2.0	.4773	.4778	.4783	.4788	.4793	.4798	.4803	.4808	.4812	.4817
2.1	.4821	.4826	.4830	.4834	.4838	.4842	.4846	.4850	.4854	.4857
2.2	.4861	.4866	.4868	.4871	.4875	.4878	.4881	.4884	.4887	.4890
2.3	.4893	.4896	.4898	.4901	.4904	.4906	.4909	.4911	.4913	.4916
2.4	.4918	.4920	.4922	.4925	.4927	.4929	.4931	.4932	.4934	.4936
2.5	.4938	.4940	.4941	.4943	.4945	.4946	.4948	.4949	.4951	.4952
2.6	.4953	.4955	.4956	.4957	.4959	.4960	.4961	.4962	.4963	.4964
2.7	.4965	.4966	.4967	.4968	.4969	.4970	.4971	.4972	.4973	.4974
2.8	.4974	.4975	.4976	.4977	.4977	.4978	.4979	.4979	.4980	.4981
2.9	.4981	.4982	.4982	.4982	.4984	.4984	.4985	.4985	.4986	.4986
3.0	.4987	.4987	.4987	.4988	.4988	.4989	.4989	.4989	.4990	.4990

$N(d)$ represents areas under the standard normal distribution function. Suppose that $d_1 = .24$. The table implies a cumulative probability of $.5000 + .0948 = .5948$. If d_1 is equal to .2452, we must estimate the probability by interpolating between $N(.25)$ and $N(.24)$.

(continued)

$d = .37$ is .1443. This value is *not* the cumulative probability of .37. We must first make an adjustment to determine cumulative probability. That is:

$$N(.37) = .50 + .1443 = .6443$$
$$N(-.37) = .50 - .1443 = .3557$$

Unfortunately, our table handles only two significant digits, whereas our value of .3742 has four significant digits. Hence we must interpolate to find $N(.3742)$. Because $N(.37) = .6443$ and $N(.38) = .6480$, the difference between the two values is .0037 ($= .6480 - .6443$). Since .3742 is 42 percent of the way between .37 and .38, we interpolate as:[8]

$$N(.3742) = .6443 + .42 \times .0037 = .6459$$

Step 3: *Calculate C.* We have:

$$
\begin{aligned}
C &= S \times [N(d_1)] - Ee^{-Rt} \times [N(d_2)] \\
&= \$50 \times [N(d_1)] - \$49 \times [e^{-.07 \times (199/365)}] \times N(d_2) \\
&= (\$50 \times .6459) - (\$49 \times .9626 \times .5607) \\
&= \$32.295 - \$26.447 \\
&= \$5.85
\end{aligned}
$$

The estimated price of \$5.85 is greater than the \$4 actual price, implying that the call option is underpriced. A trader believing in the Black–Scholes model would buy a call. Of course the Black–Scholes model is fallible. Perhaps the disparity between the model's estimate and the market price reflects error in the trader's estimate of variance.

The previous example stressed the calculations involved in using the Black–Scholes formula. Is there any intuition behind the formula? Yes, and that intuition follows from the stock purchase and borrowing strategy in our binomial example. The first line of the Black–Scholes equation is:

$$C = S \times N(d_1) - Ee^{-Rt} N(d_2)$$

which is exactly analogous to Equation 22.2:

$$\text{Value of call} = \text{Stock price} \times \text{Delta} - \text{Amount borrowed} \qquad \textbf{(22.2)}$$

Another good options calculator can be found at **www/margrabe.com/ optionpricing.html**.

We presented this equation in the binomial example. It turns out that $N(d_1)$ is the delta in the Black–Scholes model. $N(d_1)$ is .6459 in the previous example. In addition, $Ee^{-Rt} N(d_2)$ is the amount that an investor must borrow to duplicate a call. In the previous example, this value is \$26.45 ($= \$49 \times .9626 \times .5607$). Thus, the model tells us that we can duplicate the call of the preceding example by both:

1. Buying .6459 share of stock.
2. Borrowing \$26.45.

It is no exaggeration to say that the Black–Scholes formula is among the most important contributions in finance. It allows anyone to calculate the value of an option given a few parameters. The attraction of the formula is that four of the parameters are observable: the current price of stock, S; the exercise price, E; the interest rate, R; and the time to expiration date, t. Only one of the parameters must be estimated: the variance of return, σ^2.

To see how truly attractive this formula is, note what parameters are not needed. First, the investor's risk aversion does not affect value. The formula can be used by anyone,

---

[8]This method is called *linear interpolation.* It is only one of a number of possible methods of interpolation.

regardless of willingness to bear risk. Second, it does not depend on the expected return on the stock! Investors with different assessments of the stock's expected return will nevertheless agree on the call price. As in the two-state example, this is because the call depends on the stock price, and that price already balances investors' divergent views.

22.9   Stocks and Bonds as Options

The previous material in this chapter described, explained, and valued publicly traded options. This is important material to any finance student because much trading occurs in these listed options. The study of options has another purpose for the student of corporate finance.

You may have heard the one-liner about the elderly gentleman who was surprised to learn that he had been speaking prose all of his life. The same can be said about the corporate finance student and options. Although options were formally defined for the first time in this chapter, many corporate policies discussed earlier in the text were actually options in disguise. Though it is beyond the scope of this chapter to recast all of corporate finance in terms of options, the rest of the chapter considers three examples of implicit options:

1. Stocks and bonds as options.
2. Capital structure decisions as options.
3. Capital budgeting decisions as options.

We begin by illustrating the implicit options in stocks and bonds.

EXAMPLE 22.5

Stocks and Bonds as Options   The Popov Company has been awarded the concessions at next year's Olympic Games in Antarctica. Because the firm's principals live in Antarctica and because there is no other concession business in that continent, their enterprise will disband after the games. The firm has issued debt to help finance this venture. Interest and principal due on the debt next year will be $800, at which time the debt will be paid off in full. The firm's cash flows next year are forecast as follows:

	Popov's Cash Flow Schedule			
	Very Successful Games	Moderately Successful Games	Moderately Unsuccessful Games	Outright Failure
Cash flow before interest and principal	$1,000	$850	$700	$550
−interest and principal	−800	−800	−700	−550
Cash flow to stockholders	$ 200	$ 50	$ 0	$ 0

As can be seen, the principals forecast four equally likely scenarios. If either of the first two scenarios occurs, the bondholders will be paid in full. The extra cash flow goes to the stockholders. However, if either of the last two scenarios occurs, the bondholders will not be paid in full. Instead they will receive the firm's entire cash flow, leaving the stockholders with nothing.

This example is similar to the bankruptcy examples presented in our chapters about capital structure. Our new insight is that the relationship between the common stock and the firm can be expressed in terms of options. We consider call options first because the intuition is easier. The put option scenario is treated next.

Figure 22.11

Cash Flow to
Stockholders of
Popov Company as
a Function of Cash
Flow of Firm

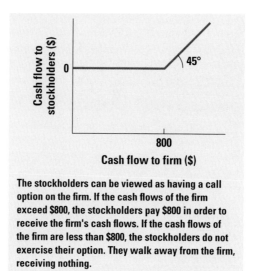

The stockholders can be viewed as having a call
option on the firm. If the cash flows of the firm
exceed $800, the stockholders pay $800 in order to
receive the firm's cash flows. If the cash flows of
the firm are less than $800, the stockholders do not
exercise their option. They walk away from the firm,
receiving nothing.

The Firm Expressed in Terms of Call Options

The Stockholders   We now show that stock can be viewed as a call option on the firm. To illustrate this, Figure 22.11 graphs the cash flow to the stockholders as a function of the cash flow to the firm. The stockholders receive nothing if the firm's cash flows are less than $800; here all of the cash flows go to the bondholders. However, the stockholders earn a dollar for every dollar that the firm receives above $800. The graph looks exactly like the call option graphs that we considered earlier in this chapter.

But what is the underlying asset upon which the stock is a call option? The underlying asset is the firm itself. That is, we can view the *bondholders* as owning the firm. However, the stockholders have a call option on the firm with an exercise price of $800.

If the firm's cash flow is above $800, the stockholders would choose to exercise this option. In other words, they would buy the firm from the bondholders for $800. Their net cash flow is the difference between the firm's cash flow and their $800 payment. This would be $200 (= $1,000−$800) if the games are very successful and $50 (= $850−$800) if the games are moderately successful.

Should the value of the firm's cash flows be less than $800, the stockholders would not choose to exercise their option. Instead, they would walk away from the firm, as any call option holder would do. The bondholders would then receive the firm's entire cash flow.

This view of the firm is a novel one, and students are frequently bothered by it on first exposure. However, we encourage students to keep looking at the firm in this way until the view becomes second nature to them.

The Bondholders   What about the bondholders? Our earlier cash flow schedule showed that they would get the entire cash flow of the firm if the firm generates less cash than $800. Should the firm earn more than $800, the bondholders would receive only $800. That is, they are entitled only to interest and principal. This schedule is graphed in Figure 22.12.

In keeping with our view that the stockholders have a call option on the firm, what does the bondholders' position consist of? The bondholders' position can be described by two claims:

1. They own the firm.
2. They have written a call on the firm with an exercise price of $800.

Figure 22.12

Cash Flow to
Bondholders of
Popov Company as
a Function of Cash
Flow of Firm

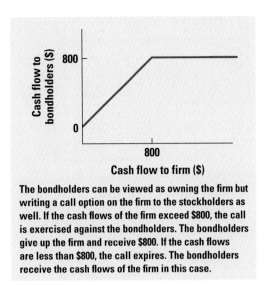

The bondholders can be viewed as owning the firm but
writing a call option on the firm to the stockholders as
well. If the cash flows of the firm exceed $800, the call
is exercised against the bondholders. The bondholders
give up the firm and receive $800. If the cash flows
are less than $800, the call expires. The bondholders
receive the cash flows of the firm in this case.

As we mentioned before, the stockholders walk away from the firm if cash flows are less than $800. Thus, the bondholders retain ownership in this case. However, if the cash flows are greater than $800, the stockholders exercise their option. They call the stock away from the bondholders for $800.

The Firm Expressed in Terms of Put Options

The preceding analysis expresses the positions of the stockholders and the bondholders in terms of call options. We can now express the situation in terms of put options.

The Stockholders   The stockholders' position can be expressed by three claims:

1. They own the firm.
2. They owe $800 in interest and principal to the bondholders.

If the debt were risk-free, these two claims would fully describe the stockholders' situation. However, because of the possibility of default, we have a third claim as well:

3. The stockholders own a put option on the firm with an exercise price of $800. The group of bondholders is the seller of the put.

Now consider two possibilities.

Cash Flow Is Less Than $800   Because the put has an exercise price of $800, the put is in the money. The stockholders "put"—that is, sell—the firm to the bondholders. Normally, the holder of a put receives the exercise price when the asset is sold. However, the stockholders already owe $800 to the bondholders. Thus, the debt of $800 is simply canceled—and no money changes hands—when the stock is delivered to the bondholders. Because the stockholders give up the stock in exchange for extinguishing the debt, the stockholders end up with nothing if the cash flow is below $800.

Cash Flow Is Greater Than $800   Because the put is out of the money here, the stockholders do not exercise. Thus, the stockholders retain ownership of the firm but pay $800 to the bondholders as interest and principal.

The Bondholders   The bondholders' position can be described by two claims:

1. The bondholders are owed $800.
2. They have sold a put option on the firm to the stockholders with an exercise price of $800.

Cash Flow Is Less Than $800   As mentioned before, the stockholders will exercise the put in this case. This means that the bondholders are obligated to pay $800 for the firm. Because they are owed $800, the two obligations offset each other. Thus, the bondholders simply end up with the firm in this case.

Cash Flow Is Greater Than $800   Here, the stockholders do not exercise the put. Thus, the bondholders merely receive the $800 that is due them.

Expressing the bondholders' position in this way is illuminating. With a riskless default-free bond, the bondholders are owed $800. Thus, we can express the risky bond in terms of a riskless bond and a put:

$$\text{Value of risky bond} = \text{Value of default-free bond} - \text{Value of put option}$$

That is, the value of the risky bond is the value of the default-free bond less the value of the stockholders' option to sell the company for $800.

A Resolution of the Two Views

We have argued that the positions of the stockholders and the bondholders can be viewed either in terms of calls or in terms of puts. These two viewpoints are summarized in Table 22.4.

We have found from experience that it is generally harder for students to think of the firm in terms of puts than in terms of calls. Thus, it would be helpful if there were a way to show that the two viewpoints are equivalent. Fortunately there is *put–call parity*. In an earlier section, we presented the put–call parity relationship as Equation 22.1, which we now repeat:

$$\text{Price of underlying stock} + \text{Price of put} = \text{Price of call} + \text{Present value of exercise price} \qquad \textbf{(22.1)}$$

Table 22.4

Positions of Stockholders and Bondholders in Popov Company in Terms of Calls and Puts

Stockholders	Bondholders
Positions viewed in terms of call options	
1. Stockholders own a call on the firm with an exercise price of $800.	1. Bondholders own the firm.
	2. Bondholders have sold a call on the firm to the stockholders.
Positions viewed in terms of put options	
1. Stockholders own the firm.	1. Bondholders are owed $800 in interest and principal.
2. Stockholders owe $800 in interest and principal to bondholders.	2. Bondholders have sold a put on the firm to the stockholders.
3. Stockholders own a put option on the firm with an exercise price of $800.	

Using the results of this section, Equation 22.1 can be rewritten like this:

$$\begin{matrix} \text{Value of call} \\ \text{on firm} \end{matrix} = \begin{matrix} \text{Value of} \\ \text{firm} \end{matrix} + \begin{matrix} \text{Value of put} \\ \text{on firm} \end{matrix} - \begin{matrix} \text{Value of} \\ \text{default-free bond} \end{matrix} \qquad \textbf{(22.3)}$$

$$\begin{matrix} \text{Stockholders'} \\ \text{position in terms} \\ \text{of call options} \end{matrix} = \begin{matrix} \text{Stockholders' position} \\ \text{in terms of put options} \end{matrix}$$

Going from Equation 22.1 to Equation 22.3 involves a few steps. First, we treat the firm, not the stock, as the underlying asset in this section. (In keeping with common convention, we refer to the *value* of the firm and the *price* of the stock.) Second, the exercise price is now $800, the principal and interest on the firm's debt. Taking the present value of this amount at the riskless rate yields the value of a default-free bond. Third, the order of the terms in Equation 22.1 is rearranged in Equation 22.3.

Note that the left side of Equation 22.3 is the stockholders' position in terms of call options, as shown in Table 22.4. The right side of Equation 22.3 is the stockholders' position in terms of put options, as shown in the table. Thus, put–call parity shows that viewing the stockholders' position in terms of call options is equivalent to viewing the stockholders' position in terms of put options.

Now let's rearrange the terms in Equation 22.3 to yield the following:

$$\begin{matrix} \text{Value of} \\ \text{firm} \end{matrix} - \begin{matrix} \text{Value of call} \\ \text{on firm} \end{matrix} = \begin{matrix} \text{Value of} \\ \text{default-free bond} \end{matrix} - \begin{matrix} \text{Value of put} \\ \text{on firm} \end{matrix} \qquad \textbf{(22.4)}$$

$$\begin{matrix} \text{Bondholders' position in} \\ \text{terms of call options} \end{matrix} = \begin{matrix} \text{Bondholders' position in} \\ \text{terms of put options} \end{matrix}$$

The left side of Equation 22.4 is the bondholders' position in terms of call options, as shown in Table 22.4. (The minus sign on this side of the equation indicates that the bondholders are *writing* a call.) The right side of the equation is the bondholders' position in terms of put options, as shown in Table 22.4. Thus, put–call parity shows that viewing the bondholders' position in terms of call options is equivalent to viewing the bondholders' position in terms of put options.

A Note about Loan Guarantees

In the Popov example given earlier, the bondholders bore the risk of default. Of course, bondholders generally ask for an interest rate that is high enough to compensate them for bearing risk. When firms experience financial distress, they can no longer attract new debt at moderate interest rates. Thus, firms experiencing distress have frequently sought loan guarantees from the government. Our framework can be used to understand these guarantees.

If the firm defaults on a guaranteed loan, the government must make up the difference. In other words, a government guarantee converts a risky bond into a riskless bond. What is the value of this guarantee?

Recall that with option pricing:

$$\begin{matrix} \text{Value of} \\ \text{default-free bond} \end{matrix} = \begin{matrix} \text{Value of} \\ \text{risky bond} \end{matrix} + \begin{matrix} \text{Value of} \\ \text{put option} \end{matrix}$$

This equation shows that the government is assuming an obligation that has a cost equal to the value of a put option.

This analysis differs from that of either politicians or company spokespeople. They generally say that the guarantee will cost the taxpayers nothing because the guarantee enables the firm to attract debt, thereby staying solvent. However, it should be pointed out that although solvency may be a strong possibility, it is never a certainty. Thus, when the guarantee is made, the government's obligation has a cost in terms of present value. To say that a government guarantee costs the government nothing is like saying a put on the stock of Microsoft has no value because the stock is *likely* to rise in price.

Actually, the U.S. government has had good fortune with loan guarantees. Its two biggest guarantees were to the Lockheed Corporation in 1971 and the Chrysler Corporation in 1980. Both firms nearly ran out of cash and defaulted on loans. In both cases, the U.S. government came to the rescue by agreeing to guarantee new loans. Under the guarantees, if Lockheed and Chrysler had defaulted on new loans, the lenders could have obtained the full value of their claims from the U.S. government. From the lender's point of view, the loans became as risk-free as Treasury bonds. These guarantees enabled Lockheed and Chrysler to borrow large amounts of cash and to get through a difficult time. As it turned out, neither firm defaulted.

Who benefits from a typical loan guarantee?

1. If existing risky bonds are guaranteed, all gains accrue to the existing bondholders. The stockholders gain nothing because the limited liability of corporations absolves the stockholders of any obligation in bankruptcy.

2. If new debt is issued and guaranteed, the new debtholders do not gain. Rather, in a competitive market, they must accept a low interest rate because of the debt's low risk. The stockholders gain here because they are able to issue debt at a low interest rate. In addition, some of the gains accrue to the old bondholders because the firm's value is greater than would otherwise be true. Therefore, if shareholders want all the gains from loan guarantees, they should renegotiate or retire existing bonds before the guarantee is in place. This happened in the Chrysler case.

22.10 Options and Corporate Decisions: Some Applications

In this section, we explore the implications of options analysis in two key areas: capital budgeting and mergers. We start with mergers and show a very surprising result. We then go on to show that the net present value rule has some important wrinkles in a leveraged firm.

Mergers and Diversification

Elsewhere in this book, we discuss mergers and acquisitions. There we mention that diversification is frequently cited as a reason for two firms to merge. Is diversification a good reason to merge? It might seem so. After all, in an earlier chapter, we spent a lot of time explaining why diversification is valuable for investors in their own portfolios because of the elimination of unsystematic risk.

To investigate this issue, let's consider two companies, Sunshine Swimwear (SS) and Polar Winterwear (PW). For obvious reasons, both companies have highly seasonal cash flows; and, in their respective off-seasons, both companies worry about cash flow. If the two companies were to merge, the combined company would have a much more stable cash flow. In other words, a merger would diversify away some of the seasonal variation and, in fact, would make bankruptcy much less likely.

Notice that the operations of the two firms are very different, so the proposed merger is a purely "financial" merger. This means that there are no "synergies" or other value-creating possibilities except, possibly, gains from risk reduction. Here is some premerger information:

	Sunshine Swimwear	Polar Winterwear
Market value of assets	$30 million	$10 million
Face value of pure discount debt	$12 million	$4 million
Debt maturity	3 years	3 years
Asset return standard deviation	50%	60%

The risk-free rate, continuously compounded, is 5 percent. Given this, we can view the equity in each firm as a call option and calculate the following using Black–Scholes to determine equity values (check these for practice):

	Sunshine Swimwear	Polar Winterwear
Market value of equity	$20.394 million	$6.992 million
Market value of debt	$ 9.606 million	$3.008 million

If you check these, you may get slightly different answers if you use Table 22.3 (we used a spreadsheet). Notice that we calculated the market value of debt using the balance sheet identity.

After the merger, the combined firm's assets will simply be the sum of the premerger values, $30 + $10 = $40, because no value was created or destroyed. Similarly, the total face value of the debt is now $16 million. However, we will assume that the combined firm's asset return standard deviation is 40 percent. This is lower than for either of the two individual firms because of the diversification effect.

So, what is the impact of this merger? To find out, we compute the postmerger value of the equity. Based on our discussion, here is the relevant information:

	Combined Firm
Market value of assets	$40 million
Face value of pure discount debt	$16 million
Debt maturity	3 years
Asset return standard deviation	40%

Once again, we can calculate equity and debt values:

	Combined Firm
Market value of equity	$26.602 million
Market value of debt	$13.398 million

What we notice is that this merger is a terrible idea, at least for the stockholders! Before the merger, the stock in the two separate firms was worth a total of $20.394 + 6.992 = $27.386 million compared to only $26.602 million postmerger; so the merger vaporized $27.386 − 26.602 = $.784 million, or almost $1 million, in equity.

Where did $1 million in equity go? It went to the bondholders. Their bonds were worth $9.606 + 3.008 = $12.614 million before the merger and $13.398 million after, a gain of exactly $.784 million. Thus this merger neither created nor destroyed value, but it shifted it from the stockholders to the bondholders.

Our example shows that pure financial mergers are a bad idea, and it also shows why. The diversification works in the sense that it reduces the volatility of the firm's return on assets. This risk reduction benefits the bondholders by making default less likely. This is sometimes called the "coinsurance" effect. Essentially, by merging, the firms insure each other's bonds. The bonds are thus less risky, and they rise in value. If the bonds increase in value, and there is no net increase in asset values, then the equity must decrease in value. Thus, pure financial mergers are good for creditors but not for stockholders.

Another way to see this is that because the equity is a call option, a reduction in return variance on the underlying asset has to reduce its value. The reduction in value in the case of a purely financial merger has an interesting interpretation. The merger makes default (and thus bankruptcy) *less* likely to happen. That is obviously a good thing from a bondholder's perspective, but why is it a bad thing from a stockholder's perspective? The answer is simple: The right to go bankrupt is a valuable stockholder option. A purely financial merger reduces the value of that option.

Options and Capital Budgeting

We now consider two issues regarding capital budgeting. What we will show is that, for a leveraged firm, the shareholders might prefer a lower NPV project to a higher one. We then show that they might even prefer a *negative* NPV project to a positive NPV project.

As usual, we will illustrate these points first with an example. Here is the basic background information for the firm:

Market value of assets	$20 million
Face value of pure discount debt	$40 million
Debt maturity	5 years
Asset return standard deviation	50%

The risk-free rate is 4 percent. As we have now done several times, we can calculate equity and debt values:

Market value of equity	$ 5.724 million
Market value of debt	$14.276 million

This firm has a fairly high degree of leverage: The debt–equity ratio based on market values is $14.276/5.724 = 2.5, or 250 percent. This is high, but not unheard of. Notice also that the option here is out of the money; as a result, the delta is .546.

The firm has two mutually exclusive investments under consideration. The projects affect both the market value of the firm's assets and the firm's asset return standard deviation as follows:

	Project A	Project B
NPV	$4	$2
Market value of firm's assets ($20 + NPV)	$24	$22
Firm's asset return standard deviation	40%	60%

Which project is better? It is obvious that project *A* has the higher NPV, but by now you are wary of the change in the firm's asset return standard deviation. One project reduces it; the other increases it. To see which project the stockholders like better, we have to go through our by now familiar calculations:

	Project A	Project B
Market value of equity	$ 5.938	$ 8.730
Market value of debt	$18.062	$13.270

There is a dramatic difference between the two projects. Project *A* benefits both the stockholders and the bondholders, but most of the gain goes to the bondholders. Project *B* has a huge impact on the value of the equity, plus it reduces the value of the debt. Clearly the stockholders prefer *B*.

What are the implications of our analysis? Basically, we have discovered two things. First, when the equity has a delta significantly smaller than 1.0, any value created will go partially to bondholders. Second, stockholders have a strong incentive to increase the variance of the return on the firm's assets. More specifically, stockholders will have a strong preference for variance-increasing projects as opposed to variance-decreasing ones, even if that means a lower NPV.

Let's do one final example. Here is a different set of numbers:

Market value of assets	$20 million
Face value of pure discount debt	$100 million
Debt maturity	5 years
Asset return standard deviation	50%

The risk-free rate is 4 percent, so the equity and debt values are these:

Market value of equity	$ 2 million
Market value of debt	$18 million

Notice that the change from our previous example is that the face value of the debt is now $100 million, so the option is far out of the money. The delta is only .24, so most of any value created will go to the bondholders.

The firm has an investment under consideration that must be taken now or never. The project affects both the market value of the firm's assets and the firm's asset return standard deviation as follows:

Project NPV	−$ 1 million
Market value of firm's assets ($20 million + NPV)	$19 million
Firm's asset return standard deviation	70%

Thus, the project has a negative NPV, but it increases the standard deviation of the firm's return on assets. If the firm takes the project, here is the result:

Market value of equity	$ 4.821 million
Market value of debt	$14.179 million

This project more than doubles the value of the equity! Once again, what we are seeing is that stockholders have a strong incentive to increase volatility, particularly when the option is far out of the money. What is happening is that the shareholders have relatively little to lose because bankruptcy is the likely outcome. As a result, there is a strong incentive to go for a long shot, even if that long shot has a negative NPV. It's a bit like using your very last dollar on a lottery ticket. It's a bad investment, but there aren't a lot of other options!

22.11 Investment in Real Projects and Options

Let us quickly review the material about capital budgeting presented earlier in the text. We first considered projects where forecasts for future cash flows were made at date 0. The expected cash flow in each future period was discounted at an appropriate risky rate, yielding an NPV calculation. For independent projects, a positive NPV meant acceptance and a negative NPV meant rejection. This approach treated risk through the discount rate.

We later considered decision tree analysis, an approach that handles risk in a more sophisticated way. We pointed out that the firm will make investment and operating decisions on a project over its entire life. We value a project today, assuming that future decisions will be optimal. However, we do not yet know what these decisions will be because much information remains to be discovered. The firm's ability to delay its investment and operating decisions until the release of information is an option. We now illustrate this option through an example.

EXAMPLE 22.6

Options and Capital Budgeting   Exoff Oil Corporation is considering the purchase of an oil field in a remote part of Alaska. The seller has listed the property for $10,000 and is eager to sell immediately. Initial drilling costs are $500,000. Exoff anticipates that 10,000 barrels of oil can be extracted each year for many decades. Because the termination date is so far in the future and so hard to estimate, the firm views the cash flow stream from the oil as a perpetuity. With oil prices at $50 per barrel and extraction costs at $46 a barrel, the firm anticipates a net margin of $4 per barrel. Because oil prices are expected to rise at the inflation rate, the firm assumes that its cash flow per barrel will always be $4 in real terms. The appropriate real discount rate is 10 percent. The firm has enough tax credits from bad years in the past that it will not need to pay taxes on any profits from the oil field. Should Exoff buy the property?

The NPV of the oil field to Exoff is:

$$-\$110,000 = -\$10,000 - \$500,000 + \frac{\$4 \times 10,000}{.10}$$

According to this analysis, Exoff should not purchase the land.

Though this approach uses the standard capital budgeting techniques of this and other textbooks, it is actually inappropriate for this situation. To see this, consider the analysis of Kirtley Thornton, a consultant to Exoff. He agrees that the price of oil is *expected* to rise at the rate of inflation. However, he points out that the next year is quite perilous for oil prices. On the one hand, OPEC is

(continued)

considering a long-term agreement that would raise oil prices to $65 per barrel in real terms for many years in the future. On the other hand, National Motors recently indicated that cars using a mixture of sand and water for fuel are currently being tested. Thornton argues that oil will be priced at $35 in real terms for many years should this development prove successful. Full information about both these developments will be released in exactly one year.

Should oil prices rise to $65 a barrel, the NPV of the project would be:

$$\$1,390,000 = -\$10,000 - \$500,000 + \frac{(\$65 - \$46) \times 10,000}{.10}$$

However, should oil prices fall to $35 a barrel, the NPV of the oil field will be even more negative than it is today.

Mr. Thornton makes two recommendations to Exoff's board. He argues that:

1. The land should be purchased.
2. The drilling decision should be delayed until information about both OPEC's new agreement and National Motors' new automobile is released.

Mr. Thornton explains his recommendations to the board by first assuming that the land has already been purchased. He argues that under this assumption, the drilling decision should be delayed. Second, he investigates his assumption that the land should have been purchased in the first place. This approach of examining the second decision (whether to drill) after assuming that the first decision (to buy the land) has been made was also used in our earlier presentation on decision trees. Let us now work through Mr. Thornton's analysis.

Assume the land has already been purchased. If the land has already been purchased, should drilling begin immediately? If drilling begins immediately, the NPV is −$110,000: If the drilling decision is delayed until new information is released in a year, the optimal choice can be made at that time. If oil prices drop to $35 a barrel, Exoff should not drill. Instead the firm should walk away from the project, losing nothing beyond its $10,000 purchase price for the land. If oil prices rise to $65, drilling should begin.

Mr. Thornton points out that by delaying, the firm will invest the $500,000 of drilling costs only if oil prices rise. Thus, by delaying, the firm saves $500,000 in the case where oil prices drop. Kirtley concludes that once the land is purchased, the drilling decision should be delayed.[9]

Should the land have been purchased in the first place? We now know that if the land has been purchased, it is optimal to defer the drilling decision until the release of information. Given that we know this optimal decision concerning drilling, should the land be purchased in the first place? Without knowing the exact probability that oil prices will rise, Mr. Thornton is nevertheless confident that the land should be purchased. The NPV of the project at $65 oil prices is $1,390,000, whereas the cost of the land is only $10,000. Mr. Thornton believes that an oil price rise is possible, though by no means probable. Even so, he argues that the high potential return is clearly worth the risk.

This example presents an approach that is similar to our decision tree analysis of the Solar Equipment Company in a previous chapter. Our purpose in this section is to discuss this type of decision in an option framework. When Exoff purchases the land, it is actually

---

[9]Actually, there are three separate effects here. First, the firm avoids drilling costs in the case of low oil prices by delaying the decision. This is the effect discussed by Mr. Thornton. Second, the present value of the $500,000 payment is less when the decision is delayed, even if drilling eventually takes place. Third, the firm loses one year of cash inflows through delay.

The first two effects support delaying the decision. The third effect supports immediate drilling. In this example, the first effect greatly outweighs the other two effects. Thus, Mr. Thornton avoided the second and third effects in his presentation.

purchasing a call option. That is, once the land has been purchased, the firm has an option to buy an active oil field at an exercise price of $500,000. As it turns out, one should generally not exercise a call option immediately.[10] In this case, the firm should delay exercise until relevant information concerning future oil prices is released.

This section points out a serious deficiency in classical capital budgeting: Net present value calculations typically ignore the flexibility that real-world firms have. In our example, the standard techniques generated a negative NPV for the land purchase. Yet, by allowing the firm the option to change its investment policy according to new information, the land purchase can easily be justified.

We encourage the reader to look for hidden options in projects. Because options are beneficial, managers are shortchanging their firm's projects if capital budgeting calculations ignore flexibility.

Summary and Conclusions

This chapter serves as an introduction to options.

1. The most familiar options are puts and calls. These options give the holder the right to sell or buy shares of common stock at a given exercise price. American options can be exercised any time up to and including the expiration date. European options can be exercised only on the expiration date.

2. We showed that a strategy of buying a stock and buying a put is equivalent to a strategy of buying a call and buying a zero coupon bond. From this, the put–call parity relationship was established:

$$\begin{array}{ccccccc} \text{Value of} \\ \text{stock} \end{array} + \begin{array}{c} \text{Value of} \\ \text{put} \end{array} - \begin{array}{c} \text{Value of} \\ \text{call} \end{array} = \begin{array}{c} \text{Present value of} \\ \text{exercise price} \end{array}$$

3. The value of an option depends on five factors:
   a. The price of the underlying asset.
   b. The exercise price.
   c. The expiration date.
   d. The variability of the underlying asset.
   e. The interest rate on risk-free bonds.

   The Black–Scholes model can determine the intrinsic price of an option from these five factors.

4. Much of corporate financial theory can be presented in terms of options. In this chapter, we pointed out that:
   a. Common stock can be represented as a call option on the firm.
   b. Stockholders enhance the value of their call by increasing the risk of their firm.
   c. Real projects have hidden options that enhance value.

Concept Questions

1. **Options**   What is a call option? A put option? Under what circumstances might you want to buy each? Which one has greater *potential* profit? Why?

---

[10] Actually, it can be shown that a call option that pays no dividend should *never* be exercised before expiration. However, for a dividend-paying stock, it may be optimal to exercise prior to the ex-dividend date. The analogy applies to our example of an option in real assets.

The firm would receive cash flows from oil earlier if drilling begins immediately. This is equivalent to the benefit from exercising a call on a stock prematurely in order to capture the dividend. However, in our example, this dividend effect is far outweighed by the benefits from waiting.

2. **Options**   Complete the following sentence for each of these investors:
   a. A buyer of call options.
   b. A buyer of put options.
   c. A seller (writer) of call options.
   d. A seller (writer) of put options.

   "The (buyer/seller) of a (put/call) option (pays/receives) money for the (right/obligation) to (buy/sell) a specified asset at a fixed price for a fixed length of time."

3. **American and European Options**   What is the difference between an American option and a European option?

4. **Intrinsic Value**   What is the intrinsic value of a call option? Of a put option? How do we interpret this value?

5. **Option Pricing**   You notice that shares of stock in the Patel Corporation are going for $50 per share. Call options with an exercise price of $35 per share are selling for $10. What's wrong here? Describe how you can take advantage of this mispricing if the option expires today.

6. **Options and Stock Risk**   If the risk of a stock increases, what is likely to happen to the price of call options on the stock? To the price of put options? Why?

7. **Option Rise**   True or false: The unsystematic risk of a share of stock is irrelevant in valuing the stock because it can be diversified away; therefore, it is also irrelevant for valuing a call option on the stock. Explain.

8. **Option Pricing**   Suppose a certain stock currently sells for £30 per share. If a put option and a call option are available with £30 exercise prices, which do you think will sell for more, the put or the call? Explain.

9. **Option Price and Interest Rates**   Suppose the interest rate on T-bills suddenly and unexpectedly rises. All other things being the same, what is the impact on call option values? On put option values?

10. **Contingent Liabilities**   When you take out an ordinary student loan, it is usually the case that whoever holds that loan is given a guarantee by the U.S. government, meaning that the government will make up any payments you skip. This is just one example of the many loan guarantees made by the U.S. government. Such guarantees don't show up in calculations of government spending or in official deficit figures. Why not? Should they show up?

11. **Options and Expiration Dates**   What is the impact of lengthening the time to expiration on an option's value? Explain.

12. **Options and Stock Price Volatility**   What is the impact of an increase in the volatility of the underlying stock's return on an option's value? Explain.

13. **Insurance as an Option**   An insurance policy is considered analogous to an option. From the policyholder's point of view, what type of option is an insurance policy? Why?

14. **Equity as a Call Option**   It is said that the equityholders of a levered firm can be thought of as holding a call option on the firm's assets. Explain what is meant by this statement.

15. **Option Valuation and NPV**   You are CEO of Titan Industries and have just been awarded a large number of employee stock options. The company has two mutually exclusive projects available. The first project has a large NPV and will reduce the total risk of the company. The second project has a small NPV and will increase the total risk of the company. You have decided to accept the first project when you remember your employee stock options. How might this affect your decision?

16. **Put–Call Parity**   You find a put and a call with the same exercise price and maturity. What do you know about the relative prices of the put and call? Prove your answer and provide an intuitive explanation.

17. **Put–Call Parity**   A put and a call have the same maturity and strike price. If they have the same price, which one is in the money? Prove your answer and provide an intuitive explanation.

www.mhhe.com/rwj

18. Put–Call Parity   One thing put-call parity tells us is that given any three of a stock, a call, a put, and a T-bill, the fourth can be synthesized or replicated using the other three. For example, how can we replicate a share of stock using a call, a put, and a T-bill?

Questions
and Problems

BASIC
(Questions 1–17)

1. Two-State Option Pricing Model   T-bills currently yield 6 percent. Stock in Tina Textiles is currently selling for €55 per share. There is no possibility that the stock will be worth less than €50 per share in one year.

  a. What is the value of a call option with a €45 exercise price? What is the intrinsic value?
  b. What is the value of a call option with a €35 exercise price? What is the intrinsic value?
  c. What is the value of a put option with a €45 exercise price? What is the intrinsic value?

2. Understanding Option Quotes   Use the option quote information shown here to answer the questions that follow. The stock is currently selling for $83.

| Option and | | Strike | Calls | | Puts | |
NY Close	Expiration	Price	Vol.	Last	Vol.	Last
DDD						
	March	80	230	2.80	160	0.80
	April	80	170	6	127	1.40
	July	80	139	8.05	43	3.90
	October	80	60	10.20	11	3.65

  a. Are the call options in the money? What is the intrinsic value of a Davidson Day Dreamer (DDD) call option?
  b. Are the put options in the money? What is the intrinsic value of a Davidson Day Dreamer (DDD) put option?
  c. Two of the options are clearly mispriced. Which ones? At a minimum, what should the mispriced options sell for? Explain how you could profit from the mispricing in each case.

3. Calculating Payoffs   Use the option quote information shown here to answer the questions that follow. The stock is currently selling for INR 114.

| Option and | | Strike | Calls | | Puts | |
NY Close	Expiration	Price	Vol.	Last	Vol.	Last
Techno						
	February	110	85	7.60	40	.60
	March	110	61	8.80	22	1.55
	May	110	22	10.25	11	2.85
	August	110	3	13.05	3	4.70

  a. Suppose you buy 10 contracts of the February 110 call option. How much will you pay, ignoring commissions?
  b. In part (a), suppose that Techno stock is selling for INR 140 per share on the expiration date. How much is your options investment worth? What if the terminal stock price is INR 125? Explain.
  c. Suppose you buy 10 contracts of the August 110 put option. What is your maximum gain? On the expiration date, Techno is selling for INR 104 per share. How much is your options investment worth? What is your net gain?
  d. In part (c), suppose you *sell* 10 of the August 110 put contracts. What is your net gain or loss if Techno is selling for INR 103 at expiration? For INR 132? What is the break-even price—that is, the terminal stock price that results in a zero profit?

4. **Two-State Option Pricing Model** The price of Zhao Fisheries stock will be either CNY 75 or CNY 95 at the end of the year. Call options are available with one year to expiration. T-bills currently yield 6 percent.
   a. Suppose the current price of Zhao stock is CNY 80. What is the value of the call option if the exercise price is CNY 70 per share?
   b. Suppose the exercise price is CNY 90 in part (a). What is the value of the call option now?

5. **Two-State Option Pricing Model** The price of Tara, Inc., stock will be either $60 or $80 at the end of the year. Call options are available with one year to expiration. T-bills currently yield 5 percent.
   a. Suppose the current price of Tara stock is $70. What is the value of the call option if the exercise price is $45 per share?
   b. Suppose the exercise price is $70 in part (a). What is the value of the call option now?

6. **Put–Call Parity** A stock is currently selling for ¥7,000 per share. A call option with an exercise price of ¥7,500 sells for ¥450 and expires in three months. If the risk-free rate of interest is 2.6 percent per year, compounded continuously, what is the price of a put option with the same exercise price?

7. **Put–Call Parity** A put option that expires in six months with an exercise price of ¥5,000 sells for ¥489. The stock is currently priced at ¥5,300, and the risk-free rate is 3.6 percent per year, compounded continuously. What is the price of a call option with the same exercise price?

8. **Put–Call Parity** A put option and a call option with an exercise price of €70 and three months to expiration sell for €2.87 and €4.68, respectively. If the risk-free rate is 4.8 percent per year, compounded continuously, what is the current stock price?

9. **Put–Call Parity** A put option and a call option with an exercise price of THB 65 expire in two months and sell for THB 2.86 and THB 4.08, respectively. If the stock is currently priced at THB 65.80, what is the annual continuously compounded rate of interest?

10. **Black–Scholes** What are the prices of a call option and a put option with the following characteristics?

    > Stock price = CAD 38
    > Exercise price = CAD 35
    > Risk-free rate = 6% per year, compounded continuously
    > Maturity = 3 months
    > Standard deviation = 54% per year

11. **Black–Scholes** What are the prices of a call option and a put option with the following characteristics?

    > Stock price = ILS 86
    > Exercise price = ILS 90
    > Risk-free rate = 4% per year, compounded continuously
    > Maturity = 8 months
    > Standard deviation = 62% per year

12. **Delta** What are the deltas of a call option and a put option with the following characteristics? What does the delta of the option tell you?

    > Stock price = LAK 87
    > Exercise price = LAK 85
    > Risk-free rate = 5% per year, compounded continuously
    > Maturity = 9 months
    > Standard deviation = 56% per year

13.   **Black–Scholes and Asset Value**   You own a lot in Rawalpindi, Pakistan that is currently unused. Similar lots have recently sold for PKR 20 million. Over the past five years, the price of land in the area has increased 12 percent per year, with an annual standard deviation of 20 percent. A buyer has recently approached you and wants an option to buy the land in the next 12 months for PKR 22 million. The risk-free rate of interest is 5 percent per year, compounded continuously. How much should you charge for the option?

14.   **Black–Scholes and Asset Value**   In the previous problem, suppose you wanted the option to sell the land to the buyer in one year. Assuming all the facts are the same, describe the transaction that would occur today. What is the price of the transaction today?

15.   **Time Value of Options**   You are given the following information concerning options on a particular stock:

> Stock price = $86
> Exercise price = $90
> Risk-free rate = 12% per year, compounded continuously
> Maturity = 6 months
> Standard deviation = 53% per year

   a. What is the intrinsic value of the call option? Of the put option?
   b. What is the time value of the call option? Of the put option?
   c. Does the call or the put have the larger time value component? Would you expect this to be true in general?

16.   **Risk-Neutral Valuation**   A stock is currently priced at NAD 75. The stock will either increase or decrease by 15 percent over the next year. There is a call option on the stock with a strike price of NAD 70 and one year until expiration. If the risk-free rate is 12 percent, what is the risk-neutral value of the call option?

17.   **Risk-Neutral Valuation**   In the previous problem, assume the risk-free rate is only 8 percent. What is the risk-neutral value of the option now? What happens to the risk-neutral probabilities of a stock price increase and a stock price decrease?

INTERMEDIATE
(Questions 18–29)

18.   **Black–Scholes**   A call option matures in six months. The underlying stock price is EGP 85, and the stock's return has a standard deviation of 20 percent per year. The risk-free rate is 4 percent per year, compounded continuously. If the exercise price is EGP 0, what is the price of the call option?

19.   **Black–Scholes**   A call option has an exercise price of €80 and matures in six months. The current stock price is €84, and the risk-free rate is 5 percent per year, compounded continuously. What is the price of the call if the standard deviation of the stock is 0 percent per year?

20.   **Black–Scholes**   A stock is currently priced at SCR 35. A call option with an expiration of one year has an exercise price of SCR 50. The risk-free rate is 12 percent per year, compounded continuously, and the standard deviation of the stock's return is infinitely large. What is the price of the call option?

21.   **Equity as an Option**   Winnipeg Entertainment has a zero coupon bond issue outstanding with a ¥10 million face value that matures in one year. The current market value of the firm's assets is ¥10.5 million. The standard deviation of the return on the firm's assets is 38 percent per year, and the annual risk-free rate is 5 percent per year, compounded continuously. Based on the Black–Scholes model, what is the market value of the firm's equity and debt?

22.   **Equity as an Option and NPV**   Suppose the firm in the previous problem is considering two mutually exclusive investments. Project A has a NPV of ¥700,000, and project B has a NPV of ¥1 million. As the result of taking project A, the standard deviation of the return on the firm's assets will increase to 55 percent per year. If project B is taken, the standard deviation will fall to 34 percent per year.
   a. What is the value of the firm's equity and debt if project A is undertaken? If project B is undertaken?

b. Which project would the stockholders prefer? Can you reconcile your answer with the NPV rule?

c. Suppose the stockholders and bondholders are in fact the same group of investors. Would this affect your answer to (b)?

d. What does this problem suggest to you about stockholder incentives?

23.   Equity as an Option   Frostbite Thermalwear has a zero coupon bond issue outstanding with a face value of ¥20 million that matures in one year. The current market value of the firm's assets is ¥22 million. The standard deviation of the return on the firm's assets is 53 percent per year, and the annual risk-free rate is 5 percent per year, compounded continuously. Based on the Black–Scholes model, what is the market value of the firm's equity and debt? What is the firm's continuously compounded cost of debt?

24.   Mergers and Equity as an Option   Suppose Winnipeg Entertainment and Frostbite Thermalwear in the previous problems have decided to merge. Because the two companies have seasonal sales, the combined firm's return on assets will have a standard deviation of 31 percent per year.

a. What is the combined value of equity in the two existing companies? The value of debt?

b. What is the value of the new firm's equity? The value of debt?

c. What was the gain or loss for shareholders? For bondholders?

d. What happened to shareholder value here?

25.   Equity as an Option and NPV   A company has a single zero coupon bond outstanding that matures in 10 years with a face value of $30 million. The current value of the company's assets is $22 million, and the standard deviation of the return on the firm's assets is 39 percent per year. The risk-free rate is 6 percent per year, compounded continuously.

a. What is the current market value of the company's equity?

b. What is the current market value of the company's debt?

c. What is the company's continuously compounded cost of debt?

d. The company has a new project available. The project has an NPV of $800,000. If the company undertakes the project, what will be the new market value of equity? Assume volatility is unchanged.

e. Assuming the company undertakes the new project and does not borrow any additional funds, what is the new continuously compounded cost of debt? What is happening here?

26.   Two-State Option Pricing Model   Wu is interested in buying a European call option written on Chengdu Airlines, Inc., a nondividend-paying common stock, with a strike price of CNY 110 and one year until expiration. Currently, Chengdu's stock sells for CNY 100 per share. In one year Wu knows that Chengdu's stock will be trading at either CNY 125 per share or CNY 80 per share. Wu is able to borrow and lend at the risk-free EAR of 2.5 percent.

a. What should the call option sell for today?

b. If no options currently trade on the stock, is there a way to create a synthetic call option with identical payoffs to the call option just described? If there is, how would you do it?

c. How much does the synthetic call option cost? Is this greater than, less than, or equal to what the actual call option costs? Does this make sense?

27.   Two-State Option Pricing Model   Khaitan wishes to buy a European put option on BioLabs, Inc., a nondividend-paying common stock, with a strike price of $40 and six months until expiration. BioLab's common stock is currently selling for $30 per share, and Khaitan expects that the stock price will either rise to $60 or fall to $15 in six months. Khaitan can borrow and lend at the risk-free EAR of 21 percent.

a. What should the put option sell for today?

b. If no options currently trade on the stock, is there a way to create a synthetic put option with identical payoffs to the put option just described? If there is, how would you do it?

c. How much does the synthetic put option cost? Is this greater than, less than, or equal to what the actual put option costs? Does this make sense?

28.   Two-State Option Pricing Model   Zighi Cutters must purchase gold in three months for use in its operations. Zighi's management has estimated that if the price of gold were to rise above

CNY 3,750 per ounce, the firm would go bankrupt. The current price of gold is CNY 3,500 per ounce. The firm's chief financial officer believes that the price of gold will either rise to CNY 4,000 per ounce or fall to CNY 3,250 per ounce over the next three months. Management wishes to eliminate any risk of the firm going bankrupt. Zighi can borrow and lend at the risk-free EAR of 16.99 percent.

a. Should the company buy a call option or a put option on gold? To avoid bankruptcy, what strike price and time to expiration would the company like this option to have?

b. How much should such an option sell for in the open market?

c. If no options currently trade on gold, is there a way for the company to create a synthetic option with identical payoffs to the option just described? If there is, how would the firm do it?

d. How much does the synthetic option cost? Is this greater than, less than, or equal to what the actual option costs? Does this make sense?

29. **Black–Scholes and Collar Cost** An investor is said to take a position in a "collar" if she buys the asset, buys an out-of-the-money put option on the asset, and sells an out-of-the-money call option on the asset. The two options should have the same time to expiration. Suppose Marie wishes to purchase a collar on Tondon Eye, a nondividend-paying common stock, with six months until expiration. She would like the put to have a strike price of £50 and the call to have a strike price of £120. The current price of Tondon's stock is £80 per share. Marie can borrow and lend at the continuously compounded risk-free rate of 10 percent per annum, and the annual standard deviation of the stock's return is 50 percent. Use the Black–Scholes model to calculate the total cost of the collar that Marie is interested in buying. What is the effect of the collar?

CHALLENGE
(Questions 30–38)

30. **Debt Valuation and Time to Maturity** Anita Textiles has a zero coupon bond issue that matures in two years with a face value of $30,000. The current value of the company's assets is $13,000, and the standard deviation of the return on assets is 60 percent per year.

a. Assume the risk-free rate is 5 percent per year, compounded continuously. What is the value of a risk-free bond with the same face value and maturity as the company's bond?

b. What price would the bondholders have to pay for a put option on the firm's assets with a strike price equal to the face value of the debt?

c. Using the answers from (a) and (b), what is the value of the firm's debt? What is the continuously compounded yield on the company's debt?

d. From an examination of the value of the assets of Anita Textiles, and the fact that the debt must be repaid in two years, it seems likely that the company will default on its debt. Management has approached bondholders and proposed a plan whereby the company would repay the same face value of debt, but the repayment would not occur for five years. What is the value of the debt under the proposed plan? What is the new continuously compounded yield on the debt? Explain why this occurs.

31. **Debt Valuation and Asset Variance** Brozik Corp. has a zero coupon bond that matures in five years with a face value of $60,000. The current value of the company's assets is $57,000, and the standard deviation of its return on assets is 50 percent per year. The risk-free rate is 6 percent per year, compounded continuously.

a. What is the value of a risk-free bond with the same face value and maturity as the current bond?

b. What is the value of a put option on the firm's assets with a strike price equal to the face value of the debt?

c. Using the answers from (a) and (b), what is the value of the firm's debt? What is the continuously compounded yield on the company's debt?

d. Assume the company can restructure its assets so that the standard deviation of its return on assets increases to 60 percent per year. What happens to the value of the debt? What is the new continuously compounded yield on the debt? Reconcile your answers in (c) and (d).

e. What happens to bondholders if the company restructures its assets? What happens to shareholders? How does this create an agency problem?

32. **Two-State Option Pricing and Corporate Valuation** Hirosaki Builders, a construction firm financed by both debt and equity, is undertaking a new project. If the project is successful, the value of the firm in one year will be ¥500 billion but if the project is a failure, the firm will

be worth only ¥320 billion. The current value of Hirosaki is ¥400 billion, a figure that includes the prospects for the new project. Hirosaki has outstanding zero coupon bonds due in one year with a face value of ¥380 billion. Treasury bills that mature in one year yield 7 percent EAR. Hirosaki pays no dividends.

  a. Use the two-state option pricing model to find the current value of Hirosaki's debt and equity.
  b. Suppose Hirosaki has 500,000 shares of common stock outstanding. What is the price per share of the firm's equity?
  c. Compare the market value of Hirosaki's debt to the present value of an equal amount of debt that is riskless with one year until maturity. Is the firm's debt worth more than, less than, or the same as the riskless debt? Does this make sense? What factors might cause these two values to be different?
  d. Suppose that in place of the proceding project, Hirosaki's management decides to undertake a project that is even more risky. The value of the firm will either increase to ¥800 billion or decrease to ¥200 billion by the end of the year. Surprisingly, management concludes that the value of the firm today will remain at exactly ¥400 billion if this risky project is substituted for the less risky one. Use the two-state option pricing model to determine the value of the firm's debt and equity if the firm plans on undertaking this new project. Which project do bondholders prefer?

33. **Black–Scholes and Dividends** In addition to the five factors discussed in the chapter, dividends also affect the price of an option. The Black–Scholes option pricing model with dividends is:

$$C = S \times e^{-dt} \times N(d_1) - E \times e^{-Rt} \times N(d_2)$$
$$d_1 = [\ln(S/E) + (R - d + \sigma^2/2) \times t]/(\sigma \times \sqrt{t})$$
$$d_2 = d_1 - \sigma \times \sqrt{t}$$

All of the variables are the same as the Black–Scholes model without dividends except for the variable d, which is the continuously compounded dividend yield on the stock.

  a. What effect do you think the dividend yield will have on the price of a call option? Explain.
  b. A stock is currently priced at £84 per share, the standard deviation of its return is 50 percent per year, and the risk-free rate is 5 percent per year compounded continuously. What is the price of a call option with a strike price of £80 and a maturity of six months if the stock has a dividend yield of 2 percent per year?

34. **Put–Call Parity and Dividends** The put–call parity condition is altered when dividends are paid. The dividend adjusted put–call parity formula is:

$$S \times e^{-dt} + P = E \times e^{-Rt} + C$$

where d is again the continuously compounded dividend yield.

  a. What effect do you think the dividend yield will have on the price of a put option? Explain.
  b. From the previous question, what is the price of a put option with the same strike price and time to expiration as the call option?

35. **Put Delta** In the chapter, we noted that the delta for a put option is $N(d_1) - 1$. Is this the same thing as $-N(-d_1)$? (*Hint*: Yes, but why?)

36. **Black–Scholes Put Pricing Model** Use the Black–Scholes model for pricing a call, put–call parity, and the previous question to show that the Black–Scholes model for directly pricing a put can be written as follows:

$$P = E \times e^{-Rt} \times N(-d_2) - S \times N(-d_1)$$

37. **Black–Scholes** A stock is currently priced at €50. The stock will never pay a dividend. The risk-free rate is 12 percent per year, compounded continuously, and the standard deviation of the stock's return is 60 percent. A European call option on the stock has a strike price of €100 and no expiration date, meaning that it has an infinite life. Based on Black-Scholes, what is the value of the call option? Do you see a paradox here? Do you see a way out of the paradox?

38. **Delta** You purchase one call and sell one put with the same strike price and expiration date. What is the delta of your portfolio? Why?

Clissold Industries Options

You are currently working for Clissold Industries. The company, which went public five years ago, engages in the design, production, and distribution of lighting equipment and specialty products worldwide. Because of recent events, Mal Clissold, the company president, is concerned about the company's risk, so he asks for your input.

In your discussion with Mal, you explain that the CAPM proposes that the market risk of the company's stock is the determinant of its expected return. Even though Mal agrees with this, he argues that his portfolio consists entirely of Clissold Industry stock and options, so he is concerned with the total risk, or standard deviation, of the company's stock. Furthermore, even though he has calculated the standard deviation of the company's stock for the past five years, he would like an estimate of the stock's volatility moving forward.

Mal states that you can find the estimated volatility of the stock for future periods by calculating the implied standard deviation of option contracts on the company stock. When you examine the factors that affect the price of an option, all of the factors except the standard deviation of the stock are directly observable in the market. You can also observe the option price as well. Mal states that because you can observe all of the option factors except the standard deviation, you can simply solve the Black–Scholes model and find the implied standard deviation.

To help you find the implied standard deviation of the company's stock, Mal has provided you with the following option prices on four call options that expire in six months. The risk-free rate is 6 percent, and the current stock price is $50.

Strike Price	Option Price
$30	$23.00
40	16.05
50	9.75
55	7.95

1. How many different volatilities would you expect to see for the stock?

2. Unfortunately, solving for the implied standard deviation is not as easy as Mal suggests. In fact, there is no direct solution for the standard deviation of the stock even if we have all other variables for the Black–Scholes model. Mal would still like you to estimate the implied standard deviation of the stock. To do this, set up a spreadsheet using the Solver function in Excel to calculate the implied volatilities for each of the options.

3. Are all of the implied volatilities for the options the same? (*Hint*: No.) What are the possible reasons that can cause different volatilities for these options?

4. After you discuss the importance of volatility on option prices, your boss mentions that he has heard of the VIX. What is the VIX and what does it represent? You might need to visit the Chicago Board Options Exchange (CBOE) at www.cboe.com to help with your answer.

5. When you are on the CBOE Web site, look for the option quotes for the VIX. What does the implied volatility of a VIX option represent?

Options and Corporate Finance

Extensions and Applications

In December 2005, Intel announced that it would reduce the number of employee stock options it granted. Instead, the company would grant restricted stock units (RSUs). An RSU is a share of stock that can't be sold or exchanged until it is vested. The vesting period can vary, but in Intel's case the vesting period was four years. When an RSU vests, the employee receives a full share of stock. The biggest advantage of RSUs for employees is that they receive the stock no matter what the stock price. In comparision, with employee stock options, the employee may receive nothing. Intel stated that moving to RSUs was due to a change in employee compensation policies.

Of course, others believed that the reason for the change in compensation policies had more to do with a new accounting rule. Prior to 2005, companies did not report option grants as an expense; but new FASB regulations require expensing of stock options. For many companies, this accounting change could dramatically affect the bottom line. Of course, Intel wasn't alone in the decision to reduce the number of employee stock options granted. Dell, McDonalds, Pfizer, and Aetna are only a few of the others that reduced employee stock option grants. This chapter explores employee stock options, as well as the application of option principles to other areas of corporate finance.

23.1 Executive Stock Options

Why Options?

Executive compensation is usually made up of base salary plus some or all of the following elements:

1. Long-term compensation.
2. Annual bonuses.
3. Retirement contributions.
4. Options.

The final component of compensation, options, is by far the biggest part of total compensation for many top executives. Table 23.1 lists the 10 CEOs who received the largest stock option grants during 2005. The rank is in terms of the *face value* of the options granted. This is the number of options times the current stock price.

Knowing the face value of an option does not automatically allow us to determine the market value of the option. We also need to know the exercise price before valuing the option

Table 23.1   2005 Top 10 Option Grants*

Company	CEO	Number of Options Granted (thousands)†	Average Stock Price	Grant Value of Options Granted (millions)‡
Wells Fargo & Co.	Richard Kovacevich	1,853	$58.71	$108.8
Gillette Company	James Kilts	2,000	39.71	79.4
United HealthGroup Inc.	William McGuire	1,300	59.40	77.2
Viacom International Inc.	Sumner Redstone	2,050	36.09	74.0
U.W. Bancorp	Jerry Grundhofer	1,720	30.40	52.3
Capital One Financial Corporation	Richard Fairbank	566	82.39	46.6
Anheuser-Busch Companies, Inc.	Patrick Stokes	900	50.29	45.3
Countrywide Financial Corporation	Angelo Mozilo	1,400	31.86	44.6
Dell Computer Corporation	Kevin Rollins	1,200	34.73	41.7
American Express Company	Kenneth Chenault	799	51.72	41.3

*Based on the 200 largest U.S. industrial and service corporations (grants from fiscal years ending 2/1/2004 to 1/31/2005).

†Stock option award includes reload/restoration options as well as other features.

‡Face value of options granted equals the number of options times the stock price.

SOURCE: Pearl Meyer & Partners.

according to either the Black–Scholes model or the binomial model. However, the exercise price is generally set equal to the market price of the stock on the date the executive receives the options. In the next section, we value options under the assumption that the exercise price is equal to the market price.

Options in the stock of the company are increasingly being granted to executives as an alternative to increases in base pay. Some of the reasons given for using options are these:

1. Options make executives share the same interests as the stockholders. By aligning interests, executives are more likely to make decisions for the benefit of the stockholders.

2. Options allow the company to lower the executive's base pay. This removes pressures on morale caused by disparities between the salaries of executives and those of other employees.

3. Options put an executive's pay at risk, rather than guaranteeing it regardless of the performance of the firm.

4. Options are a tax-efficient way to pay employees. Under current tax law, if an executive is given options to purchase company stock and the options are "at the money," they are not considered part of taxable income to the employee. The options are taxed only when and if they are eventually exercised.

EXAMPLE 23.1

Options at Starbucks Stock options are not always restricted to the highest-ranking executives. Starbucks, the coffee chain, has pushed options down to the lowest-level employees. To quote its founder, Howard Schultz, "Even though we were a private company, we would grant stock options to every employee companywide, from the top managers to the baristas, in proportion to their level of base pay. They could then, through their efforts, help make Starbucks more successful every year, and if Starbucks someday went public, their options could eventually be worth a good sum of money."

Valuing Executive Compensation

In this section, we value executive stock options. Not surprisingly, the complexity of the total compensation package often makes valuation a difficult task. The economic value of the options depends on factors such as the volatility of the underlying stock and the exact terms of the option grant.

We attempt to estimate the economic value of the options held by the executives listed in Table 23.1. To do so, we employ the Black–Scholes option pricing formula from Chapter 22. Of course, we are missing many features of the particular plans, and the best we can hope for is a rough estimate. Simple matters such as requiring the executive to hold the option for a fixed period, the freeze-out period, before exercising, can significantly diminish the value of a standard option. Equally important, the Black–Scholes formula has to be modified if the stock pays dividends and is no longer applicable if the volatility of the stock is changing randomly over time. Intuitively, a call option on a dividend-paying stock is worth less than a call on a stock that pays no dividends: All other things being equal, the dividends will lower the stock price. Nevertheless, let us see what we can do.

EXAMPLE 23.2

Options at Gillette Consider James Kilts, the chief executive officer (CEO) of Gillette, who was granted 2 million options. The average stock price at the time of the options grant was $39.71. We will assume that his options are at the money. The risk-free rate is 5 percent and the options expire in five years. The preceding information implies that:

1. The stock price (S) of $39.71 equals the exercise price (E).
2. The risk-free rate $R = 0.05$.
3. The time interval $t = 5$.

In addition, the variance of Gillette is estimated to be $(0.2168)^2 = .0470$

This information allows us to value James Kilts's options using the Black–Scholes model:

$$C = SN(d_1) - Ee^{-Rt}N(d_2)$$

$$d_1 = [(R + 1/2\sigma^2)t]/\sqrt{\sigma^2 t} = 0.758$$

$$d_2 = d_1 - \sqrt{\sigma^2 t} = 0.273$$

$$N(d_1) = 0.776$$

$$N(d_2) = 0.608$$

$$e^{-.05 \times 5} = 0.7788$$

$$C = \$39.71 \times .776 - \$39.71 \times (0.7788 \times 0.608) = \$12.03$$

Thus the value of a call option on one share of Gillette stock is $12.03. Because Mr. Kilts was granted options on 2 million shares, the market value of his options, as estimated by the Black–Scholes formula, is about $24 million (= 2 million × $12.03).

Table 23.2   Value of 2005 Top 10 Option Grants*

Company	CEO	Grant Value of Options Granted (millions)†	Annual Stock Standard Deviation (%/year)	Black–Scholes Value (millions)‡
Wells Fargo & Co.	Richard Kovacevich	$108.8	20.09	$32
Viacom International Inc.	Sumner Redstone	74.0	30.86	27
Gillette Company	James Kilts	79.4	21.68	24
United HealthGroup Inc.	William McGuire	77.2	21.77	23
Capital One Financial Corporation	Richard Fairbank	46.6	43.78	21
U.W. Bancorp	Jerry Grundhofer	52.3	25.70	17
Dell Computer Corporation	Kevin Rollins	41.7	35.79	17
Countrywide Financial Corporation	Angelo Mozilo	44.6	30.84	16
American Express Company	Kenneth Chenault	41.3	26.32	14
Anheuser-Busch Companies, Inc.	Patrick Stokes	45.3	15.05	12

*Based on the 200 largest U.S. industrial and service corporations.

†Grant value of options granted is the number of options times the stock price.

‡Stock option award includes reload/restoration options as well as other features that are not being valued here.

SOURCE: Pearl Meyer & Partners.

We assume that all of the options are "at the money," so that their exercise prices are the current stock values. The total exercise prices are thus equal to the reported face value. We take the risk-free interest rate as 5 percent and assume that the options all have a maturity of five years. Finally, we ignore the dilution from exercising them as warrants and value them as call options. The last required input, the volatility or standard deviation of the stock, σ, is estimated from the historical returns on each of the stocks. Table 23.2 lists the volatilities for each stock and the estimated value of the stock grants. As can be seen, these values, while large by ordinary standards, are significantly less than the corresponding face values. Notice that the ordering by face value is not the same as that by economic value. For example, whereas Table 23.1 indicates that Sumner Redstone of Viacom ranks fourth in grant value, Table 23.2 shows that he ranks second in Black–Scholes value—the difference being caused by Viacom's high standard deviation.

The values we have computed in Table 23.2 are the economic values of the options if they were to trade in the market. The real question is this: Whose value are we talking about? Are these the costs of the options to the company? Are they the values of the options to the executives?

Suppose a company computes the fair market value of the options as we have done in Table 23.2. For illustration, assume that the options are in the money and that they are worth $25 each. Suppose, too, that the CEO holds 1 million such options for a total value of $25 million. This is the amount that the options would trade at in the financial markets and that traders and investors would be willing to pay for them.[1] If the company were very large, it would not be unreasonable for it to view this as the cost of granting the options to the CEO. Of course, in return, the company would expect the CEO to improve the value of the company to its shareholders by more than this amount. As we have seen, perhaps the main purpose of options is to align the interests of management with those of the shareholders of the firm. Under no circumstances, though, is the $25 million necessarily a fair measure of what the options are worth to the CEO.

As an illustration, suppose that the CEO of ABC has options on 1 million shares with an exercise price of $30 per share, and the current price of ABC stock is $50 per share. If the options were exercised today, they would be worth $20 million (an underestimation of their market value). Suppose, in addition, that the CEO owns $5 million in company stock and has $5 million in other assets. The CEO clearly has a very undiversified personal portfolio. By the standards of modern portfolio theory, having 25/30 or about 83 percent of your personal wealth in one stock and its options is unnecessarily risky.

Although the CEO is wealthy by most standards, shifts in stock price impact the CEO's economic well-being. If the price drops from $50 per share to $30 per share, the current exercise value of the options on 1 million shares drops from $20 million down to zero. Ignoring the fact that if the options had more time to mature they might not lose all of this value, we nevertheless have a rather startling decline in the CEO's net worth from about $30 million to $8 million ($5 million in other assets plus stock that is now worth $3 million). But that is the purpose of giving the options and the stock holdings to the CEO—namely, to make the CEO's fortunes rise and fall with those of the company. It is why the company requires the executive to hold the options for at least a freeze-out period rather than letting the executive sell them to realize their value.

The implication is that when options are a large portion of an executive's net worth, the total value of the position to the executive is less than market value. As a purely financial matter, an executive might be happier with $5 million in cash rather than $20 million in options. At least the executive could then diversify his personal portfolio.

23.2 Valuing a Start-Up

Ralph Simmons was not your typical MBA student. Since childhood he had had one ambition: to open a restaurant that sold alligator meat. He went to business school because he realized that although he knew 101 ways to cook alligators, he didn't have the business skills necessary to run a restaurant. He was extremely focused, with each course at graduate school being important to him only to the extent that it could further his dream.

While taking his school's course in entrepreneurship, he began to develop a business plan for his restaurant, which he now called Alligator Alley. He thought about marketing; he thought about raising capital; he thought about dealing with future employees. He even devoted a great deal of time to designing the physical layout of the restaurant. Against the professor's advice in his entrepreneurship class, he designed the restaurant in the shape of an alligator, where the front door went through the animal's mouth. Of course his business

---

[1]We ignore warrant dilution in this example. See Chapter 24 for a discussion of warrant dilution.

Table 23.3 **Financial Projections for Alligator Alley**

	Year 1	Year 2	Year 3	Year 4	All Future Years
(1) Sales	$300,000	$600,000	$900,000	$1,000,000	$1,000,000
(2) Cash flows from operations	−100,000	−50,000	+75,000	+250,000	+250,000
(3) Increase in working capital	50,000	20,000	10,000	10,000	0
(4) Net cash flows [(2) − (3)]	−$150,000	−$ 70,000	$ 65,000	$ 240,000	$ 250,000
Present value of net cash flows in years 1–4 (discounted at 20%)			−$ 20,255		
Present value of terminal value	$\left[\dfrac{\$250,000}{0.20} \times \dfrac{1}{(1.20)^4} \right] =$		+$602,816		
Present value of restaurant			$582,561		
− Cost of building			−700,000		
Net present value of restaurant			−$117,439		

plan would not be complete without financial projections. After much thought, he came up with the projections shown in Table 23.3.

The table starts with sales projections, which rise from $300,000 in the first year to a steady state of $1 million a year. Cash flows from operations are shown in the next line, although we leave out the intermediate calculations needed to move from line (1) to line (2). After subtracting working capital, the table shows net cash flows in line (4). Net cash flows are negative initially, as is quite common in start-ups, but they become positive by year 3. However, the rest of the table presents the unfortunate truth. The cash flows from the restaurant yield a present value of $582,561, assuming a discount rate of 20 percent. Unfortunately, the cost of the building is greater, at $700,000, implying a negative net present value of −$117,439.

The projections indicate that Ralph's lifelong dream may not come to pass. He cannot expect to raise the capital needed to open his restaurant; and if he did obtain the funding, the restaurant would likely go under anyway. Ralph checked and rechecked the numbers, hoping vainly to discover either a numerical error or a cost-saving omission that would move his venture from the red to the black. In fact, Ralph saw that, if anything, his forecasts are generous: A 20 percent discount rate and an infinitely lived building are on the optimistic side.

It wasn't until Ralph took a course in corporate strategy that he saw the hidden value in his venture. In that course, his instructor repeatedly stated the importance of positioning a firm to take advantage of new opportunities. Although Ralph didn't see the connection at first, he finally realized the implications for Alligator Alley. His financial projections were based on expectations. There was a 50 percent probability that alligator meat would be more popular than he thought, in which case actual cash flows would exceed projections. And there was a 50 percent probability that the meat would be less popular, in which case the actual flows would fall short of projections.

If the restaurant did poorly, it would probably fold in a few years because he would not want to keep losing money forever. However, if the restaurant did well, he would be in a position to expand. With alligator meat being popular in one locale, it would likely prove popular in other locales as well. Thus, he noticed two options: the option to abandon under bad conditions and the option to expand under good conditions. Although both options can be valued according to the principles of the previous chapter, we focus on the option to expand because it is probably much more valuable.

Ralph reasoned that as much as he personally liked alligator meat, consumer resistance in some regions of the country would doom Alligator Alley. So he developed a strategy of catering only to those regions where alligator meat is somewhat popular already. He forecast that although he could expand quickly if the first restaurant proved successful, the market would limit him to 30 additional restaurants.

Ralph believes that this expansion will occur about four years from now. He believes that he will need three years of operating the first restaurant to (1) get the initial restaurant running smoothly and (2) have enough information to place an accurate value on the restaurant. If the first restaurant is successful enough, he will need another year to obtain outside capital. Thus, he will be ready to build the 30 additional units around the fourth year.

Ralph will value his enterprise, including the option to expand, according to the Black–Scholes model. From Table 23.3 we see that each unit costs $700,000, implying a total cost over the 30 additional units of $21,000,000 (= 30 × $700,000). The present value of the cash inflows from these 30 units is $17,476,830 (= 30 × $582,561), according to the table. However, because the expansion will occur around the fourth year, this present value calculation is provided from the point of view of four years in the future. The present value as of today is $8,428,255 [= $17,476,830/$(1.20)^4$], assuming a discount rate of 20 percent per year. Thus, Ralph views his potential restaurant business as an option, where the exercise price is $21,000,000 and the value of the underlying asset is $8,428,255. The option is currently out of the money, a result that follows from the negative value of a typical restaurant, as calculated in Table 23.3. Of course, Ralph is hoping that the option will move into the money within four years.

Ralph needs three additional parameters to use the Black–Scholes model: R, the continuously compounded interest rate; t, the time to maturity; and σ, the standard deviation of the underlying asset. Ralph uses the yield on a four-year zero coupon bond, which is 3.5 percent, as the estimate of the interest rate. The time to maturity is four years. The estimate of standard deviation is a little trickier because there is no historical data on alligator restaurants. Ralph finds that the average annual standard deviation of the returns on publicly traded restaurants is 0.35. Because Alligator Alley is a new venture, he reasons that the risk here would be somewhat greater. He finds that the average annual standard deviation for restaurants that have gone public in the last few years is 0.45. Ralph's restaurant is newer still, so he uses a standard deviation of 0.50.

There are now enough data to value Ralph's venture. The value according to the Black–Scholes model is $1,455,196. The actual calculations are shown in Table 23.4. Of course Ralph must start his pilot restaurant before he can take advantage of this option. Thus, the net value of the call option plus the negative present value of the pilot restaurant is $1,337,757 (= $1,455,196 − $117,439). Because this value is large and positive, Ralph decides to stay with his dream of Alligator Alley. He knows that the probability that the restaurant will fail is greater than 50 percent. Nevertheless, the option to expand is important enough that his restaurant business has value. And if he needs outside capital, he probably can attract the necessary investors.

This finding leads to the appearance of a paradox. If Ralph approaches investors to invest in a single restaurant with no possibility of expansion, he will probably not be able to attract capital. After all, Table 23.3 shows a net present value of −$117,439. However, if Ralph thinks bigger, he will likely be able to attract all the capital he needs. But this is really not a paradox at all. By thinking bigger, Ralph is offering investors the option—not the obligation—to expand.

The example we have chosen may seem frivolous, and certainly we added offbeat characteristics for interest. However, if you think that business situations involving options are unusual or unimportant, let us state emphatically that nothing is further from the truth. The notion of embedded options is at the heart of business. There are two possible outcomes

Table 23.4

Valuing a Start-Up Firm (Alligator Alley) as an Option

Facts

1. The value of a single restaurant is negative, as indicated by the net present value calculation in Table 23.3 of −$117,439. Thus, the restaurant would not be funded if there were no possibility of expansion.

2. If the pilot restaurant is successful, Ralph Simmons plans to create 30 additional restaurants around year 4. This leads to the following observations:
    a. The total cost of 30 units is $21,000,000 (= 30 × $700,000).
    b. The present value of future cash flows as of year 4 is $17,476,830 (= 30 × $582,561).
    c. The present value of these cash flows today is $8,428,255 [= $17,476,830/(1.20)^4].

    Here we assume that cash flows from the project are discounted at 20% per annum.

    Thus, the business is essentially a call option, where the exercise price is $21,000,000 and the underlying asset is worth $8,428,255.

3. Ralph Simmons estimates the standard deviation of the annual return on Alligator Alley's stock to be 0.50.

Parameters of the Black–Scholes model:

$$S \text{ (stock price)} = \$8,428,255$$
$$E \text{ (exercise price)} = \$21,000,000$$
$$t \text{ (time to maturity)} = 4 \text{ years}$$
$$\sigma \text{ (standard deviation)} = 0.50$$
$$R \text{ (continuously compounded interest rate)} = 3.5\%$$

Calculation from the Black–Scholes model:

$$C = SN(d_1) - Ee^{-Rt}N(d_2)$$
$$d_1 = [\ln(S/E) + (R + 1/2\sigma^2)t]/\sqrt{\sigma^2 t}$$
$$d_2 = d_1 - \sqrt{\sigma^2 t}$$
$$d_1 = \left[\ln \frac{8,428,255}{21,000,000} + \left(0.035 + \frac{1}{2}(0.50)^2\right)4\right] \bigg/ \sqrt{(0.50)^2 \cdot 4} = -0.27293$$
$$d_2 = -0.27293 - \sqrt{(0.50)^2 \cdot 4} = -1.27293$$
$$N(d_1) = N(-0.27293) = 0.3936$$
$$N(d_2) = N(-1.27293) = 0.1020$$
$$C = \$8,428,255 \times 0.3936 - \$21,000,000 \times e^{-0.035 \times 4} \times 0.1020$$
$$= \$1,455,196$$

Value of business including cost of pilot restaurant = $1,455,196 − $117,439
$$= \$1,337,757$$

for virtually every business idea. On the one hand, the business may fail, in which case the managers will probably try to shut it down in the most cost-efficient way. On the other hand, the business may prosper, in which case the managers will try to expand. Thus, virtually every business has both the option to abandon and the option to expand. You may have read pundits claiming that the net present value approach to capital budgeting is wrong or incomplete. Although criticism of this type frequently irritates the finance establishment, the pundits definitely have a point. If virtually all projects have embedded options, only an approach such as the one we have outlined can be appropriate. Ignoring the options is likely to lead to serious undervaluation.

23.3   More about the Binomial Model

Earlier in this chapter, we examined two applications of options: executive compensation and the start-up decision. In both cases we valued an option using the Black–Scholes model. Although this model is justifiably well known, it is not the only approach to option valuation. As mentioned in the previous chapter, the two-state or binomial model is an alternative and—in some situations—a superior approach to valuation. The rest of this chapter examines two applications of the binomial model.

Heating Oil

Two-Date Example   Consider Anthony Meyer, a typical heating oil distributor, whose business consists of buying heating oil at the wholesale level and reselling the oil to homeowners at a somewhat higher price. Most of his revenue comes from sales during the winter. Today, September 1, heating oil sells for $2.00 per gallon. Of course this price is not fixed. Rather, oil prices will vary from September 1 until December 1, the time when his customers will probably make their big winter purchases of heating oil. Let's simplify the situation by assuming that Mr. Meyer believes that oil prices will either be at $2.74 or $1.46 on December 1. Figure 23.1 portrays this possible price movement. This potential price range represents a great deal of uncertainty because Mr. Meyer has no idea which of the two possible prices will actually occur. However, this price variability does not translate into that much risk because he can pass price changes on to his customers. That is, he will charge his customers more if he ends up paying $2.74 per gallon than if he ends up paying $1.46 per gallon.

Of course, Mr. Meyer is avoiding risk by passing on that risk to his customers. His customers accept the risk, perhaps because they are each too small to negotiate a better deal. This is not the case with CECO, a large electric utility in his area. CECO approaches Mr. Meyer with the following proposition. The utility would like to be able to buy *up to* 6 million gallons of oil from him at $2.10 per gallon on December 1.

Although this arrangement represents a lot of oil, both Mr. Meyer and CECO know that Mr. Meyer can expect to lose money on it. If prices rise to $2.74 per gallon, the utility will happily buy all 6 million gallons at only $2.10 per gallon, clearly creating a loss for the distributor. However, if oil prices decline to $1.46 per gallon, the utility will not buy any oil. After all, why should CECO pay $2.10 per gallon to Mr. Meyer when the utility

Figure 23.1

Movement of Heating Oil Prices from September 1 to December 1 in a Two-Date Example

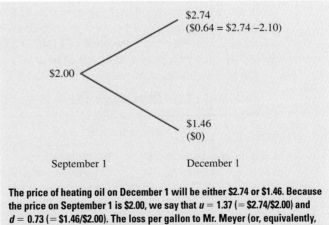

$2.74
($0.64 = $2.74 −2.10)

$2.00

$1.46
($0)

September 1   December 1

The price of heating oil on December 1 will be either $2.74 or $1.46. Because the price on September 1 is $2.00, we say that $u = 1.37$ (= $2.74/$2.00) and $d = 0.73$ (= $1.46/$2.00). The loss per gallon to Mr. Meyer (or, equivalently, the gain per gallon to CECO) of $0.64 in the up state or $0 in the down state is shown in parentheses.

can buy all the oil it wants at $1.46 per gallon in the open market? In other words, CECO is asking for a *call option* on heating oil. To compensate Mr. Meyer for the risk of loss, the two parties agree that CECO will pay him $1,000,000 up front for the right to buy up to 6 million gallons of oil at $2.10 per gallon.

Is this a fair deal? Although small distributors may evaluate a deal like this by gut feel, we can evaluate it more quantitatively by using the binomial model described in the previous chapter. In that chapter, we pointed out that option problems can be handled most easily by assuming *risk-neutral pricing*. In this approach, we first note that oil will either rise 37 percent (= $2.74/$2.00 − 1) or fall −27 percent (= $1.46/$2.00 − 1) from September 1 to December 1. We can think of these two numbers as the possible returns on heating oil. In addition, we introduce two new terms, *u* and *d*. We define *u* as 1 + 0.37 = 1.37 and *d* as 1 − 0.27 = 0.73.[2] Using the methodology of the previous chapter, we value the contract in the following two steps.

Step 1: Determining the Risk-Neutral Probabilities   We determine the probability of a price rise such that the expected return on oil exactly equals the risk-free rate. Assuming an 8 percent annual interest rate, which implies a 2 percent rate over the next three months, we can solve for the probability of a rise as follows:[3]

$$2\% = \text{Probability of rise} \times 0.37 + (1 - \text{Probability of rise}) \times (-0.27)$$

Solving this equation, we find that the probability of a rise is approximately 45 percent, implying that the probability of a fall is 55 percent. In other words, if the probability of a price rise is 45 percent, the expected return on heating oil is 2 percent. In accordance with what we said in the previous chapter, these are the probabilities that are consistent with a world of risk neutrality. That is, under risk neutrality, the expected return on any asset would equal the riskless rate of interest. No one would demand an expected return above this riskless rate, because risk-neutral individuals do not need to be compensated for bearing risk.

Step 2: Valuing the Contract   If the price of oil rises to $2.74 on December 1, CECO will want to buy oil from Mr. Meyer at $2.10 per gallon. Mr. Meyer will lose $0.64 per gallon because he buys oil in the open market at $2.74 per gallon, only to resell it to CECO at $2.10 per gallon. This loss of $0.64 is shown in parentheses in Figure 23.1. Conversely, if the market price of heating oil falls to $1.46 per gallon, CECO will not buy any oil from Mr. Meyer. That is, CECO would not want to pay $2.10 per gallon to him when the utility could buy heating oil in the open market at $1.46 per gallon. Thus, we can say that Mr. Meyer neither gains nor loses if the price drops to $1.46. The gain or loss of zero is placed in parentheses under the price of $1.46 in Figure 23.1. In addition, as mentioned earlier, Mr. Meyer receives $1,000,000 up front.

Given these numbers, the value of the contract to Mr. Meyer can be calculated as:

$$\underbrace{[0.45 \times (\$2.10 - \$2.74) \times 6 \text{ million} + 0.55 \times 0]/1.02}_{\text{Value of the call option}} + \$1,000,000 = -\$694,118$$

(23.1)

As in the previous chapter, we are valuing an option using risk-neutral pricing. The cash flows of −$0.64 (= $2.10 − $2.74) and $0 per gallon are multiplied by their risk-neutral probabilities. The entire first term in Equation 23.1 is then discounted at $1.02 because the cash flows in that term occur on December 1. The $1,000,000 is not discounted because

---

[2]As we will see later, here *u* and *d* are consistent with a standard deviation of the annual return on heating oil of 0.63.

[3]For simplicity, we ignore both storage costs and a convenience yield.

Figure 23.2

Movement of Heating Oil Prices in a Three-Date Model

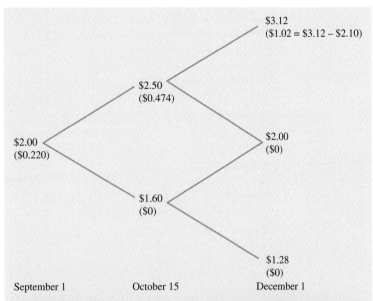

The figure shows the prices of a gallon of heating oil on three dates, given $u = 1.25$ and $d = 0.80$. There are three possible prices for heating oil on December 1. For each one of these three prices, we calculate the price on December 1 of a call option on a gallon of heating oil with an exercise price of $2.10. These numbers are in parentheses. Call prices at earlier dates are determined by the binomial model and are also shown in parentheses.

Mr. Meyer receives it today, September 1. Because the present value of the contract is negative, Mr. Meyer would be wise to reject the contract.

As stated before, the distributor has sold a call option to CECO. The first term in the preceding equation, which equals −$1,694,000, can be viewed as the value of this call option. It is a negative number because the equation looks at the option from Mr. Meyer's point of view. Therefore, the value of the call option would be +$1,694,000 to CECO. On a per-gallon basis, the value of the option to CECO is:

$$[0.45\,(\$2.74 - \$2.10) + 0.55 \times 0]/1.02 = \$0.282 \qquad \textbf{(23.2)}$$

Equation 23.2 shows that CECO will gain $0.64 (= $2.74 − $2.10) per gallon in the up state because CECO can buy heating oil worth $2.74 for only $2.10 under the contract. By contrast, the contract is worth nothing to CECO in the down state because the utility will not pay $2.10 for oil selling for only $1.46 in the open market. Using risk-neutral pricing, the formula tells us that the value of the call option on one gallon of heating oil is $0.282.

Three-Date Example   Although the preceding example captures a number of aspects of the real world, it has one deficiency. It assumes that the price of heating oil can take on only two values on December 1. This is clearly not plausible: Oil can take on essentially any value in reality. Although this deficiency seems glaring at first glance, it actually is easily correctable. All we have to do is to introduce more intervals over the three-month period of our example.

For example, consider Figure 23.2, which shows the price movement of heating oil over two intervals of 1½ months each.[4] As shown in the figure, the price will be either $2.50

---

[4]Though it is not apparent at first glance, we will see later that the price movement in Figure 23.2 is consistent with the price movement in Figure 23.1.

or $1.60 on October 15. We refer to $2.50 as the price in the *up state* and $1.60 as the price in the *down state*. Thus, heating oil has returns of 25 percent (= $2.50/$2.00) and −20 percent (= $1.60/$2) in the two states.

We assume the same variability as we move forward from October 15 to December 1. That is, given a price of $2.50 on October 15, the price on December 1 will be either $3.12 (= $2.50 × 1.25) or $2 (= $2.50 × 0.80). Similarly, given a price of $1.60 on October 15, the price on December 1 will be either $2 (= $1.60 × 1.25) or $1.28 (= $1.60 × 0.80). This assumption of constant variability is quite plausible because the rate of new information impacting heating oil (or most commodities or assets) is likely to be similar from month to month.

Note that there are three possible prices on December 1, but there are two possible prices on October 15. Also note that there are two paths to a price of $2 on December 1. The price could rise to $2.50 on October 15 before falling back down to $2 on December 1. Alternatively, the price could fall to $1.60 on October 15 before going back up to $2 on December 1. In other words, the model has symmetry, where an up movement followed by a down movement yields the same price on December 1 as a down movement followed by an up movement.

How do we value CECO's option in this three-date example? We employ the same procedure that we used in the two-date example, although we now need an extra step because of the extra date.

Step 1: Determining the Risk-Neutral Probabilities   As we did in the two-date example, we determine what the probability of a price rise would be such that the expected return on heating oil exactly equals the riskless rate. However, in this case, we work with an interval of 1½ months. Assuming an 8 percent annual rate of interest, which implies a 1 percent rate over a 1½ month interval,[5] we can solve for the probability of a rise like this:

$$1\% = \text{Probability of rise} \times 0.25 + (1 - \text{Probability of rise}) \times (-0.20)$$

Solving the equation, we find that the probability of a rise here is 47 percent, implying that the probability of a fall is 53 percent. In other words, if the probability of a rise is 47 percent, the expected return on heating oil is 1 percent per each 1½-month interval. Again these probabilities are determined under the assumption of risk-neutral pricing.

Note that the probabilities of 47 percent and 53 percent hold for both the interval from September 1 to October 15 and the interval from October 15 to December 1. This is the case because the return in the up state is 25 percent and the return in the down state is –20 percent for each of the two intervals. Thus, the preceding equation must apply to each of the intervals separately.

Step 2: Valuing the Option as of October 15   As indicated in Figure 23.2, the option to CECO will be worth $1.02 per gallon on December 1 if the price of heating oil has risen to $3.12 on that date. That is, CECO can buy oil from Mr. Meyer at $2.10 when it would otherwise have to pay $3.12 in the open market. However, the option will be worthless on December 1 if the price of a gallon of heating oil is either $2 or $1.28 on that date. Here the option is out of the money because the exercise price of $2.10 is above either $2 or $1.28.

Using these option prices on December 1, we can calculate the value of the call option on October 15. If the price of a gallon of heating oil is $2.50 on October 15, Figure 23.2

---

[5]For simplicity, we ignore interest compounding.

shows us that the call option will be worth either $1.02 or $0 on December 1. Thus if the price of heating oil is $2.50 on October 15, the value of the option on one gallon of heating oil at that time is:

$$[0.47 \times \$1.02 + 0.53 \times 0]/1.01 = \$0.474$$

Here we are valuing an option using the same risk-neutral pricing approach that we used in the earlier two-date example. This value of $0.474 is shown in parentheses in Figure 23.2.

We also want to value the option on October 15 if the price at that time is $1.60. However, the value here is clearly zero, as indicated by this calculation:

$$[0.47 \times \$0 + 0.53 \times \$0]/1.01 = 0$$

This is obvious once we look at Figure 23.2. We see from the figure that the call must end up out of the money on December 1 if the price of heating oil is $1.60 on October 15. Thus, the call must have zero value on October 15 if the price of heating oil is $1.60 on that date.

Step 3: Valuing the Option on September 1   In the previous step, we saw that the price of the call on October 15 would be $0.474 if the price of a gallon of heating oil were $2.50 on that date. Similarly, the price of the option on October 15 would be $0 if oil were selling at $1.60 on that date. From these values, we can calculate the call option value on September 1:

$$[0.47 \times \$0.474 + 0.53 \times \$0]/1.01 = \$0.220$$

Notice that this calculation is completely analogous to the calculation of the option value in the previous step, as well as the calculation of the option value in the two-date example that we presented earlier. In other words, the same approach applies regardless of the number of intervals used. As we will see later, we can move to many intervals, which produces greater realism, yet still maintain the same basic methodology.

The previous calculation has given us the value to CECO of its option on one gallon of heating oil. Now we are ready to calculate the value of the contract to Mr. Meyer. Given the calculations from the previous equation, the contract's value can be written as:

$$-\$0.220 \times 6,000,000 + \$1,000,000 = -\$320,000$$

That is, Mr. Meyer is giving away an option worth $0.220 for each of the 6 million gallons of heating oil. In return, he is receiving only $1,000,000 up front. On balance, he is losing $320,000. Of course, the value of the contract to CECO is the opposite, so the value to this utility is $320,000.

Extension to Many Dates   We have looked at the contract between CECO and Mr. Meyer using both a two-date example and a three-date example. The three-date case is more realistic because more possibilities for price movements are allowed here. However, why stop at just three dates? Moving to 4 dates, 5 dates, 50 dates, 500 dates, and so on should give us ever more realism. Note that as we move to more dates, we are merely shortening the interval between dates without increasing the overall time period of three months (September 1 to December 1).

For example, imagine a model with 90 dates over the three months. Here each interval is approximately one day long because there are about 90 days in a three-month period. The assumption of two possible outcomes in the binomial model is more plausible over a one-day interval than it is over a 1½-month interval, let alone a three-month interval. Of course, we could probably achieve greater realism still by going to an interval of, say, one hour or one minute.

Table 23.5

Value of a Call on One Gallon of Heating Oil

Number of Intervals*	Call Value
1	$0.282
2	0.220
3	0.244
4	0.232
6	0.228
10	0.228
20	0.228
30	0.228
40	0.228
50	0.226
99	0.226
Black–Scholes Infinity	0.226

In this example, the value of the call according to the binomial model varies as the number of intervals increases. However, the value of the call converges rapidly to the Black–Scholes value. Thus the binomial model, even with only a few intervals, appears to be a good approximation to Black–Scholes.

*The number of intervals is always one less than the number of dates.

How do we adjust the binomial model to accommodate increases in the number of intervals? It turns out that two simple formulas relate u and d to the standard deviation of the return of the underlying asset:[6]

$$u = e^{\sigma/\sqrt{n}} \quad \text{and} \quad d = 1/u$$

where σ is the standard deviation of the annualized return on the underlying asset (heating oil, in this case) and n is the number of intervals over a year.

When we created the heating oil example, we assumed that the annualized standard deviation of the return on heating oil was 0.63 (or, equivalently, 63 percent). Because there are four quarters in a year, $u = e^{0.63/\sqrt{4}} = 1.37$ and $d = 1/1.37 = 0.73$, as shown in the two-date example of Figure 23.1. In the three-date example of Figure 23.2, where each interval is 1½ months long, $u = e^{0.63/\sqrt{8}} = 1.25$ and $d = 1/1.25 = 0.80$. Thus the binomial model can be applied in practice if the standard deviation of the return of the underlying asset can be estimated.

We stated earlier that the value of the call option on a gallon of heating oil was estimated to be $0.282 in the two-date model and $0.220 in the three-date model. How does the value of the option change as we increase the number of intervals while keeping the time period constant at three months (from September 1 to December 1)? We have calculated the value of the call for various time intervals in Table 23.5.[7] The realism increases with the number of intervals because the restriction of only two possible outcomes is more plausible over a short interval than over a long one. Thus, the value of the call when the number of intervals is 99 or infinity is likely more realistic than this value when the number of intervals is, say, 1 or 2.

---

[6]See John C. Hull, *Options, Futures, and Other Derivatives*, 6th ed. (Upper Saddle River, NJ: Prentice Hall, 2005), for a derivation of these formulas.

[7]In this discussion we have used both *intervals* and *dates*. To keep the terminology straight, remember that the number of intervals is always one less than the number of dates. For example, if a model has two dates, it has only one interval.

However, a very interesting phenomenon can be observed from the table. Although the value of the call changes as the number of intervals increases, convergence occurs quite rapidly. The call's value with 6 intervals is almost identical to the value with 99 intervals. Thus, a small number of intervals appears serviceable for the binomial model. Six intervals in a three-month period implies that each interval is two weeks long. Of course the assumption that heating oil can take on only one of two prices in two weeks is simply not realistic. The paradox is that this unrealistic assumption still produces a realistic call price.

What happens when the number of intervals goes to infinity, implying that the length of the interval goes to zero? It can be proved mathematically that we end up with the value of the Black–Scholes model. This value is also presented in Table 23.5. Thus, we can argue that the Black–Scholes model is the best approach to value the heating oil option. It is also quite easy to apply. We can use a calculator to value options with Black–Scholes, whereas we must generally use a computer program for the binomial model. However, as shown in Table 23.5, the values from the binomial model, even with relatively few intervals, are quite close to the Black–Scholes value. Thus, although Black–Scholes may save us time, it does not materially affect our estimate of value.

At this point it seems as if the Black–Scholes model is preferable to the binomial model. Who wouldn't want to save time and still get a slightly more accurate value? However, such is not always the case. There are plenty of situations where the binomial model is preferred to the Black–Scholes model. One such situation is presented in the next section.

23.4 Shutdown and Reopening Decisions

Some of the earliest and most important examples of special options have occurred in the natural resources and mining industries.

Valuing a Gold Mine

The Woe Is Me gold mine was founded in 1878 on one of the richest veins of gold in the West. Thirty years later, by 1908, the mine had been played out; but occasionally, depending on the price of gold, it is reopened. Currently, gold is not actively mined at Woe Is Me, but its stock is still traded on the exchange under the ticker symbol WOE. WOE has no debt and, with about 20 million outstanding shares, its market value (stock price times number of shares outstanding) exceeds $1 billion. WOE owns about 160 acres of land surrounding the mine and has a 100-year government lease to mine gold there. However, land in the desert has a market value of only a few thousand dollars. WOE holds cash securities, and other assets worth about $30 million. What could possibly explain why a company with $30 million in assets and a closed gold mine with no cash flow has the market value that WOE has?

The answer lies in the options that WOE implicitly owns in the form of a gold mine. Assume that the current price of gold is about $320 per ounce, and the cost of extraction and processing at the mine is about $350 per ounce. It is no wonder that the mine is closed. Every ounce of gold extracted costs $350 and can be sold for only $320, for a loss of $30 per ounce. Presumably, if the price of gold were to rise, the mine could be opened. It costs $2 million to open the mine; when it is opened, production is 50,000 ounces per year. Geologists believe that the amount of gold in the mine is essentially unlimited, and WOE has the right to mine it for the next 100 years. Under the terms of its lease, WOE cannot stockpile gold and must sell each year all the gold it mines that year. Closing the mine, which costs $1 million, requires equipment to be mothballed and some environmental precautions to be put in place. We will refer to the $2 million required to open the mine as the entry fee or investment and the $1 million to close it as the closing or abandonment cost. (We cannot avoid the abandonment cost by simply keeping the mine open and not operating.)

From a financial perspective, WOE is really just a package of options on the price of gold disguised as a company and a mine. The basic option is a call on the price of gold where the exercise price is the $350 extraction cost. The option is complicated by having an exercise fee of $2 million—the opening cost—whenever it is exercised and a closing fee of $1 million when it is abandoned. It is also complicated by the fact that it is a perpetual option with no final maturity.

The Abandonment and Opening Decisions

Before valuing the option implicit in WOE, it is useful to see what we can say by just applying common sense. To begin with, the mine should be opened only when the price of gold is sufficiently above the extraction cost of $350 per ounce. Because it costs $2 million to open the mine, the mine should not be opened whenever the price of gold is only slightly above $350. At a gold price of, say, $350.10, the mine wouldn't be opened because the ten-cent profit per ounce translates into $5,000 per year (= 50,000 ounces × $0.10/ounce). This would not begin to cover the $2 million opening costs. More significantly, though, the mine probably would not be opened if the price rose to $360 per ounce, even though a $10 profit per ounce—$500,000 per year—would pay the $2 million opening costs at any reasonable discount rate. The reason is that here, as in all option problems, volatility (in this case the volatility of gold) plays a significant role. Because the gold price is volatile, the price has to rise sufficiently above $350 per ounce to make it worth opening the mine. If the price at which the mine is opened is too close to the extraction price of $350 per ounce, say at $360 per ounce, we would open the mine every time the price jogged above $360. Unfortunately, we would then find ourselves operating at a loss or facing a closing decision whenever gold jogged back down $10 per ounce (or only 3 percent) to $350.

The estimated volatility of the return on gold is about 15 percent per year. This means that a single annual standard deviation movement in the gold price is 15 percent of $320 or $48 per year. Surely with this amount of random movement in the gold price, a threshold of, for example, $352 is much too low at which to open the mine. A similar logic applies to the closing decision. If the mine is open, we will clearly keep it open as long as the gold price is above the extraction cost of $350 per ounce because we are profiting on every ounce of gold mined. But we also won't close the mine down simply because the gold price drops below $350 per ounce. We will tolerate a running loss because gold may later rise back above $350. If, alternatively, we closed the mine, we would pay the $1 million abandonment cost, only to pay another $2 million to reopen the mine if the price rose again.

To summarize, if the mine is currently closed, then it will be opened—at a cost of $2 million—whenever the price of gold rises *sufficiently* above the extraction cost of $350 per ounce. If the mine is currently operating, then it will be closed down—at a cost of $1 million—whenever the price of gold falls *sufficiently* below the extraction cost of $350 per ounce. WOE's problem is to find these two threshold prices at which it opens a closed mine and closes an open mine. We call these prices p*open* and p*close*, respectively, where:

$$p\mathit{open} > \$350/\text{ounce} > p\mathit{close}$$

In other words, WOE will open the mine if the gold price option is sufficiently in the money and will close it when the option is sufficiently out of the money.

We know that the more volatile the gold price, the further away p*open* and p*close* will be from $350 per ounce. We also know that the greater the cost of opening the mine, the higher p*open* will be; and the greater the cost of abandoning the mine, the lower will be p*close*. Interestingly, we should also expect that p*open* will be higher if the abandonment cost is increased. After all, if it costs more to abandon the mine, WOE will need to be more assured that the price will stay above the extraction cost when it decides to open the mine.

Otherwise WOE will face the costly choice between abandonment and operating at a loss if the price falls below $350 per ounce. Similarly, raising the cost of opening the mine will make WOE more reluctant to close an open mine. As a result, p*close* will be lower.

The preceding arguments have enabled us to reduce the problem of valuing WOE to two stages. First, we have to determine the threshold prices, p*open* and p*close*. Second, given the best choices for these thresholds, we must determine the value of a gold option that is exercised for a cost of $2 million when the gold price rises above p*open* and is shut down for a cost of $1 million whenever the gold price is below p*close*.

When the mine is open—that is, when the option is exercised—the annual cash flow is equal to the difference between the gold price and the extraction cost of $350 per ounce times 50,000 ounces. When the mine is shut down, it generates no cash flow.

The following diagram describes the decisions available at each point in time:

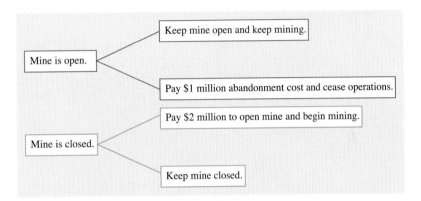

How do we determine the critical values for p*open* and p*close* and then the value of the mine? It is possible to get a good approximation by using the tools we have currently developed.

Valuing the Simple Gold Mine

Here is what has to be done both to determine p*open* and p*close* and to value the mine.

Step 1   Find the risk-free interest rate and the volatility. We assume a semiannual interest rate of 3.4 percent and a volatility of 15 percent per year for gold.

Step 2   Construct a binomial tree and fill it in with gold prices. Suppose, for example, that we set the steps of the tree six months apart. If the annual volatility is 15 percent, u is equal to $e^{0.15/\sqrt{2}}$, which is approximately equal to 1.11. The other parameter, d, is 0.90 ($= 1/1.11$). Figure 23.3 illustrates the tree. Starting at the current price of $320, the first 11 percent increase takes the price to $355 in six months. The first 10 percent decrease takes the price to $288. Subsequent steps are up 11 percent or down 10 percent from the previous price. The tree extends for the 100-year life of the lease or 200 six-month steps.

Using our analysis from the previous section, we now compute the risk-adjusted probabilities for each step. Given a semiannual interest rate of 3.4 percent, we have:

$$3.4\% = \text{Probability of a rise} \times 0.11 + (1 - \text{Probability of a rise}) \times -0.10$$

Solving this equation gives us 0.64 for the probability of a rise, implying that the probability of a fall is 0.36. These probabilities are the same for each six-month interval. In other words, if the probability of a rise is 0.64, the expected return on gold is 3.4 percent

Figure 23.3

A Binomial Tree for Gold Prices

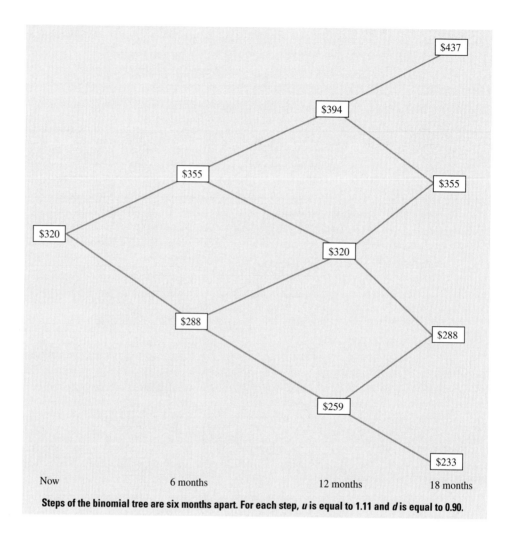

Steps of the binomial tree are six months apart. For each step, *u* is equal to 1.11 and *d* is equal to 0.90.

per each six-month interval. These probabilities are determined under the assumption of risk-neutral pricing. In other words, if investors are risk-neutral, they will be satisfied with an expected return equal to the risk-free rate because the extra risk of gold will not concern them.

Step 3   Now we turn the computer on and let it simulate, say, 5,000 possible paths through the tree. At each node, the computer has a 0.64 probability of picking an "up" movement in the price and a corresponding 0.36 probability of picking a "down" movement in the price. A typical path might be represented by whether the price rose or fell each six-month period over the next 100 years; it would be a list like:

up, up, down, up, down, down, . . . , down

where the first "up" means the price rose from $320 to $355 in the first six months, the next "up" means it again went up in the second half of the year from $355 to $394, and so on, ending with a down move in the last half of year 100.

With 5,000 such paths we will have a good sample of all the future possibilities for movement in the gold price.

Step 4   Next we consider possible choices for the threshold prices, p*open* and p*close*. For p*open*, we let the possibilities be:

$$p\textit{open} = \$360 \text{ or } \$370 \text{ or } \ldots \text{ or } \$500$$

a total of 15 values. For p*close* we let the possibilities be:

$$p\textit{close} = \$340 \text{ or } \$330 \text{ or } \ldots \text{ or } \$100$$

a total of 25 values.

We picked these choices because they seemed reasonable and because increments of $10 for each seemed sensible. To be precise, though, we should let the threshold prices change as we move through the tree and get closer to the end of 100 years. Presumably, for example, if we decided to open the mine with one year left on the lease, the price of gold should be at least high enough to cover the $2 million opening costs in the coming year. Because we mine 50,000 ounces per year, we will open the mine in year 99 only if the gold price is at least $40 above the extraction cost, or $390.

Although this will become important at the end of the lease, using a constant threshold shouldn't have too big an impact on the value with 100 years to go. Therefore, we will stick with our approximation of constant threshold prices.

Step 5   We calculate the value of the mine for each pair of choices of p*open* and p*close*. For example, if p*open* = $410 and p*close* = $290, we use the computer to keep track of the cash flows if we opened the mine whenever it was previously closed and the gold price rose to $410, and closed the mine whenever it was previously open and the gold price fell to $290. We do this for each of the 5,000 paths we simulated in Step 4.

For example, consider the path illustrated in Figure 23.4:

up, up, down, up, up, down, down, down, down

As can be seen from the figure, the price reaches a peak of $437 in 2½ years, only to fall to $288 over the following four six-month intervals. If p*open* = $410 and p*close* = $290, the mine will be opened when the price reaches $437, necessitating a cost of $2 million. However, the firm can sell 25,000 ounces of gold at $437 at that time, producing a cash flow of $2.175 million [= 25,000 × ($437 − $350)]. When the price falls to $394 six months later, the firm sells another 25,000 ounces, yielding a cash flow of $1.1 million [= 25,000 × ($394 − $350)]. The price continues to fall, reaching $320 a year later. Here, the firm experiences a cash outflow because production costs are $350 per ounce. Next, the price falls to $288. Because this price is below p*close* of $290, the mine is closed at a cost of $1 million. Of course, the price of gold will fluctuate in further years, leading to the possibility of future mine openings and closings.

This path is just a possibility. It may or may not occur in any simulation of 5,000 paths. For each of the 5,000 paths that the computer simulated, we have a sequence of semiannual cash flows using a p*open* of $410 and a p*close* of $290. We calculate the present value of each of these cash flows, discounting at the interest rate of 3.4 percent. Summing across all the cash flows, we have the present value of the gold mine for one path.

We then take the average present value of the gold mine across all the 5,000 simulated paths. This number is the expected value of the mine from following a policy of opening the mine whenever the gold price hits $410 and closing it at a price of $290.

Step 6   The final step is to compare the different expected discounted cash flows from Step 5 for the range of possible choices for p*open* and p*close* and to pick the highest one. This is the

Figure 23.4

A Possible Path for the Price of Gold

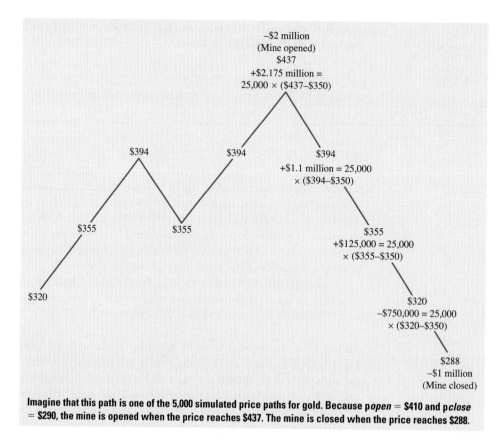

−$2 million
(Mine opened)
$437
+$2.175 million =
25,000 × ($437−$350)

$394 $394 $394
+$1.1 million = 25,000
× ($394−$350)

$355 $355 $355
+$125,000 = 25,000
× ($355−$350)

$320 $320
−$750,000 = 25,000
× ($320−$350)

$288
−$1 million
(Mine closed)

Imagine that this path is one of the 5,000 simulated price paths for gold. Because p*open* = $410 and p*close* = $290, the mine is opened when the price reaches $437. The mine is closed when the price reaches $288.

best estimate of the expected value of the mine. The values for p*close* and p*open* corresponding to this estimate are the points at which to open a closed mine and to shut an open one.

As mentioned in Step 3, there are 15 different values for p*open* and 25 different values for p*close*, implying 375 (= 15 × 25) different pairs. Consider Table 23.6, which shows the present values associated with the 20 best pairs. The table indicates that the best pair is p*open* = $400 and p*close* = $140, with a present value of $1.467 billion. This number represents the average present value across 5,000 simulations, all assuming the preceding values of p*open* and p*close*. The next best pair is p*open* = $460 and p*close* = $300, with a present value of $1.459 billion. The third best pair has a somewhat lower present value, and so on.

Of course, our estimate of the value of the mine is $1.467 billion, the present value of the best pair of choices. The market capitalization (price × number of shares outstanding) of WOE should reach this value if the market makes the same assumptions that we did. Note that the value of the firm is quite high using an option framework. However, as stated earlier, WOE would appear worthless if a regular discounted cash flow approach were used. This occurs because the initial gold price of $320 is below the extraction cost of $350.

This example is not easy, either in concepts or in implementation. However, the extra work involved in mastering this example is worth it because the example illustrates the type of modeling that actually occurs in corporate finance departments in the real world.

Furthermore, the example illustrates the benefits of the binomial approach. We merely calculate the cash flows associated with each of a number of simulations, discount the cash flows from each simulation, and average present values across the simulations. Because the Black–Scholes model is not amenable to simulations, it cannot be used for this type of problem. In addition, there are a number of other situations where the binomial model is

Table 23.6

Valuation of Woe Is Me (WOE) Gold Mine for the 20 Best Choices of p*open* and p*close*

popen	pclose	Estimated Value of Gold Mine
$400	$140	$1,466,720,900
460	300	1,459,406,200
380	290	1,457,838,700
370	100	1,455,131,900
360	190	1,449,708,200
420	150	1,448,711,400
430	340	1,448,450,200
430	110	1,445,396,500
470	200	1,435,687,400
500	320	1,427,512,000
410	290	1,426,483,500
420	290	1,423,865,300
400	160	1,423,061,900
360	320	1,420,748,700
360	180	1,419,112,000
380	280	1,417,405,400
450	310	1,416,238,000
450	280	1,409,709,800
440	220	1,408,269,100
440	240	1,403,398,100

For our simulation, WOE opens the mine whenever the gold price rises above p*open* and closes the mine whenever the gold price falls below p*close*.

more appropriate than is the Black–Scholes model. For example, it is well known that the Black–Scholes model cannot properly handle options with dividend payments prior to the expiration date. This model also does not adequately handle the valuation of an American put. By contrast, the binomial model can easily handle both of these situations.

Thus, any student of corporate finance should be well versed in both models. The Black–Scholes model should be used whenever appropriate because it is simpler to use than is the binomial model. However, for the more complex situations where the Black–Scholes model breaks down, the binomial model becomes a necessary tool.

Summary and Conclusions

Real options, which are pervasive in business, are not captured by net present value analysis. Chapter 8 valued real options via decision trees. Given the work on options in the previous chapter, we are now able to value real options according to the Black–Scholes model and the binomial model.

In this chapter, we described and valued four different types of options:

The Executive stock options, which are technically not real options.
The embedded option in a start-up company.
The option in simple business contracts.
The option to shut down and reopen a project.

We tried to keep the presentation simple and straightforward from a mathematical point of view. The binomial approach to option pricing in Chapter 22 was extended to many periods. This adjustment brings us closer to the real world because the assumption of only two prices at the end of an interval is more plausible when the interval is short.

Concept Questions

1. **Employee Stock Options** Why do companies issue options to executives if they cost the company more than they are worth to the executive? Why not just give cash and split the difference? Wouldn't that make both the company and the executive better off?

2. **Real Options** What are the two options that many businesses have?

3. **Project Analysis** Why does a strict NPV calculation typically understate the value of a company or project?

4. **Real Options** Utility companies often face a decision to build new plants that burn coal, oil, or both. If the prices of both coal and gas are highly volatile, how valuable is the decision to build a plant that can burn either coal or oil? What happens to the value of this option as the correlation between coal and oil prices increases?

5. **Real Options** Your company owns a vacant lot in a suburban area. What is the advantage of waiting to develop the lot?

6. **Real Options** Star Mining buys a gold mine, but the cost of extraction is currently too high to make the mine profitable. In option terminology, what type of option(s) does the company have on this mine?

7. **Real Options** You are discussing real options with a colleague. During the discussion, the colleague states, "Real option analysis makes no sense because it says that a real option on a risky venture is worth more than a real option on a safe venture." How should you respond to this statement?

8. **Real Options and Capital Budgeting** Your company currently uses traditional capital budgeting techniques, including net present value. After hearing about the use of real option analysis, your boss decides that your company should use real option analysis in place of net present value. How would you evaluate this decision?

9. **Insurance as an Option** Insurance, whether purchased by a corporation or an individual, is in essence an option. What type of option is an insurance policy?

10. **Real Options** How would the analysis of real options change if a company has competitors?

Questions and Problems

BASIC
(Questions 1–5)

1. **Employee Stock Options** Andrea Louis is the chief executive officer of Bourges Sports Center. The board of directors has just granted Mr. Louis 20,000 at-the-money European call options on the company's stock, which is currently trading at €50 per share. The stock pays no dividends. The options will expire in four years, and the standard deviation of the returns on the stock is 55 percent. Treasury bills that mature in four years currently yield a continuously compounded interest rate of 6 percent.
   a. Use the Black–Scholes model to calculate the value of the stock options.
   b. You are Mr. Louis's financial adviser. He must choose between the previously mentioned stock option package and an immediate €450,000 bonus. If he is risk-neutral, which would you recommend?
   c. How would your answer to (b) change if Mr. Louis were risk-averse and he could not sell the options prior to expiration?

2. **Employee Stock Options** Rashid Naqvi has just been named the new chief executive officer of Technica Pakistan Ltd. In addition to an annual salary of PKR 400,000, his three-year contract states that his compensation will include 10,000 at-the-money European call options on the company's stock that expire in three years. The current stock price is PKR 40 per share, and the standard deviation of the returns on the firm's stock is 68 percent. The company does not pay a dividend. Treasury bills that mature in three years yield a continuously compounded interest rate of 5 percent. Assume that Mr. Naqvi's annual salary payments occur at the end of the year and that these cash flows should be discounted at a rate of 9 percent. Using the Black–Scholes model to calculate the value of the stock options, determine the total value of the compensation package on the date the contract is signed.

3. **Binomial Model** Gaswoks, Inc., has been approached to sell up to 5 million gallons of gasoline in three months at a price of $1.85 per gallon. Gasoline is currently selling on the

wholesale market at \$1.65 per gallon and has a standard deviation of 46 percent. If the risk-free rate is 6 percent per year, what is the value of this option?

4. **Real Options** Calgary Developers is an international conglomerate with a real estate division that owns the right to erect an office building on a parcel of land in downtown Sacramento over the next year. This building would cost CAD 10.5 million to construct. Due to low demand for office space in the downtown area, such a building is worth approximately CAD 10 million today. If demand increases, the building would be worth CAD 12.5 million a year from today. If demand decreases, the same office building would be worth only CAD 8 million in a year. The company can borrow and lend at the risk-free rate of 2.5 percent effective annual rate. A local competitor in the real estate business has recently offered CAD 750,000 for the right to build an office building on the land. Should the company accept this offer? Use a two-state model to value the real option.

5. **Real Options** Jet Black is an international conglomerate with a petroleum division and is currently competing in an auction to win the right to drill for crude oil on a large piece of land in one year. The current market price of crude oil is \$55 per barrel, and the land is believed to contain 125,000 barrels of oil. If found, the oil would cost \$10 million to extract. Treasury bills that mature in one year yield a continuously compounded interest rate of 6.5 percent, and the standard deviation of the returns on the price of crude oil is 50 percent. Use the Black–Scholes model to calculate the maximum bid that the company should be willing to make at the auction.

INTERMEDIATE
(Questions 6–7)

6. **Real Options** Bjeorn Smelters is a large, publicly held company that is considering leasing a warehouse. One of the company's divisions specializes in manufacturing steel, and this particlar warehouse is the only facility in the area that suits the firm's operations. The current price of steel is €3,600 per ton. If the price of steel falls over the next six months, the company will purchase 400 tons of steel and produce 4,800 steel rods. Each steel rod will cost €120 to manufacture, and the company plans to sell the rods for €360 each. It will take only a matter of days to produce and sell the steel rods. If the price of steel rises or remains the same, it will not be profitable to undertake the project, and the company will allow the lease to expire without producing any steel rods. Treasury bills that mature in six months yield a continuously compounded interest rate of 4.5 percent, and the standard deviation of the returns on steel is 45 percent. Use the Black–Scholes model to determine the maximum amount that the company should be willing to pay for the lease.

7. **Real Options** Wet for the Summer, Inc., manufactures filters for swimming pools. The company is deciding whether to implement a new technology in its pool filters. One year from now the company will know whether the new technology is accepted in the market. If the demand for the new filters is high, the present value of the cash flows in one year will be \$10 million. Conversely, if the demand is low, the value of the cash flows in one year will be \$6 million. The value of the project today under these assumptions is \$9.1 million, and the risk-free rate is 6 percent. Suppose that in one year, if the demand for the new technology is low, the company can sell the technology for \$7 million. What is the value of the option to abandon?

CHALLENGE
(Questions 8–9)

8. **Binomial Model** There is an American put option on a stock that expires in two months. The stock price is £63, and the standard deviation of the stock returns is 65 percent. The option has a strike price of £70, and the risk-free interest rate is a 5 percent annual percentage rate. What is the price of the put option today using one-month steps? (*Hint*: How will you find the value of the option if it can be exercised early? When would you exercise the option early?)

9. **Real Options** You are in discussions to purchase an option on an office building with a strike price of ¥47 billion. The building is currently valued at ¥45 billion. The option will allow you to purchase the building either six months from today or one year from today. Six months from today, accrued rent payments from the building in the amount of ¥500 million will be made to the owners. If you exercise the option in six months, you will receive the accrued rent payments; otherwise the payment will be made to the current owners. A second accrued rent payment of ¥500 million will be paid one year from today with the same payment terms. The standard deviation of the value of the building is 25 percent, and the risk-free rate is an 8 percent annual percentage rate. What is the price of the option today using six-month steps? (*Hint*: The value of the building in six months will be reduced by the accrued rent payment if you do not exercise the option at that time.)

www.mhhe.com/rwj

Exotic Cuisines Employee Stock Options

As a newly minted MBA, you've taken a management position with Exotic Cuisines, Inc., a restaurant chain that just went public last year. The company's restaurants specialize in exotic main dishes, using ingredients such as alligator, buffalo, and ostrich. A concern you had going in was that the restaurant business is very risky. However, after some due diligence, you discovered a common misperception about the restaurant industry. It is widely thought that 90 percent of new restaurants close within three years; however, recent evidence suggests the failure rate is closer to 60 percent over three years. So it is a risky business, although not as risky as you originally thought.

During your interview process, one of the benefits mentioned was employee stock options. Upon signing your employment contract, you received options with a strike price of $50 for 10,000 shares of company stock. As is fairly common, your stock options have a three-year vesting period and a 10-year expiration, meaning that you cannot exercise the options for three years, and you lose them if you leave before they vest. After the three-year vesting period, you can exercise the options at any time. Thus, the employee stock options are European (and subject to forfeit) for the first three years and American afterward. Of course, you cannot sell the options, nor can you enter into any sort of hedging agreement. If you leave the company after the options vest, you must exercise within 90 days or forfeit.

Exotic Cuisines stock is currently trading at $24.38 per share, a slight increase from the initial offering price last year. There are no market-traded options on the company's stock. Because the company has been traded for only about a year, you are reluctant to use the historical returns to estimate the standard deviation of the stock's return. However, you have estimated that the average annual standard deviation for restaurant company stocks is about 55 percent. Because Exotic Cuisines is a newer restaurant chain, you decide to use a 60 percent standard deviation in your calculations. The company is relatively young, and you expect that all earnings will be reinvested back into the company for the near future. Therefore, you expect no dividends will be paid for at least the next 10 years. A three-year Treasury note currently has a yield of 3.8 percent, and a 10-year Treasury note has a yield of 4.4 percent.

1. You're trying to value your options. What minimum value would you assign? What is the maximum value you would assign?

2. Suppose that in three years the company's stock is trading at $60. At that time should you keep the options or exercise them immediately? What are some of the important determinants in making such a decision?

3. Your options, like most employee stock options, are not transferable or tradable. Does this have a significant effect on the value of the options? Why?

4. Why do you suppose employee stock options usually have a vesting provision? Why must they be exercised shortly after you depart the company even after they vest?

5. A controversial practice with employee stock options is repricing. What happens is that a company experiences a stock price decrease, which leaves employee stock options far out of the money or "underwater." In such cases, many companies have "repriced" or "restruck" the options, meaning that the company leaves the original terms of the option intact but lowers the strike price. Proponents of repricing argue that because the option is very unlikely to end in the money because of the stock price decline, the motivational force is lost. Opponents argue that repricing is in essence a reward for failure. How do you evaluate this argument? How does the possibility of repricing affect the value of an employee stock option at the time it is granted?

6. As we have seen, much of the volatility in a company's stock price is due to systematic or marketwide risks. Such risks are beyond the control of a company and its employees. What are the implications for employee stock options? In light of your answer, can you recommend an improvement over traditional employee stock options?

CHAPTER 24

Warrants and Convertibles

In February 2006, biotech giant Amgen announced the pricing on two new bond issues. The company sold $2.5 billion worth of zero coupon bonds due in 2011, with another $2.5 billion in zero coupon bonds due in 2013. What might surprise you is that the yields to maturity on the bonds when they were issued were 0.125 percent and 0.375 percent, respectively. At the same time, U.S. Treasury bonds with five years to maturity had a yield of about 4.6 percent. So how was Amgen able to issue bonds with a lower yield than U.S Treasuries?

The answer is that Amgen's bonds were convertible into shares of common stock in the company. The bonds maturing in 2011 could be converted into 12.52 shares for every $1,000 in par value, and the bonds maturing in 2013 could be converted into 12.58 shares for every $1,000 in par value. The conversion of the bonds into shares of stock is at the discretion of the bondholder. So, in essence, these convertible bonds are zero coupon bonds with an attached call option on the company stock.

How do we value a financial instrument that is a combination of a bond and a call option? This chapter explores this and other issues.

24.1 Warrants

Warrants are securities that give holders the right, but not the obligation, to buy shares of common stock directly from a company at a fixed price for a given period. Each warrant specifies the number of shares of stock that the holder can buy, the exercise price, and the expiration date.

From the preceding description of warrants, it is clear that they are similar to call options. The differences in contractual features between warrants and the call options that trade on the Chicago Board Options Exchange are small. For example, warrants have longer maturity periods.[1] Some warrants are actually perpetual, meaning that they never expire.

Warrants are referred to as *equity kickers* because they are usually issued in combination with privately placed bonds.[2] In most cases, warrants are attached to the bonds when issued. The loan agreement will state whether the warrants are detachable from the bond—that is, whether they can be sold separately. Usually, the warrant can be detached immediately.

For example, during a reorganization, famed banana company Chiquita Brands International issued warrants. Each warrant gave the holder the right to purchase one share of stock at an exercise price of $19.32. The warrants expire on March 19, 2009. On March 1, 2006, Chiquita Brands stock closed at $17.57, and the price of a warrant was $4.05.

---

[1] Warrants are usually protected against stock splits and dividends in the same way that call options are.

[2] Warrants are also issued with publicly distributed bonds and new issues of common stock.

Figure 24.1

Chiquita Warrants
on March 1, 2006

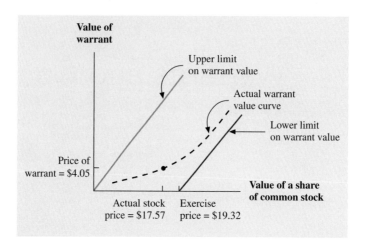

The relationship between the value of Chiquita's warrants and its stock price can be viewed as similar to the relationship between a call option and the stock price, described in a previous chapter. Figure 24.1 depicts the relationship for Chiquita's warrants. The lower limit on the value of the warrants is zero if Chiquita's stock price is below $19.32 per share. If the price of Chiquita's stock rises above $19.32 per share, the lower limit is the stock price minus $19.32. The upper limit is the price of Chiquita's stock. A warrant to buy one share of stock cannot sell at a price above the price of the underlying stock.

The price of Chiquita's warrants on March 1, 2006, was higher than the lower limit. The height of the warrant price above the lower limit will depend on the following:

1. The variance of Chiquita's stock returns.
2. The time to expiration date.
3. The risk-free rate of interest.
4. The stock price of Chiquita.
5. The exercise price.

These are the same factors that determine the value of a call option.

Warrants can also have unusual features. For example, the Montana Mills Bread Company, Inc., has warrants that expire in 2007 with an exercise price of $7.58. Each warrant can be used to purchase 0.15 shares of stock in Krispy Kreme Doughnuts. To purchase one share of Krispy Kreme stock, a holder must give up 6.66 warrants and $50.48. This means the exercise price on the stock is $50.48, not the $7.58 exercise price listed on the warrant.

24.2 The Difference between Warrants and Call Options

From the holder's point of view, warrants are similar to call options on common stock. A warrant, like a call option, gives its holder the right to buy common stock at a specified price. Warrants usually have an expiration date, though in most cases they are issued with longer lives than call options. From the firm's point of view, however, a warrant is very different from a call option on the company's common stock.

The most important difference between call options and warrants is that call options are issued by individuals and warrants are issued by firms. When a warrant is exercised, a firm must issue new shares of stock. Each time a warrant is exercised, then, the number of shares outstanding increases.

To illustrate, suppose the Endrun Company issues a warrant giving holders the right to buy one share of common stock at $25. Further, suppose the warrant is exercised. Endrun must print one new stock certificate. In exchange for the stock certificate, it receives $25 from the holder.

In contrast, when a call option is exercised, there is no change in the number of shares outstanding. Suppose Ms. Eager holds a call option on the common stock of the Endrun Company. The call option gives Ms. Eager the right to buy one share of the common stock of the Endrun Company for $25. If Ms. Eager chooses to exercise the call option, a seller, say Mr. Swift, is obligated to give her one share of Endrun's common stock in exchange for $25. If Mr. Swift does not already own a share, he must enter the stock market and buy one. The call option is a side bet between buyers and sellers on the value of the Endrun Company's common stock. When a call option is exercised, one investor gains and the other loses. The total number of shares outstanding of the Endrun Company remains constant, and no new funds are made available to the company.

EXAMPLE 24.1

Warrants and Firm Value To see how warrants affect the value of the firm, imagine that Mr. Gould and Ms. Rockefeller are two investors who have together purchased six ounces of platinum. At the time they bought the platinum, Mr. Gould and Ms. Rockefeller each contributed half of the cost, which we will assume was $3,000 for six ounces, or $500 an ounce (they each contributed $1,500). They incorporated, printed two stock certificates, and named the firm the GR Company. Each certificate represents a one-half claim to the platinum. Mr. Gould and Ms. Rockefeller each own one certificate. Mr. Gould and Ms. Rockefeller have formed a company with platinum as its only asset.

A Call Is Issued Suppose Mr. Gould later decides to sell to Ms. Fiske a call option issued on Mr. Gould's share. The call option gives Ms. Fiske the right to buy Mr. Gould's share for $1,800 within the next year. If the price of platinum rises above $600 per ounce, the firm will be worth more than $3,600, and each share will be worth more than $1,800. If Ms. Fiske decides to exercise her option, Mr. Gould must turn over his stock certificate and receive $1,800.

How would the firm be affected by the exercise? The number of shares will remain the same. There will still be two shares, now owned by Ms. Rockefeller and Ms. Fiske. If the price of platinum rises to $700 an ounce, each share will be worth $2,100 (= $4,200/2). If Ms. Fiske exercises her option at this price, she will profit by $300.

A Warrant Is Issued Instead This story changes if a warrant is issued. Suppose that Mr. Gould does not sell a call option to Ms. Fiske. Instead, Mr. Gould and Ms. Rockefeller have a stockholders' meeting. They vote that GR Company will issue a warrant and sell it to Ms. Fiske. The warrant will give Ms. Fiske the right to receive a share of the company at an exercise price of $1,800.[3] If Ms. Fiske decides to exercise the warrant, the firm will issue another stock certificate and give it to Ms. Fiske in exchange for $1,800.

From Ms. Fiske's perspective, the call option and the warrant *seem* to be the same. The exercise prices of the warrant and the call are the same: $1,800. It is still advantageous for Ms. Fiske to exercise the option when the price of platinum exceeds $600 per ounce. However, we will show that Ms. Fiske actually makes less in the warrant situation due to dilution.

(continued)

---

[3]The sale of the warrant brings cash into the firm. We assume that the sale proceeds immediately leave the firm through a cash dividend to Mr. Gould and Ms. Rockefeller. This simplifies the analysis because the firm with warrants then has the same total value as the firm without warrants.

The GR Company must also consider dilution. Suppose the price of platinum increases to $700 an ounce and Ms. Fiske exercises her warrant. Two things will occur:

1. Ms. Fiske will pay $1,800 to the firm.
2. The firm will print one stock certificate and give it to Ms. Fiske. The stock certificate will represent a one-third claim on the platinum of the firm.

Because Ms. Fiske contributes $1,800 to the firm, the value of the firm increases. It is now worth

$$\text{New value of firm} = \text{Value of platinum} + \text{Contribution to the firm by Ms. Fiske}$$
$$-\ \$4,200 \qquad + \qquad \$1,800$$
$$=\ \$6,000$$

Because Ms. Fiske has a one-third claim on the firm's value, her share is worth $2,000 (= $6,000/3). By exercising the warrant, Ms. Fiske gains $2,000 − $1,800 = $200. This is illustrated in Table 24.1.

Dilution   Why does Ms. Fiske gain only $200 in the warrant case but gain $300 in the call option case? The key is dilution—that is, the creation of another share. In the call option case, she contributes $1,800 and receives one of the two outstanding shares. That is, she receives a share worth $2,100 (= $\frac{1}{2}$ × $4,200). Her gain is $300 (= $2,100 − $1,800). We rewrite this gain like this:

Gain on Exercise of Call

$$\frac{\$4,200}{2} - \$1,800 = \$300 \tag{24.1}$$

In the warrant case, she contributes $1,800 and receives a newly created share. She now owns one of the three outstanding shares. Because the $1,800 remains in the firm, her share is worth $2,000 [(= $4,200 + $1,800)/3]. Her gain is $200 (= $2,000 − $1,800). We rewrite this gain as follows:

Table 24.1   **Effect of Call Option and Warrant on the GR Company***

	Price of Platinum per Share	
Value of Firm if	**$700**	**$600**
No warrant		
Mr. Gould's share	$2,100	$1,800
Ms. Rockefeller's share	2,100	1,800
Firm	$4,200	$3,600
Call option		
Mr. Gould's claim	$ 0	$1,800
Ms. Rockefeller's claim	2,100	1,800
Ms. Fiske's claim	2,100	0
Firm	$4,200	$3,600
Warrant		
Mr. Gould's share	$2,000	$1,800
Ms. Rockefeller's share	2,000	1,800
Ms. Fiske's share	2,000	0
Firm	$6,000	$3,600

*If the price of platinum is $700, the value of the firm is equal to the value of six ounces of platinum plus the excess dollars paid into the firm by Ms. Fiske. This amount is $4,200 + $1,800 = $6,000.

(continued)

Gain on Exercise of Warrant

$$\frac{\$4,200 + \$1,800}{2 + 1} - \$1,800 = \$200 \tag{24.2}$$

Warrants also affect accounting numbers. Warrants and (as we shall see) convertible bonds cause the number of shares to increase. This causes the firm's net income to be spread over more shares, thereby decreasing earnings per share. Firms with significant amounts of warrants and convertible issues must report earnings on a *primary* basis and a *fully diluted* basis.

How the Firm Can Hurt Warrant Holders

The platinum firm owned by Mr. Gould and Ms. Rockefeller has issued a warrant to Ms. Fiske that is *in the money* and about to expire. One way that Mr. Gould and Ms. Rockefeller can hurt Ms. Fiske is to pay themselves a large dividend. This could be funded by selling a substantial amount of platinum. The value of the firm would fall, and the warrant would be worth much less.

24.3 Warrant Pricing and the Black–Scholes Model

We now wish to express the gains from exercising a call and a warrant in more general terms. The gain on a call can be written like this:

Gain from Exercising a Single Call

$$\frac{\text{Firm's value net of debt}}{\#} - \text{Exercise price} \tag{24.3}$$

(Value of a share of stock)

Equation 24.3 generalizes Equation 24.1. We define the *firm's value net of debt* to be the total firm value less the value of the debt. The total firm value is $4,200 in our example, and there is no debt. The # stands for the number of shares outstanding, which is two in our example. The ratio on the left is the value of a share of stock. The gain on a warrant can be written as follows:

Gain from Exercising a Single Warrant

$$\frac{\text{Firm's value net of debt} + \text{Exercise price} \times \#_w}{\# + \#_w} - \text{Exercise price} \tag{24.4}$$

(Value of a share of stock after warrant is exercised)

Equation 24.4 generalizes Equation 24.2. The numerator of the left term is the firm's value net of debt *after* the warrant is exercised. It is the sum of the firm's value net of debt *prior* to the warrant's exercise plus the proceeds the firm receives from the exercise. The proceeds equal the product of the exercise price multiplied by the number of warrants. The number of warrants appears as $\#_w$. (Our analysis uses the plausible assumption that all warrants in the money will be exercised.) Note that $\#_w = 1$ in our numerical example. The denominator, $\# + \#_w$, is the number of shares outstanding *after* the exercise of the warrants. The ratio on the left is the value of a share of stock after exercise. By rearranging terms, we can rewrite Equation 24.4 as[4]

---

[4]To derive Formula 24.5, we separate "Exercise price" in Equation 24.4. This yields

$$\frac{\text{Firm's value net of debt}}{\# + \#_w} - \frac{\#}{\# + \#_w} \times \text{Exercise price}$$

By rearranging terms, we can obtain Formula 24.5.

Gain from Exercising a Single Warrant

$$\frac{\#}{\# + \#_w} \times \left(\frac{\text{Firm's value net of debt}}{\#} - \text{Exercise price} \right) \tag{24.5}$$

(Gain from a call on a firm with no warrants)

Formula 24.5 relates the gain on a warrant to the gain on a call. Note that the term within parentheses is Equation 24.3. Thus, the gain from exercising a warrant is a proportion of the gain from exercising a call in a firm without warrants. The proportion $\#/(\# + \#_w)$ is the ratio of the number of shares in the firm without warrants to the number of shares after all the warrants have been exercised. This ratio must always be less than 1. Thus, the gain on a warrant must be less than the gain on an identical call in a firm without warrants. Note that $\#/(\# + \#_w) = \frac{2}{3}$ in our example, which explains why Ms. Fiske gains \$300 on her call yet gains only \$200 on her warrant.

The preceding implies that the Black–Scholes model must be adjusted for warrants. When a call option is issued to Ms. Fiske, we know that the exercise price is \$1,800 and the time to expiration is one year. Though we have not posited the price of the stock, the variance of the stock, or the interest rate, we could easily provide these data for a real-world situation. Thus, we could use the Black–Scholes model to value Ms. Fiske's call.

Suppose that the warrant is to be issued tomorrow to Ms. Fiske. We know the number of warrants to be issued, the warrant's expiration date, and the exercise price. Using our assumption that the warrant proceeds are immediately paid out as a dividend, we could use the Black–Scholes model to value the warrant. We would first calculate the value of an identical call. The warrant price is the call price multiplied by the ratio $\#/(\# + \#_w)$. As mentioned earlier, this ratio is $\frac{2}{3}$ in our example.

24.4 Convertible Bonds

A **convertible bond** is similar to a bond with warrants. The most important difference is that a bond with warrants can be separated into distinct securities and a convertible bond cannot. A convertible bond gives the holder the right to exchange it for a given number of shares of stock anytime up to and including the maturity date of the bond.

Preferred stock can frequently be converted into common stock. A convertible preferred stock is the same as a convertible bond except that it has an infinite maturity date.

EXAMPLE 24.2

Convertibles   Oceandoor Technology is one of the most important manufacturers of rigid magnetic disk drives for computers. Its stock is traded over the counter (OTC).

On November 1, 2006, Oceandoor raised \$300 million by issuing 6.75 percent convertible subordinated debentures due in 2022. It planned to use the proceeds to invest in new plant and equipment. Like typical debentures, they had a sinking fund and were callable. Oceandoor's bonds differed from other debentures in their convertible feature: Each bond was convertible into 23.53 shares of common stock of Oceandoor anytime before maturity. The number of shares received for each bond (23.53 in this example) is called the **conversion ratio**.

Bond traders also speak of the **conversion price** of the bond. This is calculated as the ratio of the face value of the bond to the conversion ratio. Because the face value of each Oceandoor bond was \$1,000, the conversion price was \$42.50 (= \$1,000/23.53). The bondholders of Oceandoor could give up bonds with a face value of \$1,000 and receive 23.53 shares of Oceandoor common stock. This was equivalent to paying \$42.50 (= \$1,000/23.53) for each share of Oceandoor common stock received.

(continued)

When Oceandoor issued its convertible bonds, its common stock was trading at $22.625 per share. The conversion price of $42.5 was 88 percent higher than the actual common stock price. This 88 percent is referred to as the **conversion premium**. It reflects the fact that the conversion option in Oceandoor convertible bonds was *out of the money*. This conversion premium is typical.

Convertibles are almost always protected against stock splits and stock dividends. If Oceandoor's common stock had been split two for one, the conversion ratio would have been increased from 23.53 to 47.06.

Conversion ratio, conversion price, and conversion premium are well-known terms in the real world. For that reason alone, the student should master the concepts. However, conversion price and conversion premium implicitly assume that the bond is selling at par. If the bond is selling at another price, the terms have little meaning. By contrast, conversion ratio can have a meaningful interpretation regardless of the price of the bond.

To give an example of these ideas, let's look back at the Amgen bonds we discussed at the beginning of the chapter. At the time, this offering was the largest convertible bond issue in history and represented about 2 percent of all convertible bonds outstanding. The conversion ratio of the bonds maturing in 2011 is 12.52. This means the conversion price is $1,000/12.52 = $79.87. Amgen's stock was selling for about $71.93, so this represented a conversion premium of 11 percent. The bonds maturing in 2013 have a conversion ratio of 12.58. Check and see if you agree this represents a conversion premium of 10.5 percent.

24.5   The Value of Convertible Bonds

The value of a convertible bond can be described in terms of three components: straight bond value, conversion value, and option value. We examine these three components next.

Straight Bond Value

The straight bond value is what the convertible bonds would sell for if they could not be converted into common stock. It will depend on the general level of interest rates and on the default risk. Suppose that straight debentures issued by Oceandoor had been rated A, and A-rated bonds were priced to yield 4 percent per six months on November 1, 2006. The straight bond value of Oceandoor convertible bonds can be determined by discounting the $33.75 semiannual coupon payment and principal amount at 4 percent:

$$\text{Straight bond} = \sum_{t=1}^{32} \frac{\$33.75}{1.04^t} + \frac{\$1,000}{(1.04)^{32}}$$

$$= \$33.75 \times A_{0.04}^{32} + \frac{\$1,000}{(1.04)^{32}}$$

$$= \$603.23 + \$285.06$$

$$= \$888.29$$

The straight bond value of a convertible bond is a minimum value. The price of Oceandoor's convertible could not have gone lower than the straight bond value.

Figure 24.2 illustrates the relationship between straight bond value and stock price. In Figure 24.2 we have been somewhat dramatic and implicitly assumed that the convertible bond is default free. In this case, the straight bond value does not depend on the stock price, so it is graphed as a straight line.

Figure 24.2

Minimum Value of
a Convertible Bond
versus the Value of
the Stock for a Given
Interest Rate

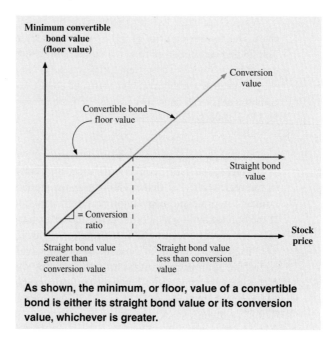

As shown, the minimum, or floor, value of a convertible
bond is either its straight bond value or its conversion
value, whichever is greater.

Conversion Value

The value of convertible bonds depends on conversion value. **Conversion value** is what the bonds would be worth if they were immediately converted into common stock at current prices. Typically, we compute conversion value by multiplying the number of shares of common stock that will be received when the bond is converted by the current price of the common stock.

On November 1, 2006, each Oceandoor convertible bond could have been converted into 23.53 shares of Oceandoor common stock. Oceandoor common stock was selling for $22.625. Thus, the conversion value was 23.53 × $22.625 = $532.37. A convertible cannot sell for less than its conversion value. Arbitrage prevents this from happening. If Oceandoor's convertible sold for less than $532.37, investors would have bought the bonds and converted them into common stock and sold the stock. The profit would have been the difference between the value of the stock sold and the bond's conversion value.

Thus, convertible bonds have two minimum values: the straight bond value and the conversion value. The conversion value is determined by the value of the firm's underlying common stock. This is illustrated in Figure 24.2. As the value of common stock rises and falls, the conversion price rises and falls with it. When the value of Oceandoor's common stock increased by $1, the conversion value of its convertible bonds increased by $23.53.

Option Value

The value of a convertible bond will generally exceed both the straight bond value and the conversion value.[5] This occurs because holders of convertibles need not convert immediately. Instead, by waiting they can take advantage of whichever is greater in the future: the straight bond value or the conversion value. This option to wait has value, and it raises the value over both the straight bond value and the conversion value.

---

[5]The most plausible exception is when conversion would provide the investor with a dividend much greater than the interest available prior to conversion. The optimal strategy here could very well be to convert immediately, implying that the market value of the bond would exactly equal the conversion value. Other exceptions occur when the firm is in default or the bondholders are forced to convert.

Figure 24.3

Value of a
Convertible Bond
versus the Value of
the Stock for a Given
Interest Rate

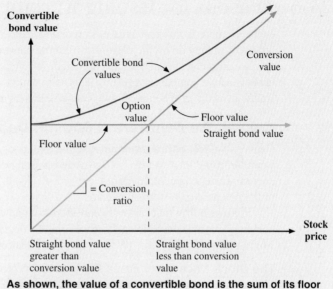

As shown, the value of a convertible bond is the sum of its floor
value and its option value.

When the value of the firm is low, the value of convertible bonds is most significantly influenced by their underlying value as straight debt. However, when the value of the firm is very high, the value of convertible bonds is mostly determined by their underlying conversion value. This is illustrated in Figure 24.3.

The bottom portion of the figure implies that the value of a convertible bond is the maximum of its straight bond value and its conversion value, plus its option value:

$$\text{Value of convertible bond} = \text{The greater of (Straight bond value, Conversion value)} + \text{Option value}$$

Conversion   Suppose the Moulton Company has outstanding 1,000 shares of common stock and 100 bonds. Each bond has a face value of $1,000 at maturity. They are discount bonds and pay no coupons. At maturity each bond can be converted into 10 shares of newly issued common stock.

What circumstances will make it advantageous for the holders of Moulton convertible bonds to convert to common stock at maturity?

If the holders of the convertible bonds convert, they will receive $100 \times 10 = 1,000$ shares of common stock. Because there were already 1,000 shares, the total number of shares outstanding becomes 2,000 upon conversion. Thus, converting bondholders own 50 percent of the value of the firm, V. If they do not convert, they will receive $100,000 or V, whichever is less. The choice for the holders of the Moulton bonds is obvious. They should convert if 50 percent of V is greater than $100,000. This will be true whenever V is greater than $200,000. This is illustrated as follows:

Payoff to Convertible Bondholders and Stockholders of the Moulton Company

	(1) $V \leq \$100,000$	(2) $\$100,000 < V \leq \$200,000$	(3) $V > \$200,000$
Decision:	Bondholders will not convert	Bondholders will not convert	Bondholders will convert
Convertible bondholders	V	$100,000	0.5V
Stockholders	0	$V - \$100,000$	0.5V

24.6 Reasons for Issuing Warrants and Convertibles

Probably there is no other area of corporate finance where real-world practitioners get as confused as they do on the reasons for issuing convertible debt. To separate fact from fantasy, we present a rather structured argument. We first compare convertible debt with straight debt. Then we compare convertible debt with equity. For each comparison, we ask in what situations is the firm better off with convertible debt and in what situations is it worse off.

Convertible Debt versus Straight Debt

Convertible debt pays a lower interest rate than does otherwise identical straight debt. For example, if the interest rate is 10 percent on straight debt, the interest rate on convertible debt might be 9 percent. Investors will accept a lower interest rate on a convertible because of the potential gain from conversion.

Imagine a firm that seriously considers both convertible debt and straight debt, finally deciding to issue convertibles. When would this decision have benefited the firm and when would it have hurt the firm? We consider two situations.

The Stock Price Later Rises So That Conversion Is Indicated   The firm clearly likes to see the stock price rise. However, it would have benefited even more had it previously issued straight debt instead of a convertible. Although the firm paid out a lower interest rate than it would have with straight debt, it was obligated to sell the convertible holders a chunk of the equity at a below-market price.

The Stock Price Later Falls or Does Not Rise Enough to Justify Conversion   The firm hates to see the stock price fall. However, as long as the stock price does fall, the firm is glad that it had previously issued convertible debt instead of straight debt. This is because the interest rate on convertible debt is lower. Because conversion does not take place, our comparison of interest rates is all that is needed.

Summary   Compared to straight debt, the firm is worse off having issued convertible debt if the underlying stock subsequently does well. The firm is better off having issued convertible debt if the underlying stock subsequently does poorly. In an efficient market, we cannot predict future stock price. Thus, we cannot argue that convertibles either dominate or are dominated by straight debt.

Convertible Debt versus Common Stock

Next, imagine a firm that seriously considers both convertible debt and common stock but finally decides to issue convertibles. When would this decision benefit the firm and when would it hurt the firm? We consider our two situations.

The Stock Price Later Rises So That Conversion Is Indicated   The firm is better off having previously issued a convertible instead of equity. To see this, consider the Oceandoor case. The firm could have issued stock for $22. Instead, by issuing a convertible, the firm effectively received $42.50 for a share upon conversion.

The Stock Price Later Falls or Does Not Rise Enough to Justify Conversion   No firm wants to see its stock price fall. However, given that the price did fall, the firm would have been better off if it had previously issued stock instead of a convertible. The firm would have benefited by issuing stock above its later market price. That is, the firm would have received more than the subsequent worth of the stock. However, the drop in stock price did not affect the value of the convertible much because the straight bond value serves as a floor.

Table 24.2

The Case for and against Convertible Bonds (CBs)

	If Firm Subsequently Does Poorly	If Firm Subsequently Prospers
Convertible bonds (CBs)	No conversion because of low stock price.	Conversion because of high stock price.
Compared to: Straight bonds	CBs provide cheap financing because coupon rate is lower.	CBs provide expensive financing because bonds are converted, which dilutes existing equity.
Common stock	CBs provide expensive financing because firm could have issued common stock at high prices.	CBs provide cheap financing because firm issues stock at high prices when bonds are converted.

Summary Compared with equity, the firm is better off having issued convertible debt if the underlying stock subsequently does well. The firm is worse off having issued convertible debt if the underlying stock subsequently does poorly. We cannot predict future stock price in an efficient market. Thus, we cannot argue that issuing convertibles is better or worse than issuing equity. The preceding analysis is summarized in Table 24.2.

Modigliani–Miller (MM) pointed out that, abstracting from taxes and bankruptcy costs, the firm is indifferent to whether it issues stock or issues debt. The MM relationship is a quite general one. Their pedagogy could be adjusted to show that the firm is indifferent to whether it issues convertibles or issues other instruments. To save space (and the patience of students) we have omitted a full-blown proof of MM in a world with convertibles. However, our results are perfectly consistent with MM. Now we turn to the real-world view of convertibles.

The "Free Lunch" Story

The preceding discussion suggests that issuing a convertible bond is no better and no worse than issuing other instruments. Unfortunately, many corporate executives fall into the trap of arguing that issuing convertible debt is actually better than issuing alternative instruments. This is a free lunch type of explanation, of which we are quite critical.

EXAMPLE 24.4

Are Convertibles Always Better? The stock price of RW Company is $20. Suppose this company can issue subordinated debentures at 10 percent. It can also issue convertible bonds at 6 percent with a conversion value of $800. The conversion value means that the holders can convert a convertible bond into 40 (= $800/$20) shares of common stock.

A company treasurer who believes in free lunches might argue that convertible bonds should be issued because they represent a cheaper source of financing than either subordinated bonds or common stock. The treasurer will point out that if the company does poorly and the price does not rise above $20, the convertible bondholders will not convert the bonds into common stock. In this case the company will have obtained debt financing at below-market rates by attaching worthless equity kickers. On the other hand, if the firm does well and the price of its common stock rises to $25 or above, convertible holders will convert. The company will issue 40 shares. The company will receive a bond with face value of $1,000 in exchange for issuing 40 shares of common stock, implying a conversion price of $25. The company will have issued common stock at $25 per share, or 20 percent above the $20 common stock price prevailing when the convertible bonds were issued. This enables it to lower its cost of equity capital. Thus, the treasurer happily points out, regardless of whether the company does well or poorly, convertible bonds are the cheapest form of financing.

(continued)

Although this argument may sound quite plausible at first, there is a flaw. The treasurer is comparing convertible financing *with straight debt* when the stock subsequently falls. However, the treasurer compares convertible financing *with common stock* when the stock subsequently rises. This is an unfair mixing of comparisons. By contrast, our analysis of Table 24.2 was fair because we examined both stock increases and decreases when comparing a convertible with each alternative instrument. We found that no single alternative dominated convertible bonds in *both* up and down markets.

The "Expensive Lunch" Story

Suppose we stand the treasurer's argument on its head by comparing (1) convertible financing with straight debt when the stock rises and (2) convertible financing with equity when the stock falls.

From Table 24.2, we see that convertible debt is more expensive than straight debt when the stock subsequently rises. The firm's obligation to sell convertible holders a chunk of equity at a below-market price more than offsets the lower interest rate on a convertible.

Also from Table 24.2, we see that convertible debt is more expensive than equity when the stock subsequently falls. Had the firm issued stock, it would have received a price higher than its subsequent worth. Therefore, the expensive lunch story implies that convertible debt is an inferior form of financing. Of course, we dismiss both the free lunch and the expensive lunch arguments.

A Reconciliation

In an efficient financial market there is neither a free lunch nor an expensive lunch. Convertible bonds can be neither cheaper nor more expensive than other instruments. A convertible bond is a package of straight debt and an option to buy common stock. The difference between the market value of a convertible bond and the value of a straight bond is the price investors pay for the call option feature. In an efficient market, this is a fair price.

In general, if a company prospers, issuing convertible bonds will turn out to be worse than issuing straight bonds and better than issuing common stock. In contrast, if a company does poorly, convertible bonds will turn out to be better than issuing straight bonds and worse than issuing common stock.

24.7   Why Are Warrants and Convertibles Issued?

From studies it is known that firms that issue convertible bonds are different from other firms. Here are some of the differences:

1. The bond ratings of firms using convertibles are lower than those of other firms.[6]
2. Convertibles tend to be used by smaller firms with high growth rates and more financial leverage.[7]
3. Convertibles are usually subordinated and unsecured.

The kind of company that uses convertibles provides clues to why they are issued. Here are some explanations that make sense.

---

[6]E. F. Brigham, "An Analysis of Convertible Debentures," *Journal of Finance* 21 (1966).

[7]W. H. Mikkelson, "Convertible Calls and Security Returns," *Journal of Financial Economics* 9 (September 1981), p. 3.

Table 24.3

A Hypothetical Case of the Yields on Convertible Bonds*

	Firm Risk	
	Low	High
Straight Bond Yield	10%	15%
Convertible Bond Yield	6	7

*The yields on straight bonds reflect the risk of default. The yields on convertibles are not sensitive to default risk.

Matching Cash Flows

If financing is costly, it makes sense to issue securities whose cash flows match those of the firm. A young, risky, and (it hopes) growing firm might prefer to issue convertibles or bonds with warrants because these will have lower initial interest costs. When the firm is successful, the convertibles (or warrants) will be converted. This causes expensive dilution, but it occurs when the firm can most afford it.

Risk Synergy

Another argument for convertible bonds and bonds with warrants is that they are useful when it is very costly to assess the risk of the issuing company. Suppose you are evaluating a new product by a start-up company. The new product is a genetically engineered virus that may increase the yields of corn crops in northern climates. It may also cause cancer. This type of product is difficult to value properly. Thus, the risk of the company is very hard to determine: It may be high, or it may be low. If you could be sure the risk of the company was high, you would price the bonds for a high yield, say 15 percent. If it was low, you would price them at a lower yield, say 10 percent.

Convertible bonds and bonds with warrants can protect somewhat against mistakes of risk evaluation. Convertible bonds and bonds with warrants have two components: straight bonds and call options on the company's underlying stock. If the company turns out to be a low-risk company, the straight bond component will have high value and the call option will have low value. However, if the company turns out to be a high-risk company, the straight bond component will have low value and the call option will have high value. This is illustrated in Table 24.3.

However, although risk has effects on value that cancel each other out in convertibles and bonds with warrants, the market and the buyer nevertheless must make an assessment of the firm's potential to value securities, and it is not clear that the effort involved is that much less than is required for a straight bond.

Agency Costs

Convertible bonds can resolve agency problems associated with raising money. In a previous chapter, we showed that straight bonds are like risk-free bonds minus a put option on the assets of the firm. This creates an incentive for creditors to force the firm into low-risk activities. In contrast, holders of common stock have incentives to adopt high-risk projects. High-risk projects with negative NPV transfer wealth from bondholders to stockholders. If these conflicts cannot be resolved, the firm may be forced to pass up profitable investment opportunities. However, because convertible bonds have an equity component, less expropriation of wealth can occur when convertible debt is issued instead of straight debt.[8] In other words, convertible bonds mitigate agency costs. One implication is that convertible

---

[8]A. Barnea, R.A. Haugen, and L. Senbet, *Agency Problems and Financial Contracting*, Prentice Hall Foundations of Science Series (New York: Prentice Hall, 1985), Chapter VI.

bonds have less restrictive debt covenants than do straight bonds in the real world. Casual empirical evidence seems to bear this out.

Backdoor Equity

A popular theory of convertibles views them as backdoor equity.[9] The basic story is that young, small, high-growth firms cannot usually issue debt on reasonable terms due to high financial distress costs. However, the owners may be unwilling to issue equity if current stock prices are too low.

Lewis, Ragolski, and Seward examine the risk shifting and backdoor equity theories of convertible bond debt. They find evidence for both theories.

24.8 Conversion Policy

There is one aspect of convertible bonds that we have omitted so far. Firms are frequently granted a call option on the bond. The typical arrangements for calling a convertible bond are simple. When the bond is called, the holder has about 30 days to choose between the following:

1. Converting the bond to common stock at the conversion ratio.
2. Surrendering the bond and receiving the call price in cash.

What should bondholders do? It should be obvious that if the conversion value of the bond is greater than the call price, conversion is better than surrender; and if the conversion value is less than the call price, surrender is better than conversion. If the conversion value is greater than the call price, the call is said to **force conversion**.

What should financial managers do? Calling the bonds does not change the value of the firm as a whole. However, an optimal call policy can benefit the stockholders at the expense of the bondholders. Because we are speaking about dividing a pie of fixed size, the optimal call policy is simple: Do whatever the bondholders do not want you to do.

Bondholders would love the stockholders to call the bonds when the bonds' market value is below the call price. Shareholders would be giving bondholders extra value. Alternatively, should the value of the bonds rise above the call price, the bondholders would love the stockholders not to call the bonds because bondholders would be allowed to hold onto a valuable asset.

There is only one policy left. This is the policy that maximizes shareholder value and minimizes bondholder value:

Call the bond when its value is equal to the call price.

It is a puzzle that firms do not always call convertible bonds when the conversion value reaches the call price. Ingersoll examined the call policies of 124 firms between 1968 and 1975.[10] In most cases he found that the company waited to call the bonds until the conversion value was much higher than the call price. The median company waited until the conversion value of its bonds was 44 percent higher than the call price. This is not even close to our optimal strategy. Why?

---

[9]J. Stein, "Convertible Bonds as Backdoor Equity Financing," *Journal of Financial Economics* 32 (1992). See also Craig M. Lewis, Richard J. Ragolski, and James K. Seward, "Understanding the Design of Convertible Debt," *The Journal of Applied Corporate Finance* (Spring 1998).

[10]J. Ingersoll, "An Examination of Corporate Call Policies on Convertible Bonds," *Journal of Finance* (May 1977). See also M. Harris and A. Raviv, "A Sequential Signalling Model of Convertible Debt Policy," *Journal of Finance* (December 1985). Harris and Raviv describe a signal equilibrium that is consistent with Ingersoll's result. They show that managers with favorable information will delay calls to avoid depressing stock prices.

One reason is that if firms attempt to implement the optimal strategy, it may not be truly optimal. Recall that bondholders have 30 days to decide whether to convert bonds to common stock or to surrender bonds for the call price in cash. In 30 days the stock price could drop, forcing the conversion value below the call price. If so, the convertible is "out of the money" and the firm is giving away money. The firm would be giving up cash for common stock worth much less. Because of this possibility, firms in the real world usually wait until the conversion value is substantially above the call price before they trigger the call.[11] This is sensible.

Summary and Conclusions

1. A warrant gives the holder the right to buy shares of common stock at an exercise price for a given period. Typically, warrants are issued in a package with privately placed bonds. Afterward they become detached and trade separately.

2. A convertible bond is a combination of a straight bond and a call option. The holder can give up the bond in exchange for shares of stock.

3. Convertible bonds and warrants are like call options. However, there are some important differences:
   a. Warrants and convertible securities are issued by corporations. Call options are traded between individual investors.
      i.   Warrants are usually issued privately and are combined with a bond. In most cases the warrants can be detached immediately after the issue. In some cases, warrants are issued with preferred stock, with common stock, or in executive compensation programs.
      ii. Convertibles are usually bonds that can be converted into common stock.
      iii. Call options are sold separately by individual investors (called *writers* of call options).
   b. Warrants and call options are exercised for cash. The holder of a warrant gives the company cash and receives new shares of the company's stock. The holder of a call option gives another individual cash in exchange for shares of stock. When someone converts a bond, it is exchanged for common stock. As a consequence, bonds with warrants and convertible bonds have different effects on corporate cash flow and capital structure.
   c. Warrants and convertibles cause dilution to the existing shareholders. When warrants are exercised and convertible bonds converted, the company must issue new shares of common stock. The percentage ownership of the existing shareholders will decline. New shares are not issued when call options are exercised.

4. Many arguments, both plausible and implausible, are given for issuing convertible bonds and bonds with warrants. One plausible rationale for such bonds has to do with risk. Convertibles and bonds with warrants are associated with risky companies. Lenders can do several things to protect themselves from high-risk companies:
   a. They can require high yields.
   b. They can lend less or not at all to firms whose risk is difficult to assess.
   c. They can impose severe restrictions on such debt.

---

[11]See Paul Asquith, "Convertible Bonds Are Not Called Late," *Journal of Finance* (September 1995). On the other hand, the stock market usually reacts negatively to the announcement of a call. For example, see A. K. Singh, A. R. Cowan, and N. Nayan, "Underwritten Calls of Convertible Bonds," *Journal of Financial Economics* (March 1991), and M. A. Mazzeo and W. T. Moore, "Liquidity Costs and Stock Price Response to Convertible Security Calls," *Journal of Business* (July 1992).

Ederington, Caton, and Campbell tested various theories about when it is optimal to call convertibles. They found evidence consistent for the preceding 30-day "safety margin" theory. They also found that calls of in-the-money convertibles are highly unlikely if dividends to be received (after conversion) exceed the company's interest payment. See Louis H. Ederington, Gary L. Caton, and Cynthia J. Campbell, "To Call or Not to Call Convertible Debt," *Financial Management* (Spring 1997).

Another useful way to protect against risk is to issue bonds with equity kickers. This gives the lenders the chance to benefit from risks and reduces the conflicts between bondholders and stockholders concerning risk.

5. A puzzle particularly vexes financial researchers: Convertible bonds usually have call provisions. Companies appear to delay calling convertibles until the conversion value greatly exceeds the call price. From the shareholders' standpoint, the optimal call policy would be to call the convertibles when the conversion value equals the call price.

Concept Questions

1. **Warrants and Options** What is the primary difference between a warrant and a traded call option?

2. **Warrants** Explain the following limits on the prices of warrants:
   a. If the stock price is below the exercise price of the warrant, the lower bound on the price of a warrant is zero.
   b. If the stock price is above the exercise price of the warrant, the lower bound on the price of a warrant is the difference between the stock price and the exercise price.
   c. An upper bound on the price of any warrant is the current value of the firm's stock.

3. **Convertible Bonds and Stock Volatility** Suppose you are evaluating a callable, convertible bond. If the stock price volatility increases, how will this affect the price of the bond?

4. **Convertible Bond Value** What happens to the price of a convertible bond if interest rates increase?

5. **Dilution** What is dilution, and why does it occur when warrants are exercised?

6. **Warrants and Convertibles** What is wrong with the simple view that it is cheaper to issue a bond with a warrant or a convertible feature because the required coupon is lower?

7. **Warrants and Convertibles** Why do firms issue convertible bonds and bonds with warrants?

8. **Convertible Bonds** Why will convertible bonds not be voluntarily converted to stock before expiration?

9. **Convertible Bonds** When should a firm force conversion of convertibles? Why?

10. **Warrant Valuation** A warrant with six months until expiration entitles its owner to buy 10 shares of the issuing firm's common stock for an exercise price of $31 per share. If the current market price of the stock is $15 per share, will the warrant be worthless?

Questions and Problems

BASIC
(Questions 1–10)

1. **Conversion Price** A convertible bond has a conversion ratio of 23.2. What is the conversion price?

2. **Conversion Ratio** A convertible bond has conversion price of £74.25. What is the conversion ratio of the bond?

3. **Conversion Value** A convertible bond has a conversion ratio of 10.5. If the stock is currently priced at $62, what is the conversion value of the bond?

4. **Conversion Premium** Eckely, Inc., recently issued bonds with a conversion ratio of 14.5. If the stock price at the bond issue was €46.24, what was the conversion premium?

5. **Convertible Bonds** Hannon Home Products, Inc., recently issued THB 430,000 worth of 8 percent convertible debentures. Each convertible bond has a face value of THB 1,000. Each convertible bond can be converted into 24.25 shares of common stock anytime before maturity. The stock price is THB 31.25, and the market value of each bond is THB 1,180.
   a. What is the conversion ratio?
   b. What is the conversion price?
   c. What is the conversion premium?

d. What is the conversion value?

e. If the stock price increases by THB 2, what is the new conversion value?

6. **Warrant Value** A warrant gives its owner the right to purchase three shares of common stock at an exercise price of $32 per share. The current market price of the stock is $38. What is the minimum value of the warrant?

7. **Convertible Bond Value** An analyst has recently informed you that at the issuance of a company's convertible bonds, one of the two following sets of relationships existed:

	Scenario A	Scenario B
Face Value of Bond	CNY 1,000	CNY 1,000
Straight Value of Convertible Bond	900	950
Market Value of Convertible Bond	1,000	900

Assume the bonds are available for immediate conversion. Which of the two scenarios do you believe is more likely? Why?

8. **Convertible Bond Value** Sportime Fitness Center, Inc., issued convertible bonds with a conversion price of $25. The bonds are available for immediate conversion. The current price of the company's common stock is $21 per share. The current market price of the convertible bonds is $990. The convertible bonds' straight value is not known.

a. What is the minimum price for the convertible bonds?

b. Explain the difference between the current market price of each convertible bond and the value of the common stock into which it can be immediately converted.

9. **Convertible Bonds** You own a callable, convertible bond with a conversion ratio of 35. The stock is currently selling for NGN 40 per share. The issuer of the bond has announced a call at a call price of 110. What are your options here? What should you do?

10. **Warrant Value** Never Say Die has five-year warrants that currently trade in the open market. Each warrant gives its owner the right to purchase one share of common stock for an exercise price of $35.

a. Suppose the stock is currently trading for $33 per share. What is the lower limit on the price of the warrant? What is the upper limit?

b. Suppose the stock is currently trading for $39 per share. What is the lower limit on the price of the warrant? What is the upper limit?

INTERMEDIATE
(Questions 11–14)

11. **Convertible Bonds** Salt N Pepper has just issued a 30-year callable, convertible bond with a coupon rate of 7 percent annual coupon payments. The bond has a conversion price of ILS 125. The company's stock is selling for ILS 32 per share. The owner of the bond will be forced to convert if the bond's conversion value is ever greater than or equal to ILS 1,100. The required return on an otherwise identical nonconvertible bond is 12 percent.

a. What is the minimum value of the bond?

b. If the stock price were to grow by 15 percent per year forever, how long would it take for the bond's conversion value to exceed ILS 1,100?

12. **Convertible Bonds** Rob Stevens is the chief executive officer of Vericon Radio, Inc., and owns 500,000 shares of stock. The company currently has 4 million shares of stock and convertible bonds with a face value of $20 million outstanding. The convertible bonds have a conversion price of $20, and the stock is currently selling for $25.

a. What percentage of the firm's common stock does Mr. Stevens own?

b. If the company decides to call the convertible bonds and force conversion, what percentage of the firm's common stock will Mr. Stevens own? He does not own any convertible bonds.

13. **Warrants** Lausanne Beauty Products, Inc., an all-equity firm, has three shares of stock outstanding. Yesterday, the firm's assets consisted of five ounces of platinum, currently worth

www.mhhe.com/rwj

€1,000 per ounce. Today, the company issued Ms. Suq a warrant for its fair value of €1,000. The warrant gives Ms. Suq the right to buy a single share of the firm's stock for €2,100 and can be exercised only on its expiration date one year from today. The firm used the proceeds from the issuance to immediately purchase an additional ounce of platinum.

a. What was the price of a single share of stock *before* the warrant was issued?

b. What was the price of a single share of stock immediately *after* the warrant was issued?

c. Suppose platinum is selling for €1,100 per ounce on the warrant's expiration date in one year. What will be the value of a single share of stock on the warrant's expiration date?

14. **Warrants** The capital structure of Ricketti Enterprises, Inc., consists of 10 million shares of common stock and 1 million warrants. Each warrant gives its owner the right to purchase one share of common stock for an exercise price of $15. The current stock price is $17, and each warrant is worth $3. What is the new stock price if all warrant holders decide to exercise today?

CHALLENGE
(Questions 15–17)

15. **Convertible Calculations** You have been hired to value a new 25-year callable, convertible bond. The bond has a 6.80 percent coupon rate, payable annually. The conversion price is £150, and the stock currently sells for £44.75. The stock price is expected to grow at 12 percent per year. The bond is callable at £1,200; but based on prior experience, it won't be called unless the conversion value is £1,300. The required return on this bond is 10 percent. What value would you assign to this bond?

16. **Warrant Value** Superior Clamps, Inc., has a capital structure consisting of 4 million shares of common stock and 500,000 warrants. Each warrant gives its owner the right to purchase one share of newly issued common stock for an exercise price of $20. The warrants are European and will expire one year from today. The market value of the company's assets is $88 million, and the annual variance of the returns on the firm's assets is 0.04. Treasury bills that mature in one year yield a continuously compounded interest rate of 7 percent. The company does not pay a dividend. Use the Black–Scholes model to determine the value of a single warrant.

17. **Warrant Value** Omega Airline's capital structure consists of 1.5 million shares of common stock and zero coupon bonds with a face value of LKR 10 million that mature in six months. The firm just announced that it will issue warrants with an exercise price of LKR 95 and six months until expiration to raise the funds to pay off its maturing debt. Each warrant can be exercised only at expiration and gives its owner the right to buy a single newly issued share of common stock. The firm will place the proceeds from the warrant issue immediately into Treasury bills. The market value balance sheet shows that the firm will have assets worth LKR 160 million after the announcement. The company does not pay dividends. The standard deviation of the returns on the firm's assets is 65 percent, and Treasury bills with a six-month maturity yield 6 percent. How many warrants must the company issue today to be able to use the proceeds from the sale to pay off the firm's debt obligation in six months?

S&S Air's Convertible Bond

Chris Guthrie was recently hired by S&S Air, Inc., to assist the company with its short-term financial planning and to evaluate the company's performance. Chris graduated from college five years ago with a finance degree. He has been employed in the finance department of a *Fortune* 500 company since then.

S&S Air was founded 10 years ago by two friends, Mark Sexton and Todd Story. The company has manufactured and sold light airplanes over this period, and the company's products have received high reviews for safety and reliability. The company has a niche market in that it sells primarily to individuals who own and fly their own airplanes. The company has two models: the Birdie, which sells for $53,000, and the Eagle, which sells for $78,000.

S&S Air is not publicly traded, but the company needs new funds for investment opportunities. In consultation with Tonisha Jones of underwriter Raines and Warren, Chris decided that a convertible bond issue with a 20-year maturity is the way to go. He met with the owners, Mark and Todd, and presented his analysis of the convertible bond issue. Because the company is not publicly traded, Chris looked at comparable publicly traded companies and determined that the average PE ratio for the industry is 12.5. Earnings per share for the company are $1.60. With this in mind, Chris concluded that the conversion price should be $25 per share.

Several days later Todd, Mark, and Chris met again to discuss the potential bond issue. Both Todd and Mark have researched convertible bonds and have questions for Chris. Todd begins by asking Chris if the convertible bond issue will have a lower coupon rate than a comparable bond without a conversion feature. Chris replies that to sell the bond at par value, the convertible bond issue would require a 6 percent coupon rate with a conversion value of $800, while a plain vanilla bond would have a 7 percent coupon rate. Todd nods in agreement, and he explains that the convertible bonds are a win–win form of financing. He states that if the value of the company stock does not rise above the conversion price, the company has issued debt at a cost below the market rate (6 percent instead of 7 percent). If the company's stock does rise to the conversion value, the company has effectively issued stock at above the current value.

Mark immediately disagrees, arguing that convertible bonds are a no-win form of financing. He argues that if the value of the company stock rises to $25, the company is forced to sell stock at the conversion price. This means the new shareholders (those who bought the convertible bonds) benefit from a bargain price. Put another way, if the company prospers, it would have been better to have issued straight debt so that the gains would not be shared.

Chris has gone back to Tonisha for help. As Tonisha's assistant, you've been asked to prepare another memo answering the following questions:

1. Why do you think Chris is suggesting a conversion price of $25? Given that the company is not publicly traded, does it even make sense to talk about a conversion price?

2. What is the floor value of the S&S Air convertible bond?

3. What is the conversion ratio of the bond?

4. What is the conversion premium of the bond?

5. What is the value of the option?

6. Is there anything wrong with Todd's argument that it is cheaper to issue a bond with a convertible feature because the required coupon is lower?

7. Is there anything wrong with Mark's argument that a convertible bond is a bad idea because it allows new shareholders to participate in gains made by the company?

8. How can you reconcile the arguments made by Todd and Mark?

9. During the debate, a question comes up concerning whether the bonds should have an ordinary (not make-whole) call feature. Chris confuses everybody by stating, "The call feature lets S&S Air force conversion, thereby minimizing the problem Mark has identified." What is he talking about? Is he making sense?

25 Derivatives and Hedging Risk

Managing risk is one of the most important tasks confronting corporate management, and financial markets are always willing to introduce new products to meet a need, either real or perceived. Consider credit derivatives, also known as credit default swaps. A credit derivative is an optionlike instrument that allows the seller of the derivative to put an underlying bond to the purchaser if a credit event, such as bankruptcy, occurs. Credit derivatives were practically unheard of in 2000, but the notional value of these instruments had grown to $12.4 trillion by the middle of 2005. Of course, the market for currency and interest rate swaps, which allows for the exchange of currencies or interest payments, had grown even larger, with a notional value of over $200 trillion. In this chapter, we explore a variety of derivative contracts that allow a company's management to control risk.

25.1 Derivatives, Hedging, and Risk

The name *derivatives* is self-explanatory. A derivative is a financial instrument whose payoffs and values are derived from, or depend on, something else. Often, we speak of the thing that the derivative depends on as the *primitive* or the *underlying*. For example, in Chapter 22 we studied how options work. An option is a derivative. The value of a call option depends on the value of the underlying stock on which it is written. Actually, call options are quite complicated examples of derivatives. The vast majority of derivatives are simpler than call options. Most derivatives are forward or futures agreements or what are called *swaps*, and we will study each of these in some detail.

Why do firms use derivatives? The answer is that derivatives are tools for changing the firm's risk exposure. Someone once said that derivatives are to finance what scalpels are to surgery. By using derivatives, the firm can cut away unwanted portions of risk exposure and even transform the exposures into quite different forms. A central point in finance is that risk is undesirable. In our chapters about risk and return, we pointed out that individuals would choose risky securities only if the expected return compensated for the risk. Similarly, a firm will accept a project with high risk only if the return on the project compensates for this risk. Not surprisingly, then, firms are usually looking for ways to reduce their risk. When the firm reduces its risk exposure with the use of derivatives, it is said to be **hedging**. Hedging offsets the firm's risk, such as the risk in a project, by one or more transactions in the financial markets.

Derivatives can also be used to merely change or even increase the firm's risk exposure. When this occurs, the firm is **speculating** on the movement of some economic variables—those that underlie the derivative. For example, if a derivative is purchased that will rise in value if interest rates rise, and if the firm has no offsetting exposure to interest rate changes, then the firm is speculating that interest rates will rise and give it a profit on its derivatives position. Using derivatives to translate an opinion about whether interest rates or some other economic variable will rise or fall is the opposite of hedging—it is risk enhancing. Speculating on your views on the economy and using derivatives to profit if that view turns out to be correct is not necessarily wrong, but the speculator should always remember that sharp tools cut deep: If the opinions on which the derivatives position is based turn out to be incorrect, then the consequences can prove costly. Efficient market theory teaches how difficult it is to predict what markets will do. Most of the sad experiences with derivatives have occurred not from their use as instruments for hedging and offsetting risk, but rather from speculation.

25.2 Forward Contracts

We can begin our discussion of hedging by considering forward contracts. You have probably been dealing in forward contracts your whole life without knowing it. Suppose you walk into a bookstore on, say, February 1 to buy the best-seller *Eating Habits of the Rich and Famous*. The cashier tells you that the book is currently sold out, but he takes your phone number, saying that he will reorder it for you. He says the book will cost $10.00. If you agree on February 1 to pick up and pay $10.00 for the book when called, you and the cashier have engaged in a **forward contract**. That is, you have agreed both to pay for the book and to pick it up when the bookstore notifies you. Because you are agreeing to buy the book at a later date, you are *buying* a forward contract on February 1. In commodity parlance, you will be taking delivery when you pick up the book. The book is called the **deliverable instrument**.

The cashier, acting on behalf of the bookstore, is selling a forward contract. (Alternatively, we say that he is writing a forward contract.) The bookstore has agreed to turn the book over to you at the predetermined price of $10.00 as soon as the book arrives. The act of turning the book over to you is called **making delivery**. Table 25.1 illustrates the book purchase. Note that the agreement takes place on February 1. The price is set and the conditions for sale are set at that time. In this case, the sale will occur when the book arrives. In other cases, an exact date of sale would be given. However, *no* cash changes hands on February 1; cash changes hands only when the book arrives.

Though forward contracts may have seemed exotic to you before you began this chapter, you can see that they are quite commonplace. Dealings in your personal life probably have involved forward contracts. Similarly, forward contracts occur all the time in business.

Table 25.1

Illustration of Book Purchase as a Forward Contract

February 1	Date When Book Arrives
Buyer	
Buyer agrees to	Buyer:
1. Pay the purchase price of $10.00.	1. Pays purchase price of $10.00.
2. Receive book when book arrives.	2. Receives book.
Seller	
Seller agrees to	Seller:
1. Give up book when book arrives.	1. Gives up book.
2. Accept payment of $10.00 when book arrives.	2. Accepts payment of $10.00.

Note that cash does not change hands on February 1. Cash changes hands when the book arrives.

Every time a firm orders an item that cannot be delivered immediately, a forward contract takes place. Sometimes, particularly when the order is small, an oral agreement will suffice. Other times, particularly when the order is larger, a written agreement is necessary.

Note that a forward contract is not an option. Both the buyer and the seller are obligated to perform under the terms of the contract. Conversely, the buyer of an option *chooses* whether to exercise the option.

A forward contract should be contrasted with a **cash transaction**—that is, a transaction where exchange is immediate. Had the book been on the bookstore's shelf, your purchase of it would constitute a cash transaction.

25.3   Futures Contracts

A variant of the forward contract takes place on financial exchanges. Contracts on exchanges are usually called **futures contracts**. There are a number of futures exchanges in the United States and elsewhere, and more are being established. The Chicago Board of Trade (CBT) is among the largest. Other notable exchanges include the Chicago Mercantile Exchange (CME), the London International Financial Futures and Options Exchange (LIFFE), and the New York Mercantile Exchange (NYM).

Table 25.2 gives a partial *Wall Street Journal* listing for selected futures contracts. Taking a look at the corn contracts in the left portion of the table, note that the contracts trade on the CBT, one contract calls for the delivery of 5,000 bushels of corn, and prices are quoted in cents per bushel. The months in which the contracts mature are given in the first column.

For the corn contract with a March maturity, the first number in the row is the opening price (223 cents per bushel), the next number is the high price for the day (224), and the following number is the low price for the day (220.75). The *settlement price* is the fourth number (221), and it essentially the closing price for the day. For purposes of marking to market, this is the figure used. The change, listed next, is the movement in the settlement price since the previous trading session (−2 cents). The highest price 276.50 and lowest price (199.50) over the life of the contract are shown next. Finally, the *open interest* (14,348), the number of contracts outstanding at the end of the day, is shown.

To see how large futures trading can be, look at the CBT Treasury bond contracts (under the interest rate heading). One contract is for long-term Treasury bonds with a face, or par, value of $100,000. The total open interest for all months is about 650,000 contracts. The total face value outstanding is therefore $650 billion for this one type of contract!

Though we are discussing a futures contract, let us work with a forward contract first. Suppose you wrote a *forward* contract for September wheat at $4.07. From our discussion of forward contracts, this would mean that you would agree to turn over an agreed-upon number of wheat bushels for $4.07 per bushel on some specified date in the remainder of the month of September.

A futures contract differs somewhat from a forward contract. First, the seller can choose to deliver the wheat on any day during the delivery month—that is, the month of September. This gives the seller leeway that he would not have with a forward contract. When the seller decides to deliver, he notifies the exchange clearinghouse that he wants to do so. The clearinghouse then notifies an individual who bought a September wheat contract that she must stand ready to accept delivery within the next few days. Though each exchange selects the buyer in a different way, the buyer is generally chosen in a random fashion. Because there are so many buyers at any one time, the buyer selected by the clearinghouse to take delivery almost certainly did not originally buy the contract from the seller now making delivery.

Table 25.2

Data on Futures Contracts, Tuesday, March 7, 2006

Published Wednesday, March 8, 2006, *The Wall Street Journal*.

FUTURES

Agriculture Futures

Corn (CBT)-5,000 bu.; cents per bu.

	OPEN	HIGH	LOW	SETTLE	CHG	LIFETIME HIGH	LIFETIME LOW	OPEN INT
Mar	223.00	224.00	220.75	221.00	-2.00	276.50	199.50	14,348
May	232.75	233.75	230.25	230.50	-2.25	276.75	208.75	506,328

Oats (CBT)-5,000 bu.; cents per bu.

	OPEN	HIGH	LOW	SETTLE	CHG	LIFETIME HIGH	LIFETIME LOW	OPEN INT
Mar	185.00	185.00	183.25	183.25	-.75	206.00	146.50	46
May	187.50	189.00	186.75	188.75	1.25	200.75	154.00	8,436

Soybeans (CBT)-5,000 bu.; cents per bu.

	OPEN	HIGH	LOW	SETTLE	CHG	LIFETIME HIGH	LIFETIME LOW	OPEN INT
Mar	586.50	592.00	578.00	578.00	-9.00	760.00	529.00	4,440
May	601.00	603.00	589.00	590.00	-10.50	742.00	530.25	188,984

Soybean Meal (CBT)-100 tons; $ per ton.

	OPEN	HIGH	LOW	SETTLE	CHG	LIFETIME HIGH	LIFETIME LOW	OPEN INT
Mar	174.90	174.90	171.80	172.50	-1.40	237.00	162.50	3,313
May	176.00	176.70	173.70	174.30	-1.60	230.50	164.80	60,721

Soybean Oil (CBT)-60,000 lbs.; cents per lb.

	OPEN	HIGH	LOW	SETTLE	CHG	LIFETIME HIGH	LIFETIME LOW	OPEN INT
Mar	24.45	24.46	23.88	23.95	-.50	26.45	19.70	2,379
May	24.82	24.85	24.20	24.31	-.48	26.35	20.00	117,981

Rough Rice (CBT)-2,000 cwt.; cents per cwt.

	OPEN	HIGH	LOW	SETTLE	CHG	LIFETIME HIGH	LIFETIME LOW	OPEN INT
Mar	835.00	839.00	828.00	839.00	10.00	875.00	690.00	31
May	858.00	865.00	853.00	865.00	9.00	901.00	719.00	6,911

Wheat (CBT)-5,000 bu.; cents per bu.

	OPEN	HIGH	LOW	SETTLE	CHG	LIFETIME HIGH	LIFETIME LOW	OPEN INT
Mar	370.00	375.00	369.50	370.50	.50	393.00	307.00	1,432
May	381.00	385.25	378.00	381.00	1.00	390.50	316.50	227,477

Wheat (KC)-5,000 bu.; cents per bu.

	OPEN	HIGH	LOW	SETTLE	CHG	LIFETIME HIGH	LIFETIME LOW	OPEN INT
Mar	436.00	440.00	433.00	433.00	-2.75	447.00	331.50	1,109
May	440.00	445.00	436.75	438.75	-.75	453.50	344.25	56,743

Wheat (MPLS)-5,000 bu.; cents per bu.

	OPEN	HIGH	LOW	SETTLE	CHG	LIFETIME HIGH	LIFETIME LOW	OPEN INT
Mar	423.25	423.50	422.00	423.00	1.00	426.00	340.75	314
May	421.75	428.00	421.00	424.75	1.75	435.50	347.00	18,539

Cattle-Feeder (CME)-50,000 lbs.; cents per lb.

	OPEN	HIGH	LOW	SETTLE	CHG	LIFETIME HIGH	LIFETIME LOW	OPEN INT
Mar	105.950	106.200	104.600	104.700	-1.250	116.100	96.000	5,922
Apr	107.200	107.400	106.050	106.200	-.750	115.000	95.500	14,007

Cattle-Live (CME)-40,000 lbs.; cents per lb.

	OPEN	HIGH	LOW	SETTLE	CHG	LIFETIME HIGH	LIFETIME LOW	OPEN INT
Apr	85.700	85.900	84.700	84.775	-.925	95.550	83.600	94,815
June	80.750	81.475	80.350	80.375	-.900	88.000	78.800	62,163

Hogs-Lean (CME)-40,000 lbs.; cents per lb.

	OPEN	HIGH	LOW	SETTLE	CHG	LIFETIME HIGH	LIFETIME LOW	OPEN INT
Apr	60.450	60.500	58.875	59.400	-1.375	71.325	55.000	74,789
June	68.900	69.150	67.950	68.650	-.875	73.450	59.500	47,790

Pork Bellies (CME)-40,000 lbs.; cents per lb.

	OPEN	HIGH	LOW	SETTLE	CHG	LIFETIME HIGH	LIFETIME LOW	OPEN INT
Mar	87.150	87.800	86.500	87.100	-1.100	98.000	72.400	220
May	87.750	89.000	87.350	87.875	-1.375	99.900	73.850	1,553

Lumber (CME)-110,000 bd. ft., $ per 1,000 bd. ft.

	OPEN	HIGH	LOW	SETTLE	CHG	LIFETIME HIGH	LIFETIME LOW	OPEN INT
Mar	337.30	337.30	334.00	335.00	-1.50	391.80	288.00	714
May	336.80	339.30	334.70	334.90	-3.90	382.80	293.00	2,869

Milk (CME)-200,000 lbs., cents per lb.

	OPEN	HIGH	LOW	SETTLE	CHG	LIFETIME HIGH	LIFETIME LOW	OPEN INT
Mar	11.08	11.15	11.06	11.11	.05	13.21	10.92	2,638
Apr	10.92	10.95	10.90	10.90	-.01	13.20	10.85	3,123

Cocoa (NYBOT)-10 metric tons; $ per ton.

	OPEN	HIGH	LOW	SETTLE	CHG	LIFETIME HIGH	LIFETIME LOW	OPEN INT
Mar	1,415	1,415	1,410	1,435	-10	1,899	1,344	50
May	1,450	1,460	1,444	1,453	-2	1,810	1,366	54,283

Coffee (NYBOT)-37,500 lbs.; cents per lb.

	OPEN	HIGH	LOW	SETTLE	CHG	LIFETIME HIGH	LIFETIME LOW	OPEN INT
Mar	109.50	109.60	106.50	106.70	-2.30	148.75	82.60	346
May	110.50	110.70	108.00	108.60	-2.25	148.50	92.10	65,218

Sugar-World (NYBOT)-112,000 lbs.; cents per lb.

	OPEN	HIGH	LOW	SETTLE	CHG	LIFETIME HIGH	LIFETIME LOW	OPEN INT
May	17.53	17.60	17.02	17.18	-.59	19.65	7.65	227,070
July	17.05	17.10	16.70	16.85	-.54	18.71	7.70	86,260

Sugar-Domestic (NYBOT)-112,000 lbs.; cents per lb.

	OPEN	HIGH	LOW	SETTLE	CHG	LIFETIME HIGH	LIFETIME LOW	OPEN INT
May	22.75	22.75	22.70	22.75	-.08	25.25	20.65	3,450
July	22.75	22.81	22.75	22.81	-.12	25.20	20.88	4,080

Cotton (NYBOT)-50,000 lbs.; cents per lb.

	OPEN	HIGH	LOW	SETTLE	CHG	LIFETIME HIGH	LIFETIME LOW	OPEN INT
Mar	54.25	54.35	53.60	53.80	-.22	69.00	48.30	2,229
May	53.90	54.45	53.75	53.75	-.18	61.20	49.25	91,003

Orange Juice (NYBOT)-15,000 lbs.; cents per lb.

	OPEN	HIGH	LOW	SETTLE	CHG	LIFETIME HIGH	LIFETIME LOW	OPEN INT
Mar	133.40	133.50	132.00	133.00	1.00	136.00	87.25	518
May	132.25	133.20	131.40	132.95	.95	135.00	95.30	22,936

Metal & Petroleum Futures

Copper-High (CMX)-25,000 lbs.; cents per lb.

	OPEN	HIGH	LOW	SETTLE	CHG	LIFETIME HIGH	LIFETIME LOW	OPEN INT
Mar	220.05	220.75	216.80	218.60	-1.50	233.90	98.00	5,083
May	219.80	220.80	215.60	217.70	-1.95	231.45	100.00	59,327

Gold (CMX)-100 troy oz.; $ per troy oz.

	OPEN	HIGH	LOW	SETTLE	CHG	LIFETIME HIGH	LIFETIME LOW	OPEN INT
Mar	554.50	554.50	554.00	552.70	-2.20	577.00	530.70	13
Apr	556.50	559.80	549.60	554.50	-2.30	579.50	418.00	225,452
June	556.90	564.30	555.00	559.70	-2.30	585.00	312.00	50,013
Oct	573.40	573.40	571.00	569.90	-2.40	592.30	436.50	10,173
Dec	578.00	580.90	570.00	575.00	-2.40	600.50	338.00	16,129
Dc07	608.00	608.00	602.00	605.60	-2.50	630.00	368.00	10,011

Platinum (NYM)-50 troy oz.; $ per troy oz.

	OPEN	HIGH	LOW	SETTLE	CHG	LIFETIME HIGH	LIFETIME LOW	OPEN INT
Apr	1046.60	1050.00	1036.00	1040.90	-2.50	1094.00	815.00	7,286
July	1051.00	1054.00	1046.00	1048.70	-2.70	1090.00	985.00	1,528

Silver (CMX)-5,000 troy oz.; cnts per troy oz.

	OPEN	HIGH	LOW	SETTLE	CHG	LIFETIME HIGH	LIFETIME LOW	OPEN INT
Mar	1002.5	1006.0	991.0	1003.5	8.2	1022.5	662.5	1,433
May	1003.5	1012.0	997.0	1010.7	8.2	1033.0	685.5	85,574

Crude Oil, Light Sweet (NYM)-1,000 bbls.; $ per bbl.

	OPEN	HIGH	LOW	SETTLE	CHG	LIFETIME HIGH	LIFETIME LOW	OPEN INT
Apr	62.32	62.75	61.10	61.58	-0.83	71.00	27.10	212,684
May	63.95	64.40	62.80	63.32	-0.73	70.33	36.86	163,365
June	64.70	65.25	63.60	64.08	-0.84	70.80	23.75	92,996
Dec	67.20	67.57	65.80	66.32	-1.10	71.70	19.10	77,871
Dc07	67.65	67.80	66.14	66.63	-1.22	70.80	19.50	59,682
Dc08	67.03	67.03	66.10	65.83	-1.27	68.60	19.75	36,045

Heating Oil No. 2 (NYM)-42,000 gal.; $ per gal.

	OPEN	HIGH	LOW	SETTLE	CHG	LIFETIME HIGH	LIFETIME LOW	OPEN INT
Apr	1.7577	1.7674	1.6970	1.7222	-.0355	2.1160	1.0954	61,222
May	1.7785	1.7898	1.7265	1.7459	-.0361	2.0300	1.0600	37,753

Gasoline-NY Unleaded (NYM)-42,000 gal.; $ per gal.

	OPEN	HIGH	LOW	SETTLE	CHG	LIFETIME HIGH	LIFETIME LOW	OPEN INT
Apr	1.6610	1.6610	1.5755	1.6334	-.0226	2.0760	1.4475	67,346
May	1.6935	1.7005	1.6210	1.6770	-.0184	2.0700	1.4710	42,028

Natural Gas (NYM)-10,000 MMBtu.; $ per MMBtu.

	OPEN	HIGH	LOW	SETTLE	CHG	LIFETIME HIGH	LIFETIME LOW	OPEN INT
Apr	6.541	6.750	6.501	6.678	.131	11.680	3.786	77,102
May	6.767	6.950	6.722	6.888	.121	11.266	3.571	59,780
June	6.961	7.140	6.925	7.085	.113	11.285	3.601	28,321
Oct	7.556	7.720	7.530	7.676	.104	11.390	3.732	37,484
Nov	8.660	8.770	8.660	8.771	.099	11.765	3.950	34,493
Ja07	10.400	10.450	10.380	10.471	.099	12.600	4.823	42,728

Interest Rate Futures

Treasury Bonds (CBT)-$100,000; pts 32nds of 100%

	OPEN	HIGH	LOW	SETTLE	CHG	LIFETIME HIGH	LIFETIME LOW	OPEN INT
Mar	110-18	110-28	110-01	110-24	..	118-19	110-01	81,587
June	110-17	110-27	109-31	110-23	..	117-24	109-31	570,473

Treasury Notes (CBT)-$100,000; pts 32nds of 100%

	OPEN	HIGH	LOW	SETTLE	CHG	LIFETIME HIGH	LIFETIME LOW	OPEN INT
Mar	106-275	107-000	106-175	106-295	1.0	112-300	106-175	182,109

Second, futures contracts are traded on an exchange, whereas forward contracts are generally traded off an exchange. Because of this, there is generally a liquid market in futures contracts. A buyer can net out her futures position with a sale. A seller can net out his futures position with a purchase. If a buyer of a futures contract does not subsequently sell her contract, she must take delivery.

Third, and most important, the prices of futures contracts are **marked to the market** daily. That is, suppose the price falls to $4.05 on Friday's close. Because all buyers lost two cents per bushel on that day, they each must turn over the two cents per bushel to their brokers within 24 hours, who subsequently remit the proceeds to the clearinghouse. All sellers gained two cents per bushel on that day, so they each receive two cents per bushel from their brokers. Their brokers are subsequently compensated by the clearinghouse. Because there is a buyer for every seller, the clearinghouse must break even every day.

Now suppose that the price rises to $4.12 on the close of the following Monday. Each buyer receives seven cents ($4.12 − $4.05) per bushel, and each seller must pay seven cents per bushel. Finally, suppose that on Monday a seller notifies his broker of his intention to deliver.[1] The delivery price will be $4.12, which is Monday's close.

There are clearly many cash flows in futures contracts. However, after all the dust settles, the *net price* to the buyer must be the price at which she bought originally. That is, an individual buying at Thursday's closing price of $4.07 and being called to take delivery on Monday pays two cents per bushel on Friday, receives seven cents per bushel on Monday, and takes

Illustration of Example Involving Marking to Market in Futures Contracts

Both buyer and seller originally transact at Thursday's closing price. Delivery takes place at Monday's closing price.*

	Thursday, September 19	Friday, September 20	Monday, September 23	Delivery (Notification Given by Seller on Monday)
Closing price	$4.07	$4.05	$4.12	
Buyer	Buyer purchases futures contract at closing price of $4.07/bushel.	Buyer must pay two cents/bushel to clearinghouse within one business day.	Buyer receives seven cents/bushel from clearinghouse within one business day.	Buyer pays $4.12 per bushel and receives grain within one business day.

Buyer's net payment of −$4.07 (= −$0.02 + $0.07 − $4.12) is the same as if buyer purchased a forward contract for $4.07/bushel.

	Thursday, September 19	Friday, September 20	Monday, September 23	Delivery (Notification Given by Seller on Monday)
Seller	Seller sells futures contract at closing price of $4.07/bushel.	Seller receives two cents/bushel from clearinghouse within one business day.	Seller pays seven cents/bushel to clearinghouse within one business day.	Seller receives $4.12 per bushel and delivers grain within one business day.

Seller's net receipts of $4.07 (= $0.02 − $0.07 + $4.12) are the same as if seller sold a forward contract for $4.07/bushel.

*For simplicity, we assume that buyer and seller both (1) initially transact at the same time and (2) meet in the delivery process. This is actually very unlikely to occur in the real world because the clearinghouse assigns the buyer to take delivery in a random manner.

---

[1] He will deliver on Wednesday, two days later.

delivery at \$4.12. Her net outflow per bushel is $-\$4.07$ ($=-\$0.02 + \$0.07 - \$4.12$), which is the price at which she contracted on Thursday. (Our analysis ignores the time value of money.) Conversely, an individual selling at Thursday's closing price of \$4.07 and notifying his broker concerning delivery the following Monday receives two cents per bushel on Friday, pays seven cents per bushel on Monday, and makes delivery at \$4.12. His net inflow per bushel is \$4.07 ($= \$0.02 - \$0.07 + \$4.12$), which is the price at which he contracted on Thursday.

These details are presented in a nearby box. For simplicity, we assumed that the buyer and seller who initially transact on Thursday's close meet in the delivery process.[2] The point in the example is that the buyer's net payment of \$4.07 per bushel is the same as if she purchased a forward contract for \$4.07. Similarly, the seller's net receipt of \$4.07 per bushel is the same as if he sold a forward contract for \$4.07 per bushel. The only difference is the timing of the cash flows. The buyer of a forward contract knows that he will make a single payment of \$4.07 on the expiration date. He will not need to worry about any other cash flows in the interim. Conversely, though the cash flows to the buyer of a futures contract will net to exactly \$4.07 as well, the pattern of cash flows is not known ahead of time.

The mark-to-the-market provision on futures contracts has two related effects. The first concerns differences in net present value. For example, a large price drop immediately following purchase means an immediate outpayment for the buyer of a futures contract. Though the net outflow of \$4.07 is still the same as under a forward contract, the present value of the cash outflows is greater to the buyer of a futures contract. Of course, the present value of the cash outflows is less to the buyer of a futures contract if a price rise follows purchase.[3] Though this effect could be substantial in certain theoretical circumstances, it appears to be of quite limited importance in the real world.[4]

Second, the firm must have extra liquidity to handle a sudden outflow prior to expiration. This added risk may make the futures contract less attractive.

Students frequently ask, "Why in the world would managers of the commodity exchanges ruin perfectly good contracts with these bizarre mark-to-the-market provisions?" Actually, the reason is a very good one. Consider the forward contract of Table 25.1 concerning the bookstore. Suppose the public quickly loses interest in *Eating Habits of the Rich and Famous*. By the time the bookstore calls the buyer, other stores may have dropped the price of the book to \$6.00. Because the forward contract was for \$10.00, the buyer has an incentive not to take delivery on the forward contract. Conversely, should the book become a hot item selling at \$15.00, the bookstore may simply not call the buyer.

As indicated, forward contracts have a big flaw. Whichever way the price of the deliverable instrument moves, one party has an incentive to default. There are many cases where defaults have occurred in the real world. One famous case concerned Coca-Cola. When the company began in the early 20th century, Coca-Cola made an agreement to supply its bottlers and distributors with cola syrup at a constant price *forever*. Of course, subsequent inflation would have caused Coca-Cola to lose large sums of money had it honored the contract. After much legal effort, Coke and its bottlers put an *inflation escalator clause* in the contract. Another famous case concerned Westinghouse. It seems the firm had promised to deliver uranium to certain utilities at a fixed price. The price of uranium skyrocketed in the 1970s, making Westinghouse lose money on every shipment. Westinghouse defaulted on its agreement. The utilities took Westinghouse to court but did not recover amounts anything near what Westinghouse owed them.

---

[2]As pointed out earlier, this is actually very unlikely to occur in the real world.

[3]The direction is reversed for the seller of a futures contract. However, the general point that the net present value of cash flows may differ between forward and futures contracts holds for sellers as well.

[4]See John C. Cox, John E. Ingersoll, and Steven A. Ross, "The Relationship between Forward and Future Prices," *Journal of Financial Economics* (1981).

Mark-to-the-market provisions minimize the chance of default on a futures contract. If the price rises, the seller has an incentive to default on a forward contract. However, after paying the clearinghouse, the seller of a futures contract has little reason to default. If the price falls, the same argument can be made for the buyer. Because changes in the value of the underlying asset are recognized daily, there is no accumulation of loss, and the incentive to default is reduced.

Because of this default issue, forward contracts generally involve individuals and institutions who know and can trust each other. But as W. C. Fields said, "Trust everybody, but cut the cards." Lawyers earn a handsome living writing supposedly airtight forward contracts, even among friends. The genius of the mark-to-the-market system is that it can prevent default where it is most likely to occur—among investors who do not know each other. Textbooks on futures contracts from decades ago usually include a statement such as "No major default has ever occurred on the commodity exchanges." No textbook published after the Hunt Brothers defaulted on silver contracts in the 1970s can make that claim. Nevertheless, the extremely low default rate in futures contracts is truly awe-inspiring.

25.4 Hedging

Now that we have determined how futures contracts work, let us talk about hedging. There are two types of hedges, long and short. We discuss the short hedge first.

EXAMPLE 25.1

Futures Hedging   In June, Bernard Abelman, a Midwestern farmer, anticipates a harvest of 50,000 bushels of wheat at the end of September. He has two alternatives.

1. Write futures contracts against his anticipated harvest. The September wheat contract on the Chicago Board of Trade is trading at $3.75 a bushel on June 1. He executes the following transaction:

Date of Transaction	Transaction	Price per Bushel
June 1	Write 10 September futures contracts	$3.75

He notes that transportation costs to the designated delivery point in Chicago are 30 cents/bushel. Thus, his net price per bushel is $3.45 = $3.75 − $0.30.

2. *Harvest the wheat without writing a futures contract.* Alternatively, Mr. Abelman could harvest the wheat without benefit of a futures contract. The risk would be quite great here because no one knows what the cash price in September will be. If prices rise, he will profit. Conversely, he will lose if prices fall.

We say that strategy 2 is an unhedged position because there is no attempt to use the futures markets to reduce risk. Conversely, strategy 1 involves a hedge. That is, a position in the futures market offsets the risk of a position in the physical—that is, in the actual—commodity.

Though hedging may seem quite sensible to you, it should be mentioned that not everyone hedges. Mr. Abelman might reject hedging for at least two reasons.

First, he may simply be uninformed about hedging. We have found that not everyone in business understands the hedging concept. Many executives have told us that they do not want to use futures markets for hedging their inventories because the risks are too great. However, we disagree. While there are large price fluctuations in these markets, hedging actually reduces the risk that an individual holding inventories bears.

(continued)

Second, Mr. Abelman may have a special insight or some special information that commodity prices will rise. He would not be wise to lock in a price of $3.75 if he expects the cash price in September to be well above this price.

The hedge of strategy 1 is called a **short hedge** because Mr. Abelman reduces his risk by *selling* a futures contract. The short hedge is very common in business. It occurs whenever someone either anticipates receiving inventory or is holding inventory. Mr. Abelman is anticipating the harvest of grain. A manufacturer of soybean meal and oil may hold large quantities of raw soybeans that are already paid for. However, the prices to be received for meal and oil are not known because no one knows what the market prices will be when the meal and oil are produced. The manufacturer may write futures contracts in meal and oil to lock in sales prices. An oil company may hold large inventories of petroleum to be processed into heating oil. The firm could sell futures contracts in heating oil to lock in the sales price. A mortgage banker may assemble mortgages slowly before selling them in bulk to a financial institution. Movements of interest rates affect the value of the mortgages while they are in inventory. The mortgage banker could sell Treasury bond futures contracts to offset this interest rate risk. (This last example is treated later in this chapter.)

More Hedging On April 1, Moon Chemical agreed to sell petrochemicals to the U.S. government in the future. The delivery dates and prices have been determined. Because oil is a basic ingredient of the production process, Moon Chemical will need to have large quantities of oil on hand. The firm can get the oil in one of two ways:

1. *Buy the oil as the firm needs it.* This is an unhedged position because, as of April 1, the firm does not know the prices it will later have to pay for the oil. Oil is quite a volatile commodity, so Moon Chemical is bearing a good bit of risk. The key to this risk bearing is that the sales price to the U.S. government has already been fixed. Thus, Moon Chemical cannot pass on increased costs to the consumer.

2. *Buy futures contracts.*[5] The firm can buy futures contracts with expiration months corresponding to the dates the firm needs inventory. The futures contracts lock in the purchase price to Moon Chemical. Because there is a crude oil futures contract for every month, selecting the correct futures contract is not difficult. Many other commodities have only five contracts per year, frequently necessitating buying contracts one month away from the month of production.

As mentioned earlier, Moon Chemical is interested in hedging the risk of fluctuating oil prices because it cannot pass any cost increases on to the consumer. Suppose, alternatively, that Moon Chemical was not selling petrochemicals on fixed contract to the U.S. government. Instead, imagine that the petrochemicals were to be sold to private industry at currently prevailing prices. The price of petrochemicals should move directly with oil price because oil is a major component of petrochemicals. Because cost increases are likely to be passed on to the consumer, Moon Chemical would probably not want to hedge in this case. Instead, the firm is likely to choose strategy 1, buying the oil as it is needed. If oil prices increase between April 1 and September 1, Moon Chemical will, of course, find that its inputs have become quite costly. However, in a competitive market, its revenues are likely to rise as well.

Strategy 2 is called a **long hedge** because one *purchases* a futures contract to reduce risk. In other words, one takes a long position in the futures market. In general, a firm institutes a long hedge when it is committed to a fixed sales price. One class of situations involves actual written contracts with customers, such as Moon Chemical had with the U.S. government. Alternatively, a firm may

---

[5]Alternatively, the firm could buy the oil on April 1 and store it. This would eliminate the risk of price movement because the firm's oil costs would be fixed upon the immediate purchase. However, this strategy would be inferior to strategy 2 in the common case where the difference between the futures contract quoted on April 1 and the April 1 cash price is less than the storage costs.

(continued)

find that it cannot easily pass on costs to consumers or does not want to pass on these costs. For example, a group of students opened a small meat market called *What's Your Beef* near the University of Pennsylvania in the late 1970s.[6] This was a time of volatile consumer prices, especially food prices. Knowing that their fellow students were particularly budget-conscious, the owners vowed to keep food prices constant, regardless of price movements in either direction. They accomplished this by purchasing futures contracts in various agricultural commodities.

25.5   Interest Rate Futures Contracts

In this section we consider interest rate futures contracts. Our examples deal with futures contracts on Treasury bonds because of their high popularity. We first price Treasury bonds and Treasury bond forward contracts. Differences between futures and forward contracts are explored. Hedging examples are provided next.

Pricing of Treasury Bonds

As mentioned earlier in the text, a Treasury bond pays semiannual interest over its life. In addition, the face value of the bond is paid at maturity. Consider a 20-year, 8 percent coupon bond that was issued on March 1. The first payment is to occur in six months—that is, on September 1. The value of the bond can be determined as follows:

Pricing of Treasury Bond

$$P_{TB} = \frac{\$40}{1 + R_1} + \frac{\$40}{(1 + R_2)^2} + \frac{\$40}{(1 + R_3)^3} + \cdots + \frac{\$40}{(1 + R_{39})^{39}} + \frac{\$1,040}{(1 + R_{40})^{40}} \qquad \textbf{(25.1)}$$

Because an 8 percent coupon bond pays interest of $80 a year, the semiannual coupon is $40. Principal and the semiannual coupons are both paid at maturity. As we mentioned in a previous chapter, the price of the Treasury bond, P_{TB}, is determined by discounting each payment on a bond at the appropriate spot rate. Because the payments are semiannual, each spot rate is expressed in semiannual terms. That is, imagine a horizontal term structure where the effective annual yield is 12 percent for all maturities. Because each spot rate, R, is expressed in semiannual terms, each spot rate is $\sqrt{1.12} - 1 = 5.83\%$. Coupon payments occur every six months, so there are 40 spot rates over the 20-year period.

Pricing of Forward Contracts

Now imagine a *forward* contract where, on March 1, you agree to buy a new 20-year, 8 percent coupon Treasury bond in six months (on September 1). As with typical forward contracts, you will pay for the bond on September 1, not March 1. The cash flows from both the Treasury bond issued on March 1 and the forward contract that you purchase on March 1 are presented in Figure 25.1. The cash flows on the Treasury bond begin exactly six months earlier than do the cash flows on the forward contract. The Treasury bond is purchased with cash on March 1 (date 0). The first coupon payment occurs on September 1 (date 1). The last coupon payment occurs at date 40, along with the face value of $1,000. The forward contract compels you to pay $P_{\text{FORW.CONT.}}$, the price of the forward contract, on September 1 (date 1). You receive a new Treasury bond at that time. The first coupon payment you receive from the bond occurs on March 1 of the following year (date 2). The last coupon payment occurs at date 41, along with the face value of $1,000.

---

[6]Ordinarily, an unusual firm name in this textbook is a tip-off that it is fictional. This, however, is a true story.

Figure 25.1

Cash Flows for Both
a Treasury Bond and
a Forward Contract
on a Treasury Bond

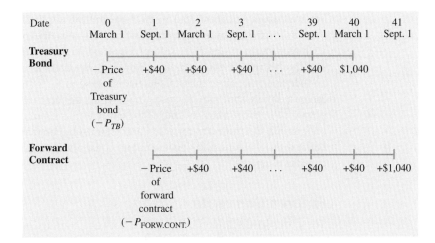

Given the 40 spot rates, Equation 25.1 showed how to price a Treasury bond. How do we price the forward contract on a Treasury bond? Just as we saw earlier in the text that net present value analysis can be used to price bonds, we will now show that net present value analysis can be used to price forward contracts. Given the cash flows for the forward contract in Figure 25.1, the price of the forward contract must satisfy the following equation:

$$\frac{P_{\text{FORW.CONT}}}{1 + R_1} = \frac{\$40}{(1 + R_2)^2} + \frac{\$40}{(1 + R_3)^3} + \frac{\$40}{(1 + R_4)^4} + \cdots + \frac{\$40}{(1 + R_{40})^{40}} + \frac{\$1,040}{(1 + R_{41})^{41}}$$

(25.2)

The right side of Equation 25.2 discounts all the cash flows from the delivery instrument (the Treasury bond issued on September 1) back to date 0 (March 1). Because the first cash flow occurs at date 2 (March 1 of the subsequent year), it is discounted by $1/(1 + R_2)^2$. The last cash flow of $1,040 occurs at date 41, so it is discounted by $1/(1 + R_{41})^{41}$. The left side represents the cost of the forward contract as of date 0. Because the actual outpayment occurs at date 1, it is discounted by $1/(1 + R_1)$.

Students often ask, "Why are we discounting everything back to date 0, when we are actually paying for the forward contract on September 1?" The answer is simply that we apply the same techniques to Equation 25.2 that we apply to all capital budgeting problems: We want to put everything in today's (date 0's) dollars. Given that the spot rates are known in the marketplace, traders should have no more trouble pricing a forward contract by Equation 25.2 than they would have pricing a Treasury bond by Equation 25.1.

Forward contracts are similar to the underlying bonds themselves. If the entire term structure of interest rates unexpectedly shifts upward on March 2, the Treasury bond issued the previous day should fall in value. This can be seen from Equation 25.1. A rise in each of the spot rates lowers the present value of each of the coupon payments. Hence, the value of the bond must fall. Conversely, a fall in the term structure of interest rates increases the value of the bond.

The same relationship holds with forward contracts, as we can see by rewriting Equation 25.2 like this:

$$P_{\text{FORW.CONT}} = \frac{\$40 \times (1 + R_1)}{(1 + R_2)^2} + \frac{\$40 \times (1 + R_1)}{(1 + R_3)^3} + \frac{\$40 \times (1 + R_1)}{(1 + R_4)^4}$$

$$+ \cdots + \frac{\$40 \times (1 + R_1)}{(1 + R_{40})^{40}} + \frac{\$1,040 \times (1 + R_1)}{(1 + R_{41})^{41}} \qquad \textbf{(25.3)}$$

We went from Equation 25.2 to 25.3 by multiplying both the left and the right sides by $(1 + R_1)$. If the entire term structure of interest rates unexpectedly shifts upward on March 2, the *first* term on the right side of Equation 25.3 should fall in value.[7] That is, both R_1 and R_2 will rise an equal amount. However, R_2 enters as a *squared* term, $1/(1 + R_2)^2$, so an increase in R_2 more than offsets the increase in R_1. As we move further to the right, an increase in any spot rate, R_i, more than offsets an increase in R_1. Here R_i enters as the ith power, $1/(1 + R_i)^i$. Thus, as long as the entire term structure shifts upward an equal amount on March 2, the value of a forward contract must fall on that date. Conversely, as long as the entire term structure shifts downward an equal amount on March 2, the value of a forward contract must rise.

Futures Contracts

The previous discussion concerned a forward contract in U.S. Treasury bonds—that is, a forward contract where the deliverable instrument is a U.S. Treasury bond. What about a futures contract on a Treasury bond?[8] We mentioned earlier that futures contracts and forward contracts are quite similar, though there are a few differences between the two. First, futures contracts are generally traded on exchanges, whereas forward contracts are not traded on an exchange. In this case, the Treasury bond futures contract is traded on the Chicago Board of Trade. Second, futures contracts generally allow the seller a period of time in which to deliver, whereas forward contracts generally call for delivery on a particular day. The seller of a Treasury bond futures contract can choose to deliver on any business day during the delivery month.[9] Third, futures contracts are subject to the mark-to-the-market convention, whereas forward contracts are not. Traders in Treasury bill futures contracts must adhere to this convention. Fourth, there is generally a liquid market for futures contracts allowing contracts to be quickly netted out. That is, a buyer can sell his futures contract at any time, and a seller can buy back her futures contract at any time. Conversely, because forward markets are generally quite illiquid, traders cannot easily net out their positions. The popularity of the Treasury bond futures contract has produced liquidity even higher than that on other futures contracts. Positions in that contract can be netted out quite easily.

This discussion is not intended to be an exhaustive list of differences between the Treasury bond forward contract and the Treasury bond futures contract. Rather, it is intended to show that both contracts share fundamental characteristics. Though there are differences, the two instruments should be viewed as variations of the same species, not different species. Thus, the pricing equation 25.3, which is exact for the forward contract, should be a decent approximation for the futures contract.

Hedging in Interest Rate Futures

Now that we have the basic institutional details under our belts, we are ready for examples of hedging using either futures contracts or forward contracts on Treasury bonds. Because the T-bond futures contract is extremely popular whereas the forward contract is traded sporadically, our examples use the futures contract.

---

[7]We are assuming that each spot rate shifts by the same amount. For example, suppose that on March 1 $R_1 = 5\%$, $R_2 = 5.4\%$, and $R_3 = 5.8\%$. Assuming that all rates increase by 1/2 percent on March 2, R_1 becomes 5.5 percent (.5% + 1/2%), R_2 becomes 5.9 percent, and R_3 becomes 6.3 percent.

[8]Futures contracts on bonds are also called *interest rate futures contracts*.

[9]Delivery occurs two days after the seller notifies the clearinghouse of her intention to deliver.

Interest Rate Hedging Ron Cooke owns a mortgage banking company. On March 1 he made a commitment to lend a total of $1 million to various homeowners on May 1. The loans are 20-year mortgages carrying a 12 percent coupon, the going interest rate on mortgages at the time. Thus, the mortgages are made at par. Though homeowners would not use the term, we could say that he is buying a *forward contract* on a mortgage. That is, he agrees on March 1 to give $1 million to his borrowers on May 1 in exchange for principal and interest from them every month for the next 20 years.

Like many mortgage bankers, he has no intention of paying the $1 million out of his own pocket. Rather, he intends to sell the mortgages to an insurance company. Thus, the insurance company will actually lend the funds and will receive principal and interest over the next 20 years. Mr. Cooke does not currently have an insurance company in mind. He plans to visit the mortgage departments of insurance companies over the next 60 days to sell the mortgages to one or many of them. He sets April 30 as a deadline for making the sale because the borrowers expect the funds on the following day.

Suppose Mr. Cooke sells the mortgages to the Acme Insurance Co. on April 15. What price will Acme pay for the bonds?

You may think the insurance company will obviously pay $1 million for the loans. However, suppose interest rates have risen above 12 percent by April 15. The insurance company will buy the mortgage at a discount. For example, suppose the insurance company agrees to pay only $940,000 for the mortgages. Because the mortgage banker agreed to lend a full $1 million to the borrowers, the mortgage banker must come up with the additional $60,000 (= $1 million − $940,000) out of his own pocket.

Alternatively, suppose interest rates fall below 12 percent by April 15. The mortgages can be sold at a premium under this scenario. If the insurance company buys the mortgages at $1.05 million, the mortgage banker will have made an unexpected profit of $50,000 (= $1.05 million − $1 million).

Because Ron Cooke is unable to forecast interest rates, this risk is something that he would like to avoid. The risk is summarized in Table 25.3.

Seeing the interest rate risk, students at this point may ask, "What does the mortgage banker get out of this loan to offset his risk bearing?" Mr. Cooke wants to sell the mortgages to the insurance company so that he can get two fees. The first is an *origination fee,* which is paid to the mortgage banker by the insurance company on April 15—that is, on the date the loan is sold. An industry standard in certain locales is 1 percent of the value of the loan, which is $10,000 (= 1% × $1 million). In addition, Mr. Cooke will act as a collection agent for the insurance company. For this service he will receive a small portion of the outstanding balance of the loan each month. For example, if he is paid 0.03 percent of the loan each month, he will receive $300 (= 0.03% × $1 million) in the first month. As the outstanding balance of the loan declines, he will receive less.

Table 25.3 Effects of Changing Interest Rates on Ron Cooke, Mortgage Banker

	Mortgage Interest Rate on April 15	
	Above 12%	**Below 12%**
Sale Price to Acme Insurance Company	Below $1 million (we assume $940,000).	Above $1 million (we assume $1.05 million).
Effect on Mortgage Banker	He loses because he must lend the full $1 million to borrowers.	He gains because he lends only $1 million to borrowers.
Dollar Gain or Loss	Loss of $60,000 (= $1 million − $940,000).	Gain of $50,000 (= $1.05 million − $1 million).

The interest rate on March 1, the date when the loan agreement was made with the borrowers, was 12 percent. April 15 is the date the mortgages were sold to Acme Insurance Company.

(continued)

Though Mr. Cooke will earn profitable fees on the loan, he bears interest rate risk. He loses money if interest rates rise after March 1, and he profits if interest rates fall after March 1. To hedge this risk, he writes June Treasury bond futures contracts on March 1. As with mortgages, Treasury bond futures contracts fall in value if interest rates rise. Because he *writes* the contract, he makes money on these contracts if they fall in value. Therefore, with an interest rate rise, the loss he endures in the mortgages is offset by the gain he earns in the futures market. Conversely, Treasury bond futures contracts rise in value if interest rates fall. Because he writes the contracts, he suffers losses on them when rates fall. With an interest rate fall, the profit he makes on the mortgages is offset by the loss he suffers in the futures markets.

The details of this hedging transaction are presented in Table 25.4. The column on the left is labeled "cash markets" because the deal in the mortgage market is transacted off an exchange. The column on the right shows the offsetting transactions in the futures market. Consider the first row. The mortgage banker enters into a forward contract on March 1. He simultaneously writes Treasury bond futures contracts. Ten contracts are written because the deliverable instrument on each contract is $100,000 of Treasury bonds. The total is $1 million ($= 10 \times $100,000$), which is equal to the value of the mortgages. Mr. Cooke would prefer to write May Treasury bond futures contracts. Here, Treasury bonds would be delivered on the futures contract during the same month that the loan is funded. Because there is no May T-bond futures contract, Mr. Cooke achieves the closest match through a June contract.

If held to maturity, the June contract would obligate the mortgage banker to deliver Treasury bonds in June. Interest rate risk ends in the cash market when the loans are sold. Interest rate risk must be terminated in the futures market at that time. Thus, Mr. Cooke nets out his position in the futures contract as soon as the loan is sold to Acme Insurance.

Table 25.4   **Illustration of Hedging Strategy for Ron Cooke, Mortgage Banker**

	Cash Markets	Futures Markets
March 1	Mortgage banker makes forward contracts to lend $1 million at 12 percent for 20 years. The loans are to be funded on May 1. No cash changes hands on March 1.	Mortgage banker writes 10 June Treasury bond futures contracts.
April 15	Loans are sold to Acme Insurance Company. Mortgage banker will receive sale price from Acme on the May 1 funding date.	Mortgage banker buys back all the futures contracts.
If interest rates rise:	Loans are sold at a price below $1 million. Mortgage banker loses because he receives less than the $1 million he must give to borrowers.	Each futures contract is bought back at a price below the sales price, resulting in *profit*. Mortgage banker's profit in futures market offsets loss in cash market.
If interest rates fall:	Loans are sold at a price above $1 million. Mortgage banker *gains* because he receives more than the $1 million he must give to borrowers.	Each futures contract is bought back at a price above the sales price, resulting in *loss*. Mortgage banker's loss in futures market offsets gain in cash market.

As our example shows, risk is clearly reduced via an offsetting transaction in the futures market. However, is risk totally eliminated? Risk would be totally eliminated if losses in the cash markets were *exactly* offset by gains in the futures markets and vice versa. This is unlikely to happen because mortgages and Treasury bonds are not identical instruments. First, mortgages may have different maturities than Treasury bonds. Second, Treasury bonds have a different payment stream than do mortgages. Principal is paid only at maturity on T-bonds, whereas principal is paid every month on mortgages. Because mortgages pay principal continuously, these instruments have a shorter *effective* time to maturity than do Treasury bonds of equal maturity.[10] Third, mortgages have default risk whereas Treasury bonds do not. The term structure applicable to instruments with default risk may change even when the term structure for risk-free assets remains constant. Fourth, mortgages may be paid off early and hence have a shorter *expected maturity* than Treasury bonds of equal maturity.

Because mortgages and Treasury bonds are not identical instruments, they are not identically affected by interest rates. If Treasury bonds are less volatile than mortgages, financial consultants may advise Mr. Cooke to write more than 10 T-bond futures contracts. Conversely, if these bonds are more volatile, the consultant may state that fewer than 10 futures contracts are indicated. An optimal ratio of futures to mortgages will reduce risk as much as possible. However, because the price movements of mortgages and Treasury bonds are not *perfectly correlated,* Mr. Cooke's hedging strategy cannot eliminate all risk.

The preceding strategy is called a *short hedge* because Mr. Cooke sells futures contracts to reduce risk. Though it involves an interest rate futures contract, this short hedge is analogous to short hedges in agricultural and metallurgical futures contracts. We argued at the beginning of this chapter that individuals and firms institute short hedges to offset inventory price fluctuation. Once Mr. Cooke makes a contract to lend money to borrowers, the mortgages effectively become his inventory. He writes a futures contract to offset the price fluctuation of his inventory.

We now consider an example where a mortgage banker institutes a long hedge.

EXAMPLE 25.4

Short versus Long Hedging   Margaret Boswell is another mortgage banker. Her firm faces problems similar to those facing Mr. Cooke's firm. However, she tackles the problems through the use of **advance commitments**, a strategy the opposite of Mr. Cooke's. That is, she promises to deliver loans to a financial institution *before* she lines up borrowers. On March 1 her firm agreed to sell mortgages to No-State Insurance Co. The agreement specifies that she must turn over 12 percent coupon mortgages with a face value of $1 million to No-State by May 1. No-State is buying the mortgages at par, implying that they will pay Ms. Boswell $1 million on May 1. As of March 1, Ms. Boswell had not signed up any borrowers. Over the next two months, she will seek out individuals who want mortgages beginning May 1.

As with Mr. Cooke, changing interest rates will affect Ms. Boswell. If interest rates fall before she signs up a borrower, the borrower will demand a premium on a 12 percent coupon loan. That is, the borrower will receive more than par on May 1.[11] Because Ms. Boswell receives par from the insurance company, she must make up the difference.

Conversely, if interest rates rise, a 12 percent coupon loan will be made at a discount. That is, the borrower will receive less than par on May 1. Because Ms. Boswell receives par from the insurance company, the difference is pure profit to her.

(continued)

---

[10]Alternatively, we can say that mortgages have shorter duration than do Treasury bonds of equal maturity. A precise definition of duration is provided later in this chapter.

[11]Alternatively, the mortgage would still be at par if a coupon rate below 12 percent were used. However, this is not done because the insurance company wants to buy only 12 percent mortgages.

Table 25.5   **Illustration of Advance Commitment for Margaret Boswell, Mortgage Banker**

	Cash Markets	Futures Markets
March 1	Mortgage banker makes a forward contract (advance commitment) to deliver $1 million of mortgages to No-State Insurance. The insurance company will pay par to Ms. Boswell for the loans on May 1. The borrowers are to receive their funding from the mortgage banker on May 1. The mortgages are to be 12 percent coupon loans for 20 years.	Mortgage banker buys 10 June Treasury bond futures contracts.
April 15	Mortgage banker signs up borrowers to 12 percent coupon, 20-year mortgages. She promises that the borrowers will receive funds on May 1.	Mortgage banker sells all futures contracts.
If interest rates rise:	Mortgage banker issues mortgages to borrowers at a discount. Mortgage banker gains because she receives par from the insurance company.	Futures contracts are sold at a price below purchase price, resulting in loss. Mortgage banker's loss in futures market offsets gain in cash market.
If interest rates fall:	Loans to borrowers are issued at a premium. Mortgage banker loses because she receives only par from insurance company.	Futures contracts are sold at a price above purchase price, resulting in gain. Mortgage banker's gain in futures market offsets loss in cash market.

The details are provided in Table 25.5. As did Mr. Cooke, Ms. Boswell finds the risk burdensome. Therefore, she offsets her advance commitment with a transaction in the futures markets. Because she *loses* in the cash market when interest rates fall, she *buys* futures contracts to reduce the risk. When interest rates fall, the value of her futures contracts increases. The gain in the futures market offsets the loss in the cash market. Conversely, she gains in the cash markets when interest rates rise. The value of her futures contracts decreases when interest rates rise, offsetting her gain.

We call this a *long hedge* because Ms. Boswell offsets risk in the cash markets by buying a futures contract. Though it involves an interest rate futures contract, this long hedge is analogous to long hedges in agricultural and metallurgical futures contracts. We argued at the beginning of this chapter that individuals and firms institute long hedges when their finished goods are to be sold at a fixed price. Once Ms. Boswell makes the advance commitment with No-State Insurance, she has fixed her sales price. She buys a futures contract to offset the price fluctuation of her raw materials—that is, her mortgages.

25.6   Duration Hedging

The last section concerned the risk of interest rate changes. We now want to explore this risk in a more precise manner. In particular, we want to show that the concept of duration is a prime determinant of interest rate risk. We begin by considering the effect of interest rate movements on bond prices.

Table 25.6

Value of a Pure Discount Bond as a Function of Interest Rate

Interest Rate	One-Year Pure Discount Bond	Five-Year Pure Discount Bond
8%	$101.85 = \dfrac{\$110}{1.08}$	$109.61 = \dfrac{\$161.05}{(1.08)^5}$
10%	$100.00 = \dfrac{\$110}{1.10}$	$100.00 = \dfrac{\$161.05}{(1.10)^5}$
12%	$98.21 = \dfrac{\$110}{1.12}$	$91.38 = \dfrac{\$161.05}{(1.12)^5}$

For a given interest rate change, a five-year pure discount bond fluctuates more in price than does a one-year pure discount bond.

The Case of Zero Coupon Bonds

Imagine a world where the interest rate is 10 percent across all maturities. A one-year pure discount bond pays $110 at maturity. A five-year pure discount bond pays $161.05 at maturity. Both of these bonds are worth $100, as given by the following:[12]

Value of One-Year Pure Discount Bond

$$\$100 = \frac{\$110}{1.10}$$

Value of Five-Year Pure Discount Bond

$$\$100 = \frac{\$161.05}{(1.10)^5}$$

Which bond will change more when interest rates move? To find out, we calculate the value of these bonds when interest rates are either 8 or 12 percent. The results are presented in Table 25.6. As can be seen, the five-year bond has greater price swings than does the one-year bond. That is, both bonds are worth $100 when interest rates are 10 percent. The five-year bond is worth more than the one-year bond when interest rates are 8 percent and worth less than the one-year bond when interest rates are 12 percent. We state that the five-year bond is subject to more price volatility. This point, which was mentioned in passing in an earlier section of the chapter, is not difficult to understand. The interest rate term in the denominator, $1 + R$, is taken to the fifth power for a five-year bond and only to the first power for the one-year bond. Thus, the effect of a changing interest rate is magnified for the five-year bond. The general rule is this:

The percentage price changes in long-term pure discount bonds are greater than the percentage price changes in short-term pure discount bonds.

The Case of Two Bonds with the Same Maturity but with Different Coupons

The previous example concerned pure discount bonds of different maturities. We now want to see the effect of different coupons on price volatility. To abstract from the effect of differing maturities, we consider two bonds with the same maturity but with different coupons.

Consider a five-year, 10 percent coupon bond and a five-year, 1 percent coupon bond. When interest rates are 10 percent, the bonds are priced like this:

---

[12]Alternatively, we could have chosen bonds that pay $100 at maturity. Their values would be $90.91 ($= \$100/1.10$) and $62.09 [$= \$100/(1.10)^5$]. However, our comparisons to come are made easier if both have the same initial price.

Value of Five-Year, 10 Percent Coupon Bond

$$\$100 = \frac{\$10}{1.10} + \frac{\$10}{(1.10)^2} + \frac{\$10}{(1.10)^3} + \frac{\$10}{(1.10)^4} + \frac{\$110}{(1.10)^5}$$

Value of Five-Year, 1 Percent Coupon Bond

$$\$65.88 = \frac{\$1}{1.10} + \frac{\$1}{(1.10)^2} + \frac{\$1}{(1.10)^3} + \frac{\$1}{(1.10)^4} + \frac{\$101}{(1.10)^5}$$

Which bond will change more in *percentage terms* if interest rates change?[13] To find out, we first calculate the value of these bonds when interest rates are either 8 or 12 percent. The results are presented in Table 25.7. As we would expect, the 10 percent coupon bond always sells for more than the 1 percent coupon bond. Also as we would expect, each bond is worth more when the interest rate is 8 percent than when the interest rate is 12 percent.

We calculate percentage price changes for both bonds as the interest rate changes from 10 to 8 percent and from 10 to 12 percent:

	10% Coupon Bond	1% Coupon Bond
Interest rate changes from 10% to 8%:	$7.99\% = \frac{\$107.99}{\$100} - 1$	$9.37\% = \frac{\$72.05}{\$65.88} - 1$
Interest rate changes from 10% to 12%:	$-7.21\% = \frac{\$92.79}{\$100} - 1$	$-8.39\% = \frac{\$60.35}{\$65.88} - 1$

As we can see, the 1 percent coupon bond has a greater percentage price increase than does the 10 percent coupon bond when the interest rate falls. Similarly, the 1 percent coupon bond has a greater percentage price decrease than does the 10 percent coupon bond when the interest rate rises. Thus, we say that the percentage price changes on the 1 percent coupon bond are greater than are the percentage price changes on the 10 percent coupon bond.

Table 25.7

Value of Coupon Bonds at Different Interest Rates

Interest Rate	Five-Year, 10% Coupon Bond
8%	$\$107.99 = \frac{\$10}{1.08} + \frac{\$10}{(1.08)^2} + \frac{\$10}{(1.08)^3} + \frac{\$10}{(\$1.08)^4} + \frac{\$110}{(1.08)^5}$
10%	$\$100.00 = \frac{\$10}{1.10} + \frac{\$10}{(1.10)^2} + \frac{\$10}{(1.10)^3} + \frac{\$10}{(1.10)^4} + \frac{\$110}{(1.10)^5}$
12%	$\$92.79 = \frac{\$10}{1.12} + \frac{\$10}{(1.12)^2} + \frac{\$10}{(1.12)^3} + \frac{\$10}{(1.12)^4} + \frac{\$110}{(1.12)^5}$

Interest Rate	Five-Year, 1% Coupon Bond
8%	$\$72.05 = \frac{\$1}{1.08} + \frac{\$1}{(1.08)^2} + \frac{\$1}{(1.08)^3} + \frac{\$1}{(1.08)^4} + \frac{\$101}{(1.08)^5}$
10%	$\$65.88 = \frac{\$1}{1.10} + \frac{\$1}{(1.10)^2} + \frac{\$1}{(1.10)^3} + \frac{\$1}{(1.10)^4} + \frac{\$101}{(1.10)^5}$
12%	$\$60.35 = \frac{\$1}{1.12} + \frac{\$1}{(1.12)^2} + \frac{\$1}{(1.12)^3} + \frac{\$1}{(1.12)^4} + \frac{\$101}{(1.12)^5}$

---

[13]The bonds are at different prices initially. Thus, we are concerned with percentage price changes, not absolute price changes.

Duration

The question, of course, is "Why?" We can answer this question only after we have explored a concept called **duration**. We begin by noticing that any coupon bond is actually a combination of pure discount bonds. For example, the five-year, 10 percent coupon bond is made up of five pure discount bonds:

1. A pure discount bond paying $10 at the end of year 1.
2. A pure discount bond paying $10 at the end of year 2.
3. A pure discount bond paying $10 at the end of year 3.
4. A pure discount bond paying $10 at the end of year 4.
5. A pure discount bond paying $110 at the end of year 5.

Similarly, the five-year, 1 percent coupon bond is made up of five pure discount bonds. Because the price volatility of a pure discount bond is determined by its maturity, we would like to determine the average maturity of the five pure discount bonds that make up a five-year coupon bond. This leads us to the concept of duration.

We calculate average maturity in three steps. For the 10 percent coupon bond, we have these:

1. *Calculate present value of each payment.* We do this as follows:

Year	Payment	Present Value of Payment by Discounting at 10%
1	$ 10	$ 9.091
2	10	8.264
3	10	7.513
4	10	6.830
5	110	68.302
		$100.00

2. *Express the present value of each payment in relative terms.* We calculate the relative value of a single payment as the ratio of the present value of the payment to the value of the bond. The value of the bond is $100. We obtain these values:

Year	Payment	Present Value of Payment	Relative Value = $\dfrac{\text{Present Value of Payment}}{\text{Value of Bond}}$
1	$ 10	$ 9.091	$9.091/$100 = 0.09091
2	10	8.264	0.08264
3	10	7.513	0.07513
4	10	6.830	0.06830
5	110	68.302	0.68302
		$100.00	1.0

The bulk of the relative value, 68.302 percent, occurs at year 5 because the principal is paid back at that time.

3. *Weight the maturity of each payment by its relative value*:

$$4.1699 \text{ years} = 1 \text{ year} \times 0.09091 + 2 \text{ years} \times 0.08264 + 3 \text{ years} \times 0.07513$$

$$+ 4 \text{ years} \times 0.06830 + 5 \text{ years} \times 0.68302$$

There are many ways to calculate the average maturity of a bond. We have calculated it by weighting the maturity of each payment by the payment's present value. We find that the *effective* maturity of the bond is 4.1699 years. *Duration* is a commonly used word for effective maturity. Thus, the bond's duration is 4.1699 years. Note that duration is expressed in units of time.[14]

Because the five-year, 10 percent coupon bond has a duration of 4.1699 years, its percentage price fluctuations should be the same as those of a zero coupon bond with a duration of 4.1699 years.[15] It turns out that the five-year, 1 percent coupon bond has a duration of 4.8742 years. Because the 1 percent coupon bond has a higher duration than the 10 percent bond, the 1 percent coupon bond should be subject to greater price fluctuations. This is exactly what we found earlier. In general we say the following:

The percentage price changes of a bond with high duration are greater than the percentage price changes of a bond with low duration.

A final question: Why *does* the 1 percent bond have a greater duration than the 10 percent bond, even though they both have the same five-year maturity? As mentioned earlier, duration is an average of the maturity of the bond's cash flows, weighted by the present value of each cash flow. The 1 percent coupon bond receives only $1 in each of the first four years. Thus the weights applied to years 1 through 4 in the duration formula will be low. Conversely, the 10 percent coupon bond receives $10 in each of the first four years. The weights applied to years 1 through 4 in the duration formula will be higher.

Matching Liabilities with Assets

Earlier in this chapter, we argued that firms can hedge risk by trading in futures. Because some firms are subject to interest rate risk, we showed how they can hedge with interest rate futures contracts. Firms may also hedge interest rate risk by matching liabilities with assets. This ability to hedge follows from our discussion of duration.

---

[14]The mathematical formula for duration is:

$$\text{Duration} = \frac{PV(C_1)1 + PV(C_2)2 + \cdots + PV(C_T)T}{PV}$$

and

$$PV = PV(C_1) + PV(C_2) + \cdots + PV(C_T)$$

$$PV(C_T) = \frac{C_T}{(1 + R)^T}$$

where C_T is the cash to be received in time T and R is the current discount rate.

Also note that in our numerical example, we discounted each payment by the interest rate of 10 percent. This was done because we wanted to calculate the duration of the bond before a change in the interest rate occurred. After a change in the rate to, say, 8 or 12 percent, all three of our steps would need to reflect the new interest rate. In other words, the duration of a bond is a function of the current interest rate.

[15]Actually, this relationship exactly holds only in the case of a one-time shift in a flat yield curve, where the change in the spot rate is identical for all maturities.

EXAMPLE 25.5

Using Duration The Physical Bank of New York has the following market value balance sheet:

PHYSICAL BANK OF NEW YORK
Market Value Balance Sheet

	Market Value	Duration
Assets		
Overnight money	$ 35 million	0
Accounts receivable–backed loans	500 million	3 months
Inventory loans	275 million	6 months
Industrial loans	40 million	2 years
Mortgages	150 million	14.8 years
	$1,000 million	
Liabilities and Owners' Equity		
Checking and savings accounts	$ 400 million	0
Certificates of deposit	300 million	1 year
Long-term financing	200 million	10 years
Equity	100 million	
	$1,000 million	

The bank has $1,000 million of assets and $900 million of liabilities. Its equity is the difference between the two: $100 million (= $1,000 million − $900 million). Both the market value and the duration of each individual item are provided in the balance sheet. Both overnight money and checking and savings accounts have a duration of zero. This is because the interest paid on these instruments adjusts immediately to changing interest rates in the economy.

The bank's managers think that interest rates are likely to move quickly in the coming months. Because they do not know the direction of the movement, they are worried that their bank is vulnerable to changing rates. They call in a consultant, James Charest, to determine a hedging strategy.

Mr. Charest first calculates the duration of the assets and the duration of the liabilities:[16]

Duration of Assets

$$2.56 \text{ years} = 0 \text{ years} \times \frac{\$35 \text{ million}}{\$1,000 \text{ million}} + \tfrac{1}{4} \text{ year} \times \frac{\$500 \text{ million}}{\$1,000 \text{ million}} \qquad \textbf{(25.4)}$$

$$+ \tfrac{1}{2} \text{ year} \times \frac{\$275 \text{ million}}{\$1,000 \text{ million}} + 2 \text{ years} \times \frac{\$40 \text{ million}}{\$1,000 \text{ million}}$$

$$+ 14.8 \text{ years} + \frac{\$150 \text{ million}}{\$1,000 \text{ million}}$$

Duration of Liabilities

$$2.56 = 0 \text{ years} \times \frac{\$400 \text{ million}}{\$900 \text{ million}} + 1 \text{ year} \times \frac{\$300 \text{ million}}{\$900 \text{ million}} + 10 \text{ years} \times \frac{\$200 \text{ million}}{\$900 \text{ million}} \qquad \textbf{(25.5)}$$

(*continued*)

---

[16]Note that the duration of a group of items is an average of the duration of the individual items, weighted by the market value of each item. This is a simplifying step that greatly increases duration's practicality.

The duration of the assets, 2.56 years, equals the duration of the liabilities. Because of this, Mr. Charest argues that the firm is immune to interest rate risk.

Just to be on the safe side, the bank calls in a second consultant, Gail Ellert. Ms. Ellert argues that it is incorrect to simply match durations because assets total $1,000 million and liabilities total only $900 million. If both assets and liabilities have the same duration, the price change on a *dollar* of assets should be equal to the price change on a dollar of liabilities. However, the *total* price change will be greater for assets than for liabilities because there are more assets than liabilities in this bank. The firm will be immune from interest rate risk only when the duration of the liabilities is greater than the duration of the assets. Ms. Ellert states that the following relationship must hold if the bank is to be **immunized**—that is, immune to interest rate risk:

$$\begin{matrix}\text{Duration of} \\ \text{assets}\end{matrix} \times \begin{matrix}\text{Market value of} \\ \text{assets}\end{matrix} = \begin{matrix}\text{Duration of} \\ \text{liabilities}\end{matrix} \times \begin{matrix}\text{Market value} \\ \text{of liabilities}\end{matrix} \qquad \textbf{(25.6)}$$

She says that the bank should not *equate* the duration of the liabilities with the duration of the assets. Rather, using Equation 25.6, the bank should match the duration of the liabilities to the duration of the assets. She suggests two ways to achieve this match.

1. *Increase the duration of the liabilities without changing the duration of the assets.* Ms. Ellert argues that the duration of the liabilities could be increased to:

$$\text{Duration of assets} \times \frac{\text{Market value of assets}}{\text{Market value of liabilities}} = 2.56 \text{ years} \times \frac{\$1,000 \text{ million}}{\$900 \text{ million}}$$

$$= 2.84 \text{ years}$$

    Equation 25.5 then becomes:

$$2.56 \times \$1 \text{ billion} = 2.84 \times \$900 \text{ million}$$

2. *Decrease the duration of the assets without changing the duration of the liabilities.* Alternatively, Ms. Ellert points out that the duration of the assets could be decreased to:

$$\text{Duration of liabilities} \times \frac{\text{Market value of liabilities}}{\text{Market value of assets}} = 2.56 \text{ years} \times \frac{\$900 \text{ million}}{\$1,000 \text{ million}}$$

$$= 2.30 \text{ years}$$

    Equation 25.6 then becomes:

$$2.30 \times \$1 \text{ billion} = 2.56 \times \$900 \text{ million}$$

Though we agree with Ms. Ellert's analysis, the bank's current mismatch was small anyway. Huge mismatches have occurred for real-world financial institutions, particularly savings and loans. S&Ls have frequently invested large portions of their assets in mortgages. The durations of these mortgages would clearly be above 10 years. Much of the funds available for mortgage lending were financed by short-term credit, especially savings accounts. As we mentioned, the duration of such instruments is quite small. A thrift institution in this situation faces a large amount of interest rate risk because any increase in interest rates would greatly reduce the value of the mortgages. Because an interest rate rise would reduce the value of the liabilities only slightly, the equity of the firm would fall. As interest rates rose over much of the 1960s and the 1970s, many S&Ls found that the market value of their equity approached zero.[17]

---

[17]Actually, the market value of the equity could easily be negative in this example. However, S&Ls in the real world have an asset not shown on our market value balance sheet: the ability to generate new, profitable loans. This should increase the market value of a thrift above the market value of its outstanding loans less its existing debt.

Duration and the accompanying immunization strategies are useful in other areas of finance. For example, many firms establish pension funds to meet obligations to retirees. If the assets of a pension fund are invested in bonds and other fixed-income securities, the duration of the assets can be computed. Similarly, the firm views the obligations to retirees as analogous to interest payments on debt. The duration of these liabilities can be calculated as well. The manager of a pension fund would commonly choose pension assets so that the duration of the assets is matched with the duration of the liabilities. In this way, changing interest rates would not affect the net worth of the pension fund.

Life insurance companies receiving premiums today are legally obligated to provide death benefits in the future. Actuaries view these future benefits as analogous to interest and principal payments of fixed-income securities. The duration of these expected benefits can be calculated. Insurance firms frequently invest in bonds where the duration of the bonds is matched to the duration of the future death benefits.

The business of a leasing company is quite simple. The firm issues debt to purchase assets, which are then leased. The lease payments have a duration, as does the debt. Leasing companies frequently structure debt financing so that the duration of the debt matches the duration of the lease. If a firm did not do this, the market value of its equity could be eliminated by a quick change in interest rates.

25.7 Swaps Contracts

Swaps are close cousins to forwards and futures contracts. Swaps are arrangements between two counterparts to exchange cash flows over time. There is enormous flexibility in the forms that swaps can take, but the two basic types are **interest rate swaps** and **currency swaps**. Often these are combined when interest received in one currency is swapped for interest in another currency.

Interest Rate Swaps

Like other derivatives, swaps are tools that firms can use to easily change their risk exposures and their balance sheets.[18] Consider a firm that has borrowed and carried on its books an obligation to repay a 10-year loan for $100 million of principal with a 9 percent coupon rate paid annually. Ignoring the possibility of calling the loan, the firm expects to have to pay coupons of $9 million every year for 10 years and a balloon payment of $100 million at the end of the 10 years. Suppose, though, that the firm is uncomfortable with having this large fixed obligation on its books. Perhaps the firm is in a cyclical business where its revenues vary and could conceivably fall to a point where it would be difficult to make the debt payment.

Suppose, too, that the firm earns a lot of its revenue from financing the purchase of its products. Typically, for example, a manufacturer might help its customers finance their purchase of its products through a leasing or credit subsidiary. Usually these loans are for relatively short periods and are financed at some premium over the prevailing short-term rate of interest. This puts the firm in the position of having revenues that move up and down with interest rates while its costs are relatively fixed.

What the firm would really prefer is to have a floating-rate loan rather than a fixed-rate loan. That way, when interest rates rise, the firm would have to pay more on the loan, but it would be making more on its product financing. An interest rate swap is ideal in this situation.

---

[18]Under current accounting rules, most derivatives do not usually show up on firms' balance sheets because they do not have a historical cost (i.e., the amount a dealer would pay on the initial transaction day).

Figure 25.2

**Fixed for Floating
Swap: Cash Flows
($ million)**

	Coupons									
Year	**1**	**2**	**3**	**4**	**5**	**6**	**7**	**8**	**9**	**10**
A. Swap										
Fixed obligation	9	9	9	9	9	9	9	9	9	9
LIBOR floating	−8.5	−9.5	−10.5	−11.5	−7.5	−7.5	−7.5	−7.5	−7.5	−7.5
B. Original loan										
Fixed obligation	−9	−9	−9	−9	−9	−9	−9	−9	−9	109
Net effect	−8.5	−9.5	10.5	11.5	7.5	7.5	7.5	7.5	7.5	−107.5

Of course, the firm could also just go into the capital markets and borrow $100 million at a variable interest rate and then use the proceeds to retire its outstanding fixed-rate loan. Although this is possible, it is generally quite expensive, requiring underwriting a new loan and the repurchase of the existing loan. The ease of entering a swap is its inherent advantage.

The particular swap would be one that exchanged its fixed obligation for an agreement to pay a floating rate. Every year it would agree to pay a coupon based on whatever the prevailing interest rate was at the time in exchange for an agreement from a counterparty to pay the firm's fixed coupon.

A common reference point for floating-rate commitments is called LIBOR. LIBOR stands for the London Interbank Offered Rate, and it is the rate that most international banks charge one another for dollar-denominated loans in the London market. LIBOR is commonly used as the reference rate for a floating-rate commitment, and, depending on the creditworthiness of the borrower, the rate can vary from LIBOR to LIBOR plus one point or more over LIBOR.

If we assume that our firm has a credit rating that requires it to pay LIBOR plus 50 basis points, then in a swap it would be exchanging its fixed 9 percent obligation for the obligation to pay whatever the prevailing LIBOR rate is plus 50 basis points. Figure 25.2 displays how the cash flows on this swap would work. In the figure, we have assumed that LIBOR starts at 8 percent and rises for three years to 11 percent and then drops to 7 percent. As the figure illustrates, the firm would owe a coupon of 8.5% × $100 million = $8.5 million in year 1, $9.5 million in year 2, $10.5 million in year 3, and $11.5 million in year 4. The precipitous drop to 7 percent lowers the annual payments to $7.5 million thereafter. In return, the firm receives the fixed payment of $9 million each year. Actually, rather than swapping the full payments, the cash flows would be netted. Because the firm is paying variable and receiving fixed—which it uses to pay its lender—in the first year, for example, the firm owes $8.5 million and is owed by its counterparty, who is paying fixed, $9 million. Hence, net, the firm would receive a payment of $.5 million. Because the firm has to pay its lender $9 million but gets a net payment from the swap of $.5 million, it really pays out only the difference, or $8.5 million. In each year, then, the firm would effectively pay only LIBOR plus 50 basis points.

Notice, too, that the entire transaction can be carried out without any need to change the terms of the original loan. In effect, by swapping, the firm has found a counterparty that is willing to pay its fixed obligation in return for the firm paying a floating obligation.

Currency Swaps

FX stands for foreign exchange, and currency swaps are sometimes called FX swaps. Currency swaps are swaps of obligations to pay cash flows in one currency for obligations to pay in another currency.

Currency swaps arise as a natural vehicle for hedging the risk in international trade. For example, suppose a U.S. firm sells a broad range of its product line in the German market. Every year the firm can count on receiving revenue from Germany in euros. We will study international finance later in this book, but for now we can just observe that because exchange rates fluctuate, this subjects the firm to considerable risk.

If the firm produces its products in the United States and exports them to Germany, then the firm has to pay its workers and its suppliers in dollars. But it is receiving some of its revenues in euros. The exchange rate between $ and euros changes over time. As the euro rises in value, the German revenues are worth more $, but as it falls they decline. Suppose the firm can count on selling 100 million euros of goods each year in Germany. If the exchange rate is 2 euros for each $, then the firm will receive $50 million. But if the exchange rate were to rise to 3 euros for each $, the firm would receive only $33.333 million for its 100 million euros. Naturally the firm would like to protect itself against these currency swings.

To do so the firm can enter a currency swap. We will learn more about exactly what the terms of such a swap might be, but for now we can assume that the swap is for five years at a fixed term of 100 million euros for $50 million each year. Now, no matter what happens to the exchange rate between euros and $ over the next five years, as long as the firm makes 100 million euros each year from the sale of its products, it will swap this for $50 million each year.

We have not addressed the question of how the market sets prices for swaps—either interest rate swaps or currency swaps. In the fixed for floating example and in the currency swap, we just quoted some terms. We won't go into great detail on exactly how it is done, but we can stress the most important points.

Swaps, like forwards and futures, are essentially zero-sum transactions, which is to say that in both cases the market sets prices at a fair level, and neither party has any substantial bargain or loss at the moment the deal is struck. For example, in the currency swap, the swap rate is some average of the market expectation of what the exchange rate will be over the life of the swap. In the interest rate swap, the rates are set as the fair floating and fixed rates for the creditor, taking into account the creditworthiness of the counterparties. We can actually price swaps fairly once we know how to price forward contracts. In our interest rate swap example, the firm swapped LIBOR plus 50 basis points for a 9 percent fixed rate, all on a principal amount of $100 million. This is equivalent to a series of forward contracts extending over the life of the swap. In year 1, for example, having made the swap, the firm is in the same position that it would be if it had sold a forward contract entitling the buyer to receive LIBOR plus 50 basis points on $100 million in return for a fixed payment of $9 million (9 percent of $100 million). Similarly, the currency swap can also be viewed as a series of forward contracts.

Exotics

Up to now we have dealt with the meat and potatoes of the derivatives markets, swaps, options, forwards, and futures. **Exotics** are the complicated blends of these that often produce surprising results for buyers.

One of the more interesting types of exotics is called an *inverse floater*. In our fixed for floating swap, the floating payments fluctuated with LIBOR. An inverse floater is one that fluctuates inversely with some rate such as LIBOR. For example, the floater might pay an interest rate of 20 percent minus LIBOR. If LIBOR is 9 percent, then the inverse pays 11 percent, and if LIBOR rises to 12 percent, the payments on the inverse would fall to 8 percent. Clearly the purchaser of an inverse profits from the inverse if interest rates fall.

Both floaters and inverse floaters have a supercharged version called *superfloaters* and *superinverses* that fluctuate more than one for one with movements in interest rates. As an example of a superinverse floater, consider a floater that pays an interest rate of 30 percent minus *twice* LIBOR. When LIBOR is 10 percent, the inverse pays

$$30\% - 2 \times 10\% = 30\% - 20\% = 10\%$$

And if LIBOR falls by 3 percent to 7 percent, then the return on the inverse rises by 6 percent from 10 percent to 16 percent:

$$30\% - 2 \times 7\% = 30\% - 14\% = 16\%$$

Sometimes derivatives are combined with options to bound the impact of interest rates. The most important of these instruments are called *caps* and *floors*. A cap is so named because it puts an upper limit or a cap on the impact of a rise in interest rates. A floor, conversely, provides a floor below which the interest rate impact is insulated.

To illustrate the impact of these, consider a firm that is borrowing short-term and is concerned that interest rates might rise. For example, using LIBOR as the reference interest rate, the firm might purchase a 7 percent cap. The cap pays the firm the difference between LIBOR and 7 percent on some principal amount, provided that LIBOR is greater than 7 percent. As long as LIBOR is below 7 percent, the holder of the cap receives no payments.

By purchasing the cap the firm has assured itself that even if interest rates rise above 7 percent, it will not have to pay more than a 7 percent rate. Suppose that interest rates rise to 9 percent. While the firm is borrowing short-term and paying 9 percent rates, this is offset by the cap, which is paying the firm the difference between 9 percent and the 7 percent limit. For any LIBOR rate above 7 percent, the firm receives the difference between LIBOR and 7 percent, and, as a consequence, it has capped its cost of borrowing at 7 percent.

On the other side, consider a financial firm that is in the business of lending short-term and is concerned that interest rates—and consequently its revenues—might fall. The firm could purchase a floor to protect itself from such declines. If the limit on the floor is 7 percent, then the floor pays the difference between 7 percent and LIBOR whenever LIBOR is below 7 percent, and nothing if LIBOR is above 7 percent. Thus, if interest rates were to fall to, say, 5 percent while the firm is receiving only 5 percent from its lending activities, the floor is paying it the difference between 7 percent and 5 percent, or an additional 2 percent. By purchasing the floor, the firm has assured itself of receiving no less than 7 percent from the combination of the floor and its lending activities.

We have only scratched the surface of what is available in the world of derivatives. Derivatives are designed to meet marketplace needs, and the only binding limitation is the human imagination. Nowhere should the buyer's warning *caveat emptor* be taken more seriously than in the derivatives markets, and this is especially true for the exotics. If swaps are the meat and potatoes of the derivatives markets, then caps and floors are the meat and potatoes of the exotics. As we have seen, they have obvious value as hedging instruments. But much attention has been focused on truly exotic derivatives, some of which appear to have arisen more as the residuals that were left over from more straightforward deals. We won't examine these in any detail, but suffice it to say that some of these are so volatile and unpredictable that market participants have dubbed them "toxic waste."

Table 25.8

Derivative Usage:
Survey Results

Companies That Use Derivatives			
	Overall	**Under $1 billion**	**Over $1 billion**
12/05	68%	53%	83%
12/04	74	67	83

Do You Use Derivatives to Manage . . .?			
	Overall	**Under $1 billion**	**Over $1 billion**
Short-Term Assets	55%	35%	68%
Long-Term Assets	29	17	37
Short-Term Liabilities	59	54	63
Long-Term Liabilities	61	67	57

In Which Asset Classes Do You Use Derivatives?				
	Overall		**Over $1 billion**	
	2005	**2004**	**2005**	**2004**
Interest-rates	70%	73%	77%	76%
Currencies	67	54	80	68
Credit	9	7	12	13
Energy	17	10	21	11
Commodities	20	11	30	13
Equities	7	12	10	16

SOURCE: Adapted from *Treasury & Risk Management* (December/January 2006). Results are based on a survey of 190 financial executives. In the sample, 30 percent of the companies had revenues under $500 million, 18 percent were between $500 million and $1 billion, 33 percent were between $1 billion and $5 billion, and 19 percent had revenues over $5 billion.

25.8   Actual Use of Derivatives

Because derivatives do not usually appear in financial statements, it is much more difficult to observe the use of derivatives by firms compared to, say, bank debt. Much of our knowledge of corporate derivative use comes from academic surveys. Most surveys report that the use of derivatives appears to vary widely among large publicly traded firms. Large firms are far more likely to use derivatives than are small firms. Table 25.8 shows that for firms that use derivatives, foreign currency and interest rate derivatives are the most frequently used.

The prevailing view is that derivatives can be very helpful in reducing the variability of firm cash flows, which, in turn, reduces the various costs associated with financial distress. Therefore, it is somewhat puzzling that large firms use derivatives more often than small firms—because large firms tend to have less cash flow variability than small firms. Also some surveys report that firms occasionally use derivatives when they want to speculate about future prices and not just to hedge risks.

However, most of the evidence is consistent with the theory that derivatives are most frequently used by firms where financial distress costs are high and access to the capital markets is constrained.

Summary and Conclusions

1. Firms hedge to reduce risk. This chapter showed a number of hedging strategies.

2. A forward contract is an agreement by two parties to sell an item for cash at a later date. The price is set at the time the agreement is signed. However, cash changes hands on the date of delivery. Forward contracts are generally not traded on organized exchanges.

3. Futures contracts are also agreements for future delivery. They have certain advantages, such as liquidity, that forward contracts do not. An unusual feature of futures contracts is the mark-to-the-market convention. If the price of a futures contract falls on a particular day, every buyer of the contract must pay money to the clearinghouse. Every seller of the contract receives money from the clearinghouse. Everything is reversed if the price rises. The mark-to-the-market convention prevents defaults on futures contracts.

4. We divided hedges into two types: short hedges and long hedges. An individual or firm that sells a futures contract to reduce risk is instituting a short hedge. Short hedges are generally appropriate for holders of inventory. An individual or firm that buys a futures contract to reduce risk is instituting a long hedge. Long hedges are typically used by firms with contracts to sell finished goods at a fixed price.

5. An interest rate futures contract employs a bond as the deliverable instrument. Because of their popularity, we worked with Treasury bond futures contracts. We showed that Treasury bond futures contracts can be priced using the same type of net present value analysis that is used to price Treasury bonds themselves.

6. Many firms face interest rate risk. They can reduce this risk by hedging with interest rate futures contracts. As with other commodities, a short hedge involves the sale of a futures contract. Firms that are committed to buying mortgages or other bonds are likely to institute short hedges. A long hedge involves the purchase of a futures contract. Firms that have agreed to sell mortgages or other bonds at a fixed price are likely to institute long hedges.

7. Duration measures the average maturity of all the cash flows in a bond. Bonds with high duration have high price variability. Firms frequently try to match the duration of their assets with the duration of their liabilities.

8. Swaps are agreements to exchange cash flows over time. The first major type is an interest rate swap in which one pattern of coupon payments, say, fixed payments, is exchanged for another, say, coupons that float with LIBOR. The second major type is a currency swap, in which an agreement is struck to swap payments denominated in one currency for payments in another currency over time.

Concept Questions

1. **Hedging Strategies**   If a firm is selling futures contracts on lumber as a hedging strategy, what must be true about the firm's exposure to lumber prices?

2. **Hedging Strategies**   If a firm is buying call options on pork belly futures as a hedging strategy, what must be true about the firm's exposure to pork belly prices?

3. **Forwards and Futures**   What is the difference between a forward contract and a futures contract? Why do you think that futures contracts are much more common? Are there any circumstances under which you might prefer to use forwards instead of futures? Explain.

4. **Hedging Commodities**   Bubbling Crude Corporation, a large Texas oil producer, would like to hedge against adverse movements in the price of oil because this is the firm's primary source of revenue. What should the firm do? Provide at least two reasons why it probably will not be possible to achieve a completely flat risk profile with respect to oil prices.

5. **Sources of Risk**   A company produces an energy-intensive product and uses natural gas as the energy source. The competition primarily uses oil. Explain why this company is exposed to fluctuations in both oil and natural gas prices.

6. **Hedging Commodities** If a textile manufacturer wanted to hedge against adverse movements in cotton prices, it could buy cotton futures contracts or buy call options on cotton futures contracts. What would be the pros and cons of the two approaches?

7. **Option** Explain why a put option on a bond is conceptually the same as a call option on interest rates.

8. **Hedging Interest Rates** A company has a large bond issue maturing in one year. When it matures, the company will float a new issue. Current interest rates are attractive, and the company is concerned that rates next year will be higher. What are some hedging strategies that the company might use in this case?

9. **Swaps** Explain why a swap is effectively a series of forward contracts. Suppose a firm enters a swap agreement with a swap dealer. Describe the nature of the default risk faced by both parties.

10. **Swaps** Suppose a firm enters a fixed for floating interest rate swap with a swap dealer. Describe the cash flows that will occur as a result of the swap.

11. **Transaction versus Economic Exposure** What is the difference between transactions and economic exposure? Which can be hedged more easily? Why?

12. **Hedging Exchange Rate Risk** If a U.S. company exports its goods to Japan, how would it use a futures contract on Japanese yen to hedge its exchange rate risk? Would it buy or sell yen futures? Does the way the exchange rate is quoted in the futures contract matter?

13. **Hedging Strategies** For the following scenarios, describe a hedging strategy using futures contracts that might be considered. If you think that a cross-hedge would be appropriate, discuss the reasons for your choice of contract.
    a. A public utility is concerned about rising costs.
    b. A candy manufacturer is concerned about rising costs.
    c. A corn farmer fears that this year's harvest will be at record high levels across the country.
    d. A manufacturer of photographic film is concerned about rising costs.
    e. A natural gas producer believes there will be excess supply in the market this year.
    f. A bank derives all its income from long-term, fixed-rate residential mortgages.
    g. A stock mutual fund invests in large, blue-chip stocks and is concerned about a decline in the stock market.
    h. A U.S. importer of Swiss army knives will pay for its order in six months in Swiss francs.
    i. A U.S. exporter of construction equipment has agreed to sell some cranes to a German construction firm. The U.S. firm will be paid in euros in three months.

14. **Swaps** In May 2004, Sysco Corporation, the distributor of food and food-related products (not to be confused with Cisco Systems), announced it had signed an interest rate swap. The interest rate swap effectively converted the company's £100 million, 4.6 percent interest rate bonds for a variable rate payment, which would be the six-month LIBOR minus 0.52 percent. Why would Sysco use a swap agreement? In other words, why didn't Sysco just go ahead and issue floating-rate bonds because the net effect of issuing fixed-rate bonds and then doing a swap is to create a variable rate bond?

15. **Hedging Strategies** William Santiago is interested in entering the import/export business. During a recent visit with his financial advisers, he said, "If we play the game right, this is the safest business in the world. By hedging all of our transactions in the foreign exchange futures market, we can eliminate all of our risk." Do you agree with Mr. Santiago's assessment of hedging? Why or why not?

16. **Hedging Strategies** Kevin Nomura is a Japanese student who is planning a one-year stay in the United States. He expects to arrive in the United States in eight months. He is worried about depreciation in the yen relative to the dollar over the next eight months and wishes to take a position in foreign exchange futures to hedge this risk. What should Mr. Nomura's hedging position be? Assume the exchange rate between Japanese and U.S. currencies is quoted as yen/dollar.

Questions and Problems

BASIC
(Questions 1–8)

1. **Futures Quotes** Refer to Table 25.2 in the text to answer this question. Suppose you purchase a May 2006 cocoa futures contract on March 7, 2006, at the last price of the day. What will your profit or loss be if cocoa prices turn out to be $1,402 per metric ton at expiration?

2. **Futures Quotes** Refer to Table 25.2 in the text to answer this question. Suppose you sell five May 2006 silver futures contracts on March 7, 2006, at the last price of the day. What will your profit or loss be if silver prices turn out to be $11.15 per ounce at expiration? What if silver prices are $9.05 per ounce at expiration?

3. **Put and Call Payoffs** Suppose a financial manager buys call options on 50,000 barrels of oil with an exercise price of €35 per barrel. She simultaneously sells a put option on 50,000 barrels of oil with the same exercise price of €35 per barrel. Consider her gains and losses if oil prices are €30, €32, €35, €38, and €40. What do you notice about the payoff profile?

4. **Marking to Market** You are long 10 gold futures contracts, established at an initial settle price of £480 per ounce, where each contract represents 100 ounces. Over the subsequent four trading days, gold settles at £473, £479, £482, and £486, respectively. Compute the cash flows at the end of each trading day, and compute your total profit or loss at the end of the trading period.

5. **Marking to Market** You are short 25 kerosene futures contracts, established at an initial settle price of ZAR 1.52 per gallon, where each contract represents 40,000 gallons. Over the subsequent four trading days, kerosene settles at ZAR 1.46, ZAR 1.55, ZAR 1.59, and ZAR 1.62, respectively. Compute the cash flows at the end of each trading day, and compute your total profit or loss at the end of the trading period.

6. **Duration** What is the duration of a bond with three years to maturity and a coupon of 8 percent paid annually if the bond sells at par?

7. **Duration** What is the duration of a bond with four years to maturity and a coupon of 8 percent paid annually if the bond sells at par?

8. **Duration** Blue Steel Community Bank has the following market value balance sheet:

Asset or Liability	Market Value (in millions)	Duration (in years)
Federal funds deposits	£ 28	0
Accounts receivable	580	0.20
Short-term loans	390	0.65
Long-term loans	84	5.25
Mortgages	315	14.25
Checking and savings deposits	520	0
Certificates of deposit	340	1.60
Long-term financing	260	11.2
Equity	277	N/A

    a. What is the duration of the assets?
    b. What is the duration of the liabilities?
    c. Is the bank immune from interest rate risk?

INTERMEDIATE
(Questions 9–15)

9. **Hedging with Futures** Refer to Table 25.2 in the text to answer this question. Suppose today is March 7, 2006, and your firm produces breakfast cereal and needs 75,000 bushels of corn in May 2006 for an upcoming promotion. You would like to lock in your costs today because you are concerned that corn prices might go up between now and May.
    a. How could you use corn futures contracts to hedge your risk exposure? What price would you effectively be locking in based on the closing price of the day?
    b. Suppose corn prices are $2.46 per bushel in May. What is the profit or loss on your futures position? Explain how your futures position has eliminated your exposure to price risk in the corn market.

10. **Interest Rate Swaps** Anil Traders and Sunil Traders need to raise funds to pay for capital improvements at their manufacturing plants. Anil Traders is a well-established firm with an excellent credit rating in the debt market; it can borrow funds either at 11 percent fixed rate or at LIBOR + 1 percent floating rate. Sunil Traders is a fledgling start-up firm without a strong credit history. It can borrow funds either at 10 percent fixed rate or at LIBOR + 3 percent floating rate.

   a. Is there an opportunity here for Anil and Sunil to benefit by means of an interest rate swap?

   b. Suppose you've just been hired at a bank that acts as a dealer in the swaps market, and your boss has shown you the borrowing rate information for your clients Anil and Sunil. Describe how you could bring these two companies together in an interest rate swap that would make both firms better off while netting your bank a 2.0 percent profit.

11. **Duration** Ted and Alice Hansel have a son who will begin college three years from today. School expenses of $30,000 will need to be paid at the beginning of each of the four years that their son plans to attend college. What is the duration of this liability to the couple if they can borrow and lend at the market interest rate of 8 percent?

12. **Duration** What is the duration of a bond with two years to maturity if the bond has a coupon rate of 9 percent paid semiannually, and the market interest rate is 7 percent?

13. **Forward Pricing** The forward price (F) of a contract on an asset with neither carrying costs nor convenience yield is the current spot price of the asset (S_0) multiplied by 1 plus the appropriate interest rate between the initiation of the contract and the delivery date of the asset. Derive this relationship by comparing the cash flows that result from the following two strategies:

   Strategy 1: Buy silver on the spot market today and hold it for one year. (*Hint*: Do not use any of your own money to purchase the silver.)

   Strategy 2: Take on a long position in a silver forward contract for delivery in one year. Assume that silver is an asset with neither carrying costs nor convenience yield.

14. **Forward Pricing** You enter into a forward contract to buy a 10-year, zero coupon bond that will be issued in one year. The face value of the bond is £1,000, and the 1-year and 11-year spot interest rates are 5 percent and 9 percent, respectively.

   a. What is the forward price of your contract?

   b. Suppose both the 1-year and 11-year spot rates unexpectedly shift downward by 2 percent. What is the new price of the forward contract?

15. **Forward Pricing** This morning you agreed to buy a one-year Treasury bond in six months. The bond has a face value of ¥1,000. Use the spot interest rates listed here to answer the following questions:

Time	EAR
6 months	7.42%
12 months	8.02%
18 months	8.79%
24 months	9.43%

   a. What is the forward price of this contract?

   b. Suppose shortly after you purchased the forward contract, all rates increased by 30 basis points. For example, the six-month rate increased from 7.42 percent to 7.72 percent. What is the price of a forward contract otherwise identical to yours given these changes?

CHALLENGE
(Question 16)

16. **Financial Engineering** Suppose there were call options and forward contracts available on coal, but no put options. Show how a financial engineer could synthesize a put option using the available contracts. What does your answer tell you about the general relationship between puts, calls, and forwards?

Williamson Mortgage, Inc.

Jennifer Williamson recently received her MBA and has decided to enter the mortgage broker-age business. Rather than work for someone else, she has decided to open her own shop. Her cousin Jerry has approached her about a mortgage for a house he is building. The house will be completed in three months, and he will need the mortgage at that time. Jerry wants a 25-year, fixed-rate mortgage in the amount of $500,000 with monthly payments.

Jennifer has agreed to lend Jerry the money in three months at the current market rate of 8 percent. Because Jennifer is just starting out, she does not have $500,000 available for the loan, so she approaches Max Cabell, the president of MC Insurance Corporation, about purchasing the mortgage from her in three months. Max has agreed to purchase the mortgage in three months, but he is unwilling to set a price on the mortgage. Instead, he has agreed in writing to purchase the mortgage at the market rate in three months. There are Treasury bond futures con-tracts available for delivery in three months. A Treasury bond contract is for $100,000 in face value of Treasury bonds.

1. What is the monthly mortgage payment on Jerry's mortgage?

2. What is the most significant risk Jennifer faces in this deal?

3. How can Jennifer hedge this risk?

4. Suppose that in the next three months the market rate of interest rises to 9 percent.
   a. How much will Max be willing to pay for the mortgage?
   b. What will happen to the value of Treasury bond futures contracts? Will the long or short position increase in value?

5. Suppose that in the next three months the market rate of interest falls to 7 percent.
   a. How much will Max be willing to pay for the mortgage?
   b. What will happen to the value of T-bond futures contracts? Will the long or short posi-tion increase in value?

6. Are there any possible risks Jennifer faces in using Treasury bond futures contracts to hedge her interest rate risk?

Short-Term Finance and Planning

On January 1, 2005, retailing giant Wal-Mart began requiring its largest 100 suppliers to put radio frequency identification (RFID) tags on cases and pallets shipped to three of its distribution centers and 100 of its stores. By October 2005, the company expanded the requirement to three additional distribution centers and 900 more stores. The next 200 largest suppliers also had to begin adding the RFID tags.

RFID tags are essentially high-tech replacements for bar codes. The advantage is that they can be read from a distance, so an entire warehouse can be scanned in seconds. RFID tag sales are expected to grow from about $1 billion in 2003 to about $4.6 billion in 2007.

So why the rapid growth in high-tech bar codes? Look no further than Wal-Mart for the answer. Specifically, the

company thought it would save $6.7 billion in labor costs by eliminating individual scans, $600 million by reducing out-of-stock items, $575 million by reducing theft, $300 million with better tracking, and $180 million by reducing inventory. The total cost savings for Wal-Mart is estimated at $8.35 billion per year! As this example suggests, proper management of short-term assets such as inventory can have a significant impact on the profitability of a company and the value investors place on it.

Short-term financial planning is one activity that concerns everyone in business. As this chapter illustrates, such planning demands, among other things, sales projections from marketing, cost numbers from accounting, and inventory requirements from operations.

26.1 Tracing Cash and Net Working Capital

In this section we trace the components of cash and net working capital as they change from one year to the next. Our goal is to describe the short-term operating activities of the firm and their impact on cash and working capital.

Current assets are cash and other assets that are expected to be converted to cash within the year. Current assets are presented in the balance sheet in order of their accounting **liquidity**—the ease with which they can be converted to cash at a fair price and the time it takes to do so. Table 26.1 gives the balance sheet and income statement of the Tradewinds Manufacturing Corporation for 2006 and 2007. The four major items found in the current asset section of the Tradewinds balance sheet are cash, marketable securities, accounts receivable, and inventories.

Analogous to their investment in current assets, firms use several kinds of short-term debt, called current liabilities. Current liabilities are obligations that are expected to require

745

Table 26.1

Financial Statements

TRADEWINDS MANUFACTURING CORPORATION
December 31, 2007, and December 31, 2006
Balance Sheet and Income Statement

	2007	2006
Assets		
Current assets:		
Cash	$ 500,000	$ 500,000
Marketable securities (at cost)	500,000	450,000
Accounts receivable less allowance for bad debts....	2,000,000	1,600,000
Inventories	3,000,000	2,000,000
Total current assets	$ 6,000,000	$ 4,550,000
Fixed assets (property, plant, and equipment):		
Land	450,000	450,000
Building	4,000,000	4,000,000
Machinery	1,500,000	800,000
Office equipment	50,000	50,000
Less: Accumulated depreciation	2,000,000	1,700,000
Net fixed assets	4,000,000	3,600,000
Prepayments and deferred charges	400,000	300,000
Intangibles	100,000	100,000
Total assets	$10,500,000	$ 8,550,000
Liabilities		
Current liabilities:		
Accounts payable	$ 1,000,000	$ 750,000
Notes payable	1,500,000	500,000
Accrued expenses payable	250,000	225,000
Taxes payable	250,000	225,000
Total current liabilities	$ 3,000,000	$ 1,700,000
Long-term liabilities:		
First mortgage bonds, 5% interest, due 2025	3,000,000	3,000,000
Deferred taxes	600,000	600,000
Total liabilities	$ 6,600,000	$ 5,300,000
Stockholders' Equity		
Common stock, $5 par value each; authorized,		
issued, and outstanding 300,000 shares	$ 1,500,000	$ 1,500,000
Capital surplus	500,000	500,000
Accumulated retained earnings	1,900,000	1,250,000
Total stockholders' equity	3,900,000	3,250,000
Total liabilities and stockholders' equity	$10,500,000	$ 8,550,000
Consolidated Income Statement		
Net sales	$11,500,000	$10,700,000
Cost of sales and operating expenses:		
Cost of goods sold	8,200,000	7,684,000
Depreciation	300,000	275,000
Selling and administration expenses	1,400,000	1,325,000
Operating profit	1,600,000	1,416,000

(continued)

Table 26.1
(Continued)

TRADEWINDS MANUFACTURING CORPORATION December 31, 2007, and December 31, 2006 Balance Sheet and Income Statement *(continued)*		
	2007	**2006**
Other income:		
Dividends and interest	50,000	50,000
Total income from operations.	1,650,000	1,466,000
Less: Interest on bonds and other liabilities	300,000	150,000
Income before provision for income tax	1,350,000	1,316,000
Provision for income tax	610,000	600,000
Net profit.	$ 740,000	$ 716,000
Dividends paid out.	$ 90,000	$ 132,000
Retained earnings.	$ 650,000	$ 584,000

cash payment within one year or within the operating cycle, whichever is shorter.[1] The three major items found as *current liabilities* are accounts payable; accrued wages, taxes, and other expenses payable; and notes payable.

26.2   Defining Cash in Terms of Other Elements

Now we will define cash in terms of the other elements of the balance sheet. The balance sheet equation is:

$$\text{Net working capital} + \text{Fixed assets} = \text{Long-term debt} + \text{Equity} \qquad (26.1)$$

Net working capital is cash plus the other elements of net working capital:

$$\text{Net working capital} = \text{Cash} + \text{Other current assets} - \text{Current liabilities} \qquad (26.2)$$

Substituting Equation 26.2 into 26.1 yields:

$$\text{Cash} + \frac{\text{Other current}}{\text{assets}} - \text{Current liabilities} = \frac{\text{Long-term}}{\text{debt}} + \text{Equity} - \frac{\text{Fixed}}{\text{assets}} \qquad (26.3)$$

and rearranging, we find that:

$$\text{Cash} = \frac{\text{Long-term}}{\text{debt}} + \text{Equity} - \frac{\text{Net working capital}}{\text{(excluding cash)}} - \frac{\text{Fixed}}{\text{assets}} \qquad (26.4)$$

The natural interpretation of Equation 26.4 is that increasing long-term debt and equity and decreasing fixed assets and net working capital (excluding cash) will increase cash to the firm.

The Sources and Uses of Cash

We first introduced the statement of cash flows in Chapter 2. This is the accounting statement that describes the sources and uses of cash. In this section we look at where cash comes from and how it is used. From the right side of Equation 26.4 we can see that an increase in long-term debt or equity leads to an increase in cash. Moreover, a decrease in net working capital or fixed assets leads to an increase in cash. In addition, the sum of net

---

[1]As we will learn in this chapter, the operating cycle begins when inventory is received and ends when cash is collected from the sale of inventory.

Table 26.2

Sources and Uses of Cash

TRADEWINDS MANUFACTURING CORPORATION Sources and Uses of Cash (in thousands)	
Sources of Cash	
Cash flow from operations:	
Net income	$ 740
Depreciation	300
Total cash flow from operations	$1,040
Decrease in net working capital:	
Increase in accounts payable	250
Increase in notes payable	1,000
Increase in accrued expenses	25
Increase in taxes payable	25
Total sources of cash	$2,340
Uses of Cash	
Increase in fixed assets	$ 700
Increase in prepayments	100
Dividends	90
Increase in net working capital:	
Investment in inventory	1,000
Increase in accounts receivable	400
Increase in marketable securities	50
Total uses of cash	$2,340
Change in cash balance	0

income and depreciation increases cash, whereas dividend payments decrease cash. This reasoning allows an accountant to create a statement of cash flows, which shows all the transactions that affect a firm's cash position.

Let us trace the changes in cash for Tradewinds during the year. Notice that Tradewinds' cash balance remained constant during 2007, even though cash flow from operations was $1.04 million (net income plus depreciation). Why did cash remain the same? The answer is simply that the sources of cash were equal to the uses of cash. From the firm's statement of cash flows (Table 26.2), we find that Tradewinds generated cash as follows:

1. It generated cash flow from operations of $1.04 million.
2. It increased its accounts payable by $250,000. This is the same as increasing borrowing from suppliers.
3. It increased its borrowing from banks by $1 million. This shows up as an increase in notes payable.
4. It increased accrued expenses by $25,000.
5. It increased taxes payable by $25,000, in effect borrowing from the IRS.

Tradewinds used cash for the following reasons:

1. It invested $700,000 in fixed assets.
2. It increased prepayments by $100,000.
3. It paid a $90,000 dividend.
4. It invested in inventory worth $1 million.

5. It lent its customers additional money. Hence, accounts receivable increased by $400,000.

6. It purchased $50,000 worth of marketable securities.

This example illustrates the difference between a firm's cash position on the balance sheet and its cash flows from operations.

26.3   The Operating Cycle and the Cash Cycle

Short-term finance is concerned with the firm's short-term **operating activities**. A typical manufacturing firm's short-term operating activities consist of a sequence of events and decisions:

Events	Decisions
1. Buying raw materials.	1. How much inventory to order?
2. Paying cash for purchases.	2. To borrow or draw down cash balance?
3. Manufacturing the product.	3. What choice of production technology?
4. Selling the product.	4. To offer cash terms or credit terms to customers?
5. Collecting cash.	5. How to collect cash?

These activities create patterns of cash inflows and cash outflows that are both unsynchronized and uncertain. They are unsynchronized because the payment of cash for raw materials does not happen at the same time as the receipt of cash from selling the product. They are uncertain because future sales and costs are not known with certainty.

Figure 26.1 depicts the short-term operating activities and cash flows for a typical manufacturing firm along the **cash flow time line**. The **operating cycle** is the interval between the arrival of inventory stock and the date when cash is collected from receivables.

Figure 26.1

Cash Flow Time Line and the Short-Term Operating Activities of a Typical Manufacturing Firm

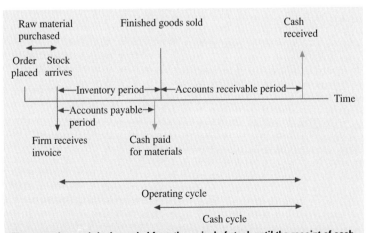

The *operating cycle* is the period from the arrival of stock until the receipt of cash. (Sometimes the operating cycle is defined to include the time from placement of the order until arrival of the stock.) The *cash cycle* begins when cash is paid for materials and ends when cash is collected from receivables.

The **cash cycle** begins when cash is paid for materials and ends when cash is collected from receivables. The cash flow time line consists of an operating cycle and a cash cycle. The need for short-term financial decision making is suggested by the gap between the cash inflows and cash outflows. This is related to the lengths of the operating cycle and the accounts payable period. This gap can be filled either by borrowing or by holding a liquidity reserve for marketable securities. The gap can be shortened by changing the inventory, receivable, and payable periods. Now we take a closer look at the operating cycle.

The length of the operating cycle is equal to the sum of the lengths of the inventory and accounts receivable periods. The inventory period is the length of time required to order raw materials, produce, and sell a product. The accounts receivable period is the length of time required to collect cash receipts.

The cash cycle is the time between cash disbursement and cash collection. It can be thought of as the operating cycle less the accounts payable period:

$$\text{Cash cycle} = \text{Operating cycle} - \text{Accounts payable period}$$

The accounts payable period is the length of time the firm is able to delay payment on the purchase of various resources, such as labor and raw materials.

In practice, the inventory period, the accounts receivable period, and the accounts payable period are measured by days in inventory, days in receivables, and days in payables, respectively. We illustrate how the operating cycle and the cash cycle can be measured in the following example.

EXAMPLE 26.1

Cash Cycle   Tradewinds Manufacturing is a diversified manufacturing firm with the balance sheet and income statement shown in Table 26.1 for 2006 and 2007. We can determine the operating cycle and the cash cycle for Tradewinds after calculating the appropriate ratios for inventory, receivables, and payables. Consider inventory first. The average inventory is

$$\text{Average inventory} = \frac{\$3 \text{ million} + \$2 \text{ million}}{2} = \$2.5 \text{ million}$$

The terms in the numerator are the ending inventory in the second and first years, respectively.

We next calculate the inventory turnover ratio:

$$\text{Inventory turnover ratio} = \frac{\text{Cost of goods sold}}{\text{Average inventory}} = \frac{\$8.2 \text{ million}}{\$2.5 \text{ million}} = 3.3$$

This implies that the inventory cycle occurs 3.3 times a year. Finally, we calculate days in inventory:

$$\text{Days in inventory} = \frac{365 \text{ days}}{3.3} = 110.6 \text{ days}$$

Our calculation implies that the inventory cycle is slightly more than 110 days.

We perform analogous calculations for receivables and payables:[2]

$$\begin{array}{c}\text{Average}\\\text{accounts receivable}\end{array} = \frac{\$2.0 \text{ million} + \$1.6 \text{ million}}{2} = \$1.8 \text{ million}$$

$$\begin{array}{c}\text{Average}\\\text{receivable turnover}\end{array} = \frac{\text{Credit sales}}{\text{Average accounts receivable}} = \frac{\$11.5 \text{ million}}{\$1.8 \text{ million}} = 6.4$$

---

[2]We assume that Tradewinds Manufacturing makes no cash sales.

(continued)

$$\text{Days in receivables} = \frac{365}{6.4} = 57 \text{ days}$$

$$\text{Average payables} = \frac{\$1.0 \text{ million} + \$0.75 \text{ million}}{2} = \$0.875 \text{ million}$$

$$\text{Accounts payable deferral period} = \frac{\text{Cost of goods sold}}{\text{Average payables}} = \frac{\$8.2 \text{ million}}{\$0.875 \text{ million}} = 9.4$$

$$\text{Days in payables} = \frac{365}{9.4} = 38.8 \text{ days}$$

The preceding calculations allow us to determine both the operating cycle and the cash cycle:

$$\text{Operating cycle} = \text{Days in inventory} + \text{Days in receivables}$$
$$= 110.6 \text{ days} + 57 \text{ days} = 167.6 \text{ days}$$
$$\text{Cash cycle} = \text{Operating cycle} - \text{Days in payables}$$
$$= 167.6 \text{ days} - 38.8 \text{ days} = 128.8 \text{ days}$$

The cash cycle is longer in some industries than in others because of different products and industry practices. Table 26.3 illustrates this point by comparing the current assets and current liabilities for four different companies. Of the four, Wal-Mart has the highest level of inventories. Does this mean Wal-Mart is less efficient? Probably not; instead, it is likely that the relatively high inventory levels are consistent with the industry. Wal-Mart needs a higher level of inventory to satisfy customers who walk into its stores. In contrast, Dell makes products to order, so its inventory levels are lower. What might seem surprising is Boeing's relatively low level of inventory, especially given that much of its inventory consists of aircraft under construction. However, notice that the current assets for Boeing are only 37 percent of total assets, implying that fixed assets are large, as you would expect from such a capital-intensive company—plus Boeing has been aggressive in recent years in reducing its inventory. In contrast, Amazon's fixed assets are small relative to its current assets, which again is what we would expect given the nature of its business.

Table 26.3

Current Assets and Current Liabilities as a Percentage of Total Assets for Selected Companies: 2006

	Amazon.com	Boeing	Dell	Wal-Mart
Cash and near cash	27.41%	11.04%	30.47%	4.56%
Marketable securities	26.70	0.94	8.72	0.00
Accounts receivable	9.82	8.17	17.69	1.43
Inventories	15.31	12.42	2.49	24.49
Other current assets	0.00	4.49	17.24	1.53
Total current assets	79.25%	37.07%	76.62%	32.02%
Accounts payable	52.19%	27.23%	42.58%	29.20%
Short-term borrowings	0.00	3.20	26.34	6.47
Other short-term liabilities	0.00	4.32	0.00	0.00
Current liabilities	52.19%	34.75%	68.92%	35.67%

26.4   Some Aspects of Short-Term Financial Policy

The policy that a firm adopts for short-term finance will be composed of at least two elements:

1. *The size of the firm's investment in current assets*: This is usually measured relative to the firm's level of total operating revenues. A flexible or accommodative short-term financial policy would maintain a high ratio of current assets to sales. A restrictive short-term financial policy would entail a low ratio of current assets to sales.

2. *The financing of current assets*: This is measured as the proportion of short-term debt to long-term debt. A restrictive short-term financial policy means a high proportion of short-term debt relative to long-term financing, and a flexible policy means less short-term debt and more long-term debt.

The Size of the Firm's Investment in Current Assets

Flexible short-term financial policies include:

1. Keeping large balances of cash and marketable securities.
2. Making large investments in inventory.
3. Granting liberal credit terms, which results in a high level of accounts receivable.

Restrictive short-term financial policies are:

1. Keeping low cash balances and no investment in marketable securities.
2. Making small investments in inventory.
3. Allowing no credit sales and no accounts receivable.

Determining the optimal investment level in short-term assets requires an identification of the different costs of alternative short-term financing policies. The objective is to trade off the cost of restrictive policies against those of the flexible ones to arrive at the best compromise.

Current asset holdings are highest with a flexible short-term financial policy and lowest with a restrictive policy. Thus, flexible short-term financial policies are costly in that they require higher cash outflows to finance cash and marketable securities, inventory, and accounts receivable. However, future cash inflows are highest with a flexible policy. Sales are stimulated by the use of a credit policy that provides liberal financing to customers. A large amount of inventory on hand ("on the shelf") provides a quick delivery service to customers and increases in sales.[3] In addition, the firm can probably charge higher prices for the quick delivery service and the liberal credit terms of flexible policies. A flexible policy also may result in fewer production stoppages because of inventory shortages.[4]

Managing current assets can be thought of as involving a trade-off between costs that rise with the level of investment and costs that fall with the level of investment. Costs that rise with the level of investment in current assets are called **carrying costs**. Costs that fall with increases in the level of investment in current assets are called **shortage costs**.

Carrying costs are generally of two types. First, because the rate of return on current assets is low compared with that of other assets, there is an opportunity cost. Second, there is the cost of maintaining the economic value of the item. For example, the cost of warehousing inventory belongs here.

---

[3]This is true of some types of finished goods.

[4]This is true of inventory of raw material but not of finished goods.

Determinants of Corporate Liquid Asset Holdings

Firms with High Holdings of Liquid Assets Will Have	Firms with Low Holdings of Liquid Assets Will Have
High-growth opportunities	Low-growth opportunities
High-risk investments	Low-risk investments
Small firms	Large firms
Low-credit firms	High-credit firms

Firms will hold more liquid assets (i.e., cash and marketable securities) to ensure that they can continue investing when cash flow is low relative to positive NPV investment opportunities. Firms that have good access to capital markets will hold less liquid assets.

SOURCE: Tim Opler, Lee Pinkowitz, René Stulz, and Rohan Williamson, "The Determinants and Implication of Corporate Cash Holdings," *Journal of Financial Economics* 52 (1999).

Shortage costs are incurred when the investment in current assets is low. If a firm runs out of cash, it will be forced to sell marketable securities. If a firm runs out of cash and cannot readily sell marketable securities, it may need to borrow or default on an obligation. (This general situation is called *cash-out*.) If a firm has no inventory (a *stockout*) or if it cannot extend credit to its customers, it will lose customers.

There are two kinds of shortage costs:

1. *Trading or order costs*: Order costs are the costs of placing an order for more cash (*brokerage costs*) or more inventory (*production setup costs*).

2. *Costs related to safety reserves*: These are costs of lost sales, lost customer goodwill, and disruption of production schedules.

Figure 26.2 illustrates the basic nature of carrying costs. The total costs of investing in current assets are determined by adding the carrying costs and the shortage costs. The minimum point on the total cost curve (CA*) reflects the optimal balance of current assets. The curve is generally quite flat at the optimum, and it is difficult, if not impossible, to find the precise optimal balance of shortage and carrying costs. Usually, we are content with a choice near the optimum.

If carrying costs are low or shortage costs are high, the optimal policy calls for substantial current assets. In other words, the optimal policy is a flexible one. This is illustrated in the middle graph of Figure 26.2.

If carrying costs are high or shortage costs are low, the optimal policy is a restrictive one. That is, the optimal policy calls for modest current assets. This is illustrated in the bottom graph of the figure.

Opler, Pinkowitz, Stulz, and Williamson examine the determinants of holdings of cash and marketable securities by publicly traded firms.[5] They find evidence that firms behave according to the static trade-off model described earlier. Their study focuses only on liquid assets (i.e., cash and market securities), so that carrying costs are the opportunity costs of holding liquid assets and shortage costs are the risks of not having cash when investment opportunities are good.

---

[5]Tim Opler, Lee Pinkowitz, René Stulz, and Rohan Williamson, "The Determinants and Implication of Corporate Cash Holdings," *Journal of Financial Economics* 52 (1999).

Figure 26.2

**Carrying Costs and
Shortage Costs**

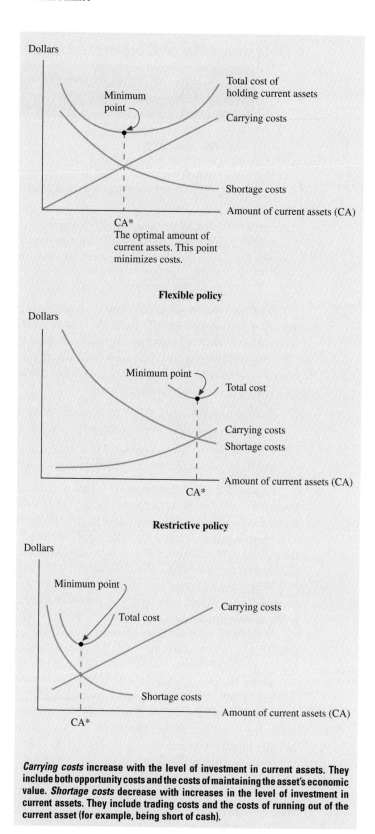

Flexible policy

Restrictive policy

Carrying costs increase with the level of investment in current assets. They
include both opportunity costs and the costs of maintaining the asset's economic
value. *Shortage costs* decrease with increases in the level of investment in
current assets. They include trading costs and the costs of running out of the
current asset (for example, being short of cash).

Figure 26.3

**Financing Policy for
an Idealized Economy**

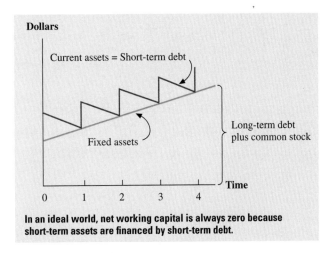

In an ideal world, net working capital is always zero because
short-term assets are financed by short-term debt.

Alternative Financing Policies for Current Assets

In the previous section, we examined the level of investment in current assets. Now we turn
to the level of current liabilities, assuming the investment in current assets is optimal.

An Ideal Model   In an ideal economy, short-term assets can always be financed with
short-term debt, and long-term assets can be financed with long-term debt and equity. In
this economy, net working capital is always zero.

Imagine the simple case of a grain elevator operator. Grain elevator operators buy
crops after harvest, store them, and sell them during the year. They have high inventories of
grain after the harvest and end with low inventories just before the next harvest.

Bank loans with maturities of less than one year are used to finance the purchase of
grain. These loans are paid with the proceeds from the sale of grain.

The situation is shown in Figure 26.3. Long-term assets are assumed to grow over
time, whereas current assets increase at the end of the harvest and then decline during the
year. Short-term assets end at zero just before the next harvest. These assets are financed
by short-term debt, and long-term assets are financed with long-term debt and equity. Net
working capital—current assets minus current liabilities—is always zero.

Different Strategies in Financing Current Assets   Current assets cannot be expected
to drop to zero in the real world because a long-term rising level of sales will result in
some permanent investment in current assets. A growing firm can be thought of as having a permanent requirement for both current assets and long-term assets. This total asset
requirement will exhibit balances over time reflecting (1) a secular growth trend, (2) a
seasonal variation around the trend, and (3) unpredictable day-to-day and month-to-month
fluctuations. This is depicted in Figure 26.4. (We have not tried to show the unpredictable
day-to-day and month-to-month variations in the total asset requirement.)

Now let us look at how this asset requirement is financed. First, consider the strategy
(strategy *F* in Figure 26.5) where long-term financing covers more than the total asset requirement, even at seasonal peaks. The firm will have excess cash available for investment
in marketable securities when the total asset requirement falls from peaks. Because this
approach implies chronic short-term cash surpluses and a large investment in net working
capital, it is considered a flexible strategy.

When long-term financing does not cover the total asset requirement, the firm must
borrow short-term to make up the deficit. This restrictive strategy is labeled strategy *R* in
Figure 26.5.

Figure 26.4

The Total Asset Requirement over Time

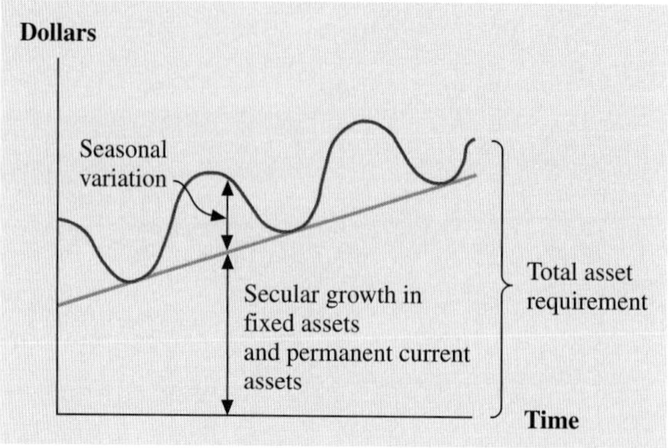

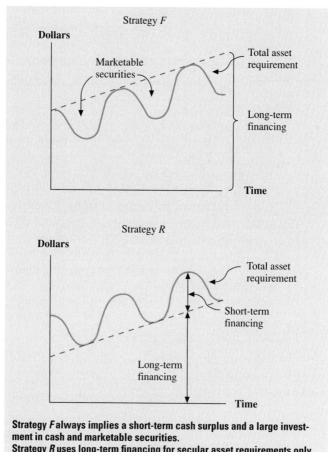

Figure 26.5

Alternative Asset Financing Policies

Strategy *F* always implies a short-term cash surplus and a large investment in cash and marketable securities.
Strategy *R* uses long-term financing for secular asset requirements only, and short-term borrowing for seasonal variations.

Which Is Best?

What is the most appropriate amount of short-term borrowing? There is no definitive answer. Several considerations must be included in a proper analysis:

1. *Cash reserves*: The flexible financing strategy implies surplus cash and little short-term borrowing. This strategy reduces the probability that a firm will experience financial distress. Firms may not need to worry as much about meeting recurring

short-term obligations. However, investments in cash and marketable securities are zero net present value investments at best.

2. *Maturity hedging*: Most firms finance inventories with short-term bank loans and fixed assets with long-term financing. Firms tend to avoid financing long-lived assets with short-term borrowing. This type of maturity mismatching would necessitate frequent financing and is inherently risky because short-term interest rates are more volatile than longer rates.

3. *Term structure*: Short-term interest rates are normally lower than long-term interest rates. This implies that, on average, it is more costly to rely on long-term borrowing than on short-term borrowing.

26.5 Cash Budgeting

The cash budget is a primary tool of short-term financial planning. It allows the financial manager to identify short-term financial needs (and opportunities). It will tell the manager the required borrowing for the short term. It is the way of identifying the cash flow gap on the cash flow time line. The idea of the cash budget is simple: It records estimates of cash receipts and disbursements. We illustrate cash budgeting with the following example of Fun Toys.

EXAMPLE 26.2

Cash Collections All of Fun Toys' cash inflows come from the sale of toys. Cash budgeting for Fun Toys starts with a sales forecast for the next year, by quarter:

	First Quarter	Second Quarter	Third Quarter	Fourth Quarter
Sales ($ millions)	$100	$200	$150	$100

Fun Toys' fiscal year starts on July 1. Fun Toys' sales are seasonal and are usually very high in the second quarter due to holiday sales. But Fun Toys sells to department stores on credit, and sales do not generate cash immediately. Instead, cash comes later from collections on accounts receivable. Fun Toys has a 90-day collection period, and 100 percent of sales are collected the following quarter. In other words

$$\text{Collections} = \text{Last quarter's sales}$$

This relationship implies that

$$\text{Accounts receivable at end of last quarter} = \text{Last quarter's sales} \qquad \textbf{(26.5)}$$

We assume that sales in the fourth quarter of the previous fiscal year were $100 million. From Equation 26.5 we know that accounts receivable at the end of the fourth quarter of the previous fiscal year were $100 million, and collections in the first quarter of the current fiscal year are $100 million.

The first quarter sales of the current fiscal year of $100 million are added to the accounts receivable, but $100 million of collections are subtracted. Therefore, Fun Toys ended the first quarter with accounts receivable of $100 million. The basic relation is

$$\frac{\text{Ending accounts}}{\text{receivable}} = \frac{\text{Starting accounts}}{\text{receivable}} + \text{Sales} - \text{Collections}$$

Table 26.4, on the next page, shows cash collections for Fun Toys for the next four quarters. Though collections are the only source of cash here, this need not always be the case. Other sources of cash could include sales of assets, investment income, and long-term financing.

(continued)

Table 26.4   Sources of Cash (in millions)

	First Quarter	Second Quarter	Third Quarter	Fourth Quarter
Sales	$100	$200	$150	$100
Cash collections	100	100	200	150
Starting receivables	100	100	200	150
Ending receivables	100	200	150	100

Cash Outflow

Next, we consider cash disbursements. They can be put into four basic categories, as shown in Table 26.5.

1. *Payments of accounts payable*: These are payments for goods or services, such as raw materials. These payments will generally be made after purchases. Purchases will depend on the sales forecast. In the case of Fun Toys, assume that:

$$\text{Payments} = \text{Last quarter's purchases}$$
$$\text{Purchases} = 1/2 \text{ next quarter's sales forecast}$$

2. *Wages, taxes, and other expenses*: This category includes all other normal costs of doing business that require actual expenditures. Depreciation, for example, is often thought of as a normal cost of business, but it requires no cash outflow.

3. *Capital expenditures*: These are payments of cash for long-lived assets. Fun Toys plans a major capital expenditure in the fourth quarter.

4. *Long-term financing*: This category includes interest and principal payments on long-term outstanding debt and dividend payments to shareholders.

The total forecast outflow appears in the last line of Table 26.5.

The Cash Balance

The net cash balance appears in Table 26.6, and a large net cash outflow is forecast in the second quarter. This large outflow is not caused by an inability to earn a profit. Rather, it results from delayed collections on sales. This results in a cumulative cash shortfall of $30 million in the second quarter.

Table 26.5

Disbursement of Cash (in millions)

	First Quarter	Second Quarter	Third Quarter	Fourth Quarter
Sales	$100	$200	$150	$100
Purchases	100	75	50	50
Uses of cash				
Payments of accounts payable	50	100	75	50
Wages, taxes, and other expenses	20	40	30	20
Capital expenditures	0	0	0	100
Long-term financing expenses:				
interest and dividends	10	10	10	10
Total uses of cash	$ 80	$150	$115	$180

Table 26.6

**The Cash Balance
(in millions)**

	First Quarter	Second Quarter	Third Quarter	Fourth Quarter
Total cash receipts	$100	$100	$200	$150
Total cash disbursements	80	150	115	180
Net cash flow	20	(50)	85	(30)
Cumulative excess cash balance	20	(30)	55	25
Minimum cash balance	5	5	5	5
Cumulative finance surplus (deficit) requirement	15	(35)	50	20

Fun Toys had established a minimum operating cash balance equal to $5 million to facilitate transactions, protect against unexpected contingencies, and maintain compensating balances at its commercial banks. This means that it has a cash shortfall in the second quarter equal to $35 million.

26.6 The Short-Term Financial Plan

Fun Toys has a short-term financing problem. It cannot meet the forecast cash outflows in the second quarter from internal sources. Its financing options include (1) unsecured bank borrowing, (2) secured borrowing, and (3) other sources.

Unsecured Loans

The most common way to finance a temporary cash deficit is to arrange a short-term unsecured bank loan. Firms that use short-term bank loans usually ask their bank for either a noncommitted or a committed *line of credit.* A *noncommitted* line is an informal arrangement that allows firms to borrow up to a previously specified limit without going through the normal paperwork. The interest rate on the line of credit is usually set equal to the bank's prime lending rate plus an additional percentage.

Committed lines of credit are formal legal arrangements and usually involve a commitment fee paid by the firm to the bank (usually the fee is approximately 0.25 percent of the total committed funds per year). For larger firms, the interest rate is often tied to the London Interbank Offered Rate (LIBOR) or to the bank's cost of funds, rather than the prime rate. Midsized and smaller firms often are required to keep compensating balances in the bank.

Compensating balances are deposits the firm keeps with the bank in low-interest or noninterest-bearing accounts. Compensating balances are commonly on the order of 2 to 5 percent of the amount used. By leaving these funds with the bank without receiving interest, the firm increases the effective interest earned by the bank on the line of credit. For example, if a firm borrowing $100,000 must keep $5,000 as a compensating balance, the firm effectively receives only $95,000. A stated interest rate of 10 percent implies yearly interest payments of $10,000 ($=$100,000 \times 0.10$). The effective interest rate is 10.53 percent ($=$10,000/$95,000$).

Secured Loans

Banks and other finance companies often require *security* for a loan. Security for short-term loans usually consists of accounts receivable or inventories.

Under **accounts receivable financing,** receivables are either *assigned* or *factored.* Under assignment, the lender not only has a lien on the receivables but also has recourse to the borrower. Factoring involves the sale of accounts receivable. The purchaser, who is called a *factor*, must then collect on the receivables. The factor assumes the full risk of default on bad accounts.

As the name implies, an **inventory loan** uses inventory as collateral. Some common types of inventory loans are:

1. *Blanket inventory lien*: The blanket inventory lien gives the lender a lien against all the borrower's inventories.

2. *Trust receipt*: Under this arrangement the borrower holds the inventory in trust for the lender. The document acknowledging the loan is called the trust receipt. Proceeds from the sale of inventory are remitted immediately to the lender.

3. *Field warehouse financing*: In field warehouse financing, a public warehouse company supervises the inventory for the lender.

Other Sources

A variety of other sources of short-term funds are employed by corporations. The most important of these are the issuance of **commercial paper** and financing through **banker's acceptances**. Commercial paper consists of short-term notes issued by large, highly rated firms. Typically these notes are of short maturity, ranging up to 270 days (beyond that limit the firm must file a registration statement with the SEC). Because the firm issues these directly and because it usually backs the issue with a special bank line of credit, the rate the firm obtains is often significantly below the prime rate the bank would charge it for a direct loan.

A banker's acceptance is an agreement by a bank to pay a sum of money. These agreements typically arise when a seller sends a bill or draft to a customer. The customer's bank *accepts* this bill and notes the acceptance on it, which makes it an obligation of the bank. In this way a firm that is buying something from a supplier can effectively arrange for the bank to pay the outstanding bill. Of course, the bank charges the customer a fee for this service.

Summary and Conclusions

1. This chapter introduced the management of short-term finance. Short-term finance involves short-lived assets and liabilities. We traced and examined the short-term sources and uses of cash as they appear on the firm's financial statements. We saw how current assets and current liabilities arise in the short-term operating activities and the cash cycle of the firm. From an accounting perspective, short-term finance involves net working capital.

2. Managing short-term cash flows involves the minimization of costs. The two major costs are carrying costs (the interest and related costs incurred by overinvesting in short-term assets such as cash) and shortage costs (the cost of running out of short-term assets). The objective of managing short-term finance and short-term financial planning is to find the optimal trade-off between these costs.

3. In an ideal economy, a firm could perfectly predict its short-term uses and sources of cash, and net working capital could be kept at zero. In the real world, net working capital provides a buffer that lets the firm meet its ongoing obligations. The financial manager seeks the optimal level of each of the current assets.

4. The financial manager can use the cash budget to identify short-term financial needs. The cash budget tells the manager what borrowing is required or what lending will be possible in the short term. The firm has a number of possible ways of acquiring funds to meet short-term shortfalls, including unsecured and secured loans.

Concept Questions

1. **Operating Cycle**   What are some of the characteristics of a firm with a long operating cycle?

2. **Cash Cycle**   What are some of the characteristics of a firm with a long cash cycle?

3. **Sources and Uses**   For the year just ended, you have gathered the following information about the Holly Corporation:
   a. A CAD 200 dividend was paid.
   b. Accounts payable increased by CAD 500.
   c. Fixed asset purchases were CAD 900.
   d. Inventories increased by CAD 625.
   e. Long-term debt decreased by CAD 1,200.

   Label each as a source or use of cash and describe its effect on the firm's cash balance.

4. **Cost of Current Assets**   Loftis Manufacturing, Inc., has recently installed a just-in-time (JIT) inventory system. Describe the effect this is likely to have on the company's carrying costs, shortage costs, and operating cycle.

5. **Operating and Cash Cycles**   Is it possible for a firm's cash cycle to be longer than its operating cycle? Explain why or why not.

6. **Shortage Costs**   What are the costs of shortages? Describe them.

7. **Reasons for Net Working Capital**   In an ideal economy, net working capital is always zero. Why might net working capital be positive in a real economy?

Use the following information to answer Questions 8–12: Last month, BlueSky Airline announced that it would stretch out its bill payments to 45 days from 30 days. The reason given was that the company wanted to "control costs and optimize cash flow." The increased payable period will be in effect for all of the company's 4,000 suppliers.

8. **Operating and Cash Cycles**   What impact did this change in payables policy have on BlueSky's operating cycle? Its cash cycle?

9. **Operating and Cash Cycles**   What impact did the announcement have on BlueSky's suppliers?

10. **Corporate Ethics**   Is it ethical for large firms to unilaterally lengthen their payable periods, particularly when dealing with smaller suppliers?

11. **Payables Period**   Why don't all firms simply increase their payables periods to shorten their cash cycles?

12. **Payables Period**   BlueSky lengthened its payables period to "control costs and optimize cash flow." Exactly what is the cash benefit to BlueSky from this change?

Questions and Problems

BASIC
(Questions 1–11)

1. **Changes in the Cash Account**   Indicate the impact of the following corporate actions on cash, using the letter *I* for an increase, *D* for a decrease, or *N* when no change occurs.
   a. A dividend is paid with funds received from a sale of debt.
   b. Real estate is purchased and paid for with short-term debt.
   c. Inventory is bought on credit.
   d. A short-term bank loan is repaid.
   e. Next year's taxes are prepaid.
   f. Preferred stock is redeemed.
   g. Sales are made on credit.
   h. Interest on long-term debt is paid.
   i. Payments for previous sales are collected.
   j. The accounts payable balance is reduced.
   k. A dividend is paid.
   l. Production supplies are purchased and paid with a short-term note.
   m. Utility bills are paid.

n. Cash is paid for raw materials purchased for inventory.

o. Marketable securities are sold.

2. **Cash Equation** Andrie Candles, Inc., has a book net worth of £9,300. Long-term debt is £1,900. Net working capital, other than cash, is £2,450. Fixed assets are £2,300. How much cash does the company have? If current liabilities are £1,250, what are current assets?

3. **Changes in the Operating Cycle** Indicate the effect that the following will have on the operating cycle. Use the letter I to indicate an increase, the letter D for a decrease, and the letter N for no change.

  a. Receivables average goes up.

  b. Credit repayment times for customers are increased.

  c. Inventory turnover goes from 3 times to 6 times.

  d. Payables turnover goes from 6 times to 11 times.

  e. Receivables turnover goes from 7 times to 9 times.

  f. Payments to suppliers are accelerated.

4. **Changes in Cycles** Indicate the impact of the following on the cash and operating cycles, respectively. Use the letter I to indicate an increase, the letter D for a decrease, and the letter N for no change.

  a. The terms of cash discounts offered to customers are made less favorable.

  b. The cash discounts offered by suppliers are increased; thus, payments are made earlier.

  c. An increased number of customers begin to pay in cash instead of with credit.

  d. Fewer raw materials than usual are purchased.

  e. A greater percentage of raw material purchases are paid for with credit.

  f. More finished goods are produced for inventory instead of for order.

5. **Calculating Cash Collections** Aero Mart Company has projected the following quarterly sales amounts for the coming year:

	Q1	Q2	Q3	Q4
Sales	€800	€760	€940	€870

  a. Accounts receivable at the beginning of the year are €300. Aero Mart has a 45-day collection period. Calculate cash collections in each of the four quarters by completing the following:

	Q1	Q2	Q3	Q4
Beginning receivables				
Sales				
Cash collections				
Ending receivables				

  b. Rework (a) assuming a collection period of 60 days.

  c. Rework (a) assuming a collection period of 30 days.

6. **Calculating Cycles** Consider the following financial statement information for the Bulldog Icers Corporation:

Item	Beginning		Ending
Inventory	$8,413		$10,158
Accounts receivable	5,108		5,439
Accounts payable	6,927		7,625
Net sales		$67,312	
Cost of goods sold		51,004	

Calculate the operating and cash cycles. How do you interpret your answer?

7. **Calculating Payments** Guangxi Products has projected the following sales for the coming year:

	Q1	Q2	Q3	Q4
Sales	CNY 540	CNY 630	CNY 710	CNY 785

Sales in the year following this one are projected to be 15 percent greater in each quarter.

a. Calculate payments to suppliers assuming that Guangxi places orders during each quarter equal to 30 percent of projected sales for the next quarter. Assume that the company pays immediately. What is the payables period in this case?

	Q1	Q2	Q3	Q4
Payment of accounts	CNY	CNY	CNY	CNY

b. Rework (a) assuming a 90-day payables period.

	Q1	Q2	Q3	Q4
Payment of accounts	CNY	CNY	CNY	CNY

c. Rework (a) assuming a 60-day payables period.

	Q1	Q2	Q3	Q4
Payment of accounts	CNY	CNY	CNY	CNY

8. **Calculating Payments** The Thakor Corporation's purchases from suppliers in a quarter are equal to 75 percent of the next quarter's forecast sales. The payables period is 60 days. Wages, taxes, and other expenses are 20 percent of sales, and interest and dividends are INR 60 per quarter. No capital expenditures are planned.

Here are the projected quarterly sales:

	Q1	Q2	Q3	Q4
Sales	INR 750	INR 920	INR 890	INR 790

Sales for the first quarter of the following year are projected at INR 970. Calculate the company's cash outlays by completing the following:

	Q1	Q2	Q3	Q4
Payment of accounts				
Wages, taxes, other expenses				
Long-term financing expenses (interest and dividends)				
Total				

9. **Calculating Cash Collections**   The following is the sales budget for Shleifer, Inc., for the first quarter of 2007:

	January	February	March
Sales budget	€150,000	€173,000	€190,000

Credit sales are collected as follows:

65 percent in the month of the sale.
20 percent in the month after the sale.
15 percent in the second month after the sale.

The accounts receivable balance at the end of the previous quarter was €57,000 (€41,000 of which was uncollected December sales).

a. Compute the sales for November.
b. Compute the sales for December.
c. Compute the cash collections from sales for each month from January through March.

10. **Calculating the Cash Budget**   Here are some important figures from the budget of Cornell, Inc., for the second quarter of 2007:

	April	May	June
Credit sales	$380,000	$396,000	$438,000
Credit purchases	147,000	175,500	200,500
Cash disbursements			
Wages, taxes, and expenses	39,750	48,210	50,300
Interest	11,400	11,400	11,400
Equipment purchases	83,000	91,000	0

The company predicts that 5 percent of its credit sales will never be collected, 35 percent of its sales will be collected in the month of the sale, and the remaining 60 percent will be collected in the following month. Credit purchases will be paid in the month following the purchase.

In March 2007, credit sales were $210,000, and credit purchases were $156,000. Using this information, complete the following cash budget:

	April	May	June
Beginning cash balance	$280,000		
Cash receipts			
Cash collections from credit sales			
Total cash available			
Cash disbursements			
Purchases			
Wages, taxes, and expenses			
Interest			
Equipment purchases			
Total cash disbursements			
Ending cash balance			

11.   Sources and Uses   Here are the most recent balance sheets for Arkudo Co. Excluding accumulated depreciation, determine whether each item is a source or a use of cash, and the amount:

ARKUDO CO. Balance Sheet December 31, 2007		
	2007	**2006**
Assets		
Cash	¥ 42,000,000	¥ 35,000,000
Accounts receivable	94,250,000	84,500,000
Inventory	78,750,000	75,000,000
Property, plant, equipment	181,475,000	168,750,000
Less: Accumulated depreciation	61,475,000	56,250,000
Total assets	¥335,000,000	¥307,000,000
Liabilities and Equity		
Accounts payable	¥ 60,500,000	¥ 55,000,000
Accrued expenses	5,150,000	8,450,000
Long-term debt	15,000,000	30,000,000
Common stock	28,000,000	25,000,000
Accumulated retained earnings	226,350,000	188,550,000
Total liabilities and equity	¥335,000,000	¥307,000,000

INTERMEDIATE
(Questions 12–15)

12.   Cash Budgeting   The sales budget for your company in the coming year is based on a 20 percent quarterly growth rate with the first-quarter sales projection at CRC 100 million. In addition to this basic trend, the seasonal adjustments for the four quarters are 0, −CRC 10, −CRC 5, and CRC 15 million, respectively. Generally, 50 percent of the sales can be collected within the quarter and 45 percent in the following quarter; the rest of sales are bad debt. The bad debts are written off in the second quarter after the sales are made. The beginning accounts payable balance is CRC 81 million. Assuming all sales are on credit, compute the cash collections from sales for each quarter.

13.   Calculating the Cash Budget   Him Jun So Co., has estimated sales (in millions) for the next four quarters as follows:

	Q1	Q2	Q3	Q4
Sales	KRW 230	KRW 195	KRW 270	KRW 295

Sales for the first quarter of the year after this one are projected at KRW 250 million. Accounts receivable at the beginning of the year were KRW 79 million. Him Jun So has a 45-day collection period.

Him Jun So's purchases from suppliers in a quarter are equal to 45 percent of the next quarter's forecast sales, and suppliers are normally paid in 36 days. Wages, taxes, and other expenses run about 30 percent of sales. Interest and dividends are KRW 15 million per quarter.

Him Jun So plans a major capital outlay in the second quarter of KRW 90 million. Finally, the company started the year with a KRW 73 million cash balance and wishes to maintain a KRW 30 million minimum balance.

a. Complete a cash budget for Him Jun So by filling in the following:

HIM JUN SO CO. Cash Budget (in millions)				
	Q1	Q2	Q3	Q4
Beginning cash balance	KRW 73			
Net cash inflow				
Ending cash balance				
Minimum cash balance	30			
Cumulative surplus (deficit)				

b. Assume that Him Jun So can borrow any needed funds on a short-term basis at a rate of 3 percent per quarter, and can invest any excess funds in short-term marketable securities at a rate of 2 percent per quarter. Prepare a short-term financial plan by filling in the following schedule. What is the net cash cost (total interest paid minus total investment income earned) for the year?

HIM JUN SO CO. Short-Term Financial Plan (in millions)				
	Q1	Q2	Q3	Q4
Beginning cash balance	KRW 73			
Net cash inflow				
New short-term investments				
Income from short-term investments				
Short-term investments sold				
New short-term borrowing				
Interest on short-term borrowing				
Short-term borrowing repaid				
Ending cash balance				
Minimum cash balance	30			
Cumulative surplus (deficit)				
Beginning short-term investments				
Ending short-term investments				
Beginning short-term debt				
Ending short-term debt				

14. **Cash Management Policy**   Rework Problem 13 assuming the following:
    a. Him Jum So maintains a minimum cash balance of KRW 45 million.
    b. Him Jum So maintains a minimum cash balance of KRW 15 million.

    Based on your answers in (a) and (b), do you think the firm can boost its profit by changing its cash management policy? Should other factors be considered as well? Explain.

15. **Short-Term Finance Policy**   Cleveland Compressor and Pnew York Pneumatic are competing manufacturing firms. Their financial statements are printed here.
    a. How are the current assets of each firm financed?
    b. Which firm has the larger investment in current assets? Why?
    c. Which firm is more likely to incur carrying costs, and which is more likely to incur shortage costs? Why?

CLEVELAND COMPRESSOR
Balance Sheet

	2007	2006
Assets		
Cash	£ 13,862	£ 16,339
Net accounts receivable	23,887	25,778
Inventory	54,867	43,287
Total current assets	£ 92,616	£ 85,404
Fixed assets:		
Plant, property, and equipment	101,543	99,615
Less: Accumulated depreciation	34,331	31,957
Net fixed assets	£ 67,212	£ 67,658
Prepaid expenses	1,914	1,791
Other assets	13,052	13,138
Total assets	£174,794	£167,991
Liabilities and Equity		
Current liabilities:		
Accounts payable	£ 6,494	£ 4,893
Notes payable	10,483	11,617
Accrued expenses	7,422	7,227
Other taxes payable	9,924	8,460
Total current liabilities	34,323	32,197
Long-term debt	22,036	22,036
Total liabilities	£ 56,359	£ 54,233
Equity:		
Common stock	38,000	38,000
Paid-in capital	12,000	12,000
Retained earnings	68,435	63,758
Total equity	118,435	113,758
Total liabilities and equity	£174,794	£167,991

CLEVELAND COMPRESSOR
Income Statement
2007

Income:	
Sales	£162,749
Other income	1,002
Total income	£163,751
Operating expenses:	
Cost of goods sold	103,570
Selling and administrative expenses	28,495
Depreciation	2,274
Total expenses	£134,339
Pretax earnings	29,412
Taxes	14,890
Net earnings	£ 14,522
Dividends	£ 9,845
Retained earnings	£ 4,677

www.mhhe.com/rwj

PNEW YORK PNEUMATIC
Balance Sheet

	2007	2006
Assets		
Cash	£ 5,794	£ 3,307
Net accounts receivable	26,177	22,133
Inventory	46,463	44,661
Total current assets	£78,434	£70,101
Fixed assets:		
Plant, property, and equipment	31,842	31,116
Less: Accumulated depreciation	19,297	18,143
Net fixed assets	£12,545	£12,973
Prepaid expenses	763	688
Other assets	1,601	1,385
Total assets	£93,343	£85,147
Liabilities and Equity		
Current liabilities:		
Accounts payable	£ 6,008	£ 5,019
Bank loans	3,722	645
Accrued expenses	4,254	3,295
Other taxes payable	5,688	4,951
Total current liabilities	£19,672	£13,910
Equity:		
Common stock	20,576	20,576
Paid-in capital	5,624	5,624
Retained earnings	48,598	46,164
Less: Treasury stock	1,127	1,127
Total equity	£73,671	£71,237
Total liabilities and equity	£93,343	£85,147

PNEW YORK PNEUMATIC
Income Statement
2007

Income:	
Sales	£91,374
Other income	1,067
Total income	£92,441
Operating expenses:	
Cost of goods sold	59,042
Selling and administrative expenses	18,068
Depreciation	1,154
Total expenses	£78,264
Pretax earnings	14,177
Taxes	6,838
Net earnings	£ 7,339
Dividends	£ 4,905
Retained earnings	£ 2,434

www.mhhe.com/rwj

S&P Problems

STANDARD &POOR'S

1. **Cash and Operating Cycles** Find the most recent financial statements for Dell Computer (DELL) and Boeing (BA). Calculate the cash and operating cycle for each company for the most recent year. Are the numbers similar for these companies? Why or why not?

2. **Cash and Operating Cycles** Download the most recent quarterly financial statements for Wal-Mart (WMT). Calculate the operating and cash cycle for Wal-Mart over each of the last four quarters. Comment on any changes in the operating or cash cycle over this period.

Mini Case

Keafer Manufacturing Working Capital Management

You have recently been hired by Keafer Manufacturing to work in its established treasury department. Keafer Manufacturing is a small company that produces highly customized cardboard boxes in a variety of sizes for different purchasers. Adam Keafer, the owner of the company, works primarily in the sales and production areas of the company. Currently, the company basically puts all receivables in one pile and all payables in another, and a part-time bookkeeper periodically comes in and attacks the piles. Because of this disorganized system, the finance area needs work, and that's what you've been brought in to do.

The company currently has a cash balance of $115,000, and it plans to purchase new machinery in the third quarter at a cost of $200,000. The purchase of the machinery will be made with cash because of the discount offered for a cash purchase. Adam wants to maintain a minimum cash balance of $90,000 to guard against unforeseen contingencies. All of Keafer's sales to customers and purchases from suppliers are made with credit, and no discounts are offered or taken.

The company had the following sales each quarter of the year just ended:

	Q1	Q2	Q3	Q4
Gross sales	$565,000	$585,000	$628,000	$545,000

After some research and discussions with customers, you're projecting that sales will be 8 percent higher in each quarter next year. Sales for the first quarter of the following year are also expected to grow at 8 percent. You calculate that Keafer currently has an accounts receivable period of 57 days and an accounts receivable balance of $426,000. However, 10 percent of the accounts receivable balance is from a company that has just entered bankruptcy, and it is likely that this portion will never be collected.

You've also calculated that Keafer typically orders supplies each quarter in the amount of 50 percent of the next quarter's projected gross sales, and suppliers are paid in 53 days on average. Wages, taxes, and other costs run about 25 percent of gross sales. The company has a quarterly interest payment of $120,000 on its long-term debt. Finally, the company uses a local bank for its short-term financial needs. It currently pays 1.2 percent per quarter on all short-term borrowing and maintains a money market account that pays .5 percent per quarter on all short-term deposits.

Adam has asked you to prepare a cash budget and short-term financial plan for the company under the current policies. He has also asked you to prepare additional plans based on changes in several inputs.

1. Use the numbers given to complete the cash budget and short-term financial plan.

2. Rework the cash budget and short-term financial plan assuming Keafer changes to a minimum cash balance of $70,000.

3. Rework the sales budget assuming an 11 percent growth rate in sales and a 5 percent growth rate in sales. Assume a $90,000 target cash balance.

4. Assuming the company maintains its target cash balance at $90,000, what sales growth rate would result in a zero need for short-term financing? To answer this question, you may need to set up a spreadsheet and use the "Solver" function.

CHAPTER 27

Cash Management

Most often, when news breaks about a firm's cash position, it's because the company is running low. That wasn't the case for many companies in early 2006. The insurance company Cigna certainly had one of the largest cash reserves relative to its size: Its cash balance was $2.15 billion. With a market capitalization of $14.77 billion, cash made up about 15 percent of the company's value. Other companies with large cash balances included IBM with $10.5 billion in cash, Dell with about $10 billion, and Pfizer with about $27.5 billion. Of course, no company came close to Microsoft. In 2004, before paying a special dividend, the cash balance for the company reached a staggering $64 billion. Why would firms such as these hold such large quantities of cash? We examine cash management in this chapter to find out.

27.1 Reasons for Holding Cash

The term *cash* is a surprisingly imprecise concept. The economic definition of cash includes currency, checking account deposits at commercial banks, and undeposited checks. However, financial managers often use the term *cash* to include short-term marketable securities. Short-term marketable securities are frequently referred to as *cash equivalents* and include Treasury bills, certificates of deposit, and repurchase agreements. (Several different types of short-term marketable securities are described at the end of this chapter.) The balance sheet item "cash" usually includes cash equivalents.

The previous chapter discussed the management of net working capital. Net working capital includes both cash and cash equivalents. This chapter is concerned with cash, not net working capital, and it focuses on the narrow economic definition of cash.

The basic elements of net working capital management such as carrying costs, shortage costs, and opportunity costs are relevant for cash management. However, cash management is more concerned with how to minimize cash balances by collecting and disbursing cash effectively.

There are two primary reasons for holding cash. First, cash is needed to satisfy the **transactions motive**. Transaction-related needs come from normal disbursement and collection activities of the firm. The disbursement of cash includes the payment of wages and salaries, trade debts, taxes, and dividends. Cash is collected from sales from operations, sales of assets, and new financing. The cash inflows (*collections*) and outflows (*disbursements*) are not perfectly synchronized, and some level of cash holdings is necessary as a buffer. If the firm maintains too small a cash balance, it may run out of cash. If so, it must sell marketable securities or borrow. Selling marketable securities and borrowing involve *trading costs*.

Another reason to hold cash is for **compensating balances**. Cash balances are kept at commercial banks to compensate for banking services rendered to the firm. A minimum required compensating balance at banks providing credit services to the firm may impose a lower limit on the level of cash a firm holds.

The cash balance for most firms can be thought of as consisting of transaction balances and compensating balances. However, it would not be correct for a firm to add the amount of cash required to satisfy its transaction needs to the amount of cash needed to satisfy its compensatory balances to produce a target cash balance. The same cash can be used to satisfy both requirements.

The cost of holding cash is, of course, the opportunity cost of lost interest. To determine the target cash balance, the firm must weigh the benefits of holding cash against the costs. It is generally a good idea for firms to figure out first how much cash to hold to satisfy transaction needs. Next, the firm must consider compensating balance requirements, which will impose a lower limit on the level of the firm's cash holdings. Because compensating balances merely provide a lower limit, we ignore compensating balances for the following discussion of the target cash balance.

27.2 Determining the Target Cash Balance

The **target cash balance** involves a trade-off between the opportunity costs of holding too much cash and the trading costs of holding too little. Figure 27.1 presents the problem graphically. If a firm tries to keep its cash holdings too low, it will find itself selling marketable securities (and perhaps later buying marketable securities to replace those sold) more frequently than if the cash balance was higher. Thus, trading costs will tend to fall as the cash balance becomes larger. In contrast, the opportunity costs of holding cash rise as the cash holdings rise. At point C^* in Figure 27.1, the sum of both costs, depicted as the total cost curve, is at a minimum. This is the target or optimal cash balance.

Figure 27.1

Costs of Holding Cash

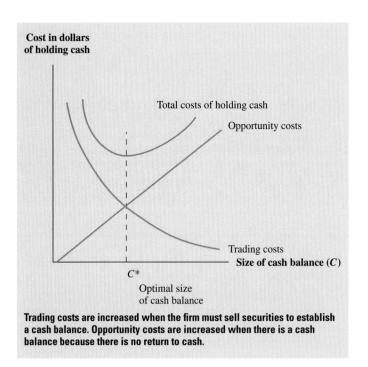

Trading costs are increased when the firm must sell securities to establish a cash balance. Opportunity costs are increased when there is a cash balance because there is no return to cash.

Figure 27.2

Cash Balances for the Golden Socks Corporation

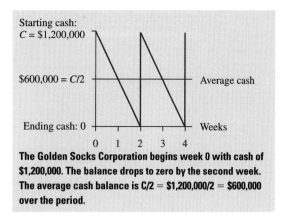

Starting cash:
$C = \$1,200,000$

$\$600,000 = C/2$ — Average cash

Ending cash: 0 — Weeks

0 1 2 3 4

The Golden Socks Corporation begins week 0 with cash of $1,200,000. The balance drops to zero by the second week. The average cash balance is C/2 = $1,200,000/2 = $600,000 over the period.

The Baumol Model

William Baumol was the first to provide a formal model of cash management incorporating opportunity costs and trading costs.[1] His model can be used to establish the target cash balance.

Suppose the Golden Socks Corporation began week 0 with a cash balance of $C = \$1.2$ million, and outflows exceed inflows by $600,000 per week. Its cash balance will drop to zero at the end of week 2, and its average cash balance will be $C/2 = \$1.2$ million$/2 = \$600,000$ over the two-week period. At the end of week 2, Golden Socks must replace its cash either by selling marketable securities or by borrowing. Figure 27.2 shows this situation.

If C were set higher, say at $2.4 million, cash would last four weeks before the firm would need to sell marketable securities, but the firm's average cash balance would increase to $1.2 million (from $600,000). If C were set at $600,000, cash would run out in one week and the firm would need to replenish cash more frequently, but its average cash balance would fall from $600,000 to $300,000.

Because transaction costs must be incurred whenever cash is replenished (for example, the brokerage costs of selling marketable securities), establishing large initial cash balances will lower the trading costs connected with cash management. However, the larger the average cash balance, the greater the opportunity cost (the return that could have been earned on marketable securities).

To solve this problem, Golden Socks needs to know the following three things:

F = The fixed cost of selling securities to replenish cash.

T = The total amount of new cash needed for transaction purposes over the relevant planning period—say, one year.

and

R = The opportunity cost of holding cash; this is the interest rate on marketable securities.

With this information, Golden Socks can determine the total costs of any particular cash-balance policy. It can then determine the optimal cash-balance policy.

The Opportunity Costs The total opportunity costs of cash balances, in dollars, must be equal to the average cash balance multiplied by the interest rate:

$$\text{Opportunity costs (\$)} = (C/2) \times R$$

[1]W. S. Baumol, "The Transactions Demand for Cash: An Inventory Theoretic Approach," *Quarterly Journal of Economics* 66 (November 1952).

The opportunity costs of various alternatives are given here:

Initial Cash Balance	Average Cash Balance	Opportunity Costs (R = 0.10)
C	C/2	(C/2) × R
$4,800,000	$2,400,000	$240,000
2,400,000	1,200,000	120,000
1,200,000	600,000	60,000
600,000	300,000	30,000
300,000	150,000	15,000

The Trading Costs   We can determine total trading costs by calculating the number of times that Golden Socks must sell marketable securities during the year. The total amount of cash disbursement during the year is $600,000 × 52 weeks = $31.2 million. If the initial cash balance is set at $1.2 million, Golden Socks will sell $1.2 million of marketable securities every two weeks. Thus, trading costs are given by:

$$\frac{\$31.2 \text{ million}}{\$1.2 \text{ million}} \times F = 26F$$

The general formula is:

$$\text{Trading costs (\$)} = (T/C) \times F$$

A schedule of alternative trading costs follows:

Total Disbursements during Relevant Period	Initial Cash Balance	Trading Costs (F = $1,000)
T	C	(T/C) × F
$31,200,000	$4,800,000	$ 6,500
31,200,000	2,400,000	13,000
31,200,000	1,200,000	26,000
31,200,000	600,000	52,000
31,200,000	300,000	104,000

The Total Cost   The total cost of cash balances consists of the opportunity costs plus the trading costs:

$$\text{Total cost} = \text{Opportunity costs} + \text{Trading costs}$$
$$= (C/2) \times R + (T/C) \times F$$

Cash Balance	Total Cost	=	Opportunity Costs	+	Trading Costs
$4,800,000	$246,500		$240,000		$ 6,500
2,400,000	133,000		120,000		13,000
1,200,000	86,000		60,000		26,000
600,000	82,000		30,000		52,000
300,000	119,000		15,000		104,000

The Solution   We can see from the preceding schedule that a $600,000 cash balance results in the lowest total cost of the possibilities presented: $82,000. But what about $700,000 or $500,000 or other possibilities? To determine minimum total costs precisely, Golden Socks must equate the marginal reduction in trading costs as balances rise with the marginal increase in opportunity costs associated with cash balance increases. The target cash balance should be the point where the two offset each other. This can be calculated with either numerical iteration or calculus. We will use calculus; but if you are unfamiliar with such an analysis, you can skip to the solution.

Recall that the total cost equation is:

$$\text{Total cost (TC)} = (C/2) \times R + (T/C) \times F$$

If we differentiate the TC equation with respect to the cash balance and set the derivative equal to zero, we will find:

$$\frac{\text{dTC}}{\text{dC}} = \frac{R}{2} - \frac{TF}{C^2} = 0$$

$$\underset{\text{total cost}}{\text{Marginal}} \quad = \quad \underset{\text{opportunity costs}}{\text{Marginal}} \quad + \quad \underset{\text{trading costs}}{\text{Marginal}^2}$$

We obtain the solution for the general cash balance, C^*, by solving this equation for C:

$$\frac{R}{2} = \frac{TF}{C^2}$$

$$C^* = \sqrt{2TF/R}$$

If $F = \$1,000$, $T = \$31,200,000$, and $R = 0.10$, then $C^* = \$789,936.71$. Given the value of C^*, opportunity costs are:

$$(C^*/2) \times R = \frac{\$789,936.71}{2} \times 0.10 = \$39,496.84$$

Trading costs are:

$$(T/C^*) \times F = \frac{\$31,200,000}{\$789,936.71} \times \$1,000 = \$39,496.84$$

Hence, total costs are:

$$\$39,496.84 + \$39,496.84 = \$78,993.68$$

Limitations   The Baumol model represents an important contribution to cash management. The limitations of the model include the following:

1. *The model assumes the firm has a constant disbursement rate.* In practice, disbursements can be only partially managed because due dates differ and costs cannot be predicted with certainty.

2. *The model assumes there are no cash receipts during the projected period.* In fact, most firms experience both cash inflows and outflows daily.

3. *No safety stock is allowed.* Firms will probably want to hold a safety stock of cash designed to reduce the possibility of a cash shortage or *cash-out.* However, to the extent that firms can sell marketable securities or borrow in a few hours, the need for a safety stock is minimal.

---

[2]Marginal trading costs are negative because trading costs are *reduced* when C is increased.

Figure 27.3

The Miller–Orr Model

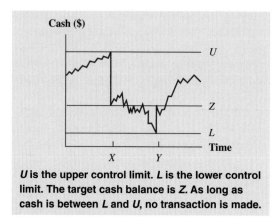

U is the upper control limit. L is the lower control limit. The target cash balance is Z. As long as cash is between L and U, no transaction is made.

The Baumol model is possibly the simplest and most stripped-down sensible model for determining the optimal cash position. Its chief weakness is that it assumes discrete, certain cash flows. We next discuss a model designed to deal with uncertainty.

The Miller–Orr Model

Merton Miller and Daniel Orr developed a cash balance model to deal with cash inflows and outflows that fluctuate randomly from day to day.[3] In the Miller–Orr model, both cash inflows and cash outflows are included. The model assumes that the distribution of daily net cash flows (cash inflow minus cash outflow) is normally distributed. On each day the net cash flow could be the expected value or some higher or lower value. We will assume that the expected net cash flow is zero.

Figure 27.3 shows how the Miller–Orr model works. The model operates in terms of upper (U) and lower (L) control limits and a target cash balance (Z). The firm allows its cash balance to wander randomly within the lower and upper limits. As long as the cash balance is between U and L, the firm makes no transaction. When the cash balance reaches U, such as at point X, the firm buys $U - Z$ units (or dollars) of marketable securities.

This action will decrease the cash balance to Z. In the same way, when cash balances fall to L, such as at point Y (the lower limit), the firm should sell $Z - L$ securities and increase the cash balance to Z. In both situations, cash balances return to Z. Management sets the lower limit, L, depending on how much risk of a cash shortfall the firm is willing to tolerate.

Like the Baumol model, the Miller–Orr model depends on trading costs and opportunity costs. The cost per transaction of buying and selling marketable securities, F, is assumed to be fixed. The percentage opportunity cost per period of holding cash, R, is the daily interest rate on marketable securities. Unlike in the Baumol model, the number of transactions per period is a random variable that varies from period to period, depending on the pattern of cash inflows and outflows.

As a consequence, trading costs per period depend on the expected number of transactions in marketable securities during the period. Similarly, the opportunity costs of holding cash are a function of the expected cash balance per period.

Given L, which is set by the firm, the Miller–Orr model solves for the target cash balance, Z, and the upper limit, U. Expected total costs of the cash balance return policy (Z, U) are equal to the sum of expected transaction costs and expected opportunity costs. The values of Z (the return cash point) and U (the upper limit) that minimize the expected

---

[3]M. H. Miller and D. Orr, "A Model of the Demand for Money by Firms," *Quarterly Journal of Economics* (August 1966).

total cost have been determined by Miller and Orr:

$$Z^* = \sqrt[3]{3F\sigma^2/(4R)} + L$$
$$U^* = 3Z^* - 2L$$

Here * denotes optimal values, and σ^2 is the variance of net daily cash flows.

The average cash balance in the Miller–Orr model is:

$$\text{Average cash balance} = \frac{4Z - L}{3}$$

EXAMPLE 27.1

Miller–Orr To clarify the Miller–Orr model, suppose $F = \$1,000$, the interest rate is 10 percent annually, and the standard deviation of daily net cash flows is $2,000. The daily opportunity cost, R, is:

$$(1 + R)^{365} - 1.0 = 0.10$$
$$1 + R = \sqrt[365]{1.10} = 1.000261$$
$$R = 0.000261$$

The variance of daily net cash flows is:

$$\sigma^2 = (2,000)^2 = 4,000,000$$

Let us assume that $L = 0$:

$$Z^* = \sqrt[3]{(3 \times \$1,000 \times 4,000,000)/(4 \times 0.000261)} + 0$$
$$= \sqrt[3]{(\$11,493,900,000,000)} = \$22,568$$
$$U^* = 3 \times \$22,568 = \$67,704$$
$$\text{Average cash balance} = \frac{4 \times \$22,568}{3} = \$30,091$$

Implications of the Miller–Orr Model To use the Miller–Orr model, the manager must do four things:

1. Set the lower control limit for the cash balance. This lower limit can be related to a minimum safety margin decided on by management.
2. Estimate the standard deviation of daily cash flows.
3. Determine the interest rate.
4. Estimate the trading costs of buying and selling marketable securities.

These four steps allow the upper limit and return point to be computed. Miller and Orr tested their model using nine months of data for cash balances for a large industrial firm. The model was able to produce average daily cash balances much lower than the averages actually obtained by the firm.[4]

The Miller–Orr model clarifies the issues of cash management. First, the model shows that the best return point, Z^*, is positively related to trading costs, F, and negatively related to R. This finding is consistent with and analogous to the Baumol model. Second, the

---

[4]D. Mullins and R. Hamonoff discuss tests of the Miller–Orr model in "Applications of Inventory Cash Management Models," in *Modern Developments in Financial Management*, ed. by S. C. Myers (New York: Praeger, 1976). They show that the model works very well when compared to the actual cash balances of several firms. However, simple rules of thumb do as good a job as the Miller–Orr model.

Miller–Orr model shows that the best return point and the average cash balance are positively related to the variability of cash flows. That is, firms whose cash flows are subject to greater uncertainty should maintain a larger average cash balance.

Other Factors Influencing the Target Cash Balance

Borrowing In our previous examples, the firm obtained cash by selling marketable securities. Another alternative is to borrow cash. Borrowing introduces additional considerations to cash management:

1. Borrowing is likely to be more expensive than selling marketable securities because the interest rate is likely to be higher.
2. The need to borrow will depend on management's desire to hold low cash balances. A firm is more likely to need to borrow to cover an unexpected cash outflow with greater cash flow variability and lower investment in marketable securities.

Compensating Balance The costs of trading securities are well below the lost income from holding cash for large firms. Consider a firm faced with either selling $2 million of Treasury bills to replenish cash or leaving the money idle overnight. The daily opportunity cost of $2 million at a 10 percent annual interest rate is $0.10/365 = 0.027$ percent per day. The daily return earned on $2 million is $0.00027 \times \$2$ million $= \$540$. The cost of selling $2 million of Treasury bills is much less than $540. As a consequence, a large firm will buy and sell securities many times a day before it will leave substantial amounts idle overnight.

However, most large firms hold more cash than cash balance models imply. Here are some possible reasons:

1. Firms have cash in the bank as a compensating balance in payment for banking services.
2. Large corporations have thousands of accounts with several dozen banks. Sometimes it makes more sense to leave cash alone than to manage each account daily.

27.3 Managing the Collection and Disbursement of Cash

A firm's cash balance as reported in its financial statements (*book cash* or *ledger cash*) is not the same thing as the balance shown in its bank account (*bank cash* or *collected bank cash*). The difference between bank cash and book cash is called **float** and represents the net effect of checks in the process of collection.

EXAMPLE 27.2

Float Imagine that General Mechanics, Inc. (GMI), currently has $100,000 on deposit with its bank. It purchases some raw materials, paying its vendors with a check written on July 8 for $100,000. The company's books (that is, ledger balances) are changed to show the $100,000 reduction in the cash balance. But the firm's bank will not find out about this check until it has been deposited at the vendor's bank and has been presented to the firm's bank for payment on, say, July 15. Until the check's presentation, the firm's bank cash is greater than its book cash, and it has *positive float*.

Position Prior to July 8

$$\text{Float} = \text{Firm's bank cash} - \text{Firm's book cash}$$
$$= \quad \$100,000 \quad - \quad \$100,000$$
$$= \quad 0$$

(continued)

Position from July 8 through July 14

$$\text{Disbursement float} = \text{Firm's bank cash} - \text{Firm's book cash}$$
$$= \$100,000 \qquad - \qquad 0$$
$$= \$100,000$$

While the check is *clearing*, GMI has a balance with the bank of $100,000 and can obtain the benefit of this cash. For example, the bank cash could be invested in marketable securities. Checks written by the firm generate *disbursement float*, causing an immediate decrease in book cash but no immediate change in bank cash.

EXAMPLE 27.3

More Float   Imagine that GMI receives a check from a customer for $100,000. Assume, as before, that the company has $100,000 deposited at its bank and has a *neutral float position*. It deposits the check and increases its book cash by $100,000 on November 8. However, the cash is not available to GMI until its bank has presented the check to the customer's bank and received $100,000 on, say, November 15. In the meantime, the cash position at GMI will reflect a collection float of $100,000.

Position Prior to November 8

$$\text{Float} = \text{Firm's bank cash} - \text{Firm's book cash}$$
$$= \$100,000 \quad - \quad \$100,000$$
$$= \quad 0$$

Position from November 8 through November 14

$$\text{Collection float} = \text{Firm's bank cash} - \text{Firm's book cash}$$
$$= \$100,000 \quad - \quad \$200,000$$
$$= -\$100,000$$

Checks received by the firm represent *collection float*, which increases book cash immediately but does not immediately change bank cash. The firm is helped by disbursement float and is hurt by collection float. The sum of disbursement float and collection float is *net float*.

A firm should be more concerned with net float and bank cash than with book cash. If a financial manager knows that a check will not clear for several days, he or she will be able to keep a lower cash balance at the bank than might be true otherwise. Good float management can generate a great deal of money. For example, suppose the average daily sales of Exxon are about $400 million. If Exxon speeds up the collection process or slows down the disbursement process by one day, it frees up $400 million, which can be invested in marketable securities. With an interest rate of 4 percent, this represents overnight interest of approximately $44,000 [= ($400 million/365) × 0.04].

Float management involves controlling the collection and disbursement of cash. The objective in cash collection is to reduce the lag between the time customers pay their bills and the time the checks are collected. The objective in cash disbursement is to slow down payments, thereby increasing the time between when checks are written and when checks are presented. In other words, collect early and pay late. Of course, to the extent that the firm succeeds in doing this, the customers and suppliers lose money, and the trade-off is the effect on the firm's relationship with them.

Collection float can be broken down into three parts: mail float, in-house processing float, and availability float:

1. *Mail float* is the part of the collection and disbursement process where checks are trapped in the postal system.

2. In-house processing float is the time it takes the receiver of a check to process the payment and deposit it in a bank for collection.

3. *Availability float* refers to the time required to clear a check through the banking system. The clearing process takes place using the Federal Reserve check collection service, using correspondent banks, or using local clearinghouses.

Float   A check for $1,000 is mailed from a customer on Monday, September 1. Because of mail, processing, and clearing delays, it is not credited as available cash in the firm's bank until the following Monday, seven days later. The float for this check is:

$$\text{Float} = \$1,000 \times 7 \text{ days} = \$7,000$$

Another check for $7,000 is mailed on September 1. It is available on the next day. The float for this check is:

$$\text{Float} = \$7,000 \times 1 \text{ day} = \$7,000$$

The measurement of float depends on the time lag and the dollars involved. The cost of float is an opportunity cost: The cash is unavailable for use while checks are tied up in the collection process. The cost of float can be determined by (1) estimating the average daily receipts, (2) calculating the average delay in obtaining the receipts, and (3) discounting the average daily receipts by the *delay-adjusted cost of capital.*

Average Float   Suppose that Concepts, Inc., has two receipts each month:

	Amount	Number of Days' Delay	Float
Item 1	$5,000,000	× 3 =	$15,000,000
Item 2	3,000,000	× 5 =	15,000,000
Total	$8,000,000		$30,000,000

Here is the average daily float over the month:

Average Daily Float

$$\frac{\text{Total float}}{\text{Total days}} = \frac{\$30,000,000}{30} = \$1,000,000$$

Another procedure we can use to calculate average daily float is to determine average daily receipts and multiply by the average daily delay:

Average Daily Receipts

$$\frac{\text{Total receipts}}{\text{Total days}} = \frac{\$8,000,000}{30} = \$266,666.67$$

$$\text{Weighted average delay} = (5/8) \times 3 + (3/8) \times 5$$

$$= 1.875 + 1.875 = 3.75 \text{ days}$$

$$\text{Average daily float} = \text{Average daily receipts} \times \text{Weighted average delay}$$

$$= \$266,666.67 \times 3.75 = \$1,000,000$$

EXAMPLE 27.6

Cost of Float   Suppose Concepts, Inc., has average daily receipts of $266,667. The float results in this amount being delayed 3.75 days. The present value of the delayed cash flow is:

$$V = \frac{\$266,667}{1 + R_B}$$

where R_B is the cost of debt capital for Concepts, adjusted to the relevant time frame. Suppose the annual cost of debt capital is 10 percent. Then:

$$R_B = 0.1 \times (3.75/365) = 0.00103$$

and

$$V = \frac{\$266,667}{1 + 0.00103} = \$266,392.62$$

Thus, the net present value of the delay float is $266,392.62 − $266,667 = − $274.38 per day. For a year, this is − $274.38 × 365 = − $100,148.70.

Accelerating Collections

The following is a depiction of the basic parts of the cash collection process:

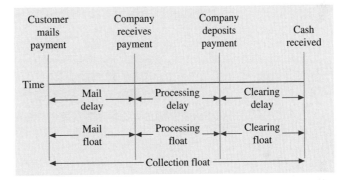

The total time in this process is made up of mailing time, check processing time, and check clearing time. The amount of time cash spends in each part of the cash collection process depends on where the firm's customers and banks are located and how efficient the firm is at collecting cash. Some of the techniques used to accelerate collections and reduce collection time are lockboxes, concentration banking, and wire transfers.

Lockboxes   The **lockbox** is the most widely used device to speed up collections of cash. It is a special post office box set up to intercept accounts receivable payments.

Figure 27.4 illustrates the lockbox system.[5] The collection process is started by customers mailing their checks to a post office box instead of sending them to the firm. The lockbox is maintained by a local bank and is typically located no more than several hundred miles away. Large corporations may maintain more than 20 lockboxes around the country. In the typical lockbox system, the local bank collects the lockbox checks from the post office several times a day. The bank deposits the checks directly to the firm's account. Details of the operation are recorded (in some computer-usable form) and sent to the firm.

---

[5]Two types of lockboxes are offered by banks. Wholesale lockboxes are used in processing a few large checks. Retail lockboxes are used for processing many smaller checks

Figure 27.4

Overview of Lockbox Processing

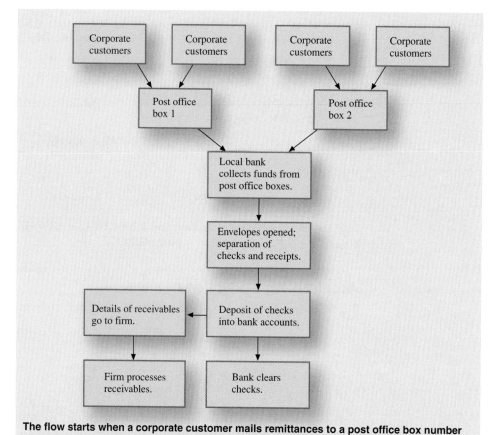

The flow starts when a corporate customer mails remittances to a post office box number instead of to the corporation. Several times a day the bank collects the lockbox receipts from the post office; the checks are then put into the company bank accounts.

A lockbox system reduces mailing time because checks are received at a nearby post office instead of at corporate headquarters. Lockboxes also reduce the firm's processing time because they reduce the time required for a corporation to physically handle receivables and to deposit checks for collection. A bank lockbox should enable a firm to get its receipts processed, deposited, and cleared faster than if it were to receive checks at its headquarters and deliver them itself to the bank for deposit and clearing.

Concentration Banking   Using lockboxes is one way firms can collect checks from customers and get them into deposit banks. Another way to speed up collection is to get the cash from the deposit banks to the firm's main bank more quickly. This is done by a method called **concentration banking**.

With a concentration banking system, the firm's sales offices are usually responsible for collecting and processing customer checks. The sales office deposits the checks into a local deposit bank account. Surplus funds are transferred from the deposit bank to the concentration bank. The purpose of concentration banking is to obtain customer checks from nearby receiving locations. Concentration banking reduces mailing time because the firm's sales office is usually nearer than corporate headquarters to the customer. Furthermore, bank clearing time will be reduced because the customer's check is usually drawn on a local bank. Figure 27.5 illustrates this process, where concentration banks are combined with lockboxes in a total cash management system.

Figure 27.5

**Lockboxes and
Concentration
Banks in a Cash
Management System**

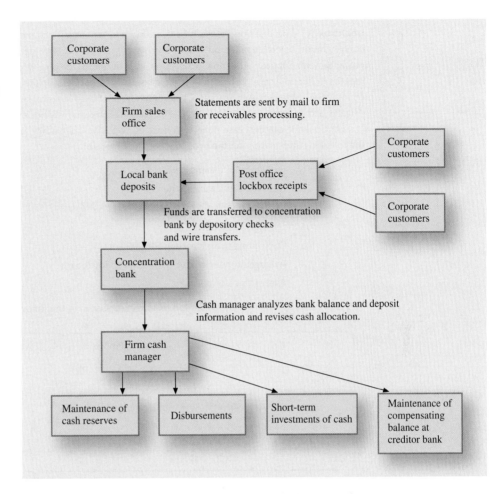

The corporate cash manager uses the pools of cash at the concentration bank for short-term investing or for some other purpose. The concentration banks usually serve as the source of short-term investments. They also serve as the focal point for transferring funds to disbursement banks.

Wire Transfers   After the customers' checks get into the local banking network, the objective is to transfer the surplus funds (funds in excess of required compensating balances) from the local deposit bank to the concentration bank. The fastest and most expensive way is by **wire transfer**.[6] Wire transfers take only a few minutes, and the cash becomes available to the firm upon receipt of a wire notice at the concentration bank. Wire transfers take place electronically, from one computer to another, and eliminate the mailing and check clearing times associated with other cash transfer methods.

Two wire services are available—Fedwire, the Federal Reserve wire service (operated by the Federal Reserve bank system) and CHIPS (Clearing House Interbank Payments System)—as well as the proprietary wire systems of the major investment banks.

---

[6]A slower and cheaper way is a depository transfer check. This is an unsigned, nonnegotiable check drawn on
the local collection bank and payable to the concentration bank.

Lockboxes   The decision to use a bank cash management service incorporating lockboxes and concentration banks depends on where a firm's customers are located and the speed of the U.S. postal system. Suppose Atlantic Corporation, located in Philadelphia, is considering a lockbox system. Its collection delay is currently eight days. It does business in the southwestern part of the country (New Mexico, Arizona, and California). The proposed lockbox system will be located in Los Angeles and operated by Pacific Bank. Pacific Bank has analyzed Atlantic's cash gathering system and has concluded it can decrease collection float by two days. Specifically, the bank has come up with the following information on the proposed lockbox system:

Reduction in mailing time	= 1.0 day
Reduction in clearing time	= 0.5 day
Reduction in firm's processing time	= 0.5 day
Total reduction	2.0 days
Daily interest on Treasury bills	= 0.03%
Average number of daily payments to lockboxes	= 200
Average size of payment	= $5,000

The cash flows for the current collection process are shown in the following cash flow time chart:

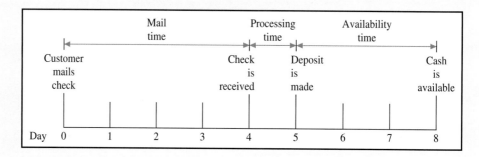

The cash flows for the lockbox collection operation will be as follows:

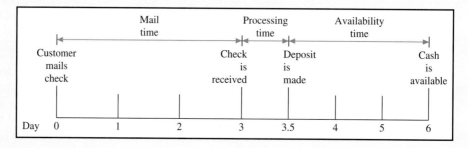

The average daily collections from the southwestern region are $1 million (= 200 × $5,000). Pacific Bank has agreed to operate a lockbox system for an annual fee of $20,000 and $0.30 per check processed.

On this basis the lockbox would increase the collected bank balance by $1 million × 2 = $2 million. The lockbox, in effect, releases $2 million to the firm by reducing processing, mailing, and clearing time by two days.

Atlantic Corporation can expect to realize a daily return of 0.0003 × $2 million = $600. The yearly savings would be $600 × 365 days = $219,000 under the lockbox system.

(continued)

Pacific Bank's charge for this lockbox service would be

Annual variable fee	365 days × 200 checks × $0.30 = $21,900
Annual fixed fee	$20,000
Total	$41,900

Because the return on released funds exceeds the lockbox system costs, Atlantic should employ Pacific Bank. (We should note, however, that this example has ignored the cost of moving funds into the concentration account.)

Delaying Disbursements

Accelerating collections is one method of cash management; paying more slowly is another. The cash disbursement process is illustrated in Figure 27.6. Techniques to slow down disbursement will attempt to increase mail time and check clearing time.

Disbursement Float ("Playing the Float Game")

Even though the cash balance at the bank may be $1 million, a firm's books may show only $500,000 because it has written $500,000 in payment checks. The disbursement float of $500,000 is available for the corporation to use until the checks are presented for payment. Float in terms of slowing down payment checks comes from mail delivery, check processing time, and collection of funds. This is illustrated in Figure 27.6. Disbursement float can be increased by writing a check on a geographically distant bank. For example, a New York supplier might be paid with checks drawn on a Los Angeles bank. This will increase the time required for the checks to clear through the banking system.

Figure 27.6

Cash Disbursement

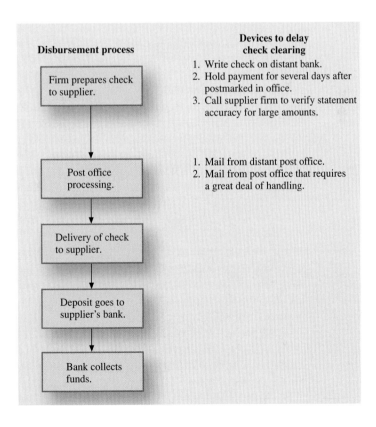

Zero-Balance Accounts

Some firms set up a **zero-balance account (ZBA)** to handle disbursement activity. The account has a zero balance as checks are written. As checks are presented to the zero-balance account for payment (causing a negative balance), funds are automatically transferred in from a central control account. The master account and the ZBA are located in the same bank. Thus, the transfer is automatic and involves only an accounting entry in the bank.

Drafts

Firms sometimes use drafts instead of checks. Drafts differ from checks because they are drawn not on a bank but on the issuer (the firm) and are payable by the issuer. The bank acts only as an agent, presenting the draft to the issuer for payment. When a draft is transmitted to a firm's bank for collection, the bank must present the draft to the issuing firm for acceptance before making payment. After the draft has been accepted, the firm must deposit the necessary cash to cover the payment. The use of drafts rather than checks allows a firm to keep lower cash balances in its disbursement accounts because cash does not need to be deposited until the drafts are presented for payment.

Ethical and Legal Questions

The cash manager must work with cash balances collected by the bank and not the firm's book balance, which reflects checks that have been deposited but not collected. If not, a cash manager could be drawing on uncollected cash as a source for making short-term investments. Most banks charge a penalty for use of uncollected funds. However, banks may not have good enough accounting and control procedures to be fully aware of the use of uncollected funds. This raises some ethical and legal questions for the firm.

In May 1985, Robert Fomon, chairman of E. F. Hutton, a large investment bank at the time, pleaded guilty to 2,000 charges of mail and wire fraud in connection with a scheme the firm had operated from 1980 to 1982. E. F. Hutton employees wrote checks totaling hundreds of millions of dollars in uncollected cash, which were invested in short-term money market assets. E. F. Hutton's systematic overdrafting of accounts is apparently not a widespread practice among corporations; and since the E. F. Hutton affair, firms have been much more careful in managing their cash accounts. Generally, firms are scrupulous in investing only the cash they actually have on hand. E. F. Hutton paid a $2 million fine, reimbursed the government (the U.S. Department of Justice) $750,000, and reserved $8 million for restitution to defrauded banks. We should emphasize that the case against E. F. Hutton was a case against not float management, but rather writing checks with no economic value other than to exploit float.

Electronic Data Interchange and Check 21: The End of Float?

Electronic data interchange (EDI) is a general term that refers to the growing practice of direct electronic information exchange between all types of businesses. One important use of EDI, often called financial EDI, or FEDI, is to electronically transfer financial information and funds between parties, thereby eliminating paper invoices, paper checks, mailing, and handling. For example, it is possible to arrange to have your checking account directly debited each month to pay many types of bills, and corporations now routinely directly deposit paychecks into employee accounts. More generally, EDI allows a seller to send a bill electronically to a buyer, thereby avoiding the mail. The buyer can then authorize payment, which also occurs electronically. Its bank then transfers the funds to the seller's account at a different bank. The net effect is that the length of time required to initiate and complete a business transaction is shortened considerably, and much of what we normally think of as float is sharply reduced or eliminated. As the use of FEDI increases (which it will), float management will evolve to focus much more on issues surrounding computerized information exchange and fund transfers.

On October 29, 2004, the Check Clearing Act for the 21st Century, also known as Check 21, took effect. Before Check 21, a bank receiving a check was required to send the physical check to the customer's bank before payment could be made. Now a bank can transmit an electronic image of the check to the customer's bank and receive payment immediately. Previously, an out-of-state check might take three days to clear, but with Check 21 the clearing time is typically one day, and often a check can clear the same day it is written. Thus, Check 21 promises to significantly reduce float.

27.4 Investing Idle Cash

If a firm has a temporary cash surplus, it can invest in short-term marketable securities. The market for short-term financial assets is called the *money market.* The maturity of short-term financial assets that trade in the money market is one year or less.

Most large firms manage their own short-term financial assets, transacting through banks and dealers. Some large firms and many small firms use money market funds. These are funds that invest in short-term financial assets for a management fee. The management fee is compensation for the professional expertise and diversification provided by the fund manager. Among the many money market mutual funds, some specialize in corporate customers. Banks also offer *sweep accounts*, where the bank takes all excess available funds at the close of each business day and invests them for the firm.

Firms have temporary cash surpluses for these reasons: to help finance seasonal or cyclical activities of the firm, to help finance planned expenditures of the firm, and to provide for unanticipated contingencies.

Seasonal or Cyclical Activities

Some firms have a predictable cash flow pattern. They have surplus cash flows during part of the year and deficit cash flows the rest of the year. For example, Toys "R" Us, a retail toy firm, has a seasonal cash flow pattern influenced by holiday sales. Such a firm may buy marketable securities when surplus cash flows occur and sell marketable securities when deficits occur. Of course bank loans are another short-term financing device. Figure 27.7 illustrates the use of bank loans and marketable securities to meet temporary financing needs.

Figure 27.7

Seasonal Cash Demands

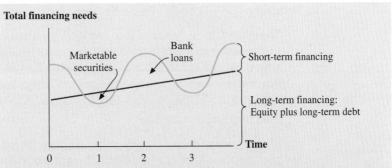

Time 1: A surplus cash flow exists. Seasonal demand for investing is low. The surplus cash flow is invested in short-term marketable securities. Time 2: A deficit cash flow exists. Seasonal demand for investing is high. The financial deficit is financed by selling marketable securities and by bank borrowing.

Planned Expenditures

Firms frequently accumulate temporary investments in marketable securities to provide the cash for a plant construction program, dividend payment, and other large expenditures. Thus, firms may issue bonds and stocks before the cash is needed, investing the proceeds in short-term marketable securities, and then selling the securities to finance the expenditures.

The important characteristics of short-term marketable securities are their maturity, default risk, marketability, and taxability.

Maturity   *Maturity* refers to the time period over which interest and principal payments are made. For a given change in the level of interest rates, the prices of longer-maturity securities will change more than those for shorter-maturity securities. As a consequence, firms that invest in long-maturity securities are accepting greater risk than firms that invest in securities with short-term maturities. This type of risk is usually called *interest rate risk.* Most firms limit their investments in marketable securities to those maturing in less than 90 days. Of course, the expected return on securities with short-term maturities is usually less than the expected return on securities with longer maturities.

Default Risk   *Default risk* refers to the probability that interest or principal will not be paid on the due date and in the promised amount. In previous chapters, we observed that various financial reporting agencies, such as Moody's and Standard & Poor's, compile and publish ratings of various corporate and public securities. These ratings are connected to default risk. Of course, some securities have negligible default risk, such as U.S. Treasury bills. Given the purposes of investing idle corporate cash, firms typically avoid investing in marketable securities with significant default risk.

Marketability   *Marketability* refers to how easy it is to convert an asset to cash. Sometimes marketability is referred to as *liquidity*. It has two characteristics:

1. *No price pressure effect*: If an asset can be sold in large amounts without changing the market price, it is marketable. Price pressure effects are those that come about when the price of an asset must be lowered to facilitate the sale.

2. *Time*: If an asset can be sold quickly at the existing market price, it is marketable. In contrast, a Renoir painting or antique desk appraised at $1 million will likely sell for much less if the owner must sell on short notice.

In general, marketability is the ability to sell an asset for its face market value quickly and in large amounts. Perhaps the most marketable of all securities are U.S. Treasury bills.

Taxability   Several kinds of securities have varying degrees of tax exemption:

1. The interest on the bonds of state and local governments is exempt from federal taxes and usually from the state and local taxes where the bonds are issued. Pretax expected returns on state and local bonds must be lower than on similar taxable investments and therefore are more attractive to corporations in high marginal tax brackets.

2. Seventy percent of the dividend income on preferred and common stock is exempt from corporate income taxes.

The market price of securities will reflect the total demand and supply of tax influences. The position of the firm may be different from that of the market.

Different Types of Money Market Securities

Money market securities are generally highly marketable and short term. They usually have low risk of default. They are issued by the U.S. government (for example, U.S. Treasury bills), domestic and foreign banks (for example, certificates of deposit), and business corporations (commercial paper, for example).

U.S. Treasury bills are obligations of the U.S. government that mature in 90, 180, 270, or 360 days. They are pure discount securities. The 90-day and 180-day bills are sold by auction every week, and 270-day and 360-day bills are sold every month.

U.S. Treasury notes and bonds have original maturities of more than one year. They are interest-bearing securities. The interest is exempt from state and local taxes.

Federal agency securities are securities issued by corporations and agencies created by the U.S. government, such as the Federal Home Loan Bank Board and the Government National Mortgage Association (*Ginnie Mae*). The interest rates on agency issues are higher than those on comparable U.S. Treasury issues. This is true because agency issues are not as marketable as U.S. Treasury issues, and they have more default risk.

Short-term tax exempts are short-term securities issued by states, municipalities, local housing agencies, and urban renewal agencies. They have more default risk than U.S. Treasury issues and are less marketable. The interest is exempt from federal income tax. As a consequence, the pretax yield on tax exempts is lower than those on comparable securities, such as U.S. Treasury bills.

Commercial paper refers to short-term securities issued by finance companies, banks, and corporations. Commercial paper typically is unsecured. Maturities range from a few weeks to 270 days. There is no active secondary market in commercial paper. As a consequence, their marketability is low. (However, firms that issue commercial paper will directly repurchase before maturity.) The default risk of commercial paper depends on the financial strength of the issuer. Moody's and Standard & Poor's publish quality ratings for commercial paper.

Certificates of deposit (CDs) are short-term loans to commercial banks. There are active markets in CDs of 3-month, 6-month, 9-month, and 12-month maturities.

Repurchase agreements are sales of government securities (for example, U.S. Treasury bills) by a bank or securities dealer with an agreement to repurchase. An investor typically buys some Treasury securities from a bond dealer and simultaneously agrees to sell them back at a later date at a specified higher price. Repurchase agreements are usually very short term—overnight to a few days.

Eurodollar CDs are deposits of dollars with foreign banks.

Banker's acceptances are time drafts (orders to pay) issued by a business firm (usually an importer) that have been accepted by a bank that guarantees payment.

Summary and Conclusions

The chapter discussed how firms manage cash.

1. A firm holds cash to conduct transactions and to compensate banks for the various services they render.

2. The optimal amount of cash for a firm to hold depends on the opportunity cost of holding cash and the uncertainty of future cash inflows and outflows. The Baumol model and the Miller–Orr model are two transaction models that provide rough guidelines for determining the optimal cash position.

3. The firm can use a variety of procedures to manage the collection and disbursement of cash to speed up the collection of cash and slow down payments. Some methods to speed collection are lockboxes, concentration banking, and wire transfers. The financial manager must always work with collected company cash balances and not with the company's book balance. To do otherwise is to use the bank's cash without the bank knowing it, raising ethical and legal questions.

4. Because of seasonal and cyclical activities, to help finance planned expenditures, or as a reserve for unanticipated needs, firms temporarily find themselves with cash surpluses. The money market offers a variety of possible vehicles for parking this idle cash.

Concept Questions

1. **Cash Management**   Is it possible for a firm to have too much cash? Why would shareholders care if a firm accumulates large amounts of cash?

2. **Cash Management**   What options are available to a firm if it believes it has too much cash? How about too little?

3. **Agency Issues**   Are stockholders and creditors likely to agree on how much cash a firm should keep on hand?

4. **Motivations for Holding Cash**   In the chapter opening, we discussed the enormous cash positions of several companies. Why would firms like these hold such large quantities of cash?

5. **Cash Management versus Liquidity Management**   What is the difference between cash management and liquidity management?

6. **Short-Term Investments**   Why is a preferred stock with a dividend tied to short-term interest rates an attractive short-term investment for corporations with excess cash?

7. **Collection and Disbursement Floats**   Which would a firm prefer: a net collection float or a net disbursement float? Why?

8. **Float**   Suppose a firm has a book balance of £2 million. At the automatic teller machine (ATM) the cash manager finds out that the bank balance is £2.5 million. What is the situation here? If this is an ongoing situation, what ethical dilemma arises?

9. **Short-Term Investments**   For each of the short-term marketable securities given here, provide an example of the potential disadvantages the investment has for meeting a corporation's cash management goals:
    a. U.S. Treasury bills.
    b. Ordinary preferred stock.
    c. Negotiable certificates of deposit (NCDs).
    d. Commercial paper.
    e. Revenue anticipation notes.
    f. Repurchase agreements.

10. **Agency Issues**   It is sometimes argued that excess cash held by a firm can aggravate agency problems (discussed in Chapter 1) and, more generally, reduce incentives for shareholder wealth maximization. How would you frame the issue here?

11. **Use of Excess Cash**   One option a firm usually has with any excess cash is to pay its suppliers more quickly. What are the advantages and disadvantages of this use of excess cash?

12. **Use of Excess Cash**   Another option usually available is to reduce the firm's outstanding debt. What are the advantages and disadvantages of this use of excess cash?

13. **Float**   An unfortunately common practice goes like this (warning—don't try this at home): Suppose you are out of money in your checking account; however, your local grocery store will, as a convenience to you as a customer, cash a check for you. So you cash a check for €200. Of course, this check will bounce unless you do something. To prevent this, you go to the grocery the next day and cash another check for €200. You take this €200 and deposit it. You repeat this process every day, and in doing so you make sure that no checks bounce. Eventually, manna from heaven arrives (perhaps in the form of money from home), and you are able to cover your outstanding checks.

To make it interesting, suppose you are absolutely certain that no checks will bounce along the way. Assuming this is true, and ignoring any question of legality (what we have described is probably illegal check kiting), is there anything unethical about this? If you say yes, then why? In particular, who is harmed?

14. **Interpreting Miller–Orr**   Based on the Miller–Orr model, describe what will happen to the lower limit, the upper limit, and the spread (the distance between the two) if the variation in net cash flow grows. Give an intuitive explanation for why this happens. What happens if the variance drops to zero?

Questions and Problems

BASIC
(Questions 1–13)

1. **Changes in Target Cash Balances**   Indicate the likely impact of each of the following on a company's target cash balance. Use the letter *I* to denote an increase and *D* to denote a decrease. Briefly explain your reasoning in each case.
   a. Commissions charged by brokers decrease.
   b. Interest rates paid on money market securities rise.
   c. The compensating balance requirement of a bank is raised.
   d. The firm's credit rating improves.
   e. The cost of borrowing increases.
   f. Direct fees for banking services are established.

2. **Using the Baumol Model**   Given the following information, calculate the target cash balance using the Baumol model:

Annual interest rate	7%
Fixed order cost	AUD 10
Total cash needed	AUD 10,000

   How do you interpret your answer?

3. **Opportunity versus Trading Costs**   White Whale Corporation has an average daily cash balance of $400. Total cash needed for the year is $25,000. The interest rate is 5 percent, and replenishing the cash costs $7 each time. What are the opportunity cost of holding cash, the trading cost, and the total cost? What do you think of White Whale's strategy?

4. **Costs and the Baumol Model**   Debit and Credit Bookkeepers needs a total of $4,000 in cash during the year for transactions and other purposes. Whenever cash runs low, it sells off $300 in securities and transfers the cash in. The interest rate is 7 percent per year, and selling off securities costs $25 per sale.
   a. What is the opportunity cost under the current policy? The trading cost? With no additional calculations, would you say that Debit and Credit keeps too much or too little cash? Explain.
   b. What is the target cash balance derived using the Baumol model?

5. **Calculating Net Float**   Each business day, on average, a company writes checks totaling €25,000 to pay its suppliers. The usual clearing time for the checks is four days. Meanwhile, the company is receiving payments from its customers each day, in the form of checks, totaling €40,000. The cash from the payments is available to the firm after two days.
   a. Calculate the company's disbursement float, collection float, and net float.
   b. How would your answer to part (a) change if the collected funds were available in one day instead of two?

6. **Costs of Float**   Jagriti Prakashan receives an average of INR 9,000 in checks per day. The delay in clearing is typically four days. The current interest rate is .025 percent per day.
   a. What is the company's float?
   b. What is the most Jagriti Prakashan should be willing to pay today to eliminate its float entirely?
   c. What is the highest daily fee the company should be willing to pay to eliminate its float entirely?

7. **Float and Weighted Average Delay**   Your neighbor goes to the post office once a month and picks up two checks, one for $16,000 and one for $2,500. The larger check takes four days to clear after it is deposited; the smaller one takes five days.
   a. What is the total float for the month?
   b. What is the average daily float?
   c. What are the average daily receipts and weighted average delay?

8. **NPV and Collection Time**   Your firm has an average receipt size of €80. A bank has approached you concerning a lockbox service that will decrease your total collection time by two days. You typically receive 12,000 checks per day. The daily interest rate is .016 percent. If the bank charges a fee of €190 per day, should the lockbox project be accepted? What would the net annual savings be if the service were adopted?

9. **Using Weighted Average Delay**   A mail-order firm processes 5,000 checks per month. Of these, 65 percent are for £50 and 35 percent are for £70. The £50 checks are delayed two days on average; the £70 checks are delayed three days on average.
   a. What is the average daily collection float? How do you interpret your answer?
   b. What is the weighted average delay? Use the result to calculate the average daily float.
   c. How much should the firm be willing to pay to eliminate the float?
   d. If the interest rate is 8 percent per year, calculate the daily cost of the float.
   e. How much should the firm be willing to pay to reduce the weighted average float by 2 days?

10. **Value of Lockboxes**   Ghiji Xua Manufacturing is investigating a lockbox system to reduce its collection time. It has determined the following:

Average number of payments per day	400
Average value of payment	CNY 1,400
Variable lockbox fee (per transaction)	CNY .75
Daily interest rate on money market securities	.02%

The total collection time will be reduced by three days if the lockbox system is adopted.
   a. What is the PV of adopting the system?
   b. What is the NPV of adopting the system?
   c. What is the net cash flow per day from adopting? Per check?

11. **Lockboxes and Collections**   It takes Cookie Cutter Modular Homes, Inc., about six days to receive and deposit checks from customers. Cookie Cutter's management is considering a lockbox system to reduce the firm's collection times. It is expected that the lockbox system will reduce receipt and deposit times to three days total. Average daily collections are $140,000, and the required rate of return is 9 percent per year.
   a. What is the reduction in outstanding cash balances as a result of implementing the lockbox system?
   b. What dollar return could be earned on these savings?
   c. What is the maximum monthly charge Cookie Cutter should pay for this lockbox system?

12. **Value of Delay**   No More Pencils, Inc., disburses checks every two weeks that average ¥20,000,000 and take seven days to clear. How much interest can the company earn annually if it delays transfer of funds from an interest-bearing account that pays .02 percent per day for these seven days? Ignore the effects of compounding interest.

13. **NPV and Reducing Float**   Zekeriya Refiners & Bottlers has an agreement with National Bank whereby the bank handles €8 million in collections a day and requires a €500,000 compensating balance. Zekeriya is contemplating canceling the agreement and dividing its eastern region so that two other banks will handle its business. Banks *A* and *B* will each handle €4 million of collections a day, and each requires a compensating balance of €300,000. Zekeriya's financial management expects that collections will be accelerated by one day if the eastern region is divided. Should the company proceed with the new system? What will be the annual net savings? Assume that the T-bill rate is 5 percent annually.

INTERMEDIATE
(Questions 14–21)

14. **Determining Optimal Cash Balances**   The Joe Elvis Company is currently holding $700,000 in cash. It projects that over the next year its cash outflows will exceed cash inflows by $360,000 per month. How much of the current cash holding should be retained, and how much should be used to increase the company's holdings of marketable securities? Each time

these securities are bought or sold through a broker, the company pays a fee of $500. The annual interest rate on money market securities is 6.5 percent. After the initial investment of excess cash, how many times during the next 12 months will securities be sold?

15. **Using Miller–Orr**   Chen & Chen Ltd. has a fixed cost associated with buying and selling marketable securities of KRW 100. The interest rate is currently .021 percent per day, and the firm has estimated that the standard deviation of its daily net cash flows is KRW 75. Management has set a lower limit of KRW 1,100 on cash holdings. Calculate the target cash balance and upper limit using the Miller–Orr model. Describe how the system will work.

16. **Using Miller–Orr**   The variance of the daily cash flows for the Pele Bicycle Shop is BRL 960,000. The opportunity cost to the firm of holding cash is 7 percent per year. What should be the target cash level and the upper limit if the tolerable lower limit has been established as BRL 150,000? The fixed cost of buying and selling securities is BRL 500 per transaction.

17. **Using Baumol**   All Night Corporation has determined that its target cash balance if it uses the Baumol model is LKR 2,200. The total cash needed for the year is LKR 21,000, and the order cost is LKR 10. What interest rate must All Night be using?

18. **Lockboxes and Collection Time**   Bird's Eye Treehouses, Inc., a Kentucky company, has determined that a majority of its customers are located in the Pennsylvania area. It therefore is considering using a lockbox system offered by a bank located in Pittsburgh. The bank has estimated that use of the system will reduce collection time by two days. Based on the following information, should the lockbox system be adopted?

Average number of payments per day	600
Average value of payment	$1,100
Variable lockbox fee (per transaction)	$.35
Annual interest rate on money market securities	6.0%

How would your answer change if there were a fixed charge of $1,000 per year in addition to the variable charge?

19. **Calculating Transactions Required**   Ismail Brothers, a large fertilizer distributor based in Islamabad, is planning to use a lockbox system to speed up collections from its customers located in Peshawar. A bank will provide this service for an annual fee of PKR 25,000 plus 10 paise per transaction. The estimated reduction in collection and processing time is one day. If the average customer payment in this region is PKR 5,500, how many customers each day, on average, are needed to make the system profitable for Ismail Brothers? Treasury bills are currently yielding 5 percent per year.

20. **Baumol Model**   Mr. Numata, CFO of Purple Rain Co., concluded from the Baumol model that the optimal cash balance for the firm is ¥10 million. The annual interest rate on marketable securities is 5.8 percent. The fixed cost of selling securities to replenish cash is ¥5,000. Purple Rain's cash flow pattern is well approximated by the Baumol model. What can you infer about Purple Rain's average weekly cash disbursement?

21. **Miller–Orr Model**   Gold Star Co. and Silver Star Co. both manage their cash flows according to the Miller–Orr model. Gold Star's daily cash flow is controlled between $95,000 and $205,000, whereas Silver Star's daily cash flow is controlled between $120,000 and $230,000. The annual interest rates Gold Star and Silver Star can get are 5.8 percent and 6.1 percent, respectively, and the costs per transaction of trading securities are $2,800 and $2,500, respectively.
   a. What are their respective target cash balances?
   b. Which firm's daily cash flow is more volatile?

Appendix 27A Adjustable Rate Preferred Stock, Auction Rate Preferred Stock, and Floating-Rate Certificates of Deposit.

To access the appendix for this chapter, please visit **www.mhhe.com/rwj**.

Mini Case

Cash Management at Richmond Corporation

Richmond Corporation was founded 20 years ago by its president, Daniel Richmond. The company originally began as a mail-order company but has grown rapidly in recent years, in large part due to its Web site. Because of the wide geographical dispersion of the company's customers, it currently employs a lockbox system with collection centers in San Francisco, St. Louis, Atlanta, and Boston.

Steve Dennis, the company's treasurer, has been examining the current cash collection policies. On average, each lockbox center handles $130,000 in payments each day. The company's current policy is to invest these payments in short-term marketable securities daily at the collection center banks. Every two weeks the investment accounts are swept, and the proceeds are wire-transferred to Richmond's headquarters in Dallas to meet the company's payroll. The investment accounts each pay 0.015 percent per day, and the wire transfers cost 0.15 percent of the amount transferred.

Steve has been approached by Third National Bank, located just outside Dallas, about the possibility of setting up a concentration banking system for Richmond Corp. Third National will accept the lockbox centers' daily payments via automated clearinghouse (ACH) transfers in lieu of wire transfers. The ACH-transferred funds will not be available for use for one day. Once cleared, the funds will be deposited in a short-term account, which will also yield 0.015 percent per day. Each ACH transfer will cost $700. Daniel has asked Steve to determine which cash management system will be the best for the company. Steve has asked you, his assistant, to answer the following questions:

1. What is Richmond Corporation's total net cash flow from the current lockbox system available to meet payroll?

2. Under the terms outlined by Third National Bank, should the company proceed with the concentration banking system?

3. What cost of ACH transfers would make the company indifferent between the two systems?

28

Credit Management

In any sale, one of the most important decisions made by the seller is whether to grant credit and, if credit is granted, the terms of the credit sale. As with many other decisions, there is variation from company to company, but credit policies tend to be similar within industries.

One way to examine a company's credit policy is to look at the days' sales in receivables, or the length of time from the sale until the company is paid. In early 2006, the receivables period for a typical firm in the S&P 500 index was about 35 days, or a little over a month. For some firms, the period is much shorter. For example, retailer Wal-Mart's was about two days and grocer Kroger's was about four days. Neither firm routinely grants credit to its customers, so these numbers come as no surprise. In contrast, in the pharmaceutical business, credit periods are longer. Pfizer, for example, had a credit period of about 68 days in 2006.

In this chapter, we examine how a firm sets its credit policy, including when to grant credit and for how long.

28.1 Terms of the Sale

The *terms of sale* refer to the period for which credit is granted, the cash discount, and the type of credit instrument. For example, suppose a customer is granted credit with terms of 2/10, net 30. This means that the customer has 30 days from the **invoice** date within which to pay.[1] In addition, a cash discount of 2 percent from the stated sales price is to be given if payment is made in 10 days. If the stated terms are net 60, the customer has 60 days from the invoice date to pay and no discount is offered for early payment.

When sales are seasonal, a firm might use seasonal dating. O. M. Scott and Sons is a manufacturer of lawn and garden products with a seasonal dating policy that is tied to the growing season. Payments for winter shipments of fertilizer might be due in the spring or summer. A firm offering 3/10, net 60, May 1 dating, is making the effective invoice date May 1. The stated amount must be paid on June 30, regardless of when the sale is made. The cash discount of 3 percent can be taken until May 10.

An account receivable is created when credit is granted; an account payable is created when a firm receives credit. These accounts are illustrated in Figure 28.1. The term "trade credit" refers to credit granted to other firms.

Credit Period

Credit periods vary among different industries. For example, a jewelry store may sell diamond engagement rings for 5/30, net 4 months. A food wholesaler, selling fresh fruit

---

[1] An *invoice* is a bill written by a seller of goods or services and submitted to the buyer. The invoice date is usually the same as the shipping date.

Figure 28.1

Trade Credit

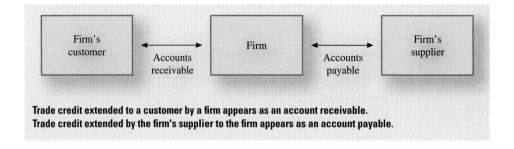

Trade credit extended to a customer by a firm appears as an account receivable.
Trade credit extended by the firm's supplier to the firm appears as an account payable.

Figure 28.2

The Cash Flows of Granting Credit

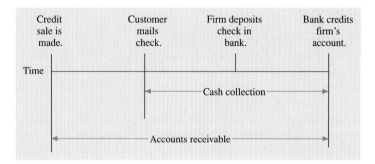

and produce, might use net 7. Generally, a firm must consider three factors in setting a credit period:

1. *The probability that the customer will not pay*: A firm whose customers are in high-risk businesses may find itself offering restrictive credit terms.

2. *The size of the account*: If the account is small, the credit period will be shorter. Small accounts are more costly to manage, and small customers are less important.

3. *The extent to which the goods are perishable*: If the collateral values of the goods are low and cannot be sustained for long periods, less credit will be granted.

Lengthening the credit period effectively reduces the price paid by the customer. Generally, this increases sales. Figure 28.2 illustrates the cash flows from granting credit.

Cash Discounts

Cash discounts are often part of the terms of sale. One reason they are offered is to speed up the collection of receivables. The firm must trade this off against the cost of the discount.

EXAMPLE 28.1

Credit Policy   Edward Manalt, the chief financial officer of Ruptbank Company, is considering the request of the company's largest customer, who wants to take a 3 percent discount for payment within 20 days on a $10,000 purchase. In other words, he intends to pay $9,700 [= $10,000 × (1 − 0.03)]. Normally, this customer pays in 30 days with no discount. The cost of debt capital for Ruptbank is 10 percent. Edward has worked out the cash flow implications illustrated in Figure 28.3. He assumes that the time required to cash the check when the customer receives it is the same under both credit arrangements. He has calculated the present value of the two proposals:

Current Policy

$$PV = \frac{\$10,000}{1 + (0.1 \times 30/365)} = \$9,918.48$$

(continued)

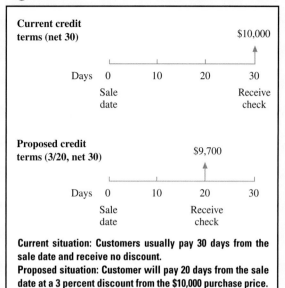

Figure 28.3   **Cash Flows for Different Credit Terms**

Current credit terms (net 30)

$10,000

Days   0   10   20   30

Sale date   Receive check

Proposed credit terms (3/20, net 30)

$9,700

Days   0   10   20   30

Sale date   Receive check

Current situation: Customers usually pay 30 days from the sale date and receive no discount.
Proposed situation: Customer will pay 20 days from the sale date at a 3 percent discount from the $10,000 purchase price.

Proposed Policy

$$PV = \frac{\$9,700}{1 + (0.1 \times 20/365)} = \$9,647.14$$

His calculation shows that granting the discount would cost the Ruptbank firm $271.34 (= $9,918.48 − $9,647.14) in present value. Consequently, Ruptbank is better off with the current credit arrangement.

In the previous example, we implicitly assumed that granting credit had no side effects. However, the decision to grant credit may generate higher sales and involve a different cost structure. The next example illustrates the impact of changes in the level of sales and costs in the credit decision.

EXAMPLE 28.2

More Credit Policy   Suppose that Ruptbank Company has variable costs of $0.50 per $1 of sales. If offered a discount of 3 percent, customers will increase their order size by 10 percent. This new information is shown in Figure 28.4. That is, the customer will increase the order size to $11,000 and, with the 3 percent discount, will remit $10,670 [= $11,000 × (1 − 0.03)] to Ruptbank in 20 days. It will cost more to fill the larger order because variable costs are $5,500. The net present values are worked out here:

Current Policy

$$NPV = -\$5,000 + \frac{\$10,000}{1 + (0.1 \times 30/365)} = \$4,918.48$$

Proposed Policy

$$NPV = -\$5,500 + \frac{\$10,670}{1 + (0.1 \times 20/365)} = \$5,111.85$$

Now it is clear that the firm is better off with the proposed credit policy. This increase is the net effect of several different factors including the larger initial costs, the earlier receipt of the cash inflows, the increased sales level, and the discount.

(continued)

Figure 28.4   **Cash Flows for Different Credit Terms: The Impact of New Sales and Costs**

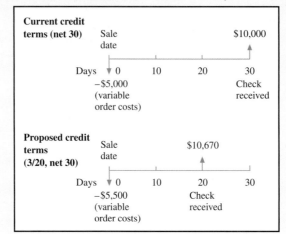

Credit Instruments

Most credit is offered on *open account.* This means that the only formal **credit instrument** is the invoice, which is sent with the shipment of goods, and which the customer signs as evidence that the goods have been received. Afterward, the firm and its customers record the exchange on their accounting books.

At times, the firm may require that the customer sign a *promissory note* or IOU. This is used when the order is large and when the firm anticipates a problem in collections. Promissory notes can eliminate controversies later about the existence of a credit agreement.

One problem with promissory notes is that they are signed after delivery of the goods. One way to obtain a credit commitment from a customer before the goods are delivered is through the use of a *commercial draft.* The selling firm typically writes a commercial draft calling for the customer to pay a specific amount by a specified date. The draft is then sent to the customer's bank with the shipping invoices. The bank has the buyer sign the draft before turning over the invoices. The goods can then be shipped to the buyer. If immediate payment is required, it is called a *sight draft.* Here, funds must be turned over to the bank before the goods are shipped.

Frequently, even a signed draft is not enough for the seller. In this case she might demand that the banker pay for the goods and collect the money from the customer. When the banker agrees to do so in writing, the document is called a *banker's acceptance.* That is, the banker *accepts* responsibility for payment. Because banks generally are well-known and well-respected institutions, the banker's acceptance becomes a liquid instrument. In other words, the seller can then sell (*discount*) the banker's acceptance in the secondary market.

A firm can also use a *conditional sales contract* as a credit instrument. This is an arrangement where the firm retains legal ownership of the goods until the customer has completed payment. Conditional sales contracts usually are paid off in installments and have interest costs built into them.

28.2   The Decision to Grant Credit: Risk and Information

Locust Industries has been in existence for two years. It is one of several successful firms that develop computer programs. The present financial managers have set out two alternative credit strategies: The firm can offer credit, or the firm can refuse credit.

Suppose Locust has determined that if it offers no credit to its customers, it can sell its existing computer software for $50 per program. It estimates that the costs to produce a typical computer program are $20 per program.

The alternative is to offer credit. In this case, customers of Locust will pay one period later. With some probability, Locust has determined that if it offers credit, it can charge higher prices and expect higher sales.

Strategy 1: Refuse Credit   If Locust refuses to grant credit, cash flows will not be delayed, and period 0 net cash flows, NCF, will be:

$$P_0 Q_0 - C_0 Q_0 = \text{NCF}$$

The subscripts denote the time when the cash flows are incurred, where:

$P_0 = $ Price per unit received at time 0.

$C_0 = $ Cost per unit paid at time 0.

$Q_0 = $ Quantity sold at time 0.

The net cash flows at period 1 are zero, and the net present value to Locust of refusing credit will simply be the period 0 net cash flow:

$$\text{NPV} = \text{NCF}$$

For example, if credit is not granted and $Q_0 = 100$, the NPV can be calculated as:

$$(\$50 \times 100) - (\$20 \times 100) = \$3,000$$

Strategy 2: Offer Credit   Alternatively, let us assume that Locust grants credit to all customers for one period. The factors that influence the decision are listed here:

	Strategy 1 Refuse Credit	Strategy 2 Offer Credit
Price per unit	$P_0 = \$50$	$P_0' = \$50$
Quantity sold	$Q_0 = 100$	$Q_0' = 200$
Cost per unit	$C_0 = \$20$	$C_0' = \$25$
Probability of payment	$h = 1$	$h = 0.90$
Credit period	0	1 period
Discount rate	0	$R_B = 0.01$

The prime (') denotes the variables under the second strategy. If the firm offers credit and the new customers pay, the firm will receive revenues of $P_0' Q_0'$ one period hence, but its costs, $C_0' Q_0'$, are incurred in period 0. If new customers do not pay, the firm incurs costs $C_0' Q_0'$ and receives no revenues. The probability that customers will pay, h, is 0.90 in the example. Quantity sold is higher with credit because new customers are attracted. The cost per unit is also higher with credit because of the costs of operating a credit policy.

The expected cash flows for each policy are set out as follows:

	Expected Cash Flows	
	Time 0	Time 1
Refuse credit	$P_0 Q_0 - C_0 Q_0$	0
Offer credit	$-C_0' Q_0'$	$h \times P_0' Q_0'$

Note that granting credit produces delayed expected cash inflows equal to $h \times P_0'Q_0'$. The costs are incurred immediately and require no discounting. The net present value if credit is offered is:

$$\text{NPV(offer)} = \frac{h \times P_0'Q_0'}{1 + R_B} - C_0'Q_0'$$

$$= \frac{0.9 \times \$50 \times 200}{1.01} - \$5,000 = \$3,910.89$$

Locust's decision should be to adopt the proposed credit policy. The NPV of granting credit is higher than that of refusing credit. This decision is very sensitive to the probability of payment. If it turns out that the probability of payment is 81 percent, Locust Software is indifferent to whether it grants credit or not. In this case, the NPV of granting credit is $3,000, which we previously found to be the NPV of not granting credit:

$$\$3,000 = h \times \frac{\$50 \times 200}{1.01} - \$5,000$$

$$\$8,000 = h \times \frac{\$50 \times 200}{1.01}$$

$$h = 80.8\%$$

The decision to grant credit depends on four factors:

1. The delayed revenues from granting credit, $P_0'Q_0'$.
2. The immediate costs of granting credit, $C_0'Q_0'$.
3. The probability of payment, h.
4. The appropriate required rate of return for delayed cash flows, R_B.

The Value of New Information about Credit Risk

Obtaining a better estimate of the probability that a customer will default can lead to a better decision. How can a firm determine when to acquire new information about the creditworthiness of its customers?

It may be sensible for Locust to determine which of its customers are most likely not to pay. The overall probability of nonpayment is 10 percent. But credit checks by an independent firm show that 90 percent of Locust's customers (computer stores) have been profitable over the last five years and that these customers have never defaulted on payments. The less profitable customers are much more likely to default. In fact, 100 percent of the less profitable customers have defaulted on previous obligations.

Locust would like to avoid offering credit to the deadbeats. Consider its projected number of customers per year of $Q_0' = 200$ if credit is granted. Of these customers, 180 have been profitable over the last five years and have never defaulted on past obligations. The remaining 20 have not been profitable. Locust Software expects that all of these less profitable customers will default. This information is set out here:

Type of Customer	Number	Probability of Nonpayment	Expected Number of Defaults
Profitable	180	0%	0
Less profitable	20	100	20
Total customers	200	10%	20

Figure 28.5

Future Sales and the Credit Decision

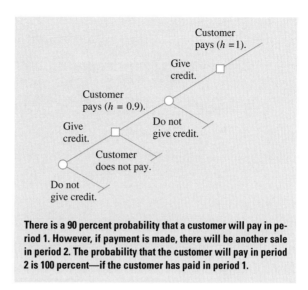

There is a 90 percent probability that a customer will pay in period 1. However, if payment is made, there will be another sale in period 2. The probability that the customer will pay in period 2 is 100 percent—if the customer has paid in period 1.

The NPV of granting credit to the customers who default is:

$$\frac{hP_0'Q_0'}{1 + R_B} - C_0'Q_0' = \frac{0 \times \$50 \times 20}{1.01} - \$25 \times 20 = -\$500$$

This is the cost of providing them with the software. If Locust can identify these customers without cost, it would certainly deny them credit.

In fact, it actually costs Locust $3 per customer to figure out whether a customer has been profitable over the last five years. The expected payoff of the credit check on its 200 customers is then:

$$\begin{array}{ccc} \text{Gain from not} & & \text{Cost of} \\ \text{extending credit} & - & \text{credit checks} \\ \$500 & - & \$3 \times 200 \end{array} = -\$100$$

For Locust, credit is not worth checking. It would need to pay $600 to avoid a $500 loss.

Future Sales

Up to this point, Locust has not considered the possibility that offering credit will permanently increase the level of sales in future periods (beyond next month). In addition, payment and nonpayment patterns in the current period will provide credit information that is useful for the next period. These two factors should be analyzed.

In the case of Locust, there is a 90 percent probability that the customer will pay in period 1. But, if payment is made, there will be another sale in period 2. The probability that the customer will pay in period 2, if the customer has paid in period 1, is 100 percent. Locust can refuse to offer credit in period 2 to customers that have refused to pay in period 1. This is diagrammed in Figure 28.5.

28.3 Optimal Credit Policy

So far, we have discussed how to compute net present value for two alternative credit policies. However, we have not discussed the optimal amount of credit. At the optimal amount of credit, the incremental cash flows from increased sales are exactly equal to the carrying costs from the increase in accounts receivable.

Figure 28.6

The Costs of Granting Credit

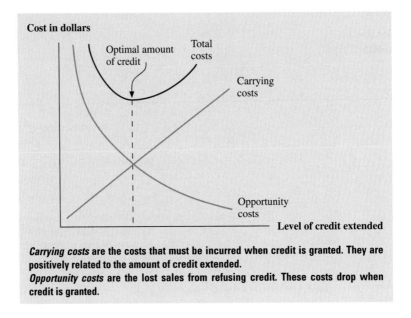

Carrying costs are the costs that must be incurred when credit is granted. They are positively related to the amount of credit extended.
Opportunity costs are the lost sales from refusing credit. These costs drop when credit is granted.

Consider a firm that does not currently grant credit. This firm has no bad debts, no credit department, and relatively few customers. Now consider another firm that grants credit. This firm has lots of customers, a credit department, and a bad debt expense account.

It is useful to think of the decision to grant credit in terms of carrying costs and opportunity costs:

1. *Carrying costs* are the costs associated with granting credit and making an investment in receivables. Carrying costs include the delay in receiving cash, the losses from bad debts, and the costs of managing credit.

2. *Opportunity costs* are the lost sales from refusing to offer credit. These costs drop as credit is granted.

We represent these costs in Figure 28.6.

The sum of the carrying costs and the opportunity costs of a particular credit policy is called the *total credit cost curve*. A point is identified as the minimum of the total credit cost curve. If the firm extends more credit than the minimum, the additional net cash flow from new customers will not cover the carrying costs of this investment in receivables.

The concept of optimal credit policy in the context of modern principles of finance should be somewhat analogous to the concept of the optimal capital structure discussed earlier in the text. In perfect financial markets, there should be no optimal credit policy. Alternative amounts of credit for a firm should not affect the value of the firm. Thus, the decision to grant credit would be a matter of indifference to financial managers.

Just as with optimal capital structure, we could expect taxes, monopoly power, bankruptcy costs, and agency costs to be important in determining an optimal credit policy in a world of imperfect financial markets. For example, customers in high tax brackets would be better off borrowing and taking advantage of cash discounts offered by firms than would customers in low tax brackets. Corporations in low tax brackets would be less able to offer credit because borrowing would be relatively more expensive than for firms in high tax brackets.

In general, a firm will extend trade credit if it has a comparative advantage in doing so. Trade credit is likely to be advantageous if the selling firm has a cost advantage over other

The Decision to Grant Credit

Trade credit is more likely to be granted by the selling firm if

1. The selling firm has a cost advantage over other lenders.

    Example: The American Manufacturing Co. produces widgets. In a default, it is easier for the American Manufacturing Co. to repossess widgets and resell them than for a finance company to arrange for it with no experience in selling widgets.

2. The selling firm can engage in price discrimination.

    Example: National Motors can offer below-market interest rates to lower-income customers that must finance a large portion of the purchase price of cars. Higher-income customers pay the list price and do not generally finance a large part of the purchase.

3. The selling firm can obtain favorable tax treatment.

    Example: The A.B. Production Company offers long-term credit to its best customers. This form of financing may qualify as an installment plan and allow the A.B. Production Co. to book profits of the sale over the life of the loan. This may save taxes because the present value of the tax payments will be lower if spread over time.

4. The selling firm has no established reputation for quality products or services.

    Example: Advanced Micro Instruments (AMI) manufactures sophisticated measurement instruments for controlling electrical systems on commercial airplanes. The firm was founded by two engineering graduates from the University of Pennsylvania in 1997. It became a public firm in 1998. To hedge their bets, aircraft manufacturers will ask for credit from AMI. It is very difficult for customers of AMI to assess the quality of its instruments until the instruments have been in place for some time.

5. The selling firm perceives a long-term strategic relationship.

    Example: Food.com is a fast-growing, cash-constrained Internet food distributor. It is currently not profitable. Acme Food will grant Food.com credit for food purchased because Food.com will generate profits in the future.

SOURCE: Shezad I. Mian and Clifford W. Smith, "Extending Trade Credit and Financing Receivables," *Journal of Applied Corporate Finance* (Spring 1994); Marc Deloof and Marc Jegers, "Trade Credit, Product Quality, and Intragroup Trade: Some European Evidence," *Financial Management* (Autumn 1996); Michael Long, I. B. Malitz, and S.A. Ravid, "Trade Credit, Quality Guarantees, and Product Marketability," *Financial Management* (Winter 1993); and Mitchell A. Petersen and Raghuram G. Rajan, "Trade Credit: Theories and Evidence," *The Review of Financial Studies* 10 (1997).

potential lenders, if the selling firm has monopoly power it can exploit, if the selling firm can reduce taxes by extending credit, and if the product quality of the selling firm is difficult to determine. Firm size may be important if there are size economies in managing credit.

The optimal credit policy depends on characteristics of particular firms. Assuming that the firm has more flexibility in its credit policy than in the prices it charges, firms with excess capacity, low variable operating costs, high tax brackets, and repeat customers should extend credit more liberally than others.

28.4   Credit Analysis

When granting credit, a firm tries to distinguish between customers that will pay and customers that will not pay. There are a number of sources of information for determining creditworthiness.

Credit Information

Information commonly used to assess creditworthiness includes the following:

1. *Financial statements*: A firm can ask a customer to supply financial statements. Rules of thumb based on calculated financial ratios can be used.

2. *Credit reports on customer's payment history with other firms*: Many organizations sell information on the credit strength of business firms. The best-known and largest firm of this type is Dun & Bradstreet, which provides subscribers with a credit reference book and credit reports on individual firms. The reference book has credit ratings on thousands of businesses.

3. *Banks*: Banks will generally provide some assistance to their business customers in acquiring information on the creditworthiness of other firms.

4. *The customer's payment history with the firm*: The most obvious way to obtain an estimate of a customer's probability of nonpayment is whether he or she has paid previous bills.

Credit Scoring

Once information has been gathered, the firm faces the hard choice of either granting or refusing credit. Many firms use the traditional and subjective guidelines referred to as the "five Cs of credit":

1. *Character*: The customer's willingness to meet credit obligations.

2. *Capacity*: The customer's ability to meet credit obligations out of operating cash flows.

3. *Capital*: The customer's financial reserves.

4. *Collateral*: A pledged asset in the case of default.

5. *Conditions*: General economic conditions.

Conversely, firms such as credit card issuers have developed elaborate statistical models (called **credit scoring** models) for determining the probability of default. Usually, all the relevant and observable characteristics of a large pool of customers are studied to find their historic relation to default. Because these models determine who is and who is not creditworthy, not surprisingly they have been the subject of government regulation. For example, if a model were to find that women default more than men, it might be used to deny women credit. Regulation removes such models from the domain of the statistician and makes them the subject of politicians.

28.5 Collection Policy

Collection refers to obtaining payment of past-due accounts. The credit manager keeps a record of payment experiences with each customer.

Average Collection Period

Acme Compact Disk Players sells 100,000 compact disk players a year at $300 each. All sales are for credit with terms of 2/20, net 60.

Suppose that 80 percent of Acme's customers take the discounts and pay on day 20; the rest pay on day 60. The **average collection period (ACP)** measures the average amount of time required to collect an account receivable. The ACP for Acme is 28 days:

$$0.8 \times 20 \text{ days} + 0.2 \times 60 \text{ days} = 28 \text{ days}$$

(The average collection period is frequently referred to as *days' sales outstanding* or *days in receivables.*)

Of course, this is an idealized example where customers pay on either one of two dates. In reality, payments arrive in a random fashion, so the average collection period must be calculated differently.

To determine the ACP in the real world, firms first calculate average daily sales. The **average daily sales (ADS)** equal annual sales divided by 365. The ADS of Acme are:

$$\text{Average daily sales} = \frac{\$300 \times 100,000}{365 \text{ days}} = \$82,192$$

If receivables today are $2,301,376, the average collection period is:

$$\text{Average collection period} = \frac{\text{Accounts receivable}}{\text{Average daily sales}}$$

$$= \frac{\$2,301,376}{\$82,192}$$

$$= 28 \text{ days}$$

In practice, firms observe sales and receivables daily. Consequently, an average collection period can be computed and compared to the stated credit terms. For example, suppose Acme had computed its ACP at 40 days for several weeks, versus its credit terms of 2/20, net 60. With a 40-day ACP, some customers are paying later than usual. Some accounts may be overdue.

However, firms with seasonal sales will often find the *calculated* ACP changing during the year, making the ACP a somewhat flawed tool. This occurs because receivables are low before the selling season and high after the season. Thus, firms may keep track of seasonal movement in the ACP over past years. In this way, they can compare the ACP for today's date with the average ACP for that date in previous years. To supplement the information in the ACP, the credit manager may make up an accounts receivable aging schedule.

Aging Schedule

The **aging schedule** tabulates receivables by age of account. In the following schedule, 75 percent of the accounts are on time, but a significant number are more than 60 days past due. This signifies that some customers are in arrears.

Aging Schedule	
Age of Account	**Percentage of Total Value of Accounts Receivable**
0–20 days	50%
21–60 days	25
61–80 days	20
Over 80 days	5
	100%

The aging schedule changes during the year. Comparatively, the ACP is a somewhat flawed tool because it gives only the yearly average. Some firms have refined it so that they can examine how it changes with peaks and valleys in their sales. Similarly, the aging schedule is often augmented by the payments pattern. The *payments pattern* describes the lagged collection pattern of receivables. Like a mortality table that describes the probability that a 23-year-old will live to be 24, the payments pattern describes the probability that a 67-day-old account will still be unpaid when it is 68 days old.

Collection Effort

The firm usually employs the following procedures for customers that are overdue:

1. Send a delinquency letter informing the customer of the past-due status of the account.
2. Make a telephone call to the customer.
3. Employ a collection agency.
4. Take legal action against the customer.

At times, a firm may refuse to grant additional credit to customers until arrearages are paid. This may antagonize a normally good customer and points to a potential conflict of interest between the collections department and the sales department.

Factoring

Factoring refers to the sale of a firm's accounts receivable to a financial institution known as a *factor*. The firm and the factor agree on the basic credit terms for each customer. The customer sends payment directly to the factor, and the factor bears the risk of nonpaying customers. The factor buys the receivables at a discount, which usually ranges from 0.35 to 4 percent of the value of the invoice amount. The average discount throughout the economy is probably about 1 percent.

One point should be stressed. We have presented the elements of credit policy as though they were somewhat independent of each other. In fact, they are closely interrelated. For example, the optimal credit policy is not independent of collection and monitoring policies. A tighter collection policy can reduce the probability of default, and this in turn can raise the NPV of a more liberal credit policy.

28.6 How to Finance Trade Credit

In addition to the unsecured debt instruments described earlier in this chapter, there are three general ways of financing accounting receivables: secured debt, a captive finance company, and securitization.

Use of secured debt is usually referred to as asset-based receivables financing. This is the predominant form of receivables financing. Many lenders will not lend without security to firms with substantive uncertainty or little equity. With secured debt, if the borrower gets into financial difficulty, the lender can repossess the asset and sell it for its fair market value.

Many large firms with good credit ratings use captive finance companies. The captive finance companies are subsidiaries of the parent firm. This is similar to the use of secured debt because the creditors of the captive finance company have a claim on its assets and, as a consequence, the accounts receivable of the parent firm. A captive finance company is attractive if economies of scale are important and if an independent subsidiary with limited liability is warranted.

Securitization occurs when the selling firm sells its accounts receivable to a financial institution. The financial institution pools the receivables with other receivables and issues securities to finance items.

Summary and Conclusions

1. The components of a firm's credit policy are the terms of sale, the credit analysis, and the collection policy.

2. The terms of sale describe the amount and period of time for which credit is granted and the type of credit instrument.

3. The decision to grant credit is a straightforward NPV decision that can be improved by additional information about customer payment characteristics. Additional information about the customers' probability of defaulting is valuable, but this value must be traded off against the expense of acquiring the information.

4. The optimal amount of credit the firm offers is a function of the competitive conditions in which it finds itself. These conditions will determine the carrying costs associated with granting credit and the opportunity costs of the lost sales from refusing to offer credit. The optimal credit policy minimizes the sum of these two costs.

5. We have seen that knowledge of the probability that customers will default is valuable. To enhance its ability to assess customers' default probability, a firm can score credit. This relates the default probability to observable characteristics of customers.

6. The collection policy is the method of dealing with past-due accounts. The first step is to analyze the average collection period and to prepare an aging schedule that relates the age of accounts to the proportion of the accounts receivable they represent. The next step is to decide on the collection method and to evaluate the possibility of factoring—that is, selling the overdue accounts.

Concept Questions

1. **Credit Instruments** Describe each of the following:
   a. Sight draft.
   b. Time draft.
   c. Banker's acceptance.
   d. Promissory note.
   e. Trade acceptance.

2. **Trade Credit Forms** In what form is trade credit most commonly offered? What is the credit instrument in this case?

3. **Receivables Costs** What are the costs associated with carrying receivables? What are the costs associated with not granting credit? What do we call the sum of the costs for different levels of receivables?

4. **Five Cs of Credit** What are the five Cs of credit? Explain why each is important.

5. **Credit Period Length** What are some factors that determine the length of the credit period? Why is the length of the buyer's operating cycle often considered an upper bound on the length of the credit period?

6. **Credit Period Length** In each of the following pairings, indicate which firm would probably have a longer credit period and explain your reasoning.
   a. Firm A sells a miracle cure for baldness; firm B sells toupees.
   b. Firm A specializes in products for landlords; firm B specializes in products for renters.
   c. Firm A sells to customers with an inventory turnover of 10 times; firm B sells to customers with an inventory turnover of 20 times.
   d. Firm A sells fresh fruit; firm B sells canned fruit.
   e. Firm A sells and installs carpeting; firm B sells area rugs.

7. **Credit Analysis** When performing an NPV analysis for the decision to grant credit, what cost of debt should be used?

8. **Granting Credit** Suppose we have a new customer who will buy from our company if we grant credit. In calculating the default rate, it is likely to be high. Why is this so? How does this compare to the decision to grant credit to a previous, cash-paying customer?

9. **Granting Credit** Suppose we are considering granting credit to a new customer who will make a one-time purchase. If we compare the default rate from this analysis with the default rate for a customer who will become a repeat customer, which default rate will be higher? Why?

10. **Granting Credit** What is the relationship between the decision to grant credit and the gross margin of the product?

Questions and Problems

BASIC
(Questions 1–14)

1. **Cash Discounts** You place an order for 200 units of inventory at a unit price of $85. The supplier offers terms of 2/10, net 30.
   a. How long do you have to pay before the account is overdue? If you take the full period, how much should you remit?
   b. What is the discount being offered? How quickly must you pay to get the discount? If you take the discount, how much should you remit?
   c. If you don't take the discount, how much interest are you paying implicitly? How many days' credit are you receiving?

2. **Size of Accounts Receivable** The Suzita Corporation has annual sales of ¥65 million. The average collection period is 48 days. What is Suzita's average investment in accounts receivable as shown on the balance sheet?

3. **ACP and Accounts Receivable** Kyoto Joe, Inc., sells earnings forecasts for Japanese securities. Its credit terms are 2/10, net 30. Based on experience, 65 percent of all customers will take the discount.
   a. What is the average collection period for Kyoto Joe?
   b. If Kyoto Joe sells 1,200 forecasts every month at a price of ¥2,200 each, what is its average balance sheet amount in accounts receivable?

4. **Size of Accounts Receivable** Vitale, Baby!, Inc., has weekly credit sales of €18,000, and the average collection period is 29 days. The cost of production is 80 percent of the selling price. What is Vitale's average accounts receivable figure?

5. **Terms of Sale** A firm offers terms of 2/9, net 40. What effective annual interest rate does the firm earn when a customer does not take the discount? Without doing any calculations, explain what will happen to this effective rate if:
   a. The discount is changed to 3 percent.
   b. The credit period is increased to 60 days.
   c. The discount period is increased to 15 days.

6. **ACP and Receivables Turnover** Music City, Inc., has an average collection period of 52 days. Its average daily investment in receivables is ZWD 46,000. What are annual credit sales? What is the receivables turnover?

7. **Size of Accounts Receivable** Essence of Skunk Fragrances, Ltd., sells 4,000 units of its perfume collection each year at a price per unit of ZAR 400. All sales are on credit with terms of 2/15, net 40. The discount is taken by 60 percent of the customers. What is the amount of the company's accounts receivable? In reaction to sales by its main competitor, Sewage Spray, Essence of Skunk is considering a change in its credit policy to terms of 4/10, net 30 to preserve its market share. How will this change in policy affect accounts receivable?

8. **Size of Accounts Receivable** The Orbison Corporation sells on credit terms of net 25. Its accounts are, on average, nine days past due. If annual credit sales are CRC 9 million, what is the company's balance sheet amount in accounts receivable?

9. **Evaluating Credit Policy** Fly Em Now is a wholesaler that stocks engine components and test equipment for the commercial aircraft industry. A new customer has placed an order for eight high-bypass turbine engines, which increase fuel economy. The variable cost is CAD 1.5 million per unit, and the credit price is CAD 1.8 million each. Credit is extended for one period, and based on historical experience, payment for about 1 out of every 200 such orders is never collected. The required return is 2.5 percent per period.

a. Assuming that this is a one-time order, should it be filled? The customer will not buy if credit is not extended.

b. What is the break-even probability of default in part (a)?

c. Suppose that customers who don't default become repeat customers and place the same order every period forever. Further assume that repeat customers never default. Should the order be filled? What is the break-even probability of default?

d. Describe in general terms why credit terms will be more liberal when repeat orders are a possibility.

10. **Credit Policy Evaluation** Champions, Inc., is considering a change in its cash-only sales policy. The new terms of sale would be net one month. Based on the following information, determine if Champions should proceed. Describe the buildup of receivables in this case. The required return is 2 percent per month.

	Current Policy	New Policy
Price per unit	$ 800	$ 800
Cost per unit	$ 475	$ 475
Unit sales per month	1,130	1,195

11. **Evaluating Credit Policy** Angaroo Collectibles is in the process of considering a change in its terms of sale. The current policy is cash only; the new policy will involve one period's credit. Sales are 70,000 units per period at a price of AUD 530 per unit. If credit is offered, the new price will be AUD 552. Unit sales are not expected to change, and all customers are expected to take the credit. Angaroo Collectibles estimates that 2 percent of credit sales will be uncollectible. If the required return is 2 percent per period, is the change a good idea?

12. **Credit Policy Evaluation** The Johnson Company sells 3,000 pairs of running shoes per month at a cash price of $90 per pair. The firm is considering a new policy that involves 30 days' credit and an increase in price to $91.84 per pair on credit sales. The cash price will remain at $90, and the new policy is not expected to affect the quantity sold. The discount period will be 10 days. The required return is 1 percent per month.

a. How would the new credit terms be quoted?

b. What is the investment in receivables required under the new policy?

c. Explain why the variable cost of manufacturing the shoes is not relevant here.

d. If the default rate is anticipated to be 12 percent, should the switch be made? What is the break-even credit price? The break-even cash discount?

13. **Factoring** The factoring department of Inter American Bank (IAB) is processing 100,000 invoices per year with an average invoice value of $1,500. IAB buys the accounts receivable at 3.5 percent off the invoice value. Currently 2 percent of the accounts receivable turns out to be bad debt. The annual operating expense of this department is $400,000. What are the EBIT for the factoring department of IAB?

14. **Factoring Receivables** Your firm has an average collection period of 35 days. Current practice is to factor all receivables immediately at a 2 percent discount. What is the effective cost of borrowing in this case? Assume that default is extremely unlikely.

INTERMEDIATE
(Questions 15–21)

15. **Credit Analysis** Silicon Wafers, Inc. (SWI), is debating whether to extend credit to a particular customer. SWI's products, primarily used in the manufacture of semiconductors, currently sell for $1,850 per unit. The variable cost is $1,200 per unit. The order under consideration is for 12 units today; payment is promised in 30 days.

a. If there is a 20 percent chance of default, should SWI fill the order? The required return is 2 percent per month. This is a one-time sale, and the customer will not buy if credit is not extended.

b. What is the break-even probability in part (a)?

c. This part is a little harder. In general terms, how do you think your answer to part (a) will be affected if the customer will purchase the merchandise for cash if the credit is refused? The cash price is $1,750 per unit.

16. **Credit Analysis**   Consider the following information about two alternative credit strategies:

	Refuse Credit	Grant Credit
Price per unit	€ 51	€ 55
Cost per unit	€ 29	€ 31
Quantity sold per quarter	3,300	3,500
Probability of payment	1.0	.90

The higher cost per unit reflects the expense associated with credit orders, and the higher price per unit reflects the existence of a cash discount. The credit period will be 90 days, and the cost of debt is .75 percent per month.

a. Based on this information, should credit be granted?

b. In part (a), what does the credit price per unit have to be to break even?

c. In part (a), suppose we can obtain a credit report for €2 per customer. Assuming that each customer buys one unit and that the credit report correctly identifies all customers who will not pay, should credit be extended?

17. **NPV of Credit Policy Switch**   Suppose a corporation currently sells Q units per month for a cash-only price of P. Under a new credit policy that allows one month's credit, the quantity sold will be Q' and the price per unit will be P'. Defaults will be π percent of credit sales. The variable cost is v per unit and is not expected to change. The percentage of customers who will take the credit is α, and the required return is R per month. What is the NPV of the decision to switch? Interpret the various parts of your answer.

18. **Credit Policy**   Simba Sports, Inc., operates a mail-order running shoe business. Management is considering dropping its policy of no credit. The credit policy under consideration is this:

	Current Policy	New Policy
Price per unit	NGN 35	NGN 40
Cost per unit	NGN 25	NGN 32
Quantity sold	2,000	3,000
Probability of payment	100%	85%
Credit period	0	1

a. If the interest rate is 3 percent per period, should the company offer credit to its customers?

b. What must the probability of payment be before the company would adopt the policy?

19. **Credit Policy**   The Silver Spokes Bicycle Shop has decided to offer credit to its customers during the spring selling season. Sales are expected to be 400 bicycles. The average cost to the shop of a bicycle is £280. The owner knows that only 97 percent of the customers will be able to make their payments. To identify the remaining 3 percent, she is considering subscribing to a credit agency. The initial charge for this service is £500, with an additional charge of £4 per individual report. Should she subscribe to the agency?

20. **Credit Policy Evaluation**   The Jungle Corporation is considering a change in its cash-only policy. The new terms would be net one period. Based on the following information, determine if Jungle should proceed. The required return is 2.5 percent per period.

	Current Policy	New Policy
Price per unit	€ 75	€ 80
Cost per unit	€ 43	€ 43
Unit sales per month	3,200	3,500

21. **Credit Policy Evaluation**   Andy's Hood currently has an all-cash credit policy. It is considering making a change in the credit policy by going to terms of net 30 days. Based on the following information, what do you recommend? The required return is 2.5 percent per month.

	Current Policy	**New Policy**
Price per unit	$ 340	$ 345
Cost per unit	$ 260	$ 265
Unit sales per month	1,800	1,850

CHALLENGE
(Questions 22–25)

22. **Break-Even Quantity** In Problem 20, what is the break-even quantity for the new credit policy?

23. **Credit Markup** In Problem 20, what is the break-even price per unit that should be charged under the new credit policy? Assume that the sales figure under the new policy is 3,300 units and all other values remain the same.

24. **Credit Markup** In Problem 21, what is the break-even price per unit under the new credit policy? Assume all other values remain the same.

25. **Credit Policy** The Tropeland Company has annual sales of ¥50 million, all of which are on credit. The current collection period is 45 days, and the credit terms are net 30. The company is considering offering terms of 2/10, net 30. It anticipates that 70 percent of its customers will take advantage of the discount. The new policy will reduce the collection period to 28 days. The appropriate interest rate is 6 percent. Should the new credit policy be adopted? How does the level of credit sales affect this decision?

Credit Policy at Braam Industries

Mini Case

Tricia Haltiwinger, the president of Braam Industries, has been exploring ways of improving the company's financial performance. Braam Industries manufactures and sells office equipment to retailers. The company's growth has been relatively slow in recent years, but with an expansion in the economy, it appears that sales may increase more quickly in the future. Tricia has asked Andrew Preston, the company's treasurer, to examine Braam's credit policy to see if a different credit policy can help increase profitability.

The company currently has a policy of net 30. As with any credit sales, default rates are always of concern. Because of Braam's screening and collection process, the default rate on credit is currently only 1.5 percent. Andrew has examined the company's credit policy in relation to other vendors, and he has determined that three options are available.

The first option is to relax the company's decision on when to grant credit. The second option is to increase the credit period to net 45, and the third option is a combination of the relaxed credit policy and the extension of the credit period to net 45. On the positive side, each of the three policies under consideration would increase sales. The three policies have the drawbacks that default rates would increase, the administrative costs of managing the firm's receivables would increase, and the receivables period would increase. The credit policy change would impact all four of these variables in different degrees. Andrew has prepared the following table outlining the effect on each of these variables:

	Annual Sales (millions)	**Default Rate (% of sales)**	**Administrative Costs (% of sales)**	**Receivables Period**
Current Policy	$120	1.5%	2.1%	38 days
Option 1	140	2.4	3.1	41
Option 2	137	1.7	2.3	51
Option 3	150	2.1	2.9	49

Braam's variable costs of production are 45 percent of sales, and the relevant interest rate is a 6 percent effective annual rate. Which credit policy should be company use? Also, notice that in option 3 the default rate and administrative costs are below those in option 2. Is this plausible? Why or why not?

Mergers and Acquisitions

In late 2005, SBC Communication's $16 billion acquisition of venerable phone company AT&T was completed. The acquisition by SBC was the end of a long, strange road for AT&T, which had been forced to split into the "Baby Bells" by regulators in 1984. SBC Communications was one of the Baby Bells split from AT&T. In a nod to AT&T's history and name brand reputation, even though SBC was the acquiring company, the new company kept the AT&T name.

So why would SBC purchase AT&T? The main reason was cost savings, which were estimated to have an NPV of $15 billion. Of course, the cost savings were only an estimate, and many times these estimates are incorrect. Fortunately for AT&T/SBC, this was the case. In February 2006, the company announced that the updated forecast for the deal's NPV was $18 billion, a 20 percent increase.

How do companies like SBC determine whether an acquisition is a good idea? This chapter explores reasons that mergers should take place—and just as important, reasons why they should not.

29.1 The Basic Forms of Acquisitions

Acquisitions follow one of three basic forms: (1) merger or consolidation, (2) acquisition of stock, and (3) acquisition of assets.

Merger or Consolidation

A **merger** refers to the absorption of one firm by another. The acquiring firm retains its name and identity, and it acquires all of the assets and liabilities of the acquired firm. After a merger, the acquired firm ceases to exist as a separate business entity.

A **consolidation** is the same as a merger except that an entirely new firm is created. In a consolidation both the acquiring firm and the acquired firm terminate their previous legal existence and become part of the new firm.

EXAMPLE 29.1

Merger Basics Suppose firm A acquires firm B in a merger. Further, suppose firm B's shareholders are given one share of firm A's stock in exchange for two shares of firm B's stock. From a legal standpoint, firm A's shareholders are not directly affected by the merger. However, firm B's shares cease to exist. In a consolidation, the shareholders of firm A and firm B exchange their shares for shares of a new firm (e.g., firm C).

Because of the similarities between mergers and consolidations, we shall refer to both types of reorganization as mergers. Here are two important points about mergers and consolidations:

1. A merger is legally straightforward and does not cost as much as other forms of acquisition. It avoids the necessity of transferring title of each individual asset of the acquired firm to the acquiring firm.

2. The stockholders of each firm must approve a merger.[1] Typically, votes of the owners of two-thirds of the shares are required for approval. In addition, shareholders of the acquired firm have *appraisal rights*. This means that they can demand that the acquiring firm purchase their shares at a fair value. Often the acquiring firm and the dissenting shareholders of the acquired firm cannot agree on a fair value, which results in expensive legal proceedings.

Acquisition of Stock

A second way to acquire another firm is to purchase the firm's voting stock in exchange for cash, shares of stock, or other securities. This process may start as a private offer from the management of one firm to another. At some point the offer is taken directly to the selling firm's stockholders, often by a tender offer. A **tender offer** is a public offer to buy shares of a target firm. It is made by one firm directly to the shareholders of another firm. The offer is communicated to the target firm's shareholders by public announcements such as newspaper advertisements. Sometimes a general mailing is used in a tender offer. However, a general mailing is difficult because the names and addresses of the stockholders of record are not usually available.

The following factors are involved in choosing between an acquisition of stock and a merger:

1. In an acquisition of stock, shareholder meetings need not be held and a vote is not required. If the shareholders of the target firm do not like the offer, they are not required to accept it and need not tender their shares.

2. In an acquisition of stock, the bidding firm can deal directly with the shareholders of a target firm via a tender offer. The target firm's management and board of directors are bypassed.

3. Target managers often resist acquisition. In such cases, acquisition of stock circumvents the target firm's management. Resistance by the target firm's management often makes the cost of acquisition by stock higher than the cost by merger.

4. Frequently a minority of shareholders will hold out in a tender offer, and thus the target firm cannot be completely absorbed.

5. Complete absorption of one firm by another requires a merger. Many acquisitions of stock end with a formal merger.

Acquisition of Assets

One firm can acquire another by buying all of its assets. The selling firm does not necessarily vanish because its "shell" can be retained. A formal vote of the target stockholders is required in an acquisition of assets. An advantage here is that although the acquirer is often

---

[1]Mergers between corporations require compliance with state laws. In virtually all states, the shareholders of each corporation must give their assent.

Figure 29.1

Varieties of Takeovers

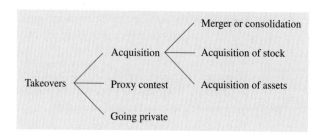

left with minority shareholders in an acquisition of stock, this does not happen in an acquisition of assets. Minority shareholders often present problems, such as holdouts. However, asset acquisition involves transferring title to individual assets, which can be costly.

A Classification Scheme

Financial analysts have typically classified acquisitions into three types:

1. *Horizontal acquisition*: Here, both the acquirer and acquired are in the same industry. Exxon's acquisition of Mobil in 1998 is an example of a horizontal merger in the oil industry.

2. *Vertical acquisition*: A vertical acquisition involves firms at different steps of the production process. The acquisition by an airline company of a travel agency would be a vertical acquisition.

3. *Conglomerate acquisition*: The acquiring firm and the acquired firm are not related to each other. The acquisition of a food products firm by a computer firm would be considered a conglomerate acquisition.

A Note about Takeovers

Takeover is a general and imprecise term referring to the transfer of control of a firm from one group of shareholders to another.[2] A firm that has decided to take over another firm is usually referred to as the **bidder**. The bidder offers to pay cash or securities to obtain the stock or assets of another company. If the offer is accepted, the **target** firm will give up control over its stock or assets to the bidder in exchange for *consideration* (i.e., its stock, its debt, or cash).

Takeovers can occur by acquisition, proxy contests, and going-private transactions. Thus, takeovers encompass a broader set of activities than acquisitions, as depicted in Figure 29.1.

If a takeover is achieved by acquisition, it will be by merger, tender offer for shares of stock, or purchase of assets. In mergers and tender offers, the acquiring firm buys the voting common stock of the acquired firm.

Proxy contests can result in takeovers as well. Proxy contests occur when a group of shareholders attempts to gain seats on the board of directors. A *proxy* is written authorization for one shareholder to vote the stock of another shareholder. In a proxy contest, an insurgent group of shareholders solicits proxies from other shareholders.

In *going-private transactions*, a small group of investors purchases all the equity shares of a public firm. The group usually includes members of incumbent management and some outside investors. The shares of the firm are delisted from stock exchanges and can no longer be purchased in the open market.

---

[2]*Control* can usually be defined as having a majority vote on the board of directors.

29.2 Synergy

The previous section discussed the basic forms of acquisition. We now examine why firms are acquired. (Although the previous section pointed out that acquisitions and mergers have different definitions, these differences will be unimportant in this, and many of the following, sections. Thus, unless otherwise stated, we will refer to acquisitions and mergers synonymously.)

Much of our thinking here can be organized around the following four questions:

1. Is there a rational reason for mergers? Yes—in a word, *synergy*.

   Suppose firm A is contemplating acquiring firm B. The value of firm A is V_A and the value of firm B is V_B. (It is reasonable to assume that for public companies, V_A and V_B can be determined by observing the market prices of the outstanding securities.) The difference between the value of the combined firm (V_{AB}) and the sum of the values of the firms as separate entities is the synergy from the acquisition:

$$\text{Synergy} = V_{AB} - (V_A + V_B)$$

   In words, synergy occurs if the value of the combined firm after the merger is greater than the sum of the value of the acquiring firm and the value of the acquired firm before the merger.

2. Where does this magic force, synergy, come from?

   Increases in cash flow create value. We define ΔCF_t as the difference between the cash flows at date t of the combined firm and the sum of the cash flows of the two separate firms. From the chapters about capital budgeting, we know that the cash flow in any period t can be written as:

$$\Delta\text{CF}_t = \Delta\text{Rev}_t - \Delta\text{Costs}_t - \Delta\text{Taxes}_t - \Delta\text{Capital Requirements}_t$$

   where ΔRev_t is the incremental revenue of the acquisition, ΔCosts_t is the incremental costs of the acquisition, ΔTaxes_t is the incremental acquisition taxes, and $\Delta\text{Capital Requirements}_t$ is the incremental new investment required in working capital and fixed assets.

   It follows from our classification of incremental cash flows that the possible sources of synergy fall into four basic categories: revenue enhancement, cost reduction, lower taxes, and lower capital requirements.[3] Improvements in at least one of these four categories create synergy. Each of these categories will be discussed in detail in the next section.

---

[3]Many reasons are given by firms to justify mergers and acquisitions. When two firms merge, the boards of directors of the two firms adopt an *agreement of merger*. The agreement of merger of U.S. Steel and Marathon Oil is typical. It lists the economic benefits that shareholders can expect from the merger (key words have been italicized):

U.S. Steel believes that the acquisition of Marathon provides U.S. Steel with an attractive opportunity to *diversify* into the energy business. Reasons for the merger include, but are not limited to, the facts that consummation of the merger will allow U.S. Steel to consolidate Marathon into U.S. Steel's federal *income tax return,* will also contribute to *greater efficiency,* and will enhance the ability to manage capital by permitting the movement of cash between U.S. Steel and Marathon. Additionally, the merger will eliminate the possibility of conflicts of interests between the interests of minority and majority shareholders and will enhance management flexibility. The acquisition will provide Marathon shareholders with a substantial premium over historical market prices for their shares. However, shareholders will no longer continue to share in the future prospects of the company.

In addition, reasons are often provided for mergers where improvements are not expected in any of these four categories. These "bad" reasons for mergers will be discussed in Section 29.4.

3. How are these synergistic gains shared? In general, the acquiring firm pays a premium for the acquired, or target, firm. For example, if the stock of the target is selling for $50, the acquirer might need to pay $60 a share, implying a premium of $10 or 20 percent. The gain to the target in this example is $10. Suppose that the synergy from the merger is $30. The gain to the acquiring firm, or bidder, would be $20 (= $30 − $10). The bidder would actually lose if the synergy were less than the premium of $10. A more detailed treatment of these gains or losses will be provided in Section 29.6.

4. Are there other motives for a merger besides synergy? Yes.

   As we have said, synergy is the source of benefit to stockholders. However, the *managers* are likely to view a potential merger differently. Even if the synergy from the merger is less than the premium paid to the target, the managers of the acquiring firm may still benefit. For example, the revenues of the combined firm after the merger will almost certainly be greater than the revenues of the bidder before the merger. The managers may receive higher compensation once they are managing a larger firm. Even beyond the increase in compensation, managers generally experience greater prestige and power when managing a larger firm. Conversely, the managers of the target could lose their jobs after the acquisition. They might very well oppose the takeover even if their stockholders would benefit from the premium. These issues will be discussed in more detail in Section 29.9.

29.3   Sources of Synergy

In this section, we discuss sources of synergy.

Revenue Enhancement

A combined firm may generate greater revenues than two separate firms. Increased revenues can come from marketing gains, strategic benefits, and market power.

Marketing Gains   It is frequently claimed that, due to improved marketing, mergers and acquisitions can increase operating revenues. Improvements can be made in the following areas:

1. Previously ineffective media programming and advertising efforts.
2. A weak existing distribution network.
3. An unbalanced product mix.

Strategic Benefits   Some acquisitions promise a *strategic* benefit, which is more like an option than a standard investment opportunity. For example, imagine that a sewing machine company acquires a computer company. The firm will be well positioned if technological advances allow computer-driven sewing machines in the future.

Michael Porter has used the word *beachhead* to denote the strategic benefits from entering a new industry.[4] He uses the example of Procter & Gamble's acquisition of the Charmin Paper Company as a beachhead that allowed Procter & Gamble to develop a highly interrelated cluster of paper products—disposable diapers, paper towels, feminine hygiene products, and bathroom tissue.

---

[4]M. Porter, *Competitive Advantage* (New York: Free Press, 1998).

Figure 29.2

Economies of Scale and the Optimal Size of the Firm

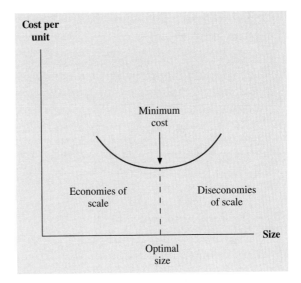

Market or Monopoly Power   One firm may acquire another to reduce competition. If so, prices can be increased, generating monopoly profits. However, mergers that reduce competition do not benefit society, and the U.S. Department of Justice or the Federal Trade Commission may challenge them.

Cost Reduction

A combined firm may operate more efficiently than two separate firms. When Bank of America agreed to acquire Security Pacific, lower costs were cited as the primary reason. A merger can increase operating efficiency in the following ways:

Economy of Scale   Economy of scale means that the average cost of production falls as the level of production increases. Figure 29.2 illustrates the relation between cost per unit and size for a typical firm. As can be seen, average cost first falls and then rises. In other words, the firm experiences economies of scale until optimal firm size is reached. Diseconomies of scale arise after that.

Though the precise nature of economies of scale is not known, it is one obvious benefit of horizontal mergers. The phrase *spreading overhead* is frequently used in connection with economies of scale. This refers to sharing central facilities such as corporate head-quarters, top management, and computer systems.

Economies of Vertical Integration   Operating economies can be gained from vertical combinations as well as from horizontal combinations. The main purpose of vertical acquisitions is to make coordination of closely related operating activities easier. This is probably why most forest product firms that cut timber also own sawmills and hauling equipment. Because petroleum is used to make plastics and other chemical products, the DuPont–Conoco merger was motivated by DuPont's need for a steady supply of oil. Economies from vertical integration probably explain why most airline companies own airplanes. They also may explain why some airline companies have purchased hotels and car rental companies.

Technology Transfer   Technology transfer is another reason for merger. An automobile manufacturer might well acquire an aircraft company if aerospace technology can improve automotive quality. This technology transfer was the motivation behind the merger of General Motors and Hughes Aircraft.

Complementary Resources   Some firms acquire others to improve usage of existing resources. A ski equipment store merging with a tennis equipment store will smooth sales over both the winter and summer seasons, thereby making better use of store capacity.

Elimination of Inefficient Management   A change in management can often increase firm value. Some managers overspend on perquisites and pet projects, making them ripe for takeover. For example, the leveraged buyout of RJR Nabisco was instituted primarily to halt the profligate behavior of CEO Ross Johnson. Alternatively, incumbent managers may not understand changing market conditions or new technology, making it difficult for them to abandon old strategies. Although the board of directors should replace these managers, the board is often unable to act independently. Thus, a merger may be needed to make the necessary replacements.

Michael C. Jensen cites the oil industry as an example of managerial inefficiency.[5] In the late 1970s, changes in the oil industry included expectation of lower oil prices, increased exploration and development costs, and higher real interest rates. As a result of these changes, substantial reductions in exploration and development were called for. However, many oil company managers were unable to downsize their firms. Acquiring companies sought out oil firms in order to reduce their investment levels. For example, T. Boone Pickens of Mesa Petroleum attempted to buy three oil companies—Unocal, Phillips, and Getty—to install more frugal management. Although he was unable to make the acquisitions, his attempts spurred existing management to reduce expenditures on exploration and development, generating huge gains to the shareholders of these firms, including himself.

Mergers and acquisitions can be viewed as part of the labor market for top management. Michael Jensen and Richard Ruback have used the phrase "market for corporate control," in which alternative management teams compete for the rights to manage corporate activities.[6]

Tax Gains

Tax reduction may be a powerful incentive for some acquisitions. This reduction can come from:

1. The use of tax losses.
2. The use of unused debt capacity.
3. The use of surplus funds.

Net Operating Losses   A firm with a profitable division and an unprofitable one will have a low tax bill because the loss in one division offsets the income in the other. However, if the two divisions are actually separate companies, the profitable firm will not be able to use the losses of the unprofitable one to offset its income. Thus, in the right circumstances, a merger can lower taxes.

Consider Table 29.1, which shows pretax income, taxes, and aftertax income for firms A and B. Firm A earns $200 in state 1 but loses money in state 2. The firm pays taxes in state 1 but is not entitled to a tax rebate in state 2. Conversely, firm B turns a profit in state 2 but not in state 1. This firm pays taxes only in state 2. The table shows that the combined tax bill of the two separate firms is always $68, regardless of which state occurs.

However, the last two columns of the table show that after a merger, the combined firm will pay taxes of only $34. Taxes drop after the merger, because a loss in one division offsets the gain in the other.

---

[5]M. C. Jensen, "Agency Costs of Free Cash Flow, Corporate Finance, and Takeovers," *American Economic Review* (1986).

[6]M. C. Jensen and R. S. Ruback, "The Market for Corporate Control: The Scientific Evidence," *Journal of Financial Economics* 11 (1983).

Table 29.1

Tax Effect of Merger of Firms *A* and *B*

| | Before Merge | | | | After Merger | |
| | Firm *A* | | Firm *B* | | Firm *AB* | |
	If State 1	If State 2	If State 1	If State 2	If State 1	If State 2
Taxable income	$200	−$100	−$100	$200	$100	$100
Taxes	68	0	0	68	34	34
Net income	$132	−$100	−$100	$132	$ 66	$ 66

Neither firm will be able to deduct its losses prior to the merger. The merger allows the losses from *A* to offset the taxable profits from *B*—and vice versa.

The message of this example is that firms need taxable profits to take advantage of potential losses. These losses are often referred to as *net operating losses* or *NOL* for short. Mergers can sometimes bring losses and profits together. However, there are two qualifications to the previous example:

1. Federal tax laws permit firms that experience alternating periods of profits and losses to equalize their taxes by carryback and carryforward provisions. A firm that has been profitable but has a loss in the current year can get refunds of income taxes paid in *three previous years* and can carry the loss *forward for 15 years*. Thus, a merger to exploit unused tax shields must offer tax savings over and above what can be accomplished by firms via carryovers.[7]

2. The IRS may disallow an acquisition if the principal purpose of the acquisition is to avoid federal tax. This is one of the Catch-22s of the Internal Revenue Code.

Debt Capacity   There are at least two cases where mergers allow for increased debt and a larger tax shield. In the first case, the target has too little debt, and the acquirer can infuse the target with the missing debt. In the second case, both target and acquirer have optimal debt levels. A merger leads to risk reduction, generating greater debt capacity and a larger tax shield. We treat each case in turn.

Case 1: Unused Debt Capacity   In Chapter 16, we pointed out that every firm has a certain amount of debt capacity. This debt capacity is beneficial because greater debt leads to a greater tax shield. More formally, every firm can borrow a certain amount before the marginal costs of financial distress equal the marginal tax shield. This debt capacity is a function of many factors, perhaps the most important being the risk of the firm. Firms with high risk generally cannot borrow as much as firms with low risk. For example, a utility or a supermarket, both firms with low risk, can have a higher debt-to-value ratio than can a technology firm.

Some firms, for whatever reason, have less debt than is optimal. Perhaps the managers are risk-averse, or perhaps the managers simply don't know how to assess debt capacity properly. Is it bad for a firm to have too little debt? The answer is yes. As we have said, the optimal level of debt occurs when the marginal cost of financial distress equals the marginal tax shield. Too little debt reduces firm value.

This is where mergers come in. A firm with little or no debt is an inviting target. An acquirer could raise the target's debt level after the merger to create a bigger tax shield.

Case 2: Increased Debt Capacity   Let's move back to the principles of modern portfolio theory, as presented in Chapter 10. Consider two stocks in different industries, where both stocks have the same risk or standard deviation. A portfolio of these two stocks has lower

---

[7]Under the 1986 Tax Reform Act, a corporation's ability to carry forward net operating losses (and other tax credits) is limited when more than 50 percent of the stock changes hands over a three-year period.

risk than that of either stock separately. In other words, the two-stock portfolio is somewhat diversified, whereas each stock by itself is completely undiversified.[8]

Now, rather than considering an individual buying both stocks, consider a merger between the two underlying firms. Because the risk of the combined firm is less than that of either one separately, banks should be willing to lend more money to the combined firm than the total of what they would lend to the two firms separately. In other words, the risk reduction that the merger generates leads to greater debt capacity.

For example, imagine that each firm can borrow $100 on its own before the merger. Perhaps the combined firm after the merger will be able to borrow $250. Debt capacity has increased by $50 (= $250 − $200).

Remember that debt generates a tax shield. If debt rises after the merger, taxes will fall. That is, simply because of the greater interest payments after the merger, the tax bill of the combined firm should be less than the sum of the tax bills of the two separate firms before the merger. In other words, the increased debt capacity from a merger can reduce taxes.

To summarize, we first considered the case where the target had too little leverage. The acquirer could infuse the target with more debt, generating a greater tax shield. Next, we considered the case where both target and acquirer began with optimal debt levels. A merger leads to more debt even here. That is, the risk reduction from the merger creates greater debt capacity and thus a greater tax shield.

Surplus Funds   Another quirk in the tax laws involves surplus funds. Consider a firm that has *free cash flow*. That is, it has cash flow available after payment of all taxes and after all positive net present value projects have been funded. In this situation, aside from purchasing securities, the firm can either pay dividends or buy back shares.

We have already seen in our previous discussion of dividend policy that an extra dividend will increase the income tax paid by some investors. Investors pay lower taxes in a share repurchase.[9] However, a share repurchase is not a legal option if the sole purpose is to avoid taxes on dividends.

Instead, the firm might make acquisitions with its excess funds. Here, the shareholders of the acquiring firm avoid the taxes they would have paid on a dividend.[10] And no taxes are paid on dividends remitted from the acquired firm.

Reduced Capital Requirements

Earlier in this chapter, we stated that due to economies of scale, mergers can reduce operating costs. It follows that mergers can reduce capital requirements as well. Accountants typically divide capital into two components: fixed capital and working capital.

When two firms merge, the managers will likely find duplicate facilities. For example, if both firms had their own headquarters, all executives in the merged firm could be moved to one headquarters building, allowing the other headquarters to be sold. Some plants might be redundant as well. Or two merging firms in the same industry might consolidate their research and development, permitting some R&D facilities to be sold.

---

[8]Although diversification is most easily explained by considering stocks in different industries, the key is really that the returns on the two stocks are less than perfectly correlated—a relationship that should occur even for stocks in the same industry.

[9]A dividend is taxable to all tax-paying recipients. A repurchase creates a tax liability only for those who choose to sell (and do so at a profit).

[10]The situation is actually a little more complex: The target's shareholders must pay taxes on their capital gains. These stockholders will likely demand a premium from the acquirer to offset this tax.

MICHAEL C. JENSEN ON MERGERS AND ACQUISITIONS

Economic analysis and evidence indicate that takeovers, LBOs, and corporate restructurings are playing an important role in helping the economy adjust to major competitive changes in the last two decades. The competition among alternative management teams and organizational structures for control of corporate assets has enabled vast economic resources to move more quickly to their highest-valued use. In the process, substantial benefits for the economy as a whole as well as for shareholders have been created. Overall gains to selling-firm shareholders from mergers, acquisitions, leveraged buyouts, and other corporate restructurings in the 12-year period 1977–1988 totaled over $500 billion in 1988 dollars. I estimate gains to buying-firm shareholders to be at least $50 billion for the same period. These gains equaled 53 percent of the total cash dividends (valued in 1988 dollars) paid to investors by the entire corporate sector in the same period.

Mergers and acquisitions are a response to new technologies or market conditions that require a strategic change in a company's direction or use of resources.

Compared to current management, a new owner is often better able to accomplish major change in the existing organizational structure. Alternatively, leveraged buyouts bring about organizational change by creating entrepreneurial incentives for management and by eliminating the centralized bureaucratic obstacles to maneuverability that are inherent in large public corporations.

When managers have a substantial ownership interest in the organization, the conflicts of interest between shareholders and managers over the payout of the company's free cash flow are reduced. Management's incentives are focused on maximizing the value of the enterprise, rather than building empires—often through poorly conceived diversification acquisitions—without regard to shareholder value. Finally, the required repayment of debt replaces management's discretion in paying dividends and the tendency to overretain cash. Substantial increases in efficiency are thereby created.

Michael C. Jensen is Jesse Isidor Professor of Business Administration Emeritus at Harvard University. An outstanding scholar and researcher, he is famous for his pathbreaking analysis of the modern corporation and its relations with its stockholders.

The same goes for working capital. The inventory-to-sale ratio and the cash-to-sales ratio often decrease as firm size increases. A merger permits these economies of scale to be realized, allowing a reduction in working capital.

29.4 Two "Bad" Reasons for Mergers

Earnings Growth

An acquisition can create the appearance of earnings growth, perhaps fooling investors into thinking that the firm is worth more than it really is. Let's consider two companies, Global Resources, Ltd., and Regional Enterprises, as depicted in the first two columns of Table 29.2. As can be seen, earnings per share are $1 for both companies. However, Global sells for $25 per share, implying a price–earnings (P/E) ratio of 25 (= 25/1). By contrast, Regional sells for $10, implying a P/E ratio of 10. This means that an investor in Global pays $25 to get $1 in earnings, whereas an investor in Regional receives the same $1 in earnings on only a $10 investment. Are investors getting a better deal with Regional? Not necessarily. Perhaps Global's earnings are expected to grow faster than are Regional's earnings. If this is the case, an investor in Global will expect to receive high earnings in later years, making up for low earnings in the short term. In fact, Chapter 5 argues that the primary determinant of a firm's P/E ratio is the market's expectation of the firm's growth rate in earnings.

Now let's imagine that Global acquires Regional, with the merger creating no value. If the market is smart, it will realize that the combined firm is worth the sum of the values

Table 29.2

Financial Positions of Global Resources, Ltd., and Regional Enterprises

	Global Resources before Merger	Regional Enterprises before Merger	Global Resources after Merger	
			The Market Is "Smart"	The Market Is "Fooled"
Earnings per share	$ 1.00	$ 1.00	$ 1.43	$ 1.43
Price per share	$ 25.00	$ 10.00	$ 25.00	$ 35.71
Price–earnings ratio	25	10	17.5	25
Number of shares	100	100	140	140
Total earnings	$ 100	$ 100	$ 200	$ 200
Total value	$2,500	$1,000	$3,500	$5,000

Exchange ratio: 1 share in Global for 2.5 shares in Regional.

of the separate firms. In this case, the market value of the combined firm will be $3,500, which is equal to the sum of the values of the separate firms before the merger.

At these values, Global will acquire Regional by exchanging 40 of its shares for 100 shares of Regional, so that Global will have 140 shares outstanding after the merger.[11] Global's stock price remains at $25 (= $3,500/140). With 140 shares outstanding and $200 of earnings after the merger, Global earns $1.43 (= $200/140) per share after the merger. Its P/E ratio becomes 17.5 (= 25/1.43), a drop from 25 before the merger. This scenario is represented by the third column of Table 29.2. Why has the P/E dropped? The combined firm's P/E will be an average of Global's high P/E and Regional's low P/E before the merger. This is common sense once you think about it. Global's P/E should drop when it takes on a new division with low growth.

Let us now consider the possibility that the market is fooled. As we just said, the acquisition enables Global to increase its earnings per share from $1 to $1.43. If the market is fooled, it might mistake the 43 percent increase in earnings per share for true growth. In this case, the price–earnings ratio of Global may not fall after the merger. Suppose the price–earnings ratio of Global remains at 25. The total value of the combined firm will increase to $5,000 (= 25 × $200), and the stock price per share of Global will increase to $35.71 (= $5,000/140). This is reflected in the last column of the table.

This is earnings growth magic. Can we expect this magic to work in the real world? Managers of a previous generation certainly thought so, with firms such as LTV Industries, ITT, and Litton Industries all trying to play the P/E-multiple game in the 1960s. However, in hindsight it looks as if they played the game without much success. These operators have all dropped out with few, if any, replacements. It appears that the market is too smart to be fooled this easily.

Diversification

Diversification often is mentioned as a benefit of one firm acquiring another. Earlier in this chapter, we noted that U.S. Steel included diversification as a benefit in its acquisition of Marathon Oil. At the time of the merger, U.S. Steel was a cash-rich company, with over 20 percent of its assets in cash and marketable securities. It is not uncommon to see firms with surplus cash articulating a need for diversification.

---

[11]This ratio implies a fair exchange because a share of Regional is selling for 40 percent (= $10/$25) of the price of a share of Global.

However, we argue that diversification, by itself, cannot produce increases in value. To see this, recall that a business's variability of return can be separated into two parts: (1) what is specific to the business and called *unsystematic* and (2) what is *systematic* because it is common to all businesses.

Systematic variability cannot be eliminated by diversification, so mergers will not eliminate this risk at all. By contrast, unsystematic risk can be diversified away through mergers. However, the investor does not need widely diversified companies such as General Electric to eliminate unsystematic risk. Shareholders can diversify more easily than corporations by simply purchasing common stock in different corporations. For example, the shareholders of U.S. Steel could have purchased shares in Marathon if they believed there would be diversification gains in doing so. Thus, diversification through conglomerate merger may not benefit shareholders.[12]

Diversification can produce gains to the acquiring firm only if one of two things is true:

1. Diversification decreases the unsystematic variability at lower costs than by investors' adjustments to personal portfolios. This seems very unlikely.

2. Diversification reduces risk and thereby increases debt capacity. This possibility was mentioned earlier in the chapter.

29.5 A Cost to Stockholders from Reduction in Risk

We considered two "bad" reasons for mergers in the previous section. However, merging for either of these two reasons will not necessarily destroy value. Rather, it is just unlikely that merging for these two reasons will increases value. In this section, we examine a byproduct of acquisitions that should actually destroy value, at least from the stockholders' point of view. As we will see, mergers increase the safety of bonds, raising the value of these bonds and hurting the stockholders.

In Chapter 10, we considered an individual adding one security after another, all of equal risk, to a portfolio. We saw that as long as the securities were less than perfectly positively correlated with each other, the risk of this portfolio fell as the number of securities rose. In a word, this risk reduction reflected *diversification*. Diversification also happens in a merger. When two firms merge, the volatility of their combined value is usually less than their volatilities as separate entities.

However, there is a surprising result here. Whereas an individual benefits from portfolio diversification, diversification from a merger may actually hurt the stockholders. The reason is that the bondholders are likely to gain from the merger because their debt is now "insured" by two firms, not just one. It turns out that this gain to the bondholders is at the stockholders' expense.

The Base Case

Consider an example where firm *A* acquires firm *B*. Panel I of Table 29.3 shows the net present values of firm *A* and firm *B* prior to the merger in the two possible states of the

---

[12]In fact, a number of scholars have argued that diversification can *reduce* firm value by weakening corporate focus, a point to be developed in a later section of this chapter.

Table 29.3

Stock-Swap Mergers

	NPV		
	State 1	State 2	Market Value
Probability	0.5	0.5	
I. Base case (no debt in either firm's capital structure)			
Values before merger:			
Firm A	$80	$20	$50
Firm B	10	40	25
Values after merger:*			
Firm AB	$90	$60	$75
II. Debt with face value of $30 in firm A's capital structure			
Debt with face value of $15 in firm B's capital structure			
Values before merger:			
Firm A	$80	$20	$50
Debt	30	20	25
Equity	50	0	25
Firm B	$10	$40	$25
Debt	10	15	12.50
Equity	0	25	12.50
Values after merger:†			
Firm AB	$90	$60	$75
Debt	45	45	45
Equity	45	15	30

Values of both firm A's debt and firm B's debt rise after merger. Values of both firm A's stock and firm B's stock fall after merger.

*Stockholders in firm A receive $50 of stock in firm AB. Stockholders in firm B receive $25 of stock in firm AB. Thus stockholders in both firms are indifferent to the merger.

†Stockholders in firm A receive stock in firm AB worth $20. Stockholders in firm B receive stock in firm AB worth $10. Gains and losses from merger are

Loss to stockholders in firm A: $20 − $25 = −$5
Loss to stockholders in firm B: $10 − $12.50 = −$2.50
Combined gain to bondholders in both firms: $45.00 − $37.50 = $7.50

economy. Because the probability of each state is 0.50, the market value of each firm is the average of its values in the two states. For example, the market value of firm A is:

$$0.5 \times \$80 + 0.5 \times \$20 = \$50$$

Now imagine that the merger of the two firms generates no synergy. The combined firm AB will have a market value of $75 (= $50 + $25), the sum of the values of firm A and firm B. Further imagine that the stockholders of firm B receive stock in AB equal to firm B's stand-alone market value of $25. In other words, firm B receives no premium. Because the value of AB is $75, the stockholders of firm A have a value of $50 (= $75 − $25) after the merger—just what they had before the merger. Thus, the stockholders of both firms A and B are indifferent to the merger.

Both Firms Have Debt

Alternatively, imagine that firm A has debt with a face value of $30 in its capital structure, as shown in Panel II of Table 29.3. Without a merger, firm A will default on its debt in state

2 because the value of firm A in this state is $20, less than the face value of the debt of $30. As a consequence, firm A cannot pay the full value of the debt claim; the bondholders receive only $20 in this state. The creditors take the possibility of default into account, valuing the debt at $25 (= 0.5 × $30 + 0.5 × $20).

Firm B's debt has a face value of $15. Firm B will default in state 1 because the value of the firm in this state is $10, less than the face value of the debt of $15. The value of firm B's debt is $12.50 (= 0.5 × $10 + 0.5 × $15). It follows that the sum of the value of firm A's debt and the value of firm B's debt is $37.50 (= $25 + $12.50).

Now let's see what happens after the merger. Firm AB is worth $90 in state 1 and $60 in state 2, implying a market value of $75 (= 0.5 × $90 + 0.5 × $60). The face value of the debt in the combined firm is $45 (= $30 + $15). Because the value of the firm is greater than $45 in either state, the bondholders always get paid in full. Thus, the value of the debt is its face value of $45. This value is $7.50 greater than the sum of the values of the two debts before the merger, which we just found to be $37.50. Therefore, the merger benefits the bondholders.

What about the stockholders? Because the equity of firm A was worth $25 and the equity of firm B was worth $12.50 before the merger, let's assume that firm AB issues two shares to firm A's stockholders for every share issued to firm B's stockholders. Firm AB's equity is $30, so firm A's shareholders get shares worth $20 and firm B's shareholders get shares worth $10. Firm A's stockholders lose $5 (= $20 − $25) from the merger. Similarly, firm B's stockholders lose $2.50 (= $10 − $12.50). The total loss to the stockholders of both firms is $7.50, exactly the gain to the bondholders from the merger.

There are a lot of numbers in this example. The point is that the bondholders gain $7.50 and the stockholders lose $7.50 from the merger. Why does this transfer of value occur? To see what is going on, notice that when the two firms are separate, firm B does not guarantee firm A's debt. That is, if firm A defaults on its debt, firm B does not help the bondholders of firm A. However, after the merger the bondholders can draw on the cash flows from both A and B. When one of the divisions of the combined firm fails, creditors can be paid from the profits of the other division. This mutual guarantee, which is called the *coinsurance effect,* makes the debt less risky and more valuable than before.

There is no net benefit to the firm as a whole. The bondholders gain the coinsurance effect, and the stockholders lose the coinsurance effect. Some general conclusions emerge from the preceding analysis:

1. Mergers usually help bondholders. The size of the gain to bondholders depends on the reduction in the probability of bankruptcy after the combination. That is, the less risky the combined firm is, the greater are the gains to bondholders.

2. Stockholders of the acquiring firm are hurt by the amount that bondholders gain.

3. Conclusion 2 applies to mergers without synergy. In practice, much depends on the size of the synergy.

How Can Shareholders Reduce Their Losses from the Coinsurance Effect?

The coinsurance effect raises bondholder values and lowers shareholder values. However, there are at least two ways in which shareholders can reduce or eliminate the coinsurance effect. First, the shareholders in firm A could retire its debt *before* the merger announcement date and reissue an equal amount of debt after the merger. Because debt is retired at the low premerger price, this type of refinancing transaction can neutralize the coinsurance effect to the bondholders.

Also, note that the debt capacity of the combined firm is likely to increase because the acquisition reduces the probability of financial distress. Thus, the shareholders' second alternative is simply to issue more debt after the merger. An increase in debt following the merger will have two effects, even without the prior action of debt retirement. The interest tax shield from new corporate debt raises firm value, as discussed in an earlier section of this chapter. In addition, an increase in debt after the merger raises the probability of financial distress, thereby reducing or eliminating the bondholders' gain from the coinsurance effect.

29.6 The NPV of a Merger

Firms typically use NPV analysis when making acquisitions. The analysis is relatively straightforward when the consideration is cash. The analysis becomes more complex when the consideration is stock.

Cash

Suppose firm A and firm B have values as separate entities of $500 and $100, respectively. They are both all-equity firms. If firm A acquires firm B, the merged firm AB will have a combined value of $700 due to synergies of $100. The board of firm B has indicated that it will sell firm B if it is offered $150 in cash.

Should firm A acquire firm B? Assuming that firm A finances the acquisition out of its own retained earnings, its value after the acquisition is:[13]

$$\text{Value of firm } A \text{ after the acquisition} = \text{Value of combined firm} - \text{Cash paid}$$
$$= \$700 - \$150$$
$$= \$550$$

Because firm A was worth $500 prior to the acquisition, the NPV to firm A's stockholders is:

$$\$50 = \$550 - \$500 \qquad \qquad \textbf{(29.1)}$$

Assuming that there are 25 shares in firm A, each share of the firm is worth $20 ($= \$500/25$) prior to the merger and $22 ($= \$550/25$) after the merger. These calculations are displayed in the first and third columns of Table 29.4. Looking at the rise in stock price, we conclude that firm A should make the acquisition.

We spoke earlier of both the synergy and the premium of a merger. We can also value the NPV of a merger to the acquirer:

$$\text{NPV of a merger to acquirer} = \text{Synergy} - \text{Premium}$$

Because the value of the combined firm is $700 and the premerger values of A and B were $500 and $100, respectively, the synergy is $100 [$= \$700 - (\$500 + \$100)$]. The premium is $50 ($= \$150 - \$100$). Thus, the NPV of the merger to the acquirer is:

$$\text{NPV of merger to firm } A = \$100 - \$50 = \$50$$

---

[13]The analysis will be essentially the same if new stock is issued. However, the analysis will differ if new debt is issued to fund the acquisition because of the tax shield to debt. An adjusted present value (APV) approach would be necessary here.

Table 29.4   **Cost of Acquisition: Cash versus Common Stock**

	Before Acquisition			After Acquisition: Firm A	
	(1)	(2)	(3)	(4) Common Stock[†] Exchange Ratio (0.75:1)	(5) Common Stock[†] Exchange Ratio (0.6819:1)
	Firm A	Firm B	Cash[*]		
Market value (V_A, V_B)	$500	$100	$550	$700	$700
Number of shares	25	10	25	32.5	31.819
Price per share	$ 20	$ 10	$ 22	$ 21.54	$ 22

[*]Value of firm A after acquisition: cash

$$V_A = V_{AB} - \text{Cash}$$
$$\$550 = \$700 - \$150$$

[†]Value of firm A after acquisition: common stock

$$V_A = V_{AB}$$
$$\$700 = \$700$$

One caveat is in order. This textbook has consistently argued that the market value of a firm is the best estimate of its true value. However, we must adjust our analysis when discussing mergers. If the true price of firm A *without the merger* is $500, the market value of firm A may actually be above $500 when merger negotiations take place. This happens because the market price reflects the possibility that the merger will occur. For example, if the probability is 60 percent that the merger will take place, the market price of firm A will be:

	Market value of firm A with merger	×	Probability of merger	+	Market value of firm A without merger	×	Probability of no merger
$530 =	$550	×	0.60	+	$500	×	0.40

The managers would underestimate the NPV from merger in Equation 29.1 if the market price of firm A is used. Thus, managers face the difficult task of valuing their own firm without the acquisition.

Common Stock

Of course, firm A could purchase firm B with common stock instead of cash. Unfortunately, the analysis is not as straightforward here. To handle this scenario, we need to know how many shares are outstanding in firm B. We assume that there are 10 shares outstanding, as indicated in column 2 of Table 29.4.

Suppose firm A exchanges 7.5 of its shares for the entire 10 shares of firm B. We call this an exchange ratio of 0.75:1. The value of each share of firm A's stock before the acquisition is $20. Because 7.5 × $20 = $150, this exchange *appears* to be the equivalent of purchasing firm B in cash for $150.

This is incorrect: The true cost to firm A is greater than $150. To see this, note that firm A has 32.5 (= 25 + 7.5) shares outstanding after the merger. Firm B shareholders own 23 percent (= 7.5/32.5) of the combined firm. Their holdings are valued at $161 (= 23% × $700). Because these stockholders receive stock in firm A worth $161, the cost of the merger to firm A's stockholders must be $161, not $150.

This result is shown in column 4 of Table 29.4. The value of each share of firm A's stock after a stock-for-stock transaction is only $21.54 (= $700/32.5). We found out earlier that the value of each share is $22 after a cash-for-stock transaction. The difference is that the cost of the stock-for-stock transaction to firm A is higher.

This nonintuitive result occurs because the exchange ratio of 7.5 shares of firm *A* for 10 shares of firm *B* was based on the *premerger* prices of the two firms. However, because the stock of firm *A* rises after the merger, firm *B* stockholders receive more than $150 in firm *A* stock.

What should the exchange ratio be so that firm *B* stockholders receive only $150 of firm *A*'s stock? We begin by defining α, the proportion of the shares in the combined firm that firm *B*'s stockholders own. Because the combined firm's value is $700, the value of firm *B* stockholders after the merger is:

Value of Firm *B* Stockholders after Merger

$$\alpha \times \$700$$

Setting $\alpha \times \$700 = \$150$, we find that $\alpha = 21.43\%$. In other words, firm *B*'s stockholders will receive stock worth $150 if they receive 21.43 percent of the firm after merger.

Now we determine the number of shares issued to firm *B*'s shareholders. The proportion, α, that firm *B*'s shareholders have in the combined firm can be expressed as follows:

$$\alpha = \frac{\text{New shares issued}}{\text{Old shares} + \text{New shares issued}} = \frac{\text{New shares issued}}{25 + \text{New shares issued}}$$

Plugging our value of α into the equation yields:

$$0.2143 = \frac{\text{New shares issued}}{25 + \text{New shares issued}}$$

Solving for the unknown, we have:

$$\text{New shares} = 6.819 \text{ shares}$$

Total shares outstanding after the merger are 31.819 (= 25 + 6.819). Because 6.819 shares of firm *A* are exchanged for 10 shares of firm *B*, the exchange ratio is 0.6819:1.

Results at the exchange ratio of 0.6819:1 are displayed in column 5 of Table 29.4. Because there are now 31.819 shares, each share of common stock is worth $22 (= $700/31.819), exactly what it is worth in the stock-for-cash transaction. Thus, given that the board of firm *B* will sell its firm for $150, this is the fair exchange ratio, not the ratio of 0.75:1 mentioned earlier.

Cash versus Common Stock

In this section, we have examined both cash deals and stock-for-stock deals. Our analysis leads to the following question: When do bidders want to pay with cash and when do they want to pay with stock? There is no easy formula: The decision hinges on a few variables, with perhaps the most important being the price of the bidder's stock.

In the example of Table 29.4, firm *A*'s market price per share prior to the merger was $20. Let's now assume that at the time firm *A*'s managers believed the "true" price was $15. In other words, the managers believed that their stock was overvalued. Is it likely for managers to have a different view than that of the market? Yes—managers often have more information than does the market. After all, managers deal with customers, suppliers, and employees daily and are likely to obtain private information.

Now imagine that firm *A*'s managers are considering acquiring firm *B* with either cash or stock. The overvaluation would have no impact on the merger terms in a cash deal; firm *B* would still receive $150 in cash. However, the overvaluation would have a big impact on a stock-for-stock deal. Although firm *B* receives $150 worth of *A*'s stock as calculated at market prices, firm *A*'s managers know that the true value of the stock is less than $150.

How should firm *A* pay for the acquisition? Clearly, firm *A* has an incentive to pay with stock because it would end up giving away less than $150 of value. This conclusion might seem rather cynical because firm *A* is, in some sense, trying to cheat firm *B*'s stockholders. However, both theory and empirical evidence suggest that firms are more likely to acquire with stock when their own stocks are overvalued.[14]

The story is not quite this simple. Just as the managers of firm *A* think strategically, firm *B*'s managers will likely think this way as well. Suppose that in the merger negotiations, firm *A*'s managers push for a stock-for-stock deal. This might tip off firm *B*'s managers that firm *A* is overpriced. Perhaps firm *B*'s managers will ask for better terms than firm *A* is currently offering. Alternatively, firm *B* may resolve to accept cash or not to sell at all.

And just as firm *B* learns from the negotiations, the market learns also. Empirical evidence shows that the acquirer's stock price generally falls upon the announcement of a stock-for-stock deal.[15]

However, this discussion does not imply that mistakes are never made. For example, consider the stock-for-stock merger in January 2001 between AOL, an Internet service provider, and Time Warner (TW), a media firm. Although the deal was presented as a merger of equals and the combined company is now called Time Warner, AOL appears, in retrospect, to have been the acquirer. The merger was one of the biggest of all time, with a combined market capitalization between the two firms of about $350 billion at the time of the announcement in January 2000. (The delay of about a year between merger announcement and merger completion was due to regulatory review.) It is also considered one of the worst deals of all time, with Time Warner having a market value of about $70 billion in mid-2006.

AOL was in a precarious position at the time of the merger, providing narrow-band Internet service when consumers were hungering for broadband. Also, at least in retrospect, Internet stocks were greatly overpriced. The deal allowed AOL to offer its inflated stock as currency for a company not in the technology industry and, therefore, not nearly as overpriced, if overpriced at all. Had TW looked at the deal in this way, it might have simply called it off. (Alternatively, it could have demanded cash, though it is unlikely that AOL had the financial resources to pay in this way.)

Just as TW's managers did not understand all the implications of the merger right away, it appears that the market did not either. TW's stock price rose over 25 percent relative to the market in the week following the merger announcement.

---

[14]The basic theoretical ideas are presented in S. Myers and N. Majluf, "Corporate Financing and Investment Decisions When Firms Have Information That Investors Do Not Have," *Journal of Financial Economics* (1984).

[15]For example, see G. Andrade, M. Mitchell, and E. Stafford, "New Evidence and Perspectives on Mergers," *Journal of Economic Perspectives* (Spring 2001); and R. Heron and E. Lie, "Operating Performance and the Method of Payment in Takeovers," *Journal of Financial and Quantitative Analysis* (2002).

29.7 Friendly versus Hostile Takeovers

Mergers are generally initiated by the acquiring, not the acquired, firm. Thus, the acquirer must decide to purchase another firm, select the tactics to effectuate the merger, determine the highest price it is willing to pay, set an initial bid price, and make contact with the target firm. Often the CEO of the acquiring firm simply calls on the CEO of the target and proposes a merger. Should the target be receptive, a merger eventually occurs. Of course there may be many meetings, with negotiations over price, terms of payment, and other parameters. The target's board of directors generally has to approve the acquisition. Sometimes the bidder's board must also give its approval. Finally, an affirmative vote by the stockholders is needed. But when all is said and done, an acquisition that proceeds in this way is viewed as *friendly*.

Of course, not all acquisitions are friendly. The target's management may resist the merger, in which case the acquirer must decide whether to pursue the merger and, if so, what tactics to use. Facing resistance, the acquirer may begin by purchasing some of the target's stock in secret. This position is often called a *toehold*. The Williams Act, passed in 1968 and one of the landmark pieces of legislation in the area, requires that the acquirer file a Schedule 13D with the Securities and Exchange Commission (SEC) within 10 days of obtaining a 5 percent holding in the target's stock. The acquirer must provide detailed information, including its intentions and its position in the target, on this schedule. Secrecy ends at this point because the acquirer must state that it plans to acquire the target. The price of the target's shares will probably rise after the filing, with the new stock price reflecting the possibility that the target will be bought out at a premium. Acquirers will, however, often make the most of this 10-day delay, buying as much stock as possible at the low prefiling price during this period.

Although the acquirer may continue to purchase shares in the open market, an acquisition is unlikely to be effectuated in this manner. Rather, the acquirer is more likely at some point to make a *tender offer* (an offer made directly to the stockholders to buy shares at a premium above the current market price). The tender offer may specify that the acquirer will purchase all shares that are tendered—that is, turned in to the acquirer. Alternatively, the offer may state that the acquirer will purchase all shares up to, say, 50 percent of the number of shares outstanding. If more shares are tendered, prorating will occur. For example, if, in the extreme case, all of the shares are tendered, each stockholder will be allowed to sell one share for every two shares tendered. The acquirer may also say that it will accept the tendered shares only if a minimum number of shares have been tendered.

Under the Williams Act, a tender offer must be held open for at least 20 days. This delay gives the target time to respond. For example, the target may want to notify its stockholders not to tender their shares. It may release statements to the press criticizing the offer. The target may also encourage other firms to enter the bidding process.

At some point, the tender offer ends, at which time the acquirer finds out how many shares have been tendered. The acquirer does not necessarily need 100 percent of the shares to obtain control of the target. In some companies, a holding of 20 percent or so may be enough for control. In others the percentage needed for control is much higher. *Control* is a vague term, but you might think of it operationally as control over the board of directors. Stockholders elect members of the board, who, in turn, appoint managers. If the acquirer receives enough stock to elect a majority of the board members, these members can appoint the managers whom the acquirer wants. And effective control can often be achieved with less than a majority. As long as some of the original board members vote with the acquirer, a few new board members can gain the acquirer a working majority.

Sometimes, once the acquirer gets working control, it proposes a merger to obtain the few remaining shares that it does not already own. The transaction is now friendly because the board of directors will approve it. Mergers of this type are often called *cleanup* mergers.

A tender offer is not the only way to gain control of a *hostile* target. Alternatively, the acquirer may continue to buy more shares in the open market until control is achieved. This strategy, often called a *street sweep*, is infrequently used, perhaps because of the difficulty of buying enough shares to obtain control. Also, as mentioned, tender offers often allow the acquirer to return the tendered shares if fewer shares than the desired number are tendered. By contrast, shares purchased in the open market cannot be returned.

Another means to obtain control is a *proxy fight*—a procedure involving corporate voting. Elections for seats on the board of directors are generally held at the annual stockholders' meeting, perhaps four to five months after the end of the firm's fiscal year. After purchasing shares in the target company, the acquirer nominates a slate of candidates to run against the current directors. The acquirer generally hires a proxy solicitor, who contacts shareholders prior to the stockholders' meeting, making a pitch for the insurgent slate. Should the acquirer's candidates win a majority of seats on the board, the acquirer will control the firm. And as with tender offers, effective control can often be achieved with less than a majority. The acquirer may just want to change a few specific policies of the firm, such as the firm's capital budgeting program or its diversification plan. Or it may simply want to replace management. If some of the original board members are sympathetic to the acquirer's plans, a few new board members can give the acquirer a working majority.

For example, consider Carl Icahn's proxy fight with Blockbuster. Carl Icahn's group was Blockbuster's biggest stockholder in early 2005, owning 9.7 percent of the firm's Class A stock and 7.7 percent of the firm's Class B shares. With the company losing over $1 billion in 2004, Mr. Icahn publicly criticized Blockbuster, calling for a number of changes involving spending cuts. He, along with two of his associates, won seats on the Blockbuster board in 2005. Though his group did not win a majority on the seven-member board, pundits argued that he would be able to move the company in his direction.

Whereas mergers end up with the acquirer owning all of the target's stock, the victor in a proxy fight does not gain additional shares. The reward to the proxy victor is simply share price appreciation if the victor's policies prove effective. In fact, just the threat of a proxy fight may raise share prices because management may improve operations to head off the fight. For example, Mr. Icahn had threatened a proxy fight with Kerr-McGee (KM), withdrawing in April 2005 when the stock price rose in response to KM's new policies.

29.8 Defensive Tactics

Target firm managers frequently resist takeover attempts. Actions to defeat a takeover may benefit the target shareholders if the bidding firm raises its offer price or another firm makes a bid. Alternatively, resistance may simply reflect self-interest at the shareholders' expense. That is, the target managers might fight a takeover to preserve their jobs. Sometimes management resists while simultaneously improving corporate policies. Stockholders can benefit in this case, even if the takeover fails.

In this section, we describe various ways in which target managers resist takeovers. A company is said to be "in play" if one or more suitors are currently interested in acquiring it. It is useful to separate defensive tactics before a company is in play from tactics after the company is in play.

Deterring Takeovers before Being in Play

Corporate Charters   The corporate charter refers to the articles of incorporation and corporate bylaws governing a firm. Among other provisions, the charter establishes conditions allowing a takeover. Firms frequently amend charters to make acquisitions more difficult. As examples, consider the following two amendments:

1. *Classified board*: In an unclassified board of directors, stockholders elect all of the directors each year. In a classified, or staggered, board, only a fraction of the board is elected each year, with terms running for multiple years. For example, one-third of the board might stand for election each year, with terms running for three years. Classified boards increase the time an acquirer needs to obtain a majority of seats on the board. In the previous example, the acquirer can gain control of only one-third of the seats in the first year after acquisition. Another year must pass before the acquirer is able to control two-thirds of the seats. Therefore, the acquirer may not be able to change management as quickly as it would like. However, some argue that classified boards are not necessarily effective because the old directors often choose to vote with the acquirer.

2. *Supermajority provisions*: Corporate charters determine the percentage of voting shares needed to approve important transactions such as mergers. A supermajority provision in the charter means that this percentage is above 50 percent. Two-thirds majorities are common, though the number can be much higher. A supermajority provision clearly increases the difficulty of acquisition in the face of hostile management. Many charters with supermajority provisions have what is known as a *board out* clause as well. Here supermajority does not apply if the board of directors approves the merger. This clause makes sure that the provision hinders only hostile takeovers.

Golden Parachutes   This colorful term refers to generous severance packages provided to management in the event of a takeover. The argument is that golden parachutes will deter takeovers by raising the cost of acquisition. However, some authorities point out that the deterrence effect is likely to be unimportant because a severance package, even a generous one, is probably a small part of the cost of acquiring a firm. In addition, some argue that golden parachutes actually *increase* the probability of a takeover. The reasoning here is that management has a natural tendency to resist any takeover because of the possibility of job loss. A large severance package softens the blow of takeover, reducing management's inclination to resist.

Although we are now discussing measures to deter a future hostile takeover, golden parachutes can also be invoked once a bid has been received. For example, when the Scotville board endorsed a $523 million tender offer from First City Properties, it arranged for 13 top executives to receive termination payments of $5 million each.

Poison Pills   The poison pill is a sophisticated defensive tactic that Martin Lipton, a well-known New York attorney, developed in the early 1980s. Since then a number of variants have surfaced, so there is no single definition of a poison pill. Perhaps the example of PeopleSoft (PS) will illustrate the general idea. At one point in 2005, PS's poison pill provision stated that once a bidder acquired 20 percent or more of PeopleSoft's shares, all stockholders except the acquirer could buy new shares from the corporation at half price.

At the time, PS had about 400 million shares outstanding. Should some bidder acquire 20 percent of the company (80 million shares), every shareholder *except the bidder* would be able to buy 16 new shares for every one previously held. If all shareholders exercised this option, PeopleSoft would have to issue 5.12 billion (=0.8 × 400 million × 16) new shares, bringing its total to 5.52 billion. The stock price would drop because the company would be selling shares at half price. The bidder's percentage of the firm would drop from 20 percent to 1.45 percent (=80 million/5.52 billion). Dilution of this magnitude causes some critics to argue that poison pills are insurmountable.

Deterring a Takeover after the Company Is in Play

Greenmail and Standstill Agreements Managers may arrange a *targeted repurchase* to forestall a takeover attempt. In a targeted repurchase, a firm buys back its own stock from a potential bidder, usually at a substantial premium, with the proviso that the seller promises not to acquire the company for a specified period. Critics of such payments label them *greenmail.*

A *standstill agreement* occurs when the acquirer, for a fee, agrees to limit its holdings in the target. As part of the agreement, the acquirer often promises to offer the target a right of first refusal in the event that the acquirer sells its shares. This promise prevents the block of shares from falling into the hands of another would-be acquirer.

EXAMPLE 29.2

Takeover Defenses On April 2, 1986, Ashland Oil, Inc., the nation's largest independent oil refiner, had 28 million shares outstanding. The company's stock price closed the day before at $49\frac{3}{4}$ per share on the New York Stock Exchange. On April 2, Ashland's board of directors made two decisions:

1. The board approved management's agreement with the Belzberg family of Canada to buy, for $51 a share, the Belzbergs' 2.6 million shares in Ashland. This was part of a greenmail agreement ending the Belzberg family's attempt to control Ashland.

2. The board authorized the company to repurchase 7.5 million shares (27 percent of the outstanding shares) of its stock. The board simultaneously established an employee stock ownership plan to be funded with 5.3 million shares of Ashland stock.

These two actions made Ashland invulnerable to unfriendly takeover attempts. In effect, the company was selling about 20 percent of its stock to the employee stock ownership plan. Earlier, Ashland had put in place a provision that said 80 percent of the stockholders have to approve a takeover. Ashland's stock price fell by $0.25 over the next two days. Because this move can probably be explained by random error, there is no evidence that Ashland's actions reduced shareholder value.

Greenmail has been a colorful part of the financial lexicon since its first application in the late 1970s. Since then, pundits have commented numerous times on either its ethical or unethical nature. Greenmail has declined in recent years, perhaps for two reasons. First, Congress has imposed a tax on the profits from greenmail. Second, the law on greenmail is currently unsettled, causing recipients to worry about potential lawsuits.

White Knight and White Squire A firm facing an unfriendly merger offer might arrange to be acquired by a friendly suitor, commonly referred to as a *white knight.* The white knight might be favored simply because it is willing to pay a higher purchase price. Alternatively, it might promise not to lay off employees, fire managers, or sell off divisions.

Management instead may wish to avoid any acquisition at all. A third party, termed a *white squire*, might be invited to make a significant investment in the firm, under the condition that it vote with management and not purchase additional shares. White squires are generally offered shares at favorable prices. Billionaire investor Warren Buffett has acted as a white squire to many firms, including Champion International and Gillette.

Recapitalizations and Repurchases   Target management will often issue debt to pay out a dividend—a transaction called a *leveraged recapitalization*. A *share repurchase,* where debt is issued to buy back shares, is a similar transaction. The two transactions fend off takeovers in a number of ways. First, the stock price may rise, perhaps because of the increased tax shield from greater debt. A rise in stock price makes the acquisition less attractive to the bidder. However, the price will rise only if the firm's debt level before the recapitalization was below the optimum, so a levered recapitalization is not recommended for every target. Consultants point out that firms with low debt but with stable cash flows are ideal candidates for "recaps." Second, as part of the recapitalization, management may issue new securities that give management greater voting control than it had before the recap. The increase in control makes a hostile takeover more difficult. Third, firms with a lot of cash on their balance sheets are often seen as attractive targets. As part of the recap, the target may use this cash to pay a dividend or buy back stock, reducing the firm's appeal as a takeover candidate.

Exclusionary Self-Tenders   An *exclusionary self-tender* is the opposite of a targeted repurchase. Here, the firm makes a tender offer for a given amount of its own stock while excluding targeted stockholders.

In a particularly celebrated case, Unocal, a large integrated oil firm, made a tender offer for 29 percent of its shares while excluding its largest shareholder, Mesa Partners II (led by T. Boone Pickens). Unocal's self-tender was for $72 per share, which was $16 over the prevailing market price. It was designed to defeat Mesa's attempted takeover of Unocal by transferring wealth, in effect, from Mesa to Unocal's other stockholders.

Asset Restructurings   In addition to altering capital structure, firms may sell off existing assets or buy new ones to avoid takeover. Targets generally sell, or divest, assets for two reasons. First, a target firm may have assembled a hodgepodge of assets in different lines of business, with the various segments fitting together poorly. Value might be increased by placing these divisions into separate firms. Academics often emphasize the concept of *corporate focus.* The idea here is that firms function best by focusing on those few businesses that they really know. A rise in stock price following a divestiture will reduce the target's appeal to a bidder.

The second reason is that a bidder might be interested in a specific division of the target. The target can reduce the bidder's interest by selling off this division. Although the strategy may fend off a merger, it can hurt the target's stockholders if the division is worth more to the target than to the division's buyer. Authorities frequently talk of selling off the *crown jewels* or pursuing a *scorched earth policy.*

While some targets divest existing assets, others buy new ones. Two reasons are generally given here. First, the bidder may like the target as is. The addition of an unrelated business makes the target less appealing to the acquirer. However, a bidder can always sell off the new business, so the purchase is likely not a strong defense. Second, antitrust legislation is designed to prohibit mergers that reduce competition. Antitrust law is enforced by both the Department of Justice (DOJ) and the Federal Trade Commission (FTC). A target may purchase a company, knowing that this new division will pose antitrust problems for the bidder. However, this strategy might not be effective because, in its filings with the DOJ and the FTC, the bidder can state its intention to sell off the unrelated business.

29.9 Do Mergers Add Value?

In Section 29.2, we stated that synergy occurs if the value of the combined firm after the merger is greater than the sum of the value of the acquiring firm and the value of the acquired firm before the merger. Section 29.3 provided a number of sources of synergy in mergers, implying that mergers *can* create value. We now want to know whether mergers actually create value in practice. This is an empirical question and must be answered by empirical evidence.

There are a number of ways to measure value creation, but many academics favor *event studies.* These studies estimate abnormal stock returns on, and around, the merger announcement date. An *abnormal return* is usually defined as the difference between an actual stock return and the return on a market index or control group of stocks. This control group is used to net out the effect of marketwide or industrywide influences.

Consider Table 29.5, where returns around the announcement days of mergers are reported. The average abnormal percentage return across all mergers from 1980 to 2001 is 0.0135. This number combines the returns on both the acquiring company and the acquired company. Because 0.0135 is positive, the market believes that mergers on average create value. The other three returns in the first column are positive as well, implying value creation in the different subperiods. Many other academic studies have provided similar results. Thus, it appears from this column that the synergies we mentioned in Section 29.3 show up in the real world.

However, the next column tells us something different. Across all mergers from 1980 to 2001, the aggregate dollar change around the day of merger announcement is −$79 billion. This means that the market is, on average, *reducing* the combined stock value of the acquiring and acquired companies around the merger announcement date. Though the difference between the two columns may seem confusing, there is an explanation. Although most mergers have created value, mergers involving the very largest firms have lost value. The abnormal percentage return is an unweighted average in which the returns on all mergers are treated equally. A positive return here reflects all those small mergers that created value. However, losses in a few large mergers cause the aggregate dollar change to be negative.

But there is more. The rest of the second column indicates that the aggregate dollar losses occurred only in the 1998 to 2001 period. While there were losses of −$134 billion in this period, there were gains of $12 billion from 1980 to 1990. And interpolation of the table indicates that there were gains of $44 billion (=$134 − $90) from 1991 through 1997. Thus, it appears that some large mergers lost a great deal of value from 1998 to 2001.

Table 29.5 Percentage and Dollar Returns for Mergers

Time Period	Gain or Loss to Merger (Both Acquired and Acquiring Firms)		Gain or Loss to Acquiring Firms	
	Abnormal Percentage Return	Aggregate Dollar Gain or Loss	Abnormal Percentage Return	Aggregate Dollar Gain or Loss
1980–2001	0.0135	−$79 billion	0.0110	−$220 billion
1980–1990	0.0241	$12 billion	0.0064	−$4 billion
1991–2001	0.0104	−$90 billion	0.0120	−$216 billion
1998–2001	0.0029	−$134 billion	0.0069	−$240 billion

SOURCE: Modified from Sara Moeller, Frederik Schlingemann, and Rene Stulz, "Wealth Destruction on a Massive Scale? A Study of Acquiring-Firm Returns in the Recent Merger Wave," *Journal of Finance* (April 2005), Table 1.

The results in a table such as Table 29.5 should have important implications for public policy because Congress is always wondering whether mergers are to be encouraged or discouraged. However, the results in that table are, unfortunately, ambiguous. On the one hand, you could focus on the first column, saying that mergers create value on average. Proponents of this view might argue that the great losses in the few large mergers were flukes, not likely to occur again. On the other hand, we cannot easily ignore the fact that over the entire period, mergers destroyed more value than they created. A proponent of this position might quote the old adage, "Except for World War I and World War II, the 20th century was quite peaceful."

Before we move on, some final thoughts are in order. Readers may be bothered that abnormal returns are taken only around the time of the acquisition, well before all of the acquisition's impact is revealed. Academics look at long-term returns but they have a special fondness for short-term returns. If markets are efficient, the short-term return provides an unbiased estimate of the total effect of the merger. Long-term returns, while capturing more information about a merger, also reflect the impact of many unrelated events.

Returns to Bidders

The preceding results combined returns on both bidders and targets. Investors want to separate the bidders from the targets. Columns 3 and 4 of Table 29.5 provide returns for acquiring companies alone. The third column shows that abnormal percentage returns for bidders have been positive for the entire sample period and for each of the individual subperiods—a result similar to that for bidders and targets combined. The fourth column indicates aggregate dollar losses, suggesting that large mergers did worse than small ones. The time pattern for these aggregate dollar losses to bidders is presented in Figure 29.3. Again, the large losses occurred from 1998 to 2001, with the greatest loss in 2000.

Let's fast-forward a few decades and imagine that you are the CEO of a company. In that position you will certainly be faced with potential acquisitions. Does the evidence in Table 29.5 and Figure 29.3 encourage you to make acquisitions or not? Again, the evidence is ambiguous. On the one hand, you could focus on the averages in Column 3 of the table, likely increasing your appetite for acquisitions. On the other hand, Column 4 of the table, as well as the figure, might give you pause.

Target Companies

Although the evidence just presented for both the combined entity and the bidder alone is ambiguous, the evidence for targets is crystal-clear. Acquisitions benefit the target's stockholders. Consider the following chart, which shows the median merger *premium* over different periods in the United States:[16]

Time Period	1973–1998	1973–1979	1980–1989	1990–1998
Premium	42.1%	47.2%	37.7%	34.5%

The premium is the difference between the acquisition price per share and the target's pre-acquisition share price, divided by the target's pre-acquisition share price. The average premium is quite high for the entire sample period and for the various subsamples. For example, a target stock selling at $100 per share before the acquisition that is later acquired for $142.1 per share generates a premium of 42.1 percent. Clearly, stockholders of any firm trading at $100 would love to be able to sell their holdings for $142.1 per share.

---

[16]Taken from Gregor Andrade, Mark Mitchell, and Erik Stafford, "New Evidence and Perspectives on Mergers," *Journal of Economic Perspectives* (Spring 2001), Table 1.

Figure 29.3

Yearly Aggregate Dollar Gain or Loss for the Shareholders of Acquiring Firms

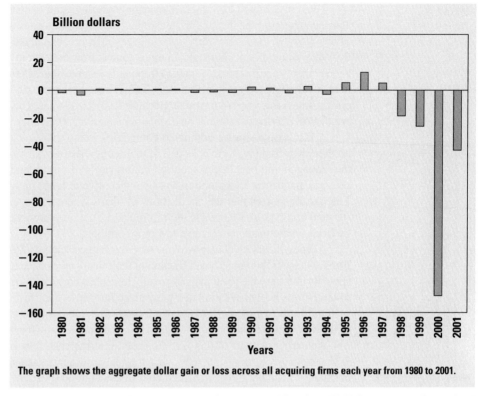

The graph shows the aggregate dollar gain or loss across all acquiring firms each year from 1980 to 2001.

SOURCE: Taken from Figure 1, Sara Moeller, Frederick Schlingemann, and Rene Stulz, "Wealth Destruction on a Massive Scale? A Study of Acquiring-Firm Returns in the Recent Merger Wave," *Journal of Finance* (April 2005).

Though other studies may provide different estimates of the average premium, all studies show positive premiums. Thus, we can conclude that mergers benefit the target stockholders. This conclusion leads to at least two implications. First, we should be somewhat skeptical of target managers who resist takeovers. These managers may claim that the target's stock price does not reflect the true value of the company. Or they may say that resistance will induce the bidder to raise its offer. These arguments could be true in certain situations, but they may also provide cover for managers who are simply scared of losing their jobs after acquisition. Second, the premium creates a hurdle for the acquiring company. Even in a merger with true synergies, the acquiring stockholders will lose if the premium exceeds the dollar value of these synergies.

The Managers versus the Stockholders

Managers of Bidding Firms   The preceding discussion was presented from the stockholders' point of view. Because, in theory, stockholders pay the salaries of managers, we might think that managers would look at things from the stockholders' point of view. However, it is important to realize that individual stockholders have little clout with managers. For example, the typical stockholder is simply not in a position to pick up the phone and give the managers a piece of her mind. It is true that the stockholders elect the board of directors, which monitors the managers. However, an elected director has little contact with individual stockholders.

Thus, it is fair to ask whether managers are held fully accountable for their actions. This question is at the heart of what economists call *agency theory.* Researchers in this area often argue that managers work less hard, get paid more, and make worse business decisions than they would if stockholders had more control over them. And there is a special place in agency theory for mergers. Managers frequently receive bonuses for acquiring other companies. In addition, their pay is often positively related to the size of their firm. Finally, managers' prestige is also tied to firm size. Because firm size increases with acquisitions, managers are disposed to look favorably on acquisitions, perhaps even ones with negative NPV.

A fascinating study[17] compared companies where managers received a lot of options on their own company's stock as part of their compensation package with companies where the managers did not. Because option values rise and fall in tandem with the firm's stock price, managers receiving options have an incentive to forgo mergers with negative NPVs. The paper reported that the acquisitions by firms where managers receive lots of options (termed *equity-based compensation* in the paper) create more value than the acquisitions by firms where managers receive few or no options.

Agency theory may also explain why the biggest merger failures have involved large firms. Managers owning a small fraction of their firm's stock have less incentive to behave responsibly because the great majority of any losses are borne by other stockholders. Managers of large firms likely have a smaller percentage interest in their firm's stock than do managers of small firms (a large percentage of a large firm is too costly to acquire). Thus, the merger failures of large acquirers may be due to the small percentage ownership of the managers.

An earlier chapter of this text discussed the free cash flow hypothesis. The idea here is that managers can spend only what they have. Managers of firms with low cash flow are likely to run out of cash before they run out of good (positive NPV) investments. Conversely, managers of firms with high cash flow are likely to have cash on hand even after all the good investments are taken. Managers are rewarded for growth, so managers with cash flow above that needed for good projects have an incentive to spend the remainder on bad (negative NPV) projects. A paper tested this conjecture, finding that "cash-rich firms are more likely than other firms to attempt acquisitions. . . . cash-rich bidders destroy seven cents in value for every dollar of cash reserves held. . . . consistent with the stock return evidence, mergers in which the bidder is cash-rich are followed by abnormal declines in operating performance."[18]

The previous discussion has considered the possibility that some managers were knaves—more interested in their own welfare than in the welfare of their stockholders. However, a recent paper entertained the idea that other managers were more fools than knaves. Malmendier and Tate[19] classified certain CEOs as overconfident, either because they refused to exercise stock options on their own company's stock when it was rational to do so or because the press portrayed them as confident or optimistic. The authors find that these overconfident managers are more likely to make acquisitions than are other managers. In addition, the stock market reacts more negatively to announcements of acquisitions when the acquiring CEO is overconfident.

Managers of Target Firms   Our discussion has just focused on the managers of acquiring firms, finding that these managers sometimes make more acquisitions than they should.

---

[17]Sudip Datta, Mai Iskandar-Datta, and Kartil Raman, "Executive Compensation and Corporate Acquisition Decisions," *Journal of Finance* (December 2001).

[18]From Jarrad Harford, "Corporate Cash Reserves and Acquisitions," *Journal of Finance* (December 1999), p. 1969.

[19]Ulrike Malmendier and Geoffrey Tate, "Who Makes Acquisitions? CEO Overconfidence and the Market's Reaction," unpublished paper, Stanford University (December 2003).

However, that is only half of the story. Stockholders of target firms may have just as hard a time controlling their managers. While there are many ways that managers of target firms can put themselves ahead of their stockholders, two seem to stand out. First, we said earlier that because premiums are positive, takeovers are beneficial to the target's stockholders. However, if managers may be fired after their firms are acquired, they may resist these takeovers.[20] Tactics employed to resist takeover, generally called defensive tactics, were discussed in an earlier section of this chapter. Second, managers who cannot avoid takeover may bargain with the bidder, getting a good deal for themselves at the expense of their shareholders.

Consider Wulf's fascinating work on *mergers of equals* (MOEs).[21] Some deals are announced as MOEs, primarily because both firms have equal ownership in and equal representation on the board of directors of the merged entity. AOL and Time Warner, Daimler-Benz and Chrysler, Morgan Stanley and Dean Witter, and Fleet Financial Group and BankBoston are generally held out as examples of MOEs. Nevertheless, authorities point out that in any deal one firm is typically "more equal" than the other. That is, the target and the bidder can usually be distinguished in practice. For example, Daimler-Benz is commonly classified as the bidder and Chrysler as the target in their merger.

Wulf finds that targets get a lower percentage of the merger gains, as measured by abnormal returns around the announcement date, in MOEs than in other mergers. And the percentage of the gains going to the target is negatively related to the representation of the target's officers and directors on the postmerger board. These and other findings lead Wulf to conclude, "They [the findings of the paper] suggest that CEOs trade power for premium in merger of equals transactions."

29.10 The Tax Forms of Acquisitions

If one firm buys another, the transaction may be taxable or tax-free. In a *taxable acquisition*, the shareholders of the acquired firm are considered to have sold their shares, and their realized capital gains or losses will be taxed. In a taxable transaction, the *appraised value* of the assets of the selling firm may be revalued, as we explain next.

In a *tax-free acquisition*, the selling shareholders are considered to have exchanged their old shares for new ones of equal value, and they have experienced no capital gains or losses. In a tax-free acquisition the assets are not revalued.

EXAMPLE 29.3

Taxes Suppose that 15 years ago Bill Evans started the Samurai Machinery (SM) Corp., which purchased plant and equipment costing $80,000. These have been the only assets of SM, and the company has no debts. Bill is the sole proprietor of SM and owns all the shares. For tax purposes the assets of SM have been depreciated using the straight-line method over 10 years and have no salvage value. The annual depreciation expense has been $8,000 (= $80,000/10). The machinery has no accounting value today (i.e., it has been written off the books). However, because of inflation, the fair market value of the machinery is $200,000. As a consequence, the S.A. Steel Company has bid $200,000 for all of the outstanding stock of Samurai.

---

[20]However, as stated earlier, managers may resist takeovers to raise the offer price, not to prevent the merger.

[21]Julie Wulf, "Do CEOs in Mergers Trade Power for Premium? Evidence From 'Mergers of Equals,'" *Journal of Law, Economics, and Organization* (Spring 2004).

Table 29.6   **The Tax Consequences of S. A. Steel Company's Acquisition of Samurai Machinery**

Buyer or Seller	Type of Acquisition	
	Taxable Acquisition	Tax-Free Acquisition
Bill Evans	Immediate tax on $120,000 ($200,000 − $80,000)	Capital gain tax not paid until Evans sells shares of S.A. Steel
S.A. Steel	S.A. Steel may elect to write up assets: 1. Assets of Samurai are written up to $200,000 (with useful life of 10 years). Annual depreciation expense is $20,000. 2. Immediate tax on $200,000 write-up of assets. Alternatively, S.A. Steel may elect not to write up assets. Here there is neither additional depreciation nor immediate tax. Typically acquirers elect *not* to write up assets.	No additional depreciation

S.A. Steel acquires Samurai Machinery for $200,000, which is the market value of Samurai's equipment. The book value of the equipment is $0. Bill Evans started Samurai Steel 15 years ago with a contribution of $80,000.

The tax consequences of a tax-free acquisition are better than the tax consequences of a taxable acquisition because the seller pays no immediate tax on a tax-free acquisition.

Tax-Free Transaction   If Bill Evans receives *shares* of S. A. Steel worth $200,000, the IRS will treat the sale as a tax-free transaction. Thus, Bill will not have to pay taxes on any gain received from the stock. In addition, S. A. Steel will be allowed the same depreciation deduction that Samurai Machinery was allowed. Because the asset has already been fully depreciated, S. A. Steel will receive no depreciation deduction.

Taxable Transaction   If S. A. Steel pays $200,000 in *cash* for Samurai Machinery, the transaction will be taxable with the following consequences:

1. In the year of the merger, Bill Evans must pay taxes on the difference between the merger price of $200,000 and his initial contribution to the firm of $80,000. Thus, his taxable income is $120,000 (= $200,000 − $80,000).

2. S. A. Steel may *elect* to *write up* the value of the machinery. In this case, S. A. Steel will be able to depreciate the machinery from an initial tax basis of $200,000. If S. A. Steel depreciates straight-line over 10 years, depreciation will be $20,000 (= $200,000/10) per year.

     If S. A. Steel elects to write up the machinery, S. A. Steel must treat the $200,000 write-up as taxable income immediately.[22]

3. Should S. A. Steel *not* elect the write-up, there is no increase in depreciation. Thus, depreciation remains zero in this example. In addition, because there is no write-up, S. A. Steel does not need to recognize any additional taxable income.

     Because the tax benefits from depreciation occur slowly over time and the taxable income is recognized immediately, the acquirer generally elects *not* to write up the value of the machinery in a taxable transaction.

Because the write-up is not allowed for tax-free transactions and is generally not chosen for taxable ones, the only real tax difference between the two types of transactions

---

[22]Technically, Samurai Machinery pays this tax. However, because Samurai is now a subsidiary of S. A. Steel, S. A. Steel is the effective taxpayer.

concerns the taxation of the selling shareholders. These individuals can defer taxes under a tax-free situation but must pay taxes immediately under a taxable situation, so the tax-free transaction has better tax consequences. The tax implications for both types of transactions are displayed in Table 29.6.

29.11 Accounting for Acquisitions

Earlier in this text we mentioned that firms keep two distinct sets of books: the stockholders' books and the tax books. The previous section concerned the effect of acquisitions on the tax books. We now consider the stockholders' books. When one firm acquires another, the buyer uses the purchase method to account for the acquisition.

The **purchase** method requires that the assets of the acquired firm be reported at their fair market value on the books of the acquiring firm. This allows the acquiring firm to establish a new cost basis for the acquired assets.

In a purchase, an accounting term called *goodwill* is created. **Goodwill** is the excess of the purchase price over the sum of the fair market values of the individual assets acquired.

EXAMPLE 29.4

Acquisitions and Accounting Suppose firm A acquires firm B, creating a new firm, AB. Firm A's and firm B's financial positions at the date of the acquisition are shown in Table 29.7. The book value of firm B on the date of the acquisition is $10 million. This is the sum of $8 million in buildings and $2 million in cash. However, an appraiser states that the sum of the fair market values of the individual buildings is $14 million. With $2 million in cash, the sum of the market values of the individual assets in firm B is $16 million. This represents the value to be received if the firm is liquidated by selling off the individual assets separately. However, the whole is often worth more than the sum of the parts in business. Firm A pays $19 million in cash for firm B. This difference of $3 million (= $19 million − $16 million) is goodwill. It represents the increase in value from keeping the firm as an ongoing business. Firm A issued $19 million in new debt to finance the acquisition.

The total assets of firm AB increase to $39 million. The buildings of firm B appear in the new balance sheet at their current market value. That is, the market value of the assets of the acquired firm becomes part of the book value of the new firm. However, the assets of the acquiring firm (firm A) remain at their old book value. They are not revalued upward when the new firm is created.

The excess of the purchase price over the sum of the fair market values of the individual assets acquired is $3 million. This amount is reported as goodwill. Financial analysts generally ignore goodwill because it has no cash flow consequences. Each year the firm must assess the value of its goodwill. If the value goes down (this is called *impairment* in accounting speak), the amount of goodwill on the balance sheet must be decreased accordingly. Otherwise no amortization is required.

Table 29.7 **Accounting for Acquisitions: Purchase (in $ millions)**

Firm A				Firm B				Firm AB			
Cash	$ 4	Equity	$20	Cash	$ 2	Equity	$10	Cash	$ 6	Debt	$19
Land	16			Land	0			Land	16	Equity	20
Buildings	0			Buildings	8			Buildings	14		
								Goodwill	3		
Total	$20		$20	Total	$10		$10	Total	$39		$39

When the purchase method is used, the assets of the acquired firm (firm B) appear in the combined firm's books at their fair market value.

29.12   Going Private and Leveraged Buyouts

Going private transactions and leveraged buyouts have much in common with mergers, and it is worthwhile to discuss them in this chapter. A publicly traded firm *goes private* when a private group, usually composed of existing management, purchases its stock. As a consequence, the firm's stock is taken off the market (if it is an exchange-traded stock, it is delisted) and is no longer traded. Thus, in going-private transactions, shareholders of publicly held firms are forced to accept cash for their shares.

Going-private transactions are frequently *leveraged buyouts* (LBOs). In a leveraged buyout the cash offer price is financed with large amounts of debt. Part of the appeal of LBOs is that the arrangement calls for little equity capital. This equity capital is generally supplied by a small group of investors, some of whom are likely to be managers of the firm being purchased.

The selling stockholders are invariably paid a premium above market price in an LBO, just as in a merger. As with a merger, the acquirer profits only if the synergy created is greater than the premium. Synergy is quite plausible in a merger of *two* firms, and we delineated a number of types of synergy earlier in the chapter. However, it is more difficult to explain synergy in an LBO because only *one* firm is involved.

Two reasons are generally given for value creation in an LBO. First, the extra debt provides a tax deduction, which, as earlier chapters suggested, leads to an increase in firm value. Most LBOs are on firms with stable earnings and with low to moderate debt. The LBO may simply increase the firm's debt to its optimum level.

The second source of value comes from increased efficiency and is often explained in terms of "the carrot and the stick." Managers become owners under an LBO, giving them an incentive to work hard. This incentive is commonly referred to as the carrot, and the carrots in some LBOs have been huge. For example, consider the LBO of Gibson Greeting Cards (GGC), previously a division of RCA, for which the management buyout group paid about $80 million. Because of the leveraged nature of the transaction, the group invested only about $1 million of its own capital. The division was taken private in 1982, but only for a brief period; GGC went public as its own company in 1984. The value of the initial public offering (IPO) was almost $300 million. One of the principals in the buyout group, William Simon, who was a former secretary of the U.S. Treasury, received $66 million from the IPO on an investment of somewhat under $350,000.

Interest payments from the high level of debt constitute the stick. Large interest payments can easily turn a profitable firm before an LBO into an unprofitable one after the LBO. Management must make changes, either through revenue increases or cost reductions, to keep the firm in the black. Agency theory, a topic mentioned earlier in this chapter, suggests that managers can be wasteful with a large free cash flow. Interest payments reduce this cash flow, forcing managers to curb the waste.

Though it is easy to measure the additional tax shields from an LBO, it is difficult to measure the gains from increased efficiency. Nevertheless, this increased efficiency is considered at least as important as the tax shield in explaining the LBO phenomenon.

Academic research suggests that LBOs have, on average, created value. First, premiums are positive, as they are with mergers, implying that selling stockholders benefit. Second, studies indicate that LBOs that eventually go public generate high returns for the management group. Finally, other studies show that operating performance increases after the LBO. However, we cannot be completely confident of value creation because researchers have difficulty obtaining data about LBOs that do not go public. If these LBOs generally destroy value, the sample of firms going public would be a biased one.

Regardless of the average performance of firms undertaking an LBO, we can be sure of one thing: Because of the great leverage involved, the risk is huge. On the one hand, LBOs have created many large fortunes, a prominent example being Gibson Greeting Cards. On the other hand, a number of bankruptcies and near-bankruptcies have occurred as well, perhaps the most infamous being Revco's LBO. Revco was taken private near the end of 1986, but it is still talked about extensively today. In retrospect, the management group overpaid (a premium almost 50 percent above market price) and overlevered (a debt-to-value ratio of 97 percent). Revco was also not an ideal LBO candidate, though it seemed to be at the time. As mentioned earlier, firms with stable cash flows can best handle the high leverage of LBOs. Revco, a chain of about 1,400 drugstores, seemed to fit the bill here because sales in this retail industry are relatively unresponsive to the business cycle. However, Revco planned to add about 100 stores a year, a strategy necessitating large capital expenditures. The combination of high leverage and large capital commitments provided little margin for error. The firm went under about a year and a half after the LBO. Perhaps the depressed Christmas season of 1987 or the rise of the discounters pushed Revco over the edge. Because of the size of the transaction (total LBO financing over $1.4 billion) and the embarrassment to the LBO specialist (it was Salomon Brothers' first large LBO), pundits are still arguing about the cause of Revco's demise.

29.13 Divestitures

This chapter has primarily been concerned with acquisitions but it is also worthwhile to consider their opposite—divestitures. Divestitures come in a number of different varieties, the most important of which we discuss next.

Sale

The most basic type of divestiture is the *sale* of a division, business unit, segment, or set of assets to another company. The buyer generally, but not always, pays in cash. A number of reasons are provided for sales. First, in an earlier section of this chapter we considered asset sales as a defense against hostile takeovers. It was pointed out in that section that sales often improve corporate focus, leading to greater overall value for the seller. This same rationale applies when the selling company is not in play. Second, asset sales provide needed cash to liquidity-poor firms. Third, it is often argued that the paucity of data about individual business segments makes large, diversified firms hard to value. Investors may discount the firm's overall value because of this lack of transparency. Sell-offs streamline a firm, making it easier to value. However, this argument is inconsistent with market efficiency because it implies that large, diversified firms sell below their true value. Fourth, firms may simply want to sell unprofitable divisions. However, unprofitable divisions are likely to have low values to anyone. A division should be sold only if its value is greater to the buyer than to the seller.

There has been a fair amount of research on sell-offs, with academics reaching two conclusions. First, event studies show that returns on the seller's stock are positive around the time of the announcement of sale, suggesting that sell-offs create value to the seller. Second, acquisitions are often sold off down the road. For example, Kaplan and Weisbach[23] found that over 40 percent of acquisitions were later divested, a result that does not reflect well on mergers. The average time between acquisition and divestiture was about seven years.

---

[23]Steven Kaplan and Michael Weisbach, "The Success of Acquisitions: Evidence from Divestitures," *Journal of Finance* (March 1992).

Spin-Off

In a spin-off a parent firm turns a division into a separate entity and distributes shares in this entity to the parent's stockholders. Spin-offs differ from sales in at least two ways. First, the parent firm receives no cash from a spin-off: Shares are sent for free to the stockholders. Second, the initial stockholders of the spun-off division are the same as the parent's stockholders. By contrast, the buyer in a sell-off is most likely another firm. However, because the shares of the division are publicly traded after the spin-off, the identities of the stockholders will change over time.

At least four reasons are generally given for a spin-off. First, as with a sell-off, the spin-off may increase corporate focus. Second, because the spun-off division is now publicly traded, the Securities and Exchange Commission requires additional information to be disseminated—so investors may find it easier to value the parent and subsidiary after the spin-off. Third, corporations often compensate executives with shares of stock in addition to cash. The stock acts as an incentive: Good performance from managers leads to stock price increases. However, prior to the spin-off, executives can receive stock only in the parent company. If the division is small relative to the entire firm, price movement in the parent's stock will be less related to the performance of the manager's division than to the performance of the rest of the firm. Thus, divisional managers may see little relation between their effort and stock appreciation. However, after the spin-off, the manager can be given stock in the subsidiary. The manager's effort should directly impact price movement in the subsidiary's stock. Fourth, the tax consequences from a spin-off are generally better than from a sale because the parent receives no cash from a spin-off.

Carve-Out

In a carve-out, the firm turns a division into a separate entity and then sells shares in the division to the public. Generally the parent retains a large interest in the division. This transaction is similar to a spin-off, and the first three benefits listed for a spin-off apply to a carve-out as well. However, the big difference is that the firm receives cash from a carve-out, but not from a spin-off. The receipt of cash can be both good and bad. On the one hand, many firms need cash. Michaely and Shaw[24] find that large, profitable firms are more likely to use carve-outs, whereas small, unprofitable firms are more likely to use spin-offs. One interpretation is that firms generally prefer the cash that comes with a carve-out. However, small and unprofitable firms have trouble issuing stock. They must resort to a spin-off, where stock in the subsidiary is merely given to their own stockholders.

Unfortunately, there is also a dark side to cash, as developed in the free cash flow hypothesis. That is, firms with cash exceeding that needed for profitable capital budgeting projects may spend it on unprofitable ones. Allen and McConnell[25] find that the stock market reacts positively to announcements of carve-outs if the cash is used to reduce debt. The market reacts neutrally if the cash is used for investment projects.

Tracking Stocks

A parent corporation issues tracking stock to "track" the performance of a specific division of the corporation. For example, if the tracking stock pays dividends, the size of the dividend

---

[24]Roni Michaely and Wayne Shaw, "The Choice of Going Public: Spinoffs vs. Carveouts," *Financial Management* (Autumn 1995).

[25]Jeffrey Allen and John McConnell, "Equity Carve-outs and Managerial Discretion," *Journal of Finance* (February 1998).

depends on the division's performance. However, although "trackers" trade separately from the parent's stock, the division stays with the parent. By contrast, the subsidiary separates from the parent in a spin-off.

The first tracking stock was tied to the performance of EDS, a subsidiary of General Motors. Later, large firms such as Walt Disney and Sony issued trackers. However, few companies have issued tracking stocks in recent years, and parents have pulled most of those issued in earlier times.

Perhaps the biggest problem with tracking stocks is their lack of clearly defined property rights. An optimistic accountant can increase the earnings of a particular division, leading to a larger dividend. A pessimistic accountant will have the reverse effect. Although accountants affect the earnings of regular companies, a change in earnings will not directly impact dividends.

Summary and Conclusions

1. One firm can acquire another in several different ways. The three legal forms of acquisition are merger and consolidation, acquisition of stock, and acquisition of assets. Mergers and consolidations are the least costly from a legal standpoint, but they require a vote of approval by the shareholders. Acquisition by stock does not require a shareholder vote and is usually done via a tender offer. However, it is difficult to obtain 100 percent control with a tender offer. Acquisition of assets is comparatively costly because it requires more difficult transfer of asset ownership.

2. The synergy from an acquisition is defined as the value of the combined firm (V_{AB}) less the value of the two firms as separate entities (V_A and V_B):

$$\text{Synergy} = V_{AB} - (V_A + V_B)$$

The shareholders of the acquiring firm will gain if the synergy from the merger is greater than the premium.

3. The possible benefits of an acquisition come from the following:
   a. Revenue enhancement.
   b. Cost reduction.
   c. Lower taxes.
   d. Reduced capital requirements.

4. Stockholders may not benefit from a merger that is done only to achieve diversification or earnings growth. And the reduction in risk from a merger may actually help bondholders and hurt stockholders.

5. A merger is said to be friendly when the managers of the target support it. A merger is said to be hostile when the target managers do not support it. Some of the most colorful language of finance stems from defensive tactics in hostile takeover battles. *Poison pills, golden parachutes, crown jewels,* and *greenmail* are terms that describe various antitakeover tactics.

6. The empirical research on mergers and acquisitions is extensive. On average, the shareholders of acquired firms fare very well. The effect of mergers on acquiring stockholders is less clear.

7. Mergers and acquisitions involve complicated tax and accounting rules. Mergers and acquisitions can be taxable or tax-free transactions. In a taxable transaction each selling shareholder must pay taxes on the stock's capital appreciation. Should the acquiring firm elect to write up the assets, additional tax implications arise. However, acquiring firms do not generally elect to write up the assets for tax purposes. The selling stockholders do not pay taxes at the time of a tax-free acquisition. The purchase method is used to account for mergers and acquisitions.

8. In a *going-private* transaction, a buyout group, usually including the firm's management, buys all the shares of the other stockholders. The stock is no longer publicly traded. A *leveraged buyout* is a going-private transaction financed by extensive leverage.

www.mhhe.com/rwj

Concept Questions

1. **Merger Accounting**   Explain the difference between purchase and pooling of interests accounting for mergers. What is the effect on cash flows of the choice of accounting method? On EPS?

2. **Merger Concepts**   Indicate whether you think the following claims regarding takeovers are true or false. In each case, provide a brief explanation for your answer.
   a. By merging competitors, takeovers have created monopolies that will raise product prices, reduce production, and harm consumers.
   b. Managers act in their own interests at times and in reality may not be answerable to shareholders. Takeovers may reflect runaway management.
   c. In an efficient market, takeovers would not occur because market price would reflect the true value of corporations. Thus, bidding firms would not be justified in paying premiums above market prices for target firms.
   d. Traders and institutional investors, having extremely short time horizons, are influenced by their perceptions of what other market traders will be thinking of stock prospects and do not value takeovers based on fundamental factors. Thus, they will sell shares in target firms despite the true value of the firms.
   e. Mergers are a way of avoiding taxes because they allow the acquiring firm to write up the value of the assets of the acquired firm.
   f. Acquisitions analysis frequently focuses on the total value of the firms involved. An acquisition, however, will usually affect relative values of stocks and bonds, as well as their total value.

3. **Merger Rationale**   Explain why diversification *per se* is probably not a good reason for merger.

4. **Corporate Split**   In May 2005, high-end retailer Nieman Marcus announced plans to sell off its private label credit card business. Unlike other credit cards, private label credit cards can be used only in a particular merchant's store. Why might a company do this? Is there a possibility of reverse synergy?

5. **Poison Pills**   Are poison pills good or bad for stockholders? How do you think acquiring firms are able to get around poison pills?

6. **Merger and Taxes**   Describe the advantages and disadvantages of a taxable merger as opposed to a tax-free exchange. What is the basic determinant of tax status in a merger? Would an LBO be taxable or nontaxable? Explain.

7. **Economies of Scale**   What does it mean to say that a proposed merger will take advantage of available economies of scale? Suppose Eastern Power Co. and Western Power Co. are located in different time zones. Both operate at 60 percent of capacity except for peak periods, when they operate at 100 percent of capacity. The peak periods begin at 9:00 a.m. and 5:00 p.m. local time and last about 45 minutes. Explain why a merger between Eastern and Western might make sense.

8. **Hostile Takeovers**   What types of actions might the management of a firm take to fight a hostile acquisition bid from an unwanted suitor? How do the target firm shareholders benefit from the defensive tactics of their management team? How are the target firm shareholders harmed by such actions? Explain.

9. **Merger Offers**   Suppose a company in which you own stock has attracted two takeover offers. Would it ever make sense for your company's management to favor the lower offer? Does the form of payment affect your answer at all?

10. **Merger Profit**   Acquiring firm stockholders seem to benefit little from takeovers. Why is this finding a puzzle? What are some of the reasons offered for it?

Questions and Problems

BASIC
(Questions 1–10)

1. **Calculating Synergy**   Evan, Inc., has offered COP 740 million cash for all of the common stock in Tanner Corporation. Based on recent market information, Tanner is worth COP 640 million as an independent operation. If the merger makes economic sense for Evan, what is the "minimum estimated value of the synergistic benefits from the merger?

2. **Balance Sheets for Mergers**   Consider the following premerger information about firm X and firm Y:

	Firm X	Firm Y
Total earnings	£40,000	£15,000
Shares outstanding	20,000	20,000
Per-share values:		
Market	£ 49	£ 18
Book	£ 20	£ 7

Assume that firm X acquires firm Y by paying cash for all the shares outstanding at a merger premium of £5 per share. Assuming that neither firm has any debt before or after the merger, construct the postmerger balance sheet for firm X assuming the use of (a) pooling of interests accounting methods and (b) purchase accounting methods.

3. **Balance Sheets for Mergers**   Assume that the following balance sheets are stated at book value. Construct a postmerger balance sheet assuming that Las Tunas Dykes purchases Moa Dykes, and the pooling of the interests method of accounting is used.

LAS TUNAS DYKES			
Current assets	CUP 10,000	Current liabilities	CUP 3,100
Net fixed assets	14,000	Long-term debt	1,900
		Equity	19,000
Total	CUP 24,000	Total	CUP 24,000

MOA DYKES			
Current assets	CUP 3,400	Current liabilities	CUP 1,600
Net fixed assets	5,600	Long-term debt	900
		Equity	6,500
Total	CUP 9,000	Total	CUP 9,000

4. **Incorporating Goodwill**   In the previous problem, suppose the fair market value of Moa's fixed assets is CUP 12,000 versus the CUP 5,600 book value shown. Las Tunas pays CUP 17,000 for Moa and raises the needed fund through an issue of long-term debt. Construct the postmerger balance sheet now, assuming that the purchase method of accounting is used.

5. **Balance Sheets for Mergers**   Silver Enterprises has acquired All Gold Mining in a merger transaction. Construct the balance sheet for the new corporation if the merger is treated as a pooling of interests for accounting purposes. The following balance sheets represents the premerger book values for both firms:

SILVER ENTERPRISES			
Current assets	YER 2,600	Current liabilities	YER 1,800
Other assets	800	Long-term debt	900
Net fixed assets	3,900	Equity	4,600
Total	YER 7,300	Total	YER 7,300

ALL GOLD MINING			
Current assets	YER 1,100	Current liabilities	YER 900
Other assets	350	Long-term debt	0
Net fixed assets	YER 2,800	Equity	3,350
Total	YER 4,250	Total	YER 4,250

6. **Incorporating Goodwill**   In the previous problem, construct the balance sheet for the new corporation assuming that the transaction is treated as a purchase for accounting purposes. The market value of All Gold Mining's fixed assets is YER 2,800; the market values for current and other assets are the same as the book values. Assume that Silver Enterprises issues YER 8,400 in new long-term debt to finance the acquisition.

7. **Cash versus Stock Payment**   Iwaki Corp. is analyzing the possible acquisition of Chiba Company. Both firms have no debt. Iwaki believes the acquisition will increase its total aftertax annual cash flows by ¥3.1 million indefinitely. The current market value of Chiba is ¥78 million, and that of Iwaki is ¥135 million. The appropriate discount rate for the incremental cash flows is 10 percent. Iwaki is trying to decide whether it should offer 40 percent of its stock or ¥94 million in cash to Chiba's shareholders.
    a. What is the cost of each alternative?
    b. What is the NPV of each alternative?
    c. Which alternative should Iwaki choose?

8. **EPS, PE, and Mergers**   The shareholders of Flannery Company have voted in favor of a buyout offer from Stultz Corporation. Information about each firm is given here:

	Flannery	Stultz
Price–earnings ratio	5.25	21
Shares outstanding	60,000	180,000
Earnings	€300,000	€675,000

    Flannery's shareholders will receive one share of Stultz stock for every four shares they hold in Flannery.
    a. What will the EPS of Stultz be after the merger? What will the PE ratio be if the NPV of the acquisition is zero?
    b. What must Stultz feel is the value of the synergy between these two firms? Explain how your answer can be reconciled with the decision to go ahead with the takeover.

9. **Merger Rationale**   Cholern Electric Company (CEC) is a public utility that provides electricity to the central Dimona area. Recent events at its Mile-High Nuclear Station have been discouraging. Several shareholders have expressed concern over last year's financial statements.

Income Statement Last Year (in millions)		Balance Sheet End of Year (in millions)	
Revenue	ILS 110	Assets	ILS 400
Fuel	50	Debt	300
Other expenses	30	Equity	100
Interest	30		
Net income	ILS 0		

    Recently, a wealthy group of individuals has offered to purchase half of CEC's assets at fair market price. Management recommends that this offer be accepted because "We believe our expertise in the energy industry can be better exploited by CEC if we sell our electricity generating and transmission assets and enter the telecommunication business. Although telecommunications is a riskier business than providing electricity as a public utility, it is also potentially very profitable."
    Should the management approve this transaction? Why or why not?

10.   Cash versus Stock as Payment   Consider the following premerger information about a bidding firm (firm B) and a target firm (firm T). Assume that both firms have no debt outstanding.

	Firm B	Firm T
Shares outstanding	1,500	900
Price per share	CYP 34	CYP 24

Firm B has estimated that the value of the synergistic benefits from acquiring firm T is CYP 3,000.

a. If firm T is willing to be acquired for CYP 27 per share in cash, what is the NPV of the merger?

b. What will the price per share of the merged firm be assuming the conditions in (a)?

c. In part (a), what is the merger premium?

d. Suppose firm T is agreeable to a merger by an exchange of stock. If B offers three of its shares for every one of T's shares, what will the price per share of the merged firm be?

e. What is the NPV of the merger assuming the conditions in (d)?

INTERMEDIATE
(Questions 11–16)

11.   Cash versus Stock as Payment   In problem 10, are the shareholders of firm T better off with the cash offer or the stock offer? At what exchange ratio of B shares to T shares would the shareholders in T be indifferent between the two offers?

12.   Effects of a Stock Exchange   Consider the following premerger information about firm A and firm B:

	Firm A	Firm B
Total earnings	DKK 900	DKK 600
Shares outstanding	550	220
Price per share	DKK 40	DKK 15

Assume that firm A acquires firm B via an exchange of stock at a price of DKK 20 for each share of B's stock. Both A and B have no debt outstanding.

a. What will the earnings per share, EPS, of firm A be after the merger?

b. What will firm A's price per share be after the merger if the market incorrectly analyzes this reported earnings growth (that is, the price–earnings ratio does not change)?

c. What will the price–earnings ratio of the postmerger firm be if the market correctly analyzes the transaction?

d. If there are no synergy gains, what will the share price of A be after the merger? What will the price–earnings ratio be? What does your answer for the share price tell you about the amount A bid for B? Was it too high? Too low? Explain.

13.   Merger NPV   Show that the NPV of a merger can be expressed as the value of the synergistic benefits, ΔV, less the merger premium.

14.   Merger NPV   Fly-By-Night Couriers is analyzing the possible acquisition of Flash-in-the-Pan Restaurants. Neither firm has debt. The forecasts of Fly-By-Night show that the purchases would increase its annual aftertax cash flow by LAK 600,000 indefinitely. The current market value of Flash-in-the-Pan is LAK 20 million. The current market value of Fly-By-Night is LAK 35 million. The appropriate discount rate for the incremental cash flows is 8 percent. Fly-By-Night is trying to decide whether it would offer 25 percent of its stock or LAK 25 million in cash to Flash-in-the-Pan.

a. What is the synergy from the merger?

b. What is the value of Flash-in-the-Pan to Fly-By-Night?

c. What is the cost to Fly-By-Night of each alternative?

d. What is the NPV to Fly-By-Night of each alternative?

e. What alternative should Fly-By-Night use?

15. **Merger NPV**   Harrods PLC has a market value of £600 million and 30 million shares outstanding. Selfridge Department Store has a market value of £200 million and 20 million shares outstanding. Harrods is contemplating acquiring Selfridge. Harrods's CFO concludes that the combined firm with synergy will be worth £1 billion, and Selfridge can be acquired at a premium of £100 million.

    a. If Harrods offers 15 million shares of its stock in exchange for the 20 million shares of Selfridge, what will the stock price of Harrods be after the acquisition?

    b. What exchange ratio between the two stocks would make the value of stock offer equivalent to a cash offer of £280 million?

16. **Mergers and Shareholder Value**   Bentley Corp. and Rolls Manufacturing are considering a merger. The possible states of the economy and each company's value in that state are shown here:

State	Probability	Bentley	Rolls
Boom	.70	$300,000	$260,000
Recession	.30	$110,000	$ 80,000

Bentley currently has a bond issue outstanding with a face value of $140,000. Rolls is an all-equity company.

    a. What is the value of each company before the merger?

    b. What are the values of each company's debt and equity before the merger?

    c. If the companies continue to operate separately, what are the total value of the companies, the total value of the equity, and the total value of the debt?

    d. What would be the value of the merged company? What would be the value of the merged company's debt and equity?

    e. Is there a transfer of wealth in this case? Why?

    f. Suppose that the face value of Bentley's debt was $120,000. Would this affect the transfer of wealth?

CHALLENGE
(Questions 17–18)

17. **Calculating NPV**   Plant, Inc., is considering making an offer to purchase Palmer Corp. Plant's vice president of finance has collected the following information:

	Plant	Palmer
Price–earnings ratio	12.5	9
Shares outstanding	1,000,000	550,000
Earnings	$2,000,000	$580,000
Dividends	600,000	290,000

Plant also knows that securities analysts expect the earnings and dividends of Palmer to grow at a constant rate of 5 percent each year. Plant management believes that the acquisition of Palmer will provide the firm with some economies of scale that will increase this growth rate to 7 percent per year.

    a. What is the value of Palmer to Plant?

    b. What would Plant's gain be from this acquisition?

    c. If Plant were to offer $18 in cash for each share of Palmer, what would the NPV of the acquisition be?

    d. What is the most Plant should be willing to pay in cash per share for the stock of Palmer?

    e. If Plant were to offer 110,000 of its shares in exchange for the outstanding stock of Palmer, what would the NPV be?

    f. Should the acquisition be attempted? If so, should it be as in (c) or as in (e)?

    g. Plant's outside financial consultants think that the 7 percent growth rate is too optimistic and a 6 percent rate is more realistic. How does this change your previous answers?

18.   **Mergers and Shareholder Value**   The Chocolate Ice Cream Company and the Vanilla Ice Cream Company have agreed to merge and form Fudge Swirl Consolidated. Both companies are exactly alike except that they are located in different towns. The end-of-period value of each firm is determined by the weather, as shown below. There will be no synergy to the merger.

State	Probability	Value
Rainy	.1	€100,000
Warm	.4	200,000
Hot	.5	400,000

    The weather conditions in each town are independent of those in the other. Furthermore, each company has an outstanding debt claim of €200,000. Assume that no premiums are paid in the merger.

    a. What are the possible values of the combined company?

    b. What are the possible values of end-of-period debt values and stock values after the merger?

    c. Show that the bondholders are better off and the stockholders are worse off in the combined firm than they would have been if the firms had remained separate.

Mini Case

The Birdie Golf–Hybrid Golf Merger

Birdie Golf, Inc., has been in merger talks with Hybrid Golf Company for the past six months. After several rounds of negotiations, the offer under discussion is a cash offer of $550 million for Hybrid Golf. Both companies have niche markets in the golf club industry, and the companies believe a merger will result in significant synergies due to economies of scale in manufacturing and marketing, as well as significant savings in general and administrative expenses.

    Bryce Bichon, the financial officer for Birdie, has been instrumental in the merger negotiations. Bryce has prepared the following pro forma financial statements for Hybrid Golf assuming the merger takes place. The financial statements include all synergistic benefits from the merger:

	2008	2009	2010	2011	2012
Sales	$800,000,000	$900,000,000	$1,000,000,000	$1,125,000,000	$1,250,000,000
Productions costs	562,000,000	630,000,000	700,000,000	790,000,000	875,000,000
Depreciation	75,000,000	80,000,000	82,000,000	83,000,000	83,000,000
Other expenses	80,000,000	90,000,000	100,000,000	113,000,000	125,000,000
EBIT	$ 83,000,000	$100,000,000	$ 118,000,000	$ 139,000,000	$ 167,000,000
Interest	19,000,000	22,000,000	24,000,000	25,000,000	27,000,000
Taxable income	$ 64,000,000	$ 78,000,000	$ 94,000,000	$ 114,000,000	$ 140,000,000
Taxes (40%)	25,600,000	31,200,000	37,600,000	45,600,000	56,000,000
Net income	$ 38,400,000	$ 46,800,000	$ 56,400,000	$ 68,400,000	$ 84,000,000

Bryce is also aware that the Hybrid Golf division will require investments each year for continuing operations, along with sources of financing. The following table outlines the required investments and sources of financing:

	2008	2009	2010	2011	2012
Investments:					
Net working capital	$20,000,000	$25,000,000	$25,000,000	$30,000,000	$30,000,000
Fixed assets	15,000,000	25,000,000	18,000,000	12,000,000	7,000,000
Total	$35,000,000	$50,000,000	$43,000,000	$42,000,000	$37,000,000
Sources of financing:					
New debt	$35,000,000	$16,000,000	$16,000,000	$15,000,000	$12,000,000
Profit retention	0	34,000,000	27,000,000	27,000,000	25,000,000
Total	$35,000,000	$50,000,000	$43,000,000	$42,000,000	$37,000,000

The management of Birdie Golf feels that the capital structure at Hybrid Golf is not optimal. If the merger take place, Hybrid Golf will immediately increase its leverage with a $110 million debt issue, which would be followed by a $150 million dividend payment to Birdie Golf. This will increase Hybrid's debt-to-equity ratio from .50 to 1.00. Birdie Golf will also be able to use a $25 million tax loss carryforward in 2009 and 2010 from Hybrid Golf's previous operations. The total value of Hybrid Golf is expected to be $900 million in five years, and the company will have $300 million in debt at that time.

Stock in Birdie Golf currently sells for $94 per share, and the company has 18 million shares of stock outstanding. Hybrid Golf has 8 million shares of stock outstanding. Both companies can borrow at an 8 percent interest rate. The risk-free rate is 6 percent, and the expected return on the market is 13 percent. Bryce believes the current cost of capital for Birdie Golf is 11 percent. The beta for Hybrid Golf stock at its current capital structure is 1.30.

Bryce has asked you to analyze the financial aspects of the potential merger. Specifically, he has asked you to answer the following questions:

1. Suppose Hybrid shareholders will agree to a merger price of $68.75 per share. Should Birdie proceed with the merger?

2. What is the highest price per share that Birdie should be willing to pay for Hybrid?

3. Suppose Birdie is unwilling to pay cash for the merger but will consider a stock exchange. What exchange ratio would make the merger terms equivalent to the original merger price of $68.75 per share?

4. What is the highest exchange ratio Birdie would be willing to pay and still undertake the merger?

CHAPTER 30

Financial Distress

In 2006, financial problems at General Motors and Ford were much in the news. Both automakers were saddled with large debt loads and legacy costs such as retiree health care benefits. In early 2006, Ford received more bad news when its debt was downgraded by Standard & Poor's to BB–. Meanwhile, GM announced that its 2005 loss was actually $2 billion larger than previously thought—$10.6 billion versus $8.6 billion—due to accounting errors. GM stock dropped nearly 5 percent on the news, shaving more than half a billion dollars off GM's market cap.

GM and Ford are examples of companies experiencing significant financial distress, the subject of this chapter. A firm that does not generate enough cash flow to make a contractually required payment, such as an interest payment, will experience financial distress. A firm that defaults on a required payment may be forced to liquidate its assets. More often, a defaulting firm will reorganize its financial structure. Financial restructuring involves replacing old financial claims with new ones and takes place with private workouts or legal bankruptcy. Private workouts are voluntary arrangements to restructure a company's debt, such as postponing a payment or reducing the size of the payment. If a private workout is not possible, formal bankruptcy is usually required.

30.1 What Is Financial Distress?

Financial distress is surprisingly hard to define precisely. This is true partly because of the variety of events befalling firms under financial distress. The list of events is almost endless, but here are some examples:

> Dividend reductions
>
> Plant closings
>
> Losses
>
> Layoffs
>
> CEO resignations
>
> Plummeting stock prices

Financial distress is a situation where a firm's operating cash flows are not sufficient to satisfy current obligations (such as trade credits or interest expenses) and the firm is forced to take corrective action.[1] Financial distress may lead a firm to default on a contract, and it may

---

[1]This definition is close to the one used by Karen Wruck, "Financial Distress: Reorganization and Organization Efficiency," *Journal of Financial Economics* 27 (1990), p. 425.

Table 30.1 The Largest U.S. Bankruptcies

Firm	Liabilities (in $ millions)	Bankruptcy Date
1 Conseco Inc.	$56,639.30	December 2, 2002
2 WorldCom Inc.	45,984.00	July 2, 2002
3 Enron Corp.	31,237.00	December 2, 2001
4 Delta Air Lines	28,546.00	September 14, 2005
5 Pacific Gas & Electric Co.	25,717.00	April 6, 2001
6 UAL Corporation	22,164.00	December 2, 2002
7 Texaco (including subsidiaries)	21,603.00	April 1, 1987
8 Conseco Finance Corp.	20,278.50	December 2, 2002
9 Olympia & York	19,800.00	May 15, 1992
10 Northwest Airlines	17,915.00	September 14, 2005
11 Adelphia Communications Corp.	17,349.10	June 1, 2002
12 Mirant Corp.	16,460.00	July 14, 2003
13 Global Crossing, Ltd.	14,639.00	January 28, 2002
14 Executive Life Insurance	14,577.00	April 1, 1991
15 NTL, Inc.	14,134.00	May 2, 2002
16 Mutual Benefit Life	13,500.00	July 1, 1991
17 Reliance Group Holdings, Inc.	12,877.47	June 12, 2001
18 Finova Group, Inc.	11,822.21	March 7, 2001
19 Swissair	11,704.50	October 1, 2001
20 NRG Energy, Inc.	11,579.89	May 3, 2003
21 US Airways Group	10,640.00	August 2, 2002
22 Kmart Corp.	10,263.00	January 22, 2002
23 United Pan-Europe Communications NV	10,086.40	December 2, 2002
24 Campeau (Allied & Federated)	9,947.00	January 1, 1990
25 First Capital Holdings	9,291.00	May 1, 1991
26 Home Holdings, Inc.	9,132.00	January 15, 1998
27 Baldwin United	9,000.00	September 1, 1983
28 PG&E National Energy Group, Inc.	8,908.00	July 8, 2003
29 US Air Inc.	8,383.00	September 1, 2004
30 Federal Mogul Corp.	8,232.70	October 1, 2001

SOURCE: Supplied by Edward I. Altman, NYU Salomon Center, Stern School of Business.

involve financial restructuring between the firm, its creditors, and its equity investors. Usually the firm is forced to take actions that it would not have taken if it had sufficient cash flow.

Our definition of financial distress can be expanded somewhat by linking it to insolvency. Insolvency is defined in *Black's Law Dictionary* as:[2]

> Inability to pay one's debts; lack of means of paying one's debts. Such a condition of a woman's (or man's) assets and liability that the former made immediately available would be insufficient to discharge the latter.

---

[2]Taken from *Black's Law Dictionary*, 5th ed. (St. Paul, Minn.: West Publishing Company), p. 716.

Figure 30.1

Insolvency

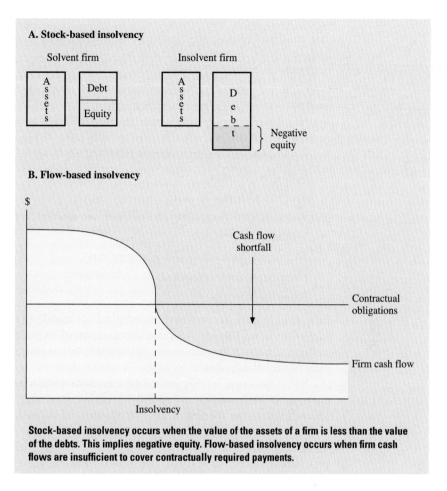

A. Stock-based insolvency

Solvent firm

Insolvent firm

Negative equity

B. Flow-based insolvency

$

Cash flow shortfall

Contractual obligations

Firm cash flow

Insolvency

Stock-based insolvency occurs when the value of the assets of a firm is less than the value of the debts. This implies negative equity. Flow-based insolvency occurs when firm cash flows are insufficient to cover contractually required payments.

This definition has two general themes: stocks and flows.[3] These two ways of thinking about insolvency are depicted in Figure 30.1. Stock-based insolvency occurs when a firm has negative net worth, so the value of assets is less than the value of its debts. Flow-based insolvency occurs when operating cash flow is insufficient to meet current obligations. Flow-based insolvency refers to the inability to pay one's debts.

30.2 What Happens in Financial Distress?

In the early 1990s, Trans World Airline, Inc. (TWA), experienced financial distress. It lost money in 1989, 1990, and 1991 and steadily lost its market share to rivals United, American, and Delta. Having seen Eastern and Pan Am disappear, airline travelers had good reason to be nervous about buying tickets from TWA.

In the summer of 1991, TWA General Counsel Mark A. Buckstein bet Carl Icahn, TWA owner and CEO, $1,000 that the airline would be forced to file involuntary bankruptcy by September 1991.[4] Icahn argued that he could arrange a private restructuring and avoid formal bankruptcy. Icahn won the bet, but TWA eventually filed for bankruptcy on January 31, 1992.

---

[3]Edward Altman was one of the first to distinguish between stock-based insolvency and flow-based insolvency. See Edward Altman, *Corporate Financial Distress: A Complete Guide to Predicting, Avoiding, and Dealing with Bankruptcy*, 2nd ed. (New York: John Wiley & Sons, 1993).

[4]The bet was reported in "Carl Has 9 Lives but He Is Betting up to 8½," *Business Week*, February 24, 1992.

Icahn was quoted as saying the bankruptcy reorganization would give TWA the time it needed to turn the firm around. The odds favored Icahn because financial distress does not usually result in a firm's death. TWA was reorganized in 1993. Icahn resigned as CEO and gave up all ownership claims. However, TWA continued to struggle and for the second time, on July 3, 1995, filed for bankruptcy. Several months later, it emerged from bankruptcy after exchanging $500 million of debt for equity. Remarkably, on January 9, 2001, the board of TWA again approved a plan to file for bankruptcy. The plan included the purchase of TWA by American Airlines for $500 million. (So far, no public firm has ever filed for bankruptcy four times.)

Firms deal with financial distress in several ways, such as these:

1. Selling major assets.
2. Merging with another firm.
3. Reducing capital spending and research and development.
4. Issuing new securities.
5. Negotiating with banks and other creditors.
6. Exchanging debt for equity.
7. Filing for bankruptcy.

Items (1), (2), and (3) concern the firm's assets. Items (4), (5), (6), and (7) involve the right side of the firm's balance sheet and are examples of financial restructuring. Financial distress may involve both asset restructuring and financial restructuring (i.e., changes on both sides of the balance sheet).

Some firms may actually benefit from financial distress by restructuring their assets. For example, in 1986, Goodyear Tire and Rubber's levered recapitalization changed the firm's behavior and forced the firm to dispose of unrelated businesses. Goodyear's cash flow was not sufficient to cover required payments, and it was forced to sell its noncore businesses. For some firms, financial distress may bring about new organizational forms and new operating strategies. However, in this chapter we focus on financial restructuring.

Financial restructuring may occur in a private workout or a bankruptcy reorganization under Chapter 11 of the U.S. bankruptcy code. Figure 30.2 shows how large public firms move through financial distress. Approximately half of the financial restructurings have been done via private workouts. As was true for TWA, most large public firms (approximately 70 percent) that file for Chapter 11 bankruptcy are able to reorganize and continue to do business.[5]

Financial distress can serve as a firm's "early warning" system for trouble. Firms with more debt will experience financial distress earlier than firms with less debt. However, firms that experience financial distress earlier will have more time for private workouts and reorganization. Firms with low leverage will experience financial distress later and, in many instances, be forced to liquidate.

30.3 Bankruptcy Liquidation and Reorganization

Firms that cannot or choose not to make contractually required payments to creditors have two basic options: liquidation or reorganization. This section discusses bankruptcy liquidation and reorganization.

Liquidation means termination of the firm as a going concern; it involves selling the assets of the firm for salvage value. The proceeds, net of transactions costs, are distributed to creditors in order of established priority.

---

[5]However, only less than 20 percent of all firms (public or private) going through a Chapter 11 bankruptcy are successfully reorganized.

Figure 30.2

What Happens in Financial Distress

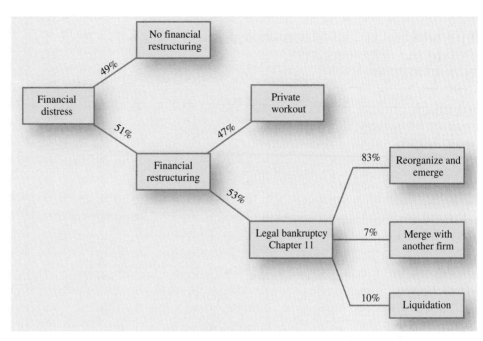

SOURCE: Karen H. Wruck, "Financial Distress: Reorganization and Organizational Efficiency," *Journal of Financial Economics* 27 (1990), Figure 2. See also Stuart C. Gilson, Kose John, and Larry N. P. Lang, "Troubled Debt Restructurings: An Empirical Study of Private Reorganization of Firms in Defaults," *Journal of Financial Economics* 27 (1990); and Lawrence A. Weiss, "Bankruptcy Resolution: Direct Costs and Violation of Priority of Claims," *Journal of Financial Economics* 27 (1990).

Reorganization is the option of keeping the firm a going concern; it sometimes involves issuing new securities to replace old securities.

Liquidation and formal reorganization may be done by bankruptcy. *Bankruptcy* is a legal proceeding and can be done voluntarily with the corporation filing the petition or involuntarily with the creditors filing the petition.

Bankruptcy Liquidation

Chapter 7 of the Bankruptcy Reform Act of 1978 deals with "straight" liquidation. The following sequence of events is typical:

1. A petition is filed in a federal court. A corporation may file a voluntary petition, or involuntary petitions may be filed against the corporation.

2. A bankruptcy trustee is elected by the creditors to take over the assets of the debtor corporation. The trustee will attempt to liquidate the assets.

3. When the assets are liquidated, after payment of the costs of administration, proceeds are distributed among the creditors.

4. If any assets remain, after expenses and payments to creditors, they are distributed to the shareholders.

Conditions Leading to Involuntary Bankruptcy An involuntary bankruptcy petition may be filed by creditors if both the following conditions are met:

1. The corporation is not paying debts as they become due.

2. If there are more than 12 creditors, at least three with claims totaling $5,000 or more must join in the filing. If there are fewer than 12 creditors, then only one with a claim of $5,000 is required to file.

In Their Own Words

EDWARD I. ALTMAN* ON CORPORATE FINANCIAL DISTRESS AND BANKRUPTCY

As we entered the new millennium, corporate distress and bankruptcy were no longer a niche area of corporate evolution. Indeed the bankruptcy rate of U.S. corporations reached record proportions in 2001/2002, with as many as 77 *large* corporations filing for protection under Chapter 11 of the bankruptcy code with *liabilities* greater than $1 billion—an unprecedented number. While telecommunication firms "lead" the way, airlines, steel companies, retailers, and, in general, a broad cross section of industrial sectors have succumbed to a combination of excessive debt and poor operating results. The average American company is far riskier today than it was just two decades ago, and the roles of the bankruptcy courts and restructuring specialists have never been more important.

Financial distress of private and public entities throughout the world is a frequent occurrence with important implications to their many stakeholders. While the role of corporate bankruptcy laws is clear—either to provide a legal procedure that permits firms, which have temporary liquidity problems, to restructure and successfully emerge as continuing entities or to provide an orderly process to liquidate assets for the benefit of creditors before asset values are dissipated—bankruptcy laws differ markedly from country to country. It is generally agreed that the U.S. Chapter 11 provisions under the Bankruptcy Reform Act of 1978 provide the most protection for bankrupt firms' assets and result in a greater likelihood of successful reorganization than is found in other countries where liquidation and sale of the assets for the benefit of creditors is more likely the result. But the U.S. code's process is usually lengthy (averaging close to two years, except where a sufficient number of creditors agree in advance via a prepackaged Chapter 11) and expensive, and the reorganized entity is not always successful in avoiding subsequent distress. If the reorganization is not successful, then liquidation under Chapter 7 will usually ensue.

Bankruptcy processes in the industrialized world outside the United States strongly favor senior creditors who obtain control of the firm and seek to enforce greater adherence to debt contracts. The U.K. process, for example, is speedy and less costly, but the reduced costs can result in undesirable liquidations, unemployment, and underinvestment. The new bankruptcy code in Germany attempts to reduce the considerable power of secured creditors but it is still closer to the U.K. system. In the United States, creditors and owners can negotiate "violations" to the "absolute priority rule"—this "rule" holds that more senior creditors must be paid in full, prior to any payments to more junior creditors or to owners. (However, the so-called "violations" to absolute priority have empirically been shown to be relatively small—such as under 10 percent of firm value.) Finally, the U.S. system gives the court the right to sanction postpetition debt financing, usually with superpriority status over existing claims, thereby facilitating the continuing operation of the firm. Recently, France has had similar successful experience.

A measure of performance of the U.S. bankruptcy system is the proportion of firms that emerge successfully. The results in the United States of late are somewhat mixed, with close to 70 percent of large firms emerging but probably less than 20 percent of smaller entities. And a not insignificant number of firms suffer subsequent distress and may file again ("Chapter 22").

Regardless of the location, one of the objectives of bankruptcy and other distressed workout arrangements is that creditors and other suppliers of capital clearly know their rights and expected recoveries in the event

---

Priority of Claims Once a corporation is determined to be bankrupt, liquidation takes place. The distribution of the proceeds of the liquidation occurs according to the following priority:

1. Administration expenses associated with liquidating the bankrupt's assets.
2. Unsecured claims arising after the filing of an involuntary bankruptcy petition.
3. Wages, salaries, and commissions.
4. Contributions to employee benefit plans arising within 180 days before the filing date.
5. Consumer claims.
6. Tax claims.

of a distressed situation. When these are not transparent and/or are based on outdated processes with arbitrary and possibly corrupt outcomes, then the entire economic system suffers and growth is inhibited. Such is the case in several emerging market countries. Revision of these outdated systems should be a priority.

In addition to the comparative benefits of different national restructuring systems, a number of intriguing theoretical and empirical issues are related to the distressed firm. Among these are corporate debt capacity, manager–creditor–owner incentives, ability to predict distress, data and computations for default rate estimation, investment in securities of distressed firms, and postreorganization performance assessment.

Corporate distress has a major impact on creditor–debtor relationships and, combined with business risk and tax considerations, affects the capital structure of companies. One key question is how costly are the *expected* distress costs compared to the *expected* tax benefits of using leverage—the so-called trade-off theory. Most analysts agree that the sum of direct (e.g., legal fees) and indirect costs is in the range of 10–20 percent of firm value.

Whether the taking of excess risk and overinvestment are examples of agency conflicts between managers and creditors rests upon one's view as to who are the true residual owners of a distressed firm—the existing equityholders or creditors who will more than likely be the new owners of a reorganized entity. Existing management has the exclusive right to file the first plan of reorganization within 120 days of filing, with exclusivity extensions possible. Their incentives and influence can be biased, however, and not always in accord with other stakeholders, primarily creditors. Limiting this exclusivity would appear to be desirable to speed up the process and restrict managerial abuse.

Distress prediction models have intrigued researchers and practitioners for more than 50 years. Models have evolved from univariate financial statement ratios to multivariate statistical classification models, to contingent claim and market value–based approaches, and finally to using artificial intelligence techniques. Most large financial institutions have one or more of these types of models in place as more sophisticated credit risk management frameworks are being introduced, sometimes combined with aggressive credit asset portfolio strategies. Increasingly, private credit assets are being treated as securities with estimates of default and recovery given default the critical inputs to their valuation.

Perhaps the most intriguing by-product of corporate distress is the development of a relatively new class of investors known as *vultures*. These money managers specialize in securities of distressed and defaulted companies. Defaulted bonds have had a small following ever since the Great Depression of the 1930s, but this has grown to more than 70 institutional "vulture" specialists, actively managing over $60 billion in 2003. The size of the distressed and defaulted market grew dramatically in recent years and by year-end 2002, estimates by this author were over $940 billion (face value) and $510 billion (market value) for the public and private markets combined (mainly public defaulted and distressed bonds and private bank loans). Distressed debt investors have target annual rates of return of 15 to 25 percent. Although these annual returns are sometimes earned, the overall annual rate of return from 1987 through 2002 has been less than 10 percent—similar to the high-yield bonds and considerably below returns in the stock market. Yet, the incredible supply of potential investment opportunities has created unprecedented interest in this *alternative asset* class.

*Edward I. Altman is Max L. Heine Professor of Finance, NYU Stern School of Business. He is widely recognized as one of the world's experts on bankruptcy and credit analysis as well as the distressed debt and high-yield bond markets.

7. Secured and unsecured creditors' claims.

8. Preferred stockholders' claims.

9. Common stockholders' claims.

The priority rule in liquidation is the **absolute priority rule** (APR).

One qualification to this list concerns secured creditors. Liens on property are outside APR ordering. However, if the secured property is liquidated and provides cash insufficient to cover the amount owed them, the secured creditors join with unsecured creditors in dividing the remaining liquidating value. In contrast, if the secured property is liquidated for proceeds greater than the secured claim, the net proceeds are used to pay unsecured creditors and others.

EXAMPLE 30.1

APR   The B. O. Drug Company is to be liquidated. Its liquidating value is $2.7 million. Bonds worth $1.5 million are secured by a mortgage on the B.O. Drug Company corporate headquarters building, which is sold for $1 million; $200,000 is used to cover administrative costs and other claims (including unpaid wages, pension benefits, consumer claims, and taxes). After paying $200,000 to the administrative priority claims, the amount available to pay secured and unsecured creditors is $2.5 million. This is less than the amount of unpaid debt of $4 million.

Under APR, all creditors must be paid before shareholders, and the mortgage bondholders have first claim on the $1 million obtained from the sale of the headquarters building.

The trustee has proposed the following distribution:

Type of Claim	Prior Claim	Cash Received under Liquidation
Bonds (secured by mortgage)	$ 1,500,000	$1,500,000
Subordinated debentures	2,500,000	1,000,000
Common stockholders	10,000,000	0
Total	$14,000,000	$2,500,000

Calculation of the Distribution		
Cash received from sale of assets available for distribution		$2,500,000
Cash paid to secured bondholders on sale of mortgaged property		1,000,000
Available to bond and debenture holders		$1,500,000
Total claims remaining ($4,000,000 less payment of $1,000,000 on secured bonds)		$3,000,000
Distribution of remaining $1,500,000 to cover total remaining claims of $3,000,000		

Type of Claim Remaining	Claim on Liquidation Proceeds	Cash Received
Bonds	$ 500,000	$ 500,000
Debentures	2,500,000	1,000,000
Total	$3,000,000	$1,500,000

Bankruptcy Reorganization

Corporate reorganization takes place under Chapter 11 of the Federal Bankruptcy Reform Act of 1978. The general objective of a proceeding under Chapter 11 is to plan to restructure the corporation with some provision for repayment of creditors. A typical sequence of events follows:

1. A voluntary petition can be filed by the corporation, or an involuntary petition can be filed by three or more creditors (or one creditor if the total creditors are fewer than 12—see the previous section). The involuntary petition must allege that the corporation is not paying its debts.

2. A federal judge either approves or denies the petition. If the petition is approved, a time for filing proofs of claims of creditors and of shareholders is set.

3. In most cases, the corporation (the "debtor in possession") continues to run the business.

4. The corporation is given 120 days to submit a reorganization plan.

5. Creditors and shareholders are divided into classes. A class of creditors accepts the plan if two-thirds of the class (in dollar amount) and one-half of the class (in number) have indicated approval.[6]

6. After acceptance by creditors, the plan is confirmed by the court.

7. Payments in cash, property, and securities are made to creditors and shareholders. The plan may provide for the issuance of new securities.

Chapter 11 Suppose B.O. Drug Co. decides to reorganize under Chapter 11. Generally senior claims are honored in full before various other claims receive anything. Assume that the "going concern" value of B.O. Drug Co. is $3 million and that its balance sheet is as shown:

Assets	$3,000,000
Liabilities	
Mortgage bonds	1,500,000
Subordinated debentures	2,500,000
Stockholders' equity	−1,000,000

The firm has proposed the following reorganization plan:

Old Security	Old Claim	New Claim with Reorganization Plan
Mortgage bonds	$1,500,000	$1,500,000
Subordinated debentures	2,500,000	1,500,000

and a distribution of new securities under a new claim with this reorganization plan:

Old Security	Received under Proposed Reorganization Plan
Mortgage bonds	$1,000,000 in 9% senior debentures $500,000 in 11% subordinated debentures
Debentures	$1,000,000 in 8% preferred stock $500,000 in common stock

However, it will be difficult for the firm to convince secured creditors (mortgage bonds) to accept unsecured debentures of equal face value. In addition, the corporation may wish to allow the old stockholders to retain some participation in the firm. Needless to say, this would be a violation of the absolute priority rule, and the holders of the debentures would not be happy.

30.4   Private Workout or Bankruptcy: Which Is Best?

A firm that defaults on its debt payments will need to restructure its financial claims. The firm will have two choices: formal bankruptcy or **private workout**. The previous section described two types of formal bankruptcies: bankruptcy liquidation and bankruptcy

---

[6]We are describing the standard events in a bankruptcy reorganization. The general rule is that a reorganization plan will be accepted by the court if all of the creditor classes accept it and it will be rejected if all of the creditor classes reject it. However, if one or more (but not all) of the classes accept it, the plan may be eligible for a "cram down" procedure. A cram down takes place if the bankruptcy court finds a plan fair and equitable and accepts the plan for all creditors.

Absolute Priority Rule (APR)

The absolute priority rule states that senior claims are fully satisfied before junior claims receive anything.

Deviation from Rule

Equityholders	Expectation: No payout
	Reality: Payout in 81 percent of cases
Unsecured creditors	Expectation: Full payout after secured creditors
	Reality: Violation in 78 percent of cases
Secured creditors	Expectation: Full payout
	Reality: Full payout in 92 percent of cases

Reasons for Violations

Creditors want to avoid the expense of litigation. Debtors are given a 120-day opportunity to cause delay and harm value.

Managers often own equity and demand to be compensated.

Bankruptcy judges like consensual plans and pressure parties to compromise.

SOURCE: Lawrence A. Weiss, "Bankruptcy Resolution: Direct Costs and Violation of Priority of Claims," *Journal of Financial Economics* 27 (1990).

---

reorganization. This section compares private workouts with bankruptcy reorganizations. Both types of financial restructuring involve exchanging new financial claims for old financial claims. Usually senior debt is replaced with junior debt and debt is replaced with equity. Much recent academic research has described what happens in private workouts and formal bankruptcies.[7]

- Historically, half of financial restructurings have been private, but recently formal bankruptcy has dominated.

- Firms that emerge from private workouts experience stock price increases that are much greater than those for firms emerging from formal bankruptcies.

- The direct costs of private workouts are much less than the costs of formal bankruptcies.

- Top management usually loses pay and sometimes jobs in both private workouts and formal bankruptcies.

These facts, when taken together, seem to suggest that a private workout is much better than a formal bankruptcy. We then ask: Why do firms ever use formal bankruptcies to restructure?

The Marginal Firm

For the average firm, a formal bankruptcy is more costly than a private workout, but for other firms formal bankruptcy is better. Formal bankruptcy allows firms to issue debt that is senior to all previously incurred debt. This new debt is "debtor in possession" (DIP)

---

[7]For example, see Stuart Gilson, "Managing Default: Some Evidence on How Firms Choose between Workouts and Bankruptcy," *Journal of Applied Corporate Finance* (Summer 1991); and Stuart C. Gilson, Kose John, and Larry N. P. Lang, "Troubled Debt Restructuring: An Empirical Study of Private Reorganization of Firms in Defaults," *Journal of Financial Economics* 27 (1990).

debt. For firms that need a temporary injection of cash, DIP debt makes bankruptcy reorganization an attractive alternative to a private workout. There are some tax advantages to bankruptcy. Firms do not lose tax carryforwards in bankruptcy, and the tax treatment of the cancellation of indebtness is better in bankruptcy. Also, interest on prebankruptcy unsecured debt stops accruing in formal bankruptcy.

Holdouts

Bankruptcy is usually better for the equity investors than it is for the creditors. Using DIP debt and stopping prebankruptcy interest on unsecured debt helps the stockholders and hurts the creditors. As a consequence, equity investors can usually hold out for a better deal in bankruptcy. The absolute priority rule, which favors creditors over equity investors, is usually violated in formal bankruptcies. One recent study found that in 81 percent of recent bankruptcies the equity investor obtained some compensation.[8] Under Chapter 11 the creditors are often forced to give up some of their seniority rights to get management and the equity investors to agree to a deal.

Complexity

A firm with a complicated capital structure will have more trouble putting together a private workout. Firms with secured creditors and trade creditors such as Macy's and Carter Hale will usually use formal bankruptcy because it is too hard to reach an agreement with many different types of creditors.

Lack of Information

There is an inherent conflict of interest between equity investors and creditors, and the conflict is accentuated when both have incomplete information about the circumstances of financial distress. When a firm initially experiences a cash flow shortfall, it may not know whether the shortfall is permanent or temporary. If the shortfall is permanent, creditors will push for a formal reorganization or liquidation. However, if the cash flow shortfall is temporary, formal reorganization or liquidation may not be necessary. Equity investors will push for this viewpoint. This conflict of interest cannot easily be resolved.

These last two points are especially important. They suggest that financial distress will be more expensive (cheaper) if complexity is high (low) and information is incomplete (complete). Complexity and lack of information make cheap workouts less likely.

30.5   Prepackaged Bankruptcy[9]

On October 5, 2004, Choice One Communications, a broadband data, Internet services, and phone company, filed for Chapter 11 reorganization under the U.S. bankruptcy code. At the time of the filing, the company had about $1 billion in debt. A firm in this situation could reasonably be expected to spend a year or longer in bankruptcy. Not so with Choice

---

[8]Lawrence A. Weiss, "Bankruptcy Dissolution: Direct Costs and Violation of Priority and Claims," *Journal of Financial Economics* 23 (1990). However, W. Beranek, R. Boehmer, and B. Smith, in "Much Ado about Nothing: Absolute Priority Deviations in Chapter 11," *Financial Management* (Autumn 1996), find that 33.8 percent of bankruptcy reorganizations leave the stockholders with nothing. They also point out that deviations from the absolute priority rule are to be expected because the bankruptcy code allows creditors to waive their rights if they perceive a waiver to be in their best interests. A rejoinder can be found in Allan C. Eberhart and Lawrence A. Weiss, "The Importance of Deviations from the Absolute Priority Rule in Chapter 11 Bankruptcy Proceedings," *Financial Management* 27 (1998).

[9]John McConnell and Henri Servaes, "The Economics of Prepackaged Bankruptcy," *Journal of Applied Corporate Finance* (Summer 1991), describe prepackaged bankruptcy.

One. Its reorganization plan was confirmed by the U.S Bankruptcy Court on November 10, 2004, six weeks after the date of filing!

Firms typically file bankruptcy to seek protection from their creditors, essentially admitting that they cannot meet their financial obligations as they are presently structured. Once in bankruptcy, the firm attempts to reorganize its financial picture so that it can survive. A key to this process is that the creditors must ultimately give their approval to the restructuring plan. The time a firm spends in Chapter 11 depends on many things, but it usually depends most on the time it takes to get creditors to agree to a plan of reorganization.

Prepackaged bankruptcy is a combination of a private workout and legal bankruptcy. Prior to filing bankruptcy, the firm approaches its creditors with a plan for reorganization. The two sides negotiate a settlement and agree on the details of how the firm's finances will be restructured in bankruptcy. Then, the firm puts together the necessary paperwork for the bankruptcy court before filing for bankruptcy. A filing is a prepack if the firm essentially walks into court and, at the same time, files a reorganization plan complete with the documentation of the approval of its creditors, which is exactly what Choice One did.

The key to the prepackaged reorganization process is that both sides have something to gain and something to lose. If bankruptcy is imminent, it may make sense for the creditors to expedite the process even though they are likely to take a financial loss in the restructuring. Choice One's bankruptcy was relatively painless for most creditors. Interest payments were made on its debt while in bankruptcy, and all vendors were paid. The prepack for Choice One was approved by 100 percent of creditors. Two sets of bondholders were involved. The senior bondholders exchanged $404 million worth of long-term debt for $175 million in new notes and 90 percent of the new stock in the company. The subordinated bondholders had their $252 million worth of bonds converted to 10 percent of the new stock and the ability to purchase more common stock in the future. Of course, stockholders received nothing and, in fact, had their shares canceled.

Prepackaged bankruptcy arrangements require that most creditors reach agreement privately. Prepackaged bankruptcy doesn't seem to work when there are thousands of reluctant trade creditors, such as in the case of a retail trading firm like Macy's and Revco D. S.[10]

The main benefit of prepackaged bankruptcy is that it forces holdouts to accept a bankruptcy reorganization. If a large fraction of a firm's creditors can agree privately to a reorganization plan, the holdout problem may be avoided. It makes a reorganization plan in formal bankruptcy easier to put together.[11]

A study by McConnell, Lease, and Tashjian reports that prepackaged bankruptcies offer many of the advantages of a formal bankruptcy, but they are also more efficient. Their results suggest that the time spent and the direct costs of resolving financial distress are less in a prepackaged bankruptcy than in a formal bankruptcy.[12]

---

[10]S. Chattergee, U. S. Dhillon, and G. G. Ramirez, in "Prepackaged Bankruptcies and Workouts," *Financial Management* (Spring 1996), find that firms using prepackaged bankruptcy arrangements are smaller and in better financial shape and have greater short-term liquidity problems than firms using private workouts or Chapter 11.

[11]During bankruptcy, a proposed plan can be "crammed down" on a class of creditors. A bankruptcy court can force creditors to participate in a reorganization if it can be shown that the plan is "fair and equitable."

[12]John J. McConnell, Ronald Lease, and Elizabeth Tashjian, "Prepacks as a Mechanism for Resolving Financial Distress: The Evidence," *Journal of Applied Corporate Finance* 8 (1996).

Summary and Conclusions

This chapter examined what happens when firms experience financial distress.

1. Financial distress is a situation where a firm's operating cash flow is not sufficient to cover contractual obligations. Financially distressed firms are often forced to take corrective action and undergo financial restructuring. Financial restructuring involves exchanging new financial claims for old ones.

2. Financial restructuring can be accomplished with a private workout or formal bankruptcy. Financial restructuring can involve liquidation or reorganization. However, liquidation is not common.

3. Corporate bankruptcy involves Chapter 7 liquidation or Chapter 11 reorganization. An essential feature of the U.S. bankruptcy code is the absolute priority rule. The absolute priority rule states that senior creditors are paid in full before junior creditors receive anything. However, in practice the absolute priority rule is often violated.

4. A new form of financial restructuring is prepackaged bankruptcy. It is a hybrid of a private workout and formal bankruptcy.

Concept Questions

1. **Financial Distress**   Define *financial distress* using the stock-based and flow-based approaches.

2. **Financial Distress**   What are some benefits of financial distress?

3. **Prepackaged Bankruptcy**   What is prepackaged bankruptcy? What is the main benefit of prepackaged bankruptcy?

4. **Financial Distress**   Why doesn't financial distress always cause firms to die?

5. **Liquidation versus Reorganization**   What is the difference between liquidation and reorganization?

6. **APR**   What is the absolute priority rule?

7. **DIP Loans**   What are DIP loans? Where do DIP loans fall in the APR?

8. **Bankruptcy Ethics**   Firms sometimes use the threat of a bankruptcy filing to force creditors to renegotiate terms. Critics argue that in such cases the firm is using bankruptcy laws "as a sword rather than a shield." Is this an ethical tactic?

9. **Bankruptcy Ethics**   Several firms have entered bankruptcy, or threatened to enter bankruptcy, at least in part, as a means of reducing labor costs. Whether this move is ethical, or proper, is hotly debated. Is this an ethical use of bankruptcy?

10. **Bankruptcy versus Private Workouts**   Why do so many firms file for legal bankruptcy when private workouts are so much less expensive?

Questions and Problems

BASIC
(Questions 1–2)

1. **Chapter 7**   When getrichfast.com filed for bankruptcy under Chapter 7 of the U.S. bankruptcy code, it had the following balance sheet information:

Liquidating Value		Claims	
		Trade credit	$3,000
		Secured mortgage notes	6,000
		Senior debentures	5,000
		Junior debentures	9,000
Total assets	$15,500	Book equity	−7,500

Assuming there are no legal fees associated with the bankruptcy, as trustee, what distribution of liquidating value do you propose?

2. Chapter 11   When the Sorry Brothers filed for bankruptcy, it filed under Chapter 11 of the U.S. bankruptcy code. Key information is shown here:

Assets		Claims	
		Mortgage bonds	$10,000
		Senior debentures	6,000
		Junior debentures	4,000
Going concern value	$15,500	Book equity	−5,000

As trustee, what reorganization plan would you accept?

Appendix 30A   Predicting Corporate Bankruptcy: The Z-Score Model

To access the appendix for this chapter, please visit **www.mhhe.com/rwj**.

International Corporate Finance

Relatively few large companies operate in a single country, and companies based in the United States are no exception. In 2005, multinational companies based in the United States received a significant tax break with the passage of the American Jobs Creation Act. The act allowed multinational companies to return or "repatriate" profits earned overseas prior to 2003 back to the United States at a tax rate of only 5.25 percent. Previously, the tax rates on repatriated profits were as high as 35 percent, which encouraged companies to invest profits from foreign operations in other countries, thereby avoiding the tax. The goal of the act was to encourage companies to move resources from foreign operations to the United States. Economists estimated that the total amount repatriated could reach as much as $300 billion. Pharmaceutical giant Pfizer, for example, was expected to repatriate as much as $38 billion, and Johnson & Johnson said it would bring home $11 billion. Of course, taxes are only one of the intricacies involved in global operations. In this chapter, we explore the roles played by currencies and exchange rates, along with a number of other key topics in international finance.

Corporations with significant foreign operations are often called *international corporations* or *multinationals*. Such corporations must consider many financial factors that do not directly affect purely domestic firms. These include foreign exchange rates, differing interest rates from country to country, complex accounting methods for foreign operations, foreign tax rates, and foreign government intervention.

The basic principles of corporate finance still apply to international corporations; like domestic companies, these firms seek to invest in projects that create more value for the shareholders than they cost and to arrange financing that raises cash at the lowest possible cost. In other words, the net present value principle holds for both foreign and domestic operations, although it is usually more complicated to apply the NPV rule to foreign investments.

One of the most significant complications of international finance is foreign exchange. The foreign exchange markets provide important information and opportunities for an international corporation when it undertakes capital budgeting and financing decisions. As we will discuss, international exchange rates, interest rates, and inflation rates are closely related. We will spend much of this chapter exploring the connection between these financial variables.

We won't have much to say here about the role of cultural and social differences in international business. Neither will we be discussing the implications of differing political and economic systems. These factors are of great importance to international businesses, but it would take another book to do them justice. Consequently we will focus only on some purely financial considerations in international finance and some key aspects of foreign exchange markets.

31.1 Terminology

A common buzzword for the student of business finance is *globalization*. The first step in learning about the globalization of financial markets is to conquer the new vocabulary. As with any specialty, international finance is rich in jargon. Accordingly, we get started on the subject with a highly eclectic vocabulary exercise.

The terms that follow are presented alphabetically, and they are not all of equal importance. We choose these particular ones because they appear frequently in the financial press or because they illustrate the colorful nature of the language of international finance.

See **www.adr.com** for more.

1. An **American depositary receipt (ADR)** is a security issued in the United States that represents shares of a foreign stock, allowing that stock to be traded in the United States. Foreign companies use ADRs, which are issued in U.S. dollars, to expand the pool of potential U.S. investors. ADRs are available in two forms for a large and growing number of foreign companies: company sponsored, which are listed on an exchange, and unsponsored, which usually are held by the investment bank that makes a market in the ADR. Both forms are available to individual investors, but only company-sponsored issues are quoted daily in newspapers.

2. The **cross-rate** is the implicit exchange rate between two currencies (usually non-U.S.) when both are quoted in some third currency, usually the U.S. dollar.

3. A **Eurobond** is a bond issued in multiple countries but denominated in a single currency, usually the issuer's home currency. Such bonds have become an important way to raise capital for many international companies and governments. Eurobonds are issued outside the restrictions that apply to domestic offerings and are syndicated and traded mostly from London. Trading can and does take place anywhere there are buyers and sellers.

4. **Eurocurrency** is money deposited in a financial center outside of the country whose currency is involved. For instance, Eurodollars—the most widely used Eurocurrency—are U.S. dollars deposited in banks outside the U.S. banking system.

5. **Foreign bonds**, unlike Eurobonds, are issued in a single country and are usually denominated in that country's currency. Often, the country in which these bonds are issued will draw distinctions between them and bonds issued by domestic issuers—including different tax laws, restrictions on the amount issued, and tougher disclosure rules.

   Foreign bonds often are nicknamed for the country where they are issued: Yankee bonds (United States), Samurai bonds (Japan), Rembrandt bonds (the Netherlands), Bulldog bonds (Britain). Partly because of tougher regulations and disclosure requirements, the foreign bond market hasn't grown in past years with the vigor of the Eurobond market.

6. **Gilts**, technically, are British and Irish government securities, although the term also includes issues of local British authorities and some overseas public-sector offerings.

For current LIBOR rates, see **www.bloomberg.com**.

7. The **London Interbank Offer Rate (LIBOR)** is the rate that most international banks charge one another for overnight loans of Eurodollars in the London market. LIBOR is a cornerstone in the pricing of money market issues and other short-term debt issues by both government and corporate borrowers. Interest rates are frequently quoted as some spread over LIBOR, and they then float with the LIBOR rate.

8. There are two basic kinds of **swaps**: interest rate and currency. An interest rate swap occurs when two parties exchange a floating-rate payment for a fixed-rate payment or vice versa. Currency swaps are agreements to deliver one currency in exchange for another. Often, both types of swaps are used in the same transaction when debt denominated in different currencies is swapped.

31.2 Foreign Exchange Markets and Exchange Rates

The **foreign exchange market** is undoubtedly the world's largest financial market. It is the market where one country's currency is traded for another's. Most of the trading takes place in a few currencies: the U.S. dollar ($), the British pound sterling (£), the Japanese yen (¥), and the euro (€). Table 31.1 lists some of the more common currencies and their symbols.

The foreign exchange market is an over-the-counter market, so there is no single location where traders get together. Instead, market participants are located in the major commercial and investment banks around the world. They communicate using computers, telephones, and other telecommunications devices. For example, one communications network for foreign transactions is maintained by the Society for Worldwide Interbank Financial Telecommunications (SWIFT), a Belgian not-for-profit cooperative. Using data transmission lines, a bank in New York can send messages to a bank in London via SWIFT regional processing centers.

The many different types of participants in the foreign exchange market include the following:

Visit SWIFT at
www.swift.com.

1. Importers who pay for goods using foreign currencies.
2. Exporters who receive foreign currency and may want to convert to the domestic currency.
3. Portfolio managers who buy or sell foreign stocks and bonds.
4. Foreign exchange brokers who match buy and sell orders.
5. Traders who "make a market" in foreign currencies.
6. Speculators who try to profit from changes in exchange rates.

Exchange Rates

An **exchange rate** is simply the price of one country's currency expressed in terms of another country's currency. In practice, almost all trading of currencies takes place in terms

Table 31.1

International Currency Symbols

Country	Currency	Symbol
Australia	Dollar	A$
Canada	Dollar	Can$
Denmark	Krone	DKr
EMU	Euro	€
India	Rupee	Rs
Iran	Rial	RI
Japan	Yen	¥
Kuwait	Dinar	KD
Mexico	Peso	Ps
Norway	Krone	NKr
Saudi Arabia	Riyal	SR
Singapore	Dollar	S$
South Africa	Rand	R
Sweden	Krona	SKr
Switzerland	Franc	SF
United Kingdom	Pound	£
United States	Dollar	$

of the U.S. dollar. For example, both the Swiss franc and the Japanese yen are traded with their prices quoted in U.S. dollars. Exchange rates are constantly changing.

Exchange Rate Quotations   Figure 31.1 reproduces exchange rate quotations as they appeared in *The Wall Street Journal* in 2006. The first two columns (labeled "U.S. $ equivalent") give the number of dollars it takes to buy one unit of foreign currency. Because this is the price in dollars of a foreign currency, it is called a *direct* or *American quote* (remember that "Americans are direct"). For example, the Australian dollar is quoted at .7385, which means that you can buy one Australian dollar with U.S. $.7385.

The third and fourth columns show the *indirect*, or *European*, *exchange rate* (even though the currency may not be European). This is the amount of foreign currency per U.S. dollar. The Australian dollar is quoted here at 1.3541, so you can get 1.3541 Australian dollars for one U.S. dollar. Naturally this second exchange rate is just the reciprocal of the first one (possibly with a little rounding error): $1/.7385 = 1.3541$.

Get up-to-the-minute exchange rates at **www.xe.com** and **www. exchangerate.com**.

Figure 31.1

Exchange Rate Quotations

Key Currency Cross Rates
Late New York Trading Thursday, February 23, 2006

	Dollar	Euro	Pound	SFranc	Peso	Yen	CdnDlr
Canada	1.1529	1.3741	2.0194	0.8807	.10995	.00984	...
Japan	117.16	139.65	205.23	89.502	11.174	...	101.629
Mexico	10.4855	12.4976	18.366	8.0099	...	.08949	9.0951
Switzerland	1.3091	1.5603	2.2930	...	.12485	.01117	1.1355
U.K.	.57090	.6805	...	.4361	.05445	.00487	.49520
Euro	.83900	...	1.4696	.64091	.08002	.00716	.72775
U.S.	...	1.1919	1.7516	.76390	.09537	.00854	.86740

Source: Reuters

Exchange Rates
February 23, 2006

The foreign exchange mid-range rates below apply to trading among banks in amounts of $1 million and more, as quoted at 4 p.m. Eastern time by Reuters and other sources. Retail transactions provide fewer units of foreign currency per dollar.

Country	U.S. $ EQUIVALENT		CURRENCY PER U.S. $	
	Thu	Wed	Thu	Wed
Argentina (Peso)-y	.3253	.3256	3.0741	3.0713
Australia (Dollar)	.7385	.7364	1.3541	1.3580
Bahrain (Dinar)	2.6534	2.6529	.3769	.3769
Brazil (Real)	.4681	.4692	2.1363	2.1313
Canada (Dollar)	.8674	.8705	1.1529	1.1488
1-month forward	.8680	.8711	1.1521	1.1480
3-months forward	.8695	.8726	1.1501	1.1460
6-months forward	.8716	.8747	1.1473	1.1432
Chile (Peso)	.001933	.001926	517.33	519.21
China (Renminbi)	.1243	.1243	8.0475	8.0476
Colombia (Peso)	.0004447	.0004444	2248.71	2250.23
Czech. Rep. (Koruna)				
Commercial rate	.04198	.04170	23.821	23.981
Denmark (Krone)	.1597	.1595	6.2617	6.2696
Ecuador (US Dollar)	1.0000	1.0000	1.0000	1.0000
Egypt (Pound)-y	.1741	.1742	5.7425	5.7399
Hong Kong (Dollar)	.1289	.1288	7.7591	7.7611
Hungary (Forint)	.004705	.004689	212.54	213.27
India (Rupee)	.02254	.02245	44.366	44.543
Indonesia (Rupiah)	.0001079	.0001069	9268	9355
Israel (Shekel)	.2120	.2117	4.7170	4.7237
Japan (Yen)	.008535	.008435	117.16	118.55
1-month forward	.008565	.008465	116.75	118.13
3-months forward	.008638	.008534	115.77	117.18
6-months forward	.008745	.008641	114.35	115.73
Jordan (Dinar)	1.4098	1.4102	.7093	.7091
Kuwait (Dinar)	3.4230	3.4231	.2921	.2921
Lebanon (Pound)	.0006634	.0006634	1507.39	1507.39
Malaysia (Ringgit)-b	.2692	.2687	3.7147	3.7216
Malta (Lira)	2.7765	2.7730	.3602	.3606

Country	U.S. $ EQUIVALENT		CURRENCY PER U.S. $	
	Thu	Wed	Thu	Wed
Mexico (Peso)				
Floating rate	.0954	.0955	10.4855	10.4668
New Zealand (Dollar)	.6609	.6587	1.5131	1.5181
Norway (Krone)	.1482	.1476	6.7476	6.7751
Pakistan (Rupee)	.01664	.01666	60.096	60.024
Peru (new Sol)	.3045	.3045	3.2841	3.2841
Philippines (Peso)	.01935	.01928	51.680	51.867
Poland (Zloty)	.3141	.3133	3.1837	3.1918
Russia (Ruble)-a	.03547	.03543	28.193	28.225
Saudi Arabia (Riyal)	.2667	.2666	3.7495	3.7509
Singapore (Dollar)	.6154	.6128	1.6250	1.6319
Slovak Rep. (Koruna)	.03196	.03186	31.289	31.387
South Africa (Rand)	.1639	.1646	6.1013	6.0753
South Korea (Won)	.0010357	.0010261	965.53	974.56
Sweden (Krona)	.1269	.1271	7.8802	7.8678
Switzerland (Franc)	.7639	.7623	1.3091	1.3118
1-month forward	.7660	.7644	1.3055	1.3082
3-months forward	.7711	.7692	1.2968	1.3001
6-months forward	.7781	.7764	1.2852	1.2880
Taiwan (Dollar)	.03071	.03064	32.563	32.637
Thailand (Baht)	.02544	.02528	39.308	39.557
Turkey (New Lira)-d	.7568	.7553	1.3213	1.3240
U.K. (Pound)	1.7516	1.7435	.5709	.5736
1-month forward	1.7517	1.7436	.5709	.5735
3-months forward	1.7529	1.7447	.5705	.5732
6-months forward	1.7555	1.7473	.5696	.5723
United Arab (Dirham)	.2723	.2722	3.6724	3.6738
Uruguay (Peso)				
Financial	.04120	.04120	24.272	24.272
Venezuela (Bolivar)	.000466	.000466	2145.92	2145.92
SDR	1.4376	1.4310	.6956	.6988
Euro	1.1919	1.1903	.8390	.8401

Special Drawing Rights (SDR) are based on exchange rates for the U.S., British, and Japanese currencies. Source: International Monetary Fund.

a-Russian Central Bank rate. b-Government rate. d-Rebased as of Jan. 1, 2005. y-Floating rate.

You can also find exchange rates on a number of Web sites. Suppose you have just returned from your dream vacation to Jamaica and feel rich because you have 10,000 Jamaican dollars left over. You now need to convert these to U.S. dollars. How much will you have? We went to www.xe.com and used the currency converter on the site to find out. This is what we found:

xe.com Universal Currency Converter® Results
Live mid-market rates as of 2006.03.01 18:42:29 UTC.
10,000.00 JMD **＝** **153.645 USD**
Jamaica Dollars   United States Dollars
1 JMD = 0.0153645 USD   1 USD = 65.0850 JMD
Another Conversion? · Bookmark Us

Looks like you left Jamaica just before you ran out of money.

EXAMPLE 31.1

A Yen for Euros Suppose you have $1,000. Based on the rates in Figure 31.1, how many Japanese yen can you get? Alternatively, if a Porsche costs € 100,000 (recall that € is the symbol for the euro), how many dollars will you need to buy it?

The exchange rate in terms of yen per dollar (third column) is 117.16. Your $1,000 will thus get you

$$\$1,000 \times 117.16 \text{ yen per } \$1 = 117,160 \text{ yen}$$

Because the exchange rate in terms of dollars per euro (first column) is 1.1919, you will need

$$€100,000 \times \$1.1919 \text{ per } € = \$119,190$$

Cross-Rates and Triangle Arbitrage Using the U.S. dollar as the common denominator in quoting exchange rates greatly reduces the number of possible cross-currency quotes. For example, with five major currencies, there would potentially be 10 exchange rates instead of just 4.[1] Also, the fact that the dollar is used throughout cuts down on inconsistencies in the exchange rate quotations.

Earlier, we defined the cross-rate as the exchange rate for a non-U.S. currency expressed in terms of another non-U.S. currency. For example, suppose we observe the following for the euro (€) and the Swiss franc (SF):

$$€ \text{ per } \$1 = 1.00$$
$$SF \text{ per } \$1 = 2.00$$

Suppose the cross-rate is quoted as:

$$€ \text{ per } SF = .40$$

What do you think?

The cross-rate here is inconsistent with the exchange rates. To see this, suppose you have $100. If you convert this to Swiss francs, you will receive:

$$\$100 \times SF \ 2 \text{ per } \$1 = SF \ 200$$

---

[1]There are four exchange rates instead of five because one exchange rate would involve the exchange of a currency for itself. More generally, it might seem that there should be 25 exchange rates with five currencies. There are 25 different combinations, but, of these, 5 involve the exchange of a currency for itself. Of the remaining 20, half are redundant because they are just the reciprocals of another exchange rate. Of the remaining 10, 6 can be eliminated by using a common denominator.

If you convert this to euros at the cross-rate, you will have:

$$SF\ 200 \times €.4\ per\ SF\ 1 = €80$$

However, if you just convert your dollars to euros without going through Swiss francs, you will have:

$$\$100 \times €1\ per\ \$1 = €100$$

What we see is that the euro has two prices, €1 per $1 and €.80 per $1, with the price we pay depending on how we get the euros.

To make money, we want to buy low and sell high. The important thing to note is that euros are cheaper if you buy them with dollars because you get 1 euro instead of just .8. You should proceed as follows:

1. Buy 100 euros for $100.
2. Use the 100 euros to buy Swiss francs at the cross-rate. Because it takes .4 euros to buy a Swiss franc, you will receive €100/.4 = SF 250.
3. Use the SF 250 to buy dollars. Because the exchange rate is SF 2 per dollar, you receive SF 250/2 = $125, for a round-trip profit of $25.
4. Repeat steps 1 through 3.

This particular activity is called *triangle arbitrage* because the arbitrage involves moving through three different exchange rates:

To prevent such opportunities, it is not difficult to see that because a dollar will buy you either one euro or two Swiss francs, the cross-rate must be:

$$(€1/\$1)/(SF\ 2/\$1) = €1/SF\ 2$$

That is, the cross-rate must be one euro per two Swiss francs. If it were anything else, there would be a triangle arbitrage opportunity.

Shedding Some Pounds   Suppose the exchange rates for the British pound and Swiss franc are:
Pounds per $1 = .60
SF per $1 = 2.00

The cross-rate is three francs per pound. Is this consistent? Explain how to go about making some money.

The cross-rate should be SF 2.00/£.60 = SF 3.33 per pound. You can buy a pound for SF 3 in one market, and you can sell a pound for SF 3.33 in another. So we want to first get some francs, then use the francs to buy some pounds, and then sell the pounds. Assuming you have $100, you could:

1. Exchange dollars for francs: $100 × 2 = SF 200.
2. Exchange francs for pounds: SF 200/3 = £66.67.
3. Exchange pounds for dollars: £66.67/.60 = $111.12.

This would result in an $11.12 round-trip profit.

Types of Transactions There are two basic types of trades in the foreign exchange market: spot trades and forward trades. A **spot trade** is an agreement to exchange currency "on the spot," which actually means that the transaction will be completed or settled within two business days. The exchange rate on a spot trade is called the **spot exchange rate**. Implicitly, all of the exchange rates and transactions we have discussed so far have referred to the spot market.

A **forward trade** is an agreement to exchange currency at some time in the future. The exchange rate that will be used is agreed upon today and is called the **forward exchange rate**. A forward trade will normally be settled sometime in the next 12 months.

If you look back at Figure 31.1, you will see forward exchange rates quoted for some of the major currencies. For example, the spot exchange rate for the Swiss franc is SF 1 = $.7639. The 180-day (6-month) forward exchange rate is SF 1 = $.7781. This means that you can buy a Swiss franc today for $.7639, or you can agree to take delivery of a Swiss franc in 180 days and pay $.7781 at that time.

Notice that the Swiss franc is more expensive in the forward market ($.7781 versus $.7639). Because the Swiss franc is more expensive in the future than it is today, it is said to be selling at a *premium* relative to the dollar. For the same reason, the dollar is said to be selling at a *discount* relative to the Swiss franc.

Why does the forward market exist? One answer is that it allows businesses and individuals to lock in a future exchange rate today, thereby eliminating any risk from unfavorable shifts in the exchange rate.

EXAMPLE 31.3

Looking Forward Suppose you are expecting to receive a million British pounds in six months, and you agree to a forward trade to exchange your pounds for dollars. Based on Figure 31.1, how many dollars will you get in six months? Is the pound selling at a discount or a premium relative to the dollar?

In Figure 31.1, the spot exchange rate and the 180-day forward rate in terms of dollars per pound are $1.7516 = £1 and $1.7555 = £1, respectively. If you expect £1 million in 180 days, then you will get £1 million × $1.7555 per pound = $1.7555 million. Because it is more expensive to buy a pound in the forward market than in the spot market ($1.7555 versus $1.7516), the pound is said to be selling at a premium relative to the dollar.

As we mentioned earlier, it is standard practice around the world (with a few exceptions) to quote exchange rates in terms of the U.S. dollar. This means that rates are quoted as the amount of currency per U.S. dollar. For the remainder of this chapter, we will stick with this form. Things can get extremely confusing if you forget this. Thus, when we say things like "the exchange rate is expected to rise," it is important to remember that we are talking about the exchange rate quoted as units of foreign currency per dollar.

31.3 Purchasing Power Parity

Now that we have discussed what exchange rate quotations mean, we can address an obvious question: What determines the level of the spot exchange rate? In addition, because we know that exchange rates change through time, we can ask the related question, What determines the rate of change in exchange rates? At least part of the answer in both cases goes by the name of **purchasing power parity (PPP)**, the idea that the exchange rate adjusts to keep purchasing power constant among currencies. As we discuss next, there are two forms of PPP, *absolute* and *relative*.

Absolute Purchasing Power Parity

The basic idea behind *absolute purchasing power* parity is that a commodity costs the same regardless of what currency is used to purchase it or where it is selling. This is a very straightforward concept. If a beer costs £2 in London, and the exchange rate is £.60 per dollar, then a beer costs £2/.60 = $3.33 in New York. In other words, absolute PPP says that $1 will buy you the same number of, say, cheeseburgers anywhere in the world.

More formally, let S_0 be the spot exchange rate between the British pound and the U.S. dollar today (time 0), and remember that we are quoting exchange rates as the amount of foreign currency per dollar. Let P_{US} and P_{UK} be the current U.S. and British prices, respectively, on a particular commodity, say, apples. Absolute PPP simply says that:

$$P_{UK} = S_0 \times P_{US}$$

This tells us that the British price for something is equal to the U.S. price for that same something multiplied by the exchange rate.

The rationale behind PPP is similar to that behind triangle arbitrage. If PPP did not hold, arbitrage would be possible (in principle) if apples were moved from one country to another. For example, suppose apples are selling in New York for $4 per bushel, whereas in London the price is £2.40 per bushel. Absolute PPP implies that:

$$P_{UK} = S_0 \times P_{US}$$
$$£2.40 = S_0 \times \$4$$
$$S_0 = £2.40/\$4 = £.60$$

That is, the implied spot exchange rate is £.60 per dollar. Equivalently, a pound is worth $1/£.60 = $1.67.

Suppose instead that the actual exchange rate is £.50. Starting with $4, a trader could buy a bushel of apples in New York, ship it to London, and sell it there for £2.40. Our trader could then convert the £2.40 into dollars at the prevailing exchange rate, $S_0 = £.50$, yielding a total of £2.40/.50 = $4.80. The round-trip gain would be 80 cents.

Because of this profit potential, forces are set in motion to change the exchange rate and/or the price of apples. In our example, apples would begin moving from New York to London. The reduced supply of apples in New York would raise the price of apples there, and the increased supply in Britain would lower the price of apples in London.

In addition to moving apples around, apple traders would be busily converting pounds back into dollars to buy more apples. This activity would increase the supply of pounds and simultaneously increase the demand for dollars. We would expect the value of a pound to fall. This means that the dollar would be getting more valuable, so it would take more pounds to buy one dollar. Because the exchange rate is quoted as pounds per dollar, we would expect the exchange rate to rise from £.50.

For absolute PPP to hold absolutely, several things must be true:

1. The transaction costs of trading apples—shipping, insurance, spoilage, and so on—must be zero.

2. There must be no barriers to trading apples—no tariffs, taxes, or other political barriers.

3. Finally, an apple in New York must be identical to an apple in London. It won't do for you to send red apples to London if the English eat only green apples.

Given the fact that the transaction costs are not zero and that the other conditions are rarely met exactly, it is not surprising that absolute PPP is really applicable only to traded goods, and then only to very uniform ones.

For this reason, absolute PPP does not imply that a Mercedes costs the same as a Ford or that a nuclear power plant in France costs the same as one in New York. In the case of the cars, they are not identical. In the case of the power plants, even if they were identical, they are expensive and would be very difficult to ship. On the other hand, we would be very surprised to see a significant violation of absolute PPP for gold.

As an example of a violation of absolute PPP, in late 2003, the euro was going for about $1.30. Porsche's new (and very desirable) Carrera GT sold for about $440,000 in the United States. This converted to a euro price of €338,462 before tax and €392,615 after tax. The price of the car in Germany was €452,690, which meant that if German residents could ship the car for less than €60,000 they would be better off buying it in the United States.

Violations of PPP are actually sought out by corporations. For example, in the middle of 2004, Alcoa announced that it would build a $1 billion aluminum smelter plant on the Caribbean island of Trinidad. At the same time, the company was breaking ground on another $1 billion plant in Iceland and looking into other locations including China, Brunei, Bahrain, Brazil, and Canada. In all cases, low energy costs were the attraction (aluminum smelting is very energy-intensive). Meanwhile, the company had several plants in the Pacific Northwest that were closed because higher electricity prices in this region made the plants unprofitable.

One of the more famous violations of absolute PPP is the Big Mac Index constructed by *The Economist*. To construct the index, prices for a Big Mac in different countries are gathered from McDonald's. Nearby you will find the January 2006 Big Mac index from www.economist.com. (We will leave it to you to find the most recent index.)

As you can see from the index, absolute PPP does not seem to hold, at least for the Big Mac. In fact, in only 5 of the 29 currencies surveyed by *The Economist* is the exchange rate within 10 percent of that predicted by absolute PPP. The largest disparity is in Switzerland, where the currency is apparently overvalued by about 60 percent. And 11 of the 29 currencies are "incorrectly" priced by more than 40 percent. Why?

There are several reasons. First, a Big Mac is not really transportable. Yes, you can load a ship with Big Macs and send it to Denmark where the currency is supposedly overvalued by more than 40 percent. But do you really think people would buy your Big Macs? Probably not. Even though it is relatively easy to transport a Big Mac, it would be relatively expensive, and the hamburger would suffer in quality along the way.

Also, if you look, the price of the Big Mac is the average price from New York, Chicago, San Franciso, and Atlanta. The reason is that Big Macs do not sell for the same price in the United States, where presumably they are all purchased with the dollar. The cost of living and competition are only a few of the factors that affect the price of a Big Mac in the United States. If Big Macs are not priced the same in the same currency, would we expect absolute PPP to hold across currencies?

Finally, differing tastes can account for the apparent discrepancy. In the United States, hamburgers and fast food have become a staple of the American diet. In other countries, hamburgers have not become as entrenched. We would expect the price of the Big Mac to be lower in the United States because there is much more competition.

Having examined the Big Mac, we should say that absolute PPP should hold more closely for more easily transportable items. For instance, there are many companies with stock listed on both the NYSE and the stock exchange of another country. If you examine the share prices on the two exchanges you will find that the price of the stock is almost exactly what absolute PPP would predict. The reason is that a share of stock in a particular company is (usually) the same wherever you buy it and whatever currency you use.

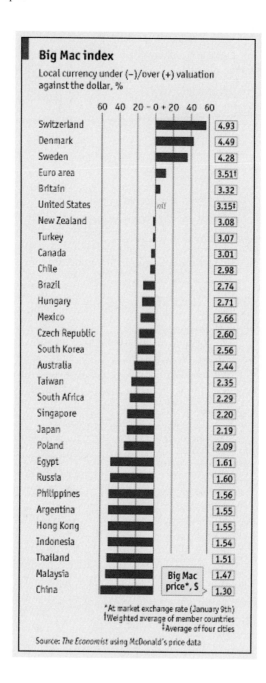

Relative Purchasing Power Parity

As a practical matter, a relative version of purchasing power parity has evolved. *Relative purchasing power parity* does not tell us what determines the absolute level of the exchange rate. Instead, it tells us what determines the *change* in the exchange rate over time.

The Basic Idea   Suppose the British pound–U.S. dollar exchange rate is currently $S_0 = £.50$. Further suppose that the inflation rate in Britain is predicted to be 10 percent over the coming year, and (for the moment) the inflation rate in the United States is predicted to be zero. What do you think the exchange rate will be in a year?

If you think about it, you see that a dollar currently costs .50 pounds in Britain. With 10 percent inflation, we expect prices in Britain to generally rise by 10 percent. So we expect that the price of a dollar will go up by 10 percent, and the exchange rate should rise to £.50 × 1.1 = £.55.

If the inflation rate in the United States is not zero, then we need to worry about the *relative* inflation rates in the two countries. For example, suppose the U.S. inflation rate is predicted to be 4 percent. Relative to prices in the United States, prices in Britain are rising at a rate of 10 percent − 4 percent = 6 percent per year. So we expect the price of the dollar to rise by 6 percent, and the predicted exchange rate is £.50 × 1.06 = £.53.

The Result   In general, relative PPP says that the change in the exchange rate is determined by the difference in the inflation rates of the two countries. To be more specific, we will use the following notation:

S_0 = Current (Time 0) spot exchange rate (foreign currency per dollar).

$E(S_t)$ = Expected exchange rate in t periods.

h_{US} = Inflation rate in the United States.

h_{FC} = Foreign country inflation rate.

Based on our discussion just preceding, relative PPP says that the expected percentage change in the exchange rate over the next year, $[E(S_1) - S_0]/S_0$, is:

$$[E(S_1) - S_0]/S_0 = h_{FC} - h_{US} \qquad \textbf{(31.1)}$$

In words, relative PPP simply says that the expected percentage change in the exchange rate is equal to the difference in inflation rates. If we rearrange this slightly, we get:

$$E(S_1) = S_0 \times [1 + (h_{FC} - h_{US})] \qquad \textbf{(31.2)}$$

This result makes a certain amount of sense, but care must be used in quoting the exchange rate.

In our example involving Britain and the United States, relative PPP tells us that the exchange rate will rise by $h_{FC} - h_{US}$ = 10 percent − 4 percent = 6 percent per year. Assuming the difference in inflation rates doesn't change, the expected exchange rate in two years, $E(S_2)$, will therefore be:

$$E(S_2) = E(S_1) \times (1 + .06)$$
$$= .53 \times 1.06$$
$$= .562$$

Notice that we could have written this as:

$$E(S_2) = .53 \times 1.06$$
$$= .50 \times (1.06 \times 1.06)$$
$$= .50 \times 1.06^2$$

In general, relative PPP says that the expected exchange rate at some time in the future, $E(S_t)$, is:

$$E(S_t) = S_0 \times [1 + (h_{FC} - h_{US})]^t \qquad \textbf{(31.3)}$$

As we will see, this is a very useful relationship.

Because we don't really expect absolute PPP to hold for most goods, we will focus on relative PPP in our following discussion. Henceforth, when we refer to PPP without further qualification, we mean relative PPP.

EXAMPLE 31.4

It's All Relative   Suppose the Japanese exchange rate is currently 105 yen per dollar. The inflation rate in Japan over the next three years will run, say, 2 percent per year, whereas the U.S. inflation rate will be 6 percent. Based on relative PPP, what will the exchange rate be in three years?

Because the U.S. inflation rate is higher, we expect that a dollar will become less valuable. The exchange rate change will be 2 percent − 6 percent = −4 percent per year. Over three years the exchange rate will fall to:

$$E(S_3) = S_0 \times [1 + (h_{FC} - h_{US})]^3$$
$$= 105 \times [1 + (-.04)]^3$$
$$= 92.90$$

Currency Appreciation and Depreciation   We frequently hear things like "the dollar strengthened (or weakened) in financial markets today" or "the dollar is expected to appreciate (or depreciate) relative to the pound." When we say that the dollar strengthens or appreciates, we mean that the value of a dollar rises, so it takes more foreign currency to buy a dollar.

What happens to the exchange rates as currencies fluctuate in value depends on how exchange rates are quoted. Because we are quoting them as units of foreign currency per dollar, the exchange rate moves in the same direction as the value of the dollar: It rises as the dollar strengthens, and it falls as the dollar weakens.

Relative PPP tells us that the exchange rate will rise if the U.S. inflation rate is lower than the foreign country's. This happens because the foreign currency depreciates in value and therefore weakens relative to the dollar.

31.4   Interest Rate Parity, Unbiased Forward Rates, and the International Fisher Effect

The next issue we need to address is the relationship between spot exchange rates, forward exchange rates, and interest rates. To get started, we need some additional notation:

F_t = Forward exchange rate for settlement at time t.

R_{US} = U.S. nominal risk-free interest rate.

R_{FC} = Foreign country nominal risk-free interest rate.

As before, we will use S_0 to stand for the spot exchange rate. You can take the U.S. nominal risk-free rate, R_{US}, to be the T-bill rate.

Covered Interest Arbitrage

Suppose we observe the following information about U.S. and Swiss currencies in the market:

$$S_0 = \text{SF } 2.00$$
$$F_1 = \text{SF } 1.90$$
$$R_{US} = 10\%$$
$$R_S = 5\%$$

where R_S is the nominal risk-free rate in Switzerland. The period is one year, so F_1 is the 360-day forward rate.

Do you see an arbitrage opportunity here? There is one. Suppose you have $1 to invest, and you want a riskless investment. One option you have is to invest the $1 in a riskless U.S. investment such as a 360-day T-bill. If you do this, then in one period your $1 will be worth:

$$\$ \text{ value in 1 period} = \$1 \times (1 + R_{US})$$
$$= \$1.10$$

Alternatively, you can invest in the Swiss risk-free investment. To do this, you need to convert your $1 to Swiss francs and simultaneously execute a forward trade to convert francs back to dollars in one year. The necessary steps would be as follows:

1. Convert your $1 to $1 \times S_0 = SF 2.00.

2. At the same time, enter into a forward agreement to convert Swiss francs back to dollars in one year. Because the forward rate is SF 1.90, you will get $1 for every SF 1.90 that you have in one year.

3. Invest your SF 2.00 in Switzerland at R_S. In one year, you will have:

$$SF \text{ value in 1 year} = SF\ 2.00 \times (1 + R_S)$$
$$= SF\ 2.00 \times 1.05$$
$$= SF\ 2.10$$

4. Convert your SF 2.10 back to dollars at the agreed-upon rate of SF 1.90 = $1. You end up with:

$$\$ \text{ value in 1 year} = SF\ 2.10/1.90$$
$$= \$1.1053$$

Notice that the value in one year resulting from this strategy can be written as:

$$\$ \text{ value in 1 year} = \$1 \times S_0 \times (1 + R_S)/F_1$$
$$= \$1 \times 2 \times 1.05/1.90$$
$$= \$1.1053$$

The return on this investment is apparently 10.53 percent. This is higher than the 10 percent we get from investing in the United States. Because both investments are risk-free, there is an arbitrage opportunity.

To exploit the difference in interest rates, you need to borrow, say, $5 million at the lower U.S. rate and invest it at the higher Swiss rate. What is the round-trip profit from doing this? To find out, we can work through the steps outlined previously:

1. Convert the $5 million at SF 2 = $1 to get SF 10 million.

2. Agree to exchange Swiss francs for dollars in one year at SF 1.90 to the dollar.

3. Invest the SF 10 million for one year at $R_S = 5$ percent. You end up with SF 10.5 million.

4. Convert the SF 10.5 million back to dollars to fulfill the forward contract. You receive SF 10.5 million/1.90 = $5,526,316.

5. Repay the loan with interest. You owe $5 million plus 10 percent interest, for a total of $5.5 million. You have $5,526,316, so your round-trip profit is a risk-free $26,316.

The activity that we have illustrated here goes by the name of *covered interest arbitrage*. The term *covered* refers to the fact that we are covered in the event of a change in the exchange rate because we lock in the forward exchange rate today.

Interest Rate Parity

If we assume that significant covered interest arbitrage opportunities do not exist, then there must be some relationship between spot exchange rates, forward exchange rates, and relative interest rates. To see what this relationship is, note that in general strategy 1 from the preceding discussion, investing in a riskless U.S. investment, gives us $1 + R_{US}$ for every dollar we invest. Strategy 2, investing in a foreign risk-free investment, gives us $S_0 \times (1 + R_{FC})/F_1$ for every dollar we invest. Because these have to be equal to prevent arbitrage, it must be the case that:

$$1 + R_{US} = S_0 \times (1 + R_{FC})/F_1$$

Rearranging this a bit gets us the famous **interest rate parity (IRP)** condition:

$$F_1/S_0 = (1 + R_{FC})/(1 - R_{US}) \tag{31.4}$$

There is a very useful approximation for IRP that illustrates clearly what is going on and is not difficult to remember. If we define the percentage forward premium or discount as $(F_1 - S_0)/S_0$, then IRP says that this percentage premium or discount is *approximately* equal to the difference in interest rates:

$$(F_1 - S_0)/S_0 = R_{FC} - R_{US} \tag{31.5}$$

Loosely, what IRP says is that any difference in interest rates between two countries for some period is just offset by the change in the relative value of the currencies, thereby eliminating any arbitrage possibilities. Notice that we could also write:

$$F_1 = S_0 \times [1 + (R_{FC} - R_{US})] \tag{31.6}$$

In general, if we have t periods instead of just one, the IRP approximation is written like this:

$$F_t = S_0 \times [1 + (R_{FC} - R_{US})]^t \tag{31.7}$$

EXAMPLE 31.5

Parity Check   Suppose the exchange rate for Japanese yen, S_0, is currently ¥120 = $1. If the interest rate in the United States is $R_{US} = 10$ percent and the interest rate in Japan is $R_J = 5$ percent, then what must the forward rate be to prevent covered interest arbitrage?

From IRP, we have

$$
\begin{aligned}
F_1 &= S_0 \times [1 + (R_J - R_{US})] \\
    &= ¥120 \times [1 + (.05 - .10)] \\
    &= ¥120 \times .95 \\
    &= ¥114
\end{aligned}
$$

Notice that the yen will sell at a premium relative to the dollar. (Why?)

Forward Rates and Future Spot Rates

In addition to PPP and IRP, there is one more basic relationship we need to discuss. What is the connection between the forward rate and the expected future spot rate? The **unbiased forward rates (UFR)** condition says that the forward rate, F_1, is equal to the *expected* future spot rate, $E(S_1)$:

$$F_1 = E(S_1)$$

With t periods, UFR would be written as:

$$F_t = E(S_t)$$

Loosely, the UFR condition says that, on average, the forward exchange rate is equal to the future spot exchange rate.

   If we ignore risk, then the UFR condition should hold. Suppose the forward rate for the Japanese yen is consistently lower than the future spot rate by, say, 10 yen. This means that anyone who wanted to convert dollars to yen in the future would consistently get more yen by not agreeing to a forward exchange. The forward rate would have to rise to get anyone interested in a forward exchange.

   Similarly, if the forward rate were consistently higher than the future spot rate, then anyone who wanted to convert yen to dollars would get more dollars per yen by not agreeing to a forward trade. The forward exchange rate would have to fall to attract such traders.

   For these reasons, the forward and actual future spot rates should be equal to each other on average. What the future spot rate will actually be is uncertain, of course. The UFR condition may not hold if traders are willing to pay a premium to avoid this uncertainty. If the condition does hold, then the 180-day forward rate that we see today should be an unbiased predictor of what the exchange rate will actually be in 180 days.

Putting It All Together

We have developed three relationships—PPP, IRP, and UFR—that describe the interactions between key financial variables such as interest rates, exchange rates, and inflation rates. We now explore the implications of these relationships as a group.

Uncovered Interest Parity   To start, it is useful to collect our international financial market relationships in one place:

$$\begin{aligned} \text{PPP:} \quad & E(S_1) = S_0 \times [1 + (h_{FC} - h_{US})] \\ \text{IRP:} \quad & F_1 = S_0 \times [1 + (R_{FC} - R_{US})] \\ \text{UFR:} \quad & F_1 = E(S_1) \end{aligned}$$

   We begin by combining UFR and IRP. Because we know that $F_1 = E(S_1)$ from the UFR condition, we can substitute $E(S_1)$ for F_1 in IRP. The result is:

$$\text{UIP: } E(S_1) = S_0 \times [1 + (R_{FC} - R_{US})] \qquad \textbf{(31.8)}$$

This important relationship is called **uncovered interest parity (UIP)**, and it will play a key role in our international capital budgeting discussion that follows. With t periods, UIP becomes:

$$E(S_t) = S_0 \times [1 + (R_{FC} - R_{US})]^t \qquad \textbf{(31.9)}$$

The International Fisher Effect   Next we compare PPP and UIP. Both of them have $E(S_1)$ on the left side, so their right sides must be equal. We thus have:

$$S_0 \times [1 + (h_{FC} - h_{US})] = S_0 \times [1 + (R_{FC} - R_{US})]$$
$$h_{FC} - h_{US} = R_{FC} - R_{US}$$

This tells us that the difference in returns between the United States and a foreign country is just equal to the difference in inflation rates. Rearranging this slightly gives us the **international Fisher effect (IFE)**:

$$\text{IFE: } R_{US} - h_{US} = R_{FC} - h_{FC} \qquad \textbf{(31.10)}$$

The IFE says that *real* rates are equal across countries.[2]

The conclusion that real returns are equal across countries is really basic economics. If real returns were higher in, say, Brazil than in the United States, money would flow out of U.S. financial markets and into Brazilian markets. Asset prices in Brazil would rise and their returns would fall. At the same time, asset prices in the United States would fall and their returns would rise. This process acts to equalize real returns.

Having said all this, we need to note a couple of things. First, we really haven't explicitly dealt with risk in our discussion. We might reach a different conclusion about real returns once we do, particularly if people in different countries have different tastes and attitudes toward risk. Second, there are many barriers to the movement of money and capital around the world. Real returns might be different in two different countries for long periods if money can't move freely between them.

Despite these problems, we expect that capital markets will become increasingly internationalized. As this occurs, any differences in real rates will probably diminish. The laws of economics have little respect for national boundaries.

31.5 International Capital Budgeting

Kihlstrom Equipment, a U.S.-based international company, is evaluating an overseas investment. Kihlstrom's exports of drill bits have increased to such a degree that it is considering building a distribution center in France. The project will cost €2 million to launch. The cash flows are expected to be €.9 million a year for the next three years.

The current spot exchange rate for euros is €.5. Recall that this is euros per dollar, so a euro is worth $1/.5 = $2. The risk-free rate in the United States is 5 percent, and the risk-free rate in France is 7 percent. Note that the exchange rate and the two interest rates are observed in financial markets, not estimated.[3] Kihlstrom's required return on dollar investments of this sort is 10 percent.

Should Kihlstrom take this investment? As always, the answer depends on the NPV; but how do we calculate the net present value of this project in U.S. dollars? There are two basic methods:

1. *The home currency approach*: Convert all the euro cash flows into dollars, and then discount at 10 percent to find the NPV in dollars. Notice that for this approach we have to come up with the future exchange rates to convert the future projected euro cash flows into dollars.

2. *The foreign currency approach*: Determine the required return on euro investments, and then discount the euro cash flows to find the NPV in euros. Then convert this euro NPV to a dollar NPV. This approach requires us to somehow convert the 10 percent dollar required return to the equivalent euro required return.

The difference between these two approaches is primarily a matter of when we convert from euros to dollars. In the first case, we convert before estimating the NPV. In the second case, we convert after estimating NPV.

It might appear that the second approach is superior because for it we have to come up with only one number, the euro discount rate. Furthermore, because the first approach

---

[2]Notice that our result here is in terms of the approximate real rate, $R - h$ (see Chapter 7), because we used approximations for PPP and IRP. For the exact result, see Problem 17 at the end of the chapter.
[3]For example, the interest rates might be the short-term Eurodollar and euro deposit rates offered by large banks.

requires us to forecast future exchange rates, it probably seems that there is greater room for error with this approach. As we illustrate next, however, based on our previous results, the two approaches are really the same.

Method 1: The Home Currency Approach

To convert the project future cash flows into dollars, we will invoke the uncovered interest parity, or UIP, relation to come up with the projected exchange rates. Based on our earlier discussion, the expected exchange rate at time t, $E(S_t)$, is:

$$E(S_t) = S_0 \times [1 + (R_\text{€} - R_{US})]^t$$

where $R_\text{€}$ stands for the nominal risk-free rate in France. Because $R_\text{€}$ is 7 percent, R_{US} is 5 percent, and the current exchange rate (S_0) is €.5:

$$E(S_t) = .5 \times [1 + (.07 - .05)]^t$$
$$= .5 \times 1.02^t$$

The projected exchange rates for the drill bit project are thus as shown here:

Year	Expected Exchange Rate
1	€.5 × 1.02^1 = €.5100
2	€.5 × 1.02^2 = €.5202
3	€.5 × 1.02^3 = €.5306

Using these exchange rates, along with the current exchange rate, we can convert all of the euro cash flows to dollars (note that all of the cash flows in this example are in millions):

Year	(1) Cash Flow in €mil	(2) Expected Exchange Rate	(3) Cash Flow in $mil (1)/(2)
0	−€2.0	€.5000	−$4.00
1	.9	.5100	1.76
2	.9	.5202	1.73
3	.9	.5306	1.70

To finish off, we calculate the NPV in the ordinary way:

$$NPV_\$ = -\$4 + \$1.76/1.10 + \$1.73/1.10^2 + \$1.70/1.10^3$$
$$= \$.3 \text{ million}$$

So, the project appears to be profitable.

Method 2: The Foreign Currency Approach

Kihlstrom requires a nominal return of 10 percent on the dollar-denominated cash flows. We need to convert this to a rate suitable for euro-denominated cash flows. Based on the international Fisher effect, we know that the difference in the nominal rates is:

$$R_\text{€} - R_{US} = h_\text{€} - h_{US}$$
$$= 7\% - 5\% = 2\%$$

The appropriate discount rate for estimating the euro cash flows from the drill bit project is approximately equal to 10 percent plus an extra 2 percent to compensate for the greater euro inflation rate.

If we calculate the NPV of the euro cash flows at this rate, we get:

$$NPV_{\euro} = -\euro 2 + \euro.9/1.12 + \euro.9/1.12^2 + \euro.9/1.12^3$$
$$= \euro.16 \text{ million}$$

The NPV of this project is €.16 million. Taking this project makes us €.16 million richer today. What is this in dollars? Because the exchange rate today is €.5, the dollar NPV of the project is

$$NPV_{\$} = NPV_{\euro}/S_0 = \euro.16/.5 = \$.3 \text{ million}$$

This is the same dollar NPV that we previously calculated.

The important thing to recognize from our example is that the two capital budgeting procedures are actually the same and will always give the same answer.[4] In this second approach, the fact that we are implicitly forecasting exchange rates is simply hidden. Even so, the foreign currency approach is computationally a little easier.

Unremitted Cash Flows

The previous example assumed that all aftertax cash flows from the foreign investment could be remitted to (paid out to) the parent firm. Actually, substantial differences can exist between the cash flows generated by a foreign project and the amount that can be remitted, or "repatriated," to the parent firm.

A foreign subsidiary can remit funds to a parent in many forms, including the following:

1. Dividends.
2. Management fees for central services.
3. Royalties on the use of trade names and patents.

However cash flows are repatriated, international firms must pay special attention to remittances because there may be current and future controls on remittances. Many governments are sensitive to the charge of being exploited by foreign national firms. In such cases, governments are tempted to limit the ability of international firms to remit cash flows. Funds that cannot currently be remitted are sometimes said to be *blocked*.

31.6 Exchange Rate Risk

Exchange rate risk is the natural consequence of international operations in a world where relative currency values move up and down. Managing exchange rate risk is an important part of international finance. As we discuss next, there are three different types of exchange rate risk or exposure: short-term exposure, long-term exposure, and translation exposure.

Short-Term Exposure

The day-to-day fluctuations in exchange rates create short-term risks for international firms. Most such firms have contractual agreements to buy and sell goods in the near future at set prices. When different currencies are involved, such transactions have an extra element of risk.

---

[4]Actually, there will be a slight difference because we are using the approximate relationships. If we calculate the required return as $1.10 \times (1 + .02) - 1 = 12.2\%$, then we get exactly the same NPV. See Problem 17 for more detail.

For example, imagine that you are importing imitation pasta from Italy and reselling it in the United States under the Impasta brand name. Your largest customer has ordered 10,000 cases of Impasta. You place the order with your supplier today, but you won't pay until the goods arrive in 60 days. Your selling price is $6 per case. Your cost is 8.4 euros per case, and the exchange rate is currently €1.50, so it takes 1.50 euros to buy $1.

At the current exchange rate, your cost in dollars of filling the order is €8.4/1.5 = $5.60 per case, so your pretax profit on the order is 10,000 × ($6 − 5.60) = $4,000. However, the exchange rate in 60 days will probably be different, so your profit will depend on what the future exchange rate turns out to be.

For example, if the rate goes to €1.6, your cost is €8.4/1.6 = $5.25 per case. Your profit goes to $7,500. If the exchange rate goes to, say, €1.4, then your cost is €8.4/1.4 = $6, and your profit is zero.

The short-term exposure in our example can be reduced or eliminated in several ways. The most obvious way is by entering into a forward exchange agreement to lock in an exchange rate. For example, suppose the 60-day forward rate is €1.58. What will be your profit if you hedge? What profit should you expect if you don't?

If you hedge, you lock in an exchange rate of €1.58. Your cost in dollars will thus be €8.4/1.58 = $5.32 per case, so your profit will be 10,000 × ($6 − 5.32) = $6,800. If you don't hedge, then, assuming that the forward rate is an unbiased predictor (in other words, assuming the UFR condition holds), you should expect that the exchange rate will actually be €1.58 in 60 days. You should expect to make $6,800.

Alternatively, if this strategy is not feasible, you could simply borrow the dollars today, convert them into euros, and invest the euros for 60 days to earn some interest. Based on IRP, this amounts to entering into a forward contract.

Long-Term Exposure

In the long term, the value of a foreign operation can fluctuate because of unanticipated changes in relative economic conditions. For example, imagine that we own a labor-intensive assembly operation located in another country to take advantage of lower wages. Through time, unexpected changes in economic conditions can raise the foreign wage levels to the point where the cost advantage is eliminated or even becomes negative.

The impact of changes in exchange rate levels can be substantial. For example, during 2005, the U.S. dollar continued to weaken against other currencies. This meant domestic manufacturers took home more for each dollar's worth of sales they made, which can lead to big profit swings. For example, during 2005, Pepsico estimated that it gained about $251 million due to currency swings. The dramatic effect of exchange rate movements on profitability is also shown by the analysis done by Iluka Resources, Ltd., an Australian mining company, which stated that a one-cent movement in the Australian dollar–U.S. dollar exchange rate would change its net income by $5 million.

Hedging long-term exposure is more difficult than hedging short-term risks. For one thing, organized forward markets don't exist for such long-term needs. Instead, the primary option that firms have is to try to match up foreign currency inflows and outflows. The same thing goes for matching foreign currency–denominated assets and liabilities. For example, a firm that sells in a foreign country might try to concentrate its raw material purchases and labor expense in that country. That way, the dollar values of its revenues and costs will move up and down together. Probably the best examples of this type of hedging are the so-called transplant auto manufacturers such as BMW, Honda, Mercedes, and Toyota, which now build a substantial portion of the cars they sell in the United States at plants located in the United States, thereby obtaining some degree of immunization against exchange rate movements.

In Their Own Words

RICHARD M. LEVICH ON FORWARD EXCHANGE RATES

What is the relationship between today's three-month forward exchange rate, which can be observed in the market, and the spot exchange rate of three months from today, which cannot be observed until the future? One popular answer is that there is no relationship. As every bank trader knows, the possibility of covered interest arbitrage between domestic and foreign securities establishes a close link between the forward premium and the interest rate differential. At any moment, a trader can check a screen and observe that the forward premium and the interest rate differentials are nearly identical, especially when Eurocurrency interest rates are used. Thus, the trader might say, "The forward rate reflects today's interest differential. It has nothing to do with expectations."

To check the second popular belief, that the forward rate reflects exchange rate expectations, takes a bit more work. Take today's three-month forward rate as of January 15 and compare it to the spot exchange rate that actually exists three months later on April 15. This produces one observation of the forward rate as a forecaster—not enough to accept or reject a theory. The idea that the forward rate might be an unbiased predictor of the future spot rate suggests that, on average and looking at many observations, the prediction error is small. So collect more data using the forward rate of April 15 and match it with the spot rate

of July 15, and then the forward rate of July 15 matched to the spot rate of October 15, and so no. Look at the data for 8–10 years to have a large sample of observations.

The data suggest that in the early 1980s when the dollar was very strong, the forward rate significantly *under*estimated the strength of the dollar, and the forward rate was a biased predictor. But from 1985 to 1987 when the dollar depreciated sharply, the forward rate tended to *over*estimate the strength of the dollar, and the forward rate was again a biased predictor, but with the opposite sign as the earlier period. Looking at all of the 1980s—you guessed it—the forward rate was on average very close to the future spot exchange rate.

There are two messages here. First, even if there were "no relationship" between the forward rate and the future spot rate, the treasurer of General Motors would want to know exactly what that "nonrelationship" was. Because if the forward rate were *consistently* 3 percent higher than, or *consistently* 5 percent lower than, the future spot rate, the treasurer would be facing a tantalizing profit opportunity. A watch that is three minutes fast or five minutes slow is a very useful watch as long as the bias is known and consistent.

Richard M. Levich is Professor of Finance and International Business at New York University. He has written extensively on exchange rates and other issues in international economics and finance.

For example, BMW produces 160,000 cars in South Carolina and exports about 100,000 of them. The costs of manufacturing the cars are paid mostly in dollars, and, when BMW exports the cars to Europe, it receives euros. When the dollar weakens, these vehicles become more profitable for BMW. At the same time, BMW exports about 217,000 cars to the United States each year. The costs of manufacturing these imported cars are mostly in euros, so they become less profitable when the dollar weakens. Taken together, these gains and losses tend to offset each other and give BMW a natural hedge.

Similarly, a firm can reduce its long-term exchange rate risk by borrowing in the foreign country. Fluctuations in the value of the foreign subsidiary's assets will then be at least partially offset by changes in the value of the liabilities.

Translation Exposure

When a U.S. company calculates its accounting net income and EPS for some period, it must translate everything into dollars. This can create some problems for the accountants when there are significant foreign operations. In particular, two issues arise:

1. What is the appropriate exchange rate to use for translating each balance sheet account?

2. How should balance sheet accounting gains and losses from foreign currency translation be handled?

To illustrate the accounting problem, suppose we started a small foreign subsidiary in Lilliputia a year ago. The local currency is the gulliver, abbreviated GL. At the beginning of the year, the exchange rate was GL 2 = $1, and the balance sheet in gullivers looked like this:

Assets	GL 1,000	Liabilities	GL 500
		Equity	500

At 2 gullivers to the dollar, the beginning balance sheet in dollars was as follows:

Assets	$500	Liabilities	$250
		Equity	250

Lilliputia is a quiet place, and nothing at all actually happened during the year. As a result, net income was zero (before consideration of exchange rate changes). However, the exchange rate did change to 4 gullivers = $1 purely because the Lilliputian inflation rate is much higher than the U.S. inflation rate.

Because nothing happened, the accounting ending balance sheet in gullivers is the same as the beginning one. However, if we convert it to dollars at the new exchange rate, we get these figures:

Assets	$250	Liabilities	$125
		Equity	125

Notice that the value of the equity has gone down by $125, even though net income was exactly zero. Despite the fact that absolutely nothing happened, there is a $125 accounting loss. How to handle this $125 loss has been a controversial accounting question.

One obvious and consistent way to handle this loss is simply to report the loss on the parent's income statement. During periods of volatile exchange rates, this kind of treatment can dramatically impact an international company's reported EPS. This is a purely accounting phenomenon, but even so, such fluctuations are disliked by some financial managers.

The current approach to handling translation gains and losses is based on rules set out in the Financial Accounting Standards Board (FASB) *Statement of Financial Accounting Standards No. 52 (FASB 52)*, issued in December 1981. For the most part, *FASB 52* requires that all assets and liabilities be translated from the subsidiary's currency into the parent's currency using the exchange rate that currently prevails.

Any translation gains and losses that occur are accumulated in a special account within the shareholders' equity section of the balance sheet. This account might be labeled something like "unrealized foreign exchange gains (losses)." The amounts involved can be substantial, at least from an accounting standpoint. For example, IBM's December 31, 2005, fiscal year-end balance sheet shows a loss from equity in the amount of $1.15 billion for translation adjustments related to assets and liabilities of non-U.S. subsidiaries. These gains and losses are not reported on the income statement. As a result, the impact of translation gains and losses will not be recognized explicitly in net income until the underlying assets and liabilities are sold or otherwise liquidated.

Managing Exchange Rate Risk

For a large multinational firm, the management of exchange rate risk is complicated by the fact that there can be many different currencies involved in many different subsidiaries. It is likely that a change in some exchange rate will benefit some subsidiaries and hurt others. The net effect on the overall firm depends on its net exposure.

For example, suppose a firm has two divisions. Division *A* buys goods in the United States for dollars and sells them in Britain for pounds. Division *B* buys goods in Britain for pounds and sells them in the United States for dollars. If these two divisions are of roughly equal size in terms of their inflows and outflows, then the overall firm obviously has little exchange rate risk.

In our example, the firm's net position in pounds (the amount coming in less the amount going out) is small, so the exchange rate risk is small. However, if one division, acting on its own, were to start hedging its exchange rate risk, then the overall firm's exchange rate risk would go up. The moral of the story is that multinational firms have to be conscious of the overall position that the firm has in a foreign currency. For this reason, management of exchange rate risk is probably best handled on a centralized basis.

31.7 Political Risk

One final element of risk in international investing is **political risk**: changes in value that arise as a consequence of political actions. This is not a problem faced exclusively by international firms. For example, changes in U.S. tax laws and regulations may benefit some U.S. firms and hurt others, so political risk exists nationally as well as internationally.

Some countries have more political risk than others, however. When firms have operations in these riskier countries, the extra political risk may lead the firms to require higher returns on overseas investments to compensate for the possibility that funds may be blocked, critical operations interrupted, and contracts abrogated. In the most extreme case, the possibility of outright confiscation may be a concern in countries with relatively unstable political environments.

Political risk also depends on the nature of the business: Some businesses are less likely to be confiscated because they are not particularly valuable in the hands of a different owner. An assembly operation supplying subcomponents that only the parent company uses would not be an attractive takeover target, for example. Similarly, a manufacturing operation that requires the use of specialized components from the parent is of little value without the parent company's cooperation.

Natural resource developments, such as copper mining or oil drilling, are just the opposite. Once the operation is in place, much of the value is in the commodity. The political risk for such investments is much higher for this reason. Also, the issue of exploitation is more pronounced with such investments, again increasing the political risk.

Political risk can be hedged in several ways, particularly when confiscation or nationalization is a concern. The use of local financing, perhaps from the government of the foreign country in question, reduces the possible loss because the company can refuse to pay the debt in the event of unfavorable political activities. Based on our discussion in this section, structuring the operation in such a way that it requires significant parent company involvement to function is another way to reduce political risk.

Summary and Conclusions

The international firm has a more complicated life than the purely domestic firm. Management must understand the connection between interest rates, foreign currency exchange rates, and inflation, and it must become aware of many different financial market regulations and tax systems. This chapter is intended to be a concise introduction to some of the financial issues that come up in international investing.

Our coverage has been necessarily brief. The main topics we discussed are the following:

1. **Some basic vocabulary**: We briefly defined some exotic terms such as *LIBOR* and *Eurocurrency*.

2. **The basic mechanics of exchange rate quotations**: We discussed the spot and forward markets and how exchange rates are interpreted.

3. **The fundamental relationships between international financial variables**:
   a. Absolute and relative purchasing power parity, PPP.
   b. Interest rate parity, IRP.
   c. Unbiased forward rates, UFR.

   Absolute purchasing power parity states that $1 should have the same purchasing power in each country. This means that an orange costs the same whether you buy it in New York or in Tokyo.

   Relative purchasing power parity means that the expected percentage change in exchange rates between the currencies of two countries is equal to the difference in their inflation rates.

   Interest rate parity implies that the percentage difference between the forward exchange rate and the spot exchange rate is equal to the interest rate differential. We showed how covered interest arbitrage forces this relationship to hold.

   The unbiased forward rates condition indicates that the current forward rate is a good predictor of the future spot exchange rate.

4. **International capital budgeting**: We showed that the basic foreign exchange relationships imply two other conditions:
   a. Uncovered interest parity.
   b. The international Fisher effect.

   By invoking these two conditions, we learned how to estimate NPVs in foreign currencies and how to convert foreign currencies into dollars to estimate NPV in the usual way.

5. **Exchange rate and political risk**: We described the various types of exchange rate risk and discussed some common approaches to managing the effect of fluctuating exchange rates on the cash flows and value of the international firm. We also discussed political risk and some ways of managing exposure to it.

Concept Questions

1. **Spot and Forward Rates**   Suppose the exchange rate for the Swiss franc is quoted as SF 1.50 in the spot market and SF 1.53 in the 90-day forward market.
   a. Is the dollar selling at a premium or a discount relative to the franc?
   b. Does the financial market expect the franc to strengthen relative to the dollar? Explain.
   c. What do you suspect is true about relative economic conditions in the United States and Switzerland?

2. **Purchasing Power Parity**   Suppose the rate of inflation in Mexico will run about 3 percent higher than the U.S. inflation rate over the next several years. All other things being the same, what will happen to the Mexican peso versus dollar exchange rate? What relationship are you relying on in answering?

3. **Exchange Rates**   The exchange rate for the Australian dollar is currently A$1.40. This exchange rate is expected to rise by 10 percent over the next year.
   a. Is the Australian dollar expected to get stronger or weaker?
   b. What do you think about the relative inflation rates in the United States and Australia?
   c. What do you think about the relative nominal interest rates in the United States and Australia? Relative real rates?

4. **Yankee Bonds**   Which of the following most accurately describes a Yankee bond?
   a. A bond issued by General Motors in Japan with the interest payable in U.S. dollars.
   b. A bond issued by General Motors in Japan with the interest payable in yen.
   c. A bond issued by Toyota in the United States with the interest payable in yen.
   d. A bond issued by Toyota in the United States with the interest payable in dollars.
   e. A bond issued by Toyota worldwide with the interest payable in dollars.

5. **Exchange Rates**   Are exchange rate changes necessarily good or bad for a particular company?

6. **International Risks**   At one point, Duracell International confirmed that it was planning to open battery manufacturing plants in China and India. Manufacturing in these countries allows Duracell to avoid import duties of between 30 and 35 percent that have made alkaline batteries prohibitively expensive for some consumers. What additional advantages might Duracell see in this proposal? What are some of the risks to Duracell?

7. **Multinational Corporations**   Given that many multinationals based in many countries have much greater sales outside their domestic markets than within them, what is the particular relevance of their domestic currency?

8. **Exchange Rate Movements**   Are the following statements true or false? Explain why.
    a. If the general price index in Great Britain rises faster than that in the United States, we would expect the pound to appreciate relative to the dollar.
    b. Suppose you are a German machine tool exporter, and you invoice all of your sales in foreign currency. Further suppose that the euro monetary authorities begin to undertake an expansionary monetary policy. If it is certain that the easy money policy will result in higher inflation rates in Germany relative to those in other countries, then you should use the forward markets to protect yourself against future losses resulting from the deterioration in the value of the euro.
    c. If you could accurately estimate differences in the relative inflation rates of two countries over a long period while other market participants were unable to do so, you could successfully speculate in spot currency markets.

9. **Exchange Rate Movements**   Some countries encourage movements in their exchange rate relative to those of some other country as a short-term means of addressing foreign trade imbalances. For each of the following scenarios, evaluate the impact the announcement would have on an American importer and an American exporter doing business with the foreign country:
    a. Officials in the administration of the U.S. government announce that they are comfortable with a rising euro relative to the dollar.
    b. British monetary authorities announce that they feel the pound has been driven too low by currency speculators relative to the dollar.
    c. The Brazilian government announces that it will print billions of new reais and inject them into the economy in an effort to reduce the country's unemployment rate.

10. **International Capital Market Relationships**   We discussed five international capital market relationships: relative PPP, IRP, UFR, UIP, and the international Fisher effect. Which of these would you expect to hold most closely? Which do you think would be most likely to be violated?

11. **Exchange Rate Risk**   If you are an exporter who must make payments in foreign currency three months after receiving each shipment and you predict that the domestic currency will appreciate in value over this period, is there any value in hedging your currency exposure?

12. **International Capital Budgeting**   Suppose it is your task to evaluate two different investments in new subsidiaries for your company, one in your own country and the other in a foreign country. You calculate the cash flows of both projects to be identical after exchange rate differences. Under what circumstances might you choose to invest in the foreign subsidiary? Give an example of a country where certain factors might influence you to alter this decision and invest at home.

13. **International Capital Budgeting**   An investment in a foreign subsidiary is estimated to have a positive NPV after the discount rate used in the calculations is adjusted for political risk and any advantages from diversification. Does this mean the project is acceptable? Why or why not?

14. **International Borrowing**   If a U.S. firm raises funds for a foreign subsidiary, what are the disadvantages to borrowing in the United States? How would you overcome them?

15. **International Investment**   If financial markets are perfectly competitive and the Eurodollar rate is above that offered in the U.S. loan market, you would immediately want to borrow money in the United States and invest it in Eurodollars. True or false? Explain.

16. **Eurobonds**   What distinguishes a Eurobond from a foreign bond? Which particular feature makes the Eurobond more popular than the foreign bond?

Questions and Problems

BASIC
(Questions 1–14)

1. **Using Exchange Rates**   Take a look back at Figure 31.1 to answer the following questions:
   a. If you have $100, how many euros can you get?
   b. How much is one euro worth?
   c. If you have 10 million euros, how many dollars do you have?
   d. Which is worth more, a New Zealand dollar or a Singapore dollar?
   e. Which is worth more, a Mexican peso or a Chilean peso?
   f. How many Mexican pesos can you get for a euro? What do you call this rate?
   g. Per unit, what is the most valuable currency of those listed? The least valuable?

2. **Using the Cross-Rate**   Use the information in Figure 31.1 to answer the following questions:
   a. Which would you rather have, $100 or £100? Why?
   b. Which would you rather have, 100 Swiss francs (SF) or £100? Why?
   c. What is the cross-rate for Swiss francs in terms of British pounds? For British pounds in terms of Swiss francs?

3. **Forward Exchange Rates**   Use the information in Figure 31.1 to answer the following questions:
   a. What is the six-month forward rate for the Japanese yen in yen per U.S. dollar? Is the yen selling at a premium or a discount? Explain.
   b. What is the three-month forward rate for British pounds in U.S. dollars per pound? Is the dollar selling at a premium or a discount? Explain.
   c. What do you think will happen to the value of the dollar relative to the yen and the pound, based on the information in the figure? Explain.

4. **Using Spot and Forward Exchange Rates**   Suppose the spot exchange rate for the Canadian dollar is Can$1.26 and the six-month forward rate is Can$1.22.
   a. Which is worth more, a U.S. dollar or a Canadian dollar?
   b. Assuming absolute PPP holds, what is the cost in the United States of an Elkhead beer if the price in Canada is Can$2.19? Why might the beer actually sell at a different price in the United States?
   c. Is the U.S. dollar selling at a premium or a discount relative to the Canadian dollar?
   d. Which currency is expected to appreciate in value?
   e. Which country do you think has higher interest rates—the United States or Canada? Explain.

5. **Cross-Rates and Arbitrage**   Suppose the Japanese yen exchange rate is ¥115 = $1, and the British pound exchange rate is £1 = $1.70.
   a. What is the cross-rate in terms of yen per pound?
   b. Suppose the cross-rate is ¥180 = £1. Is there an arbitrage opportunity here? If there is, explain how to take advantage of the mispricing.

6. **Interest Rate Parity**   Use Figure 31.1 to answer the following questions. Suppose interest rate parity holds, and the current six-month risk-free rate in the United States is 3.8 percent. What must the six-month risk-free rate be in Great Britain? In Japan? In Switzerland?

7. **Interest Rates and Arbitrage**   The treasurer of a major U.S. firm has $30 million to invest for three months. The annual interest rate in the United States is .45 percent per month. The interest rate in Great Britain is .6 percent per month. The spot exchange rate is £.56, and the three-month forward rate is £.59. Ignoring transaction costs, in which country would the treasurer want to invest the company's funds? Why?

8. **Inflation and Exchange Rates**   Suppose the current exchange rate for the Polish zloty is Z 3.84. The expected exchange rate in three years is Z 3.92. What is the difference in

the annual inflation rates for the United States and Poland over this period? Assume that the anticipated rate is constant for both countries. What relationship are you relying on in answering?

9.   **Exchange Rate Risk**   Suppose your company imports computer motherboards from Singapore. The exchange rate is given in Figure 31.1. You have just placed an order for 30,000 motherboards at a cost to you of 168.5 Singapore dollars each. You will pay for the shipment when it arrives in 90 days. You can sell the motherboards for $145 each. Calculate your profit if the exchange rate goes up or down by 10 percent over the next 90 days. What is the break-even exchange rate? What percentage rise or fall does this represent in terms of the Singapore dollar versus the U.S. dollar?

10.   **Exchange Rates and Arbitrage**   Suppose the spot and six-month forward rates on the Norwegian krone are Kr 6.43 and Kr 6.56, respectively. The annual risk-free rate in the United States is 5 percent, and the annual risk-free rate in Norway is 8 percent.
   a. Is there an arbitrage opportunity here? If so, how would you exploit it?
   b. What must the six-month forward rate be to prevent arbitrage?

11.   **The International Fisher Effect**   You observe that the inflation rate in the United States is 3.5 percent per year and that T-bills currently yield 3.9 percent annually. What do you estimate the inflation rate to be in
   a. Australia if short-term Australian government securities yield 5 percent per year?
   b. Canada if short-term Canadian government securities yield 7 percent per year?
   c. Taiwan if short-term Taiwanese government securities yield 10 percent per year?

12.   **Spot versus Forward Rates**   Suppose the spot and three-month forward rates for the yen are ¥131.30 and ¥129.76, respectively.
   a. Is the yen expected to get stronger or weaker?
   b. What would you estimate is the difference between the inflation rates of the United States and Japan?

13.   **Expected Spot Rates**   Suppose the spot exchange rate for the Hungarian forint is HUF 215. The inflation rate in the United States are 3.5 percent per year. They are 8.6 percent in Hungary. What do you predict the exchange rate will be in one year? In two years? In five years? What relationship are you using?

14.   **Forward Rates**   The spot rate of foreign exchange between the United States and the United Kingdom is $1.50/£. If the interest rate in the United States is 13 percent and it is 9 percent in the United Kingdom, what would you expect the one-year forward rate to be if no immediate arbitrage opportunities existed?

INTERMEDIATE
(Questions 15–16)

15.   **Capital Budgeting**   Lakonishok Equipment has an investment opportunity in Europe. The project costs €12 million and is expected to produce cash flows of €2.7 million in year 1, €3.5 million in year 2, and €3.3 million in year 3. The current spot exchange rate is $1.22/€ and the current risk-free rate in the United States is 4.8 percent, compared to that in Europe of 4.1 percent. The appropriate discount rate for the project is estimated to be 13 percent, the U.S. cost of capital for the company. In addition, the subsidiary can be sold at the end of three years for an estimated €7.4 million. What is the NPV of the project?

16.   **Capital Budgeting**   You are evaluating a proposed expansion of an existing subsidiary located in Switzerland. The cost of the expansion would be SF 27.0 million. The cash flows from the project would be SF 7.5 million per year for the next five years. The dollar required return is 13 percent per year, and the current exchange rate is SF 1.72. The going rate on Eurodollars is 8 percent per year. It is 7 percent per year on Swiss francs.
   a. What do you project will happen to exchange rates over the next four years?
   b. Based on your answer in (a), convert the projected franc flows into dollar flows and calculate the NPV.
   c. What is the required return on franc flows? Based on your answer, calculate the NPV in francs and then convert to dollars.

CHALLENGE
(Question 17)

17. **Using the Exact International Fisher Effect**   From our discussion of the Fisher effect in Chapter 7, we know that the actual relationship between a nominal rate, R, a real rate, r, and an inflation rate, h, can be written as follows:

$$1 + r = (1 + R)/(1 + h)$$

This is the *domestic* Fisher effect.
   a. What is the nonapproximate form of the international Fisher effect?
   b. Based on your answer in (a), what is the exact form for UIP? (*Hint*: Recall the exact form of IRP and use UFR.)
   c. What is the exact form for relative PPP? (*Hint*: Combine your previous two answers.)
   d. Recalculate the NPV for the Kihlstrom drill bit project (discussed in Section 31.5) using the exact forms for the UIP and the international Fisher effect. Verify that you get precisely the same answer either way.

S&P Problem

STANDARD &POOR'S

www.mhhe.com/edumarketinsight

1. **American Depositary Receipts**   Nestlé S. A. has American depositary receipts listed on the over-the-counter market. Many ADRs listed on U.S. exchanges are for fractional shares. In the case of Nestlé, four ADRs are equal to one registered share of stock. Find the information for Nestlé using the ticker symbol "3NSRGY."
   a. Click on the "Mthly. Adj. Prices" link and find Nestlé's closing price for April 2006. Assume the exchange rate on that day was \$/SF = 1.231 and Nestlé shares traded for SF 14.65. Is there an arbitrage opportunity available? If so, how would you take advantage of it?
   b. What exchange rate is necessary to eliminate the arbitrage opportunity available in (a)?
   c. Dividend payments made to ADR shareholders are in U.S. dollars. Suppose you own 90 Nestlé ADRs. Assume the current exchange rate is the rate you calculated in (b). Nestlé declares a dividend of SF 1.15. What U.S. dollar dividend payment will you receive?

Mini Case

East Coast Yachts Goes International

Larissa Warren, the owner of East Coast Yachts, has been in discussions with a yacht dealer in Monaco about selling the company's yachts in Europe. Jarek Jachowicz, the dealer, wants to add East Coast Yachts to his current retail line. Jarek has told Larissa that he feels the retail sales will be approximately €5 million per month. All sales will be made in euros, and Jarek will retain 5 percent of the retail sales as commission, which will be paid in euros. Because the yachts will be customized to order, the first sales will take place in one month. Jarek will pay East Coast Yachts for the order 90 days after it is filled. This payment schedule will continue for the length of the contract between the two companies.

Larissa is confident the company can handle the extra volume with its existing facilities, but she is unsure about any potential financial risks of selling yachts in Europe. In her discussion with Jarek she found that the current exchange rate is \$1.20/€. At this exchange rate the company would spend 70 percent of the sales income on production costs. This number does not reflect the sales commission to be paid to Jarek.

Larissa has decided to ask Dan Ervin, the company's financial analyst, to prepare an analysis of the proposed international sales. Specifically she asks Dan to answer the following questions:

1. What are the pros and cons of the international sales plan? What additional risks will the company face?

2. What will happen to the company's profits if the dollar strengthens? What if the dollar weakens?

3. Ignoring taxes, what are East Coast Yacht's projected gains or losses from this proposed arrangement at the current exchange rate of $1.20/€? What will happen to profits if the exchange rate changes to $1.30/€? At what exchange rate will the company break even?

4. How can the company hedge its exchange rate risk? What are the implications for this approach?

5. Taking all factors into account, should the company pursue international sales further? Why or why not?

Appendix A
Mathematical Tables

Table A.1
Present Value of $1 to Be Received after T Periods $= 1/(1 + r)^T$

Table A.2
Present Value of an Annuity of $1 per Period for T Periods $= [1 - 1/(1 + r)^T]/r$

Table A.3
Future Value of $1 at the End of T Periods $= (1 + r)^T$

Table A.4
Future Value of an Annuity of $1 per Period for T Periods $= [(1 + r)^T - 1]/r$

Table A.5
Future Value of $1 with a Continuously Compounded Rate r for T Periods:
Values of e^{rT}

Table A.6
Present Value of $1 with a Continuous Discount Rate r for T Periods: Values of e^{-rT}

Table A.1 Present Value of $1 to Be Received after T Periods $= 1/(1 + r)^T$

Period	1%	2%	3%	4%	5%	6%	7%	8%	9%
1	.9901	.9804	.9709	.9615	.9524	.9434	.9346	.9259	.9174
2	.9803	.9612	.9426	.9246	.9070	.8900	.8734	.8573	.8417
3	.9706	.9423	.9151	.8890	.8638	.8396	.8163	.7938	.7722
4	.9610	.9238	.8885	.8548	.8227	.7921	.7629	.7350	.7084
5	.9515	.9057	.8626	.8219	.7835	.7473	.7130	.6806	.6499
6	.9420	.8880	.8375	.7903	.7462	.7050	.6663	.6302	.5963
7	.9327	.8706	.8131	.7599	.7107	.6651	.6227	.5835	.5470
8	.9235	.8535	.7894	.7307	.6768	.6274	.5820	.5403	.5019
9	.9143	.8368	.7664	.7026	.6446	.5919	.5439	.5002	.4604
10	.9053	.8203	.7441	.6756	.6139	.5584	.5083	.4632	.4224
11	.8963	.8043	.7224	.6496	.5847	.5268	.4751	.4289	.3875
12	.8874	.7885	.7014	.6246	.5568	.4970	.4440	.3971	.3555
13	.8787	.7730	.6810	.6006	.5303	.4688	.4150	.3677	.3262
14	.8700	.7579	.6611	.5775	.5051	.4423	.3878	.3405	.2992
15	.8613	.7430	.6419	.5553	.4810	.4173	.3624	.3152	.2745
16	.8528	.7284	.6232	.5339	.4581	.3936	.3387	.2919	.2519
17	.8444	.7142	.6050	.5134	.4363	.3714	.3166	.2703	.2311
18	.8360	.7002	.5874	.4936	.4155	.3503	.2959	.2502	.2120
19	.8277	.6864	.5703	.4746	.3957	.3305	.2765	.2317	.1945
20	.8195	.6730	.5537	.4564	.3769	.3118	.2584	.2145	.1784
21	.8114	.6598	.5375	.4388	.3589	.2942	.2415	.1987	.1637
22	.8034	.6468	.5219	.4220	.3418	.2775	.2257	.1839	.1502
23	.7954	.6342	.5067	.4057	.3256	.2618	.2109	.1703	.1378
24	.7876	.6217	.4919	.3901	.3101	.2470	.1971	.1577	.1264
25	.7798	.6095	.4776	.3751	.2953	.2330	.1842	.1460	.1160
30	.7419	.5521	.4120	.3083	.2314	.1741	.1314	.0994	.0754
40	.6717	.4529	.3066	.2083	.1420	.0972	.0668	.0460	.0318
50	.6080	.3715	.2281	.1407	.0872	.0543	.0339	.0213	.0134

Period	10%	12%	14%	15%	16%	18%	20%	24%	28%	32%	36%
1	.9091	.8929	.8772	.8696	.8621	.8475	.8333	.8065	.7813	.7576	.7353
2	.8264	.7972	.7695	.7561	.7432	.7182	.6944	.6504	.6104	.5739	.5407
3	.7513	.7118	.6750	.6575	.6407	.6086	.5787	.5245	.4768	.4348	.3975
4	.6830	.6355	.5921	.5718	.5523	.5158	.4823	.4230	.3725	.3294	.2923
5	.6209	.5674	.5194	.4972	.4761	.4371	.4019	.3411	.2910	.2495	.2149
6	.5645	.5066	.4556	.4323	.4104	.3704	.3349	.2751	.2274	.1890	.1580
7	.5132	.4523	.3996	.3759	.3538	.3139	.2791	.2218	.1776	.1432	.1162
8	.4665	.4039	.3506	.3269	.3050	.2660	.2326	.1789	.1388	.1085	.0854
9	.4241	.3606	.3075	.2843	.2630	.2255	.1938	.1443	.1084	.0822	.0628
10	.3855	.3220	.2697	.2472	.2267	.1911	.1615	.1164	.0847	.0623	.0462
11	.3505	.2875	.2366	.2149	.1954	.1619	.1346	.0938	.0662	.0472	.0340
12	.3186	.2567	.2076	.1869	.1685	.1372	.1122	.0757	.0517	.0357	.0250
13	.2897	.2292	.1821	.1625	.1452	.1163	.0935	.0610	.0404	.0271	.0184
14	.2633	.2046	.1597	.1413	.1252	.0985	.0779	.0492	.0316	.0205	.0135
15	.2394	.1827	.1401	.1229	.1079	.0835	.0649	.0397	.0247	.0155	.0099
16	.2176	.1631	.1229	.1069	.0930	.0708	.0541	.0320	.0193	.0118	.0073
17	.1978	.1456	.1078	.0929	.0802	.0600	.0451	.0258	.0150	.0089	.0054
18	.1799	.1300	.0946	.0808	.0691	.0508	.0376	.0208	.0118	.0068	.0039
19	.1635	.1161	.0829	.0703	.0596	.0431	.0313	.0168	.0092	.0051	.0029
20	.1486	.1037	.0728	.0611	.0514	.0365	.0261	.0135	.0072	.0039	.0021
21	.1351	.0926	.0638	.0531	.0443	.0309	.0217	.0109	.0056	.0029	.0016
22	.1228	.0826	.0560	.0462	.0382	.0262	.0181	.0088	.0044	.0022	.0012
23	.1117	.0738	.0491	.0402	.0329	.0222	.0151	.0071	.0034	.0017	.0008
24	.1015	.0659	.0431	.0349	.0284	.0188	.0126	.0057	.0027	.0013	.0006
25	.0923	.0588	.0378	.0304	.0245	.0160	.0105	.0046	.0021	.0010	.0005
30	.0573	.0334	.0196	.0151	.0116	.0070	.0042	.0016	.0006	.0002	.0001
40	.0221	.0107	.0053	.0037	.0026	.0013	.0007	.0002	.0001	*	*
50	.0085	.0035	.0014	.0009	.0006	.0003	.0001	*	*	*	*

*The factor is zero to four decimal places.

Table A.2 Present Value of an Annuity of $1 per Period for T Periods $= [1 - 1/(1 + r)^T]/r$

Number of Periods	1%	2%	3%	4%	5%	6%	7%	8%	9%
1	.9901	.9804	.9709	.9615	.9524	.9434	.9346	.9259	.9174
2	1.9704	1.9416	1.9135	1.8861	1.8594	1.8334	1.8080	1.7833	1.7591
3	2.9410	2.8839	2.8286	2.7751	2.7232	2.6730	2.6243	2.5771	2.5313
4	3.9020	3.8077	3.7171	3.6299	3.5460	3.4651	3.3872	3.3121	3.2397
5	4.8534	4.7135	4.5797	4.4518	4.3295	4.2124	4.1002	3.9927	3.8897
6	5.7955	5.6014	5.4172	5.2421	5.0757	4.9173	4.7665	4.6229	4.4859
7	6.7282	6.4720	6.2303	6.0021	5.7864	5.5824	5.3893	5.2064	5.0330
8	7.6517	7.3255	7.0197	6.7327	6.4632	6.2098	5.9713	5.7466	5.5348
9	8.5660	8.1622	7.7861	7.4353	7.1078	6.8017	6.5152	6.2469	5.9952
10	9.4713	8.9826	8.5302	8.1109	7.7217	7.3601	7.0236	6.7101	6.4177
11	10.3676	9.7868	9.2526	8.7605	8.3064	7.8869	7.4987	7.1390	6.8052
12	11.2551	10.5753	9.9540	9.3851	8.8633	8.3838	7.9427	7.5361	7.1607
13	12.1337	11.3484	10.6350	9.9856	9.3936	8.8527	8.3577	7.9038	7.4869
14	13.0037	12.1062	11.2961	10.5631	9.8986	9.2950	8.7455	8.2442	7.7862
15	13.8651	12.8493	11.9379	11.1184	10.3797	9.7122	9.1079	8.5595	8.0607
16	14.7179	13.5777	12.5611	11.6523	10.8378	10.1059	9.4466	8.8514	8.3126
17	15.5623	14.2919	13.1661	12.1657	11.2741	10.4773	9.7632	9.1216	8.5436
18	16.3983	14.9920	13.7535	12.6593	11.6896	10.8276	10.0591	9.3719	8.7556
19	17.2260	15.6785	14.3238	13.1339	12.0853	11.1581	10.3356	9.6036	8.9501
20	18.0456	16.3514	14.8775	13.5903	12.4622	11.4699	10.5940	9.8181	9.1285
21	18.8570	17.0112	15.4150	14.0292	12.8212	11.7641	10.8355	10.0168	9.2922
22	19.6604	17.6580	15.9369	14.4511	13.1630	12.0416	11.0612	10.2007	9.4424
23	20.4558	18.2922	16.4436	14.8568	13.4886	12.3034	11.2722	10.3741	9.5802
24	21.2434	18.9139	16.9355	15.2470	13.7986	12.5504	11.4693	10.5288	9.7066
25	22.0232	19.5235	17.4131	15.6221	14.0939	12.7834	11.6536	10.6748	9.8226
30	25.8077	22.3965	19.6004	17.2920	15.3725	13.7648	12.4090	11.2578	10.2737
40	32.8347	27.3555	23.1148	19.7928	17.1591	15.0463	13.3317	11.9246	10.7574
50	39.1961	31.4236	25.7298	21.4822	18.2559	15.7619	13.8007	12.2335	10.9617

Number of Periods	10%	12%	14%	15%	16%	18%	20%	24%	28%	32%
1	.9091	.8929	.8772	.8696	.8621	.8475	.8333	.8065	.7813	.7576
2	1.7355	1.6901	1.6467	1.6257	1.6052	1.5656	1.5278	1.4568	1.3916	1.3315
3	2.4869	2.4018	2.3216	2.2832	2.2459	2.1743	2.1065	1.9813	1.8684	1.7663
4	3.1699	3.0373	2.9137	2.8550	2.7982	2.6901	2.5887	2.4043	2.2410	2.0957
5	3.7908	3.6048	3.4331	3.3522	3.2743	3.1272	2.9906	2.7454	2.5320	2.3452
6	4.3553	4.1114	3.8887	3.7845	3.6847	3.4976	3.3255	3.0205	2.7594	2.5342
7	4.8684	4.5638	4.2883	4.1604	4.0386	3.8115	3.6046	3.2423	2.9370	2.6775
8	5.3349	4.9676	4.6389	4.4873	4.3436	4.0776	3.8372	3.4212	3.0758	2.7860
9	5.7590	5.3282	4.9464	4.7716	4.6065	4.3030	4.0310	3.5655	3.1842	2.8681
10	6.1446	5.6502	5.2161	5.0188	4.8332	4.4941	4.1925	3.6819	3.2689	2.9304
11	6.4951	5.9377	5.4527	5.2337	5.0286	4.6560	4.3271	3.7757	3.3351	2.9776
12	6.8137	6.1944	5.6603	5.4206	5.1971	4.7932	4.4392	3.8514	3.3868	3.0133
13	7.1034	6.4235	5.8424	5.5831	5.3423	4.9095	4.5327	3.9124	3.4272	3.0404
14	7.3667	6.6282	6.0021	5.7245	5.4675	5.0081	4.6106	3.9616	3.4587	3.0609
15	7.6061	6.8109	6.1422	5.8474	5.5755	5.0916	4.6755	4.0013	3.4834	3.0764
16	7.8237	6.9740	6.2651	5.9542	5.6685	5.1624	4.7296	4.0333	3.5026	3.0882
17	8.0216	7.1196	6.3729	6.0472	5.7487	5.2223	4.7746	4.0591	3.5177	3.0971
18	8.2014	7.2497	6.4674	6.1280	5.8178	5.2732	4.8122	4.0799	3.5294	3.1039
19	8.3649	7.3658	6.5504	6.1982	5.8775	5.3162	4.8435	4.0967	3.5386	3.1090
20	8.5136	7.4694	6.6231	6.2593	5.9288	5.3527	4.8696	4.1103	3.5458	3.1129
21	8.6487	7.5620	6.6870	6.3125	5.9731	5.3837	4.8913	4.1212	3.5514	3.1158
22	8.7715	7.6446	6.7429	6.3587	6.0113	5.4099	4.9094	4.1300	3.5558	3.1180
23	8.8832	7.7184	6.7921	6.3988	6.0442	5.4321	4.9245	4.1371	3.5592	3.1197
24	8.9847	7.7843	6.8351	6.4338	6.0726	5.4509	4.9371	4.1428	3.5619	3.1210
25	9.0770	7.8431	6.8729	6.4641	6.0971	5.4669	4.9476	4.1474	3.5640	3.1220
30	9.4269	8.0552	7.0027	6.5660	6.1772	5.5168	4.9789	4.1601	3.5693	3.1242
40	9.7791	8.2438	7.1050	6.6418	6.2335	5.5482	4.9966	4.1659	3.5712	3.1250
50	9.9148	8.3045	7.1327	6.6605	6.2463	5.5541	4.9995	4.1666	3.5714	3.1250

Table A.3 Future Value of $1 at the End of T Periods $= (1 + r)^T$

					Interest Rate				
Period	1%	2%	3%	4%	5%	6%	7%	8%	9%
1	1.0100	1.0200	1.0300	1.0400	1.0500	1.0600	1.0700	1.0800	1.0900
2	1.0201	1.0404	1.0609	1.0816	1.1025	1.1236	1.1449	1.1664	1.1881
3	1.0303	1.0612	1.0927	1.1249	1.1576	1.1910	1.2250	1.2597	1.2950
4	1.0406	1.0824	1.1255	1.1699	1.2155	1.2625	1.3108	1.3605	1.4116
5	1.0510	1.1041	1.1593	1.2167	1.2763	1.3382	1.4026	1.4693	1.5386
6	1.0615	1.1262	1.1941	1.2653	1.3401	1.4185	1.5007	1.5869	1.6771
7	1.0721	1.1487	1.2299	1.3159	1.4071	1.5036	1.6058	1.7138	1.8280
8	1.0829	1.1717	1.2668	1.3686	1.4775	1.5938	1.7182	1.8509	1.9926
9	1.0937	1.1951	1.3048	1.4233	1.5513	1.6895	1.8385	1.9990	2.1719
10	1.1046	1.2190	1.3439	1.4802	1.6289	1.7908	1.9672	2.1589	2.3674
11	1.1157	1.2434	1.3842	1.5395	1.7103	1.8983	2.1049	2.3316	2.5804
12	1.1268	1.2682	1.4258	1.6010	1.7959	2.0122	2.2522	2.5182	2.8127
13	1.1381	1.2936	1.4685	1.6651	1.8856	2.1329	2.4098	2.7196	3.0658
14	1.1495	1.3195	1.5126	1.7317	1.9799	2.2609	2.5785	2.9372	3.3417
15	1.1610	1.3459	1.5580	1.8009	2.0789	2.3966	2.7590	3.1722	3.6425
16	1.1726	1.3728	1.6047	1.8730	2.1829	2.5404	2.9522	3.4259	3.9703
17	1.1843	1.4002	1.6528	1.9479	2.2920	2.6928	3.1588	3.7000	4.3276
18	1.1961	1.4282	1.7024	2.0258	2.4066	2.8543	3.3799	3.9960	4.7171
19	1.2081	1.4568	1.7535	2.1068	2.5270	3.0256	3.6165	4.3157	5.1417
20	1.2202	1.4859	1.8061	2.1911	2.6533	3.2071	3.8697	4.6610	5.6044
21	1.2324	1.5157	1.8603	2.2788	2.7860	3.3996	4.1406	5.0338	6.1088
22	1.2447	1.5460	1.9161	2.3699	2.9253	3.6035	4.4304	5.4365	6.6586
23	1.2572	1.5769	1.9736	2.4647	3.0715	3.8197	4.7405	5.8715	7.2579
24	1.2697	1.6084	2.0328	2.5633	3.2251	4.0489	5.0724	6.3412	7.9111
25	1.2824	1.6406	2.0938	2.6658	3.3864	4.2919	5.4274	6.8485	8.6231
30	1.3478	1.8114	2.4273	3.2434	4.3219	5.7435	7.6123	10.063	13.268
40	1.4889	2.2080	3.2620	4.8010	7.0400	10.286	14.974	21.725	31.409
50	1.6446	2.6916	4.3839	7.1067	11.467	18.420	29.457	46.902	74.358
60	1.8167	3.2810	5.8916	10.520	18.679	32.988	57.946	101.26	176.03

Period	10%	12%	14%	15%	16%	18%	20%	24%	28%	32%	36%
1	1.1000	1.1200	1.1400	1.1500	1.1600	1.1800	1.2000	1.2400	1.2800	1.3200	1.3600
2	1.2100	1.2544	1.2996	1.3225	1.3456	1.3924	1.4400	1.5376	1.6384	1.7424	1.8496
3	1.3310	1.4049	1.4815	1.5209	1.5609	1.6430	1.7280	1.9066	2.0972	2.3000	2.5155
4	1.4641	1.5735	1.6890	1.7490	1.8106	1.9388	2.0736	2.3642	2.6844	3.0360	3.4210
5	1.6105	1.7623	1.9254	2.0114	2.1003	2.2878	2.4883	2.9316	3.4360	4.0075	4.6526
6	1.7716	1.9738	2.1950	2.3131	2.4364	2.6996	2.9860	3.6352	4.3980	5.2899	6.3275
7	1.9487	2.2107	2.5023	2.6600	2.8262	3.1855	3.5832	4.5077	5.6295	6.9826	8.6054
8	2.1436	2.4760	2.8526	3.0590	3.2784	3.7589	4.2998	5.5895	7.2058	9.2170	11.703
9	2.3579	2.7731	3.2519	3.5179	3.8030	4.4355	5.1598	6.9310	9.2234	12.166	15.917
10	2.5937	3.1058	3.7072	4.0456	4.4114	5.2338	6.1917	8.5944	11.806	16.060	21.647
11	2.8531	3.4785	4.2262	4.6524	5.1173	6.1759	7.4301	10.657	15.112	21.199	29.439
12	3.1384	3.8960	4.8179	5.3503	5.9360	7.2876	8.9161	13.215	19.343	27.983	40.037
13	3.4523	4.3635	5.4924	6.1528	6.8858	8.5994	10.699	16.386	24.759	36.937	54.451
14	3.7975	4.8871	6.2613	7.0757	7.9875	10.147	12.839	20.319	31.691	48.757	74.053
15	4.1772	5.4736	7.1379	8.1371	9.2655	11.974	15.407	25.196	40.565	64.359	100.71
16	4.5950	6.1304	8.1372	9.3576	10.748	14.129	18.488	31.243	51.923	84.954	136.97
17	5.0545	6.8660	9.2765	10.761	12.468	16.672	22.186	38.741	66.461	112.14	186.28
18	5.5599	7.6900	10.575	12.375	14.463	19.673	26.623	48.039	86.071	148.02	253.34
19	6.1159	8.6128	12.056	14.232	16.777	23.214	31.948	59.568	108.89	195.39	344.54
20	6.7275	9.6463	13.743	16.367	19.461	27.393	38.338	73.864	139.38	257.92	468.57
21	7.4002	10.804	15.668	18.822	22.574	32.324	46.005	91.592	178.41	340.45	637.26
22	8.1403	12.100	17.861	21.645	26.186	38.142	55.206	113.57	228.36	449.39	866.67
23	8.9543	13.552	20.362	24.891	30.376	45.008	66.247	140.83	292.30	593.20	1178.7
24	9.8497	15.179	23.212	28.625	35.236	53.109	79.497	174.63	374.14	783.02	1603.0
25	10.835	17.000	26.462	32.919	40.874	62.669	95.396	216.54	478.90	1033.6	2180.1
30	17.449	29.960	50.950	66.212	85.850	143.37	237.38	634.82	1645.5	4142.1	10143.
40	45.259	93.051	188.88	267.86	378.72	750.38	1469.8	5455.9	19427.	66521.	*
50	117.39	289.00	700.23	1083.7	1670.7	3927.4	9100.4	46890.	*	*	*
60	304.48	897.60	2595.9	4384.0	7370.2	20555.	56348.	*	*	*	*

*FVIV > 99,999.

Table A.4 Future Value of an Annuity of $1 per Period for T Periods $= [(1 + r)^T - 1]/r$

Number of Periods	Interest Rate								
	1%	2%	3%	4%	5%	6%	7%	8%	9%
1	1.0000	1.0000	1.0000	1.0000	1.0000	1.0000	1.0000	1.0000	1.0000
2	2.0100	2.0200	2.0300	2.0400	2.0500	2.0600	2.0700	2.0800	2.0900
3	3.0301	3.0604	3.0909	3.1216	3.1525	3.1836	3.2149	3.2464	3.2781
4	4.0604	4.1216	4.1836	4.2465	4.3101	4.3746	4.4399	4.5061	4.5731
5	5.1010	5.2040	5.3091	5.4163	5.5256	5.6371	5.7507	5.8666	5.9847
6	6.1520	6.3081	6.4684	6.6330	6.8019	6.9753	7.1533	7.3359	7.5233
7	7.2135	7.4343	7.6625	7.8983	8.1420	8.3938	8.6540	8.9228	9.2004
8	8.2857	8.5830	8.8932	9.2142	9.5491	9.8975	10.260	10.637	11.028
9	9.3685	9.7546	10.159	10.583	11.027	11.491	11.978	12.488	13.021
10	10.462	10.950	11.464	12.006	12.578	13.181	13.816	14.487	15.193
11	11.567	12.169	12.808	13.486	14.207	14.972	15.784	16.645	17.560
12	12.683	13.412	14.192	15.026	15.917	16.870	17.888	18.977	20.141
13	13.809	14.680	15.618	16.627	17.713	18.882	20.141	21.495	22.953
14	14.947	15.974	17.086	18.292	19.599	21.015	22.550	24.215	26.019
15	16.097	17.293	18.599	20.024	21.579	23.276	25.129	27.152	29.361
16	17.258	18.639	20.157	21.825	23.657	25.673	27.888	30.324	33.003
17	18.430	20.012	21.762	23.698	25.840	28.213	30.840	33.750	36.974
18	19.615	21.412	23.414	25.645	28.132	30.906	33.999	37.450	41.301
19	20.811	22.841	25.117	27.671	30.539	33.760	37.379	41.446	46.018
20	22.019	24.297	26.870	29.778	33.066	36.786	40.995	45.762	51.160
21	23.239	25.783	28.676	31.969	35.719	39.993	44.865	50.423	56.765
22	24.472	27.299	30.537	34.248	38.505	43.392	49.006	55.457	62.873
23	25.716	28.845	32.453	36.618	41.430	46.996	53.436	60.893	69.532
24	26.973	30.422	34.426	39.083	44.502	50.816	58.177	66.765	76.790
25	28.243	32.030	36.459	41.646	47.727	54.865	63.249	73.106	84.701
30	34.785	40.568	47.575	56.085	66.439	79.058	94.461	113.28	136.31
40	48.886	60.402	75.401	95.026	120.80	154.76	199.64	259.06	337.88
50	64.463	84.579	112.80	152.67	209.35	290.34	406.53	573.77	815.08
60	81.670	114.05	163.05	237.99	353.58	533.13	813.52	1253.2	1944.8

Number of Periods	10%	12%	14%	15%	16%	18%	20%	24%	28%	32%	36%
1	1.0000	1.0000	1.0000	1.0000	1.0000	1.0000	1.0000	1.0000	1.0000	1.0000	1.0000
2	2.1000	2.1200	2.1400	2.1500	2.1600	2.1800	2.2000	2.2400	2.2800	2.3200	2.3600
3	3.3100	3.3744	3.4396	3.4725	3.5056	3.5724	3.6400	3.7776	3.9184	4.0624	4.2096
4	3.6410	4.7793	4.9211	4.9934	5.0665	5.2154	5.3680	5.6842	6.0156	6.3624	6.7251
5	6.1051	6.3528	6.6101	6.7424	6.8771	7.1542	7.4416	8.0484	8.6999	9.3983	10.146
6	7.7156	8.1152	8.5355	8.7537	8.9775	9.4420	9.9299	10.980	12.136	13.406	14.799
7	9.4872	10.089	10.730	11.067	11.414	12.142	12.916	14.615	16.534	18.696	21.126
8	11.436	12.300	13.233	13.727	14.240	15.327	16.499	19.123	22.163	25.678	29.732
9	13.579	14.776	16.085	16.786	17.519	19.086	20.799	24.712	29.369	34.895	41.435
10	15.937	17.549	19.337	20.304	21.321	23.521	25.959	31.643	38.593	47.062	57.352
11	18.531	20.655	23.045	24.349	25.733	28.755	32.150	40.238	50.398	63.122	78.998
12	21.384	24.133	27.271	29.002	30.850	34.931	39.581	50.895	65.510	84.320	108.44
13	24.523	28.029	32.089	34.352	36.786	42.219	48.497	64.110	84.853	112.30	148.47
14	27.975	32.393	37.581	40.505	43.672	50.818	59.196	80.496	109.61	149.24	202.93
15	31.772	37.280	43.842	47.580	51.660	60.965	72.035	100.82	141.30	198.00	276.98
16	35.950	42.753	50.980	55.717	60.925	72.939	87.442	126.01	181.87	262.36	377.69
17	40.545	48.884	59.118	65.075	71.673	87.068	105.93	157.25	233.79	347.31	514.66
18	45.599	55.750	68.394	75.836	84.141	103.74	128.12	195.99	300.25	459.45	700.94
19	51.159	64.440	78.969	88.212	98.603	123.41	154.74	244.03	385.32	607.47	954.28
20	57.275	72.052	91.025	102.44	115.38	146.63	186.69	303.60	494.21	802.86	1298.8
21	64.002	81.699	104.77	118.81	134.84	174.02	225.03	377.46	633.59	1060.8	1767.4
22	71.403	92.503	120.44	137.63	157.41	206.34	271.03	469.06	812.00	1401.2	2404.7
23	79.543	104.60	138.30	159.28	183.60	244.49	326.24	582.63	1040.4	1850.6	3271.3
24	88.497	118.16	158.66	184.17	213.98	289.49	392.48	723.46	1332.7	2443.8	4450.0
25	98.347	133.33	181.87	212.79	249.21	342.60	471.98	898.09	1706.8	3226.8	6053.0
30	164.49	241.33	356.79	434.75	530.31	790.95	1181.9	2640.9	5873.2	12941.	28172.3
40	442.59	767.09	1342.0	1779.1	2360.8	4163.2	7343.9	22729.	69377.	*	*
50	1163.9	2400.0	4994.5	7217.7	10436.	21813.	45497.	*	*	*	*
60	3034.8	7471.6	18535.	29220.	46058.	*	*	*	*	*	*

*FVIFA > 99,999.

Table A.5 Future Value of $1 with a Continuously Compounded Rate r for T Periods: Values of e^{rT}

Period (T)							Continuously Compounded Rate (r)							
	1%	2%	3%	4%	5%	6%	7%	8%	9%	10%	11%	12%	13%	14%
1	1.0101	1.0202	1.0305	1.0408	1.0513	1.0618	1.0725	1.0833	1.0942	1.1052	1.1163	1.1275	1.1388	1.1503
2	1.0202	1.0408	1.0618	1.0833	1.1052	1.1275	1.1503	1.1735	1.1972	1.2214	1.2461	1.2712	1.2969	1.3231
3	1.0305	1.0618	1.0942	1.1275	1.1618	1.1972	1.2337	1.2712	1.3100	1.3499	1.3910	1.4333	1.4770	1.5220
4	1.0408	1.0833	1.1275	1.1735	1.2214	1.2712	1.3231	1.3771	1.4333	1.4918	1.5527	1.6161	1.6820	1.7507
5	1.0513	1.1052	1.1618	1.2214	1.2840	1.3499	1.4191	1.4918	1.5683	1.6487	1.7333	1.8221	1.9155	2.0138
6	1.0618	1.1275	1.1972	1.2712	1.3499	1.4333	1.5220	1.6161	1.7160	1.8221	1.9348	2.0544	2.1815	2.3164
7	1.0725	1.1503	1.2337	1.3231	1.4191	1.5220	1.6323	1.7507	1.8776	2.0138	2.1598	2.3164	2.4843	2.6645
8	1.0833	1.1735	1.2712	1.3771	1.4918	1.6160	1.7507	1.8965	2.0544	2.2255	2.4109	2.6117	2.8292	3.0649
9	1.0942	1.1972	1.3100	1.4333	1.5683	1.7160	1.8776	2.0544	2.2479	2.4596	2.6912	2.9447	3.2220	3.5254
10	1.1052	1.2214	1.3499	1.4918	1.6487	1.8221	2.0138	2.2255	2.4596	2.7183	3.0042	3.3201	3.6693	4.0552
11	1.1163	1.2461	1.3910	1.5527	1.7333	1.9348	2.1598	2.4109	2.6912	3.0042	3.3535	3.7434	4.1787	4.6646
12	1.1275	1.2712	1.4333	1.6161	1.8221	2.0544	2.3164	2.6117	2.9447	3.3201	3.7434	4.2207	4.7588	5.3656
13	1.1388	1.2969	1.4770	1.6820	1.9155	2.1815	2.4843	2.8292	3.2220	3.6693	4.1787	4.7588	5.4195	6.1719
14	1.1503	1.3231	1.5220	1.7507	2.0138	2.3164	2.6645	3.0649	3.5254	4.0552	4.6646	5.3656	6.1719	7.0993
15	1.1618	1.3499	1.5683	1.8221	2.1170	2.4596	2.8577	3.3201	3.8574	4.4817	5.2070	6.0496	7.0287	8.1662
16	1.1735	1.3771	1.6161	1.8965	2.2255	2.6117	3.0649	3.5966	4.2207	4.9530	5.8124	6.8210	8.0045	9.3933
17	1.1853	1.4049	1.6653	1.9739	2.3396	2.7732	3.2871	3.8962	4.6182	5.4739	6.4883	7.6906	9.1157	10.8049
18	1.1972	1.4333	1.7160	2.0544	2.4596	2.9447	3.5254	4.2207	5.0531	6.0496	7.2427	8.6711	10.3812	12.4286
19	1.2092	1.4623	1.7683	2.1383	2.5857	3.1268	3.7810	4.5722	5.5290	6.6859	8.0849	9.7767	11.8224	14.2963
20	1.2214	1.4918	1.8221	2.2255	2.7183	3.3201	4.0552	4.9530	6.0496	7.3891	9.0250	11.0232	13.4637	16.4446
21	1.2337	1.5220	1.8776	2.3164	2.8577	3.5254	4.3492	5.3656	6.6194	8.1662	10.0744	12.4286	15.3329	18.9158
22	1.2461	1.5527	1.9348	2.4109	3.0042	3.7434	4.6646	5.8124	7.2427	9.0250	11.2459	14.0132	17.4615	21.7584
23	1.2586	1.5841	1.9937	2.5093	3.1582	3.9749	5.0028	6.2965	7.9248	9.9742	12.5535	15.7998	19.8857	25.0281
24	1.2712	1.6161	2.0544	2.6117	3.3201	4.2207	5.3656	6.8210	8.6711	11.0232	14.0132	17.8143	22.6464	28.7892
25	1.2840	1.6487	2.1170	2.7183	3.4903	4.4817	5.7546	7.3891	9.4877	12.1825	15.6426	20.0855	25.7903	33.1155
30	1.3499	1.8221	2.4596	3.3204	4.4817	6.0496	8.1662	11.0232	14.8797	20.0855	27.1126	36.5982	49.4024	66.6863
35	1.4191	2.0138	2.8577	4.0552	5.7546	8.1662	11.5883	16.4446	23.3361	33.1155	46.9931	66.6863	94.6324	134.2898
40	1.4918	2.2255	3.3201	4.9530	7.3891	11.0232	16.4446	24.5235	36.5982	54.5982	81.4509	121.5104	181.2722	270.4264
45	1.5683	2.4596	3.8574	6.0496	9.4877	14.8797	23.3361	36.5982	57.3975	90.0171	141.1750	221.4064	347.2344	544.5719
50	1.6487	2.7183	4.4817	7.3891	12.1825	20.0855	33.1155	54.5982	90.0171	148.4132	244.6919	403.4288	665.1416	1096.633
55	1.7333	3.0042	5.2070	9.0250	15.6426	27.1126	46.9931	81.4509	141.1750	244.6919	424.1130	735.0952	1274.106	2208.348
60	1.8221	3.3201	6.0496	11.0232	20.0855	36.5982	66.6863	121.5104	221.4064	403.4288	735.0952	1339.431	2440.602	4447.067

Continuously Compounded Rate (r)

Period (T)	15%	16%	17%	18%	19%	20%	21%	22%	23%	24%	25%	26%	27%	28%
1	1.1618	1.1735	1.1853	1.1972	1.2092	1.2214	1.2337	1.2461	1.2586	1.2712	1.2840	1.2969	1.3100	1.3231
2	1.3499	1.3771	1.4049	1.4333	1.4623	1.4918	1.5220	1.5527	1.5841	1.6161	1.6487	1.6820	1.7160	1.7507
3	1.5683	1.6161	1.6653	1.7160	1.7683	1.8221	1.8776	1.9348	1.9937	2.0544	2.1170	2.1815	2.2479	2.3164
4	1.8221	1.8965	1.9739	2.0544	2.1383	2.2255	2.3164	2.4109	2.5093	2.6117	2.7183	2.8292	2.9447	3.0649
5	2.1170	2.2255	2.3396	2.4596	2.5857	2.7183	2.8577	3.0042	3.1582	3.3201	3.4903	3.6693	3.8574	4.0552
6	2.4596	2.6117	2.7732	2.9447	3.1268	3.3201	3.5254	3.7434	3.9749	4.2207	4.4817	4.7588	5.0351	5.3656
7	2.8577	3.0649	3.2871	3.5254	3.7810	4.0552	4.3492	4.6646	5.0028	5.3656	5.7546	6.1719	6.6194	7.0993
8	3.3201	3.5966	3.8962	4.2207	4.5722	4.9530	5.3656	5.8124	6.2965	6.8210	7.3891	8.0045	8.6711	9.3933
9	3.8574	4.2207	4.6182	5.0531	5.5290	6.0496	6.6194	7.2427	7.9248	8.6711	9.4877	10.3812	11.3589	12.4286
10	4.4817	4.9530	5.4739	6.0496	6.6859	7.3891	8.1662	9.0250	9.9742	11.0232	12.1825	13.4637	14.8797	16.4446
11	5.2070	5.8124	6.4883	7.2427	8.0849	9.0250	10.0744	11.2459	12.5535	14.0132	15.6426	17.4615	19.4919	21.7584
12	6.0496	6.8210	7.6906	8.6711	9.7767	11.0232	12.4286	14.0132	15.7998	17.8143	20.0855	22.6464	25.5337	28.7892
13	7.0287	8.0045	9.1157	10.3812	11.8224	13.4637	15.3329	17.4615	19.8857	22.6464	25.7903	29.3708	33.4483	38.0918
14	8.1662	9.3933	10.8049	12.4286	14.2963	16.4446	18.9158	21.7584	25.0281	28.7892	33.1155	38.0918	43.8160	50.4004
15	9.4877	11.0232	12.8071	14.8797	17.2878	20.0855	23.3361	27.1126	31.5004	36.5982	42.5211	49.4024	57.3975	66.6863
16	11.0232	12.9358	15.1803	17.8143	20.9052	24.5325	28.7892	33.7844	39.6464	46.5255	54.5982	64.0715	75.1886	88.2347
17	12.8071	15.1803	17.9933	21.3276	25.2797	29.9641	35.5166	42.0980	49.8990	59.1455	70.1054	83.0963	98.4944	116.7459
18	14.8797	17.8143	21.3276	25.5337	30.5694	36.5982	43.8160	52.4573	62.8028	75.1886	90.0171	107.7701	129.0242	154.4700
19	17.2878	20.9052	25.2797	30.5694	36.9661	44.7012	54.0549	65.3659	79.0436	95.5835	115.5843	139.7702	169.0171	204.3839
20	20.0855	24.5325	29.9641	36.5982	44.7012	54.5982	66.6863	81.4509	99.4843	121.5104	148.4132	181.2722	221.4064	270.4264
21	23.3361	28.7892	35.5166	43.8160	54.0549	66.6863	82.2695	101.4940	125.2110	154.4700	190.5663	235.0974	290.0345	357.8092
22	27.1126	33.7844	42.0980	52.4573	65.3659	81.4509	101.4940	126.4694	157.5905	196.3699	244.6919	304.9049	379.9349	473.4281
23	31.5004	39.6464	49.8990	62.8028	79.0436	99.4843	125.2110	157.5905	198.3434	249.6350	314.1907	395.4404	497.7013	626.4068
24	36.5982	46.5255	59.1455	75.1886	95.5835	121.5104	154.4700	196.3699	249.6350	317.3483	403.4288	512.8585	651.9709	828.8175
25	42.5211	54.5982	70.1054	90.0171	115.5843	148.4132	190.5663	244.6919	314.1907	403.4288	518.0128	665.1416	854.0588	1096.633
30	90.0171	121.5104	164.0219	221.4064	298.8674	403.4288	544.5719	735.0952	992.2747	1339.431	1808.042	2440.602	3294.468	4447.067
35	190.5663	270.4264	383.7533	544.5719	772.7843	1096.633	1556.197	2208.348	3133.795	4447.067	6310.688	8955.293	12708.17	18033.74
40	403.4288	601.8450	897.8473	1339.431	1998.196	2980.958	4447.067	6634.244	9897.129	14764.78	22026.47	32859.63	49020.80	73130.44
45	854.0588	1339.431	2100.646	3294.468	5166.754	8103.084	12708.17	19930.37	31257.04	49020.80	76879.92	120571.7	189094.1	296558.6
50	1808.042	2980.958	4914.769	8103.084	13359.73	22026.47	36315.50	59874.14	98715.77	162754.8	268337.3	442413.4	729416.4	1202604.
55	3827.626	6634.244	11498.82	19930.37	34544.37	59874.14	103777.0	179871.9	311763.4	540364.9	936589.2	1623346.	2813669.	4876801.
60	8103.084	14764.78	26903.19	49020.80	89321.72	162754.8	296558.6	540364.9	984609.1	1794075.	3269017.	5956538.	10853520.	19776403.

Table A.6   Present Value of \$1 with a Continuous Discount Rate r for T Periods: Values of e^{-rT}

Period (T)	1%	2%	3%	4%	5%	6%	7%	8%	9%	10%	11%	12%	13%	14%	15%	16%	17%
1	.9900	.9802	.9704	.9608	.9512	.9418	.9324	.9231	.9139	.9048	.8958	.8869	.8781	.8694	.8607	.8521	.8437
2	.9802	.9608	.9418	.9231	.9048	.8869	.8694	.8521	.8353	.8187	.8025	.7866	.7711	.7558	.7408	.7261	.7118
3	.9704	.9418	.9139	.8869	.8607	.8353	.8106	.7866	.7634	.7408	.7189	.6977	.6771	.6570	.6376	.6188	.6005
4	.9608	.9231	.8869	.8521	.8187	.7866	.7558	.7261	.6977	.6703	.6440	.6188	.5945	.5712	.5488	.5273	.5066
5	.9512	.9048	.8607	.8187	.7788	.7408	.7047	.6703	.6376	.6065	.5769	.5488	.5220	.4966	.4724	.4493	.4274
6	.9418	.8869	.8353	.7866	.7408	.6977	.6570	.6188	.5827	.5488	.5169	.4868	.4584	.4317	.4066	.3829	.3606
7	.9324	.8694	.8106	.7558	.7047	.6570	.6126	.5712	.5326	.4966	.4630	.4317	.4025	.3753	.3499	.3263	.3042
8	.9231	.8521	.7866	.7261	.6703	.6188	.5712	.5273	.4868	.4493	.4148	.3829	.3535	.3263	.3012	.2780	.2576
9	.9139	.8353	.7634	.6977	.6376	.5827	.5326	.4868	.4449	.4066	.3716	.3396	.3104	.2837	.2592	.2369	.2165
10	.9048	.8187	.7408	.6703	.6065	.5488	.4966	.4493	.4066	.3679	.3329	.3012	.2725	.2466	.2231	.2019	.1827
11	.8958	.8025	.7189	.6440	.5769	.5169	.4630	.4148	.3716	.3329	.2982	.2671	.2393	.2144	.1920	.1720	.1541
12	.8869	.7866	.6977	.6188	.5488	.4868	.4317	.3829	.3396	.3012	.2671	.2369	.2101	.1864	.1653	.1466	.1300
13	.8781	.7711	.6771	.5945	.5220	.4584	.4025	.3535	.3104	.2725	.2393	.2101	.1845	.1620	.1423	.1249	.1097
14	.8694	.7558	.6570	.5712	.4966	.4317	.3753	.3263	.2837	.2466	.2144	.1864	.1620	.1409	.1225	.1065	.0926
15	.8607	.7408	.6376	.5488	.4724	.4066	.3499	.3012	.2592	.2231	.1920	.1653	.1423	.1225	.1054	.0907	.0781
16	.8521	.7261	.6188	.5273	.4493	.3829	.3263	.2780	.2369	.2019	.1720	.1466	.1249	.1065	.0907	.0773	.0659
17	.8437	.7118	.6005	.5066	.4274	.3606	.3042	.2567	.2165	.1827	.1541	.1300	.1097	.0926	.0781	.0659	.0556
18	.8353	.6977	.5827	.4868	.4066	.3396	.2837	.2369	.1979	.1653	.1381	.1153	.0963	.0805	.0672	.0561	.0469
19	.8270	.6839	.5655	.4677	.3867	.3198	.2645	.2187	.1809	.1496	.1237	.1023	.0846	.0699	.0578	.0478	.0396
20	.8187	.6703	.5488	.4493	.3679	.3012	.2466	.2019	.1653	.1353	.1108	.0907	.0743	.0608	.0498	.0408	.0334
21	.8106	.6570	.5326	.4317	.3499	.2837	.2299	.1864	.1511	.1225	.0993	.0805	.0652	.0529	.0429	.0347	.0282
22	.8025	.6440	.5169	.4148	.3329	.2671	.2144	.1720	.1381	.1108	.0889	.0714	.0573	.0460	.0369	.0296	.0238
23	.7945	.6313	.5016	.3985	.3166	.2516	.1999	.1588	.1262	.1003	.0797	.0633	.0503	.0400	.0317	.0252	.0200
24	.7866	.6188	.4868	.3829	.3012	.2369	.1864	.1466	.1153	.0907	.0714	.0561	.0442	.0347	.0273	.0215	.0169
25	.7788	.6065	.4724	.3679	.2865	.2231	.1738	.1353	.1054	.0821	.0639	.0498	.0388	.0302	.0235	.0183	.0143
30	.7408	.5488	.4066	.3012	.2231	.1653	.1225	.0907	.0672	.0498	.0369	.0273	.0202	.0150	.0111	.0082	.0061
35	.7047	.4966	.3499	.2466	.1738	.1225	.0863	.0608	.0429	.0302	.0213	.0150	.0106	.0074	.0052	.0037	.0026
40	.6703	.4493	.3012	.2019	.1353	.0907	.0608	.0408	.0273	.0183	.0123	.0082	.0055	.0037	.0025	.0017	.0011
45	.6376	.4066	.2592	.1653	.1054	.0672	.0429	.0273	.0174	.0111	.0071	.0045	.0029	.0018	.0012	.0007	.0005
50	.6065	.3679	.2231	.1353	.0821	.0498	.0302	.0183	.0111	.0067	.0041	.0025	.0015	.0009	.0006	.0003	.0002
55	.5769	.3329	.1920	.1108	.0639	.0369	.0213	.0123	.0071	.0041	.0024	.0014	.0008	.0005	.0003	.0002	.0001
60	.5488	.3012	.1653	.0907	.0498	.0273	.0150	.0082	.0045	.0025	.0014	.0007	.0004	.0002	.0001	.0001	.0000

Continuous Discount Rate (r)

Continuous Discount Rate (r)

Period (T)	18%	19%	20%	21%	22%	23%	24%	25%	26%	27%	28%	29%	30%	31%	32%	33%	34%	35%
1	.8353	.8270	.8187	.8106	.8025	.7945	.7866	.7788	.7711	.7634	.7558	.7483	.7408	.7334	.7261	.7189	.7118	.7047
2	.6977	.6839	.6703	.6570	.6440	.6313	.6188	.6065	.5945	.5827	.5712	.5599	.5488	.5379	.5273	.5169	.5066	.4966
3	.5827	.5655	.5488	.5326	.5169	.5016	.4868	.4724	.4584	.4449	.4317	.4190	.4066	.3946	.3829	.3716	.3606	.3499
4	.4868	.4677	.4493	.4317	.4148	.3985	.3829	.3679	.3535	.3396	.3263	.3135	.3012	.2894	.2780	.2671	.2567	.2466
5	.4066	.3867	.3679	.3499	.3329	.3166	.3012	.2865	.2725	.2592	.2466	.2346	.2231	.2122	.2019	.1920	.1827	.1738
6	.3396	.3198	.3012	.2837	.2671	.2516	.2369	.2231	.2101	.1979	.1864	.1755	.1653	.1557	.1466	.1381	.1300	.1225
7	.2837	.2645	.2466	.2299	.2144	.1999	.1864	.1738	.1620	.1511	.1409	.1313	.1225	.1142	.1065	.0993	.0926	.0863
8	.2369	.2187	.2019	.1864	.1720	.1588	.1466	.1353	.1249	.1153	.1065	.0983	.0907	.0837	.0773	.0714	.0659	.0608
9	.1979	.1809	.1653	.1511	.1381	.1262	.1153	.1054	.0963	.0880	.0805	.0735	.0672	.0614	.0561	.0513	.0469	.0429
10	.1653	.1496	.1353	.1225	.1108	.1003	.0907	.0821	.0743	.0672	.0608	.0550	.0498	.0450	.0408	.0369	.0334	.0302
11	.1381	.1237	.1108	.0993	.0889	.0797	.0714	.0639	.0573	.0513	.0460	.0412	.0369	.0330	.0296	.0265	.0238	.0213
12	.1154	.1023	.0907	.0805	.0714	.0633	.0561	.0498	.0442	.0392	.0347	.0308	.0273	.0242	.0215	.0191	.0169	.0150
13	.0963	.0846	.0743	.0652	.0573	.0503	.0442	.0388	.0340	.0299	.0263	.0231	.0202	.0178	.0156	.0137	.0120	.0106
14	.0805	.0699	.0608	.0529	.0460	.0400	.0347	.0302	.0263	.0228	.0198	.0172	.0150	.0130	.0113	.0099	.0086	.0074
15	.0672	.0578	.0498	.0429	.0369	.0317	.0273	.0235	.0202	.0174	.0150	.0129	.0111	.0096	.0082	.0071	.0061	.0052
16	.0561	.0478	.0408	.0347	.0296	.0252	.0215	.0183	.0156	.0133	.0113	.0097	.0082	.0070	.0060	.0051	.0043	.0037
17	.0469	.0396	.0334	.0282	.0238	.0200	.0169	.0143	.0120	.0102	.0086	.0072	.0061	.0051	.0043	.0037	.0031	.0026
18	.0392	.0327	.0273	.0228	.0191	.0159	.0133	.0111	.0093	.0078	.0065	.0054	.0045	.0038	.0032	.0026	.0022	.0018
19	.0327	.0271	.0224	.0185	.0153	.0127	.0105	.0087	.0072	.0059	.0049	.0040	.0033	.0028	.0023	.0019	.0016	.0013
20	.0273	.0224	.0183	.0150	.0123	.0101	.0082	.0067	.0055	.0045	.0037	.0030	.0025	.0020	.0017	.0014	.0011	.0009
21	.0228	.0185	.0150	.0122	.0099	.0080	.0065	.0052	.0043	.0034	.0028	.0023	.0018	.0015	.0012	.0010	.0008	.0006
22	.0191	.0153	.0123	.0099	.0079	.0063	.0051	.0041	.0033	.0026	.0021	.0017	.0014	.0011	.0009	.0007	.0006	.0005
23	.0159	.0127	.0101	.0080	.0063	.0050	.0040	.0032	.0025	.0020	.0016	.0013	.0010	.0008	.0006	.0005	.0004	.0003
24	.0133	.0105	.0082	.0065	.0051	.0040	.0032	.0025	.0019	.0015	.0012	.0009	.0007	.0006	.0005	.0004	.0003	.0002
25	.0111	.0087	.0067	.0052	.0041	.0032	.0025	.0019	.0015	.0012	.0009	.0007	.0006	.0004	.0003	.0003	.0002	.0002
30	.0045	.0033	.0025	.0018	.0014	.0010	.0007	.0006	.0004	.0003	.0002	.0002	.0001	.0001	.0001	.0001	.0000	.0000
35	.0018	.0013	.0009	.0006	.0005	.0003	.0002	.0002	.0001	.0001	.0001	.0000	.0000	.0000	.0000	.0000	.0000	.0000
40	.0007	.0005	.0003	.0002	.0002	.0001	.0001	.0000	.0000	.0000	.0000	.0000	.0000	.0000	.0000	.0000	.0000	.0000
45	.0003	.0002	.0001	.0001	.0001	.0000	.0000	.0000	.0000	.0000	.0000	.0000	.0000	.0000	.0000	.0000	.0000	.0000
50	.0001	.0001	.0000	.0000	.0000	.0000	.0000	.0000	.0000	.0000	.0000	.0000	.0000	.0000	.0000	.0000	.0000	.0000
55	.0001	.0000	.0000	.0000	.0000	.0000	.0000	.0000	.0000	.0000	.0000	.0000	.0000	.0000	.0000	.0000	.0000	.0000
60	.0000	.0000	.0000	.0000	.0000	.0000	.0000	.0000	.0000	.0000	.0000	.0000	.0000	.0000	.0000	.0000	.0000	.0000

Appendix B

Solutions to Selected End-of-Chapter Problems

CHAPTER 2

2 Net income = £126,100
   Add. to RE = £79,100

6 ₩1,425,000

10 Rs. 730,000

14 **a.** ₪41,260
   b. ₪1,500
   c. ₪2,250
   d. ₪5,510

18 **a.** $\text{Tax}_{\text{Growth}} = \$17,150$
   $\text{Tax}_{\text{Income}} = \$2,890,000$
   b. $3,400

CHAPTER 3

2 Equity multiplier = 2.30 times
   ROE = 20.01%
   Net income = $104,052

6 15.34%

10 5.85%

14 37.12 days

19 Ca$84,353

CHAPTER 4

2 **a.** €1,790.05
   b. €1,967.15
   c. €3,207.14

6 11.90 years; 23.79 years

10 **a.** $1,822.12
   b. $1,349.86
   c. $1,648.72
   d. $1,750.67

14 $187,500; 7.69%

18 EAR = 176.68%

22 First Complex rate = 6.05%

26 Rs. 3,636,363.64

30 ㍍29,125,663

34 SAR 3,520,088.18

38 $356,387.10

42 Profit = $7,700.77
   Breakeven rate = 16.89%

46 $29,700.29

50 Au$1,361.82

CHAPTER 5

2 **a.** £1,000.00
   b. £828.41
   c. £1,231.15

6 Rs. 42.35

14 ㍍25.27

18 Rs. 2.75

22 ¥47,621.45

26 Rs. 4.16

CHAPTER 6

2 3.57 years; 5.95 years; Never

6 41.48%

10 $\text{PI}_{\text{Alpha}} = 2.60$
   $\text{PI}_{\text{Beta}} = 1.52$

14 **a.** $\text{PI}_{\text{I}} = 1.24$
   $\text{PI}_{\text{II}} = 1.39$
   b. $\text{NPV}_{\text{I}} = \text{Ca}\$7,302.78$
   $\text{NPV}_{\text{II}} = \text{Ca}\$1,963.19$

18 **a.** AZM payback = 1 year
   AZF payback = 2 years
   b. $\text{NPV}_{\text{AZM}} = ¢218,482$
   $\text{NPV}_{\text{AZF}} = ¢155,147$
   c. $\text{IRR}_{\text{AZM}} = 70.04\%$
   $\text{IRR}_{\text{AZF}} = 25.70\%$

CHAPTER 7

2 NPV = $2,294.67

6 IRR = 23.85%

10 Techron I EAC = −£84,274
   Techron II EAC = −£83,794

14 $\text{EAC}_{\text{A}} = -€2,504,676$
   $\text{EAC}_{\text{B}} = -€2,426,382$

18 Ca$666,667

CHAPTER 8

2 $\text{NPV}_{\text{Best}} = £3,109,608$
   $\text{NPV}_{\text{Worst}} = -£1,848,883$

6 Go to market NPV = ¥12,500,000
   Test market NPV = ¥11,541,666,67

10 3,518 units

14 Payback = 2.95 years
   NPV = $9,103,637
   IRR = 28.24%

18 a. 元237,730
    b. 元126,909

CHAPTER 9

2 Dividend yield = 1.69%
    Capital gains yield = 13.25%

6 Government bonds = 2.62%
    Corporate bonds = 3.01%

10 a. 48.94%
    b. 50.10%

14 1.37%

22 Arithmetic average = 7.5%
    Geometric average = 6.5%

CHAPTER 10

2 13.68%

6 $E(R_A) = 8.10\%$
    $\sigma_A = 1.92\%$
    $E(R_B) = 15.70\%$
    $\sigma_B = 14.89\%$

10 a. 13.29%
    b. 17.81%

14 1.67

18 Market risk premium = 8.46%

CHAPTER 11

2 a. 0.80%
    b. 7.77%

5 $F_1 = 5.80\%$
    $F_2 = 6.38\%$

CHAPTER 12

2 5.16%

6 13.28%

10 a. 7.50%
    b. 13.78%

14 $42,385,321

CHAPTER 14

2 a. Common stock = £1,000
    Total equity = £1,001,000
    b. Common stock = £11,000
    Capital suprlus = £390,000

6 Rs. 210,000,420

CHAPTER 15

2 a. $1.01; $3.36; $4.70
    b. $.48; $4.40; $6.64

6 a. $7.59; $8.06; $7.14
    b. $7,700
    c. $7,700
    d. $4.55; $4.83; $4.29
        Breakeven = $7,700

10 $5,250,000

16 increase of €725,000,000

CHAPTER 16

1 a. DOP 3,775,000

4 $650,000

8 a. ¥100,000,000
    b. 37.70%
    c. 19.34%

CHAPTER 17

2 $106,169.85

6 a. $3,465,535
    c. $3,075,306

10 £3,219,442

14 a. $113,750,000; $75.83
    b. $127,750,000; $85.17
    c. Share repurchased = 469,667
        Value = $87,750,000
        Share price = $85.17

CHAPTER 18

2 a. New shares issued = 1,000
    b. New shares issued = 2,500

6 9,770; $17.50

10 €600; €1,350

14 a. $95.00
    b. $100.00
    c. 20,000

18 a. Rs. 1,412,000
    b. Rs. 138.00
    c. Rs. 1,412,000
    d. 76.67 shares

CHAPTER 19

2 a. $40; anything > $0
    b. 1,428,571; 3.64
    c. $38.92; $1.08
    d. $4,000; $4,000

6 207,488

10 Book value per share = $40.65
    New earnings = $500,000
    New EPS = $1.45
    New share price = $48.29

Old market-to-book = 1.25 times
New market-to-book = 1.19 times
NPV = −$18,333,333

14 **a.** Price ex-rights = $10.00
Subscription price = $4.00
Value of a right = $3.00
b. Price ex-rights = $12.00
Subscription price = $8.00
Value of a right = $1.00

CHAPTER 20

2 £881.25

6 **a.** $1,164.61
b. 7.76%
c. $130.15

9 $119.73

CHAPTER 21

2 NAL = −€64,508.39

6 €37,884.90

10 Au$1,314,738.31

14 **a.** Kr 51,438.43
c. Kr 1,221,502

CHAPTER 22

4 **a.** 元13.96
b. 元2.31

6 ¥901.41

10 Call = Ca$5.90
Put = Ca$2.38

14 Rs. 22,000,000

18 £85.00

22 Equity$_A$ = ¥3,183.37
Debt$_A$ = ¥8,016.63
Equity$_B$ = ¥2,624.54
Debt$_B$ = ¥8,875.46

26 **a.** 元7.32
b. Shares to buy = 1/3
Borrow 元26.02
c. 元7.32

CHAPTER 23

2 Rs. 1,206,821

6 €50,789.29

CHAPTER 24

2 13.47

6 $18.00

10 **a.** Lower bound = $0
Upper bound = $33.00
b. Lower bound = $4.00
Upper bound = $39.00

14 $17.09

CHAPTER 25

2 At $11.15, loss of $26,075
At $9.05, gain of $24,425

6 2.783 years

14 **a.** £406.91
b. £489.35

CHAPTER 26

2 Cash = £6,450
Current assets = $10,150

6 Operating cycle = 95.05 days
Cash cycle = 42.98 days

10 Ending balance
April: $248,850
May: $317,840
June: $471,540

CHAPTER 27

2 Au$1,690.31

6 **a.** Rs. 36,000
b. Rs. 36,000
c. Rs. 9.00

10 **a.** 元1,680,000
b. 元180,000
c. Cash flow per day = 元36.00
Cash flow per check = 元0.09

14 16.76 times

CHAPTER 28

2 ¥8,547,945

6 7.02 times; $322,844.62

10 $121,375.00

14 23.45%

18 **a.** NPV of current policy = ₦20,000
NPV of new policy = ₦9,583.33
b. 96.49%

CHAPTER 29

2 **a.** Assets = £540,000
b. Assets = £860,000

6 Goodwill = YER 4,150

10 **a.** £300
   b. £34.20
   c. £2,700
   d. £75,600

14 **a.** ¥7,500,000
   b. ¥27,500,000
   c. ¥15,625,000
   d. NPV_{Cash} = ¥2,500,000
       NPV_{Stock} = ¥11,875,000

CHAPTER 31

2 £ = $57.09
   SF/£ = 229.2970
   £/SF = 0.4361

6 Great Britian = 3.57%
   Japan = 1.40%
   Switzerland = 1.97%

10 Kr/$ = 6.5257

14 $F(0,1)$ = $1.56/£

Name Index

Page numbers followed by n indicate notes.

Page numbers followed by n indicate notes.